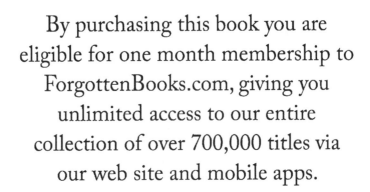

ISBN 978-0-428-61897-1
PIBN 10670538

### Palmer's Company Precedents.—Conveyancing and other
Forms and Precedents for use in relation to Companies subject to the Companies Acts, 1862 to 1890. Arranged as follows:—Promoters, Prospectuses, Agreements, Memoranda and Articles of Association, Resolutions, Notices, Certificates, Private Companies, Power of Attorney, Debentures and Debenture Stock, Petitions, Writs, Pleadings, Judgments and Orders, Reconstruction, Amalgamation, Arrangements, Special Acts, Provisional Orders, Winding-up. With Copious Notes and an Appendix containing the Acts and Rules. *Fifth Edition.* By FRANCIS BEAUFORT PALMER, assisted by CHARLES MACNAGHTEN, Esqrs., Barristers-at-Law. *Royal 8vo.* 1891.
" In company drafting it stands unrivalled."—*Law Times.* *Price 36s. cloth*

### Hamilton's Manual of Company Law for the Use of.
Directors and Promoters. By WM. FREDK. HAMILTON, LL.D. (Lond.): assisted by KENNARD GOLBORNE METCALFE, M.A., Barristers-at-Law. *Demy 8vo.* 1891. *Price 12s. 6d. cloth.*

### Williams' Law and Practice in Bankruptcy.—Comprising
the Bankruptcy Acts, 1883 to 1890, the Bankruptcy Rules, 1886, 1890, the Debtors Acts, 1869, 1878, the Bankruptcy (Discharge and Closure) Act, 1887, and the Deeds of Arrangement Act, 1887. By the Hon. SIR ROLAND VAUGHAN WILLIAMS, a Justice of the High Court. *Fifth Edition.* By EDWARD WM. HANSELL, Esq., Barrister-at-Law. *Royal 8vo.* 1891. *Price 25s. cloth.*
" A safe and useful guide to practitioners."—*Law Quarterly Review.*

### Godefroi's Law relating to Trusts and Trustees.—*Second Edit.*
By HENRY GODEFROI, Esq., Barrister-at-Law. *Royal 8vo.* 1891. *Price 32s. cloth.*

### Pollock's Digest of the Law of Partnership.—Incorporating
the Partnership Act, 1890. *Fifth Edition.* By SIR FREDERICK POLLOCK, Bart., Barrister-at-Law. *Demy 8vo.* 1890. *Price 8s. 6d. cloth.*

### Pollock's Law of Torts.—A Treatise on the Principles of
Obligations arising from Civil Wrongs in the Common Law. *Second Edition,* to which is added the draft of a Code of Civil Wrongs, prepared for the Government of India. By SIR FREDERICK POLLOCK, Bart., of Lincoln's Inn, Barrister-at-Law. *Demy 8vo.* 1890. *Price 1l. 1s. cloth.*

### Pollock's Principles of Contract.—Being a Treatise on
the General Principles relating to the Validity of Agreements in the Law of England. *Fifth Edition.* With a New Chapter. By SIR FREDERICK POLLOCK, Bart., M.A., LL.D., Barrister-at-Law. *Demy 8vo.* 1889. *Price 1l. 8s. cloth.*

### Smith's Compendium of Mercantile Law.—*Tenth Edition.*
By JOHN MACDONELL, Esq., one of the Masters of the Supreme Court, assisted by GEO. HUMPHREYS, Esq., Barrister-at-Law. 2 *Vols.* *Royal 8vo.* 1890. *Price 2l. 2s. cloth.*
" Of the greatest value to the mercantile lawyer."—*Law Times.*

### Prideaux's Precedents in Conveyancing.—With Disserta-
tions on its Law and Practice. *Fourteenth Edition.* By FREDERICK PRIDEAUX, late Professor of the Law of Real and Personal Property to the Inns of Court, and JOHN WHITCOMBE, Esqrs., Barristers-at-Law. 2 *Vols.* *Royal 8vo.* 1889. *Price 3l. 10s. cloth.*
" The most useful work out on Conveyancing."—*Law Journal.*

### Greenwood's Practice of Conveyancing, with Concise Prece-
dents.—A Manual of the Practice of Conveyancing. Showing the present Practice relating to the daily routine of Conveyancing in Solicitors' Offices, to which are added Concise Common Forms and Precedents in Conveyancing. *Eighth Edition.* By HARRY GREENWOOD, Barrister-at-Law. *Demy 8vo.* 1891. *Price 16s. cloth.*
" One of those books which no lawyer's bookshelf should be without. . . . A complete guide to Conveyancing.—*Law Gazette.*

## Goddard's Treatise on the Law of Easements.—By
JOHN LEYBOURN GODDARD, Esq., Barrister-at-Law. *Fourth Edition. Demy 8vo.* 1891. *Price 21s. cloth.*
" An indispensable part of the lawyer's library."—*Solicitors' Journal.*

## Pitt-Lewis' Winding-up Practice.—A Manual of the
Practice as to Winding-up in the High Court and in the County Court; being the Companies (Winding-up) Act, 1890, and the Winding-up of Companies and Associations (Part IV. of the Companies Act, 1862), as now amended, with Notes, and the Companies Winding-up Rules, 1890. Forming a Supplement to "A Complete Practice of the County Courts." By G. PITT-LEWIS, Q.C., M.P., Recorder of Poole. *Demy 8vo.* 1891. *Price 7s. 6d. cloth.*

## Pitt-Lewis' Complete Practice of the County Courts,
including that in Admiralty and Bankruptcy, embodying the County Courts Act, 1888, and other existing Acts, Rules, Forms, and Costs, with Full Alphabetical Index to Official Forms, Additional Forms, and General Index. *Fourth Edition,* with Supplementary Volume containing New Winding-up Practice. By G. PITT-LEWIS, Esq., Q.C , M.P., Recorder of Poole. 3 *Vols. Demy 8vo.* 1890-91. *Price 2l. 10s. cloth.*
" The Standard County Court Practice."—*Solicitors' Journal.*

## Roscoe's Criminal Law.—A Digest of the Law of Evidence
in Criminal Cases. *Eleventh Edit.* By HORACE SMITH and GILBERT GEORGE KENNEDY, Esqrs., Metropolitan Police Magistrates. *Demy 8vo.* 1890. *Price* 1l. 11s. 6d. cloth.
" What Roscoe says, most judges will accept without question."—*Law Times.*

## Roscoe's Nisi Prius.—A Digest of the Law of Evidence on
the Trial of Actions at Nisi Prius.—*Fifteenth Edition.* By MAURICE POWELL, Esq., Barrister-at-Law. 2 vols. *Demy 8vo.* 1891.                    (*Nearly ready.*)

## Edmunds on Patents.—The Law and Practice of Letters
Patent for Inventions. with the Patent Acts and Rules annotated, and the International Convention ; a full Collection of Statutes, Forms and Precedents, and an Outline of Foreign and Colonial Patent Laws, &c. By LEWIS EDMUNDS. assisted by A. WOOD RENTON. Esqrs., Barristers-at-Law. *Royal 8vo.* (992 *pp.*) 1890. *Price* 1l. 12s. cloth.
" We have nothing but commendation for the book. Conceived in a large and comprehensive spirit, it is well and thoroughly carried out. . . . . The statement of the existing law is accurate and clear. . . . . The book is one to be recommended."—*Solicitors' Journal.*

## Sebastian's Law of Trade Marks and their Registration,
and matters connected therewith, including a Chapter on Goodwill. Together with the Patents, Designs, and Trade Marks Acts, 1883-8, and the Trade Marks Rules and Instructions thereunder, Forms and Precedents; the Merchandise Marks Act, 1887, and other Statutory enactments; and the United States Statutes, 1870 to 1881, and the Rules and Forms thereunder, and the Treaty with the United States, 1877. *Thir·' Edition.* By LEWIS BOYD SEBASTIAN, B.C.L., M.A., of Lincoln's Inn, Esq., Barrister-at-Law. *Demy 8vo.* 1890. *Price* 1l. 5s. cloth.
" The work stands alone as an authority upon the law of trade marks."—*Law Journal.*

## Chitty's Index to all the Reported Cases decided in the
several Courts of Equity in England, the Privy Council, and the House of Lords, with a Selection of Irish Cases on or relating to the Principles, Pleading and Practice of Equity and Bankruptcy from the Earliest Period. *Fourth Edition.* Wholly Revised, Re-classified, and brought down to the end of 1883. By HENRY EDWARD HIRST, Esq., Barrister-at-Law. *Complete in 9 Vols. Royal 8vo,* 1883-89. *Price 12l. 12s. cloth.*      *** *The Volumes may be had separately to complete Sets.*
" The work is thoroughly well done."—*Law Quarterly Review.*

## Fisher's Digest of the Reported Decisions of the Courts of
Common Law, Bankruptcy, Probate, Admiralty, and Divorce, together with a selection from those of the Court of Chancery and Irish Courts. From 1756 to 1883 inclusive. Founded on Fisher's Digest. By JOHN MEWS, Assisted by C. M. CHAPMAN, HARRY H. W. SPARHAM, and A. H. TODD, Barristers-at-Law. *In 7 Vols. Royal 8vo.* 1884. *Price 12l. 12s. cloth.*

## Mews' Consolidated Digest of all the Reports in all the
Courts for the Years 1884-88 inclusive. By JOHN MEWS, Barrister-at-Law. *Royal 8vo.* 1889. *Price 1l. 11s. 6d. cloth.*

## The Annual Digest for 1889 and 1890.   By JOHN MEWS,
Barrister-at-Law. *Royal 8vo. Price each 15s. cloth.*      *** *The above works bring Fisher's Common Law and Chitty's Equity Digests down to the end of* 1890.

*** *All Standard Law Works are kept in stock, in law calf and other bindings.*

A

# COMPENDIUM

OF

# MERCANTILE LAW

BY

## JOHN WILLIAM SMITH,

LATE OF THE INNER TEMPLE, ESQUIRE, BARRISTER-AT-LAW.

## TENTH EDITION

EDITED BY

## JOHN MACDONELL, M.A.,

A MASTER OF THE SUPREME COURT OF JUDICATURE.

ASSISTED BY

## GEORGE HUMPHREYS, B.A.,

OF THE MIDDLE TEMPLE, ESQUIRE, BARRISTER-AT-LAW.

IN TWO VOLUMES.
VOL. II.

LONDON:

STEVENS AND SONS, LIMITED, 119 & 120, CHANCERY LANE,

SWEET AND MAXWELL, LIMITED, 3, CHANCERY LANE,

Law Publishers and Booksellers.

1890.

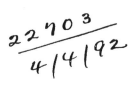

22703

4/4/92

LONDON :

PRINTED BY C. F. ROWORTH, GREAT NEW STREET, FETTER LANE—E.C.

# CONTENTS OF VOL. II.

## BOOK IV.

### OF MERCANTILE REMEDIES.

# BOOK THE FOURTH.

———◆———

## OF MERCANTILE REMEDIES.

It is proposed to treat, in this Book, of *Mercantile Remedies:* that is, omitting all consideration of those universal ones, by action, which are open to merchants in common with the rest of her Majesty's subjects, to speak of such as are, from their very nature, exclusively, or almost exclusively, appropriated to that class of the community, with whom we are, in this Treatise, chiefly concerned.

---

## CHAPTER I.

### STOPPAGE IN TRANSITU.

———

### Section I.—*Right to stop in Transitu—what.*

The first subject which we shall place under this head is that of Stoppage in Transitu, which is, indeed, a measure rather of prevention than of cure; but yet sufficiently entitled to the epithet *remedial* to justify its present collocation.

When goods are consigned on credit by one merchant to another, it sometimes happens that the consignee becomes

Right to stop in transitu— what.

bankrupt or insolvent (*a*) while the goods are on their way to him, and before they are delivered. In such case, as it would be hard that the goods of the consignor should be applied in payment of the debts of the consignee, the former is allowed by law to resume possession (*c*) of them, if he can succeed in doing so while they are on their way, and before they have got into the purchaser's possession. This resumption is called stoppage *in transitu* (*d*), and the doctrine of stoppage *in transitu* has always been construed favourably to the unpaid vendor (*e*). *Insolvency* is understood generally by merchants as having a popular and not a technical meaning, and it has been frequently construed by the Courts in its larger sense. The term insolvency (when used with reference to this branch of the law) is satisfied by general inability to pay, evidenced by stoppage of payment. In *Biddlecombe* v. *Bond* (*f*), it was held in a contract to mean general inability to pay debts. It seems that there is no necessity that the vendee should have become bankrupt, or that a receiving order should have been made against him, but that general inability to pay, evidenced by stoppage of payment, is sufficient (*g*). Mere failure by the vendee to comply with a condition subsequent, as the sending, in accordance with the contract, of a banker's draft for the price, does not give the vendor the right to resume possession after the property has vested in the vendee (*h*).

(*a*) For history of the right, see Lord *Abinger*'s judgment in *Gibson* v. *Carruthers*, 8 M. & W. 321. In *Wilmshurst* v. *Bowker*, 2 M. & G. at p. 812, *Tindal*, C. J., says, "The ordinary right of countermanding the actual delivery of goods shipped to a consignee is limited to the cases in which the *bankruptcy* or *insolvency* of the consignee has taken place."

(*c*) See *The Tigress*, 32 L. J. Adm. 97.

(d) In former editions it was said that this right "was first allowed by equity," alluding to *Wiseman* v. *Vandeput* (1690), 2 Vern. 203; *Snee* v. *Prescott*, 1 Atk. 246, and *D'Aquila* v. *Lambert*, 2 Eden, 75; Ambl. 399.

But the right seems to have existed as part of the lex mercatoria : Blackburn on Sale, 2nd ed., p. 318.

(*e*) *Bethell* v. *Clark*, 20 Q. B. D. at p. 617, per Lord *Esher*, M. R.

(*f*) 4 Ad. & E. 332. See per *James*, V.-C., in *Re European Assurance Society*, L. R. 9 Eq. at p. 128.

(*g*) See *Vertue* v. *Jewell*, 4 Camp. 31 ; *Newsom* v. *Thornton*, 6 East, 17 (in both of which cases the stoppage in transitu was effected before the bankruptcy of the vendee).

(*h*) *Wilmshurst* v. *Bowker*, 7 M. & G. 882 (Exch. Ch.); and see *Key* v. *Cotesworth*, 7 Exch. 595, and *R.* v. *Saddlers' Co.*, 10 H. L. Cas. 404, at p. 425, per *Willes*, J.

Whether its effect be or be not to dissolve the contract of sale between the consignor and consignee of the goods stopped, has been much discussed (i). Lord *Kenyon* was of opinion that it did not rescind the sale, but was an "*equitable* (j) lien, adopted by the law for the purposes of substantial justice" (k); an opinion which certainly consists best with the decisions which have taken place, that payment of part of the price (unless the contract be apportionable (l)), or acceptance of a bill for the whole of it, by the vendee, will not defeat the vendor's right to stop *in transitu*, if the vendee become insolvent before the remainder of the price has been liquidated, or the bill taken up (m), and that the vendor is not, when he stops *in transitu*, obliged to tender back a bill he has received on account of the price (n). Mr. Justice *Bayley*, in *Bloxam* v. *Saunders* (o), gave a descrip-

Right to stop in transitu— what.

---

(i) In *Stephens* v. *Wilkinson*, 2 B. & Ad. 320. In *Edwards* v. *Brewer*, 2 M. & W. 375, and *Gibson* v. *Carruthers*, 8 M. & W. 321, the Court adverted to it as undetermined. And see *Wilmshurst* v. *Bowker*, 5 Bing. N. C. 541. In Bell's Comm. it is treated as a rescission (3rd ed. I. 2, p. 2, c. 1).

(j) *Schotsmans* v. *Lancashire and Yorkshire Rail. Co.*, L. R. 2 Ch. 332.

(k) *Hodgson* v. *Loy*, 7 T. R. at p. 445.

(l) See *Merchant Banking Co.* v. *Phœnix Bessemer Steel Co.*, 5 Ch. D. at p. 220.

(m) *Hodgson* v. *Loy*, 7 T. R. 440; *Feise* v. *Wray*, 3 East, 93. Compare *Cowasjee* v. *Thompson*, 5 Moo. P. C. 165.

(n) *Edwards* v. *Brewer*, 2 M. & W. 375; *Jenkyns* v. *Usborne*, 7 M. & G. 678.

(o) 4 B. & C. at p. 948. "The buyer's right," said his Lordship, "in respect of the price is not a mere lien, which he will forfeit if he parts with the possession, but grows out of his original ownership and dominion. If the seller has despatched the goods to the buyer, and insolvency occurs, he has a right, in virtue of his original ownership, to stop them in transitu.—Why? Because the *property* is vested in the buyer, so as to subject him to the risk of any accident, but he has not an indefeasible right to the *possession*; and his insolvency, without payment of the price, defeats that right. And if this be the case after he has despatched the goods, and whilst they are in transitu, à fortiori is it when he has never parted with the goods, and when no transitus has begun? The buyer, or those who stand in his place, may still obtain the right of *possession*, if they will pay or tender the price; or they may still act upon their right of *property*, if anything unwarrantable is done to that right. If, for instance, the original vendor sell when he ought not, they may bring a special action against him for the injury they sustain by such wrongful sale, and recover damages to the extent of that injury; but they can maintain no action in which the right of *property* and right of *possession* are both requisite, unless they have both those rights." See also *Valpy* v. *Oakeley*, 16 Q. B. 941; *Wilmshurst* v. *Bowker*, 5 Bing. N. C. 541. See, also, *Milgate* v. *Kebble*, 3 M. & G. 100, where it was held that the vendee could not maintain trover against the vendor for taking the goods

tion of the nature of a vendor's lien for his price, wide enough to include the right of stoppage *in transitu*, and seemingly opposed to the idea that the exercise of that right operates as a rescission of the contract of sale. In *Edwards* v. *Brewer* (*p*), *Parke*, B., says, " the effect is the same as if the consignor had not delivered them on board ship. Then, if so, he has a right to retain them till payment of the whole price." There is now a general consensus of opinion that the effect of stoppage *in transitu* is not to rescind the contract (*q*).

In *Vertue* v. *Jewell* (*r*), Lord *Ellenborough* held that although the vendee may have become insolvent, still if the state of his accounts with the vendor be such that the vendor is, upon the whole, indebted to the vendee, he cannot stop *in transitu* goods of less value consigned to the vendee, on account of the balance ; for the delivery of them to the vendee's representatives can, in that case, be productive of no injustice ; and if the balance against him be occasioned by the vendee being under acceptances for his accommodation, he cannot stop *in transitu* until the bills are paid. This view was confirmed by the Court in banc. But it has often been questioned.

---

away, the plaintiff not being in actual possession, and the price, *which was to be paid before removal*, unpaid. And see Lord v. *Price*, L. R. 9 Ex. 54 ; *Johnson* v. *Stear*, 15 C. B. N. S. 330 ; *Halliday* v. *Holgate*, L. R. 3 Ex. 299.

(*p*) Ubi supra.

(*q*) See per *Brett*, L. J., in *Kendal* v. *Marshall*, *Stevens & Co.*, 11 Q. B. D. 356, at p. 364 ; where he observes, " where the goods are in the course of transit from the vendor to the vendee, although the property has passed to vendee, and although he has the con-

structive possession of them, the right to stop prevails." In *Phelps, Stokes & Co.* v. *Comber*, 29 Ch. D. 813, at p. 821, *Cotton*, L. J., thus describes the right : " *It is a retaking by the unpaid vendor*, either on the cancellation of the contract, as some people say, or, as I should rather say, *on resuming possession for the purpose of insisting on his lien for the price, at any time while the goods are in the hands of the carrier, &c.*" Benjamin on Sale, 4th ed. 898.

(r) 4 Camp. 31.

## Section II.—*Who possesses it.*

Lord *Ellenborough* stated, in *Siffken* v. *Wray* (s), that the person Who possesses it. who stopped goods *in transitu* must not be a mere surety for their price; one, for instance, who had, at the request of the vendee, accepted bills drawn by the vendor for their purchase-money. But since the passing of the Mercantile Law Amendment Act (19 & 20 Vict. c. 97, s. 5) this is not necessarily the case ; a surety who has paid may exercise the right. In *The Imperial Bank* v. *The London and St. Katharine's Dock Co.* (t), a broker who purchased for an undisclosed principal, and who was liable to pay the payee in the event of default, was held entitled to exercise the right; and a person abroad, who, in pursuance of orders sent him by a British merchant, purchases goods, on his own credit, of others whose names are unknown to the merchant, and charges a commission on the price, is a consignor, and is entitled to stop the goods *in transitu* if the merchants fail while they are on their passage; for he stands in the light of a vendor, and the British merchant of *his* vendee (u). So is a person who consigns goods to be sold on the joint account of himself and the consignee (v). The right belongs to a buyer who resells his interest in the goods (w).

If the stoppage be made by an unauthorized person on behalf of vendor, the act must be ratified before the transit is over (x), otherwise it will not be effectual.

---

(s) 6 East, 371. See *Sweet* v. *Pym*, 1 East, 4.

(t) 5 Ch. D. 195.

(u) *Feise* v. *Wray*, 3 East, 93 ; *The Tigress*, 32 L. J. Adm. 97. See *Ireland* v. *Livingston*, L. R. 5 H. L. 395 ; *Ex parte Banner*, 2 Ch. D. 278 ; *Ex parte Cooper*, 11 Ch. D. 68.

(v) *Newsom* v. *Thornton*, 6 East, 17. As to the authority of an agent to stop goods in transitu, and the effect of a ratification, see *Nicholls* v. *Le Feuvre*, 2 Bing. N. C. 81 ; *Whitehead* v. *Anderson*, 9 M. & W. 518 ; *Bird* v. *Brown*, 4 Exch. 786 ; *Hutchings* v. *Nunes*, 1 Moore, P. C. N. S. 243.

(w) *Jenkyns* v. *Usborne*, 7 M. & G. 678.

(x) *Bird* v. *Brown*, 4 Ex. 786.

## SECTION III.—*How long it continues.*

The period during which the right to stop the goods continues is, as we have seen, co-extensive with that of their transit
from the vendor to the purchaser. Hence, in cases where the
propriety of a resumption of this sort is questioned, the point
disputed generally is, whether, at the time of seizure by the
vendor, the transit of the goods had or had not determined.
Such cases always mainly depend upon their own peculiar
circumstances, but the general rule to be collected from all the
decisions is, that goods are to be deemed *in transitu* till they get
into the hands of the purchaser, his servants or agents.

Most of the cases fall into the following groups :—

(a) *Where the goods, after sale, remain in the possession of the
vendor.*—These, which are scarcely cases of stoppage *in transitu*,
have already been discussed with reference to the Statute of
Frauds; the purchaser not having acquired the actual possession, the vendor's lien exists (y).

(b) *Where the goods are in the possession of a carrier, or railway company, or a general ship not belonging to or chartered by the
vendee.*—Goods are to be deemed *in transitu* so long as they
remain in the possession of carriers as such, whether by water or
land (z), even though such carrier may have been appointed by
the consignee himself (a); and until they come into the actual

---

(y) *Hurry* v. *Mangles*, 1 Camp. 452;
*Miles* v. *Gorton*, 2 C. & M. 504;
*Townley* v. *Crump*, 1 A. & E. 58;
*Lackington* v. *Atherton*, 8 Scott, N. S.
38; *Grice* v. *Richardson*, 3 App. Cas.
319.

(z) *Mills* v. *Ball*, 2 B. & P. 457.
Per *James*, L. J., in *Ex parte Rosevear
China Clay Co.*, 11 Ch. D. at p. 568.

(a) *Holst* v. *Pawnal*, 1 Esp. 240;
*Northey* v. *Field*, 2 Esp. 613; *Hodgson*
v. *Loy*, 7 T. R. 440; *Jackson* v. *Nichol*,

5 Bing. N. C. 508; *Berndtson* v. *Strang*,
L. R. 4 Eq. 481; 3 Ch. 588; *Rodger* v.
*The Comptoir d'Escompte de Paris*, L. R.
2 P. C. 393; *Ex parte Rosevear China
Clay Co.*, 11 Ch. D. 560; *Ex parte
Barrow*, 6 Ch. D. 783; *Stokes* v. *La
Riviere*, cited in *Bothlingk* v. *Inglis*,
3 East, 381; *Smith* v. *Goss*, 1 Camp.
282; *Coates* v. *Railton*, 6 B. & C. 422;
*Nicholls* v. *Le Feuvre*, 2 Bing. N. C.
81; *Turner* v. *Trustees of Liverpool
Dock Co.*, 6 Exch. 593; *James* v.

or constructive possession of the consignee, who may require How long it continues.
the goods to be delivered to him at any stage of the journey (b).

(c) *Where the goods are in any place of deposit connected with the transmission and delivery of them.*—Such goods are still in transit. Thus, if they be landed at a seaport town, and there deposited with a wharfinger appointed by the consignee to forward them by land to his own residence, while in the hands of the wharfinger they are subject to the consignor's right of stoppage (c). "Nothing is clearer than that it is not delivery to any agent which terminates the transit" (d). But the *transitus* is completely at an end when the goods arrive at an agent's, who is to keep them till he receives the further orders of the vendee (e). The warehouse of the intermediary may really be the warehouse of the vendee; a carrier or wharfinger may hold the goods for him. If a consignee be in the habit, with the consent of the owner, of using the warehouse of a carrier, packer, wharfinger, or other person as his own, for instance, by making it the repository of his goods, and disposing of them there, the transit will be considered as at an end when they have arrived at such warehouse (f). Where the right of stoppage *in transitu* is to be defeated by a constructive possession through the medium of the carrier,

*Griffin*, 2 M. & W. 623; *Bolton* v. *The L. & Y. Rail. Co.*, L. R. 1 C. P. 431; *Edwards* v. *Brewer*, 2 M. & W. 375. See *Whitehead* v. *Anderson*, 9 M. & W. 518; *Nicholson* v. *Bower*, 1 E. & E. 172.

(b) *London and North Western Rail. Co.* v. *Bartlett*, 7 H. & N. 400; *Fraser* v. *Witt*, L. R. 7 Eq. 64.

(c) *Mills* v. *Ball*, 2 B. & P. 457; *Ex parte Barrow*, 6 Ch. D. 787; *Kendal* v. *Marshall*, 11 Q. B. D. 356, 365.

(d) *Fry*, L. J., in *Bethell* v. *Clarke*, 20 Q. B. D. at p. 619.

(e) Per Lord *Ellenborough*, in *Dixon* v. *Baldwin*, 5 East, 175; and *Parke*, B., in *Wentworth* v. *Outhwaite*, 10 M. & W. at p. 450; *Bethell* v. *Clarke*, 20 Q. B.

D. at pp. 619, 620. The right to stop will not be revived by a re-delivery to the vendor for a special purpose, *e.g.*, to repack: *Valpy* v. *Gibson*, 4 C. B. 837.

(f) *Richardson* v. *Goss*, 3 B. & P. 119; *Scott* v. *Pettit*, 3 B. & P. 469; *Foster* v. *Frampton*, 6 B. & C. 107; *Allan* v. *Gripper*, 2 C. & J. 218; *Wentworth* v. *Outhwaite*, 10 M. & W. 436; *Dodson* v. *Wentworth*, 4 M. & G. 1080; *Rowe* v. *Pickford*, 8 Taunt. 83. See *James* v. *Griffin*, 2 M. & W. 623, and the judgment in *Whitehead* v. *Anderson*, 9 M. & W. 518; *Nicholson* v. *Bower*, 1 E. & E. 172; *Smith* v. *Hudson*, 6 B. & S. 431; and compare *Bethell* v. *Clarke*, supra.

acts of dominion exercised by the vendee over the goods while
in the carrier's hands (as, for instance, by taking samples),
will not have the effect of creating such a constructive possession, unless they be accompanied by such circumstances as
denote that the carrier was intended to keep, and assented to
keep, the goods in the nature of an agent for custody (g).

(d) *Where goods are put on board the vendee's ship.*—This will
be a delivery to the vendee, unless the vendor stipulates by the
form of bills of lading or otherwise to the contrary, so as to
show that the master is an agent for carriage, and not an agent
to receive possession for the vendee (h), *e.g.*, where goods are put
on board a vessel chartered by vendee. If the charter be of the
ordinary character, not operating as a demise of the ship, and
not giving the charterers for the time being complete control of
the ship and crew, this will not take away the vendor's right of
stoppage (i).

(e) *Agreement as to destination.*—The vendor and vendee may
agree as to the transit, as in *Ex parte Watson, In re Love* (j) ;
and in this case the transit will continue until the goods reach
their agreed destination.

The following observations of *Bowen*, L. J., in *Kendal v.
Marshall, Stevens & Co.* (k), explain the law where no destination is named :—

"In *Ex parte Watson* (l), it was held that the right to stop *in transitu* continued, because, wherever it is part of the bargain between
the vendor and the vendee that the transit shall last up to a certain
time, the transit continues until that time has arrived (m). But when
goods are bought to be afterwards despatched as the vendee shall
direct, and it is not part of the bargain that the goods shall be sent

(g) *Whitehead* v. *Anderson,* 9 M. &
W. 518 ; *Coventry* v. *Gladstone,* L. R.
6 Eq. 44 ; *London and North Western
Rail. Co.* v. *Bartlett,* 7 H. & N. 400.
See *Merchant Banking Co.* v. *Phœnix
Bessemer Steel Co.,* 5 Ch. D. 205.

(h) *Rodger* v. *Comptoir d'Escompte,*
L. R. 2 P. C. 393 ; *Schotsmans* v.
*Lancashire and Yorkshire Rail. Co.,*
L. R. 2 Ch. 332 ; *Ex parte Francis,*

56 L. T. 577.

(i) *Berndtson* v. *Strang,* L. R. 3 Ch.
588 ; *Ex parte Rosevear China Clay Co.,*
11 Ch. D. 560.

(j) 5 Ch. D. 35 ; *Ex parte Miles, Re
Isaacs,* 15 Q. B. D. 39. See, however,
*Whitehead* v. *Anderson,* 9 M. & W. 518.

(k) 11 Q. B. D. 356, at p. 369.

(l) 5 Ch. D. 35.

(m) See *Bethell* v. *Clarke,* supra.

to any particular place, in that case the transit only ends when the How long it continues. goods reach the place ultimately named by the vendee as their destination. In *Coates* v. *Railton* (n), several cases were cited by *Bayley*, J., in the course of his judgment, and the principle to be deduced from them is that, where goods are sold to be sent to a particular destination, the *transitus* is not at an end until the goods have reached the place named by the vendee to the vendor as their destination. One exception, at least, is to be found to the principle here laid down : the vendee can always anticipate the place of destination, if he can succeed in getting the goods out of the hands of the carrier. In that case the transit is at an end, whatever may have been said as to the place of destination, and this shows that the real test is not what is said, but what is done. But it has never been decided that where the goods have reached the place of destination named to the vendor by the vendee, to be there held by an agent to the vendee at the vendee's disposal, the right to stop continues " (o).

Though goods may not have reached their ultimate destination, yet if they "have so far gotten to the end of their journey that they [wait] for new orders from the purchaser to put them again in motion, to communicate to them another substantive destination, and that without such orders they would continue stationary " (p), the *transitus* is at an end.

(n) 6 B. & C. 422.

(o) See *Bethell* v. *Clark*, 20 Q. B. D. 615. See also the remarks of *Brett*, M. R., in *Ex parte Miles*, 15 Q. B. D. at p. 43.

(p) Per Lord *Ellenborough*, C. J., in *Dixon* v. *Baldwin*, 5 East, at p. 186 ; cited by Lord *Esher*, M. R., in *Ex parte Miles*, 15 Q. B. D. at p. 44, and *Bethell* v. *Clark*, 20 Q. B. D. at p. 619.

The following is an analysis of recent cases on this subject, in order of date :—

*Ex parte Watson, In re Love*, 5 Ch. D. 35 (1877).—Goods sold by W., a Bradford manufacturer, to L., a London merchant ; L. to ship the goods to R., at *Shanghai*, for sale on L.'s account ; W. to have lien on bills of lading and goods on transit outwards ; goods packed by W.'s packer, who forwarded them by rail to London in bales marked

for *Shanghai*, addressed to ship designated by L. ; the packer, advising L. of despatch of goods, said they were "at L.'s disposal," and the railway company, advising L. of the arrival of the goods in London, told him they remained at his order, and were held by the railway company as warehouse-men, at his risk, but said " will be sent to ship." Held, by Court of Appeal, that the transit was from Bradford to Shanghai. See also *Rodger* v. *Comptoir d'Escompte de Paris*, L. R. 2 P. C. 393.

*Ex parte Rosevear Clay Co., In re Cock*, 11 Ch. D. 560 (1879).—Sale by Rosevear Co. to C., a merchant at *Roche*, near *St. Austell*, of 80 to 100 tons of clay at 15s. per ton, f. o. b. *Fowey*; C. agreed verbally to charter a ship to call at *Fowey*, to convey the clay to *Glasgow* to his agent there for sale ; clay delivered by Rosevear Co.

How long it
continues.
It has been decided that, where part of the goods sold by one entire contract is taken possession of by the vendee, without any intention on the vendor's part of retaining the rest, but as a step towards and in progress of the delivery of the whole, that is to be deemed a taking possession of the whole (*q*); though it is otherwise if there were such an intention (*r*). It has been said that, *primâ facie*, a delivery of part imports an intention to deliver the whole (*s*). But this is open to grave doubt (*t*).

on board ship at *Fowey*, and invoice and bill of exchange for acceptance sent to C. The Rosevear Co. know nothing as to the destination of the ship. *Held*, by Court of Appeal (reversing *Bacon*, C. J.), that vendor's right to stop existed after ship had left *Fowey* for *Glasgow*. "The mere fact that the port of destination was left uncertain, or was changed after the contract of sale, can make no difference." Per *James*, L. J., at p. 568. See, also, *Berndtson* v. *Strang*, L. R. 3 Ch. 588.

*Kemp* v. *Falk*, 7 App. Cas. 573 (1882).—Falk, a Liverpool merchant, sold to Kiell, a London merchant, a cargo of salt at 13*s*. 5*d*. per ton, f. o. b. The salt was intended for Calcutta, and was shipped by Falk on board a vessel, chartered by Kiell, for the voyage to Calcutta. Thereupon Falk forwarded invoices and bills of lading to Kiell. The salt was consigned to W. at Calcutta. Kiell obtained from a bank an advance upon the bill of lading, and the salt was sold by W. "to arrive." *Held*, by the House of Lords, affirming Court of Appeal, that the transit was not at an end until the arrival of the ship at Calcutta.

*Kendal* v. *Marshall, Stevens & Co.*, 11 Q. B. D. 356 (1883.)—L. bought goods of W., a merchant at Bolton, nothing being said as to the place of delivery. L. arranged with M. & Co., shipping agents and carriers at Garston in Lancashire, that the goods should be sent to them at Garston and conveyed by them to Rouen, at a through rate

from Bolton to Rouen. L. then instructed W. to send the goods to M. & Co. W. sent the goods by railway to M. & Co. The railway company gave notice to M. & Co. of the arrival of the goods, and stated that they would hold the goods as warehousemen. *Held* by Court of Appeal (reversing the decision of *Mathew*, J.), that the transit was at an end when the goods came into the possession of M. & Co.

*Bethell* v. *Clark*, 20 Q. B. D. 615 (1888).—Goods were purchased by London merchants from manufacturers at Wolverhampton, the purchasers directed the vendors to consign the goods "to the 'Darling Downs,' to Melbourne, loading in the East India Docks," the vendors delivered the goods to carriers to be forwarded to the ship. *Held*, by Court of Appeal (affirming *Mathew*, J., and *Cave*, J.) that the transit was not at an end till the goods reached Melbourne.

(*q*) *Hammond* v. *Anderson*, 1 B. & P. N. R. 69. And see *Slubey* v. *Heyward*, 2 H. Bl. 504, and the remarks on these cases in *Ex parte Cooper*, 11 Ch. D. 68.

(*r*) *Bunney* v. *Poyntz*, 4 B. & Ad. 568; *Dixon* v. *Yates*, 5 B. & Ad. 313; *Tanner* v. *Scovell*, 14 M. & W. 28.

(*s*) Per *Taunton*, J., *Betts* v. *Gibbins*, 2 Ad. & E. 57, but quære. And in *Tanner* v. *Scovell*, 14 M. & W. 28, the Court of Exchequer dissented from the dictum of *Taunton*, J., and approved of this quære.

(*t*) See *Ex parte Cooper*, 11 Ch. D. 68.

## SECTION IV.—*How defeated.*

It has been already observed, that the delivery of goods to a carrier named by the vendee, though a delivery to the vendee himself for many purposes, is not such a one as to put an end to the right to stop them *in transitu ;* and it has been thought that the vendee, when a particular place of delivery has been appointed, cannot anticipate the regular determination of the transit by going to meet the goods upon their journey (*u*). This, however, as a general rule, has been much questioned and seems overruled (*x*). " If," said Baron *Parke*, in *Whitehead* v. *Anderson* (*y*), " the vendee take them out of the possession of the carrier into his own before their arrival, with or without the consent of the carrier, there seems to be no doubt that the transit would be at an end." But at all events, whatever may be the effect of the receipt of goods by the vendee before the regular determination of the transit, it seems clear that the vendor's right to stop them cannot be taken away by the vendee making a demand of them, while on their journey, with which the carrier, whether rightly or wrongly, refuses to comply (*z*). At the termination of the journey, however, if the vendee demand the goods, the carrier cannot by wrongfully detaining them, prolong the right of the vendor to stop them (*a*). The vendor's right also will not be defeated by the exercise of any claim against the consignee, such, for instance, as process of foreign attachment at the suit of a creditor of the vendee (*b*), or the carrier's claim of a general lien for the balance due to him by the vendee (*c*), or (generally speaking) by his vendee's selling

(*u*) *Holst* v. *Pownall*, 1 Esp. 240, Lord *Kenyon*. But see the observations of Lord *Alvanley* in *Mills* v. *Ball*, 2 B. & P. 461, and those of *Chambre*, J., in *Oppenheim* v. *Russel*, 3 B. & P. 54. See, too, *Foster* v. *Frampton*, 6 B. & C. 107.

(*x*) See *Kendal* v. *Marshall, Stevens & Co.*, L. R. 11 Q. B. D. 356, at pp. 366, 369.

(*y*) 9 M. & W. at p. 534.

(*z*) *Jackson* v. *Nichol*, 5 Bing. N. C. 508 ; *Whitehead* v. *Anderson*, 9 M. & W. 518 ; *Coventry* v. *Gladstone*, L. R. 6 Eq. 44.

(*a*) *Bird* v. *Brown*, 4 Exch. 786.

(*b*) *Smith* v. *Goss*, 1 Camp. 282.

(*c*) *Butler* v. *Woolcot*, 2 B. & P. N. R. 64 ; *Nicholls* v. *Le Feuvre*, 2 Bing. N. C. 81.

How defeated. them again to a third party, the ordinary rule of law being
that the second vendee of a chattel cannot stand in a better
situation than his vendor (d). Purchasers on credit of a cargo
of salt consigned it abroad to W. M. & Co. They obtained
upon the security of the bills of lading an advance from a
bank. The consignees sold the goods "to arrive" to sub-
purchasers, to whom they were delivered. On the purchasers
going into liquidation, the seller gave notice to the master, after
the sub-sale but before delivery and payment of the freight, to
stop the goods *in transitu*. It was contended that the sub-sale
displaced the right of stoppage. "But," said Lord *Selborne*,
"the original purchaser can transfer no greater or better right
than he has; and the right which he has is a right subject to a
stoppage *in transitu*, in all cases in which the right of stoppage *in
transitu* remains in favour of the original seller of the goods" (e).
We have, however, seen that the negotiation of a bill of lading
for valuable consideration (f) will defeat the vendor's right to
stop *in transitu* (g); and the Factors Act, 1889, as we have also
seen (h), confers similar efficacy on the transfer of documents of
title (i).

It must, however, be observed that the negotiation of a bill of
lading or other instrument by way of pledge, defeats only the
*legal* right to stop *in transitu*; for, in equity, the vendor may,
by giving notice to the pledgee, resume his former interest in
the goods, subject to the pledgee's claim, and will be entitled to
the residue of their proceeds after the pledgee's demand has
been satisfied out of them, or to the goods themselves, if it be
satisfied *aliunde*, notwithstanding the pledgee may have other
demands against the consignee (k). The indorsement, therefore,
of a bill of lading as a pledge for a specific sum, though it

(d) *Dixon* v. *Yates*, 5 B. & Ad. 313.

(e) *Kemp* v. *Falk*, 7 App. Cas. 573,
577; but see *Ex parte Golding, Davis &
Co.*, 13 Ch. D. 628.

(f) *Rodger* v. *The Comptoir d'Escompte de Paris*, L. R. 2 P. C. 393.

(g) See ante, p. 346; *Gurney* v.
*Behrend*, 3 E. & B. 622; *The Marie
Joseph*, L. R. 1 P. C. 219.

(h) Ante, B. I. Chap. 4, sect. 4,
pp. 145 *et seq.*

(i) See Appendix.

(k) *In re Westzinthus*, 5 B. & Ad.
817; *Kemp* v. *Falk*, 7 App. Cas. 573.
And see *Berndtson* v. *Strang*, L. R. 3
Ch. 588; *Rodger* v. *The Comptoir
d'Escompte de Paris*, L. R. 2 P. C. 393.

transfers the property in the goods, will only bar the right of How defeated.
the consignor to stop *in transitu* to that extent. " It [the
right of stoppage] is a qualified right in the circumstances
which I have mentioned; because it cannot be asserted as
against the holder of the bill of lading without paying him off;
but the instant his claim is discharged it is exactly the same
right as if there had been no security as against the original
purchaser, and as against, in my opinion, everyone claiming
under him" (*l*). The vendor may recover from the indorsee the
difference between the sum for which the pledge was made and
the sum realised by their sale, although the indorsee has other
claims upon the consignee (*m*).


## Section V.—*How exercised.*

A consignor who is desirous, and who has a right, to stop his     How
goods *in transitu*, is not obliged to make an actual seizure of   exercised.
them while upon their road; it is sufficient to give notice (*n*) to
the carrier or other person in whose hands they are, on the
delivery of which notice it becomes that person's duty *to retain
the goods;* so that if he afterwards, by mistake, deliver them to
the vendee, the vendor may bring trover for them, even against
the vendee's assignees, if he himself have become bankrupt (*o*);
and the carrier who, after the receipt of such a notice, delivers
the goods to the vendee, is guilty of a tortious act, for which
he may, of course, be held responsible (*p*). This right to stop
extends, not only to countermand delivery to the vendee, but to
require re-delivery to the vendor, who may, therefore, at once
demand the goods (*q*). The *notice* must, however, that it may

---

(1) *Selborne*, L. C., in *Kemp* v. *Falk*,
7 App. Cas. at p. 577.

(*m*) *Spalding* v. *Ruding*, 6 Beav. 376;
*Coventry* v. *Gladstone*, L. R. 6 Eq. 44;
*Ex parte Golding, Davis & Co.*, 13 Ch. D.
628.

(*n*) As to what notice will suffice,
see *Phelps Stokes* v. *Comber*, 29 Ch. D.
813.

(*o*) *Litt* v. *Cowley*, 7 Taunt. 169.

(*p*) *Stokes* v. *La Riviere* (Lord *Mansfield*), cited in *Bothlingk* v. *Inglis*, 3
East, 381; *Hunter* v. *Beale* (Lord
*Mansfield*), cited 3 T. R. 466; *Schotsmans* v. *The Lancashire and Yorkshire
Railway Co.* L. R. 1 Eq. 349; 2 Ch.
332.

(*q*) *The Tigress*, 32 L. J. Adm. 97.

be effectual, be given to the person who has the immediate
custody of the goods : if given to a principal whose servant has
such custody, it must be given at such a time, and under such
circumstances, that the principal, by the exercise of reasonable
diligence, may communicate it to his servant in time to prevent
the delivery to the consignee (r).  It has been stated by Lord
*Blackburn*, that it is the duty of the shipowner who receives such
a notice to forward it to the master (s) : " I had always myself
understood that the law was, that when you became aware that
a man, to whom you had sold goods which had been shipped,
had become insolvent, your best way, or at least a good way,
of stopping them *in transitu*, was to give notice to the shipowner in order that he might send it on.  He knew where his
master was likely to be, and he might send it on ; and I have
always been under the belief that although such a notice, if
sent, cast upon the shipowner who received it an obligation to
send it on with reasonable diligence, yet if, though he used
reasonable diligence, somehow or other the goods were delivered
before it reached, he would not be responsible.  I have always
thought that a stoppage, if effected thus, was a sufficient stoppage *in transitu*."

(r) *Whitehead* v. *Anderson*, 9 M. &      (s) *Kemp* v. *Falk*, 7 App. Cas. p.
W. 518.                                                585.

# CHAPTER II.

## LIEN.

---

SECTION I.—*Lien—what.*

A POSSESSORY lien (*a*) is a right to retain property until a debt due to the person retaining has been satisfied (*b*). It is not incompatible with a right on the part of the person claiming it to sue for the same debt; but he is allowed to do so, retaining his lien as a collateral security (*c*). There are two species of liens known to the common law, viz., *Particular* and *General*. *Particular liens* are where persons claim to retain the goods in respect of which the debt arises; and these are favoured by the law. *General liens* are claimed in respect of a general balance of account; and these are to be taken strictly (*d*). Where a lien exists, it is available, although the debt for which the party retaining claims to hold the goods be of more than six years'

*Lien—what.*

---

(*a*) Under the name of lien are included rights really diverse. Lien properly means, as the above definition states, a right to retain until the claim be satisfied. But the banker's general lien gives him a right to realise the security. His rights resemble those of a pawnee : *Donald* v. *Suckling*, L. R. 1 Q. B. at p. 604.

(*b*) *Hammond* v. *Barclay*, 2 East, at p. 235; 2 Rose, 357. In *Sunbolf* v. *Alford*, 3 M. & W. 248, an innkeeper set up a claim of lien on his guest's *person*, which was, however, negatived by the Court without hesitation, as was his claim of a right to take the guest's coat from his person and detain it.

(*c*) *Hughes* v. *Lenny*, 5 M. & W. 183.

(*d*) Per *Heath*, J. in *Houghton* v. *Matthews*, 3 B. & P. at p. 494 ; *Bock* v. *Gorrissen*, 2 De G. F. & J. 434, at p. 443.

standing, and the remedy by action at law barred in consequence by the Statute of Limitations (e). A creditor who elects to exercise his right of lien cannot exercise it as security for the expense of keeping or taking care of the property (f).

The goods, while they continue in the possession of a person entitled to a lien, cannot be seized in execution for the real owner's debt (g).


## Section II.—*How acquired.*

The doctrine of lien originated in certain principles of the common law, by which a party who was *compelled* to receive the goods of another was also entitled to retain them for his indemnity. Thus carriers (h) and innkeepers (i) had, by the common law, a lien on the goods entrusted to their charge. The rescuer of goods from perils of the sea has, as we have already remarked, on grounds of public policy, a lien at common law for salvage (j); and it is a principle, that, where an individual has bestowed labour and skill in the alteration and improvement of the properties of the subject delivered to him, he has a lien on it for his charge. Thus a miller and a shipwright (k) have each a lien; so has a trainer, for the expense of keeping and training a race-horse (l), for he has, by his instruction, wrought an essential

---

(e) *Spears* v. *Hartley*, 3 Esp. 81; *Higgins* v. *Scott*, 2 B. & Ad. 413; *Re Broomhead*, 16 L. J. Q. B. 355.

(f) *Somes* v. *British Empire Shipping Co.*, 8 H. L. Ca. 338.

(g) *Legg* v. *Evans*, 6 M. & W. 36.

(h) *Skinner* v. *Upshaw*, Ld. Raym. 752. As to lien for freight, see ante, pp. 372 *et seq.*

(i) In the case of an innkeeper, the lien is confined to the goods entrusted to his charge by his *guest: Smith* v. *Dearlove*, 6 C. B. 132; but they may belong to a third person: *Threfall* v. *Borwick*, L. R. 7 Q. B. 711; 10 Q. B. 210; *Turrill* v. *Crawley*, 13 Q. B. 197; *Snead* v. *Watkins*, 1 C. B. N. S. 267; *Allen* v. *Smith*, 12 C. B. N. S. 638. But see *Broadwood* v. *Granara*, 10 Exch.

417. As to his power to sell the goods, see infra, p. 706, n. (u).

(j) *Hingston* v. *Wendt*, 1 Q. B. D. 367.

(k) *Ex parte Ockenden*, 1 Atk. 235; *Franklin* v. *Hosier*, 4 B. & Ald. 341; and *Chase* v. *Westmore*, 6 M. & S. 180. See *Ex parte Bland*, 2 Rose, 91; *British Empire Shipping Co.* v. *Somes*, E. B. & E. 353.

(l) *Bevan* v. *Waters*, M. & M. 236; unless the usual right of the owner to run him when he pleases be inconsistent with a continuing possession of the trainer. See per *Parke*, B., in *Jackson* v. *Cummins*, 5 M. & W. at p. 350, 351; *Forth* v. *Simpson*, 13 Q. B. 680.

improvement in the animal's character and capabilities, unless by usage or contract the owner has a right inconsistent with it, as, for instance, of sending the horse to run for any race he pleases, and selecting the jockey to ride him (*m*). And if the owner of a stallion receive a mare for the purpose of being covered, he has a lien on her for his charge, for she will be rendered more valuable by proving in foal (*n*). So, too, an auctioneer and a factor have liens (though not general) on goods sold by them (*o*). But here the rule appears to stop, and not to include cases wherein expense has been bestowed upon the object claimed to be retained without producing any alteration in it ( *p* ). Thus it has been decided that a livery-stable keeper has no lien for the keep of a horse (*q*) ; nor an agister of a horse or cow (*r*) for its agistment.

Such is the description of a lien at common law. Whenever a lien of any other kind is sought to be established, the claim to it is not to be deduced from principles of common law, but founded upon the agreement of the parties, either expressed or to be inferred from usage or course of business (*s*), and will fail if some such contract be not shown to have existed (*t*).

*By special agreement.*—With respect to liens by express agreement, little need be said; the question, whether one has or has not been created, depends upon the special terms of each individual contract. Where the intention of the parties to create one is plain, there can be no doubt of their legal right to

How acquired.

---

(*m*) *Forth* v. *Simpson*, 13 Q. B. 680.

(*n*) *Scarfe* v. *Morgan*, 4 M. & W. 270.

(*o*) *Webb* v. *Smell*, 30 Ch. D. 192; *In re Hermann Loog, Limited*, W. N. (1887), 180, 191.

(*p*) *Stone* v. *Lingwood*, 1 Str. 651; and see 8 C. & P. 6; but see 1 H. Bl. 85.

(*q*) *Wallace* v. *Woodgate*, R. & M. 193; *Judson* v. *Etheridge*, 1 C. & M. 743; *Orchard* v. *Rackstraw*, 9 C. B. 698. But see *Taylor* v. *James*, 2 Roll. Abr. 92, M. pl. 3; *Lenton* v. *Cook*, B. N. P. 45. See *Sanderson* v. *Bell*, 2

C. & M. 304.

(*r*) *Jackson* v. *Cummins*, 5 M. & W. 342. An auctioneer has a lien on the goods which he sells: *Webb* v. *Smell*, 30 Ch. D. 192.

(*s*) See *Naylor* v. *Mangles*, 1 Esp. 109 ; *Kirkman* v. *Shawcross*, 6 T. R. 14. The lien of an unpaid vendor for the price subsists till delivery to the vendee: *Cooper* v. *Bill*, 3 H. & C. 722.

(*t*) *Pratt* v. *Vizard*, 5 B. & Ad. 808. See also *Ogle* v. *Story*, 4 B. & Ad. 735 ; and quære, if that case be law; see *Harrington* v. *Price*, 3 B. & Ad. 170 ; *Cumpston* v. *Haigh*, 2 Bing. N. C. 449.

carry it into effect (*u*), and, as they can deal as they please with their own property, they may, of course, frame their contract so as to exclude the right of lien, as well as to create or to extend it : and this may be done, either by direct words, or the insertion of some stipulation incompatible with the existence of a right of lien (*v*), or a similar usage or course of trade, consistent with, and incorporated by implication into, the contract (*x*). Indeed, it once was thought, that, wherever there was an agreement for the payment of a fixed sum, the right of lien must be taken to have been abandoned (*y*). But this doctrine, which seems unreasonable, has been overturned ; and the rule now is, that the mere existence of a special agreement will not, of itself, exclude the right of lien ; but that if any of its terms be inconsistent with such right, it will do so (*z*). Thus, an agreement stipulating for payment in a particular manner and out of a particular fund, might possibly be held inconsistent with the right of lien (*a*). So would an agreement to deliver goods at a certain time, or whenever demanded (*b*). Where a customer deposited with his bankers a policy of assurance accompanied by a memorandum to secure over-drafts not exceeding at any one time 4,000*l.*, it was held that the bankers might not retain the policy in respect of over-drafts in excess of the amount (*c*). Thus, too, it was remarked by Baron *Parke*, in his judg-

---

(*u*) See *Small* v. *Moates*, 9 Bing. 574 ; *Ward* v. *Bell*, 1 C. & M. 848.

(*v*) *Owenson* v. *Morse*, 7 T. R. 64 ; *Boardman* v. *Sill*, 1 Camp. 410, n. ; *Walker* v. *Birch*, 6 T. R. 258 ; *Weymouth* v. *Boyer*, 1 Ves. jun. 416. See *Lucas* v. *Nockells*, 10 Bing. 157 ; *Crawshay* v. *Homfray*, 4 B. & Ald. 50.

(*x*) *Raitt* v. *Mitchell*, 4 Camp. 146.

(*y*) *Brenan* v. *Currint*, Say. 224 ; B. N. P. 45 ; *Collins* v. *Ongley*, there cited. In *Chambers* v. *Davidson*, L. R. 1 P. C. 296, Lord *Westbury* says : "But lien is not the result of an express contract ; it is given by implication of law. If, therefore, a mercantile relation, which might involve a lien, is created by a written contract, and security given for the result of

the dealings in that relation, the express stipulation and agreement of the parties for security excludes lien, and limits their rights by the extent of the express contract that they have made. Expressum facit cessare tacitum. If a consignee takes an express security, it excludes general lien." But quære, whether these words are not too wide.

(*z*) *Chase* v. *Harrison*, 5 M. & S. 180 ; *Hutton* v. *Bragg*, 7 Taunt. 15 ; *Fisher* v. *Smith*, 4 App. Cas. 1.

(*a*) See *Pinnock* v. *Harrison*, 3 M. & W. 532.

(*b*) Lord *Selborne*, in *Fisher* v. *Smith*, 4 App. Cas. at p. 12 ; and *Crawshay* v. *Homfray*, 4 B. & Ad. 50.

(*c*) *In re Bowes*, 33 Ch. D. 586.

How
acquired.

ment in *Jackson* v. *Cummins* (*d*), that, even if a lien could
have been claimed at common law in respect of agistment
generally, it would be excluded in a case of agistment of milch
cows, by a necessary implication arising from the nature of the
subject-matter, since the owner must have possession of them
during the time of milking, which establishes that it was not
intended the agister should have the entire control. His Lordship observed that a similar implication would arise in the case
of a livery-stable keeper, since it must be his intention that the
owner of the horse should take him out; and that, even in such
a case as *Bevan* v. *Waters* (*dd*), there might be a distinction, as it
has since been held there is (*e*), between the situation of the
trainer of a horse for ordinary purposes and the trainer of a
race-horse, which, according to usage, may be taken away to run
for various plates during his training.

*By Usage or Course of Business.*—As to liens resulting from
usage, these depend upon *implied*, as those last mentioned upon
*express*, contract (*f*). The usage whence such agreement may
be implied is either the common usage of trade, or that of the
parties themselves in their previous dealings with each other (*g*).
Of this description are most general liens, none of which existed
at common law, but all depend upon the agreement of the
parties themselves, either expressed, or to be inferred from their
previous dealings, or from the usage of trade and the decisions
of the courts of law thereon (*h*). It has been settled, that an
attorney has a lien for his general balance on papers of his
clients, which come to his hands in the course of his professional
employment (*i*). So a banker, who has advanced money to a

(*d*) 5 M. & W. at pp. 350, 351.

(*dd*) M. & M. 236.

(*e*) *Forth* v. *Simpson*, 13 Q. B. 680.

(*f*) *Rushworth* v. *Hadfield*, 6 East, 519; 7 East, 224; *Kirkman* v. *Shawcross*, 6 T. R. 14; *Brandao*, v. *Barnett* 12 Cl. & F. 787.

(*g*) *Holderness* v. *Collinson*, 7 B. & C. 212; *Ex parte Ockenden*, 1 Atk. 235; *Kirkman* v. *Shawcross*, 6 T. R. 14; *In re Spotten*, 11 Ir. Rep. Eq. 412.

(*h*) See *Leuckhart* v. *Cooper*, 3 Bing. N. C. 99, in which defendant claimed a lien by the custom of London, which was, however, held to be unreasonable: *Bock* v. *Gorrissen*, 30 L. J. Ch. 39.

(*i*) *Stevenson* v. *Blacklock*, 1 M. & S. 535. If he be the town-clerk of a corporation, or steward of a manor, he will have a lien for work done in his *professional*, though not for work done in his *official*, capacity: *Rex* v.

customer, has a lien for his general balance upon securities belonging to such customer, which come into his hands (*k*), but not on muniments pledged for a specific sum (*l*), or deposited for a defined purpose (*m*), or left by mistake or casually in the banker's possession, after his own refusal to advance money on them (*n*), or negotiable instruments belonging to a third person, left in the banker's hands by his customer (*o*), or locked-up boxes left for safe custody, though containing securities (*p*). The lien belongs to the bankers as such; it does not therefore extend to articles received not by them as such, but as gratuitous bailees or otherwise (*q*). Packers (*r*), calico-printers (*s*), and wharfingers (*t*), have liens for their general balance, but not fullers (*u*), millers (*v*), or dyers (*w*).

However, notwithstanding these decisions, it does not appear certain that the right of lien may not, even with respect to some of the above trades, be hereafter contested, for the Court has remarked, with respect to wharfingers, that there may be a usage in one place varying from that which prevails in another (*x*). The party, therefore, claiming to retain goods for a general balance, should, in almost every instance, be prepared

*Sankey,* 5 Ad. & E. 423; *Worrall v. Johnson,* 2 J. & W. 214; *Newington Local Board* v. *Eldridge,* 12 Ch. D. 349.

(*k*) *London Chartered Bank of Australia* v. *White,* 4 App. Cas. 413; *Brandao* v. *Barnett,* 12 Cl. & F. 787; *In re United Service Co.,* L. R. 6 Ch. 217; *Marten* v. *Roche,* 53 L. T. 946; *Roxburghe* v. *Cox,* 17 Ch. D. 520.

(*l*) *Vanderzee* v. *Willis,* 3 Bro. C. C. 21; *Wolstenholm* v. *Sheffield Banking Co.,* 54 L. T. N. S. 746.

(*m*) *In re Bowes,* 33 Ch. D. 586; *Wolstenholm* v. *Sheffield Banking Co.,* 54 L. T. 746.

(*n*) *Lucas* v. *Dorrein,* 7 Taunt. 278.

(*o*) *Brandao* v. *Barnett,* 12 C. & F. 787.

(*p*) *Leese* v. *Martin,* L. R. 17 Eq. 224; *Giblin* v. *McMullen,* L. R. 2 P. C. 317.

(*q*) See judgment of Lord *Campbell*

in *Brandao* v. *Barnett,* 12 C. & F. at p. 809; *Leese* v. *Martin,* L. R. 17 Eq. 224.

(*r*) *Ex parte Deeze,* 1 Atk. 228; *In re Witt,* 2 Ch. D. 489.

(*s*) *Weldon* v. *Gould,* 3 Esp. 268.

(*t*) *Naylor* v. *Mangles,* 1 Esp. 109; *Spears* v. *Hartly,* 3 Esp. 81; *Dresser* v. *Bosanquet,* 4 B. & S. 460; *Moet* v. *Pickering,* 8 Ch. D. 372. The lien of wharfingers was said by Lord *Kenyon,* in *Naylor* v. *Mangles,* to have been proved so often that it was a settled point.

(*u*) *Rose* v. *Hart,* 8 Taunt. 499; 2 Moore, 547.

(*v*) *Ex parte Ockenden,* 1 Atk. 235.

(*w*) *Green* v. *Farmer,* 4 Burr. 2214; *Close* v. *Waterhouse,* 6 East, 523, n.; *Bennett* v. *Johnson,* 2 Chitty, 455; but see *Savill* v. *Barchard,* 4 Esp. 53.

(*x*) *Holderness* v. *Collinson,* 7 B. & C. 212.

with evidence of the usage applicable to his own case. It is, however, established too well for dispute that a factor has a lien upon all goods in his hands, *as factor* (y), for the balance of his general account (z), whether or not he be authorized to sell in his own name or has any discretion as to the price (a). His lien extends to the *price* of goods with the possession of which he has parted. Thus, where A. consigned goods to B. a factor, to whom he owed more than their value, and B. sold them to C., to whom he was himself indebted, the factor having become bankrupt, it was decided that he had a lien on the whole price due from C., which must consequently be placed to the credit of his assignees in winding up his account with C., and that A. was not entitled to any portion of it (b). But a factor has not a lien for debts which accrued before his character as such commenced (c). Policy brokers have also a general lien, and may avail themselves of it to obtain payment of the balance due to them from their employer, though he be merely an agent, if he did not disclose his principal (d), but not if they know, or there is enough to indicate to them, his representative character (e).

In *Mildred* v. *Maspons* (f), the appellants, merchants in London, acting upon instructions of shipping agents at Havannah, effected policies of insurance on a cargo of tobacco for all whom it might concern. The Havannah agents shipped and consigned

(y) *Dixon* v. *Stansfield*, 10 C. B. 398.

(z) *Houghton* v. *Matthews*, 3 B. & P. 485; *Kruger* v. *Wilcox*, Ambler, 252; *Gardiner* v. *Coleman*, cited 1 Burr. 494; 6 East, 28, n.; *Man* v. *Shiffner*, 2 East, 523.

(a) *Stevens* v. *Biller*, 25 Ch. D. 31.

(b) *Hudson* v. *Granger*, 5 B. & Ald. 27. See *Drinkwater* v. *Goodwin*, Cowp. 251, and ante, Book i. Ch. 4.

(c) *Houghton* v. *Matthews*, 3 B. & P. 485. See *Walker* v. *Birch*, 6 T. R. 258, per *Lawrence*, J.; *Olive* v. *Smith*, 5 Taunt. 56; *Weldon* v. *Gould*, 3 Esp. 268.

(d) *Mann* v. *Forrester*, 4 Camp. 60; *Westwood* v. *Bell*, Id. 349; *Bell* v. *Jutting*, 1 Moore, 155.

(e) *Maans* v. *Henderson*, 1 East, 335; *Snook* v. *Davidson*, 2 Camp. 218; *Sweeting* v. *Pearce*, 7 C. B. N. S. 449. See *Man* v. *Shiffner*, 2 East, 523, 529, where a broker employed by a factor to insure, was held to have a lien on the policy to the extent of the factor's balance against his principal; this was on the ground that the factor had a lien, and that the broker might be considered his servant to retain the goods. See *M'Combie* v. *Davies*, 7 East, 5. Therefore, the right of a sub-agent to retain against the principal can never extend beyond that of the immediate agent: *Solly* v. *Rathbone*, 2 M. & S. 298. See *Jackson* v. *Clarke*, 1 Y. & J. 216.

(f) 8 App. Cas. 874.

How<br>
acquired.

the tobacco in their own names, but they were in fact commission agents for Havannah merchants to whom the tobacco
belonged.  The plaintiffs, who had notice that the Havannah
agents had unnamed principals, were held not entitled to a
general lien on the policy money in their hands for the balance
of their general account with the Havannah agents.  "On this
question," said the Court of Appeal, referring to *McFarlane*
v. *Norris* (*g*), and *Meyer* v. *Dresser* (*h*), " according to our law
the right of the defendants to a lien or set-off depends on a
question of fact—viz., whether the defendants did or did not
know that Demestre & Co. (the Havannah agents) were acting
for an undisclosed principal before the defendants' alleged lien
or right of set-off accrued " (*i*).

Where a general lien is claimed by carriers founded on the
usage of trade, strong evidence of the usage is required (*j*).


## SECTION III.—*How Lost.*

How lost

As a possessory lien is a right to *retain* possession, it follows
of course that where there is no possession there can be no
lien (*k*).  It also follows, that, where the possession of the goods
has once been abandoned, the lien is gone; but when the master
of a ship, in obedience to revenue regulations, lands goods at a
particular wharf or dock, he does not thereby lose his lien on
them for the freight (*l*), and, where they are not required to
be landed at any particular dock, the common practice is to

---

(*g*) 2 B. & S. 783.

(*h*) 16 C. B. N. S. 646, at p. 665.

(*i*) *Maspons* v. *Mildred*, 9 Q. B. D.
530, at p. 543.  Lord *Blackburn*, with
reference to the same case in the House
of Lords (8 App. Cas. at p. 885), sug-
gests that the Factors Act of 1823 (4
Geo. 4, c. 83), s. 1, may have modified
the rule as to consignees, so that knowledge, however obtained, that the
goods were not the property of the
person dealing with them would not
necessarily deprive the agent of his
lien.

(*j*) *Rushforth* v. *Hadfield*, 6 East,
519; 7 East, 224; *Holderness* v. *Collinson*, 7 B. & C. 212; *Wright* v. *Enell*,
5 B. & Ald. 350; *Butler* v. *Woolcott*,
2 B. & P. 6; but see *Aspinall* v. *Pickford*, 3 B. & P. 44, n. (*a*).

(*k*) *Hutton* v. *Bragg*, 7 Taunt. 14;
*Kruger* v. *Wilcox*, Amb. 254; 1 Burr.
494; *Sweet* v. *Pym*, 1 East, 4.  The
peculiarity, in this respect, of a vendor's lien, if it can properly be so
called, for his price, has been treated
of in the last chapter.

(*l*) *Wilson* v. *Kymer*, 1 M. & S. 157.

land them at a public wharf and direct the wharfinger not to part with them till the charges upon them are paid (*m*) ; in this case the wharfinger is the shipmaster's agent, and the goods remain in the constructive possession of the latter: the Merchant Shipping Act, 1862, s. 67, directs what course the shipowner is to follow (*n*). But, otherwise, the rule concerning possession is so strict, that if a party having a lien on goods cause them to be taken in execution at his own suit and purchase them, he so alters the nature of the possession that his lien is destroyed, though the goods may never have left his premises (*o*). And if, when the goods are demanded from him, he claim to retain them on some different ground, and make no mention of his lien, he will be considered as having waived it, and the owner of the goods may sue him without tendering a satisfaction for the debt which created his lien (*p*). For it is to be remembered that in all cases the owner of the goods, on tendering such satisfaction, has a right to his property ; and if the creditor refuse after such tender to restore it, he does so at his peril, for if the tender were sufficient in amount, he is a wrongdoer, and answerable for his misconduct in an action (*q*). Nor, indeed, is an actual tender strictly so called necessary, if the person in whose possession the goods are have signified his refusal to accept the amount really due (*r*). Moreover, the possession must be *lawful*. A creditor cannot tortiously seize upon his debtor's goods and then claim to retain them by virtue of a lien (*s*); so if he abuse the

(*m*) Abbott on Shipping, 323, 12th ed.; Carver on Carriage by Sea, s. 475 ; *Mors-le-Blanch* v. *Wilson*, L. R. 8 C. P. 227.

(*n*) See Appendix.

(*o*) *Jacobs* v. *Latour*, 5 Bing. 130.

(*p*) *Boardman* v. *Sill*, 1 Camp. 410, n.; accord. *Weeks* v. *Coode*, 6 C. B. N. S. 367. And see *Knight* v. *Harrison*, 2 Saund. on Pl. and Evidence, 641, and *Thompson* v. *Trail*, 6 B. & C. 36; *Jones* v. *Tarleton*, 9 M. & W. 675 ; *Dirks* v. *Richards*, 4 M. & G. 574 ; *Caunce* v. *Spanton*, 7 M. & G. 903.

(*q*) *Chilton* v. *Carrington*, 16 C. B. 206 ; and the owner paying the over-charge under protest may recover it : *Somes* v. *British E. S. Co.*, 8 H. L. Ca. 338.

(*r*) *Jones* v. *Tarleton*, 9 M. & W. 675 ; *The Norway*, Brown. & Lush. 377, 404.

(*s*) *Taylor* v. *Robinson*, 2 Moore, 730. So it would seem from the judgment in *Sanderson* v. *Bell*, 2 C. & M. 304, that, if he claim a lien of too large a description, the whole detainer becomes tortious, though he really possesses one of a narrower description. But *Scarfe* v. *Morgan*, 4 M. & W. 270, is contrary to this notion. As to whether an excessive

How lost. goods, as, for instance, by selling or pledging them, his lien is forfeited (t). In the case of a simple lien there is no power of sale or disposition of the goods; whereas, in the case of a pledge or pawn of goods, to secure the payment of money at a certain day, the pawnee, on default by the pawnor, may sell the goods deposited, realize the amount, and become a trustee for the overplus for the pawnor. Even if no day of payment be named, he may, upon waiting a reasonable time, and taking the proper steps, realize his debt in like manner (u).

A right of lien is not, however, determined by an alteration in the property of the goods over which it is exercised (v). Thus, where the lading of a ship belongs to the charterer, and such lading is subject to the shipowner's lien for the freight reserved by the charterparty, such lading, if it be sold by the charterer, after it is put on board, will pass to the purchaser, subject to the lien which the shipowner had before the sale (x).

If a security is taken for the debt for which the party has a lien upon the property of the debtor, such security being payable at a distant day, the lien is gone (y). So, too, if the parties come to a new arrangement and agree that the debt shall be paid in a particular manner. But it is doubtful whether the taking of a security not in its nature inconsistent with the existence of a lien will destroy a lien (z). A mere right of set-off to an amount equal to that for which the lien

claim will dispense with a tender, see *Allen* v. *Smith*, 12 C. B. N. S. 638.

(t) *Johnson* v. *Stear*, 15 C. B. N. S. 330; *Scott* v. *Newington*, 1 M. & Rob. 252; *Jones* v. *Cliff*, 1 C. & M. 540. As to the difference between a lien and a pledge, in this respect, see *Donald* v. *Suckling*, L. R. 1 Q. B. 585; *Halliday* v. *Holgate*, L. R. 3 Exch. 299.

(u) *Thames Ironworks Co.* v. *Patent Derrick Co.*, 1 J. & H. 93. Innkeepers, by 41 & 42 Vict. c. 38, have the right to sell goods upon which they have a lien.

(v) *Small* v. *Moates*, 9 Bing. 574; *Dixon* v. *Yates*, 5 B. & Ad. 313.

(x) *Mitchell* v. *Scaife*, 4 Camp. 298; *Small* v. *Moates*, 9 Bing. 574, at p. 592. But see, when bills of lading are given at a different rate of freight, *Gilkison* v. *Middleton*, 2 C. B. N. S. 134; but as to the latter case, see *Kirchner* v. *Venus*, 12 Moo. P. C. Ca. 361.

(y) *Hewison* v. *Guthrie*, 2 Bing. N. C. 755; or if the creditor executes a composition deed which includes a release of the original debt without a reserve of the lien, the lien is gone: *Cowper* v. *Green*, 7 M. & W. 633; *Buck* v. *Shippam*, 1 Phillips, 694.

(z) *Angus* v. *McLachlan*, 23 Ch. D. 330.

is claimed does not destroy it, for in that case there are two
parties having mutual claims on one another, with this difference, that one has a security and the other has not; and, in the
absence of special agreement to that effect, it would be obviously
unjust to deprive the former of his advantage (a).

## Section IV.—*Maritime Liens.*

A maritime lien does not, like a lien at common law, depend
upon the possession by the party asserting it of the thing in
respect of which the claim arises (b). It is the right to enforce
by action in the Admiralty Courts a claim against the *res*. It
exists in the case of bottomry (c), claims for salvage (d), for
damage done by collision (e), and for wages of seamen (f).
Material men, or persons who have supplied necessaries to a
ship, have no maritime lien on the ship (h). But they may
take proceedings *in rem* under 3 & 4 Vict. c. 65, s. 6, against
the ship. The difference is thus explained in the judgment
of the Court of Appeal in *The Heinrich Bjorn* (i) :—

"But if the material man may thus arrest the property to enforce
his claim, how does his claim differ from a maritime lien? The
answer is, that a maritime lien arises the moment the event occurs
which creates it; the proceeding *in rem* which perfects the inchoate
right relates back to the period when it first attached; the maritime
lien travels with the thing into whosesoever possession it may come

---

(a) See *Pinnock* v. *Harrison*, 3 M. &
W. 532; *Clarke* v. *Fell*, 4 B. & Ad.
at p. 408. See *Roxburghe* v. *Cox*, 17
Ch. D. 520.

(b) *The Cella*, 57 L. J. Adm. at p. 56;
13 P. D. at p. 87, per Lord *Esher*,
M. R.

(c) *The Royal Arch*, Swab. 269. See
*The Druid*, 1 W. Rob. at p. 399.

(d) *The Gustaf*, Lush. 506.

(e) *The Bold Buccleugh*, 7 Moo. P.
C. 267; *The Charles Amelia*, L. R.
2 A. & E. 330.

(f) *The Neptune*, 1 Hagg. at p. 238.
See as to the master's wages, 17 & 18
Vict. c. 104, s. 191. Now by 52 & 53

Vict. c. 46, s. 1, the master, "and
every person lawfully acting as master
by reason of the decease or incapacity from illness of the master,"
have "the same rights, liens, and
remedies for the recovery of disbursements and liabilities properly incurred by him on account of the ship
as the master has for the recovery of
his wages." This alters the law as
laid down in *The Sara*, 14 App. Cas.
209.

(h) *The Heinrich Bjorn*, 11 App. Cas.
270.

(i) 10 P. D. at p. 54; affirmed, 11
App. Cas. 270.

(*The Bold Buccleugh* (*k*)), and the arrest can extend only to the ship subject to the lien. But, on the contrary, the arrest of a vessel under the statute is only one of several possible alternative proceedings *ad fundandam jurisdictionem;* no right in the ship or against the ship is created at any time before the arrest; it has no relation back to any earlier period; it is available only against the property of the person who owes the debt for necessaries, and the arrest need not be of the ship in question, but may be of any property of the defendant within the realm. The two proceedings, therefore, though approaching one another in form, are different in substance; in the one case, the arrest is to give effect to a pre-existent lien; in the other, the arrest is only one of several alternative modes of procedure, because, to use the language of Dr. *Lushington* in *The Volant* (*l*), 'it offers the greatest security for obtaining substantial justice in furnishing a security for prompt and immediate payment.' "

A maritime lien attaches to the *res* as soon as the act is done which gives rise to the claim, and prevails against subsequent purchasers, mortgagees, judgment creditors, or persons into whose possession the ship may afterwards come (*m*).

"The position of a creditor who has a proper maritime lien differs from that of a creditor in an unsecured claim in this respect, that the former, unless he has forfeited the right by his own laches, can proceed against the ship notwithstanding any change in her ownership, whereas the latter cannot have an action *in rem*, unless at the time of its institution the *res* is the property of his debtor " (*n*).

The lien may, as above stated, be lost by laches on the part of the person claiming it (*o*).

(*k*) 7 Moo. P. C. 267, 284, 285.

(l) 1 Wm. Rob. 383.

(*m*) *The Mellona*, 3 W. Rob. at p. 21 ; *The Charles Amelia*, supra. See *The Bold Buccleugh*, supra.

(*n*) *The Heinrich Björn*, 11 App. Cas. at p. 277, per Lord *Watson*. But where the unsecured creditor has brought an action *in rem*, and the ship has been arrested by the Admiralty Court, the ship is held by the Court as a security for whatever may be found to be due to the creditors. See *The Cella*, supra.

(*o*) See *The Bold Buccleugh*, supra.

# CHAPTER III.

## BANKRUPTCY.

---

PRIOR to 1861 only traders were subject to the bankruptcy Bankruptcy. laws. The Bankruptcy Acts of 1861 and 1869 (*a*) subjected non-traders under certain circumstances to their operation, and the Bankruptcy Act, 1883 (*b*), has removed all distinctions

---

(*a*) 24 & 25 Vict. c. 134; 32 & 33     (*b*) 46 & 47 Vict. c. 52.
Vict. c. 71.

Bankruptcy. between traders and non-traders, as regards liability to be made
bankrupt. It is proposed to consider briefly the law of bankruptcy in the order of topics mentioned at the head of this
chapter.

SECTION I.—Who may be a Bankrupt.

Who may be
a bankrupt.　　Any person whatever, who is capable of binding himself by
contracts, as for instance, a person having privilege of parliament (c), a clergyman (d), a public officer, a foreigner who is
domiciled in England, or who, within a year before the date of
the presentation of the petition, ordinarily resided or had a
dwelling-house or place of business there (f), and a convicted
felon (g), may become bankrupt.

An infant can be made bankrupt only, if at all, in respect of
debts for necessaries (h). Formerly a married woman could
have been made bankrupt only if she were a sole trader by the
custom of the City of London, or if her husband were a convict (i), or when she could otherwise have been sued personally
as if a *feme sole*. But now, by virtue of the Married Women's
Property Act, 1882, if she carry on a trade separately from
her husband, in respect of her separate property (k), she is
subject to the bankruptcy laws in the same way as if she were
a *feme sole* (l). Apparently a lunatic may be made bankrupt,
since he may act for all the purposes of the Act by his com-

---

(c) B. A. 1883, s. 124; *Re Duke of
Newcastle*, L. R. 5 Ch. 172; and as to
the disqualifications resulting from
adjudication, s. 32 (1).

(d) *Ex parte Meymot*, 1 Atk. 196;
*Cobb* v. *Symonds*, 5 B. & Ald. 516. As
to sequestration of benefice, s. 52.

(f) *Re Mitchell*, 13 Q. B. D. 418;
*Re Barne*, 16 Q. B. D. 522.

(g) *Ex parte Graves*, *Re Harris*, 19
Ch. D. 1.

(h) 37 & 38 Vict. c. 62. See *Ex
parte Kibble*, *Re Onslow*, L. R. 10 Ch.
373; *Ex parte Jones*, 18 Ch. D. 109.

(i) *Lavie* v. *Phillips*, 3 Bur. 1776;

*Ex parte Franks*, 7 Bing. 762.

(k) "Separate property" does not
include an unexercised power of appointment: *Ex parte Gilchrist, In re
Armstrong*, 17 Q. B. D. 521.

(l) 45 & 46 Vict. c. 75, s. 1, sub-s. 5;
B. A. 1883, s. 152. See *Ex parte
Gilchrist, In re Armstrong*, supra.
But a married woman cannot be com-
mitted to prison under sect. 5 of the
Debtors Act, 1869, for non-payment
of a judgment recovered against her in
an action under the Married Women's
Property Act: *In re Morley, Ex parte
Morley*, 4 Morrell, 286.

mittee or *curator bonis*, and in the case of a lunatic not so Who may be a bankrupt.
found by inquisition the Court may appoint a person to act
for him (*m*).


SECTION II.—*How a Person may become Bankrupt.*

Any person indebted may become a bankrupt by committing How a person may become bankrupt.
one of the acts which the law has denominated *acts of bank-*
*ruptcy* (*n*).   These we will now enumerate in the order in which
they occur in the statute (*o*).   A debtor commits an act of
bankruptcy—

(a) If in England or elsewhere he makes a conveyance or assign- Acts of bankruptcy.
ment of his property to a trustee or trustees for the benefit of his
creditors generally.

This sub-section seems to contemplate a conveyance of the
whole of the debtor's property, which has always been held an
act of bankruptcy (*p*).   The conveyance may be executed
abroad, but it must be intended to operate according to English
law (*q*).

It has been long since held that an assignment of the whole
property, or of the whole with some exception merely nominal
and insufficient to prevent insolvency, for the benefit of one or
more of the creditors to the exclusion of the rest, upon account
of a bygone and before-contracted debt, carries in itself evidence
of fraud, and is an act of bankruptcy (*r*).   So far did this doctrine

---

(*m*) B. A. 1883, s. 148; B. R. 1886, r. 271; *Ex parte Cahen*, 10 Ch. D. 183; *Re Lee*, 23 Ch. D. 216; *Re James*, 12 Q. B. D. 332.

(*n*) See as to the distinction between acts which are necessarily acts of bankruptcy, and acts which are so when coupled with an intent, *Mellish*, L. J., in *Re Wood*, L. R. 7 Ch. at p. 306; *Ex parte Chaplin*, 26 Ch. D. 319.

(*o*) B. A. 1883, s. 4.

(*p*) *Kettle* v. *Hammond*, Cooke, 86; *Ex parte Alsop*, 29 L. J. Bank. 7.

(*q*) *Ex parte Crispin*, L. R. 8 Ch. 374.   Evidence may be given of such

an assignment, though not stamped in accordance with the Bankruptcy Act, 1877, s. 5.   *In re Hollingshead*, 6 Morrell, 66.

(*r*) *Worsley* v. *De Mattos*, 1 Burr. 467; *Re Wood*, *Ex parte Lückes*, L. R. 7 Ch. 302; *Ex parte Hawker*, *Re Keely*, L. R. 7 Ch. 214; *Smith* v. *Cannan*, 2 E. & B. 35; *Oriental Bank* v. *Coleman*, 30 L. J. Ch. 635; *Woodhouse* v. *Murray*, L. R. 2 Q. B. 634; 4 Q. B. 27; *Ex parte Foxley*, L. R. 3 Ch. 515; *Young* v. *Fletcher*, 3 H. & C. 732; *Ex parte Trevor*, 1 Ch. D. 297; *Ex parte Burton*, 13 Ch. D. 102.

extend, that if a debtor conveyed his property to trustees, such conveyance, though it were for the benefit of all his creditors, and had never passed out of the debtor's hands (s), was an act of bankruptcy (t); nor would such its effect be prevented·by the fact of its non-execution by the trustees (u); if, however, it could not operate at all till executed by three persons, it was not an act of bankruptcy when executed only by one, though, when it operated immediately as to that one, it constituted an act of bankruptcy by him (x). The transfer must convey, or purport to convey, an interest to the transferee (y). Neither a creditor who has executed, or been privy to, or acted under, such a deed, nor any person as his representative, can afterwards set it up as an act of bankruptcy (z). Such an assignment for a present consideration—*e.g.*, an advance of money—is not void, unless a fraudulent intent is proved (a).

An assignment of part of a debtor's effects, even on account of a bygone and before-contracted debt, does not, like an assignment of the whole, carry with it any intrinsic evidence of fraud; since everybody must, in the course of business, have power to make over some part of his property to creditors (b). But though not fraudulent or void *per se*, yet if made in contemplation of bankruptcy, and with an intent to give the transferee an undue advantage over other creditors, it is fraudulent and void (c).

It is to be observed that all the cases, without a single exception, where the assignment of his property by a debtor has

(s) *Botcherby* v. *Lancaster*, 1 Ad. & E. 77.

(t) *Kettle* v. *Hammond*, Co. B. L. 90; *Eckhardt* v. *Wilson*, 8 T. R. 140; *Stewart* v. *Moody*, 1 C. M. & R. 777; *Bowker* v. *Burdekin*, 11 M. & W. 128.

(u) *Simpson* v. *Sikes*, 6 M. & S. 295.

(x) *Dutton* v. *Morrison*, 17 Ves. 190; *Bowker* v. *Burdekin*, 11 M. & W. 128; *Bannatyne* v. *Leader*, 10 Sim. 350.

(y) *Isitt* v. *Beeston*, L. R. 4 Ex. 159.

(z) *Ex parte Stray*, L. R. 2 Ch. 374; *Bamford* v. *Baron*, 2 T. R. 594, n.; *Ex parte Cawkell*, 1 Rose, 313; *Ex parte*

*Crawford*, 1 Christ. 137, 182; *Ex parte Shaw*, 1 Madd. 598; *Ex parte Kilner*, Buck, 104; *Ex parte Tealdi*, 1 M. D. & De G. 210; *Marshall* v. *Barkworth*, 4 B. & Ad. 508.

(a) *Golden* v. *Gillam*, 20 Ch. D. 389.

(b) *Hale* v. *Allnutt*, 18 C. B. 505; *Smith* v. *Timms*, 1 H. & C. 849; *Edwards* v. *Glyn*, 28 L. J. Q. B. 350; *Dills* v. *Smith*, 34 L. J. Q. B. 68.

(c) *Ex parte Pearson, Re Mortimer*, L. R. 8 Ch. 667; *Lacon* v. *Liffen*, 32 L. J. Ch. 315.

been deemed fraudulent and an act of bankruptcy, are cases
where the assignment was made, either without consideration, or
for a *bygone* and before-contracted debt. But it is clear that a
trader may *sell* the whole, or any part, of his stock, to a fair
and *bonâ fide* purchaser, without thereby committing an act of
bankruptcy. Nay, even though the intention of the debtor
when he sells be to abscond and carry off the purchase-money,
still, if the purchaser was not aware of that intent, but dealt
fairly and *bonâ fide*, such sale is not an act of bankruptcy (d).
And an assignment by a debtor of all his effects, executed to
secure a bygone debt in consideration of an advance (e) by a
person lending *bonâ fide* or agreeing *bonâ fide* to make advances
or any fair present equivalent, with the object of enabling the
debtor to continue his business (f), would be supported on the
like grounds. So, too, would a *bonâ fide* sale of goods, though
the proceeds of the sale were used in making a voluntary payment (g).

(b) If in England or elsewhere he makes a fraudulent conveyance, gift, delivery, or transfer of his property, or of any part
thereof.

A conveyance, gift, delivery, or transfer, if fraudulent, which
we observe it must be to constitute an act of bankruptcy within
this section, is either fraudulent within stat. 13 Eliz. c. 5, or
fraudulent on account of its contravening the policy of the
bankrupt laws, which seeks, as we must recollect, the equal
distribution of the bankrupt's property among his creditors.

How a person may become bankrupt.
<hr>
Acts of bank-ruptcy.

---

(d) *Harwood* v. *Bartlett*, 6 Bing. N. C. 61.

(e) *Lomax* v. *Buxton*, L. R. 6 C. P. 107; *Ex parte Snowball*, L. R. 7 Ch. 534; *Ex parte Norton*, L. R. 16 Eq. 397; *Whitmore* v. *Claridge*, 33 L. J. Q. B. 87 (Exch. Ch.); *Mercer* v. *Peterson*, L. R. 2 Ex. 304; 3 Ex. 104; *Pennell* v. *Reynolds*, 11 C. B. N. S. 709; *Baxter* v. *Pritchard*, 1 Ad. & E. 456; *Rose* v. *Haycock*, Id. 460; *Bittlestone* v. *Cook*, 6 E. & B. 296; *Carr* v. *Burdiss*, 1 C. M. & R. 443; *Whitwell* v. *Thompson*, 1 Esp. 68; *Ex parte Izard*, L. R. 9 Ch. 271; *Ex parte Ellis*, 2 Ch. D. 797; *Ex parte Winder*, 1 Ch. D. 290; *Ex parte King*, 2 Ch. D. 256.

(f) *Ex parte Reed*, L. R. 14 Eq. 586; *Ex parte Sheen*, 1 Ch. D. 560; *Ex parte Wilkinson*, *Re Berry*, 22 Ch. D. 788; *Ex parte Johnson*, *Re Chapman*, 26 Ch. D. 338; *Ex parte Stubbins*, *Re Wilkinson*, 17 Ch. D. 58; *Ex parte Hauxwell*, *Re Hemingway*, 23 Ch. D. 626; *Ex parte Chaplin*, *Re Sinclair*, 26 Ch. D. 319.

(g) *Ex parte Stubbins*, 17 Ch. D. 58; *Ex parte Helder*, 24 Ch. D. 339.

How a person may become bankrupt.

Acts of bank-ruptcy.

With respect to the cases on the statute of Elizabeth, they depend each on its own particular circumstances. Where there has been a transfer or assignment of goods, but the transferor or assignor continues in possession of them after such transfer or assignment, that is a badge or evidence of fraud if the continuance of possession be inconsistent with the purport of the assignment (*h*); and it was once held by Lord *Ellenborough* that the transferor remaining in possession, even concurrently with the transferee, would be a mark of fraud (*i*). However, the want of transfer of possession, though evidence, is in no case conclusive evidence of fraud (*k*), and, if consistent with the purport of the assignment, seems not to warrant any imputation thereof (*l*). And there are many other ways of rebutting the imputation of fraud; *e.g.*, if the assignment to the transferee take place under circumstances of such notoriety as occur at a sheriff's sale (*m*), or at an auction (*n*). In short, though there is always reason for suspicion where an assignor who is under pecuniary embarrassments remains in possession of the property assigned, such suspicion of fraud is open to be rebutted, and if it can be rebutted, the assignment is not void (*o*). We shall, however, presently see that property in this situation may become lost to the transferee and pass to the bankrupt's trustee upon another ground, namely, that of its

---

(*h*) *Twyne's Case*, 3 Rep. 80 b; 1 Smith, L. C. 1; *Edwards* v. *Harben*, 2 T. R. 587; *Freeman* v. *Pope*, L. R. 5 Ch. 538; *Mackay* v. *Douglas*, L. R. 14 Eq. 106; *Ex parte Mercer*, *Re Wise*, 17 Q. B. D. 290; *Taylor* v. *Coenen*, 1 Ch. D. 636; *Ex parte Stephens*, *Re Pearson*, 3 Ch. D. 807; *Spenser* v. *Slater*, 4 Q. B. D. 13; *Boldero* v. *London and Westminster Discount Co.*, 5 Ex. D. 47; *Re Ridler*, *Ridler* v. *Ridler*, 22 Ch. D. 74.

(*i*) *Wordall* v. *Smith*, 1 Camp. 332. But see *Benton* v. *Thornhill*, 7 Taunt. 149; *Latimer* v. *Batson*, 4 B. & C. 652; *Eastwood* v. *Brown*, R. & M. 312.

(*k*) *Martindale* v. *Booth*, 3 B. & Ad.

498; *Carr* v. *Burdiss*, 1 C. M. & R. 782.

(*l*) *Martindale* v. *Booth*, ubi sup.; *Reed* v. *Wilmot*, 7 Bing. 577. See B. N. P. 258; *Steele* v. *Brown*, 1 Taunt. 381. See *Spackman* v. *Miller*, 12 C. B. N. S. 659.

(*m*) *Kidd* v. *Rawlinson*, 2 B. & P. 59; *Watkins* v. *Birch*, 4 Taunt. 823; *Latimer* v. *Batson*, 4 B. & C. 652. See *Willies* v. *Farley*, 3 C. & P. 395.

(*n*) *Leonard* v. *Baker*, 1 M. & S. 251; *Jezeph* v. *Ingram*, 1 Moore, 189. See *Guthrie* v. *Wood*, 1 Stark. 367.

(*o*) See *Eastwood* v. *Brown*, R. & M. 312; *Hoffman* v. *Pitt*, 5 Esp. 22; *Benton* v. *Thornhill*, 7 Taunt. 149; *Manton* v. *Moore*, 7 T. R. 67.

being in his possession, order, or disposition at the time of bankruptcy.

Generally speaking, a debtor has, at common law, a right to prefer one creditor to another (*p*); and therefore, though an assignment by a debtor of all his effects, or of all with a nominal exception, to a creditor is void and an act of bankruptcy, on the ground of its contravening the policy of the bankruptcy law, yet it would not be necessarily void under the Statute of Elizabeth (*q*); and we shall see that an assignment of *part* of his property to a creditor is good, unless the debtor made it voluntarily and in contemplation of bankruptcy.

*How a person may become bankrupt.*

*Acts of bankruptcy.*

(c) If in England or elsewhere he makes any conveyance or transfer of his property or any part thereof, or creates any charge thereon which would, under this or any other Act, be void as a fraudulent preference if he were adjudged bankrupt.

Sect. 48 (1) thus defines a fraudulent preference:

" Every conveyance or transfer of property, or charge thereon made, every payment made, every obligation incurred, and every judicial proceeding taken or suffered by any person unable to pay his debts as they become due from his own money in favour of any creditor, or any person in trust for any creditor, with a view of giving such creditor a preference over the other creditors, shall, if the person making, taking, paying, or suffering the same is adjudged bankrupt on a bankruptcy petition presented within three months after the date of making, taking, paying, or suffering the same, be deemed fraudulent and void as against the trustee in bankruptcy."

To constitute a fraudulent preference, the conveyance must have been made by a person unable to pay his debts as they become due from his own money, with a view of giving his creditor (or some person in trust for him) a preference over the other creditors, and it must have been made within three months prior to the presentation of the petition on which he has been

---

(*p*) *Pickstock* v. *Lyster*, 3 M. & S. 371; *Holbird* v. *Anderson*, 5 T. R. 235; *Meux* v. *Howell*, 4 East, 1; *Estwick* v. *Caillaud*, 5 T. R. 420; *Bowen* v. *Bramidge*, 6 C. & P. 140. See s. 48.

(*q*) *Alton* v. *Harrison*, L. R. 4 Ch. 622; *Ex parte Games, Re Bamford*, 12 Ch. D. 314.

**How a person may become bankrupt.**

---

**Acts of bankruptcy.**

adjudged bankrupt (*r*). The person preferring must, therefore, have been insolvent at the time of making the preference, and must have had a view to prefer (*s*), which seems to imply a voluntary act (*t*) ; so that it was formerly in many cases held that pressure, or even a demand, would negative fraudulent preference. The Court will now, however, be governed by the statutory definition rather than by the earlier decisions (*u*), and will pay little regard to pressure or demand, at all events unless the debtor was in such a position that it might really induce him to make the payment or conveyance (*x*). If the motive of preferring the creditor is the real, effective, or dominant view of the debtor in making the payment or conveyance, the transaction will be a fraudulent preference; the presence in the debtor's mind of other motives will not save it ; it is unnecessary to show that the desire to prefer was the sole motive under which he acted (*y*). The person preferred must be, strictly speaking, a creditor (*z*). Where, however, there is real pressure which influences the debtor (*a*), or where the payment is made in the ordinary course of business, the transaction will not be regarded as a fraudulent preference (*b*).

(d) If with intent to defeat or delay his creditors he departs out of England, or being out of England remains out of England, or departs from his dwelling-house, or otherwise absents himself, or begins to keep house.

The departure from England must be coupled with an intent, at the moment of departure, to delay creditors (*c*). If such an

---

(*r*) B. A. 1883, s. 48.

(*s*) *In re Lane*, 23 Q. B. D. at p. 77.

(*t*) *Ex parte Bolland, Re Cherry*, L. R. 7 Ch. 24 ; *Ex parte Topham, Re Walker*, L. R. 8 Ch. 614 ; *Butcher* v. *Stead*, L. R. 7 H. L. 839, at p. 846.

(*u*) *Ex parte Griffith, Re Wilcoxon*, 23 Ch. D. 69 (C. A.)

(*x*) *Ex parte Wheatley, Re Grimes*, 45 L. T. 80 ; *Ex parte Hall, Re Cooper*, 19 Ch. D. 580.

(*y*) *Ex parte Hill, Re Bird*, 23 Ch. D. 695 ; and compare *Ex parte Taylor, Re Goldsmid*, 18 Q. B. D. 295.

(*z*) *Ex parte Kelly & Co., Re Smith, Fleming & Co.*, 11 Ch. D. 306 ; *Ex parte Taylor, Re Goldsmid*, supra.

(*a*) *Ex parte Topham*, L. R. 8 Ch. 614 ; *Ex parte Tempest*, L. R. 6 Ch. 70 ; *Smith* v. *Pilgrim*, 2 Ch. D. 127 ; *Ex parte Saffery*, 3 App. Cas. 213.

(*b*) *Tomkins* v. *Saffery*, 3 App. Cas. p. 235.

(*c*) *In re Wood*, L. R. 7 Ch. 302 ; *In re McKeand*, 6 Morrell, 240. Where the person is a foreigner, see *Ex parte Crispin*, L. R. 8 Ch. 374 ; *Ex parte Gutierrez*, 11 Ch. D. 298.

intention exist, it is not necessary that a delay should actually have taken place (*d*). In some cases, where the debtor has gone abroad under circumstances which rendered it highly improbable that he would return to this country, *ex. gr.*, where he had committed murder, it will be inferred that he must have intended to delay his creditors, such being the necessary consequence of his behaviour (*e*).

*How a person may become bankrupt.*

*Acts of bankruptcy.*

Where a domiciled Englishman has his permanent home abroad no such intent will be inferred (*f*).

As in the case of departure from the realm, so in the case of departure from the dwelling-house, there must be an intent, at the moment of departure, to delay creditors ; and if there be such an intent, there need not be an actual delay (*g*). It seems, that if a person were to depart from his dwelling-house, with intent to delay creditors in case a certain event should happen, which event, however, did not happen, that might not be an act of bankruptcy (*h*).

The words "otherwise absents himself" are extensive in their signification. They are not confined to an absenting from the dwelling-house. If the debtor absent himself from any place, in order to delay his creditors, such an absenting will constitute an act of bankruptcy within this phrase (*i*). Thus a debtor may commit an act of bankruptcy by absenting himself from his own regular place of business in which a man would be expected to be, or from some other place where he expected to meet those to whom he was indebted—for instance, the Royal Exchange (*k*)—in order to delay his creditors. But

(*d*) *Robertson* v. *Liddell*, 9 East, 487.

(*e*) *Woodier's Case*, B. N. P. 39 ; *Raikes* v. *Poreau*, Co. B. L. 73 ; *Vernon* v. *Hankey*, Co. B. L. 73. See these cases explained in *Fowler* v. *Padget*, 7 T. R. 509.

(*f*) *Ex parte Brandon, Re Trench*, 25 Ch. D. 500.

(*g*) *Wilson* v. *Norman*, 1 Esp. 334 ; *Hammond* v. *Hincks*, 5 Esp. 139 ; *Holroyd* v. *Whitehead*, 3 Camp. 530 ; *Ex parte Wydown*, 14 Ves. 84 ; *Ex parte Bamford*, 15 Ves. 449 ; *Deffle* v. *Desanges*, 8 Taunt. 671. See Holroyd

v. *Gwynne*, 2 Taunt. 176 (length of absence immaterial) ; *Spencer* v. *Billing*, 3 Camp. 310 ; *Bigg* v. *Spooner*, 2 Esp. 651 ; *Ex parte Birch*, 2 M. D. & De G. 659 ; *Ex parte Barney*, 32 L. J. Bk. 41.

(*h*) *Fisher* v. *Boucher*, 10 B. & C. 705.

(*i*) *Robson* v. *Rolls*, 9 Bing. 648.

(*k*) See *Maylin* v. *Eyloe*, Str. 809 ; *Bigg* v. *Spooner*, 2 Esp. 651 ; *Bayly* v. *Schofield*, 1 M. & S. 338 ; *Judine* v. *Da Cossen*, 1 B. & P. N. R. 234 ; *Chenoweth* v. *Hay*, 1 M. & S. 676 ; *Gillingham* v. *Laing*, 6 Taunt. 532.

How a person
may become
bankrupt.
_____
Acts of bank-
ruptcy.

the mere fact of a trader's absenting himself from a place where, though he had once transacted business, it did not appear that he had any business to transact at the time of his staying away from it, and at which, therefore, he would not, in the ordinary course of things, be expected to be present, will not warrant the conclusion that he had committed an act of bankruptcy by absenting himself in order to delay creditors (*l*). Nor will mere failure to keep an appointment with a creditor, apart from intention to delay, be an act of bankruptcy (*m*).

The keeping house must be with the intention to delay a creditor; in the absence of such intention it is not sufficient to make it an act of bankruptcy that a creditor has in fact been delayed. But if there be such an intention, it is an act of bankruptcy, whether the debtor keep house for an hour or a day, and whether any creditor was delayed or no (*n*). The usual evidence of this act is a denial to a creditor. Such denial is not in itself an act of bankruptcy, it is only evidence of one, and therefore may be explained. For instance, it may be shown that he was sick in bed or engaged with company (*o*); on the other hand, it is not the only evidence, and the debtor may therefore be shown to have *kept house* by other means. Thus, if he shut himself up in his house, debarring all access to it, whereby his creditors are delayed, an act of bankruptcy may be established by proof of his having done so. And generally, if a trader seclude himself in his house to avoid the fair importunity of his creditors, who are thus deprived of the means of communicating with him, he begins to keep his house, and commits an act of bankruptcy (*p*). A mere direction by a debtor to deny him to a creditor, if he do no further act

---

(*l*) *Bernasconi* v. *Farebrother*, 10 B. & C. 549; *Lees* v. *Marton*, 1 M. & Rob. 210; *Ex parte Barney*, 32 L. J. Bkcy. 41.

(*m*) *Lees* v. *Marton*, 1 M. & Rob. 210; *Ex parte Meyer*, *Re Stephany*, L. R. 7 Ch. 188; *Ex parte Lopez*, *Re Brelaz*, L. R. 6 Ch. 894; *Ex parte Geisel*, *Re Stanger*, 22 Ch. D. 436.

(*n*) See *Heyler* v. *Hall*, Palmer, 325.

(*o*) *Round* v. *Hope Byde*, Co. B. L.

94; B. N. P. 39, 40; *Ex parte Preston*, 1 Rose, 21; *Ex parte Hall*, 1 Atk. 201; *Smith* v. *Currie*, 3 Camp. 349; *Shew* v. *Thompson*, 1 Holt, 159. But see *Lazarus* v. *Waithman*, 5 Moore, 313.

(*p*) See *Dudley* v. *Vaughan*, 1 Camp. 271; *Bayly* v. *Schofield*, 1 M. & S. 338; *Cumming* v. *Baily*, 6 Bing. 363; *Fisher* v. *Boucher*, 10 B. & C. 705; *Key* v. *Shaw*, 8 Bing. 320.

indicative of keeping house, such, for instance, as secluding How a person
himself, is not, *per se*, an act of bankruptcy (q) ; neither, on may become<br>bankrupt.
the other hand, is a denial, if he did not order it (r).   And Acts of bank-
it has been laid down that such denial must be to a cre- ruptcy.
ditor (s) who has a debt actually due, and that a denial to a
creditor whose debt is payable *in futuro* is not sufficient (t).
If a debtor order himself to be *generally* denied, and be in
consequence denied to a creditor, that is sufficient, though it
was not that creditor, but another, whom he intended to
avoid (u).

(e) If execution issued against him has been levied by seizure
and sale of his goods under process in an action in any Court, or in
any civil proceeding in the High Court.

In order to render the levying of such an execution an act of
bankruptcy, there must be not only a seizure but a sale (x).
The act of bankruptcy not being complete till the sale has
divested the debtor of the property, the proceeds would belong
to the creditor; but by a subsequent section (y) the officer
executing the process, if the judgment on which execution has
issued exceeds twenty pounds, is to retain them for fourteen
days, and in the event of notice of a petition in bankruptcy
being served on him within that period, and the debtor being
adjudged a bankrupt, he is to hold them, after deducting
expenses, for the trustee.

(f) If he files in the Court a declaration of his inability to pay
his debts, or presents a bankruptcy petition against himself.

The declaration must be in proper form (z), and filed,

(q) *Fisher* v. *Boucher*, 10 B. & C.
705 ; *Garret* v. *Moule*, 5 T. R. 575 ;
*Hare* v. *Waring*, 3 M. & W. 362.

(r) *Dudley* v. *Vaughan*, 1 Camp.
271 ; *Ex parte Foster*, 17 Ves. 416.

(s) *Clements* v. *M'Kibben*, 2 H. & N.
62.

(t) See *Ex parte Levi*, 7 Vin. Abr. 61,
pl. 14 ; *Colkett* v. *Freeman*, 2 T. R. 59 ;
*Jackman* v. *Nightingale*, B. N. P. 40 ;

*Jeffs* v. *Smith*, 2 Taunt. 401 ; *Ex parte
Bamford*, 15 Ves. 449.

(u) *Mucklow* v. *May*, 1 Taunt. 479.

(x) *Ex parte Brooke, Re Hassall*, L. R.
9 Ch. 301 ; *Stock* v. *Holland*, L. R. 9
Ex. 147.

(y) B. A. 1883, s. 46; *Ex parte
Crossthwaite*, 14 Q. B. D. 966.

(z) B. R. 1886, Rule 135.

that is, delivered to the proper officer for that purpose (*a*).   A
debtor may now present a petition against himself; and the
presentation thereof will be deemed an act of bankruptcy
without the previous filing of any declaration of inability to
pay debts (*b*).

(g) If a creditor has obtained a final judgment against him for
any amount, and execution thereon not having been stayed, has
served on him in England, or, by leave of the Court, elsewhere, a
bankruptcy notice under this Act, requiring him to pay the judgment debt in accordance with the terms of the judgment, or to
secure or compound for it to the satisfaction of the creditor or the
Court, and he does not, within seven days after service of the notice
in case the service is effected in England, and in case the service is
effected elsewhere then within the time limited in that behalf by
the order giving leave to effect the service, either comply with the
requirements of the notice, or satisfy the Court that he has a
counter-claim, set-off, or cross demand which equals or exceeds the
amount of the judgment debt, and which he could not set up in the
action in which the judgment was obtained.

A bankruptcy notice under this sub-section can be issued only
by the creditor who has obtained the judgment, or his legal
personal representative (*c*).   On the act of bankruptcy, however,
which is complete upon the failure of the judgment debtor to
comply with the notice, any creditor may found a petition (*d*).
The judgment must be a final one, strictly so called, upon which
the creditor may at once issue execution (*e*).   A garnishee order

---

(*a*) *Ransford* v. *Maule*, L. R. 8 C. P.
672.

(*b*) B. A. 1883, s. 8.

(*c*) *Ex parte Blanchett, Re Keeling*,
17 Q. B. D. 303; *Ex parte Woodall*,
13 Q. B. D. 479.   As to form of
notice, No. 6.

(*d*) *Ex parte Dearle, Re Hastings*, 14
Q. B. D. 184.

(*e*) *Ex parte Feast*, 4 Mor. 37; *Ex
parte Woodall*, supra; *Ex parte Chinery*,
12 Q. B. D. 342; *Ex parte Schmitz,
Re Cohen*, 12 Q. B. D. 509; *Ex
parte Moore, Re Faithfull*, 14 Q. B.
D. 627; *Ex parte Whinney, Re Sanders*,
13 Q. B. D. 476; *Ex parte Grimwade*,

*Re Tennent*, 17 Q. B. D. 357; *Ex parte
Ide*, 17 Q. B. D. 755; *Ex parte Ford*,
3 Mor. 283; *In re Connon*, 5 Morrell,
80; *In re Reddell*, 5 Mor. 59.

In *Ex parte Woodall*, supra, it was
said, that the executrix (i. e., the *legal
personal representative*) of a judgment
creditor would be included in the
words "creditor who has obtained a
final judgment," if she had obtained
leave to issue execution; but in *Ex
parte Blanchett*, 17 Q. B. D. 303,
the Court of Appeal decided that they
did not apply to the assignee of a
judgment debt; and in *In re Goldring*,
22 Q. B. D. 87, that they did not

absolute is not a final judgment within the section (*f*). Satisfaction may be made under the provision in the latter part of
the sub-section, by giving a note or bill, during the currency
of which the creditor would not be entitled to proceed on the
notice (*g*).

(h) If the debtor gives notice to any of his creditors that he has
suspended, or that he is about to suspend, payment of his debts.

The notice may be given by word of mouth (*h*), but must be
formal and deliberate (*i*), such as business men would under-
stand to denote an intention to suspend payment.

### SECTION III.—*Who may be petitioning Creditor.*

In order to found proceedings in bankruptcy there must be a
liquidated debt or debts amounting to 50*l.* payable either immediately or at some certain future time (*k*), an act of bankruptcy must have been committed by the debtor within three
months before the presentation of the petition, and the debtor
must be domiciled in England, or within a year before the
presentation of the petition have ordinarily resided or had a
dwelling-house or place of business in England (*l*). We must
now consider who may be petitioning creditor, and of what
nature must be his debt.

A single creditor or two or more creditors may petition (*m*).
In the case of a debt due to a company or co-partnership authorized to sue and be sued in the name of a public officer or agent,
the petition and affidavit may be filed by any such officer or

---

apply to the trustee in the bankruptcy of a judgment creditor.

(*f*) *Ex parte Chinery,* 12 Q. B. D. 342.

(*g*) *Ex parte Matthew,* 12 Q. B. D. 506.

(*h*) *Ex parte Nickoll, Re Walker,* 13 Q. B. D. 469.

(i) *Ex parte Oastler, Re Friedlander,* 13 Q. B. D. 471. But compare *In re Lamb, Ex parte Gibson,* 4 Morrell, 25.

(*k*) A judgment recovered against the debtor is not necessarily conclu-
sive; and, if sufficient reasons are given, the Court of Bankruptcy will inquire into the validity of the judgment: *In re Lennox, Ex parte Lennox,* 16 Q. B. D. 315; *In re Saville, Ex parte Saville,* 4 Morrell, 277.

(l) B. A. 1883, s. 6.

(*m*) B. A. 1883, s. 6, sub-s. 1 (a).

agent (*n*).  A married woman in cases where she can sue
alone (*o*), an infant (*p*), an executor (*q*), and a factor who has
sold goods in his own name (*r*), can all be petitioning creditors;
so can a trustee provided the *cestui que trust* joins in the petition (*s*).  But a receiver appointed by the Chancery Division to
collect certain property cannot (*t*).

We have seen that the debt or debts must amount to fifty
pounds, and that they must be liquidated and payable either
immediately or at some certain future time (*u*).  Though, in the
present Act, there are no express words, as there were in the
preceding one, to the effect that a debt " due in equity" will
suffice, it would seem that such a debt will still support a petition.  Apparently, however, there may be, in equity, liabilities
to pay money which would not constitute debts (*x*).

The debt may be on account, if the creditor swear to a sufficient balance (*y*), or a sum awarded, notwithstanding a motion
to set aside the award (*z*), or a solicitor's bill, though not signed,
or delivered, or taxed (*a*), or the debt of a surety (*b*).  Differences
on the Stock Exchange, as fixed by the official assignee according to the rules of the Stock Exchange, will be a good petitioning debt (*c*).  But not a mere security for a contingent
demand (*d*), nor unliquidated damages on a covenant, or for a
tort before judgment (*e*); nor a cross-acceptance, unless the
creditor have paid his own (*f*); nor can the husband petition

(*n*) B. A. 1883, s. 148 ; B. R. 1886,
r. 258.

(*o*) 45 & 46 Vict. c. 75, s. 1 ; 20 & 21
Vict. c. 85.

(*p*) *Ex parte Brocklebank*, 6 Ch. D.
358.

(*q*) *Ex parte Paddy*, 3 Madd. 241.

(*r*) *Sadler* v. *Leigh*, 4 Camp. 195.

(*s*) *Ex parte Culley*, *Re Adams*, 9
Ch. D. 307 ; *Ex parte Dearle, Re Hastings*, 14 Q. B. D. 184.

(*t*) *In re Sacker*, 22 Q. B. D. 179.

(*u*) B. A. 1883, s. 6, sub-s. 1 (a), (b).

(*x*) *Ex parte Jones*, 18 Ch. D. 109 ;
and *Unity Banking Association*, 3 De G.
& J. 63.

(*y*) *Flower* v. *Herbert*, 2 Ves. sen. 327 ;

*Re Scott Russell*, 31 L. J. B. 37.  But
see *Ex parte Bowes*, 4 Ves. 168.

(*z*) *Ex parte Lingwood*, 1 Atk. 240 ;
*Marson* v. *Barber*, Gow, 17.

(*a*) *Ex parte Sutton*, 11 Ves. 163 ; *Ex
parte Steel*, 16 Ves. 166 ; *Ex parte Howell*,
1 Rose, 312.  See *Ex parte Prideaux*, 1
G. & J. 28.

(*b*) *Heylor* v. *Hall*, Palm. 325 ; *Den-
ham's case*, Stone, 183.

(*c*) *Ex parte Ward*, 22 Ch. D. 132.

(*d*) *Ex parte Page*, 1 G. & J. 100.

(*e*) *Re Broadhurst*, 22 L. J. Bank.
21 ; *Ex parte Charles*, 16 Ves. 256 ;
*Beavan* v. *Walker*, 12 C. B. 480.

(*f*) *Sarratt* v. *Austin*, 4 Taunt. 200.
See *Hope* v. *Meek*, 10 Exch. 829.

alone on a debt due to his wife *dum sola* (*g*) ; unless it be a Who may be petitioning creditor.
bill or note payable to bearer or order (*h*). Of course, the debt
must not be void for illegality (*i*). It must not be a debt
barred by the Statute of Limitations (*k*); nor will a sum assessed
as damages against a co-respondent, and ordered by the Court
to be paid by him to the husband, be a good petitioning creditor's debt (*l*).

A secured creditor (*m*) must either state in his petition that he
is willing to give up his security, or must estimate its value, and
petition only in respect of the balance remaining after deducting
the amount of such estimate (*n*). By omitting to observe these
regulations, he will not, however, forfeit his security (*o*), nor
will such an omission be fatal to the petition; it will be treated
as a formal defect, and amended (*p*).

The debt, in order to support a petition, must have been due
from the debtor before an act of bankruptcy (*q*). As a bill of
exchange is a debt from the time of issuing it, as against the
drawer, it is sufficient to constitute a petitioning creditor's debt,
though not indorsed to the creditor till after an act of bankruptcy (*r*) ; but if the creditor be indorsee, it must appear that
it was indorsed to him before the petition was filed (*s*). Such a
bill was held sufficient to support a fiat against the drawer,
though paid by the acceptor after fiat issued (*t*). Upon such a
bill it is, for obvious reasons, necessary to prove presentment
and notice of dishonour (*u*).

The costs of all proceedings, down to the making of a receiv-

---

(*g*) *Rumsey* v. *George*, 1 M. & S. 176.

(*h*) *Ex parte Barber, Re Shaw*, 1 G.
& J. 1. See *M'Neilage* v. *Holloway*,
1 B. & Ald. 218; but see *Sherrington*
v. *Yates*, 12 M. & W. 855.

(*i*) *M'Connell* v. *Hector*, 3 B. & P.
113; *Ex parte Randleson*, 1 Mont. &
M'A. 86.

(*k*) *Quantock* v. *England*, 2 W. Bl.
703; *Ex parte Tynte*, 15 Ch. D. 125.

(*l*) *Ex parte Muirhead*, 2 Ch. D. 22.

(*m*) Sect. 168.

(*n*) B. A. 1883, s. 6, sub-s. (2).

(*o*) *Moor* v. *Anglo-Italian Bank*, 10
Ch. D. 681.

(*p*) *Ex parte Vanderlinden, Re Pogose*,
20 Ch. D. 289.

(*q*) *Ex parte Hayward*, L. R. 6 Ch.
546; *Ex parte Waimman*, Co. B. L. 31;
*Hill* v. *Harris*, M. & M. 448; *Mavor*
v. *Pyne*, 2 C. & P. 91.

(*r*) *Macarty* v. *Barrow*, 2 Str. 949;
*Glaister* v. *Hewer*, 7 T. R. 498; *Anon.*
2 Wils. 135; *Ex parte Cyrus*, L. R. 5
Ch. 176.

(*s*) *Rose* v. *Rowcroft*, 4 Camp. 245;
*Cowie* v. *Harris*, Moo. & M. 141.

(*t*) *Ex parte Douthat*, 4 B. & Ald. 67.

(*u*) *Cooper* v. *Machin*, 1 Bing. 426.

Who may be
petitioning
creditor.
ing order, will have to be borne by the petitioning creditor;
but he will be entitled to be recouped out of the debtor's estate
as soon as the actual expenses of the official receiver, the prescribed fees and percentages, the fees and costs of the official
receiver, repayment of deposits, and the remuneration of the
special manager, have been provided for ($x$). Two or more
petitions presented against the same debtor may be consolidated ($y$). A stay of proceedings under a petition may be
ordered ($z$), and if the petitioning creditor does not proceed
with due diligence, another creditor may be substituted for
him ($a$).

Where the debt is due from a firm, any creditor, who could
petition against all, may petition against one or more of the
partners ($b$) ; and the Court may dismiss a joint petition as to
one or more of the partners, without affecting the proceedings
as to the others ($c$).


SECTION IV.—*The Petition, and the Court to which it is
presented.*

The petition,
and the Court
to which it is
presented.
A petition in bankruptcy must be fairly written or printed,
or partly written and partly printed, and it must not be altered
without leave of the registrar ($d$). It must be attested ($e$), and
must set out the residence and place of business of the debtor,
and any former residence or place of business which he occupied
at the time of contracting the debt ($f$). Where the debtor
resides and carries on business in different districts, the petition
should be presented to the Court in district of which he carries
on business ($g$). The petitioning creditor must make a deposit
of five pounds, and such further sum as the Court may,
from time to time, direct ($h$), and he will have to verify the

($x$) B. R. 1886, rr. 125, 183.    (d) B. R. 1886, r. 143.
($y$) B. A. 1883, s. 106.    (e) B. R. 1886, r. 146.
($z$) B. A. 1883, s. 109.    ($f$) B. R. 1886, r. 144.
($a$) B. A. 1883, s. 107.    ($g$) B. R. 1886, r. 145.
($b$) B. A. 1883, s. 110.    ($h$) B. R. 1886, r. 147.
(c) B. A. 1883, s. 111.

petition by the affidavit of himself or of some person who can depose to the facts (i).

The petition will be investigated by the registrar (k), after which two sealed copies will be delivered to the petitioner (l). He must then serve the debtor *personally* with one of the sealed copies (m), unless substituted service be ordered by the Court (n). A time and place are appointed for the hearing of the petition (o), and the debtor will be entitled to show cause (p). At the hearing, the petitioner must be prepared to prove the debt, the act of bankruptcy, and service of the petition (q). If satisfied with such proof, the Court may make a receiving order (r), or it may, in certain cases, order proceedings in the petition to be stayed (s). If not satisfied with the proof, the Court may dismiss the petition (t). In the case of a petition presented by the debtor himself, a receiving order will be made forthwith (u).

Where it is necessary for the protection of the estate, the Court may, at any time after presentation of a petition, appoint the official receiver interim receiver of the property of the debtor (x), and it may also stay any action, execution, or other legal process against the property or person of the debtor (y).

The Act does not provide any remedy or punishment for maliciously and without reasonable and probable cause taking proceedings in bankruptcy. But such an action would lie at the instance of a person who could show that the proceedings had been set aside or dismissed (z).

*The petition, and the Court to which it is presented.*

(i) B. R. 1886, rr. 149, 150; B. A. 1883, s. 7, sub-s. 1. The petition may be signed by his duly constituted attorney: *Ex parte Wallace*, 14 Q. B. D. 22. As to amending the petition, *Ex parte Dearle*, 14 Q. B. D. 184.

(k) B. R. 1886, r. 152.

(l) B. R. 1886, rr. 149, 153.

(m) B. R. 1886, r. 149.

(n) B. R. 1886, r. 154.

(o) B. R. 1886, r. 158.

(p) B. R. 1886, rr. 160, 162.

(q) B. A. 1883, s. 7, sub-s. (1).

(r) B. A. 1883, ss. 5, 7, sub-s. (1).

(s) B. A. 1883, s. 7, sub-sects. (4) and (5).

(t) B. A. 1883, s. 7, sub-s. (3).

(u) B. A. 1883, s. 8; B. R. 1886, r. 157.

(x) B. A. 1883, s. 10, sub-s. (1); B. R. 1886, rr. 170—175.

(y) B. A. 1883, s. 10, sub-s. (2).

(z) *Whitworth* v. *Hall*, 2 B. & Ad. 695; *Johnson* v. *Emerson*, L. R. 6 Ex. 329; *Quartz Hill Gold Mining Co.* v. *Eyre*, 11 Q. B. D. 674; *Metropolitan Bank* v. *Pooley*, 10 App. Cas. 210.

Where the debtor dies, proceedings will be continued as if he were alive, unless the Court otherwise orders (*a*).

The Courts which have jurisdiction in bankruptcy are the High Court of Justice, the district of which includes the City of London and the liberties thereof, and the districts of the Metropolitan County Courts, enumerated in Schedule III. of the Act, and elsewhere the County Courts (*b*). In the High Court the bankruptcy business is assigned to the Queen's Bench Division (*c*), and is transacted before a judge of that Division and the Bankruptcy Registrars (*d*). A County Court has in bankruptcy all the powers and jurisdiction of the High Court (*e*).

Persons aggrieved have a right of appeal from the High Court to the Court of Appeal, and, by leave, thence to the House of Lords (*f*); from the County Courts to a Divisional Court in bankruptcy of the High Court of Justice, and thence, by leave, to the Court of Appeal, whose decision in such cases is final (*g*). The official receiver should not appear on an appeal unless there are special circumstances to bring before the Court (*h*).

In order to enable these Courts to carry into effect the purpose for which they are intended, a general power is given them in the following terms :—

"Sect. 102.—(1.) Subject to the provisions of this Act, every Court having jurisdiction in bankruptcy under this Act shall have full power to decide all questions of priorities (*i*), and all other questions whatsoever (*k*), whether of law or fact, which may arise in any case of bankruptcy (*l*) coming within the cognizance of the Court,

(*a*) B. A. 1883, s. 108 ; *In re Walker*, 3 Morrell, 69.

(*b*) See B. A. 1883, ss. 92—96, and Sched. 3.

(*c*) Order of Lord Chancellor, dated 1st January, 1884.

(*d*) B. A. 1883, s. 99.

(*e*) B. A. 1883, s. 100.

(*f*) B. A. 1883, s. 104, sub-s. (2). As to who is and is not a person aggrieved, see *Ex parte Learoyd*, *Re Foulds*, 10 Ch. D. 3 ; *Ex parte Ditton*, *Re Woods*, 11 Ch. D. 56 ; *Ex parte Mason*, *Re White*, 14 Ch. D. 71 ; *Ex parte Sidebotham*, 14 Ch. D. 458 ; *Ex*

*parte Castle Mail Packet Co.*, 3 Morrell, 270 ; *In re Batten*, *Ex parte Milne*, 22 Q. B. D. 685 (trustee under deed of arrangement).

(*g*) 47 Vict. c. 9, s. 2.

(*h*) *Ex parte Dixon*, 13 Q. B. D. 118 ; *Ex parte White*, 14 Q. B. D. 600 ; *Ex parte Reed and Bowen*, 17 Q. B. D. 244.

(*i*) *Ex parte Payne*, 11 Ch. D. 539.

(*k*) *Ex parte Streeter*, 19 Ch. D. 216.

(*l*) Including a composition : *Ex parte Rumboll*, L. R. 6 Ch. 843 ; *In re Thorpe*, L. R. 8 Ch. 743 ; *In re Hawke*, 3 Morrell, 1.

or which the Court may deem it expedient or necessary to decide for the purpose of doing complete justice or making a complete distribution of property in any such case (m).

" Provided that the jurisdiction hereby given shall not be exercised by the County Court for the purpose of adjudicating upon any claim, not arising out of the bankruptcy, which might heretofore have been enforced by action in the High Court, unless all parties to the proceeding consent thereto, or the money, money's worth, or right in dispute does not in the opinion of the judge exceed in value 200*l.*

"(2.) A Court having jurisdiction in bankruptcy under this Act shall not be subject to be restrained in the execution of its powers under this Act by the order of any other Court, nor shall any appeal lie from its decisions, except in manner directed by this Act.

"(3.) If in any proceeding in bankruptcy there arises any question of fact which either of the parties desire to be tried before a jury instead of by the Court itself, or which the Court thinks ought to be tried by a jury, the Court may, if it thinks fit, direct. the trial to be had with a jury, and the trial may be had accordingly in the High Court in the same manner as if it were the trial of an issue of fact in an action, and in the County Court in the manner in which jury trials in ordinary cases are by law held in that Court.

"(4.) Where a receiving order has been made in the High Court under this Act, the judge by whom such order was made shall have power, if he sees fit, without any further consent, to order the transfer to such judge of any action pending in any other division, brought or continued by or against the bankrupt.

"(5.) Where default is made by a trustee, debtor, or other person, in obeying any order or direction given by the Board of Trade or by an official receiver, or any other officer of the Board of Trade, under any power conferred by this Act, the Court may, on the application of the Board of Trade or an official receiver, or other duly authorized person, order such defaulting trustee, debtor, or person to comply with the order or direction so given; and the Court may also, if it shall think fit, upon any such application, make an immediate order for the committal of such defaulting trustee, debtor, or other person ; provided that the power given by this sub-section shall be deemed to be in addition to and not in substitution for any other right or remedy in respect of such default."

The powers thus conferred are very wide, and if the trustee or other party resort to them he will be deemed to have made

---

(*m*) *Ex parte Great Western Ry. Co.*, 22 Ch. D. 470; *Ex parte Hirst*, 11 Ch. D. 278.

The petition,
and the Court
to which it is
presented.
his election, and cannot proceed for the same matter elsewhere.
But they do not exclude the jurisdiction of other tribunals, and
therefore the trustee may still assert his rights in the ordinary
course against strangers (p). .

Where the case falls within this section (q), the Court has a
discretion whether it shall act upon it or leave the matter to be
decided in the ordinary course (r) ; but if it determines to act
under the section, it may restrain parties from resorting to any
other tribunal (s).

The debtor is bound to give every assistance in the realization
and discovery of his property under pain of being held guilty of
contempt of Court (t). Wide powers are given to the Court, if
it be necessary to prevent his making away with or con-
cealing his property or in any way delaying the proceedings
against him, to order his arrest and the seizure of his papers (u).
The Court may also summon and cause to be examined any
debtor against whom a receiving order has been made, or his
wife or any person known or suspected to have in his possession
any of the debtor's property, or supposed to be indebted to
him, or to be capable of giving information as to him, his
dealings, or property (x). Production of documents may also
be ordered (y).

The orders and warrants of these Courts may be enforced in
any part of her Majesty's dominions (z).

These several Courts, and the Courts of Bankruptcy in
Scotland and Ireland, and every like British Court elsewhere,
are to act in aid of, and be auxiliary to each other in all matters
of bankruptcy (a).

(p) Ellis v. Silber, L. R. 8 Ch. 83 ;
In re Thorpe, Ibid. 743 ; Jenney v. Bell,
2 Ch. D. 547.

(q) Smith v. Baker, L. R. 8 C. P.
350.

(r) Ex parte Reynolds, Re Barnett, 15
Q. B. D. 169 ; Ex parte Armitage, 17
Ch. D. 13.

(s) Ex parte Cohen, Re Sparke, L. R.
7 Ch. 20 ; Morley v. White, L. R. 8 Ch.
214.

(t) B. A. 1883, s. 24.

(u) B. A. 1883, s. 25.

(x) B. A. 1883, s. 27.

(y) B. R. 1886, r. 69.

(z) B. A. 1883, ss. 117, 119.

(a) B. A. 1883, s. 118.

## Section V.—*Receiving Order, and Proceedings thereupon.*

### (A) *Receiving Order and its Consequences.*

If satisfied with the proof by the petitioning creditor of his debt and the act of bankruptcy, and service of the petition, the Court will make a receiving order. This order will be served on the debtor (*b*), and gazetted and advertised in a local paper (*c*). The result of the order will be that the official receiver will be constituted receiver of the debtor's property, and that after it is made no creditor will have any remedy against the debtor's property or person in respect of any provable debt other than those provided by the Act, or be able to commence any action or other legal proceedings without leave of the Court (*d*). The debtor, for example, will be protected from the day on which the order is pronounced (*e*) as regards the remedies given to creditors by the Debtors Act, 1869 (*f*). But the receiving order, it is important to observe, will not in any way affect the power of secured creditors to realize or otherwise deal with their securities (*g*). A secured creditor is defined as one who holds a mortgage, charge, or lien on the property of the debtor, or any part thereof, as a security for a debt due to him from the debtor (*h*). Creditors who have issued execution against the goods or land of their debtor, or who have attached any debt due to them, will be allowed, as against a trustee in bankruptcy, to retain the benefit of the execution or attachment only if they have completed it before the date of the receiving order, and before notice of any bankruptcy petition presented by or against the debtor, or the commission of any available act of bankruptcy by the debtor (*i*). That is to say, in the case of execution against goods, there must

*Receiving order, and proceedings thereupon.*

---

(*b*) B. R. 1886, r. 179.

(*c*) B. A. 1883, s. 13; B. R. 1886, r. 182.

(*d*) B. A. 1883, s. 9, sub-s. 1.

(*e*) *Re Manning*, 30 Ch. D. 480.

(*f*) 32 & 33 Vict. c. 62, s. 4; *Cobham* v. *Dalton*, L. R. 10 Ch. 655; *Earl of Lewes* v. *Barnett*, 6 Ch. D. 252; *Re Ryley, Ex parte Official Receiver*, 15 Q. B. D. 329.

(*g*) B. A. 1883, s. 9, sub-s. (2).

(*h*) B. A. 1883, s. 168, sub-s. (1).

(*i*) B. A. 1883, s. 45, sub-s. (1).

have been seizure and sale $(j)$, and against land, seizure or the
appointment of a receiver $(k)$, and in the case of attachment, the
debt attached must have been received $(l)$. An available act of
bankruptcy is one available for a petition at the date of the
presentation of the petition on which the receiving order is
made $(m)$; in other words, an act of bankruptcy committed
within three months next preceding the date of presentation of
the petition $(n)$.

(B) *Public Examination of the Debtor, and Meetings of Creditors.*

Every debtor must undergo a public examination on oath in
open Court $(o)$. An appointment for this purpose is made by the
Court on the application of the official receiver when the receiving order has been made $(p)$, and notice thereof is given to the
creditors $(q)$. Any creditor who has tendered a proof, or his
representative authorized in writing, may question the debtor
concerning his affairs and the causes of his failure $(r)$. Notes
of the examination are taken, and are open to the inspection
of creditors at all reasonable times $(s)$. The first meeting of
creditors is held within fourteen days after the date of the
receiving order $(t)$. Notice of the meeting is gazetted and
advertised, and sent to each creditor, together with a summary
of the debtor's statement of affairs $(u)$. At the first meeting,
the creditors consider any proposal made by the debtor for a
composition or scheme of arrangement, or the question whether
the debtor should be adjudged bankrupt, and will also consider
the mode of dealing with the debtor's property $(x)$. A creditor will not be able to vote unless he has proved his debt and
lodged his proof with the official receiver at the time specified
in the notice convening the meeting $(y)$. Nor can he vote in

$(j)$ *Jones* v. *Parcell*, 11 Q. B. D. 430.

$(k)$ *Ex parte Evans*, 13 Ch. D. 252;
*Smith* v. *Cowell*, 6 Q. B. D. 75.

$(l)$ B. A. 1883, s. 45, sub-s. (2).

$(m)$ B. A. 1883, s. 168, sub-s. (1).

$(n)$ B. A. 1883, s. 6, sub-s. (1) (c.).

$(o)$ B. A. 1883, s. 17; B. R. 1886,
r. 6.

$(p)$ B. R. 1886, r. 184.

$(q)$ B. R. 1886, r. 186.

$(r)$ B. A. 1883, s. 17, sub-s. (4).

$(s)$ B. A. 1883, s. 17, sub-s. (8).

$(t)$ B. A. 1883, s. 15, Sched. I.,
r. 1.

$(u)$ B. A. 1883, Sched. I., rr. 2, 3.

$(x)$ B. A. 1883, s. 15.

$(y)$ B. A. 1883, Sched. I., r. 8; B.
R. 1886, r. 222.

respect of any unliquidated, contingent or unascertained debt (z). Receiving order, and proceedings thereupon.
Creditors may vote by proxy and give a general proxy to their
manager, clerk, or any other person in their regular employ (a),
and a special proxy to vote at any specified meeting for any
specific resolution (b). Proxies may also be given to the official
receiver (c), and, if given by a firm or person carrying on
business, may be signed by any person in the employ of the
firm or by any person having a written general authority to
sign for the firm or person (d). Subsequent meetings are
summoned by notice (e). The costs of any meeting summoned
by any person other than the official receiver or trustee will be
borne by him, but may be repaid to him out of the estate by
direction of the Court or the creditors (f).

Every debtor must make out a statement of affairs, and any
person stating himself in writing to be a creditor will be
entitled, personally or by agent, to inspect and take a copy of
or extracts from it; but any person who untruthfully so states
himself to be a creditor, will be guilty of contempt of Court (g).

### (c) Composition or Scheme of Arrangement.

A composition or scheme of arrangement, the terms of which
must be settled at the first meeting, or an adjournment of it (h),
may be resolved on by a resolution passed by a majority in
number, and three-fourths in value, of the creditors present
personally or by proxy, and voting (i), and must be confirmed
at a subsequent meeting held after the debtor's public examination is concluded, by a resolution passed by a majority in
number representing three-fourths in value of all the creditors
who have proved (k). At the subsequent meeting a creditor

(z) B. A. 1883, Sched. I., r. 9.
(a) B. A. 1883, Sched. I., rr. 15, 17; B. R. 1886, r. 245.
(b) B. A. 1883, Sched. I., r. 18.
(c) B. A. 1883, Sched. I., r. 21.
(d) B. R. 1886, r. 246. As to proxies generally, see B. A. 1883, Sched. I., rr. 15—21; B. R. 1886, rr. 245—248.
(e) B. A. 1883, Sched. I., r. 6; B. R. 1886, r. 251.
(f) B. R. 1886, r. 254.
(g) B. A. 1883, s. 16.
(h) B. R. 1886, r. 195.
(i) B. A. 1883, s. 18, sub-s. (1); s. 168, sub-s. (1).
(k) B. A. 1883, s. 18, sub-sects. (2) and (3).

may vote by letter, witnessed and sent to the official receiver not later than the day before the meeting (*m*). Before the composition or scheme becomes binding on the creditors, however, it must be approved by the Court, which will have regard to the interests of the creditors and the conduct of the debtor, and exercise discretion as to approving it (*n*), on application by the debtor or official receiver, notice of the hearing of which will be given to every creditor who has proved (*o*). On the application, the official receiver will make a report, and any creditor may object to the approval (*p*).

If the composition or scheme is approved, the debtor or trustee appointed thereunder (if any) will be put in possession of the debtor's property, and the receiving order will be rescinded (*q*). The release to the debtor will be the same as if he had obtained a discharge in bankruptcy (*r*). If default is made in payment of any instalment under the composition or scheme, or if the Court thinks that it cannot be carried out without injustice or undue delay to the creditors or debtor, or that the approval was obtained by fraud, the Court may adjudge the debtor a bankrupt (*s*). It may also do so if, between the first and the subsequent meetings, the debtor informs the official receiver in writing that he cannot carry out the composition or scheme; or if the composition or scheme is not confirmed at the subsequent meeting (*t*). Default in payment of a composition under the Act will not, apparently, restore a creditor to his original rights in respect of the debt, his remedy being by application to the Court (*u*). Compositions or schemes of arrangement may also be accepted after adjudication (*x*), in which cases the rules relating thereto will apply as if they had been accepted in the first instance (*y*).

(*m*) B. A. 1883, s. 18, sub-s. (2); B. R. 1886, r. 245.

(*n*) *In re Genese*, 3 Morrell, 274; *In re Barlow*, 3 Morrell, 304; *In re Postlethwaite*, 3 Morrell, 169; see *Lucas* v. *Martin*, 37 Ch. D. 597, in which the Court declined to carry out an agreement which had been approved.

(*o*) B. A. 1883, s. 18, sub-s. (4); B. R. 1886, rr. 197—199.

(*p*) B. A. 1883, s. 18, sub-s. (5).

(*q*) B. R. 1886, r. 208.

(*r*) B. A. 1883, s. 18, sub-s. (8); *Flint* v. *Barnard*, 22 Q. B. D. 90.

(*s*) B. A. 1883, s. 18, sub-s. (11).

(*t*) B. R. 1886, r. 192.

(*u*) B. R. 1886, r. 211.

(*x*) B. A. 1883, s. 23.

(*y*) B. R. 1886, r. 216.

## (D) *Adjudication.*

If the creditors so resolve at the first meeting, or if they pass no resolution, or if a composition or scheme is not accepted or approved within fourteen days after the conclusion of the public examination, the debtor will be adjudged bankrupt by the Court; and his property will forthwith become divisible amongst his creditors, and vest in a trustee (*z*). There is also power to adjudge the debtor a bankrupt at the time of making the receiving order, or at any time thereafter on his own application (*a*), and on the application of a creditor or the official receiver after the receiving order if there is no quorum of creditors at the first meeting or one adjournment thereof, or if the debtor has absconded or does not propose any composition or scheme (*b*).

The Court has power, notwithstanding the adoption of a composition or scheme (*c*), to adjudge the debtor bankrupt if it cannot, owing to legal difficulties, or for any sufficient reason, proceed without injustice or undue delay to the creditors, or if the approval of the Court was obtained by fraud. In *Re Moon* (*d*), the debtor represented that his assets were sufficient to pay twenty shillings in the pound, and the creditors adopted a scheme of arrangement for the payment of such sum, and assigned to a trustee all his property, except certain property included in a post-nuptial settlement. The value of the property assigned was greatly over-estimated ; although no charge of fraud was made against the debtor, the Court, under this section, adjudicated him bankrupt.

An adjudication operates not merely from its date or the date of the petition, but retrospectively, it being enacted by s. 43 :—

"The bankruptcy of a debtor, whether the same takes place on the debtor's own petition or upon that of a creditor or creditors, shall be deemed to have relation back to, and to commence at, the time of the act of bankruptcy being committed on which a receiving order is made against him ; or, if the bankrupt is proved to have committed more acts of bankruptcy than one, to have relation back.

---

(*z*) B. A. 1883, s. 20.  
(*a*) B. R. 1886, r. 190.  
(*b*) B. R. 1886, r. 191.  
(*c*) Sect. 18, sub-s. (11).  
(*d*) 19 Q. B. D. 669.

to, and to commence at, the time of the first of the acts of bankruptcy proved to have been committed by the bankrupt within
three months next preceding the date of the presentation of the
bankruptcy petition; but no bankruptcy petition, receiving order,
or adjudication shall be rendered invalid by reason of any act of
bankruptcy anterior to the debt of the petitioning creditor" (e).


## Section VI.—*Remedies of Creditors.*

### (A.) *Proof of Debts.*

Remedies of
creditors.
First, with regard to the mode of proof. A debt is to be
proved as soon as may be after the receiving order by affidavit
sent to the official receiver or trustee by post, and made by the
creditor or some person authorised by him (f). The affidavit
should contain or refer to an account showing the particulars of
the debt; and trade discounts must be deducted, but not discounts for cash not exceeding 5*l.* per cent. per annum (g). As
the jurisdiction in this matter is both legal and equitable, the
consideration of the alleged debt can always be looked into, notwithstanding an award, a verdict, or a judgment (h).

The Court may examine into the validity of a judgment
upon evidence of fraud, collusion, or miscarriage of justice (i);
and it has been laid down that when the only evidence of a debt
is a judgment, and the judgment has been recovered after the
act of bankruptcy, the judgment debt cannot be proved in the
bankruptcy (k).

A bill of exchange, promissory note, or other negotiable
instrument or security must be produced before a proof of it can

---

(e) *Ex parte Kelder*, 24 Ch. D. 339;
*Ex parte Edwards*, 13 Q. B. D. 747.

(f) B. A. 1883, Scbed. II., rr. 1—3;
B. R. 1886, r. 219.

(g) B. A. 1883, Sched. II., rr. 4, 8.

(h) *Ex parte Butterfill*, 1 Rose, 192;
*Ex parte Kemshead*, 1 Rose, 149. See *Ex
parte Mudie*, 3 M. D. & De G. 66; *Ex
parte Thornthwaite*, 1 De G. M. & G. Bk.
App. 407; *Ex parte Kibble, Re Onslow*,
L. R. 10 Ch. 373; *Ex parte Banner,
Re Blythe*, 17 Ch. D. 480; *Ex parte*

*Revell, Re Tollemache*, 13 Q. B. D. 720;
*Ex parte Lennox*, 16 Q. B. D. 315; *Ex
parte Anderson, Re Tollemache*, 14 Q.
B. D. 606; *Ex parte Bonham, Re Tol-
lemache*, 14 Q. B. D. 604; *Ex parte
Revell, Re Tollemache*, 13 Q. B. D. 727;
*In re Savile*, 4 Morrell, 277.

(i) *In re Flatau*, 22 Q. B. D. 83.

(k) *Ex parte Bonham, Re Tollemache*,
14 Q. B. D. 604; *In re Lopes*, 6 Morrell, 245.

be admitted (*l*). In respect of periodical payments the creditor may prove for the proportionate part due down to the date of the receiving order (*m*). Debts payable in future may be proved for, but a rebate of interest at five per cent. will be deducted from the dividend (*n*). The creditor may prove for interest at four per cent. from the date when the debt became due down to the date of the receiving order if the debt was payable by virtue of a written instrument at a certain time, and if otherwise from the date of notice in writing to the debtor that interest would thenceforth be claimed (*o*). The official receiver or trustee will examine every proof, and in writing reject or admit it wholly or in part not later than seven days from the latest date specified in the notice to declare a dividend (*p*). Any decision as to a proof is subject to an appeal by the creditor to the Court within twenty-one days from the decision (*q*). The Court may expunge or reduce a proof on the application of the trustee or a creditor if the trustee declines to interfere (*r*). The cost of proof is borne by the creditor, unless the Court otherwise order (*s*).

There are some peculiar rules respecting the admission to proof of creditors holding securities for their debts. Such persons have, as will be more fully explained in a subsequent part of this chapter, considerable advantages over the bankrupt's other creditors; they are able to avail themselves of their securities as far as they will go, toward payment of their demands. A secured creditor may, as we have seen, deal with his security just as if no receiving order had been made (*t*). He may, therefore, realize his security if it be sufficient, and not prove at all. If, however, his security is insufficient, he may either realize it, and prove for the balance after deducting the net proceeds (*u*), or he may surrender his security for the benefit of the creditors and prove for the whole debt (*x*) ; or he may assess its value in

(1) B. R. 1886, r. 221. See as to proofs on bills not due, B. A. Sched. II., r. 21.

(*m*) B. A. Sched. II., r. 19.
(*n*) B. A. Sched. II., r. 21.
(*o*) B. A. Sched. II., r. 20.
(*p*) B. A. Sched. II., rr. 22, 27; B. R. 1886, rr. 227, 228.

(*q*) B. A. Sched. II., r. 24; B. R. 1886, r. 230.
(*r*) B. A. Sched. II., rr. 23, 25.
(*s*) B. A. 1883, Sched. II., r. 6.
(*t*) B. A. 1883, s. 9.
(*u*) B. A. 1883, Sched. II., r. 9.
(*x*) B. A. 1883, Sched. II., r. 10.

his proof and receive a dividend on the balance in respect of the balance after deducting such assessed value (*y*). There are provisions in such a case for amendment of the valuation and enabling the trustee to redeem the security at the value put upon it by the creditor (*z*). The penalty for non-compliance with these rules is exclusion from dividend (*a*).

For the purpose of voting at any meeting of creditors, a secured creditor is to be deemed a creditor only for the balance of his debt after allowing for the value of his security, and if he votes in respect of the whole debt he will be deemed to have surrendered his security (*b*). A secured creditor means one holding a mortgage, charge or lien on any part of the bankrupt's property as security for a debt due to him from the debtor (*c*). A creditor, therefore, holding the security of a third person is not obliged to give it up, or sell it, before proving ; and as the separate estates of partners are considered as distinct from the joint estate of the firm, it would seem that a joint creditor, holding a separate security, from one of the co-debtors, or separate securities from both of them (*d*), may prove against the joint estate, without surrender or sale of his security (*e*). And so the holder of a joint security may prove against the separate estate of one debtor, and recover what he can against the other. But more than twenty shillings in the pound must not be received in the whole (*f*). Where a security is deposited generally, and the creditor has two demands, one provable, the other not, he may apply his security to the demand which is not provable (*g*).

*What debts provable.*—Having considered the *mode of proof*, the next question that occurs under the head of proof is, *what*

(*y*) B. A. 1883, Sched. II., r. 11.

(*z*) B. A. 1883, Sched. II., rr. 12—15 ; *Ex parte Norris*, *Re Sadler*, 17 Q. B. D. 728 ; 3 Morrell, 260.

(*a*) B. A. 1883, Sched. II., r. 16.

(*b*) B. A. 1883, Sched. II., r. 10 ; *Baines* v. *Wright*, 15 Q. B. D. 102.

(*c*) B. A. 1883, s. 168, sub-s. 1.

(*d*) *Re Plummer*, 1 Ph. 56.

(*e*) *Ex parte Peacock*, 2 G. & J. 27.

See *Ex parte Freen*, Id. 250 ; *Ex parte M'Kenna*, 30 L. J. Bkcy. 25 ; *Ex parte West Riding*, 19 Ch. D. 105 ; *Ex parte Caldicott*, 25 Ch. D. 716.

(*f*) B. A. 1883, Sched. II., r. 17 ; *Ex parte Bennet*, 2 Atk. 527 ; *Ex parte Parr*, 1 Rose, 76 ; *Ex parte Taylor*, 26 L. J. Bkcy. 58.

(*g*) *Ex parte Havard*, Co. B. L. 124 ; *Ex parte Hunter*, 6 Ves. 94.

*debts are provable.* No debt can be so, if it arise out of an Remedies of creditors. illegal contract, or is barred by the Statute of Limitations (*h*), or if there be no consideration for it.

A debt founded in felony will probably be provable unless the creditor is shown to be omitting some duty, as that of taking proceedings for a prosecution, in regard to prosecuting the felon (*i*). Demands in the nature of unliquidated damages arising otherwise than by reason of a contract, promise or breach of trust are not provable ; nor can a creditor who has notice of an act of bankruptcy available against the debtor prove for any debt or liability contracted subsequently to the date of his having notice (*k*). Thus, a demand of damages for the commission of a tort is not provable, unless judgment has been signed for them before the receiving order, or they have been liquidated by agreement before bankruptcy (*l*).

Except demands for unliquidated damages and debts contracted after notice of an act of bankruptcy (which, as we have seen, are not provable), all debts and liabilities, present or future, certain or contingent, to which the debtor is subject at the date of the receiving order, or to which he may become subject before his discharge by reason of any liability incurred before such date, are provable (*m*). The value of contingent debts will be estimated; if incapable of valuation such debts will not be provable (*n*).

The word " liability " includes any compensation for work or labour done, any obligation or possibility of an obligation to pay money or money's worth on the breach of any express or implied covenant, contract, agreement, or undertaking, whether the breach does or does not occur, or is or is not likely to occur

(*h*) *Ex parte Dewdney,* 15 Ves. 498 ; *Ex parte Roffey,* 2 Rose, 245 ; *Ex parte Bell,* 1 M. & S. 751 ; *Ex parte Chavasse,* 34 L. J. Bktcy. 17 ; *Ex parte Mather,* 3 Ves. 373.

(*i*) See *Ex parte Ball, Re Shepherd,* 10 Ch. D. 667 ; *Midland Insurance Co.* v. *Smith,* 6 Q. B. D. 561 ; *Ex parte Leslie, Re Guerrier,* 20 Ch. D. 131 ; *Roope* v. *D'Avigdor,* 10 Q. B. D. 412.

(*k*) B. A. 1883, s. 37.

(*l*) *Ex parte Baum, Re Edwards,* L. R. 9 Ch. 673 ; *Ex parte Brook, Re Newman,* 3 Ch. D. 494 ; *Ex parte Mumford,* 15 Ves. 289 ; *Ex parte Harding, Re Pickering,* 23 L. J. Bktcy. 22 ; *Watson* v. *Holliday,* 20 Ch. D. 780 ; *In re Giles,* 6 Morrell, 158.

(*m*) B. A. 1883, s. 37, sub-s. 3.

(*n*) B. A. 1883, s. 37, sub-ss. 4, 6 ; *Linton* v. *Linton,* 15 Q. B. D. 239.

or capable of occurring before the discharge of the debtor, and generally it includes any express or implied engagement, agreement, or undertaking, to pay, or capable of resulting in the payment of money or money's worth, whether the payment is, as respects amount, fixed or unliquidated ; as respects time, present or future, certain or dependent on any one contingency, or on two or more contingencies ; as to mode of valuation capable of being ascertained by fixed rules, or as matter of opinion (o).

These terms are exceedingly comprehensive (p)—indeed it is impossible that wider terms should have been employed—and the Court is disposed to give them an operation which shall relieve the bankrupt " from any liability under any contract he had ever entered into " (q).

Thus, debts arising from fraud or breach of trust (r), money paid for a lost bet or for differences on the Stock Exchange (s), liability for calls in a winding-up (t), voluntary bonds (u), may all form the subject of a proof. The holder of a bill of exchange may, in general, prove against all the parties liable upon it for the full amount of the bill, and he may prove against the estate of the drawer or acceptor before the bill is dishonoured (x). Where, however, the bill is a fraud on the bankruptcy law, and the holder knew or ought to have known that it was so, he can only prove at most for the amount which he has paid to obtain the bill (y). In the case of accommodation acceptances, if one of the parties only becomes bankrupt, the other may prove for the amount he has paid for the bankrupt's accommodation (z), but if both are bankrupt, only the

---

(o) B. A. 1883, s. 37, sub-s. 8.

(p) Ex parte Naden, Re Wood, L. R. 9 Ch. 670 ; Ex parte Peacock, Re Duffield, L. R. 8 Ch. 682.

(q) Ex parte Llynvi C. & I. Co., L. R. 7 Ch. 28 ; Ex parte Waters, L. R. 8 Ch. 562 ; Robinson v. Ommanney, 23 Ch. D. 285.

(r) B. A. 1883, s. 37, sub-ss. (1) and (3) ; Emma Silver Mining Co. v. Grant, 17 Ch. D. 122 ; Jack v. Kipping, 9 Q. B. D. 113.

(s) Ex parte Pyke, Re Lister, 8 Ch. D. 754 ; Ex parte Rogers, 15 Ch. D. 207.

(t) Re Mercantile Marine Assurance Co., 25 Ch. D. 415.

(u) Ex parte Pottinger, Re Stewart, 8 Ch. D. 621.

(x) Ex parte Brymer, Co. B. L. 165 ; Cowley v. Dunlop, 7 T. R. 565 ; Ex parte Bartlett, 3 De G. & J. 378 ; Ex parte Hayward, L. R. 6 Ch. 546 ; Ex parte Newton, 16 Ch. D. 330. As to the right of voting, see B. A. 1883, Sched. I. rr. 11, 12, in Appendix.

(y) Jones v. Gordon, 2 App. Cas. 616.

(z) Re Bowness, Co. B. L. 162.

cash balance on the one side or the other can be proved for (a). A party who has negotiated a bill of exchange cannot prove against the acceptor's estate, unless he takes up the bill (b). A surety can only prove against his co-surety's estate if he has paid more than his proportion of the debt (c). Persons who have made loans under Bovill's Act, without becoming partners (d), and married women who have lent money to their husbands, cannot prove at all until the other creditors have been paid in full (e).

There are certain debts directed to be paid in priority to all others, viz. : —

All parochial or other local rates due from the bankrupt at the date of the receiving order, and having become due and payable within twelve months next before such time, and all assessed taxes, land tax, property or income tax, assessed on him up to the 5th day of April next before the date of the receiving order, and not exceeding in the whole one year's assessment (f) ;

All wages or salary of any clerk or servant in respect of services rendered to the bankrupt during four months before the date of the receiving order, not exceeding 50l. (g) ;

All wages of any labourer or workman, not exceeding 25l., whether payable for time or piece-work, in respect of services

(a) Ex parte Walker, 4 Ves. 373 ; Ex parte Macredie, Re Charles, L. R. 8 Ch. 535 ; Ex parte Cama, Re London, Bombay, and Mediterranean Bank, L. R. 9 Ch. 686. As to outstanding acceptances, see Ex parte Solarte, 2 D. & C. 261 ; Ex parte Newton, Re Bunyard, 16 Ch. D. 330.

(b) Ex parte Macredie, L. R. 8 Ch. 535 ; Ex parte Mann, 5 Ch. D. 367.

(c) Ex parte Snowdon, 17 Ch. D. 44 ; as to the rights of a surety who has paid the debt as regards the estate of the principal debtor, see Ex parte Rushworth, 10 Ves. 409 ; Gray v. Seckham, L. R. 7 Ch. 680 ; Ellis v. Emmanuel, 1 Ex. D. 157 ; Duncan,

Fox & Co. v. N. & S. Wales Bank, 6 App. Cas. 1 ; Ex parte National Provincial Bank, Re Rees, 17 Ch. D. 98.

(d) 28 & 29 Vict. c. 86, s. 5, in Appendix. See supra, p. 14.

(e) Ex parte District Bank, 16 Q. B. D. 700 ; Ex parte Taylor, Re Grason, 12 Ch. D. 366 ; 45 & 46 Vict. c. 75, s. 3 ; Ex parte Fox, L. R. 17 Q. B. D. 4 ("four months before," that is, next before).

(f) 51 & 52 Vict. c. 62, s. 1, sub-s. 1 (a) ; In re Thomas, Ex parte Ystradfodwg Local Board, 4 Morrell, 295.

(g) 51 & 52 Vict. c. 62, s. 1, sub-s. 1 (b).

rendered to the bankrupt during two months before the date of
the receiving order (*h*).

These will be paid in full forthwith. They are a first charge
on goods distrained by the landlord. But if the property is
insufficient to meet them, the debts of such creditors will abate
in equal proportions between themselves (*i*). A labourer in
husbandry who has contracted for a lump sum at the end of the
year of hiring will have priority as to the whole sum, or as to
such proportionate part as the Court may decide to be the proportion due for services to the date of the receiving order (*j*).
There are also provisions giving preferential claims to apprentices
and articled clerks of the bankrupt (*k*). With the above exceptions, and with the exception of priorities under the Friendly
Societies Act, 1875 (*l*), and of the postponement of certain debts
by virtue of Bovill's Act as to loans by persons not partners (*m*),
and the Married Women's Property Act (*n*), all provable debts
are paid *pari passu* (*o*).

There remains to be considered proof for interest and for
costs. With respect to *interest*, the general rule was that no
interest was provable, save that which was reserved by contract (*p*). Now, however, it is provided that on any debt or
sum certain, payable at a certain time or otherwise, whereon
interest is not reserved or agreed for, and which is overdue at
the date of the receiving order and provable in bankruptcy,
interest may be proved for not exceeding 4 per cent. per annum
to the date of the order from the time the debt or sum is payable,
if payable under a written instrument at a certain time, and if
not, from the time when written notice has been given to the

(*h*) 51 & 52 Vict. c. 62, s. 1, sub-s.
1 (c).

(*i*) 51 & 52 Vict. c. 62, s. 1, sub-ss.
2, 3, 4.

(*j*) 51 & 52 Vict. c. 62, s. 1, sub-s.
1 (c).

(*k*) B. A. 1883, s. 41.

(*l*) 38 & 39 Vict. c. 60 ; B. A. 1883,
s. 40, sub-s. 6.

(*m*) 28 & 29 Vict. c. 86, s. 5 ; B. A.
1883, s. 40, sub-s. 6.

(*n*) 45 & 46 Vict. c. 75, s. 3 ; B. A.
1883, s. 152.

(*o*) B. A. 1883, s. 40, sub-s. 4.

(*p*) *Ex parte Furneaux*, 2 Cox, 219 ;
*Ex parte Hankey*, 3 Bro. C. C. 504 ;
*Ex parte Williams*, 1 Rose, 399 ; *Ex
parte Brooke*, cited 12 Ves. 128 ; *Dornford* v. *Dornford*, 12 Ves. 127 ; *Bromley* v. *Goodere*, 1 Atk. 79 ; *Ex parte
Bennett*, 2 Atk. 527 ; *Ex parte Furber*,
17 Ch. D. 191.

debtor claiming interest (q). Interest after the receiving order Remedies of creditors.
can only be given if there is a surplus (r).

*Costs.*—As the law formerly stood, costs in equity could not
be proved unless taxed at the time of the bankruptcy (s). With
respect to costs at law in actions *ex contractu*, where the debt for
which the action was brought was originally provable, and the
bankruptcy had occurred after verdict though before judgment,
the costs *de incremento* are said to have been provable, being
considered as incorporated by the verdict with the original
debt, although not ascertained till judgment (t) ; and where
interlocutory judgment had been signed against the drawer of
a bill, who became bankrupt before a bill to compute had been
carried out and costs taxed, the plaintiff was allowed to prove
for the costs, the amount of the bill having been paid by the
acceptor (u). But where the verdict was not obtained till after
bankruptcy, the costs were not provable (v). Now, however, a
liability to pay costs accruing from debts or demands for unliquidated damages arising by reason of a contract or promise
before the date of the adjudication, or to which the bankrupt
may even become subject during the continuance of the bankruptcy, by reason of any obligation incurred previously to that
date, appears to be provable (w). But in actions *ex delicto*, in
case of a bankruptcy before judgment, though after verdict,
there being no debt with which the costs could be incorporated,
they could not be proved (x). And now, if judgment have not
been signed before the adjudication in actions of tort or for

(q) B. A. 1883, Sched. II., r.20 ; *Re
European Central Rail. Co.*, 4 Ch. D.
33 ; *Ex parte Fewings, Re Sneyd*, 25 Ch.
D. 338.

(r) B. A. 1883, s. 40, sub-s. 5 ;
*Ex parte Bath, Re Phillips*, 22 Ch. D.
450 ; 27 Ch. D. 509.

(s) Co. B. L. 195 ; *R.* v. *Davis*, 9
East, 318 ; *Ex parte Eicke*, 1 G. & J.
261.

(t) See *Ex parte Poucher*, 1 G. & J.
385 ; *Aylett* v. *Harford*, 2 W. Bl.
1317 ; *Ex parte Helm*, 1 Mont. & M.
70.

(u) *Ex parte Cocks*, De G. 446.

(v) *Ex parte Hill*, 11 Ves. 646 ;
*Southgate* v. *Saunders*, 5 Exch. 565.
But see *Simpson* v. *Mirabita*, L. R. 4
Q. B. 257.

(w) *Ex parte Peacock, Re Duffield*, L.
R. 8 Ch. 682.

(x) *Ex parte Newman, Re Brooke*, 3
Ch. D. 494 ; *Buss* v. *Gilbert*, 2 M. & S.
70. See *Ex parte Poucher*, 1 G. & J.
385 ; *Biré* v. *Moreau*, 4 Bing. 57 ;
*Oxlade* v. *N. E. R. Co.*, 15 C. B. N. S.
695.

demands in the nature of unliquidated damages arising otherwise than by reason of some contract or promise, proof cannot
be made for costs. But if judgment has been signed before
adjudication the costs may be proved as part of the judgment (*y*). So where an action was compromised, the defendant
apologising and agreeing by rule of Court to pay the plaintiff's
costs, it was held that the Master's allocatur rendered these
costs provable under the defendant's bankruptcy, which afterwards took place (*z*); and so were interlocutory costs held
provable which were awarded and taxed against the bankrupt
for not proceeding to trial before his bankruptcy (*a*). Proof
may be made for costs before taxation if the creditor swear to
a certain amount " and upwards " (*b*).

*Partnership Debts.*—There are some peculiar considerations
applicable to the proof of debts where a firm has wholly or in
part become involved in bankruptcy. These considerations
relate either to demands by third persons against the firm or
some of its members, or else to demands made by the partners or
their respective representatives against each other. We will
consider these two cases successively ; and, first, with respect to
demands by third persons upon a partnership or its individual
members.

All the partners in a firm may become bankrupt together, or
some or one only may become bankrupt, the rest remaining
solvent. For acts of bankruptcy are, we have seen, not to be
raised by implication, and a partner cannot become a bankrupt
unless he personally commit an act of bankruptcy (*c*) ; therefore, when the resident partner in a bank shut up the house and
absented himself and the bank stopped payment, this was held
evidence of his own bankruptcy, not of that of the non-resident
partner (*d*). Of course the separate creditor of one partner

(*y*) *Ex parte Newman, Re Brooke,*
3 Ch. D. 494.

(*z*) *Riley* v. *Byrne,* 2 B. & Ad. 779 ;
*Ex parte Harding, Re Pickering,* 5 De G.
M. & G. 367.

(*a*) *Jacobs* v. *Phillips,* 1 C. M. & R.
195.

(*b*) *Ex parte Ruffle, Re Dummelow,*
L. R. 8 Ch. 997. See *Ex parte Ditton,
Re Woods,* 13 Ch. D. 318.

(*c*) See ss. 115, 148, rr. 259—264.

(*d*) *Mills* v. *Bennett,* 2 M. & S. 555 ;
*Ex parte Mavor,* 19 Ves. 538. For
cases where the whole firm became

cannot present a joint petition (e), but we have seen that a Remedies of creditors. creditor of the firm may present a joint petition against all the partners, or against one or more of the partners without including the others (f). Where a receiving order has been made against one partner, a petition against another partner is to be filed in or transferred to the same Court, and the same receiver or trustee shall be appointed, unless it be otherwise ordered, and the proceedings may be consolidated (g). A receiving order against a firm will operate as a receiving order against each of the persons who was a partner at the date of the order (h); and no order of adjudication is to be made in the firm name, but it must be made individually against the partners (i).

Where the whole firm has become bankrupt and a petition has been presented by or against it, the whole of the joint property of the firm, and of the separate property of each of its members, is to be administered and passes to the trustee (j). But under a separate bankruptcy the property to be administered consists of the separate estate of the bankrupt, together with such part of the joint property as the bankrupt himself would be entitled to (k). And as the bankruptcy occasions a dissolution of the partnership, the trustee of the bankrupt partner becomes tenant in common with the solvent partner of the partnership effects, and holds the bankrupt's undivided share thereof, subject to the state of the partnership accounts (l).

bankrupt, see *Spencer* v. *Billing*, 3 Camp. 310; *Capper* v. *Desanges*, 3 Moore, 4; *Deffle* v. *Desanges*, 8 Taunt. 671; *Ex parte Gardner*, 1 V. & B. 74; *Eckhardt* v. *Wilson*, 8 T. R. 140; *Dutton* v. *Morrison*, 17 Ves. 193.

(e) *Prosser* v. *Smith*, Holt, 442.

(f) B. A. 1883, ss. 110, 115.

(g) B. A. 1883, s. 112. *Ex parte Green*, 3 De G. & J. 50; *In re Trott*, 7 L. T. N. S. 699.

(h) B. R. 1886, r. 262.

(i) B. R. 1886, r. 264, and see generally, rr. 259—270.

(j) See *Ex parte Cook*, 2 P. Wms. 500; *Ex parte Baudier*, 1 Atk. 98; *Hague* v. *Rolleston*, 4 Burr. 2174; *Jer-*vis v. *Tayleur*, 3 B. & Ald. 557.

(k) *Horsey's case*, 3 P. Wms. 23; *Eddie* v. *Davidson*, Dougl. 627; *Bolton* v. *Puller*, 1 B. & P. 539; *Barker* v. *Goodair*, 11 Ves. 85.

(l) *West* v. *Skip*, 1 Ves. sen. 239; *Fox* v. *Hanbury*, Cowp. 445; *Taylor* v. *Field*, 4 Ves. 396; *Smith* v. *Stokes*, 1 East, 363; *Smith* v. *Oriel*, 1 East, 368; *Holderness* v. *Shackels*, 8 B. & C. 612; *Lewis* v. *Edwards*, 7 M. & W. 300; *Morgan* v. *Marquis*, 9 Exch. 145; *Ex parte Gordon*, *Re Dixon*, L. R. 8 Ch. 555; *Ex parte Owen*, 13 Q. B. D. 113; *Turquand* v. *Board of Trade*, 11 App. Cas. 286.

_____

Hence it follows that, in case of the bankruptcy of part of an entire firm, it is necessary to take an account of the whole state of the partnership affairs, in order to ascertain *what* is to be administered (*m*) ; and in case of the bankruptcy of an entire firm it is also, as we shall immediately see, necessary to take such an account, in order to ascertain *how* the assets are to be administered (*n*). For the rule as to the application of joint and separate property to the payment of creditors is, that the joint estate shall be applied to the joint debts, the separate to the separate debts, and the surplus of each reciprocally to the creditors remaining on the other (*o*).

This rule was qualified by some exceptions which established that in the following cases (*p*) a joint creditor might prove against the separate estate *pari passu* with the separate creditors. Whether these exceptions now exist is doubtful (*q*).

*First.* A joint creditor who was the petitioning creditor in a separate petition might so prove, for the petition was in the nature of an execution for his debt against the separate estate of the bankrupt partner (*r*), and this held, though he might have a separate debt due to him sufficient to support the petition, as well as the joint debt (*s*). But it was otherwise where a joint creditor presented a petition against A. as surviving partner of B., for then the above reason ceased to apply (*t*).

*Secondly.* Joint creditors might prove against the separate estate, where there was no joint estate *and* no solvent partner (*u*).

(*m*) B. R. 1886, r. 293.

(*n*) See *Ex parte Elton*, 3 Ves. 238; *Barker* v. *Goodair*, 11 Ves. 85; *Dutton* v. *Morrison*, 17 Ves. 193; *Ex parte Farlow*, 1 Rose, 421.

(*o*) B. A. 1883, s. 40, sub-s. 3; *Ex parte Cook*, 2 P. Wms. 500; *Ex parte Elton*, 3 Ves. 238; *Ex parte Wilson*, 3 M. D. & De G. 57. See *Ex parte Clay*, 6 Ves. 814; *Ex parte Alcock*, 11 Ves. 603; *Ex parte Taitt*, 16 Ves. 193; *Ex parte Wood*, 2 M. D. & De G. 283; *Ex parte Christie*, 3 M. D. & De G. 736; *Ex parte Dear*, 1 Ch. D. 514; *Re Collie*, 3 Ch. D. 481.

(*p*) As to double proof in cases of breach of trust, see *Ex parte Barnewall*, 6 De G. M. & G. 801, Id. 795.

(*q*) See ss. 40 (3), 59.

(*r*) *Ex parte Hall*, 9 Ves. 349; *Ex parte Ackermann*, 14 Ves. 604; *Ex parte De Tastet*, 1 Rose, 10.

(*s*) *Ex parte Burnett*, coram Lord Lyndhurst, C., on appeal 2 M. D. & De G. 357.

(*t*) *Ex parte Barned*, 1 G. & J. 309.

(*u*) *Ex parte Sadler*, 15 Ves. 52; *Ex parte Machell*, 2 V. & B. 216. See *Ex parte Wylie*, 2 Rose, 393; *Ex parte Nolte*, 2 G. & J. 295. See *Lodge* v.

These two conditions must have been strictly observed, for the exception did not apply if there were a joint estate, however small (*v*), unless it were utterly incapable of being realized (*w*); nor if there were a solvent partner, *i.e.*, a partner who had not become bankrupt, even though there was no joint property (*x*), unless, indeed, it were impossible that he should be reached (*y*); the principle being, that, while there is any other fund, however small, to which they might resort, the joint creditors cannot compete with the separate ones.

*Thirdly.* Where there were no separate debts, or, which is the same thing, where the joint creditors undertook to pay them (*z*).

However, though the above are the rules respecting proof in order to a dividend, if a receiving order is made against one partner, any creditor of the firm may prove for the purpose of voting (*a*).

Where there are distinct contracts on which the bankrupt is liable, either as a member of two or more distinct firms, or as a sole contractor, and also as a member of a firm, proof may be made against the several estates liable in respect of such contracts (*b*). Thus, W. P., one of the firm of P. & P., placed trust funds in the hands of P. & P., and the firm wrongfully converted the money, it was held that, as the partners were jointly and severally liable, the proof might be made against both the joint and separate estate.

*Proof between Partners.*—The next case to be considered is

---

*Prichard*, 32 L. J. Chanc. 775. If a judgment had been obtained against one only, then he must have proved on that estate alone: *Ex parte Higgins*, 27 L. J. Bkcy. 27.

. (*v*) *Ex parte Peake*, 2 Rose, 54; *In re Lee*, Ibid. n.; *Ex parte Kennedy*, 2 De G. M. & G. 228.

(*w*) Per Lord *Eldon*, 2 Rose, 54; *Ex parte Hill*, 2 B. & P. N. R. 191, n.

(*x*) *Ex parte Kensington*, 14 Ves. 447; *Ex parte Janson*, 3 Madd. 229; Buck, 227. See *Ex parte Bauerman*, 3 Deac. 476. And this doctrine applies to the case of co-contractors as

well as of partners: *Ex parte Field*, 3 M. D. & De G. 95.

(*y*) See *Ex parte Pinkerton*, 6 Ves. 814, n.

(*z*) *Ex parte Chandler*, 9 Ves. 35; *Ex parte Hubbard*, 13 Ves. 424.

(*a*) B. A. 1883, Sched. I., r. 13.

(*b*) B. A. 1883, Sched. II., r. 18. See *Ex parte Honey, Re Jeffery*, L. R. 7 Ch. 178; *Ex parte Stone, Re Welsh*, L. R. 8 Ch. 914; *Ex parte Wilson, Re Douglas*, L. R. 7 Ch. 490; *Banco de Portugal* v. *Waddell*, 5 App. Cas. 161; *Ex parte Shephard, Re Parker*, 4 Morrell, 135.

that of demands by partners or their representatives upon each
other. It sometimes happens, that a partner is indebted to the
firm, or the firm to one of its partners; in such case, the rule
is, that an individual partner cannot prove against the joint
estate in competition with the joint creditors; for, as they are
his own creditors also, he has no right to withdraw any part of
the funds available for the payment of their debts, unless his
separate estate has been fraudulently converted to the use of the
joint estate (c), and the executor of a deceased partner is in no˙
better position (d). But the rule only applies if a joint debt
has been actually proved (e). Nor can those partners of a firm·
who remain solvent prove against the separate estate of a
member of that firm, in competition with his separate creditors,
unless the joint creditors be first paid twenty shillings in the
pound and interest; for they might, by doing so, prevent a
surplus of the separate estate from accruing, which surplus
would be available towards payment of the joint creditors (f).
Indeed, if the solvent partner will pay all the joint debts, he
may then prove against the separate estate in competition with
the separate creditors of his bankrupt copartner (g). But to
bring him within this class of creditors, there must have been
an actual satisfaction of the joint debts, either by payment of
the whole, or part in discharge of the whole. Nothing less will
be sufficient (h).

Where a solvent partner pays all the joint debts, and proves

---

(c) *Ex parte Ellis*, 2 Gl. & J. 312;
*Ex parte Blyth*, 16 Ch. D. 620; *Ex
parte Sillitoe*, 1 Gl. & J. 374; conversely where joint estate has been
fraudulently converted into separate
estate: *Read* v. *Bailey*, 3 App. Cas. 94.

(d) *Ex parte Carter*, 2 Gl. & J. 233;
*Nanson* v. *Gordon*, 1 App. Cas. 195.

(e) *Ex parte Andrews, Re Wilcoxon*,
25 Ch. D. 505; *Re Hepburn, Ex parte
Smith*, 14 Q. B. D. 394.

(f) *Ex parte Reeve*, 9 Ves. 588; *Ex
parte Ogle*, Mont. 350; *Ex parte Broome*,
1 Rose, 69; *Ex parte Rawson*, Jac. 277;
Co. B. L. 503, 505; *Ex parte Collinge*,
33 L. J. Bktcy. 9; *Ex parte Maude*,
L. R. 2 Ch. 550.

(g) *Ex parte Bass*, 36 L. J. Bktcy.
39. But see an exception, *Ex parte
Topping*, 34 L. J. Bktcy. 13; *Ex parte
Watson*, 4 Madd. 477; *Wood* v. *Dodgson*,
2 M. & S. 195; *Aflalo* v. *Fourdrinier*,·
6 Bing. 306; *Ex parte King*, 17 Ves.
115; *Ex parte Rix*, Mont. 237; *Ex
parte Taylor*, 2 Rose, 175; *Ex parte
Young*, 2 Rose, 40; 3 V. & B. 31.

(h) *Ex parte Moore*, 2 G. & J. 166;
*Ex parte Carter*,· 2 G. & J. 233; *Ex
parte Ellis*, 2 G. & J. 312;. *Ex parte
Collinge*, 33 L. J. Bktcy. 9; *In re
Dixon*, L. R. 10 Ch. 160.

against the separate estates of his copartners (more than one Remedies of creditors. having become bankrupt) for the respective sums each is bound to contribute, it has been made a question whether, if the estate of one of the bankrupts is insufficient to pay his share of the debts, the solvent partner can come upon the other bankrupt's estates for his proportion of the deficiency. Sir *John Leach* decided in the negative (i), on the ground that proof is equivalent to payment; and, therefore, that the solvent partner, having proved for each bankrupt's whole quota, must be regarded as having been paid it. Lord *Eldon* dissented from this case (k), and from the reason on which it was founded, saying, he agreed that proof was equivalent to payment when it produced payment, but doubted whether it was payment when it produced nothing.

*Proof between Estates.*—In analogy to the rule above stated, it is also held, that where all the members of a firm become bankrupt, the separate estate of one partner cannot claim against the joint estate of the firm in competition with joint creditors; nor the joint estate against the separate estate in competition with separate creditors (l). Where money or effects have been fraudulently abstracted from one estate to benefit the others, there is, as we have seen, an exception: for instance, if one partner were, in violation of the partnership articles, to draw more than his share out of a bank in which the money of the firm had been deposited, the sum so drawn by him in fraud of the partnership articles would be considered in the light of property stolen from the joint estate, and would be provable by the joint estate against his separate estate, the question, whether a case be one of fraud, of course, depending upon its peculiar circumstances (m).

---

(i) *Ex parte Watson*, Buck, 449; *Ex parte Smith*, Id. 492.

(k) *Ex parte Hunter*, Buck, 552; *Ex parte Moore*, 2 G. & J. 166.

(l) *Ex parte Burrell*, *Ex parte Pine*, Co. B. L. 532; *Ex parte Grill*, Id. 534; *Ex parte Ogle*, Mont. 350.

(m) *Ex parte Cust*, Co. B. L. 535.

See *Ex parte Harris*, 2 V. & B. 210; *Ex parte Emly*, 1 Rose, 61; *Ex parte Assignees of Lodge and Fendall*, 1 Ves. jun. 166; *Ex parte Yonge*, 3 V. & B. 31; *Ex parte Smith*, 1 G. & J. 74; *Ex parte Watkins*, Mon. & Mac. 57. See also *Ex parte Graham*, 2 M. D. & De G. 781; *Ex parte Walker*, 31 L. J.

Where one or more members of a firm carry on a distinct
trade, proof will be admitted between the estates of the general
and particular firm *pari passu* with the creditors, when the debt
sought to be proved is for goods furnished in the same way as if
they had been wholly unconnected in trade, by the one firm to
the other (*n*), at least if the estate, against which proof is admitted, is not liable with that of the firm proving to any
joint debts.   But, excepting in the case of bankers (*o*), this
rule will not be applicable where the debt has arisen only from
money advanced by the one firm to the other (*p*).

By sect. 3 of the Married Women's Property Act, the claim
of a wife for money lent to her husband for purposes of trade or
business carried on by him, or otherwise, is postponed until the
claims of all other creditors for value are satisfied.   But she may,
it would seem, receive a dividend concurrently with other creditors where the money has been lent for private purposes (*q*).

*Contributions between Estates.*—As there may be proof between
estates, so there may be contribution between them, where one
has been subjected to an undue proportion of a charge, which
ought to have fallen equally on both (*r*).

### (B.) *Remedies without Proof.*

Having now touched on the principal rules concerning *proof*,
let us proceed to notice certain cases in which the creditor has
a remedy without proving.   Under this head we comprehend
the cases, 1. of a creditor who owes to the bankrupt's estate a debt

Bktcy. 69; *Read* v. *Bailey*, 3 App.
Cas. 94.

(*n*) B. R. 1886, r. 269; *Cases of
Shakeshaft, Stirrup, and Salisbury*, 6
Ves. 123, 743, 747; *Ex parte Har-
greaves*, 1 Cox, 440; *Ex parte St.
Barbe*, 11 Ves. 413; *Ex parte Johns*,
Co. B. L. 538; *Ex parte Castell, Ex
parte Stroud*, 2 G. & J. 124, at p. 127;
*Ex parte Sillitoe*, 1 G. & J. 374;
*Ex parte Cook*, Mont. 228; *Ex parte
Williams*, 3 M. D. & De G. 433; *Ex
parte Maude*, L. R. 2 Ch. 550; *Ex
parte Glidden*, 13 Q. B. D. 43.

(*o*) *Ex parte Castell*, ubi sup. But
the case of bankers will only form an
exception where money has been advanced by them in the course of their
business as such: *Ex parte Williams*,
ubi sup.

(*p*) *Ex parte Sillitoe*, ubi supra.

(*q*) *Ex parte Tidswell, In re Tidswell*,
4 Morrell, 219.

(*r*) *Ex parte Willock*, 2 Rose, 392;
*Ex parte Wylie*, Id. 393. See *Rogers*
v. *Mackenzie*, 4 Ves. 752.   As to costs,
see B. R. 1886, r. 128.

which is entitled to set off against his demand upon it.  2. Of a Remedies of creditors.
creditor who is in possession of a security or lien upon some
portion of the bankrupt's property.  3. That of a landlord
availing himself of his right of distress in order to obtain payment of his rent.  We will consider these in order.

1. *Set-off.*—Sect. 38 of the Bankruptcy Act, 1883, provides
that :—

"Where there have been mutual credits, mutual debts, or other
mutual dealings between a debtor against whom a receiving order
shall be made under this Act and any other person proving or
claiming to prove a debt under such receiving order, an account
shall be taken of what is due from the one party to the other in
respect of such mutual dealings, and the sum due from the one
party shall be set off against any sum due from the other party,
and the balance of the account, and no more, shall be claimed or
paid on either side respectively; but a person shall not be entitled
under this section to claim the benefit of any set-off against the
property of a debtor in any case where he had, at the time of
giving credit to the debtor, notice of an act of bankruptcy committed by the debtor, and available against him."

It will be perceived that the right of set-off given by this
section is not confined to cases where there are *mutual debts*,
but comprehends cases of *mutual credits*, including not only
pecuniary demands, but also cases where that which will terminate in a debt exists on both sides (*s*), and the still wider
class of "*other mutual dealings*" (*t*).  And if the credit given

---

(*s*) *Gibson* v. *Bell*, 1 Bing. N. C.
743; *Rose* v. *Hart*, 8 Taunt. 449;
*Groom* v. *West*, 8 Ad. & E. 758;
*Easum* v. *Cato*, 5 B. & Ald. 861,
*Smith* v. *Hodson*, 4 T. R. 211; *Hankey*
v. *Smith*, 3 T. R. 507; *Ex parte Pres-
cott*, 1 Atk. 230; *Olive* v. *Smith*, 5
Taunt. 56; *Ex parte Deeze*, 1 Atk.
228; *Atkinson* v. *Elliott*, 7 T. R. 378;
*Naoroji* v. *Chartered Bank of India*,
L. R. 3 C. P. 444; *Astley* v. *Gurney*,
L. R. 4 C. P. 714; *Young* v. *Bank of
Bengal*, 1 Moo. P. C. C. 150.

(*t*) See, as to what claims fall within
these words, *Krehl* v. *Great Central*

S. C., L. R. 5 Ex. 289. See *Make-
ham* v. *Crow*, 15 C. B. N. S. 847;
*Booth* v. *Hutchinson*, L. R. 15 Eq.
30; *Peat* v. *Jones*, 8 Q. B. D. 147;
*Jack* v. *Kipping*, 9 Q. B. D. 113;
*Mersey Steel and Iron Co.* v. *Naylor*, 9
App. Cas. 434; *Ex parte Price*, *Re
Lankester*, L. R. 10 Ch. 648; *Re
Winter*, *Ex parte Bolland*, 8 Ch. D.
225; *Ex parte Keys*, 25 Ch. D. 587;
*Ex parte Caldicott*, *Re Hart*, 25 Ch.
D. 716; *Ex parte Morier*, *Re Willis*,
*Percival & Co.*, 12 Ch. D. 491; *Eberle's
Hotels and Restaurant Co.* v. *Jonas*,
18 Q. B. D. 459. At p. 465, *Brett*,

by the bankrupt existed before the bankruptcy, or before notice
of an act of bankruptcy available for adjudication, it is sufficient, although the debt to the bankrupt's estate arising from
such credit may not have accrued till afterwards (*u*). Whoever takes a bill is to be considered as giving a credit to
the acceptor, and whoever takes a note, a credit to the
maker (*x*). But, under the terms mutual debts and mutual
credits in a similar provision, it was held otherwise where a bill
was deposited with the party who attempted to set it off, not in
order to create a debt, but for some specific purpose (*y*) ; and
that no case was within those in which there was not either a
debt, or something which was, from its nature, likely to end in a
debt (*z*). It was further held that the Act (*a*) did not authorize
a set-off " where the debt, though *legally* due to the debtor from
the bankrupt, was really due to him as a trustee for another,
and, though recoverable in a cross-action, would not have been
recovered for his own benefit" (*b*). But, on the other hand, a
person who has an equitable debt due to him is as much entitled
to set it off as a legal demand (*c*). Moreover, in order to constitute such a *mutuality* as this section intends, the debts from
and to the bankrupt must be due *in the same right* (*d*). Thus,
there can be no set-off between joint and separate debts (*e*). So

M. R., says, "In my opinion, wherever in the result the dealings on each
side would end in a money claim, its
provisions would be applicable."

(*u*) *Bittlestone* v. *Timmis*, 1 C. B. 389 ;
*Hulme* v. *Mugglestone*, 3 M. & W. 30.

(*x*) Per *Bayley*, J., in *Collins* v. *Jones*,
10 B. & C. 777.

(*y*) *Key* v. *Flint*, 8 Taunt. 21. And
see *Belcher* v. *Lloyd*, 10 Bing. 310;
and *Forster* v. *Wilson*, 12 M. & W.
191 ; and the observations of *Parke*,
B., in *Alsager* v. *Currie*, 12 M. & W.
at p. 758.

(*z*) *Rose* v. *Sims*, 1 B. & Ad. 521 ;
*Sampson* v. *Burton*, 2 B. & B. 89 ;
*Rose* v. *Hart*, 8 Taunt. 499 ; *Ex parte
Ockenden*, 1 Atk. 235 ; *Bell* v. *Carey*, 8
C. B. 887.

(*n*) 6 Geo. 4, c. 16, s. 50.

(*b*) *Forster* v. *Wilson*, 12 M. & W.
191, see p. 204 ; *Belcher* v. *Lloyd*, 10
Bing. 310 ; *De Mattos* v. *Saunders*,
L. R. 7 C. P. 570 ; *Lackington* v.
*Combes*, 6 Bing. N. C. 71 ; *De Pass* v.
*Bell*, 10 C. B. N. S. 517 ; *Ex parte
Kingston*, L. R. 6 Ch. 632.

(*c*) *Ex parte Deeze*, 1 Atk. 228 ;
*Bailey* v. *Johnson*, L. R. 6 Ex. 279 ; 7
Ex. 263 ; *Elkin* v. *Baker*, 11 C. B.
N. S. 526 ; *Thornton* v. *Maynard*, L. R.
10 C. P. 695 ; *Bailey* v. *Finch*, L. R.
7 Q. B. 34.

(*d*) *Ex parte Whitehead*, 1 G. & J.
39 ; *West* v. *Pryce*, 2 Bing. 455 ; *The
New Quebrada Co.* v. *Carr*, L. R. 4
C. P. 651.

(*e*) *Ex parte Christie*, 10 Ves. 105 ;
*Ex parte Twogood*, 11 Ves. 517 ; *Ex
parte Ross*, Buck, 125.

in an action by a trustee upon a note given to the bankrupt's wife *dum sola*, a debt due from the bankrupt cannot be set off (*f*); nor can a debt arising after bankruptcy to or from the trustee be set off against a debt from or to the bankrupt before bankruptcy (*g*), even though the debt on which the trustee claims, though arising after bankruptcy, was founded on a contract made by the bankrupt before bankruptcy (*h*). The set-off is equivalent to payment, and will put an end to a lien for a sum so set off (*i*).

The only qualification imposed on the right of set-off by sect. 38 of the Act of 1883 is contained in the words, "*but a person shall not be entitled under this section to claim the benefit of any set-off against the property of a debtor in any case where he had at the time of giving credit to the debtor notice of an act of bankruptcy committed by the debtor and available against him*" (*j*). Notice of the act of bankruptcy is, therefore, the criterion; so that where the defendant, in an action brought by the assignees of certain bankers, claimed to set off notes which he had industriously obtained after the bank had stopped payment, it was held that he had a right to do so, the notes having been taken before he knew of the commission of an act of bankruptcy (*k*). But a debtor to the firm was not allowed to set off notes which he had taken after notice that three out of four partners had committed acts of bankruptcy (*l*). The act of bankruptcy, too, of which the claimant had notice, must be "available," *i. e.*, it must have been committed within three months next before the presentation of the petition on which the receiving order is made, and during the subsistence of a sufficient debt. The mutual account ought, as a rule, to be taken down to the commencement of the bankruptcy (*m*), but if the act of bank-

---

(*f*) *Yates* v. *Sherrington*, 11 M. & W. 42.

(*g*) *West* v. *Pryce*, 2 Bing. 455; *Alloway* v. *Steere*, 10 Q. B. D. 22; *Sankey Brook Coal Co.* v. *Marsh*, L. R. 6 Ex. 185.

(*h*) *Ince Hall Rolling Mills Co.* v. *Douglas Forge Co.*, 8 Q. B. D. 179.

(i) *Ex parte Barnett*, L. R. 9 Ch. 293.

(*j*) B. A. 1883, s. 38.

(*k*) *Hawkins* v. *Whitten*, 10 B. & C. 217; *Dickson* v. *Cass*, 1 B. & Ad. 343. See also *Forster* v. *Wilson*, 12 M. & W. 191.

(*l*) *Dickson* v. *Cass*, 1 B. & Ad. 343.

(*m*) *Re Milan Tramways Co.*, 25 Ch. D. 587; *Re Gillespie, Ex parte Reid*, 14 Q. B. D. 963.

ruptcy is secret, down to the time when the person claiming to set off had notice of it (*n*). It may be doubted whether any agreement can exclude the operation of this section (*o*).

The effect of this provision is to confer a much more comprehensive right of set-off than the party would otherwise have, and also to give effect to it, notwithstanding an available act of bankruptcy, if he had not notice of it.

2. *Securities and Liens on the Bankrupt's Property.*—There are certain cases in which a creditor is allowed to satisfy himself out of some part of the bankrupt's property on which he has obtained a security. These cases will be dealt with separately, first observing that the statute gives validity to many transactions entered into by or with a bankrupt before the date of the receiving order by a person dealing *bonâ fide*, and without notice of a prior available act of bankruptcy ( *p* ).

*Executions.*—To entitle a creditor to retain, as against the trustee, the benefit of an execution issued by him against the goods or land of a debtor, he must, before the receiving order, and before notice of the presentation of a petition by or against the debtor, or of the commission of any available act of bankruptcy by him, have completed his execution ; *i.e.*, in the case of goods he must have seized and sold; and in the case of land, he must have seized (*q*).

As to what "seizure" is, there is sometimes doubt; the delivery of land in execution under a writ of *elegit* appears to be sufficient (*r*).

Although seizure and sale for any amount is an act of bankruptcy (*s*), the creditor will be entitled to retain the benefit of his execution ; although an act of bankruptcy, the sale is valid (*t*).

(*n*) *Elliott* v. *Turquand*, 7 App. Cas. 79.

(*o*) *Ex parte Fletcher, Re Vaughan*, 6 Ch. D. 350; *Ex parte Barnett, Re Deveze*, L. R. 9 Ch. 293.

(*p*) B. A. 1883, s. 49; *Ex parte Helder*, 24 Ch. D. 339.

(*q*) B. A. 1883, s. 45; *Mackay* v. *Merrit*, 34 W. R. 433.

(r) *In re Hobson*, 33 Ch. D. 493. As to equitable executions, see *In re Dickson*, 6 Morrell, 1.

(*s*) B. A. 1883, s. 4, sub-s. (1) (e).

(*t*) B. A. 1883, s. 46, sub-s. (3); *Ex parte Villars, Re Rogers*, L. R. 9 Ch. 432.

Mere notice that an available act of bankruptcy has been committed by the debtor is enough, though the creditor may not have notice of the particular act relied on (*u*) ; but this notice must be to the person on whose account the execution was issued ; and notice to the sheriff's officer in possession under an execution is not equivalent to notice to him (*v*). Notice, however, to the solicitor, or his clerk or agent issuing, or having the conduct of the execution, is, it appears, sufficient (*x*).

A sheriff who has seized goods, and who has before sale been served with notice of a receiving order made against the debtor, must deliver the goods to the official receiver ; and the costs of the execution will be a charge on them (*y*). If, however, the goods are sold in respect of execution on a judgment for a sum exceeding twenty pounds, the sheriff, after deducting costs, must retain the balance for fourteen days ; and if within that time he is served with notice of a bankruptcy petition by or against the debtor, and the debtor is adjudged bankrupt on that or any other petition of which the sheriff has notice, he must pay such balance to the trustee instead of to the creditor (*z*).

The sale, as we have seen, is valid ; and if no notice of a petition be served at the end of the fourteen days, the sheriff may hand over the proceeds to the creditor, who will be entitled to retain them (*a*), if he had not notice of any prior act of bankruptcy (*b*). The notice thus given should afford sufficient information to the sheriff that the person against whom the petition is presented is the execution debtor, and must be served on the sheriff or his recognized agent for such purpose (*c*). If, in order to prevent a seizure or a sale, the debtor pay money to

(*u*) *Ramsey* v. *Eaton*, 10 M. & W. 22 ; *Udal* v. *Walton*, 14 M. & W. 254 ; *Turner* v. *Hardcastle*, 11 C. B. N. S. 683.

(*v*) *Ramsay* v. *Eaton*, supra.

(*x*) *Bird* v. *Bass*, 6 M. & G. 143 ; *Rothwell* v. *Timbrell*, 1 Dowl. N. S. 778 ; *Pike* v. *Stephens*, 12 Q. B. 465 ; *Brewin* v. *Briscoe*, 2 E. & E. 116 ; *Pennell* v. *Stephens*, 7 C. B. 987.

(*y*) B. A. 1883, s. 46, sub-s. (1).

(*z*) B. A. 1883, s. 46, sub-s. (2).

(*a*) *Ex parte Villars*, *Re Rogers*, L. R. 9 Ch. 432 ; *Ex parte James*, L. R. 9 Ch. 609.

(*b*) *Ex parte Dawes*, L. R. 19 Eq. 438.

(*c*) *Ex parte Spooner*, L. R. 10 Ch. 168 ; *Ex parte Warren*, *Re Holland*, 15 Q. B. D. 48.

the sheriff, with the assent of the creditor, the latter is entitled
to it (*d*).

The creditor may abandon part of his claim, so as to avoid
the operation of the section (*e*). The fourteen days are to be
reckoned from the completion of the whole sale (*f*). An execution is not invalid by reason of its being an act of bankruptcy;
and a purchaser in good faith of the goods under a sale by the
sheriff in all cases acquires a good title against the trustee (*g*).

The provisions as to remedies against the property of a debtor
are binding on the Crown (*h*).

*Mortgages and Pledges.*—A legal mortgage gives the mortgagee a right to retain the property mortgaged until his debt
is satisfied, nor can the trustee redeem without paying interest
up to the time of redemption (*i*). And an equitable mortgage
by agreement, or by deposit of title deeds, is in like manner
upheld in Courts of Bankruptcy (*j*). A mortgagee of leasehold
premises is not affected by disclaimer (*k*).

In one case, where the bankrupt, not then being insolvent or in
contemplation of insolvency, had given a voluntary bond, and
had afterwards deposited title deeds as a security for the amount
of the bond, Vice-Chancellor *Knight Bruce* held, that parties
who had made the bond a subject of settlement were entitled to
the benefit of the deposit (*l*). A pledge of personal property is

(*d*) *Stock* v. *Holland*, L. R. 9 Ex.
147 ; *Ex parte Brooke, Re Hassall*, L. R.
9 Ch. 301. See, however, *Ex parte
Pearson, Re Mortimer*, L. R. 8 Ch. 667.

(*e*) *Ex parte Rega, Re Salinger*, 6 Ch.
D. 332 ; *Re Hinks, Ex parte Berthier*,
7 Ch. D. 882 ; *Turner* v. *Bridgett*, 8
Q. B. D. 392 ; *Mostyn* v. *Stock*, 9 Q.
B. D. 432.

(*f*) *Jones* v. *Parcell*, 11 Q. B. D. 430.

(*g*) B. A. 1883, s. 46, sub-s. (3).

(*h*) B. A. 1883, s. 150; *Ex parte
Postmaster-General*, 10 Ch. D. 595 ;
*Ex parte Commissioners of Woods and
Forests*, 21 Q. B. D. 380.

(*i*) See *Ex parte Barnes*, 3 Deac. 223 ;

*Ex parte Bignold*, Ibid. 121 ; 7 Vin.
Abr. 100. As to the mode and terms
by and on which a mortgagee may
procure a sale of the property, see
B. R. 1886, rr. 73—77.

(*j*) *Ex parte Orett*, 3 M. & A. 153 ;
*Ex parte Whitbread*, 19 Ves. 209. But
see *Ex parte Perry*, De Gex, 252 ; *Ex
parte Rogers*, 25 L. J. Bank. 41 ; *Ex
parte Littledale*, 24 L. J. Bank. 9 ; *Ex
parte Union Bank of Manchester*, L. R.
12 Eq. 354.

(*k*) *Ex parte Watton*, 17 Ch. D. 746,
753.

(*l*) *Meggison* v. *Forster*, 2 Y. & C.
C. C. 336.

in the nature of a mortgage, and can only be redeemed by payment of the sum advanced upon it (*m*). Mortgages of personal chattels are generally effected by bills of sale, which are now subject to special enactments (*n*).

*Liens.*—A *lien*, such as we have described in the preceding chapter, is available against the trustee (*o*); so is a vendor's legal lien on a thing sold but not paid for, and his right of stoppage *in transitu* (*p*); so also is the equitable right of a vendor of real estate to a lien for his unpaid purchase-money (*q*) against the vendee, volunteers, purchasers with notice, or persons claiming equitable interests under the vendee (*r*).

An equitable assignment of an interest in personalty (not being a fraudulent preference) is available against the trustee. A distinction, however, must be drawn between an equitable assignment and a mere licence to seize (*s*). Where the agreement to assign does not come into existence till after bankruptcy, the creditor will get no title and be left to prove for breach of the contract to assign (*t*); but a charge on money earned before but not payable till after bankruptcy will be

*Remedies of creditors.*

(*m*) *Demandray* v. *Metcalf*, Prec. Chanc. 419 ; 2 Vern. 691 ; *Maughan* v. *Sharpe*, 17 C. B. N. S. 443.

(*n*) 41 & 42 Vict. c. 31 ; 45 & 46 Vict. c. 43.

(*o*) *Ex parte Underwood*, De Gex, 190. It would seem that a general lien on goods coming into the hands of a party before the fiat, without notice, was protected by Stat. 2 & 3 Vict. c. 29: *Bowman* v. *Malcolm*, 11 M. & W. 833. Neither a security arising by seizure of bills, notes, or bonds, under 1 & 2 Vict. c. 110, nor an order binding a debt under the garnishee clause of the Common Law Procedure Act, 1854, or the Rules of Court, 1883, constitutes a lien : *Holmes* v. *Tutton*, 5 E. & B. 65 ; *Tilbury* v. *Brown*, 30 L. J. Q. B. 46 ; *Wood* v. *Dunn*, L. R. 1 Q. B. 77 ; 2 Q. B. 73.

(*p*) *Ex parte Chalmers, Re Edwards*, L. R. 8 Ch. 289 ; *Valpy* v. *Oakeley*, 16

Q. B. 941 ; *Kendal* v. *Marshall & Co.*, 11 Q. B. D. 356 ; *Ex parte Miles, Re Isaacs*, 15 Q. B. D. 39.

(*q*) *Ex parte Loaring*, 2 Rose, 79 ; *Ex parte Peake*, 1 Mad. 346 ; *Ex parte Parkes*, 1 G. & J. 228 ; *Ex parte Dicken*, Buck, 115 ; *Rose* v. *Watson*, 33 L. J. Ch. 385.

(*r*) See Sugden, V. & P. Chap. 12 ; *Blackburne* v. *Gregson*, 1 Bro. C. C. 419.

(*s*) *Holyroyd* v. *Marshall*, 10 H. of L. Cas. 191 ; *Reeve* v. *Whitmore*, 33 L. J. Ch. 63 ; *Brown* v. *Bateman*, L. R. 2 C. P. 272 ; *Thompson* v. *Cohen*, L. R. 7 Q. B. 527 ; *Cole* v. *Kernot*, L. R. 7 Q. B. 534 ; *Clements* v. *Mathews*, 11 Q. B. D. 808 ; *Tailby* v. *Official Receiver*, 13 App. Cas. 523.

(*t*) *Collyer* v. *Isaacs*, 19 Ch. D. 342 ; *Ex parte Nichols, Re Jones*, 22 Ch. D. 782.

good (*u*). If the assignment is conditional, and the condition has not happened before the bankruptcy, the assignment will be defeated by that event, and will not take effect even though the condition afterwards happen (*v*) ; and if the condition be the occurrence of a bankruptcy, it appears to be void as against public policy (*x*). With regard to money, the rule seems to be, that it is sufficient to render the assignment valid if the debt assigned be not larger than the sum due from the party assigning (*y*). But it would appear that a contract entered into by a bankrupt that certain of his goods should, *in case of his bankruptcy*, become the property of other persons, if they should so choose, would not be binding on his trustee, for that he cannot make a contract which would have the effect of vesting in others *after his bank-ruptcy* the property which *on* his bankruptcy had vested in his trustee (*z*).

The Bills of Sale Act, 1882 (*a*), renders a bill of sale void, as to all goods (save certain growing crops and substituted plant and machinery) which are not specifically described in the schedule thereto, or of which the grantor was not the true owner at the time of its execution.

3. *Distress.*—A landlord or other person to whom any rent is due from the bankrupt may distrain therefor either before or after the commencement of the bankruptcy (*b*). Debts, however, entitled to preferential payment are a first charge on the goods distrained or their proceeds (see ante, p. 739). If the distress is made after the commencement of the bankruptcy, it will only be available for one year's rent due prior to the adju-

(*u*) *Ex parte Moss, Re Toward*, 14 Q. B. D. 310.

(*v*) *Burn* v. *Carvalho*, 1 Ad. & E. 883.

(*x*) See *Tripp* v. *Armitage*, 4 M. & W. 687, per Ld. *Abinger*. But see *Ex parte Wright*, 2 Deac. 551.

(*y*) *Crowfoot* v. *Gurney*, 9 Bing. 372; *Tibbits* v. *George*, 5 Ad. & E. 107; *Hutchinson* v. *Heyworth*, 9 Ad. & E. 375; *Walker* v. *Rostron*, 9 M. & W.

411.

(*z*) Per Lord *Abinger* in *Tripp* v. *Armitage*, 4 M. & W. 687; *Whitmore* v. *Mason*, 2 J. & H. 204. But see *Hawthorne* v. *Newcastle and South Shields Rail. Co.*, 3 Q. B. 734, n.; *In re Waugh*, 4 Ch. D. 524; *Ex parte Newitt, Re Garrud*, 16 Ch. D. 522.

(*a*) 45 & 46 Vict. c. 43, ss. 4, 5, 6.

(*b*) Sect. 42 (1).

dication, and the landlord must prove for the surplus (c). The Remedies of creditors.
rent must be a real rent (d), although it may be one reserved
by an attornment clause in a mortgage deed (e). A distress is
not liable to be restrained (f). A company with statutory
powers similar to those of a landlord may distrain in the same
way as a landlord under this section (g).

If the distress be made before the commencement of the
bankruptcy, the landlord is, subject to the provisions of the
Agricultural Holdings Act, 1883 (h), entitled to six years' rent,
if so much be in arrear, though *the sale* be made after the tenant
has been adjudged a bankrupt (i).

It has been held that if the goods distrained be a stranger's,
the landlord may hold them as a security for more than a year's
rent; inasmuch as the rent is not released by the bankrupt's
discharge, and the bankrupt's discharge from it is merely personal (k). If, too, the landlord, having made a distress, withdraw from possession of the goods upon being paid the entire
rent by a person who claims them under a bill of sale, the
trustee cannot sue the landlord for money had and received (l).

### SECTION VII.—*Official Receivers and Trustees.*

*Official Receivers.*—On the making of a receiving order, an Official receivers and trustees.
official receiver of the debtor's property (m) is, as we have seen,

---

(c) B. A. 1883, s. 42. See, as to
rent accruing due *after* the adjudication, *Ex parte Hale,* 1 Ch. D. 285.

(d) *Ex parte Williams, Re Thompson,*
7 Ch. D. 138; *Re Stockton Iron Fur-
nace Co.,* 10 Ch. D. 335; *Ex parte
Jackson, Re Bowes,* 14 Ch. D. 725; *Ex
parte Voisey, Re Knight,* 21 Ch. D. 442.

(e) *Ex parte Punnett, Re Kitchin,* 16
Ch. D. 226; *Ex parte Queen's Benefit
Building Society, Re Threlfall,* 16 Ch. D.
274; *Ex parte Voisey, Re Knight,* 21
Ch. D. 442; *In re Tryman's Estate,*
38 Ch. D. 468.

(f) *Ex parte Birmingham Gas Co.,
Re Fanshaw,* L. R. 11 Eq. 615.

(g) *Ex parte Birmingham Gas Co.,
Re Fanshaw,* supra; *Ex parte Harrison, Re Peake,* 13 Q. B. D. 753; and
see *Ex parte Hill, Re Roberts,* 6 Ch. D.
63.

(h) 46 & 47 Vict. c. 61, s. 44.

(i) *Ex parte Bayly,* 22 L. J. Bank. 26.

(k) *Brocklehurst* v. *Lawe,* 7 E. & B.
176. See *Newton* v. *Scott,* 9 M. & W.
434; 10 M. & W. 471. The words,
too, of B. A. 1883, s. 42, are limited
to the goods of the bankrupt.

(l) *Lackington* v. *Elliott,* 7 M. & G.
538.

(m) B. A. 1883, s. 9.

Official receivers and trustees.

appointed. Official receivers are officers of, and appointed by, the Board of Trade (*n*), who may also appoint deputies (*o*). Their duties relate both to the conduct of the debtor and the administration of his estate (*p*). As regards the debtor, the official receiver is to investigate his conduct, and report thereon to the Court, and to take part in his public examination, and in the prosecution of a fraudulent debtor (*q*). As regards the debtor's estate, the official receiver's duty is to act as trustee pending the appointment of trustee during any vacancy in the office of trustee; and, in small bankruptcies (*r*), to summon and preside at the first meeting, to issue proxies, to report to the creditors any proposal made by the debtor, and to advertise the receiving order, &c. (*s*). He has the powers of a receiver of the High Court. He is bound, as far as possible, to consult the wishes of creditors (*t*). He must assist the debtor in preparing his statements of affairs (*u*), and may, if he see fit, appoint a special manager of the estate, and authorize him to raise money (*v*), and apply to the Court without formality for directions (*w*). The costs and expenses to which he is put will be provided for out of the debtor's estate (*x*). He may make an allowance out of the estate for the subsistence of the debtor and his family (*y*). After adjudication, the official receiver possesses the powers of a trustee until one is appointed, and may, under s. 56 (1), sell any portion of the debtor's property (*z*).

Having seen towards the payment of what debts the bankrupt's property is applicable, let us inquire by whom it is to be collected, and in whom vested, for the purpose of such

---

(*n*) B. A. 1883, s. 66; B. R. 1886, r. 321.

(*o*) B. A. 1883, s. 67; B. R. 1886, r. 329.

(*p*) B. A. 1883, s. 68.

(*q*) B. A. 1883, s. 69.

(*r*) B. A. 1883, s. 70, sub-ss. 1 (a) and (g); s. 87, sub-s. 4; s. 121.

(*s*) B. A. 1883, s. 70, sub-ss. 1 (b) to (f).

(*t*) B. A. 1883, s. 70, sub-s. 2.

(*u*) B. R. 1886, rr. 324, 326; B. A. 1883, s. 70, sub-s. 2.

(*v*) B. A. 1883, ss. 12, 70, sub-s. 1 (b). The official receiver has complete discretion as to the appointment: *Re Whittaker*, 50 L. T. 510.

(*w*) B. R. 1886, rr. 332—334.

(*x*) See B. R. 1886, rr. 108, 125, 231, 339.

(*y*) B. R. 1886, r. 325.

(*z*) *Turquand* v. *Board of Trade*, 11 App. Cas. 286.

application. This brings us to the office, rights, and duties of Official receivers and trustees. the trustee.

*Trustees.*—When the debtor is adjudged bankrupt, or the creditors have resolved on adjudication, they may by ordinary resolution, appoint a trustee (*a*). The trustee will have to give security to the Board of Trade, who may, subject to the decision of the High Court (*b*), object to the appointment. The Board of Trade will, if they do not object to the trustee, give him a certificate, which will be conclusive evidence of his appointment (*c*). They have power, in case of neglect by the creditors, to appoint a trustee, subject to the right of the creditors subsequently to appoint their own trustee in his place (*d*). The creditors have also the power to appoint a committee of inspection, consisting of not more than five or less than three persons chosen from the creditors entitled to vote, or the holders of general proxies or powers of attorney from such creditors (*e*). Joint trustees may be appointed; the creditors declaring whether any act is to be done by one or more of such persons. They will be joint tenants of the bankrupt's property. And persons may be appointed to act as trustees in succession in case of the one first named declining to act or failing to satisfy the Board of Trade (*f*).

The remuneration of the trustee will be fixed by an ordinary resolution of the creditors, and must be in the form of a percentage, half on the amount realized and half on the amount distributed in dividend (*g*). No vote of the trustee or his partner, clerk, solicitor, or solicitor's clerk, either as creditor or proxy, is to be reckoned in the majority required for passing any resolution affecting his remuneration or conduct (*h*). The Court may order any trustee who has solicited proxies or the office of trustee to be deprived of his remuneration (*i*). There are special provisions as to a trustee's costs (*k*), receipts, payments, and

(*a*) B. A. 1883, s. 21, sub-s. 1.
(*b*) B. A. 1883, s. 21, sub-ss. 2, 3.
(*c*) B. A. 1883, s. 21, sub-ss. 2, 4.
(*d*) B. A. 1883, s. 21, sub-ss. 6, 7.
(*e*) B. A. 1883, s. 22.
(*f*) B. A. 1883, s. 84.

(*g*) B. A. 1883, s. 72; B. R. 1886, rr. 305—307.
(*h*) B. A. 1883, s. 88.
(i) B. A. 1883, Scbed I. r. 20.
(*k*) B. A. 1883, s. 73; B. R. 1886, rr. 108, 125.

accounts (*l*), as to the books to be kept by him (*m*), the control
which the creditors (*n*) and the Board of Trade (*o*) have over
him, his release on the termination or resignation of his office (*p*),
and his removal from office (*q*).

A trustee may sue and be sued in his official name (*r*). He
may apply to the Court for directions (*s*). Any decision or act of
his may be the subject of an appeal to the Court by any person
aggrieved thereby (*t*).

A trustee has power to sell the property, give receipts, prove
for any debt due to the bankrupt, exercise powers, and deal with
property to which the bankrupt is beneficially entitled as tenant
in tail (*u*). He may not, without leave of the Court, nor may
any member of the committee of inspection, purchase the estate
or any part of it (*x*). He has power further, but only with the
leave of the committee of inspection given for the specific
purpose in each case, to carry on the bankrupt's business, to
bring or defend actions, to employ a solicitor or agent, to sell
the property for a sum to be paid at a future time, to mortgage
the property, to refer disputes to arbitration, and make
compromises, and to divide property in its existing form among
creditors. And it is his duty, as soon as may be, to take possession of the bankrupt's deeds, books, and documents, and all
other parts of his property capable of manual delivery (*y*).

*Interest of Trustee in Bankrupt's Property.*—Such being the
duties and rights of the trustee, it remains to ascertain about
what *property* these duties and rights are to be exercised, and
the manner in which it is to be dealt with.

Upon the debtor being adjudged bankrupt his property

(l) B. A. 1883, ss. 74—78, 81; B. R.
1886, rr. 285—296, 314.

(m) B. A. 1883, s. 80; B. R. 1886,
rr. 285—288.

(n) B. A. 1883, s. 89; B. R. 1886,
rr. 311, 319.

(o) B. A. 1883, s. 91.

(p) B. A. 1883, s. 82; B. R. 1886,
rr. 292, 304, 309, 310.

(q) B. A. 1883, s. 86; B. R. 1886,
rr. 302, 303.

(r) B. A. 1883, s. 83.

(s) B. A. 1883, s. 89, sub-s. 3; B. R.
1886, r. 213.

(t) B. A. 1883, s. 90.

(u) B. A. 1883, s. 56.

(x) B. R. 1886, r. 316.

(y) B. A. 1883, s. 50, sub-s. 1; s. 57;
B. R. 1886, r. 349.

becomes divisible among his creditors and vests in the trustee (z). The property passes from trustee to trustee, including in this term the official receiver, and vests in the trustee for the time being without any conveyance, assignment, or transfer (a).

Let us therefore inquire—1st. What property of the bankrupt vests in the trustee. 2nd. What property, belonging at the time of the bankruptcy to other persons, vests in him.

The word "property" includes money, goods, things in action, land, and every description of property, whether real or personal, and whether situate in England or elsewhere; also, obligations, easements, and every description of estate, interest and profit, present or future, vested or contingent, arising out of or incident to property as above defined (b). It is further provided that it shall comprise *all* such property as may belong to, or be vested in, the bankrupt at the commencement of the bankruptcy, or may be acquired by, or devolve on, him before his discharge, and the capacity to exercise, and take proceedings for exercising, all such powers in respect of property as might have been exercised by the bankrupt for his own benefit at the commencement of the bankruptcy, or before his discharge, except the right of nomination to a vacant ecclesiastical benefice (c). There are two exceptions—viz., of trust property, and tools, apparel and bedding—to which attention will be presently called.

We will now advert to some special portions of this property.

*Estates Tail and Base Fees.*—The trustee is entitled " to deal with any property to which the bankrupt is beneficially entitled as tenant in tail in the same manner as the bankrupt might have dealt with it; and sections 56 to 73 (both inclusive) of the Act of the session of the 3rd and 4th years of the reign of King William the Fourth, chapter 74, ' for the abolition of

---

(z) B. A. 1883, s. 20, sub-s. 1; s. 54, sub-s. 1.

(a) B. A. 1883, s. 54, sub-s. 3.

(b) B. A. 1883, s. 168, sub-s. 1; *Ex parte Rogers*, 16 Ch. D. 665.

(c) B. A. 1883, s. 44.

fines and recoveries, and the substitution of more simple modes of assurance,' shall extend and apply to proceedings under this Act as if those sections were here re-enacted and made applicable in terms to those proceedings " (d).

*Copyholds.*—With regard to these, the statute enacts that, " where any part of the property of the bankrupt is of copyhold or customary tenure, or is any like property passing by surrender and admittance, or in any similar manner, the trustee shall not be compellable to be admitted to the property, but may deal with it in the same manner as if it had been capable of being and had been duly surrendered or otherwise conveyed to such uses as the trustee may appoint; and any appointee of the trustee shall be admitted to or otherwise invested with the property accordingly " (e).

*Contingent Interests.*—These pass under the express words contained in the statute; but the possibility of an heir during the lifetime of his ancestor does not (f). So the possibility of a husband becoming entitled as tenant by the curtesy to real property left contingently to his wife (g).

*Advowsons—Benefices.*—The advowson itself may be sold for the benefit of the creditors; but if the church fall void before the sale, the bankrupt shall present, for the law does not consider the void turn as of any pecuniary value (h), and the Act therefore excepts from its operation " the right of nomination to a vacant ecclesiastical benefice "(i). If the bankrupt be the incumbent he cannot be removed. The profits, however, of the living are rendered available for the payment of his creditors by sect. 52, which enables the trustee to obtain a sequestration of

(d) B. A. 1883, s. 56, sub-s. 5.

(e) B. A. 1883, s. 50, sub-s. 4.

(f) *Moth* v. *Frome*, Amb. 394. See *Carleton* v. *Leighton*, 3 Mer. 667 ; *Re Vizard's Trust*, L. R. 1 Ch. 588.

(g) *Gibbins* v. *Eyden*, L. R. 7 Eq. 371.

(h) Co. B. L. 297 ; *Ex parte Meymot*, 1 Atk. 200 ; *Gally* v. *Selby*, 1 Str. 403.

(i) B. A, 1883, s. 44.

the profits of the benefice, subject to the right of the bishop to appoint a stipend to the bankrupt in respect of the performance of the duties of the benefice, and to the claim of any licensed curate for salary for duties performed during four months prior to the receiving order, not exceeding fifty pounds (k).

*Officers—Half-pay—Pensions—Salary, &c.*—Where the bankrupt is an officer in the army or navy, or an officer or clerk or civil servant of the Crown, the trustee may obtain an order for the payment to him of such portion of the bankrupt's pay or salary as the Court, with the concurrence of the chief officer of the department, may direct; and where he is in receipt of a salary or income other than these, or is entitled to any half-pay or pension, or compensation granted by the Treasury, the trustee may, in like manner, obtain an order for payment to him of such portion thereof as the Court may direct (m). Where the allowance is purely voluntary, the section does not apply.

*Choses in Action.*—The trustee takes all the bankrupt's choses in action and obligations as part of the bankrupt's property (n). He has thus a right to sue upon beneficial contracts made with the bankrupt, where pecuniary loss is the substantial and primary cause of action, and for injuries affecting his property, so far as they do not involve a claim for personal damages for which he would be entitled to a remedy whether his property was impaired or not (o). Under former statutes, which transferred to the assignees all the personal estate, effects, and debts due to the bankrupt, it was held that actions for mere personal wrongs (p), or breaches of contracts having relation to the bank-

(k) See *Hopkins* v. *Clarke*, 5 B. & S. 753.

(m) B. A. 1883, s. 53; *Ex parte Huggins*, 21 Ch. D. 85; *Ex parte Benwell, Re Hutton*, 14 Q. B. D. 301; *Ex parte Wicks*, 17 Ch. D. 70; *In re Webber*, 3 Morrell, 288.

(n) B. A. 1883, s. 44 (i), and sect.

168.

(o) *Rogers* v. *Spence*, 12 C. & F. 700; *Brewer* v. *Dew*, 11 M. & W. 625.

(p) *Wright* v. *Fairfield*, 2 B. & Ad. 727; *Hancock* v. *Caffyn*, 8 Bing. 358; *Porter* v. *Vorleg*, 9 Bing. 93 (disapproved, *Ashdown* v. *Ingamells*, 5 Ex. D. 280); *Whitworth* v. *Davis*, 1 V. &

rupt's person and the breach of what would affect him personally,
and not by way of diminishing his personal estate, such, for
instance, as a contract to marry him or to cure him of a wound
or disease (*q*), or contracts from which his estate could derive no
possible advantage, did not pass (*r*).

There are some cases in which the trustee may elect whether
he will affirm a contract made with the bankrupt, and sue on it,
or proceed in his own right in tort; for instance, where the
defendant sold the bankrupt's goods after an act of bankruptcy,
and with notice of it, the assignees in bankruptcy were allowed
to sue for the price as money had and received to their use (*s*);
but could also have sued in trover for the goods.

A trustee who carries out a contract of the bankrupt is entitled
at any time, on finding it unprofitable, to cease to continue it;
the other party to the contract being left to his remedy by proof
for damages for the breach (*t*). Contracts involving the personal
skill of the bankrupt (*u*), and, as a rule, his personal earnings (*x*),
do not pass to the trustee, though the latter might possibly be
made the subject of an order of the Court, as being salary or
income (*y*). Personal earnings, however, of the bankrupt, arising
from a trade carried on by him after bankruptcy, and before
discharge, will, if the trustee chooses to interfere, and to that

---

B. 545; *Sloper* v. *Fish*, 2 V. & B.
145; *Howard* v. *Crowther*, 8 M. & W.
601; *Ex parte Vine, Re Wilson*, 8 Ch.
D. 364.

(*q*) *Beckham* v. *Drake*, 2 H. of L.
Cas. 579; *Boddington* v. *Castelli*, 1 E.
& B. 879; *Wetherell* v. *Julius*, 10
C. B. 267; *North* v. *Gurney*, 1 J. & H.
509; *Morgan* v. *Steble*, L. R. 7 Q. B.
611; but see *Hodgson* v. *Sidney*, L. R.
1 Ex. 313; *Wadling* v. *Oliphant*, 1
Q. B. D. 145.

(r) *Trott* v. *Smith*, 12 M. & W. 688;
*Wright* v. *Fairfield*, 2 B. & Ad. 727;
and see *Hill* v. *Smith*, 12 M. & W.
618; *Alder* v. *Keighley*, 15 M. & W.
117.

(*s*) *King* v. *Leith*, 2 T. R. 141;
*Clark* v. *Gilbert*, 2 Bing. N. C. 343.
See *Gye* v. *Hitchcock*, 4 Ad. & E. 84;
*Russell* v. *Bell*, 10 M. & W. 340; *Gib-
son* v. *Carruthers*, 8 M. & W. 321.

(*t*) *Re Sneezum, Ex parte Davis*, 3
Ch. D. 463 (on B. A. 1869). But any
person interested may require him to
give notice within twenty-eight days
whether he will disclaim the contract
or not, and if he does not do so, he
will be deemed to have adopted it:
B. A. 1883, s. 55, sub-s. 4.

(*u*) *Knight* v. *Burgess*, 33 L. J. Ch.
727.

(*x*) *Chippendale* v. *Tomlinson*, 1 Co.
B. L. 431.

(*y*) See B. A. 1883, s. 53, sub-s. 2.

extent only, pass to the trustee (z), as will damages in lieu of notice of dismissal (a).

When bills belonging to a bankrupt were at the time of the bankruptcy in the hands of an agent, it was held that the agent was not guilty of a conversion by receiving the money due upon them; for though the title to the bills, as well as to the bankrupt's other choses in action, had passed to the assignees, yet it was the duty of the agent to receive the money when due, to whomsoever it might belong (b); but it would have been otherwise if he had renewed or changed the acceptances—that would have amounted to a conversion for which he would have been liable in trover (c).

As the right to bring an action at law upon the bankrupt's contract passes to his trustee, so does the right to have specific performance decreed by equity (d).

*Foreign Property.*—According to the law of England, and of almost every other country, personal property has no locality, but is subject to the law governing the person of the owner. It follows that, unless there be a positive law there to prevent it, the bankrupt's personal property in foreign countries passes to his trustee (e). His real property, so situated, will pass only according to the law of the country where it is situated (f). "Property" now includes all real and personal property, whether in England or elsewhere, and it may be that the Court would, where the bankrupt is within its jurisdiction, order him to execute a conveyance of the property sufficient to vest it in the trustee, according to the law of the country where it is

---

(z) *Ex parte Banks, Re Dowling*, 4 Ch. D. 689 ; *Emden* v. *Carte*, 17 Ch. D. 768; *Jameson* v. *Brick and Stone Co.*, 4 Q. B. D. 208.

(a) *Wadling* v. *Oliphant*, 1 Q. B. D. 145.

(b) *Jones* v. *Fort*, 9 B. & C. 764.

(c) *Robson* v. *Rolls*, 1 M. & Rob. 239.

(d) See *Whitworth* v. *Davis*, 1 V. & B. 545; *Sloper* v. *Fish*, 2 V. & B. 145 ;

*Brooke* v. *Hewitt*, 3 Ves. 253.

(e) See *Sill* v. *Worswick*, 1 H. Bl. at p. 690; Cullen, 240; 2 Bell's Comm. 685; Story on Conflict of Laws; *Hunter* v. *Potts*, 4 T. R. 182; *Phillips* v. *Hunter*, 2 H. Bl. 402; *Selkrig* v. *Davies*, 2 Rose, 291 ; 2 Dow. 230 ; *Cockerell* v. *Dickens*, 1 M., D. & De G. 45.

(f) *Ex parte Rogers, Re Boustead*, 16 Ch. D. 665.

Official re-
ceivers and
trustees.

situated (*g*). Conversely, real estate in England will not vest in a foreign assignee or trustee (*h*).

The capacity to exercise, and to take proceedings for exercising, the powers which the bankrupt might have exercised for his own benefit at the commencement of the bankruptcy or before discharge (except the right of nomination to a vacant ecclesiastical benefice), vests in the trustee (*i*).

*Onerous property.*—This class of property vests in the trustee, but it may be disclaimed by him (*j*). This right of disclaimer extends to land of any tenure burdened with onerous covenants, shares or stock in companies, unprofitable contracts, and any property unsaleable or not readily saleable, by reason of its binding the possessor thereof to the performance of onerous acts, or to payment of any sum of money. It may be exercised by written notice of disclaimer, signed by the trustee (*k*), notwithstanding any act of ownership, within three months from his appointment, or within two months from his becoming aware of the existence of the property, if it first comes to his knowledge more than a month after his appointment (*l*).

To make a valid disclaimer of a lease, the leave of the Court, except in certain specified cases, is required (*m*), and the trustee may be required by any person interested in the property, to give notice within twenty-eight days whether he disclaims or not, on pain of losing his right to disclaim (*n*). Various powers are given enabling the Court to make orders, as, for instance, an order vesting the disclaimed property in any person entitled thereto, or giving compensation to a landlord to prevent the disclaimer working injustice to other persons (*o*). Any person who is injured by a disclaimer has a right of proof against the estate in respect of such injury (*p*). The effect of a disclaimer

---

(*g*) See B. A. 1883, s. 168, sub-s. 1, and s. 24.

(*h*) *Waite* v. *Bingley*, 21 Ch. D. 674.

(i) B. A. 1883, s. 44 (ii).

(*j*) B. A. 1883, s. 55.

(*k*) *Wilson* v. *Wallani*, 5 Ex. D. 155.

(l) B. A. 1883, s. 55, sub-s. 1.

(*m*) B. A. 1883, s. 55, sub-s. 3; B. R. 1886, r. 320.

(*n*) B. A. 1883, s. 55, sub-s. 4.

(*o*) B. A. 1883, s. 55, sub-ss. 3, 5, 6. See *Re Morgan*, 22 Q. B. D. 592, as to service of notice of application for vesting order.

(*p*) B. A. 1883, s. 55, sub-s. 7.

will be to determine, as from its date, the rights, interests, and liabilities of the bankrupt and his property in relation to the disclaimed property, to relieve the trustee from all personal liability in respect thereof as from the date when the property vested in him, but will not affect the rights or liabilities of others, except so far as necessary to release the bankrupt and his property and the trustee from liability (*q*). Official re-ceivers and trustees.

If the trustee has omitted to disclaim a lease, he can relieve himself from future liability by assignment to a pauper (*r*). In ordering compensation to a landlord, the Court will consider two things, whether the occupation by the trustee has either in fact produced a benefit to the bankrupt's estate, or was contemplated as likely to produce a benefit (*s*).

*Stock—Shares, &c.*—The right to transfer stock, shares in ships, shares, or other property transferable in the books of any company, office, or person, belonging to the bankrupt, is abso-lutely vested in the trustee to the same extent as the bankrupt could have exercised it (*t*).

*Trust Property.*—Property held by the bankrupt in trust for others does not pass to his trustee, it being provided that the property referred to in the Act as divisible among his creditors shall not include " property held by the bankrupt on trust for any other person" (*u*). This will include *bonâ fide* express or implied trusts, cases where the bankrupt is legal owner, or has no interest, or only a partial beneficial interest (*x*), and where the bankrupt holds property as an agent or factor (*y*).

---

(*q*) B. A. 1883, s. 55, sub-s. 2. See *Lowrey* v. *Barker*, 5 Ex. D. 170.

(*r*) *Hopkinson* v. *Lovering*, 11 Q. B. D. 92.

(*s*) *Ex parte Isherwood, Re Knight*, 22 Ch. D. 384; *Ex parte Arnal, Re Witton*, 24 Ch. D. 26; *Ex parte Good, Re Salkeld*, 13 Q. B. D. 731.

(*t*) B. A. 1883, s. 50, sub-s. 3.

(*u*) B. A. 1883, s. 44, sub-s. 1.

(*x*) *Ex parte Gennys*, Mont. & M'A. 258; *Carvalho* v. *Burn*, 4 B. & Ad. 382;

*Winch* v. *Keely*, 1 T. R. 619; *Bodding-ton* v. *Castelli*, 1 E. & B. 879; *Ex parte Cooke, Re Strachan*, 4 Ch. D. 123; *Re Hallett's Estate*, 13 Ch. D. 696; *Re Blakeway and Thomas, Ex parte Ran-kart*, 52 L. T. 630; *Harris* v. *Truman & Co.*, 9 Q. B. D. 264.

(*y*) *Whitcomb* v. *Jacob*, 1 Salk. 160; *Scott* v. *Surnam*, Wils. 400; *Frith* v. *Cartland*, 34 L. J. Ch. 301; *Pennell* v. *Deffell*, 23 L. J. Ch. 115; *Taylor* v. *Plumer*, 3 M. & S. 562.

*Tools of Trade, Apparel, and Bedding.*—By sect. 44 (2), are excepted, " the tools (if any) of his trade and the necessary wearing apparel and bedding of himself, his wife and children, to a value, inclusive of tools and apparel and bedding, not exceeding twenty pounds in the whole."

*Property in Right of Wife.*—Whatever beneficial interest the bankrupt has in his wife's property goes to his trustee (a). But property which she possesses as a sole trader by the custom of London (b), or which is settled to her separate use (c), or falls within the provisions of the Married Women's Property Act, 1882, does not come within that denomination. As the trustee takes the same beneficial interest which the bankrupt possessed, it follows that if the bankrupt die before he has reduced the wife's choses in action into possession, the wife will take those by survivorship (d). The right to bring an action for the recovery of real property in right of the wife passes to the trustee, and he may join her in an action for the recovery of damages done to her personal property before her marriage (e). If the trustee be able to obtain the wife's property at law, equity will not interfere with the legal title, but if he be obliged to apply to equity for its assistance, the Court will impose terms upon him, by stipulating that a provision be made for her out of the fund (f). This equity is personal to her; she may, if she think fit, waive it, and defeat her children, but if she do not, it will enure for their benefit also (g).

(a) *Mitchell* v. *Hughes*, 6 Bing. 689; *Caunt* v. *Ward*, 7 Bing. 608; *Pringle* v. *Hodson*, 3 Ves. 617; *Robinson* v. *Taylor*, 2 Bro. C. C. 589; *Doe* d. *Shaw* v. *Steward*, 1 Ad. & E. 300.

(b) *Lavie* v. *Phillips*, 3 Burr. 1776.

(c) *Vandenanker* v. *Desbrough*, 2 Vern. 96; *Bennet* v. *Davis*, 2 P. Wms. 316; *Parnham* v. *Hurst*, 8 M. & W. 743.

(d) *Mitford* v. *Mitford*, 9 Ves. 87; *Hornsby* v. *Lee*, 2 Madd. 16; *Purdew* v. *Jackson*, 1 Russ. 1; *Sherrington* v. *Yates*, 12 M. & W. 855; *Pierce* v. *Thornley*, 2 Sim. 167; *Nicholson* v.

*Drury Buildings Co.*, 7 Ch. D. 48.

(e) *Richbell* v. *Alexander*, 10 C. B. N. S. 324; *Mitchell* v. *Hughes*, 6 Bing. 689; *Smith* v. *Coffin*, 2 H. Bl. 444.

(f) *Worrall* v. *Marlar*, 1 Cox, 153; *Burdon* v. *Dean*, 2 Ves. jun. 607; *Brown* v. *Clark*, 3 Ves. 166; *Lumb* v. *Milnes*, 5 Ves. 517; *Carr* v. *Taylor*, 10 Ves. 574; *Elibank* v. *Montolieu*, 5 Ves. 737; *Basevi* v. *Serra*, 3 Meriv. 674; *Scott* v. *Spashett*, 21 L. J. Chanc. 349; *Lloyd* v. *Mason*, 5 Hare, 149; *In re Cutler's Trust*, 20 L. J. Chanc. 504; *Ex parte Norton*, 25 L. J. Bank. 43.

(g) *Murray* v. *Lord Elibank*, 10 Ves.

*Future Property.*—The trustee takes not merely the bank- rupt's present property, but also all such "as may be acquired by or devolve on him before his discharge" (*h*).

As to the time from which the bankrupt's property vests in his trustee, although the trustee has no title till his appointment, when he is appointed, his title relates back to the commencement of the bankruptcy; that is, to the time of the act of bankruptcy being committed on which the receiving order is made, or if the bankrupt is proved to have committed more acts of bankruptcy than one, to the first act of bankruptcy proved to have been committed within three months next preceding the date of the presentation of the petition (*i*). Subject, however, to the provisions in the act relating to executions, settlements and fraudulent preferences (*k*), there are certain transactions which, although within the period of relation back, are protected and valid as against the trustee. These are:—any payment by the bankrupt to any of his creditors; any payment or delivery to the bankrupt; any conveyance or assignment by, or contract, dealing, or transaction by or with the bankrupt for valuable consideration; provided that the payment, delivery, conveyance, &c., takes place before the receiving order, and before the party to the transaction, other than the debtor, has notice of any prior available act of bankruptcy (*l*).

With regard to payments, it was held that when A. lent the bankrupt his acceptance, and afterwards purchased four horses from him, agreeing that their price should be set off against the amount of the acceptance, this was not a payment (*m*); nor was the loan of a sum of money to the bankrupt upon a mortgage of

at pp. 88 and 91; *Scriven* v. *Tapley*, 2 Eden, 337; *Lloyd* v. *Williams*, 1 Madd. 450. But see *Fenner* v. *Taylor*, 1 Sim. 169; *Steinmetz* v. *Halthin*, 1 G. & J. 64; *Rowe* v. *Jackson*, 2 Dick. 604; *Carter* v. *Taggart*, 21 L. J. Chanc. 216.

(*h*) B. A. 1883, s. 44. *Ex parte Ansell*, 19 Ves. 208; *Re Birch's Legacy*, 2 Kay & J. 328.

(*i*) B. A. 1883, s. 43.
(*k*) B. A. 1883, ss. 45, 47, 48.
(*l*) B. A. 1883, s. 49.
(*m*) *Carter* v. *Breton*, 6 Bing. 617; *Wilkins* v. *Casey*, 7 T. R. 711; *Bishop* v. *Crawshay*, 3 B. & C. 415; *Copland* v. *Stein*, 8 T. R. 199; *Hurst* v. *Gwennap*, 2 Stark. 306.

his property (*q*). A payment may be a fraudulent preference (*r*) and not made in good faith within this clause, though it was not the intention of the bankrupt to benefit the person to whom it was made, but some other person, *e.g.*, relieving an estate settled on his wife from incumbrance, or exonerating a surety (*s*).

With regard to *conveyances*, it was held, under 6 Geo. 4, c. 16, s. 81, that a voluntary transfer, which was in itself an act of bankruptcy, could not be considered *bonâ fide* so as to be protected (*t*).

The most extensive exception to the general rule is that which comprises any *contract, dealing* or *transaction* by or with the bankrupt for a valuable consideration. These terms are extremely large (*u*).

The protection afforded by these provisions, it will be observed, is upon the condition that the person so dealing had not, at the time, notice of any prior available act of bankruptcy ; and under this section the onus of proof is on the person relying on the want of notice (*x*).

In the first place, therefore, the person whose interest is to be affected must have this notice. Now, it has been held that, in the case of an execution, it must be brought home to the execution creditor or his solicitor (*y*) employed in issuing it, and that

---

(*q*) *Cannan* v. *Denew*, 10 Bing. 292 ; *Crowfoot* v. *London Dock Co.*, 4 Tyr. 986 ; *Wright* v. *Fearnley*, 5 Bing. N. C. 89 ; *Fearnley* v. *Wright* (in error), 6 Bing. N. C. 446. See further as to the meaning of payment, *Ferrall* v. *Alexander*, 1 Dowl. 132 ; *Cannan* v. *Wood*, 2 M. & W. 465. See *Bowes* v. *Foster*, 2 H. & N. 779 ; *Hill* v. *Farnell*, 9 B. & C. 45. See *Cash* v. *Young*, 2 B. & C. 413 ; *Willis* v. *Bank of England*, 4 Ad. & E. 21 ; *Shaw* v. *Batley*, 4 B. & Ad. 801 ; *Tope* v. *Hockin*, 7 B. & C. 101 ; *Kynaston* v. *Crouch*, 14 M. & W. 266 ; *Gibson* v. *Muskett*, 4 M. & G. 170.

(*r*) See *Groom* v. *Watts*, 4 Exch. 727.

(*s*) *Marshall* v. *Lamb*, 5 Q. B. 115.

(*t*) *Bevan* v. *Nunn*, 9 Bing. 107. See *Hall* v. *Wallace*, 7 M. & W. 356 ; *Belcher* v. *Magnay*, 12 M. & W. 102.

(*u*) *Krehl* v. *Great Central Gas Co.*, L. R. 5 Ex. 289, 295. See *Young* v. *Hope*, 2 Exch. 105 ; *Brewin* v. *Short*, 5 E. & B. 227 ; *Ex parte Norton*, L. R. 16 Eq. 397.

(*x*) *Ex parte Schulte*, *Re Matanle*, L. R. 9 Ch. 409 ; *Ex parte Cartwright*, *Re Joy*, 44 L. T. 883 ; *Ex parte Revell*, *Re Tollemache*, 13 Q. B. D. 727.

(*y*) *Bird* v. *Bass*, 6 M. & G. 143 ; *Green* v. *Steer*, 1 Q. B. 707 ; *Pennell* v. *Stephens*, 7 C. B. 987 ; *Rothwell* v. *Timbrell*, 1 Dowl. N. S. 526 ; *Ex parte Schulte*, *Re Matanle*, supra ; *Pike* v. *Stephens*, 12 Q. B. 465.

notice to the sheriff or sheriff's officer in possession is insuffi- cient (z). It has also been questioned whether notice to the bailiff of a landlord in possession under a distress for rent would be enough (a).

Secondly, there must be notice of an act of bankruptcy prior to the transaction (b), not simply of facts which possibly may not constitute it (c). The word "notice " here means knowledge, and not the mere means of knowledge; therefore the bare receipt of a letter containing a notice, which the party has not read, does not satisfy the statute (d). Notice may be given by telegram (e).

Thirdly, the notice must be of a prior act of bankruptcy by such bankrupt committed. A knowledge, therefore, that the trader was in embarrassed circumstances, if a sale were bonâ fide, will not invalidate it (f). Notice that a trader has executed a bill of sale of all his property for the benefit of his creditors, is enough (g). But it is not necessary that there should be notice of any specific act; and, therefore, a general notice (h) that the trader has committed an act of bankruptcy, given to the party, if true, will avoid any such subsequent dealing. It has also been held that a person having notice of a previous act of bankruptcy, obtains no title by an assignment from the sheriff under an execution by a creditor who had no notice (i).

Fourthly, the notice must be of a prior act of bankruptcy available for a bankruptcy petition at the date of the pre-

(z) *Ramsey* v. *Eaton*, 10 M. & W. 22; *Brewin* v. *Briscoe*, 2 E. & E. 116; *Ex parte Schulte*, *Re Matanle*, L. R. 9 Ch. 409.

(a) *Lackington* v. *Elliott*, 7 M. & G. 539.

(b) *Ex parte Schulte*, *Re Matanle*, supra.

(c) *Evans* v. *Hallam*, L. R. 6 Q. B. 713; *Ex parte Snowball*, *Re Douglas*, L. R. 7 Ch. 534. Notice that a petition has been filed is sufficient: *Lucas* v. *Dicker*, 6 Q. B. D. 84.

(d) *Bird* v. *Bass*, 6 M. & G. 143.

(e) *Ex parte Langley*, *Re Bishop*, 13 Ch. D. 110.

(f) *Tucker* v. *Barrow*, M. & M. 137; *Spratt* v. *Hobhouse*, 4 Bing. 173.

(g) *Lindon* v. *Sharpe*, 6 M. & G. 895; B. A. 1883, s. 6, sub-s. 1 ; *Evans* v. *Hallam*, supra.

(h) *Hocking* v. *Acraman*, 12 M. & W. 170; *Ramsey* v. *Eaton*, 10 M. & W. 22; *Udal* v. *Walton*, 14 M. & W. 254; *Hope* v. *Meek*, 10 Exch. 829; *Turner* v. *Hardcastle*, 11 C. B. N. S. 683.

(i) *Fawcett* v. *Fearne*, 6 Q. B. 20.

sentation of the petition on which the receiving order is made (*m*).

Where none of these statutory exceptions apply, the trustee takes the bankrupt's property by relation back to the commencement of the bankruptcy, but the relation will not be carried back to an act of bankruptcy committed more than three months before the date of presentation of the petition, nor will it be available against the Crown (*n*).

Money received by the solicitor of a petitioning creditor from the debtor pending proceedings, and by him handed over to his client, must be refunded to the trustee by the solicitor; but money paid to a solicitor by the debtor for the expenses of opposing bankruptcy proceedings (*o*), need not be so refunded.

Where one member of a firm has become bankrupt, he cannot afterwards transfer the partnership effects, or pay partnership debts out of the joint funds to a creditor with notice of his bankruptcy (*p*).

*What Property other than the Bankrupt's passes to his Trustee.*—Certain property which could not have been retained by the bankrupt himself, or could not have been claimed by him, had he continued solvent, may become vested in his trustee upon his bankruptcy. Thus, there will pass to the trustee all goods being, at the commencement of the bankruptcy, in the possession, order or disposition of the bankrupt, in his trade or business, by the consent and permission of the true owner, under such circumstances that he is the reputed owner thereof, except things in action other than debts due or growing due to the bankrupt in the course of his trade or business, which are not deemed goods within this provision (*q*).

It will be observed that the operation of this provision is confined to cases in which there is a reputed ownership of *goods*.

---

(*m*) B. A. 1883, s. 168, sub-s. 1.

(*n*) B. A. 1883, ss. 30, 43, 150; *Ex parte Postmaster-General, Re Bonham*, 10 Ch. D. 595.

(*o*) *Ex parte Edwards, Re Chapman*, 13 Q. B. D. 747; *Re Sinclair, Ex parte Payne*, 15 Q. B. D. 616.

(*p*) *Thomason* v. *Frere*, 10 East, 418; *Craven* v. *Edmondson*, 6 Bing. 734; *Burt* v. *Moult*, 1 Cr. & M. 525; *New Quebrada Co.* v. *Carr*, L. R. 4 C. P. 651.

(*q*) B. A. 1883, s. 44 (iii.).

Such are ships (*r*), furniture (*s*), utensils in trade (*t*) (unless such furniture and utensils are let in conformity to a usage of trade (*u*)), and stock (*x*) and shares in a newspaper (*y*). Bonds, debentures, bills of exchange and promissory notes (*z*), policies of insurance (*a*), debts (*b*), and shares in companies (*c*), are choses in action within the terms of the proviso, unless they constitute debts due (*d*) or growing due to the bankrupt in the way of his trade or business, they will not vest in the trustee. Chattel interests in real property, fixtures, or shares in a company seised of real estate, have been held not to come within these words (*e*).

The section, it will be observed, only extends to goods which are in the bankrupt's possession, order or disposition in his trade or business (*f*).

(*r*) *Stephens* v. *Sole*, cited 1 Ves. sen. 352; *Ex parte Burn*, 1 J. & W. 378. But see in case of British ships, 17 & 18 Vict. c. 104, ss. 72, 80, and 81, in Appendix; and *Swainston* v. *Clay*, 32 L. J. Chanc. 503.

(*s*) *Lingham* v. *Biggs*, 1 B. & P. 82.

(*t*) *Lingard* v. *Messiter*, 1 B. & C. 808; *Sinclair* v. *Stevenson*, 2 Bing. 514; *Trappes* v. *Harter*, 2 Cr. & M. 153. See *Coombs* v. *Beaumont*, 5 B. & Ad. 72.

(*u*) *Horn* v. *Baker*, 9 East, 215, at p. 239; *Lingham* v. *Biggs*, 1 B. & P. at p. 88 (furniture in furnished house); *Storer* v. *Hunter*, 3 B. & C. 368; *Spackman* v. *Miller*, 12 C. B. N. S. 659; *In re Jensen*, 4 Morrell, 1 (custom to hire vans); *Crawcour* v. *Salter*, 18 Ch. D. 30 (custom to hire furniture); *Ex parte Turquand*, *Re Parker*, 14 Q. B. D. 636; but see *Ex parte Brooks*, *Re Fowler*, 23 Ch. D. 261.

(*x*) *Ex parte Richardson*, Buck, 480.

(*y*) *Longman* v. *Tripp*, 2 B. & P. N. R. 67.

(*z*) *Hornblower* v. *Proud*, 2 B. & Ald. 327; *Re Pryce*, *Ex parte Rensberg*, 4 Ch. D. 685; *Ex parte Ibbetson*, *Re Moore*, 8 Ch. D. 519; *Re Bainbridge*, *Ex parte Fletcher*, 8 Ch. D. 218.

(*a*) *Falkener* v. *Case*, 1 Bro. C. C. 125; *Edwards* v. *Scott*, 1 M. & G. 962; *West* v. *Reid*, 2 Hare, 249; *Thompson* v. *Speirs*, 13 Sim. 469; *In re Bromley*, Id. 475; *Green* v. *Ingham*, L. R. 2 C. P. 525.

(*b*) *Cooke* v. *Hemming*, L. R. 3 C. P. 334.

(*c*) *Colonial Bank* v. *Whinney*, 11 App. Cas. 426.

(*d*) *Ex parte Kemp*, *Re Fastnedge*, L. R. 9 Ch. 383; *Re Pryce*, *Ex parte Rensberg*, supra.

(*e*) *Ryall* v. *Rolle*, 1 Atk. 165; *Horn* v. *Baker*, 9 East, 215; *Ex parte Vauxhall Bridge Co.*, 1 G. & J. 101; *Clark* v. *Crownshaw*, 3 B. & Ad. 804; *Hubbard* v. *Bagshaw*, 4 Sim. 326; *Trappes* v. *Harter*, 3 Tyr. 603; *Coombs* v. *Beaumont*, 5 B. & Ad. 72. See also *Boydell* v. *M'Michael*, 1 C. M. & R. 177; *Ex parte Barclay*, 5 De G. M. & G. 403, 410; *Thompson* v. *Pettit*, 10 Q. B. 101; *Hitchman* v. *Walton*, 4 M. & W. 409; *Ex parte Scarth*, 1 M. D. & De G. 240; *Ex parte Heathcote*, 2 M. D. & De G. 711; *Whitmore* v. *Empson*, 23 Beav. 313; *Climie* v. *Wood*, L. R. 3 Ex. 257; 4 Ex. 328; *Ex parte Astbury*, L. R. 4 Ch. 630. But see *Waterfall* v. *Penistone*, 6 E. & B. 876.

(*f*) *Ex parte Nottingham Bank*, *Re*

The goods must be in the possession, order, or disposition of
the bankrupt alone (*g*), and that with the consent and permission,
express or implied, of the true owner (*h*).  And so the property
of infants who cannot consent is not within this clause (*i*) ; nor
is it enough that they were in the possession of the bankrupt
with the consent of a person who himself held them only by the
sufferance of the true owner (*k*).  But goods belonging to the
assignees under a former bankruptcy, remaining in the possession of the bankrupt at the time of a subsequent one, are within
this section (*l*).  Constructive possession of the bankrupt however—for instance, that of a servant—is sufficient to make the
section apply (*m*).  The wrongful seizure of the goods by a
wrongdoer would seem sufficient to take the goods out of the
possession, order, or disposition of the bankrupt (*n*).  Moreover,
such consent and permission, together with the possession of the
bankrupt, must continue up to the commencement of the bankruptcy.

The circumstances must also be such that the bankrupt is the
reputed, and not the real, owner of the goods, and the real
owner must consent to the apparent ownership as such.  Therefore, goods in the possession of an ostensible partner (*o*) of the
bankrupt, under a purchase by him, which the vendors subsequently to the act of bankruptcy discovered to have been

---

*Jenkinson*, 15 Q. B. D. 441 ; *Ex parte
McGeorge*, 20 Ch. D. 697 ; *Colonial
Bank* v. *Whinney*, 30 Ch. D. 261, at
pp. 274, 281 (reversed on other points,
11 App. Cas. 426) ; *Ex parte Sully, Re
Wallis*, 14 Q. B. D. 950.

(*g*) *Ex parte Dorman, Re Lake*, L. R.
8 Ch. 51 ; *Ex parte Fletcher, Re Bainbridge*, 8 Ch. D. 218.

(*h*) *Ex parte Richardson*, Buck, 480 ;
*Ex parte Dale*, Buck, 365 ; *Re Rawbone*,
3 Jur. N. S. 837 Ch. ; *Ex parte Union
Bank of Manchester*, L. R. 12 Eq. 354 ;
*Re Bankhead's Trust*, 2 K. & J. 560 ;
*Ex parte Cox, Re Reed*, 1 Ch. D. 302.
See *Ex parte Hayman, Re Pulsford*, 8
Ch. D. 11 ; *Reynolds* v. *Bowley*, L. R.
2 Q. B. 474.

(*i*) *Viner* v. *Cadell*, 3 Esp. 88.

(*k*) *Fraser* v. *Swansea Canal Co.*, 1
Ad. & E. 354.  But see *In re Thomas*,
1 Ph. 159.

(*l*) *Butler* v. *Hobson*, 5 Bing. N. C.
128.  See *Re Rawbone*, 3 Jur. N. S.
837 Ch.

(*m*) *Ex parte Bolland, Re Gatehouse*,
24 L. T. 335 ; *Ex parte Roy, Re Sil-
lence*, 7 Ch. D. 70 ; *Hornsby* v. *Miller*,
28 L. J. Q. B. 99 ; *Hervey* v. *Liddiard*,
1 Stark. 123.

(*n*) *Meggy* v. *Imperial Discount Co.*,
3 Q. B. D. 711, at p. 716.

(*o*) *Reynolds* v. *Bowley*, L. R. 2 Q. B.
474 ; *Ex parte Hayman, Re Pulsford*, 8
Ch. D. 11.

fraudulent, and in consequence annulled, will not pass to the trustee (*p*).

The principal difficulty in deciding questions on this clause is that of ascertaining whether the bankrupt was or was not reputed owner, and this is a question of fact; nor is it easy to lay down rules for its solution. Where the bankrupt has once been the real owner of the property in question, the mere fact of possession may raise a presumption that he continues in possession as reputed owner. But where the bankrupt has never been the real owner, possession may not of itself show him to be reputed owner; some additional evidence may be requisite for that purpose (*q*). A servant's possession of goods has been held to be that of his master for the purposes of this clause (*r*); a carrier's that of his employer (*s*); and a factor's that of the principal, unless the relationship be notorious (*t*). But the pawnee's is not that of the pawnor (*u*). Where the purchaser transferred his purchase to a particular bin in the vendor's cellar, sealed it, and had an entry made in the vendor's books, the statute was held not to apply (*x*); but it was otherwise where he only marked the goods with his initials (*y*). A symbolical delivery will be sufficient to take the case out of this clause, if, from the nature of the goods, no other can be made (*z*); and so will the taking possession of a part (*a*). The usage of trade is sometimes of importance, and if the bankrupt's possession of another person's goods be consistent with such usage, they may be exempted from the operation of this clause, under circumstances which

(*p*) *Load* v. *Green*, 15 M. & W. 216; *Holderness* v. *Rankin*, 2 De G. F. & J. 258; *Smith* v. *Hudson*, 6 B. & S. 431.

(*q*) *Lingard* v. *Messiter*, 1 B. & C. 308; *Ex parte Castle*, 3 M. D. & De G. 117; *Hornsby* v. *Miller*, supra. But see *Re Wallworth*, 26 L. J. Bank. 61.

(*r*) *Jackson* v. *Irvin*, 2 Camp. 48; *Toussaint* v. *Hartop*, Holt, 335.

(*s*) *Hervey* v. *Liddiard*, 1 Stark. 123.

(*t*) *Re Fawcus, Ex parte Buck*, 3 Ch. D. 795; *Ex parte Bright, Re Smith*, 10 Ch. D. 566.

(*u*) *Greening* v. *Clark*, 4 B. & C. 316.

(*x*) *Ex parte Marrable*, 1 G. & J. 402; *Carruthers* v. *Payne*, 5 Bing. 270; *Sinclair* v. *Wilson*, 24 L. J. Ch. 537. See *Wilkins* v. *Bromhead*, 6 M. & G. 963.

(*y*) *Knowles* v. *Horsfall*, 5 B. & Ald. 134; *Lingard* v. *Messiter*, 1 B. & C. 308.

(*z*) *Manton* v. *Moore*, 7 T. R. 67; *Mair* v. *Glennie*, 4 M. & S. 240.

(*a*) *Re Eslick, Ex parte Phillips*, 4 Ch. D. 496.

otherwise would have brought them within it (*b*). Thus, in *Ex parte Watkins; Re Couston* (*c*), the Court gave effect to a custom in the wine trade to allow wine to remain in the warehouse of the vendor or a third person (*d*). In such cases the question is, whether the custom be so general that all should know it who had dealings, or were likely to have dealings, with the bankrupt (*e*).

There are certain cases, also, where property which the bankrupt has parted with, by way of settlement, for the benefit of his wife or children, passes to the trustee, the Act providing (sect. 47) (*f*)—

(1.) "Any settlement of property not being a settlement made before and in consideration of marriage, or made in favour of a purchaser or incumbrancer in good faith and for valuable consideration, or a settlement made on or for the wife or children of the settlor of property which has accrued to the settlor after marriage in right of his wife, shall, if the settlor becomes bankrupt within two years after the date of the settlement, be void against the trustee in the bankruptcy, and shall, if the settlor becomes bankrupt at any subsequent time within ten years after the date of the settlement, be void against the trustee in the bankruptcy, unless the parties claiming under the settlement can prove that the settlor (*g*) was at the time of making the settlement able to pay all his debts without the aid of the property comprised in the settlement (*h*), and

---

(*b*) See *Storer* v. *Hunter*, 3 B. & C. 368; *Hamilton* v. *Bell*, 10 Exch. 545; *Thackthwaite* v. *Cock*, 3 Taunt. 487; *Horn* v. *Baker*, 9 East, 215, at p. 239; *Watson* v. *Peache*, 1 Bing. N. C. 327; *Whitfield* v. *Brand*, 16 M. & W. 282; *Carruthers* v. *Payne*, 5 Bing. 270; *Re Terry*, 11 W. R. 113; *Ex parte Watkins, Re Couston*, L. R. 8 Ch. 520; *Crawcour* v. *Salter*, 18 Ch. D. 30; *Re Lay, Ex parte Woodward*, 54 L. T. 683; *Re Blanshard, Ex parte Hattersley*, 8 Ch. D. 601; *Ex parte Wingfield, Re Florence*, 10 Ch. D. 591; *Harris* v. *Truman & Co.*, 9 Q. B. D. 264; *Re Taylor, Ex parte Dyer*, 53 L. T. 768; *Ex parte Bright, Re Smith*, 10 Ch. D. 566.

(*c*) L. R. 8 Ch. 520; *Ex parte Vaux, In re Couston*, L. R. 9 Ch. 602.

(*d*) *Ex parte Turquand*, 14 Q. B. D. 636.

(*e*) *Watson* v. *Peache*, 1 Bing. N. C. 327; *Ex parte Watkins, Re Couston*, L. R. 8 Ch. 520; *Ex parte Vaux, Re Couston*, L. R. 9 Ch. 602. See *Re Wallworth*, 26 L. J. Bank. 61; *Ex parte Powell, Re Matthews*, 1 Ch. D. 501; *In re Hill*, ib. 503, n.; *Priestley* v. *Pratt*, L. R. 2 Ex. 101; *Ex parte Brooks*, 23 Ch. D. 201; *Crawcour* v. *Salter*, L. R. 18 Ch. D. 30.

(*f*) B. A. 1883, s. 47; see *Ex parte Mercer*, 17 Q. B. D. 290.

(*g*) *Ex parte Russell*, 19 Ch. D. 588; *Ex parte Huxtable*, 2 Ch. D. 54.

(*h*) "It seems to us that the section must be read to mean 'without the aid of the property which, by the settlement, passes to other persons'": *Ex parte Official Receiver, In re Lowndes*, 4 Morrell, 139, at p. 143.

that the interest of the settlor in such property had passed to the trustee of such settlement on the execution thereof.

(2.) "Any covenant or contract made in consideration of marriage, for the future settlement on or for the settlor's wife or children of any money or property wherein he had not at the date of his marriage any estate or interest, whether vested or contingent, in possession or remainder (i), and not being money or property of or in right of his wife, shall, on his becoming bankrupt before the property or money has been actually transferred or paid pursuant to the contract or covenant, be void against the trustee in the bankruptcy.

(3.) "'Settlement' shall for the purposes of this section include any conveyance or transfer of property" (k).

A voluntary settlement, though not impeachable under the above section, may be void under 13 Eliz. c. 5, as intended to defeat creditors.

This section, it would appear, is retrospective so far as regards "traders," to whom the corresponding section in the Act of 1869 applied, but not as regards non-traders (l).

Lastly, fraudulent preferences of particular creditors, which have been dealt with in an earlier part of this chapter as constituting an act of bankruptcy, are void as against the trustee if the debtor is adjudged bankrupt on a petition presented within three months after it is made (m).


## Section VIII.—*Evidence.*

Every Court in bankruptcy has a seal of which judicial notice is taken (n), and a copy of any document used in a bankruptcy proceeding is, if sealed, or signed by the judge, receivable in evidence in all legal proceedings (o). A certificate by the Board of Trade is conclusive evidence of the appointment of a

---

(i) *Ex parte Bishop*, L. R. 8 Ch. 718 ; *Ex parte Dawson*, L. R. 19 Eq. 433.

(k) *Ex parte Harvey*, 15 Q. B. D. 682.

(l) *In re Ashcroft, Ex parte Todd*, 4 Morrell, 209.

(m) B. A. 1883, s. 4, sub-s. 1 (c).

(n) B. A. 1883, s. 137; B. R. 1886, r. 14.

(o) B. A. 1883, s. 134.

trustee (*l*). A copy of the *London Gazette* is evidence of the facts stated ·in any notice therein, and it is conclusive evidence in the case of a receiving order or order of adjudication that the order is duly made and of its date (*m*). The proceedings at meetings of creditors are evidenced by a minute signed by the chairman (*n*).

Should the debtor or his wife, or any witness who has been examined by the Court, die, the deposition, sealed by the Court, is receivable in evidence (*o*). Deeds and other documents relating to the property of the bankrupt, or to any proceeding in the bankruptcy, are, except as regards the fees imposed by the Act and rules, exempt from stamp duty (*p*).

## SECTION IX.—*Dividend and Audit.*

The first dividend under a bankruptcy must be declared and distributed within four months from the conclusion of the first meeting, unless the trustee satisfies the committee of inspection that there is sufficient reason for postponing it. Subsequent dividends must, unless there be sufficient reason to the contrary, be declared and distributed at intervals of not more than six months (*q*). Notice of an intention to declare a dividend must be gazetted, and sent to any creditor mentioned in the statement of affairs who has not proved his debt (*r*). When the dividend has been declared, notice of the particulars of time and place of payment will be sent to each creditor who has proved (*s*). Dividends may, at the creditor's request and at his risk, be sent by post (*t*). In the case of joint and separate estates, dividends will, as a rule, be declared together (*u*). The trustee will make provision for creditors residing at a distance who have not had

(*l*) B. A. 1883, s. 138.
(*m*) B. A. 1883, s. 132.
(*n*) B. A. 1883, s. 133. As to evidence of orders, &c. by the Board of Trade, see s. 140.
(*o*) B. A. 1883, s. 136; see also B. R. 1886, rr. 61—71.
(*p*) B. A. 1883, s. 144; B. R. 1886, r. 60.
(*q*) B. A. 1883, s. 58, sub-ss. (2) and (3).
(*r*) B. R. 1886, r. 232.
(*s*) B. A. 1883, s. 58, sub-ss.· (4) and (5).
(*t*) B. R. 1886, r. 234.
(*u*) B. A. 1883, s. 59.

opportunity of establishing their debts, and also for undetermined and disputed claims (*u*). Any creditor who has not proved before dividend will be entitled to the amount out of any money in hand, but he cannot disturb the distribution of any dividend which has been declared (*x*).

Creditors will have notice of the final dividend (*y*) when the property has been realized. No action lies for a dividend ; the remedy is by application to the Court (*z*). At least twice a year the trustee must submit his accounts to the Board of Trade for audit (*a*), and will have to submit, also, an annual statement of the proceedings in the bankruptcy (*b*).

SECTION X.—*Small Bankruptcies and Administration of Estates of deceased Insolvents.*

Where the Court·is satisfied, or the official receiver reports, that the estate of the debtor is not likely to exceed in value 300*l.*, the Court will make an order for summary administration (*c*). The official receiver is trustee, unless the creditors otherwise determine, and there is no committee of inspection. Powers are also given to County Courts, in the case of a judgment-debtor whose whole indebtedness does not exceed 50*l.*, to make orders for the administration of his estate in lieu of an order for payment by instalments (*d*). The estates of deceased insolvents may also be administered by the Court on petition by any creditor whose debt would have been sufficient to support a bankruptcy petition had the debtor been alive (*e*) ; and all the provisions of Part III. of the Bankruptcy Act shall, so far as applicable, apply to such an administration

(*u*) B. A. 1883, s. 60.

(*x*) B. A. 1883, s. 61.

(*y*) B. A. 1883, s. 62.

(*z*) B. A. 1883, s. 63. See *Re Prager, Ex parte Societé Cockerill*, 3 Ch. D. 115 ; *Ex parte Carter, Re Ware*, 8 Ch. D. 731. As to unclaimed and undistributed dividends, see sect. 162.

(*a*) B. A. 1883, s. 78 ; B. R. 1886, rr. 289—291.

(*b*) B. A. 1883, s. 81.

(*c*) B. A. 1883, s. 121 ; B. R. 1886, rr. 272, 273.

(*d*) B. A. 1883, s. 122. Special rules are provided under this section.

(*e*) B. A. 1883, s. 125 ; B. R. 1886, rr. 274—279 ; *Ex parte May*, 13 Q. B. D. 552 ; *Higgs* v. *Weaver*, 29 Q. B. D. 236.

Small bankruptcies and administration of estates of deceased insolvents.

order. Such provisions do not include those relating to the property of persons other than the bankrupt; for example, sect. 47, relating to the avoidance of voluntary settlement (*f*).

SECTION XI.—*Consequences to Debtor himself—Examination— Punishment for Misconduct—Allowance—Surplus.*

Consequences to debtor himself, &c.

It has been explained that at any time after the making of a receiving order the Court may order the examination of the debtor or his wife touching his dealings or property, and the production of documents relating thereto (*g*). If he refuses to answer, the registrar will report such refusal to the judge who will deal with the matter as if the default had been made in answering before him (*h*). It will be no ground for a debtor to refuse to answer any question relating to his property that the answer would tend to criminate him (*i*). The Court may also, after a receiving order has been made, order a debtor's letters to be re-directed to the official receiver or trustee (*j*). A debtor may be arrested and his papers seized if, after the issue of a bankruptcy notice or presentation of a petition, it appears probable to the Court that he will abscond; or if after presentation of a petition it appears probable that he will remove, conceal, or destroy any of his goods; or if, after service of a petition on him or the making of a receiving order, he removes goods above the value of 5*l*. without leave; or if without good cause he fails to attend any examination ordered by the Court (*k*).

The debtor is bound to assist in every way in the discovery and realization of his property; and if he fails to do so, he will be guilty of a contempt of Court (*l*).

There are besides severe punishments which may be inflicted on him for misdemeanours in neglecting to make the proper

(*f*) *Ex parte Official Receiver, In re Gould,* 4 Morrell, 202.

(*g*) B. A. 1883, s. 27 ; *Reg.* v. *County Court of Surrey,* 13 Q. B. D. 963.

(*h*) B. R. 1886, r. 88.

(*i*) *Ex parte Schofield, Re Frith,* 6 Ch. D. 230.

(*j*) B. A. 1883, s. 26.

(*k*) B. A. 1883, s. 25.

(*l*) B. A. 1883, s. 24.

disclosures, as well as for fraudulent and dishonest conduct, either after his bankruptcy or within a limited period before the presentation of the petition, which are enumerated in sects. 11, 12, and 13, of the Debtors Act, 1869 (32 & 33 Vict. c. 62), which enacts—

*Consequences to debtor himself, &c.*

Sect 11. "Any person adjudged bankrupt, and any person whose affairs are liquidated by arrangement in pursuance of the Bankruptcy Act, 1869, shall, in each of the cases following, be deemed guilty of a misdemeanour, and on conviction thereof shall be liable to be imprisoned for any time not exceeding two years, with or without hard labour; that is to say,

(1.) "If he does not, to the best of his knowledge and belief, fully and truly discover to the trustee administering his estate for the benefit of his creditors all his property (*m*), real and personal, and how, and to whom, and for what consideration, and when he disposed of any part thereof, except such part as has been disposed of in the ordinary way of his trade, if any, or laid out in the ordinary expense of his family, unless the jury is satisfied that he had no intent to defraud:

(2.) "If he does not deliver up to such trustee, or as he directs, all such part of his real and personal property as is in his custody or under his control, and which he is required by law to deliver up, unless the jury is satisfied that he had no intent to defraud:

(3.) "If he does not deliver up to such trustee, or as he directs, all books, documents, papers, and writings in his custody or under his control relating to his property or affairs, unless the jury is satisfied that he had no intent to defraud:

(4.) "If after the presentation of a bankruptcy petition [by or (*n*)] against him or the commencement of the liquidation, or within four months next before such presentation or commencement, he conceals any part of his property (*o*) to the value of ten pounds or upwards, or conceals any debt due to or from him, unless the jury is satisfied that he had no intent to defraud:

(5.) "If after the presentation of a bankruptcy petition [by or (*n*)] against him (*n*) or the commencement of the

(*m*) *Reg.* v. *Michell*, 43 L. T. 572.  (*o*) *Reg.* v. *Creese*, L. R. 2 C. C. R.
(*n*) See B. A. 1883, s. 163 (1).  105.

liquidation, or within four months next before such presentation or commencement, he fraudulently removes any
part of his property of the value of ten pounds or upwards :

(6.) "If he makes any material omission in any statement relating to his affairs, unless the jury is satisfied that he had
no intent to defraud :

(7.) "If, knowing or believing that a false debt has been proved
by any person under the bankruptcy or liquidation, he
fail for the period of a month to inform such trustee as
aforesaid thereof :

(8.) "If after the presentation of a bankruptcy petition [by
or (n)] against him or the commencement of the liquidation he prevents the production of any book, document,
paper, or writing, affecting or relating to his property or
affairs, unless the jury is satisfied that he had no intent
to conceal the state of his affairs or to defeat the law :

(9.) "If after the presentation of a bankruptcy petition [by
or (n)] against him or the commencement of the liquidation, or within four months next before such presentation
or commencement, he conceals, destroys, mutilates, or
falsifies, or is privy to the concealment, destruction,
mutilation, or falsification of any book or document affecting or relating to his property or affairs, unless the jury
is satisfied that he had no intent to conceal the state of
his affairs or to defeat the law :

(10.) "If after the presentation of a bankruptcy petition [by
or (n)] against him or the commencement of the liquidation, or within four months next before such presentation
or commencement, he makes or is privy to the making
of any false entry in any book or document affecting or
relating to his property or affairs, unless the jury is satisfied that he had no intent to conceal the state of his affairs
or to defeat the law :

(11.) "If after the presentation of a bankruptcy petition [by
or (n)] against him or the commencement of the liquidation, or within four months next before such presentation
or commencement, he fraudulently parts with, alters, or
makes any omission, or is privy to the fraudulently parting
with, altering, or making any omission in any document
affecting or relating to his property or affairs :

(12.) "If after the presentation of a bankruptcy petition [by
or (n)] against him or the commencement of the liquidation, or at any meeting of his creditors within four

(n) See B. A. 1883, s. 163 (1).

months next before such presentation or commencement, he attempts to account for any part of his property by fictitious losses or expenses : Consequences to debtor himself, &c.

(13.) " If within four months next before the presentation of a bankruptcy petition against him or the commencement of the liquidation, he, by any false representation or other fraud, has obtained any property on credit and has not paid for the same :

(14.) " If within four months next before the presentation of a bankruptcy petition against him or the commencement of the liquidation, he, being a trader (*o*), obtains, under the false pretence of carrying on business and dealing in the ordinary way of his trade, any property on credit and has not paid for the same, unless the jury is satisfied that he had no intent to defraud :

(15.) " If within four months next before the presentation of a bankruptcy petition against him or the commencement of the liquidation, he, being a trader, pawns, pledges, or disposes of otherwise than in the ordinary way of his trade, any property which he has obtained on credit and has not paid for, unless the jury is satisfied that he had no intent to defraud :

(16.) " If he is guilty of any false representation or other fraud for the purpose of obtaining the consent of his creditors or any of them to any agreement with reference to his affairs or his bankruptcy or liquidation."

Sect. 12. " If any person who is adjudged a bankrupt or has his affairs liquidated by arrangement after the presentation of a bankruptcy petition against him or the commencement of the liquidation, or within four months before such presentation or commencement, quits England and takes with him, or attempts or makes preparation for quitting England and for taking with him, any part of his property to the amount of twenty pounds or upwards, which ought by law to be divided amongst his creditors, he shall (unless the jury is satisfied that he had no intent to defraud) be guilty of felony, punishable with imprisonment for a time not exceeding two years, with or without hard labour."

Sect. 13. " Any person shall in each of the cases following be deemed guilty of a misdemeanor, and on conviction thereof shall be liable to be imprisoned for any time not exceeding one year, with or without hard labour ; that is to say,

(1.) " If in incurring any debt or liability he has obtained credit under false pretences, or by means of any other fraud :

(*o*) Sect. 163 (2).

(2.) "If he has, with intent to defraud his creditors, or any of them, made or caused to be made any gift, delivery, or transfer of or any charge on his property:

(3.) "If he has, with intent to defraud his creditors, concealed or removed any part of his property since or within two months before the date of any unsatisfied judgment or order for payment of money obtained against him."

If an undischarged bankrupt obtains credit to the extent of 20*l.* or upwards without informing the person from whom he obtains it that he is an undischarged bankrupt, he will be guilty of a misdemeanor and punishable as for a misdemeanor under the Debtors Act, 1869 (*l*). The above provisions of the Debtors Act will be applicable to any person whether a trader or not, against whom a receiving order has been made on a petition presented either by or against him (*m*).

The Court may commit for trial (*n*); and the public prosecutor will act where the Court orders a prosecution (*o*). An order of discharge, or the acceptance of a composition or scheme, will not relieve the debtor from liability to prosecution for a criminal offence (*p*).

The powers under the Debtors Act, 1869 (*q*), formerly vested in the Superior Courts, of committing to prison for default in payment of a judgment debt, are now vested in the judge to whom bankruptcy business is assigned (*r*). That Act, by sect. 4, abolished imprisonment for debt (*s*); but by sect. 5 enacted that—

" Any Court may commit to prison for a term not exceeding six

---

(l) B. A. 1883, s. 31.

(*m*) B. A. 1883, s. 163.

(*n*) B. A. 1883, s. 165.

(*o*) B. A. 1883, s. 166. See sect. 164, and the Debtors Act, 1869, s. 16.

(*p*) B. A. 1883, s. 167.

(*q*) 32 & 33 Vict. c. 62.

(*r*) B. A. 1883, s. 103; Order, Jan. 1, 1884.

(s) The following cases are excepted from the operation of the Act by sect. 4, viz.:—

"(1.) Default in payment of a penalty, or sum in the nature of a penalty, other than a penalty in respect of any contract: (2.) Default in payment of any sum recoverable summarily before a justice or justices of the peace: (3.) Default by a trustee or person acting in a fiduciary capacity and ordered to pay by a Court of Equity any sum in his possession or under his control (see 41 & 42 Vict. c. 54): (4.) Default by an attorney or solicitor in payment of costs when ordered to pay costs for misconduct as such, or in payment of

weeks, or until payment of the sum due, any person who makes Consequences default in payment of any debt or instalment of any debt due from to debtor<br>himself, &c. him in pursuance of any order or judgment of that or any other competent Court."

This jurisdiction may, however, only be exercised where " it is proved to the satisfaction of the Court that the person making default either has, or has had since the date of the order or judgment, the means (*t*) to pay the sum in respect of which he has made default, and has refused or neglected, or refuses or neglects, to pay the same" (*u*). Proof of "means" may be given in such manner as the Court thinks just; and for that purpose the debtor and witnesses may be summoned and examined on oath (*x*).

Jurisdiction under the section may be exercised by the judge sitting in chambers (*x*).

Instead of committing the debtor in the first instance, the judge may direct the debt to be paid by instalments (*y*). But in that case the judge has power to commit upon failure to pay each instalment (*z*). The order to pay by instalments may be from time to time varied or rescinded (*a*).

Imprisonment under the section does not operate as a satisfaction or extinguishment of the debt or demand or cause of action, or deprive any person of any right to take out execution against the lands, goods, or chattels of the person imprisoned, in

a sum of money when ordered to pay the same in his character of an officer of the Court making the order (see 41 & 42 Vict. c. 54) : (5.) Default in payment for the benefit of creditors of any portion of a salary or other income in respect of the payment of which any Court having jurisdiction in bankruptcy is authorized to make an order: Provided that no person shall be imprisoned in any case excepted from the operation of the section for a longer period than one year."

(*t*) See *Chard* v. *Jervis*, 9 Q. B. D. 178. It is not necessary that the "means" should be derived from the debtor's earnings, or a fixed income : *Ex parte Koster*, 14 Q. B. D. 597.

(*u*) 32 & 33 Vict. c. 62, s. 5.

(*x*) Ibid.

(*y*) Ibid. The order for payment by instalments may be made without any proof of means: *Dillon* v. *Cunningham*, L. R. 8 Ex. 23. The Court if satisfied of the debtor's means may make an order for commitment, but direct the warrant to be suspended if the debtor pay the debt by instalments: *Stonor* v. *Fowle*, 13 App. Cas. 20.

(*z*) *Evans* v. *Wills*, 1 C. P. D. 229.

(*a*) 32 & 33 Vict. c. 62, s. 5.

the same manner as if the imprisonment had not taken place (c). The person imprisoned will be discharged out of custody upon a certificate signed in the prescribed manner to the effect that he has satisfied the debt or instalment of a debt in respect of which he was imprisoned, together with the prescribed costs (if any) (d).

Where the debt is due upon a judgment in a County Court, the jurisdiction given by the section can only be exercised by a County Court (e).

County Courts within the jurisdiction of which a judgment debtor is or resides, have now jurisdiction under the section, although the amount of the judgment debt exceeds 50l. (f); but jurisdiction can be exercised in the County Court only by a judge or his deputy, and by an order showing on its face the ground on which it is issued (g).

*Allowance.*—An allowance in money may be made by the trustee, with the permission of the committee of inspection, to the bankrupt for the support of himself and his family, or in consideration of his services (h). The bankrupt may also be appointed in like manner to superintend the management of the property, or to carry on his trade (i).

*Surplus.*—The bankrupt is entitled to any surplus after payment in full of the creditors, with interest, and the costs of the bankruptcy (k).

The Bankruptcy Discharge and Closure Act, 1887 (50 & 51 Vict. c. 66), provides for the discharge of bankrupts under repealed Bankruptcy Acts, for closing bankruptcies, and for the release of trustees.

(c) 32 & 33 Vict. c. 62, s. 5.
(d) Ibid.
(e) Ibid.
(f) B. A. 1883, s. 104 (4); *Ex parte Addington*, 16 Q. B. D. 665.

(g) 32 & 33 Vict. c. 62, s. 5.
(h) B. A. 1883, s. 64; B. R. 1886, r. 296.
(i) Ibid.
(k) B. A. 1883, s. 65.

## Section XII.—*Discharge of Debtor and Annulment of Bankruptcy.*

*Discharge.*—At any time after adjudication, an application for discharge, which must be made in open Court, may be made by the bankrupt; but it will not be heard till after the public examination is concluded (*l*). The Court will consider a report of the official receiver, and will hear the official receiver, trustee, and any creditor on the subject. Fourteen days' notice of the day for hearing must be given to each creditor (*m*). The Court may either grant or refuse an absolute order, or suspend the operation of the order for a specified time, or impose conditions as to future earnings and property. But an order of discharge must be refused where the debtor has committed a misdemeanor under the Act, or the Debtors Act, 1869; and it must either be refused, or suspended, or made conditional, if the bankrupt has not kept proper books (*n*) relating to his business, and showing his business transactions and financial position for three years prior to his bankruptcy, or if he has traded after knowing himself to be insolvent, or if he has contracted any provable debt without reasonable or probable expectation of being able to pay it (*o*), or if he has brought on his bankruptcy by rash and hazardous speculation (*p*), or by unjustifiable extravagance in living, or if he has put a creditor to expense by frivolous or vexatious defence of an action, or if he has, within three months before the receiving order and while insolvent, given an undue preference to any creditor, or if he has been previously adjudicated, or made any statutory composition or arrangement with creditors, or if he has been guilty of any fraud or fraudulent breach of trust (*q*).

If any of the above facts are proved, the Court cannot grant an unconditional discharge; it must either refuse the discharge, suspend it, or make it conditional (*r*). The Court cannot make

*Discharge of debtor and annulment of bankruptcy.*

---

(1) B. A. 1883, s. 28, sub-s. 1. See B. R. 1886, rr. 235—244.

(*m*) B. A. 1883, s. 28, sub-ss. 2, 4, 5.

(*n*) *Ex parte Reed*, 17 Q. B. D. 244.

(*o*) *Ex parte White*, 14 Q. B. D. 600.

(*p*) *Ex parte Salaman*, 14 Q. B. D. 936.

(*q*) B. A. 1883, s. 28, sub-s. 2.

(*r*) *In re Heap, Ex parte Board of Trade*, 4 Morrell, 314.

Discharge of debtor and annulment of bankruptcy.

a conditional order of discharge and also suspend the order— e. g., require as a condition of discharge that the debtor consent to judgment being entered against him under sect. 23 (6), and also suspend the order of discharge for six months (s).

The effect of the order of discharge is to release the bankrupt from all provable debts, except debts on a recognizance, debts at the suit of the Crown, or chargeable against the bankrupt for any offence against a statute relating to any branch of the public revenue, or at the suit of the sheriff or other public officer, on a bail bond for the appearance of any person prosecuted for such offence (unless the Treasury consent in writing to his being discharged therefrom), and except debts or liabilities incurred by means of any fraud or fraudulent breach of trust (t) to which he was a party, or debts or liabilities whereof he has obtained forbearance by any fraud to which he was a party (u). An order of discharge is conclusive evidence of the bankruptcy, and of the validity of the proceedings therein (x). It will not release any person who, at the date of the receiving order, was a partner or co-trustee with the bankrupt, or who was jointly bound or had made any joint contract with him, or any person who was surety or in the nature of surety for him (y).

*Annulment of Adjudication.*—If, in the opinion of the Court, the debtor ought not to have been adjudicated, or if the debts are proved to have been paid in full, an order of adjudication may be annulled (z). In such case, all sales and dispositions of property and payments made, and acts done, by the official receiver, trustee, or other person acting under their authority, or by the Court, will be valid; but the property of the bankrupt will vest in such person as the Court may appoint, or, in default of appointment, in the debtor, subject to any conditions that the Court may impose (a). A receiving order may also, in similar

---

(s) *In re Huggins*, 6 Morrell, 38.

(t) *Emma Silver Mining Co.* v. *Grant*, 17 Ch. D. 122; *Ramshill* v. *Edwards*, 31 Ch. D. 100.

(u) B. A. 1883, s. 30, sub-ss. 1, 2. ; *Cooper* v. *Prichard*, 11 Q. B. D. 351.

(x) B. A. 1883, s. 30, sub-s. 3.

(y) B. A. 1883, s. 30, sub-s. 4.

(z) B. A. 1883, s. 35, sub-s. 1 ; *In re Gyll*, 5 Morrell, 272. As to payment in full, see sect. 36.

(a) B. A. 1883, s. 35, sub-s. 2.

circumstances, be set aside by the Court. But the consent of the creditors to its annulment will not be decisive (*b*).

By the Deeds of Arrangement Act, 1887 (50 & 51 Vict. c. 57) (*c*), deeds of arrangement made in respect of the affairs of a debtor for the benefit of his creditors generally (*d*), must be registered with the registrar of bills of sale within seven clear days after the first execution thereof by the debtor or any creditor, otherwise they are void (*e*). Registration under the Act does not make the deed valid, if bankruptcy proceedings are taken within three months of the execution of the deed. If, however, no such proceedings are taken within the three months, then the deed if duly registered stands good against the world (*f*).

A deed of arrangement, whether under seal or not, within the meaning of the Act, includes ( *g* ) :—

" (a) An assignment of property;

" (b) A deed of or agreement for composition;

"And in cases where creditors of a debtor obtain any control over his property or business :—

"(c) A deed of inspectorship entered into for the purpose of carrying on or winding up a business;

"(d) A letter of licence authorising the debtor or any other person to manage, carry on, realize or dispose of a business, with a view to the payment of debts; and

"(e) Any agreement or instrument entered into for the purpose of carrying on or winding up the debtor's business, or authorising the debtor or any other person to manage, carry on, realize, or dispose of the debtor's business with a view to the payment of his debts."

Registration is effected by filing in like manner as a bill of sale given by way of security for the payment of money a true copy of the deed and of every schedule or inventory thereto

*Marginal note:* Discharge of debtor and annulment of bankruptcy.

---

(*b*) *In re Hester*, 22 Q. B. D. 632.

(*c*) See the Act in the Appendix.

(*d*) The Act does not appear to extend to a case where the debtor deals individually with each creditor, or the creditor executes a separate release.

(*e*) Sects. 5, 8. Where the time for registration expires on a Sunday, or day on which the office is closed, registration may be made on the next day the office is open: sect. 10.

(*f*) Sect. 4, sub-s. 2. See *In re Batten, Ex parte Milne*, 58 L. J. Q. B. at p. 335, per Lord *Esher*, M. R., 22 Q. B. D. at p. 691.

(*g*) Sect. 4.

annexed, or therein referred to, together with an affidavit verifying the time of execution, and containing a description of the residence and occupation of the debtor, and of the place or places where his business is carried on, and an affidavit by the debtor stating the total estimated amount of property and liabilities included under the deed, the total amount of the composition (if any) payable thereunder, and the names and addresses of his creditors (*h*) ; the deed must be produced to the registrar at the time of registration duly stamped, not only with the proper inland revenue duty, but with a stamp denoting duty at the rate of 1*s*. in the pound for every 100*l*. or fraction of 100*l*. of the sworn value of the property passing, or, if none passes, of the amount of composition payable under the deed (*i*).

Registration is not invalidated by reason of the execution of the deed by creditors subsequent to registration (*k*).

Where the place of business or residence of the debtor is outside the London Bankruptcy District, the registrar must, within three days of registration, transmit a copy of the deed to the registrar of the County Court of the district where the debtor carries on business or resides (*l*).

Office copies of the deed may be obtained (*m*), and inspection had of the register (*n*).

---

(*h*) Sect. 6, sub-s. 1.

(i) Sect. 6, sub-s. 2.

(*k*) *In re Batten, Ex parte Milne*, 58 L. J. Q. B. 335 ; L. R. 22 Q. B. D.

685.

(l) Sect. 13.

(*m*) Sect. 11, and sect. 13, sub-s. 2.

(*n*) Sect. 12, and sect. 13, sub-s. 2.

# APPENDIX.

# APPENDIX

OF THE

## PRINCIPAL STATUTES ON COMMERCIAL SUBJECTS.

———◆———

### CONTENTS.

# APPENDIX

#### OF THE

## PRINCIPAL STATUTES ON COMMERCIAL SUBJECTS.

### 29 Car. II. c. 3.

*An Act for Prevention of Frauds and Perjuries.*

IV. And be it further enacted by the authority aforesaid, that from and after the said four and twentieth day of June no action shall be brought whereby to charge any executor or administrator upon any special promise to answer damages out of his own estate, or whereby to charge the defendant upon any special promise (a) to answer for the debt, default, or miscarriages of another person; or to charge any person upon any agreement made upon consideration of marriage; or upon any contract or* sale of lands, tenements, or hereditaments, or any interest in or concerning them; or upon any agreement that is not to be performed within the space of one year from the making thereof; unless the agreement upon which such action shall be brought or some memorandum or note thereof, shall be in writing, and signed by the party to be charged therewith, or some other person thereunto by him lawfully authorised.

*Promises and agreements by parol.*

\* *Sic.*

XVII. (b) And be it further enacted by the authority aforesaid, that from and after the said four and twentieth day of June no contract for the sale of any goods, wares, and merchandises (c), for the price of ten pounds sterling or upwards, shall be allowed to be good, except the buyer shall accept part of the goods so sold, and actually receive the same, or give something in earnest to bind the bargain or in part of payment, or that some note or memorandum in writing of the said bargain be made and signed by the parties to be charged by such contracts, or their agents thereunto lawfully authorised.

*Contracts for sales of goods for 10l. or more.*

### 29 Car. II. c. 7.

*An Act for the better Observation of the Lord's Day, commonly called Sunday.*

For the better observation and keeping holy the Lord's day, commonly called Sunday, be it enacted by the King's most excellent Majesty, by and with the advice and consent of the lords spiritual and temporal, and of the commons, in this present parliament assembled, and by the authority of the same, That all the laws enacted and in force concerning the observation of the Lord's day, and repairing to the church thereon, be carefully put in execution; and that all and every person and persons whatsoever shall on every Lord's day apply themselves to the observation of the same, by exercising themselves thereon in the duties of piety and true religion, publicly and privately; and that no tradesman, artificer, workman, labourer, or other

*3 Car. 1, c. 1.*

(a) See as to this 19 & 20 Vict. c. 97, s. 3, *infra*
(b) See 9 Geo. 4, c. 94, s. 7, *infra.*
(c) This section is in the Revised Edition of the Statutes printed as sect. 16.

Tradesmen, artificers, and labourers.

person whatsoever, shall do or exercise any worldly labour, business, or work of their ordinary callings upon the Lord's day, or any part thereof (works of necessity and charity only excepted) ; and that every person being of the age of fourteen years or upwards, offending in the premises, shall for every such offence forfeit the sum of five shillings; and that no person or persons whatsoever shall publicly cry, shew forth, or expose to sale, any wares, merchandises, fruit, herbs, goods, or chattels whatsoever, upon the Lord's day, or any part thereof, upon pain that every person so offending shall forfeit the same goods so cried, or shewed forth, or exposed to sale.

None shall cry or expose to sale wares.

---

## 19 GEO. II. c. 37.

*An Act to regulate Insurance on Ships belonging to the Subjects of Great Britain, and on Merchandises or Effects laden thereon.*

Preamble.

WHEREAS it hath been found by experience, that the making assurances, interest or no interest, or without further proof of interest than the policy, hath been productive of many pernicious practices, whereby great numbers of ships, with their cargoes, have either been fraudulently lost and destroyed, or taken by the enemy in time of war, and such assurances have encouraged the exportation of wool, and the carrying on many other prohibited and clandestine trades, which by means of such assurances have been concealed, and the parties concerned secured from loss, as well to the diminution of the public revenue as to the great detriment of fair traders ; and by introducing a mischievous kind of gaming or wagering, under the pretence of assuring the risk on shipping and fair trade, the institution and laudable design of making assurances hath been perverted, and that which was intended for the encouragement of trade and navigation has, in many instances, become hurtful of and destructive to the same: for remedy whereof, be it enacted by the King's most excellent Majesty, by and with the advice and consent of the lords spiritual and temporal, and commons, in this present parliament assembled, and by the authority of the same, that from and after the first day of August, one thousand seven hundred and forty-six, no assurance or assurances shall be made by any person or persons, bodies corporate or politic, on any ship or ships belonging to his Majesty, or any of his subjects, or on any goods, merchandises, or effects, laden or to be laden on board of any such ship or ships, interest or no interest, or without further proof or* interest than the policy, or by way of gaming or wagering, or without benefit of salvage to the assurer ; and that every such assurance shall be null and void to all intents and purposes.

No assurance to be made on ships or effects, &c., of subjects, interest or no interest.

\* *Sic.*

Assurance on private ships of war may be made for the owners, interest or no interest.

II. Provided always, that assurance on private ships of war, fitted out by any of his Majesty's subjects solely to cruise against his Majesty's enemies, may be made by or for the owners thereof, interest or no interest, free of average, and without benefit of salvage to the assurer ; anything herein contained to the contrary thereof in anywise notwithstanding.

Assurance on effects from Spain or Portugal.

III. Provided also, that any merchandises or effects from any ports or places in Europe or America, in the possession of the Crowns of Spain or Portugal, may be assured in such way and manner as if this Act had not been made.

IV. and V. [Repealed 30 & 31 Vict. c. 59, as to all the Queen's dominions.]

In all actions plaintiff to declare w.thin fifteen days what sums he hath assured.

VI. In all actions or suits brought or commenced, after the said first day of August, by the assured, upon any policy of assurance, the plaintiff in such action or suit, or his attorney or agent, shall, within fifteen days after he or they shall be required so to do in writing by the defendant, or his attorney or agent, declare in writing what sum or sums he hath assured or caused to be assured in the whole, and what sums he hath borrowed at respondentia or bottom-ree, for the voyage, or any part of the voyage in question in such suit or action.

VII. [Repealed by 42 & 43 Vict. c. 59, as to the Supreme Court of Judicature in England.]

VIII. Provided always, that this Act shall not extend to or be in force against any persons residing in any parts or places in Europe out of his Majesty's dominions, for whose account any assurance or assurances shall be made before the 29th day of September, in the year of our Lord one thousand seven hundred and forty-six ; nor extend to or be in force against any persons residing in any parts or places in Turkey, or in Asia, Africa, or America, for whose account any assurance or assurances shall be made before the twenty-fifth day of March, in the year of our Lord one thousand seven hundred and forty-seven ; anything herein contained to the contrary thereof in anywise notwithstanding (a).

(a) Repealed as to the Queen's dominions, 30 & 31 Vict. c. 59.

---

## 14 GEO. III. c. 48.

*An Act for regulating Insurances upon Lives, and for prohibiting all such Insurance, except in cases where the Persons insuring shall have an Interest in the Life or Death of the Persons insured.*

WHEREAS it hath been found by experience, that the making insurances on lives or other events, wherein the assured shall have no interest, hath introduced a mischievous kind of gaming : for remedy whereof, be it enacted by the King's most excellent Majesty, by and with the advice and consent of the lords spiritual and temporal, and commons, in this present parliament assembled, and by the authority of the same, that from and after the passing of this Act, no insurance shall be made by any person or persons, bodies politic or corporate, on the life or lives of any person or persons, or on any other event or events whatsoever, wherein the person or persons for whose use, benefit, or on whose account such policy or policies shall be made, shall have no interest, or by way of gaming or wagering ; and that every assurance made, contrary to the true intent and meaning hereof, shall be null and void, to all intents and purposes whatsoever. *Preamble.*

*No insurance to be made on the lives of persons having no interest, &c.*

II. It shall not be lawful to make any policy or policies on the life or lives of any person or persons, or other event or events, without inserting in such policy or policies the person or persons' name or names interested therein, or for whose use, benefit, or on whose account such policy is so made or underwrote. *No policies on lives without inserting the persons' names, &c.*

III. In all cases where the insured hath interest in such life or lives, event or events, no greater sum shall be recovered or received from the insurer or insurers than the amount or value of the interest of the insured in such life or lives, or other event or events. *How much may be recovered where the insured hath interest in lives.*

IV. Provided always, that nothing herein contained shall extend, or be construed to extend, to insurances bonâ fide made by any person or persons, on ships, goods, or merchandises ; but every such insurance shall be as valid and effectual in the law, as if this Act had not been made. *Not to extend to insurances on ships, goods, &c.*

---

7 Geo. IV. c. 46.

*An Act for the better regulating Copartnerships of certain Bankers in England ; and for amending so much of an Act of the Thirty-ninth and Fortieth Years of the Reign of his late Majesty King George the Third, intituled "An Act for establishing an Agreement with the Governor and Company of the Bank of England, for advancing the Sum of Three Millions towards the Supply for the Service of the Year One Thousand eight hundred," as relates to the same.*

[*26th May*, 1826.]

Preamble.
39 & 40 Geo.
c. 28.

WHEREAS an Act was passed in the thirty-ninth and fortieth years of the reign of his late Majesty King George the Third, intituled "An Act for establishing an Agreement with the Governor and Company of the Bank of England, for advancing the sum of Three Millions towards the Supply for the Service of the Year One Thousand eight hundred : " And whereas it was, to prevent doubts as to the privilege of the said governor and company, enacted and declared in the said recited Act, that no other bank should be erected, established, or allowed by Parliament ; and that it should not be lawful for any body politic or corporate whatsoever, erected or to be erected, or for any other persons united or to be united in covenants or partnership, exceeding the number of six persons, in that part of Great Britain called England, to borrow, owe, or take up any sum or sums of money, on their bills or notes payable on demand, or at any less time than six months from the borrowing thereof, during the continuance of the said privilege to the said governor and company, who were thereby declared to be and remain a corporation, with the privilege of exclusive banking, as before recited ; but subject nevertheless to redemption on the terms and conditions in the said Act specified : And whereas the governor and company of the Bank of England have consented to relinquish so much of their exclusive privilege as prohibits any body politic or corporate, or any number of persons exceeding six in England, acting in copartnership, from borrowing, owing, or taking up any sum or sums of money on their bills or notes payable on demand, or at any less time than six months from the borrowing thereof ; provided that such body politic or corporate, or persons united in covenants or partnerships, exceeding the number of six persons in each copartnerships, shall have the whole of their banking establishments, and carry on their business as bankers, at any place or places in England exceeding the distance of sixty-five miles from London, and that all the individuals composing such corporations or copartnerships, carrying on such business, shall be liable to and responsible for the due payment of all bills and notes issued by such corporations or copartnerships respectively : Be it therefore enacted by the King's most excellent Majesty, by and with the advice and consent of the lords spiritual and temporal, and commons, in this present parliament assembled, and by the authority of the same, that from and after the passing of this Act, it shall and may be lawful for any bodies politic or corporate erected for the purposes of banking, or for any number of persons united in covenants or copartnership, although such persons so united or carrying on business together shall consist of more than six in number, to carry on the trade or

Copartnerships of more than six in number may carry on business as bankers in England sixty-five miles from London, provided they have no establishment

business of bankers in England, in like manner as copartnerships of bankers consisting of not more than six persons in number may lawfully do ; and for such bodies politic or corporate, or such persons so united as aforesaid, to make and issue their bills or notes at any place or places in England, exceeding the distance of sixty-five miles from London, payable on demand, or otherwise at some place or places specified upon such bills or notes, exceeding the distance of sixty-five miles from London, and not elsewhere, and to borrow, owe, or take up any sum or sums of money on their bills or notes so made and issued at any such place or places as aforesaid : Provided always, that such corporations or persons carrying on such trade or business of bankers in copartnership shall not have any house of business or establishment as bankers in London, or at any place or places not exceeding the distance of sixty-five miles from London ; and that every member of any such corporation or copartnership shall be liable to and responsible for the due payment of all bills and notes which shall be issued, and for all sums of money which shall be borrowed, owed, or taken up by the corporation or copartnership of which such person shall be a member, such person being a member at the period of the date of the bills or notes, or becoming or being a member before or at the time of the bills or notes being payable, or being such member at the time of the borrowing, owing, or taking up of any sum or sums of money upon any bills or notes by the corporation or copartnership, or while any sum of money on any bills or notes is owing or unpaid, or at the time the same became due from the corporation or copartnership ; any agreement, covenant, or contract to the contrary notwithstanding. *{as bankers in London, and that every member shall be liable for the payment of all bills, &c.}*

II. Provided always, and be it further enacted, that nothing in this Act contained shall extend or be construed to extend to enable or authorise any such corporation or copartnership exceeding the number of six persons, so carrying on the trade or business of bankers as aforesaid, either by any member of or person belonging to any such corporation or copartnership, or by any agent or agents, or any other person or persons on behalf of any such corporation or copartnership, to issue or re-issue in London, or at any place or places not exceeding the distance of sixty-five miles from London, any bill or note of such corporation or copartnership, which shall be payable to bearer on demand, or any bank post bill ; nor to draw upon any partner or agent, or other person or persons who may be resident in London, or at any place or places not exceeding the distance of sixty-five miles from London, any bill of exchange which shall be payable on demand, or which shall be for a less amount than fifty pounds : Provided also, that it shall be lawful, notwithstanding anything herein, or in the said recited Act contained, for any such corporation or copartnership to draw any bill of exchange for any sum of money amounting to the sum of fifty pounds or upwards, payable either in London or elsewhere, at any period after date or after sight. *{This Act not to authorise copartnerships to issue within the limits mentioned, any bills payable on demand ; nor to draw bills upon any partner, &c., so resident for less than 50l. ;}*

III. Provided also, and be it further enacted, that nothing in this Act contained shall extend or be construed to extend to enable or authorise any such corporation or copartnership exceeding the number of six persons, so carrying on the trade or business of bankers in England as aforesaid, or any member, agent, or agents of any such corporation or copartnership, to borrow, owe, or take up in London, or at any place or places not exceeding the distance of sixty-five miles from London, any sum or sums of money on any bill or promissory note of any such corporation or copartnership payable on demand, or at any time less than six months from the borrowing thereof, nor to make or issue any bill or bills of exchange or promissory note or notes of such corporation or copartnership contrary to the provisions of the said recited Act of the thirty-ninth and fortieth years of King George the Third, save as provided by this Act in that behalf : Provided also, that nothing herein contained shall extend or be construed to extend to prevent any such corporation or copartnership, by any agent or person authorised by them, from discounting in London, or elsewhere, any bill or bills of exchange not drawn by or upon such corporation or copartnership, or by or upon any person on their behalf. *{nor to borrow money, or take up or issue bills of exchange contrary to the provisions of the recited Act, except as herein provided.}*

IV. And be it further enacted, that before any such corporation or copartnership exceeding the number of six persons, in England, shall begin to issue any bills or notes, or borrow, owe or take up any money on their bills or notes, an account or return shall be made out, according to the form contained in the schedule marked (A) to this Act annexed, wherein shall be set forth the true names, title or firm of such intended or existing corporation or *{Such copartnerships shall, before issuing any notes, &c., deliver at the Stamp Office in London an account contain-}*

ing the name of the firm, &c. copartnership, and also the names and places of abode of all the members of such corporation, or of all the partners concerned or engaged in such copartnership, as the same respectively shall appear on the books of such corporation or copartnership, and the name or firm of every bank or banks established or to be established by such corporation or copartnership, and also the names and places of abode of two or more persons, being members of such corporation or copartnership, and being resident in England, who shall have been appointed public officers of such corporation or copartnership, together with the title of office or other description of every such public officer respectively, in the name of any one of whom such corporation shall sue and be sued as hereinafter provided, and also the name of every town and place where any of the bills or notes of such corporation or copartnership shall be issued by

* *Sic.* any such corporation or by their agent or agents ; and every such amount* or return shall be delivered to the commissioners of stamps at the Stamp Office in London, who shall cause the same to be filed and kept in the said stamp office, and an entry and registry thereof to be made in a book or books to be there kept for that purpose by some person or persons to be appointed by the said commissioners in that behalf, and which book or books any person or persons shall from time to time have liberty to search and inspect on payment of the sum of one shilling for every search.

Governor and Company of the Bank of England may empower agents to carry on banking business at any place in England. XV. And to prevent any doubts that might arise whether the said governor and company, under and by virtue of their charter, and the several Acts of Parliament which have been made and passed in relation to the affairs of the said governor and company, can lawfully carry on the trade or business of banking, otherwise than under the immediate order, management and direction of the court of directors of the said governor and company : Be it therefore enacted, that it shall and may be lawful for the said governor and company to authorise and empower any committee or committees, agent or agents, to carry on the trade and business of banking, for and on behalf of the said governor and company, at any place or places in that part of the United Kingdom called England, and for that purpose to invest such committee or committees, agent or agents with such powers of management and superintendence, and such authority to appoint cashiers and other officers and servants as may be necessary or convenient for carrying on such trade and business as aforesaid : and for the same purpose to issue to such committee or committees, agent or agents, cashier or cashiers, or other officer or officers, servant or servants, cash, bills of exchange, bank post bills, bank notes, promissory notes, and other securities for payment of money : Provided always, that all such acts of the said governor and company shall be done and exercised in such manner as may be appointed by any bye-laws, constitutions, orders, rules, and directions from time to time hereafter to be made by the general court of the said governor and company in that behalf, such bye-laws not being repugnant to the laws of that part of the United Kingdom called England; and in all cases where such bye-laws, constitutions, orders, rules or directions of the said general court shall be wanting, in such manner as the governor, deputy governor, and directors, or the major part of them assembled, whereof the said governor or deputy governor is always to be one, shall or may direct, such directions not being repugnant to the laws of that part of the United Kingdom called England; anything in the said charter or Acts of Parliament, or other law, usage, matter, or thing to the contrary thereof notwithstand-

Proviso for payment of notes in coin. ing : Provided always, that in any place where the trade and business of banking shall be carried on for and on behalf of the said governor and company of the Bank of England, any promissory note issued on their account in such place shall be made payable in coin in such place as well as in London.

Copartnerships may issue unstamped notes on giving bond. XVI. And be it further enacted, that if any corporation or copartnership carrying on the trade or business of bankers under the authority of this Act, shall be desirous of issuing and reissuing notes in the nature of bank notes, payable to the bearer on demand, without the same being stamped as by law is required, it shall be lawful for them so to do on giving security by bond to his Majesty, his heirs and successors, in which bond two of the directors, members, or partners of such corporation or copartnership shall be the obligors, together with the cashier or cashiers, or accountant or accountants employed by such corporation or copartnership as the said commissioners of stamps shall require; and such bonds shall be taken in such reasonable sums as the duties may amount unto during the period of one year, with condition to deliver to the said commissioners of stamps, within fourteen days after the fifth day of January, the fifth day of April, the fifth day of July, and the tenth day of October in every year, whilst the present stamp duties shall remain in force, a just and true account, verified upon the oaths or affirmations of two directors, members or partners of such corporation or copartnership, and of the said cashier or cashiers, accountant or accountants, or such of them as the said commissioners of stamps shall require, such oaths or affirmations to be taken before any justice of the peace and which oaths or affirmations any justice of the peace is hereby authorised and empowered to administer, of the amount or value of all their promissory notes in circulation on some given day in every week, for the space of one quarter of a year, prior to the quarter day immediately preceding the delivery of such account, together with the average amount or value thereof according to such account; and also to pay or cause to be paid into the hands of the receivers general of stamp duties in Great Britain, as a composition for the duties which would otherwise have been payable for such promissory notes issued within the space of one year, the sum of seven shillings for every one hundred pounds, and also for the fractional part of one hundred pounds of the said average amount or value of such notes in circulation, according to the true intent and meaning of this Act; and on due performance thereof such bond shall be void; and it shall be lawful for the said commissioners to fix the time or times of making such payment, and to specify the same in the condition to every such bond; and every such bond may be required to be renewed from time to time at the discretion of the said commissioners or the major part of them, and as often as the same shall be forfeited, or the party or parties to the same, or any of them, shall die, become bankrupt or insolvent, or reside in parts beyond the sea.

XVII. Provided always, and be it further enacted, that no such corporation or copartnership shall be obliged to take out more than four licences for the issuing of any promissory notes for money payable to the bearer on demand, allowed by law to be re-issued in all for any number of towns or places in England ; and in case any such corporation or copartnership shall issue such promissory notes as aforesaid, by themselves or their agents, at more than four different towns or places in England, then, after taking out three distinct licences for three of such towns or places, such corporation or copartnership shall be entitled to have all the rest of such towns or places included in a fourth licence. *No corporation compelled to take out more than four licences.*

XVIII. And be it further enacted, that if any such corporation or copartnership exceeding the number of six persons in England shall begin to issue any bills or notes, or to borrow, owe, or take up any money on their bills or notes, without having caused such account or return as aforesaid to be made out and delivered in the manner and form directed by this Act, or shall neglect or omit to cause such account or return to be renewed yearly, and every year, between the days or times hereinbefore appointed for that purpose, such corporation or copartnership so offending shall, for each and every week they shall neglect so to make* such account and return, forfeit the sum of five hundred pounds; and if any secretary or other officer of such corporation or copartnership shall make out or sign any false account or return, or any account or return which shall not truly set forth all the several particulars by this Act required to be contained or inserted in such account or return, the corporation or copartnership to which such secretary or other officer so offending shall belong, shall for every such offence forfeit the sum of five hundred pounds, and the said secretary or other officer so offending shall also for every such offence forfeit the sum of one hundred pounds ; and if any such secretary or other officer making out or signing any such account or return as aforesaid shall knowingly and wilfully make a false oath of or concerning any of the matters to be therein specified and set forth, every such secretary or other officer so offending, and being thereof lawfully convicted, shall be subject and liable to such pains and penalties as by any law now in force persons convicted of wilful and corrupt perjury are subject and liable to. *Penalty on copartnership neglecting to send returns, 500l.*

*\* Sic.*

*Penalties for making false returns.*

*False oath, perjury.*

XIX. And be it further enacted, that if any such corporation or copartnership exceeding the number of six persons, so carrying on the trade or business of bankers as aforesaid, shall, either by any member of or person belonging to any such corporation or copartnership, or by any agent or agents, or any other person or persons on behalf of any such corporation or *Penalty on copartnership for issuing bills payable on demand;*

copartnership, issue or re-issue in London, or at any place or places not
exceeding the distance of sixty-five miles from London, any bill or note of
*or drawing bills* such corporation or copartnership which shall be payable on demand ; or
*of exchange pay-* shall draw upon any partner or agent, or other person or persons who may
*able on demand,* be resident in London, or at any place or places not exceeding the distance
*or for less than* of sixty-five miles from London, any bill of exchange which shall be
*50l. ;* payable on demand, or which shall be for a less amount than fifty pounds ;
*or borrowing* or if any such corporation or copartnership exceeding the number of six
*money on bills,* persons, so carrying on the trade or business of bankers in England as afore-
*except as herein* said, or any member, agent or agents of any such corporation or copartner-
*provided.* ship, shall borrow, owe, or take up in London, or at any place or places not
exceeding the distance of sixty-five miles from London, any sum or sums
of money on any bill or promissory note of any such corporation or copartnership payable on demand, or at any less time than six months from the
borrowing thereof, or shall make or issue any bill or bills of exchange or
promissory note or notes of such corporation or copartnership contrary to the
provisions of the said recited Act of the thirty-ninth and fortieth years of
King George the Third, save as provided by this Act, such corporation or
copartnership so offending, or on whose account or behalf any such offence
as aforesaid shall be committed, shall for every such offence forfeit the sum
of fifty pounds.

---

## 9 GEO. IV. c. 14.

*An Act for rendering a written Memorandum necessary to the validity
of certain Promises and Engagements.* [*9th May,* 1828.]

*Confirmation of* V. And be it further enacted, that no action shall be maintained whereby
*promises made* to charge any person upon any promise made after full age to pay any debt
*by infants.* contracted during infancy, or upon any ratification after full age of any
promise or simple contract made during infancy, unless such promise or
ratification shall be made by some writing signed by the party to be charged
therewith (*a*).

*Representations* VI. And be it further enacted, that no action shall be brought whereby to
*of character.* charge any person upon or by reason of any representation or assurance
made or given concerning or relating to the character, conduct, credit,
ability, trade, or dealings of any other person, to the intent or purpose that
*\* Sic.* such other person may obtain credit, money, or goods upon\*, unless such
representation or assurance be made in writing, signed by the party to be
charged therewith.

*29 Car. 2, c. 3.* VII. And whereas by an Act passed in England in the twenty-ninth year
*Statute of* of the reign of King Charles the Second, intituled "An Act for the
*Frauds.* Prevention of Frauds and Perjuries," it is among other things enacted, that
from and after the twenty-fourth day of June, one thousand six hundred
and seventy-seven, no contract for the sale of any goods, wares, and
merchandises, for the price of ten pounds sterling or upwards, shall be
allowed to be good, except the buyer shall accept part of the goods so sold,
and actually receive the same, or give something in earnest to bind the
bargain, or in part of payment, or that some note or memorandum in
writing of the said bargain be made and signed by the parties to be charged
by such contract, or their agents thereunto lawfully authorised : And whereas
*Irish Act, 7 Will.* a similar enactment is contained in an Act passed in Ireland in the seventh
*3, c. 12.* year of the reign of King William the Third : And whereas it has been
held, that the said recited enactments do not extend to certain executory
contracts for the sale of goods, which nevertheless are within the mischief
thereby intended to be remedied ; and it is expedient to extend the said
*Powers of recited* enactments to such executory contracts : Be it enacted, that the said enact-
*Acts extended to* ments shall extend to all contracts for the sale of goods of the value of ten
*contracts for*
*goods of 10l., &c.*

(*a*) This section is repealed by Statute Law Revision Act, 1875, **38 & 39**
Vict. c. 66. See now 37 & 38 Vict. c. 62, s. 1, *infra.*

pounds sterling and upwards, notwithstanding the goods may be intended to be delivered at some future time, or may not at the time of such contract be actually made, procured or provided, or fit or ready for delivery, or some act may be requisite for the making or completing thereof, or rendering the same fit for delivery.

---

## 11 GEO. IV. & 1 WILL. IV. c. 68.

*An Act for the more effectual Protection of Mail Contractors, Stage Coach Proprietors and other Common Carriers for Hire, against the Loss of or Injury to Parcels or Packages delivered to them for Conveyance or Custody, the Value and Contents of which shall not be declared to them by the Owners thereof.* [23rd July, 1830.]

WHEREAS by reason of the frequent practice of bankers and others of sending by the public mails, stage coaches, waggons, vans, and other public conveyances by land for hire, parcels and packages containing money, bills, notes, jewellery and other articles of great value in small compass, much valuable property is rendered liable to depredation, and the responsibility of mail contractors, stage coach proprietors and common carriers for hire is greatly increased: And whereas through the frequent omission by persons sending such parcels and packages to notify the value and nature of the contents thereof, so as to enable such mail contractors, stage coach proprietors and other common carriers, by due diligence, to protect themselves against losses arising from their legal responsibility, and the difficulty of fixing parties with knowledge of notices published by such mail contractors, stage coach proprietors, and other common carriers, with the intent to limit such responsibility, they have become exposed to great and unavoidable risks, and have thereby sustained heavy losses: Be it therefore enacted by the King's most excellent Majesty, by and with the advice and consent of the lords spiritual and temporal, and commons, in this present parliament assembled, and by the authority of the same, that from and after the passing of this Act no mail contractor, stage coach proprietor, or other common carrier by land for hire shall be liable for the loss of or injury to any article or articles or property of the descriptions following; (that is to say,) gold or silver coin of this realm or of any foreign state, or any gold or silver in a manufactured or unmanufactured state, or any precious stones, jewellery, watches, clocks or time-pieces of any description, trinkets, bills, notes of the governor and company of the Banks of England, Scotland and Ireland respectively, or of any other bank in Great Britain or Ireland, orders, notes or securities for payment of money, English or foreign, stamps, maps, writings, title-deeds, paintings, engravings, pictures, gold or silver plate, or plated articles, glass, china, silks in a manufactured and unmanufactured state, and whether wrought up or not wrought up with other materials, furs or lace (a), or any of them, contained in any parcel or package which shall have been delivered, either to be carried for hire or to accompany the person of any passenger in any mail or stage coach or other public conveyance, when the value of such article or articles or property aforesaid contained in such parcel or package shall exceed the sum of ten pounds, unless at the time of the delivery thereof at the office, warehouse or receiving house of such mail contractor, stage coach proprietor or other common carrier, or to his, her or their book-keeper, coachman or other servant, for the purpose of being carried or of accompanying the person of any passenger as aforesaid, the value and nature of such article or articles or property shall have been declared by the person or persons sending or delivering the same, and such increased charge as hereinafter mentioned, or an engagement to pay the same, be accepted by the person receiving such parcel or package.

*Preamble.*

*Mail contractors, coach proprietors and carriers not to be liable for loss of certain goods above the value of 10l., unless declared as such and increased charge accepted.*

(a) This does not include machine-made lace. See Carriers Act Amendment Act, 1865 (28 & 29 Vict. c. 94).

When parcel so delivered increased rate of charge may be demanded.

II. And be it further enacted, that when any parcel or package containing any of the articles above specified shall be so delivered, and its value and contents declared as aforesaid, and such value shall exceed the sum of ten pounds, it shall be lawful for such mail contractors, stage coach proprietors, and other common carriers to demand and receive an increased rate of charge,

Notice of the same to be affixed in offices or warehouses.

to be notified by some notice affixed in legible characters in some public and conspicuous part of the office, warehouse, or other receiving house where such parcels or packages are received by them for the purpose of conveyance, stating the increased rates of charge required to be paid over and above the ordinary rate of carriage as a compensation for the greater risk and care to be taken for the safe conveyance of such valuable articles; and all persons sending or delivering parcels or packages containing such valuable articles as aforesaid at such office shall be bound by such notice without further proof of the same having come to their knowledge.

Carriers to give receipts, acknowledging increased rate.

In case of neglect to give receipt, &c.

III. Provided always, and be it further enacted, that when the value shall have been so declared, and the increased rate of charge paid, or an engagement to pay the same shall have been accepted as hereinbefore mentioned, the person receiving such increased rate of charge or accepting such agreement shall, if thereto required, sign a receipt for the package or parcel, acknowledging the same to have been insured, which receipt shall not be liable to any stamp duty; and if such receipt shall not be given when required, or such notice as aforesaid shall not have been affixed, the mail contractor, stage coach proprietor, or other common carrier as aforesaid shall not have or be entitled to any benefit or advantage under this Act, but shall be liable and responsible as at the common law, and be liable to refund the increased rate of charge.

Publication of notices not to limit the liability of proprietors, &c , in respect of any other goods conveyed.

* Sic.

IV. Provided always, and be it enacted, that from and after the first day of September now next ensuing no public notice or declaration heretofore made or hereafter to be made, shall be deemed or construed to limit or in anywise affect the liability at common law of any such mail contractors, stage coach proprietors, or other public common carriers as aforesaid, for or in respect of any articles or goods to be carried and conveyed by them; but that all and every such mail contractors, stage coach proprietors, and other common carriers as aforesaid shall from and after the said first day of September be liable, as at the common law, to answer for the loss of* any injury to any articles and goods in respect whereof they may not be entitled to the benefit of this Act; any public notice or declaration by them made and given contrary thereto, or in anywise limiting such liability, notwithstanding.

Every office used to be deemed a receiving house;

and any one coach proprietor or carrier shall be liable to be sued.

V. And be it further enacted, that for the purposes of this Act every office, warehouse, or receiving house which shall be used or appointed by any mail contractor, or stage coach proprietor, or other such common carrier as aforesaid for the receiving of parcels to be conveyed as aforesaid, shall be deemed and taken to be the receiving house, warehouse, or office of such mail contractor, stage coach proprietor, or other common carrier: and that any one or more of such mail contractors, stage coach proprietors, or common carriers shall be liable to be sued by his, her, or their name or names only; and that no action or suit commenced to recover damages for loss or injury to any parcel, package, or person shall abate for the want of joining any co-proprietor or co-partner in such mail, stage coach, or other public conveyance by land for hire as aforesaid.

Not to affect contracts.

VI. Provided always, and be it further enacted, that nothing in this Act contained shall extend or be construed to annul or in anywise affect any special contract between such mail contractor, stage coach proprietor, or common carrier, and any other parties, for the conveyance of goods and merchandises.

Parties entitled to damages for loss may also recover back extra charges.

VII. Provided also, and be it further enacted, that where any parcel or package shall have been delivered at any such office, and the value and contents declared as aforesaid, and the increased rate of charges been paid, and such parcels or packages shall have been lost or damaged, the party entitled to recover damages in respect of such loss or damage shall also be entitled to recover back such increased charges so paid as aforesaid, in addition to the value of such parcel or package.

Nothing herein to protect felonious acts.

VIII. Provided also, and be it further enacted, that nothing in this Act shall be deemed to protect any mail contractor, stage coach proprietor, or other common carrier for hire, from liability to answer for loss or injury to any goods or articles whatsoever, arising from the felonious acts of any coachman, guard, book-keeper, porter, or other servant in his or their employ, nor to protect any such coachman, guard, book-keeper, or other servant from liability for any loss or injury occasioned by his or their own personal neglect or misconduct.

IX. Provided also, and be it further enacted, that such mail contractors, stage coach proprietors, or other common carriers for hire shall not be concluded as to the value of any such parcel or package by the value so declared as aforesaid, but that he or they shall in all cases be entitled to require, from the party suing in respect of any loss or injury, proof of the actual value of the contents by the ordinary legal evidence, and that the mail contractors, stage coach proprietors, or other common carriers as aforesaid shall be liable to such damages only as shall be so proved as aforesaid, not exceeding the declared value, together with the increased charges as before mentioned. *Coach proprietors and carrier liable only to such damages as are proved.*

X. And be it further enacted, that in all actions to be brought against any such mail contractor, stage coach proprietor, or other common carrier as aforesaid for the loss of or injury to any goods delivered to be carried, whether the value of such goods shall have been declared or not, it shall be lawful for the defendant or defendants to pay money into court in the same manner and with the same effect as the money may be paid into court in any other action. *Money may be paid into court in all actions for loss of goods.*

XI. And be it further enacted, that this Act shall be deemed and taken to be a public Act, and shall be judicially taken notice of as such by all judges, justices, and others, without being specially pleaded. *Public Act.*

---

## 1 & 2 WILL. IV. c. 37.

*An Act to prohibit the Payment, in certain Trades, of Wages in Goods, or otherwise than in the current Coin of the Realm.*

[*15th October*, 1831.]

WHEREAS it is necessary to prohibit the payment, in certain trades, of wages in goods, or otherwise than in the current coin of the realm; be it therefore enacted by the King's most excellent Majesty, by and with the advice and consent of the lords spiritual and temporal, and commons, in this present parliament assembled, and by the authority of the same, that in all contracts hereafter to be made for the hiring of any artificer in any of the trades (a) hereinafter enumerated, or for the performance by any artificer of any labour in any of the said trades, the wages of such artificer shall be made payable in the current coin of this realm only, and not otherwise; and that if in any such contract the whole or any part of such wages shall be made payable in any manner other than in the current coin aforesaid, such contract shall be and is hereby declared illegal, null, and void. *Preamble.* *Contracts for the hiring of artificers must be made in the current coin of the realm;*

II. If in any contract hereafter to be made between any artificer in any of the trades hereinafter enumerated, and his employer, any provision shall be made directly or indirectly respecting the place where, or the manner in which, or the person or persons with whom, the whole or any part of the wages due or to become due to any such artificer shall be laid out or expended, such contract shall be and is hereby declared illegal, null, and void. *and must not contain any stipulations, &c.*

III. The entire amount of the wages earned by or payable to any artificer in any of the trades hereinafter enumerated, in respect of any labour by him done in any such trade, shall be actually paid to such artificer in the current coin of this realm (b), and not otherwise; and every payment made to any such artificer by his employer, of or in respect of any such wages, by the delivering to him of goods, or otherwise than in the current coin aforesaid, except as hereinafter mentioned, shall be and is hereby declared illegal, null, and void. *All wages must be paid in coin.* *Payment in goods declared illegal.*

---

(a) See 50 & 51 Vict. c. 46, s. 2; *Ingram* v. *Barnes*, 7 E. & B. 115.    (b) See *Smith* v. *Walton*, 3 C. P. D. 109.

3 H 2

Artificers may recover wages if not paid in the current coin.

IV. Every artificer in any of the trades hereinafter enumerated shall be entitled to recover from his employer in any such trade, in the manner by law provided for the recovery of servants' wages, or by any other lawful ways and means, the whole or so much of the wages earned by such artificer in such trade as shall not have been actually paid to him by such his employer in the current coin of this realm.

In an action brought for wages no set-off shall be allowed for goods supplied by the employer, &c.

V. In any action, suit, or other proceeding to be hereafter brought or commenced by any such artificer as aforesaid, against his employer, for the recovery of any sum of money due to any such artificer as the wages of his labour in any of the trades hereinafter enumerated, the defendant shall not be allowed to make any set-off, nor to claim any reduction (c) of the plaintiff's demand, by reason or in respect of any goods, wares or merchandise had or received by the plaintiff as or on account of his wages or in reward for his labour, or by reason or in respect of any goods, wares or merchandise sold, delivered, or supplied to such artificer at any shop or warehouse kept by or belonging to such employer, or in the profits of which such employer shall have any share or interest.

No employer, shall have any action against his artificer for goods supplied to him on account of wages.

VI. No employer of any artificer in any of the trades hereinafter enumerated shall have or be entitled to maintain any suit or action in any court of law or equity, against any such artificer, for or in respect of any goods, wares, or merchandise sold, delivered, or supplied to any such artificer by any such employer, whilst in his employment, as or on account of his wages or reward for his labour, or for or in respect of any goods, wares, or merchandise sold, delivered, or supplied to such artificer at any shop or warehouse kept by or belonging to such employer, or in the profits of which such employer shall have any share or interest.

Not to invalidate the payment of wages in bank notes, if artificer consents.

VIII. Nothing herein contained shall be construed to prevent or to render invalid any contract for the payment, or any actual payment, to any such artificer as aforesaid, of the whole or any part of his wages, either in the notes of the governor and company of the Bank of England, or in the notes of any person or persons carrying on the business of a banker, and duly licensed to issue such notes in pursuance of the laws relating to his Majesty's revenue of stamps, or in drafts or orders for the payment of money to the bearer on demand, drawn upon any person or persons carrying on the business of a banker, being duly licensed as aforesaid, within fifteen miles of the place where such drafts or order shall be so paid, if such artificer shall be freely consenting to receive such drafts or orders as aforesaid, but all payments so made, with such consent as aforesaid, in any such notes, drafts, or orders as aforesaid, shall for the purposes of this Act be as valid and effectual as if such payments had been made in the current coin of the realm.

IX. Any employer of any artificer in any of the trades hereinafter enumerated who shall by himself or by the agency of any other person or persons, directly or indirectly, enter into any contract or make any payment hereby declared illegal shall for the first offence forfeit a sum not exceeding 10l. nor less than 5l., and for the second offence any sum not exceeding 20l. nor less than 10l.; and in the case of a third offence any such employer shall be and be deemed guilty of a misdemeanor, and being thereof convicted shall be punished by fine only at the discretion of the Court, so that the fines shall not in any case exceed the sum of 100l.

XIX. [Repealed by 50 & 51 Vict. c. 46.]

Domestics.

XX. Nothing herein contained shall extend to any domestic servant (d) [or servant in husbandry] (e).

Particular exceptions to the generality to the law.

XXIII. Nothing herein contained shall extend or be construed to extend to prevent any employer of any artificer, or agent of any such employer, from supplying or contracting to supply to any such artificer any medicine or medical attendance, or any fuel, or any materials, tools, or implements to be by such artificer employed in his trade or occupation, if such artificers be employed in mining, or any hay, corn, or other provender to be consumed by any horse or other beast of burden employed by any such artificer in his trade and occupation; nor from demising to any artificer, workman, or

(c) See *Archer* v. *James*, 2 B. & S. 61.

(d) Sect. 4 of 50 & 51 Vict. c. 46,

*infra.*

(e) Words in brackets repealed by 50 & 51 Vict. c. 46, *infra.*

labourer employed in any of the trades or occupations enumerated in this Act, the whole or any part of any tenement at any rent to be thereon reserved; nor from supplying or contracting to supply to any such artificer any victuals dressed or prepared under the roof of any such employer, and there consumed by such artificer; nor from making or contracting to make any stoppage or deduction from the wages of any such artificer for or in respect of any such rent; or for or in respect of any such medicine or medical attendance; or for or in respect of any such fuel, materials, tools, implements, hay, corn, or provender, or of any such victuals dressed and prepared under the roof of any such employer; or for or in respect of any money advanced to such artificer for any such purpose as aforesaid : provided always, that such stoppage or deduction shall not exceed the real and true value of such fuel, materials, tools, implements, hay, corn, and provender, and shall not be in any case made from the wages of such artificer, unless the agreement or contract for such stoppage or deduction shall be in writing, and signed by such artificer (*f*).

XXIV. Nothing herein contained shall extend or be construed to extend to prevent any such employer from advancing to any such artificer any money to be by him contributed to any friendly society or bank for savings duly established according to law, nor from advancing to any such artificer any money for his relief in sickness, or for the education of any child or children of such artificer, nor from deducting or contracting to deduct any sum or sums of money from the wages of such artificers for the education of any such child or children of such artificer [and unless the agreement or contract for such deduction shall be in writing, and signed by such artificer] (*g*).

*Employers may advance money to artificers for certain purposes.*

XXV. In the meaning and for the purposes of this Act [all workmen, labourers, and other persons in any manner engaged in the performance of any work, employment, or operation of what nature soever, in or about the several trades and occupations aforesaid, shall be and be deemed "artificers;" and that within the meaning and for the purposes aforesaid all masters, bailiffs, foremen, managers, clerks, and other persons engaged in the hiring, employment, or superintendence of the labour of any such artificers, shall be and be deemed to be "employers;" and that within the meaning and for the purposes of this Act any money or other thing had or contracted to be paid, delivered, or given as a recompense, reward, or remuneration for any labour, done or to be done, whether within a certain time or to a certain amount, or for a time or an amount uncertain, shall be deemed and taken to be the "wages" of such labour; and that within the meaning and for the purposes aforesaid] (*g*) any agreement, understanding, device, contrivance, collusion or arrangement whatsoever on the subject of wages, whether written or oral, whether direct or indirect, to which the employer and artificer are parties or are assenting, or by which they are mutually bound to each other or whereby either of them shall have endeavoured to impose an obligation on the other of them, shall be and be deemed a "contract."

*Definition of terms.*

---

### 3 & 4 WILL. IV. c. 98.

*An Act for giving to the Corporation of the Governor and Company of the Bank of England certain Privileges, for a limited Period, under certain Conditions.* [29th August, 1833.]

WHEREAS an Act was passed in the thirty-ninth and fortieth years of the reign of his Majesty King George the Third, intituled "An Act for establishing an Agreement with the Governor and Company of the Bank of England for advancing the sum of Three Millions towards the Supply for the Service of the Year One thousand eight hundred:" and whereas it was by the said recited Act declared and enacted, that the said governor and company should be and continue a corporation, with such powers, autho-

*Preamble recites. 39 & 40 Geo. 3, c. 28.*

---

(*f*) See 50 & 51 Vict. c. 46, s. 5, *infra.*

(*g*) Words within brackets repealed by 50 & 51 Vict. c. 46, *infra.*

rities, emoluments, profits, and advantages, and such privileges of exclusive banking, as are in the said recited Act specified, subject nevertheless to the powers and conditions of redemption and on the terms in the said Act mentioned : and whereas an Act passed in the seventh year of the reign of his

7 Geo. 4, c. 46.

late Majesty King George the Fourth, intituled "An Act for the better regulating Copartnership of certain Bankers in England, and for amending so much of an Act of the thirty-ninth and fortieth years of the reign of his late Majesty King George the Third, intituled 'An Act for establishing an Agreement with the Governor and Company of the Bank of England for advancing the sum of Three Millions towards the Supply for the Service of the Year One thousand eight hundred,' as relates to the same:'" and whereas it is expedient that certain privileges of exclusive banking should be continued to the said governor and company for a further limited period upon certain conditions : and whereas the said governor and company of the Bank of England are willing to deduct and allow to the public, from the sums now payable to the said governor and company for the charges of management of the public unredeemed debt, the annual sum hereinafter mentioned, and for the period in this Act specified, provided the privilege of exclusive banking specified in this Act is continued to the said governor and company for the period specified in this Act : may it therefore please your Majesty that it may be enacted : and be it enacted by the King's most excellent Majesty, by and with the advice and consent of the lords spiritual and temporal, and commons, in this present parliament assembled, and by the authority of the

Bank of England to enjoy an exclusive privilege of banking, &c.

same, that the said governor and company of the Bank of England shall have and enjoy such exclusive privilege of banking as is given by this Act, as a body corporate, for the period and upon the terms and conditions hereinafter mentioned, and subject to termination of such exclusive privilege at the time and in the manner in this Act specified.

During such privilege, no banking company of more than six persons to issue notes payable on demand within London, or sixty-five miles thereof.

II. And be it further enacted, that during the continuance of the said privilege, no body politic or corporate, and no society or company, or persons united or to be united in covenants or partnerships, exceeding six persons, shall make or issue in London, or within sixty-five miles thereof, any bill of exchange or promissory note, or engagement for the payment of money on demand, or upon which any person holding the same may obtain payment on demand : Provided always, that nothing herein or in the said recited Act of the seventh year of the reign of his late Majesty King George the Fourth contained shall be construed to prevent any body politic or corporate, or any society or company, or incorporated company or corporation, or copartnership, carrying on and transacting banking business at any greater distance than sixty-five miles from London, and not having any house of business or establishment as bankers in London, or within sixty-five miles thereof (except

7 & 8 Vict. c. 32.

as hereinafter mentioned), to make and issue their bills and notes, payable on demand or otherwise, at the place at which the same shall be issued, being more than sixty-five miles from London, and also in London, and to have an agent or agents in London, or at any other place at which such bills or notes shall be made payable, for the purpose of payment only, but no such bill or note shall be for any sum less than five pounds, or be re-issued in London or within sixty-five miles thereof.

Any company or partnership may carry on business of banking in London or within sixty-five miles thereof, upon the terms herein mentioned.

III. And whereas the intention of this Act is, that the governor and company of the Bank of England should, during the period stated in this Act (subject nevertheless to such redemption as is described in this Act), continue to hold and enjoy all the exclusive privileges of banking given by the said recited Act of the thirty-ninth and fortieth years of the reign of his Majesty King George the Third aforesaid, as regulated by the said recited Act of the seventh year of his late Majesty King George the Fourth, or any prior or subsequent Act or Acts of Parliament, but no other or further exclusive privilege of banking : and whereas doubts have arisen as to the construction of the said Acts, and as to the extent of such exclusive privilege; and it is expedient that all such doubts should be removed : be it therefore declared and enacted, that any body politic or corporate, or society, or company, or partnership, although consisting of more than six persons, may carry on the trade or business of banking in London, or within sixty-five miles thereof, provided that such body politic or corporate, or society, or company, or partnership, do not borrow, owe, or take up in England any sum or sums of

7 & 8 Vict. c. 32, s. 26.

money on their bills or notes payable on demand or at any less time than six months from the borrowing thereof, during the continuance of the privileges granted by this Act to the said governor and company of the Bank of England.

IV. Provided always, and be it further enacted, that from and after the first day of August, One thousand eight hundred and thirty-four, all promissory notes payable on demand of the governor and company of the Bank of England, which shall be issued at any place in that part of the United Kingdom called England out of London, where the trade and business of banking shall be carried on for and on behalf of the said governor and company of the Bank of England, shall be made payable at the place where such promissory notes shall be issued ; and it shall not be lawful for the said governor and company, or any committee, agent, cashier, officer or servant of the said governor and company to issue, at any such place out of London, any promissory note payable on demand which shall not be made payable at the place where the same shall be issued ; anything in the said recited Act of the seventh year aforesaid to the contrary notwithstanding. *All notes of the Bank of England payable on demand which shall be issued out of London shall be payable at the place where issued, &c.*

V. [Repealed by Statute Law Revision Act, 1874.]

VI. And be it further enacted, that from and after the first day of August, One thousand eight hundred and thirty-four, unless and until Parliament shall otherwise direct, a tender of a note or notes of the governor and company of the Bank of England, expressed to be payable to bearer on demand, shall be a legal tender to the amount expressed in such note or notes, and shall be taken to be valid as a tender to such amount for all sums above five pounds on all occasions on which any tender of money may be legally made, so long as the Bank of England shall continue to pay on demand their said notes in legal coin : Provided always, that no such note or notes shall be deemed a legal tender of payment by the governor and company of the Bank of England, or any branch bank of the said governor and company ; but the said governor and company are not to become liable or be required to pay and satisfy, at any branch bank of the said governor and company, any note or notes of the said governor and company, not made specially payable at such branch bank ; but the said governor and company shall be liable to pay and satisfy at the Bank of England in London all notes of the said governor and company, or of any branch thereof. *Bank notes to be a legal tender, except at the Bank and branch banks.*

---

## 5 & 6 WILL. IV. c. 41.

*An Act to amend the Law relating to Securities given for Considerations arising out of gaming, usurious, and certain other illegal Transactions (a).* [31st August, 1835.]

WHEREAS by an Act passed in the sixteenth year of the reign of his late Majesty King Charles the Second, and by an Act passed in the parliament of Ireland in the tenth year of the reign of his late Majesty King William the Third, each of such Acts being intituled "An Act against deceitful, disorderly, and excessive Gaming," it was enacted that all and singular judgments, statutes, recognizances, mortgages, conveyances, assurances, bonds, bills, specialties, promises, covenants, agreements, and other acts, deeds and securities whatsoever, which should be obtained, made, given, acknowledged, or entered into for security or satisfaction of or for any money or other thing lost at play or otherwise as in the said Acts respectively is mentioned, or for any part thereof, should be utterly void and of none effect : and whereas by an Act passed in the ninth year of the reign of her late Majesty Queen Anne, and also by an Act passed in the parliament of Ireland in the eleventh year of the reign of her said late Majesty, each of such Acts being intituled "An Act for the better preventing of excessive and deceitful Gaming," it was enacted, that from and after the several days therein respectively mentioned all notes, bills, bonds, judgments, mortgages, or other securities or conveyances whatsoever, given, granted, drawn or entered into *Preamble recites 16 Car. 2, c. 7. 10 Will. 3 (I.). 9 Anne, c. 14. 11 Anne (I.).*

(a) Repealed, except so much of sects. 1 and 2 as relates to the Acts 9 and 11 Anne, by Statute Law Revision Act, 1874.

or executed by any person or persons whatsoever, where the whole or any part of the consideration of such conveyances or securities should be for any money or other valuable thing whatsoever won by gaming or playing at cards, dice, tables, tennis, bowls, or other game or games whatsoever, or by betting on the sides or hands of such as did game at any of the games aforesaid, or for the reimbursing or repaying any money knowingly lent or advanced for such gaming or betting as aforesaid, or lent or advanced at the time and place of such play, to any person or persons so gaming or betting as aforesaid, or that should, during such play, so play or bet, should be utterly void, frustrate, and of none effect, to all intents and purposes whatsoever : and that where such mortgages, securities, or other conveyances should be of lands, tenements, or hereditaments, or should be such as should incumber or affect the same, such mortgages, securities, or other conveyances should enure and be to and for the sole use and benefit of and should devolve upon such person or persons as should or might have or be entitled to such lands or hereditaments in case the said grantor or grantors thereof, or the person or persons so incumbering the same had been naturally dead, and as if such mortgages, securities, or other conveyances had been made to such person or persons so to be entitled after the decease of the person or persons so incumbering the same ; and that all grants or conveyances to be made for the preventing of such lands, tenements, or hereditaments from coming to or devolving upon such person or persons thereby intended to enjoy the same as aforesaid should be deemed fraudulent and void and of

12 Anne, st. 2, c. 16.

none effect, to all intents and purposes whatsoever : And whereas by an Act passed in the twelfth year of the reign of her said late Majesty Queen Anne, intituled "An Act to reduce the Rate of Interest without any Prejudice to Parliamentary Securities," it was enacted that all bonds, contracts, and assurances whatsoever made after the twenty-ninth day of September, one thousand seven hundred and fourteen, for payment of any principal or money to be lent or covenanted to be performed upon or for any usury, whereupon or whereby there should be reserved or taken above the rate of five pounds in the hundred, as therein mentioned, should be utterly void :

5 Geo. 2 (I.).

And whereas by an Act passed in the parliament of Ireland in the fifth year of the reign of his late Majesty King George the Second, intituled "An Act for reducing the Interest of Money to six per cent.," it was enacted, that all bonds, contracts, and assurances whatsoever made after the first day of May, one thousand seven hundred and thirty-two, for payments of any principal or money to be lent or covenant to be performed upon or for any loan, whereupon or whereby there should be taken or reserved above the rate of six pounds in the hundred, should be utterly void : And whereas by an Act passed in the fifty-eighth year of the reign of his late Majesty King George

58 Geo. 3, c. 93.

the Third, intituled, "An Act to afford Relief to the bonâ fide Holders of Negotiable Securities without Notice that they were given for a usurious Consideration," it was enacted that no bill of exchange or promissory note that should be drawn or made after the passing of that Act should, though it might have been given for a usurious consideration or upon a usurious contract, be void in the hands of an indorsee for valuable consideration, unless such indorsee had at the time of discounting or paying such consideration for the same, actual notice that such bill of exchange or promissory note had been originally given for a usurious consideration or upon a usurious contract : And whereas by an Act passed in the parliament of Ireland in the eleventh and twelfth years of the reign of his said late Majesty King George

11 & 12 Geo. 3 (I.).

the Third, intituled "An Act to prevent Frauds committed by Bankrupts," it was enacted, that every bond, bill, note, contract, agreement, or other security whatsoever to be made or given by any bankrupt or by any other person unto or to the use of or in trust for any creditor or creditors, or for the security of the payment of any debt or sum of money due from such bankrupt at the time of his becoming bankrupt, or any part thereof, between the time of his becoming bankrupt, and such bankrupt's discharge, as a consideration or to the intent to persuade him, her, or them to consent to or sign any such allowance or certificate, should be wholly void and of no effect, and the moneys there secured or agreed to be paid should not be recovered

45 Geo. 3, c. 72.

or recoverable : And whereas by an Act passed in the forty-fifth year of the reign of his said late Majesty King George the Third, intituled "An Act for the Encouragement of Seamen and for the better and more effectually manning his Majesty's Navy during the present War," it was enacted, that all contracts and agreements which should be entered into, and all bills, notes, and other securities which should be given, by any person or persons for ransom of any ship or vessel, or of any merchandise or goods on board the same, contrary to that Act, should be absolutely null and void in law, and of no effect whatsoever: And whereas by an Act passed in the sixth year of the reign of his late Majesty King George the Fourth, intituled "An Act to amend the Laws relating to Bankrupts," it was enacted, that any contract or security made or given by any bankrupt or other person unto or in trust for any creditor, or for securing the payment of any money due by such bankrupt, at his bankruptcy, as a consideration or with intent to persuade such creditor to consent to or sign the certificate of any such bankrupt, should be void, and the money thereby secured or agreed to be paid should not be recoverable, and the party sued on such contract or security might plead the general issue, and give that Act and the special matter in evidence: And whereas securities and instruments made void by virtue of the several hereinbefore recited Acts of the sixteenth year of the reign of his said late Majesty King Charles the Second, the tenth year of the reign of his said late Majesty King William the Third, the ninth and eleventh years of the reign of her said late Majesty Queen Anne, the eleventh and twelfth years of the reign of his said late Majesty King George the Third, the forty-fifth year of the reign of his said late Majesty King George the Third, and the sixth year of the reign of his said late Majesty King George the Fourth, and securities and instruments made void by virtue of the said Act of the twelfth year of the reign of her said late Majesty Queen Anne, and the fifth year of the reign of his said late Majesty King George the Second, other than bills of exchange or promissory notes made valid by the said Act of the fifty-eighth year of the reign of his said late Majesty King George the Third, are sometimes indorsed, transferred, assigned, or conveyed to purchasers or other persons for a valuable consideration, without notice of the original consideration for which such securities or instruments were given, and the avoidance of such securities or instruments in the hands of such purchasers or other persons is often attended with great hardship and injustice: for remedy thereof be it enacted by the King's most excellent Majesty, by and with the advice and consent of the lords spiritual and temporal, and commons, in this present parliament assembled, and by the authority of the same, that so much of the hereinbefore-recited Acts of the sixteenth year of the reign of his said late Majesty King Charles the Second, the tenth year of the reign of his said late Majesty King William the Third, the ninth, eleventh, and twelfth years of the reign of her said late Majesty Queen Anne, the fifth year of the reign of his said late Majesty King George the Second, the eleventh and twelfth, and the forty-fifth years of the reign of his said late Majesty King George the Third, and the sixth year of the reign of his said late Majesty King George the Fourth, as enacts that any note, bill, or mortgage shall be absolutely void, shall be and the same is hereby repealed; but nevertheless every note, bill, or mortgage which if this Act had not been passed would, by virtue of the said several lastly hereinbefore-mentioned Acts or any of them, have been absolutely void, shall be deemed and taken to have been made, drawn, accepted, given or executed for an illegal consideration, and the said several Acts shall have the same force and effect which they would respectively have had if instead of enacting that any such note, bill, or mortgage should be absolutely void, such Acts had respectively provided that every such note, bill, or mortgage should be deemed and taken to have been made, drawn, accepted, given, or executed for an illegal consideration: provided always, that nothing herein contained shall prejudice or affect any note, bill or mortgage which would have been good and valid if this Act had not been passed.

*6 Geo. 4, c. 16.*

*Securities given for considerations arising out of illegal transactions not to be void, but to be deemed to have been given for an illegal consideration.*

II. And be it further enacted, that in case any person shall, after the passing of this Act, make, draw, give, or execute any note, bill, or mortgage for any consideration on account of which the same is by the hereinbefore-recited Acts of the sixteenth year of the reign of his said late Majesty King Charles the Second, the tenth year of the reign of his said late Majesty King William the Third, and the ninth and eleventh years of the reign of her said late Majesty Queen Anne, or by one or more of such Acts, declared to be void, and such person shall actually pay to any indorsee, holder, or assignee of such note, bill, or mortgage the amount of the money thereby secured, or any part thereof, such money so paid shall be deemed and taken

*Money paid to the holder of such securities shall be deemed to be paid on account of the person to whom the same was originally given.*

to have been paid for and on account of the person to whom such note, bill, or mortgage was originally given upon such illegal consideration as aforesaid, and shall be deemed and taken to be a debt due and owing from such last-named person to the person who shall so have paid such money, and shall accordingly be recoverable by action at law in any of his Majesty's Courts of Record.

---

1 & 2 VICT. c. 106.

*An Act to abridge the holding of Benefices in Plurality, and to make better Provision for the Residence of the Clergy.*

[*14th August*, 1838.]

No spiritual person beneficed or performing ecclesiastical duty shall engage in trade, or buy to sell again for profit or gain.

XXIX. And be it enacted, that it shall not be lawful for any spiritual person holding any such cathedral preferment, benefice, curacy or lectureship, or who shall be licensed or allowed to perform such duties as aforesaid, by himself or by any other for him or to his use, to engage in or carry on any trade or dealing for gain or profit, or to deal in any goods, wares or merchandise, unless in any case in which such trading or dealing shall have been or shall be carried on by or on behalf of any number of partners exceeding the number of six, or in any case in which any trade or dealing, or any share in any trade or dealing, shall have devolved or shall devolve upon any spiritual person, or upon any other person for him or to his use, under or by virtue of any devise, bequest, inheritance, intestacy, settlement, marriage, bankruptcy or insolvency; but in none of the foregoing excepted cases shall it be lawful for such spiritual person to act as a director or managing partner, or to carry on such trade or dealing as aforesaid in person (*a*).

Not to extend to spiritual persons engaged in keeping schools or as tutors, &c., in respect of anything done, or any buying or selling in such employment; or to selling anything bonâ fide bought for the use of the family, or to being a manager, &c., in any benefit or life or fire assurance society, or buying and selling cattle, &c. for the use of his own lands, &c.

XXX. Provided always, and be it enacted, that nothing hereinbefore contained shall subject to any penalty or forfeiture any spiritual person for keeping a school or seminary, or acting as a schoolmaster or tutor or instructor, or being in any manner concerned or engaged in giving instruction or education for profit or reward, or for buying or selling or doing any other thing in relation to the management of any such school, seminary or employment, or to any spiritual person whatever for the buying of any goods, wares, or merchandises, or articles of any description, which shall without fraud be bought with intent at the buying thereof to be used by the spiritual person buying the same for his family or in his household, and after the buying of any such goods, wares or merchandises or articles, selling the same again or any parts thereof which such person may not want or choose to keep, although the same shall be sold at an advanced price beyond that which may have been given for the same; or for disposing of any books or other works to or by means of any bookseller or publisher; or for being a manager, director, partner or shareholder in any benefit society, or fire or life assurance society, by whatever name or designation such society may have been constituted; or for any buying or selling again for gain or profit, of any cattle or corn or other articles necessary or convenient to be bought, sold, kept or maintained by any spiritual person, or any other person for him or to his use, for the occupation, manuring, improving, pasturage or profit of any glebe, demesne lands, or other lands or hereditaments which may be lawfully held and occupied, possessed or enjoyed by such spiritual person or any other for him or to his use; or for selling any minerals the produce of mines situated on his own lands; so nevertheless that no such spiritual person shall buy or sell any cattle or corn or other articles as aforesaid in person in any market, fair, or place of public sale.

(*a*) *Lewis* v. *Bright*, 4 El. & B. 917.

XXXI. And be it enacted, that if any spiritual person shall trade or deal in any manner contrary to the provisions of this Act, it shall be lawful for the bishop of the diocese where such person shall hold any cathedral preferment, benefice, curacy or lectureship, or shall be licensed or otherwise allowed to perform the duties of any ecclesiastical office whatever, to cause such person to be cited before his chancellor or other competent judge, and it shall be lawful for such chancellor or other judge, on proof in due course of law of such trading, to suspend such spiritual person for his first offence for such time not exceeding one year as to such judge shall seem fit; and on proof in like manner before such or any other competent ecclesiastical judge of a second offence committed by such spiritual person subsequent to such sentence of suspension, such spiritual person shall for such second offence be suspended for such time as to the judge shall seem fit; and for his third offence be deprived ab officio et beneficio; and thereupon it shall be lawful for the patron or patrons of any such cathedral preferment, benefice, lectureship or office, to make donation or to present or nominate to the same as if the person so deprived were actually dead; and in all such cases of suspension the bishop, during such suspension, shall sequester the profits of any cathedral preferment, benefice, lectureship, or office of which such spiritual person may be in possession, and by an order under his hand direct the application of the profits of the same respectively, after deducting the necessary expenses of providing for the due performance of the duties of the same respectively, towards the same purposes and in the same order, as near as the difference of circumstances will admit, as are hereinafter directed with respect to the profits of a benefice sequestered in case of noncompliance after monition with an order requiring a spiritual person to proceed and reside on his benefice, save that no part of such profits shall be paid to the spiritual person so suspended, nor applied in satisfaction of a sequestration at the suit of a creditor; and in case of deprivation, the bishop shall forthwith give notice thereof in writing under his hand to the patron or patrons of any cathedral preferment, benefice, lectureship or office which the said spiritual person may have holden in the manner hereinafter required with respect to notice to the patron of a benefice continuing under sequestration for one whole year, and thereby becoming void, and any such cathedral preferment or benefice shall lapse at such period after the said notice as any such last-mentioned benefice would under the provisions of this Act lapse: Provided always, that no contract shall be deemed to be void by reason only of the same having been entered into by a spiritual person trading or dealing, either solely or jointly with any other person or persons contrary to the provisions of this Act, but every such contract may be enforced by or against such spiritual person, either solely, or jointly with any other person or persons, as the case may be, in the same way as if no spiritual person had been party to such contract.

*Spiritual persons illegally trading may be suspended, and for the third offence deprived.*

7 & 8 Vict. c. 32.

*An Act to regulate the Issue of Bank Notes, and for giving to the Governor and Company of the Bank of England certain Privileges for a limited Period.* [19th July, 1844.]

All persons may demand of the issue department notes for gold bullion.

IV. And be it enacted, that from and after the thirty-first day of August, one thousand eight hundred and forty-four, all persons shall be entitled to demand from the issue department of the Bank of England Bank of England notes in exchange for gold bullion, at the rate of three pounds seventeen shillings and nine-pence per ounce of standard gold: Provided always, that the said governor and company shall in all cases be entitled to require such gold bullion to be melted and assayed by persons approved by the said governor and company at the expense of the parties tendering such gold bullion.

No new bank of issue.

X. And be it enacted, that from and after the passing of this Act no person other than a banker, who, on the sixth day of May, one thousand eight hundred and forty-four, was lawfully issuing his own bank notes, shall make or issue bank notes in any part of the United Kingdom.

Restriction against issue of bank notes.

XI. And be it enacted, that from and after the passing of this Act it shall not be lawful for any banker to draw, accept, make, or issue, in England or Wales, any bill of exchange or promissory note, or engagement for the payment of money payable to bearer on demand, or to borrow, owe, or take up, in England or Wales, any sums or sum of money on the bills or notes of such banker payable to bearer on demand, save and except that it shall be lawful for any banker who was on the sixth day of May, one thousand eight hundred and forty-four, carrying on the business of a banker in England or Wales, and was then lawfully issuing, in England or Wales, his own bank notes, under the authority of a license to that effect, to continue to issue such notes to the extent and under the conditions hereinafter mentioned, but not further or otherwise; and the right of any company or partnership to continue to issue such notes shall not be in any manner prejudiced or affected by any change which may hereafter take place in the personal composition of such company or partnership, either by the transfer of any shares or share therein, or by the admission of any new partner or member thereto, or by the retirement of any present partner or member therefrom: Provided always, that it shall not be lawful for any company or partnership now consisting of only six or less than six persons to issue bank notes at any time after the number of partners therein shall exceed six in the whole.

Bankers ceasing to issue notes may not resume.

XII. And be it enacted, that if any banker in any part of the United Kingdom, who, after the passing of this Act, shall be entitled to issue bank notes, shall become bankrupt, or shall cease to carry on the business of a banker, or shall discontinue the issue of bank notes, either by agreement with the governor and company of the Bank of England or otherwise, it shall not be lawful for such banker at any time thereafter to issue any such notes.

Existing banks of issue to continue under

XIII. And be it enacted, that every banker claiming under this Act to continue to issue bank notes in England or Wales, shall, within one month

next after the passing of this Act, give notice in writing to the commissioners certain limitations.
of stamps and taxes at their head office in London of such claim, and of the
place and name and firm at and under which such banker has issued such
notes during the twelve weeks next preceding the twenty-seventh day of
April last; and thereupon the said commissioners shall ascertain if such
banker was, on the sixth day of May, one thousand eight hundred and forty-
four, carrying on the business of a banker, and lawfully issuing his own bank
notes in England or Wales, and if it shall so appear, then the said commissioners shall proceed to ascertain the average amount of the bank notes of
such banker which were in circulation during the said period of twelve weeks
preceding the twenty-seventh day of April last, according to the returns
made by such banker in pursuance of the Act passed in the fourth and fifth 4 & 5 Vict. c. 50.
years of the reign of her present Majesty, intituled, "An Act to make further
provisions relative to the returns to be made by banks of the amount of their
notes in circulation;" and the said commissioners, or any two of them, shall
certify under their hands to such banker the said average amount, when so
ascertained as aforesaid; and it shall be lawful for every such banker to continue to issue his own bank notes after the passing of this Act: Provided
nevertheless, that such banker shall not at any time after the tenth day of
October, one thousand eight hundred and forty-four, have in circulation upon
the average of a period of four weeks, to be ascertained as hereinafter mentioned, a greater amount of notes than the amount so certified.

XIV. Provided always, and be it enacted, that if it shall be made to appear Provision for united banks.
to the commissioners of stamps and taxes that any two or more banks have,
by written contract or agreement (which contract or agreement shall be produced to the said commissioners), become united within the twelve weeks next
preceding such twenty-seventh day of April as aforesaid, it shall be lawful
for the said commissioners to ascertain the average amount of the notes of
each such bank in the manner hereinbefore directed, and to certify the average
amount of the notes of the two or more banks so united as the amount which
the united bank shall thereafter be authorized to issue, subject to the regulations of this Act.

XV. And be it enacted, that the commissioners of stamps and taxes shall, Duplicate certificate to be published in the Gazette.
at the time of certifying to any banker such particulars as they are herein-
before required to certify, also publish a duplicate of their certificate thereof
in the next succeeding London Gazette in which the same may be conve- Gazette to be evidence.
niently inserted; and the Gazette in which such publication shall be made,
shall be conclusive evidence in all courts whatsoever of the amount of bank
notes which the banker named in such certificate or duplicate is by law authorized to issue and to have in circulation as aforesaid.

XVI. And be it enacted, that in case it shall be made to appear to the In case banks become united, commissioners to certify the amount of bank notes which each bank was authorised to issue.
commissioners of stamps and taxes, at any time hereafter, that any two or
more banks, each such bank consisting of not more than six persons, have, by
written contract or agreement (which contract or agreement shall be produced to the said commissioners), become united subsequently to the passing
of this Act, it shall be lawful to the said commissioners, upon the application
of such united bank, to certify, in manner hereinbefore mentioned, the aggregate of the amounts of bank notes which such separate banks were previously
authorized to issue, and so from time to time; and every such certificate
shall be published in manner hereinbefore directed; and from and after such
publication the amount therein stated shall be and be deemed to be the limit
of the amount of bank notes which such united bank may have in circulation
Provided always, that it shall not be lawful for any such united bank to issue
bank notes at any time after the number of partners therein shall exceed six
in the whole.

XVII. And be it enacted, that if the monthly average circulation of bank Penalty on banks issuing in excess.
notes of any banker, taken in the manner hereinafter directed, shall at any
time exceed the amount which such banker is authorized to issue and to have
in circulation under the provisions of this Act, such banker shall in every
such case forfeit a sum equal to the amount by which the average monthly
circulation, taken as aforesaid, shall have exceeded the amount which such
banker was authorized to issue and to have in circulation as aforesaid.

XVIII. And be it enacted, that every banker in England and Wales who, Issuing banks to render accounts.
after the tenth day of October one thousand eight hundred and forty-four,
shall issue bank notes, shall, on some one day in every week after the nineteenth day of October, one thousand eight hundred and forty-four (such day

to be fixed by the commissioners of stamps and taxes), transmit to the said commissioners an account of the amount of the bank notes of such banker in circulation on every day during the week ending on the next preceding Saturday, and also an account of the average amount of the bank notes of such banker in circulation during the same week; and on completing the first period of four weeks, and so on completing each successive period of four week, every such banker shall annex to such account the average amount of bank notes of such banker in circulation during the said four weeks, and also the amount of bank notes which such banker is authorized to issue under the provisions of this Act; and every such account shall be verified by the signature of such banker or his chief cashier, cr in the case of a company or partnership, by the signature of a managing director or partner or chief cashier of such company or partnership, and shall be made in the form of this Act annexed marked (B); and so much of the said return as states the weekly average amount of the notes of such bank shall be published by the said commissioners in the next succeeding London Gazette in which the same may be conveniently inserted; and if any such banker shall neglect or refuse to render any such account in the form and at the time required by this Act, or shall at any time render a false account, such banker shall forfeit the sum of one hundred pounds for every such offence.

Mode of ascertaining the average amount of bank notes of each banker in circulation during the first four weeks after the 10th October, 1844.

XIX. And be it enacted, that for the purpose of ascertaining the monthly average amount of bank notes of each banker in circulation, the aggregate of the amount of bank notes of each such banker in circulation on every day of business during the first complete period of four weeks next after the tenth day of October, one thousand eight hundred and forty-four, such period ending on a Saturday, shall be divided by the number of days of business in such four weeks, and the average so ascertained shall be deemed to be the average of bank notes of each such banker in circulation during such period of four weeks, and so in each successive period of four weeks, and such average is not to exceed the amount certified by the commissioners of stamps and taxes as aforesaid.

Commissioners of stamps and taxes empowered to cause the books of bankers containing accounts of their bank notes in circulation to be inspected.

XX. And whereas, in order to insure the rendering of true and faithful accounts of the amount of bank notes in circulation, as directed by this Act, it is necessary that the commissioners of stamps and taxes should be empowered to cause the books of bankers issuing such notes to be inspected, as hereinafter mentioned; be it therefore enacted, that all and every the book and books of any banker who shall issue bank notes under the provisions of this Act, in which shall be kept, contained or entered any account, minute or memorandum of or relating to the bank notes issued or to be issued by such banker, or of or relating to the amount of such notes in circulation from time to time, or any account, minute, or memorandum, the sight or inspection whereof may tend to secure the rendering of true accounts of the average amount of such notes in circulation, as directed by this Act, or to test the truth of any such account, shall be open for the inspection and examination, at all seasonable times, of any officer of stamp duties authorized in that behalf by writing, signed by the commissioners of stamps and taxes, or any two of them; and every such officer shall be at liberty to take copies of or

Penalty for refusing to allow such inspection.

extracts from any such book or account as aforesaid; and if any banker or other person keeping any such book, or having the custody or possession thereof, or power to produce the same, shall, upon demand made by any such officer, showing (if required) his authority in that behalf, refuse to produce any such book to such officer for his inspection and examination, or to permit him to inspect and examine the same, or to take copies thereof or extracts therefrom, or of or from such account, minute or memorandum as aforesaid kept, contained or entered therein, every such banker or other person so offending shall for every such offence forfeit the sum of one hundred pounds; provided always, that the said commissioners shall not exercise the powers aforesaid without the consent of the commissioners of her Majesty's treasury.

All bankers to return names once a year to the stamp office.

XXI. And be it enacted, that every banker in England and Wales who is now carrying on or shall hereafter carry on business as such shall on the first day of January, in each year or within fifteen days thereafter, make a return to the commissioners of stamps and taxes at their head office in London of his name, residence and occupation, or, in the case of a company or partnership, of the name, residence and occupation of every person composing or being a member of such company or partnership, and also the name of the firm under which such banker, company or partnership carry on the business of banking and of every place where such business is carried on ; and if any such banker, company or partnership shall omit or refuse to make such return within fifteen days after the said first day of January, or shall wilfully make other than a true return of the persons as herein required, every banker, company or partnership so offending shall forfeit and pay the sum of fifty pounds ; and the said commissioners of stamps and taxes shall, on or before the first day of March in every year, publish in some newspaper circulating within each town or county respectively a copy of the return so made by every banker, company or partnership carrying on the business of bankers within such town or county respectively, as the case may be.

XXII. And be it enacted, that every banker who shall be liable by law to take out a licence from the commissioners of stamps and taxes to authorize the issuing of notes or bills shall take a separate and distinct licence for every town or place at which he shall, by himself or his agent, issue any notes or bills requiring such licence to authorize the issuing thereof, anything in any former Act contained to the contrary thereof notwithstanding : Provided always, that no banker who on or before the sixth day of May, one thousand eight hundred and forty-four, had taken out four such licences, which on the said last-mentioned day were respectively in force, for the issuing of any such notes or bills at more than four separate towns or places, shall at any time hereafter be required to take out or to have in force at one and the same time more than four such licences to authorize the issuing of such notes or bills at all or any of the same towns or places specified in such licences in force on the said sixth day of May, one thousand eight hundred and forty-four, and at which towns or places respectively such bankers had on or before the said last-mentioned day issued such notes or bills in pursuance of such licences or any of them respectively.

*Bankers to take out a separate licence for every place at which they issue notes or bills.*

*Proviso in favour of bankers who had four such licences in force on the 6th of May, 1844.*

XXIV. And be it enacted, that it shall be lawful for the said governor and company to agree with every banker who, under the provisions of this Act, shall be entitled to issue bank notes, to allow to such banker a composition at the rate of one per centum per annum on the amount of Bank of England notes which shall be issued and kept in circulation by such banker, as a consideration for his relinquishment of the privilege of issuing his own bank notes ; and all the provisions herein contained for the ascertaining and determining the amount of composition payable to the several bankers named in the Schedule hereto marked (C), shall apply to all such other bankers with whom the said governor and company are hereby authorized to agree as aforesaid ; provided that the amount of composition payable to such bankers as last aforesaid shall, in every case in which an increase of securities in the issue department shall have been authorized by any order in council, be deducted out of the amount payable by the said governor and company to the public under the provisions herein contained : Provided always, that the total sum payable to any banker, under the provisions herein contained, by way of composition as aforesaid, in any one year, shall not exceed, in case of the bankers mentioned in the Schedule hereto marked (C), one per centum on the several sums set against the names of such bankers respectively in the list and statement delivered to the commissioners of stamps as aforesaid, and in the case of other bankers shall not exceed one per centum on the amount of bank notes which such bankers respectively would otherwise be entitled to issue under the provisions herein contained.

*Bank of England to be allowed to compound with issuing banks.*

*Limitation of compositions.*

XXV. [Repealed by 19 Vict. c. 20, s. 1.]

XXVI. And be it enacted, that from and after the passing of this Act it shall be lawful for any society or company or any persons in partnership, though exceeding six in number, carrying on the business of banking in London, or within sixty-five miles thereof, to draw, accept or indorse bills of exchange, not being payable to bearer on demand, anything in the hereinbefore recited Act passed in the fourth year of the reign of his said Majesty King William the Fourth, or in any other Act, to the contrary notwithstanding.

*Banks within sixty-five miles of London may accept, &c., bills.*

## SCHEDULE (B).

Name and title as set forth in }
the licence    .    .    .  } _____ Bank.
Name of the firm    .    .    . _____ Firm.
Insert head office or principal }
place of issue    .    .    .  } _____ Place.

An Account pursuant to the Act 7 & 8 Vict. c. 32, of the notes of the said bank in circulation during the week ending Saturday, the —— day of ——, 18—.

Monday    .    .    .
Tuesday    .    .    .
Wednesday .    .    .
Thursday    .    .    .
Friday    .    .    .
Saturday    .    .    .
_____
6)
_____

Average of the week
_____

*[To be annexed to this Account at the End of the Period of Four Weeks.]*

Amount of notes authorized by law    .    .    .    £
Average amount in circulation during the four }    £
weeks ending as above    .    .    .  }

I, being [the banker, chief cashier, managing director *or* partner of the —— Bank, *as the case may be*], do hereby certify, that the above is a true account of the notes of the said bank in circulation during the week above written.

(Signed)

Dated the —— day of ——, 18—.

---

## 17 & 18 Vict. c. 31.

*An Act for the better Regulation of the Traffic on Railways and Canals (a).*
[*10th July*, 1854.]

WHEREAS it is expedient to make better provision for regulating the traffic on railways and canals: Be it enacted by the Queen's most excellent Majesty, by and with the advice and consent of the lords spiritual and temporal, and commons, in this present parliament assembled, and by the authority of the same, as follows:

"Board of Trade;"
I. In the construction of this Act, "the Board of Trade" shall mean the Lords of the Committee of her Majesty's Privy Council for Trade and Foreign Plantations:

"Traffic,"
The word "traffic" shall include not only passengers, and their luggage, and goods, animals and other things conveyed by any railway company or canal company, or railway and canal company, but also carriages, waggons, trucks, boats and vehicles of every description adapted for running or passing on the railway or canal of any such company:

"Railway;"
The word "railway" shall include every station of or belonging to such railway used for the purposes of public traffic: and,

"Canal;"
The word "canal" shall include any navigation whereon tolls are levied by authority of parliament, and also the wharves and landing places of and belonging to such canal or navigation, and used for the purposes of public traffic:

"Company."
The expression "railway company," "canal company" or "railway and canal company," shall include any person being the owner or lessee of

(a) See 51 & 52 Vict. c. 25, *infra*, p. 1190.

or any contractor working any railway or canal or navigation, constructed or carried on under the powers of any Act of Parliament:

A station, terminus or wharf shall be deemed to be near another station, terminus or wharf when the distance between such stations, termini or wharves shall not exceed one mile, such stations not being situate within five miles from St. Paul's Church, in London. *Stations.*

II. Every railway company, canal company and railway and canal company shall, according to their respective powers, afford all reasonable facilities for the receiving and forwarding and delivering of traffic upon and from the several railways and canals belonging to or worked by such companies respectively, and for the return of carriages, trucks, boats and other vehicles, and no such company shall make or give any undue or unreasonable preference or advantage to or in favour of any particular person or company, or any particular description of traffic in any respect whatsoever, nor shall any such company subject any particular person or company, or any particular description of traffic, to any undue or unreasonable prejudice or disadvantage in any respect whatsoever; and every railway company and canal company and railway and canal company having or working railways or canals which form part of a continuous line of railway or canal or railway and canal communication, or which have the terminus, station or wharf of the one near the terminus, station or wharf of the other, shall afford all due and reasonable facilities for receiving and forwarding all the traffic arriving by one of such railways or canals by the other, without any reasonable delay, and without any such preference or advantage, or prejudice or disadvantage, as aforesaid, and so that no obstruction may be offered to the public desirous of using such railways or canals or railways and canals as a continuous line of communication, and so that all reasonable accommodation may, by means of the railways and canals of the several companies, be at all times afforded to the public in that behalf. *Duty of railway companies to make arrangements for receiving and forwarding traffic without unreasonable delay, and without partiality.*

III. It shall be lawful for any company or person complaining against any such companies or company of anything done, or of any omission made in violation or contravention of this Act, to apply in a summary way, by motion or summons, in England, to her Majesty's Court of Common Pleas at Westminster, or in Ireland to any of her Majesty's superior courts in Dublin, or in Scotland to the Court of Session in Scotland, as the case may be, or to any judge of any such court (a): and, upon the certificate to her Majesty's Attorney-General in England or Ireland, or her Majesty's Lord Advocate in Scotland, of the Board of Trade alleging any such violation or contravention of this Act by any such companies or company, it shall also be lawful for the said Attorney-General or Lord Advocate to apply in like manner to any such court or judge, and in either of such cases it shall be lawful for such court or judge to hear and determine the matter of such complaint; and for that purpose, if such court or judge shall think fit, to direct and prosecute, in such mode and by such engineers, barristers or other persons, as they shall think proper, all such inquiries as may be deemed necessary to enable such court or judge to form a just judgment on the matter of such complaint; and if it be made to appear to such court or judge on such hearing, or on the report of any such person, that anything has been done or omission made, in violation or contravention of this Act, by such company or companies, it shall be lawful for such court or judge to issue a writ of injunction or interdict, restraining such company or companies from further continuing such violation or contravention of this Act, and enjoining obedience to the same; and in case of disobedience of any such writ of injunction or interdict, it shall be lawful for such court or judge to order that a writ or writs of attachment or any other process of such court incident or applicable to writs of injunction or interdict, shall issue against any one or more of the directors of any company, or against any owner, lessee, contractor or other person failing to obey such writ of injunction or interdict; and such court or judge may also, if they or he shall think fit, make an order directing the payment by any one or more of such companies of such sum of money as such court or judge shall determine, not exceeding for each company the sum of two hundred pounds for every day, after a day to be named in the order, that such com- *Parties complaining that reasonable facilities for forwarding traffic, &c., are withheld, may apply by motion or summons to the superior courts.*

(a) See Regulation of Railways Act, 1873 (36 & 37 Vict. c. 48), and Railway and Canal Traffic Act, 1888 (51 & 52 Vict. c. 25), s. 8, *infra*.

pany or companies shall fail to obey such injunction or interdict: and such moneys shall be payable as the court or judge may direct, either to the party complaining, or into court to abide the ultimate decision of the court, or to her Majesty, and payment thereof may, without prejudice to any other mode of recovering the same, be enforced by attachment or order in the nature of a writ of execution, in like manner as if the same had been recovered by decree or judgment in any superior court at Westminster or Dublin in England or Ireland, and in Scotland by such diligence as is competent on an extracted decree of the Court of Session; and in any such proceeding as aforesaid, such court or judge may order and determine that all or any costs thereon incurred shall and may be paid by or to the one party or the other, as such court or judge shall think fit; and it shall be lawful for any such engineer, barrister or other person, if directed so to do by such court or judge, to receive evidence on oath relating to the matter of any such inquiry, and to administer such oath.

Judges may make such regulations as may be necessary for proceedings under this Act.

IV. It shall be lawful for the said Court of Common Pleas at Westminster, or any three of the judges thereof, of whom the Chief Justice shall be one, and it shall be lawful for the said courts in Dublin, or any nine of the judges thereof, of whom the Lord Chancellor, the Master of the Rolls, the Lords Chief Justice of the Queen's Bench and Common Pleas, and the Lord Chief Baron of the Exchequer, shall be five, from time to time to make all such general rules and orders as to the forms of proceedings and process, and all other matters and things touching the practice and otherwise in carrying this Act into execution before such courts and judges, as they may think fit, in England or Ireland, and in Scotland it shall be lawful for the Court of Session to make such Acts of sederunt for the like purpose as they shall think fit.

Court or judge may order a re-hearing.

V. Upon the application of any party aggrieved by the order made upon any such motion or summons as aforesaid, it shall be lawful for the court or judge by whom such order was made to direct, if they think fit so to do, such motion or application on summons to be reheard before such court or judge, and upon such rehearing to rescind or vary such order.

Mode of proceeding under this Act.

VI. No proceeding shall be taken for any violation or contravention of the above enactments, except in the manner herein provided; but nothing herein contained shall take away or diminish any rights, remedies or privileges of any person or company against any railway or canal or railway and canal company under the existing law.

Company to be liable for neglect or default in the carriage of goods, notwithstanding notice to the contrary.

VII. Every such company as aforesaid shall be liable for the loss of, or for any injury done to any horses, cattle or other animals, or to any articles, goods or things, in the receiving, forwarding or delivering thereof, occasioned by the neglect or default of such company or its servants, notwithstanding any notice, condition or declaration made and given by such company contrary thereto, or in anywise limiting such liability: every such notice, condition or declaration being hereby declared to be null and void: provided always, that nothing herein contained shall be construed to prevent the said companies from making such conditions with respect to the receiving, forwarding and delivering of any of the said animals, articles, goods or things as shall be adjudged by the court or judge before whom any question relating

Company not to be liable beyond a limited amount in certain cases, unless the value declared and extra payment made.

thereto shall be tried to be just and reasonable: provided always, that no greater damages shall be recovered for the loss of or for any injury done to any of such animals, beyond the sums hereinafter mentioned; (that is to say,) for any horse fifty pounds; for any neat cattle, per head, fifteen pounds; for any sheep or pigs, per head, two pounds; unless the person sending or delivering the same to such company shall, at the time of such delivery, have declared them to be respectively of higher value than as above mentioned; in which case it shall be lawful for such company to demand and receive, by way of compensation for the increased risk and care thereby occasioned, a reasonable per-centage upon the excess of the value so declared above the respective sums so limited as aforesaid, and which shall be paid in addition to the ordinary rate of charge; and such per-centage or increased rate of charge shall be notified in the manner prescribed in the statute 11 Geo. 4 & 1 Will. 4, c. 68, and shall be binding upon such company in the

Proof of value to be on the person claiming compensation.

manner therein mentioned: provided also, that the proof of the value of such animals, articles, goods, and things, and the amount of the injury done thereto, shall in all cases lie upon the person claiming compensation for such loss or injury: provided also, that no special contract between such company and any other parties respecting the receiving, forwarding or delivering of any animals, articles, goods, or things as aforesaid, shall be binding upon or affect any such party unless the same be signed by him or by the person delivering such animals, articles, goods, or things respectively for carriage: provided also, that nothing herein contained shall alter or affect the rights, privileges or liabilities of any such company under the said Act of the 11 Geo. 4 & 1 Will. 4, c. 68, with respect to articles of the descriptions mentioned in the said Act.

No special contract to be binding unless signed.

Saving of Carriers Act, 11 Geo. 4 & 1 Will. 4, c. 68.

VIII. This Act may be cited for all purposes as "The Railway and Canal Traffic Act, 1854."

Short title.

---

### 17 & 18 VICT. C. 104.

*An Act to amend and consolidate the Acts relating to Merchant Shipping.*　　　　　　　　　　　　　　　[*10th August,* 1854.]

WHEREAS it is expedient to amend and consolidate (*a*) the Acts relating to Merchant Shipping: Be it therefore enacted by the Queen's most excellent Majesty, by and with the advice and consent of the lords spiritual and temporal, and commons, in this present parliament assembled, and by the authority of the same, as follows:

#### *Preliminary.*

*Preliminary.*

. This Act may be cited for all purposes as "The Merchant Shipping Act, 1854."

Short title of Act.

II. In the construction and for the purposes of this Act (if not inconsistent with the context or subject-matter) the following terms shall have the respective meanings hereinafter assigned to them: that is to say,

Interpretation of certain terms in this Act.

"Her Majesty's Dominions" shall mean her Majesty's dominions strictly so called, and all territories under the government of the East India Company, and all other territories (if any) governed by any charter or licence from the crown or parliament of the United Kingdom:

"The United Kingdom" shall mean Great Britain and Ireland:

"British Possession" shall mean any colony, plantation, island, territory, or settlement within her Majesty's dominions, and not within the "United Kingdom" (*b*):

"The Treasury" shall mean the commissioners of her Majesty's treasury:

"The Admiralty" shall mean the lord high admiral or the commissioners for executing his office:

"The Board of Trade" shall mean the lords of the committee of privy council appointed for the consideration of matters relating to trade and foreign plantations:

"The Trinity House" shall mean the master, wardens, and assistants of the guild, fraternity, or brotherhood of the most glorious and undivided Trinity and of St. Clement in the parish of Deptford Strond, in the county of Kent, commonly called the corporation of the Trinity House of Deptford Strond:

"The Port of Dublin Corporation" shall mean the corporation for preserving and improving the port of Dublin:

"Consular Officer" shall include consul-general, consul, and vice-consul, and any person for the time being discharging the duties of consul-general, consul, or vice-consul:

---

(*a*) The previous provisions upon this subject were repealed by statute 17 & 18 Vict. c. 120, from the time this statute came into operation. Only those parts of this long enactment have been inserted which relate to the matters discussed in this Treatise, and they have been inserted entire. This Act has, in some respects, been amended and repealed by 25 & 26 Vict. c. 63; 30 & 31 Vict. c. 124; 34 & 35 Vict. c. 110; 35 & 36 Vict. c. 73; 36 & 37 Vict. c. 85, 39 & 40 Vict. c. 80, and 42 & 43 Vict. c. 72, *post.*

(*b*) See 32 Vict. c. 11, s. 7.

"Receiver" shall mean any person appointed in pursuance of this Act receiver of wreck:

"Pilotage Authority" shall include all bodies and persons authorized to appoint or license pilots, or to fix or alter rates of pilotage, or to exercise any jurisdiction in respect of pilotage:

"Pilot" shall mean any person not belonging to a ship who has the conduct thereof:

"Qualified Pilot" shall mean any person duly licensed by any pilotage authority to conduct ships to which he does not belong:

"Master" shall include every person (except a pilot) having command or charge of any ship:

"Seamen" shall include every person (except masters, pilots and apprentices duly indentured and registered), employed or engaged in any capacity on board any ship:

"Salvor" shall, in the case of salvage services rendered by the officers or crew or part of the crew of any ship belonging to her Majesty, mean the person in command of such ship:

"Person" shall include body corporate:

"Ship" shall include every description of vessel used in navigation not propelled by oars:

"Foreign-going Ship" shall include every ship employed in trading or going between some place or places in the United Kingdom, and some place or places situate beyond the following limits: that is to say, the coasts of the United Kingdom, the islands of Guernsey, Jersey, Sark, Alderney and Man, and the continent of Europe between the river Elbe and Brest inclusive:

"Home-trade Ship" shall include every ship employed in trading or going within the following limits: that is to say, the United Kingdom, the islands of Guernsey, Jersey, Sark, Alderney and Man, and the continent of Europe between the river Elbe and Brest inclusive:

"Home-trade Passenger Ship" shall mean every home-trade ship employed in carrying passengers:

"Lighthouses" shall, in addition to the ordinary meaning of the word, include floating and other lights exhibited for the guidance of ships, and "buoys and beacons" shall include all other marks and signs of the sea:

"Wreck" shall include jetsam, flotsam, lagan and derelict found in or on the shores of the sea or any tidal water (c).

III. This Act shall come into operation on the first day of May, one thousand eight hundred and fifty-five.

IV. This Act shall not, except as hereinafter specially provided, apply to ships belonging to Her Majesty.

V. This Act shall be divided into eleven parts:

The First Part relating to the Board of Trade: its general functions.
The Second Part to British Ships: their ownership, measurement and registry:
The Third Part to Masters and Seamen:
The Fourth Part to Safety and Prevention of Accidents:
The Fifth Part to Pilotage:
The Sixth Part to Lighthouses:
The Seventh Part to the Mercantile Marine Fund:
The Eighth Part to Wrecks, Casualties and Salvage:
The Ninth Part to Liability of Shipowners:
The Tenth Part to Legal Procedure:
The Eleventh Part to Miscellaneous Matters.

(c) See 31 & 32 Vict. c. 45, s. 2.

## PART I.

### THE BOARD OF TRADE: ITS GENERAL FUNCTIONS.

VI. The Board of Trade shall be the department to undertake the general superintendence of matters relating to merchant ships and seamen, and shall be authorised to carry into execution the provisions of this Act, and of all other Acts relating to merchant ships and seamen in force for the time being, other than such Acts as relate to the revenue.

VII. All documents whatever purporting to be issued or written by or under the direction of the Board of Trade, and purporting either to be sealed with the seal of such board, or to be signed by one of the secretaries or assistant secretaries to such board, shall be received in evidence and shall be deemed to be issued or written by or under the direction of the said board, without further proof, unless the contrary be shown; and all documents purporting to be certificates issued by the Board of Trade in pursuance of this Act, and to be sealed with the seal of such board, or to be signed by one of the officers of the marine department of such board, shall be received in evidence and shall be deemed to be such certificates, without further proof, unless the contrary be shown.

VIII. The Board of Trade may from time to time prepare and sanction forms of the various books, instruments, and papers required by this Act other than those required by the second part thereof, and may from time to time make such alterations therein as it deems requisite; and shall before finally issuing or altering any such form, give such public notice thereof as it deems necessary in order to prevent inconvenience; and shall cause every such form to be sealed with such seal as aforesaid, or marked with some other distinguishing mark, and to be supplied at the custom houses and shipping offices of the United Kingdom free of charge, or at such moderate prices as it may from time to time fix, or may license any persons to print and sell the same; and every such book, instrument and paper as aforesaid, shall be made in the form issued by the Board of Trade, and sanctioned by it as the proper form for the time being; and no such book, instrument or paper as aforesaid, unless made in such form, shall be admissible in evidence in any civil proceeding on the part of any owner or master of any ship; and every such book, instrument or paper, if made in a form purporting to be a proper form, and to be sealed or marked as aforesaid, shall be taken to be made in the form hereby required, unless the contrary is proved.

IX. All instruments used in carrying into effect the second part of this Act, if not already exempted from stamp duty, and all instruments which by the third, fourth, sixth, or seventh parts of this Act are required to be made in forms sanctioned by the Board of Trade, if made in such forms, and all instruments used by or under the direction of the Board of Trade in carrying such parts of this Act into effect, shall be exempt from stamp duty.

X. Every person who forges, assists in forging, or procures to be forged, such seal or other distinguishing mark as aforesaid, or who fraudulently alters, assists in fraudulently altering, or procures to be fraudulently altered, any form issued by the Board of Trade, with the view of evading any of the provisions of this Act or any condition contained in such form, shall for each offence be deemed guilty of a misdemeanour; and every person who, in any case in which a form sanctioned by the Board of Trade is by the third part of this Act required to be used, uses without reasonable excuse any form not purporting to be so sanctioned, or who prints, sells or uses any document purporting to be a form so sanctioned, knowing the same not to be so sanctioned for the time being, or not to have been prepared and issued by the Board of Trade, shall for each such offence incur a penalty not exceeding ten pounds.

XI. Subject to the provisions hereinafter contained, all fees and payments (other than fines) coming to the hands of the Board of Trade under the third and fourth parts of this Act, shall be carried to the account of the Mercantile Marine Fund hereinafter mentioned (d), and shall be dealt with as herein prescribed in that behalf; and all fines coming to the hands of the Board of Trade under this Act shall be paid into the receipt of her Majesty's

(d) See s. 417.

I. *Functions of Board of Trade.*

exchequer in such manner as the treasury may direct, and shall be carried to and form part of the Consolidated Fund of the United Kingdom.

Returns to Board of Trade.

XII. All consular officers (*e*), and all officers of customs abroad, and all local marine boards and shipping masters, shall make and send to the Board of Trade such returns or reports on any matter relating to British merchant shipping or seamen as such board requires ; and all shipping masters shall, whenever required by the Board of Trade, produce to such board or to its officers all official log-books and other documents which, in pursuance of this Act, are delivered to them.

Officers of Board of Trade, naval officers, consuls, the registrar-general of seamen, officers of customs and shipping masters, may inspect documents and muster crews.

XIII. Every officer of the Board of Trade, and every commissioned officer of any of her Majesty's ships on full pay, and every British consular officer, and the registrar-general of seamen and his assistant, and every chief officer of customs in any place in her Majesty's dominions, and every shipping master, may, in cases where he has reason to suspect that the provisions of this Act or the laws for the time being relating to merchant seamen and to navigation are not complied with, exercise the following powers ; (that is to say,)

He may require the owner, master, or any of the crew of any British ship to produce any official log-books or other documents relating to such crew or any member thereof in their respective possession or control :

He may require any such master to produce a list of all persons on board his ship, and take copies of all official log-books or documents, or of any part thereof :

He may muster the crew of any such ship :

He may summon the master to appear and give any explanation concerning such ship or her crew or the said official log-book or documents :

And if upon requisition duly made by any person so authorised in that behalf as aforesaid, any person refuses or neglects to produce any such official log-book or document as he is hereinbefore required to produce, or to allow the same to be inspected or copied as aforesaid, or impedes any such master of a crew as aforesaid, or refuses or neglects to give any explanation which he is hereinbefore required to give, or knowingly misleads or deceives any person hereinbefore authorised to demand any such explanation, he shall for each such offence incur a penalty not exceeding twenty pounds.

Board of Trade may appoint inspectors.

XIV. The Board of Trade may, from time to time, whenever it seems expedient to them so to do, appoint any person, as an inspector to report to them upon the following matters : (that is to say,)

(1.) Upon the nature and causes of any accident or damage which any ship ha sustained or caused, or is alleged to have sustained or caused :s

(2.) Whether the p     n of this Act, or any regulations made under or by virtue of this Acts have been complied with :

(3.) Whether the hull and machinery of any steam ship are sufficient and in good condition ;

Powers of inspectors.

XV. Every such inspector as aforesaid shall have the following powers : (that is to say,)

(1.) He may go on board any ship, and may inspect the same or any part thereof, or any of the machinery, boats, equipments, or articles on board thereof to which the provisions of this Act apply, not unnecessarily detaining or delaying her from proceeding on any voyage :

(2.) He may enter and inspect any premises the entry or inspection of which appears to him to be requisite for the purpose of the report which he is directed to make :

(3.) He may, by summons under his hand, require the attendance of all such persons as he thinks fit to call before him and examine for such purpose, and may require answers or returns to any inquiries he thinks fit to make :

(4.) He may require and enforce the production of all books, papers or documents which he considers important for such purpose :

(5.) He may administer oaths, or may, in lieu of requiring or administering an oath, require every person examined by him to make and subscribe a declaration of the truth of the statements made by him in his examination :

(*e*) See s. 2.

Any every witness so summoned as aforesaid shall be allowed such expenses as would be allowed to any witness attending on subpœna to give evidence before any court of record, or if in Scotland to any witness attending on citation the Court of Justiciary ; and in case of any dispute as to the amount of such expenses, the same shall be referred by the inspector to one of the masters of her Majesty's Court of Queen's Bench in England or Ireland, or to the Queen's and lord treasurer's remembrancer in Scotland, who on a request made to him for that purpose under the hand of the said inspector, shall ascertain and certify the proper amount of such expenses ; and every person who refuses to attend as a witness before any such inspector, after having been required so to do in the manner hereby directed, and after having had a tender made to him of the expenses (if any) to which he is entitled as aforesaid, or who refuses or neglects to make any answer, or to give any return, or to produce any document in his possession, or to make or subscribe any declarations which any such inspector is hereby empowered to require, shall for each such offence incur a penalty not exceeding ten pounds.

*I. Functions of Board of Trade.*

*Witnesses to be allowed expenses.*

*Penalty for refusing to give evidence.*

XVI. Every person who wilfully impedes any such inspector appointed by the Board of Trade as aforesaid in the execution of his duty, whether on board any ship or elsewhere, shall incur a penalty not exceeding ten pounds, and may be seized and detained by such inspector or other person or by any person or persons whom he may call to his assistance until such offender can be conveniently taken before some justice of the peace or other officer having proper jurisdiction.

*Penalty for obstructing inspectors in the execution of their duty.*

---

## PART II. (*f*).

### BRITISH SHIPS : THEIR OWNERSHIP, MEASUREMENT, AND REGISTRY.

#### Application.

XVII. The second part of this Act shall apply to the whole of her Majesty's dominions.

*Application.*

*Application of Part 2 of Act.*

#### Description and Ownership of British Vessels.

XVIII. No ship shall be deemed to be a British ship unless she belongs wholly to owners of the following description : (that is to say,)

*II. Description and Ownership of British Ships.*

*Description and ownership of British ships.*

(1.) Natural-born British subjects :

*Who may be owners.*

> Provided, that no natural-born subject who has taken the oath of allegiance to any foreign sovereign or state shall be entitled to be such owner as aforesaid, unless he has subsequently to taking such last-mentioned oath, taken the oath of allegiance to her Majesty, and is and continues to be during the whole period of his so being an owner resident in some place within her Majesty's dominions, or if not so resident, member of a British factory, or partner in a house actually carrying on business in the United Kingdom, or in some other place within her Majesty's dominions :

(2.) Persons made denizens by letters of denization, or naturalized by or pursuant to any Act of the Imperial Legislature, or by or pursuant to any Act or ordinance of the proper legislative authority in any British possession :

> Provided that such persons are and continue to be during the whole period of their so being owners resident in some place within her Majesty's dominions, or if not so resident, members of a British factory, or partners in a house actually carrying on business in the United Kingdom or in some other place within her Majesty's dominions, and have taken the oath of allegiance to her Majesty subsequently to the period of their being so made denizens or naturalized :

(3.) Bodies corporate established under, subject to the laws of, and having their principal place of business in the United Kingdom or some British possession.

(*f*) See 18 & 19 Vict. c. 91, s. 9, *infra*.

II. *Description and Ownership of British Ships.*

British ships with certain exceptions must be registered.

XIX. Every British ship must be registered in manner hereinafter mentioned, except,

(1.) Ships duly registered before this Act comes into operation:

(2.) Ships not exceeding fifteen tons burden employed solely in navigation on the rivers or coasts of the United Kingdom, or on the rivers or coasts of some British possession within which the managing owners of such ships are resident:

(3.) Ships not exceeding thirty tons burden, and not having a whole or fixed deck, and employed solely in fishing or trading coastwise on the shores of Newfoundland, or parts adjacent thereto, or in the Gulf of St. Lawrence, or on such portion of the coasts of Canada, Nova Scotia, or New Brunswick as lie bordering on such Gulf:

And no ship hereby required to be registered shall, unless registered, be recognized as a British ship; and no officer of customs shall grant a clearance or transire to any ship hereby required to be registered for the purpose of enabling her to proceed to sea as a British ship, unless the master of such ship, upon being required so to do, produces to him such certificate of registry as is hereinafter mentioned; and if such ship attempts to proceed to sea as a British ship without a clearance or transire, such officer may detain such ship until such certificate is produced to him.

## Measurement of Tonnage (f).

*Measurement of Tonnage.*

Tonnage deck; feet; decimals.

XX. Throughout the following rules the tonnage deck shall be taken to be the upper deck in ships which have less than three decks, and to be the second deck from below in all other ships; and in carrying such rules into effect all measurements shall be taken in feet and fractions of feet, and all fractions of feet shall be expressed in decimals.

RULE I.

For ships to be registered and other ships of which the hold is clear.

Lengths.

XXI. The tonnage of every ship to be registered, with the exceptions mentioned in the next section, shall, previously to her being registered, be ascertained by the following rule, hereinafter called Rule I. (g); and the tonnage of every ship to which such rule can be applied, whether she is about to be registered or not, shall be ascertained by the same rule:—

(1.) Measure the length of the ship in a straight line along the upper side of the tonnage deck from the inside of the inner plank (average thickness) at the inside of the stem to the inside of the midship stern timber or plank there, as the case may be (average thickness), deducting from this length what is due to the rake of the bow in the thickness of the deck, and what is due to the rake of the stern timber in the thickness of the deck, and also what is due to the rake of the stern timber in one-third of the round of the beam; divide the length so taken into the number of equal parts required by the following table, according to the class in such table to which the ship belongs:

### TABLE.

Class 1. Ships of which the tonnage deck is according to the above measurement 50 feet long or under, into four equal parts:

,, 2. Ships of which the tonnage deck is according to the above measurement above 50 feet long and not exceeding 120, into six equal parts:

,, 3. Ships of which the tonnage deck is according to the above measurement above 120 feet long and not exceeding 180, into eight equal parts:

,, 4. Ships of which the tonnage deck is according to the above measurement above 180 feet long and not exceeding 225, into ten equal parts:

,, 5. Ships of which the tonnage deck is according to the above measurement above 225 feet long, into twelve equal parts.

Transverse areas.

(2.) Then, the hold being first sufficiently cleared to admit of the required depths and breadths being properly taken, find the transverse area of such ship at each point of division of the length as follows:—

(f) See the Merchant Shipping (Tonnage) Act, 1889 (52 & 53 Vict. c. 43).
(g) See 18 & 19 Vict. c. 91, s. 14.

Measure the depth at each point of division, from a point at a  II. *Measurement*
distance of one-third of the round of the beam below such deck,  *of Tonnage.*
or, in case of a break, below a line stretched in continuation
thereof, to the upper side of the floor timber at the inside of the
limber strake, after deducting the average thickness of the ceiling
which is between the bilge planks and limber strake : then, if the
depth at the midship division of the length do not exceed sixteen
feet, divide each depth into four equal parts ; then measure the
inside horizontal breadth at each of the three points of division,
and also at the upper and lower points of the depth, extending each
measurement to the average thickness of that part of the ceiling
which is between the points of measurement ; number those breadths
from above (i. *e.* numbering the upper breadth one, and so on down
to the lowest breadth) ; multiply the second and fourth by four,
and the third by two ; add these products together, and to the sum
add the first breadth and the fifth : multiply the quantity thus
obtained by one-third of the common interval between the breadths,
and the product shall be deemed the transverse area ; but if the
midship depth exceed sixteen feet, divide each depth into six equal
parts instead of four, and measure as before directed the horizontal
breadths at the five points of division, and also at the upper and
lower points of the depth ; number them from above as before ;
multiply the second, fourth, and sixth by four, and the third and
fifth by two ; add these products together, and to the sum add the
first breadth and the seventh ; multiply the quantity thus obtained
by one-third of the common interval between the breadths, and the
product shall be deemed the transverse area.

(3.) Having thus ascertained the transverse area at each point of division  Computation
to ascertain the register tonnage of the ship in the following  from areas.
of the length of the ship as required by the above table, proceed
manner :—Number the areas successively, 1, 2, 3, &c., No. 1 being
at the extreme limit of the length at the bow, and the last number
at the extreme limit of the length at the stern : then, whether the
length be divided according to the table into four or twelve parts as
in classes 1 and 5, or any intermediate number as in classes 2, 3,
and 4, multiply the second and every even numbered area by four,
and the third and every odd numbered area (except the first and
last) by two ; add these products together, and to the sum add the
first and last if they yield anything ; multiply the quantity thus
obtained by one-third of the common interval between the areas,
and the product will be the cubical contents of the space under the
tonnage deck ; divide this product by one hundred, and the quotient
being the tonnage under the tonnage deck shall be deemed to be
the register tonnage of the ship, subject to the additions and deductions hereinafter mentioned.

(4.) If there be a break, a poop, or any other permanent closed-in space  Poop and any
on the upper deck, available for cargo or stores, or for the berthing  other closed-in
or accommodation of passengers or crew, the tonnage of such space  space.
shall be ascertained as follows :—Measure the internal mean length
of such space in feet, and divide it into two equal parts ; measure
at the middle of its height three inside breadths, namely, one at
each end and the other at the middle of the length ; then to the
sum of the end breadths add four times the middle breadth, and
multiply the whole sum by one-third of the common interval
between the breadths : the product will give the mean horizontal
area of such space ; then measure the mean height, and multiply it
by the mean horizontal area ; divide the product by one hundred,
and the quotient shall be deemed to be the tonnage of such space,
and shall be added to the tonnage under the tonnage deck, ascertained as aforesaid, subject to the following provisions :—[First,
that nothing shall be added for a closed-in space solely appropriated
to the berthing of the crew, unless such space exceeds one-twentieth
of the remaining tonnage of the ship, and in case of such excess
the excess only shall be added ; and, secondly (*h*)], that nothing shall

(*h*) Repealed : 52 & 53 Vict. c. 43, s. 1 (2).

be added in respect of any building erected for the shelter of deck passengers, and approved by the Board of Trade.

(5.) If the ship has a third deck, commonly called a spar deck, the tonnage of the space between it and the tonnage deck shall be ascertained as follows :—Measure in feet the inside length of the space at the middle of its height from the plank at the side of the stem to the lining on the timbers at the stern, and divide the length into the same number of equal parts into which the length of the tonnage deck is divided as above directed ; measure (also at the middle of its height) the inside breadth of the space at each of the points of division, also the breadth of the stem and the breadth of the stern ; number them successively 1, 2, 3, &c., commencing at the stem ; multiply the second and all the other even numbered breadths by four ; and the third and all the other odd numbered (except the first and last) by two ; to the sum of these products add the first and last breadths ; multiply the whole sum by one-third of the common interval between the breadths, and the result will give in superficial feet the mean horizontal area of such space ; measure the mean height of such space, and multiply by it the mean horizontal area, and the product will be the cubical contents of the space ; divide this product by one hundred, and the quotient shall be deemed to be the tonnage of such space, and shall be added to the other tonnage of the ship ascertained as aforesaid ; and if the ship has more than three decks, the tonnage of each space between decks above the tonnage deck shall be severally ascertained in manner above described, and shall be added to the tonnage of the ship ascertained as aforesaid.

XXII. Ships which, requiring to be measured for any purpose other than registry, have cargo on board, and ships which, requiring to be measured for the purpose of registry, cannot be measured by the rule above given, shall be measured by the following rule, hereinafter called Rule II. :—

(1.) Measure the length on the upper deck from the outside of the outer plank at the stem to the aftside of the stern post, deducting therefrom the distance between the aftside of the stern post and the rabbet of the stern post at the point where the counter plank crosses it ; measure also the greatest breadth of the ship to the outside of the outer planking or wales, and then, having first marked on the outside of the ship on both sides thereof the height of the upper deck at the ship's sides, girt the ship at the greatest breadth in a direction perpendicular to the keel from the height so marked on the outside of the ship on the one side to the height so marked on the other side by passing a chain under the keel ; to half the girth thus taken add half the main breadth ; square the sum ; multiply the result by the length of the ship taken as aforesaid ; then multiply this product by the factor ·0018 (eighteen ten-thousandths) in the case of ships built of wood, and by ·0021 (twenty-one ten-thousandths) in the case of ships built of iron, and the products shall be deemed the register tonnage of the ship* subject to the additions and deductions hereinafter mentioned.

(2.) If there be a break, a poop, or other closed-in space on the upper deck, the tonnage of such space shall be ascertained by multiplying together the mean length, breadth, and depth of such space and dividing the product by one hundred, and the quotient so obtained shall be deemed to be the tonnage of such space, and shall, [subject to the deduction for a closed-in space appropriated to the crew as mentioned in Rule I. (*i*)], be added to the tonnage of the ship ascertained as aforesaid.

XXIII. In every ship propelled by steam or other power requiring engine-room, an allowance shall be made for the space occupied by the propelling power, and the amount so allowed shall be deducted from the gross tonnage of the ship ascertained as aforesaid, and the remainder shall be deemed to be the register tonnage of such ship ; and such deduction shall be estimated as follows ; (that is to say,)

(*a.*) As regards ships propelled by paddle wheels in which the tonnage of the space solely occupied by and necessary for the proper working of the boilers and machinery is above twenty per cent. and under thirty per

(i) Repealed : 52 & 53 Vict. c. 43, s. 1 (2).

cent. of the gross tonnage of the ship, such deduction shall be thirty-seven one-hundredths of such gross tonnage; and in ships propelled by screws in which the tonnage of such space is above thirteen per cent. and under twenty per cent. of such gross tonnage, such deduction shall be thirty-two one hundredths of such gross tonnage. *II. Measurement of Tonnage.*

(*b.*) As regards all other ships, the deduction shall, if the commissioners of customs(*k*) and the owner both agree thereto, be estimated in the same manner; but either they or he may in their or his discretion require the space to be measured and the deduction estimated accordingly; and whenever such measurement is so required, the deduction shall consist of the tonnage of the space actually occupied by or required to be inclosed for the proper working of the boilers and machinery, with the addition in the case of ships propelled by paddle-wheels of one-half, and in the case of ships propelled by screws of three-fourths of the tonnage of such space; and the measurement and use of such space shall be governed by the following rules; (that is to say,) May be measured where the space is unusually large or small.

(1.) Measure the mean depth of the space from its crown to the ceiling at the limber strake, measure also three, or if necessary, more than three breadths of the space at the middle of its depth, taking one of such measurements at each end, and another at the middle of the length; take the mean of such breadths; measure also the mean length of the space between the foremost and aftermost bulkheads or limits of its length, excluding such parts, if any, as are not actually occupied by or required for the proper working of the machinery; multiply together these three dimensions of length, breadth, and depth, and the product will be the cubical contents of the space below the crown; then find the cubical contents of the space or spaces, if any, above the crown aforesaid, which are framed in for the machinery or for the admission of light and air, by multiplying together the length, depth and breadth thereof; add such contents to the cubical contents of the space below the crown; divide the sum by 100; and the result shall be deemed to be the tonnage of the said space: Mode of measurement.

(2.) If in any ship in which the space aforesaid is to be measured the engines and boilers are fitted in separate compartments, the contents of each shall be measured severally in like manner, according to the above rules, and the sum of their several results shall be deemed to be the tonnage of the said space: In case of separate compartments.

(3.) In the case of screw steamers in which the space aforesaid is to be measured, the contents of the shaft trunk shall be added to and deemed to form part of such space, and shall be ascertained by multiplying together the mean length, breadth, and depth of the trunk, and dividing the product by 100: Shaft trunk of screw steamer.

(4.) If in any ship in which the space aforesaid is to be measured any alteration be made in the length or capacity of such space, or if any cabins be fitted in such space, such ship shall be deemed to be a ship not registered until remeasurement: Alteration of engine room.

(5.) If in any ship in which the space aforesaid is to be measured any goods or stores are stowed or carried in such space, the master and owner each shall be liable to a penalty not exceeding one hundred pounds. Penalty for carrying goods in such space.

XXIV. In ascertaining the tonnage of open ships the upper edge of the upper strake is to form the boundary line of measurement, and the depths shall be taken from an athwartship line, extending from upper edge to upper edge of the said strake at each division of the length. RULE IV. Open ships, how measured.

XXV. Repealed by 34 & 35 Vict. c. 110, s. 12, and see 36 & 37 Vict. c. 85, s. 3.

XXVI. Whenever the tonnage of any ship has been ascertained and registered in accordance with the provisions of this Act, the same shall thenceforth be deemed to be the tonnage of such ship, and be repeated in every subsequent registry thereof, unless any alteration is made in the form or capacity of such ship, or unless it is discovered that the tonnage of such ship has been erroneously computed; and in either of such cases such ship shall Tonnage when once ascertained to be ever after deemed the tonnage.

(*k*) Now the Board of Trade, 35 & 36 Vict. c. 73, s. 3.

II. *Measurement of Tonnage.*

Remeasurement of ships already registered may be made, but not to be compulsory.

Power to remeasure engine-rooms improperly extended.

Officers may be appointed and regulations made for measurement of ships.

be measured, and her tonnage determined and registered according to the rules hereinbefore contained in that behalf.

XXVII. The rules for the measurement of tonnage herein contained shall not make it necessary to alter the present registered tonnage of any British ship registered before this Act comes into operation; but if the owner of any such ship desires to have the same remeasured according to these rules, he may apply to the commissioners of customs (*j*) for the purpose, and such commissioners shall thereupon, and on payment of such reasonable charge for the expenses of remeasurement, not exceeding the sum of seven shillings and sixpence for each transverse section, as they may authorise, direct such remeasurement to be made, and such ship shall thereupon be remeasured according to such rules as aforesaid, or according to such of them as may be applicable; and the number denoting the register tonnage shall be altered accordingly.

XXVIII. If it appears to the commissioners of customs (*j*) that in any steam ship measured before this Act comes into operation, store rooms or coal bunkers have been introduced into or thrown across the engine-room, so that the deduction from the tonnage on account of the engine-room is larger than it ought to be, the said commissioners may, if they think fit, direct such engine-room to be remeasured according to the rules in force before this Act comes into operation, excluding the space occupied by such store rooms or coal bunkers, or may, if the owners so desire, cause the ship to be remeasured according to the rules hereinbefore contained, and subject to the conditions contained in the last preceding section; and, after remeasurement, the said commissioners shall cause the ship to be registered anew, or the registry thereof to be altered, as the case may require.

XXIX. The commissioners of customs (*j*) may, with the sanction of the treasury, appoint such persons to superintend the survey and admeasurement of ships as they think fit; and may, with the approval of the Board of Trade, make such regulations for that purpose as may be necessary; and also, with the like approval, make such modifications and alterations as from time to time become necessary in the tonnage rules hereby prescribed, in order to the more accurate and uniform application thereof, and the effectual carrying out of the principle of admeasurement therein adopted.

*Registry of British Ships.*

Registrars of British ships.

## Registry of British Ships.

XXX. The following persons are required to register British ships, and shall be deemed registrars for the purposes of this Act (*k*); (that is to say,)

(1.) At any port or other place in the United Kingdom or Isle of Man approved by the commissioners of customs for the registry of ships, the collector, comptroller, or other principal officer of customs for the time being:

(2.) In the islands of Guernsey and Jersey, the principal officers of her Majesty's customs, together with the governor, lieutenant-governor, or other person administering the government of such islands respectively:

(3.) In Malta, Gibraltar, and Heligoland, the governor, lieutenant-governor, or other person administering the government of such places respectively:

(4.) At any port or place so approved as aforesaid within the limits of the charter but not under the government of the East India Company, and at which no custom house is established, the collector of duties, together with the governor, lieutenant-governor, or other person administering the government:

(5.) At the ports of Calcutta, Madras, and Bombay, the master attendants, and at any other port or place so approved, as aforesaid, within the limits of the charter and under the government of the East India Company, the collector of duties, or any other person of six years' standing in the civil service of the said company who is appointed by any of the governments of the said company to act for this purpose:

(*j*) By 35 & 36 Vict. c. 73, s. 3, the Board of Trade.
(*k*) See 32 Vict. c. 11, s. 6.

(6.) At every other port or place so approved as aforesaid within her Majesty's dominions abroad, the collector, the collector, comptroller, or other principal officer of customs or of navigation laws, or if there is no such officer resident at such port or place, the governor, lieutenant-governor, or other person administering the government of the possession in which such port or place is situate.

XXXI. The governor, lieutenant-governor, or other person administering the government in any British possession where any ship is registered under the authority of this Act shall, with regard to the performance of any act or thing relating to the registry of a ship or of any interest therein, be considered in all respects as occupying the place of the commissioners of customs; and any British consular officer shall, in any place where there is no justice of the peace, be authorized to take any declaration hereby required or permitted to be made in the presence of a justice of the peace (*l*).

XXXII. Every registrar shall keep a book, to be called "the Register Book," and enter therein the particulars hereinafter required to be registered.

XXXIII. The port or place at which any British ship is registered for the time being shall be considered her port of registry, or the port to which she belongs.

XXXIV. Repealed by 34 & 35 Vict. c. 110, s. 12; and see 36 & 37 Vict. c. 85, s. 3.

XXXV. Every application for the registry of a ship shall, in the case of individuals, be made by the person requiring to be registered as owner, or by some one or more of such persons if more than one, or by his or their duly authorized agent, and in the case of bodies corporate by their duly authorized agent; the authority of such agent, if appointed by individuals, to be testified by some writing under the hands of the appointors, and if appointed by a body corporate, by some instrument under the common seal of such body corporate.

XXXVI. Before registry the ship shall be surveyed by a person duly appointed under this Act; and such surveyor shall grant a certificate in the form marked (A) in the schedule hereto, specifying her tonnage, build, and such other particulars descriptive of the identity of the ship, as may from time to time be required by the Board of Trade; and such certificate shall be delivered to the registrar before registry.

XXXVII. The following rules shall be observed with respect to entries in the register book; (that is to say,)

(1.) The property in a ship shall be divided into sixty-four shares:

(2.) Subject to the provisions with respect to joint owners or owner by transmission hereinafter contained, not more than thirty-two (*m*) individuals shall be entitled to be registered at the same time as owners of any one ship; but this rule shall not affect the beneficial title of any number of persons or of any company represented by or claiming under or through any registered owner or joint owner:

(3.) No person shall be entitled to be registered as owner of any fractional part of a share in a ship; but any number of persons, not exceeding five, may be registered as joint owners of a ship or of a share or shares therein:

(4.) Joint owners shall be considered as constituting one person only as regards the foregoing rule relating to the number of persons entitled to be registered as owners, and shall not be entitled to dispose in severalty of any interest in any ship or in any share or shares therein in respect of which they are registered:

(5.) A body corporate may be registered as owner by its corporate name.

XXXVIII. No person shall be entitled to be registered as owner of a ship or any share therein until he has made and subscribed a declaration in the form marked (B) in the schedule hereto, referring to the ship as described in the certificate of the surveyor, and containing the following particulars; (that is to say,)

(1.) A statement of his qualification to be an owner of a share in a British ship:

*Side notes:*

II. *Registry of British Ships.*

Substitution of governor abroad for commissioners of customs, and of consul for justice.

Registrar to keep register books.

Port of registry of British ship.

Application for registry, by whom to be made.

Survey of ship.

Rules as to entries in register book.

Declaration of ownership by individual owner.

(*l*) See 50 & 51 Vict. c. 62, s. 3, *infra*.
(*m*) Sixty-four by 43 & 44 Vict. c. 18, s. 2.

(2.) A statement of the time when and the place where such ship was built, or (if the ship is foreign built, and the time and place of building not known) a statement that she is foreign built, and that he does not know the time or place of her building ; and, in addition thereto, in the case of a foreign ship, a statement of her foreign name, or (in the case of a ship condemned) a statement of the time, place and court at and by which she was condemned :

(3.) A statement of the name of the master :

(4.) A statement of the number of shares in such ship of which he is entitled to be registered as owner :

(5.) A denial that, to the best of his knowledge and belief, any unqualified person or body of persons is entitled as owner to any legal or beneficial (*n*) interest in such ship or any share therein :

The above declaration of ownership shall be made and subscribed in the presence of the registrar if the declarant reside within five miles of the custom house of the port of registry, but if beyond that distance, in the presence of any registrar or of any justice of the peace.

**Declaration of ownership by body corporate.**

XXXIX. No body corporate shall be entitled to be registered as owner of a ship or of any share therein until the secretary or other duly appointed public officer of such body corporate has made and subscribed in the presence of the registrar of the port of registry a declaration in the form marked (C) in the Schedule hereto, referring to the ship as described in the certificate of the surveyor, and containing the following particulars; (that is to say,)

(1.) A statement of such circumstances of the constitution and business of such body corporate as prove it to be qualified to own a British ship :

(2.) A statement of the time when and the place where such ship was built, or (if the ship is foreign built, and the time and place of building unknown) a statement that she is foreign built, and that he does not know the time or place of her building; and, in addition thereto, in the case of a foreign ship, a statement of her foreign name, or (in the case of a ship condemned) a statement of the time, place and court at and by which she was condemned :

(3.) A statement of the name of the master :

(4.) A statement of the number of shares in such ship of which such body corporate is owner:

(5.) A denial that, to the best of his knowledge and belief, any unqualified person or body of persons is entitled as owner to any legal or beneficial (*n*) interest in such ship, or any share therein.

**Evidence to be produced on registry.**

XL. Upon the first registry of a ship there shall, in addition to the declaration of ownership, be produced the following evidence; (that is to say,)

(1.) In the case of a British-built ship, a certificate (which the builder is hereby required to grant under his hand) containing a true account of the proper denomination and of the tonnage of such ship as estimated by him, and of the time when and of the place where such ship was built, together with the name of the party (if any) on whose account he has built the same, and, if any sale or sales have taken place, the bill or bills of sale under which the ship or share therein has become vested in the party requiring to be registered as owner:

(2.) In the case of a foreign-built ship, the same evidence as in the case of a British-built ship, unless the person requiring to be registered as owner, or, in the case of a body corporate, the duly appointed officer, declares that the time or place of her building is unknown, or that the builder's certificate cannot be procured, in which case there shall be required only the bill or bills of sale under which the ship or share therein became vested in the party requiring to be registered as owner thereof:

(3.) In the case of a ship condemned by any competent court, an official copy of the condemnation of such ship.

**Penalty on builder for false certificate.**

XLI. If any builder wilfully makes a false statement in any certificate hereby required to be granted by him, he shall for every such offence incur a penalty not exceeding one hundred pounds.

(*n*) See 25 & 26 Vict. c. 63, s. 3, *infra*.

**XLII.** As soon as the foregoing requisites to the due registry of a ship have been complied with, the registrar shall enter in the register book the following particulars relating to such ship ; (that is to say,)

(1.) The name of the ship and of the port to which she belongs :

(2.) The details as to her tonnage, build and description comprised in the certificate hereinbefore directed to be given by the surveyor :

(3.) The several particulars as to her origin stated in the declaration or declarations of ownership :

(4.) The names and descriptions of her registered owner or owners, and if there is more than one such owner, the proportions in which they are interested in such ship.

*II. Registry of British Ships.*

Particulars of entry in register book.

**XLIII.** No notice of any trust, express, implied or constructive, shall be entered in the register book, or receivable by the registrar ; and, subject to any rights and powers appearing by the register book to be vested in any other party, the registered owner of any ship or share therein shall have power absolutely to dispose, in manner hereinafter mentioned, of such ship or share, and to give effectual receipts for any money paid or advanced by way of consideration (*o*).

No notice taken of trusts.

### *Certificate of Registry.*

Certificate of Registry.

**XLIV.** Upon the completion of the registry of any ship the registrar shall grant a certificate of registry in the form marked (D) in the Schedule hereto, comprising the following particulars ; (that is to say,)

(1.) The name of the ship and of the port to which she belongs :

(2.) The details as to her tonnage, build, and description comprised in the certificate hereinbefore directed to be given by the surveyor :

(3.) The name of her master :

(4.) The several particulars as to her origin stated in the declaration or declarations of ownership :

(5.) The names and descriptions of her registered owner or owners, and if there is more than one such owner, the proportions in which they are respectively interested, indorsed upon such certificate.

Certificate of registry to be granted.

**XLV.** Whenever any change takes place in the registered ownership of any ship, then, if such change occurs at a time when the ship is at her port of registry, the master shall forthwith deliver the certificate of registry to the registrar, and he shall indorse thereon a memorandum of such change ; but if such change occurs during the absence of the ship from her port of registry, then upon her first return to such port the master shall deliver the certificate of registry to the registrar, and he shall indorse thereon a like memorandum of the change ; or if she previously arrives at any port where there is a British registrar, such registrar shall, upon being advised by the registrar of her port of registry of the change having taken place, indorse a like memorandum thereof on the certificate of registry, and may for that purpose require the certificate to be delivered to him, so that the ship be not thereby detained ; and any master who fails to deliver to the registrar the certificate of registry as hereinbefore required shall incur a penalty not exceeding one hundred pounds.

Change of owners to be indorsed on certificate of registry.

**XLVI.** Whenever the master of any British registered ship is changed, the following persons, that is to say, if such change is made in consequence of the sentence of any naval court, the presiding officer of such court, but if the change takes place from any other cause, the registrar, or if there is no registrar the British consular officer resident at the port where such change takes place, shall indorse on the certificate of registry a memorandum of such change, and subscribe his name to such indorsement, and forthwith report the change of master to the commissioners of customs (*p*) in London ; and the officers of customs at any port situate within her Majesty's dominions may refuse to admit any person to do any act at such port as master of any British ship unless his name is inserted in or indorsed upon the certificate of registry of such ship as the last appointed master thereof.

Change of master to be indorsed on certificate of registry.

**XLVII.** The registrar may, with the sanction of the commissioners of customs, upon the delivery up to him of the former certificate of registry, grant a new certificate in the place of the one so delivered up.

Power to grant new certificate.

(*o*) See 25 & 26 Vict. c. 63, s. 3, *infra.*

(*p*) Now a registrar-general of seamen : 35 & 36 Vict. c. 73, *infra.*

II. *Certificate of Registry.*

Provision in case of loss of certificate.

XLVIII. In the event of the certificate of registry of any ship being mislaid, lost or destroyed, if such event occurs at any port in the United Kingdom, the ship being registered in the United Kingdom, or at any port in any British possession, the ship being registered in the same British possession, then the registrar of her port of registry shall grant a new certificate of registry in lieu of and as a substitute for her original certificate of registry; but if such event occurs elsewhere, the master or some other person having knowledge of the circumstances shall make a declaration before the registrar of any port having a British registrar at which such ship is at the time or first arrives after such mislaying, loss or destruction; and such declaration shall state the facts of the case, and the names and descriptions of the registered owners of such ship, to the best of the declarant's knowledge and belief; and the registrar shall thereupon grant a provisional certificate as near to the form appointed by this Act as circumstances permit, and shall insert therein a statement of the circumstances under which such provisional certificate is granted.

Provisional certificate to be delivered up.

XLIX. Every such provisional certificate shall, within ten days after the first subsequent arrival of the ship at her port of discharge in the United Kingdom, if registered in the United Kingdom, or, if registered elsewhere, at her port of discharge in the British possession within which her port of registry is situate, be delivered up to the registrar thereof, who shall thereupon grant a new one, as near to the form appointed by this Act as circumstances permit; and if the master neglects to deliver up such certificate within such time he shall incur a penalty not exceeding fifty pounds.

Custody of certificate.

Delivery of certificate may be required.

Penalty for detention.

L. The certificate of registry shall be used only for the lawful navigation of the ship, and shall not be subject to detention by reason of any title, lien, charge or interest whatsoever, which any owner, mortgagee or other person may have or claim to have on or in the ship described in such certificate; and if any person whatever, whether interested or not in the ship, refuses on request to deliver up such certificate when in his possession or under his control to the person for the time being entitled to the custody thereof for the purposes of such lawful navigation as aforesaid, or to any registrar, officer of the customs or other person legally entitled to require such delivery, it shall be lawful for any justice, by warrant under his hand and seal, or for any court capable of taking cognisance of such matter, to cause the person so refusing to appear before him and to be examined touching such refusal; and unless it is proved to the satisfaction of such justice or court that there was reasonable cause for such refusal, the offender shall incur a penalty not exceeding one hundred pounds; but if it is made to appear to such justice or court that the certificate is lost, the party complained of shall be discharged, and such justice or court shall thereupon certify that the certificate of registry is lost.

Mode of proceeding, if detaining party abscond.

LI. If the person charged with such detainer or refusal is proved to have absconded, so that the warrant of the justice or process of the court cannot be served upon him, or if he persists in his refusal to deliver the certificate, such justice or court shall certify the fact, and the same proceedings may then be taken as in the case of a certificate of registry mislaid, lost or destroyed, or as near thereto as circumstances permit.

Penalty for using improper certificate.

LII. If the master or owner of any ship uses or attempts to use for the navigation of such ship a certificate of registry not legally granted in respect of such ship, he shall be guilty of misdemeanor, and it shall be lawful for any commissioned officer on full pay in the military or naval service of her Majesty, or any British officer of customs, or any British consular officer, to seize and detain such ship, and to bring her for adjudication before the High Court of Admiralty in England or Ireland or any Court having Admiralty jurisdiction in her Majesty's dominions; and if such court is of opinion that such use or attempt at use has taken place, it shall pronounce such ship, with her tackle, apparel and furniture to be forfeited to her Majesty, and may award such portion of the proceeds arising from the sale of such ship as it may think just to the officer so bringing in the same for adjudication.

Certificate of ship lost or ceasing to be British to be delivered up.

LIII. If any registered ship is either actually or constructively lost, taken by the enemy, burnt or broken up, or if by reason of a transfer to any persons not qualified to be owners of British ships, or of any other matter or thing, any such ship as aforesaid ceases to be a British ship, every person who at the time of the occurrence of any of the aforesaid events owns such ship or any share therein shall, immediately upon obtaining knowledge of any such occurrence, if no notice thereof has already been given to the registrar at the port of registry of such ship, give such notice to him, and he shall make an entry thereof in his register book; and, except in cases where the certificate of registry is lost or destroyed, the master of every ship so circumstanced as aforesaid shall immediately, if such event occurs in port, but if the same occurs elsewhere, then within ten days after his arrival in port, deliver the certificate of registry of such ship to the registrar, or if there be no registrar, to the British consular officer at such port, and such registrar, if he is not himself the registrar of her port of registry, or such British consular officer, shall forthwith forward the certificate so delivered to him to the registrar of the port of registry of the ship; and every owner and master who, without reasonable cause, makes default in obeying the provisions of this section, shall for each offence incur a penalty not exceeding one hundred pounds.

LIV. If any ship becomes the property of persons qualified to be owners of British ships at any foreign port, the British consular officer resident at such port may grant the master of such ship, upon his application, a provisional certificate stating—

The name of the ship;

The time and place of her purchase, and the names of her purchasers;

The name of her master;

The best particulars as to her tonnage, build, and description that he is able to obtain;

And he shall forward a copy of such certificate, at the first convenient opportunity, to the commissioners of customs (*q*) in London: the certificate so granted shall possess the same force as a certificate of registry until the expiration of six months, or until such earlier time as the ship arrives at some port where there is a British registrar; but upon the expiration of such period, or upon arrival at such port, shall be void to all intents.

### Transfers and Transmissions.

LV. A registered ship or any share therein, when disposed of to persons qualified to be owners of British ships, shall be transferred by bill of sale; and such bill of sale shall contain such description of the ship as is contained in the certificate of the surveyor, or such other description as may be sufficient to identify the ship to the satisfaction of the registrar, and shall be according to the form marked (E) in the Schedule hereto, or as near thereto as circumstances permit, and shall be executed by the transferor in the presence of and be attested by one or more witnesses.

LVI. No individual shall be entitled to be registered as transferee of a ship or any share therein until he has made a declaration in the form marked (F) in the Schedule hereto, stating his qualification to be registered as owner of a share in a British ship, and containing a denial similar to the denial hereinbefore required to be contained in a declaration of ownership by an original owner; and no body corporate shall be entitled to be registered as transferee of a ship or any share therein until the secretary or other duly appointed public officer of such body corporate has made a declaration in the form marked (G) in the Schedule hereto, stating the name of such body corporate, and such circumstances of its constitution and business as may prove it to be qualified to own a British ship, and containing a denial similar to the denial hereinbefore required to be contained in a declaration of ownership made on behalf of a body corporate; in the case of an individual, the above declaration shall be made, if he resides within five miles of the custom house of the port of registry in the presence of the registrar, but if beyond that distance in the presence of any registrar or of any justice of the peace; in the case of a body corporate the declaration shall be made in the presence of the registrar of the port of registry.

LVII. Every bill of sale for the transfer of any registered ship, or of any share therein, when duly executed, shall be produced to the registrar of the port at which the ship is registered, together with the declaration hereinbefore required to be made by a transferee; and the registrar shall thereupon enter in the register book the name of the transferee, as owner of the ship or share comprised in such bill of sale, and shall indorse on the bill of sale the

*Marginal notes:*

II. *Certificate of Registry.*

Provisional certificate for ship becoming vested in British owners at foreign port.

*Transfers and Transmissions.*

Transfer of ships or shares therein.

Declaration to be made by transferee.

Registration of transfer.

(*q*) Now the Registrar-General of Seamen: 35 & 36 Vict. c. 73, s. 4, *infra.*

II. *Transfers and Transmissions.*

fact of such entry having been made, with the date and hour thereof ; and all bills of sale of any ship or shares in a ship shall be entered in the registry book in the order of their production to the registrar.

Transmission of shares by death, bankruptcy, or marriage.

LVIII. If the property in any ship, or in any share therein, becomes transmitted in consequence of the death or bankruptcy or insolvency of any registered owner, or in consequence of the marriage of any female registered owner, or by any lawful means other than by a transfer according to the provisions of this Act, such transmission shall be authenticated by a declaration of the person to whom such property has been transmitted, made in the form marked (H) in the Schedule hereto, and containing the several statements hereinbefore required to be contained in the declaration of a transferee, or as near thereto as circumstances permit, and in addition, a statement describing the manner in which and the party to whom such property has been transmitted ; and such declaration shall be made and subscribed, if the declarant resides at or within five miles of the custom house of the port of registry, in the presence of the registrar, but if beyond that distance in the presence of any registrar or of any justice of the peace.

Proof of transmission by bankruptcy, marriage, will, or an intestacy.

LIX. If such transmission has taken place by virtue of the bankruptcy or insolvency of any registered owner, the said declaration shall be accompanied by such evidence as may for the time being be receivable in courts of justice as proof of the title of parties claiming under any bankruptcy or insolvency ; and if such transmission has taken place by virtue of the marriage of a female owner, the said declaration shall be accompanied by a copy of the register of such marriage or other legal evidence of the celebration thereof, and shall declare the identity of the said female owner ; and if such transmission has taken place by virtue of any testamentary instrument or by intestacy, then in England, Wales, and Ireland the said declaration shall be accompanied by the probate of the will, or the letters of administration or an official extract therefrom, and in Scotland, or in any British possession, by the will or any copy thereof that may be evidence by the laws of Scotland or of such possession, or by letters of administration or any copy thereof, or by such other document as may by the laws of Scotland or of such possession be receivable in the courts of judicature thereof as proof of the person entitled upon an intestacy.

Registration of transmitted share.

LX. The registrar, upon the receipt of such declaration so accompanied as aforesaid, shall enter the name of the person or persons entitled under such transmission in the register book as owner or owners of the ship or share therein in respect of which such transmission has taken place ; and such persons, if more than one, shall, however numerous, be considered as one person only as regards the rule hereinbefore contained relating to the number of persons entitled to be registered as owners.

Registrar to retain certain evidence.

LXI. Of the documents hereby required to be produced to the registrar, he shall retain in his possession the following ; that is to say, the surveyor's certificate, the builder's certificate, the copy of the condemnation, and all declarations of ownership.

Unqualified owner entitled by transmission may apply to court for sale of ship.

LXII. Whenever any property in a ship or share in a ship becomes vested by transmission on the death of any owner or on the marriage of any female owner in any person not qualified to be the owner of British ships, it shall be lawful, if such ship is registered in England or Ireland for the Court of Chancery, if in Scotland for the Court of Session, or if in any British possession for any court possessing the principal civil jurisdiction within such possession, upon an application made by or on behalf of such unqualified person, to order a sale to be made of the property so transmitted, and to direct the proceeds of such sale, after deducting the expenses thereof, to be paid to the person entitled under such transmission, or otherwise as the court may direct ; and it shall be in the discretion of any such court as aforesaid to make or refuse any such order for sale, and to annex thereto any terms or conditions, and to require any evidence in support of such application it may think fit, and generally to act in the premises in such manner as the justice of the case requires.

Order to be made by court.

LXIII. Every order for a sale made by such court as aforesaid shall contain a declaration vesting the right to transfer the ship or share so to be sold in some person or persons named by the court, and such nominee or nominees shall thereupon be entitled to transfer such ship or share in the same manner and to the same extent, as if he or they were the registered owner or owners of the same ; and every registrar shall obey the requisition of such nominee or nominees as aforesaid in respect of any transfer to the same extent as he would be compellable to obey the requisition of any registered owner or owners of such ship or share.

**II. *Transfers and Transmissions.***

LXIV. Every such application as aforesaid for sale shall be made within four weeks after the occurrence of the event on which such transmission has taken place, or within such further time as such court as aforesaid may allow, such time not in any case to exceed the space of one year from the date of such occurrence as aforesaid; and in the event of no such application being made within such period as aforesaid, or of such court refusing to accede thereto, the ship or share so transmitted shall thereupon be forfeited in manner hereinafter directed with respect to interests acquired by unqualified owners in ships using a British flag and assuming the British character.

**Limit of time for application.**

LXV. It shall be lawful in England or Ireland for the Court of Chancery (r), in Scotland for the Court of Session, in any British possession for any court, possessing the principal civil jurisdiction within such possession, without prejudice to the exercise of any other power such court may possess, upon the summary application of any interested person made either by petition or otherwise, and either ex parte, or upon service of notice on any other person, as the court may direct, to issue an order prohibiting for a time to be named in such order any dealing with such ship or share; and it shall be in the discretion of such court to make or refuse any such order, and to annex thereto any terms or conditions it may think fit, and to discharge such order when granted with or without costs, and generally to act in the premises in such manner as the justice of the case requires; and every registrar, without being made a party to the proceedings, upon being served with such order, or an official copy thereof, shall obey the same.

**Power of courts to prohibit transfers.**

### *Mortgages.*

**Mortgages.**

LXVI. A registered ship or any share therein may be made a security for a loan or other valuable consideration; and the instrument creating such security, hereinafter termed a "mortgage," shall be in the form marked (I) in the Schedule hereto, or as near thereto as circumstances permit; and on the production of such instrument the registrar of the port at which the ship is registered shall record the same in the register book (s).

**Mortgage of ships and shares therein.**

LXVII. Every such mortgage shall be recorded by the registrar in the order of time in which the same is produced to him for that purpose; and the registrar shall, by memorandum under his hand, notify on the instrument of mortgage that the same has been recorded by him, stating the date and hour of such record.

**Mortgages to be registered in order of time of production.**

LXVIII. Whenever any registered mortgage has been discharged, the registrar shall, on the production of the mortgage deed, with a receipt for the mortgage money indorsed thereon, duly signed and attested, make an entry in the register book to the effect that such mortgage has been discharged; and upon such entry being made, the estate, if any, which passed to the mortgagee shall vest in the same person or persons in whom the same would, having regard to intervening acts and circumstances, if any, have vested if no such mortgage had ever been made.

**Entry of discharge of mortgage.**

LXIX. If there is more than one mortgage registered of the same ship or share therein, the mortgagees shall, notwithstanding any express, implied, or constructive notice, be entitled in priority one over the other according to the date at which each instrument is recorded in the register books, and not according to the date of each instrument itself.

**Priority of mortgages.**

LXX. A mortgagee shall not by reason of his mortgage be deemed to be the owner of a ship or any share therein, nor shall the mortgagor be deemed to have ceased to be owner of such mortgaged ship or share, except in so far as may be necessary for making such ship or share available as a security for the mortgage debt.

**Mortgagee not to be deemed owner.**

LXXI. Every registered mortgagee shall have power absolutely to dispose of the ship or share in respect of which he is registered, and to give effectual receipts for the purchase-money: but if there are more persons than

**Mortgagee to have power of sale.**

(r) See 24 Vict. c. 10, s. 12.          (s) See 8 & 9 Vict. c. 89, s. 45.

3 K 2

II. *Mortgages.*

one registered as mortgagees of the same ship or share, no subsequent mortgagee shall, except under the order of some court capable of taking cognizance of such matters, sell such ship or share without the concurrence of every prior mortgagee.

Rights of mortgagee not affected by any act of bankruptcy of mortgagor.

LXXII. No registered mortgage of any ship or of any share therein shall be affected by any act of bankruptcy committed by the mortgagor after the date of the record of such mortgage, notwithstanding such mortgagor at the time of his becoming bankrupt may have in his possession and disposition and be reputed owner of such ship or share thereof ; and such mortgage shall be preferred to any right, claim or interest in such ship or any share thereof which may belong to the assignees of such bankrupt.

Transfer of mortgages.

LXXIII. A registered mortgage of any ship or share in a ship may be transferred to any person, and the instrument creating such transfer shall be in the form marked (K) in the Schedule hereto, and on the production of such instrument the registrar shall enter in the register book the name of the transferee as mortgagee of the ship or shares therein mentioned, and shall by memorandum under his hand record on the instrument of transfer that the same has been recorded by him, stating the date and hour of such record.

Transmission of interest of mortgagee by death, bankruptcy, or marriage.

LXXIV. If the interest of any mortgagee in any ship or in any share therein becomes transmitted in consequence of death, bankruptcy or insolvency, or in consequence of the marriage of any female mortgagee, or by any lawful means other than by a transfer according to the provisions of this Act, such transmission shall be authenticated by a declaration of the person to whom such interest has been transmitted, made in the form marked (L) in the Schedule hereto, and containing a statement describing the manner in which and the party to whom such property has been transmitted ; and such declaration shall be made and subscribed, if the declarant resides at or within five miles of the custom house of the port of registry, in the presence of the registrar, but if beyond that distance, in the presence of any registrar or of any justice of the peace, and shall be accompanied by such evidence as is hereinbefore required to authenticate a corresponding transmission of property from one registered owner to another.

Entry of transmitted mortgage.

LXXV. The registrar, upon the receipt of such declaration, and the production of such evidence as aforesaid, shall enter the name of the person or persons entitled under such transmission in the register book as mortgagee or mortgagees of the ship or share in respect of which such transmission has taken place.

*Certificates of Mortgage and Sale.*

## Certificates of Mortgage and Sale.

Powers of mortgage and sale may be conferred by certificate.

LXXVI. Any registered owner, if desirous of disposing by way of mortgage or sale of the ship or share in respect of which he is registered at any place out of the country or possession in which the port of registry of such ship is situate, may apply to the registrar, who shall thereupon enable him to do so by granting such certificates as are hereinafter mentioned, to be called respectively certificates of mortgage or certificates of sale, according as they purport to give a power to mortgage or a power to sell.

Requisites for certificates of mortgage and sale.

LXXVII. Previously to any certificate of mortgage or sale being granted, the applicant shall state to the registrar, to be by him entered in the register book, the following particulars ; (that is to say,)

(1). The names of the persons by whom the power mentioned in such certificate is to be exercised, and in the case of a mortgage the maximum amount of charge to be created, if it is intended to fix any such maximum, and in the case of a sale the minimum price at which a sale is to be made, if it is intended to fix any such minimum :

(2). The specific place or places where such power is to be exercised, or if no place be specified, then that it may be exercised anywhere, subject to the provisions hereinafter contained : ·

(3). The limit of time within which such power may be exercised.

Restrictions on certificates of mortgage and sale.

LXXVIII. No certificate of mortgage or sale shall be granted so as to authorise any mortgage or sale to be made—

At any place within the United Kingdom, if the port of registry of the ship be situate in the United Kingdom ; or at any place within the same

British possession if the port of registry is situate within a British possession ; or,

By any person not named in the certificate.

LXXIX. Certificates of mortgage and sale shall be in the forms marked respectively (M) and (N) in the Schedule hereto, and shall contain a statement of the several particulars hereinbefore directed to be entered in the register book, and in addition thereto an enumeration of any registered mortgages or certificates of mortgage or sale affecting the ships or shares in respect of which such certificates are given.

LXXX. The following rules shall be observed as to certificates of mortgage ; (that is to say,)

(1). The power shall be exercised in conformity with the directions contained in the certificate :

(2). A record of every mortgage made thereunder shall be indorsed thereon by a registrar or British consular officer :

(3). No mortgage bonâ fide made thereunder shall be impeached by reason of the person by whom the power was given dying before the making of such mortgage :

(4). Whenever the certificate contains a specification of the place or places at which, and a limit of time not exceeding twelve months within which, the power is to be exercised, no mortgage bonâ fide made to a mortgagee without notice shall be impeached by reason of the bankruptcy or insolvency of the person by whom the power was given :

(5). Every mortgage which is so registered as aforesaid on the certificate shall have priority over all mortgages of the same ship or share created subsequently to the date of the entry of the certificate in the register book ; and if there be more mortgages than one so indorsed, the respective mortgagees claiming thereunder shall, notwithstanding any express, implied or constructive notice, be entitled one before the other according to the date at which a record of each instrument is indorsed on the certificate, and not according to the date of the instrument creating the mortgage :

(6). Subject to the foregoing rules every mortgagee whose mortgage is registered on the certificate shall have the same rights and powers, and be subject to the same liabilities as he would have had and been subject to if his mortgage had been registered in the register book instead of on the certificate :

(7). The discharge of any mortgage so registered on the certificate may be indorsed thereon by any registrar or British consular officer, upon the production of such evidence as is hereby required to be produced to the registrar on the entry of the discharge of a mortgage in the register book ; and upon such indorsement being made, the estate, if any, which passed to the mortgagee shall vest in the same person or persons in whom the same would, having regard to intervening acts and circumstances, if any, have vested if no such mortgage had been made :

(8). Upon the delivery of any certificate of mortgage to the registrar by whom it was granted, he shall, after recording in the register book in such manner as to preserve its priority any unsatisfied mortgage registered thereon, cancel such certificate, and enter the fact of such cancellation in the register book ; and every certificate so cancelled shall be void to all intents.

LXXXI. The following rules shall be observed as to certificates of sale ; (that is to say,)

(1). No such certificate shall be granted except for the sale of an entire ship :

(2). The power shall be exercised in conformity with the directions contained in the certificate :

(3). No sale bonâ fide made to a purchaser for valuable consideration shall be impeached by reason of the person by whom the power was given dying before the making of such sale :

(4). Whenever the certificate contains a specification of the place or places at which, and a limit of time not exceeding twelve months within which, the power is to be exercised, no sale bonâ fide made to a purchaser for valuable consideration without notice shall be impeached by reason of the bankruptcy or insolvency of the person by whom the power was given:

(5). Any transfer made to a person qualified to be the owner of British ships, shall be by bill of sale in the form hereinbefore mentioned, or as near thereto as circumstances permit:

(6). If the ship is sold to a party qualified to hold British ships, the ship shall be registered anew, but notice of all mortgages enumerated on the certificate of sale shall be entered in the register book:

(7). Previously to such registry anew there shall be produced to the registrar required to make the same the bill of sale by which the ship is transferred, the certificate of sale and the certificate of registry of such ship:

(8). Such last-mentioned registrar shall retain the certificates of sale and registry, and after having indorsed on both of such instruments an entry of the fact of a sale having taken place, shall forward the said certificates to the registrar of the port appearing on such certificates to be the former port of registry of the ship, and such last-mentioned registrar shall thereupon make a memorandum of the sale in his register book, and the registry of the ship in such book shall be considered as closed, except as far as relates to any unsatisfied mortgages or existing certificates of mortgage entered therein:

(9). On such registry anew the description of the ship contained in her original certificate of registry may be transferred to the new register book, without her being re-surveyed, and the declaration to be made by the purchaser shall be the same as would be required to be made by an ordinary transferee:

(10). If the ship is sold to a party not qualified to be the owner of a British ship, the bill of sale by which the ship is transferred, the certificate of sale, and the certificate of registry shall be produced to some registrar or consular officer, who shall retain the certificates of sale and registry, and having indorsed thereon the fact of such ship having been sold to persons not qualified to be owners of British ships, shall forward such certificates to the registrar of the port appearing on the certificate of registry to be the port of registry of such ship; and such last-mentioned registrar shall thereupon make a memorandum of the sale in his register book, and the registry of the ship in such book shall be considered as closed, except so far as relates to any unsatisfied mortgages or existing certificates of mortgage entered therein:

(11). If upon a sale being made to an unqualified person default is made in the production of such certificates as are mentioned in the last rule, such unqualified person shall be considered by British law as having acquired no title to or interest in the ship; and further, the party upon whose application such certificate was granted, and the persons exercising the power, shall each incur a penalty not exceeding one hundred pounds:

(12). If no sale is made in conformity with the certificate of sale, such certificate shall be delivered to the registrar by whom the same was granted; and such registrar shall thereupon cancel it, and enter the fact of such cancellation in the register book; and every certificate so cancelled shall be void to all intents.

LXXXII. Upon proof at any time to the satisfaction of the commissioners of customs that any certificate of mortgage or sale is lost or so obliterated as to be useless, and that the powers thereby given have never been exercised, or if they have been exercised, then upon proof of the several matters and things that have been done thereunder, it shall be lawful for the registrar, with the sanction of the said commissioners, as circumstances may require, either to issue a new certificate, or to direct such entries to be made in the register book, or such other matter or thing to be done as might have been made or done if no such loss or obliteration had taken place.

LXXXIII. The registered owner for the time being of any ship or share therein in respect of which a certificate of mortgage or sale has been granted, specifying the place or places where the power thereby given is to be exercised, may, by an instrument under his hand made in the form (O) in the Schedule hereto, or as near thereto as circumstances permit, authorise the registrar by whom such certificate was granted to give notice to the registrar or consular officer, registrars or consular officers, at such place or places, that such certificate is revoked; and notice shall be given accordingly; and all registrars or consular officers receiving such notice shall record the same, and shall exhibit the same to all persons who may apply to them for the purpose of effecting or obtaining a mortgage or transfer under the said certificate of mortgage or sale; and after such notice has been so recorded the said certificate shall, so far as concerns any mortgage or sale to be thereafter made at such place, be deemed to be revoked and of no effect; and every registrar or consular officer recording any such notice shall thereupon state to the registrar by whom the certificate was granted whether any previous exercise of the power to which such certificate refers has been taken.

*II. Certificates of Mortgage and Sale.*

### *Registry anew, and Transfer of Registry.*

*Registry anew, and Transfer of Registry.*

LXXXIV. Whenever any registered ship is so altered as not to correspond with the particulars relating to her tonnage or description contained in the register book, then if such alteration is made at a port where there is a registrar, the registrar of such port, but if made elsewhere, the registrar of the first port having a registrar at which the ship arrives after her alteration, shall, on application made to him, and on the receipt of a certificate from the proper surveyor specifying the nature of such alteration, either retain the old certificate of registry and grant a new certificate of registry containing a description of the ship as altered, or indorse on the existing certificate a memorandum of such alteration, and subscribe his name to such indorsement; and the registrar to whom such application as aforesaid is made, if he is the registrar of the port of registry of the ship, shall himself enter in his register book the particulars of the alteration so made, and the fact of such new certificate having been granted or indorsement having been made on the existing certificate; but if he is not such last-mentioned registrar, he shall forthwith report such particulars and facts as aforesaid, accompanied by the old certificate of registry in cases where a new one has been granted, to the registrar of the port of registry of the ship, who shall retain such old certificate (if any), and enter such particulars and facts in his register book accordingly.

*Alteration in ship to be registered.*

LXXXV. When the registrar, to whom application is made in respect of any such alteration as aforesaid, is the registrar of the port of registry, he may, if he thinks fit, instead of registering such alteration, require such ship to be registered anew in manner hereinbefore directed on the first registry of a ship, and if he is not such registrar as lastly hereinbefore mentioned he may nevertheless require such ship to be registered anew, but he shall in such last-mentioned case grant a provisional certificate or make a provisional indorsement of the alteration made in manner hereinbefore directed in cases where no registry anew is required, taking care to add to such certificate or indorsement a statement that the same is made provisionally, and to insert in his report to the registrar of the port of registry of the ship a like statement.

*On alteration registry anew may be required.*

LXXXVI. Every such provisional certificate, or certificate provisionally indorsed, shall, within ten days after the first subsequent arrival of the ship at her port of discharge in the United Kingdom, if registered in the United Kingdom, or if registered elsewhere, at her port of discharge, in the British possession within which her port of registry is situate, be delivered up to the registrar thereof, who shall thereupon cause such ship to be registered anew in the same manner in all respects as hereinbefore required on the first registry of any ship.

*Grant of provisional certificate in respect of alteration.*

LXXXVII. On failure of such registry anew of any ship or registry of alteration of any ship so altered as aforesaid, such ship shall be deemed not duly registered, and shall no longer be recognised as a British ship.

*Consequence of omission to register anew.*

LXXXVIII. If upon any change of ownership in any ship the owner or owners desire to have such ship registered anew, although such registry anew is not required by this Act, it shall be lawful for the registrar of the port at which such ship is already registered, on the delivery up to him of the existing certificate of registry, and on the other requisites to registry, or such of them as the registrar thinks material, being duly complied with, to make such registry anew, and grant a certificate thereof.

*On change of owners, registry anew may be granted if required.*

II. *Registry anew, and Transfer of Registry.*

Registry may be transferred from port to port.

**LXXXIX.** The registry of any ship may be transferred from one port to another upon the application of all parties appearing on the register to be interested in such ship, whether as owners or mortgagees, such application to be expressed by a declaration in writing made and subscribed, if the party so required to make and subscribe the same resides at or within five miles of the custom house of the port from which such ship is to be transferred, in the presence of the registrar of such port, but if beyond that distance in the presence of any registrar or of any justice of the peace.

Manner of transfer of registry.

**XC.** Upon such application being made as is hereinbefore mentioned, and upon the delivery to him of the certificate of registry, the registrar of the port at which such ship is already registered (a) shall transmit to the registrar of the port at which such ship is intended to be registered, notice of such application having been made to him, together with a true copy of all particulars relating to such ship, and the names of all the parties appearing by his book to be interested as owners or mortgagees in such ship; and such last-mentioned registrar shall, upon the receipt of such notice, enter all such particulars and names in his book of registry, and grant a fresh certificate of registry, and thenceforth such ship shall be considered as registered at and belonging to such last-mentioned port, and the name of such last-mentioned port shall be substituted on the stern of such ship in lieu of the name of the port previously appearing thereon.

Transfer of registry not to affect rights of owners.

**XCI.** The transfer of the registry of any ship in manner aforesaid shall not in any way affect the rights of the several persons interested either as owners or mortgagees in such ship, but such rights shall in all respects be maintained and continue in the same manner as if no such transfer had been effected.

*Registry Miscellaneous.*

### Registry Miscellaneous.

Inspection of register books.

**XCII.** Every person may, upon payment of a fee to be fixed by the commissioners of customs (b) not exceeding one shilling, have access to the register book for the purpose of inspection at any reasonable time during the hours of official attendance of the registrar.

Indemnity to registrar.

**XCIII.** No registrar shall be liable to damages or otherwise for any loss accruing to any person by reason of any act done or default made by him in his character of registrar, unless the same has happened through his neglect or wilful act.

Return to be made by registrars to commissioners of customs.

**XCIV.** Every registrar in the United Kingdom shall at the expiration of every month, and every other registrar shall without delay, or at such stated times as may be fixed by the commissioners of customs, transmit to the custom house in London (c) a full return in such form as they may direct of all registries, transfers, transmissions, mortgages and other dealings with ships which have been registered by or communicated to them in their character of registrars, and the names of the persons who have been concerned in the same, and such other particulars as may be directed by the said commissioners.

Application of fees.

**XCV.** All fees authorised to be taken under the Second Part of this Act shall, if taken in any part of the United Kingdom, be applied in payment of the general expenses of carrying into effect the purposes of such Second Part, or otherwise as the treasury may direct, but if taken elsewhere shall be disposed of in such way as the executive government of the British possession in which they are taken may direct.

Commissioners of customs to provide, and with consent of Board of Trade may alter forms and issue instructions.

**XCVI.** The commissioners of customs shall cause the several forms (d) required or authorised to be used by the Second Part of this Act, and contained in the Schedule hereto, to be supplied to all registrars within her Majesty's dominions for distribution to the several persons requiring to use the same, either free of charge, or at such moderate prices as they may from time to time direct, and the said commissioners, with the consent of the Board of Trade, may from time to time make such alterations in the forms contained in the Schedule hereto as it may deem requisite, but shall, before issuing any altered form, give such public notice thereof as may be necessary in order to prevent inconvenience; and the said commissioners may also, with such consent as aforesaid, for the purposes of carrying into effect the

(a) See 18 & 19 Vict. c. 91, s. 112, *infra*.

(b) Registrar-General of Seamen: 35 & 36 Vict. c. 73, s. 4, *infra*.

(c) See 35 & 36 Vict. c. 73, s. 4, *infra*.

(d) 18 & 19 Vict. c. 91, s. 11, and 35 & 36 Vict. c. 73, s. 4, *infra*.

provisions contained in the Second Part of this Act, give such instructions as to the manner of making entries in the register book, as to the execution and attestation of powers of attorney, as to any evidence to be required for identifying any person, and generally as to any act or thing to be done in pursuance of the Second Part of this Act, as they may think fit. II. *Registry Miscellaneous.*

XCVII. Whenever in any case in which under the Second Part of this Act any person is required to make a declaration on behalf of himself or of any body corporate, or any evidence is required to be produced to the registrar, it is shown to the satisfaction of the registrar that from any reasonable cause such person is unable to make the declaration, or that such evidence cannot be produced, it shall be lawful for the registrar, with the sanction of the commissioners of customs, and upon the production of such other evidence, and subject to such terms as they may think fit, to dispense with any such declaration or evidence. Power to registrar to dispense with declarations and other evidence.

XCVIII. In cases where it appears to the commissioners of customs, or to the governor or other person administering the government of any British possession, that by reason of special circumstances it would be desirable that permission should be granted to any British ship to pass, without being previously registered, from one port or place in her Majesty's dominions to any other port or place within the same, it shall be lawful for such commissioners or governor or other person to grant a pass accordingly, and such pass shall for the time and within the limits therein mentioned have the same effect as a certificate of registry. Power for commissioners or governor in special cases to grant a pass to a ship not registered.

XCIX. If any person interested in any ship or any share therein, is by reason of infancy, lunacy or other inability, incapable of making any declaration or doing anything required or permitted by this Act to be made or done by such incapable person in respect of registry, then the guardian or committee, if any, of such incapable person, or, if there be none, any person appointed by any court or judge possessing jurisdiction in respect of the property of incapable persons, upon the petition of any person on behalf of such incapable person, or of any other person interested in the making such declaration or doing such thing, may make such declaration, or a declaration as nearly corresponding thereto as circumstances permit, and do such thing in the name and on behalf of such incapable person ; and all acts done by such substitute shall be as effectual as if done by the person for whom he is substituted. Provision for cases of infancy or other incapacity.

C. Whenever any person is beneficially interested, otherwise than by way of mortgage, in any ship or share therein registered in the name of some other person as owner, the person so interested shall, as well as the registered owner, be subject to all pecuniary penalties imposed by this or by any other Act on owners of ships or shares therein, so nevertheless that proceedings may be taken for the enforcement of any such pecuniary penalties against both or either of the aforesaid parties, with or without joining the other of them. Liabilities of owners.

### Forgery.
*Forgery.*

CI. Any person who forges, assists in forging, or procures to be forged, fraudulently alters, assists in fraudulently altering, or procures to be fraudulently altered, any register book, certificate of surveyor, certificate of registry, declaration of ownership, bill of sale, instrument of mortgage, certificate of mortgage or sale, or any entry or indorsement required by the Second Part of this Act to be made in or on any of the above documents, shall for every such offence be deemed to be guilty of felony. Punishment for forgery.

### National Character.
*National Character.*

CII. No officer of customs shall grant a clearance or transire for any ship until the master of such ship has declared to such officer the name of the nation to which he claims that she belongs, and such officer shall thereupon inscribe such name on the clearance or transire ; and if any ship attempts to proceed to sea without such clearance or transire, any such officer may detain her until such declaration is made. National character of ship to be declared before clearance.

CIII. The offences hereinafter mentioned shall be punishable as follows; (that is to say,) Penalties:

(1). If any person uses the British flag and assumes the British national character on board any ship owned in whole or in part by any persons not entitled by law to own British ships, for the purpose of making such ship appear to be a British ship, such ship shall be for- For unduly assuming a British character.

II. *National Character.*

feited to her Majesty, unless such assumption has been made for the purpose of escaping capture by an enemy or by a foreign ship of war in exercise of some belligerent right; and in any proceeding for enforcing any such forfeiture the burden of proving a title to use the British flag and assume the British national character shall lie upon the person using and assuming the same:

For concealment of British or assumption of foreign character.

(2). If the master or owner of any British ship does or permits to be done any matter or thing, or carries or permits to be carried any papers or documents, with intent to conceal the British character of such ship from any person entitled by British law to inquire into the same, or to assume a foreign character, or with intent to deceive any such person as lastly hereinbefore mentioned, such ship shall be forfeited to her Majesty; and the master, if he commits or is privy to the commission of the offence, shall be guilty of a misdemeanor:

For acquiring ownership if unqualified.

(3). If any qualified person, except in the case of such transmitted interests as are hereinbefore mentioned, acquires as owner any interest, either legal or beneficial, in a ship using a British flag and assuming the British character, such interest shall be forfeited to her Majesty:

For false declaration of ownership.

(4). If any person, on behalf of himself or any other person or body of persons, wilfully makes a false declaration touching the qualification of himself or such other person or body of persons to own British ships or any share therein, the declarant shall be guilty of a misdemeanor; and the ship or share in respect of which such declaration is made, if the same has not been forfeited under the foregoing provision, shall, to the extent of the interest therein of the person making the declaration, and, unless it is shown that he had no authority to make the same, of the parties on behalf of whom such declaration is made, be forfeited to her Majesty:

And in order that the above provisions as to forfeitures may be carried into effect it shall be lawful for any commissioned officer on full pay in the military or naval service of her Majesty, or any British officer of customs, or any British consular officer, to seize and detain any ship which has, either wholly or as to any share therein, become subject to forfeiture as aforesaid, and to bring her for adjudication before the High Court of Admiralty in England or Ireland, or any court having Admiralty jurisdiction in her Majesty's dominions; and such court may thereupon make such order in the case as it may think fit, and may award to the officer bringing in the same for adjudication such portion of the proceeds of the sale of any forfeited ship or share as it may think right.

Officer not liable for any seizure made on reasonable grounds.

CIV. No such officer as aforesaid shall be responsible, either civilly or criminally, to any person whomsoever, in respect of the seizure or detention of any ship that has been seized or detained by him in pursuance of the provisions herein contained, notwithstanding that such ship is not brought in for adjudication, or, if so brought in, is declared not to be liable to forfeiture, if it is shown to the satisfaction of the judge, or court before whom any trial relating to such ship or such seizure or detention is held that there were reasonable grounds for such seizure or detention; but if no such grounds are shown, such judge or court may award payment of costs and damages to any party aggrieved, and make such other order in the premises as it thinks just.

Penalty for carrying improper colours.

CV. If any colours usually worn by her Majesty's ships, or any colours resembling those of her Majesty, or any distinctive national colours, except the red ensign usually worn by merchant ships (*c*), or except the union jack with a white border, or if the pendant usually carried by her Majesty's ships or any pendant in anywise resembling such pendant, are or is hoisted on board any ship or boat belonging to any subject of her Majesty without warrant for so doing from her Majesty or from the Admiralty, the master of such ship or boat, or the owner thereof, if on board the same, and every other person hoisting or joining or assisting in hoisting the same, shall for every such offence incur a penalty not exceeding five hundred pounds (*d*); and

(*c*) See the Merchant Shipping (Colours) Act, 1889 (52 & 53 Vict. c. 73).

(*d*) As to the recovery of the penalty, see 52 & 53 Vict. c. 73, s. 3.

it shall be lawful for any officer on full pay in the military or naval service of her Majesty, or any British officer of the customs, or any British consular officer, to board any such ship or boat, and to take away any such jack, colours, or pendant ; and such jack, colours or pendant shall be forfeited to her Majesty.

CVI. Whenever it is declared by this Act that a ship belonging to any person or body corporate qualified according to this Act to be owners of British ships shall not be recognized as a British ship, such ship shall not be entitled to any benefits, privileges, advantages or protection usually enjoyed by British ships, and shall not be entitled to use the British flag, or assume the British national character ; but, so far as regards the payment of dues, the liability to pains and penalties, and the punishment of offences committed on board such ship or by any persons belonging to her, such ship shall be dealt with in the same manner in all respects as if she were a recognized British ship.

*II. National Character.*

*Effect of declaration in the Act that a ship shall not be recognized as a British ship.*

### Evidence.

*Evidence.*

CVII. Every register of or declaration made in pursuance of the Second Part of this Act in respect of any British ship may be proved in any court of justice, or before any person having by law or by consent of parties authority to receive evidence, either by the production of the original or by an examined copy thereof, or by a copy thereof purporting to be certified under the hand of the registrar or other person having the charge of the original ; which certified copies he is hereby required to furnish to any person applying at a reasonable time for the same, upon payment of one shilling for each such certified copy ; and every such register or copy of a register, and also every certificate of registry of any British ship, purporting to be signed by the registrar or other proper officer, shall be received in evidence in any court of justice or before any person having by law or by consent of parties authority to receive evidence as primâ facie proof of all the matters contained or recited in such register when the register or such copy is produced, and of all the matters contained in or indorsed on such certificate of registry, and purporting to be authenticated by the signature of a registrar, when such certificate is produced.

*Copies of registers and declarations to be admissible in evidence, and to be primâ facie proof of certain things (e).*

### Saving Clause.

*Saving Clause.*

CVIII. Nothing in this Act contained shall repeal or affect an Act passed in the session of Parliament holden in the third and fourth years of the reign of her present Majesty, chapter fifty-six, intituled "An Act further to regulate the Trade of Ships built and trading within the Limits of the East India Company's Charter."

*Saving of 3 & 4 Vict. c. 56, relating to East Indian ships.*

---

# PART III.

## MASTERS AND SEAMEN (f).

### Application.

*Application.*

CIX. The various provisions of the Third Part of this Act shall have the following applications, unless the context or subject-matter requires a different application ; (that is to say,)

So much of the Third Part of this Act as relates to the delivery or transmission of lists of crews to the registrar-general of seamen shall apply to all fishing vessels belonging to the United Kingdom, whether employed exclusively on the coasts of the United Kingdom or not ; to all ships belonging to the Trinity House, or the commissioners of northern lighthouses, constituted, as hereinafter mentioned, or the port of Dublin corporation, and to all pleasure yachts, and to the owners, masters and crews of such ships (f).

*Application of Part III. of Act.*

*Returns for certain ships belonging to the United Kingdom.*

So much of the Third Part of this Act as relates to the delivery and transmission of lists of crews, and to the wages and effects of deceased seamen and apprentices, shall apply to all-seagoing British ships,

*Returns and wages of deceased seamen in certain colonial ships.*

(e) See ss. 9 and 15 of 18 & 19 Vict. c. 91, *infra.*

(f) See 25 & 26 Vict. c. 63, s. 13, *infra.*

III. *Application.*

wherever registered, of which the crews are discharged, or whose final port of destination is in the United Kingdom, and to the owners, masters and crews of such ships :

Shipping and discharging men in the United Kingdom.

So much of the Third Part of this Act as relates to the shipping and discharge of seamen in the United Kingdom, shall apply to all sea-going British ships, wherever registered, and to the owners, masters and crews of such ships :

Volunteering into the navy.

So much of the Third Part of this Act as relates to seamen volunteering into the royal navy shall apply to all sea-going British ships wherever registered, and to the owners, masters and crews of such ships, wherever the same may be :

Provisions applicable to colonial ships.

So much of the Third Part of this Act as relates to rights to wages and remedies for the recovery thereof ; to the shipping and discharge of seamen in foreign ports ; to leaving seamen abroad, and to the relief of seamen in distress in foreign ports ; to the provisions, health and accommodation of seamen ; to the power of seamen to make complaints ; to the protection of seamen from imposition ; to discipline ; to naval courts on the high seas and abroad ; and to crimes committed abroad ; shall apply to all ships registered in any of her Majesty's dominions abroad, when such ships are out of the jurisdiction of their respective governments, and to the owners, masters and crews of such ships :

As to whole of Part III. of Act.

And the whole of the Third Part of this Act shall apply to all sea-going ships registered in the United Kingdom (except such as are exclusively employed in fishing on the coasts of the United Kingdom, and such as belong to the Trinity House, the commissioners of northern lighthouses, or the port of Dublin corporation, and also except pleasure yachts), and also to all ships registered in any British possession and employed in trading or going between any place in the United Kingdom and any place or places not situate in the possession in which such ships are registered, and to the owners, masters and crews of such ships respectively, wherever the same may be (*g*).

*Local Marine Boards.*

## Local Marine Boards.

Constitution of local marine boards.

CX. There shall be local marine boards for carrying into effect the provisions of this Act under the superintendence of the board of trade at those seaports of the United Kingdom at which local marine boards have heretofore been established, and at such other places as the board of trade appoints for this purpose ; and each of such local marine boards shall be constituted as follows : (that is to say,) the mayor or provost and the stipendiary magistrate or such of the mayors or provosts and stipendiary magistrates of the place (if more than one) as the board of trade appoints shall be a member or members ex officio ; the board of trade shall appoint four members from persons residing or having places of business at the port or within seven miles thereof ; and the owners of foreign-going ships and of home-trade passenger ships registered at the port shall elect six members ; and such elections as aforesaid shall take place on the twenty-fifth day of January, one thousand eight hundred and fifty-seven, and on the twenty-fifth day of January in every third succeeding year, and such appointments as aforesaid shall take place within one month after such elections ; and upon the conclusion of such month and the constitution of a new board the functions of the then existing board shall cease, and the board consisting of the members then newly elected and appointed shall take its place ; and any occasional vacancy caused in the intervals between the general elections and appointments, by death, resignation, disqualification, or otherwise, shall be filled up within one month after it occurs ; and every person elected or appointed on an occasional vacancy shall continue a member until the next constitution of a new board ; and the mayor or provost shall fix the place and mode of conducting all such elections as aforesaid, and also on occasional vacancies the day of election, and shall give at least ten days' notice thereof ; and the board of trade shall have power to decide any questions raised concerning any such elections.

Qualification of voters for

CXI. Owners of foreign-going ships and of home-trade passenger ships registered at any seaport of which there is a local marine board shall have

(*g*) See 25 & 26 Vict. c. 63, s. 13, *infra*.

votes at the election of members of such board as follows : (that is to say,) every registered owner of not less than two hundred and fifty tons in the whole of such shipping shall at every election have one vote for each member for every two hundred and fifty tons owned by him, so that his votes for any one member do not exceed ten : And for the purpose of ascertaining the qualification of such electors the following rules shall be observed ; (that is to say,) in the case of a ship registered in the name of one person, such person shall be deemed to be the owner, and in the case of a ship registered in distinct and several shares in the names of more persons than one, the tonnage shall be apportioned among the owners as nearly as may be in proportion to their respective shares, and each of such persons shall be deemed to be the owner of the tonnage so apportioned to him ; and in the case of a ship or shares of a ship registered jointly without severance of interest in the names of more persons than one, the tonnage shall, if it is sufficient, either alone or together with other tonnage (if any) owned by such joint owners, to give a qualification to each of them, be apportioned equally between the joint owners, and each of such joint owners shall be deemed to be the owner of the equal share so apportioned to him, but if it is not so sufficient, the whole of such tonnage shall be deemed to be owned by such one of the joint owners resident or having a place of business at the port or within seven miles thereof as is first named on the register ; and in making any such apportionment as aforesaid any portion may be struck off so as to obtain a divisible amount ; and the whole amount of tonnage so owned by each person, whether in ships or shares of or interests in ships, shall be added together, and, if sufficient, shall constitute his qualification.

CXII. The collector or comptroller of customs in every seaport of the United Kingdom at which there is a local marine board, shall, with the assistance of the registrar-general of seamen, on or before the twenty-fifth day of December in the year one thousand eight hundred and fifty-six, and in every third succeeding year, make out an alphabetical list of the persons entitled by virtue of this Act to vote at the election of members of such local marine board, containing the Christian name, surname and residence of each such person, and the number of votes to which he is entitled, and shall sign such list, and cause a sufficient number of copies thereof to be printed, and to be fixed on or near the doors of the custom-house of such seaport for two entire weeks next after such list has been made, and shall keep true copies of such list, and permit the same to be perused by any person, without payment of any fee, at all reasonable hours during such two weeks.

CXIII. The mayor or provost of every seaport at which there is a local marine board, or such of them, if more than one, as is or are for the time being so appointed as aforesaid, shall at least twenty days before the twenty-fifth day of January in the year one thousand eight hundred and fifty-seven, and in each succeeding third year, nominate two justices of the peace to revise the said lists ; and such justices shall, between the eighth and fifteenth days of January both inclusive in the year in which they are so nominated, revise the said list at the custom-house of the port, or in some convenient place near thereto, to be hired, if necessary, by the said collector or comptroller, and shall give three clear days' notice of such revision by advertising the same in some local newspaper, and by affixing a notice thereof on or near to the doors of such custom-house, and shall make such revision by inserting in such list the name of every person who claims to be inserted therein and gives proof satisfactory to the said revisors of his right to have his name so inserted, and by striking out therefrom the name of every person to the insertion of which an objection is made by any other person named in such list who gives proof satisfactory to the said revisors that the name of the person so objected to ought not to have been inserted therein ; and the decision of the said revisors with respect to every such claim or objection shall be conclusive ; and the said revisors shall immediately after such revision sign their names at the foot of the list so revised ; and such list so revised shall be the register of voters at elections of members of the local marine board of such seaport for three years from the twenty-fifth day of January then next ensuing inclusive to the twenty-fourth day of January inclusive in the third succeeding year ; and the said revised list, when so signed, shall be delivered to such mayor or provost as aforesaid of the place, who shall, if necessary, cause a sufficient number of copies thereof to be printed, and shall cause a copy to be delivered to every voter applying for the same.

*III. Local Marine Boards.*

members of local marine boards.

Lists of such voters to be made.

Revision of list of voters.

III. *Local Marine Boards.*

Registers to be produced.

CXIV. The said collector, or comptroller, if required, shall for the assistance of the said revisors in revising the said list produce to them the books containing the register of ships registered at such seaport; and the registrar-general of seamen, if required, shall also produce or transmit to such revisors such certified extracts or returns from the books in his custody as may be necessary for the same purpose.

Expenses to be paid by board of trade.

CXV. The two justices aforesaid shall certify all expenses properly incurred by any such collector or comptroller as aforesaid in making and printing the said list and in the revision thereof, and the board of trade shall pay the same, and also all expenses properly incurred by any such mayor or provost as aforesaid in printing the same or in elections taking place under this Act; and the said board may disallow any items of any such expenses as aforesaid which it deems to have been improperly incurred.

Persons on revised list qualified to vote.

CXVI. Every person whose name appears on such revised list, and no other person,'shall be qualified to vote at the election of members of the local marine board at such seaport to be held on the twenty-fifth day of January next after the revision of such list, and at any occasional election held at any time between that day and the next ordinary triennial election of the members of such board.

Qualification of members of local marine boards.

CXVII. Every male person who is according to such revised list of the voters at any seaport entitled to a vote, shall be qualified to be elected a member of the local marine board of such seaport, and no other person shall be so qualified; and if any person elected as a member after such election ceases to be an owner of such quantity of tonnage as would entitle him to a vote, he shall no longer continue to act or be considered as a member, and thereupon another member shall be elected in his place.

Error in elections not to vitiate acts done.

CXVIII. No act of any local marine board shall be vitiated or prejudiced by reason of any irregularity in the election of any of its members, or of any error in the list of voters herein mentioned, or of any irregularity in the making or revising of such list, or by reason of any person who is not duly qualified as hereinbefore directed acting upon such board.

Minutes and business of local marine boards.

CXIX. Every local marine board shall keep minutes of its proceedings, and the same shall be kept in such mode (if any) as the board of trade prescribes; and such minutes, and all books or documents used or kept by any local marine board, or by any examiners, shipping masters, or other officers or servants under the control of any local marine board, shall be open to the inspection of the board of trade and its officers; and every local marine board shall make and send to the board of trade such reports and returns as it requires; but, subject as aforesaid, every local marine board may regulate the mode in which its meetings are to be held and its business conducted (*h*).

If any local marine board fails to discharge its duties, board of trade may assume its duties, or direct a new election.

CXX. If any local marine board, by reason of any election not taking place, or of the simultaneous resignation or continued non-attendance of all or the greater part of the members, or from any other cause, fails to meet or to discharge its duties, the board of trade may, in its discretion, either take into its own hands the performance of the duties of such local marine board until the next triennial appointment and election thereof, or direct that a new appointment and election of such local marine board shall take place immediately.

Board of trade, on complaint, may alter arrangements made by local marine boards.

CXXI. If upon complaint made to the board of trade, it appears to such board that any appointments or arrangements made by any local marine board under the powers hereby given to it are not such as to meet the wants of the port, or are in any respect unsatisfactory or improper, the board of trade may annul, alter, or rectify such appointments or arrangements in such manner as, having regard to the intentions of this Act and to the wants of the port, it deems to be expedient.

### *Shipping Offices* (i).

*Shipping Offices.*

Local marine boards to establish shipping offices.

CXXII. In every seaport in the United Kingdom in which there is a local marine board such board shall establish a shipping office or shipping offices, and may for that purpose, subject as herein mentioned, procure the requisite premises, and appoint and from time to time remove and re-appoint

(*h*) See 25 & 26 Vict. c. 63, s. 14, *infra*.

(i) Now termed mercantile marine offices: 25 & 26 Vict. c. 63, s. 15, *infra*.

superintendents of such offices, to be called shipping masters, with any necessary deputies, clerks, and servants, and regulate the mode of conducting business at such offices, and shall, subject as herein mentioned, have complete control over the same; and every act done by or before any deputy duly appointed shall have the same effect as if done by or before a shipping-master (*k*).

CXXIII. The sanction of the board of trade shall be necessary so far as regards the number of persons so appointed by any such local marine board, and the amount of their salaries and wages and all other expenses; and the board of trade shall have the immediate control of such shipping offices, so far as regards the receipt and payment of money thereat; and all shipping masters, deputies, clerks, and servants so appointed as aforesaid shall before entering upon their duties give such security (if any) for the due performance thereof as the board of trade requires; and if in any case the board of trade has reason to believe that any shipping master, deputy clerk or servant appointed by any local marine board does not properly discharge his duties, the board of trade may cause the case to be invested, and may, if it thinks fit so to do, remove him from his office, and may provide for the proper performance of his duties until another person is properly appointed in his place.

*Board of trade to have partial control over shipping offices.*

CXXIV. It shall be the general business of shipping masters appointed as aforesaid—

*Business of such offices generally.*

To afford facilities for engaging seamen by keeping registries of their names and characters;

To superintend and facilitate their engagement and discharge in manner hereinafter mentioned;

To provide means for securing the presence on board at the proper times of men who are so engaged;

To facilitate the making apprenticeships to the sea service;

To perform such other duties relating to merchant seamen and merchant ships as are hereby or may hereafter under the powers herein contained be committed to them.

CXXV. Such fees, not exceeding the sums specified in the table marked (P) in the Schedule hereto, as are from time to time fixed by the board of trade, shall be payable upon all engagements and discharges effected before shipping masters as hereinafter mentioned, and the board of trade shall cause scales of the fees payable for the time being to be prepared and to be conspicuously placed in the shipping offices; and all shipping masters, their deputies, clerks and servants, may refuse to proceed with any engagement or discharge unless the fees payable thereon are first paid.

*Fees to be paid upon engagements and discharges.*

CXXVI. Every owner or master of a ship engaging or discharging any seamen or seaman in a shipping office or before a shipping master shall pay to the shipping master the whole of the fees hereby made payable in respect of such engagement or discharge, and may, for the purpose of in part reimbursing himself, deduct in respect of each such engagement or discharge from the wages of all persons (except apprentices) so engaged or discharged, and retain any sums not exceeding the sum specified in that behalf in the table marked (Q) in the Schedule hereto: Provided that, if in any cases the sums which the owner is so entitled to deduct exceed the amount of the fee payable by him, such excess shall be paid by him to the shipping master in addition to such fee.

*Masters to pay fees, and to deduct part from wages.*

*Proviso as to excess.*

CXXVII. Any shipping master, deputy shipping master, or any clerk or servant in any shipping office, who demands or receives any remuneration whatever, either directly or indirectly, for hiring or supplying any seaman for any merchant ship, excepting the lawful fees payable under this Act, shall for every such offence incur a penalty not exceeding twenty pounds, and shall also be liable to be dismissed from his office by the board of trade.

*Penalty on shipping masters taking other remuneration.*

CXXVIII. The board of trade may, with the consent of the commissioners of customs, direct that at any place in which no separate shipping office is established the whole or any part of the business of the shipping office shall be conducted at the custom house, and thereupon the same shall be there conducted accordingly; and in respect of such business such custom house shall for all purposes be deemed to be a shipping office, and the officer of

*Business of shipping offices may be transacted at custom houses.*

(*k*) See 25 & 26 Vict. c. 63, s. 15, *infra.*

III. *Shipping Offices.*

In London sailors' homes may be shipping offices.

customs there to whom such business is committed shall for all purposes be deemed to be a shipping master within the meaning of this Act.

CXXIX. The board of trade may appoint any superintendent of or other person connected with any sailors' home in the port of London to be a shipping master, with any necessary deputies, clerks and servants, and may appoint any office in any such home to be a shipping office; and all shipping masters and shipping offices so appointed shall be subject to the immediate control of the board of trade and not of the local marine board of the port.

Dispensation with shipping master's superintendence.

CXXX. The board of trade may from time to time dispense with the transaction before a shipping master or in a shipping office of any matters required by this Act to be so transacted; and thereupon such matters shall, if otherwise duly transacted as required by law, be as valid as if transacted before a shipping master or in a shipping office.

*Certificates of Masters and Mates.*

*Examinations and Certificates of Masters and Mates.*

Examinations to be instituted for masters and mates (*l*).

CXXXI. Examinations shall be instituted for persons who intend to become masters or mates of foreign-going ships, or of home-trade passenger ships, or who wish to procure certificates of competency hereinafter mentioned (l); and, subject as herein mentioned, the local marine boards shall provide for the examinations at their respective ports, and may appoint and from time to time remove and re-appoint examiners to conduct the same, and may regulate the same; and any members of the local marine board of the place where the examination is held may be present and assist at any such examination.

Powers of board of trade over examinations.

CXXXII. The board of trade may from time to time lay down rules as to the conduct of such examinations and as to the qualifications of the applicants, and such rules shall be strictly adhered to by all examiners; and no examiner shall be appointed unless he possesses a certificate of qualification, to be from time to time granted or renewed by the board of trade; and the sanction of the board of trade shall be necessary, so far as regards the number of examiners to be appointed and the amount of their remuneration; and the board of trade may at any time depute any of its officers to be present and assist at any examination; and if it appears to the board of trade that the examinations for any two or more ports can be conducted without inconvenience by the same examiners, it may require and authorize the local marine boards of such ports to act together as one board in providing for and regulating examinations and appointing and removing examiners for such ports.

Fees to be paid by applicants for examination.

CXXXIII. All applicants for examination shall pay such fees, not exceeding the sums specified in the table marked (R) in the Schedule hereto, as the board of trade directs; and such fees shall be paid to such persons as the said board appoints for that purpose.

Certificates of competency to be granted to those who pass.

CXXXIV. Subject to the proviso hereinafter contained, the board of trade shall deliver to every applicant who is duly reported by the local examiners to have passed the examination satisfactorily, and to have given satisfactory evidence of his sobriety, experience, ability and general good conduct on board ship, a certificate (hereinafter called a "certificate of competency") to the effect that he is competent to act as master, or as first, second or only mate of a foreign-going ship, or as master or mate of a home-trade passenger ship, as the case may be: Provided that in every case in which the board of trade has reason to believe such report to have been unduly made, such board may remit the case either to the same or to any other examiners, and may require a re-examination of the applicant, or a further inquiry into his testimonials and character, before granting him a certificate.

Certificates of service to be delivered to persons who served as masters or mates before 1851, and to certain naval officers; and

CXXXV. Certificates of service, differing in form from certificates of competency, shall be granted as follows; (that is to say),

(1). Every person who before the first day of January, one thousand eight hundred and fifty-one, served as master in the British merchant service, or who has attained or attains the rank of lieutenant, master, passed mate or second master, or any higher rank in the service of Her Majesty or of the East India Company, shall

(*l*) As to certificates of engineers, which are required in certain cases, see 25 & 26 Vict. c. 63, s. 5 *et seq.*, *infra*.

be entitled to a certificate of service as master for foreign-going ships:

(2). Every person who before the first day of January, one thousand eight hundred and fifty-one, served as mate in the British merchant service, shall be entitled to a certificate of service as mate for foreign-going ships:

(3). Every person who before the first day of January, one thousand eight hundred and fifty-four, has served as master of a home-trade passenger ship, shall be entitled to a certificate of service as master for home-trade passenger ships:

(4). Every person who before the first day of January, one thousand eight hundred and fifty-four, has served as mate of a home-trade passenger ship, shall be entitled to a certificate of service as mate for home-trade passenger ships:

And each of such certificates of service shall contain particulars of the name, place, and time of birth, and of the length and nature of the previous service of the person to whom the same is delivered; and the board of trade shall deliver such certificates of service to the various persons so respectively entitled thereto, upon their proving themselves to have attained such rank or to have served as aforesaid, and upon their giving a full and satisfactory account of the particulars aforesaid.

CXXXVI. No foreign-going ship or home-trade passenger ship shall go to sea from any port in the United Kingdom unless the master thereof, and in the case of a foreign-going ship the first and second mates or only mate (as the case may be), and in the case of a home-trade passenger ship the first or only mate (as the case may be), have obtained and possess valid certificates either of competency or service appropriate to their several stations in such ship, or of a higher grade; and no such ship, if of one hundred tons burden or upwards, shall go to sea as aforesaid, unless at least one officer besides the master has obtained and possesses a valid certificate appropriate to the grade of only mate therein or to a higher grade; and every person who, having been engaged to serve as master or as first or second or only mate of any foreign-going ship, or as master or first or only mate of a home-trade passenger ship, goes to sea as aforesaid as such master or mate without being at the time entitled to and possessed of such a certificate as hereinbefore required, or who employs any person as master or first, second or only mate of any foreign-going ship, or as master or first or only mate of a home-trade passenger ship, without ascertaining that he is at the time entitled to and possessed of such certificate, shall for each such offence incur a penalty not exceeding fifty pounds.

CXXXVII. Every certificate of competency for a foreign-going ship shall be deemed to be of a higher grade than the corresponding certificate for a home-trade passenger ship, and shall entitle the lawful holder thereof to go to sea in the corresponding grade in such last-mentioned ship; but no certificate for a home-trade passenger ship shall entitle the holder to go to sea as master or mate of a foreign-going ship.

CXXXVIII. All certificates, whether of competency or service, shall be made in duplicate, and one part shall be delivered to the person entitled to the certificate, and the other shall be kept and recorded by the registrar-general of seamen or by such other person as the board of trade appoints for that purpose; and the board of trade shall give to such registrar or such other person immediate notice of all orders made by it for cancelling, suspending, altering, or otherwise affecting any certificate in pursuance of the powers herein contained; and the registrar or such other person as aforesaid shall thereupon make a corresponding entry in the record of certificates; and a copy purporting to be certified by such registrar or his assistant or by such person as aforesaid of any certificate shall be primâ facie evidence of such certificate, and a copy purporting to be so certified as aforesaid of any entry made as aforesaid in respect of any certificate shall be primâ facie evidence of the truth of the matters stated in such entry.

CXXXIX. Whenever any master or mate proves to the satisfaction of the board of trade that he has, without fault on his part, lost or been deprived of any certificate already granted to him, the board of trade shall, upon payment of such fee (if any) as it directs, cause a copy of the certificate to which by the record so kept as aforesaid he appears to be entitled, to be made out and certified as aforesaid, and to be delivered to him; and any

*Side notes:*

III. *Certificates of Masters and Mates.*

certificates of service for home-trade passenger ships to be delivered to persons who have served as masters or mates in such ships before 1st January, 1854.

No foreign-going ship or home-trade passenger ship to proceed to sea without certificates of the master and mates.

Certificates for foreign-going ships available for home-trade passenger ships.

The registrar to record grants, cancellations, &c., of certificates.

Duplicates and entries to be evidence.

In case of loss a copy to be granted.

copy which purports to be so made and certified as aforesaid shall have all the effect of the original.

CXL. Every person who makes, or procures to be made, or assists in making any false representation for the purpose of obtaining for himself or for any other person a certificate either of competency or service, or who forges, assists in forging, or procures to be forged, or fraudulently alters, assists in fraudulently altering, or procures to be fraudulently altered, any such certificate or any official copy of any such certificate, or who fraudulently makes use of any such certificate or any copy of any such certificate which is forged, altered, cancelled, suspended, or to which he is not justly entitled, or who fraudulently lends his certificate to or allows the same to be used by any other person, shall for each offence be deemed guilty of a misdemeanor.

## Apprenticeships to the Sea Service.

CXLI. All shipping masters appointed under this Act shall, if applied to for the purpose, give to any board of guardians, overseers, or other persons desirous of apprenticing boys to the sea service, and to masters and owners of ships requiring apprentices, such assistance as is in their power for facilitating the making of such apprenticeships, and may receive from persons availing themselves of such assistance such fees as may be determined in that behalf by the board of trade, with the concurrence, so far as relates to pauper apprentices in England, of the poor law board in England, and so far as relates to pauper apprentices in Ireland, of the poor law commissioners in Ireland.

CXLII. In the case of every boy bound apprentice to the sea service by any guardians or overseers of the poor, or other persons having the authority of guardians of the poor, the indentures shall be executed by the boy and the person to whom he is bound in the presence of and shall be attested by two justices of the peace, who shall ascertain that the boy has consented to be bound, and has attained the age of twelve years, and is of sufficient health and strength, and that the master to whom the boy is to be bound is a proper person for the purpose.

CXLIII. All indentures of apprenticeship to the sea service shall be exempt from stamp duty ; and all such indentures shall be in duplicate : and every person to whom any boy whatever is bound as an apprentice to the sea service in the United Kingdom shall within seven days after the execution of the indentures take or transmit the same to the registrar-general of seamen or to some shipping master; and the said registrar or shipping master shall retain and record one copy, and shall indorse on the other that the same has been recorded, and shall re-deliver the same to the master of the apprentice; and whenever any such indenture is assigned or cancelled, and whenever any such apprentice dies or deserts, the master of the apprentice shall, within seven days after such assignment, cancellation, death, or desertion, if the same happens within the United Kingdom, or if the same happens elsewhere, so soon afterwards as circumstances permit, notify the same either to the said registrar of seamen, or to some shipping master, to be recorded ; and every person who fails to comply with the provisions of this section shall incur a penalty not exceeding ten pounds.

CXLIV. Subject to the provisions hereinbefore contained, all apprenticeships to the sea service made by any guardians or overseers of the poor, or persons having the authority of guardians of the poor, shall, if made in Great Britain, be made in the same manner and be subject to the same laws and regulations as other apprenticeships made by the same persons, and if made in Ireland shall be subject to the following rules ; (that is to say,)

   (1). In every union the guardians of the poor, or other persons duly appointed to carry into execution the Acts for the relief of the destitute poor and having the authority of guardians of the poor, may put out and bind as an apprentice to the sea service any boy who or whose parent or parents is or are receiving relief in such union, and who has attained the age of twelve years, and is of sufficient health and strength, and who consents to be so bound :

   (2). If the cost of relieving any such boy is chargeable to an electoral division of a union, then (except in cases in which paid officers act in place of guardians) he shall not be bound as aforesaid unless the consent in writing of the guardians of such electoral division or of a majority of the guardians (if more than one) be first obtained, such consent to be, when possible, indorsed upon the indentures : *III. Apprenticeships to Sea Service.*

(3). The expense incurred in the binding and outfit of any such apprentice shall be charged to the union or electoral division (as the case may be) to which the boy or his parent or parents is or are chargeable at the time of his being apprenticed :

(4). All indentures made in any union may be sued upon by the guardians of the union or persons having the authority of guardians therein for the time being, by their name of office, and actions brought by them upon such indentures shall not abate by reason of death or change in the persons holding the office ; but no such action shall be commenced without the consent of the Irish poor law commissioners :

(5). The amount of the costs incurred in any such action and not recovered from the defendant therein, may be charged upon the union or electoral division (as the case may be) to which the boy or his parent or parents was or were chargeable at the time of his being apprenticed.

CXLV. The master of every foreign-going ship shall, before carrying any apprentice to sea from any place in the United Kingdom, cause such apprentice to appear before the shipping master before whom the crew is engaged, and shall produce to him the indenture by which such apprentice is bound, and the assignment or assignments thereof (if any) ; and the name of such apprentice, with the date of the indenture and of the assignment or assignments thereof (if any), and the name of the port or ports at which the same have been registered, shall be entered on the agreement ; and for any default in obeying the provisions of this section the master shall for each offence incur a penalty not exceeding five pounds. *Apprentices and their indentures to be brought before shipping master before each voyage, in a foreign-going ship.*

## Engagement of Seamen.

*Engagement of Seamen.*

CXLVI. The board of trade may grant to such persons as it thinks fit licences to engage or supply seamen or apprentices for merchant ships in the United Kingdom, to continue for such periods, to be upon such terms, and to be revocable upon such conditions, as such board thinks proper. *Board of trade may license persons to procure seamen.*

CXLVII. The following offences shall be punishable as hereinafter mentioned ; (that is to say,) *Penalties :*

(1). If any person not licensed as aforesaid, other than the owner or master or a mate of the ship, or some person who is bonâ fide the servant and in the constant employ of the owner, or a shipping master duly appointed as aforesaid, engages or supplies any seaman or apprentice to be entered on board any ship in the United Kingdom, he shall for each seaman or apprentice so engaged or supplied incur a penalty not exceeding twenty pounds : *for supplying seamen without licence ;*

(2). If any person employs any unlicensed person other than persons so excepted as aforesaid, for the purpose of engaging or supplying any seaman or apprentice to be entered on board any ship in the United Kingdom, he shall for each seaman or apprentice so engaged or supplied incur a penalty not exceeding twenty pounds, and if licensed shall in addition forfeit his licence : *for employing unlicensed persons ;*

(3). If any person knowingly receives or accepts to be entered on board any ship any seaman or apprentice who has been engaged or supplied contrary to the provisions of this Act, he shall for every seaman or apprentice so engaged or supplied incur a penalty not exceeding twenty pounds. *for receiving seamen illegally supplied.*

CXLVIII. If any person demands or receives either directly or indirectly, from any seaman or apprentice, or from any person seeking employment as a seaman or apprentice, or from any person on his behalf, any remuneration whatever, other than the fees hereby authorised, for providing him with employment, he shall for every such offence incur a penalty not exceeding five pounds. *Penalty for receiving remuneration from seamen for shipping them.*

III. *Engagement of Seamen.*

Agreements to be made with seamen, containing certain particulars.

CXLIX. The master of every ship, except ships of less than eighty tons registered tonnage exclusively employed in trading between different ports on the coasts of the United Kingdom, shall enter into an agreement with every seaman whom he carries to sea from any port in the United Kingdom, as one of his crew in the manner hereinafter mentioned; and every such agreement shall be in a form sanctioned by the board of trade, and shall be dated at the time of the first signature thereof, and shall be signed by the master before any seaman signs the same, and shall contain the following particulars as terms thereof : (that is to say,)

(1). The nature and, as far as practicable, the duration of the intended voyage or engagement (*m*) :

(2). The number and description of the crew, specifying how many are engaged as sailors :

(3). The time at which each seaman is to be on board or to begin work :

(4). The capacity in which each seaman is to serve ;

(5). The amount of wages which each seaman is to receive :

(6). A scale of the provisions which are to be furnished to each seaman :

(7). Any regulations as to conduct on board, and as to fines, short allowance of provisions, or other lawful punishments for misconduct, which have been sanctioned by the board of trade as regulations proper to be adopted, and which the parties agree to adopt :

And every such agreement shall be so framed as to admit of stipulations to be adopted at the will of the master and seaman in each case, as to advance and allotment of wages (*n*), and may contain any other stipulations which are

Proviso as to forms for colonial ships.

not contrary to law : Provided, that if the master of any ship belonging to any British possession has an agreement with his crew made in due form according to the law of the possession to which such ship belongs, or in which her crew were engaged, and engages single seamen in the United Kingdom, such seamen may sign the agreement so made, and it shall not be necessary for them to sign an agreement in the form sanctioned by the board of trade.

For foreign-going ships such agreements, when made in the U. K., except in special cases, to be made before and attested by a shipping master;

CL. In the case of all foreign-going ships, in whatever part of her Majesty's dominions the same are registered, the following rules shall be observed with respect to agreements ; (that is to say,)

(1). Every agreement made in the United Kingdom (except in such cases of agreements with substitutes as are hereinafter specially provided for) shall be signed by each seaman in the presence of a shipping master :

(2). Such shipping master shall cause the agreement to be read over and explained to each seaman, or otherwise ascertain that each seaman understands the same before he signs it, and shall attest each signature :

to be in duplicate;

(3). When the crew is first engaged the agreement shall be signed in duplicate, and one part shall be retained by the shipping master, and the other part shall contain a special place or form for the descriptions and signatures of substitutes or persons engaged subsequently to the first departure of the ship, and shall be delivered to the master :

provision for substitutes.

(4). In the case of substitutes engaged in the place of seamen who have duly signed the agreement, and whose services are lost within twenty-four hours of the ship's putting to sea by death, desertion, or other unforeseen cause, the engagement shall, when practicable, be made before some shipping master duly appointed in the manner hereinbefore specified ; and whenever such last-mentioned engagement cannot be so made, the master shall, before the ship puts to sea, if practicable, and if not, as soon afterwards as possible, cause the agreement to be read over and explained to the seamen; and the seamen shall thereupon sign the same in the presence of a witness, who shall attest their signatures :

Foreign-going ships making short voyages

CLI. In the case of foreign-going ships making voyages averaging less than six months in duration, running agreements with the crew may be made to extend over two or more voyages, so that no such agreement

(*m*) See 36 & 37 Vict. c. 85, s. 7, *infra,*
as to agreements with fishermen.

(*n*) See 52 & 53 Vict. c. 46, s. 2.

shall extend beyond the next following thirtieth day of June or thirty-first day of December or the first arrival of the ship at her port of destination in the United Kingdom after such date, or the discharge of cargo consequent upon such arrival; and every person entering into such agreement, whether engaged upon the first commencement thereof or otherwise, shall enter into and sign the same in the manner hereby required for other foreign-going ships; and every person engaged thereunder, if discharged in the United Kingdom, shall be discharged in the manner hereby required for the discharge of seamen belonging to other foreign-going ships.

*III. Engagement of Seamen.* may have running agreements.

CLII. The master of every foreign-going ship for which such a running agreement as aforesaid is made shall, upon every return to any port in the United Kingdom before the final termination of the agreement, discharge or engage before the shipping master at such port any seaman whom he is required by law so to discharge or engage, and shall upon every such return indorse on the agreement a statement (as the case may be) either that no such discharges or engagements have been made or are intended to be made before the ship again leaves port, or that all such discharges or engagements have been duly made as hereinbefore required, and shall deliver the agreement so indorsed to the shipping master; and any master who wilfully makes a false statement in such indorsement shall incur a penalty not exceeding twenty pounds; and the shipping master shall also sign an indorsement on the agreement to the effect that the provisions of this Act relating to such agreement have been complied with, and shall re-deliver the agreement so indorsed to the master.

Engagement and discharge of seamen in the meantime.

CLIII. In cases in which such running agreements are made, the duplicate agreement retained by the shipping master upon the first engagement of the crew shall either be transmitted to the registrar-general of seamen immediately, or be kept by the shipping master until the expiration of the agreement, as the board of trade directs.

Duplicates of running agreements, how to be dealt with.

CLIV. For the purpose of determining the fees to be paid upon the engagement and discharge of seamen belonging to foreign-going ships which have running agreements as aforesaid, the crew shall be considered to be engaged when the agreement is first signed, and to be discharged when the agreement finally terminates, and all intermediate engagements and discharges shall be considered to be engagements and discharges of single seamen.

Fees to be paid on such running agreements.

CLV. In the case of home-trade ships, crews or single seamen may, if the master thinks fit, be engaged before a shipping master in the manner hereinbefore directed with respect to foreign-going ships; and in every case in which the engagement is not so made, the master shall, before the ship puts to sea, if practicable, and if not, as soon afterwards as possible, cause the agreement to be read over and explained to each seaman, and the seaman shall thereupon sign the same in the presence of a witness who shall attest his signature.

In home-trade ships agreement to be entered into before a shipping master or other witness.

CLVI. In cases where several home-trade ships belong to the same owner, the agreement with the seamen may, notwithstanding anything herein contained, be made by the owner instead of by the master, and the seamen may be engaged to serve in any two or more of such ships, provided that the names of the ships and the nature of the service are specified in the agreement; but with the foregoing exception all provisions herein contained which relate to ordinary agreements for home-trade ships shall be applicable to agreements made in pursuance of this section.

Special agreements for home-trade ships belonging to same owners.

CLVII. If in any case a master carries any seaman to sea without entering into an agreement with him in the form and manner and at the place and time hereby in such case required, the master in the case of a foreign-going ship, and the master or owner in the case of a home-trade ship, shall for each such offence incur a penalty not exceeding five pounds.

Penalty for shipping seamen without agreement duly executed.

CLVIII. The master of every foreign-going ship of which the crew has been engaged before a shipping master shall before finally leaving the United Kingdom sign and send to the nearest shipping master a full and accurate statement in a form sanctioned by the board of trade of every change which takes place in his crew before finally leaving the United Kingdom, and in default shall for each offence incur a penalty not exceeding five pounds; and such statement shall be admissible in evidence, subject to all just exceptions.

Changes in crew to be reported.

III. *Engagement of Seamen.*

Seamen engaged in the colonies to be shipped before some shipping master or officer of customs.

CLIX. Every master of a ship who, if such ship be registered in the United Kingdom, engages any seaman in any British possession, or if such ship belongs to any British possession engages any seaman in any British possession other than that to which the ship belongs, shall, if there is at the place where such seaman is engaged any official shipping master or other officer duly appointed for the purpose of shipping seamen, engage such seaman before such shipping master, and if there is no such shipping master or officer, then before some officer of customs; and the same rules, qualifications, and penalties as are hereinbefore specified with respect to the engagement of seamen before shipping masters in the United Kingdom shall apply to such engagements in a British possession; and upon every such engagement such shipping master or officer as aforesaid shall indorse upon the agreement an attestation to the effect that the same has been signed in his presence, and otherwise made as hereby required; and if in any case such attestation is not made, the burden of proving that the seaman was duly engaged as hereby required shall lie upon the master.

Seamen engaged in foreign port to be shipped with the sanction and in the presence of the consul.

CLX. Every master of a British ship who engages any seaman at any place out of Her Majesty's dominions in which there is a British consular officer shall, before carrying such seaman to sea, procure the sanction of such officer, and shall engage such seaman before such officer; and the same rules as are hereinbefore contained with respect to the engagement of seamen before shipping masters in the United Kingdom shall apply to such engagements made before consular officers; and upon every such engagement the consular officer shall indorse upon the agreement his sanction thereof, and an attestation to the effect that the same has been signed in his presence, and otherwise made, as hereby required; and every master who engages any seaman in any place in which there is a consular officer, otherwise than as hereinbefore required, shall incur a penalty not exceeding twenty pounds; and if in any case the indorsement and attestation hereby required is not made upon the agreement, the burden of proving the engagement to have been made as hereinbefore required shall lie upon the master.

Rules as to production of agreements and certificates of masters and mates of foreign-going ships.

CLXI. The following rules shall be observed with respect to the production of agreements and certificates of competency or service for foreign-going ships; (that is to say,)

(1). The master of every foreign-going ship shall, on signing the agreement with his crew, produce to the shipping master before whom the same is signed the certificates of competency or service which the said master and his first and second mate or only mate, as the case may be, are hereby required to possess; and upon such production being duly made, and the agreement being duly executed as hereby required, the shipping master shall sign and give to the master a certificate to that effect:

(2). In the case of running agreements for foreign-going ships the shipping master shall, before the second and every subsequent voyage made after the first commencement of the agreement, sign and give to the master, on his complying with the provisions herein contained with respect to such agreements, and producing to the shipping master the certificate of competency or service of any first, second, or only mate then first engaged by him, a certificate to that effect:

(3). The master of every foreign-going ship shall, before proceeding to sea, produce the certificate so to be given to him by the shipping master as aforesaid, to the collector or comptroller of customs, and no officer of customs shall clear any such ship outwards without such production; and if any such ship attempts to go to sea without a clearance, any such officer may detain her until such certificate as aforesaid is produced:

(4). The master of every foreign-going ship shall, within forty-eight hours after the ship's arrival at her final port of destination in the United Kingdom, or upon the discharge of the crew, whichever first happens, deliver such agreement to a shipping master at the place; and such shipping master shall thereupon give to the master a certificate of such delivery; and no officer of customs shall clear any foreign-going ship inwards without the production of such certificate:

And if the master of any foreign-going ship fails to deliver the agreement to a shipping master at the time and in the manner hereby directed, he shall for every default incur a penalty not exceeding five pounds.

CLXII. The following rules shall be observed with respect to the production of agreements and certificates or competency of service for home-trade ships ; (that is to say,)

III. *Engagement of Seamen.*

Rules as to production of agreements and certificates for home-trade ships.

  (1). In the case of home-trade ships of more than eighty tons burden, no agreement shall extend beyond the next following thirtieth day of June or thirty-first day of December, or the first arrival of the ship at her final port of destination in the United Kingdom after such date, or the discharge of cargo consequent upon such arrival (*n*).

  (2). The master or owner of every such ship shall, within twenty-one days after the thirtieth day of June and the thirty-first day of December in every year, transmit or deliver to some shipping master in the United Kingdom every agreement made within the six calendar months next preceding such days respectively, and shall also in the case of home-trade passenger ships produce to the shipping master the certificates of competency or service which the said master, and his first or only mate, as the case may be, are hereby required to possess :

  (3). The shipping master shall thereupon give to the master or owner a certificate of such delivery and production ; and no officer of customs shall grant a clearance or transire for any such ship as last aforesaid without the production of such certificate ; and if any such ship attempts to ply or go to sea without such clearance or transire, any such officer may detain her until the said certificate is produced :

And if the agreement for any home-trade ship is not delivered or transmitted by the master or owner to a shipping master at the time and in the manner hereby directed, such master or owner shall for every default incur a penalty not exceeding five pounds.

CLXIII. Every erasure, interlineation, or alteration in any such agreement with seamen as is required by the Third Part of this Act (except additions so made as hereinbefore directed for shipping substitutes or persons engaged subsequently to the first departure of the ship) shall be wholly inoperative, unless proved to have been made with the consent of all the persons interested in such erasure, interlineation, or alteration by the written attestation (if made in Her Majesty's dominions) of some shipping master, justice, officer of customs, or other public functionary, or (if made out of Her Majesty's dominions) of a British consular officer, or, where there is no such officer, of two respectable British merchants.

CLXIV. Every person who fraudulently alters, assists in fraudulently altering, or procures to be fraudulently altered, or makes, or assists in making, or procures to be made, any false entry in, or delivers, assists in delivering, or procures to be delivered, a false copy of any agreement, shall for each such offence be deemed guilty of a misdemeanor.

CLXV. Any seaman may bring forward evidence to prove the contents of any agreement or otherwise to support his case, without producing or giving notice to produce the agreement or any copy thereof.

CLXVI. The master shall at the commencement of every voyage or engagement cause a legible copy of the agreement (omitting the signatures) to be placed or posted up in such part of the ship, as to be accessible of the crew, and in default shall for each offence incur a penalty not exceeding five pounds.

CLXVII. Any seaman who has signed an agreement, and is afterwards discharged before the commencement of the voyage, or before one month's wages are earned, without fault on his part justifying such discharge, and without his consent, shall be entitled to receive from the master or owner, in addition to any wages he may have earned, due compensation for the damage thereby caused to him, not exceeding one month's wages, and may, on adducing such evidence as the court hearing the case deems satisfactory of his having been so improperly discharged as aforesaid, recover such compensation as if it were wages duly earned.

(*n*) 35 & 36 Vict. c. 73, s. 16, *infra.*

III. *Allotment of Wages.*

## Allotment of Wages.

Regulations as to allotment notes.

CLXVIII. All stipulations for the allotment of any part of the wages of a seaman during his absence which are made at the commencement of the voyage shall be inserted in the agreement, and shall state the amounts and times of the payments to be made; and all allotment notes shall be in forms sanctioned by the board of trade.

Allotment notes may be sued on summarily by certain persons and under certain conditions (*o*).

CLXIX. The wife, or the father or mother, or the grandfather or grandmother, or any child or grandchild, or any brother or sister of any seaman in whose favour an allotment note of part of the wages of such seaman is made, may, unless the seaman is shown in manner hereinafter mentioned to have forfeited or ceased to be entitled to the wages out of which the allotment is to be paid, and subject, as to the wife, to the provision hereinafter contained, sue for and recover the sums allotted by the note when and as the same are made payable, with costs, from the owner or any agent who has authorized the drawing of the note, either in the county court or in the summary manner in which seamen are by this Act enabled to sue for and recover wages not exceeding fifty pounds; and in any such proceeding it shall be sufficient for the claimant to prove that he or she is the person mentioned in the note, and that the note was given by the owner or by the master or some other authorized agent; and the seaman shall be presumed to be duly earning his wages, unless the contrary is shown to the satisfaction of the court, either by the official statement of the change in the crew caused by his absence made and signed by the master, as by this Act is required, or by a duly certified copy of some entry in the official log book to the effect that he has left the ship, or by a credible letter from the master of the ship to the same effect, or by such other evidence, of whatever description, as the court in its absolute discretion considers sufficient to show satisfactorily that the seaman has ceased to be entitled to the wages out of which the allotment is to be paid: Provided that the wife of any seaman who deserts her children, or so misconducts herself as to be undeserving of support from her husband, shall thereupon forfeit all right to further payments of any allotment of his wages which has been made in her favour.

*Discharge and Payment of Wages.*

## Discharge and Payment of Wages.

Discharge from foreign-going ships to be made before shipping master.

CLXX. In the case of all British foreign-going ships, in whatever part of her Majesty's dominions the same are registered, all seamen discharged in the United Kingdom shall be discharged and receive their wages in the presence of a shipping master duly appointed under this Act, except in cases where some competent court otherwise directs; and any master or owner of any such ship who discharges any seaman belonging thereto, or, except as aforesaid, pays his wages within the United Kingdom in any other manner, shall incur a penalty not exceeding ten pounds; and in the case of home-trade ships seamen may, if the owner or master so desires, be discharged and receive their wages in like manner.

Master to deliver account of wages.

CLXXI. Every master shall, not less than twenty-four hours before paying off or discharging any seaman, deliver to him, or if he is to be discharged before a shipping master, to such shipping master (*p*), a full and true account in a form sanctioned by the board of trade of his wages and of all deductions to be made therefrom on any account whatever, and in default shall for each offence incur a penalty not exceeding five pounds; and no deduction from the wages of any seaman (except in respect of any matter happening after such delivery) shall be allowed unless it is included in the account so delivered; and the master shall during the voyage enter the various matters in respect of which such deductions are made, with the amounts of the respective deductions as they occur, in a book to be kept for that purpose, and shall, if required, produce such book at the time of the payment of wages, and also upon the hearing before any competent authority of any complaint or question relating to such payments.

On discharge, masters to give seamen certificates of discharge, and re-

CLXXII. Upon the discharge of any seaman, or upon payment of his wages, the master shall sign and give him a certificate of his discharge, in a form sanctioned by the board of trade, specifying the period of his service and the time and place of his discharge; and if any master fails to

(*o*) See 43 & 44 Vict. c. 16, ss. 2, 3, *infra*.          (*p*) See 43 & 44 Vict. c. 16, s. 4 (2), *infra*.

sign and give to any such seaman such certificate of discharge he shall for each such offence incur a penalty not exceeding ten pounds; and the master shall also, upon the discharge of every certificated mate whose certificate of competency or service has been delivered to and retained by him, return such certificate, and shall in default incur a penalty not exceeding twenty pounds.

*III. Discharge and Payment of Wages.*

turn certificates of competency or service to mates.

CLXXIII. Every shipping master shall hear and decide any question whatever between a master or owner and any of his crew which both parties agree in writing to submit to him: and every award so made by him shall be binding on both parties, and shall in any legal proceeding which may be taken in the matter before any court of justice be deemed to be conclusive as to the right of the parties; and no such submission or award shall require a stamp; and any document purporting to be such submission or award shall be primâ facie evidence thereof.

Shipping master may decide questions which parties refer to him.

CLXXIV. In any proceeding relating to the wages, claims, or discharge of any seaman carried on before any shipping master under the provisions of this Act, such shipping master may call upon the owner or his agent, or upon the master or any mate or other member of the crew, to produce any log books, papers, or other documents in their respective possession or power relating to any matter in question in such proceeding, and may call before him and examine any of such persons being then at or near the place on any such matter; and every owner, agent, master, mate, or other member of the crew who when called upon by the shipping master does not produce any such paper or document as aforesaid, if in his possession or power, or does not appear and give evidence, shall, unless he shows some reasonable excuse for such default for each such offence incur a penalty not exceeding five pounds.

Master and others to produce ship's papers to shipping masters, and give evidence.

CLXXV. The following rules shall be observed with respect to the settlement of wages (*q*); (that is to say,)

Settlement of wages.

(1). Upon the completion before a shipping master of any discharge and settlement, the master or owner and each seaman shall respectively in the presence of the shipping master sign in a form sanctioned by the board of trade a mutual release of all claims in respect of the past voyage or engagement, and the shipping master shall also sign and attest it, and shall retain and transmit it as herein directed:

Release to be signed before and attested by the shipping master;

(2). Such release so signed and attested shall operate as a mutual discharge and settlement of all demands between the parties thereto in respect of the past voyage or engagement:

to be discharge;

(3). A copy of such release certified under the hand of such shipping master to be a true copy shall be given by him to any party thereto requiring the same; and such copy shall be receivable in evidence upon any future question touching such claims as aforesaid, and shall have all the effect of the original of which it purports to be a copy:

and to be evidence.

(4). In cases in which discharge and settlement before a shipping master are hereby required, no payment, receipt, settlement, or discharge otherwise made shall operate or be admitted as evidence of the release or satisfaction of any claim:

No other receipt to be a discharge.

(5). Upon any payment being made by a master before a shipping master, the shipping master shall, if required, sign and give to such master a statement of the whole amount so paid, and such statement shall as between the master and his employer be received as evidence that he has made the payments therein mentioned.

Voucher to be given to master, and to be evidence.

CLXXVI. Upon every discharge effected before a shipping master the master shall make and sign in a form sanctioned by the board of trade a report of the conduct, character, and qualifications of the persons discharged, or may state in a column to be left for that purpose in the said form that he declines to give any opinion upon such particulars or upon any of them: and the shipping master shall transmit the same to the registrar-general of seamen, or to such other person as the board of trade directs, to be recorded, and shall, if desired so to do by any seaman, give to him or indorse on his certificate of discharge a copy of so much of such report as concerns him;

Master to make reports of character.

(*q*) 43 & 44 Vict. c. 16, s. 4 (3), *infra.*

III. *Discharge and Payment of Wages.*

and every person who makes, assists in making, or procures to be made any false certificate or report of the service, qualifications, conduct, or character of any seaman, knowing the same to be false, or who forges, assists in forging, or procures to be forged, or fraudulently alters, assists in fraudulently altering, or procures to be fraudulently altered, any such certificate or report, or who fraudulently makes use of any certificate or report or of any copy of any certificate or report which is forged or altered or does not belong to him, shall for each such offence be deemed guilty of a misdemeanor.

*Remittance of Wages and Savings Banks for Seamen.*

### Remittance of Wages and Savings Banks for Seamen.

Facilities may be given for remitting seamen's wages.

CLXXVII. Facilities shall, if the board of trade so directs, be given for remitting the wages and other monies of seamen and apprentices to their relatives or other persons by means of money orders issued by shipping masters ; and the board of trade may make regulations concerning such orders, and the persons by or to whom, and the mode and time in and at which, the same are to be paid, and may from time to time repeal or alter any such regulations ; and all such regulations, so long as they are in force, shall be binding upon all persons interested or claiming to be interested in such orders, as well as upon the officers employed in issuing or paying the same ; and no legal proceeding shall be instituted against the board of trade, or against any shipping master or other public officer employed about such orders, on account of any such regulations, or on account of any act done or left undone in pursuance thereof, or on account of any refusal, neglect, or omission to pay any such money order, unless such refusal, neglect, or emission arise from fraud or wilful misbehaviour on the part of the person against whom proceedings are instituted.

Power to pay when order is lost.

CLXXVIII. The board of trade may, in any case in which it thinks fit so to do, cause the amount of any such money order as aforesaid to be paid to the person to whom or in whose favour the same may have been granted, or to his personal representatives, legatees, or next of kin, notwithstanding that such order may not be in his or their possession ; and in all such cases from and after such payment the board of trade and every shipping master or other officer of the board of trade shall be freed from all liability in respect of such order.

Penalty for issuing money orders with fraudulent intent.

CLXXIX. Every shipping master or other public officer who grants or issues any money order with a fraudulent intent shall in England or Ireland be deemed guilty of felony, and in Scotland of a high crime and offence, and shall be liable to be kept in penal servitude for a term not exceeding four years.

Savings banks for seamen may be established (*r*).

CLXXX. The commissioners for the reduction of the national debt, or the comptroller-general acting under them, may, on the application and recommendation of the board of trade, establish savings banks at such ports and places within the United Kingdom, either of the shipping offices established in such ports or elsewhere, as may appear to be expedient, and may appoint treasurers to receive from or on account of seamen, or the wives and families of seamen desirous to become depositors in such savings banks, deposits to an amount not exceeding one hundred and fifty pounds in the whole in respect of any one account, under such regulations as may be prescribed by the said commissioners or comptroller-general ; and such regulations shall be binding on all such treasurers and depositors ; and the said commissioners may remove such treasurers, and appoint others in their place ; and all the provisions of the Acts now in force relating to savings banks, except so far as relates to the annual amount of deposit, shall apply to all savings banks which may be established under the authority of this Act, and to such treasurers and depositors as aforesaid.

*Legal Rights to Wages.*

### Legal Rights to Wages.

Right to wages and provisions, when to begin.

CLXXXI. A seaman's right to wages and provisions shall be taken to commence either at the time at which he commences work or at the times specified in the agreement for his commencement of work or presence on board, whichever first happens.

(*r*) Extended to seamen in navy by 18 & 19 Vict. c. 91, s. 17, *infra.*

CLXXXII. No seaman shall by any agreement forfeit his lien upon the ship or be deprived of any remedy for the recovery of his wages to which he would otherwise have been entitled; and every stipulation in any agreement inconsistent with any provision of this Act, and every stipulation by which any seaman consents to abandon his right to wages in the case of the loss of the ship, or to abandon any right which he may have or obtain in the nature of salvage, shall be wholly inoperative (t).

III. *Legal rights to Wages.*

Seamen not to give up certain rights (s).

CLXXXIII. No right to wages shall be dependent on the earning of freight; and every seaman and apprentice who would be entitled to demand and recover any wages if the ship in which he has served had earned freight, shall, subject to all other rules of law and conditions applicable to the case, be entitled to claim and recover the same, notwithstanding that freight has not been earned: but in all cases of wreck or loss of the ship, proof that he has not exerted himself to the utmost to save the ship, cargo, and stores shall bar his claim.

Wages not to be dependent on the earning of freight.

CLXXXIV. If any seaman or apprentice to whom wages are due under the last-preceding enactment dies before the same are paid, they shall be paid and applied in the manner hereinafter specified with regard to the wages of seamen who die during a voyage.

In case of death such wages to be paid as after mentioned.

CLXXXV. In cases where the service of any seaman terminates before the period contemplated in the agreement by reason of the wreck or loss of the ship, and also in cases where such service terminates before such period as aforesaid by reason of his being left on shore at any place abroad under a certificate of his unfitness or inability to proceed on the voyage granted as hereinafter mentioned, such seaman shall be entitled to wages for the time of service prior to such termination as aforesaid, but not for any further period.

Rights to wages in case of termination of service by wreck or illness.

CLXXXVI. No seaman or apprentice shall be entitled to wages for any period during which he unlawfully refuses or neglects to work when required, whether before or after the time fixed by the agreement for his beginning work, nor, unless the court hearing the case otherwise directs, for any period during which he is lawfully imprisoned for any offence committed by him.

Wages not to accrue during refusal to work or imprisonment.

CLXXXVII. The master or owner of any ship shall pay to every seaman his wages within the respective periods following; (that is to say,) in the case of a home-trade ship within two days after the termination of the agreement or at the time when such seaman is discharged, whichever first happens; and in the case of all other ships (except ships employed in the southern whale fishery or on other voyages for which seamen by the terms of their agreement are wholly compensated by shares in the profits of the adventure) within three days after the cargo has been delivered, or within five days after the seaman's discharge, whichever first happens; and in all cases the seaman shall at the time of his discharge be entitled to be paid on account a sum equal to one-fourth part of the balance due to him; and every master or owner who neglects or refuses to make payment in manner aforesaid, without sufficient cause, shall pay to the seaman a sum not exceeding the amount of two days' pay for each of the days, not exceeding ten days, during which payment is delayed beyond the respective periods aforesaid, and such sum shall be recoverable as wages.

Period within which wages are to be paid.

### Mode of recovering Wages.

*Mode of recovering Wages.*

CLXXXVIII. Any seaman or apprentice, or any person duly authorised on his behalf, may sue in a summary manner before any two justices of the peace acting in or near to the place at which the service has terminated, or at which the seaman or apprentice has been discharged, or at which any person upon whom the claim is made is or resides, or in Scotland either before any such justices or before the sheriff of the county within which any such place is situated, for any amount of wages due to such seaman or apprentice not exceeding fifty pounds over and above the costs of any proceeding for the recovery thereof, so soon as the same becomes payable; and every order made by such justices or sheriff in the matter shall be final.

Seaman may sue for wages in a summary manner.

(s) See 25 & 26 Vict. c. 63, s. 18, *infra*.

(t) As to fishermen, see 36 & 37 Vict. c. 85, s. 8, *infra*.

III. *Mode of recovering Wages.*

Restrictions on suits for wages in superior courts.

CLXXXIX. No suit or proceeding for the recovery of wages under the sum of fifty pounds shall be instituted by or on behalf of any seaman or apprentice in any court of admiralty or vice-admiralty (*u*), or in the court of session in Scotland, or in any superior court of record in her Majesty's dominions, unless the owner of the ship is adjudged bankrupt or declared insolvent, or unless the ship is under arrest or is sold by the authority of any such court as aforesaid, or unless any justices acting under the authority of this Act refer the case to be adjudged by such court, or unless neither the owner nor master is or resides within twenty miles of the place where the seaman or apprentice is discharged or put ashore.

No seaman to sue for wages abroad, except in cases of discharge or of danger to life.

CXC. No seaman who is engaged for a voyage or engagement which is to terminate in the United Kingdom shall be entitled to sue in any court abroad for wages, unless he is discharged with such sanction as herein required and with the written consent of the master, or proves such ill-usage on the part of the master or by his authority as to warrant reasonable apprehension of danger to the life of such seaman if he were to remain on board; but if any seaman on his return to the United Kingdom proves that the master or owner has been guilty of any conduct or default which but for this enactment would have entitled the seaman to sue for wages before the termination of the voyage or engagement, he shall be entitled to recover in addition to his wages such compensation not exceeding twenty pounds as the court hearing the case thinks reasonable.

Master to have same remedies for wages as seamen.

CXCI. Every master of a ship shall, so far as the case permits, have the same rights, liens, and remedies for the recovery of his wages which by this Act or by any law or custom any seaman, not being a master, has for the recovery of his wages; and if in any proceeding in any court of admiralty or vice-admiralty touching the claim of a master to wages any right of set-off or counter claim is set up, it shall be lawful for such court to enter into and adjudicate upon all questions, and to settle all accounts then arising or outstanding and unsettled between the parties to the proceeding, and to direct payment of any balance which is found to be due.

*Relief to Seamen's Families out of Poor Rates.*

*Relief to Seamen's Families out of Poor Rates.*

Relief to seamen's families to be chargeable on a certain proportion of their wages.

CXCII. Whenever during the absence of any seaman on a voyage his wife, children, and step-children, or any of them, become or becomes chargeable to any union or parish in the United Kingdom, such union or parish shall be entitled to be reimbursed out of the wages of such seaman earned during such voyage any sums properly expended during his absence in the maintenance of his said relations, or any of them, so that such sums do not exceed the following proportions of his said wages; (that is to say,)
(1). If only one of such relations is chargeable, one half of such wages:
(2). If two or more of such relations are chargeable, two thirds of such wages. But if during the absence of the seaman any sums have been paid by the owner to or on behalf of any such relation as aforesaid, under an allotment note given by the seaman in his, her, or their favour, any such claim for reimbursement as aforesaid shall be limited to the excess (if any) of the proportion of the wages hereinbefore mentioned over the sums so paid.

Notice to be given to owner, and charge to be enforced on the return of the seaman.

CXCIII. For the purpose of obtaining such reimbursement as aforesaid, the guardians of the union or parish, where the relief of the poor is administered by guardians, and the overseers of the poor of any other parish in England, and the guardians or other persons having the authority of guardians in any union in Ireland, and the inspector of the poor in Scotland, may give to the owner of the ship in which the seaman is serving a notice in writing stating the proportion of the seaman's wages upon which it is intended to make the claim, and requiring the owner to retain such proportion in his hands for a period to be therein mentioned, not exceeding twenty-one days from the time of the seaman's return to his port of discharge, and also requiring such owner immediately on such return to give to such guardians, overseers, persons, or inspector notice in writing of such return; and such owner, after receiving such notice as aforesaid, shall be bound to retain the said proportion of wages, and to give notice of the seaman's return accordingly, and shall likewise give to the seaman notice of

(*u*) See, however, 24 Vict. c. 10, s. 10, and the County Courts (Admiralty) Jurisdiction Act, 31 & 32 Vict. c. 71, ss. 3 and 9.

the intended claim ; and the said guardians, overseers, persons, or inspector may upon the seaman's return apply in a summary way in England or Ireland to any two justices having jurisdiction in such union or parish as aforesaid, and in Scotland to the sheriff of the county, for an order for such reimbursement as aforesaid ; and such justices or sheriff may hear the case, and may make an order for such reimbursement to the whole extent aforesaid, or to such lesser amount as they or he may under the circumstances think fit, and the owner shall pay to such guardians, overseers, persons, or inspector, out of the seaman's wages, the amount so ordered to be paid by way of reimbursement, and shall pay the remainder of the said wages to the seaman ; and if no such order as aforesaid is obtained within the period mentioned in the notice so to be given to the owner as aforesaid, the proportion of wages so to be retained by him as aforesaid shall immediately on the expiration of such period, and without deduction, be payable to the seaman.

III. Relief to Seamen's Families out of Poor Rates.

Wages and Effects of deceased Seamen.

CXCIV. Whenever any seaman or apprentice belonging to or sent home in any British ship, whether a foreign-going ship or a home-trade ship, employed on a voyage which is to terminate in the United Kingdom, dies during such voyage, the master shall take charge of all money, clothes and effects which he leaves on board, and shall, if he thinks fit, cause all or any of the said clothes and effects to be sold by auction at the mast or other public auction, and shall thereupon sign an entry in the official log-book containing the following particulars ; (that is to say,)

Wages and Effects of deceased Seamen.

Masters to take charge of or sell effects of deceased seamen which are on board, and enter the same and wages due in the official log.

(1). A statement of the amount of the money, and a description of the effects so left by the deceased :

(2). In case of a sale, a description of each article sold, and the sum received for each :

(3). A statement of the sum due to the deceased as wages, and the total amount of the deductions (if any) to be made therefrom $(x)$.

And shall cause such entry to be attested by a mate and by one of the crew.

CXCV. In the cases provided for by the last preceding section the following rules shall be observed ; (that is to say,)

Such effects and wages to be paid either to consul or to shipping master, with full accounts.

(1). If the ship proceeds at once to any port in the United Kingdom without touching on the way at any foreign port, the master shall within forty-eight hours after his arrival deliver any such effects as aforesaid remaining unsold, and pay any money which he has taken charge of or received from such sale as aforesaid, and also the balance of wages due to the deceased, to the shipping master at the port of destination in the United Kingdom :

(2). If the ship touches and remains for forty-eight hours at some foreign port or at some port in her Majesty's dominions abroad before coming to any port in the United Kingdom, the master shall report the case to the British consular officer or officer of customs there, as the case may be, and shall give to such officer any information he requires as to the destination of the ship and probable length of the voyage ; and such officer may thereupon, if he considers it expedient so to do, require the said effects, money and wages to be delivered and paid to him, and shall upon such delivery and payment give to the master a receipt, and the master shall within forty-eight hours after his arrival at his port of destination in the United Kingdom produce the same to the shipping master there ; and such consular officer or officer of customs shall in such case indorse and certify upon the agreement with the crew such particulars with respect to such delivery and payment as the board of trade requires :

(3). If such officer as aforesaid does not require such payment and delivery to be made to him, the master shall take charge of the said effects, money and wages, and shall within forty-eight hours after his arrival at his port of destination in the United Kingdom deliver and pay the same to the shipping master there :

(4). The master shall in all cases in which any seaman or apprentice dies during the progress of a voyage or engagement give to the board

$(x)$ 25 & 26 Vict. c. 63, s. 21, *infra.*

III. *Wages and Effects of deceased Seamen.*

of trade, or to such officer or shipping master as aforesaid, an account in such form as they respectively require of the effects, money and wages so to be delivered and paid ; and no deductions claimed in such account shall be allowed unless verified, if there is any official log-book, by such entry therein as hereinbefore required, and also by such other vouchers (if any) as may be reasonably required by the board of trade, or by the officer or shipping master to whom the account is rendered :

(5). Upon due compliance with such of the provisions of this section as relate to acts to be done at the port of destination in the United Kingdom, the shipping master shall grant to the master a certificate to that effect, and no officer of customs shall clear inwards any foreign-going ship without the production of such certificate.

Penalties for not taking charge of, remitting, or accounting for such moneys and effects.

CXCVI. If any master fails to take such charge of the money or other effects of a seaman or apprentice dying during a voyage, or to make such entries in respect thereof, or to procure such attestation to such entries, or to make such payment or delivery of any money, wages or effects of any seaman or apprentice dying during a voyage, or to give such account in respect thereof as hereinbefore respectively directed, he shall be accountable for the money, wages and effects of the seaman or apprentice to the board of trade, and shall pay and deliver the same accordingly ; and such master shall in addition for every such offence incur a penalty not exceeding treble the value of the money or effects not accounted for, or if such value is not ascertained, not exceeding fifty pounds; and if any such money, wages or effects are not duly paid, delivered or accounted for by the master, the owner of the ship shall pay, deliver and account for the same, and such money and wages and the value of such effects shall be recoverable from him accordingly ; and if he fails to account for and pay the same, he shall, in addition to his liability for the said money and value, incur the same penalty which is hereinbefore mentioned as incurred by the master for the like offence ; and all money, wages and effects of any seaman or apprentice dying during a voyage shall be recoverable in the same courts and by the same modes of proceeding by which seamen are hereby enabled to recover wages due to them (*y*).

Officers of customs and consuls to take charge of effects left by seamen abroad, and to remit the same and their wages to board of trade.

CXCVII. If any such seaman or apprentice as last aforesaid dies abroad at any place either in or out of her Majesty's dominions leaving any money or effects not on board his ship, the chief officer of customs or the British consular officer at or nearest to the place, as the case may be, shall claim and take charge of such money and effects; and such officer shall, if he thinks fit, sell all or any of such effects, or any effects of any deceased seaman or apprentice delivered to him under the provisions hereinbefore contained ; and every such officer shall, quarterly or at such other times as the board of trade directs, remit to her Majesty's paymaster-general all moneys belonging to or arising from the sale of the effects of or paid as the wages of any deceased seaman or apprentices which have to come to his hands under the provisions hereinbefore contained, and shall render such accounts in respect thereof as the board of trade requires.

Wages and effects of seamen dying at home to be paid in certain cases to board of trade.

CXCVIII. Whenever any seaman or apprentice dies in the United Kingdom, and is at the time of his death entitled to claim from the master or owner of any ship in which he has served any unpaid wages or effects, such master or owner shall pay and deliver or account for the same to the shipping master at the port where the seaman or apprentice was discharged, or was to have been discharged, or to the board of trade, or as it directs.

If less than 50*l.* wages and property of deceased seamen may be paid over without probate or administration to the persons entitled.

CXCIX. If the money and effects of any deceased seaman or apprentice paid, delivered, or remitted to the board of trade or its agents, including the moneys received for any part of the said effects which have been sold either before delivery to the board of trade or by its direction, do not exceed in value the sum of fifty pounds, then, subject to the provisions hereinafter contained, and to all such deductions for expenses incurred in respect of the seaman or apprentice or of his said money and effects as the said board thinks proper to allow, the said board may, if it thinks fit so to do, pay and deliver the said money and effects either to any claimants who can prove themselves to the satisfaction of the said board either to be his widow or children, or to be entitled to the effects of the deceased under his will (if any), or under the statutes for the distribution of the effects of intestates, or under

(*y*) See 25 & 26 Vict. c. 63, s. 20, *infra.*

any other statute, or at common law, or to be entitled to procure probate or take out letters of administration or confirmation, although no probate or letters of administration or confirmation have been taken out, and shall be thereby discharged from all further liability in respect of the money and effects so paid and delivered, or may, if it thinks fit so to do, require probate or letters of administration or confirmation to be taken out, and thereupon pay and deliver the said money and effects to the legal personal representatives of the deceased ; and all claimants to whom such money or effects are so paid or delivered shall apply the same in due course of administration ; and if such money and effects exceed in value the sum of fifty pounds, then, subject to the provisions hereinafter contained and to deduction for expenses, the board of trade shall pay and deliver the same to the legal personal representatives of the deceased.

CC. In cases where the deceased seaman or apprentice has left a will, the board of trade shall have the following powers ; (that is to say,)

(1.) It may in its discretion refuse to pay or deliver any such wages or effects as aforesaid to any person claiming to be entitled thereto under a will made on board ship unless such will is in writing, and is signed or acknowledged by the testator in the presence of the master or first or only mate of the ship, and is attested by such master or mate :

(2.) It may in its discretion refuse to pay or deliver any such wages or effects as aforesaid to any person not being related to the testator by blood or marriage who claims to be entitled thereto under a will made elsewhere than on board ship, unless such will is in writing, and is signed or acknowledged by the testator in the presence of two witnesses, one of whom is some shipping master appointed under this Act, or some minister or officiating minister or curate of the place in which the same is made, or in a place where there are no such persons, some justice of the peace, or some British consular officer, or some officer of customs, and is attested by such witnesses :

Whenever any claim made under a will is rejected by the board of trade on account of the said will not being made and attested as hereinbefore required, the wages and effects of the deceased shall be dealt with as if no will had been made.

CCI. The following rules shall be observed with respect to creditors of deceased seamen and apprentices ; (that is to say,)

(1.) No such creditor shall be entitled to claim from the board of trade the wages or effects of any such seaman or apprentice or any part thereof by virtue of letters of administration taken out by him, or by virtue of confirmation in Scotland as executor creditor :

(2.) No such creditor shall be entitled by any means whatever to payment of his debt out of such wages and effects, if the debt accrued more than three years before the death of the deceased, or if the demand is not made within two years after such death :

(3.) Subject as aforesaid, the steps to be taken for procuring payment of such debts shall be as follows; (that is to say,) Every person making a demand as creditor shall deliver to the board of trade an account in writing in such form as it requires, subscribed with his name, stating the particulars of his demand and the place of his abode, and verified by his declaration made before a justice :

(4.) If before such demand is made any claim to the wages and effects of the deceased made by any person interested therein as his widow or child, or under a will or under the statutes for the distribution of the effects of intestates, or under any other statute, or at common law, has been allowed, the board of trade shall give notice to the creditor of the allowance of such person's claim, and the creditor shall thereupon have the same rights and remedies against such person as if he or she had received the said wages and effects as the legal personal representative of the deceased :

(5.) If no claim by any such person has been allowed, the board of trade shall proceed to investigate the creditor's account, and may for that purpose require him to prove the same, and to produce all books, accounts, vouchers and papers relating thereto ; and if by such means the creditor duly satisfies the board of trade of the justice of

III. *Wages and Effects of deceased Seamen.*

the demand, either in the whole or in part, the same shall be allowed and paid accordingly, so far as the assets in the hands of the board of trade will extend for that purpose, and such payment shall discharge the board of trade from all further liability in respect of the money so paid ; but if such board is not so satisfied, or if such books, accounts, vouchers or papers as aforesaid are not produced, and no sufficient reason is assigned for not producing them, the demand shall be disallowed :

(6.) In any case whatever the board of trade may delay the investigation of any demand made by a creditor for the payment of his debt for one year from the time of the first delivery of the demand ; and if in the course of that time a claim to the wages and effects of the deceased is made and substantiated as hereinbefore required by any person interested therein as a widow or child, or under a will, or under the statutes for the distribution of the effects of intestates, or under any other statute, or at common law, the board of trade may pay and deliver the same to such person ; and thereupon the creditor shall have the same rights and remedies against such persons as if he or she had received the same as the legal personal representative of the deceased.

Mode of dealing with unclaimed wages of deceased seamen.

CCII. In cases of wages or effects of deceased seamen or apprentices received by the board of trade to which no claim is substantiated within six years after the receipt thereof by such board, it shall be in the absolute discretion of such board, if any subsequent claim is made, either to allow or to refuse the same ; [and, subject to the provision hereinafter contained, the board of trade shall from time to time pay any moneys arising from the unclaimed wages and effects of deceased seamen, which in the opinion of such board it is not necessary to retain for the purpose of satisfying claims, into the receipt of her Majesty's Exchequer in such manner as the Treasury directs, and such moneys shall be carried to and form part of the consolidated fund of the United Kingdom (z)].

Punishment for forgery and false representations in order to obtain wages and property of deceased seamen.

CCIII. Every person who, for the purpose of obtaining, either for himself or for another, any money or effects of any deceased seaman or apprentice, forges, assists in forging, or procures to be forged, or fraudulently alters, assists in fraudulently altering, or procures to be fraudulently altered, any document purporting to show or assist in showing a right to such wages or effects, and every person who for the purpose aforesaid makes use of any such forged or altered document as aforesaid, or who for the purpose aforesaid gives or makes or procures to be given or made, or assists in giving or making or procuring to be given or made, any false evidence or representation, knowing the same to be false, shall be punishable with penal servitude for a term not exceeding four years, or with imprisonment with or without hard labour for any period not exceeding two years, or if summarily prosecuted and convicted by imprisonment, with or without hard labour, for any period not exceeding six months.

Effects of seamen discharged from navy to be disposed of by accountant-general of navy.

CCIV. In the case of seamen invalided or discharged from any of her Majesty's ships, and sent home in merchant ships, any moneys or effects belonging to them which are paid, remitted or delivered to. the board of trade, or its agents, under the provisions hereinbefore contained, shall be paid over and disposed of in such manner as the accountant-general of her Majesty's navy directs.

*Leaving Seamen abroad.*

## Leaving Seamen abroad.

On discharge of seamen abroad, by sale of ship or otherwise, certificates of discharge to be given, and seamen to be sent home at expense of owner.

CCV. Whenever any British ship is transferred or disposed of at any place out of her Majesty's dominions, and any seaman or apprentice belonging thereto does not in the presence of some British consular officer, or, if there is no such consular officer there, in the presence of one or more respectable British merchants residing at the place, and not interested in the said ship, signify his consent in writing to complete the voyage if continued, and whenever the service of any seaman or apprentice belonging to any British ship terminates at any place out of her Majesty's dominions, the master shall give to each such seaman or apprentice a certificate of discharge in the form sanctioned by the board of trade as aforesaid, and in the case of any

(z) Words within brackets repealed by 45 & 46 Vict. c. 56, s. 10.

certificated mate whose certificate he has retained shall return such certificate to him, and shall also, besides paying the wages to which such seaman or apprentice is entitled, either provide him with adequate employment on board some other British ship bound to the port in her Majesty's dominions at which he was originally shipped, or to such other port in the United Kingdom as is agreed upon by him, or furnish the means of sending him back to such port, or provide him with a passage home, or deposit with such consular officer or such merchant or merchants as aforesaid such a sum of money as is by such officer or merchants deemed sufficient to defray the expenses of his subsistence and passage home; and such consular officer or merchants shall indorse upon the agreement of the ship which the seaman or apprentice is leaving the particulars of such payment, provision or deposit; and if the master refuses or neglects to comply with the requirements of this section, such expenses as last aforesaid, if defrayed by such consular officer or by any other person, shall, unless such seaman or apprentice has been guilty of barratry, be a charge upon the ship to which such seaman or apprentice belonged and upon the owner for the time being thereof, and may be recovered against such owners, with costs, at the suit of the consular officer or other person defraying such expenses, or, in case the same has been allowed to the consular officer out of the public moneys, as a debt due to her Majesty either by ordinary process of law, or in the manner in which seamen are hereby enabled to recover wages; and such expenses, if defrayed by the seaman or apprentice, shall be recoverable as wages due to him.

*III. Leaving Seamen abroad.*

CCVI. If the master or any other person belonging to any British ship wrongfully forces on shore and leaves behind, or otherwise wilfully and wrongfully leaves behind, in any place, on shore or at sea, in or out of her Majesty's dominions, any seaman or apprentice belonging to such ship before the completion of the voyage for which such person was engaged or the return of the ship to the United Kingdom, he shall for each such offence be deemed guilty of a misdemeanor.

Forcing seamen on shore a misdemeanor.

CCVII. If the master of any British ship does any of the following things; (that is to say,)

No seamen to be discharged or left abroad without certificate of some functionary.

(1.) Discharges any seaman or apprentice in any place situate in any British possession abroad (except the possession in which he was shipped), without previously obtaining the sanction in writing indorsed on the agreement of some public shipping master or other officer duly appointed by the local government in that behalf, or (in the absence of any such functionary) of the chief officer of customs resident at or near the place where the discharge takes place:

(2.) Discharges any seaman or apprentice at any place out of her Majesty's dominions without previously obtaining the sanction so indorsed as aforesaid of the British consular officer there, or (in his absence) of two respectable merchants resident there:

(3.) Leaves behind any seaman or apprentice at any place situate in any British possession abroad on any ground whatever, without previously obtaining a certificate in writing so indorsed as aforesaid from such officer or person as aforesaid, stating the fact and the cause thereof, whether such cause be unfitness or inability to proceed to sea, or desertion or disappearance:

(4.) Leaves behind any seaman or apprentice at any place out of her Majesty's dominions, on shore or at sea, on any ground whatever, without previously obtaining the certificate indorsed in manner and to the effect last aforesaid of the British consular officer there, or (in his absence) of two respectable merchants, if there is any such at or near the place where the ship then is:

He shall for each such default be deemed guilty of a misdemeanor; and the said functionaries shall and the said merchants may examine into the grounds of such proposed discharge, or into the allegation of such unfitness, inability, desertion, or disappearance as aforesaid, in a summary way, and may for that purpose, if they think fit so to do, administer oaths, and may either grant or refuse such sanction or certificate as appears to them to be just.

CCVIII. Upon the trial of any information, indictment, or other proceeding against any person for discharging or leaving behind any seaman or apprentice contrary to the provisions of this Act, it shall lie upon such person either to produce the sanction or certificate hereby required, or to

Proof of such certificate to be upon the master.

III. *Leaving Seamen abroad.*

prove that he had obtained the same previously to having discharged or left such seaman or apprentice, or that it was impracticable for him to obtain such sanction or certificate.

Wages to be paid when seamen are left behind on ground of inability (*a*).

CCIX. Every master of any British ship who leaves any seaman or apprentice on shore at any place abroad in or out of her Majesty's dominions, under a certificate of his unfitness or inability to proceed on the voyage, shall deliver to one of the functionaries aforesaid, or (in the absence of such functionaries) to the merchants by whom such certificate is signed, or, if there be but one respectable merchant resident at such place, to him, a full and true account of the wages due to such seaman or apprentice, such account when delivered to a consular officer to be in duplicate, and shall pay the same either in money or by a bill drawn upon the owner (*a*) ; and in the case of every bill so drawn, such functionary, merchants or merchant as aforesaid, shall by indorsement certify thereon that the same is drawn for money due on account of a seaman's wages, and shall also indorse the amount for which such bill is drawn, with such further particulars in respect of the case as the board of trade requires, upon the agreement of the ship ; and every such master as aforesaid who refuses or neglects to deliver a full account of such wages, and pay the amount thereof in money or by bill, as hereinbefore required, shall for every such offence or default be liable, in addition to the payment of the wages, to a penalty not exceeding ten pounds ; and every such master who delivers a false account of such wages shall for every such offence, in addition to the payment of the wages, incur a penalty not exceeding twenty pounds.

Such wages to be treated as money due to the seamen, subject to payment of expense of their subsistence and passage home.

CCX. Every such payment as last aforesaid, whether by bill or in money, shall, if made in any British possession, be made to the seaman or apprentice himself, and, if made out of her Majesty's dominions, to the consular officer, who shall, if satisfied with the account, indorse on one of the duplicates thereof a receipt for the amount paid or bill delivered, and shall return the same to the master ; and the master shall within forty-eight hours after his return to his port of destination in the United Kingdom, deliver the same to the shipping master there ; and the consular officer shall retain the other duplicate of the said account, and shall, if the seaman or apprentice subsequently obtains employment at or otherwise quits the port, deduct out of the sum received by him as aforesaid any expenses which have been incurred by him in respect of the subsistence of the seaman or apprentice under the provisions herein contained, except such as the master or owner of the ship is hereby required to pay, and shall pay the remainder to the seaman or apprentice, and shall also deliver to him an account of the sums so received and expended on his behalf ; and shall, if the seaman or apprentice dies before his ship quits the port, deal with the same in the manner hereinafter specified in that behalf, and shall, if the seaman or apprentice is sent home at the public expense under the provisions herein contained, account for the amount received to the board of trade ; and such amount shall, after deducting any expenses which have been duly incurred in respect of such seaman or apprentice, except such as the master or owner of the ship is hereby required to pay, be dealt with as wages to which he is entitled, and shall be paid accordingly.

Distressed seamen found abroad may be relieved and sent home at the public expense (*b*).

CCXI. The governors, consular officers, and other officers of her Majesty in foreign countries shall, and in places where there are no such governors or officers, any two resident British merchants may, provide for the subsistence of all seamen or apprentices, being subjects of her Majesty, who have been shipwrecked, discharged, or left behind at any place abroad, whether from any ship employed in the merchant service or from any of her Majesty's ships, or who have been engaged by any person acting either as principal or agent to serve in any ship belonging to any foreign power or to the subject of any foreign state, and who are in distress in any place abroad, until such time as they are able to provide them with a passage home, and for that purpose shall cause such seamen or apprentices to be put on board some ship belonging to any subject of her Majesty bound to any port of the United Kingdom, or to the British possession to which they belong (as the case requires), which is in want of men to make up its complement, and in

(*a*) See 25 & 26 Vict. c. 63, s. 19, *infra.*

(*b*) See 18 & 19 Vict. c. 91, s. 16, and 25 & 26 Vict. c. 63, s. 22, *infra.*

default of any such ship shall provide them with a passage home as soon as possible in some ship belonging to a subject of her Majesty so bound as aforesaid, and shall indorse on the agreement of any ship on board of which any seaman or apprentice is so taken or sent the name of every person so sent on board thereof, with such particulars concerning the case as the board of trade requires, and shall be allowed for the subsistence of any such seaman or apprentice such sum per diem as the board of trade from time to time appoints; and the amount due in respect of such allowance shall be paid [out of any moneys applicable to the relief of distressed British seamen, and granted by Parliament for the purpose] (c), on the production of the bills of the disbursements, with the proper vouchers.

III. *Leaving Seamen abroad.*

CCXII. The master of every British ship so bound as aforesaid shall receive and afford a passage and subsistence to all seamen or apprentices whom he is required to take on board his ship under the provisions hereinbefore contained, not exceeding one for every fifty tons burden, and shall during the passage provide every such seaman or apprentice with a proper berth or sleeping place effectually protected against sea and weather; and on the production of a certificate signed by any governor, consular officer, or merchants by whose directions any such seaman or apprentice was received on board, specifying the number and names of such seamen or apprentices, and the time when each of them respectively was received on board, and on a declaration made by such person before a justice, and verified by the registrar-general of seamen, stating the number of days during which each seaman or apprentice received subsistence and was provided for as aforesaid on board his ship, and stating also the number of men and boys forming the complement of his crew; and the number of seamen and apprentices employed on board his ship during such time, and every variation (if any) of such number, such person shall be entitled to be paid out of the same moneys applicable to the relief of distressed British seamen, in respect of the subsistence and passage of every seaman or apprentice so conveyed, subsisted, and provided for by him exceeding the number (if any) wanted to make up the complement of his crew, such sum per diem as the board of trade from time to time appoints; and if any person having charge of any such ship fails or refuses to receive on board his ship, or to give a passage home, or subsistence to, or to provide for any such seaman or apprentice as aforesaid, contrary to the provisions of this Act, he shall incur a penalty not exceeding one hundred pounds for each seaman or apprentice with respect to whom he makes such default or refusal.

Masters of British ships compelled to take them (d).

CCXIII. If any seaman or apprentice belonging to any British ship is discharged or left behind at any place out of the United Kingdom, without full compliance on the part of the master with all the provisions in that behalf in this Act contained, and becomes distressed and is relieved under the provisions of this Act, or if any subject of her Majesty, after having been engaged by any person (whether acting as principal or agent) to serve in any ship belonging to any foreign power, or to the subject of any foreign power, becomes distressed and is relieved as aforesaid, the wages (if any) due to such seaman or apprentice, and all expenses incurred for his subsistence, necessary clothing, conveyance home, and burial, in case he should die abroad before reaching home, shall be a charge upon the ship, whether British or foreign, to which he so belonged as aforesaid; and the board of trade may in the name of her Majesty (besides suing for any penalties which may have been incurred) sue for and recover the said wages and expenses, with costs, either from the master of such ship as aforesaid, or from the person who is owner thereof for the time being, or, in the case of such engagement as aforesaid for service in a foreign ship, from such master or owner, or from the person by whom such engagement was so made as aforesaid; and such sums shall be recoverable either in the same manner as other debts due to her Majesty, or in the same manner and by the same form and process in which wages due to the seaman would be recoverable by him; and in any proceedings for that purpose production of the account (if any) to be furnished as hereinbefore is provided in such cases, together with proof of payment by the board of trade or by the paymaster-general of the charges incurred on account of any such seaman, apprentice, or other person, shall

Power to sue for the amount advanced for the relief of seamen left abroad.

(c) Words within brackets repealed by 45 & 46 Vict. c. 55, s. 10.

(d) See 25 & 26 Vict. c. 63, s. 22, *infra.*

3 M 2

be sufficient evidence that he was relieved, conveyed home, or buried (as the case may be) at her Majesty's expense.

## Volunteering into the Navy.

*Volunteering into the Navy.*

*Seamen allowed to leave their ships in order to enter the navy.*

CCXIV. Any seaman may leave his ship for the purpose of forthwith entering into the naval service of her Majesty, and such leaving his ship shall not be deemed a desertion therefrom, and shall not render him liable to any punishment or forfeiture whatever ; and all stipulations introduced into any agreement whereby any seaman is declared to incur any forfeiture or be exposed to any loss in case he enters into her Majesty's naval service shall be void, and every master or owner who causes any such stipulation to be so introduced shall incur a penalty not exceeding twenty pounds.

*Clothes to be delivered at once.*

*Wages to be given to the Queen's officer on account of the seamen.*

CCXV. Whenever any seaman, without having previously committed any act amounting to and treated by the master as desertion, leaves his ship in order to enter into the naval service of her Majesty and is received into such service, the master shall deliver to him his clothes and effects on board such ship, and shall pay the proportionate amount of his wages down to the time of such entry, subject to all just deductions, as follows ; (that is to say,) the master of the said ship shall pay the same to the officer authorized to receive such seaman into her Majesty's service, either in money or by bill drawn upon the owner and payable at sight to the order of the accountant-general of the navy : and the receipt of such officer shall be a discharge for the money or bill so given ; and such bill shall be exempt from stamp duty ; and if such wages are paid in money, such money shall be credited in the muster book of the ship to the account of the said seaman ; and if such wages are paid by bill, such bill shall be noted in the said muster book and shall be sent to the said accountant-general, who shall present the same or cause the same to be presented for payment, and shall credit the produce thereof to the account of the said seaman ; and such money or produce (as the case may be) shall not be paid to the said seaman until the time at which he would have been entitled to receive the same if he had remained in the service of the ship which he had so quitted as aforesaid ; and if any such bill is not duly paid when presented, the said accountant-general or the seaman on whose behalf the same is given may sue thereon or may recover the wages due by all or any of the means by which wages due to merchant seamen are recoverable ; and if upon any seaman leaving his ship in the manner and for the purpose aforesaid, the master fails to deliver his clothes and effects, or to pay his wages as hereinbefore required, he shall, in addition to his liability to pay and deliver the same, incur a penalty not exceeding twenty pounds ; provided that no officer who receives any such bill as aforesaid shall be subject to any liability in respect thereof, except for the safe custody thereof until sent to the said accountant-general as aforesaid.

*Repayment to owner of advance paid and not duly earned.*

CCXVI. If upon any seaman leaving his ship for the purpose of entering the naval service of her Majesty, the owner or master of such ship shows to the satisfaction of the Admiralty that he has paid or properly rendered himself liable to pay an advance of wages to or on account of such seaman, and that such seaman has not at the time of quitting his ship duly earned such advance by service therein, and, in the case of such liability as aforesaid, if such owner or master actually satisfies the same, it shall be lawful for the Admiralty to pay to such owner or master so much of such advance as has not been duly earned, and to deduct the sum so paid from the wages of the seaman earned or to be earned in the naval service of her Majesty.

*If new seamen are engaged instead of the original seamen, the owner may apply for repayment of any extra expense he has been put to.*

CCXVII. If, in consequence of any seaman so leaving his ship without the consent of the master or owner thereof, it becomes necessary for the safety and proper navigation of the said ship to engage a substitute or substitutes, and if the wages or other remuneration paid to such substitute or substitutes for subsequent service exceed the wages or remuneration which would have been payable to the said seaman under his agreement for similar service, the master or owner of the said ship may apply to the registrar of the High Court of Admiralty in England for a certificate authorizing the repayment of such excess ; and such application shall be in such form, and shall be accompanied by such documents, and by such statements, whether on oath or otherwise, as the judge of the said court from time to time directs.

*Application how to be decided on, and amount of*

CCXVIII. The said registrar shall, upon receiving any such application as aforesaid, give notice thereof in writing, and of the sum claimed, to the secretary to the admiralty, and shall proceed to examine the said application, and may call upon the registrar-general of seamen to produce any papers in his possession relating thereto, and may call for further evidence ; and if the whole of the claim appears to him to be just, he shall give a certificate accordingly ; but if he considers that such claim or any part thereof is not just, he shall give notice of such his opinion in writing under his hand to the person making the said application, or his attorney or agent ; and if within sixteen days from the giving of such notice such person does not leave or cause to be left at the office of the registrar of the said court a written notice demanding that the said application shall be referred to the judge of the said court, then the said registrar shall finally decide thereon, and certify accordingly ; but if such notice is left as aforesaid, then the said application shall stand referred to the said judge in his chambers, and his decision thereon shall be final, and the said registrar shall certify the same accordingly ; and the said registrar and judge respectively shall in every proceeding under this Act have full power to administer oaths, and to exercise all the ordinary powers of the court, as in any other proceeding within its jurisdiction ; and the said registrar or judge (as the case may be) may, if he think fit, allow for the costs of any proceeding under this Act any sum not exceeding five pounds for each seaman so quitting his ship as aforesaid ; and such sum shall be added to the sum allowed, and shall be certified by the said registrar accordingly.

III. *Volunteering into the Navy.*

repayment how to be ascertained.

CCXIX. Every certificate so given shall be sent by post or otherwise to the person making the application, his attorney or agent, and a copy thereof shall be sent to the accountant-general of the navy ; and such accountant-general shall, upon delivery to him of the said original certificate, together with a receipt in writing purporting to be a receipt from the master or owner making the application, pay to the person delivering the same out of the moneys applicable to the naval service of her Majesty, and granted by Parliament for the purpose, the amount mentioned in such certificate ; and such certificate and receipt shall absolutely discharge the said accountant-general and her Majesty from all liability in respect of the moneys so paid or of the said application.

Accountant-general to pay sums when ascertained.

CCXX. Every person who, in making or supporting any such application as aforesaid to the registrar of the High Court of Admiralty, forges, assists in forging or procures to be forged, or fraudulently alters, assists in fraudulently altering or procures to be fraudulently altered, any document, and every person who in making or supporting any such application presents or makes use of any such forged or altered document, or who in making or supporting any such application makes or gives, or assists in making or giving, or procures to be made or given, any false evidence or representation, knowing the same to be false, shall be deemed guilty of a misdemeanor.

Penalty for forgery and false representations in support of such application.

### *Provisions, Health and Accommodation.*

CCXXI. Any three or more of the crew of any British ship may complain to any officer in command of any of her Majesty's ships, or any British consular officer, or any shipping master, or any chief officer of customs, that the provisions or water for the use of the crew are at any time of bad quality, unfit for use or deficient in quantity ; and such officer may thereupon examine the said provisions or water, or cause them to be examined; and if on examination such provisions or water are found to be of bad quality and unfit for use, or to be deficient in quantity, the person making such examination shall signify the same in writing to the master of the ship ; and if such master does not thereupon provide other proper provisions or water in lieu of any so signified to be of a bad quality and unfit for use, or does not procure the requisite quantity of any so signified to be insufficient in quantity, or uses any provisions or water which have been so signified as aforesaid to be of a bad quality and unfit for use, he shall in every such case incur a penalty not exceeding twenty pounds ; and upon every such examination as aforesaid the officers making or directing the same shall enter a statement of the result of the examination in the official log, and shall send a report thereof to the Board of Trade, and such report, if produced out of the custody of such Board or its officers, shall be received in evidence in any legal proceeding.

*Provisions, Health and Accommodation.*

Survey of provisions and water on complaint made.

CCXXII. If the officer to whom any such complaint as last aforesaid is made certifies in such statement as aforesaid that there was no reasonable

Forfeiture for frivolous complaint.

III. *Provisions, Health and Accommodation.*

Allowance for short or bad provisions.

ground for such complaint, each of the parties so complaining shall be liable to forfeit to the owners out of his wages a sum not exceeding one week's wages.

CCXXIII. In the following cases ; (that is to say,)

(1.) If during a voyage the allowance of any of the provisions which any seaman has by his agreement stipulated for is reduced (except in accordance with any regulations for reduction by way of punishment contained in the agreement, and also except for any time during which such seaman wilfully and without sufficient cause refuses or neglects to perform his duty, or is lawfully under confinement for misconduct, either on board or on shore) ;

(2.) If it is shown that any of such provisions are or have during the voyage been bad in quality and unfit for use ;

The seaman shall receive by way of compensation for such reduction or bad quality, according to the time of its continuance, the following sums, to be paid to him in addition to and to be recoverable as wages ; (that is to say,)

(1.) If his allowance is reduced by any quantity not exceeding one third of the quantity specified in the agreement, a sum not exceeding fourpence a day ;

(2.) If his allowance is reduced by more than one third of such quantity, eightpence a day ;

(3.) In respect of such bad quality as aforesaid, a sum not exceeding one shilling a day ;

But if it is shown to the satisfaction of the court before which the case is tried that any provisions, the allowance of which has been reduced, could not be procured or supplied in proper quantities, and that proper and equivalent substitutes were supplied in lieu thereof, the court shall take such circumstances into consideration, and shall notify or refuse compensation as the justice of the case may require.

CCXXIV. Repealed, 30 & 31 Vict. c. 124, s. 3.

Masters to keep weights and measures on board.

CCXXV. Every master shall keep on board proper weights and measures for the purpose of determining the quantities of the several provisions and articles served out, and shall allow the same to be used at the time of serving out such provisions and articles in the presence of a witness whenever any dispute arises about such quantities, and in default shall for every offence incur a penalty not exceeding ten pounds.

Board of trade and local boards may appoint inspectors of medicines who are to see that ships are properly provided.

CCXXVI. Any local marine board may, upon being required by the board of trade so to do, appoint and remove a medical inspector of ships for the port, and may fix his remuneration, such remuneration to be subject to the control of the board of trade ; and at ports where there are no local marine boards the board of trade may appoint and remove such inspectors, and fix their remuneration ; and it shall be the duty of such inspectors to inspect the medicines, medical stores, lime or lemon juice or other articles, sugar and vinegar, required to be kept on board any such ships as aforesaid ; and such inspection, if made at places where there are local marine boards, shall be made under their direction, and also in any special cases under the direction of the board of trade, and if made at places where there are no local marine boards, shall be made under the direction of the board of trade ; and such medical inspectors shall for the purposes of such inspection have the same powers as the inspectors appointed by the board of trade under the First Part of this Act ; but every such inspector, if required by timely notice in writing from the master, owner or consignee, shall make his inspection three days at least before the ship proceeds to sea, and if the result of the inspection is satisfactory shall not again make inspection before the commencement of the voyage, unless he has reason to suspect that some of the articles inspected have been subsequently removed, injured or destroyed ; and whenever any such medical inspector is of opinion that in any ship hereby required to carry such articles as aforesaid the same or any of them are deficient in quantity or quality, or are placed in improper vessels, he shall signify the same in writing to the chief officer of customs of the port where such ship is lying, and also to the master, owner or consignee thereof, and thereupon the master of such ship, before proceeding to sea, shall produce to such chief officer of customs a certificate under the hand of such medical inspector or of some other medical inspector, to the effect that such deficiency has been supplied or remedied, or that such improper vessels have been replaced by proper vessels, as the case may require ; and such chief officer of customs shall not grant a clearance for such ship without the production of such certificate, and if such ship attempts to go to sea without a clearance, may detain her until such certificate is produced ; and if such ship proceeds to sea without the production of such certificate, the owner, master or consignee thereof shall incur a penalty not exceeding twenty pounds.

*III. Provisions, Health and Accommodation.*

CCXXVII. Repealed, 30 & 31 Vict. c. 124, s. 3.

CCXXVIII. The following rules shall be observed with respect to expenses attendant on illness and death ; (that is to say,)

Expense of medical attendance and subsistence in cases of illness, and of burial in case of death, how to be defrayed.

(1.) If the master or any seaman or apprentice receives any hurt or injury in the service of the ship to which he belongs, the expense of providing the necessary surgical and medical advice, with attendance and medicines, and of his subsistence until he is cured, or dies, or is brought back to some port in the United Kingdom, if shipped in the United Kingdom, or if shipped in some British possession to some port in such possession, and of his conveyance to such port, and the expense (if any) of his burial, shall be defrayed by the owner of such ship, without any deduction on that account from the wages of such master, seaman or apprentice :

(2.) If the master or any seaman or apprentice is on account of any illness temporarily removed from his ship for the purpose of preventing infection, or otherwise for the convenience of the ship, and subsequently returns to his duty, the expense of such removal and of providing the necessary advice with attendance and medicines and of his subsistence whilst away from the ship, shall be defrayed in like manner :

(3.) The expense of all medicines and surgical or medical advice and attendance given to any master, seaman or apprentice whilst on board his ship shall be defrayed in like manner :

(4.) In all other cases any reasonable expenses duly incurred by the owner for any seaman in respect of illness, and also any reasonable expenses duly incurred by the owner in respect of the burial of any seaman or apprentice who dies whilst on service, shall if duly proved, be deducted from the wages of such seaman or apprentice.

CCXXIX. If any such expenses in respect of the illness, injury or hurt of any seaman or apprentice, as are to be borne by the owner, are paid by any consular officer or other person on behalf of her Majesty, or if any other expenses in respect of the illness, injury or hurt of any seaman or apprentice whose wages are not accounted for to such officer under the provisions hereinbefore contained in that behalf are so paid, such expenses shall be repaid to such officer or other person by the master of the ship, and if not so repaid, the amount thereof, with costs, shall be a charge upon the ship, and be recoverable from the said master or from the owner of the ship for the time being as a debt due to her Majesty, and shall be recoverable either by ordinary process of law or in the manner in which seamen are hereby enabled to recover wages : and in any proceeding for the recovery thereof the production of a certificate of the facts, signed by such officer or other person, together with such vouchers (if any) as the case requires, shall be sufficient proof that the said expenses were duly paid by such consular officer or other person as aforesaid.

Expenses, if paid by consul, to be recoverable from owner.

CCXXX. Every foreign-going ship having one hundred persons or upwards on board shall carry on board as part of her complement some person duly authorized by law to practise as physician, surgeon or apothecary ; and in default the owner shall for every voyage of any such ship made without such medical practitioner incur a penalty not exceeding one hundred pounds : provided that nothing herein contained shall in anywise affect any provision contained in the "Passengers Act, 1852" (e), concerning the carriage of medical practitioners by the class of ships therein named passenger ships, nor shall any such passenger ship, if not thereby required to carry a medical practitioner, be hereby required to do so.

Certain ships to carry medical practitioners.

CCXXXI. Repealed, 30 & 31 Vict. c. 124, s. 3.

(e) Repealed by Passengers Act, 1855, 18 & 19 Vict. c. 119.

III. *Power of making Complaint.*

Seamen to be allowed to go ashore to make complaint to a justice.

## Power of making Complaint.

**CCXXXII.** If any seaman or apprentice whilst on board any ship states to the master that he desires to make complaint to a justice of the peace or consular officer, or naval officer in command of any of her Majesty's ships, against the master or any of the crew, the said master shall, if the ship is then at a place where there is a justice or any such officer as aforesaid, as soon as the service of the ship will permit, and if the ship is not then at such a place, so soon after her arrival at such a place as the service of the ship will permit, allow such seaman or apprentice to go ashore or send him ashore in proper custody so that he may be enabled to make such complaint, and shall, in default, incur a penalty not exceeding ten pounds.

Protection of Seamen from Imposition.

Sale of and charge upon wages to be invalid.

## Protection of Seamen from Imposition.

**CCXXXIII.** No wages due or accruing to any seaman or apprentice shall be subject to attachment or arrestment from any court ; and every payment of wages to a seamen or apprentice shall be valid in law, notwithstanding any previous sale or assignment of such wages, or of any attachment, incumbrance or arrestment thereon ; and no assignment or sale of such wages or of salvage made prior to the accruing thereof shall bind the party making the same ; and no power of attorney or authority for the receipt of any such wages or salvage shall be irrevocable.

No debt exceeding 5s. recoverable till end of voyage.

**CCXXXIV.** No debt exceeding in amount five shillings, incurred by any seaman after he has engaged to serve, shall be recoverable until the service agreed for is concluded.

Penalty for overcharges by lodging-house keepers.

**CCXXXV.** If any person demands or receives from any seaman or apprentice to the sea service payment in respect of his board or lodging in the house of such person for a longer period than such seaman or apprentice has actually resided or boarded therein, he shall incur a penalty not exceeding ten pounds.

Penalty for detaining seamen's effects.

**CCXXXVI.** If any person receives or takes into his possession or under his control any moneys, documents or effects of any seaman or apprentice to the sea service, and does not return the same or pay the value thereof, when required by such seaman or apprentice, subject to such deduction as may be justly due to him from such seaman or apprentice in respect of board or lodging or otherwise, or absconds therewith, he shall incur a penalty not exceeding ten pounds, and any two justices may, besides inflicting such penalty, by summary order direct the amount or value of such moneys, documents or effects, subject to such deduction as aforesaid, to be forthwith paid to such seaman or apprentice.

Persons not to go on board before the final arrival of ship without permission.

**CCXXXVII.** Every person who, not being in her Majesty's service, and not being duly authorized by law for the purpose, goes on board any ship about to arrive at the place of her destination (*f*), before her actual arrival in dock or at the place of her discharge, without the permission of the master, shall for every such offence incur a penalty not exceeding twenty pounds ; and the master or person in charge of such ship may take any such person so going on board as aforesaid into custody, and deliver him up forthwith to any constable or peace officer, to be by him taken before a justice or justices or the sheriff of the county in Scotland, and to be dealt with according to the provisions of this Act.

Penalty for soliciting by lodging-house keepers.

**CCXXXVIII.** If, within twenty-four hours after the arrival of any ship at any port in the United Kingdom, any person then being on board such ship solicits any seaman to become a lodger at the house of any person letting lodgings for hire, or takes out of such ship any effects of any seaman, except under his personal direction and with the permission of the master, he shall for every such offence incur a penalty not exceeding five pounds.

Discipline.

Misconduct endangering ship or life or

## Discipline.

**CCXXXIX.** Any master of or any seaman or apprentice belonging to any British ship who by wilful breach of duty, or by neglect of duty, or by reason of drunkenness, does any act tending to the immediate loss, destruc-

(*f*) See 43 & 44 Vict. c. 16, s. 5 ; *Atwood* v. *Cave*, L. R. 1 Q. B. D. 134.

tion, or serious damage of such ship, or tending immediately to endanger the life or limb of any person belonging to or on board of such ship, or who by wilful breach of duty, or by neglect of duty, or by reason of drunkenness, refuses or omits to do any lawful act proper and requisite to be done by him for preserving such ship from immediate loss, destruction, or serious damage, or for preserving any person belonging to or on board of such ship from immediate danger to life or limb, shall for every such offence be deemed guilty of a misdemeanor (*g*).

III. *Discipline.*

limb a misdemeanor.

CCXL. Any court having admiralty jurisdiction in any of her Majesty's dominions may, upon application by the owner of any ship being within the jurisdiction of such court, or by the part owner or consignee, or by the agent of the owner, or by any certificated mate, or by one third or more of the crew of such ship, and upon proof on oath to the satisfaction of such court that the removal of the master of such ship is necessary, remove him accordingly; and may also, with the consent of the owner or his agent, or the consignee of the ship, or if there is no owner or agent of the owner or consignee of the ship within the jurisdiction of the court, then without such consent, appoint a new master in his stead ; and may also make such order, and may require such security in respect of costs in the matter, as it thinks fit.

Power of admiralty courts to remove master.

CCXLI. If the board of trade or any local marine board has reason to believe that any master or mate is from incompetency or misconduct unfit to discharge his duties, the board of trade may either institute an investigation or may direct the local marine board at or nearest to the place at which it may be convenient for the parties and witnesses to attend to institute the same, and thereupon such persons as the board of trade may appoint for the purpose, or, as the case may be, the local marine board, shall, with the assistance of a local stipendiary magistrate (if any), and if there is no such magistrate, of a competent legal assistant to be appointed by the board of trade, conduct the investigation, and may summon the master or mate to appear, and shall give him full opportunity of making a defence either in person or otherwise, and shall for the purpose of such investigation have all the powers given by the first part of this Act to inspectors appointed by the board of trade, and may make such order with respect to the costs of such investigation as they may deem just; and shall on the conclusion of the investigation make a report upon the case to the board of trade ; and in cases where there is no local marine board before which the parties and witnesses can conveniently attend, or where such local marine board is unwilling to institute the investigation, the board of trade may direct the same to be instituted before two justices or a stipendiary magistrate ; and thereupon such investigation shall be conducted, and the results thereof reported, in the same manner and with the same powers in and with which formal investigations into wrecks and casualties are directed to be conducted, and the results thereof reported, under the provisions contained in the Eighth Part of this Act, save only that, if the board of trade so directs, the person bringing the charge of incompetency or misconduct to the notice of the board of trade shall be deemed to be the party having the conduct of the case.

Power to investigate cases of alleged incompetency and misconduct (*h*).

CCXLII. The board of trade may suspend or cancel the certificate (whether of competency or service) of any master or mate in the following cases; (that is to say,)

Board of trade may cancel or suspend certificate in certain cases (*i*).

(1.) If upon any investigation made in pursuance of the last preceding section, he is reported to be incompetent, or to have been guilty of any gross act of misconduct, drunkenness or tyranny :

(2.) If upon any investigation conducted under the provisions contained in the Eighth Part of this Act, or upon any investigation made by a naval court constituted as hereinafter mentioned, it is reported that the loss or abandonment of or serious damage to any ship or loss of life has been caused by his wrongful act or default :

(3.) If he is superseded by the order of any admiralty court or of any naval court constituted as hereinafter mentioned :

(4.) If he is shown to have been convicted of any offence :

(5.) If upon any investigation made by any court or tribunal authorized

(*g*) 43 & 44 Vict. c. 16, s. 10, *infra.*
(*h*) 25 & 26 Vict. c. 63, s. 11, *infra.*

(*i*) 25 & 26 Vict. c. 63, s. 23, and 39 & 40 Vict. c. 80, s. 29, *infra.*

III. *Discipline.*

or hereafter to be authorized by the legislative authority in any British possession to make inquiry into charges of incompetency or misconduct, on the part of masters or mates of ships, or as to shipwrecks or other casualties affecting ships, a report is made by such court or tribunal to the effect that he has been guilty of any gross act of misconduct, drunkenness or tyranny, or that the loss or abandonment of or serious damage to any ship or loss of life has been caused by his wrongful act or default [and such report is confirmed by the governor or person administering the government of such possession] (*k*) :

And every master or mate whose certificate is cancelled or suspended shall deliver it to the board of trade or as it directs, and in default shall for each offence incur a penalty not exceeding fifty pounds ; and the board of trade may at any subsequent time grant to any person whose certificate has been cancelled a new certificate of the same or of any lower grade.

Offences of seamen and apprentices and their punishments.

CCXLIII. Whenever any seaman who has been lawfully engaged or any apprentice to the sea service commits any of the following offences he shall be liable to be punished summarily as follows (that is to say) :

Desertion:

(1.) For desertion he shall be liable [to imprisonment for any period not exceeding twelve weeks, with or without hard labour, and also] (*l*) forfeit all or any part of the clothes and effects he leaves on board, and all or any part of the wages or emoluments which he has then earned, and also, if such desertion takes place abroad, at the discretion of the court, to forfeit all or any part of the wages or emoluments he may earn in any other ship in which he may be employed until his next return to the United Kingdom, and to satisfy any excess of wages paid by the master or owner of the ship from which he deserts to any substitute engaged in his place at a higher rate of wages than the rate stipulated to be paid to him:

Neglecting or refusing to join, or to proceed to sea, absence within twenty-four hours before sailing, and absence without leave:

(2.) For neglecting or refusing, without reasonable cause (*m*), to join his ship, or to proceed to sea in his ship, or for absence without leave at any time within twenty-four hours of the ship's sailing from any port either at the commencement or during the progress of any voyage, or for absence at any time without leave and without sufficient reason from his ship or from his duty not amounting to desertion or not treated as such by the master, he shall be liable [to imprisonment for any period not exceeding ten weeks, with or without hard labour, and also] (*l*) at the discretion of the court, to forfeit out of his wages a sum not exceeding the amount of two days' pay, and in addition for every twenty-four hours of absence either a sum not exceeding six days' pay, or any expenses which have been properly incurred in hiring a substitute:

Quitting without leave before ship is secured:

(3.) For quitting the ship without leave after arrival at her port of delivery and before she is placed in security, he shall be liable to forfeit out of his wages a sum not exceeding one month's pay:

Act of disobedience:

(4.) For wilful disobedience to any lawful command he shall be liable to imprisonment for any period not exceeding four weeks, with or without hard labour, and also, at the discretion of the court, to forfeit out of his wages a sum not exceeding two days' pay:

Continued disobedience:

(5.) For continued wilful disobedience to lawful commands, or continued wilful neglect of duty, he shall be liable to imprisonment for any period not exceeding twelve weeks, with or without hard labour, and also, at the discretion of the court, to forfeit for every twenty-four hours' continuance of such disobedience or neglect either a sum not exceeding six days' pay, or any expenses which have been properly incurred in hiring a substitute:

Assault on officers:

(6.) For assaulting any master or mate he shall be liable to imprisoment for any period not exceeding twelve weeks, with or without hard labour:

Combining to disobey:

(7.) For combining with any other or others of the crew to disobey lawful commands, or to neglect duty, or to impede the navigation of the

(*k*) The words within brackets are repealed by 45 & 46 Vict. c. 76, s. 7.
(*l*) The words within brackets re-

pealed by 43 & 44 Vict. c. 16, s. 12.
(*m*) See 34 & 35 Vict. c. 110, ss. 7 and 8, *infra*.

ship or the progress of the voyage, he shall be liable to imprison-<br>
ment for any period not exceeding twelve weeks, with or without<br>
hard labour:

(8.) For wilfully damaging the ship, or embezzling or wilfully damaging any of her stores or cargo, he shall be liable to forfeit out of his wages a sum equal in amount to the loss thereby sustained, and also, at the discretion of the court, to imprisonment for any period not exceeding twelve weeks, with or without hard labour:

*Wilful damage and embezzlement:*

(9.) For any act of smuggling of which he is convicted, and whereby loss or damage is occasioned to the master or owner, he shall be liable to pay to such master or owner such a sum as is sufficient to reimburse the master or owner for such loss or damage; and the whole or a proportionate part of his wages may be retained in satisfaction or on account of such liability, without prejudice to any further remedy.

*Acts of smuggling causing loss to owner.*

CCXLIV. Upon the commission of any of the offences enumerated in the last preceding section an entry thereof shall be made in the official log-book, and shall be signed by the master and also by the mate or one of the crew; and the offender, if still in the ship, shall before the next subsequent arrival of the ship at any port, or if she is at the time in port, before her departure therefrom, either be furnished with a copy of such entry or have the same read over distinctly and audibly to him, and may thereupon make such reply thereto as he thinks fit; and a statement that a copy of the said entry has been so furnished, or that the same has been so read over as aforesaid, and the reply (if any) made by the offender, shall likewise be entered and signed in manner aforesaid; and in any subsequent legal proceedings the entries hereinbefore required shall, if practicable, be produced or proved, and in default of such production or proof the court hearing the case may, at its discretion, refuse to receive evidence of the offence.

*Entry of offences to be made in official log, and to be read over or a copy given to the offender, and his reply, if any, to be also entered.*

CCXLV. Every seafaring person whom the master of any ship is, under the authority of this Act or of any other Act of Parliament, compelled to take on board and convey, and every person who goes to sea in any ship without the consent of the master or owner or other person entitled to give such consent, shall, so long as he remains in such ship, be subject to the same laws and regulations for preserving discipline, and to the same penalties and punishments for offences constituting or tending to a breach of discipline, to which he would be subject if he were a member of the crew and had signed the agreement.

*Seamen whom masters of ships are compelled to convey, and persons going in ships without leave to be subject to penalties for breach of discipline.*

CCXLVI. Repealed by 43 & 44 Vict. c. 16, s. 12.

CCXLVII. Whenever any seaman or apprentice is brought before any court on the ground of his having neglected or refused to join or to proceed to sea in any ship in which he is engaged to serve, or of having deserted or otherwise absented himself therefrom without leave, such court may, if the master or the owner or his agent so requires [instead of committing the offender to prison] (*n*), cause him to be conveyed on board for the purpose of proceeding on the voyage, or deliver him to the master or any mate of the ship, or the owner or his agent, to be by them so conveyed, and may in such case order any costs and expenses properly incurred by or on behalf of the master or owner by reason of the offence to be paid by the offender, and, if necessary, to be deducted from any wages which he has then earned, or which by virtue of his then existing engagement he may afterwards earn.

*Deserters may be sent on board in lieu of being imprisoned.*

CCXLVIII. Repealed by 43 & 44 Vict. c. 16, s. 12.

CCXLIX. In all cases of desertion from any ship in any place abroad the master shall produce the entry of such desertion in the official log-book to the person or persons hereby required to indorse on the agreement a certificate of such desertion; and such person or persons shall thereupon make and certify a copy of such entry and also a copy of the said certificate of desertion; and if such person is a public functionary he shall, and in other cases the said master shall forthwith transmit such copies to the registrar-general of seamen in England (*o*); and the said registrar shall, if required, cause the same to be produced in any legal proceeding; and such copies, if purporting to be so made and certified as aforesaid, and certified to have come from the custody

*Entries and certificates of desertion abroad to be copied, sent home, and admitted in evidence.*

---

(*n*) See 43 & 44 Vict. c. 16, s. 10, *infra.*

(*o*) Now called Registrar-General of Shipping and Seamen: 35 & 36 Vict. c. 73, s. 4, *infra.*

III. *Discipline.*

Facilities for proving desertion, so far as concerns forfeiture of wages.

Costs of procuring imprisonment may to the extent of 3*l.* be deducted from wages.

Amount of forfeiture how to be ascertained when seamen contract for the voyage.

Application of forfeitures.

Questions of forfeiture may be decided in suits for wages.

Penalty for false statement as to last ship or name.

Fines to be deducted from wages, and paid to shipping master.

of the said registrar, shall in any legal proceeding relating to such desertion be received as evidence of the entries therein appearing.

CCL. Whenever a question arises whether the wages of any seaman or apprentice are forfeited for desertion, it shall be sufficient for the party insisting on the forfeiture to show that such seaman or apprentice was duly engaged in or that he belonged to the ship from which he is alleged to have deserted, and that he quitted such ship before the completion of the voyage or engagement, or if such voyage was to terminate in the United Kingdom and the ship has not returned, that he is absent from her, and that an entry of the desertion has been duly made in the official log-book ; and thereupon the desertion shall, so far as relates to any forfeiture of wages or emoluments under the provisions hereinbefore contained, be deemed to be proved, unless the seaman or apprentice can produce a proper certificate of discharge, or can otherwise show to the satisfaction of the court that he had sufficient reasons for leaving his ship.

CCLI. Whenever in any proceeding relating to seamen's wages it is shown that any seaman or apprentice has in the course of the voyage been convicted of any offence by any competent tribunal and rightfully punished therefor by imprisonment or otherwise, the court hearing the case may direct a part of the wages due to such seaman, not exceeding three pounds, to be applied in reimbursing any costs properly incurred by the master in procuring such conviction and punishment.

CCLII. Whenever any seaman contracts for wages by the voyage or by the run or by the share and not by the month or other stated period of time, the amount of forfeiture to be incurred under this Act shall be taken to be an amount bearing the same proportion to the whole wages or share as a calendar month or other the period hereinbefore mentioned in fixing the amount of such forfeiture (as the case may be) bears to the whole time spent in the voyage ; and if the whole time spent in the voyage does not exceed the period for which the pay is to be forfeited, the forfeit shall extend to the whole wages or share.

CCLIII. All clothes, effects, wages and emoluments which under the provisions hereinbefore contained are forfeited for desertion shall be applied in the first instance in or towards the reimbursement of the expenses occasioned by such desertion to the master or owner of the ship from which the desertion has taken place ; and may, if earned subsequently to the desertion, be recovered by such master, or by the owner or his agent, in the same manner as the deserter might have recovered the same if they had not been forfeited ; and in any legal proceeding relating to such wages the court may order the same to be paid accordingly ; and subject to such reimbursements the same shall be paid into the receipt of her Majesty's exchequer in such manner as the treasury may direct, and shall be carried to and form part of the consolidated fund of the United Kingdom ; and in all other cases of forfeiture of wages under the provisions hereinbefore contained the forfeiture shall, in the absence of any specific directions to the contrary, be for the benefit of the master or owner by whom the wages are payable.

CCLIV. Any question concerning the forfeiture of or deductions from the wages of any seaman or apprentice may be determined in any proceeding lawfully instituted with respect to such wages, notwithstanding that the offence in respect of which such question arises, though hereby made punishable by imprisonment as well as forfeiture, has not been made the subject of any criminal proceeding.

CCLV. If any seaman on or before being engaged wilfully and fraudulently makes a false statement of the name of his last ship or last alleged ship, or wilfully and fraudulently makes a false statement of his own name, he shall incur a penalty not exceeding five pounds ; and such penalty may be deducted from any wages he may earn by virtue of such engagement as aforesaid, and shall, subject to reimbursement of the loss and expenses (if any) occasioned by any previous desertion, be paid and applied in the same manner as other penalties payable under this Act.

CCLVI. Whenever any seaman commits an act of misconduct for which his agreement imposes a fine, and which it is intended to punish by enforcing such fine, an entry thereof shall be made in the official log-book, and a copy of such entry shall be furnished or the same shall be read over to the offender, and an entry of such reading over, and of the reply (if any) made by the offender, shall be made, in the manner and subject to the conditions hereinbefore specified with respect to the offences against discipline specified in and punishable under this Act ; and such fine shall be deducted and paid over as follows, (that is to say,) if the offender is discharged in the United Kingdom, and the offence and such entries in respect thereof as aforesaid are proved, in the case of a foreign-going ship to the satisfaction of the shipping master before whom the offender is discharged, and in the case of a home trade ship to the satisfaction of the shipping master at or nearest to the place at which the crew is discharged, the master or owner shall deduct such fine from the wages of the offender, and pay the same over to such shipping master ; and if before the final discharge of the crew in the United Kingdom any such offender as aforesaid enters into any of her Majesty's ships, or is discharged abroad, and the offence and such entries as aforesaid are proved to the satisfaction of the officer in command of the ship into which he so enters, or of the consular officer, officer of customs, or other person by whose sanction he is so discharged, the fine shall thereupon be deducted as aforesaid, and an entry of such deduction shall then be made in the official log book (if any) and signed by such officer or other person ; and on the return of the ship to the United Kingdom the master or owner shall pay over such fine, in the case of foreign-going ships, to the shipping master before whom the crew is discharged, and in the case of home trade ships to the shipping master at or nearest to the place at which the crew is discharged ; and if any master or owner neglects or refuses to pay over any such fine in manner aforesaid, he shall for each such offence incur a penalty not exceeding six times the amount of the fine retained by him : provided that no act or misconduct for which any such fine as aforesaid has been inflicted and paid shall be otherwise punished under the provisions of this Act.

CCLVII. Every person who by any means whatever persuades or attempts to persuade any seaman or apprentice to neglect or refuse to join or to proceed to sea in or to desert from his ship, or otherwise to absent himself from his duty, shall for each such offence in respect of each such seaman or apprentice incur a penalty not exceeding ten pounds ; and every person who wilfully harbours or secretes any seaman or apprentice who has deserted from his ship, or who has wilfully neglected or refused to join, or has deserted from his ship, knowing or having reason to believe such seaman or apprentice to have so done, shall for every such seaman or apprentice so harboured or secreted incur a penalty not exceeding twenty pounds.

CCLVIII. Any person who secretes himself and goes to sea in any ship without the consent of either the owner, consignee or master, or of a mate or of any person in charge of such ship, or of any other person entitled to give such consent, shall incur a penalty not exceeding twenty pounds, or be liable to imprisonment with or without hard labour, for any period not exceeding four weeks (*p*).

CCLIX. If during the progress of a voyage the master is superseded or for any other reason quits the ship and is succeeded in command by some other person, he shall deliver to his successor the various documents relating to the navigation of the ship and to the crew thereof which are in his custody, and shall in default incur a penalty not exceeding one hundred pounds ; and such successor shall immediately, on assuming the command of the ship, enter in the official log a list of the documents so delivered to him.

*Naval Courts on the High Seas and Abroad.*

CCLX. Any officer in command of any ship of her Majesty on any foreign station, or, in the absence of such officer, any consular officer, may summon a court, to be termed a "Naval Court," in the following cases (that is to say) :

(1.) Whenever a complaint which appears to such officer to require immediate investigation is made to him by the master of any British ship, or by any certificated mate, or by one or more of the seamen belonging to any such ship :

(2.) Whenever the interest of the owner of any British ship or of the cargo of any such ship appears to such officer to require it :

*Marginal notes:*
III. *Discipline.*

Penalty for enticing to desert, and harbouring deserters.

Penalty for obtaining passage surreptitiously.

On change of masters, documents hereby required to be handed over to successor.

*Naval Courts.*

Naval courts may be summoned for hearing complaints and investigating wrecks on the high seas or abroad.

(*p*) As to persons secreting themselves on passenger vessels, 18 & 19 Vict. c. 119, s. 18.

III. *Naval Courts.*

(3.) Whenever any British ship is wrecked or abandoned or otherwise lost at or near the place where such officer may be, or whenever the crew or part of the crew of any British ship which has been wrecked, abandoned, or lost abroad, arrives at such place.

Constitution of such courts.

CCLXI. Every such naval court as aforesaid shall consist of not more than five and not less than three members, of whom, if possible, one shall be an officer in the naval service of her Majesty not below the rank of lieutenant, one a consular officer, and one a master of a British merchant ship, and the rest shall be either officers in the naval service of her Majesty, masters of British merchant ships or British merchants ; and such court may include the naval consular officer summoning the same, but shall not include the master or consignee of the ship to which the parties complaining or complained against may belong ; and the naval or consular officer in such court, if there is only one such officer in the court, or if there is more than one, the naval or consular officer who, according to any regulations for settling their respective ranks for the time being in force, is of the highest rank, shall be president of such court (*q*).

General functions and mode of action of such courts.

CCLXII. Every such naval court shall hear and investigate the complaint brought before it, or the cause of the wreck or abandonment (as the case may be), and may for that purpose summon and compel the attendance of parties and witnesses, and administer oaths, and order the production of documents, and shall conduct the investigation in such manner as to give any person against whom any charge is made an opportunity of making a defence.

Powers of such courts :

CCLXIII. Every such naval court may, after hearing the case, exercise the following powers ; (that is to say,)

To supersede the master :

(1.) It may, if unanimous that the safety of the ship or crew, or the interest of the owner, absolutely requires it, supersede the master, and may appoint another person to act in his stead ; but no such appointment shall be made without the consent of the consignee of the ship, if then at the place :

To discharge a seaman :

(2.) It may discharge any seaman from his ship :

To forfeit wages :

(3.) It may order the wages of any seaman so discharged or any part of such wages to be forfeited, and may direct the same either to be retained by way of compensation to the owner, or to be paid into the receipt of her Majesty's exchequer in the same manner as other penalties and forfeitures under this Act :

To decide disputes as to wages, &c. :

(4.) It may decide any questions as to wages, or fines, or forfeitures, arising between any of the parties to the proceedings :

To direct costs of imprisonment to be paid out of wages :

(5.) It may direct that all or any of the costs incurred by the master or owner of any ship in procuring the imprisonment of any seaman or apprentice in a foreign port, or in his maintenance whilst so imprisoned, shall be paid out of and deducted from the wages of such seaman or apprentice, whether then or subsequently earned :

To send home offenders for trial :

(6.) It may exercise the same powers with regard to persons charged before it with the commission of offences at sea or aboard as are by this Act given to British consular officers :

To order payment of costs, &c.

(7.) It may order the costs of the proceeding before it (if any), or any portion thereof, to be paid by any of the parties thereto, and may order any person making a frivolous or vexatious complaint to pay compensation for any loss or delay caused thereby ; and any cost or compensation so ordered shall be paid by such person accordingly, and may be recovered in the same manner in which the wages of seamen are recoverable, or may, if the case admits, be deducted from his wages :

And all orders duly made by any such court under the powers hereby given to it shall in any subsequent legal proceedings be deemed conclusive as to the rights of the parties.

Orders to be entered in official log.

CCLXIV. All orders made by any such naval court shall, whenever practicable, be entered in the official log-book of the ship to which the parties to the proceedings before it belong, and shall be signed by the president of the court.

Report to be made of proceedings of naval courts.

CCLXV. Every such naval court shall make a report to the board of trade, containing the following particulars ; (that is to say,)

(*q*) See sect. 8 of 35 & 36 Vict. c. 73, *infra.*

(1.) A statement of the proceedings, with the order made by the court, and a report of the evidence:

(2.) An account of the wages of any seaman or apprentice who is discharged from his ship by such court:

(3.) If summoned in order to inquire into a case of wreck or abandonment, a statement of the opinion of the court as to the cause of such wreck or abandonment, with such remarks on the conduct of the master and crew as the circumstances require:

And every such report shall be signed by the president of the court ; and every document purporting to be such a report and to be so signed as aforesaid shall, if produced out of the custody of some officer of the board of trade, be deemed to be such report, unless the contrary be proved, and shall be received in evidence subject to all just exceptions.

CCLXVI. Any person who wilfully and without due cause prevents or obstructs the making of any such complaint as last aforesaid, or the conduct of any case or investigation by any naval court, shall for each such offence incur a penalty not exceeding fifty pounds, or be liable to imprisonment with or without hard labour for any period not exceeding twelve weeks.

*III. Naval Courts.*

*Penalty for preventing complaint or obstructing investigation.*

### *Crimes committed on the High Seas and Abroad.*

*Crimes committed Abroad.*

CCLXVII. All offences against property or person committed in or at any place either ashore or afloat out of her Majesty's dominions by any master, seaman or apprentice who at the time when the offence is committed is or within three months previously has been employed in any British ship shall be deemed to be offences of the same nature respectively, and be liable to the same punishments respectively, and be inquired of, heard, tried, determined and adjudged in the same manner and by the same courts and in the same places as if such offences had been committed within the jurisdiction of the admiralty of England ; and the costs and expenses of the prosecution of any such offence may be directed to be paid as in the case of costs and expenses of prosecutions for offences committed within the jurisdiction of the admiralty of England.

*Offences committed by British seamen at foreign ports to be within admiralty jurisdiction.*

CCLXVIII. The following rules shall be observed with respect to offences committed on the high seas or abroad (that is to say) :

*Conveyance of offenders and witnesses to United Kingdom or some British possession.*

(1.) Whenever any complaint is made to any British consular officer of any of the offences mentioned in the last preceding section ; or of any offence on the high seas having been committed by any master, seaman or apprentice belonging to any British ship, such consular officer may inquire into the case upon oath, and may, if the case so requires, take any steps in his power for the purpose of placing the offender under necessary restraint, and of sending him as soon as practicable in safe custody to the United Kingdom, or to any British possession in which there is a court capable of taking cognisance of the offence, in any ship belonging to her Majesty or to any of her subjects, to be there proceeded against according to law :

(2.) For the purpose aforesaid such consular officer may order the master of any ship belonging to any subject of her Majesty bound to the United Kingdom, or to such British possession as aforesaid, to receive and afford a passage and subsistence during the voyage to any such offender as aforesaid, and to the witnesses, so that such master be not required to receive more than one offender for every one hundred tons of his ship's registered tonnage, or more than one witness for every fifty tons of such tonnage ; and such consular officer shall indorse upon the agreement of the ship such particulars with respect to any offenders or witnesses sent in her as the board of trade requires :

(3.) Every such master shall on his ship's arrival in the United Kingdom, or in such British possession as aforesaid, give every offender so committed to his charge into the custody of some police officer or constable, who shall take the offender before a justice of the peace or other magistrate by law empowered to deal with the matter, and such justice or magistrate shall deal with the matter as in cases of offences committed upon the high seas.

And any such master as aforesaid who, when required by any British consular officer to receive and afford a passage and subsistence to any offender

III. *Crimes committed Abroad.*

or witness, does not receive him and afford such passage and subsistence to him, or who does not deliver any offender committed to his charge into the custody of some police officer or constable as hereinbefore directed, shall for each such offence incur a penalty not exceeding fifty pounds, [and the expense of imprisoning any such offender and of conveying him and the witnesses to the United Kingdom or to such British possession as aforesaid in any manner other than in the ship to which they respectively belong, shall be part of the costs of the prosecution, or be paid as costs incurred on account of seafaring subjects of her Majesty left in distress in foreign parts(r).]

Inquiry into cause of death on board.

CCLXIX. Whenever any case of death happens on board any foreign-going ship, the shipping master shall on the arrival of such ship at the port where the crew is discharged inquire into the cause of such death, and shall make on the list of the crew delivered to him as herein required an indorsement to the effect either that the statement of the cause of death therein contained is in his opinion true or otherwise, as the result of the inquiry requires; and every such shipping master shall for the purpose of such inquiry have the powers hereby given to inspectors appointed by the board of trade under the first part of this Act; and if in the course of such inquiry it appears to him that any such death as aforesaid has been caused by violence or other improper means, he shall either report the matter to the board of trade, or, if the emergency of the case so require, shall take immediate steps for bringing the offender or offenders to justice.

Depositions to be received in evidence when witness cannot be produced.

CCLXX. Whenever in the course of any legal proceedings instituted in any part of her Majesty's dominions before any judge or magistrate, or before any person authorized by law or by consent of parties to receive evidence, the testimony of any witness is required in relation to the subject-matter of such proceeding, then upon due proof, if such proceeding is instituted in the United Kingdom, that such witness cannot be found in that kingdom, or if in any British possession, that he cannot be found in the same possession, any deposition that such witness may have previously made on oath in relation to the same subject-matter before any justice or magistrate in her Majesty's dominions, or any British consular officer elsewhere, shall be admissible in evidence, subject to the following restrictions; (that is to say,)

(1.) If such deposition was made in the United Kingdom, it shall not be admissible in any proceeding instituted in the United Kingdom:

(2.) If such a deposition was made in any British possession, it shall not be admissible in any proceeding instituted in the same British possession:

(3.) If the proceeding is criminal it shall not be admissible, unless it was made in the presence of the person accused:

Every deposition so made as aforesaid shall be authenticated by the signature of the judge, magistrate or consular officer before whom the same is made: and such judge, magistrate or consular officer shall, when the same is taken in a criminal matter, certify if the fact is so, and that the accused was present at the taking thereof, but it shall not be necessary in any case to prove the signature or official character of the person appearing to have signed any such deposition; and in any criminal proceeding such certificate as aforesaid shall, unless the contrary is proved, be sufficient evidence of the accused having been present in manner thereby certified; but nothing herein contained shall affect any case in which depositions taken in any proceeding are rendered admissible in evidence by any Act of Parliament, or by any Act or ordinance of the legislature of any colony, so far as regards such colony, or to interfere with the power of any colonial legislature to make such depositions admissible in evidence, or to interfere with the practice of any court in which depositions not authenticated as hereinbefore mentioned are admissible.

*Registration and Returns respecting Seamen.*

### Registration of and Returns respecting Seamen.

Establishment of register office.

CCLXXI. There shall be in the port of London an office, to be called the "General Register and Record Office of Seamen," and the board of trade shall have control over the same, and may appoint and from time to time remove a registrar-general, and such assistants, clerks and servants as

(r) Words within brackets repealed by 45 & 46 Vict. c. 55, s. 10.

may be necessary, and may from time to time, with the consent of the treasury, regulate their salaries and allowances: and such salaries and allowances, and all other necessary expenses, shall be paid by the treasury out of any monies to be granted by Parliament for that purpose; and the board of trade may direct the business of the register office at any of the outports to be transacted at the shipping office, or with the consent of the commissioners of customs at the custom house of the port, and may appoint the shipping master, or with such consent as aforesaid some officer of customs to conduct the same; and such business shall thereupon be conducted accordingly, but shall in all cases be subject to the immediate control of the board of trade.

CCLXXII. The said registrar-general of seamen shall by means of the agreements, lists and other papers to be transmitted to him as herein directed, or by such other means as are in his power, keep a register of all persons who serve in ships subject to the provisions of this Act.

CCLXXIII. Every master of every foreign-going ship of which the crew is discharged in the United Kingdom, in whatever part of her Majesty's dominions the same is registered, and of every home trade ship, shall make out and sign a list in a form sanctioned by the board of trade, containing the following particulars; (that is to say,)

(1.) The number and date of the ship's register and her registered tonnage:
(2.) The length and general nature of the voyage or employment:
(3.) The christian names, surnames, ages and places of birth of all the crew, including the master and apprentices; their qualities on board, their last ships or other employments, and the dates and places of their joining the ship:
(4.) The names of any members of the crew who have died or otherwise ceased to belong to the ship, with the times, places, causes and circumstances thereof:
(5.) The names of any members of the crew who have been maimed or hurt, with the times, places, causes and circumstances thereof:
(6.) The wages due to any of the crew who have died, at the times of their respective deaths:
(7.) The clothes and other effects belonging to any of the crew who have died, with a statement of the manner in which they have been dealt with, and the money for which any of them have been sold:
(8.) The name, age and sex of every person, not being one of the crew, who dies on board, with the date and the cause thereof (s):
(9.) Every birth which happens on board, with the date thereof, the sex of the infant, and the names of the parents (s):
(10.) Every marriage which takes place on board, with the date thereof, and the names and ages of the parties.

CCLXXIV. In the case of foreign-going ships the master shall, within forty-eight hours after the ship's arrival at her final port of destination in the United Kingdom, or upon the discharge of the crew, which ever first happens, deliver to the shipping master before whom the crew is discharged such list as hereinbefore required, and if he fails so to do shall for every default incur a penalty not exceeding five pounds; and such shipping master shall thereupon give to the master a certificate of such delivery; and no officer of customs shall clear inwards any foreign-going ship without the production of such certificate, and any such officer may detain any such ship until the same is produced.

CCLXXV. The master or owner of every home trade ship shall, within twenty-one days after the thirtieth day of June and the thirty-first day of December in every year, transmit or deliver to some shipping master in the United Kingdom such list as hereinbefore required for the preceding half-year, and shall in default incur a penalty not exceeding five pounds; and such shipping master shall give to the master or owner a certificate of such transmission or delivery; and no officer of customs shall grant a clearance or transire for any home trade ship without the production of such certificate, and any such officer may detain any such ship until the same is produced.

CCLXXVI. If any ship ceases by reason of transfer of ownership or change of employment to fall within the definition of a foreign-going or of a

*Marginal notes:*

III. *Registration and Returns respecting Seamen.*

Register of seamen to be kept.

Lists to be made for all ships containing certain particulars.

Lists for foreign going ships to be delivered to shipping master on arrival.

Lists to be delivered by home trade ships half-yearly.

Lists to be sent home in case of transfer of ship,

(s) See 37 & 38 Vict. c. 88, s. 54.

III. *Registration and Returns respecting Seamen.*

and in case of loss.

home trade ship, the master or owner thereof shall, if such ship is then in the United Kingdom, within one month, and if she is elsewhere, within six months, deliver or transmit to the shipping master at the port to which the ship has belonged such list as hereinbefore mentioned, duly made out to the time at which she ceased to be a foreign-going or home trade ship, and in default shall for each offence incur a penalty not exceeding ten pounds ; and if any ship is lost or abandoned, the master or owner thereof shall, if practicable and as soon as possible, deliver or transmit to the shipping master at the port to which the ship belonged such list as hereinbefore mentioned duly made out to the time of such loss or abandonment, and in default shall for each offence incur a penalty not exceeding ten pounds.

Shipping masters and other officers to transmit documents to registrar.

Registrar to permit inspection, to produce originals and give copies.

CCLXXVII. All shipping masters and officers of customs shall take charge of all documents which are delivered or transmitted to or retained by them in pursuance of this Act, and shall keep them for such time (if any) as may be necessary for the purpose of settling any business arising at the place where such documents come into their hands, or for any other proper purpose, and shall, if required, produce them for any of such purposes, and shall then transmit them to the registrar-general of seamen, to be by him recorded and preserved (*t*) ; and the said registrar shall, on payment of a moderate fee to be fixed by the board of trade, or without payment of any fee if the board of trade so directs, allow any person to inspect the same ; and in cases in which the production of the original of any such document in any court of justice or elsewhere is essential, shall produce the same, and in other cases shall make and deliver to any person requiring it a certified copy of any such document or of any part thereof ; and every copy purporting to be so made and certified shall be received in evidence, and shall have all the effect of the original of which it purports to be a copy.

Officers of customs to make returns of ships to registrar.

CCLXXVIII. The collector or comptroller of customs at every port in the United Kingdom shall on or before the first day of February and the first day of August in every year transmit to the registrar-general of seamen a list of all ships registered in such port, and also of all ships whose registers have been transferred or cancelled in such port since the last preceding return.

Agreements, indentures, and assignments, on arrival at a foreign port, to be deposited with the consul, and at a colony with the officers of customs.

CCLXXIX. The following rules shall be observed with respect to the delivery of documents to British consular officers ; (that is to say,)

(1.) Whenever any ship, in whatever part of her Majesty's dominions the same is registered (except ships whose business for the time being is to carry passengers), arrives at any foreign port where there is a British consular officer, or at any port in any British possession abroad, and remains thereat for forty-eight hours, the master shall, within forty-eight hours of the ship's arrival, deliver to such consular officer, or to the chief officer of customs (as the case may be), the agreement with the crew, and also all indentures and assignments of apprenticeships, or in the case of a ship belonging to a British possession, such of the said documents as such ship is provided with :

(2.) Such officer shall keep such documents during the ship's stay in such port, and, in cases where any indorsements upon the agreement are hereby required, shall duly make the same, and shall return the said documents to the master a reasonable time before his departure, with a certificate indorsed on the agreement, stating when the same were respectively delivered and returned :

(3.) If it appears that the required forms have been neglected, or that the existing laws have been transgressed, such officer shall make an indorsement to that effect on the agreement, and forthwith transmit a copy of such indorsement, with the fullest information he can collect regarding such neglect or transgression, to the registrar-general of seamen :

And if any master fails to deliver any such document as aforesaid he shall for every such default incur a penalty not exceeding twenty pounds ; and in any prosecution for such penalty it shall lie upon the master either to produce the certificate of the consular officer or officer of customs hereinbefore required, or to prove that he duly obtained the same, or that it was impracticable for him so to do.

(*t*) See 50 & 51 Vict. c. 62, s. 4.

*Official Logs.*

CCLXXX. The board of trade shall sanction forms of official log books which may be different for different classes of ships, so that each such form contains blanks for the entries hereinafter required ; and an official log of every ship (except ships employed exclusively in trading between ports on the coasts of the United Kingdom) shall be kept in the appropriate sanctioned form ; and such official log may, at the discretion of the master or owner, either be kept distinct from the ordinary ship's log or united therewith, so that in all cases all the blanks in the official log be duly filled up.

Official logs to be kept in forms sanctioned by board of trade.

CCLXXXI. Every entry in every official log shall be made as soon as possible after the occurrence to which it relates, and if not made on the same day as the occurrence to which it relates, shall be made and dated so as to show the date of the occurrence and of the entry respecting it ; and in no case shall any entry therein in respect of any occurrence happening previously to the arrival of the ship at her final port of discharge be made more than twenty-four hours after such arrival.

Entries to be made in due time. .

CCLXXXII. Every master of a ship for which an official log book is hereby required shall make or cause to be made therein entries of the following matters ; (that is to say,)

Entries required in official log.

(1.) Every legal conviction of any member of his crew and the punishment inflicted :

Convictions.

(2.) Every offence committed by any member of his crew for which it is intended to prosecute, or to enforce a forfeiture, or to exact a fine, together with such statement concerning the reading over such entry, and concerning the reply (if any) made to the charge, as hereinbefore required (*u*) :

Offences.

(3.) Every offence for which punishment is inflicted on board, and the punishment inflicted.

Punishments.

(4.) A statement of the conduct, character, and qualifications of each of his crew, or a statement that he declines to give an opinion on such particulars :

Conduct, &c., of crew.

(5.) Every case of illness or injury happening to any member of the crew, with the nature thereof, and the medical treatment adopted (if any) :

Illnesses and injuries.

(6.) Every case of death happening on board, and of the cause thereof (*v*) :

Deaths.

(7.) Every birth happening on board, with the sex of the infant and the names of the parents (*v*) :

Births.]

(8.) Every marriage taking place on board, with the names and ages of the parties :

Marriages.

(9.) The name of every seaman or apprentice who ceases to be a member of the crew, otherwise than by death, with the place, time, manner and cause thereof :

Quitting ship.

(10.) The amount of wages due to any seaman who enters her Majesty's service during the voyage :

Wages of men entering navy.

(11.) The wages due to any seaman or apprentice who dies during the voyage, and the gross amount of all deductions to be made therefrom :

Wages of deceased seamen.

(12.) The sale of the effects of any seaman or apprentice who dies during the voyage, including a statement of each article sold, and of the sum received for it :

Sale of deceased men's effects.

(13.) Every collision with any other ship, and the circumstances under which the same occurred.

Collisions.

CCLXXXIII. The entries hereby required to be made in official log books shall be signed as follows ; that is to say, every such entry shall be signed by the master and by the mate or some other of the crew, and every entry of illness, injury or death shall be also signed by the surgeon or medical practitioner on board (if any) ; and every entry of wages due to or of the sale of the effects of, any seaman or apprentice who dies shall be signed by the master and by the mate and some other member of the crew ; and every entry of wages due to any seaman who enters her Majesty's service shall be signed

Entries, how to be signed.

(*u*) See sect. 244, *supra*, p. 877.     (*v*) See 37 & 38 Vict. c. 88, s. 54.

III. *Official Logs.*

Penalties in respect of official logs.

by the master, and by the seaman or by the officer authorized to receive the seaman into such service.

CCLXXXIV. The following offences in respect of official log books shall be punishable as hereinafter mentioned ; (that is to say,)

(1.) If in any case an official log book is not kept in the manner hereby required, or if any entry hereby directed to be made in any such log book is not made at the time and in the manner hereby directed, the master shall for each such offence incur the specific penalty herein mentioned in respect thereof, or where there is no such specific penalty, a penalty not exceeding five pounds :

(2.) Every person who makes or procures to be made or assists in making any entry in any official log book in respect of any occurrence happening previously to the arrival of the ship at her final port of discharge more than twenty-four hours after such arrival, shall for each such offence incur a penalty not exceeding thirty pounds :

(3.) Every person who wilfully destroys or mutilates or renders illegible any entry in any official log book, or who wilfully makes or procures to be made or assists in making any false or fraudulent entry or omission in any such log book, shall for each such offence be deemed guilty of a misdemeanor.

Entries in official logs to be received in evidence.

CCLXXXV. All entries made in any official log book as hereinbefore directed shall be received in evidence in any proceeding in any court of justice, subject to all just exceptions.

Official logs to be delivered to shipping master.

CCLXXXVI. In the case of foreign-going ships the master shall, within forty-eight hours after the ship's arrival at her final port of destination in the United Kingdom or upon the discharge of the crew, whichever first happens, deliver to the shipping master before whom the crew is discharged the official log book of the voyage ; and the master or owner of every home trade ship, not exclusively employed in trading between ports on the coasts in the United Kingdom, shall within twenty-one days after the thirtieth day of June and the thirty-first day of December in every year transmit or deliver to some shipping master in the United Kingdom the official log book for the preceding half-year ; and every master or owner who refuses or neglects to deliver his official log book as hereby required, shall be subject to the same consequences and liabilities to which he is hereby made subject for the non-delivery of the list of his crew hereinbefore mentioned.

Official logs to be sent home in case of transfer of ship, and in case of loss.

CCLXXXVII. If any ship ceases by reason of transfer of ownership or change of employment to fall within the definition of a foreign-going or of a home trade ship, the master or owner thereof shall, if such ship is then in the United Kingdom, within one month, and if she is elsewhere within six months, deliver or transmit to the shipping master at the port to which the ship belonged the official log book (if any) duly made out to the time at which she ceased to be a foreign-going or home trade ship, and in default shall for each offence incur a penalty not exceeding ten pounds ; and if any ship is lost or abandoned, the master or owner thereof shall, if practicable, and as soon as possible, deliver or transmit to the shipping master at the port to which the ship belonged the official log book (if any) duly made out to the time of such loss or abandonment, and in default shall for each offence incur a penalty not exceeding ten pounds.

*East Indies and Colonies.*

## East Indies and Colonies.

Provisions of Act, as applied by East Indian and colonial governments to their own ships may be enforced throughout the empire.

CCLXXXVIII. If the governor-general of India in council, or the respective legislative authorities in any British possession abroad, by any acts, ordinances or other appropriate legal means, apply or adapt any of the provisions in the Third Part of this Act contained to any British ships registered at, trading with, or being at any place within their respective jurisdictions, and to the owners, masters, mates and crews thereof, such provisions, when so applied and adapted as aforesaid, and as long as they remain in force, shall in respect of the ships and persons to which the same are applied be enforced, and penalties and punishments for the breach thereof shall be recovered and inflicted, throughout her Majesty's dominions, in the same manner as if such provisions had been hereby so adopted and applied, and such penalties and punishments had been hereby expressly imposed.

CCLXXXIX. Every act, ordinance or other form of law to be passed or promulgated by the governor-general of India in council, or by any other legislative authority in pursuance of this Act, shall respectively be subject to the same right of disallowance or repeal, and require the same sanction or other acts and formalities, and be subject to the same conditions in all respects as exist and are required in order to the validity of any other act, ordinance or other form of law passed by such governor-general in council or other legislative authority respectively. *III. East Indies and Colonies.*

East Indian and colonial Acts to be subject to disallowance, and require sanction as in other cases.

CCXC. If in any matter relating to any ship or to any person belonging to any ship there appears to be a conflict of laws, then, if there is in the Third Part of this Act any provision on the subject which is hereby expressly made to extend to such ship, the case shall be governed by such provision, and if there is no such provision, the case shall be governed by the law of the place in which such ship is registered. Conflict of laws.

---

## PART IV.

### Safety and Prevention of Accidents.

Sects. CCXCI. to CCCXXIX.

---

## PART V.

### Pilotage (x).

Sects. CCCXXX. to CCCLXXXVII.

*Saving of Owners' and Masters' Rights.* *V. Saving of Owners' and Masters' Rights.*

CCCLXXXVIII. No owner or master of any ship shall be answerable to any person whatever for any loss or damage occasioned by the fault or incapacity of any qualified pilot acting in charge of such ship, within any district where the employment of such pilot is compulsory by law. Limitation of liability of owner where pilotage is compulsory.

---

## PART VI.

### Lighthouses.

Sects. CCCLXXXIX. to CCCCXVI.

---

## PART VII.

### Mercantile Marine Fund.

Sects. CCCCXVII. to CCCCXXXI.

---

(x) See the Merchant Shipping (Pilotage) Act, 1889 (52 & 53 Vict. c. 68).

## PART VIII.

### Wrecks, Casualties and Salvage (y).

*Inquiries into Wrecks.*

VIII. *Inquiries into Wrecks.*

Inquiries to be instituted in cases of wreck and casualty (z).

CCCCXXXII. In any of the cases following; (that is to say,)

Whenever any ship is lost, abandoned or materially damaged on or near the coasts of the United Kingdom;

Whenever any ship causes loss or material damage to any other ship on or near such coasts;

Whenever by reason of any casualty happening to or on board of any ship on or near such coasts loss of life ensues;

Whenever any such loss, abandonment, damage or casualty happens elsewhere, and any competent witnesses thereof arrive or are found at any place in the United Kingdom:

It shall be lawful for the inspecting officer of the coast guard or the principal officer of customs residing at or near the place where such loss, abandonment, damage or casualty occurred, if the same occurred on or near the coasts of the United Kingdom, but if elsewhere, at or near the place where such witnesses as aforesaid arrive or are found or can be conveniently examined, or for any other person appointed for the purpose by the board of trade to make inquiry respecting such loss, abandonment, damage or casualty; and he shall for that purpose have all the powers given by the First Part of this Act to inspectors appointed by the said board.

Formal investigation before justices.

CCCCXXXIII. If it appears to such officer or person as aforesaid, either upon or without any such preliminary inquiry as aforesaid, that a formal investigation is requisite or expedient, or if the board of trade so directs, he shall apply to any two justices or to a stipendiary magistrate to hear the case; and such justices or magistrates shall thereupon proceed to hear and try the same, and shall for that purpose, so far as it relates to the summoning of parties, compelling the attendance of witnesses and the regulation of the proceedings, have the same powers as if the same were a proceeding relating to an offence or cause of complaint upon which they or he have power to make a summary conviction or order, or as near thereto as circumstances permit, and it shall be the duty of such officer or person as aforesaid to superintend the management of the case, and to render such assistance to the said justices or magistrate as is in his power; and, upon the conclusion of the case, the said justices or magistrate shall send a report to the board of trade, containing a full statement of the case and of their or his opinion thereon, accompanied by such report of or extracts from the evidence, and such observations (if any) as they or he may think fit.

CCCCXXXIV. Repealed by 39 & 40 Vict. c. 80, s. 45.

Stipendiary magistrate to be the magistrate who is member of local marine board, and to be paid.

CCCCXXXV. In places where there is a local marine board, and where a stipendiary magistrate is a member of such board, all such investigations as aforesaid shall, whenever he happens to be present, be made before such magistrate; and there shall be paid to such magistrate in respect of his services under this Act, such remuneration, whether by way of annual increase of salary or otherwise as her Majesty's secretary of state for the home department, with the consent of the board of trade, may direct; and such remuneration shall be paid out of the mercantile marine fund.

Costs of such investigations.

CCCCXXXVI. The said justices or magistrate may make such order with respect to the costs of any such investigation or any portion thereof as they or he may deem just, and such costs shall be paid accordingly, and shall be recoverable in the same manner as other costs incurred in summary proceedings before them or him; and the board of trade may, if in any case it thinks fit so to do, pay the expense of any such investigation, and may pay to such assessor as aforesaid such remuneration as it thinks fit.

Investigations in Scotland.

CCCCXXXVII. In the case of any such investigation as aforesaid to be held in Scotland, the board of trade may, if it so think fit, remit the same to the lord advocate, to be prosecuted in such manner as he may direct [and in

---

(y) See 18 & 19 Vict. c. 91, ss. 19, 20, and 39 & 40 Vict. c. 80, s. 29, *infra*.

(z) See 39 & 40 Vict. c. 80, s. 29, *infra*.

case he so requires, with the assistance of such person of nautical skill and knowledge as the board of trade may appoint for the purpose] (a).

CCCCXXXVIII. Such justices or magistrate as aforesaid may, or in Scotland such person or persons as is or are directed by the lord advocate to conduct the investigation may, if they or he think fit, require any master or mate possessing a certificate of competency or service whose conduct is called in question or appears to them or him likely to be called in question in the course of such investigation, to deliver such certificate to them or him, and they or he shall hold the certificate so delivered until the conclusion of the investigation, and shall then either return the same to such master or mate, or, if their report is such as to enable the board of trade to cancel or suspend such certificate under the powers given to such board by the Third Part of this Act, shall forward the same to the board of trade, to be dealt with as such board thinks fit; and if any master or mate fails so to deliver his certificate when so required, he shall incur a penalty not exceeding fifty pounds.

*Master or mate may be required to deliver certificates to be held until close of inquiry.*

### *Appointment and Duties of Receivers.*

*Appointment and Duties of Receivers.*

CCCCXXXIX. The board of trade shall throughout the United Kingdom have the general superintendence of all matters relating to wreck; and it may, with the consent of the commissioners of her Majesty's treasury, appoint any officer of customs or of the coast guard, or any officer of inland revenue, or when it appears to such board to be more convenient, any other person to be a receiver of wreck in any district, and to perform such duties as are hereinafter mentioned, and shall give due notice of every such appointment.

*Board of trade superintendents of wreck, with power to appoint receivers.*

CCCCXL. No admiral, vice-admiral, or other person, under whatever denomination, exercising admiralty jurisdiction, shall as such, by himself, or his agents, receive, take, or interfere with any wreck except as hereinafter mentioned.

*Admiral not to interfere with wreck.*

CCCCXLI. Whenever any ship or boat is stranded or in distress at any place on the shore of the sea or of any tidal water within the limits of the United Kingdom, the receiver of the district within which such place is situate shall, upon being made acquainted with such accident, forthwith proceed to such place, and upon his arrival there he shall take the command of all persons present, and assign such duties to each person, and issue such directions, as he may think fit with a view to the preservation of such ship or boat, and the lives of the persons belonging thereto, and the cargo and apparel thereof; and if any person wilfully disobeys such directions he shall forfeit a sum not exceeding fifty pounds; but it shall not be lawful for such receiver to interfere between the master of such ship or boat and his crew in matters relating to the management thereof, unless he is requested so to do by such master.

*Duty of receiver whenever any ship is stranded or in distress.*

CCCCXLII. The receiver may, with a view to such preservation as aforesaid of the ship or boat, persons, cargo and apparel, do the following things; (that is to say,)

(1.) Summon such number of men as he thinks necessary to assist him:

(2.) Require the master or other person having the charge of any ship or boat near at hand to give such aid with his men, ship or boats as may be in his power:

(3.) Demand the use of any waggon, cart or horses that may be near at hand:

*Powers of receiver in case of such accident to any ship or boat.*

And any person refusing without reasonable cause to comply with any summons, requisition or demand so made as aforesaid, shall for every such refusal incur a penalty not exceeding one hundred pounds; but no person shall be liable to pay any duty of assessed taxes in respect of any such waggon, cart or horses, by reason of the user of the same under this section.

CCCCXLIII. All cargo and other articles belonging to such ship or boat as aforesaid as may be washed on shore, or otherwise be lost or taken from such ship or boat, shall be delivered to the receiver; and any person, whether he is the owner or not, who secretes or keeps possession of any such cargo or article, or refuses to deliver the same to the receiver or to any person authorised by him to demand the same, shall incur a penalty not

*All articles washed on shore or lost, or taken from any ship or boat, to be delivered to the receiver.*

(a) Words within brackets repealed by 39 & 40 Vict. c. 80, s. 45.

VIII. *Appointment and Duties of Receivers.*

exceeding one hundred pounds; and it shall be lawful for such receiver or other person as aforesaid to take such cargo or article by force from the person so refusing to deliver the same.

**Power of receiver to suppress plunder and disorder by force.**

CCCCXLIV. Whenever any accident as aforesaid occurs to any ship or boat, and any person plunders, creates disorder or obstructs the preservation of such ship, boat, lives or cargo as aforesaid, it shall be lawful for the receiver to cause such person to be apprehended, and to use force for the suppression of any such plundering, disorder or obstruction as aforesaid, with power to command all her Majesty's subjects to assist him in the use of such force; and if any person is killed, maimed or hurt by reason of his resisting the receiver in the execution of the duties hereby committed to him, or any person acting under his orders, such receiver or any other person shall be free and fully indemnified as well against the Queen's Majesty, her heirs and successors, as against all persons so killed, maimed or hurt.

**Certain officers to exercise powers of receiver in his absence.**

CCCCXLV. During the absence of the receiver from the place where any such accident as aforesaid occurs, or in places where no receiver has been appointed under this Act, the following officers in succession, each in the absence of the other, in the order in which they are named, that is to say, any principal officer of customs or of the coast guard, or officer of inland revenue, and also any sheriff, justice of the peace, commissioned officer on full pay in the naval service of her Majesty, or commissioned officer on full pay in the military service of her Majesty, may do all matters and things hereby authorised to be done by the receiver, with this exception, that with respect to any goods or articles belonging to any such ship or boat, the delivery up of which to the receiver is hereinbefore required, any officer so acting shall be considered as the agent of the receiver, and shall place the same in the custody of the receiver, and no person so acting as substitute for any receiver shall be entitled to any fees payable to receivers, or be deprived by reason of his so acting of any right to salvage to which he would otherwise be entitled.

**Power in case of a ship being in distress to pass over adjoining lands with carriages.**

CCCCXLVI. Whenever any such accident as aforesaid occurs to any ship or boat, all persons may, for the purpose of rendering assistance to such ship or boat, or saving the lives of the persons on board the same, or the cargo or apparel thereof, unless there is some public road equally convenient, pass and repass either with or without carriages or horses over any adjoining lands, without being subject to interruption by the owner or occupier, so that they do as little damage as possible, and may also, on the like condition, deposit on such lands any cargo or other article recovered from such ship or boat; and all damage that may be sustained by any owner or occupier in consequence of any such passing or repassing or deposit as aforesaid shall be a charge on the ship, boat, cargo or articles in respect of or by which such damage was occasioned, and shall, in default of payment, be recoverable in the same manner as salvage is hereby made recoverable; and the amount payable in respect thereof, if disputed, shall be determined in the same manner as the amount of salvage is hereby in case of dispute directed to be determined.

**Penalty on owners and occupiers of land refusing to allow carriages, &c., to pass over their land.**

CCCCXLVII. If the owner or occupier of any land over which any person is hereby authorised to pass or repass, for any of the purposes hereinbefore mentioned does any of the following things; (that is to say,)

(1.) Impedes or hinders any such person from so passing or repassing, with or without carriages, horses and servants, by locking his gates, refusing upon request to open the same or otherwise however:

(2.) Impedes or hinders the deposit of any cargo or other article recovered from any such ship or boat, as hereinbefore mentioned:

(3 ) Prevents such cargo or other article from remaining so deposited for a reasonable time, until the same can be removed to a safe place of public deposit:

he shall for every such offence incur a penalty not exceeding one hundred pounds.

**Power of receiver to institute examination with respect to ships in distress (b).**

CCCCXLVIII. Any receiver, or in his absence any justice of the peace, shall, as soon as conveniently may be, examine upon oath (which oath they are hereby respectively empowered to administer) any person belonging to any ship which may be or may have been in distress on the coasts of the

---

(b) 39 & 40 Vict. c. 80, ss. 31, 32, 33, *infra.*

United Kingdom, or any other person who may be able to give any account thereof, or of the cargo or stores thereof, as to the following matters; (that is to say,)

 (1.) The name and description of the ship :
 (2.) The name of the master and of the owners :
 (3.) The names of the owners of the cargo :
 (4.) The ports or places from and to which the ship was bound :
 (5.) The occasion of the distress of the ship :
 (6.) The services rendered :
 (7.) Such other matters or circumstances relating to such ship, or to the cargo on board the same, as the receiver or justice thinks necessary ;

and such receiver or justice shall take the examination down in writing, and shall make two copies of the same, of which he shall send one to the board of trade, and the other to the secretary of the committee for managing the affairs of Lloyd's in London, and such last-mentioned copy shall be placed by the said secretary in some conspicuous situation for the inspection of persons desirous of examining the same; and for the purposes of such examination every such receiver or justice as aforesaid shall have all the powers given by the First Part of this Act to inspectors appointed by the board of trade.

CCCCXLIX. Repealed by 39 & 40 Vict. c. 80.

CCCCL. The following rules shall be observed by any person finding or taking possession of wreck within the United Kingdom : (that is to say,)

 (1.) If the person so finding or taking possession of the same is the owner, he shall as soon as possible give notice to the receiver of the district within which such wreck is found, stating that he had so found or taken possession of the same ; and he shall describe in such notice the marks by which such wreck is distinguished :
 (2.) If any person not being the owner finds or takes possession of any wreck, he shall as soon as possible deliver the same to such receiver as aforesaid :

and any person making default in obeying the provisions of this section shall incur the following penalties ; (that is to say,)

 (3.) If he is the owner, and makes default in performing the several things the performance of which is hereby imposed on an owner, he shall incur a penalty not exceeding one hundred pounds :
 (4.) If he is not the owner, and makes default in performing the several things, the performance of which is hereby imposed on any person not being an owner,
He shall forfeit all claim to salvage ;
He shall pay to the owner of such wreck, if the same is claimed, but if the same is unclaimed then to the person entitled to such unclaimed wreck, double the value of such wreck (such value to be recovered in the same way as a penalty of like amount) ; and
He shall incur a penalty not exceeding one hundred pounds.

CCCCLI. If any receiver suspects or receives information that any wreck is secreted, or in the possession of some person who is not the owner thereof, or otherwise improperly dealt with, he may apply to any justice of the peace for a warrant, and such justice shall have power to grant a warrant, by virtue whereof it shall be lawful for the receiver to enter into any house or other place wherever situate, and also into any ship or boat, and to search for, and to seize and detain any such wreck as aforesaid there found ; and if any such seizure is made in consequence of information that may have been given by any person to the receiver, the informer shall be entitled by way of salvage to such sum not exceeding in any case five pounds as the receiver may allow.

CCCCLII. Every receiver shall within forty-eight hours after taking possession of any wreck cause to be posted up in the custom-house of the port nearest to the place where such wreck was found or seized a description of the same and of any marks by which it is distinguished, and shall also, if the value of such wreck exceeds twenty pounds, but not otherwise, transmit a similar description to the secretary of the committee of Lloyd's aforesaid ; and such secretary shall post up the description so sent, or a copy thereof, in some conspicuous place, for the inspection of all persons desirous of examining the same.

VIII. *Appointment and Duties of Receivers.*

Goods deemed perishable or of small value may be sold immediately.

CCCCLIII. In cases where any wreck in the custody of any receiver is under the value of five pounds, or is of so perishable a nature or so much damaged that the same cannot, in his opinion, be advantageously kept, or if the value thereof is not sufficient to defray the charge of warehousing, the receiver may sell the same before the expiration of the period hereinafter mentioned, and the money raised by such sale, after defraying the expenses thereof, shall be held by the receiver for the same purposes and subject to the same claims for and to which the article sold would have been held and liable if it had remained unsold.

In cases where any lord of the manor or other person is entitled to unclaimed wreck, receiver to give notice to him.

CCCCLIV. In cases where any admiral, vice-admiral, lord of the manor or other person is entitled for his own use to unclaimed wreck found on any place situate within a district for which a receiver is appointed, such admiral, vice-admiral, lord of the manor, or other person shall deliver to such receiver a statement containing the particulars of his title, and the address to which notices are to be sent; and upon such statement being so delivered, and proof made to the satisfaction of the receiver of the validity of such title, it shall be his duty, whenever he takes possession of any wreck found at any such place, to send within forty-eight hours thereafter a description of the same and of any marks by which it is distinguished, directed to such address as aforesaid.

Payments to be made to receiver.

CCCCLV. There shall be paid to all receivers appointed under this Act the expenses properly incurred by them in the performance of their duties, and also in respect of the several matters specified in the table marked (V) in the Schedule hereto, such fees, not exceeding the amounts therein mentioned, as may from time to time be directed by the board of trade; and the receiver shall have the same lien, and be entitled to the same remedies for the recovery of such expenses and fees as a salvor has or is entitled to in respect of salvage due to him: but, save as aforesaid, no receiver appointed under this Act shall, as such, be entitled to any remuneration whatsoever.

Disputes as to sums payable to receiver to be determined by board of trade.

CCCCLVI. Whenever any dispute arises in any part of the United Kingdom as to the amount payable to any receiver in respect of expenses or fees, such dispute shall be determined by the board of trade, whose decision shall be final.

Application of fees.

CCCCLVII. All fees received by any receiver appointed under this Act, in respect of any services performed by him as receiver, shall be carried to and form part of the mercantile marine fund, and a separate account thereof shall be kept, and the moneys arising therefrom shall be applied in defraying any expenses duly incurred in carrying into effect the purposes of the Eighth Part of this Act, in such manner as the board of trade directs.

*Salvage in the United Kingdom.*

## Salvage in the United Kingdom (c).

Salvage in respect of services rendered in the United Kingdom.

CCCCLVIII. In the following cases (that is to say,)
Whenever any ship or boat is stranded or otherwise in distress on the shore of any sea or tidal water situate within the limits of the United Kingdom, and services are rendered by any person,
(1.) In assisting such ship or boat:
(2.) In saving the lives of the persons belonging to such ship or boat:
(3.) In saving the cargo or apparel of such ship or boat, or any portion thereof:
And whenever any wreck is saved by any person other than a receiver within the United Kingdom;
There shall be payable by the owners of such ship or boat, cargo, apparel or wreck, to the person by whom such services or any of them are rendered or by whom such wreck is saved, a reasonable amount of salvage, together with all expenses properly incurred by him in the performance of such services or the saving of such wreck, the amount of such salvage and expense (which expenses are hereinafter included under the term salvage) to be determined in case of dispute in manner hereinafter mentioned.

Salvage for life may be paid by board of trade out of mercantile marine fund.

CCCCLIX. Salvage in respect of the preservation of the life or lives of any person or persons belonging to any such ship or boat, as aforesaid shall be payable by the owners of the ship or boat in priority to all other claims for salvage; and in cases where such ship or boat is destroyed, or where the value thereof is insufficient, after payment of the actual expenses incurred,

(c) See 18 & 19 Vict. c. 91, s. 20, *infra*.

to pay the amount of salvage due in respect of any life or lives, the board of trade may in its discretion award to the salvors of such life or lives, out of the mercantile marine fund, such sum or sums as it deems fit, in whole or part satisfaction of any amount of salvage so left unpaid in respect of such life or lives.

CCCCLX. Disputes with respect to salvage arising within the boundaries of the cinque ports shall be determined in the manner in which the same have hitherto been determined ; but whenever any dispute arises elsewhere in the United Kingdom between the owners of any such ship, boat, cargo, apparel or wreck as aforesaid, and the salvors, as to the amount of salvage, and the parties to the dispute cannot agree as to the settlement thereof by arbitration or otherwise,

Then, if the sum claimed does not exceed two hundred pounds (d),

Such dispute shall be referred to the arbitration of any two justices of the peace resident as follows ; (that is to say,)

In case of wreck, resident at or near the place where such wreck is found :

In case of services rendered to any ship or boat, or to the persons, cargo or apparel belonging thereto, resident at or near the place where such ship or boat is lying, or at or near the first port or place in the United Kingdom into which such ship or boat is brought after the occurrence of the accident by reason whereof the claim to salvage arises :

But if the sum claimed exceeds two hundred pounds (d),

Such dispute may, with the consent of the parties, be referred to the arbitration of such justices as aforesaid, but if they do not consent shall in England be decided by the high court of admiralty of England, in Ireland by the high court of admiralty of Ireland (e), and in Scotland by the court of session ; subject to this proviso, that if the claimants in such dispute do not recover in such court of admiralty or court of session a greater sum than two hundred pounds, they shall not, unless the court certifies that the case is a fit one to be tried in a superior court, recover any costs, charges or expenses incurred by them in the prosecution of their claim (f) :

And every dispute with respect to salvage may be heard and adjudicated upon on the application either of the salvor or of the owner of the property salved, or of their respective agents.

CCCCLXI. Whenever in pursuance of this Act any dispute as to salvage is referred to the arbitration of two justices, they may either themselves determine the same, with power to call to their assistance any person conversant with maritime affairs as assessor, or they may, if a difference of opinion arises between them, or without such difference if they think fit, appoint some person conversant with maritime affairs as umpire to decide the point in dispute ; and such justices or their umpire shall make an award as to the amount of salvage payable, within the following times, that is to say, the said justices within forty-eight hours after such dispute has been referred to them, and the said umpire within forty-eight hours after his appointment, with power nevertheless for such justice or umpire by writing under their or his hands or hand to extend the time within which they and he are hereby respectively directed to make their or his award.

CCCCLXII. There shall be paid to every assessor and umpire who may be so appointed as aforesaid in respect of his services such sum not exceeding five pounds as the board of trade may from time to time direct ; and all the costs of such arbitration, including any such payments as aforesaid, shall be paid by the parties to the dispute, in such manner and in such shares and proportions as the said justices or as the said umpire may direct by their or his award.

CCCCLXIII. The said justices or their umpire may call for the production of any documents in the possession or power of either party, which they or he may think necessary for determining the question in dispute, and may examine the parties or their witnesses on oath, and administer the oaths necessary for that purpose.

*VIII. Salvage in the United Kingdom.*

Disputes as to salvage, how to be settled.

Manner in which justices may decide disputes.

Costs of arbitration.

Justices may call for documents and administer oaths.

(d) But see now 25 & 26 Vict. c. 63, s. 49, *infra.*

(e) 30 & 31 Vict. c. 114, s. 27.
(f) 31 & 32 Vict. c. 71, s. 3.

CCCCLXIV. If any person is aggrieved by the award made by such justices or such umpire as aforesaid, he may in England appeal to the high court of admiralty of England, in Ireland to the high court of admiralty of Ireland, and in Scotland to the court of session ; but no such appeal shall be allowed unless the sum in dispute exceeds fifty pounds, nor unless within ten days after the date of the award the appellant gives notice to the justices to whom the matter was referred of his intention to appeal, nor unless the appellant proceeds to take out a monition or to take such other proceeding as according to the practice of the court of appeal is necessary for the institution of an appeal, within twenty days from the date of the award.

CCCCLXV. Whenever any appeal is made in manner hereinbefore provided, the justices shall transmit to the proper officer of the court of appeal a copy on unstamped paper certified under their hands to be a true copy of the proceedings had before such justices or their umpire, if any, and of the award so made by them or him, accompanied by their or his certificate in writing of the gross value of the article respecting which salvage is claimed ; and such copy and certificate shall be admitted in the court of appeal as evidence in the cause.

CCCCLXVI. Whenever the aggregate amount of salvage payable in respect of salvage services rendered in the United Kingdom has been finally ascertained either by agreement or by the award of such justices or their umpire, but a dispute arises as to the apportionment thereof amongst several claimants, then, if the amount does not exceed two hundred pounds, it shall be lawful for the party liable to pay the amount so due to apply to the receiver of the district for liberty to pay the amount so ascertained to him ; and he shall, if he thinks fit, receive the same accordingly, and grant a certificate under his hand, stating the fact of such payment and the services in respect of which it is made ; and such certificate shall be a full discharge and indemnity to the person or persons to whom it is given and to their ship, boats, cargo, apparel and effects, against the claims of all persons whomsoever in respect of the services therein mentioned ; but if the amount exceeds two hundred pounds it shall be apportioned in manner hereinafter mentioned.

CCCCLXVII. Upon the receipt of any such amount as aforesaid the receiver shall with all convenient speed proceed to distribute the same among the several persons entitled thereto, upon such evidence and in such shares and proportions as he thinks fit, with power to retain any moneys that may appear to him to be payable to any absent parties ; but any distribution made in pursuance of this section shall be final and conclusive against the rights of all persons claiming to be entitled to any portion of the moneys so distributed.

CCCCLXVIII. Whenever any salvage is due to any person under this Act, the receiver shall act as follows ; (that is to say,)

> (1.) If the same is due in respect of services rendered in assisting any ship or boat, or in saving the lives of persons belonging to the same, or the cargo or apparel thereof,
>> He shall detain such ship or boat and the cargo and apparel belonging thereto until payment is made, or process has been issued by some competent court for the detention of such ship, boat, cargo or apparel :
>
> (2.) If the same is due in respect of the saving of any wreck, and such wreck is not sold as unclaimed in pursuance of the provisions hereinafter contained,
>> He shall detain such wreck until payment is made, or process has been issued in manner aforesaid :

But it shall be lawful for the receiver, if at any time previously to the issue of such process security is given to his satisfaction for the amount **of salvage** due, to release from his custody any ship, boat, cargo, apparel, or wreck so detained by him as aforesaid (g) : and in cases where the claim for salvage exceeds two hundred pounds, it shall be lawful in England for the high court of admiralty of England, in Ireland for the high court of admiralty of Ireland, and in Scotland for the court of session (h), to determine any question that may arise concerning the amount of the security to be given or the sufficiency of the sureties ; and in all cases where bond or other security

---

(g) 25 & 26 Vict. c. 63, s. 50, *infra.*          (h) Id. s. 51, *infra.*

is given to the receiver for an amount exceeding two hundred pounds, it shall be lawful for the salvor or for the owner of the property salved, or their respective agents, to institute proceedings in such last-mentioned courts for the purpose of having the questions arising between them adjudicated upon, and the said courts may enforce payment of the said bond or other security, in the same manner as if bail had been given in the said courts. VIII. *Salvage in the United Kingdom.*

CCCCLXIX. Whenever any ship, boat, cargo, apparel or wreck is detained by any receiver for non-payment of any sums so due as aforesaid, and the parties liable to pay the same are aware of such detention, then, in the following cases, (that is to say,) Power of receiver to sell property salved in cases of non-payment.

(1.) In cases where the amount is not disputed, and payment thereof is not made within twenty days after the same has become due :

(2.) In cases where the amount is disputed, but no appeal lies from the first tribunal to which the dispute is referred, and payment thereof is not made within twenty days after the decision of such first tribunal :

(3.) In cases where the amount is disputed, and an appeal lies from the decision of the first tribunal to some other tribunal, and payment thereof is not made within such twenty days as last aforesaid, or such monition as hereinbefore mentioned is not taken out within such twenty days, or such other proceedings as are according to the practice of such other tribunal necessary for the prosecution of an appeal are not instituted within such twenty days :

The receiver may forthwith sell such ship, boat, cargo, apparel or wreck, or a sufficient part thereof, and out of the proceeds of the sale, after payment of all expenses thereof, defray all sums of money due in respect of expenses, fees and salvage, paying the surplus, if any, to the owners of the property sold, or other the parties entitled to receive the same.

CCCCLXX. Subject to the payment of such expenses, fees and salvage as aforesaid, the owner of any wreck who establishes his claim thereto to the satisfaction of the receiver within one year from the date at which such wreck has come into the possession of the receiver, shall be entitled to have the same delivered up to him (i). Subject to payment of expenses, fees and salvage, owner entitled to wreck.

### *Unclaimed Wreck in the United Kingdom.* *Unclaimed Wreck in the United Kingdom.*

CCCCLXXI. In the event of no owner (k) establishing a claim to a wreck found in any place in the United Kingdom before the expiration of a year from the date at which the same has come into the possession of the receiver, then, if any such admiral, vice-admiral, lord of any manor, or other person as aforesaid has given notice to and has proved to the satisfaction of the receiver, that he is entitled to wreck found at such place, the receiver shall, upon payment of all expenses, fees and salvage due in respect of such wreck, deliver up possession thereof to such admiral, vice-admiral, lord of the manor, or other person (l); and in case of dispute as to the amount of the sums so payable, and also in case of default being made in payment thereof, such dispute shall be determined and payment enforced in the manner in which such amount and payment is hereby directed to be determined and enforced in cases where any owner establishes his claim to wreck. Receiver to deliver up possession of unclaimed wreck to lord of manor or other person entitled.

CCCCLXXII. If any dispute arises between the receiver and any such admiral, vice-admiral, lord of any manor, or other person as aforesaid, as to the validity of his title to wreck, or if divers persons claim to be entitled to wreck found at the same place, the matter in dispute may be decided by two justices in the same manner in which disputes as to salvage coming within the jurisdiction of justices are hereinbefore directed to be determined. Disputed title to wreck, how to be decided.

CCCCLXXIII. If any party to such dispute is unwilling to refer the same to two justices, or, having so referred the same, is dissatisfied with their decision, he may within three months from the expiration of such year as aforesaid, or from the date of such decision as aforesaid, as the case may be, take such proceedings as he may be advised in any court of law, equity, or admiralty having jurisdiction in the matter, for establishing his title. Appeal from decision of justices.

CCCCLXXIV. The board of trade shall have power, with the consent of Power of the board of trade

---

(i) See 18 & 19 Vict. c. 91, s. 19, *infra.*

(k) 25 & 26 Vict. c. 63, s. 52, *infra.*

(l) Id. s. 53, *infra.*

**VIII.** *Unclaimed Wreck in the United Kingdom.*

*on behalf of the Crown to purchase right to wreck.*

the Treasury, out of the revenue arising under the Eighth Part of this Act, for and on behalf of her Majesty, her heirs and successors, to purchase all such rights to wreck as may be possessed by any person or body corporate other than her Majesty ; and for the purpose of facilitating such purposes the provisions of the Lands Clauses Consolidation Act, 1845, and the Lands Clauses Consolidation (Scotland) Act, 1845, relating to the purchase of lands by agreement, shall be incorporated with this Act ; and in the construction of this Act and the said incorporated Acts this Act shall be considered to be the " special Act ; " and any such rights to wreck as aforesaid shall be considered as an interest in land authorized to be taken by the special Act, and her Majesty, her heirs and successors, shall be considered as the promoters of the undertaking.

*Unclaimed wreck to be sold (m).*

CCCCLXXV. If no owner establishes his claim to wreck found at any place before the expiration of such period of a year as aforesaid, and if no admiral, vice-admiral, lord of any manor, or person other than her Majesty, her heirs and successors, is proved to be entitled to such wreck, the receiver shall forthwith sell the same, and after payment of all expenses attending such sale, and deducting therefrom his fees and all expenses (if any) incurred by him, and paying to the salvors such amount of salvage as the board of trade may in each case or by any general rule determine, pay the same into the receipt of her Majesty's Exchequer in such manner as the Treasury may direct, and the same shall be carried to and form part of the consolidated fund of the United Kingdom.

*Jurisdiction of the High Court of Admiralty.*

### Jurisdiction of the High Court of Admiralty.

*High court of admiralty may decide on all salvage cases, whether on sea or land.*

CCCCLXXVI. Subject to the provisions of this Act, the High Court of Admiralty shall have jurisdiction to decide upon all claims whatsoever relating to salvage, whether the services in respect of which salvage is claimed were performed upon the high seas, or within the body of any county, or partly in one place and partly in the other, and whether the wreck is found at sea or cast upon the land, or partly in the sea and partly on land (n).

*Offences in respect of Wreck.*

### Offences in respect of Wreck.

*In case of ship wrecked being plundered by a tumultuous assemblage, the hundred to be liable for damages.*

CCCCLXXVII. Whenever any ship or boat is stranded or otherwise in distress on or near the shore of any sea or tidal water in the United Kingdom, and such ship or boat, or any part of the cargo or apparel thereof, is plundered, damaged or destroyed by any persons riotously and tumultuously assembled together, whether on shore or afloat, full compensation shall be made to the owner of such ship, boat, cargo, or apparel, as follows ; (that is to say,)

In England, by the inhabitants of the hundred, wapentake, ward, or district in the nature of a hundred, by whatever name denominated, in or nearest to which the said offence is committed, in manner provided by an Act of the eighth year of the reign of King George the Fourth, chapter thirty-one, in case of the destruction of churches and other buildings by a riotous assemblage, or as near thereto as circumstances permit :

In Ireland, by the inhabitants of the county, county of a city or town barony, town or towns, parish or parishes, in or nearest to which such offence is committed, in manner provided by an Act of the fourth year of the reign of King William the Fourth, chapter thirty-seven, for the recovery of satisfaction and amends for the malicious demolition of or injury to churches, chapels and other buildings used for religious worship, according to the usage of the United Church of England, and Ireland, or as near thereto as circumstances permit.

In Scotland, by the inhabitants of the county, city or borough in or nearest to which such offence is committed, in manner provided by an Act of the first year of King George the First, statute two, chapter five, with respect to prosecutions for repairing the damages

---

(m) See 25 & 26 Vict. c. 63, s. 53, *infra.*

(n) Extended by 24 Vict. c. 10, s. 9, to claims for salvage of life.

of any churches and other buildings, or as near thereto as circumstances permit.

CCCCLXXVIII. Every person who does any of the following acts; (that is to say,)

(1.) Wrongfully carries away or removes any part of any ship or boat stranded or in danger of being stranded or otherwise in distress on or near the shore of any sea or tidal water, or any part of the cargo or apparel thereof, or any wreck ; or

(2.) Endeavours in any way to impede or hinder the saving of such ship, boat, cargo, apparel or wreck ; or

(3.) Secretes any wreck, or obliterates or defaces any marks thereon ;

Shall, in addition to any other penalty or punishment he may be subject to under this or any other act or law, for each such offence incur a penalty not exceeding fifty pounds ; and every person, not being a receiver or a person hereinbefore authorized to take the command in cases of ships being stranded or in distress, or not acting under the orders of such receiver or person, who without the leave of the master, endeavours to board any such ship or boat as aforesaid, shall for each offence incur a penalty not exceeding fifty pounds ; and it shall be lawful for the master of such ship or boat to repel by force any such person so attempting to board the same (*o*).

CCCCLXXIX. If any person takes into any foreign port or place any ship or boat stranded, derelict, or otherwise in distress on or near the shore of the sea or of any tidal water situate within the limits of the United Kingdom, or any part of the cargo or apparel thereof, or anything belonging thereto, or any wreck found within such limits as aforesaid, and there sells the same, he shall be guilty of felony, and be subject to penal servitude for a term not exceeding four years.

*Dealers in Marine Stores and Manufacturers of Anchors.*

CCCCLXXX. Every person dealing in, buying and selling anchors, cables, sails or old junk, old iron, or marine stores of any description, shall conform to the following regulations ; (that is to say,)

(1.) He shall have his name, together with the words " Dealer in Marine Stores," painted distinctly in letters of not less than six inches in length on every warehouse or other place of deposit belonging to him ;

If he does not he shall incur a penalty not exceeding twenty pounds :

(2.) He shall keep a book or books, fairly written, and shall enter therein an account of all such marine stores as he may from time to time become possessed of, stating, in respect of each article, the time at which and the person from whom he purchased or received the same, adding, in the case of every such last-mentioned person, a description of his business and place of abode :

If he does not he shall incur for the first offence a penalty not exceeding twenty pounds, and for every subsequent offence a penalty not exceeding fifty pounds :

(3.) He shall not, by himself or his agents, purchase marine stores of any description from any person apparently under the age of sixteen years ;

If he does so he shall incur for the first offence a penalty not exceeding five pounds, and for every subsequent offence a penalty not exceeding twenty pounds :

(4.) He shall not cut up any cable, or any similar article exceeding five fathoms in length, or unlay the same into twine or paper stuff, on any pretence whatever, without obtaining such permit and publishing such notice of his having so obtained the same as is hereinafter mentioned ;

If he does so he shall incur for the first offence a penalty not exceeding twenty pounds, and for every subsequent offence a penalty not exceeding fifty pounds (*p*).

(*o*) 24 & 25 Vict. c. 96, ss. 65, 66, *infra;* 24 & 25 Vict. c. 100, ss. 17, 37.　　(*p*) 38 & 39 Vict. c. 25.

VIII. *Dealers in Marine Stores and Manufacturers of Anchors.*

Manner of obtaining permit to cut up cables.

CCCCLXXXI. In order to obtain such permit as aforesaid, a dealer in marine stores shall make a declaration before some justice of the peace, having jurisdiction over the place where such dealer resides, containing the following particulars : (that is to say,)

(1.) A statement of the quality and description of the cable or other like article about to be cut up or unlaid :

(2.) A statement that he purchased or otherwise acquired the same bonâ fide and without fraud, and without any knowledge or suspicion that the same had been come by dishonestly :

(3.) A statement of the name and description of the person from whom he purchased or received the same :

And it shall be lawful for the justice before whom any such declaration is made, or for the receiver of the district in which such dealer in marine stores resides, upon the production of any such declaration as aforesaid, to grant a permit authorizing him to cut up or unlay such cable or other like article.

Permit to be advertised before dealer proceeds to act thereon.

CCCCLXXXII. No dealer in marine stores who has obtained such permit as aforesaid shall proceed by virtue thereof to cut up or unlay any cable or other like article until he has for the space of one week at the least before doing any such act published in some newspaper published nearest to the place where he resides one or more advertisements notifying the fact of his having so obtained a permit, and specifying the nature of the cable or other article mentioned in the permit, and the place where the same is deposited, and the time at which the same is intended to be so cut up or unlaid ; and if any person suspects or believes that such cable or other article is his property, he may apply to any justice of the peace for a warrant ; and such justice of the peace may, on the applicant making oath, or, if a person entitled to make an affirmation, making an affirmation, in support of such his suspicion or belief, grant a warrant by virtue whereof the applicant shall be entitled to require the production by such dealer as aforesaid of the cable or other article mentioned in the permit, and also of the book of entries hereinbefore directed to be kept by every dealer in marine stores ; and upon such cable or other article and book of entries being produced, to inspect and examine the same ; and if any dealer in marine stores makes default in complying with any of the provisions of this section, he shall for the first offence incur a penalty not exceeding twenty pounds, and for every subsequent offence a penalty not exceeding fifty pounds.

Manufacturers to place marks on anchors.

CCCCLXXXIII. Every manufacturer of anchors shall, in case of each anchor which he manufactures, mark in legible characters on the crown and also on the shank under the stock his name or initials, with the addition of a progressive number and the weight of such anchor ; and if he makes default in doing so he shall for each offence incur a penalty not exceeding five pounds.

## Salvage by Her Majesty's Ships.

Salvage by H. M. Ships.

No claim for salvage services to be allowed in respect of loss or risk of her Majesty's ships or property.

CCCCLXXXIV. In cases where salvage services are rendered by any ship belonging to her Majesty or by the commander or crew thereof, no claim shall be made or allowed for any loss, damage or risk thereby caused to such ship, or to the stores, tackle or furniture thereof, or for the use of any stores or other articles belonging to her Majesty supplied in order to effect such services, or for any other expense or loss sustained by her Majesty by reason of such services.

Claims for salvage by her Majesty's officers not to be determined without consent of admiralty.

CCCCLXXXV. No claim whatever on account of any salvage services rendered to any ship or cargo or to any appurtenances of any ship by the commander or crew or part of the crew of any of her Majesty's ships shall be finally adjudicated upon unless the consent of the admiralty has been first obtained, such consent to be signified by writing under the hand of the secretary to the admiralty ; and if any person who has originated proceedings in respect of any such claim fails to prove such consent to the satisfaction of the court, his suit shall stand dismissed and he shall pay all the costs of such proceedings ; provided that any document purporting to give such consent and to be signed by the secretary to the admiralty shall be primâ facie evidence of such consent having been given.

Steps to be taken when salvage services have been rendered by her

CCCCLXXXVI. Whenever services for which salvage is claimed are rendered to any ship or cargo, or to any part of any ship or cargo, or to any appurtenances of any ship, at any place out of the United Kingdom and the four seas adjoining thereto, by the commander or crew or part of the crew of any of her Majesty's ships, the property alleged to be salved shall, if the VIII. *Salvage by*<br>*H. M. Ships.* salvor is justified by the circumstances of the case in detaining it at all, be taken to some port where there is either a consular officer or a vice-admiralty Majesty's ships court ; and within twenty-four hours after arriving at such port the said abroad. salvor and the master or other person in charge of the property alleged to be salved shall each deliver to the consular officer or vice-admiralty judge there a statement verified on oath, specifying, so far as they respectively can, and so far as the particulars required apply to the case,

(1.) The place, condition, and circumstances in which the said ship, cargo, or property was at the time when the services were rendered for which salvage is claimed :

(2.) The nature and duration of the services rendered :

And the salvor shall add to his statement,

(3.) The proportion of the value of the said ship, cargo, and property, and of the freight which he claims for salvage, or the values at which he estimates the said ship, freight, cargo, and property respectively, and the several amounts that he claims for salvage in respect of the same :

(4.) Any other circumstances he thinks relevant to the said claim :

And the said master or other person in charge of the said ship, cargo, or property shall add to his statement,

(3.) A copy of the certificate of registry of the said ship, and of the indorsements thereon, stating any change which (to his knowledge or belief) has occurred in the particulars contained in such certificate; and stating also, to the best of his knowledge and belief, the state of the title to the ship for the time being, and of the incumbrances and certificates of mortgage or sale, if any, affecting the same, and the names and places of business of the owners and incumbrancers :

(4.) The name and place of business or residence of the freighter (if any) of the said ship, and the freight to be paid for the voyage she is then on :

(5.) A general account of the quantity and nature of the cargo at the time the salvage services were rendered :

(6.) The name and place of business or residence of the owner of such cargo, and of the consignee thereof :

(7.) The value at which the said master estimates the said ship, cargo, and property, and the freight respectively, or, if he thinks fit, in lieu of such estimated value of the cargo, a copy of the ship's manifest :

(8.) The amounts which the master thinks should be paid as salvage for the services rendered :

(9.) An accurate list of the property saved, in cases where the ship is not saved :

(10.) An account of the proceeds of the sale of the said ship, cargo, or property, in cases where the same or any of them are sold at such port as aforesaid :

(11.) The number, capacities, and condition of the crew of the said ship at the time the said services were rendered :

(12.) Any other circumstances he thinks relevant to the matters in question :

(13.) A statement of his willingness to execute a bond, in the form in the table marked (W) in the Schedule hereto, in such amount as the said consular officer or vice-admiralty judge may fix.

CCCCLXXXVII. The said consular officer or judge, as the case may be, Consular officer shall within four days after receiving the aforesaid statements, fix the amount or judge to fix to be inserted in the said bond at such sum as he thinks sufficient to answer amount for<br>which a bond is the demand for the salvage services rendered ; but such sum shall not exceed to be given. one-half of the value which in his estimation the said ship, freight, and cargo, or any parts thereof in respect of which salvage is claimed, are worth ; and the said consular officer or judge may, if either of the aforesaid statements is not delivered to him within the time hereby required, proceed ex parte, but he shall in no case under this Act require the cargo to be unladen ; and the said consular officer may in any proceeding under this Act relating to salvage, take affidavits and receive affirmations.

VIII. *Salvage by H. M. Ships.*

On master executing bond, the right of detention to cease.

CCCCLXXXVIII. The said consular officer or judge shall send notice of the sum which he has so fixed as aforesaid to the said salvor and the said master ; and upon such master executing a bond in such form as aforesaid, with the said sum inserted therein, in the presence of the said officer or judge (who shall attest the same), and delivering the same to the said salvor, the right of the said salvor to detain or retain possession of the said ship, cargo, or property, or any of them, in respect of the said salvage claim, shall cease.

Provision for additional security in the case of ships owned by persons resident out of her Majesty's dominions.

CCCCLXXXIX. If the ship, cargo, or property in respect of which the claim for salvage is made is not owned by persons domiciled in her Majesty's dominions, the right of the salvor to detain or retain possession thereof shall not cease unless the master procures, in addition to the said bond, such security for the due performance of the conditions thereof as the said officer or judge considers sufficient for the purpose, and places the same in the possession or custody of the said officer or judge, or, if the salvor so desires, in the possession or custody of the said officer or judge jointly with any other person whom the said salvor appoints for the purpose.

Documents to be sent to England.

CCCCXC. The said consular officer or judge shall at the earliest opportunity transmit the said statements and documents so sent to him as aforesaid, and a notice of the sum he has so fixed as aforesaid, to the high court of admiralty of England, or if the said salvor and the said master or other person in charge as aforesaid agree that the said bond shall be adjudicated upon by any vice-admiralty court, to such Court.

Whom the bond shall bind.

CCCCXCI. The said bond shall bind the respective owners of the said ship, freight, and cargo, and their respective heirs, executors, and administrators, for the salvage adjudged to be payable in respect of the said ship, freight, and cargo respectively.

Court in which it is to be adjudicated on.

CCCCXCII. The said bond shall be adjudicated on and enforced by the high court of admiralty in England, or if the said salvor and master at the time of the execution of the said bond agree upon any vice-admiralty court, then by such vice-admiralty court ; and any such vice-admiralty court may in every proceeding under this Act have and exercise all powers and authorities whatsoever which the said high court of admiralty now has or at any time may have in any proceeding whatsoever before it ; and in cases where any security for the due performance of the conditions of the said bond has been placed in the possession or custody of the said consular officer or vice-admiralty judge or of such officer or judge jointly with any other person, the person or persons having the custody of such security shall respectively deal with the same in such manner as the court that adjudicates on the bond directs.

Power of high court of admiralty to enforce bonds.

CCCCXCIII. The said high court of admiralty shall have power to enforce any bond given in pursuance of this Act in any vice-admiralty court in any part of her Majesty's dominions ; and all courts in Scotland, Ireland, and the islands of Jersey, Guernsey, Alderney, Sark, and Man exercising admiralty jurisdiction shall, upon application, aid and assist the high court of admiralty in enforcing the said bonds.

Saving clause.

CCCCXCIV. Any such salvor as aforesaid of any ship, cargo, or property who elects not to proceed under this Act shall have no power to detain the said ship, cargo, or property, but may proceed otherwise for the enforcement of his salvage claim as if this Act had not been passed ; and nothing in this Act contained shall abridge or affect the rights of salvors, except in the cases by it provided for.

Documents free from duty.

CCCCXCV. All bonds, statements, agreements and other documents made or executed in pursuance of the Eighth Part of this Act shall, if so made or executed out of the United Kingdom, be exempt from stamp duty.

Punishment for forgery and false representations.

CCCCXCVI. Every person who, in any proceeding under provisions contained in the Eighth Part of this Act relating to salvage by her Majesty's ships, forges, assists in forging, or procures to be forged, fraudulently alters, assists in fraudulently altering, or procures to be fraudulently altered, any document, and every person who in any such proceeding puts off or makes use of any such forged or altered document, knowing the same to be so forged or altered, or who in any such proceeding gives or makes, or assists in giving or making, or procures to be given or made, any false evidence or representation, knowing the same to be false, shall be punishable with imprisonment, with or without hard labour, for any period not exceeding two years, or, if summarily prosecuted and convicted, by imprisonment, with or without hard labour, for any period not exceeding six months.

### Salvage (General).

CCCCXCVII. Whenever services for which salvage is claimed are rendered either by the commander or crew or part of the crew of any of her Majesty's ships, or of any other ship, and the salvor voluntarily agrees to abandon his lien upon the ship, cargo and property alleged to be salved, upon the master or other person in charge thereof entering into a written agreement attested by two witnesses to abide the decision of the said high court of admiralty or of any vice-admiralty court, and thereby giving security in that behalf to such amount as may be agreed on by the parties to the said agreement, such agreement shall bind the said ship and the said cargo and the freight payable therefor respectively, and the respective owners of the said ship, freight and cargo for the time being, and their respective heirs, executors and administrators, for the salvage which may be adjudged to be payable in respect of the said ship, cargo and freight respectively to the extent of the security so given as aforesaid, and may be adjudicated upon and enforced in the same manner as the bonds provided for by the Eighth Part of this Act, in the case of detention for salvage services rendered by her Majesty's ships; and upon such agreement being made the salvor and the master or other person in charge as aforesaid shall respectively make such statements as are hereinbefore required to be made by them in case of a bond being given, except that such statements need not be made upon oath; and the salvor shall, as soon as practicable, transmit the said agreement and the said statements to the court in which the said agreement is to be adjudicated upon.

CCCCXCVIII. Whenever the aggregate amount of salvage payable in respect of salvage services rendered in the United Kingdom has been finally ascertained, and exceeds two hundred pounds, and whenever the aggregate amount of salvage payable in respect of salvage services rendered elsewhere has been finally ascertained, whatever such amount may be, then if any delay or dispute arise as to the apportionment thereof, any court having admiralty jurisdiction may cause the same to be apportioned amongst the persons entitled thereto in such manner as it thinks just; and may for that purpose, if it thinks fit, appoint any person to carry such apportionment into effect, and may compel any person in whose hands or under whose control such amount may be to distribute the same, or to bring the same into court, to be there dealt with as the court may direct, and may for the purpose aforesaid issue such monitions or other processes as it thinks fit.

### Miscellaneous.

CCCCXCIX. All wreck, being foreign goods brought or coming into the United Kingdom or the Isle of Man, shall be subject to the same duties as if the same were imported into the United Kingdom or the Isle of Man respectively; and if any question arises as to the origin of such goods, they shall be deemed to be the produce of such country as the commissioners of customs may upon investigation determine.

D. The commissioners of customs and excise shall permit all goods, wares, and merchandise saved from any ship stranded or wrecked on its homeward voyage to be forwarded to the port of its original destination, and all goods, wares, and merchandise saved from any ship stranded or wrecked on its outward voyage to be returned to the port at which the same were shipped; but such commissioners are to take security for the due protection of the revenue in respect of such goods, wares, and merchandise.

DI. All matters and things that may in pursuance of the Eighth Part of this Act be done by or to any justice, or any two justices, may in Scotland be done also by or to the sheriff of the county, including the sheriff substitute; and the expression "lord or lady of a manor" shall in the Eighth Part of this Act, so far as regards Scotland, include "heritable proprietor duly infeft."

## PART IX.

### Liability to Shipowners (q).

IX. *Application.*

### *Application.*

Application of
Part IX. of Act. DII. The Ninth Part of this Act shall apply to the whole of her Majesty's dominions.

*Limitation of
Liability.*

### *Limitation of Liability.*

Owner not liable
in respect of
certain articles. DIII. No owner of any sea-going ship or share therein shall be liable to make good any loss or damage that may happen without his actual fault or privity of or to any of the following things; (that is to say,)

> (1.) Of or to any goods, merchandise, or other things whatsoever taken in or put on board any such ship, by reason of any fire happening on board such ship:
>
> (2.) Of or to any gold, silver, diamonds, watches, jewels, or precious stones taken in or put on board any such ship, by reason of any robbery, embezzlement, making away with or secreting thereof, unless the owner or shipper thereof has, at the time of shipping the same, inserted in his bills of lading or otherwise declared in writing, to the master or owner of such ship the true nature and value of such articles,

To any extent whatever.

DIV. Repealed, 25 & 26 Vict. c. 63, s. 2, and see s. 54 of that statute, *post.*

DV. Repealed, 25 & 26 Vict. c. 63, s. 2.

Provision
for separate
losses (r). DVI. The owner of every sea-going ship or share therein shall be liable in respect of every such loss of life (s), personal injury, loss of or damage to goods as aforesaid arising on distinct occasions to the same extent as if no other loss, injury or damage had arisen.

*Mode of Pro-
cedure.*

### *Mode of Procedure.*

In case of loss of
life or personal
injury, board of
trade may
direct pro-
ceedings. DVII. Whenever any such liability as aforesaid has been or is alleged to have been incurred in respect of loss of life or personal injury, the board of trade may, in its discretion, after giving not less than three days' notice by post or otherwise to the party to be made defendant or defender, by warrant sealed with the seal of such board or signed by one of its secretaries or assistant secretaries, require the sheriff having jurisdiction over any place in the United Kingdom to summon a jury at a time and place to be specified in such warrant for the purpose of determining the following question; (that is to say,)

> The number, names and descriptions of all persons killed or injured by reason of any wrongful act, neglect or default:

And upon the receipt of such warrant the sheriff shall summon a jury of twenty-four indifferent persons, duly qualified to act as common jurymen in the superior courts, to meet at such time and place as aforesaid.

Either party
may require
question to be
tried by a
special jury. DVIII. If either party to the inquiry desire any such question as aforesaid to be tried before a special jury, such question shall be so tried, provided that notice of such desire, if coming from the other party, is given to the board of trade before it has issued its warrant to the sheriff; and for that purpose the board of trade shall, by its warrant to the sheriff, require him to nominate a special jury for such trial; and thereupon the sheriff shall, as soon as conveniently may be after the receipt by him of such warrant, summon both the parties to appear before him by themselves or their attorneys or agents at some convenient time and place appointed by him for the purpose of nominating a special jury; and at the place and time so appointed the sheriff shall proceed to nominate and strike a special jury in the manner in which such juries are required by the laws for the time being in force to be nominated or struck by the proper officers of the superior courts; and the sheriff shall appoint a day and shall on the day so appointed proceed to

---

(q) Amended by 25 & 26 Vict. c. 63, s. 54, *infra.*

(r) See 53 Geo. 3, c. 159, s. 53.

(s) 25 & 26 Vict. c. 63, s. 56, *infra.*

reduce the said special jury to the number of twenty, in the manner used and accustomed by the proper officers of the superior courts.

DIX. The following provisions shall be applicable to the conduct of proceedings by the board of trade ; (that is to say,)

(1.) The sheriff shall preside at such inquiry ; and the board of trade shall be deemed in England and Ireland to be the plaintiff, and in Scotland the pursuer, both of which terms are hereinafter included in the term plaintiff, with power to appoint any agent to act on its behalf, and shall have all such rights and privileges as the plaintiff is entitled to in actions at law ; and the owner or owners of the ship or ships by whom such liability as last aforesaid is alleged to have been incurred shall be deemed in England and Ireland to be the defendant, and in Scotland the defender, both of which terms are hereinafter included in the term defendant :

(2.) Not less than ten days' notice of the time and place of the inquiry shall be served by the board of trade on the defendant :

(3.) Service on the master of any ship shall be deemed good service on the owner thereof, and the master shall, in respect of the proceedings on such inquiry, be deemed the agent and representative of the owner, with power to appear for him on such inquiry, and to do all matters and things which he might himself have done :

(4.) If the defendant does not appear at the time of such inquiry, the same shall be proceeded with as if he had appeared, upon due proof of service of notice having been made on him in pursuance of this Act :

(5.) The empannelling of the jury and the summoning and attendance of witnesses shall be conducted and enforced in England and Ireland in manner provided by the Lands Clauses Consolidation Act, 1845, in cases of disputed compensation as to land, and in Scotland in manner provided by the Lands Clauses Consolidation (Scotland) Act, 1845, in like cases, or as near thereto as circumstances permit ; and all provisions in the said acts having reference to cases where any question of dispute and compensation requires to be determined by the verdict of a jury shall, with the requisite alterations, be considered as incorporated with this Act, and to have reference to cases where the question of the liability of any owner in respect of any such accident as aforesaid require to be determined by the verdict of a jury :

(6.) In England and Ireland the sheriff shall, if the board of trade so requires, or if the defendant so requires and the board of trade consents thereto, appoint as assessor a barrister at law of competent knowledge and standing :

(7.) The costs incurred by all parties in and incidental to any such inquiry as aforesaid shall in England and Ireland be taxed by the master of one of her Majesty's superior courts of common law as between attorney and client, and in Scotland by the auditor of the court of session as between agent and client ; and shall, if the verdict in any inquiry is in favour of the plaintiff, be paid by the defendant, but if such verdict is in favour of the defendant, be paid by the board of trade out of the mercantile marine fund :

(8.) The payment of all damages and costs in any such inquiry as aforesaid shall, upon application made to such superior court as aforesaid by the party entitled thereto, be enforced by the rule or order of such court or a judge thereof, or otherwise as such court or judge thinks fit :

(9.) The board of trade may make any compromise it thinks fit as to the damages payable in respect of personal injury, or of the death of any person ; and any damages received in pursuance of such compromise shall, so far as the same extend, be applied in the same manner and be subject to the same rules as if the same were damages recovered on an inquiry instituted by the board of trade.

DX. The following rules shall be observed as to the damages recovered in any such inquiry, and the application thereof ; (that is to say,)

(1.) The damages payable in each case of death or injury shall be assessed at thirty pounds :

(2.) The damages found due on any such inquiry as aforesaid shall be the first charge on the aggregate amount for which the owner is liable, and shall be paid thereout in priority to all other claims:

(3.) All such damages as aforesaid shall be paid to her Majesty's paymaster general, and shall be distributed and dealt with by him in such manner as the board of trade directs; and in directing such distribution the board of trade shall have power in the first place to deduct and retain any costs incidental thereto; and in the next place, as regards the sums paid in respect of injuries, shall direct payment to each person injured of such compensation, not exceeding in any case the statutory amount, as the said board thinks fit; and as regards the sums paid in respect of deaths shall direct payment thereof for the benefit of the husband, wife, parent and child of the deceased, or any of them, in such shares, upon such evidence, and in such manner as the said board thinks fit:

(4.) The board of trade shall refund to the owner any surplus remaining under its control after making such distribution as aforesaid, and the sum so refunded shall form part of the residue hereinafter mentioned:

(5.) The board of trade shall not, nor shall any person acting under it, be liable to any action, suit, account, claim or demand whatsoever for or in respect of any act or matter done, or omitted to be done, in the distribution of such damages as aforesaid:

(6.) If the amount paid to her Majesty's paymaster general in manner aforesaid is insufficient to meet the demands upon it, the several claims thereon shall abate proportionally.

Any person who is dissatisfied with the amount of statutory damage may bring an action on his own account.

DXI. After the completion of such inquiry as aforesaid, if any person injured estimates the damages payable in respect of such injury, or if the executor or administrator of any deceased person estimates the damages payable in respect of his death at a greater sum than such statutory amount, or, in case of a compromise having been made by the board of trade, than the amount accepted by such board by way of compensation for such injury or such death as aforesaid, the person so estimating the same shall, upon repaying or obtaining the repayment by the board of trade to the owner of the amount paid by him to the board of trade in respect of such injury or death, be at liberty to bring an action for the recovery of damages in the same manner as if no power of instituting an inquiry had hereinbefore been given to the board of trade, subject to the following proviso; (that is to say,) that any damages recoverable by such person shall be payable only out of the residue, if any, of the aggregate amount for which the owner is liable, after deducting all sums paid to her Majesty's paymaster general in manner aforesaid; and if the damages recovered in such action do not exceed double the statutory amount, such person shall pay to the defendant in such action all the costs thereof, such costs to be taxed in England and Ireland as between attorney and client, and in Scotland as between agent and client.

If board of trade decline to institute proceedings individuals may bring actions.

DXII. In cases where loss of life or personal injury has occurred by any accident in respect of which the owner of any such ship as aforesaid is or is alleged to be liable in damages, no person shall be entitled to bring any action or institute any suit or other legal proceeding in the United Kingdom, until the completion of the inquiry (if any) instituted by the board of trade, or until the board of trade has refused to institute the same; and the board of trade shall, for the purpose of entitling any person to bring an action or institute a suit or other legal proceeding, be deemed to have refused to institute such inquiry whenever notice has been served on it by any person of his desire to bring such action or institute such suit or other legal proceeding, and no inquiry is instituted by the board of trade in respect of the subject-matter of such intended action, suit or proceeding for the space of one month after the service of such notice.

Proceedings by board of trade after refusal.

DXIII. Whenever the board of trade, having refused in manner aforesaid to institute any inquiry, afterwards determines to institute the same, the damages and costs (if any) recovered on such inquiry shall be payable rateably with and not in priority to the costs and damages recovered in any other action, suit or legal proceeding.

Proceedings in case of several claims being made on owner of ship.

DXIV. In cases where any liability has been or is alleged to have been incurred by any owner in respect of loss of life, personal injury or loss of or damage to ships, boats or goods, and several claims are made or apprehended in respect of such liability, then subject to the right hereinbefore given to the board of trade of recovering damages in the United Kingdom in respect of loss of life or personal injury, it shall be lawful in England (*t*) or Ireland (*u*) for the High Court of Chancery, and in Scotland for the Court of Session, and in any British possession for any competent court, to entertain proceedings at the suit of any owner for the purpose of determining the amount of such liability subject as aforesaid, and for the distribution of such amount rateably amongst the several claimants, with power for any such court to stop all actions and suits pending in any other court in relation to the same subject-matter ; and any proceeding entertained by such Court of Chancery or Court of Session, or other competent court, may be conducted in such manner and subject to such regulations as to making any persons interested parties to the same, and as to the exclusion of any claimants who do not come in within a certain time, and as to requiring security from the owner, and as to payment of costs, as the court thinks just.

*IX. Mode of Procedure.*

DXV. All sums of money paid for or on account of any loss or damage in respect whereof the liability of the owners of any ship is limited by the Ninth Part of this Act, and all costs incurred in relation thereto, may be brought into account among part owners of the same ship in the same manner as money disbursed for the use thereof.

Money paid for damage how to be accounted for between part owners.

*Saving Clause.*

*Saving Clause.*

DXVI. Nothing in the Ninth Part of this Act contained shall be construed—

Saving clause.

To lessen or take away any liability to which any master or seaman, being also owner or part owner of the ship to which he belongs, is subject in his capacity of master or seaman ; or

To extend to any British ship not being a recognized British ship within the meaning of this Act.

---

## PART X.

### LEGAL PROCEDURE (*x*).

---

## PART XI.

### MISCELLANEOUS.

---

### Table V.—(See Section 455.)

#### FEES AND REMUNERATION OF RECEIVERS.

£　*s.*　*d.*

For every examination on oath instituted by a receiver with respect to any ship or boat which may be or may have been in distress, a fee not exceeding　.　.　.　.　.　.　.　.　1　0　0

But so that in no case shall a larger fee than two pounds be charged for examination taken in respect of the same ship and the same occurrence, whatever may be the number of the deponents.

(*t*) See 24 Vict. c. 10, s. 13.　　　(*x*) See 18 & 19 Vict. c. 91, s. 21,
(*u*) 30 & 31 Vict. c. 114, s. 36.　　*infra.*

For every report required to be sent by the receiver to the secre- £ *s. d.*
tary of the committee for managing the affairs of Lloyd's in
London, the sum of . . . . . . . . . . . 0 10  0
For wreck taken by the receiver into his custody, a percentage of
five per cent. upon the value thereof,
But so that in no case shall the whole amount of percentage so
payable exceed twenty pounds.
In cases where any services are rendered by a receiver, in respect
of any ship or boat in distress, not being wreck, or in respect of
the cargo or other articles belonging thereto, the following fees
instead of a percentage ; (that is to say,)
If such ship or boat with her cargo equals or exceeds in
value six hundred pounds, the sum of two pounds for the
first, and the sum of one pound for every subsequent day
during which the receiver is employed on such service ;
but if such ship or boat with her cargo is less in value than
six hundred pounds, one moiety of the above-mentioned
sum.

---

Table W.—(See Section 486.)

SALVAGE BOND.

[*N.B.—Any of the Particulars not known, or not required, by reason of
the Claim being only against the Cargo, &c., may be omitted.*]

WHEREAS certain salvage services are alleged to have been rendered by the
ship [*insert names of ship and of commander*], commander, to the merchant ship
[*insert names of ship and master*], master, belonging to [*name of place of business
or residence of owner of ship*], freighted by [*the same of the freighter*], and to the
cargo therein, consisting of [*state very shortly the descriptions and quantities of
the goods, and the names and addresses of their owners and consignees*].
And whereas the said ship and cargo have been brought into the port of
[*insert name and situation of port*], and a statement of the salvage claim has
been sent to [*insert the name of the consular officer or vice-admiralty judge, and of
the office he fills*], and he has fixed the amount to be inserted in this bond at
the sum of [*state the sum*] :
Now I, the said [*master's name*], do hereby, in pursuance of the Merchant
Shipping Act, 1854, bind the several owners for the time being of the said
ship and of the cargo therein, and of the freight payable in respect of such
cargo, and their respective heirs, executors, and administrators, to pay among
them such sum not exceeding the said sum of [*state the sum fixed*] in such proportions and to such persons as [*if the parties agree on any other court, substitute the name of it here*], the high court of admiralty in England shall adjudge
to be payable as salvage for the services so alleged to have been rendered as
aforesaid.
In witness whereof I have hereunto set my hand and seal, this [*insert
the date*] day of
Signed, sealed, and delivered by the said [*master's name*],
(L.S.)
In the presence of [*name of consular officer or vice-admiralty judge, and
of the office he fills*].

---

18 & 19 Vict. c. 91.

*An Act to facilitate the Erection and Maintenance of Colonial Light-
houses, and otherwise to amend the Merchant Shipping Act, 1854.*
[*14th August,* 1855.]

*Registry of
Ships.*

PART II. of
Merchant
Shipping Act,
1854.

Penalty on false

IX. Any person who, in any declaration made in the presence of or produced to any registrar of shipping, in pursuance of the Second Part of the

Merchant Shipping Act, 1854, or in any documents or other evidence produced to such registrar, wilfully makes, or assists in making or procures to be made, any false statement concerning the title to or the ownership of or the interests existing in any ship, or any share or shares in any ship, or who utters, produces or makes use of any declaration or document containing any such false statement, knowing the same to be false, shall be guilty of a misdemeanor. declarations under Part II. of Merchant Shipping Act, 17 & 18 Vict. c. 104, s. 103.

X. Shares in ships registered under the said Merchant Shipping Act, 1854, shall be deemed to be included in the word "stock," as defined by the Trustee Act, 1850, and the provisions of such last mentioned Act shall be applicable to such shares accordingly. Shares in shipping within the Trustee Act, 1850, 13 & 14 Vict. c. 60.

XI. In any case in which any bill of sale, mortgage or other instrument for the disposal or transfer of any ship or any share or shares therein, or of any interest therein, is made in any form or contains any particulars other than the form and particulars prescribed and approved for the purpose by or in pursuance of the Merchant Shipping Act, 1854, no registrar shall be required to record the same without the express direction of the commissioners of her Majesty's customs. Forms of instruments. 17 & 18 Vict. c. 104, s. 96.

XII. Upon the transfer of the registry of a ship from one port to another, the certificate of registry required by the nineteenth section of the Merchant Shipping Act, 1854, to be delivered up for that purpose, may be delivered up to the registrar of either of such ports. Delivery of certificate upon transfer of registry. 17 & 18 Vict. c. 104, s. 90.

XIII. [Repealed by 34 & 35 Vict. c. 110, s. 12 (y).]

XIV. The owner of any ship which is measured under Rule II. contained in the twenty-second section of the Merchant Shipping Act, 1854, may at any subsequent period apply to the commissioners of customs (z) to have the said ship remeasured under Rule I. contained in the twenty-first section of the same Act, and the said commissioners may thereupon and upon payment of such fee not exceeding seven shillings and sixpence for each transverse section as they may authorize, direct the said ship to be remeasured accordingly, and the number denoting the register tonnage shall be altered accordingly. Ships measured under Rule II. may be measured under Rule I. 17 & 18 Vict. c. 104, ss. 21 & 22.

XV. The copy or transcript of the register of any British ship which is kept by the chief registrar of shipping at the Custom House in London, or by the registrar-general of seamen, under the direction of her Majesty's commissioners of customs or of the board of trade, shall have the same effect to all intents and purposes as the original register of which the same is a copy or transcript. General register books in London. 17 & 18 Vict. c. 104, s. 107.

*Masters and Seamen.*

PART III. of Merchant Shipping Act, 1854.

XVI. The board of trade may issue instructions concerning the relief to be administered to distressed seamen and apprentices, in pursuance of the two hundred and eleventh and two hundred and twelfth sections of the Merchant Shipping Act, 1854, and may by such instructions determine in what cases and under what circumstances and conditions such relief is to be administered; and all powers of recovering expenses incurred with respect to distressed seamen and apprentices, which by the two hundred and thirteenth section of the said Act are given to the board of trade, shall extend to all expenses incurred by any foreign government for the purposes aforesaid, and repaid to such government by her Majesty's government, and shall likewise extend to any expenses incurred by the conveying home such seamen or apprentices in foreign as well as British ships; and all provisions concerning the relief of distressed seamen and apprentices, being subjects of her Majesty, which are contained in the said sections of the said Act, and in this section shall extend to such seamen and apprentices, not being subjects of her Majesty, as are reduced to distress in foreign parts by reason of their having been shipwrecked, discharged, or left behind from any British ship; subject nevertheless to such modifications and directions concerning the cases in which relief is to be given to such foreigners, and the country to which they are to be sent, as the board of trade may, under the circumstances, think fit to make and issue. Extension of provisions concerning the relief of destitute seamen. 17 & 18 Vict. c. 104, ss. 211, 212, and 213.

XVII. The enactment of the Merchant Shipping Act, 1854, relating to saving banks shall apply to all seamen, and to their wives and families, whether such seamen belong to the royal navy or to the merchant service, or to any other sea service. Enactment concerning savings banks extended to seamen in the navy. 17 & 18 Vict. c. 104, s. 180.

(y) See 36 & 37 Vict. c. 85, s. 3, *infra.*

(z) See 35 & 36 Vict. c. 73, s. 4, *infra.*

Additional powers of naval courts. 17 & 18 Vict. c. 104, ss. 260 to 266.

XVIII. Any naval court summoned, under the provisions of the Merchant Shipping Act, 1854, to hear any complaint touching the conduct of the master or any of the crew of any ship, shall, in addition to the powers given to it by the said Act, have power to try the said master or any of the said crew for any offences against the Merchant Shipping Act, 1854, in respect of which two justices would, if the case were tried in the United Kingdom, have power to convict summarily, and by order duly made to inflict the same punishments for such offences which two justices might in the case aforesaid inflict upon summary conviction ; provided, that in cases where an offender is sentenced to imprisonment the sentence shall be confirmed in writing by the senior naval or consular officer present at the place where the court is held, and the place of imprisonment, whether on land or on board ship, shall be approved by him as a proper place for the purpose, and copies of all sentences made by any naval court summoned to hear any such complaint as aforesaid shall be sent to the commander-in-chief or senior naval officer of the station.

*Wrecks, Casualties, and Salvage.*

PART VIII. of Merchant Shipping Act, 1854.

In case of wreck of foreign ships consul general to be deemed agent of owner.

XIX. Whenever any articles belonging to or forming part of any foreign ship which has been wrecked on or near the coasts of the United Kingdom, or belonging to or forming part of the cargo thereof, are found on or near such coasts, or are brought into any port in the United Kingdom, the consul general of the country to which such ship, or, in the case of cargo, to which the owners of such cargo, may have belonged, or any consular officer of such country, authorized in that behalf by any treaty or agreement with such country, shall, in the absence of the owner of such ship or articles, and of the master or other agent of the owner, be deemed to be the agent of the owner, so far as relates to the custody and disposal of such articles.

Remuneration for services by coast guard.

XX. In cases where services are rendered by officers or men of the coast guard service in watching or protecting shipwrecked property, then, unless it can be shown that such services have been declined by the owner of such property or his agent at the time they were tendered, or that salvage has been claimed and awarded for such services, the owner of the shipwrecked property shall pay in respect of the said services remuneration according to a scale to be fixed by the board of trade, so, however, that such scale shall not exceed any scale by which payment to officers and men of the coast guard for extra duties in the ordinary service of the commissioners of customs is for the time being regulated ; and such remuneration shall be recoverable by the same means and shall be paid to the same persons and accounted for and applied in the same manner as fees received by receivers appointed under the Merchant Shipping Act, 1854.

---

## 18 & 19 VICT. c. 111.

*An Act to amend the Law relating to Bills of Lading.*
[*11th August*, 1855.]

WHEREAS by the custom of merchants a bill of lading of goods being transferable by indorsement the property in the goods may thereby pass to the indorsee, but nevertheless all rights in respect of the contract contained in the bill of lading continue in the original shipper or owner, and it is expedient that such rights should pass with the property : and whereas it frequently happens that the goods in respect of which bills of lading purport to be signed have not been laden on board, and it is proper that such bills of lading in the hands of a bonâ fide holder for value should not be questioned by the master or other person signing the same on the ground of the goods not having been laden as aforesaid : be it therefore enacted by the Queen's most excellent Majesty, by and with the advice and consent of the Lords spiritual and temporal, and Commons, in this present Parliament assembled, and by the authority of the same, as follows :

Rights under bills of lading to vest in consignee or indorsee.

I. Every consignee of goods named in a bill of lading, and every indorsee of a bill of lading to whom the property in the goods therein mentioned shall pass, upon or by reason of such consignment or indorsement, shall have transferred to and vested in him all rights of suit, and be subject to the same liabilities in respect of such goods as if the contract contained in the bill of lading had been made with himself.

II. Nothing herein contained shall prejudice or affect any right of stoppage in transitu, or any right to claim freight against the original shipper or owner, or any liability of the consignee or indorsee by reason or in consequence of his being such consignee or indorsee, or of his receipt of the goods by reason or in consequence of such consignment or indorsement.

*Not to affect right of stoppage in transitu or claims for freight.*

III. Every bill of lading in the hands of a consignee or indorsee for valuable consideration representing goods to have been shipped on board a vessel, shall be conclusive evidence of such shipment as against the master or other person signing the same, notwithstanding that such goods or some part thereof may not have been so shipped, unless such holder of the bill of lading shall have had actual notice at the time of receiving the same that the goods had not been in fact laden on board: Provided that the master or other person so signing may exonerate himself in respect of such misrepresentation by showing that it was caused without any default on his part, and wholly by the fraud of the shipper, or of the holder, or some person under whom the holder claims.

*Bill of lading in hands of consignee, &c., conclusive evidence of the shipment as against master, &c.*

*Proviso.*

---

## 18 & 19 Vict. c. 119.

*An Act to amend the Law relating to carriage of Passengers by Sea.*
[*14th August,* 1855.]

---

## 19 & 20 Vict. c. 97.

*An Act to amend the Laws of England and Ireland affecting Trade and Commerce.*  [*29th July,* 1856.]

WHEREAS inconvenience is felt by persons engaged in trade by reason of the laws of England and Ireland being in some particulars different from those of Scotland in matters of common occurrence in the course of such trade, and with a view to remedy such inconvenience it is expedient to amend the laws of England and Ireland as hereinafter is mentioned; be it enacted by the Queen's most excellent Majesty, by and with the advice and consent of the Lords spiritual and temporal, and Commons, in this present Parliament assembled, and by the authority of the same, as follows:

I. No writ of fieri facias or other writ of execution, and no writ of attachment against the goods of a debtor, shall prejudice the title to such goods acquired by any person bonâ fide and for a valuable consideration before the actual seizure or attachment thereof by virtue of such writ: Provided such person had not, at the time when he acquired such title, notice that such writ, or any other writ by virtue of which the goods of such owner might be seized or attached, had been delivered to and remained unexecuted in the hands of the sheriff, under-sheriff, or coroner.

*Persons acquiring title to goods before they have been seized or attached under a writ against the seller protected.*

II. In all actions and suits in any of the superior courts of common law at Westminster or Dublin, or in any court of record in England, Wales or Ireland, for breach of contract to deliver specific goods for a price in money, on the application of the plaintiff, and by leave of the judge before whom the cause is tried, the jury shall, if they find the plaintiff entitled to recover, find by their verdict what are the goods in respect of the non-delivery of which the plaintiff is entitled to recover, and which remain undelivered; what (if

*Specific delivery of goods sold.*

any) is the sum the plaintiff would have been liable to pay for the delivery thereof; what damages (if any) the plaintiff would have sustained if the goods should be delivered under execution, as hereinafter mentioned, and what damages if not so delivered; and thereupon, if judgment shall be given for the plaintiff, the court, or any judge thereof, at their or his discretion, on the application of the plaintiff, shall have power to order execution to issue for the delivery, on payment of such sum (if any) as shall have been found to be payable by the plaintiff as aforesaid, of the said goods, without giving the defendant the option of retaining the same upon paying the damages assessed; and such writ of execution may be for the delivery of such goods; and if such goods so ordered to be delivered, or any part thereof, cannot be found, and unless the court, or such judge or baron as aforesaid, shall otherwise order, the sheriff, or other officer of such court of record, shall distrain the defendant by all his lands and chattels, in the said sheriff's bailiwick, or within the jurisdiction of such other court of record, till the defendant deliver such goods, or, at the option of the plaintiff, cause to be made of the defendant's goods the assessed value or damages, or a due proportion thereof; provided that the plaintiff shall, either by the same or a separate writ of execution, be entitled to have made of the defendant's goods the damages, costs and interest in such action or suit. ·

*Consideration for guarantee need not appear by writing.* III. No special promise to be made by any person after the passing of this Act to answer for the debt, default or miscarriage of another person, being in writing, and signed by the party to be charged therewith, or some other person by him thereunto lawfully authorized, shall be deemed invalid to support an action, suit or other proceeding to charge the person by whom such promise shall have been made, by reason only that the consideration for such promise does not appear in writing, or by necessary inference from a written document.

*Guarantee to or for a firm to cease upon a change in the firm except in special cases.* IV. No promise to answer for the debt, default or miscarriage of another made to a firm consisting of two or more persons, or to a single person trading under the name of a firm, and no promise to answer for the debt, default or miscarriage of a firm consisting of two or more persons, or of a single person trading under the name of a firm, shall be binding on the person making such promise in respect of anything done or omitted to be done after a change shall have taken place in any one or more of the persons constituting the firm, or in the person trading under the name of a firm, unless the intention of the parties that such promise shall continue to be binding notwithstanding such change shall appear either by express stipulation or by necessary implication from the nature of the firm or otherwise.

*A surety who discharges the liability to be entitled to assignment of all securities held by the creditor.* V. Every person, who being surety for the debt or duty of another, or being liable with another for any debt or duty, shall pay such debt or perform such duty, shall be entitled to have assigned to him, or to a trustee for him, every judgment, specialty or other security which shall be held by the creditor in respect of such debt or duty, whether such judgment, specialty or other security shall or shall not be deemed at law to have been satisfied by the payment of the debt or performance of the duty, and such person shall be entitled to stand in the place of the creditor, and to use all the remedies, and, if need be, and upon a proper indemnity, to use the name of the creditor, in any action or other proceeding, at law or in equity, in order to obtain from the principal debtor, or any co-surety, co-contractor or co-debtor, as the case may be, indemnification for the advances made and loss sustained by the person who shall have so paid such debt or performed such duty, and such payment or performance so made by such surety shall not be pleadable in bar of any such action or other proceeding by him: Provided always, that no co-surety, co-contractor or co-debtor shall be entitled to recover from any other co-surety, co-contractor or co-debtor, by the means aforesaid, more than the just proportion to which, as between those parties themselves, such last-mentioned person shall be justly liable.

VI. [Repealed by 45 & 46 Vict. c. 61, s. 96.]

VII. [Repealed by 45 & 46 Vict. c. 61, s. 96.]

*With reference to the repairs of ships, every port within the United Kingdom, &c., a home port.* VIII. In relation to the rights and remedies of persons having claims for repairs done to, or supplies furnished to or for, ships, every port within the United Kingdom of Great Britain and Ireland, the Islands of Man, Guernsey, Jersey, Alderney and Sark, and the islands adjacent to any of them, being part of the dominions of her Majesty, shall be deemed a home port.

IX. All actions of account, or for not accounting, and suits for such accounts as concern the trade of merchandise between merchant and merchant, their factors or servants, shall be commenced and sued within six years after the cause of such actions or suits, or when such cause has already arisen, then within six years after the passing of this Act; and no claim in respect of a matter which arose more than six years before the commencement of such action or suit shall be enforceable by action or suit by reason only of some other matter of claim comprised in the same account having arisen within six years next before the commencement of such action or suit. *Limitation of actions for "Merchants' Accounts."*

X. No person or persons who shall be entitled to any action or suit with respect to which the period of limitation within which the same shall be brought is fixed by the Act of the twenty-first year of the reign of King James the First, chapter sixteen, section three, or by the Act of the fourth year of the reign of Queen Anne, chapter sixteen, section seventeen, or by the Act of the fifty-third year of the reign of King George the Third, chapter one hundred and twenty-seven, section five, or by the Acts of the third and fourth years of the reign of King William the Fourth, chapter twenty-seven, sections forty, forty-one and forty-two, and chapter forty-two, section three, or by the Act of the sixteenth and seventeenth years of the reign of her present Majesty, chapter one hundred and thirteen, section twenty, shall be entitled to any time within which to commence and sue such action or suit beyond the period so fixed for the same by the enactments aforesaid, by reason only of such person or some one or more of such persons, being at the time of such cause of action or suit accrued beyond the seas, or in the cases in which by virtue of any of the aforesaid enactments imprisonment is now a disability, by reason of such person or some one or more of such persons being imprisoned at the time of such cause of action or suit accrued. *Absence beyond seas or imprisonment of creditor not a disability.*

XI. Where such cause of action or suit with respect to which the period of limitation is fixed by the enactments aforesaid, or any of them, lies against two or more joint debtors, the person or persons who shall be entitled to the same shall not be entitled to any time within which to commence and sue any such action or suit against any one or more of such joint debtors who shall not be beyond the seas at the time such cause of action or suit accrued, by reason only that some other one or more of such joint debtors was or were at the time such cause of action accrued beyond the seas, and such person or persons so entitled as aforesaid shall not be barred from commencing and suing any action or suit against the joint debtor or joint debtors who was or were beyond seas at the time the cause of action or suit accrued after his or their return from beyond seas, by reason only that judgment was already recovered against any one or more of such joint debtors who was not or were not beyond seas at the time aforesaid. *Period of limitation to run as to joint debtors in the kingdom though some beyond seas.*

*Judgment recovered against joint debtors no bar to proceeding against others beyond seas after their return.*

XII. No part of the United Kingdom of Great Britain and Ireland, nor the Islands of Man, Guernsey, Jersey, Alderney, and Sark, nor any islands adjacent to any of them, being part of the dominions of her Majesty, shall be deemed to be beyond seas within the meaning of the Act of the fourth and fifth years of the reign of Queen Anne, chapter sixteen, or of this Act. *Definition of "beyond seas," within 4 & 5 Anne, c. 16, and this Act.*

XIII. In reference to the provisions of the Acts of the ninth year of the reign of King George the Fourth, chapter fourteen, sections one and eight, and the sixteenth and seventeenth years of the reign of her present Majesty, chapter one hundred and thirteen, sections twenty-four and twenty-seven, an acknowledgment or promise made or contained by or in a writing signed by an agent of the party chargeable thereby, duly authorised to make such acknowledgment or promise, shall have the same effect as if such writing had been signed by such party himself. *Provisions of 9 Geo. 4, c. 14, ss. 1 and 8, and 16 & 17 Vict. c. 113, ss. 24 and 27, extended to acknowledgments by agents.*

XIV. In reference to the provisions of the Acts of the twenty-first year of the reign of King James the First, chapter sixteen, section three, and of the Act of the third and fourth years of the reign of King William the Fourth, chapter forty-two, section three, and of the Act of the sixteenth and seventeenth years of the reign of her present Majesty, chapter one hundred and thirteen, section twenty, when there shall be two or more co-contractors or co-debtors, whether bound or liable jointly only or jointly and severally, or executors or administrators of any contractor, no such co-contractor or co-debtor, executor or administrator, shall lose the benefit of the said enactments or any of them, so as to be chargeable in respect or by reason only of payment of any principal, interest, or other money, by any other or others of such co-contractors or co-debtors, executors or administrators. *Part payment by one contractor, &c. not to prevent bar by certain statutes of limitations in favour of another contractor, &c.*

Rules and
regulations may
be made and
writs and pro-
ceedings framed
for the purposes
of this Act.

XV. In order to enable the superior courts of common law at Westminster and Dublin, and the judges thereof respectively, to make rules and regulations, and to frame writs and proceedings, for the purpose of giving effect to this Act, the two hundred and twenty-third and two hundred and twenty-fourth sections of "The Common Law Procedure Act, 1852," shall, so far as this Act is to take effect in England, and the two hundred and thirty-third and two hundred and fortieth sections of "The Common Law Procedure Amendment Act (Ireland), 1853," shall, so far as this Act is to take effect in Ireland, be incorporated with this Act, as if those provisions had been severally herein repeated and made to apply to this Act (a).

Short title.

XVI. In citing this Act it shall be sufficient to use the expression "The Mercantile Law Amendment Act, 1856."

Extent of Act.

XVII. Nothing in this Act shall extend to Scotland (b).

---

### 20 & 21 Vict. c. 54.

*An Act to make better Provision for the Punishment of Frauds committed by Trustees, Bankers, and other Persons intrusted with Property (c).*
[*17th August, 1857.*]

---

### 24 Vict. c. 10.

*An Act to extend the Jurisdiction and improve the Practice of the High Court of Admiralty.*
[*17th May, 1861.*]

---

### 24 & 25 Vict. c. 96.

*An Act to consolidate and amend the Statute Law of England and Ireland relating to Larceny and other similar Offences.*
[*6th August, 1861.*]

As to frauds by agents, bankers or factors:

Agent, banker,
&c., embezzling
money or selling
securities, &c.,
intrusted to
him;

75. Whosoever, having been intrusted, either solely, or jointly with any other person, as a banker, merchant, broker, attorney or other agent, with any money or security for the payment of money, with any direction in writing to apply, pay or deliver such money or security or any part thereof respectively, or the proceeds or any part of the proceeds of such security, for any purpose, or to any person specified in such direction, shall, in violation of good faith, and contrary to the terms of such direction, in anywise convert to his own use or benefit, or the use or benefit of any person other than the person by whom he shall have been so intrusted, such money, security,

or goods, &c.,
intrusted to him
for safe custody.

or proceeds or any part thereof respectively; and whosoever, having been intrusted, either solely, or jointly with any other person, as a banker, merchant, broker, attorney or other agent, with any chattel or valuable security, or any power of attorney for the sale or transfer of any share or interest in any public stock or fund, whether of the United Kingdom, or any part thereof, or of any foreign state, or in any stock or fund of any body corporate, company or society, for safe custody or for any special purpose, without any authority to sell, negotiate, transfer, or pledge, shall, in violation of good faith, and contrary to the object or purpose for which such chattel, security, or power of attorney shall have been intrusted to him, sell, negotiate, transfer, pledge, or in any manner convert to his own use or benefit, or the use or benefit of any person other than the person by whom he shall have been so intrusted, such chattel or security, or the proceeds of the same, or any part thereof, or the share or interest in the stock or fund to which such power of

---

(a) See 42 & 43 Vict. c. 78, s. 29.        (c) Repealed by 24 & 25 Vict. c.
(b) See 19 & 20 Vict. c. 60.                95, s. 1.

attorney shall relate, or any part thereof, shall be guilty of a misdemeanor, and being convicted thereof shall be liable, at the discretion of the court, to be kept in penal servitude for any term not exceeding seven years and not less than three years, or to be imprisoned for any term not exceeding two years, with or without hard labour, and with or without solitary confinement; but nothing in this section contained relating to agents shall affect any trustee in or under any instrument whatsoever, or any mortgagee or any property, real or personal, in respect of any act done by such trustee or mortgagee in relation to the property comprised in or affected by any such trust or mortgage; nor shall restrain any banker, merchant, broker, attorney or other agent from receiving any money which shall be or become actually due and payable upon or by virtue of any valuable security, according to the tenor and effect thereof, in such manner as he might have done if this Act had not been passed; nor for selling, transferring or otherwise disposing of any securities or effects in his possession upon which he shall have any lien, claim or demand entitling him by law so to do, unless such sale, transfer or other disposal shall extend to a greater number or part of such securities or effects than shall be requisite for satisfying such lien, claim or demand. *Punishment.* *Not to affect trustees or mortgagees;* *nor bankers, &c. receiving money due on securities;* *or disposing of securities on which they have a lien.*

76. Whosoever being a banker, merchant, broker, attorney or agent, and being intrusted, either solely, or jointly with any other person, with the property of any other person for safe custody, shall, with intent to defraud, sell, negotiate, transfer, pledge or in any manner convert or appropriate the same or any part thereof to or for his own use or benefit, or the use or benefit of any person other than the person by whom he was so intrusted, shall be guilty of a misdemeanor, and being convicted thereof shall be liable, at the discretion of the court, to any of the punishments which the court may award as hereinbefore last mentioned. *Bankers, &c., fraudulently selling, &c., property intrusted to their care.*

77. Whosoever, being intrusted, either solely, or jointly with any other person, with any power of attorney for the sale or transfer of any property, shall fraudulently sell or transfer or otherwise convert the same or any part thereof to his own use or benefit, or the use or benefit of any person other than the person by whom he was so intrusted, shall be guilty of a misdemeanor and being convicted thereof shall be liable, at the discretion of the court, to any of the punishments which the court may award as hereinbefore last mentioned. *Persons under powers of attorney fraudulently selling property.*

78. Whosoever, being a factor or agent intrusted, either solely, or jointly with any other person, for the purpose of sale or otherwise, with the possession of any goods, or of any document of title to goods, shall, contrary to or without the authority of his principal in that behalf, for his own use or benefit, or the use or benefit of any person other than the person by whom he was so intrusted, and in violation of good faith, make any consignment, deposit, transfer or delivery of any goods or document of title so intrusted to him as in this section before mentioned, as and by way of a pledge, lien or security for any money or valuable security borrowed or received by such factor or agent at or before the time of making such consignment, deposit, transfer or delivery, or intended to be thereafter borrowed or received, or shall, contrary to or without such authority, for his own use or benefit, or the use or benefit of any person other than the person by whom he was so intrusted, and in violation of good faith, accept any advance of any money or valuable security on the faith of any contract or agreement to consign, deposit, transfer or deliver any such goods or document of title, shall be guilty of a misdemeanor, and being convicted thereof shall be liable, at the discretion of the court, to any of the punishments which the court may award as hereinbefore last mentioned; and every clerk or other person who shall knowingly and wilfully act and assist in making any such consignment, deposit, transfer or delivery, or in accepting or procuring such advance as aforesaid, shall be guilty of a misdemeanor, and being convicted thereof shall be liable, at the discretion of the court, to any of the same punishments: Provided, that no such factor or agent shall be liable to any prosecution for consigning, depositing, transferring or delivering any such goods or documents of title, in case the same shall not be made a security for or subject to the payment of any greater sum of money than the amount which at the time of such consignment, deposit, transfer or delivery was justly due and owing to such agent from his principal, together with the amount of any bill of exchange drawn by or on account of such principal, and accepted by such factor or agent. *Factors obtaining advances on the property of their principals.* *Clerks wilfully assisting.* *Cases excepted where the pledge does not exceed the amount of their lien.*

Definitions of terms:
" intrusted :"

"pledge :"

" possessed:"

" advance :"

" contract or agreement:"

" advance."
Possession to be evidence of intrusting.

79. Any factor or agent intrusted as aforesaid, and possessed of any such document of title, whether derived immediately from the owner of such goods or obtained by reason of such factor or agent having been intrusted with the possession of the goods, or of any other document of title thereto, shall be deemed to have been intrusted with the possession of the goods represented by such document of title ; and every contract pledging or giving a lien upon such document of title as aforesaid shall be deemed to be a pledge of and lien upon the goods to which the same relates ; and such factor or agent shall be deemed to be possessed of such goods or document, whether the same shall be in his actual custody, or shall be held by any other person subject to his control, or for him or on his behalf ; and where any loan or advance shall be bonâ fide made to any factor or agent intrusted with and in possession of any such goods or document of title, on the faith of any contract or agreement in writing to consign, deposit, transfer or deliver such goods or document of title, and such goods or document of title shall actually be received by the person making such loan or advance, without notice that such factor or agent was not authorised to make such pledge or security, every such loan or advance shall be deemed to be a loan or advance on the security of such goods or document of title within the meaning of the last preceding section, though such goods or document of title shall not actually be received by the person making such loan or advance till the period subsequent thereto ; and any contract or agreement, whether made direct with such factor or agent, or with any clerk or other person on his behalf, shall be deemed a contract or agreement with such factor or agent ; and any payment made, whether by money or bill of exchange or other negotiable security, shall be deemed to be an advance within the meaning of the last preceding section ; and a factor or agent in possession as aforesaid of such goods or document shall be taken, for the purposes of the last preceding section, to have been intrusted therewith by the owner thereof, unless the contrary be shown in evidence.

Trustees, fraudulently disposing of property, guilty of a misdemeanor.

No prosecution shall be commenced without the sanction of some judge or the attorney-general.

80. Whosoever, being a trustee of any property for the use or benefit, either wholly or partially, of some other person, or for any public or charitable purpose, shall, with intent to defraud, convert or appropriate the same or any part thereof to or for his own use or benefit, or the use or benefit of any person other than such person as aforesaid, or for any purpose other than such public or charitable purpose as aforesaid, or otherwise dispose of or destroy such property or any part thereof, shall be guilty of a misdemeanor, and being convicted thereof shall be liable, at the discretion of the court, to any of the punishments which the court may award as hereinbefore last mentioned : Provided that no proceeding or prosecution for any offence included in this section shall be commenced without the sanction of her Majesty's attorney-general, or, in case that office be vacant, of her Majesty's solicitor-general: Provided, also, that where any civil proceedings shall have been taken against any person to whom the provisions of this section may apply, no person who shall have taken such civil proceeding shall commence any prosecution under this section without the sanction of the court or judge before whom such civil proceeding shall have been had or shall be pending.

Directors, &c. of any body corporate or public company fraudulently appropriating property ;

81. Whosoever, being a director, member or public officer of any body corporate or public company, shall fraudulently take or apply for his own use or benefit, or for any use or purposes other than the use or purposes of such body corporate or public company, any of the property of such body corporate or public company, shall be guilty of a misdemeanor, and being convicted thereof shall be liable, at the discretion of the court, to any of the punishments which the court may award as hereinbefore last mentioned.

or keeping fraudulent accounts ;

82. Whosoever, being a director, public officer or manager of any body corporate or public company, shall as such receive or possess himself of any of the property of such body corporate or public company otherwise than in payment of a just debt or demand, and shall, with intent to defraud, omit to make or to cause or direct to be made a full and true entry thereof in the books and accounts of such body corporate or public company, shall be guilty of a misdemeanor, and being convicted thereof shall be liable, at the discretion of the court, to any of the punishments which the court may award as hereinbefore last mentioned.

or wilfully destroying books, &c.;

83. Whosoever, being a director, manager, public officer or member of any body corporate or public company, shall, with intent to defraud, destroy, alter, mutilate or falsify any book, paper, writing or valuable security belonging to the body corporate or public company, or make or concur in the

making of any false entry, or omit or concur in omitting any material particular, in any book of account or other document, shall be guilty of a misdemeanor, and being convicted thereof shall be liable, at the discretion of the court, to any of the punishments which the court may award, as hereinbefore last mentioned.

84. Whosoever, being a director, manager or public officer of any body corporate or public company, shall make, circulate or publish, or concur in making, circulating, or publishing, any written statement or account which he shall know to be false in any material particular, with intent to deceive or defraud any member, shareholder or creditor of such body corporate or public company, or with intent to induce any person to become a shareholder or partner therein, or to intrust or advance any property to such body corporate or public company, or to enter into any security for the benefit thereof, shall be guilty of a misdemeanor, and being convicted thereof shall be liable, at the discretion of the court, to any of the punishments which the court may award, as hereinbefore last mentioned. *or publishing fraudulent statements.*

85. Nothing in any of the last ten preceding sections of this Act contained shall enable or entitle any person to refuse to make a full and complete discovery by answer to any bill in equity, or to answer any question or interrogatory in any civil proceeding in any court, or upon the hearing of any matter in bankruptcy or insolvency ; and no person shall be liable to be convicted of any of the misdemeanors in any of the said sections mentioned by any evidence whatever in respect of any act done by him, if he shall at any time previously to his being charged with such offence have first disclosed such act on oath, in consequence of any compulsory process of any court of law or equity, in any action, suit or proceeding which shall have been bonâ fide instituted by any party aggrieved, or if he shall have first disclosed the same in any compulsory examination or deposition before any court upon the hearing of any matter in bankruptcy or insolvency. *No person to be exempt from answering questions in any court, but no person making a disclosure in any compulsory proceeding to be liable to prosecution.*

86. Nothing in any of the last eleven preceding sections of this Act contained, nor any proceeding, conviction or judgment to be had or taken thereon against any person under any of the said sections, shall prevent, lessen or impeach any remedy at law or in equity which any party aggrieved by any offence against any of the said sections might have had if this Act had not been passed ; but no conviction of any such offender shall be received in evidence in any action at law or suit in equity against him ; and nothing in the said sections contained shall affect or prejudice any agreement entered into or security given by any trustee, having for its object the restoration or repayment of any trust property misappropriated. *No remedy at law or in equity shall be affected.*

*Convictions shall not be received in evidence in civil suits.*

87. No misdemeanor against any of the last twelve preceding sections of this Act shall be prosecuted or tried at any court of general or quarter session of the peace. *Certain misdemeanors not triable at sessions.*

---

## 25 & 26 VICT. c. 63.

*An Act to amend " The Merchant Shipping Act, 1854," " The Merchant Shipping Act Amendment Act, 1855," and " The Customs Consolidation Act, 1853."*          [29th July, 1862.]

WHEREAS it is expedient further to amend "The Merchant Shipping Act, 1854," "The Merchant Shipping Act Amendment Act, 1855," and "The Customs Consolidation Act, 1853 : " Be it enacted by the Queen's most excellent Majesty, by and with the advice and consent of the lords spiritual and temporal, and commons in this present parliament assembled, and by the authority of the same, as follows : *17 & 18 Vict. c. 104. 18 & 19 Vict. c. 91. 16 & 17 Vict. c. 107.*

1. This Act may be cited as "The Merchant Shipping Act Amendment Act, 1862," and shall be construed with and as part of " The Merchant Shipping Act, 1854," hereinafter termed the principal Act. *Short title.*

2. The enactments described in table (A) in the schedule to this Act, shall be repealed as therein mentioned, except as to any liabilities incurred before such repeal. *Enactments in Table (A) repealed.*

*Registry and Measurement of Tonnage (Part II. of Merchant Shipping Act, 1854).*

**Equities not excluded by Merchant Shipping Act.**

3. It is hereby declared that the expression "beneficial interest," whenever used in the Second Part of the principal Act, includes interests arising under contract and other equitable interests; and the intention of the said Act is that, without prejudice to the provisions contained in the said Act for preventing notice of trusts from being entered in the register book or received by the registrar, and without prejudice to the powers of disposition and of giving receipts conferred by the said Act on registered owners and mortgagees, and without prejudice to the provisions contained in the said Act relating to the exclusion of unqualified persons from the ownership of British ships, equities may be enforced against owners and mortgagees of ships in respect of their interest therein, in the same manner as equities may be enforced against them in respect of any other personal property (a).

**Tonnage rates under local Acts may be levied on the registered tonnage.**

4. Any body corporate or persons having power to levy tonnage rates on ships may, if they think fit, with the consent of the board of trade, levy such tonnage rates upon the registered tonnage of the ships as determined by the rules for the measurement of tonnage for the time being in force under the principal Act, notwithstanding that the local Act or Acts under which such rates are levied provides for levying the same upon some different system of tonnage measurement.

*Certificates for Engineers (Part III. of Merchant Shipping Act, 1854).*

**Steam ships to carry certificated engineers.**

5. On and after the first day of June, one thousand eight hundred and sixty-three, every steam ship which is required by the principal Act to have a master possessing a certificate from the board of trade shall also have an engineer or engineers possessing a certificate or certificates from the board of trade as follows; (that is to say,)

(1.) Engineers' certificates shall be of two grades, viz., "first-class engineers' certificates," and "second-class engineers' certificates:"

(2.) Every foreign-going steam ship of one hundred nominal horse power or upwards shall have as its first and second engineers two certificated engineers, the first possessing a "first-class engineers' certificate," and the second possessing a "second-class engineers' certificate," or a certificate of the higher grade:

(3.) Every foreign-going steam ship of less than one hundred nominal horse power shall have as its only or first engineer an engineer possessing a "second-class engineers' certificate," or a certificate of the higher grade:

(4.) Every sea-going home-trade passenger steam ship shall have as its only or first engineer an engineer possessing a "second-class engineers' certificate" or a certificate of the higher grade:

(5.) Every person who, having been engaged to serve in any of the above capacities in any such steam ship as aforesaid, goes to sea in that capacity without being at the time entitled to and possessed of such certificate as is required by this section, and every person who employs any person in any of the above capacities in such ship without ascertaining that he is at the time entitled to and possessed of such certificate as is required by this section, shall for each such offence incur a penalty not exceeding fifty pounds.

**Examinations for engineers' certificates of competency.**

6. The board of trade shall from time to time cause examinations to be held of persons who may be desirous of obtaining certificates of competency as engineers: for the purpose of such examinations the board of trade shall from time to time appoint and remove examiners, and award the remuneration to be paid to them; lay down rules as to the qualification of applicants, and as to the times and places of examination, and generally do all such acts as it thinks expedient in order to carry into effect the examination of such engineers as aforesaid.

**Fees to be paid by applicants for examination.**

7. All applicants for examination shall pay such fees, not exceeding the sums specified in the table marked (B) in the schedule hereto, as the board of

(a) *The Innisfallen,* L. R. 1 A. & E. 72; *The Cathcart,* L. R. 1 A. & E. 314.

trade directs (*b*) ; and such fees shall be paid to such persons as the said board appoints for that purpose, and shall be carried to the account of the mercantile marine fund.

**8.** The board of trade shall deliver to every applicant who is duly reported to have passed the examination satisfactorily, and to have given satisfactory evidence of his sobriety, experience and ability, a certificate of competency as first-class engineer or as second-class engineer, as the case may be.

*Certificates of competency to be granted to those who pass.*

**9.** Certificates of service for engineers, differing in form from certificates of competency, shall be granted as follows : (that is to say,)

*Engineers' certificates of service to be delivered on proof of certain service.*

(1.) Every person who before the first day of April, one thousand eight hundred and sixty-two, has served as first engineer in any foreign-going steam-ship of one hundred nominal horse-power or upwards, or who has attained or attains the rank of engineer in the service of her Majesty or of the East India Company, shall be entitled to a " first-class engineers' certificate " of service :

(2.) Every person who before the first day of April, one thousand eight hundred and sixty-two, has served as second engineer in any foreign-going steam-ship of one hundred nominal horse power or upwards, or as first or only engineer in any other steam-ship, or who has attained or attains the rank of first-class assistant engineer in the service of her Majesty, shall be entitled to a " second-class engineers' certificate " of service :

Each of such certificates of service shall contain particulars of the name, place and time of birth, and the length and nature of the previous service of the person to whom the same is delivered ; and the board of trade shall deliver such certificates of service to the various persons so respectively entitled thereto, upon their proving themselves to have attained such rank or to have served as aforesaid, and upon their giving a full and satisfactory account of the particulars aforesaid.

**10.** The provisions of the principal Act, with respect to the certificates of competency or service of masters and mates, contained in the 138th, 139th, 140th, 161st and 162nd sections of the said Act, shall apply to certificates of competency or service granted under this Act in the same manner as if certificates of competency and service to be granted to engineers under this Act were specially mentioned and included in the said section.

*Certain provisions of Merchant Shipping Act to apply to engineers' certificates.*

**11.** The power by the 241st section of the principal Act given to the board of trade (*c*), or to any local marine board of instituting investigations into the conduct of any master or mate whom it has reason to believe to be from incompetency or misconduct unfit to discharge his duties, shall extend to any certificated engineer whom the board of trade or any local marine board has reason to believe to be from incompetency or misconduct unfit to discharge his duties in the same manner as if in the said section the words " certificated engineer " had been inserted after " master " wherever " master " occurs in such section.

*Power of board of trade and local marine board to investigate conduct of certificated engineers.*

**12.** The declaration required to be given by the engineer surveyor under section 309 of the principal Act shall, in the case of a ship by this Act required to have a certificated engineer, contain, in addition to the statements in the said section mentioned, a statement that the certificate or certificates of the engineer or engineers of such ship is or are such and in such condition as is required by this Act.

*Declaration of engineer surveyor to contain statement concerning engineers' certificate.*

*Masters and Seamen (Part III. of Merchant Shipping Act, 1854).*

**13.** The following vessels ; (that is to say,)

[(1.) Registered sea-going ships exclusively employed in fishing on the coasts of the United Kingdom (*d*) :]

*Third Part of Act to apply to fishing boats, lighthouse vessels and pleasure yachts, with certain exceptions.*

(2.) Sea-going ships belonging to any of the three general lighthouse boards :

(3.) Sea-going ships being pleasure yachts ;

Shall be subject to the whole of the Third Part of the principal Act ; except sections 136, 143, 145, 147, 149, 150, 151, 152, 153, 154, 155, 157, 158, 161, 162, 166, 170, 171, 231, 256, 279, 280, 281, 282, 283, 284, 285, 286 and 287.

(*b*) See s. 4 of 43 & 44 Vict. c. 22.   (*d*) Repealed by 46 & 47 Vict. c. 41,
(*c*) See 39 & 40 Vict. c. 80, s. 29,  s. 55.
*infra.*

Local marine
board may
determine
number of
quorum.

**14.** Whereas doubts have been entertained whether local marine boards have the power of declaring a quorum: it is hereby declared, that the power by the 119th section of the principal Act given to every local marine board of regulating the mode in which its meetings are to be held and its business conducted includes the power of determining a quorum; nevertheless, after the passing of this Act such quorum shall never consist of less than three members.

Titles of
shipping
masters.

**15.** The offices termed shipping offices in the principal Act shall be termed mercantile marine offices, and the officers termed shipping masters and deputy shipping masters in the principal Act shall be termed superintendents and deputy superintendents of such offices; but nothing in this section contained shall invalidate or affect any act which may be done at any such office under the title of a shipping office, or any act which may be done by, with or to any of the said officers under the title of shipping master or deputy shipping master.

Punishment for
embezzlement
in shipping
offices.

**16.** Any person appointed to any office or service by or under any local marine board shall be deemed to be a clerk or servant within the meaning of the sixty-eighth section of the Act of the twenty-fifth year of the reign of her present Majesty, chapter ninety-six:

If any such person fraudulently applies or disposes of any chattel, money or valuable security received by him whilst employed in such office or service for or on account of any such local marine board, or for or on account of any other public board or department, to his own use or any use or purpose other than that for which the same was paid, entrusted to or received by him, or fraudulently withholds, retains or keeps back the same or any part thereof contrary to any lawful directions or instructions which he is required to obey in relation to such office or service, he shall be deemed guilty of embezzlement within the meaning of the said section:

Any such person shall, on conviction of such offence as aforesaid, be liable to the same pains and penalties as are thereby imposed upon any clerk or servant for embezzlement:

In any indictment against such person for such offence, it shall be sufficient to charge any such chattel, money, or valuable security as the property either of the board by which he was appointed, or of the board or department for or on account of which he may have received the same; and no greater particularity in the description of the property shall be required in such indictment in order to sustain the same, or in proof of the offence alleged, than is required in respect of an indictment or the subject-matter thereof by the seventy-first section of the said last-mentioned Act.

Examinations of
masters and
mates at ports
where there are
no local marine
boards.

**17.** Whereas it is expedient to make provision in certain cases for holding examinations of applicants for certificates of competency at places where there are no local marine boards: be it enacted, that the board of trade, if satisfied that serious inconvenience exists at any port in consequence of the distance which applicants for certificates have to travel in order to be examined, may with the concurrence of any local marine board, send the examiner or examiners of that local marine board to the port where such inconvenience exists: and thereupon the said examiner or examiners shall proceed to such port, and shall there examine the applicants in the presence of such person or persons (if any) as the board of trade may appoint for the purpose; and such examinations shall be conducted in the same manner and shall have the same effect as other examinations under the said Act.

Construction of
sect. 182 of
principal Act.
Stipulations
concerning
salvage.

**18.** It is hereby declared, that the 182nd section of the principal Act does not apply to the case of any stipulation made by the seamen belonging to any ship, which according to the terms of the agreement is to be employed on salvage service, with respect to the remuneration to be paid to them for salvage services to be rendered by such ship to any other ship or ships (e).

Payment of
wages to seamen
abroad under
sect. 209 of
principal Act.

**19.** The payment of seamen's wages required by the 209th section of the principal Act shall, whenever it is practicable so to do, be made in money and not by bill; and in cases where payment is made by bill drawn by the master, the owner of the ship shall be liable to pay the amount for which the same is drawn to the holder or indorsee thereof; and it shall not be necessary in any proceeding against the owner upon such bill to prove that the master had authority to draw the same; and any bill purporting to be drawn in pursuance of the said section, and to be indorsed as therein

(e) *The Ganges*, L. R. 2 A. & E. 370.

required, if produced out of the custody of the board of trade or of the registrar-general of seamen, or of any superintendent of any mercantile marine office, shall be received in evidence; and any indorsement on any such bill purporting to be made in pursuance of the said section, and to be signed by one of the functionaries therein mentioned, shall also be received in evidence, and shall be deemed to be primâ facie evidence of the facts stated in such indorsement.

20. The 197th section of the principal Act shall extend to seamen or apprentices who within the six months immediately preceding their death have belonged to a British ship; and such section shall be construed as if there were inserted in the first line thereof after the words "such seamen or apprentice as last aforesaid" the words "or if any seaman or apprentice who has within the six months immediately preceding his death belonged to a British ship." *Wages and effects of deceased seamen.*

21. The wages of seamen or apprentices who are lost with the ship to which they belong shall be dealt with as follows; (that is to say,) *Recovery of wages, &c., of seamen lost with their ship.*

(1.) The board of trade may recover the same from the owner of the ship in the same manner in which seamen's wages are recoverable:

(2.) In any proceedings for the recovery of such wages, if it is shown by some official return produced out of the custody of the registrar-general of seamen or by other evidence that the ship has twelve months or upwards before the institution of the proceedings left a port of departure, and if it is not shown that she has been heard of within twelve months after such departure, she shall be deemed to have been lost with all hands on board, either immediately after the time she was last heard of or at such later time as the court hearing the case may think probable:

(3.) The production out of the custody of the registrar-general of seamen or of the board of trade of any duplicate agreement or list of the crew made out at the time of the last departure of the ship from the United Kingdom, or of a certificate purporting to be a certificate from a consular or other public officer at any port abroad, stating that certain seamen or apprentices were shipped in the ship from the said port, shall, in the absence of proof to the contrary, be sufficient proof that the seamen or apprentices therein named were on board at the time of the loss:

(4.) The board of trade shall deal with such wages in the manner in which they deal with the wages of other deceased seamen and apprentices under the principal Act.

22. Whereas under the 211th and 212th sections of the principal Act, and the 16th section of "The Merchant Shipping Act Amendment Act, 1855," provision is made for relieving and sending home seamen found in distress abroad: and whereas doubts are entertained whether power exists under the said sections of making regulations and imposing conditions which are necessary for the prevention of desertion and misconduct and the undue expenditure of public money: be it enacted, and it is hereby declared, that the claims of seamen to be relieved or sent home in pursuance of the said sections or any of them, shall be subject to such regulations and dependent on such conditions as the board of trade may from time to time make or impose; and no seamen shall have any right to demand to be relieved or sent home except in the cases and to the extent provided for by such regulations and conditions. *Relief of distressed seamen to be regulated by board of trade.*

23. The following rules shall be observed with respect to the cancellation and suspension of certificates; (that is to say): *Power of cancelling certificate to rest with the court which hears the case.*

(1.) The power of cancelling or suspending the certificate of a master or mate by the 242nd section of the principal Act conferred on the board of trade shall (except in the case provided for by the fourth paragraph of the said section) vest in and be exercised by the local marine board, magistrates, naval court, admiralty court, or other court or tribunal by which the case is investigated or tried, and shall not in future vest in or be exercised by the board of trade:

(2.) Such power shall extend to cancelling or suspending the certificates of engineers in the same manner as if "certificated engineer" or "certificated engineers" were inserted throughout such section after "master" or "masters:"

(3.) Every such board, court or tribunal shall at the conclusion of the case, or as soon afterwards as possible, state in open court the decision to which they may have come with respect to cancelling or suspending certificates, and shall in all cases send a full report upon the case with the evidence to the board of trade, and shall also, if they determine to cancel or suspend any certificate, forward such certificate to the board of trade with their report:

(4.) It shall be lawful for the board of trade, if they think the justice of the case required it, to re-issue and return any certificate which has been cancelled or suspended, or shorten the time for which it is suspended, or grant a new certificate of the same or any lower grade in place of any certificate which has been cancelled or suspended:

[(5.) The 434th and 437th sections of the principal Act shall be read as if for the word "nautical" were substituted the words "nautical or engineering," and as if for the word "person" and "assessor" respectively were substituted the words "person or persons" and "assessor or assessors" respectively (f):]

(6.) No certificate shall be cancelled or suspended under this section unless a copy of the report or a statement of the case upon which the investigation is ordered has been furnished to the owner of the certificate before the commencement of the investigation, nor in the case of investigations conducted by justices or a stipendiary magistrate, unless one assessor at least expresses his concurrence in the report.

**Certificate to be delivered up.**      **24.** Every master or mate or engineer whose certificate is or is to be suspended or cancelled in pursuance of this Act shall, upon demand of the board, court or tribunal by which the case is investigated or tried, deliver his certificate to them, or, if it is not demanded by such board, court or tribunal, shall, upon demand, deliver it to the board of trade, or as it directs, and in default shall for each offence incur a penalty not exceeding fifty pounds.

**25—38.** [*Safety (Part IV. of Merchant Shipping Act,* 1854).]

**39—42.** [*Pilotage (Part V. of Merchant Shipping Act,* 1854).]

**43—48.** [*Lighthouses (Part VI. of Merchant Shipping Act,* 1854).]

*Wreck and Salvage (Part VIII. of Merchant Shipping Act,* 1854).

**Extension and amendment of summary jurisdiction in small salvage cases.**      **49.** The provisions contained in the Eighth Part of the principal Act for giving summary jurisdiction to two justices in salvage cases, and for preventing unnecessary appeals and litigation in such cases, shall be amended as follows: (that is to say,)

(1.) Such provision shall extend to all cases in which the value of the property saved does not exceed one thousand pounds, as well as to the cases provided for by the principal Act:

(2.) Such provisions shall be held to apply whether the salvage service has been rendered within the limits of the United Kingdom or not:

(3.) It shall be lawful for one of her Majesty's principal secretaries of state, or in Ireland for the lord lieutenant or other chief governor or governors to appoint out of the justices for any borough or county a rota of justices by whom jurisdiction in salvage cases shall be exercised:

(4.) When no such rota is appointed, it shall be lawful for the salvors, by writing addressed to the justice's clerk, to name one justice, and for the owner of the property saved in like manner to name the other:

(5.) If either party fails to name a justice within a reasonable time, the case may be tried by two or more justices at petty sessions:

(6.) It shall be competent for any stipendiary magistrate, and also in England for any county court judge, in Scotland for the sheriff or sheriff-substitute of any county, and in Ireland for the recorder of any borough in which there is a recorder, or for the chairmen of quarter sessions in any county, to exercise the same jurisdiction in salvage cases as is given to two justices:

(f) Repealed by Statute Law Revision Act, 1878. See 39 & 40 Vict. c. 80, s. 45, *infra.*

(7.) It shall be lawful for one of her Majesty's principal secretaries of state to determine a scale of costs to be awarded in salvage cases by any such justices or court as aforesaid (g):

(8.) All the provisions of the principal Act relating to summary proceedings in salvage cases, and to the prevention of unnecessary appeals in such cases, shall, except so far as the same are altered by this Act, extend and apply to all such proceedings, whether under the principal Act or this Act, or both of such Acts.

50. Whenever any salvage question arises the receiver of wreck for the district may, upon application from either of the parties, appoint a valuer to value the property in respect of which the salvage claim is made, and shall, when the valuation has been returned to him, give a copy of the valuation to both parties; and any copy of such valuation, purporting to be signed by the valuer and to be attested by the receiver, shall be received in evidence in any subsequent proceeding; and there shall be paid in respect of such valuation, by the party applying for the same, such fee as the board of trade may direct. *Receiver may appoint a valuer in salvage cases.*

51. The words "court of session" in the four hundred and sixty-eighth section of the principal Act shall be deemed to mean and include either division of the court of session or the lord ordinary officiating on the bills during vacation. *Jurisdiction of court of session in salvage cases.*

52. Upon delivery of wreck or of the proceeds of wreck by any receiver to any person in pursuance of the provisions of the Eighth Part of the principal Act, such receiver shall be discharged from all liability in respect thereof, but such delivery shall not be deemed to prejudice or affect any question concerning the right or title to the said wreck which may be raised by third parties, nor shall any such delivery prejudice or affect any question concerning the title to the soil on which the wreck may have been found. *Delivery of wreck by receiver not to prejudice title.*

53. Whereas by the principal Act it is provided that the proceeds of wreck, if the same is not claimed by the owner within a year, and if no person other than her Majesty, her heirs and successors, is proved to be entitled thereto, shall, subject to certain deductions, be paid into the receipt of her Majesty's exchequer in such manner as the commissioners of the treasury may direct, and that the same shall be carried to and form part of the consolidated fund of the United Kingdom (h): *Crown rights to wreck.*

And whereas doubts have been entertained whether the said last-recited provision is consistent with the arrangements concerning the hereditary revenues of the crown effected by the Act of the first year of her present Majesty, chapter two: And whereas doubts have also been entertained whether due provision is made by the said Act for paying to the revenues of the duchies of Lancaster and Cornwall respectively such of the said proceeds as may belong to those duchies: *1 Vict. c. 2.*

It is hereby declared, that such of the said proceeds of wreck as belong to her Majesty in right of her crown shall, during the life of her present Majesty (whom God long preserve), be carried to and form part of the consolidated fund of the United Kingdom, and shall after the decease of her present Majesty (whom God long preserve) be payable and paid to her Majesty's heirs and successors:

And it is hereby further declared, that such of the said proceeds of wreck as belong to her Majesty in right of her duchy of Lancaster shall be paid to the receiver-general of the said duchy, or his sufficient deputy or deputies, as part of the revenues of the said duchy, and be dealt with accordingly:

And it is hereby further declared and enacted, that the provision in the principal Act contained regarding the sale of unclaimed wreck to which no owner establishes his claim within the period of one year, and to which no admiral, vice-admiral, lord of any manor, or person other than her Majesty, her heirs and successors, is proved to be entitled, is intended and shall be construed to apply to wreck of the sea belonging to her Majesty, her heirs and successors, in respect of the duchy of Cornwall, or to the Duke of Cornwall for the time being in respect of his duchy of Cornwall; but that the proceeds of such wreck shall, subject to such deductions as are in the same Act mentioned, form part of the revenues of the duchy of Cornwall, and be dealt with accordingly.

(g) See Maude & Pollock's Merchant Shipping, 4th ed., 2, ccccxxxvi.
(h) See 45 & 46 Vict. c. 55, s. 4.

*Liability of Shipowners (Part IX. of Merchant Shipping Act, 1854).*

Shipowners' liability limited.

**54.** The owners of any ship, whether British or foreign, shall not, in cases where all or any of the following events occur without their actual fault or privity : (that is to say,)

(1.) Where any loss of life or personal injury is caused to any person being carried in such ship :

(2.) Where any damage or loss is caused to any goods, merchandise or other things whatsoever on board any such ship :

(3.) Where any loss of life or personal injury is by reason of the improper navigation of such ship as aforesaid caused to any person carried in any other ship or boat :

(4.) Where any loss or damage is by reason of the improper navigation of such ship as aforesaid caused to any other ship or boat, or to any goods, merchandise or other things whatsoever on board any other ship or boat :

be answerable in damages in respect of loss of life or personal injury, either alone or together with loss or damage to ships, boats, goods, merchandise or other things, to an aggregate amount exceeding fifteen pounds for each ton of their ship's tonnage ; nor in respect of loss or damage to ships, goods, merchandise or other things, whether there be in addition loss of life or personal injury or not to an aggregate amount exceeding eight pounds for each ton of the ship's tonnage ; such tonnage to be the registered tonnage in the case of sailing ships, and in the case of steam ships the gross tonnage without deduction on account of engine-room :

In the case of any foreign ship which has been or can be measured according to British law, the tonnage as ascertained by such measurement shall, for the purposes of this section, be deemed to be the tonnage of such ship :

In the case of any foreign ship which has not been and cannot be measured under British law, the surveyor-general of tonnage in the United Kingdom, and the chief measuring officer in any British possession abroad, shall, on receiving from or by direction of the court hearing the case such evidence concerning the dimensions of the ship as it may be found practicable to furnish, give a certificate under his hand stating what would in his opinion have been the tonnage of such ship if she had been duly measured according to British law, and the tonnage so stated in such certificate shall, for the purposes of this section, be deemed to be the tonnage of such ship.

**55.** Insurances effected against any or all of the events enumerated in the section last preceding, and occurring without such actual fault or privity as therein mentioned, shall not be invalid by reason of the nature of the risk (i).

Limitation of invalidity of insurances.
Proof of passengers on board lost ship.

**56.** In any proceeding under the 506th section of the principal Act or any Act amending the same against the owner of any ship or share therein in respect of loss of life, the master's list or the duplicate list of passengers delivered to the proper officer of customs under the sixteenth section of " The Passengers Act, 1855," shall, in the absence of proof to the contrary, be sufficient proof that the persons in respect of whose death any such prosecution or proceeding is instituted were passengers on board such ship at the time of their deaths.

*Arrangements concerning Lights, Sailing Rules, Salvage and Measurement of Tonnage in the case of Foreign Ships.*

Foreign ships in British jurisdiction to be subject to regulations in Table (C) in schedule.

**57.** Whenever foreign ships are within British jurisdiction, the regulations for preventing collision contained in table (C) in the schedule to this Act, or such other regulations for preventing collision as are for the time being in force under this Act, and all provisions of this Act relating to such regulations, or otherwise relating to collisions, shall apply to such foreign ships ; and in any cases arising in any British court of justice concerning matters happening within British jurisdiction, foreign ships shall, so far as regards such regulations and provisions be treated as if they were British ships.

Regulations, when adopted by a foreign

**58.** Whenever it is made to appear to her Majesty that the government of any foreign country is willing that the regulations for preventing collision

(i) See 30 Vict. c. 23, s. 7.

contained in table (C) in the schedule to this Act (k), or such other regulations for preventing collision as are for the time being in force under this Act, or any of the said regulations, or any provisions of this Act relating to collisions, should apply to the ships of such country when beyond the limits of British jurisdiction, her Majesty may, by order in council, direct that such regulations, and all provisions of this Act which relate to such regulations, and all such other provisions as aforesaid, shall apply to the ships of the said foreign country, whether within British jurisdiction or not. *country, may be applied to its ships on the high seas.*

59. Whenever it is made to appear to her Majesty that the government of any foreign country is willing that salvage shall be awarded by British courts for services rendered in saving life from any ship belonging to such country when such ship is beyond the limits of British jurisdiction, her Majesty may, by order in council, direct that the provisions of the principal Act and of this Act, with respect to salvage for services rendered in saving life from British ships, shall in all British courts be held to apply to services rendered in saving life from the ships of such foreign country, whether such services are rendered within British jurisdiction or not. *Provisions concerning salvage of life may, with the consent of any foreign country, be applied to its ships on the high seas.*

60. Whenever it is made to appear to her Majesty that the rules concerning the measurement of tonnage of merchant ships for the time being in force under the principal Act have been adopted by the government of any foreign country, and are in force in that country, it shall be lawful for her Majesty by order in council to direct that the ships of such foreign country shall be deemed to be of the tonnage denoted in their certificates of registry or other national papers; and thereupon it shall no longer be necessary for such ships to be remeasured in any port or place in her Majesty's dominions, but such ships shall be deemed to be of the tonnage denoted in their certificates of registry or other papers, in the same manner, to the same extent and for the same purposes in, to and for which the tonnage denoted in the certificates of registry of British ships is deemed to be the tonnage of such ships. *Ships of foreign countries adopting the rule for measurement of tonnage need not be remeasured in this country*

61. Whenever an order in council has been issued under this Act, applying any provision of this Act or any regulation made by or in pursuance of this Act to the ships of any foreign country, such ships shall in all cases arising in any British court be deemed to be subject to such provision or regulation, and shall for the purpose of such provision or regulation be treated as if they were British ships. *Effect of order in council.*

62. In issuing any order in council under this Act her Majesty may limit the time during which it is to remain in operation, and may make the same, subject to such conditions and qualifications, if any, as may be deemed expedient, and thereupon the operation of the said order shall be limited and modified accordingly. *Orders in council may be limited as to time, and qualified.*

63. Her Majesty may, by order in council, from time to time revoke or alter any order previously made under this Act (l). *Orders in council may be revoked and altered.*

64. Every order in council to be made under this Act shall be published in the London Gazette as soon as may be after the making thereof; and the production of a copy of the London Gazette containing such order shall be received in evidence, and shall be proof that the order therein published has been duly made and issued; and it shall not be necessary to plead such order specially. *Orders in council to be published in "London Gazette."*

### Legal Procedure.

65. Nothing in the third section of the Act passed in the twentieth and twenty-first years of the reign of her present Majesty, chapter forty-three, except so much thereof as provides for the payment of any fees that may be due to the clerk of the justices, shall be deemed to apply to extend to any proceeding under the direction of the board of trade, or under or by virtue of the provisions of the principal Act or this Act, or any Act amending the same. *20 & 21 Vict. c. 43, s. 3, not to apply to proceedings under board of trade or this Act, &c.*

### Delivery of Goods and Lien for Freight.

66. The following terms used in the sections of this Act hereinafter con- *Interpretation of terms.*

(k) Superseded by Order in Council, 14th August, 1879. Maude & Pollock, pp. 2, 173.

(l) 39 & 40 Vict. c. 80, s. 38, *infra.*

tained, shall have the respective meanings hereby assigned to them, if not inconsistent with the context or subject-matter; (that is to say,)

"Report:" The word "report" shall mean the report required by the customs laws to be made by the master of any importing ship:

"Entry:" The word "entry" shall mean the entry required by the customs laws to be made for the landing or discharge of goods from an importing ship:

"Goods:" The word "goods" shall include every description of wares and merchandise:

"Wharf:" The word "wharf" shall include all wharves, quays, docks and premises in or upon which any goods when landed from ships may be lawfully placed:

"Warehouse:" The word "warehouse" shall include all warehouses, buildings and premises in which goods when landed from ships may be lawfully placed:

"Wharf owner:" The expression "wharf owner" shall mean the occupier of any wharf, as hereinbefore defined:

"Warehouse owner:" The expression "warehouse owner" shall mean the occupier of any warehouse as hereinbefore defined:

"Shipowner:" The word "shipowner" shall include the master of the ship and every other person authorised to act as agent for the owner, or entitled to receive the freight, demurrage, or other charges payable in respect of such ship:

"Owner of goods." The expression "owner of goods" shall include every person who is for the time being entitled, either as owner or agent for the owner, to the possession of the goods, subject in the case of a lien, if any, to such lien:

Power to shipowner to enter and land goods in default of entry and landing by owner of goods.
**67.** Where the owner of any goods imported in any ships from foreign parts into the United Kingdom fails to make entry thereof, or having made entry thereof to land the same or take delivery thereof and to proceed therewith with all convenient speed, by the times severally hereinafter mentioned, the shipowner may make entry of and land or unship the said goods at the times, in the manner, and subject to the conditions following; (that is to say,)

(1.) If a time for the delivery of the goods is expressed in the charter party, bill of lading, or agreement, then at any time after the time so expressed:

(2.) If no time for the delivery of the goods is expressed in the charter party, bill of lading, or agreement, then at any time after the expiration of seventy-two hours, exclusive of a Sunday or holiday, after the report of the ship:

(3.) If any wharf or warehouse is named in the charter party, bill of lading, or agreement, as the wharf or warehouse where the goods are to be placed, and if they can be conveniently there received, the shipowner in landing them by virtue of this enactment shall cause them to be placed on such wharf or in such warehouse:

(4.) In other cases the shipowner in landing goods by virtue of this enactment shall place them in or on some wharf or warehouse on or in which goods of a like nature are usually placed; such wharf or warehouse being, if the goods are dutiable, a wharf or warehouse duly approved by the commissioners of customs for the landing of dutiable goods:

(5.) If at any time before the goods are landed or unshipped the owner of the goods is ready and offers to land or take delivery of the same, he shall be allowed so to do, and his entry shall in such case be preferred to any entry which may have been made by the shipowner:

(6.) If any goods are, for the purpose of convenience in assorting the same, landed at the wharf where the ship is discharged, and the owner of the goods at the time of such landing has made entry and is ready and offers to take delivery thereof, and to convey the same to some other wharf or warehouse, such goods shall be assorted at landing, and shall if demanded, be delivered to the owner thereof within twenty-four hours after assortment; and the expense of and consequent on such landing and assortment shall be borne by the shipowner:

(7.) If at any time before the goods are landed or unshipped the owner thereof has made entry for the landing and warehousing thereof at any particular wharf or warehouse other than that at which the ship is discharging, and has offered and been ready to take delivery thereof, and the shipowner has failed to make such delivery, and has also failed at the time of such offer to give the owner of the goods correct information of the time at which such goods can be delivered, then the shipowner shall, before landing or unshipping such goods under the power hereby given to him, give to the owner of the goods or of such wharf or warehouse as last aforesaid twenty-four hours' notice in writing of his readiness to deliver the goods, and shall, if he lands or unships the same without such notice, do so at his own risk and expense.

**68.** If, at the time when any goods are landed from any ship, and placed in the custody of any person as a wharf or warehouse owner, the shipowner gives to the wharf or warehouse owner notice in writing that the goods are to remain subject to a lien for freight or other charges payable to the shipowner to an amount to be mentioned in such notice, the goods so landed shall, in the hands of the wharf or warehouse owner, continue liable to the same lien, if any, for such charges as they were subject to before the landing thereof; and the wharf or warehouse owner receiving such goods shall retain them until the lien is discharged as hereinafter mentioned, and shall, if he fail so to do, make good to the shipowner any loss thereby occasioned to him. *If, when goods are landed, the shipowner give notice for that purpose, the lien for freight is to continue.*

**69.** Upon the production to the wharf or warehouse owner of a receipt for the amount claimed as due, and delivery to the wharf or warehouse owner of a copy thereof, or of a release of freight from the shipowner, the said lien shall be discharged. *Lien to be discharged on proof of payment.*

**70.** The owner of the goods may deposit with the wharf or warehouse owner a sum of money equal in amount to the sum so claimed as aforesaid by the shipowner, and thereupon the lien shall be discharged, but without prejudice to any other remedy which the shipowner may have for the recovery of the freight. *Lien to be discharged on deposit with warehouse owner.*

**71.** If such deposit as aforesaid is made with the wharf or warehouse owner, and the person making the same does not within fifteen days after making it give to the wharf or warehouse owner notice in writing to retain it, stating in such notice the sum, if any, which he admits to be payable to the shipowner, or, as the case may be, that he does not admit any sum to be so payable, the wharf or warehouse owner may, at the expiration of such fifteen days, pay the sum so deposited over to the shipowner, and shall by such payment be discharged from all liability in respect thereof. *Warehouse owner may at the end of fifteen days, if no notice is given, pay deposit to shipowner.*

**72.** If such deposit as aforesaid is made with the wharf or warehouse owner, and the person making the same does within fifteen days after making it give to the wharf or warehouse owner such notice in writing as aforesaid, the wharf or warehouse owner shall immediately apprise the shipowner of such notice, and shall pay or tender to him out of the sum deposited the sum, if any, admitted by such notice to be payable, and shall retain the remainder or balance, or, if no sum is admitted to be payable, the whole of the sum deposited for thirty days from the date of the said notice ; and at the expiration of such thirty days, unless legal proceedings have in the meantime been instituted by the shipowner against the owner of the goods to recover the said balance or sum or otherwise for the settlement of any disputes which may have arisen between them concerning such freight or other charges as aforesaid, and notice in writing of such proceedings has been served on him, the wharf or warehouse owner shall pay the said balance or sum over to the owner of the goods, and shall by such payment be discharged from all liability in respect thereof. *Course to be taken if notice to retain is given.*

**73.** If the lien is not discharged, and no deposit is made, as hereinbefore mentioned, the wharf or warehouse owner may, and, if required by the shipowner, shall, at the expiration of ninety days from the time when the goods were placed in his custody, or if the goods are of a perishable nature, at such earlier period as he in his discretion thinks fit, sell by public auction, either for home use or exportation, the said goods, or so much thereof as may be necessary to satisfy the charges hereinafter mentioned. *After ninety days warehouse owner may sell goods by public auction.*

**74.** Before making such sale the wharf or warehouse owner shall give notice thereof by advertisment in two newspapers circulating in the neighbourhood, or in one daily newspaper published in London and in one local newspaper, and also, if the address of the owner of the goods has been stated on the manifest of the cargo, or on any of the documents which have come into the possession of the wharf or warehouse owner, or is otherwise known *Notice of sale to be given.*

to him, give notice of the sale to the owner of the goods by letter sent by the post : but the title of a bonâ fide purchaser of such goods shall not be invalidated by reason of the omission to send notice as hereinbefore mentioned, nor shall any such purchaser be bound to enquire whether such notice has been sent.

*Moneys arising from sale, how to be applied.* **75.** In every case of any such sale as aforesaid the wharf or warehouse owner shall apply the moneys received from the sale as follows, and in the following order :

(1.) If the goods are sold for home use in payment of any customs or excise duties owing in respect thereof :

(2.) In payment of the expenses of the sale :

(3.) In the absence of any agreement between the wharf or warehouse owner and the shipowner concerning the priority of their respective charges, in payment of the rent, rates and other charges due to the wharf or warehouse owner in respect of the said goods :

(4.) In payment of the amount claimed by the shipowner as due for freight or other charges in respect of the said goods :

(5.) But in case of any agreement between the wharf or warehouse owner and the shipowner concerning the priority of their respective charges then such charges shall have priority according to the terms of such agreement :

and the surplus, if any, shall be paid to the owner of the goods.

*Warehouse owner's rent and expenses.* **76.** Whenever goods are placed in the custody of a wharf or warehouse owner under the authority of this Act, the said wharf or warehouse owner shall be entitled to rent in respect of the same, and shall also have power from time to time at the expense of the owner of the goods, to do all such reasonable acts as in the judgment of the said wharf or warehouse owner are necessary for the proper custody and preservation of the said goods, and shall have a lien on the said goods for the said rent and expenses.

*Warehouse owner's protection.* **77.** Nothing in this Act contained shall compel any wharf or warehouse owner to take charge of any goods which he would not be liable to take charge of if this Act had not passed ; nor shall he be bound to see to the validity of any lien claimed by any shipowner under this Act.

*Saving powers under local Acts.* **78.** Nothing in this Act contained shall take away or abridge any powers given by any local Act to any harbour trust, body corporate or persons whereby they are enabled to expedite the discharge of ships or the landing or delivery of goods ; nor shall anything in this Act contained take away or diminish any rights or remedies given to any shipowner or wharf or warehouse owner by any local Act.

---

### The SCHEDULE referred to in this Act.

---

#### Table (A).  See Sect. 2 (*m*).

#### Table (B).  See Sect. 6 (*n*).

*Fees to be charged on Examination of Engineers.*

| | | |
|---|---|---|
| For a first-class engineer's certificate . . . | £2 | 0 0 |
| For a second-class engineer's certificate . . | 1 | 0 0 |

---

(*m*) Repealed by Statute Law Revision Act, 1875.

(*n*) For table of fees payable at Mercantile Marine Offices on examination for certificate, see Maude & Pollock, 4th ed. p. cccxciii.

25 & 26 VICT. C. 89.

*An Act for the Incorporation, Regulation, and Winding-up of Trading Companies and other Associations (o).* [*7th August*, 1862.]

WHEREAS it is expedient that the laws relating to the incorporation, regulation, and winding-up of trading companies and other associations should be consolidated and amended: Be it therefore enacted by the Queen's most excellent Majesty, by and with the advice and consent of the Lords Spiritual and Temporal, and Commons, in this present Parliament assembled, and by the authority of the same, as follows:

### Preliminary.

*Preliminary.*

**1.** This Act may be cited for all purposes as " The Companies Act, 1862." Short title.

**2.** This Act, with the exception of such temporary enactment as is hereinafter declared to come into operation immediately, shall not come into operation until the second day of November, one thousand eight hundred and sixty-two, and the time at which it so comes into operation is hereinafter referred to as the commencement of this Act. *Commencement of Act.*

**3.** For the purposes of this Act a company that carries on the business of insurance in common with any other business or businesses shall be deemed to be an insurance company (*p*). *Definition of insurance company.*

**4.** No company, association, or partnership consisting of more than ten persons shall be formed, after the commencement of this Act, for the purpose of carrying on the business of banking, unless it is registered as a company under this Act, or is formed in pursuance of some other Act of Parliament, or of letters patent; and no company, association, or partnership consisting of more than twenty persons shall be formed after the commencement of this Act, for the purpose of carrying on any other business that has for its object the acquisition of gain by the company, association, or partnership, or by the individual members thereof, unless it is registered as a company under this Act, or is formed in pursuance of some other Act of Parliament, or of letters patent, or is a company engaged in working mines within and subject to the jurisdiction of the Stannaries. *Prohibition of partnerships exceeding certain number.*

**5.** This Act is divided into nine parts, relating to the following subject-matters: *Division of Act.*

The first part,—to the constitution and incorporation of companies and associations under this Act:

The second part,—to the distribution of the capital and liability of members of companies and associations under this Act:

The third part,—to the management and administration of companies and associations under this Act:

The fourth part,—to the winding-up of companies and associations under this Act:

The fifth part,—to the registration office:

The sixth part,—to application of this Act to companies registered under the Joint Stock Companies Act:

The seventh part,—to companies authorized to register under this Act:

The eighth part,—to application of this Act to unregistered companies:

The ninth part,—to repeal of Acts, and temporary provisions.

---

## PART I.

### CONSTITUTION AND INCORPORATION OF COMPANIES AND ASSOCIATIONS UNDER THIS ACT.

#### Memorandum of Association.

*Memorandum of Association.*

**6.** Any seven or more persons associated for any lawful purpose may, by subscribing their names to a memorandum of association (*q*), and otherwise complying with the requisitions of this Act in respect to registration, form an incorporated company, with or without limited liability. *Mode of forming company.*

---

(*o*) See 30 Vict. c. 29, and 30 & 31 Vict. c. 131, *infra.*

(*p*) See sect. 44.
(*q*) See Schedule II.

I. *Memorandum of Association.*

**Mode of limiting liability of members.**

**7.** The liability of the members of a company formed under this Act may, according to the memorandum of association, be limited either to the amount, if any, unpaid on the shares respectively held by them, or to such amount as the members may respectively undertake by the memorandum of association to contribute to the assets of the company in the event of its being wound up (r).

**Memorandum of association of a company limited by shares.**

**8.** Where a company is formed on the principle of having the liability of its members limited to the amount unpaid on their shares, hereinafter referred to as a company limited by shares, the memorandum of association shall contain the following things; (that is to say,)

(1.) The name of the proposed company, with the addition of the word "limited" as the last word in such name (s):

(2.) The part of the United Kingdom, whether England, Scotland, or Ireland, in which the registered office of the company is proposed to be situate:

(3.) The objects for which the proposed company is to be established:

(4.) A declaration that the liability of the members is limited:

(5.) The amount of capital with which the company proposes to be registered divided into shares of a certain fixed amount:

Subject to the following regulations:

(1.) That no subscriber shall take less than one share:

(2.) That each subscriber of the memorandum of association shall write opposite to his name the number of shares he takes.

**Memorandum of association of a company limited by guarantee.**

**9.** Where a company is formed on the principle of having the liability of its members limited to such amount as the members respectively undertake to contribute to the assets of the company in the event of the same being wound up, hereinafter referred to as a company limited by guarantee, the memorandum of association shall contain the following things; (that is to say,)

(1.) The name of the proposed company, with the addition of the word "limited" as the last word in such name:

(2.) The part of the United Kingdom, whether England, Scotland, or Ireland, in which the registered office of the company is proposed to be situate:

(3.) The objects for which the proposed company is to be established:

(4.) A declaration that each member undertakes to contribute to the assets of the company, in the event of the same being wound up during the time that he is a member, or within one year afterwards, for payment of the debts and liabilities of the company contracted before the time at which he ceases to be a member, and of the costs, charges, and expenses of winding-up the company, and for the adjustment of the rights of the contributories amongst themselves, such amount as may be required, not exceeding a specified amount.

**Memorandum of association of an unlimited company.**

**10.** Where a company is formed on the principle of having no limit placed on the liability of its members, hereinafter referred to as an unlimited company, the memorandum of association shall contain the following things; (that is to say),

(1.) The name of the proposed company:

(2.) The part of the United Kingdom, whether England, Scotland, or Ireland, in which the registered office of the company is proposed to be situate:

(3.) The objects for which the proposed company is to be established.

**Stamp, signature, and effect of memorandum of association.**

**11.** The memorandum of association shall bear the same stamp as if it were a deed, and shall be signed by each subscriber in the presence of, and be attested by, one witness at the least, and that attestation shall be a sufficient attestation in Scotland as well as in England and Ireland: it shall, when registered, bind the company and the members thereof to the same extent as if each member had subscribed his name and affixed his seal thereto, and there were in the memorandum contained, on the part of himself, his heirs, executors, and administrators, a covenant to observe all the conditions of such memorandum, subject to the provisions of this Act.

(r) By sect. 4 of 30 & 31 Vict. c. 131, *infra*, companies may have directors with unlimited liability.

(s) See sect. 23 of 30 & 31 Vict. c. 131, *infra*.

12. Any company limited by shares may so far modify the conditions contained in its memorandum of association, if authorized to do so by its regulations as originally framed, or as altered by special resolution in manner hereinafter mentioned, as to increase its capital, by the issue of new shares of such amount as it thinks expedient, or to consolidate and divide its capital into shares of larger amount than its existing shares, or to convert its paid-up shares into stock, but, save as aforesaid, and save as is hereinafter provided in the case of a change of name, no alteration shall be made by any company in the conditions contained in its memorandum of association (t). *I. Memorandum of Association.*

Power of certain companies to alter memorandum of association.

13. Any company under this Act, with the sanction of a special resolution of the company passed in manner hereinafter mentioned, and with the approval of the Board of Trade, testified in writing under the hand of one of its secretaries or assistant secretaries, may change its name, and upon such change being made the registrar shall enter the new name on the register in the place of the former name, and shall issue a certificate of incorporation altered to meet the circumstances of the case; but no such alteration of name shall affect any rights or obligations of the company, or render defective any legal proceedings instituted or to be instituted by or against the company, and any legal proceedings may be continued or commenced against the company by its new name that might have been continued or commenced against the company by its former name. Power of companies to change name.

### *Articles of Association.*

*Articles of Association.*

14. The memorandum of association may, in the case of a company limited by shares, and shall, in the case of a company limited by guarantee or unlimited, be accompanied, when registered, by articles of association signed by the subscribers to the memorandum of association, and prescribing such regulations for the company as the subscribers to the memorandum of association deem expedient: the articles shall be expressed in separate paragraphs, numbered arithmetically: they may adopt all or any of the provisions contained in the Table marked A in the first schedule hereto; they shall, in the case of a company, whether limited by guarantee or unlimited, that has a capital divided into shares, state the amount of capital with which the company preposes to be registered; and in the case of a company, whether limited by guarantee or unlimited, that has not a capital divided into shares, state the number of members with which the company proposes to be registered, for the purpose of enabling the registrar to determine the fees payable on registration: in a company limited by guarantee or unlimited, and having a capital divided into shares, each subscriber shall take one share at the least, and shall write opposite to his name in the memorandum of association the number of shares he takes. Regulations to be prescribed by articles of association.

15. In the case of a company limited by shares, if the memorandum of association is not accompanied by articles of association, or in so far as the articles do not exclude or modify the regulations contained in the Table marked A in the first schedule hereto, the last-mentioned regulations shall, so far as the same are applicable, be deemed to be the regulations of the company, in the same manner and to the same extent as if they had been inserted in articles of association, and the articles had been duly registered. Application of Table A.

16. The articles of association shall be printed, they shall bear the same stamp as if they were contained in a deed, and shall be signed by each subscriber in the presence of, and be attested by, one witness at the least, and such attestation shall be a sufficient attestation in Scotland as well as in England and Ireland; when registered, they shall bind the company and the members thereof to the same extent as if each member had subscribed his name and affixed his seal thereto, and there were in such articles contained a covenant on the part of himself, his heirs, executors, and administrators, to conform to all the regulations contained in such articles, subject to the provisions of this Act; and all moneys payable by any member of the company, in pursuance of the conditions and regulations of the company, or any of such conditions or regulations, shall be deemed to be a debt due from such member to the company, and in England and Ireland to be in the nature of a specialty debt. Stamp, signature, and effect of articles of association.

(t) See 30 & 31 Vict. c. 131, ss. 8—20; 40 & 41 Vict. c. 26, s. 4; 43 Vict. c. 19, s. 4, *infra.*

Registration of memorandum of association and articles of association, with fees as in Table B.

Effect of registration.

Copies of memorandum and articles to be given to members.

Prohibition against identity of names in companies.

Prohibition against certain companies holding land.

## General Provisions.

**17.** The memorandum of association and the articles of association, if any, shall be delivered to the registrar of joint stock companies hereinafter mentioned (*u*), who shall retain and register the same : there shall be paid to the registrar by a company having a capital divided into shares, in respect of the several matters mentioned in the table marked B in the first schedule hereto, the several fees therein specified, or such smaller fees as the Board of Trade may from time to time direct (*x*) ; and by a company not having a capital divided into shares, in respect of the several matters mentioned in the table marked C in the first schedule hereto, the several fees therein specified, or such smaller fees as the Board of Trade may from time to time direct : all fees paid to the said registrar in pursuance of this Act shall be paid into the receipt of her Majesty's Exchequer, and be carried to the account of the Consolidated Fund of the United Kingdom of Great Britain and Ireland.

**18.** Upon the registration of the memorandum of association, and of the articles of association in cases where articles of association are required by this Act or by the desire of the parties to be registered, the registrar shall certify, under his hand, that the company is incorporated, and in the case of a limited company that the company is limited : the subscribers of the memorandum of association, together with such other persons as may from time to time become members of the company, shall thereupon be a body corporate by the name contained in the memorandum of association, capable forthwith of exercising all the functions of an incorporated company, and having perpetual succession and a common seal, with power to hold lands, but with such liability on the part of the members to contribute to the assets of the company in the event of the same being wound up as hereinafter mentioned (*y*) : a certificate of the incorporation of any company given by the registrar, shall be conclusive evidence that all the requisitions of this Act in respect of registration have been complied with.

**19.** A copy of the memorandum of association, having annexed thereto the articles of association, if any, shall be forwarded to every member, at his request, on payment of the sum of one shilling, or such less sum as may be prescribed by the company for each copy ; and if any company makes default in forwarding a copy of the memorandum of association and articles of association, if any, to a member, in pursuance of this section, the company so making default shall, for each offence, incur a penalty not exceeding one pound.

**20.** No company shall be registered under a name identical with that by which a subsisting company is already registered, or so nearly resembling the same as to be calculated to deceive, except in a case where such subsisting company is in the course of being dissolved, and testifies its consent in such manner as the registrar requires ; and if any company, through inadvertence or otherwise, is, without such consent as aforesaid, registered by a name identical with that by which a subsisting company is registered, or so nearly resembling the same as to be calculated to deceive, such first-mentioned company may, with the sanction of the registrar, change its name, and upon such change being made, the registrar shall enter the new name on the register in the place of the former name, and shall issue a certificate of incorporation, altered to meet the circumstances of the case ; but no such alteration of name shall affect any rights or obligations of the company, or render defective any legal proceedings instituted, or to be instituted, by or against the company, and any legal proceedings may be continued or commenced against the company by its new name that might have been continued or commenced against the company by its former name.

**21.** No company formed for the purpose of promoting art, science, religion, charity, or any other like object, not involving the acquisition of gain by the company or by the individual members thereof, shall, without the sanction of the Board of Trade, hold more than two acres of land ; but the Board of Trade may, by licence (*z*) under the hand of one of their principal secretaries or assistant secretaries, empower any such company to hold lands in such quantity and subject to such conditions as they think fit.

---

(*u*) Sect. 174.                                    (*y*) Sect. 38.
(*x*) Sect. 71 ; Schedule I., Table (B).            (*z*) Sebed. II., Form F.

## PART II.

DISTRIBUTION OF CAPITAL AND LIABILITY OF MEMBERS OF COMPANIES AND
ASSOCIATIONS UNDER THIS ACT.

### *Distribution of Capital.*

22. The shares or other interest of any member in a company under this Act shall be personal estate, capable of being transferred in manner provided by the regulations of the company, and shall not be of the nature of real estate, and each share shall, in the case of a company having a capital divided into shares be distinguished by its appropriate number. *Nature of interest in company.*

23. The subscribers of the memorandum of association of any company under this act shall be deemed to have agreed to become members of the company whose memorandum they have subscribed, and upon the registration of the company shall be entered as members on the register of members hereinafter mentioned ; and every other person who has agreed to become a member of a company under this Act, and whose name is entered on the register of members, shall be deemed to be a member of the company (a). *Definition of "member."*

24. Any transfer of the share or other interest of a deceased member of a company under this Act, made by his personal representative, shall, notwithstanding such personal representative may not himself be a member, be of the same validity as if he had been a member at the time of the execution of the instrument of transfer. *Transfer by personal representative.*

25. Every company under this Act shall cause to be kept in one or more books a register of its members (b), and there shall be entered therein the following particulars :— *Register of members.*

    (1.) The names and addresses, and the occupations, if any, of the members of the company, with the addition, in the case of a company having a capital divided into shares, of a statement of the shares held by each member, distinguishing each share by its number ; and of the amount paid or agreed to be considered as paid on the shares of each member :

    (2.) The date at which the name of any person was entered in the register as a member :

    (3.) The date at which any person ceased to be a member :

And any company acting in contravention of this section shall incur a penalty not exceeding five pounds for every day during which its default in complying with the provisions of this section continues, and every director or manager of the company who shall knowingly and wilfully authorize or permit such contravention shall incur the like penalty.

26. Every company under this Act, and having a capital divided into shares (c), shall make, once at least in every year, a list of all persons who, on the fourteenth day succeeding the day on which the ordinary general meeting, or if there is more than one ordinary meeting in each year, the first of such ordinary general meetings is held, are members of the company ; and such list shall state the names, addresses, and occupations of all the members therein mentioned, and the number of shares held by each of them, and shall contain a summary specifying the following particulars :— *Annual list of members.*

    (1.) The amount of the capital of the company, and the number of shares into which it is divided :

    (2.) The number of shares taken from the commencement of the company up to the date of the summary :

    (3.) The amount of calls made on each share :

    (4.) The total amount of calls received :

    (5.) The total amount of calls unpaid :

    (6.) The total amount of shares forfeited :

    (7.) The names, addresses, and occupations of the persons who have ceased to be members since the last list was made, and the number of shares held by each of them.

The above list and summary shall be contained in a separate part of the register, and shall be completed within seven days after such fourteenth day

(a) Sect. 37.            Vict. c. 131, *infra.*
(b) Compare sect. 31 of 30 & 31      (c) See sect. 12 of this Act.

II. *Distribution of Capital.*

**Penalty on company, &c., not keeping a proper register.**

**Company to give notice of consolidation or of conversion of capital into stock.**

**Effect of conversion of shares into stock.**

**Entry of trusts on register.**

**Certificate of shares or stock.**

**Inspection of register.**

**Power to close register.**

**Notice of increase of capital and of members to be given to registrar.**

as is mentioned in this section, and a copy shall forthwith be forwarded to the registrar of joint stock companies (d).

27. If any company under this Act, and having a capital divided into shares, makes default in complying with the provisions of this Act with respect to forwarding such list of members or summary as is hereinbefore mentioned to the registrar, such company shall incur a penalty not exceeding five pounds for every day during which such default continues, and every director and manager of the company who shall knowingly and wilfully authorize or permit such default shall incur the like penalty.

28. Every company under this Act, and having a capital divided into shares that has consolidated and divided its capital into shares of larger amount than its existing shares, or converted any portion of its capital into stock, shall give notice to the registrar of joint stock companies of such consolidation, division, or conversion, specifying the shares so consolidated, divided, or converted.

29. Where any company under this Act, and having a capital divided into shares, has converted any portion of its capital into stock, and given notice of such conversion to the registrar, all the provisions of this Act which are applicable to shares only shall cease as to so much of the capital as is converted into stock ; and the register of members hereby required to be kept by the company, and the list of members to be forwarded to the registrar, shall show the amount of stock held by each member in the list instead of the amount of shares and the particulars relating to shares hereinbefore required.

30. No notice of any trust, expressed, implied, or constructive, shall be entered on the register, or be receivable by the registrar, in the case of companies under this Act, and registered in England or Ireland.

31. A certificate, under the common seal of the company, specifying any share or shares or stock held by any member of a company, shall be *primâ facie* evidence of the title of the member to the share or shares or stock therein specified.

32. The register of members, commencing from the date of the registration of the company, shall be kept at the registered office of the company hereinafter mentioned (e) ; except when closed, as hereinafter mentioned (f), it shall during business hours, but subject to such reasonable restrictions as the company in general meeting may impose, so that not less than two hours in each day be appointed for inspection, be open to the inspection of any member gratis, and to the inspection of any other person on the payment of one shilling, or such less sum as the company may prescribe, for each inspection ; and every such member or other person may require a copy of such register, or of any part thereof, or of such list or summary of members as is hereinbefore mentioned, on payment of sixpence for every hundred words required to be copied ; if such inspection or copy is refused, the company shall incur for each refusal a penalty not exceeding two pounds, and a further penalty not exceeding two pounds for every day during which such refusal continues, and every director and manager of the company who shall knowingly authorize or permit such refusal shall incur the like penalty ; and in addition to the above penalty, as respects companies registered in England and Ireland, any judge sitting in chambers, or the vice-warden of the stannaries, in the case of companies subject to his jurisdiction, may by order compel an immediate inspection of the register.

33. Any company under this Act may, upon giving notice by advertisement in some newspaper circulating in the district in which the registered office of the company is situated, close the register of members for any time or times not exceeding in the whole thirty days in each year.

34. Where a company has a capital divided into shares, whether such shares may or may not have been converted into stock, notice of any increase in such capital beyond the registered capital, and where a company has not a capital divided into shares, notice of any increase in the number of members beyond the registered number, shall be given to the registrar in the case of an increase of capital, within fifteen days from the date of the passing of the resolution by which such increase has been authorized ; and in the case of an increase of members, within fifteen days from the time at which

(d) See 43 Vict. c. 19, s. 6, *infra*.     (f) Sect. 33.
(e) Sect. 39.

such increase of members has been resolved on or has taken place, and the registrar shall forthwith record the amount of such increase of capital or members: if such notice is not given within the period aforesaid, the company in default shall incur a penalty not exceeding five pounds for every day during which such neglect to give notice continues, and every director and manager of the company who shall knowingly and wilfully authorize or permit such default shall incur the like penalty.

**35.** If the name of any person is, without sufficient cause, entered in or omitted from the register of members of any company under this Act, or if default is made, or unnecessary delay takes place in entering on the register the fact of any person having ceased to be a member of the company, the person or member aggrieved, or any member of the company, or the company itself, may, as respects companies registered in England or Ireland, by motion in any of her Majesty's superior courts of law or equity, or by application to a judge sitting in chambers, or to the vice-warden of the stannaries in the case of companies subject to his jurisdiction, and as respects companies registered in Scotland by summary petition to the court of session, or in such other manner as the said courts may direct, apply for an order of the court that the register may be rectified; and the court may either refuse such application, with or without cost, to be paid by the applicant, or it may, if satisfied of the justice of the case, make an order for the rectification of the register, and may direct the company to pay all the costs of such motion, application, or petition, and any damages the party aggrieved may have sustained: the court may, in any proceeding under this section, decide on any question relating to the title of any person who is a party to such proceeding to have his name entered in or omitted from the register, whether such question arises between two or more members or alleged members, or between any members or alleged members and the company, and generally the court may in any such proceeding decide any question that it may be necessary or expedient to decide for the rectification of the register; provided that the court [if a court of common law, may direct an issue to be tried, in which any question of law may be raised, and a writ of error or appeal, in the manner directed by "The Common Law Procedure Act, 1854," shall lie] (*g*).

**36.** Whenever any order has been made rectifying the register, in the case of a company hereby required to send a list of its members to the registrar, the court shall, by its order, direct that due notice of such rectification be given to the registrar.

**37.** The register of members shall be *primâ facie* evidence of any matters by this Act directed or authorized to be inserted therein (*h*).

### Liability of Members.

*Remedy for improper entry or omission of entry in register.*

*Notice to registrar of rectification of registrar.*

*Register to be evidence.*

*Liability of Members.*

**38.** In the event of a company formed under this Act being wound up, every present and past member (*i*) of such company shall be liable to contribute to the assets of the company to an amount sufficient for payment of the debts and liabilities of the company, and the costs, charges, and expenses of the winding-up, and for the payment of such sums as may be required for the adjustment of the rights of the contributories amongst themselves, with the qualifications following; (that is to say) (*k*),

*Liability of present and past members of company.*

(1.) No past member shall be liable to contribute to the assets of the company if he has ceased to be a member for a period of one year or upwards prior to the commencement (*l*) of the winding-up:

(2.) No past member shall be liable to contribute in respect of any debt or liability of the company contracted after the time at which he ceased to be a member:

(3.) No past member shall be liable to contribute to the assets of the company unless it appears to the Court that the existing members are unable to satisfy the contributions required to be made by them in pursuance of this Act:

(4.) In the case of a company limited by shares, no contribution shall be

(*g*) Words within brackets repealed by 44 & 45 Vict. c. 59.
(*h*) See sect. 25.
(*i*) Sect. 23. As to shares stand-

ing in the name of a married woman, see 45 & 46 Vict. c. 75, ss. 6—9.
(*k*) Sect. 109.
(*l*) Sects. 84, 130.

required from any member exceeding the amount, if any, unpaid on the shares in respect of which he is liable as a present or past member:

(5.) In the case of a company limited by guarantee, no contribution shall be required from any member exceeding the amount of the undertaking entered into on his behalf by the memorandum of association (*m*):

(6.) Nothing in this Act contained shall invalidate any provision contained in any policy of insurance or other contract whereby the liability of individual members upon any such policy or contract is restricted, or whereby the funds of the company are alone made liable in respect of such policy or contract:

(7.) No sum due to any member of a company, in his character of a member, by way of dividends, profits, or otherwise, shall be deemed to be a debt of the company, payable to such member in a case of competition between himself and any other creditor not being a member of the company; but any such sum may be taken into account, for the purposes of the final adjustment of the rights of the contributories amongst themselves (*n*).

---

# PART III.

## MANAGEMENT AND ADMINISTRATION OF COMPANIES AND ASSOCIATIONS UNDER THIS ACT.

### Provisions for Protection of Creditors.

**39.** Every company under this Act shall have a registered office to which all communications and notices may be addressed (*o*). If any company under this Act carries on business without having such an office, it shall incur a penalty not exceeding five pounds for every day during which business is so carried on.

**40.** Notice of the situation of such registered office, and of any change therein, shall be given to the registrar, and recorded by him: until such notice is given the company shall not be deemed to have complied with the provisions of this Act with respect to having a registered office.

**41.** Every limited company under this Act, whether limited by shares or by guarantee, shall paint or affix, and shall keep painted or affixed, its name on the outside of every office or place in which the business of the company is carried on, in a conspicuous position, in letters easily legible, and shall have its name engraven in legible characters on its seal, and shall have its name mentioned in legible characters in all notices, advertisements, and other official publications of such company, and in all bills of exchange, promissory notes, indorsements, cheques, and orders for money or goods purporting to be signed by or on behalf of such company, and in all bills of parcels, invoices, receipts, and letters of credit of the company.

**42.** If any limited company under this Act does not paint or affix, and keep painted or affixed, its name in manner directed by this Act, it shall be liable to a penalty not exceeding five pounds for not so painting or affixing its name, and for every day during which such name is not so kept painted or affixed, and every director and manager of the company who shall knowingly and wilfully authorize or permit such default shall be liable to the like penalty; and if any director, manager, or officer of such company, or any person on its behalf, uses or authorizes the use of any seal purporting to be a seal of the company whereon its name is not so engraven as aforesaid, or issues or authorizes the issue of any notice, advertisement, or other official publication of such company, or signs or authorizes to be signed on behalf of such company any bill of exchange, promissory note, indorsement, cheque, order for money or goods, or issues or authorizes to be issued any bill of parcels, invoice, receipt, or letter of credit of the company, wherein its

---

(*m*) Sect. 9 (4).      (*n*) Sect. 101.      (*o*) Sect. 62.

name is not mentioned in manner aforesaid, he shall be liable to a penalty of fifty pounds, and shall further be personally liable to the holder of any such bill of exchange, promissory note, cheque, or order for money or goods, for the amount thereof, unless the same is duly paid by the company.

*III. Provisions for Protection of Creditors.*

43. Every limited company under this Act shall keep a register of all mortgages and charges specifically affecting property of the company, and shall enter in such register in respect of each mortgage or charge a short description of the property mortgaged or charged, the amount of charge created, and the names of the mortgagees or persons entitled to such charge : if any property of the company is mortgaged or charged without such entry as aforesaid being made, every director, manager, or other officer of the company who knowingly and wilfully authorizes or permits the omission of such entry, shall incur a penalty not exceeding fifty pounds : the register of mortgages required by this section shall be open to inspection by any creditor or member of the company at all reasonable times ; and if such inspection is refused, any officer of the company refusing the same, and every director and manager of the company authorizing or knowingly and wilfully permitting such refusal, shall incur a penalty not exceeding five pounds, and a further penalty not exceeding two pounds for every day during which such refusal continues ; and in addition to the above penalty, as respects companies registered in England and Ireland, any judge sitting in chambers, or the Vice-Warden of the Stannaries, in the case of companies subject to his jurisdiction (*p*), may by order compel an immediate inspection of the register.

Register of mortgages.

44. Every limited banking company, and every insurance company, and deposit, provident, or benefit society under this Act shall, before it commences business, and also on the first Monday in February and the first Monday in August in every year during which it carries on business, make a statement in the Form marked D. in the first schedule hereto, or as near thereto as circumstances will admit, and a copy of such statement shall be put up in a conspicuous place in the registered office of the company, and in every branch office or place where the business of the company is carried on, and if default is made in compliance with the provisions of this section, the company shall be liable to a penalty not exceeding five pounds for every day during which such default continues, and every director and manager of the company who shall knowingly and wilfully authorize or permit such default shall incur the like penalty.

Certain companies to publish statement entered in Schedule.

Every member and every creditor of any company mentioned in this section shall be entitled to a copy of the above-mentioned statement on payment of a sum not exceeding sixpence.

45. Every company under this Act, and not having a capital divided into shares, shall keep at its registered office a register containing the names and addresses and the occupations of its directors or managers, and shall send to the Registrar of Joint Stock Companies a copy of such register, and shall from time to time notify to the registrar any change that takes place in such directors or managers.

List of directors to be sent to registrar.

46. If any company under this Act, and not having a capital divided into shares, makes default in keeping a register of its directors or managers, or in sending a copy of such register to the registrar in compliance with the foregoing rules, or in notifying to the registrar any change that takes place in such directors or managers, such delinquent company shall incur a penalty not exceeding five pounds for every day during which such default continues, and every director and manager of the company who shall knowingly and wilfully authorize or permit such default shall incur the like penalty.

Penalty on company not keeping register of directors.

47. A promissory note or bill of exchange shall be deemed to have been made, accepted, or indorsed on behalf of any company under this Act, if made, accepted, or indorsed in the name of the company by any person acting under the authority of the company, or if made, accepted or indorsed by or on behalf or on account of the company, by any person acting under the authority of the company (*q*).

Promissory notes and bills of exchange.

48. If any company under this Act carries on business when the number of its members is less than seven (*r*), for a period of six months after the number has been so reduced, every person who is a member of such company during the time that it so carries on business after such period of six

Prohibition against carrying on business with less than seven members.

(*p*) Sect. 35.      (*q*) Sect. 95 (3).      (*r*) Sect. 6.

III. *Provisions for Protection of Creditors.*

*Provisions for Protection of Members.*

General meeting of company.

Power to alter regulations by special resolution.

Definition of special resolution.

Provision where no regulations as to meetings.

Registry of special resolutions.

months, and is cognisant of the fact that it is so carrying on business with fewer than seven members, shall be severally liable for the payment of the whole debts of the company contracted during such time, and may be sued for the same, without the joinder in the action or suit of any other member.

### Provisions for Protection of Members.

**49.** A general meeting of every company under this Act shall be held once at the least in every year (*r*).

**50.** Subject to the provisions of this Act, and to the conditions contained in the memorandum of association (*s*), any company formed under this Act may, in general meeting, from time to time, by passing a special resolution in manner hereinafter mentioned, alter all or any of the regulations of the company contained in the articles of association or in the Table marked A in the first schedule, where such table is applicable to the company, or make new regulations to the exclusion of or in addition to all or any of the regulations of the company; and any regulations so made by special resolution shall be deemed to be regulations of the company of the same validity as if they had been originally contained in the articles of association, and shall be subject in like manner to be altered or modified by any subsequent special resolution.

**51.** A resolution passed by a company under this Act shall be deemed to be special whenever a resolution has been passed by a majority of not less than three-fourths of such members of the company for the time being entitled, according to the regulations of the company, to vote as may be present, in person or by proxy (in cases where by the regulations of the company proxies are allowed), at any general meeting of which notice specifying the intention to propose such resolution has been duly given, and such resolution has been confirmed by a majority of such members for the time being entitled, according to the regulations of the company, to vote as may be present, in person or by proxy, at a subsequent general meeting, of which notice has been duly given, and held at an interval of not less than fourteen days, nor more than one month from the date of the meeting at which such resolution was first passed; at any meeting mentioned in this section, unless a poll is demanded by at least five members, a declaration of the chairman that the resolution has been carried shall be deemed conclusive evidence of the fact, without proof of the number or proportion of the votes recorded in favour of or against the same : notice of any meeting shall, for the purposes of this section, be deemed to be duly given and the meeting to be duly held, whenever such notice is given and meeting held in manner prescribed by the regulations of the company : in computing the majority under this section, when a poll is demanded, reference shall be had to the number of votes to which each member is entitled by the regulations of the company.

**52.** In default of any regulations as to voting every member shall have one vote (*t*), and in default of any regulations as to summoning general meetings a meeting shall be held to be duly summoned of which seven days' notice in writing has been served on every member in manner in which notices are required to be served by the table marked A in the first schedule hereto, and in default of any regulations as to the persons to summon meetings five members shall be competent to summon the same, and in default of any regulations as to who is to be chairman of such meeting, it shall be competent for any person elected by the members present to preside.

**53.** A copy of any special resolution that is passed by any company under this Act, shall be printed and forwarded to the registrar of joint stock companies, and be recorded by him : if such copy is not so forwarded within fifteen days from the date of the confirmation of the resolution, the company shall incur a penalty not exceeding two pounds for every day after the expiration of such fifteen days during which such copy is omitted to be forwarded, and every director and manager of the company who shall knowingly and wilfully authorize or permit such default shall incur the like penalty.

---

(*r*) See First Schedule, Table A. (29), and sect. 39 of 30 & 31 Vict. c. 131, *infra*.

(*s*) Sect. 6.
(*t*) Sched. I. Table A. (44).

**54.** Where articles of association have been registered, a copy of every special resolution for the time being in force shall be annexed to or embodied in every copy of the articles of association that may be issued after the passing of such resolution; where no articles of association have been registered, a copy of any special resolution shall be forwarded in print to any member requesting the same on payment of one shilling or such less sum as the company may direct; and if any company makes default in complying with the provisions of this section it shall incur a penalty not exceeding one pound for each copy in respect of which such default is made; and every director and manager of the company who shall knowingly and wilfully authorize or permit such default shall incur the like penalty. *III. Provisions for Protection of Members.* Copies of special resolutions.

**55.** Any company under this Act may, by instrument in writing under its common seal, empower any person, either generally or in respect of any specified matter, as its attorney, to execute deeds on its behalf in any place not situate in the United Kingdom (*u*); and every deed signed by such attorney, on behalf of the company, and under his seal, shall be binding on the company, and have the same effect as if it were under the common seal of the company. Execution of deeds abroad.

**56.** The board of trade may appoint one or more competent inspectors to examine into the affairs of any company under this Act, and to report thereon, in such manner as the board may direct, upon the applications following; (that is to say,) Examination of affairs of company by inspectors.

    (1.) In the case of a banking company that has a capital divided into shares, upon the application of members holding not less than one-third part of the whole shares of the company for the time being issued:

    (2.) In the case of any other company that has a capital divided into shares, upon the application of members holding not less than one-fifth part of the whole shares of the company for the time being issued:

    (3.) In the case of any company not having a capital divided into shares, upon the application of members being in number not less than one-fifth of the whole number of persons for the time being entered on the register of the company as members.

**57.** The application shall be supported by such evidence as the board of trade may require for the purpose of showing that the applicants have good reason for requiring such investigation to be made, and that they are not actuated by malicious motives in instituting the same; the board of trade may also require the applicants to give security for payment of the costs of the inquiry before appointing any inspector or inspectors. Application for inspection to be supported by evidence.

**58.** It shall be the duty of all officers and agents of the company to produce for the examination of the inspectors all books and documents in their custody or power: any inspector may examine upon oath the officers and agents of the company in relation to its business, and may administer such oath accordingly: if any officer or agent refuses to produce any book or document hereby directed to be produced, or to answer any question relating to the affairs of the company, he shall incur a penalty not exceeding five pounds in respect of each offence (*x*). Inspection of books.

**59.** Upon the conclusion of the examination the inspectors shall report their opinion to the board of trade; such report shall be written or printed, as the board of trade directs; a copy shall be forwarded by the board of trade to the registered office of the company, and a further copy shall, at the request of the members upon whose application the inspection was made, be delivered to them or to any one or more of them: all expenses of and incidental to any such examination as aforesaid shall be defrayed by the members upon whose applications the inspectors were appointed, unless the board of trade shall direct the same to be paid out of the assets of the company, which it is hereby authorized to do. Result of examination, how dealt with.

**60.** Any company under this Act may by special resolution appoint inspectors for the purpose of examining into the affairs of the company: the inspectors so appointed shall have the same powers and perform the Power of company to appoint inspectors.

(*u*) See 27 Vict. c. 19, "An Act to enable Joint Stock Companies carrying on Business in Foreign Countries to have Official Seals to be used for such Countries."

(*x*) Schedule I., Table A. (78).

III. *Provisions for Protection of Members.*

same duties as inspectors appointed by the board of trade, with this exception, that, instead of making their report to the board of trade, they shall make the same in such manner and to such persons as the company in general meeting directs; and the officers and agents of the company shall incur the same penalties, in case of any refusal to produce any book or document hereby required to be produced to such inspectors, or to answer any question, as they would have incurred if such inspector had been appointed by the board of trade.

Report of inspectors to be evidence.

**61.** A copy of the report of any inspectors appointed under this Act, authenticated by the seal of the company into whose affairs they have made inspection, shall be admissible in any legal proceeding, as evidence of the opinion of the inspectors in relation to any matter contained in such report.

*Notices.*

## Notices.

Service of notices on company.

**62.** Any summons, notice, order, or other document required to be served upon the company may be served by leaving the same, or sending it through the post in a prepaid letter addressed to the company, at their registered office (*y*).

Rules as to notices by letter.

**63.** Any document to be served by post on the company shall be posted in such time as to admit of its being delivered in the due course of delivery within the period (if any) prescribed for the service thereof; and in proving service of such document it shall be sufficient to prove that such document was properly directed, and that it was put as a prepaid letter into the post office.

Authentication of notices of company.

**64.** Any summons, notice, order or proceeding requiring authentication by the company, may be signed by any director, secretary, or other authorized officer of the company, and need not be under the common seal of the company, and the same may be in writing or in print, or partly in writing and partly in print.

*Legal Proceedings.*

## Legal Proceedings.

Recovery of penalties.

**65.** All offences under this Act made punishable by any penalty may be prosecuted summarily before two or more justices, as to England, in manner directed by an Act passed in the session holden in the eleventh and twelfth years of the reign of her Majesty Queen Victoria, chapter forty-three, intituled "An Act to facilitate the Performance of the Duties of Justices of the Peace out of Sessions within England and Wales with respect to Summary Convictions and Orders," or any Act amending the same; and as to Scotland, before two or more justices or the sheriff of the county, in manner directed by the Act passed in the session of Parliament holden in the seventeenth and eighteenth years of the reign of Her Majesty Queen Victoria, chapter one hundred and four, intituled "An Act to amend and consolidate the Acts relating to Merchant Shipping," or any Act amending the same, as regards offences in Scotland against that Act, not being offences by that Act described as felonies or misdemeanors; and as to Ireland, in manner directed by the Act passed in the session holden in the fourteenth and fifteenth years of the reign of her Majesty Queen Victoria, chapter ninety-three, intituled "An Act to consolidate and amend the Acts regulating the Proceedings of Petty Sessions and the Duties of Justices of the Peace out of Quarter Sessions in Ireland," or any Act amending the same.

Application of penalties.

**66.** The justices or sheriff imposing any penalty under this Act may direct the whole or any part thereof to be applied in or towards payment of the costs of the proceedings, or in or towards the rewarding the person upon whose information or at whose suit such penalty has been recovered; and subject to such direction, all penalties shall be paid into the receipt of her Majesty's Exchequer in such manner as the Treasury may direct, and shall be carried to and form part of the consolidated fund of the United Kingdom.

Evidence of proceedings at meetings.

**67.** Every company under this Act shall cause minutes of all resolutions and proceedings of general meetings of the company, and of the directors or managers of the company in cases where there are directors or managers, to be duly entered in books to be from time to time provided for the purpose, and any such minute as aforesaid, if purporting to be signed by the chairman of the meeting at which such resolutions were passed or proceedings had, or

(*y*) Sect. 39.

by the chairman of the next succeeding meeting, shall be received as evidence in all legal proceedings (z) ; and until the contrary is proved, every general meeting of the company or meeting of directors or managers in respect of the proceedings of which minutes have been so made shall be deemed to have been duly held and convened, and all resolutions passed thereat or proceedings had to have been duly passed and had, and all appointments of directors, managers or liquidators shall be deemed to be valid, and all acts done by such directors, managers or liquidators shall be valid, notwithstanding any defect that may afterwards be discovered in their appointments or qualifications.

**68.** In the case of companies under this Act, and engaged in working mines within and subject to the jurisdiction of the stannaries, the court of the vice-warden of the stannaries shall have and exercise the like jurisdiction and powers, as well on the common law as the equity side thereof, which it now possesses by custom, usages or statute in the case of unincorporated companies, but only so far as such jurisdiction or powers are consistent with the provisions of this Act and with the constitution of companies as prescribed or required by this Act ; and for the purpose of giving fuller effect to such jurisdiction in all actions, suits or legal proceedings instituted in the said court in causes or matters whereof the court has cognizance, all process issuing out of the same, and all orders, rules, demands, notices, warrants and summons required or authorized by the practice of the court to be served on any company, whether registered or not registered, or any member or contributory thereof, or any officer, agent, director, manager or servant thereof, may be served in any part of England without any special order of the vice-warden for that purpose, or by such special order may be served in any part of the United Kingdom of Great Britain and Ireland, or in the adjacent islands, parcel of the dominions of the crown, on such terms and conditions as the court shall think fit ; and all decrees, orders and judgments of the said court made or pronounced in such causes or matters may be enforced in the same manner in which degrees, orders and judgments of the court may now by law be enforced, whether within or beyond the local limits of the stannaries ; and the seal of the said court, and the signature of the registrar thereof, shall be judicially noticed by all other courts and judges in England, and shall require no other proof than the production thereof ; the registrar of the said court, or the assistant registrar, in making sales under any decrees or order of the court shall be entitled to the same privilege of selling by auction or competition without a licence, and without being liable to duty, as a judge of the court of chancery is entitled to in pursuance of the Acts in that behalf.

**69.** Where a limited company is plaintiff or pursuer in any action, suit, or other legal proceeding, any judge having jurisdiction in the matter may, if it appears by any credible testimony that there is reason to believe that if the defendant be successful in his defence the assets of the company will be insufficient to pay his costs, require sufficient security to be given for such costs, and may stay all proceedings until such security is given.

**70.** In any action or suit brought by the company against any member to recover any call or other moneys due from such member in his character of member, it shall not be necessary to set forth the special matter, but it shall be sufficient to allege that the defendant is a member of the company, and is indebted to the company in respect of a call made or other moneys due whereby an action or suit hath accrued to the company.

### Alteration of Forms.

**71.** The forms set forth in the second schedule hereto, or forms as near thereto as circumstances admit, shall be used in all matters to which such forms refer ; the board of trade may from time to time make such alterations in the tables and forms contained in the first schedule hereto, so that it does not increase the amount of fees payable to the registrar in the said schedule mentioned, and in the forms in the second schedule, or make such additions to the last-mentioned forms as it deems requisite : any such table or form, when altered, shall be published in the London Gazette, and upon such publication being made such table or form shall have the same force as if it

*III. Legal Proceedings.*

*Jurisdiction of vice-warden of stannaries.*

*Provision as to costs in actions brought by certain limited companies.*

*Declaration in action against members.*

*Alteration of Forms.*

*Board of Trade may alter forms in Schedule.*

(z) Sect. 154.

III. *Alteration of Forms.*

were included in the schedule to this Act, but no alteration made by the board of trade in the table marked A. contained in the first schedule shall affect any company registered prior to the date of such alteration, or repeal, as respects such company, any portion of such table.

*Arbitrations.*

### *Arbitrations.*

Power for companies to refer matters to arbitration.

72. Any company under this Act may from time to time, by writing under its common seal, agree to refer and may refer to arbitration, in accordance with "The Railway Companies Arbitration Act, 1859," any existing or future difference, question, or other matter whatsoever in dispute between itself and any other company or person, and the companies parties to the arbitration may delegate to the person or persons to whom the reference is made power to settle any terms or to determine any matter capable of being lawfully settled or determined by the companies themselves, or by the directors or other managing body of such companies.

Provisions of 22 & 23 Vict. c. 59, to apply.

73. All the provisions of "The Railway Companies Arbitrations Act, 1859," shall be deemed to apply to arbitrations between companies and persons in pursuance of this Act; and in the construction of such provisions "the companies" shall be deemed to include companies authorized by this Act to refer disputes to arbitration.

---

## PART IV.

### WINDING UP OF COMPANIES AND ASSOCIATIONS UNDER THIS ACT.

*Preliminary.*

### *Preliminary.*

Meaning of contributory.

74. The term "contributory" shall mean every person liable to contribute to the assets of a company under this Act, in the event of the same being wound up (*a*): it shall also, in all proceedings for determining the persons who are to be deemed contributories, and in all proceedings prior to the final determination of such persons, include any person alleged to be a contributory.

Nature of liability of contributory.

75. The liability of any person to contribute to the assets of a company under this Act in the event of the same being wound up, shall be deemed to create a debt (in England and Ireland of the nature of a specialty) accruing due from such person at the time when his liability commenced (*b*), but payable at the time or respective times when calls are made as hereinafter mentioned for enforcing such liability; and it shall be lawful in the case of the bankruptcy of any contributory to prove against his estate the estimated value of his liability to future calls, as well as calls already made.

Contributories in case of death.

76. If any contributory dies either before or after he has been placed on the list of contributories hereinafter mentioned, his personal representatives, heirs, and devisees shall be liable in a due course of administration to contribute to the assets of the company in discharge of the liability of such deceased contributory, and such personal representative, heirs, and devisees shall be deemed to be contributories accordingly.

Contributories in case of bankruptcy.

77. If any contributory becomes bankrupt, either before or after he has been placed on the list of contributories, his assignees shall be deemed to represent such bankrupt for all the purposes of the winding-up, and shall be deemed to be contributories accordingly, and may be called upon to admit to proof against the estate of such bankrupt, or otherwise to allow to be paid out of his assets in due course of law, any moneys due from such bankrupt in respect of his liability to contribute to the assets of the company being wound up; and for the purposes of this section any person who may have taken the benefit of any Act for the relief of insolvent debtors before the eleventh day of October one thousand eight hundred and sixty-one shall be deemed to have become bankrupt.

Contributories in case of marriage.

78. If any female contributory marries, either before or after she has been placed on the list of contributories, her husband shall during the continuance

---

(*a*) Sect. 38. As to shares standing in the name of a married woman, see

45 & 46 Vict. c. 75, ss. 6—9.
(*b*) Sect. 38.

of the marriage be liable to contribute to the assets of the company the same sum as she would have been liable to contribute if she had not married, and he shall be deemed to be a contributory accordingly (*c*).

*IV. Preliminary.*

### Winding up by Court.

*Winding up by Court.*

**79.** A company under this Act may be wound up by the court as hereinafter defined (*d*), under the following circumstances; (that is to say,)

(1.) Whenever the company has passed a special resolution (*e*) requiring the company to be wound up by the court:

(2.) Whenever the company does not commence its business within a year from its incorporation, or suspends its business for the space of a whole year:

(3.) Whenever the members are reduced in number to less than seven (*f*):

(4.) Whenever the company is unable to pay its debts:

(5.) Whenever the court is of opinion that it is just and equitable that the company should be wound up.

*Circumstances under which company may be wound up by court.*

**80.** A company under this Act shall be deemed to be unable to pay its debts,

*Company when deemed unable to pay its debts.*

(1.) Whenever a creditor, by assignment or otherwise, to whom the company is indebted, at law or in equity, in a sum exceeding fifty pounds then due, has served on the company, by leaving the same at their registered office, a demand under his hand requiring the company to pay the sum so due, and the company has for the space of three weeks succeeding the service of such demand neglected to pay such sum, or to secure or compound for the same to the reasonable satisfaction of the creditor:

(2.) Whenever, in England and Ireland, execution or other process issued on a judgment, decree or order obtained in any court in favour of any creditor, at law or in equity, in any proceeding instituted by such creditor against the company, is returned unsatisfied in whole or in part:

(3.) Whenever, in Scotland, the induciæ of a charge for payment on an extract decree, or an extract registered bond, or an extract registered protest have expired without payment being made:

(4.) Whenever it is proved to the satisfaction of the court that the company is unable to pay its debts.

**81.** The expression "the court," as used in this part of this Act, shall mean the following authorities; (that is to say,)

*Definition of "the court."*

In the case of a company engaged in working any mine within and subject to the jurisdiction of the stannaries,—the court of the vice-warden of the stannaries, unless the vice-warden certifies that in his opinion the company would be more advantageously wound up in the high court of chancery, in which case "the court" shall mean the high court of chancery:

In the case of a company registered in England, that is not engaged in working any such mine as aforesaid,—the high court of chancery:

In the case of a company registered in Ireland,—the court of chancery in Ireland:

In all cases of companies registered in Scotland,—the court of session in either division thereof:

Provided that where the court of chancery in England or Ireland makes an order for winding up a company under this Act, it may, if it thinks fit, direct all subsequent proceedings for winding up (*g*) the same to be had in the court of bankruptcy having jurisdiction in the place in which the registered office of the company is situate; and thereupon such last-mentioned court of bankruptcy shall, for the purposes of winding up the company, be deemed to be "the court" within the meaning of the Act, and shall have for the purposes of such winding up all the powers of the high court of chancery, or of the court of chancery in Ireland, as the case may require.

**82.** Any application to the court for the winding up of a company under this Act shall be by petition; it may be presented by the company, or by

*Application for winding up to be made by petition.*

(*c*) See 45 & 46 Vict. c. 75, ss. 6—9.
(*d*) Sect. 81.
(*e*) Sect. 51.
(*f*) Sects. 6 and 48.
(*g*) Sect. 12 of 30 & 31 Vict. c. 131, *infra.*

IV. *Winding up by Court.*

any one or more creditor or creditors (*h*), contributory or contributories (*i*), of the company, or by all or any of the above parties, together or separately; and every order which may be made on any such petition shall operate in favour of all the creditors and all the contributories of the company in the same manner as if it had been made upon the joint petition of a creditor and a contributory.

Power of court.

**83.** Any judge of the high court of chancery may do in chambers any act which the court is hereby authorized to do; and the vice-warden of the stannaries may direct that a petition for winding up a company be heard by him at such time and at such place within the jurisdiction of the stannaries, or within or near to the place where the registered office of the company is situated, as he may deem to be convenient to the parties concerned, or (with the consent of the parties concerned) at any place in England; and all orders made thereupon shall have the same force and effect as if they had been made by the vice-warden sitting at Truro or elsewhere within the jurisdiction of the court, and all parties and persons summoned to attend at the hearing of any such petition shall be compellable to give their attendance before the vice-warden by like process, and in like manner as at the hearing of any cause or matter at the usual sitting of the said court; and the registrar of the court may, subject to exception or appeal to the vice-warden as heretofore used, do and exercise such and the like acts and powers in the matter of winding up (*j*) as he is now used to do and exercise in a suit on the equity side of the said court.

Commencement of winding up by court.

**84.** A winding up of a company by the court shall be deemed to commence at the time of the presentation of the petition for the winding up (*k*).

Court may grant injunction.

**85.** The court may at any time after the presentation of a petition for winding up a company under this Act, and before making an order for winding up the company, upon the application of the company, or of any creditor or contributory of the company, restrain further proceedings in any action, suit, or proceeding against the company, upon such terms as the court thinks fit; the court may also at any time after the presentation of such petition, and before the first appointment of liquidators, appoint provisionally an official liquidator of the estate and effects of the company.

Course to be pursued by court on hearing petition.

**86.** Upon hearing the petition the court may dismiss the same with or without costs, may adjourn the hearing conditionally or unconditionally, and may make any interim order, or any other order that it deems just.

Actions and suits to be stayed after order for winding up.

**87.** When an order has been made for winding up a company under this Act, no suit, action, or other proceeding shall be proceeded with or commenced against the company, except with the leave of the court, and subject to such terms as the court may impose (*l*).

Copy of order to be forwarded to registrar.

**88.** When an order has been made for winding up a company under this Act, a copy of such order shall forthwith be forwarded by the company to the registrar of joint stock companies, who shall make a minute thereof in his books relating to the company.

Power of court to stay proceedings.

**89.** The court may at any time after an order has been made for winding up a company, upon the application by motion of any creditor or contributory of the company, and upon proof to the satisfaction of the court that all proceedings in relation to such winding up ought to be stayed, make an order staying the same, either altogether or for a limited time, on such terms and subject to such conditions as it deems fit.

Effect of order on share capital of company limited by guarantee.

**90.** When an order has been made for winding up a company limited by guarantee and having a capital divided into shares, any share capital that may not have been called up shall be deemed to be assets of the company, and to be a debt (in England and Ireland of the nature of a specialty (*m*)) due to the company from each member to the extent of any sums that may be unpaid on any shares held by him, and payable at such time as may be appointed by the court.

Court may have regard to wishes of creditors or contributories.

**91.** The court may, as to all matters relating to the winding up, have regard to the wishes of the creditors or contributories, as proved to it by any sufficient evidence, and may, if it thinks it expedient, direct meetings of the

(*h*) See 33 & 34 Vict. c. 61, ss. 2, 21. *infra.*
(*i*) But see s. 40 of 30 & 31 Vict. c. 131, *infra.*
(*j*) Sect. 12 of 30 & 31 Vict. c. 131,

(*k*) See sect. 130.
(*l*) See sect. 160.
(*m*) Sects. 75, 134.

creditors or contributories to be summoned, held and conducted in such manner as the court directs, for the purpose of ascertaining their wishes, and may appoint a person to act as chairman of any such meeting, and to report the result of such meeting to the court : in the case of creditors, regard is to be had to the value of the debts due to each creditor, and in the case of contributories to the number of votes conferred on each contributory by the regulations of the company.

### *Official Liquidators.*

92. For the purpose of conducting the proceedings in winding up a company and assisting the court therein, there may be appointed a person or persons to be called an official liquidator or official liquidators; and the court having jurisdiction may appoint such person or persons, either provisionally or otherwise, as it thinks fit, to the office of official liquidator or official liquidators (*n*) ; in all cases if more persons than one are appointed to the office of official liquidator, the court shall declare whether any act hereby required or authorized to be done by the official liquidator is to be done by all or any one or more of such persons. The court may also determine whether any and what security is to be given by any official liquidator on his appointment ; if no official liquidator is appointed, or during any vacancy in such appointment, all the property of the company shall be deemed to be in the custody of the court.

93. Any official liquidator may resign or be removed by the court on due cause shown : and any vacancy in the office of an official liquidator appointed by the court shall be filled by the court (*o*) : there shall be paid to the official liquidator such salary or remuneration, by way of per centage or otherwise, as the court may direct ; and if more liquidators than one are appointed, such remuneration shall be distributed amongst them in such proportions as the court directs.

Style and duties
of official liqui-
dator.

94. The official liquidator or liquidators shall be described by the style of the official liquidator or official liquidators of the particular company in respect of which he is or they are appointed, and not by his or their individual name or names; he or they shall take into his or their custody, or under his or their control, all the property, effects, and things in actions to which the company is or appears to be entitled, and shall perform such duties in reference to the winding up of the company as may be imposed by the court (*p*).

95. The official liquidator shall have power, with the sanction of the court, to do the following things (*q*) :

To bring or defend any action, suit, or prosecution, or other legal proceeding, civil or criminal, in the name and on behalf of the company :

To carry on the business of the company, so far as may be necessary, for the beneficial winding-up of the same (*r*) :

To sell the real and personal and heritable and moveable property, effects, and things in action of the company by public auction or private contract, with power to transfer the whole thereof to any person or company, or to sell the same in parcels :

To do all acts, and to execute, in the name and on behalf of the company, all deeds, receipts, and other documents, and for that purpose to use, when necessary, the company's seal :

To prove, rank, claim, and draw a dividend, in the matter of the bankruptcy or insolvency or sequestration of any contributory, for any balance against the estate of such contributory, and to take and receive dividends in respect of such balance, in the matter of bankruptcy or insolvency, or sequestration, as a separate debt due from such bankrupt or insolvent, and rateably with the other separate creditors :

To draw, accept, make, and indorse any bill of exchange or promissory note in the name and on behalf of the company, also to raise upon the security of the assets of the company from time to time any requisite sum or sums of money (*s*) ; and the drawing, accepting, making, or indorsing of every such bill of exchange or promissory note as aforesaid

(*n*) Sect. 85.
(*o*) Sect. 133 (3).
(*p*) Sect. 203.

(*q*) Sect. 96.
(*r*) Sects. 131, 153.
(*s*) Sect. 47.

25 & 26 VICT. CAP. 89.

on behalf of the company shall have the same effect with respect to the liability of such company as if such bill or note had been drawn, accepted, made, or endorsed by or on behalf of such company in the course of carrying on the business thereof :

To take out, if necessary, in his official name, letters of administration to any deceased contributory, and to do in his official name any other act that may be necessary for obtaining payment of any moneys due from a contributory or from his estate, and which act cannot be conveniently done in the name of the company ; and in all cases where he takes out letters of administration, or otherwise uses his official name for obtaining payment of any moneys due from a contributory, such moneys shall for the purpose of enabling him to take out such letters or recover such moneys, be deemed to be due to the official liquidator himself :

To do and execute all such other things as may be necessary for winding up the affairs of the company and distributing its assets (t).

**Discretion of official liquidator.**

**96.** The court may provide by any order that the official liquidator may exercise any of the above powers without the sanction or intervention of the court, and where an official liquidator is provisionally appointed (u), may limit and restrict his powers by the order appointing him (x).

**Appointment of solicitor to official liquidator.**

**97.** The official liquidator may, with the sanction of the court, appoint a solicitor or law agent to assist him in the performance of his duties.

*Ordinary Powers of Court.*

**Collection and application of assets.**

**98.** As soon as may be after making an order for winding up the company, the court shall settle a list of contributories (y), with power to rectify the register of members in all cases where such rectification is required in pursuance of this Act (z), and shall cause the assets of the company to be collected and applied in discharge of its liabilities (a).

**Provision as to representative contributories.**

**99.** In settling the list of contributories, the court shall distinguish between persons who are contributories in their own right and persons who are contributories as being representatives of or being liable to the debts of others (b) ; it shall not be necessary, where the personal representative of any deceased contributory is placed on the list, to add the heirs or devisees of such contributory, nevertheless such heirs or devisees may be added as and when the court thinks fit.

**Power of court to require delivery of property.**

**100.** The court may, at any time after making an order for winding up a company, require any contributory for the time being settled on the list of contributories, trustee, receiver, banker, or agent, or officer of the company, to pay, deliver, convey, surrender, or transfer forthwith, or within such time as the court directs, to or into the hands of the official liquidator (c), any sum or balance, books, papers, estate or effects which happen to be in his hands for the time being, and to which the company is primâ facie entitled.

**Power of court to order payment of debts by contributory.**

**101.** The court may, at any time after making an order for winding up the company, make an order on any contributory for the time being settled on the list of contributories, directing payment to be made, in manner in the said order mentioned, of any moneys due from him or from the estate of the person whom he represents to the company, exclusive of any moneys which he or the estate of the person whom he represents may be liable to contribute by virtue of any call made or to be made by the court in pursuance of this part of this Act (d) ; and it may, in making such order when the company is not limited, allow to such contributory by way of set-off any moneys due to him or the estate which he represents from the company on any independent dealing or contract with the company, but not any moneys due to him as a member of the company in respect of any dividend or profit (e).

Provided, that when all the creditors of any company, whether limited or unlimited, are paid in full, any moneys due on any account whatever to any contributory from the company may be allowed to him by way of set-off against any subsequent call or calls (f).

(t) Sects. 159, 160, 161.
(u) Sect. 85.
(x) Sect. 151.
(y) Sect. 38.
(z) Sect. 35.
(a) Sect. 133.
(b) Sects. 76, 106.
(c) Sect. 103.
(d) Sect. 102.
(e) Sect. 6 of 30 & 31 Vict. c. 131, *infra.*
(f) Sect. 38 (7).

102. The court may, at any time after making an order for winding up a company, and either before or after it has ascertained the sufficiency of the assets of the company, make calls on and order payment thereof by all or any of the contributories for the time being settled on the list of contributories, to the extent of their liability, for payment of all or any sums it deems necessary to satisfy the debts and liabilities of the company, and the costs, charges, and expenses of winding it up, and for the adjustment of the rights of the contributories amongst themselves, and it may, in making a call, take into consideration the probability that some of the contributories upon whom the same is made may partly or wholly fail to pay their respective portions of the same (*g*). **IV.** *Ordinary Powers of Court.*<br>Power of court to make calls.

103. The court may order any contributory, purchaser or other person from whom money is due to the company to pay the same into the Bank of England or any branch thereof to the account of the official liquidator instead of to the official liquidator, and such order may be enforced, in the same manner as if it had directed payment to the official liquidator (*h*). Power of court to order payment into bank.

104. All moneys, bills, notes and other securities paid and delivered into the Bank of England or any branch thereof, in the event of a company being wound up by the court, shall be subject to such order and regulation for the keeping of the account of such moneys and other effects, and for the payment and delivery in, or investment and payment and delivery out of the same as the court may direct. Regulation of account with court.

105. If any person made a contributory as personal representative of a deceased contributory makes default in paying any sum ordered to be paid by him, proceedings may be taken for administering the personal and real estates of such deceased contributory, or either of such estates, and of compelling payment thereout of the moneys due (*i*). Provision in case of representative contributory not paying moneys ordered.

106. Any order made by the court in pursuance of this Act upon any contributory shall, subject to the provisions herein contained for appealing against such order (*k*), be conclusive evidence that the moneys, if any, thereby appearing to be due or ordered to be paid are due, and all other pertinent matters stated in such order are to be taken to be truly stated as against all persons and in all proceedings whatsoever, with the exception of proceedings taken against the real estate of such deceased contributory, in which case such order shall only be primâ facie evidence for the purpose of charging his real estate, unless his heirs or devisees were on the list of contributories at the time of the order being made (*l*). Order conclusive evidence.

107. The court may fix a certain day or certain days on or within which creditors of the company are to prove their debts or claims, or to be excluded from the benefit of any distribution made before such debts are proved. Court may exclude creditors not proving within certain time.

108. If in the course of proving the debts and claims of creditors in the court of the vice-warden of the stannaries any debt or claim is disputed by the official liquidator or by any creditor or contributory, or appears to the court to be open to question, the court shall have power, subject to appeal as hereinafter provided (*m*), to adjudicate upon it, and for that purpose the said court shall have and exercise all needful powers of inquiry touching the same by affidavit or by oral examination of witnesses or of parties, whether voluntarily offering themselves for examination or summoned to attend by compulsory process of the court, or to produce documents before the court: and the court shall also have power, incidentally, to decide on the validity and extent of any lien or charge claimed by any creditor on any property of the company in respect of such debt, and to make declarations of right binding on all persons interested; and for the more satisfactory determination of any question of fact, or mixed question of law and fact arising on such inquiry, the vice-warden shall have power, if he thinks fit, to direct and settle any action or issue to be tried either on the common law side of his court, or by a common or special jury, before the justices of assize in and for the counties of Cornwall or Devon, or at any sitting of one of the superior courts in London or Middlesex, which action or issue shall accordingly be tried in due course of law, and without other or further consent of parties; and the finding of the jury in such action or issue shall be con- Proceedings in the court of the vice-warden of the stannaries on proof of debts.

(*g*) Sect. 133 (9).  
(*h*) Sect. 100.  
(*i*) Sects. 76, 95, 106.  

(*k*) Sect. 124.  
(*l*) Sect. 99.  
(*m*) Sect. 124.

IV. *Ordinary Powers of Court.*

elusive of the facts found, unless the judge who tried it makes known to the vice-warden that he was not satisfied with the finding, or unless it appears to the vice-warden that, in consequence of miscarriage, accident, or the subsequent discovery of fresh material evidence, such finding ought not to be conclusive.

Court to adjust rights of contributories.

109. The court shall adjust the rights of the contributories amongst themselves, and distribute any surplus that may remain amongst the parties entitled thereto.

Court to order costs.

110. The court may, in the event of the assets being insufficient to satisfy the liabilities, make an order as to the payment out of the estate of the company of the costs, charges and expenses incurred in winding up any company in such order of priority as the court thinks just (*n*).

Dissolution of company.

111. When the affairs of the company have been completely wound up, the court shall make an order that the company be dissolved from the date of such order, and the company shall be dissolved accordingly (*o*).

Registrar to make minute of dissolution of company.

112. Any order so made shall be reported by the official liquidator to the registrar, who shall make a minute accordingly in his books of the dissolution of such company.

Penalty on not reporting dissolution of company.

113. If the official liquidator makes default in reporting to the registrar, in the case of a company being wound up by the court, the order that the company be dissolved, he shall be liable to a penalty not exceeding five pounds for every day during which he is so in default.

114. Repealed, 30 & 31 Vict. c. 47, s. 2.

*Extraordinary Powers of Court.*

### Extraordinary Powers of Court.

Power of court to summon persons before it suspected of having property of company.

115. The court may, after it has made an order for winding up the company, summon before it any officer of the company or person known or suspected to have in his possession any of the estate or effects of the company, or supposed to be indebted to the company, or any person whom the court may deem capable of giving information concerning the trade, dealings, estate or effects of the company (*p*); and the court may require any such officer or person to produce any books, papers, deeds, writings or other documents in his custody or power relating to the company ; and if any person so summoned, after being tendered a reasonable sum for his expenses, refuses to come before the court at the time appointed, having no lawful impediments (made known to the court at the time of its sitting, and allowed by it), the court may cause such person to be apprehended, and brought before the court for examination ; nevertheless, in cases where any person claims any lien on papers, deeds or writings produced by him, such production shall be without prejudice to such lien, and the court shall have jurisdiction in the winding up to determine all questions relating to such lien.

Special provisions as to court of vice-warden of the stannaries.

116. If, after an order for winding up in the court of the vice-warden of the stannaries, it appears that any person claims property in, or any lien, legal or equitable, upon any of the machinery, materials, ores or effects on the mine, or on premises occupied by the company in connexion with the mine, or to which the company was at the time of the order primâ facie entitled, it shall be lawful for the vice-warden or the registrar to adjudicate upon such claim on interpleader in the manner provided by section eleven of the Act passed in the eighteenth year of the reign of her present Majesty, chapter thirty-two ; and any action or issue directed upon such interpleader may, if the vice-warden think fit, be tried in his court or at the assizes or the sittings in London or Middlesex, before a judge of one of the superior courts, in the manner and on the terms and conditions hereinbefore provided in the case of disputed debts and claims of creditors (*q*).

Examination of parties by court.

117. The court may examine upon oath, either by word of mouth or upon written interrogatories, any person appearing or brought before them in manner aforesaid (*r*) concerning the affairs, dealings, estate or effects of the company, and may reduce into writing the answers of every such person, and require him to subscribe the same.

Power to arrest contributory about to

118. The court may at any time before or after it has made an order for winding up a company, upon proof being given that there is probable cause

(*n*) Sect. 144.
(*o*) Sect. 143.
(*p*) Sects. 117, 127.

(*q*) Sect. 108.
(*r*) Sect. 115.

for believing that any contributory to such company is about to quit the United Kingdom, or otherwise abscond, or to remove or conceal any of his goods or chattels, for the purpose of evading payment of calls, or for avoiding examination in respect of the affairs of the company, cause such contributory to be arrested, and his books, papers, moneys, securities for moneys, goods and chattels to be seized, and him and them to be safely kept until such time as the court may order.

IV. *Extraordinary Powers of Court.*

abscond, or to remove or conceal any of his property.

**119.** Any powers by this Act conferred on the court shall be deemed to be in addition to and not in restriction of any other powers subsisting either at law or in equity, of instituting proceedings against any contributory, or the estate of any contributory, or against any debtor of the company for the recovery of any call or other sums due from such contributory or debtor, or his estate, and such proceedings may be instituted accordingly.

Powers of court cumulative.

*Enforcement of and Appeal from Orders.*

### Enforcement of and Appeal from Orders.

**120.** All orders made by the court of chancery in England or Ireland under this Act may be enforced in the same manner in which orders of such court of chancery made in any suit pending therein may be enforced, and for the purposes of this part of this Act the court of the vice-warden of the stannaries shall, in addition to its ordinary powers, have the same power of enforcing any orders made by it as the court of chancery in England has in relation to matters within the jurisdiction of such court, and for the last-mentioned purposes the jurisdiction of the vice-warden of the stannaries shall be deemed to be co-extensive in local limits with the jurisdiction of the court of chancery in England.

Power to enforce orders.

**121.** Where an order, interlocutor, or decree has been made in Scotland for winding up a company by the court, it shall be competent to the court in Scotland during session, and to the lord ordinary on the bills during vacation, on production by the liquidators of a list certified by them of the names of the contributories liable in payment of any calls which they may wish to enforce, and of the amount due by each contributory respectively, and of the date when the same became due, to pronounce forthwith a decree against such contributories for payment of the sums so certified to be due by each of them respectively, with interest from the said date till payment, at the rate of five pounds per centum per annum, in the same way and to the same effect as if they had severally consented to registration for execution, on a charge of six days, of a legal obligation to pay such calls and interest; and such decree may be extracted immediately, and no suspension thereof shall be competent, except on caution or consignation, unless with special leave of the court or lord ordinary.

Power to order contributories in Scotland to pay calls.

**122.** Any order made by the court in England for or in the course of the winding-up of a company under this Act shall be enforced in Scotland and Ireland in the courts that would respectively have had jurisdiction in respect of such company if the registered office of the company had been situate in Scotland or Ireland, and in the same manner in all respects as if such order had been made by the courts that are hereby required to enforce the same; and in like manner orders, interlocutors, and decrees made by the court in Scotland for or in the course of the winding-up of a company shall be enforced in England and Ireland, and orders made by the court in Ireland for or in the course of winding up a company shall be enforced in England and Scotland by the courts which would respectively have had jurisdiction in the matter of such company if the registered office of the company were situate in the division of the United Kingdom where the order is required to be enforced, and in the same manner in all respects as if such order had been made by the court required to enforce the same in the case of a company within its own jurisdiction.

Order made in England to be enforced in Ireland and Scotland.

**123.** Where any order, interlocutor, or decree made by one court is required to be enforced by another court, as hereinbefore provided (s), an office copy of the order, interlocutor, or decree so made shall be produced to the proper officer of the court required to enforce the same, and the production of such office copy shall be sufficient evidence of such order, interlocutor, or decree having been made, and thereupon such last-mentioned court shall take such steps in the matter as may be requisite for enforcing such order, interlocutor,

Mode of dealing with orders to be enforced by other courts.

(s) Sect. 122.

IV. *Enforcement of and Appeal from Orders.*

Appeals from orders.

or decree, in the same manner as if it were the order, interlocutor, or decree of the court enforcing the same.

124. Rehearings of and appeals from any order or decision made or given in the matter of the winding-up of a company by any court having jurisdiction under this Act, may be had in the same manner and subject to the same conditions in and subject to which appeals may be had from any order or decision of the same court in cases within its ordinary jurisdiction ; subject to this restriction, that no such rehearing or appeal shall be heard unless notice of the same is given within three weeks after any order complained of has been made, in manner in which notices of appeal are ordinarily given, according to the practice of the court appealed from, unless such time is extended by the court of appeal : Provided that it shall be lawful for the lord warden of the stannaries, by a special or general order, to remit at once any appeal allowed and regularly lodged with him against any order or decision of the vice-warden made in the matter of a winding-up to the court of appeal in chancery, which court shall thereupon hear and determine such appeal, and have power to require all such certificates of the vice-warden, records of proceedings below, documents and papers as the lord warden would or might have required upon the hearing of such appeal, and to exercise all other the jurisdiction and powers of the lord warden specified in the Act of Parliament passed in the eighteenth year of the reign of her present Majesty, chapter thirty-two, and any order so made by the court of appeal in chancery shall be final, without any further appeal.

Judicial notice to be taken of signature of officers.

125. In all proceedings under this part of this Act, all courts, judges and persons judicially acting, and all other officers, judicial or ministerial, of any court, or employed in enforcing the process of any court, shall take judicial notice of the signature of any officer of the courts of chancery or bankruptcy in England or in Ireland, or of the court of session in Scotland, or of the registrar of the court of the vice-warden of the stannaries, and also of the official seal or stamp of the several offices of the courts of chancery or bankruptcy in England or Ireland, or of the court of session in Scotland, or of the court of the vice-warden of the stannaries, when such seal or stamp is appended to or impressed on any document made, issued, or signed under the provisions of this part of the Act, or any official copy thereof.

Special commissioners for receiving evidence.

126. [The commissioners of the court of bankruptcy (*t*)] and the judges of the county courts in England who sit at places more than twenty miles from the General Post Office, and the commissioners of bankrupt and the assistant barristers and recorders in Ireland, and the sheriffs of counties in Scotland, shall be commissioners for the purpose of taking evidence under this Act in cases where any company is wound up in any part of the United Kingdom, and it shall be lawful for the court to refer the whole or any part of the examination of any witnesses under this Act to any person hereby appointed commissioner although such commissioner is out of the jurisdiction of the court that made the order or decree for winding up the company ; and every such commissioner shall, in addition to any power of summoning and examining witnesses, and requiring the production or delivery of documents, and certifying or punishing defaults by witnesses, which he might lawfully exercise as a [commissioner of the court of bankruptcy (*t*)], judge of a county court, commissioner of bankrupt, assistant barrister or recorder, or as a sheriff of a county, have in the matter so referred to him all the same powers of summoning and examining witnesses, and requiring the production or delivery of documents, and punishing defaults by witnesses, and allowing costs and charges and expenses to witnesses, as the court which made the order for winding up the company has ; and the examination so taken shall be returned or reported to such last-mentioned court in such manner as it directs.

Court may order the examination of persons in Scotland.

127. The court may direct the examination in Scotland of any person for the time being in Scotland, whether a contributory of the company or not, in regard to the estate, dealings or affairs of any company in the course of being wound up, or in regard to the estate, dealings or affairs of any person being a contributory of the company, so far as the company may be interested therein by reason of his being such contributory, and the order or commission to take such examination shall be directed to the sheriff of the county in which the person to be examined is residing or happens to be for the time, and the

(*t*) Words within brackets repealed by Statute Law Revision Act, 1875.

sheriff shall summon such person to appear before him at a time and place to be specified in the summons for examination upon oath as a witness or as a haver, and to produce any books, papers, deeds or documents called for which may be in his possession or power, and the sheriff may take such examination either orally or upon written interrogatories, and shall report the same in writing in the usual form to the court, and shall transmit with such report the books, papers, deeds or documents produced, if the originals thereof are required and specified by the order, or otherwise such copies thereof or extracts therefrom, authenticated by the sheriff, as may be necessary ; and in case any person so summoned fails to appear at the time and place specified, or appearing refuses to be examined or to make the production required, the sheriff shall proceed against such person as a witness or haver duly cited, and failing to appear or refusing to give evidence or make production may be proceeded against by the law of Scotland ; and the sheriff shall be entitled to such and the like fees, and the witness shall be entitled to such and the like allowances, as sheriffs when acting as commissioners under appointment from the court of session and as witnesses and havers are entitled to in the like cases according to the law and practice of Scotland : If any objection is stated to the sheriff by the witness, either on the ground of his incompetency as a witness, or as to the production required to be made, or on any other ground whatever, the sheriff may, if he thinks fit, report such objection to the court, and suspend the examination of such witness until such objection has been disposed of by the court.

IV. *Enforcement of and Appeal from Orders.*

128. Any affidavit, affirmation, or declaration required to be sworn or made under the provisions or for the purposes of this part of this Act, may be lawfully sworn or made in Great Britain or Ireland, or in any colony, island, plantation or place under the dominion of her Majesty in foreign parts, before any court, judge or person lawfully authorized to take and receive affidavits affirmations or declarations, or before any of her Majesty's consuls or vice-consuls, in any foreign parts out of her Majesty's dominions, and all courts, judges, justices, commissioners and persons acting judicially shall take judicial notice of the seal or stamp or signature (as the case may be) of any such court, judge, person, consul or vice-consul attached, appended, or subscribed to any such affidavit, affirmation or declaration, or to any other document to be used for the purposes of this part of this Act.

Affidavits, &c., may be sworn in Ireland, Scotland, or the colonies, before any competent court or person.

### Voluntary Winding up of Company.

*Voluntary Winding up of Company.*

129. A company under this Act (*u*) may be wound up voluntarily,

(1.) Whenever the period, if any, fixed for the duration of the company by the articles of association expires, or whenever the event, if any, occurs, upon the occurrence of which it is provided by the articles of association that the company is to be dissolved, and the company in general meeting has passed a resolution requiring the company to be wound up voluntarily :

(2.) Whenever the company has passed a special resolution (*x*) requiring the company to be wound up voluntarily :

(3.) Whenever the company has passed an extraordinary resolution to the effect that it has been proved to their satisfaction that the company cannot by reason of its liabilities continue its business, and that it is advisable to wind up the same :

Circumstances under which company may be wound up voluntarily.

For the purposes of this Act any resolution shall be deemed to be extraordinary which is passed in such manner as would, if it had been confirmed by a subsequent meeting, have constituted a special resolution as hereinbefore defined.

130. A voluntary winding up (*y*) shall be deemed to commence at the time of the passing of the resolution authorizing such winding up.

Commencement of voluntary winding up.

131. Whenever a company is wound up voluntarily the company shall, from the date of the commencement of such winding up, cease to carry on its business, except in so far as may be required for the beneficial winding up thereof (*z*), and all transfers of shares, except transfers made to or with the sanction of the liquidators, or alteration in the status of the members of the company, taking place after the commencement of such winding up shall be

Effect of voluntary winding up on status of company.

(*u*) See sect. 199 (2).      (*y*) See sect. 84.
(*x*) Sect. 51.      (*z*) Sect. 95.

IV. *Voluntary Winding up of Company.*

void (*a*), but its corporate state and all its corporate powers shall, notwithstanding it is otherwise provided by its regulations, continue until the affairs of the company are wound up.

Notice of resolution to wind up voluntarily.

**132.** Notice of any special resolution or extraordinary resolution passed for winding up a company voluntarily shall be given by advertisment as respects companies registered in England in the London Gazette, as respects companies registered in Scotland in the Edinburgh Gazette, and as respects companies registered in Ireland in the Dublin Gazette.

Consequences of voluntarily winding up.

**133.** The following consequences shall ensue upon the voluntary winding up of a company :—

(1.) The property of the company shall be applied in satisfaction of its liabilities pari passu (*h*), and subject thereto shall, unless it be otherwise provided by the regulations of the company, be distributed amongst the members according to their rights and interests in the company :

(2.) Liquidators shall be appointed for the purpose of winding up the affairs of the company and distributing the property (*c*):

(3.) The company in general meeting shall appoint such persons or person as it thinks fit to be liquidators or a liquidator, and may fix the remuneration to be paid to them or him :

(4.) If one person only is appointed, all the provisions herein contained in reference to several liquidators shall apply to him :

(5.) Upon the appointment of liquidators all the power of the directors shall cease, except in so far as the company in general meeting or the liquidators may sanction the continuance of such powers :

(6.) When several liquidators are appointed, every power hereby given may be exercised by such one or more of them as may be determined at the time of their appointment, or in default of such determination by any number not less than two :

(7.) The liquidators may, without the sanction of the court, exercise all powers by this Act given to the official liquidator (*d*) :

(8.) The liquidators may exercise the powers hereinbefore given to the court of settling the list of contributories of the company (*e*), and any list so settled shall be primâ facie evidence of the liability of the persons named therein to be contributories :

(9.) The liquidators may at any time after the passing of the resolution for winding up the company, and before they have ascertained the sufficiency of the assets of the company, call on all or any of the contributories for the time being settled on the list of contributories to the extent of their liability to pay all or any sums they deem necessary to satisfy the debts and liabilities of the company, and the costs, charges and expenses of winding it up, and for the adjustment of the rights of the contributories amongst themselves, and the liquidators may in making a call take into consideration the probability that some of the contributories upon whom the same is made may partly or wholly fail to pay their respective portions of the same (*f*) :

(10.) The liquidators shall pay the debts of the company, and adjust the rights of the contributories amongst themselves (*g*) :

Effect of winding up on share capital of company limited by guarantee.

**134.** Where a company limited by guarantee, and having a capital divided into shares, is being wound up voluntarily, any share capital that may not have been called up shall be deemed to be assets of the company, and to be a specialty debt (*h*) due from each member to the company to the extent of any sums that may be unpaid on any shares held by him, and payable at such time as may be appointed by the liquidators.

Power of company to delegate authority to appoint liquidators.

**135.** A company about to be wound up voluntarily, or in the course of being wound up voluntarily, may, by an extraordinary resolution (*i*), delegate to its creditors, or to any committee of its creditors, the power of appointing liquidators, or any of them, and supplying any vacancies in the appointment

(*a*) Sect. 153.
(*b*) Sect. 159.
(*c*) Sect. 92.
(*d*) Sects. 95, 96, 97.
(*e*) Sect. 98.

(*f*) Sect. 102.
(*g*) Sects. 38, 101, 109, 158.
(*h*) Sects. 75, 90.
(*i*) Sect. 129.

of liquidators, or may by a like resolution enter into any arrangement with respect to the powers to be exercised by the liquidators, and the manner in which they are to be exercised ; and any act done by the creditors in pursuance of such delegated power shall have the same effect as if it had been done by the company (*j*).

**IV.** *Voluntary Winding-up of Company.*

**136.** Any arrangement entered into between a company about to be wound up voluntarily, or in the course of being wound up voluntarily, and its creditors (*k*) shall be binding on the company if sanctioned by an extraordinary resolution, and on the creditors if acceded to by three-fourths in number and value of the creditors, subject to such right of appeal as is hereinafter mentioned.

Arrangement, when binding on creditors.

**137.** Any creditor or contributory of a company that has in manner aforesaid entered into any arrangement with its creditors may, within three weeks from the date of the completion of such arrangement, appeal to the court against such arrangement, and the court may thereupon, as it thinks just, amend, vary or confirm the same.

Powers of creditor or contributory to appeal.

**138.** Where a company is being wound up voluntarily the liquidators or any contributory of the company may apply to the court in England, Ireland or Scotland, or to the lord ordinary on the bills in Scotland in time of vacation, to determine any question arising in the matter of such winding up, or to exercise, as respects the enforcing of calls, or in respect of any other matter, all or any of the powers which the court might exercise if the company were being wound up by the court ; and the court or lord ordinary, in the case aforesaid, if satisfied that the determination of such question, or the required exercise of power, will be just and beneficial, may accede wholly or partially to such application on such terms and subject to such conditions as the court thinks fit, or it may make such other order, interlocutor or decree on such application as the court thinks just.

Power of liquidators or contributories in voluntary winding up to apply to court.

**139.** Where a company is being wound up voluntarily the liquidators may from time to time, during the continuance of such winding up, summon general meetings of the company for the purpose of obtaining the sanction of the company by special resolution (*l*) or extraordinary resolution (*m*), or for any other purposes they think fit ; and in the event of the winding up continuing for more than one year the liquidators shall summon a general meeting of the company at the end of the first year, and of each succeeding year from the commencement of the winding up, or as soon thereafter as may be convenient, and shall lay before such meeting an account showing their acts and dealings, and the manner in which the winding up has been conducted during the preceding year.

Power of liquidators to call general meeting.

**140.** If any vacancy occurs in the office of liquidators appointed by the company, by death, resignation or otherwise, the company in general meeting may, subject to any arrangement they may have entered into with their creditors (*n*), fill up such vacancy, and a general meeting for the purpose of filling up such vacancy may be convened by the continuing liquidators, if any, or by any contributory of the company, and shall be deemed to have been duly held if held in manner prescribed by the regulations of the company, or in such other manner as may, on application by the continuing liquidators, if any, or by any contributory of the company, be determined by the court.

Power to fill up vacancy in liquidators.

**141.** If from any cause whatever there is no liquidator acting in the case of a voluntary winding up, the court may, on the application of a contributory, appoint a liquidator or liquidators ; the court may also, on due cause shown (*o*), remove any liquidator, and appoint another liquidator to act in the matter of a voluntary winding up (*p*).

Power of court to appoint liquidators.

**142.** As soon as the affairs of the company are fully wound up, the liquidators shall make up an account showing the manner in which such winding up has been conducted, and the property of the company disposed of ; and thereupon they shall call a general meeting of the company for the purpose of having the account laid before them, and hearing any explanation that may be given by the liquidators : the meeting shall be called by advertisement, specifying the time, place, and object of such meeting ; and such

Liquidators on conclusion of winding up to make up an account.

(*j*) Sect. 133.
(*k*) Sect. 159, and sect. 2 of Joint Stock Companies Arrangement Act, 1870 (33 & 34 Vict. c. 104).
(*l*) Sect. 51.

(*m*) Sect. 129.
(*n*) Sect. 135.
(*o*) Sect. 93.
(*p*) Sect. 152.

IV. *Voluntary Winding-up of Company.*

advertisement shall be published one month at least previously to the meeting, as respects companies registered in England in the London Gazette, and as respects companies registered in Scotland in the Edinburgh Gazette, and as respects companies registered in Ireland in the Dublin Gazette.

Liquidators to report meeting to registrar.

**143.** The liquidators shall make a return to the registrar of such meeting having been held, and of the date at which the same was held, and on the expiration of three months from the date of the registration of such return the company shall be deemed to be dissolved; if the liquidators make default in making such return to the registrar, they shall incur a penalty not exceeding five pounds for every day during which such default continues.

Costs of voluntary liquidation.

**144.** All costs, charges and expenses properly incurred in the voluntary winding up of a company, including the remuneration of the liquidators, shall be payable out of the assets of the company in priority to all other claims.

Saving of rights of creditors.

**145.** The voluntary winding up of a company shall not be a bar to the right of any creditor of such company to have the same wound up by the court, if the court is of opinion that the rights of such creditor will be prejudiced by a voluntary winding up.

Power of court to adopt proceedings of voluntary winding up.

**146.** Where a company is in course of being wound up voluntarily, and proceedings are taken for the purpose of having the same wound up by the court (*q*), the court may, if it thinks fit, notwithstanding that it makes an order directing the company to be wound up by the court, provide in such order or in any other order for the adoption of all or any of the proceedings taken in the course of the voluntary winding up.

*Winding up subject to the Supervision of the Court.*

*Winding up subject to the Supervision of the Court.*

Power of court on application to direct winding up subject to supervision.

**147.** When a resolution has been passed by a company to wind up voluntarily (*r*), the court may make an order directing that the voluntary winding up should continue, but subject to such supervision of the court, and with such liberty for creditors, contributories, or others, to apply to the court, and generally upon such terms and subject to such conditions as the court thinks just.

Petition for winding up, subject to supervision.

**148.** A petition, praying wholly or in part that a voluntary winding up should continue, but subject to the supervision of the court, and which winding up is hereinafter referred to as a winding up subject to the supervision of the court, shall, for the purpose of giving jurisdiction to the court over suits and actions, be deemed to be a petition for winding up the company by the Court (*s*).

Court may have regard to wishes of creditors.

**149.** The court may, in determining whether a company is to be wound up altogether by the court or subject to the supervision of the court, in the appointment of liquidator or liquidators, and in all other matters relating to the winding up subject to supervision, have regard to the wishes of the creditors or contributories as proved to it by any sufficient evidence, and may direct meetings of the creditors or contributories to be summoned, held and regulated in such manner as the court directs for the purpose of ascertaining their wishes, and may appoint a person to act as chairman of any such meeting, and to report the result of such meeting to the court: in the case of creditors, regard shall be had to the value of the debts due to each creditor, and in the case of contributories to the number of votes conferred on each contributory by the regulations of the company (*t*).

Power to court to appoint additional liquidators in winding up subject to supervision.

**150.** Where any order is made by the court for a winding up subject to the supervision of the court (*u*), the court may, in such order or in any subsequent order, appoint any additional liquidator or liquidators; and any liquidators so appointed by the court shall have the same powers, be subject to the same obligations, and in all respects stand in the same position as if they had been appointed by the company (*x*): the Court may from time to time remove any liquidators so appointed by the court, and fill up any vacancy occasioned by such removal, or by death or resignation (*y*).

Effect of order of court for winding up subject to supervision.

**151.** Where an order is made for a winding up subject to the supervision of the court (*z*), the liquidators appointed to conduct such winding up may,

(*q*) Sects. 79, 145.
(*r*) Sect. 129.
(*s*) Sects. 85, 87.
(*t*) Sects. 91, 147.

(*u*) Sect. 147.
(*x*) Sect. 133.
(*y*) Sects. 147, 152.
(*z*) Sect. 147.

subject to any restrictions imposed by the court (*a*), exercise all their powers, without the sanction or intervention of the court, in the same manner as if the company were being wound up altogether voluntarily (*b*) ; but save as aforesaid, any order made by the court for a winding up, subject to the supervision of the court shall for all purposes, including the staying of actions, suits and other proceedings, be deemed to be an order of the court for winding up the company by the court, and shall confer full authority on the court to make calls (*c*), or to enforce calls made by the liquidators, and to exercise all other powers which it might have exercised if an order had been made for winding up the company altogether by the court, and in the construction of the provisions whereby the court is empowered to direct any act or thing to be done to or in favour of the official liquidators, the expression official liquidators shall be deemed to mean the liquidators conducting the winding up, subject to the supervision of the court.

*IV. Winding up subject to Supervision of the Court.*

**152.** Where an order has been made for the winding up of a company subject to the supervision of the court, and such order is afterwards superseded by an order directing the company to be wound up compulsorily (*d*), the court may in such last-mentioned order, or in any subsequent order, appoint the voluntary liquidators or any of them, either provisionally (*e*) or permanently, and either with or without the addition of any other persons, to be official liquidators.

*Appointment in certain cases of voluntary liquidators to office of official liquidators.*

*Supplemental Provisions.*

**153.** Where any company is being wound up by the court or subject to the supervision of the court, all dispositions of the property, effects and things in action of the company, and every transfer of shares, or alteration in the status of the members of the company made between the commencement of the winding up (*f*) and the order for winding up, shall, unless the court otherwise orders, be void (*g*).

*Supplemental Provisions.*

*Dispositions after the commencement of the winding up avoided.*

**154.** Where any company is being wound up, all books, accounts, and documents of the company and of the liquidators shall, as between the contributories of the company, be primâ facie evidence of the truth of all matters purporting to be therein recorded.

*The books of the company to be evidence.*

**155.** Where any company has been wound up under this Act, and is about to be dissolved (*h*), the books, accounts, and documents of the company and of the liquidators may be disposed of in the following way ; that is to say, where the company has been wound up by or subject to the supervision of the court, in such way as the court directs, and where the company has been wound up voluntarily, in such way as the company by an extraordinary resolution (*i*) directs ; but after the lapse of five years from the date of such dissolution, no responsibility shall rest on the company, or the liquidators, or any one to whom the custody of such books, accounts, and documents has been committed, by reason that the same, or any of them, cannot be made forthcoming to any party or parties claiming to be interested therein.

*As to disposal of books, accounts and documents of the company.*

**156.** Where an order has been made for winding up a company by the court, or subject to the supervision of the court, the court may make such order for the inspection by the creditors and contributories of the company of its books and papers as the court thinks just, and any books and papers in the possession of the company may be inspected by creditors or contributories, in conformity with the order of the court, but not further or otherwise (*k*).

*Inspection of books.*

**157.** Any person to whom anything in action belonging to the company is assigned, in pursuance of this Act, may bring or defend any action or suit relating to such thing in action in his own name (*l*).

*Power of assignee to sue.*

**158.** In the event of any company being wound up under this Act, all debts payable on a contingency, and all claims against the company, present or future, certain or contingent, ascertained or sounding only in damages,

*Debts of all descriptions to be proved.*

(*a*) Sect. 96.
(*b*) Sect. 133.
(*c*) Sect. 102.
(*d*) Sect. 79.
(*e*) Sects. 85, 92.
(*f*) Sects. 84, 130.

(*g*) Sects. 131, 163, 164.
(*h*) Sect. 143.
(*i*) Sect. 129.
(*k*) Sched. I. Table A. (79).
(*l*) Judicature Act, 1873, s. 25 (6).

IV. *Supplemental Provisions.*

shall be admissible to proof against the company, a just estimate being made, so far as is possible, of the value of all such debts or claims as may be subject to any contingency or sound only in damages, or for some other reason do not bear a certain value.

General scheme of liquidation may be sanctioned.

**159.** The liquidators may, with the sanction of the court, where the company is being wound up by the court, or subject to the supervision of the court, and with the sanction of an extraordinary resolution of the company where the company is being wound up altogether voluntarily, pay any classes of creditors in full, or make such compromise or other arrangement as the liquidators may deem expedient with creditors, or persons claiming to be creditors, or persons having or alleging themselves to have any claim, present or future, certain or contingent, ascertained or sounding only in damages against the company, or whereby the company may be rendered liable (*m*).

Power to compromise.

**160.** The liquidators may, with the sanction of the court, where the company is being wound up by the court, or subject to the supervision of the court, and with the sanction of an extraordinary resolution of the company where the company is being wound up altogether voluntarily, compromise all calls and liabilities to calls, debts, and liabilities capable of resulting in debts, and all claims, whether present or future, certain or contingent, ascertained or sounding only in damages, subsisting or supposed to subsist between the company and any contributory or alleged contributory, or other debtor or person apprehending liability to the company, and all questions in any way relating to or affecting the assets of the company or the winding up of the company, upon the receipt of such sums, payable at such times, and generally upon such terms as may be agreed upon, with power for the liquidators to take any security for the discharge of such debts or liabilities, and to give complete discharges in respect of all or any such calls, debts, or liabilities.

Power for liquidators to accept shares, &c., as a consideration for sale of property of company.

**161.** Where any company is proposed to be or is in the course of being wound up altogether voluntarily, and the whole or a portion of its business or property is proposed to be transferred or sold to another company, the liquidators of the first-mentioned company may, with the sanction of a special resolution of the company by whom they were appointed, conferring either a general authority on the liquidators or an authority in respect of any particular arrangement, receive in compensation or part compensation for such transfer or sale, shares, policies or other like interests in such other company for the purpose of distribution amongst the members of the company being wound up, or may enter into any other arrangement whereby the members of the company being wound up, may, in lieu of receiving cash, shares, policies or other like interests, or in addition thereto, participate in the profits of or receive any other benefit from the purchasing company : and any sale made or arrangement entered into by the liquidators in pursuance of this section shall be binding on the members of the company being wound up ; subject to this proviso, that if any member of the company being wound up who has not voted in favour of the special resolution passed by the company of which he is a member at either of the meetings held for passing the same expresses his dissent from any such special resolution in writing addressed to the liquidators or one of them, and left at the registered office of the company not later than seven days after the date of the meeting at which such special resolution was passed, such dissentient member may require the liquidators to do one of the following things as the liquidators may prefer ; that is to say, either to abstain from carrying such resolution into effect, or to purchase the interest held by such dissentient member at a price to be determined in manner hereinafter mentioned, such purchase-money to be paid before the company is dissolved, and to be raised by the liquidators in such manner as may be determined by special resolution : no special resolution shall be deemed invalid for the purposes of this section by reason that it is passed antecedently to or concurrently with any resolution for winding up the company, or for appointing liquidators ; but if an order be made within a year for winding up the company by or subject to the supervision of the court, such resolution shall not be of any validity unless it is sanctioned by the court.

Mode of determining price.

**162.** The price to be paid for the purchase of the interest of any dissentient member may be determined by agreement, but if the parties dispute about the same, such dispute shall be settled by arbitration, and for the pur-

(*m*) Sect. 136 and 33 & 34 Vict. c. 104, s. 2.

poses of such arbitration the provisions of "The Companies Clauses Consoli- *IV. Supplemental Provisions.*
dation Act, 1845," with respect to the settlement of disputes by arbitration (n)
shall be incorporated with this Act; and in the construction of such provisions
this Act shall be deemed to be the special Act, and "the company" shall
mean the company that is being wound up, and any appointment by the said
incorporated provisions directed to be made under the hand of the secretary,
or any two of the directors, may be made under the hand of the liquidator,
if only one, or any two or more of the liquidators if more than one.

163. Where any company is being wound up by the court, or subject to *Certain attach-ments, seques-trations, and executions to be void.*
the supervision of the court, any attachment, sequestration, distress, or exe-
cution put in force against the estate or effects of the company after the
commencement of the winding up shall be void to all intents.

164. Any such conveyance, mortgage, delivery of goods, payment, exe- *Fraudulent preference.*
cution, or other act relating to property as would, if made or done by or
against any individual trader, be deemed, in the event of his bankruptcy,
to have been made or done by way of undue or fraudulent preference of the
creditors of such trader (o), shall, if made or done by or against any company,
be deemed, in the event of such company being wound up under this Act, to
have been made or done by way of undue or fraudulent preference of the
creditors of such company, and shall be invalid accordingly; and for the
purposes of this section the presentation of a petition for winding up a company shall, in the case of a company being wound up by the court, or subject to the supervision of the court, and a resolution for winding up the
company shall, in the case of a voluntary winding up, be deemed to correspond with the act of bankruptcy in the case of an individual trader; and
any conveyance or assignment made by any company formed under this Act of
all its estate and effects to trustees for the benefit of all its creditors shall be
void to all intents.

165. Where, in the course of the winding-up of any company under this *Power of court to assess damages against delinquent directors and officers.*
Act, it appears that any past or present director, manager, official or other
liquidator, or any officer of such company, has misapplied or retained in his
own hands or become liable or accountable for any moneys of the company,
or been guilty of any misfeasance or breach of trust in relation to the company, the court may, on the application of any liquidator, or of any creditor
or contributory of the company, notwithstanding that the offence is one for
which the offender is criminally responsible, examine into the conduct of
such director, manager, or other officer, and compel him to repay any moneys
so misapplied or retained, or for which he has become liable or accountable,
together with interest after such rate as the court thinks just, or to contribute such sums of money to the assets of the company by way of compensation in respect of such misapplication, retainer, misfeasance, or breach
of trust, as the court thinks just.

166. If any director, officer, or contributory of any company wound up *Penalty on falsification of books.*
under this Act destroys, mutilates, alters, or falsifies any books, papers,
writings, or securities, or makes or is privy to the making of any false or
fraudulent entry in any register, book of account, or other document belonging to the company with intent to defraud or deceive any person, every
person so offending shall be deemed to be guilty of a misdemeanor, and upon
being convicted shall be liable to imprisonment for any term not exceeding
two years, with or without hard labour (p).

167. Where any order is made for winding up a company by the court or *Prosecution of delinquent directors in the case of winding up by court.*
subject to the supervision of the court, if it appear in the course of such
winding up that any past or present director, manager, officer, or member of
such company has been guilty of any offence in relation to the company for
which he is criminally responsible, the court may, on the application of any
person interested in such winding up, or of its own motion, direct the official
liquidators, or the liquidators (as the case may be), to institute and conduct
a prosecution or prosecutions for such offence, and may order the costs and
expenses to be paid out of the assets of the company.

168. Where a company is being wound up altogether voluntarily, if it *Prosecution of delinquent ·*
appear to the liquidators conducting such winding up that any past or

(n) 8 & 9 Vict. c. 16, sects. 128— 1883, *infra.*
134. (p) See 24 & 25 Vict. c. 96, s. 83,
(o) See sect. 48 of Bankruptcy Act, *supra.*

IV. *Supplemental Provisions.*

*directors, &c., in case of voluntary winding up.*

present director, manager, officer, or member of such company has been guilty of any offence in relation to the company for which he is criminally responsible, it shall be lawful for the liquidators, with the previous sanction of the court, to prosecute such offender, and all expenses properly incurred by them in such prosecution shall be payable out of the assets of the company in priority to all other liabilities.

*Penalty of perjury.*

169. If any person, upon any examination upon oath or affirmation authorized under this Act, or in any affidavit, deposition, or solemn affirmation in or about the winding up of any company under this Act, or otherwise in or about any matter arising under this Act, wilfully and corruptly gives false evidence, he shall, upon conviction, be liable to the penalties of wilful perjury.

*Power of Courts to make Rules.*

*Power of Courts to make Rules.*

170. [Repealed by 44 & 45 Vict. c. 59.]

*Power of court of session in Scotland to make rules.*

171. In Scotland the court of session may make such rules concerning the mode of winding up as may be necessary by Act of Sederunt; but, until such rules are made, the general practice of the court of session in suits pending in such court shall, so far as the same is applicable, and not inconsistent with this Act, apply to all proceedings for winding up a company, and official liquidators shall in all respects be considered as possessing the same powers as any trustee on a bankrupt estate (*q*).

*Power to make rules in stannaries court.*

172. The vice-warden of the stannaries may from time to time, with the consent provided for by section twenty-three of the Act of eighteenth of Victoria, chapter thirty-two, make rules for carrying into effect the powers conferred by this Act upon the court of the vice-warden, but, subject to such rules, the general practice of the said court and of the registrar's office in the said court, including the present practice of the said court in winding up companies, may be applied to all proceedings under this Act; the said vice-warden may likewise, with the same consent, make from time to time rules for specifying the fees to be taken in his said court in proceedings under this Act; and any rules so made shall be of the same force as if they had been enacted in the body of this Act; and the fees paid in respect of proceedings taken under this Act, including fees taken under "The Joint Stock Companies Act, 1856," in the matter of winding up companies, shall be applied exclusively towards payment of such additional officers, or such increase of the salaries of existing officers, or pensions to retired officers, or such other needful expenses of the court, as the lord warden of the stannaries shall from time to time, on the application of the vice-warden or otherwise, think fit to direct, sanction, or assign, and meanwhile shall be kept as a separate fund apart from the ordinary fees of the court arising from other business, to await such direction and order of the lord warden herein, and to accumulate by investment in government securities until the whole shall have been so appropriated (*r*).

*Power of lord chancellor of Ireland to make rules.*

173. In Ireland the lord chancellor of Ireland may, as respects the winding up of companies in Ireland, with the advice and consent of the master of the rolls in Ireland, exercise the same power of making rules as is by this Act hereinbefore given to the lord chancellor of Great Britain; but until such rules are made the general practice of the court of chancery in Ireland, including the practice hitherto in use in Ireland in winding up companies, shall, so far as the same is applicable, and not inconsistent with this Act, apply to all proceedings for winding up a company (*r*).

## PART V.

### REGISTRATION OFFICE.

*Constitution of registration office.*

174. The registration of companies under this Act shall be conducted as follows: (that is to say,)

    (1.) The board of trade may from time to time appoint such registrars, assistant registrars, clerks, and servants as they may think neces-

(*q*) Sect. 20 of 30 & 31 Vict. c. 131.       (*r*) *Ibid.*

sary for the registration of companies under this Act, and remove them at pleasure :

V. *Registration Office.*

(2.) The board of trade may make such regulations as they think fit with respect to the duties to be performed by any such registrars, assistant registrars, clerks, and servants as aforesaid :

(3.) The board of trade may from time to time determine the places at which offices for the registration of companies are to be established, so that there be at all times maintained in each of the three parts of the United Kingdom at least one such office, and that no company shall be registered except at an office within that part of the United Kingdom in which by the memorandum of association the registered office of the company is declared to be established ; and the board may require that the registrar's office of the court of the vice-warden of the stannaries shall be one of the offices for the registration of companies formed for working mines within the jurisdiction of the court :

(4.) The board of trade may from time to time direct a seal or seals to be prepared for the authentication of any documents required for or connected with the registration of companies :

(5.) Every person may inspect the documents kept by the registrar of joint stock companies ; and there shall be paid for such inspection such fees as may be appointed by the board of trade, not exceeding one shilling for each inspection ; and any person may require a certificate of the incorporation of any company, or a copy or extract of any other document or any part of any other document, to be certified by the registrar ; and there shall be paid for such certificate of incorporation, certified copy or extract, such fees as the board of trade may appoint, not exceeding five shillings for the certificate of incorporation, and not exceeding sixpence for each folio of such copy or extract, or in Scotland for each sheet of two hundred words :

(6.) The existing registrar, assistant registrars, clerks, and other officers and servants in the office for the registration of joint stock companies shall, during the pleasure of the board of trade, hold the offices and receive the salaries hitherto held and received by them, but they shall in the execution of their duties conform to any regulations that may be issued by the board of trade :

(7.) There shall be paid to any registrar, assistant-registrar, clerk or servant that may hereafter be employed in the registration of joint stock companies such salary as the board of trade may, with the sanction of the commissioners of the treasury, direct :

(8.) Whenever any act is herein directed to be done to or by the registrar of joint stock companies, such act shall, until the board of trade otherwise directs, be done in England to or by the existing registrar of joint stock companies, or in his absence to or by such person as the board of trade may for the time being authorize ; in Scotland to or by the existing registrar of joint stock companies in Scotland ; and in Ireland to or by the existing assistant-registrar of joint stock companies for Ireland, or by such person as the board of trade may for the time being authorize in Scotland or Ireland in the absence of the registrar ; but in the event of the board of trade altering the constitution of the existing registry office, such act shall be done to or by such officer or officers and at such place or places with reference to the local situation of the registered offices of the companies to be registered as the board of trade may appoint.

---

## PART VI.

### APPLICATION OF ACT TO COMPANIES REGISTERED UNDER THE JOINT STOCK COMPANIES ACTS.

**175.** The expression " Joint Stock Companies Acts," as used in this Act shall mean " The Joint Stock Companies Act, 1856," " The Joint Stock Companies Acts, 1856, 1857," " The Joint Stock Banking Companies Act, 1857," and " The Act to enable Joint Stock Banking Companies to be formed on the

Definition of Joint Stock Companies Acts.

VI. *Application of Act to Companies registered under the Joint Stock Companies Act.*

Principle of Limited Liability," or any one or more of such Acts, as the case may require ; but shall not include the Act passed in the eighth year of the reign of her present Majesty, chapter one hundred and ten, and intituled " An Act for the Registration, Incorporation and Regulation of Joint Stock Companies."

Application of Act to companies formed under Joint Stock Companies Acts.

**176.** Subject as hereinafter mentioned, this Act, with the exception of table (A) in the first schedule, shall apply to companies formed and registered under the said Joint Stock Companies Acts, or any of them, in the same manner in the case of a limited company as if such company had been formed and registered under this Act as a company limited by shares, and in the case of a company other than a limited company as if such company had been formed and registered as an unlimited company under this Act with this qualification, that whenever reference is made expressly or impliedly to the date of registration, such date shall be deemed to refer to the date at which such companies were respectively registered under the said Joint Stock Companies Acts or any of them, and the power of altering regulations by special resolution given by this Act shall, in the case of any company formed and registered under the said Joint Stock Companies Acts, or any of them, extend to altering any provisions contained in the table marked (B) annexed to " The Joint Stock Companies Act, 1856," and shall also in the case of an unlimited company formed and registered as last aforesaid extend to altering any regulations relating to the amount of capital or its distribution into shares, notwithstanding such regulations are contained in the memorandum of association.

Application of Act to companies registered under Joint Stock Companies Acts.

**177.** This Act shall apply to companies registered but not formed under the said Joint Stock Companies Acts or any of them in the same manner as it is hereinafter declared to apply to companies registered but not formed under this Act, with this qualification, that wherever reference is made expressly or impliedly to the date of registration, such date shall be deemed to refer to the date at which such companies were respectively registered under the said Joint Stock Companies Acts or any of them.

Mode of transferring shares.

**178.** Any company registered under the said Joint Stock Companies Acts or any of them may cause its shares to be transferred in manner hitherto in use, or in such other manner as the company may direct.

---

## PART VII.

### COMPANIES AUTHORIZED TO REGISTER UNDER THIS ACT.

Regulations as to registration of existing companies.

**179.** The following regulations shall be observed with respect to the registration of companies under this part of this Act ; (that is to say,)

(1.) No company having the liability of its members limited by Act of Parliament or letters patent, and not being a joint stock company as hereinafter defined, shall register under this Act in pursuance of this part thereof :

(2.) No company having the liability of its members limited by Act of Parliament or by letters patent, shall register under this Act in pursuance of this part thereof as an unlimited company, or as a company limited by guarantee :

(3.) No company that is not a joint stock company as hereinafter defined (*u*) shall in pursuance of this part of this Act register under this Act as a company limited by shares :

(4.) No company shall register under this Act in pursuance of this part thereof unless an assent to its so registering is given by a majority of such of its members as may be present, personally or by proxy, in cases where proxies are allowed by the regulations of the company, at some general meeting summoned for the purpose :

(5.) Where a company not having the liability of its members limited by Act of Parliament or letters patent is about to register as a limited company, the majority required to assent as aforesaid shall consist

(*u*) Sect. 181.

of not less than three-fourths of the members present, personally or by proxy, at such last-mentioned general meeting :

(6.) Where a company is about to register as a company limited by guarantee, the assent to its being so registered shall be accompanied by a resolution declaring that each member undertakes to contribute to the assets of the company, in the event of the same being wound up, during the time that he is a member, or within one year afterwards, for payment of the debts and liabilities of the company contracted before the time at which he ceased to be a member, and of the costs, charges and expenses of winding up the company, and for the adjustment of the rights of the contributories amongst themselves, such amount as may be required, not exceeding a specified amount (*x*).

In computing any majority under this section when a poll is demanded regard shall be had to the number of votes to which each member is entitled according to the regulations of the company of which he is a member.

*VII. Companies authorized to register under this Act.*

180. With the above exceptions, and subject to the foregoing regulations, every company existing at the time of the commencement of this Act (*y*), including any company registered under the said Joint Stock Companies Acts, consisting of seven or more members, and any company hereafter formed in pursuance of any Act of Parliament other than this Act, or of letters patent, or being a company engaged in working mines within and subject to the jurisdiction of the stannaries, or being otherwise duly constituted by law, and consisting of seven or more members, may at any time hereafter register itself under this Act as an unlimited company, or a company limited by shares, or a company limited by guarantee ; and no such registration shall be invalid by reason that it has taken place with a view to the company being wound up.

*Companies capable of being registered.*

181. For the purposes of this part of this Act, so far as the same relates to the description of companies empowered to register as companies limited by shares, a joint stock company shall be deemed to be a company having a permanent paid-up or nominal capital of fixed amount, divided into shares, also of fixed amount, or held and transferable as stock, or divided and held partly in one way and partly in the other, and formed on the principle of having for its members the holders of shares in such capital, or the holders of such stock, and no other persons; and such company when registered with limited liability under this Act shall be deemed to be a company limited by shares.

*Definition of joint stock company.*

182. [Repealed by 42 & 43 Vict. c. 76, s. 6.]

183. Previously to the registration in pursuance of this part of this Act of any joint stock company there shall be delivered to the registrar the following documents ; (that is to say,)

*Requisitions for registration by companies.*

(1.) A list showing the names, addresses and occupations of all persons who on a day named in such list, and not being more than six clear days before the day of registration, were members of such company, with the addition of the shares held by such persons respectively, distinguishing, in cases where such shares are numbered, each share by its number :

(2.) A copy of any Act of Parliament, royal charter, letters patent, deed of settlement, contract of copartnery, cost book regulations or other instrument constituting or regulating the company :

(3.) If any such joint stock company is intended to be registered as a limited company, the above list and copy shall be accompanied by a statement specifying the following particulars ; (that is to say,)

The nominal capital of the company and the number of shares into which it is divided :

The number of shares taken and the amount paid on each share :

The name of the company, with the addition of the word " limited " as the last word thereof:

With the addition, in the case of the company intended to be registered as a company limited by guarantee, of the resolution declaring the amount of the guarantee.

(*x*) Sect. 9 (4).        (*y*) Sect. 176.

VII. *Companies authorized to register under this Act.*

184. Previously to the registration in pursuance of this part of this Act of any company not being a joint stock company (a) there shall be delivered to the registrar a list showing the names, addresses and occupations of the directors or other managers (if any) of the company, also a copy of any Act of Parliament, letters patent, deed of settlement, contract of copartnery, cost book regulations, or other instrument constituting or regulating the company, with the addition, in the case of a company intended to be registered as a company limited by guarantee, of the resolution declaring the amount of guarantee (b).

Requisitions for registration by existing company not being a joint stock company.

Power for existing company to register amount of stock instead of shares.

185. Where a joint stock company authorized to register under this Act has had the whole or any portion of its capital converted into stock, such company shall, as to the capital so converted, instead of delivering to the registrar a statement of shares, deliver to the registrar a statement of the amount of stock belonging to the company, and the names of the persons who were holders of such stock, on some day to be named in the statement, not more than six clear days before the day of registration.

Authentication of statements of existing companies.

186. The lists of members and directors and any other particulars relating to the company hereby required to be delivered to the registrar shall be verified by a declaration of the directors of the company delivering the same, or any two of them, or of any two other principal officers of the company, made in pursuance of the Act passed in the sixth year of the reign of his late majesty King William the Fourth, chapter sixty-two.

Registrar may require evidence as to nature of company.

187. The registrar may require such evidence as he thinks necessary for the purpose of satisfying himself whether an existing company is or not a joint stock company as hereinbefore defined (c).

On registration of banking company with limited liability notice to be given to customers.

188. Every banking company (d) existing at the date of the passing of this Act which registers itself as a limited company shall, at least thirty days previous to obtaining a certificate of registration with limited liability, give notice that it is intended so to register the same to every person and partnership firm who have a banking account with the company, and such notice shall be given either by delivering the same to such person or firm, or leaving the same or putting the same into the post addressed to him or them at such address as shall have been last communicated or otherwise become known as his or their address to or by the company ; and in case the company omits to give any such notice as is hereinbefore required to be given, then as between the company and the person or persons only who are for the time being interested in the account in respect of which such notice ought to have been given, and so far as respects such account and all variations thereof down to the time at which such notice shall be given, but not further or otherwise, the certificate of registration with limited liability shall have no operation (e).

Exemption of certain companies from payment of fees.

189. No fees shall be charged in respect of the registration in pursuance of this part of this Act of any company in cases where such company is not registered as a limited company, or where previously to its being registered as a limited company the liability of the shareholders was limited by some other Act of Parliament or by letters patent.

Power to company to change name.

190. Any company authorized by this part of this Act to register with limited liability shall, for the purpose of obtaining registration with limited liability, change its name, by adding thereto the word "limited."

Certificate of registration of existing companies.

191. Upon compliance with the requisitions in this part of this Act contained with respect to registration, and on payment of such fees, if any, as are payable under the tables marked (B) and (C) in the first schedule hereto, the registrar shall certify under his hand that the company so applying for registration is incorporated as a company under this Act, and, in the case of a limited company, that it is limited, and thereupon such company shall be incorporated, and shall have perpetual succession and a common seal, with power to hold lands ; and any banking company in Scotland so incorporated shall be deemed and taken to be a bank incorporated, constituted, or established by or under Act of Parliament.

Certificate to be evidence of compliance with Act.

192. A certificate of incorporation given at any time to any company registered in pursuance of this part of this Act, shall be conclusive evidence

(a) Sect. 181.
(b) 42 & 43 Vict. c. 76, s. 9.
(c) Sect. 181.

(d) 42 & 43 Vict. c. 76, s. 6.
(e) Sect. 18.

that all the requisitions herein contained in respect of registration under this Act have been complied with, and that the company is authorized to be registered under this Act as a limited or unlimited company, as the case may be, and the date of incorporation mentioned in such certificate shall be deemed to be the date at which the company is incorporated under this Act. *VII. Companies authorized to register under this Act.*

193. All such property, real and personal, including all interests and rights in, to, and out of property, real and personal, and including obligations and things in action, as may belong to or be vested in the company at the date of its registration under this Act, shall on registration pass to and vest in the company as incorporated under this Act for all the estate and interest of the company therein. Transfer of property to company.

194. The registration in pursuance of this part of this Act of any company shall not affect or prejudice the liability of such company to have enforced against it, or its right to enforce any debt or obligation incurred, or any contract entered into, by, to, with, or on behalf of such company previously to such registration. Registration under this Act not to affect obligations incurred previously to registration.

195. All such actions, suits, and other legal proceedings as may at the time of the registration of any company registered in pursuance of this part of this Act have been commenced by or against such company, or the public officer or any member thereof, may be continued in the same manner as if such registration had not taken place; nevertheless, execution shall not issue against the effects of any individual member of such company upon any judgment, decree, or order obtained in any action, suit, or proceeding so commenced as aforesaid; but in the event of the property and effects of the company being insufficient to satisfy such judgment, decree, or order, an order may be obtained for winding up the company. Continuation of existing actions and suits.

196. When a company is registered under this Act in pursuance of this part thereof, all provisions contained in any Act of Parliament, deed of settlement, contract of copartnery, cost book regulations, letters patent, or other instrument constituting or regulating the company, including, in the case of a company registered as a company limited by guarantee, the resolution declaring the amount of the guarantee, shall be deemed to be conditions and regulations of the company, in the same manner and with the same incidents as if they were contained in a registered memorandum of association and articles of association; and all the provisions of this Act shall apply to such company and the members, contributories, and creditors thereof, in the same manner in all respects as if it had been formed under this Act, subject to the provisions following; (that is to say,) Effect of registration under Act.

(1.) That table (A) in the first schedule to this Act shall not, unless adopted by special resolution (*f*), apply to any company registered under this Act in pursuance of this part thereof:

(2.) That the provisions of this Act relating to the numbering of shares (*g*) shall not apply to any joint stock company whose shares are not numbered:

(3.) That no company shall have power to alter any provision contained in any Act of Parliament relating to the company (*h*):

(4.) That no company shall have power, without the sanction of the board of trade, to alter any provision contained in any letters patent relating to the company:

(5.) That in the event of the company being wound up, every person shall be a contributory, in respect of the debts and liabilities of the company contracted prior to registration, who is liable, at law or in equity, to pay or contribute to the payment of any debt or liability of the company contracted prior to registration, or to pay or contribute to the payment of any sum for the adjustment of the rights of the members amongst themselves, in respect of any such debt or liability; or to pay or contribute to the payment of the costs, charges, and expenses of winding up the company so far as relates to such debts or liabilities as aforesaid (*i*); and every such contributory shall be liable to contribute to the assets of the company, in the course of the winding up, all sums due from him in respect of any such liability as aforesaid; and in the event of the death, bank-

(*f*) Sect. 51.
(*g*) Sect. 22.

(*h*) 30 & 31 Vict. c. 131, s. 47.
(*i*) Sects. 38, 200.

VII. *Companies authorized to register under this Act.*

ruptcy, or insolvency of any such contributory as last aforesaid, or marriage of any such contributory being a female, the provisions hereinbefore contained (i) with respect to the representatives, heirs, and devisees of deceased contributories, and with reference to the assignees of bankrupt or insolvent contributories, and to the husbands of married contributories, shall apply ;

(6.) That nothing herein contained shall authorize any company to alter any such provisions contained in any deed of settlement, contract of copartnery, cost book regulations, letters patent, or other instrument constituting or regulating the company, as would, if such company had originally been formed under this Act, have been contained in the memorandum of association (k) ; and are not authorized to be altered by this Act :

But nothing herein contained shall derogate from any power of altering its constitution or regulations which may be vested in any company registering under this Act in pursuance of this part thereof by virtue of any Act of Parliament, deed of settlement, contract of copartnery, letters patent, or other instrument constituting or regulating the company.

Power of court to restrain further proceedings.

**197.** The court may, at any time after the presentation of a petition for winding up a company registered in pursuance of this part of this Act, and before making an order for winding up the company, upon the application by motion of any creditor of the company, restrain further proceedings in any action, suit, or legal proceeding against any contributory of the company, as well as against the company as hereinbefore provided, upon such terms as the court thinks fit (l).

Order for winding up company.

**198.** Where an order has been made for winding up a company registered in pursuance of this part of the Act, in addition to the provisions hereinbefore contained (m), it is hereby further provided that no suit, action, or other legal proceeding shall be commenced or proceeded with against any contributory of the company in respect of any debt of the company, except with the leave of the court, and subject to such terms as the court may impose.

---

## PART VIII.

### APPLICATION OF ACT TO UNREGISTERED COMPANIES.

Winding up of unregistered companies.

**199.** Subject as hereinafter mentioned, any partnership, association, or company, except railway companies incorporated by Act of Parliament, consisting of more than seven members (n), and not registered under this Act (o), and hereinafter included under the term unregistered company, may be wound up under this Act, and all the provisions of this Act with respect to winding up shall apply to such company, with the following exceptions and additions :

(1.) An unregistered company shall, for the purpose of determining the court having jurisdiction in the matter of the winding up, be deemed to be registered in that part of the United Kingdom where its principal place of business is situate ; or, if it has a principal place of business situate in more than one part of the United Kingdom, then in each part of the United Kingdom where it has a principal place of business ; moreover the principal place of business of an unregistered company, or (where it has a principal place of business situate in more than one part of the United Kingdom) such one of its principal places of business as is situate in that part of the United Kingdom in which proceedings are being instituted, shall for all the purposes of the winding up of such company be deemed to be the registered office of the company (p) :

(2.) No unregistered company shall be wound up under this Act voluntarily or subject to the supervision of the court :

(i) Sects. 76, 77, 78, 105, 106.       (n) Sect 79 (3).
(k) Sects. 8, 9, 10.                    (o) Sects. 176, 177.
(l) Sect. 201.                          (p) Sect. 39.
(m) Sect. 195.

(3.) The circumstances under which an unregistered company may be wound up are as follows; (that is to say,)

(a) Whenever the company is dissolved, or has ceased to carry on business, or is carrying on business only for the purpose of winding up its affairs:

(b) Whenever the company is unable to pay its debts:

(c) Whenever the court is of opinion that it is just and equitable that the company should be wound up:

(4.) An unregistered company shall, for the purposes of this Act, be deemed to be unable to pay its debts *(q)*,

(a) Whenever a creditor to whom the company is indebted, at law or in equity, by assignment or otherwise, in a sum exceeding fifty pounds then due, has served on the company, by leaving the same at the principal place of business of the company, or by delivering to the secretary or some director or principal officer of the company, or by otherwise serving the same in such manner as the court may approve or direct, a demand under his hand requiring the company to pay the sum so due, and the company has for the space of three weeks succeeding the service of such demand neglected to pay such sum, or to secure or compound for the same to the satisfaction of the creditor:

(b) Whenever any action, suit, or other proceeding has been instituted against any member of the company for any debt or demand due, or claimed to be due, from the company, or from him in his character of member of the company, and notice in writing of the institution of such action, suit, or other legal proceeding having been served upon the company by leaving the same at the principal place of business of the company, or by delivering it to the secretary, or some director, manager, or principal officer of the company, or by otherwise serving the same in such manner as the court may approve or direct, the company has not within ten days after service of such notice paid, secured, or compounded for such debt or demand, or procured such action, suit, or other legal proceeding to be stayed, or indemnified the defendant to his reasonable satisfaction against such action, suit, or other legal proceeding, and against all costs, damages, and expenses to be incurred by him by reason of the same:

(c) Whenever in England or Ireland execution or other process issued on a judgment, decree, or order obtained in any court in favour of any creditor in any proceeding at law or in equity instituted by such creditor against the company, or any member thereof as such, or against any person authorized to be sued as nominal defendant on behalf of the company, is returned unsatisfied:

(d) Whenever, in the case of an unregistered company engaged in working mines within and subject to the jurisdiction of the stannaries, a customary decree or order absolute for the sale of the machinery, materials, and effects of such mine has been made in a creditor's suit in the court of the vice-warden:

(e) Whenever in Scotland the induciæ of a charge for payment on an extract decree, or an extract registered bond, or an extract registered protest, have expired without payment being made:

(f) Whenever it is otherwise proved to the satisfaction of the court that the company is unable to pay its debts.

200. In the event of an unregistered company being wound up every person shall be deemed to be a contributory *(r)* who is liable at law or in equity to pay or contribute to the payment of any debt or liability of the company, or to pay or contribute to the payment of any sum for the adjustment of the rights of the members amongst themselves, or to pay or contribute to the payment of the costs, charges, and expenses of winding up the company, and every such contributory shall be liable to contribute to the assets of the company in the course of the winding up all sums due from him in respect of any such liability as aforesaid; but in the event of the death, bankruptcy, or insolvency of any contributory, or marriage of any female

VIII. *Application of Act to unregistered Companies.*

contributory, the provisions hereinbefore contained with respect to the personal representatives, heirs, and devisees of a deceased contributory, and to the assignees of a bankrupt or insolvent contributory, and to the husbands of married contributories, shall apply.

Power of court to restrain further proceedings.

**201.** The court may, at any time after the presentation of a petition for winding up an unregistered company, and before making an order for winding up the company, upon the application of any creditor of the company, restrain further proceedings in any action, suit, or proceeding against any contributory of the company, or against the company as hereinbefore provided (*s*), upon such terms as the court thinks fit.

Effect of order for winding up company.

**202.** When an order has been made for winding up an unregistered company in addition to the provisions hereinbefore contained in the case of companies formed under this Act (*t*), it is hereby further provided that no suit, action, or other legal proceeding shall be commenced or proceeded with against any contributory of the company in respect of any debt of the company, except with the leave of the court, and subject to such terms as the court may impose.

Provision in case of unregistered company.

**203.** If any unregistered company has no power to sue and be sued in a common name, or if for any reason it appears expedient, the court may by the order made for winding up such company, or by any subsequent order, direct that all such property, real and personal, including all interest, claims, and rights into and out of property, real and personal, and including things in action, as may belong to or be vested in the company, or to or in any person or persons on trust for or on behalf of the company or any part of such property, is to vest in the official liquidator or official liquidators by his or their official name or names, and thereupon the same or such part thereof as may be specified in the order shall vest accordingly, and the official liquidator or official liquidators may, in his or their official name or names, or in such name or names and after giving such indemnity as the court directs, bring or defend any actions, suits, or other legal proceedings relating to any property vested in him or them, or any actions, suits, or other legal proceedings necessary to be brought or defended for the purposes of effectually winding up the company and recovering the property thereof.

Provisions in this part of Act cumulative.

**204.** The provisions made by this part of the Act with respect to unregistered companies shall be deemed to be made in addition to and not in restriction of any provisions hereinbefore contained (*u*) with respect to winding up companies by the court, and the court or official liquidator may, in addition to anything contained in this part of the Act. exercise any powers or do any act in the case of unregistered companies which might be exercised or done by it or him in winding up companies formed under this Act, but an unregistered company shall not, except in the event of its being wound up, be deemed to be a company under this Act, and then only to the extent provided by this part of this Act.

---

# PART IX.

## REPEAL OF ACTS AND TEMPORARY PROVISIONS.

Repeal of Acts.

**205.** After the commencement of this Act there shall be repealed the several Acts specified in the first part of the third schedule hereto, with this qualification, that so much of the said Act as is set forth in the second part of the said third schedule shall be hereby re-enacted and continue in force as if unrepealed.

Saving clause as to repeals.

**206.** No repeal hereby enacted shall affect,

(1.) Anything duly done under any Acts hereby repealed :

(2.) The incorporation of any company registered under any Act hereby repealed :

(3.) Any right or privilege acquired or liability incurred under any Act hereby repealed (*x*) :

---

(*s*) Sect. 85.
(*t*) Sect. 87.
(*u*) Sects. 79—128, 153—173.

(*x*) Sub-sect. (3) repealed by Statute Law Revision Act, 1875.

(4.) Any penalty, forfeiture, or other punishment incurred in respect of any offence against any Act hereby repealed :

(5.) Table B in the schedule annexed to the Joint Stock Companies Act, 1856, or any part thereof, so far as the same applies to any company existing at the time of the commencement of this Act.

**207.** [Repealed by Statute Law Revision Act, 1875.]

**208.** Where previously to the commencement of this Act any conveyance, mortgage or other deed has been made in pursuance of any Act hereby repealed, such deed shall be of the same force as if this Act had not passed, and for the purposes of such deed such repealed Act shall be deemed to remain in full force.

**209.** Every insurance company completely registered under the Act passed in the eighth year of the reign of her present Majesty, chapter one hundred and ten, intituled " An Act for the Registration, Incorporation, and Regulation of Joint Stock Companies," shall on or before the second day of November, one thousand eight hundred and sixty-two, and every other company required by any Act hereby repealed to register under the said Joint Stock Companies Acts, or one of such Acts, and which has not so registered, shall, on or before the expiration of the thirty-first day from the commencement of this Act, register itself as a company under this Act in manner and subject to the regulations hereinbefore contained (*y*), with this exception, that no company completely registered under the said Act of the eighth year of the reign of her present Majesty shall be required to deliver to the registrar a copy of its deed of settlement ; and for the purpose of enabling such insurance companies as are mentioned in this section to register under this Act, this Act shall be deemed to come into operation immediately on the passing thereof (*z*) ; nevertheless the registration of such companies shall not have any effect until the time of the commencement of this Act. No fees shall be charged in respect of the registration of any company required to register by this section.

**210.** If any company required by the last section to register under this Act makes default in complying with the provisions thereof, then, from and after the day upon which such company is required to register under this Act until the day on which such company is registered under this Act (which it is empowered to do at any time), the following consequences shall ensue ; (that is to say,)

(1.) The company shall be incapable of suing either at law or in equity, but shall not be incapable of being made a defendant to a suit either at law or in equity :

(2.) No dividend shall be payable to any shareholder in such company :

(3.) Each director or manager of the company shall for each day during which the company so being in default carries on business incur a penalty not exceeding five pounds, and such penalty may be recovered by any person, whether a shareholder or not in the company, and be applied by him to his own use :

Nevertheless, such default shall not render the company so being in default illegal, nor subject it to any penalty or disability, other than as specified in this section ; and registration under this Act shall cancel any penalty or forfeiture, and put an end to any disability which any company may have incurred under any Act hereby repealed by reason of its not having registered under the said Joint Stock Companies Acts, 1856, 1857, or one of them.

**211.** [Repealed by Statute Law Revision Act, 1875.]

**212.** [Repealed by Statute Law Revision Act, 1875.]

(*y*) Sect. 179.                    (*z*) Sect. 2.

## FIRST SCHEDULE.

### TABLE A.

##### REGULATIONS FOR MANAGEMENT OF A COMPANY LIMITED BY SHARES.

*Shares.*

(1.) If several persons are registered as joint holders of any share, any one of such persons may give effectual receipts for any dividend payable in respect of such share.

(2.) Every member shall, on payment of one shilling, or such less sum as the company in general meeting may prescribe, be entitled to a certificate (*a*), under the common seal of the company, specifying the share or shares held by him, and the amount paid up thereon.

(3.) If such certificate is worn out or lost, it may be renewed on payment of one shilling, or such less sum as the company in general meeting may prescribe.

*Calls on Shares.*

(4.) The directors may from time to time make such calls upon the members in respect of all monies unpaid on their shares as they think fit, provided that twenty-one days' notice at least is given of each call, and each member shall be liable to pay the amount of the calls so made to the persons and at the times and places appointed by the directors.

(5.) A call shall be deemed to have been made at the time when the resolution of the directors authorising such call was passed.

(6.) If the call payable in respect of any share is not paid before or on the day appointed for payment thereof, the holder for the time being of such share shall be liable to pay interest for the same at the rate of five pounds per cent. per annum from the day appointed for the payment thereof to the time of the actual payment.

(7.) The directors may, if they think fit, receive from any member willing to advance the same all or any part of the monies due upon the shares held by him beyond the sums actually called for; and upon the monies so paid in advance, or so much thereof as from time to time exceeds the amount of the calls then made upon the shares in respect of which such advance has been made, the company may pay interest at such rate as the member paying such sum in advance and the directors agree upon.

*Transfers of Shares.*

(8.) The instrument of transfer of any share in the company shall be executed both by the transferor and transferee, and the transferor shall be deemed to remain a holder of such share until the name of the transferee is entered in the register book in respect thereof (*b*).

(9.) Shares in the company shall be transferred in the following form :—
I, *A. B.* of ————, in consideration of the sum of ———— pounds paid to me by *C. D.* of ————, do hereby transfer to the said *C. D.* the share [*or* shares] numbered ———— standing in my name in the books of the ———— company, to hold unto the said *C. D.*, his executors, administrators, and assigns, subject to the several conditions on which I held the same at the time of the execution thereof; and I the said *C. D.* do hereby agree to take the said share [*or* shares] subject to the same conditions. As witness our hands the ———— day of ————.

(10.) The company may decline to register any transfer of shares made by a member who is indebted to them.

(11.) The transfer books shall be closed during the fourteen days immediately preceding the ordinary general meeting in each year.

(*a*) Sect. 31.                    (*b*) Sect. 22.

*Transmission of Shares.*

(12.) The executors or administrators of a deceased member shall be the only persons recognized by the company as having any title to his share.

(13.) Any person becoming entitled to a share in consequence of the death, bankruptcy (*c*) or insolvency of any member, or in consequence of the marriage of any female member (*d*), may be registered as a member upon such evidence being produced as may from time to time be required by the company.

(14.) Any person who has become entitled to a share in consequence of the death, bankruptcy or insolvency of any member, or in consequence of the marriage of any female member, may, instead of being registered himself, elect to have some person to be named by him registered as a transferee of such share.

(15.) The person so becoming entitled shall testify such election by executing to his nominee an instrument of transfer of such share.

(16.) The instrument of transfer shall be presented to the company, accompanied with such evidence as the directors may require to prove the title of the transferor, and thereupon the company shall register the transferee as a member.

*Forfeiture of Shares.*

(17.) If any member fails to pay any call on the day appointed for payment thereof, the directors may at any time thereafter during such time as the call remains unpaid, serve a notice on him, requiring him to pay such call, together with interest and any expenses that may have accrued by reason of such non-payment.

(18.) The notice shall name a further day on or before which such call, and all interest and expenses that have accrued by reason of such non-payment, are to be paid. It shall also name the place where payment is to be made (the place so named being either the registered office of the company or some other place at which calls of the company are usually made payable). The notice shall also state that in the event of non-payment at or before the time and at the place appointed the shares in respect of which such call was made will be liable to be forfeited.

(19.) If the requisitions of any such notice as aforesaid are not complied with, any share in respect of which such notice has been given may, at any time thereafter, before payment of all calls, interest and expenses due in respect thereof has been made, be forfeited, by a resolution of the directors to that effect.

(20.) Any share so forfeited shall be deemed to be the property of the company, and may be disposed of in such manner as the company in general meeting thinks fit.

(21.) Any member whose shares have been forfeited shall notwithstanding be liable to pay to the company all calls owing upon such shares at the time of the forfeiture.

(22.) A statutory declaration in writing, that the call in respect of a share was made and notice thereof given, and that default in payment of the call was made, and that the forfeiture of the share was made by a resolution of the directors to that effect, shall be sufficient evidence of the facts therein stated, as against all persons entitled to such share, and such declaration and the receipt of the company for the price of such share shall constitute a good title to such share, and a certificate of proprietorship shall be delivered to a purchaser, and thereupon he shall be deemed the holder of such share discharged from all calls due prior to such purchase ; and he shall not be bound to see to the application of the purchase money, nor shall his title to such share be affected by any irregularity in the proceedings in reference to such sale.

*Conversion of Shares into Stock.*

(23.) The directors may, with the sanction of the company previously given in general meeting, convert any paid-up shares into stock (*e*).

(*c*) Sect. 75.  (*d*) Sect. 78.  (*e*) Sect. 12.

(24.) When any shares have been converted into stock, the several holders of such stock may thenceforth transfer their respective interests therein, or any part of such interests, in the same manner and subject to the same regulations as and subject to which any shares in the capital of the company may be transferred, or as near thereto as circumstances admit.

(25.) The several holders of stock shall be entitled to participate in the dividends and profits of the company according to the amount of their respective interests in such stock ; and such interests shall, in proportion to the amount thereof, confer on the holders thereof respectively the same privileges and advantages for the purpose of voting at meetings of the company, and for other purposes, as would have been conferred by shares of equal amount in the capital of the company ; but so that none of such privileges or advantages, except the participation in the dividends and profits of the company, shall be conferred by any such aliquot part of consolidated stock as would not, if existing in shares, have conferred such privileges or advantages.

### Increase in Capital.

(26.) The directors may, with the sanction of a special resolution of the company previously given in general meeting, increase its capital by the issue of new shares, such aggregate increase to be of such amount and to be divided into shares of such respective amounts, as the company in general meeting directs, or, if no direction is given, as the directors think expedient.

(27.) Subject to any direction to the contrary that may be given by the meeting that sanctions the increase of capital, all new shares shall be offered to the members in proportion to the existing shares held by them, and such offer shall be made by notice specifying the number of shares to which the member is entitled, and limiting a time within which the offer, if not accepted, will be deemed to be declined, and after the expiration of such time, or on the receipt of an intimation from the member to whom such notice is given that he declines to accept the shares offered, the directors may dispose of the same in such manner as they think most beneficial to the company.

(28.) Any capital raised by the creation of new shares shall be considered as part of the original capital, and shall be subject to the same provisions with reference to the payment of calls, and the forfeiture of shares on non-payment of calls or otherwise, as if it had been part of the original capital.

### General Meetings.

(29.) The first general meeting shall be held at such time, not being more than six months (*f*) after the registration of the company, and at such place, as the directors may determine.

(30.) Subsequent general meetings shall be held at such time and place as may be prescribed by the company in general meeting ; and if no other time or place is prescribed, a general meeting shall be held on the first Monday in February in every year, at such place as may be determined by the directors.

(31.) The above-mentioned general meetings shall be called ordinary meetings ; all other general meetings shall be called extraordinary.

(32.) The directors may, whenever they think fit, and they shall upon a requisition made in writing by not less than one-fifth in number of the members of the company, convene an extraordinary general meeting.

(33.) Any requisition made by the members shall express the object of the meeting proposed to be called, and shall be left at the registered office of the company.

(34.) Upon the receipt of such requisition the directors shall forthwith proceed to convene an extraordinary general meeting. If they do not proceed to convene the same within twenty-one days from the

(*f*) Now four months : 30 & 31 Vict. c. 131, s. 39.

date of the requisition, the requisitionists, or any other members amounting to the required number, may themselves convene an extraordinary general meeting.

*Proceedings at General Meetings.*

(35.) Seven days' notice at the least (*g*), specifying the place, the day and the hour of meeting, and in case of special business the general nature of such business (*h*), shall be given to the members in manner hereinafter mentioned, or in such other manner (if any), as may be prescribed by the company in general meeting ; but the non-receipt of such notice by any member shall not invalidate the proceedings at any general meeting.

(36.) All business shall be deemed special that is transacted at an extraordinary meeting (*i*), and all that is transacted at an ordinary meeting, with the exception of sanctioning a dividend and the consideration of the accounts, balance sheets and the ordinary report of the directors.

(37.) No business shall be transacted at any general meeting except the declaration of a dividend, unless a quorum of members is present at the time when the meeting proceeds to business ; and such quorum shall be ascertained as follows ; that is to say, if the persons who have taken shares in the company at the time of the meeting do not exceed ten in number, the quorum shall be five ; if they exceed ten there shall be added to the above quorum one for every five additional members up to fifty, and one for every ten additional members after fifty, with this limitation, that no quorum shall in any case exceed twenty.

(38.) If within one hour from the time appointed for the meeting a quorum is not present, the meeting, if convened upon the requisition of members, shall be dissolved : in any other case it shall stand adjourned to the same day in the next week, at the same time and place ; and if at such adjourned meeting a quorum is not present it shall be adjourned sine die.

(39.) The chairman (if any) (*k*) of the board of directors shall preside as chairman at every general meeting of the company.

(40.) If there is no such chairman (*k*), or if at any meeting he is not present within fifteen minutes after the time appointed for holding the meeting, the members present shall choose some one of their number to be chairman.

(41.) The chairman may, with the consent of the meeting, adjourn any meeting from time to time and from place to place, but no business shall be transacted at any adjourned meeting other than the business left unfinished at the meeting from which the adjournment took place.

(42.) At any general meeting, unless a poll is demanded by at least five members, a declaration by the chairman that a resolution has been carried, and an entry to that effect in the book of proceedings of the company (*l*), shall be sufficient evidence of the fact, without proof of the number or proportion of the votes recorded in favour of or against such resolution.

(43.) If a poll is demanded by five or more members it shall be taken in such manner as the chairman directs, and the result of such poll shall be deemed to be the resolution of the company in general meeting. In the case of an equality of votes at any general meeting, the chairman shall be entitled to a second or casting vote.

*Votes of Members.*

(44.) Every member shall have one vote for every share up to ten (*m*) : he shall have an additional vote for every five shares beyond the first ten shares up to one hundred, and an additional vote for every ten shares beyond the first hundred shares.

| | |
|---|---|
| (*g*) Sect. 52. | (*k*) Sect. 52. |
| (*h*) Arts. (95)—(97). | (*l*) Sect. 67. |
| (*i*) Art. (31). | (*m*) Sect. 52. |

(45.) If any member is a lunatic or idiot he may vote by his committee, curator bonis or other legal curator.

(46.) If one or more persons are jointly entitled to a share or shares, the member whose name stands first in the register of members as one of the holders of such share or shares, and no other, shall be entitled to vote in respect of the same.

(47.) No member shall be entitled to vote at any general meeting unless all calls due from him have been paid, and no member shall be entitled to vote in respect of any share that he has acquired by transfer at any meeting held after the expiration of three months from the registration of the company, unless he has been possessed of the share in respect of which he claims to vote for at least three months previously to the time of holding the meeting at which he proposes to vote.

(48.) Votes may be given either personally or by proxy.

(49.) The instrument appointing a proxy shall be in writing, under the hand of the appointor, or if such appointor is a corporation, under their common seal, and shall be attested by one or more witness or witnesses : no person shall be appointed a proxy who is not a member of the company.

(50.) The instrument appointing a proxy shall be deposited at the registered office of the company not less than seventy-two hours before the time for holding the meeting at which the person named in such instrument proposes to vote, but no instrument appointing a proxy shall be valid after the expiration of twelve months from the date of its execution.

(51.) Any instrument appointing a proxy shall be in the following form (*n*) :—

—— Company, Limited.

I —— of —— in the county of —— being a member of the —— company, limited, and entitled to —— vote *or* —— votes, hereby appoint —— of —— as my proxy, to vote for me and on my behalf at the [ordinary *or* extraordinary, *as the case may be*] general meeting of the company to be held on the —— day of ——, and at any adjournment thereof [*or*, at any meeting of the company that may be held in the year ——].

As witness my hand this —— day of ——.

Signed by the said —— in the presence of ——.

### *Directors.*

(52.) The number of the directors, and the names of the first directors, shall be determined by the subscribers of the memorandum of association.

(53.) Until directors are appointed, the subscribers of the memorandum of association shall be deemed to be directors.

(54.) The future remuneration of the directors, and their remuneration for services performed previously to the first general meeting, shall be determined by the company in general meeting.

### *Powers of Directors.*

(55.) The business of the company shall be managed by the directors, who may pay all expenses incurred in getting up and registering the company, and may exercise all such powers of the company as are not by the foregoing Act, or by these articles, required to be exercised by the company in general meeting, subject nevertheless to any regulations of these articles, to the provisions of the foregoing Act, and to such regulations, being not inconsistent with the aforesaid regulations or provisions, as may be prescribed by the company in general meeting; but no regulation made by the company in general meeting shall invalidate any prior act of the directors which would have been valid if such regulation had not been made.

(*n*) This instrument is charged with a duty of 1*d.*, which may be denoted by an adhesive stamp. It may not be stamped after execution : 33 & 34 Vict. c. 97, s. 102.

(56.) The continuing directors may act notwithstanding any vacancy in their body.

### Disqualification of Directors.

(57.) The office of director shall be vacated,—
If he holds any other office or place of profit under the company ;
If he becomes bankrupt or insolvent ;
If he is concerned in or participates in the profits of any contract with the company ;
But the above rules shall be subject to the following exceptions : That no director shall vacate his office by reason of his being a member of any company which has entered into contracts with or done any work for the company of which he is director ; nevertheless he shall not vote in respect of such contract or work ; and if he does so vote his vote shall not be counted.

### Rotation of Directors.

(58.) At the first ordinary meeting after the registration of the company the whole of the directors shall retire from office ; and at the first ordinary meeting in every subsequent year one-third of the directors for the time being, or if their number is not a multiple of three, then the number nearest to one-third shall retire from office.

(59.) The one-third or other nearest number to retire during the first and second years ensuing the first ordinary meeting of the company shall, unless the directors agree among themselves, be determined by ballot : in every subsequent year the one-third or other nearest number who have been longest in office shall retire.

(60.) A retiring director shall be re-eligible.

(61.) The company at the general meeting at which any directors retire in manner aforesaid shall fill up the vacated offices by electing a like number of persons.

(62.) If at any meeting at which an election of directors ought to take place the places of the vacating directors are not filled up, the meeting shall stand adjourned till the same day in the next week, at the same time and place ; and if at such adjourned meeting the places of the vacating directors are not filled up, the vacating directors, or such of them as have not had their places filled up, shall continue in office until the ordinary meeting in the next year, and so on from time to time until their places are filled up.

(63.) The company may from time to time, in general meeting, increase or reduce the number of directors, and may also determine in what rotation such increased or reduced number is to go out of office.

(64.) Any casual vacancy occurring in the board of directors may be filled up by the directors, but any person so chosen shall retain his office so long only as the vacating director would have retained the same if no vacancy had occurred.

(65.) The company, in general meeting, may, by a special resolution, remove any director before the expiration of his period of office, and may by an ordinary resolution appoint another person in his stead : the person so appointed shall hold office during such time only as the director in whose place he is appointed would have held the same if he had not been removed.

### Proceedings of Directors.

(66.) The directors may meet together for the dispatch of business, adjourn, and otherwise regulate their meetings as they think fit, and determine the quorum necessary for the transaction of business : questions arising at any meeting shall be decided by a majority of votes : in case of an equality of votes the chairman shall have a second or casting vote : a director may at any time summon a meeting of the directors.

(67.) The directors may elect a chairman of their meetings, and determine the period for which he is to hold office ; but if no such chairman is elected, or if at any meeting the chairman is not present at the time appointed for holding the same, the directors present shall choose some one of their number to be chairman of such meeting.

(68.) The directors may delegate any of their powers to committees consisting of such member or members of their body as they think fit: any committee so formed shall, in the exercise of the powers so delegated, conform to any regulations that may be imposed on them by the directors.

(69.) A committee may elect a chairman of their meetings: if no such chairman is elected, or if he is not present at the time appointed for holding the same, the members present shall choose one of their number to be chairman of such meeting.

(70.) A committee may meet and adjourn as they think proper: questions arising at any meeting shall be determined by a majority of votes of the members present; and in case of an equality of votes the chairman shall have a second or casting vote.

(71.) All acts done, by any meeting of the directors, or of a committee of directors, or by any person acting as a director, shall, notwithstanding that it be afterwards discovered that there was some defect in the appointment of any such directors or persons acting as aforesaid, or that they or any of them were disqualified, be as valid as if every such person had been duly appointed and was qualified to be a director (o).

### Dividends.

(72.) The directors may, with the sanction of the company in general meeting, declare a dividend to be paid to the members in proportion to their shares.

(73.) No dividend shall be payable except out of the profits arising from the business of the company.

(74.) The directors may, before recommending any dividend, set aside out of the profits of the company such sum as they think proper as a reserved fund to meet contingencies, or for equalizing dividends, or for repairing or maintaining the works connected with the business of the company, or any part thereof; and the directors may invest the sum so set apart as a reserved fund upon such securities as they may select.

(75.) The directors may deduct from the dividends payable to any member all such sums of money as may be due from him to the company on account of calls or otherwise.

(76.) Notice of any dividend that may have been declared shall be given to each member in manner hereinafter mentioned (p); and all dividends unclaimed for three years, after having been declared, may be forfeited by the directors for the benefit of the company.

(77.) No dividend shall bear interest as against the company.

### Accounts.

(78.) The directors shall cause true accounts to be kept,—
Of the stock in trade of the company;
Of the sums of money received and expended by the company, and the matter in respect of which such receipt and expenditure takes place: and,
Of the credits and liabilities of the company;
The books of account shall be kept at the registered office of the company, and subject to any reasonable restrictions as to the time and manner of inspecting the same that may be imposed by the company in general meeting, shall be open to the inspection of the members during the hours of business.

(79.) Once at the least in every year the directors shall lay before the company in general meeting a statement of the income and expenditure for the past year, made up to a date not more than three months before such meeting.

(80.) The statement so made shall show, arranged under the most convenient heads, the amount of gross income, distinguishing the several

(o) Sect. 67.                     (p) Arts. (95)—(97).

sources from which it has been derived, and the amount of gross expenditure, distinguishing the expenses of the establishment, salaries, and other like matters : Every item of expenditure fairly chargeable against the year's income shall be brought into account, so that a just balance of profit and loss may be laid before the meeting ; and in cases where any item of expenditure which may in fairness be distributed over several years has been incurred in any one year the whole amount of such item shall be stated, with the addition of the reasons why only a portion of such expenditure is charged against the income of the year.

(81.) A balance sheet shall be made out in every year, and laid before the company in general meeting, and such balance sheet shall contain a summary of the property and liabilities of the company arranged under the heads appearing in the form annexed to this table (*q*), or as near thereto as circumstances admit.

(82.) A printed copy of such balance sheet shall, seven days previously to such meeting, be served on every member in the manner in which notices are hereinafter directed to be served (*r*).

### *Audit.*

(83.) Once at the least in every year the accounts of the company shall be examined, and the correctness of the balance sheet ascertained by one or more auditor or auditors.

(84.) The first auditors shall be appointed by the directors : Subsequent auditors shall be appointed by the company in general meeting.

(85.) If one auditor only is appointed, all the provisions herein contained relating to auditors shall apply to him.

(86.) The auditors may be members of the company ; but no person is eligible as an auditor who is interested otherwise than as a member in any transaction of the company ; and no director or other officer of the company is eligible during his continuance in office.

(87.) The election of auditors shall be made by the company at their ordinary meeting in each year.

(88.) The remuneration of the first auditors shall be fixed by the directors ; that of subsequent auditors shall be fixed by the company in general meeting.

(89.) Any auditor shall be re-eligible on his quitting office.

(90.) If any casual vacancy occurs in the office of any auditor appointed by the company, the directors shall forthwith call an extraordinary general meeting for the purpose of supplying the same.

(91.) If no election of auditors is made in manner aforesaid the board of trade may, on the application of not less than five members of the company, appoint an auditor for the current year, and fix the remuneration to be paid to him by the company for his services.

(92.) Every auditor shall be supplied with a copy of the balance sheet, and it shall be his duty to examine the same, with the accounts and vouchers relating thereto.

(93.) Every auditor shall have a list delivered to him of all books kept by the company, and shall at all reasonable times have access to the books and accounts of the company : He may at the expense of the company, employ accountants or other persons to assist him in investigating such accounts, and he may in relation to such accounts examine the directors or any other officer of the company.

(94.) The auditors shall make a report to the members upon the balance sheet and accounts, and in every such report they shall state whether, in their opinion, the balance sheet is a full and fair balance sheet, containing the particulars required by these regulations, and properly drawn up so as to exhibit a true and correct view of the state of the company's affairs, and in case they have called for explanations or information from the directors, whether such explanations or information have been given by the directors, and whether they have been satisfactory ; and such report shall be read, together with the report of the directors, at the ordinary meeting.

(*q*) *Infra.*                      (*r*) Arts. (95)—(97).

*Notices.*

(95.) A notice may be served by the company upon any member either personally or by sending it through the post in a prepaid letter addressed to such member at his registered place of abode.

(96.) All notices directed to be given to the members shall with respect to any share to which persons are jointly entitled, be given to whichever of such persons is named first in the register of members ; and notice so given shall be sufficient notice to all the holders of such share.

(97.) Any notice, if served by post, shall be deemed to have been served at the time when the letter containing the same would be delivered in the ordinary course of the post ; and in proving such service it shall be sufficient to prove that the letter containing the notices was properly addressed and put into the post office.

Dr.     BALANCE SHEET of the     Co. made up to     18 *     Cr.

## CAPITAL AND LIABILITIES.

£ s. d. | £ s. d.

**I. CAPITAL**

Showing:
1. The Number of Shares
2. The Amount paid per Share
3. If any Arrears of Calls, the Nature of the Arrear, and the Names of the Defaulters.
4. The Particulars of any forfeited Shares

**II. DEBTS AND LIABILITIES of the Company.**

Showing:
5. The Amount of Loans on Mortgages or Debenture Bonds.
6. The ... of Debts owing by the Company, distinguishing—
 (a) Debts for which Acceptances have been given.
 (b) Debts to Tradesmen for Supplies of Stock in ... or ... Articles.
 (c) Debts for Law Expenses.
 (d) Debts for Interest on Debentures or other Loans.
 (e) Unclaimed Dividends.
 (f) Debts not enumerated above.

**VI. RESERVE FUND.**

Showing:
The ... set aside ... Profits to meet Contingencies.

**VII. PROFIT AND LOSS.**

Showing:
The disposable Balance for Payment of Dividend, &c.

**CONTINGENT LIABILITIES.**

Claims against the Company not acknowledged as Debts.
Monies for which the Company is contingently liable.

## PROPERTY AND ASSETS.

£ s. d. | £ s. d.

**III. PROPERTY held by the Company.**

Showing:
7. Immoveable Property, distinguishing—
 (a) Freehold Land
 (b) ,, Buildings
 (c) Leasehold
8. Moveable Property, distinguishing—
 (d) Stock in Trade
 (e) Plant
 The Cost to be stated with Deductions for Deterioration in Value as charged to the Reserve Fund or Profit and Loss.

**IV. DEBTS owing to the Company.**

Showing:
9. Debts ... good for which the Company hold Bills or other Securities.
10. Debts considered good for which the Company hold no Security.
11. Debts considered doubtful and bad.
 Any Debt due from a ... or other Officer of the Company to be separately stated.

**V. CASH AND INVESTMENTS.**

Showing:
12. The Nature of Investment and Rate of Interest.
13. The Amount of Cash, where lodged, and if bearing interest.

* See Art. (81).

## TABLE B (s).

TABLE OF FEES to be paid to the REGISTRAR OF JOINT STOCK COMPANIES by a Company having a Capital divided into Shares.

| | £ | s. | d. |
|---|---|---|---|
| For registration of a Company whose nominal capital (t) does not exceed 2,000l., a fee of .. .. .. .. .. .. .. | 2 | 0 | 0 |

For registration of a company whose nominal capital (t) exceeds 2,000l., the above fee of 2l., with the following additional fees, regulated according to the amount of nominal capital, (that is to say,)

| | £ | s. | d. |
|---|---|---|---|
| For every 1,000l. of nominal capital, or part of 1,000l., after the first 2,000l., up to 5,000l. .. | 1 | 0 | 0 |
| For every 1,000l. of nominal capital, or part of 1,000l., after the first 5,000l., up to 100,000l. .. | 0 | 5 | 0 |
| For every 1,000l., of nominal capital, or part of 1,000l. after the first 10,000l. .. .. .. .. | 0 | 1 | 0 |

For registration of any increase of capital made after the first registration of the company, the same fees per 1,000l., or part of 1,000l., as would have been payable if such increased capital had formed part of the original capital at the time of registration.

Provided that no company shall be liable to pay in respect of nominal capital on registration, or afterwards, any greater amount of fees than 50l., taking into account in the case of fees payable on an increase of capital after registration fees paid on registration.

For registration of any existing company, except such companies as are by this Act exempted from payment of fees in respect of registration under this Act, the same fee as is charged for registering a new company.

| | £ | s. | d. |
|---|---|---|---|
| For registering any document hereby required or authorized to be registered, other than the memorandum of association .. .. | 0 | 5 | 0 |
| For making a record of any fact hereby authorized or required to be recorded by the registrar of companies, a fee of .. .. | 0 | 5 | 0 |

---

## TABLE C.

TABLE OF FEES to be paid to the REGISTRAR OF JOINT STOCK COMPANIES by a Company not having a Capital divided into Shares.

| | £ | s. | d. |
|---|---|---|---|
| For registration of a company whose number of members as stated in the articles of association does not exceed 20 .. .. .. | 2 | 0 | 0 |
| For registration of a company whose number of members, as stated in the articles of association, exceeds 20, but does not exceed 100 | 5 | 0 | 0 |

For registration of a company, whose number of members, as stated in the articles of association, exceeds 100, but is not stated to be unlimited, the above fee of 5l., with an additional 5s. for every 50 members or less number than 50 members after the first 100.

| | £ | s. | d. |
|---|---|---|---|
| For registration of a company in which the number of members is stated in the articles of association to be unlimited, a fee of .. | 20 | 0 | 0 |
| For registration of an increase on the number of members made after the registration of the company in respect of every 50 members, or less than 50 members, of such increase .. .. .. | 0 | 5 | 0 |

Provided that no one company shall be liable to pay on the whole a greater fee than 20l. in respect of its number of members, taking into account the fee paid on the first registration of the company.

For registration of any existing company, except such companies as are by this Act exempted from payment of fees in respect of registration under this Act, the same fee as is charged for registering a new company.

| | £ | s. | d. |
|---|---|---|---|
| For registering any document hereby required or authorized to be registered, other than the memorandum of association . ... | 0 | 5 | 0 |
| For making a record of any fact hereby authorized or required to be recorded by the registrar of companies, a fee of .. .. | 0 | 5 | 0 |

(s) See sects. 17, 71.                         51 Vict. c. 8, s. 11 ; and 52 Vict. c. 7,
(t) See as to ad valorem stamp duty,     s. 16.

## FORM D (u).

FORM OF STATEMENT referred to in Part III. of the Act.

\* The capital of the company is ——, divided into —— shares of —— each. The number of shares issued is ——.

Calls to the amount of —— pounds per share have been made, under which the sum of —— pounds has been received.

The liabilities of the company on the first day of January [or July] were,—

Debts owing to sundry persons by the company :

On judgment, £——.
On specialty, £——.
On notes or bills, £——.
On simple contracts, £——.
On estimated liabilities £——.

The assets of the company on that day were,—

Government securities [stating them], £——.
Bills of exchange and promissory notes, £——.
Cash at the bankers, £——.
Other securities, £——.

\* If the company has no capital divided into shares the portion of the statement relating to capital and shares must be omitted.

---

## SECOND SCHEDULE.

### FORM A (v).

MEMORANDUM OF ASSOCIATION of a Company limited by Shares (x).

1st. The name of the company is "The Eastern Steam Packet Company Limited."

2nd. The registered office of the company will be situate in England.

3rd. The objects for which the company is established are "the conveyance of passengers and goods in ships or boats between such places as the company may from time to time determine, and the doing all such other things as are incidental or conducive to the attainment of the above object."

4th. The liability of the members is limited.

5th. The capital of the company is two hundred thousand pounds, divided into one thousand shares of two hundred pounds each.

WE, the several persons whose names and addresses are subscribed, are desirous of being formed into a company in pursuance of this memorandum of association, and we respectively agree to take the number of shares in the capital of the company set opposite our respective names.

| Names, Addresses, and Descriptions of Subscribers. | Number of Shares taken by each Subscriber. |
|---|---|
| "1. John Jones of ——, in the county of ——, merchant .. | 200 |
| "2. John Smith of ——, in the county of —— .. .. | 25 |
| "3. Thomas Green of ——, in the county of —— .. .. | 30 |
| "4. John Thompson of ——, in the county of —— .. .. | 40 |
| "5. Caleb White of ——, in the county of - —— .. .. | 15 |
| "6. Andrew Brown of ——, in the county of —— .. .. | 5 |
| "7. Cæsar White of ——, in the county of —— .. .. | 10 |
| Total shares taken .. .. .. | 325 |

Dated the 22nd day of November, 1861.

Witness to the above signatures,

A. B., No. 13, Hute Street, Clerkenwell, Middlesex.

(u) Sects. 44, 71.          (v) Sect. 71.          (x) Sect. 8.

## FORM B.

Memorandum and Articles of Association of a company limited by Guarantee, and not having a Capital divided into Shares (y).

### Memorandum of Association.

1st. The name of the company is " The Mutual London Marine Association Limited."

2nd. The registered office of the company will be situate in England.

3rd. The objects for which the company is established are, " the mutual insurance of ships belonging to members of the company, and the doing all such other things as are incidental or conducive to the attainment of the above objects."

4th. Every member of the company undertakes to contribute to the assets of the company in the event of the same being wound up during the time that he is a member, or within one year afterwards, for payment of the debts and liabilities of the company contracted before the time at which he ceases to be a member, and the costs, charges and expenses of winding up the same, and for the adjustment of the rights of the contributories amongst themselves, such amount as may be required not exceeding ten pounds.

We, the several persons whose names and addresses are subscribed, are desirous of being formed into a company, in pursuance of this memorandum of association.

Names, addresses, and descriptions of subscribers.

" 1. John Jones of ——, in the county of ——, merchant.
" 2. John Smith of ——, in the county of ——
" 3. Thomas Green of ——, in the county of ——
" 4. John Thompson of ——, in the county of ——
" 5. Caleb White of ——, in the county of ——
" 6. Andrew Brown of ——, in the county of ——
" 7. Cæsar White of ——, in the county of ——

Dated the 22nd day of November, 1861.

Witness to the above signatures,
A. B., No. 13, Hute Street, Clerkenwell, Middlesex.

———

Articles of Association to accompany preceding Memorandum of Association (z).

(1.) The company, for the purpose of registration, is declared to consist of five hundred members.

(2.) The directors hereinafter mentioned may, whenever the business of the association requires it, register an increase of members.

### Definition of Members.

(3.) Every person shall be deemed to have agreed to become a member of the company who insures any ship or share in a ship in pursuance of the regulations hereinafter contained.

### General Meetings.

(4.) The first general meeting shall be held at such time, not being more than three months after the incorporation of the company, and at such place as the directors may determine.

(5.) Subsequent general meetings shall be held at such time and place, as may be prescribed by the company in general meeting (a); and if no other time or place is prescribed, a general meeting shall be held on the first Monday in February in every year, at such place as may be determined by the directors.

(6.) The above-mentioned general meetings shall be called ordinary meetings; all other general meetings shall be called extraordinary.

(7.) The directors may, whenever they think fit, and they shall, upon a requisition made in writing by any five or more members, convene an extraordinary general meeting.

(8.) Any requisition made by the members shall express the object of the meeting proposed to be called, and shall be left at the registered office of the company.

(9.) Upon the receipt of such requisition the directors shall forthwith proceed to convene a general meeting: If they do not proceed to convene the same within twenty-one days from the date of the requisition, the requisitionists or any other five members may themselves convene a meeting.

*Proceedings at General Meetings.*

(10.) Seven days' notice at the least, specifying the place, the day and the hour of meeting, and in case of special business the general nature of such business, shall be given to the members in manner hereinafter mentioned or in such other manner (if any) as may be prescribed by the company in general meeting; but the non-receipt of such notice by any member shall not invalidate the proceedings at any general meeting.

(11.) All business shall be deemed special that is transacted at an extraordinary meeting, and all that is transacted at an ordinary meeting, with the exception of the consideration of the accounts, balance sheets, and the ordinary report of the directors.

(12.) No business shall be transacted at any meeting except the declaration of a dividend, unless a quorum of members is present at the commencement of such business; and such quorum shall be ascertained as follows; that is to say, if the members of the company at the time of the meeting do not exceed ten in number, the quorum shall be five; if they exceed ten there shall be added to the above quorum one for every five additional members up to fifty, and one for every ten additional members after fifty, with this limitation, that no quorum shall in any case exceed thirty.

(13.) If within one hour from the time appointed for the meeting a quorum of members is not present, the meeting if convened upon the requisition of the members, shall be dissolved: In any other case it shall stand adjourned to the same day in the following week at the same time and place; and if at such adjourned meeting a quorum of members is not present, it shall be adjourned sine die.

(14.) The chairman (if any) of the directors shall preside as chairman at every general meeting of the company.

(15.) If there is no such chairman, or if at any meeting he is not present at the time of holding the same, the members present shall choose some one of their number to be chairman of such meeting.

(16.) The chairman may, with the consent of the meeting, adjourn any meeting from time to time, and from place to place, but no business shall be transacted at any adjourned meeting other than the business left unfinished at the meeting from which the adjournment took place.

(17.) At any general meeting, unless a poll is demanded by at least five members, a declaration by the chairman that a resolution has been carried, and an entry to that effect in the book of proceedings of the company, shall be sufficient evidence of the fact, without proof of the number or proportion of the votes recorded in favour of or against such resolution.

(18.) If a poll is demanded in manner aforesaid, the same shall be taken in such manner as the chairman directs, and the result of such poll shall be deemed to be the resolution of the company in general meeting.

*Votes of Members.*

(19.) Every member shall have one vote and no more.

(20.) If any member is a lunatic or idiot he may vote by his committee, curator bonis, or other legal curator.

(21.) No member shall be entitled to vote at any meeting unless all monies due from him to the company have been paid

(22.) Votes may be given either personally or by proxies : A proxy shall be appointed in writing under the hand of the appointor, or if such appointor is a corporation under its common seal.

(23.) No person shall be appointed a proxy who is not a member, and the instrument appointing him shall be deposited at the registered office of the company not less than forty-eight hours before the time of holding the meeting at which he proposes to vote.

(24.) Any instrument appointing a proxy shall be in the following form :

—— Company Limited.

I —— of —— in the county of —— being a member of the —— Company Limited, hereby appoint —— of —— as my proxy, to vote for me and on my behalf at the [ordinary *or* extraordinary, *as the case may be*] general meeting of the company, to be held on the —— day of ——, and at any adjournment thereof to be held on the —— day of —— next [*or* at any meeting of the company that may be held in the year ——].

As witness my hand this —— day of ——.

Signed by the said —— in the presence of —— (*b*).

*Directors.*

(25.) The number of the directors, and the names of the first directors, shall be determined by the subscribers of the memorandum of association.

(26.) Until directors are appointed, the subscribers of the memorandum of the association shall for all the purposes of this Act be deemed to be directors.

*Powers of Directors.*

(27.) The business of the company shall be managed by the directors, who may exercise all such powers of the company as are not hereby required to be exercised by the company in general meeting ; but no regulation made by the company in general meeting shall invalidate any prior act of the directors which would have been valid if such regulation had not been made.

*Election of Directors.*

(28.) The directors shall be elected annually by the company in general meeting.

*Business of Company.*

[*Here insert rules as to mode in which business of insurance is to be conducted* (*c*).]

*Accounts.*

(29.) The accounts of the company shall be audited by a committee of five members, to be called the audit committee.

(30.) The first audit committee shall be nominated by the directors out of the body of members.

(31.) Subsequent audit committees shall be nominated by the members at the ordinary general meeting in each year.

(32.) The audit committee shall be supplied with a copy of the balance sheet, and it shall be their duty to examine the same with the accounts and vouchers relating thereto.

(33.) The audit committee shall have a list delivered to them of all books kept by the company, and they shall at all reasonable times have access to the books and accounts of the company ; they may, at the expense of the company, employ accountants or other persons to assist them in investigating such accounts, and they may in relation to such accounts examine the directors or any other officer of the company.

(*b*) See 33 & 34 Vict. c. 99, and s. 102 of the Stamp Act, 1870.

(*c*) Palmer's Company Precedents, 151.

(34.) The audit committee shall make a report to the members upon the balance sheet and accounts, and in every such report they shall state whether in their opinion the balance sheet is a full and fair balance sheet, containing the particulars required by these regulations of the company, and properly drawn up, so as to exhibit a true and correct view of the state of the company's affairs, and in case they have called for explanation or information from the directors, whether such explanations or information have been given by the directors, and whether they have been satisfactory, and such report shall be read together with the report of the directors at the ordinary meeting.

*Notices.*

(35.) A notice may be served by the company upon any member either personally, or by sending it through the post in a prepaid letter addressed to such member at his registered place of abode.

(36.) Any notice, if served by post, shall be deemed to have been served at the time when the letter containing the same would be delivered in the ordinary course of the post ; and in proving such service it shall be sufficient to prove that the letter containing the notice was properly addressed and put into the post office.

*Winding up.*

(37.) The company shall be wound up voluntarily whenever an extraordinary resolution, as defined by the Companies Act, 1862, is passed, requiring the company to be wound up voluntarily.

Names, addresses, and descriptions of subscribers.

"1. John Jones of ——, in the county of ——, merchant.
"2. John Smith of ——, in the county of ——
"3. Thomas Green of ——, in the county of ——
"4. John Thompson of ——, in the county of ——
"5. Caleb White of ——, in the county of ——
"6. Andrew Brown of ——, in the county of ——
"7. Cæsar White of ——, in the county of ——

Dated the 22nd day of November, 1861.
Witness to the above signatures,
A. B., No. 13, Hute Street, Clerkenwell, Middlesex.

———

FORM C.

MEMORANDUM AND ARTICLES OF ASSOCIATION of a company limited by Guarantee, and having a Capital divided into Shares (*d*).

*Memorandum of Association.*

1st. The name of the company is " The Highland Hotel Company, Limited."

2nd. The registered office of the company will be situate in Scotland.

3rd. The objects for which the company is established are " the facilitating travelling in the highlands of Scotland, by providing hotels and conveyances by sea and by land for the accommodation of travellers, and the doing all such other things as are incidental or conducive to the attainment of the above object."

4th. Every member of the company undertakes to contribute to the assets of the company in the event of the same being wound up during the time that he is a member, or within one year afterwards, for payment of the debts and liabilities of the company contracted before the time at which he ceases to be a member, and the costs, charges and expenses of winding up the same,

(*d*) Sects. 9, 14.

and for the adjustment of the rights of the contributories amongst themselves such amount as may be required not exceeding twenty pounds.

We, the several persons whose names and addresses are subscribed, are desirous of being formed into a company, in pursuance of this memorandum of association.

Names, addresses, and descriptions of subscribers.

" 1. John Jones of ——, in the county of ——, merchant.
" 2. John Smith of ——, in the county of ——
" 3. Thomas Green of ——, in the county of ——
" 4. John Thompson of ——, in the county of ——
" 5. Caleb White of ——, in the county of ——
" 6. Andrew Brown of ——, in the county of ——
" 7. Cæsar White of ——, in the county of ——

Dated the 22nd day of November, 1861.

Witness to the above signatures,
A. B., No. 13, Hute Street, Clerkenwell, Middlesex.

*Articles of Association to accompany preceding Memorandum of Association.*

1. The capital of the company shall consist of five hundred thousand pounds divided into five thousand shares of one hundred pounds each.

2. The directors may, with the sanction of the company in general meeting, reduce the amount of shares.

3. The directors may, with the sanction of the company in general meeting, cancel any shares belonging to the company.

4. All the articles of Table A shall be deemed to be incorporated with these articles, and to apply to the company.

We, the several persons whose names and addresses are subscribed, agree to take the number of shares in the capital of the company set opposite our respective names.

| Names, Addresses, and Descriptions of Subscribers. | Number of Shares taken by each Subscriber. |
|---|---|
| " 1. John Jones of ——, in the county of ——    ..    .. | 200 |
| " 2. John Smith of ——, in the county of ——    ...    .. | 25 |
| " 3. Thomas Green of ——, in the county of —— ..    .. | 30 |
| " 4. John Thompson of ——, in the county of ——    .. | 40 |
| " 5. Caleb White of ——, in the county of ——    ..    .. | 15 |
| " 6. Andrew Brown of ——, in the county of——..    .. | 5 |
| " 7. Cæsar White of ——, in the county of ——    ..    .. | 10 |
| Total shares taken    ..    ..    .. | 325 |

Dated the 22nd day of November, 1861.

Witness to the above signatures,
A. B., No. 13, Hute Street, Clerkenwell, Middlesex.

## FORM D.

MEMORANDUM AND ARTICLES OF ASSOCIATION of an unlimited Company, having a Capital divided into Shares (e).

*Memorandum of Association.*

1st. The name of the company is " The Patent Stereotype Company."

2nd. The registered office of the company will be situate in England.

3rd. The objects for which the company is established are " the working of a patent method of founding and casting stereotype plates, of which method John Smith of London, is the sole patentee."

We, the several persons whose names are subscribed, are desirous of being formed into a company, in pursuance of this Memorandum of Association.

Names, addresses, and descriptions of subscribers.

" 1. John Jones of ——, in the county of ——, merchant.

" 2. John Smith of ——, in the county of ——

" 3. Thomas Green of ——, in the county of ——

" 4. John Thompson of ——, in the county of ——

" 5. Caleb White of ——, in the county of ——

" 6. Andrew Brown of ——, in the county of ——

" 7. Abel Brown of ——, in the county of ——

Dated the 22nd day of November, 1861.

Witness to the above signatures,

A. B., No. 20, Bond Street, Middlesex.

*Articles of Association to accompany the preceding Memorandum of Association.*

### Capital of the Company.

The capital of the company is two thousand pounds divided into twenty shares of one hundred pounds each.

### Application of Table A.

All the articles of Table A. shall be deemed to be incorporated with these articles, and to apply to the company.

We, the several persons whose names and addresses are subscribed, agree to take the number of shares in the capital of the company set opposite our respective names.

| Names, Addresses, and Descriptions of Subscribers. | Number of Shares taken by each Subscriber. |
|---|---|
| " 1. John Jones of ——, in the county of ——, merchant.. | 1 |
| " 2. John Smith of ——, in the county of —— | 5 |
| " 3. Thomas Green of ——, in the county of —— | 2 |
| " 4. John Thompson of ——, in the county of —— | 2 |
| " 5. Caleb White of ——, in the county of —— | 3 |
| " 6. Andrew Brown of ——, in the county of —— | 4 |
| " 7. Abel Brown of ——, in the county of —— | 1 |
| Total shares taken | 18 |

Dated the 22nd day of November, 1861.

Witness to the above signatures,

A. B., No. 20, Bond Street, Middlesex.

(e) Sects. 10, 14.

FORM E. as required by the Second Part of the Act (*f*).

SUMMARY OF CAPITAL AND SHARES of the —— COMPANY, made up to the —— day of ——.

Nominal capital £——, divided into —— shares of £—— each.
Number of shares taken up to the —— day of ——.
There has been called up on each share £——.
Total amount of calls received £——.
Total amount of calls unpaid £——.

LIST OF PERSONS holding shares in the —— company on the —— day of ——, and of persons who have held shares thereon at any time during the year immediately preceding the said —— day of ——, showing their names and addresses, and an account of the shares so held.

| Folio in Register Ledger containing Particulars. | NAMES, ADDRESSES AND OCCUPATIONS. | | | | ACCOUNT OF SHARES. | | | | | | Remarks. |
|---|---|---|---|---|---|---|---|---|---|---|---|
| | Surname. | Christian Name. | Address. | Occupation. | Shares held by existing Members on the —— day of ——. | Additional Shares held by existing Members during preceding year. | | Shares held by Persons no longer Members. | | | |
| | | | | | | Number. | Date of Transfer. | Number. | Date of Transfer. | | |
| | | | | | | | | | | | |

## FORM F.

### LICENCE to hold LANDS (*g*).

The lords of the committee of privy council appointed for the consideration of matters relating to trade and foreign plantations hereby license the —— association, limited, to hold the lands hereunder described [*insert description of lands*]. The conditions of this licence are [*insert conditions, if any*].

## THIRD SCHEDULE.

### FIRST PART (*h*).

*(Repeals certain Acts enumerated.)*

### SECOND PART (*h*).

#### 7 & 8 Vict. c. 113, s. 47.

Existing companies to have the powers of suing and being sued.

Every company of more than six persons established on the sixth day of May, one thousand eight hundred and forty-four, for the purpose of carrying on the trade or business of bankers within the distance of sixty-five miles from London, and not within the provisions of the Act passed in the session holden in the seventh and eighth years of the reign of her present Majesty, chapter one hundred and thirteen, shall have the same powers and privileges

(*f*) Sect. 26.        (*g*) Sect. 21.        (*h*) Sect. 205.

of suing and being sued in the name of any one of the public officers of such copartnership as the nominal plaintiff, petitioner or defendant on behalf of such copartnership; and all judgments, decrees and orders made and obtained in any such suit may be enforced in like manner as is provided with respect to such companies carrying on the said trade or business at any place in England exceeding the distance of sixty-five miles from London, under the provisions of an Act passed in the seventh year of the reign of King George the Fourth, chapter forty-six, intituled "An Act for the better regulating Copartnerships of certain Bankers in England, and for amending so much of an Act of the thirty-ninth and fortieth years of the reign of his late Majesty King George the Third, intituled 'An Act for establishing an Agreement with the Governor and Company of the Bank of England for advancing the Sum of Three Millions towards the Supply for the Service of the Year One thousand eight hundred,' as relates to the same," provided that such first-mentioned company shall make out and deliver from time to time to the Commissioners of Stamps and Taxes the several accounts or returns required by the last-mentioned Act, and all the provisions of the last-recited Act, as to such accounts or returns shall be taken to apply to the accounts or returns so made out and delivered by such first mentioned companies as if they had been originally included in the provisions of the last-recited Act.

## 20 & 21 Vict. c. 49, Part of Section XII.

Notwithstanding anything contained in any Act passed in the session holden in the seventh and eighth years of the reign of her present Majesty, chapter one hundred and thirteen, and intituled "An Act to regulate Joint Stock Banks in England," or in any other Act, it shall be lawful for any number of persons, not exceeding ten, to carry on in partnership the business of banking, in the same manner and upon the same conditions in all respects as any company of not more than six persons could before the passing of this Act have carried on such business.

*Power to form banking partnerships of ten persons.*

------

## 28 & 29 VICT. C. 86.

### *An Act to amend the Law of Partnership.*
[*5th July*, 1865.]

WHEREAS it is expedient to amend the law relating to partnership: Be it therefore enacted by the Queen's most excellent Majesty, by and with the advice and consent of the Lords spiritual and temporal, and Commons, in this present Parliament assembled, and by the authority of the same, as follows:

1. The advance of money by way of loan to a person engaged or about to engage in any trade or undertaking upon a contract in writing with such person that the lender shall receive a rate of interest varying with the profits, or shall receive a share of the profits arising from carrying on such trade or undertaking, shall not, of itself, constitute the lender a partner with the person or the persons carrying on such trade or undertaking, or render him responsible as such.

*The advance of money on contract to receive a share of profits not to constitute the lender a partner.*

2. No contract for the remuneration of a servant or agent of any person engaged in any trade or undertaking by a share of the profits of such trade or undertaking shall of itself render such servant or agent responsible as a partner therein, nor give him the rights of a partner.

*The remuneration of agents, &c., by share of profits not to make them partners.*

3. No person being the widow or child of the deceased partner of a trader, and receiving by way of annuity a portion of the profits made by such trader in his business, shall, by reason only of such receipt, be deemed to be a partner of or to be subject to any liabilities incurred by such trader.

*Certain annuitants not to be deemed partners.*

4. No person receiving by way of annuity or otherwise a portion of the profits of any business, in consideration of the sale by him of the goodwill of such business, shall, by reason only of such receipt, be deemed to be a

*Receipt of profits in consideration of sale of good-*

partner of or be subject to the liabilities of the person carrying on such business.

**5.** In the event of any such trader as aforesaid being adjudged a bankrupt, or taking the benefit of any Act for the relief of insolvent debtors, or entering into an arrangement to pay his creditors less than twenty shillings in the pound, or dying in insolvent circumstances, the lender of any such loan as aforesaid shall not be entitled to recover any portion of his principal, or of the profits or interest payable in respect of such loan, nor shall any such vendor of a goodwill as aforesaid be entitled to recover any such profits as aforesaid until the claims of the other creditors of the said trader for valuable consideration in money or money's worth have been satisfied.

**6.** In the construction of this Act the word "person" shall include a partnership firm, a joint stock company, and a corporation.

---

## 30 Vict. c. 29.

*An Act to amend the Law in respect of the Sale and Purchase of Shares in Joint Stock Banking Companies.*

[*17th June,* 1867.]

WHEREAS it is expedient to make provision for the prevention of contracts for the sale and purchase of shares and stock in Joint Stock Banking Companies of which the sellers are not possessed or over which they have no control :

May it therefore please your Majesty that it may be enacted ; and be it enacted by the Queen's most excellent Majesty, by and with the advice and consent of the Lords spiritual and temporal, and Commons, in this present Parliament assembled, and by the authority of the same :

**1.** That all contracts, agreements, and tokens of sale and purchase which shall, from and after the first day of July, one thousand eight hundred and sixty-seven, be made or entered into for the sale or transfer, or purporting to be for the sale or transfer, of any share or shares, or of any stock or other interest, in any Joint Stock Banking Company in the United Kingdom of Great Britain and Ireland constituted under or regulated by the provisions of any Act of Parliament, Royal Charter, or letters patent, issuing shares or stock transferable by any deed or written instrument, shall be null and void to all intents and purposes whatsoever, unless such contract, agreement, or other token shall set forth and designate in writing such shares, stock, or interest by the respective numbers by which the same are distinguished at the making of such contract, agreement. or token on the register or books of such banking company as aforesaid, or where there is no such register of shares or stock by distinguishing numbers, then unless such contract, agreement, or other token shall set forth the person or persons in whose name or names such shares, stock, or interest shall at the time of making such contract stand as the registered proprietor thereof in the books of such banking company ; and every person, whether principal, broker, or agent, who shall wilfully insert in any such contract, agreement, or other token any false entry of such numbers, or any name or names other than that of the person or persons in whose name such shares, stock, or interest shall stand as aforesaid, shall be guilty of a misdemeanor, and be punished accordingly, and, if in Scotland, shall be guilty of an offence punishable by fine or imprisonment.

**2.** Joint Stock Banking Companies shall be bound to show their list of shareholders to any registered shareholder during business hours, from ten of the clock to four of the clock.

**3.** This Act shall not extend to shares or stock in the Bank of England or the Bank of Ireland.

30 & 31 VICT. C. 131.

*An Act to amend The Companies Act, 1862.*

[*20th August, 1867.*]

BE it enacted by the Queen's most excellent Majesty, by and with the advice and consent of the Lords spiritual and temporal, and Commons, in this present Parliament assembled, and by the authority of the same, as follows:

### Preliminary.

*Preliminary.*

1. This Act may be cited for all purposes as "The Companies Act, 1867."    *Short title.*

2. The Companies Act, 1862, is hereinafter referred to as "The Principal Act;" and the principal Act and this Act are hereinafter distinguished as and may be cited for all purposes as "The Companies Acts, 1862 and 1867;" and this Act shall, so far as is consistent with the tenor thereof, be construed as one with the principal Act; and the expression "this Act" in the principal Act, and any expression referring to the principal Act which occurs in any Act or other document, shall be construed to mean the principal Act as amended by this Act.    *Act to be construed as one with 25 & 26 Vict. c. 89.*

3. This Act shall come into force on the first day of September one thousand eight hundred and sixty-seven, which date is hereinafter referred to as the commencement of this Act.    *Commencement of Act.*

### Unlimited Liability of Directors.

*Unlimited Liability of Directors.*

4. Where after the commencement of this Act a company is formed as a limited company under the principal Act, the liability of the directors or managers of such company, or the managing director, may, if so provided by the memorandum of association, be unlimited.    *Company may have directors with unlimited liability.*

5. The following modifications shall be made in the thirty-eighth section of the principal Act, with respect to the contributions to be required in the event of the winding up of a limited company under the principal Act, from any director or manager whose liability is, in pursuance of this Act, unlimited:    *Liability of director, past and present, where liability is unlimited.*

  (1.) Subject to the provisions hereinafter contained, any such director or manager, whether past or present, shall, in addition to his liability (if any) to contribute as an ordinary member, be liable to contribute as if he were at the date of the commencement of such winding up a member of an unlimited company:

  (2.) No contribution required from any past director or manager who has ceased to hold such office for a period of one year or upwards prior to the commencement of the winding up shall exceed the amount (if any) which he is liable to contribute as an ordinary member of the company:

  (3.) No contribution required from any past director or manager in respect of any debt or liability of the company contracted after the time at which he ceased to hold such office shall exceed the amount (if any) which he is liable to contribute as an ordinary member of the company:

  (4.) Subject to the provisions contained in the regulations of the company no contribution required from any director or manager shall exceed the amount (if any) which he is liable to contribute as an ordinary member, unless the court deems it necessary to require such contribution in order to satisfy the debts and liabilities of the company, and the costs, charges, and expenses of the winding up.

6. In the event of the winding up of any limited company, the court, if it think fit, may make to any director or manager of such company whose liability is unlimited the same allowance by way of set-off as under the one hundred and first section of the principal Act it may make to a contributory where the company is not limited.    *Director with unlimited liability may have set-off as under sect. 101 of 25 & 26 Vict. c. 89.*

7. In any limited company in which, in pursuance of this Act, the liability of a director or manager is unlimited, the directors or managers of the company (if any), and the member who proposes any person for election or ap-    *Notice to be given to director on his election*

*Unlimited Liability of Directors.*

*that his liability will be unlimited.*

pointment to such office, shall add to such proposal a statement that the liability of the person holding such office will be unlimited, and the promoters, directors, managers, and secretary (if any) of such company, or one of them, shall, before such person accepts such office or acts therein, give him notice in writing that his liability will be unlimited.

If any director, manager, or proposer make default in adding such statement, or if any promoter, director, manager, or secretary make default in giving such notice, he shall be liable to a penalty not exceeding one hundred pounds, and shall also be liable for any damage which the person so elected or appointed may sustain from such default, but the liability of the person elected or appointed shall not be affected by such default.

*Existing limited company may, by special resolution, make liability of directors unlimited.*

**8.** Any limited company under the principal Act, whether formed before or after the commencement of this Act, may, by a special resolution (a), if authorized so to do by its regulations, as originally framed or as altered by special resolution, from time to time modify the conditions contained in its memorandum of association so far as to render unlimited the liability of its directors or managers, or of the managing director ; and such special resolution shall be of the same validity as if it had been originally contained in the memorandum of association, and a copy thereof shall be embodied in or annexed to every copy of the memorandum of association which is issued after the passing of the resolution, and any default in this respect shall be deemed to be a default in complying with the provisions of the fifty-fourth section of the principal Act, and shall be punished accordingly.

## Reduction of Capital (b) and Shares.

*Reduction of Capital and Shares.*

*Power to company to reduce capital.*

**9.** Any company limited by shares may, by special resolution, so far modify the conditions contained in its memorandum of association, if authorized so to do by its regulations as originally framed or as altered by special resolution, as to reduce its capital (b) ; but no such resolution for reducing the capital of any company shall come into operation until an order of the court is registered by the Registrar of Joint Stock Companies, as is hereinafter mentioned (c).

*Company to add "and reduced" to its name for a limited period.*

**10.** The company shall, after the date of the passing of any special resolution for reducing its capital add to its name, until such date as the court may fix, the words "and reduced" (d), as the last words in its name, and those words shall, until such date, be deemed to be part of the name of the company within the meaning of the principal Act.

*Company to apply to the court for an order confirming reduction.*

**11.** A company which has passed a special resolution for reducing its capital, may apply to the court by petition for an order confirming the reduction, and on the hearing of the petition the court, if satisfied that with respect to every creditor of the company who under the provisions of this Act is entitled to object to the reduction, either his consent to the reduction has been obtained, or his debt or claim has been discharged or has determined, or has been secured as hereinafter provided (e), may make an order confirming the reduction on such terms and subject to such conditions as it deems fit.

*Definition of the court.*

**12.** The expression "the court," shall in this Act mean the court which has jurisdiction to make an order for winding up the petitioning company, and the eighty-first and eighty-third sections of the principal Act shall be construed as if the term "winding-up" in those sections included proceedings under this Act, and the court, may in any proceedings under this Act make such order as to costs as it deems fit.

*Creditors may object to reduction, and list of objecting creditors to be settled by the court.*

**13.** Where a company proposes to reduce its capital, every creditor of the company who at the date fixed by the court is entitled to any debt or claim which, if that date of the commencement of the winding up of the company would be admissible in proof against the company (f) shall be entitled to object to the proposed reduction, and to be entered in the list of creditors who are so entitled to object.

The court shall settle a list of such creditors, and for that purpose shall

---

(a) 25 & 26 Vict. c. 89, s. 51, *supra.*
(b) See 40 & 41 Vict. c. 26, s. 3, *infra.*
(c) *Infra,* s. 15.

(d) But see 40 & 41 Vict. c. 26, s. 4 (2), *infra.*
(e) *Infra,* s. 14.
(f) 25 & 26 Vict. c. 89, s. 158, *supra.*

ascertain as far as possible without requiring an application from any creditor the name of such creditors and the nature and amount of their debts or claims, and may publish notices fixing a certain day or days within which creditors of the company who are not entered on the list are to claim to be so entered or to be excluded from the right of objecting to the proposed reduction. *Reduction of Capital and Shares.*

14. Where a creditor whose name is entered on the list of creditors, and whose debt or claim is not discharged or determined, does not consent to the proposed reduction, the court may (if it think fit) dispense with such consent on the company securing the payment of the debt or claim of such creditor by setting apart and appropriating in such manner as the court may direct, a sum of such amount as is hereinafter mentioned : (that is to say,) Court may dispense with consent of creditor on security being given for his debt.

    (1.) If the full amount of the debt or claim of the creditor is admitted by the company, or, though not admitted, is such as the company are willing to set apart and appropriate, then the full amount of the debt or claim shall be set apart and appropriated.

    (2.) If the full amount of the debt or claim of the creditor is not admitted by the company, and is not such as the company are willing to set apart and appropriate, or if the amount is contingent or not ascertained, then the court may, if it think fit, inquire into and adjudicate upon the validity of such debt or claim, and the amount for which the company may be liable in respect thereof, in the same manner as if the company were being wound up by the court, and the amount fixed by the court on such inquiry and adjudication shall be set apart and appropriated.

15. The Registrar of Joint Stock Companies, upon the production to him of an order of the court confirming the reduction of the capital of a company, and the delivery to him of a copy of the order and of a minute (approved by the court), showing with respect to the capital of the company, as altered by the order, the amount of such capital, the number of shares in which it is to be divided, and the amount of each share (*g*), shall register the order and minute, and on the registration the special resolution confirmed by the order so registered shall take effect. Order and minute to be registered.

Notice of such registration shall be published in such manner as the court may direct.

The registrar shall certify under his hand the registration of the order and minute, and his certificate shall be conclusive evidence that all the requisitions of this Act with respect to the reduction of capital have been complied with and that the capital of the company is such as is stated in the minute.

16. The minute when registered shall be deemed to be substituted for the corresponding part of the memorandum of association of the company, and shall be of the same validity and subject to the same alterations as if it had been originally contained in the memorandum of association ; and, subject as in this Act mentioned, no member of the company, whether past or present, shall be liable in respect of any share to any call or contribution exceeding in amount the difference (if any) between the amount which has been paid on such share and the amount of the share as fixed by the minute. Minute to form part of memorandum of association.

17. If any creditor who is entitled in respect of any debt or claim to object to the reduction of the capital of a company under this Act is, in consequence of his ignorance of the proceeding taken with a view to such reduction, or of their nature and effect with respect to his claim, not entered on the list of creditors, and after such reduction the company is unable, within the meaning of the eightieth section of the principal Act, to pay to the creditor the amount of such debt or claim, every person who was a member of the company at the date of the registration of the order and minute relating to the reduction of the capital of the company, shall be liable to contribute for the payment of such debt or claim an amount not exceeding the amount which he would have been liable to contribute if the company had commenced to be wound up on the day prior to such registration, and on the company being wound up, the court, on the application of such creditor, and on proof that he was ignorant of the proceedings taken with a view to the reduction, or of their nature and effect with respect to his claim, may, if it think fit, settle a list of such contributories accordingly, and make and enforce calls and orders on the contributories settled on such list in the same Saving of rights of creditors who are ignorant of proceedings.

(*g*) See 40 & 41 Vict. c. 26, s. 4, *infra.*

*Reduction of Capital and Shares.*

manner in all respects as if they were ordinary contributories in a winding up; but the provisions of this section shall not affect the rights of the contributories of the company among themselves.

Copy of registered minute.

**18.** A minute when registered shall be embodied in every copy of the memorandum of association issued after its registration; and if any company makes default in complying with the provisions of this section it shall incur a penalty not exceeding one pound for each copy in respect of which such default is made, and every director and manager of the company who shall knowingly and wilfully authorize or permit such default shall incur the like penalty.

Penalty on concealment of name of creditor.

**19.** If any director, manager, or officer of the company wilfully conceals the name of any creditor of the company who is entitled to object to the proposed reduction, or wilfully misrepresents the nature or amount of the debt or claim of any creditor of the company, or if any director or manager of the company aids or abets in or is privy to any such concealment or misrepresentation as aforesaid, every such director, manager, or officer shall be guilty of a misdemeanor.

Power to make rules extended to making rules concerning matters in this Act.

**20.** The powers of making rules concerning winding up conferred by the [one hundred and seventieth](h) one hundred and seventy-first, one hundred and seventy-second, and one hundred and seventy-third sections of the principal Act shall respectively extend to making rules concerning matters in which jurisdiction is by this Act given to the court which has the power of making an order to wind up a company, and until such rules are made the practice of the court in matters of the same nature shall, so far as the same is applicable, be followed.

*Subdivision of Shares.*

## Subdivision of Shares.

Shares may be divided into shares of smaller amount.

**21.** Any company limited by shares may by special resolution so far modify the conditions contained in its memorandum of association, if authorized so to do by its regulations as originally framed or as altered by special resolution, as by subdivision of its existing shares or any of them, to divide its capital, or any part thereof, into shares of smaller amount than is fixed by its memorandum of association (i).

Provided, that in the subdivision of the existing shares the proportion between the amount which is paid and the amount (if any) which is unpaid on each share of reduced amount shall be the same as it was in the case of the existing share or shares from which the share of reduced amount is derived.

Special resolution to be embodied in memorandum of association.

**22.** The statement of the number and amount of the shares into which the capital of the company is divided contained in every copy of the memorandum of association issued after the passing of any such special resolution, shall be in accordance with such resolution; and any company which makes default in complying with the provisions of this section shall incur a penalty not exceeding one pound for each copy in respect of which such default is made; and every director and manager of the company who knowingly or wilfully authorizes or permits such default shall incur the like penalty.

*Associations not for Profit.*

## Associations not for Profit.

Special provisions as to associations formed for purposes not of gain.

**23.** Where any association is about to be formed under the principal Act as a limited company, if it proves to the Board of Trade that it is formed for the purpose of promoting commerce, art, science, religion, charity, or any other useful object, and that it is the intention of such association to apply the profits, if any, or other income of the association, in promoting its objects, and to prohibit the payment of any dividend to the members of the association, the Board of Trade may by licence, under the hand of one of the secretaries or assistant secretaries, direct such association to be registered with limited liability, without the addition of the word limited to its name (k), and such association may be registered accordingly, and upon registration shall enjoy all the privileges and be subject to the obligations by this Act imposed on limited companies, with the exceptions that none of the provisions of this Act that require a limited company to use the word

---

(h) Words within brackets repealed by 44 & 45 Vict. c. 59.

(i) See 25 & 26 Vict. c. 89, s. 12.
(k) *Ibid.*, s. 8.

lïmited as any part of its name, or to publish its name, or to send a list o f its members, directors, or managers to the registrar, shall apply to an association so registered. *Associations not for Profit.*

The licence by the Board of Trade may be granted upon such conditions and subject to such regulations as the Board think fit to impose, and such conditions and regulations shall be binding on the association, and may, at the option of the said Board, be inserted in the memorandum and articles of association, or in both or one of such documents.

### Calls upon Shares.

*Calls upon Shares.*

**24.** Nothing contained in the principal Act shall be deemed to prevent any company under that Act, if authorized by its regulations as originally framed or as altered by special resolution, from doing any one or more of the following things : namely,— *Company may have some shares fully paid and others not.*

(1.) Making arrangements on the issue of shares for a difference between the holders of such shares in the amount of calls to be paid, and in the time of payment of such calls :

(2.) Accepting from any member of the company who assents thereto the whole or a part of the amount remaining unpaid on any share or shares held by him, either in discharge of the amount of a call payable in respect of any other share or shares held by him or without any call having been made :

(3.) Paying dividend in proportion to the amount paid up on each share in cases where a larger amount is paid upon some shares than on others.

**25.** Every share in any company shall be deemed and taken to have been issued and to be held subject to the payment of the whole amount thereof in cash, unless the same shall have been otherwise determined by a contract duly made in writing, and filed with the Registrar of Joint Stock Companies at or before the issue of such shares. *Manner in which shares are to be issued and held.*

### Transfer of Shares.

*Transfer of Shares.*

**26.** A company shall on the application of a transferor of any share or interest in the company enter in its register of members the name of the transferee of such share or interest, in the same manner and subject to the same conditions as if the application for such entry were made by the transferee (*l*). *Transfer may be registered at request of transferor.*

### Share Warrants to Bearer.

*Share Warrants to Bearer.*

**27.** In the case of a company limited by shares the company, if authorized so to do by its regulations as originally framed, or as altered by special resolution, and subject to the provisions of such regulations, may, with respect to any share which is fully paid up, or with respect to stock, issue under their common seal a warrant stating that the bearer of the warrant is entitled to the share or shares or stock therein specified, and may provide by coupons or otherwise, for the payment of the future dividends on the share or shares or stock included in such warrant, hereinafter referred to as a share warrant. *Warrant of limited shares fully paid up may be issued in name of bearer.*

**28.** A share warrant shall entitle the bearer of such warrant to the shares or stock specified in it, and such shares or stock may be transferred by the delivery of the share warrant. *Effect of share warrant.*

**29.** The bearer of a share warrant shall, subject to the regulations of the company, be entitled, on surrendering such warrant for cancellation, to have his name entered as a member in the register of members, and the company shall be responsible for any loss incurred by any person by reason of the company entering in its register of members the name of any bearer of a share warrant in respect of the shares or stock specified therein without the share warrant being surrendered and cancelled. *Re-registration of bearer of a share warrant in the register.*

**30.** The bearer of a share warrant may, if the regulations of the company so provide, be deemed to be a member of the company within the meaning of the principal Act (*m*), either to the full extent or for such purposes as may be prescribed by the regulations : *Regulations of the company may make the bearer of a share warrant a member.*

---

(*l*) 25 & 26 Vict. c. 89, s. 22.　　(*m*) *Ibid.* s. 23.　See Palmer's Company Precedents, 128.

*Share Warrants to Bearer.*

Provided that the bearer of a share warrant shall not be qualified in respect of the shares or stock specified in such warrant for being a director or manager of the company in cases where such a qualification is prescribed by the regulations of the company.

Entries in register where share warrants issued.

31. On the issue of a share warrant in respect of any share or stock the company shall strike out of its register of members the name of the member then entered therein as holding such share or stock as if he had ceased to be a member, and shall enter in the register the following particulars :

(1.) The fact of the issue of the warrant :

(2.) A statement of the shares or stock included in the warrant, distinguishing each share by its number :

(3.) The date of the issue of the warrant :

And until the warrant is surrendered the above particulars shall be deemed to be the particulars which are required by the twenty-fifth section of the principal Act to be entered in the register of members of a company ; and on the surrender of a warrant the date of such surrender shall be entered as if it were the date at which a person ceased to be a member.

Particulars to be contained in annual summary.

32. After the issue by the company of a share warrant the annual summary required by the twenty-sixth section of the principal Act shall contain the following particulars : the total amount of shares or stock for which share warrants are outstanding at the date of the summary, and the total amount of share warrants which have been issued and surrendered respectively since the last summary was made, and the number of shares or amount of stock comprised in each warrant.

Stamps on share warrants.

33. There shall be charged on every share warrant a stamp duty of an amount equal to three times the amount of the *ad valorem* stamp duty which would be chargeable on a deed transferring the share or shares or stock specified in the warrant, if the consideration for the transfer were the nominal value of such share or shares or stock (*n*).

Penalties on persons committing forgery.

34. Whosoever forges or alters, or offers, utters, disposes of, or puts off, knowing the same to be forged or altered, any share warrant or coupon, or any document purporting to be a share warrant or coupon, issued in pursuance of this Act, or demands or endeavours to obtain or receive any share or interest of or in any company under the principal Act, or to receive any dividend or money payable in respect thereof, by virtue of any such forged or altered share warrant, coupon, or document, purporting as aforesaid, knowing the same to be forged or altered, with intent in any of the cases aforesaid to defraud, shall be guilty of felony, and being convicted thereof shall be liable, at the discretion of the court, to be kept in penal servitude for life or for any term not less than five years, or to be imprisoned for any term not exceeding two years, with or without hard labour, and with or without solitary confinement.

Penalties on persons falsely personating owner of shares.

35. Whosoever falsely and deceitfully personates any owner of any share or interest of or in any company, or of any share warrant or coupon issued in pursuance of this Act, and thereby obtains or endeavours to obtain any such share or interest, or share warrant or coupon, or receives or endeavours to receive any money due to any such owner, as if such offender were the true and lawful owner, shall be guilty of felony, and being convicted thereof shall be liable, at the discretion of the court, to be kept in penal servitude for life or for any term not less than five years, or to be imprisoned for any term not exceeding two years, with or without hard labour, and with or without solitary confinement.

Penalties on persons engraving plates, &c.

36. Whosoever, without lawful authority or excuse, the proof whereof shall be on the party accused, engraves or makes upon any plate, wood, stone, or other material, any share warrant or coupon purporting to be a share warrant or coupon issued or made by any particular company under and in pursuance of this Act, or to be a blank share warrant or coupon issued or made as aforesaid, or to be a part of such share warrant or coupon, or uses any such plate, wood, stone, or other material, for the making or printing any such share warrant or coupon, or any such blank share warrant or coupon, or any part thereof respectively, or knowingly has in his custody or possession any such plate, wood, stone, or other material, shall be guilty of felony, and being convicted thereof shall be liable, at the discretion of the

(*n*) By 33 & 34 Vict. c. 127, a penalty of 50*l.* is imposed for issuing a share warrant not duly stamped.

court, to be kept in penal servitude for any term not exceeding fourteen years and not less than five years, or to be imprisoned for any term not exceeding two years, with or without hard labour, and with or without solitary confinement.

*Share Warrants to Bearer.*

### Contracts.

*Contracts.*

**37.** Contracts on behalf of any company under the principal Act may be made as follows ; (that is to say,)

Contracts, how made.

(1.) Any contract which if made between private persons would be by law required to be in writing, and if made according to English law to be under seal, may be made on behalf of the company in writing under the common seal of the company, and such contract may be in the same manner varied or discharged :

(2.) Any contract which if made between private persons would be by law required to be in writing, and signed by the parties to be charged therewith, may be made on behalf of .the company in writing signed by any person acting under the express or implied authority of the company, and such contract may in the same manner be varied or discharged :

(3.) Any contract which if made between private persons would by law be valid although made by parol only, and not reduced into writing, may be made by parol on behalf of the company by any person acting under the express or implied authority of the company, and such contract may in the same way be varied or discharged :

And all contracts made according to the provisions herein contained shall be effectual in law, and shall be binding upon the company and their successors and all other parties thereto, their heirs, executors, or administrators, as the case may be.

**38.** Every prospectus of a company, and every notice inviting persons to subscribe for shares in any joint stock company, shall specify the dates and the names of the parties to any contract entered into by the company, or the promoters, directors, or trustees thereof, before the issue of such prospectus or notice, whether subject to adoption by the directors or the company, or otherwise ; and any prospectus or notice not specifying the same shall be deemed fraudulent on the part of the promoters, directors, and officers of the company knowingly issuing the same, as regards any person taking shares in the company on the faith of such prospectus, unless he shall have had notice of such contract.

Prospectus, &c., to specify dates and names of parties to any contracts made prior to issue of such prospectus, &c.

### Meetings.

*Meetings.*

**39.** Every company formed under the principal Act after the commencement of this Act shall hold a general meeting within four months after its memorandum of association is registered ; and if such meeting is not held the company shall be liable to a penalty not exceeding five pounds a day for every day after the expiration of such four months until the meeting is held ; and every director or manager of the company, and every subscriber of the memorandum of association, who knowingly authorizes or permits such default, shall be liable to the same penalty.

Company to hold meeting within four months after registration.

### Winding-up.

*Winding-up.*

**40.** No contributory of a company under the principal Act shall be capable of presenting a petition for winding-up such company (*o*) unless the shares in respect of which he is a contributory, or some of them, either were originally allotted to him or have been held by him, and registered in his name, for a period of at least six months during the eighteen months previously to the commencement of the winding-up, or have devolved upon him through the death of a former holder :

Contributory when not qualified to present winding-up petition.

Provided that where a share has during the whole or any part of the six months been held by or registered in the name of the wife of a contributory either before or after her marriage, or by or in the name of any trustee or trustees for such wife or for the contributory, such share shall for the purposes of this section be deemed to have been held by and registered in the name of the contributory.

**41.** Where the High Court of Chancery in England makes an order for winding-up a company under the principal Act, it may, if it thinks fit, direct all subsequent proceedings to be had in a county court held under an Act of

Winding-up may be referred to county court.

(*o*) 25 & 26 Vict. c. 89, s. 82.

the session of the ninth and tenth years of the reign of her present Majesty chapter ninety-five, and the Acts amending the same; and thereupon such county court shall, for the purpose of winding-up the company, be deemed to be "the court" within the meaning of the principal Act (*p*), and shall have, for the purposes of such winding-up, all the jurisdiction and powers of the High Court of Chancery.

**As to transfer of suit from one county court to another.**

**42.** If during the progress of a winding-up it is made to appear to the High Court of Chancery that the same could be more conveniently prosecuted in any other county court, it shall be competent for the High Court of Chancery to transfer the same to such other county court, and thereupon the winding-up shall proceed in such other county court.

**Parties aggrieved may appeal.**

**43.** If any party in a winding-up under this Act is dissatisfied with the determination or direction of a judge of a county court on any matter in such winding-up, such party may appeal (*q*) from the same to the Vice-Chancellor named for that purpose by the Lord Chancellor by general order; provided that such party shall, within thirty days after such determination or direction, give notice of such appeal to the other party or his attorney, and also deposit with the registrar of the county court the sum of ten pounds as security for the costs of the appeal; and the said court of appeal may make such final or other decree or order as it thinks fit, and may also make such order with respect to the costs of the said appeal as such court may think proper, and such orders shall be final.

**Powers to frame rules and orders under sect. 32 of 19 & 20 Vict. c. 108.**

**44.** The county court judges appointed or to be appointed by the Lord Chancellor from time to time to frame rules and orders for regulating the practice of the courts, and forms of proceedings therein, under the thirty-second section of an Act passed in the nineteenth and twentieth year of the reign of her present Majesty, chapter one hundred and eight, shall frame the rules and orders for regulating the practice of the county courts under this Act, and forms of proceedings therein, and from time to time may amend such rules, orders, and forms; and such rules, orders, and forms, or amended rules, orders, and forms, certified under the hands of such judges or of any three or more of them, shall be submitted to the Lord Chancellor, who may allow or disallow or alter the same, and so from time to time; and the rules, orders, and forms, or amended rules, orders, and forms, so allowed or altered, shall from a day to be named by the Lord Chancellor be in force in every county court.

**Scale of costs to be framed by the judges.**

**45.** The county court judges mentioned in the last section shall be empowered to frame a scale of costs and charges to be paid to counsel and attorneys with respect to all proceedings in a winding-up under this Act, and from time to time to amend such scale; and such scale or amended scale, certified under the hands of such judges or any three or more of them, shall be submitted to the Lord Chancellor, who from time to time may allow or disallow or alter the same; and the scale or amended scale so allowed or altered shall, from a day to be named by the Lord Chancellor, be in force in every county court.

**Remuneration of registrars and high bailiffs in winding-up of companies.**

**46.** The registrars and high bailiffs of the county courts shall be remunerated for the duties to be performed by them under this Act, by receiving, for their own use, such fees as may be from time to time authorized to be taken by any orders to be made by the Commissioners of the Treasury, with the consent of the Lord Chancellor; and the Commissioners of the Treasury are hereby authorized and empowered, with such consent as aforesaid, from time to time to make such orders; provided that it shall be lawful for the said Commissioners, with the like consent as aforesaid, by an order to direct that after the date named in the order any registrar or high bailiff shall, in lieu of receiving such fees, be paid such fixed or fluctuating allowance as may in each case be thought just, and after such date the said fees shall be accounted for and paid over by such registrar or high bailiff in such manner as may be directed in the order.

**Not to exempt companies from provisions of sect. 196 of 25 & 26 Vict. c. 89.**

**47.** Nothing in this Act contained shall exempt any company from the second or third provisions of the one hundred and ninety-sixth section of the principal Act restraining the alteration of any provision in any Act of Parliament or charter.

(*p*) 25 & 26 Vict. c. 89, s. 81.          (*q*) See Judicature Act, 1873, s. 45.

## 30 VICT. C. 15.

*An Act for the abolition of certain Exemptions from Local Dues on Shipping and on Goods carried in Ships.*
[*12th April, 1867.*]

## 30 & 31 VICT. C. 124.

*An Act to amend the Merchant Shipping Act, 1854.*
[*20th August, 1867.*]

## 31 & 32 VICT. C. 86.

*An Act to enable Assignees of Mortgage Policies to sue thereon in their own Names.*
[*31st July, 1868.*]

## 31 & 32 VICT. C. 129.

*An Act to amend the Law relating to the Registration of Ships in British Possessions.*
[*31st July, 1868.*]

## 32 VICT. C. 11.

*An Act for amending the Law relating to the Coasting Trade and Merchant Shipping in British Possessions.*
[*13th May, 1869.*]

## 33 & 34 VICT. C. 104.

*An Act to facilitate Compromises and Arrangements between Creditors and Shareholders of Joint Stock and other Companies in Liquidation.*
[*10th August, 1870.*]

## 34 & 35 VICT. CAP. 110.

*An Act to amend the Merchant Shipping Acts.*
[*21st August, 1871.*]

WHEREAS it is expedient to amend the Merchant Shipping Acts :
Be it enacted by the Queen's most excellent Majesty, by and with the advice and consent of the Lords spiritual and temporal, and Commons, in this present Parliament assembled, and by the authority of the same, as follows :

### *Preliminary.*

1. This Act may be cited as the Merchant Shipping Act, 1871. *Short title.*
2. This Act shall be construed as one with the Merchant Shipping Act, 1854, and the Acts amending the same, and the said Acts and this Act may be cited collectively as the Merchant Shipping Acts, 1854 to 1871. *Act to be construed with Merchant Shipping Acts.*
3. This Act shall come into operation on the first day of January one thousand eight hundred and seventy-two. *Commencement of Act.*

### *Registry (Part II. of Merchant Shipping Act, 1854).*

4. [Repealed by 36 & 37 Vict. c. 85, s. 33.]
5. The Board of Trade may, in any case or class of cases in which they think it expedient so to do, direct any person appointed by them for the purpose to record, in such manner and with such particulars as the Board of Trade direct, the draught of water of any sea-going ship (a), as shown on the scale of feet on her stem and on her stern post, upon her leaving any *Ship's draught of water to be recorded.*

(a) See 36 & 37 Vict. c. 85, s. 4.

dock, wharf, port, or harbour for the purpose of proceeding to sea ; and such person shall thereupon keep such record, and shall from time to time forward the same, or a copy thereof, to the Board of Trade ; and such record, or any copy thereof, if produced by or out of the custody of the Board of Trade, shall be admissible in evidence of the draught of water of the ship at the time specified in the record (b).

The master of every British sea-going ship shall, upon her leaving any dock, wharf, port, or harbour for the purpose of proceeding to sea, record her draught of water in the official logbook (if any), and shall produce such record to any principal officer of Customs whenever required by him so to do, or in default of such production shall incur a penalty not exceeding twenty pounds.

**Rules to be observed in naming of ships.** 6. With respect to the names of British ships, the following rules shall be observed :

(1.) A ship shall not be described by any name other than that by which she is for the time being registered :

(2.) No change shall be made in the name of a ship without the previous permission of the Board of Trade signified in writing under their seal, or under the hand of one of their secretaries or assistant secretaries. Upon such permission being granted, the ship's name shall forthwith be altered in the register book, to the ship's certificate of registry, and on her bows and stern (c) :

(3.) If in any case it is shown to the satisfaction of the Board of Trade that the name of any ship has been changed without such permission as aforesaid, they shall direct that her name be altered into that which she bore before such change, and the name shall be altered in the register book, in the ship's certificate of registry, and on her bows and stern accordingly :

(4.) Where a ship having once been registered has ceased to be so registered no person, unless ignorant of such previous registry (proof whereof shall lie on him), shall apply to register, and no registrar shall knowingly register such ship except by the name by which she was previously registered, unless with the permission of the Board of Trade granted as aforesaid.

Every person who acts or suffers any person under his control to act in contravention of this section, or who omits to do, or suffers any person under his control to omit to do, anything required by this section, shall for each offence incur a penalty not exceeding one hundred pounds, and any principal officer of customs may detain the ship until the provisions of this section are complied with.

Application for a change of name shall be made in writing to the Board of Trade. If the Board are of opinion that the application is made on reasonable grounds they may entertain the same, and shall thereupon require notice thereof to be published in such form and manner as they think fit.

*Masters and Seamen (Part III. of Merchant Shipping Act, 1854).*

**Survey of ships alleged by seamen to be unseaworthy.** 7. Whenever in any proceeding against any seaman or apprentice belonging to any ship for desertion, or for neglecting or refusing to join or to proceed to sea in his ship, or for being absent from or quitting the same, without leave, it is alleged by one-fourth of the seamen belonging to such ship, or, if the number of such seamen exceed twenty, by not less than five such seamen, that such ship is by reason of unseaworthiness, overloading, improper loading, defective equipment, or for any other reason, not in a fit condition to proceed to sea, or that the accommodation in such ship is insufficient, the court having cognizance of the case shall take such means as may be in their power to satisfy themselves concerning the truth or untruth of such allegation, and shall for that purpose receive the evidence of the person or persons making the same, and shall have power to summon any other witnesses whose evidence they may think it desirable to hear ; the court shall thereupon, if satisfied that the allegation is groundless, proceed to adjudicate, but if not so satisfied shall cause such ship to be surveyed (d).

(b) As to notice by master of kind and quantity of grain cargo, see 43 & 44 Vict. c. 43, s. 6.

(c) 36 & 37 Vict. c. 85, s. 3.
(d) 39 & 40 Vict. c. 80, ss. 6—12.

Provided that no seaman or apprentice charged with desertion, or with quitting his ship without leave, shall have any right to apply for a survey under this section unless previously to his quitting his ship he has complained to the master of the circumstances so alleged in justification.

For the purposes of this section, the court shall require any of the surveyors appointed by the Board of Trade, under the Merchant Shipping Act, 1854, or any person appointed for the purpose by the Board of Trade, or, if such surveyor or person cannot be obtained without reasonable expense or delay, or is not, in the opinion of the court, competent to deal with the special circumstances of the case, then any other impartial surveyor appointed by the court (e), and having no interest in the ship, her freight, or cargo, to survey the ship and to answer any question concerning her which the court may think fit to put. Such surveyor or other person shall survey the ship, and make his report in writing to the court, including an answer to every question put to him by the court. The court shall cause such report to be communicated to the parties, and unless it is proved to the satisfaction of the court that the opinions expressed in such report are erroneous, the court shall determine the questions before them in accordance with those opinions.

For the purposes of such survey, a surveyor shall have all the powers of an inspector appointed by the Board of Trade, under the Merchant Shipping Act, 1854.

The costs (if any) of the survey shall be determined by the Board of Trade according to a scale of fees to be fixed by them, and shall be paid in the first instance out of the Mercantile Marine Fund.

If it is proved to the satisfaction of the court that the ship is in a fit condition to proceed to sea, or, as the case may be, that the accommodation is sufficient, the costs of the survey shall be paid by the person or persons upon whose demand, or in consequence of whose allegation, the survey was made, and may be deducted by the master or owner out of the wages due or to become due to such person or persons, and shall be paid over to the Board of Trade.

If it is proved that the ship is not in a fit condition to proceed to sea, or, as the case may be, that the accommodation is insufficient, the costs of the survey shall be paid to the Board of Trade by the master or owner (f).

8. Any naval court may, if they think fit, direct a survey of any ship which is the subject of an investigation held before them, and such survey shall be made in the same way, and the surveyor who makes the same shall have the same powers, as if the survey had been directed by a competent court in the course of proceedings against a seaman or apprentice for desertion or a kindred offence. *Power for naval courts to direct survey of ships.*

*Safety (Part IV. of Merchant Shipping Act, 1854).*

9, 10. [Repealed by 36 & 37 Vict. c. 85, s. 33.]
11. [Repealed by 39 & 40 Vict. c. 80, s. 45.]
12. [Repealed by Statute Law Revision Act, 1883.]

---

35 & 36 Vict. cap. 73.

*An Act to amend the Merchant Shipping Acts and the Passenger Acts.*
[*10th August, 1872.*]

Whereas it is expedient to amend the Merchant Shipping Acts and the Passenger Acts:

Be it enacted by the Queen's most excellent Majesty, by and with the advice and consent of the Lords spiritual and temporal, and Commons, in this present Parliament assembled, and by the authority of the same, as follows:

*Preliminary.*

1. This Act may be cited as the Merchant Shipping Act, 1872.  Short title.
2. This Act shall come into operation on the first day of January one thousand eight hundred and seventy-three.  Commencement of Act.

(e) 35 & 36 Vict. c. 73, s. 13.        (f) 36 & 37 Vict. c. 85, s. 9; and
                                        39 & 40 Vict. c. 80, s. 11.

## Measurement of Ships.

Transfer to Board of Trade of duties of Commissioners of Customs with respect to measurement of ships.

3. The twenty-third, twenty-seventh, twenty-eighth, and twenty-ninth sections of the Merchant Shipping Act, 1854, the fourteenth section of the Merchant Shipping Act Amendment Act, 1855 [and the fourth section of the Merchant Shipping Act, 1871] (*g*), shall be read and construed as if the Board of Trade were therein named instead of the Commissioners of Customs.

## Registry.

Transfer to registrar-general of seamen of duties of Commissioners of Customs with respect to registry of ships.

4. The forty-sixth, fifty-fourth, ninety-second, and ninety-fourth sections of the Merchant Shipping Act, 1854, shall be read and construed as if the Registrar-General of Seamen were therein named instead of the Commissioners of Customs, and the returns required to be transmitted by the said ninety-fourth section of the Merchant Shipping Act, 1854, shall be transmitted to the Registrar-General of Seamen, and not to the Custom House in London, and the Registrar-General of Seamen shall be called the Registrar-General of Shipping and Seamen.

## Pilotage.

Trinity House may modify rules as to pilotage rates.

9. Notwithstanding anything in the three hundred and fifty-eighth section of the Merchant Shipping Act, 1854, the Trinity House may, by bye-law made with the sanction of her Majesty in Council, repeal or relax the provisions of that section within the whole or any part of their district so far as to allow any pilot or class of pilots under their jurisdiction to demand or receive and any master to offer or pay any rate less than the rate for the time being demandable by law (*h*).

Alteration of payments made to Trinity House pilotage fund by Cinque Ports pilots.

10. Whereas in pursuance of the Pilotage Law Amendment Act, 1853, the several funds then belonging to the Cinque Ports pilots were merged into the common fund called the Trinity House Pilotage Fund, and by the same Act power was given to the Trinity House of Deptford Strond, with the approval of the Board of Trade, from time to time to make regulations for altering and determining the payments and contributions to be made to the said pilotage fund by Cinque Ports pilots licensed before the said Act came into operation: And whereas by one of the regulations made under the authority of the said Act it was provided that each of the said Cinque Ports pilots should pay towards the said fund eleven shillings for each turn: And whereas it has proved that the turns have been more numerous than was expected, and that the sums paid to the Trinity House, and carried to the credit of the said fund, in respect of the said turns have been larger than was assumed in making the calculations upon which the said regulation was based: And whereas it is expedient that in lieu of the said sum of eleven shillings per turn the fixed annual sum of thirteen pounds four shillings should for the future be paid by or in respect of each of the said pilots so long as he remains unsuperannuated, and that the excess of the sum heretofore paid in each year by each pilot over the sum of thirteen pounds four shillings should be returned: And whereas doubts have been entertained whether the purposes aforesaid can be effected without the authority of Parliament: Be it enacted, that [the Trinity House of Deptford Strond shall, out of the Trinity House Pilotage Fund, repay to each of the Cinque Ports pilots licensed before the Pilotage Law Amendment Act, 1853, came into operation, or if he be deceased, to his executors or administrators, the aggregate sum by which the sum of eleven shillings per turn heretofore paid by him exceeds the sum which he would have paid if he had paid thirteen pounds four shillings per annum: and that] (*i*) each of the said pilots shall, while he continues to act as pilot, pay to the said Trinity House the sum of eleven shillings per turn as heretofore, from the first day of January in each year, until the sums contributed in the same year amount to an aggregate sum equal to the product of thirteen pounds four shillings multiplied by the number of pilots licensed as above who are then surviving and unsuperannuated, and that when such aggregate sum is made up no further contributions shall be required from the said pilots until after the thirty-first day of December in the same year; and if the said contributions

(*g*) Words within brackets repealed by Statute Law Revision Act, 1883.

(*h*) 2 Maude and Pollock's Merchant Shipping, 4th ed., 68, 180—190.

(*i*) Words within brackets repealed by Statute Law Revision Act, 1883.

during any one year fall short of the said aggregate sum, the said pilots then surviving and unsuperannuated shall, at such time and in such manner as the Trinity House may direct, make good such deficiency by payment of an additional contribution per man, to be calculated pro rata upon the number of turns which each may have carried during the said year, and any such pilot failing to pay such additional contribution shall, in default of such payment, become liable to immediate removal from active service and superannuation upon such proportion of the full pension payable to such pilot as the Trinity House may see fit.

**11.** Any pilotage authority may, if authorized in that behalf by Order in Council, grant special licences qualifying the persons to whom they are granted to act as pilots for any part of the sea or channels beyond the limits of any pilotage authority, so, however, that no pilot so licensed be entitled to supersede an unlicensed pilot outside the limits of the authority by which he is licensed. Pilotage authority may grant special sea licences.

### Chain Cables.

**12.** [Repealed by 37 & 38 Vict. c. 51, s. 8.]

### General.

**·13·** All duties in relation to the survey and measurement of ships under this Act or the Acts amended hereby shall be performed by the surveyors appointed under the Fourth Part of the Merchant Shipping Act, 1854, in accordance with such regulations as may be from time to time made by the Board of Trade. Duties of surveyors.

**14.** [Repealed by 39 & 40 Vict. c. 80, s. 45.]

**15.** If any surveyor, or any person employed under the authority of the Passengers Act, 1855, demands or receives directly or indirectly, otherwise than by the direction of the Board of Trade, any fee, remuneration, or gratuity whatever in respect of any of the duties performed by him under this Act or Acts amended hereby, he shall for every such offence incur a penalty not exceeding fifty pounds. Penalty on surveyor, &c., receiving gratuity &c., for duties performed under this Act.

**16.** The owner of home-trade ships or his agent may enter into time agreements, in forms to be sanctioned by the Board of Trade, with individual seamen to serve in any one or more ships belonging to him, which agreements need not expire on either the thirtieth day of June or the thirty-first day of December, anything in the Merchant Shipping Act to the contrary notwithstanding: Provided always, that a duplicate of each agreement entered into under the provisions of the section be forwarded to the Registrar General of Shipping within forty-eight hours after it has been entered into. Owner or agent of home-trade ships may enter into time agreements which need not expire half yearly.

**17.** It shall be lawful for her Majesty to accept from time to time the offers of any person whom the Lord High Admiral or the Commissioners for executing his office may recommend, to serve as officers of reserve in the Royal Navy, upon such terms and conditions as to her Majesty may from time to time seem fit, and the officers of the Royal Naval Reserve Act, 1863, shall be read and construed as if this clause formed part of the said Act. Her Majesty may accept offers of persons recomended by the Admiralty to serve as officers of the Royal Naval Reserve.

---

### 36 & 37 VICT. CAP. 48.

*An Act to make better provision for carrying into effect the Railway and Canal Traffic Act, 1854, and for other purposes connected therewith.*
[*21st July*, 1873.]

### Preliminary.

**1.** This Act may be cited as the Regulation of Railways Act, 1873. Short title

**3.** In this Act— Definitions.

The term "railway company" includes any person being the owner or lessee of or working any railway in the United Kingdom constructed or carried on under the powers of any Act of Parliament:

The term "canal company" includes any person being the owner or lessee of, or working, or entitled to charge tolls for the use of any canal in the United Kingdom constructed or carried on under the powers of any Act of Parliament:

The term "person" includes a body of persons corporate or unincorporate:

The term "railway" includes every station, siding, wharf, or dock of or belonging to such railway and used for the purposes of public traffic:

The term "canal" includes any navigation which has been made under or upon which tolls may be levied by authority of Parliament, and also the wharves and landing-places of and belonging to such canal or navigation, and used for the purposes of public traffic :

The term "traffic" includes not only p          and their luggage, goods, animals, and other things conveyed by any railway company or canal company, but also carriages, wagons, trucks, boats, and vehicles of every description adapted for running or passing on the railway or canal of any such company :

The term "mails" includes mail-bags and post-letter bags :

The term "special Act" means a local or local and personal Act, or an Act of a local and personal nature, and includes a Provisional Order of the Board of Trade confirmed by Act of Parliament, and a certificate granted by the Board of Trade under the Railways Construction Facilities Act, 1864 :

The term "the Treasury" means the Commissioners of Her Majesty's Treasury for the time being.

*Explanation and Amendment of Law.*

Publication of rates.

**14.** Every railway company and canal company shall keep at each of their stations and wharves a book or books showing every rate for the time being charged for the carriage of traffic, other than passengers and their luggage, from that station or wharf to any place to which they book, including any rates charged under any special contract, and stating the distance from that station or wharf of every station, wharf, siding, or place to which any such rate is charged.

Every such book shall during all reasonable hours be open to the inspection of any person without the payment of any fee.

The commissioners may from time to time, on the application of any person interested, make orders with respect to any particular description of traffic, requiring a railway company or canal company to distinguish in such book how much of each rate is for the conveyance of the traffic on the railway or canal, including therein tolls for the use of the railway or canal, for the use of carriages or vessels, or for locomotive power, and how much is for other expenses, specifying the nature and detail of such other expenses.

Any company failing to comply with the provisions of this section shall for each offence, and in the case of a continuing offence, for every day during which the offence continues, be liable to a penalty not exceeding five pounds, and such penalty shall be recovered and applied in the same manner as penalties imposed by the Railways Clauses Consolidation Act, 1845, and the Railways Clauses Consolidation (Scotland) Act, 1845, (as the case may require,) are for the time being recoverable and applicable.

Power to commissioners to fix terminal charges.

**15.** The commissioners shall have power to hear and determine any question or dispute which may arise with respect to the terminal charges of any railway company, where such charges have not been fixed by any Act of Parliament, and to decide what is a reasonable sum to be paid to any company for loading and unloading, covering, collection, delivery, and other services of a like nature; any decision of the commissioners under this section shall be binding on all courts and in all legal proceedings whatsoever.

Arrangements between railway companies and canal companies.

**16.** No railway company or canal company, unless expressly authorized thereto by any Act passed before the passing of this Act, shall, without the sanction of the commissioners, to be signified in such manner as they may by general order or otherwise direct, enter into any agreement whereby any control over or right to interfere in or concerning the traffic carried or rates or tolls levied on any part of a canal is given to the railway company, or any persons managing or connected with the management of any railway ; and any such agreement made after the commencement of this Act without such sanction shall be void.

The commissioners shall withhold their sanction from any such agreement which is in their opinion prejudicial to the interests of the public.

Not less than one month before any such agreement is so sanctioned, copies of the intended agreement certified under the hand of the secretary of the railway company or one of the railway companies party or parties thereto, shall be deposited for public inspection at the office of the commissioners, and also at the office of the clerk of the peace of the county, riding, or division in England or Ireland in which the head office of any canal company party to the agreement is situate, and at the office of the principal sheriff clerk of every such county in Scotland, and notice of the intended agreement, setting forth the parties between whom or on whose behalf the same is intended to be made, and such further particulars with respect thereto as the commissioners may require, shall be given by advertisement in the London, Edinburgh, or Dublin Gazette, according as the head office of any canal company party to the agreement is situate in England, Scotland, or Ireland, and shall be sent to the secretary or principal officer of every canal company any of whose canals communicates with the canal of any company party to the agreement; and shall be published in such other way, if any, as the commissioners for the purpose of giving notice to all parties interested therein by order direct.

17. Every railway company owning or having the management of any canal or part of a canal shall at all times keep and maintain such canal or part, and all the reservoirs, works, and conveniences thereto belonging, thoroughly repaired and dredged and in good working condition, and shall preserve the supplies of water to the same, so that the whole of such canal or part may be at all times kept open and navigable for the use of all persons desirous to use and navigate the same without any unnecessary hindrance, interruption, or delay. *Maintenance of canals by railway companies.*

26. Any decision or any order made by the commissioners for the purpose of carrying into effect any of the provisions of this Act may be made a rule or order of any superior court, and shall be enforced either in the manner directed by section three of the Railway and Canal Traffic Act, 1854, as to the writs and orders therein mentioned, or in like manner as any rule or order of such court. *Orders of commissioners.*

For the purpose of carrying into effect this section, general rules and orders may be made by any superior court in the same manner as general rules and orders may be made with respect to any other proceedings in such court.

30. Every document purporting to be signed by the commissioners, or any one of them, shall be received in evidence without proof of such signature, and until the contrary is proved shall be deemed to have been so signed and to have been duly executed or issued by the commissioners. *Evidence of documents.*

31. The commissioners shall, once in every year, make a report to her Majesty of their proceedings under this Act during the past year, and such report shall be laid before both Houses of Parliament within fourteen days after the making thereof if Parliament is then sitting, and if not, then within fourteen days after the next meeting of Parliament. *Commissioners to make annual reports.*

---

## 36 & 37 VICT. CAP. 85.

### An Act to amend the Merchant Shipping Acts.
[*5th August*, 1873.]

BE it enacted by the Queen's most excellent Majesty, by and with the advice and consent of the Lords spiritual and temporal, and Commons, in this present Parliament assembled, and by the authority of the same, as follows:

#### Preliminary.

1. This Act may be cited as the Merchant Shipping Act, 1873. *Short title.*

2. This Act shall be construed as one with the Merchant Shipping Act, 1854, and the Acts amending the same, and the said Acts and this Act may be cited collectively as the Merchant Shipping Acts, 1854 to 1873. *Construction of Act.*

#### Registry (Part II. of Merchant Shipping Act, 1854.)

3. Every British ship registered after the passing of this Act shall before registry, and every British ship registered before the passing of this Act shall, on or before the first day of January one thousand eight hundred and seventy-four, be permanently and conspicuously marked to the satisfaction of the Board of Trade, as follows (k):— *Particulars to be marked on British ships.*

Her name shall be marked on each of her bows, and her name and the name of her port of registry shall be marked on her stern, on a dark ground in white or yellow letters, or on a light ground in black letters, such letters to be of a length not less than four inches, and of proportionate breadth:

(k) See 39 & 40 Vict. c. 80, ss. 25—28.

Her official number and the number denoting her registered tonnage shall be cut in on her main beam:

A scale of feet denoting her draught of water shall be marked on each side of her stem and of her stern post in Roman capital letters or in figures not less than six inches in length, the lower line of such letters or figures to coincide with the draught line denoted thereby. Such letters or figures shall be marked by being cut in and painted white or yellow on a dark ground, or in such other way as the Board of Trade may from time to time approve.

The Board of Trade may, however, exempt any class of ships from the requirements of this section, or any of them.

If the scale of feet showing the ship's draught of water is in any respect inaccurate, so as to be likely to mislead, the owner of the ship shall incur a penalty not exceeding one hundred pounds.

The marks required by this section shall be permanently continued, and no alteration shall be made therein, except in the event of any of the particulars thereby denoted being altered in the manner provided by the Merchant Shipping Acts, 1854 to 1873.

Any owner or master of a British ship who neglects to cause his ship to be marked as aforesaid, or to keep her so marked, and any person who conceals, removes, alters, defaces, or obliterates, or suffers any person under his control to conceal, remove, alter, deface, or obliterate any of the said marks, except in the event aforesaid, or except for the purpose of escaping capture by an enemy, shall for each offence incur a penalty not exceeding one hundred pounds, and any officer of customs on receipt of a certificate from a surveyor or inspector of the Board of Trade that a ship is insufficiently or inaccurately marked may detain the same until the insufficiency or inaccuracy has been remedied.

Provided that no fishing vessel duly registered, lettered, and numbered in pursuance of the Sea Fisheries Act, 1868, shall be required to have her name and port of registry marked under this section.

Provided also, that if any registered British ship is not within a port of the United Kingdom at any time before the first day of January one thousand eight hundred and seventy-four, she shall be marked as by this section required within one month after her next return to a British port of registry subsequent to that date.

**Particulars to be entered in record of draught of water.** 4. The record of the draught of water of any sea-going ship required under section five of the Merchant Shipping Act, 1871, shall, in addition to the particulars thereby required, specify the extent of her clear side in feet and inches.

The term " clear side" means the height from the water to the upper side of the plank of the deck from which the depth of hold as stated in the register is measured, and the measurement of the clear side is to be taken at the lowest part of the side (*l*).

Every master of a sea-going ship shall, upon the request of any person appointed to record the ship's draught of water, permit such person to enter the ship and to make such inspections and take such measurements as may be requisite for the purpose of such record, and any master who fails so to do, or impedes or suffers any one under his control to impede any person so appointed in the execution of his duty, shall for each offence incur a penalty not exceeding five pounds.

**Rules as to names of foreign ships placed on British register.** 5. Where a foreign ship, not having at any previous time been registered as a British ship, becomes a British ship, no person shall apply to register, and no registrar shall knowingly register such ship, except by the name which she bore as a foreign ship immediately before becoming a British ship, unless with the permission of the Board of Trade granted in manner directed by section six of the Merchant Shipping Act, 1871.

Any person who acts or suffers any person under his control to act in contravention of this section, shall for each offence incur a penalty not exceeding one hundred pounds.

**Restrictions on re-registration of abandoned ships.** 6. Where a ship has ceased to be registered as a British ship by reason of having been wrecked or abandoned, or for any reason other than capture by the enemy or transfer to a person not qualified to own a British ship, such ship shall not be re-registered until she has, at the expense of the applicant for registration, been surveyed by one of the surveyors appointed by the Board of Trade and certified by him to be seaworthy.

(*l*) See 43 & 44 Vict. c. 43, s. 6.

*Masters and Seamen (Part III. of Merchant Shipping Act, 1854).*

**7.** Any agreement with a seaman made under section one hundred and forty-nine of the Merchant Shipping Act, 1854, may, instead of stating the nature and duration of the intended voyage or engagement as by that section required, state the maximum period of the voyage or engagement, and the places or parts of the world (if any) to which the voyage or engagement is not to extend.

*Agreements with seamen.*

**8.** [Repealed, except as to Scotland, by 46 & 47 Vict. c. 41, s. 55.]

**9.** If a seaman or apprentice belonging to any ship is detained on a charge of desertion or any kindred offence, and if upon a survey of the ship being made under section seven of the Merchant Shipping Act, 1871, it is proved that she is not in a fit condition to proceed to sea, or that her accommodation is insufficient, the owner or master of the ship shall be liable to pay to such seaman or apprentice such compensation for his detention as the court having cognizance of the proceedings may award.

*Compensation to seamen for unnecessary detention on charge of desertion.*

**10.** In any case where the business of a mercantile marine office is conducted otherwise than under a local marine board, the Board of Trade may, if they think fit, instead of conducting such business at a custom-house or otherwise, establish a mercantile marine office, and for that purpose procure the requisite buildings and property, and from time to time appoint and remove all the requisite superintendents, deputies, clerks and servants. They may also in the like case make all such provisions and exercise all such powers with respect to the holding of examinations for the purpose of granting certificates of competency as masters, mates, or engineers, to persons desirous of obtaining the same, as might have been made or exercised by a local marine board.

*Power for Board of Trade to establish mercantile marine offices and to hold examinations at certain ports.*

**11.** [Repealed by 39 & 40 Vict. c. 80, s. 45.]

*Safety and Prevention of Accidents (Part IV. of Merchant Shipping Act, 1854).*

**12, 13, 14.** [Repealed by 39 & 40 Vict. c. 80, s. 45.]

**15.** In the case of any ship surveyed under the Fourth Part of the Merchant Shipping Act, 1854, the Board of Trade may at the request of the owner authorize the reduction of the number and the variation of the dimensions of the boats required for the ship by section two hundred and ninety-two of that Act, and also the substitution of rafts or other appliances for saving life for any such boats, so nevertheless that the boats so reduced or varied, and the rafts or other appliances so substituted be sufficient for the persons carried on board the ship (*m*).

*Power for Board of Trade to vary requirements as to boats.*

Section two hundred and ninety-three of the said Act shall extend to any such rafts or appliances in the same manner as if they were boats.

**16.** In every case of collision between two vessels it shall be the duty of the master or person in charge of each vessel, if and so far as he can do so without danger to his own vessel, crew, and passengers (if any), to stay by the other vessel until he has ascertained that she has no need of further assistance, and to render to the other vessel, her master, crew, and passengers (if any), such assistance as may be practicable and as may be necessary in order to save them from any danger caused by the collision ; and also to give to the master or person in charge of the other vessel the name of his own vessel, and of her port of registry, or of the port or place to which she belongs, and also the names of the ports and places from which and to which she is bound.

*Duties of masters in case of collision.*

If he fails so to do, and no reasonable cause for such failure is shown, the collision shall, in the absence of proof to the contrary, be deemed to have been caused by his wrongful act, neglect, or default.

Every master or person in charge of a British vessel who fails, without reasonable cause, to render such assistance or give such information as aforesaid shall be deemed guilty of a misdemeanor, and if he is a certificated officer an inquiry into his conduct may be held and his certificate may be cancelled or suspended.

(*m*) 2 Maude and Pollock's Merchant Shipping, 4th ed., ccccxli.

Liability for
infringement of
regulations in
case of collision.
**17.** If in any case of collision it is proved to the court before which the case is tried that any of the regulations for preventing collision contained in or made under the Merchant Shipping Acts, 1854 to 1873, has been infringed, the ship by which such regulation has been infringed shall be deemed to be in fault, unless it is shown to the satisfaction of the court that the circumstances of the case made departure from the regulation necessary.

Signals of dis-
tress.
**18.** The signals specified in the First Schedule to this Act shall be deemed to be signals of distress.

Any master of a vessel who uses or displays, or causes or permits any person under his authority to use or display, any of the said signals, except in the case of a vessel being in distress, shall be liable to pay compensation for any labour undertaken, risk incurred, or loss sustained in consequence of such signal having been supposed to be a signal of distress, and such compensation may, without prejudice to any other remedy, be recovered in the same manner in which salvage is recoverable.

Signals for
pilots.
**19.** If a vessel requires the service of a pilot, the signals to be used and displayed shall be those specified in the Second Schedule to this Act.

Any master of a vessel who uses or displays, or causes or permits any person under his authority to use or display, any of the said signals for any other purpose than that of summoning a pilot, or uses or causes or permits any person under his authority to use any other signal for a pilot, shall incur a penalty not exceeding twenty pounds.

Power to alter
rules as to
signals.
**20.** Her Majesty may from time to time by Order in Council repeal or alter the rules as to signals contained in the Schedules to this Act, or make new rules in addition thereto, or in substitution therefor, and any alterations in or additions to such rules made in manner aforesaid shall be of the same force as the rules in the said Schedules.

Private signals.
**21.** Any shipowner who is desirous of using, for the purposes of a private code, any rockets, lights, or other similar signals, may register such signals with the Board of Trade, and the Board shall give public notice of the signals so registered in such manner as they may think requisite for preventing such signals from being mistaken for signals of distress or signals for pilots.

The Board may refuse to register any signals which in their opinion cannot easily be distinguished from signals of distress or signals for pilots.

When any signal has been so registered the use or display thereof by any person acting under the authority of the shipowner in whose name it is registered shall not subject any person to any of the penalties or liabilities by this Act imposed upon persons using or displaying signals improperly.

Notice to be
given of appre-
hended loss of
ship.
**22.** If the managing owner, or, in the event of there being no managing owner, the ship's husband of any British ship have reason, owing to the non-appearance of such ship, or to any other circumstance, to apprehend that such ship has been wholly lost, he shall, as soon as conveniently may be, send to the Board of Trade notice in writing of such loss and of the probable occasion thereof, stating the name of the ship and her official number (if any), and the port to which she belongs, and if he neglect to do so within a reasonable time he shall incur a penalty not exceeding fifty pounds.

Restrictions on
carriage of dan-
gerous goods.
**23.** If any person sends or attempts to send by, or not being the master or owner of the vessel carries or attempts to carry in any vessel, British, or foreign, any dangerous goods (that is to say,) aquafortis, vitriol, naphtha, benzine, gunpowder, lucifer matches, nitro-glycerine, petroleum, or any other goods of a dangerous nature, without distinctly marking their nature on the outside of the package containing the same, and giving written notice of the nature of such goods and of the name and address of the sender or carrier thereof to the master or owner of the vessel at or before the time of sending the same to be shipped or taking the same on board the vessel, he shall for every such offence incur a penalty not exceeding one hundred pounds : Provided that if such person show that he was merely an agent in the shipment of any such goods as aforesaid, and was not aware and did not suspect and had no reason to suspect that the goods shipped by him were of a dangerous nature, the penalty which he incurs shall not exceed ten pounds.

Penalty for mis-
description of
dangerous
goods.
**24.** If any person knowingly sends or attempts to send by, or carries or attempts to carry in any vessel, British or foreign, any dangerous goods or goods of a dangerous nature, under a false description, or falsely describes the sender or carrier thereof, he shall incur a penalty not exceeding five hundred pounds.

**25.** The master or owner of any vessel, British or foreign, may refuse to take on board any package or parcel which he suspects to contain goods of a dangerous nature, and may require it to be opened to ascertain the fact.

*Power to refuse to carry goods suspected of being dangerous.*

**26.** Where any dangerous goods as defined in this Act, or any goods which, in the judgment of the master or owner of the vessel, are of a dangerous nature, have been sent or brought aboard any vessel, British or foreign, without being marked as aforesaid, or without such notice having been given as aforesaid, the master or owner of the vessel may cause such goods to be thrown overboard, together with any package or receptacle in which they are contained ; and neither the master nor owner of the vessel shall, in respect of such throwing overboard, be subject to any liability, civil or criminal, in any court.

*Power to throw overboard dangerous goods.*

**27.** Where any dangerous goods have been sent or carried, or attempted to be sent or carried, on board any vessel, British or foreign, without being marked as aforesaid, or without such notice having been given as aforesaid, and where any such goods have been sent or carried, or attempted to be sent or carried, under a false description, or the sender or carrier thereof has been falsely described, it shall be lawful for any court having Admiralty jurisdiction to declare such goods, and any package or receptacle in which they are contained, to be and they shall thereupon be forfeited, and when forfeited shall be disposed of as the court directs.

*Forfeiture of dangerous goods improperly sent.*

The court shall have and may exercise the aforesaid powers of forfeiture and disposal notwithstanding that the owner of the goods have not committed any offence under the provisions of this Act relating to dangerous goods, and be not before the court, and have not notice of the proceedings, and notwithstanding that there be no evidence to show to whom the goods belong ; nevertheless the court may, in its discretion, require such notice as it may direct to be given to the owner or shipper of the goods before the same are forfeited.

**28.** The provisions of this Act relating to the carriage of dangerous goods shall be deemed to be in addition to and not in substitution for or in restraint of any other enactment for the like object, so nevertheless that nothing in the said provisions shall be deemed to authorise that any person be sued or prosecuted twice in the same matter (*n*).

*Saving as to Dangerous Goods Acts.*

### *Miscellaneous and Repeal.*

**29.** Where, in accordance with the Foreign Jurisdiction Acts, her Majesty exercises jurisdiction without any port out of her Majesty's dominions, it shall be lawful for her Majesty, by Order in Council, to declare such port a port of registry (in this Act referred to as a foreign port of registry), and by the same or any subsequent Order in Council to declare the description of persons who are to be the registrars of British ships at such foreign port of registry, and to make regulations with respect to the registry of British ships thereat.

*Her Majesty may, by order in Council, declare certain foreign ports ports of registry.*

Upon such order coming into operation it shall have effect as if it were enacted in the Merchant Shipping Acts, 1854 to 1873, and shall, subject to any exceptions and regulations contained in the order, apply in the same manner, as near as may be, as if the port mentioned in the order were an ordinary port of registry.

**30.** There shall be paid in respect of the several measurements, inspections, and surveys mentioned in the Third Schedule hereto such fees, not exceeding those specified in that behalf in the said Schedule, as the Board of Trade may from time to time determine.

*Fees in respect of surveyors, &c.*

**31.** In any legal proceedings under the Merchant Shipping Acts, 1854 to 1873, the Board of Trade may take proceedings in the name of any of their officers.

*Board of Trade may sue in name of its officers.*

**32.** The following sections of this Act, that is to say, sections sixteen, eighteen, nineteen, twenty, twenty-one, twenty-two, twenty-three, twenty-four, twenty-five, twenty-six, twenty-seven, twenty-eight, shall not come into operation until the first day of November one thousand eight hundred and seventy-three.

*Certain sections not to come into force until 1st November, 1873.*

**33.** [Repealed by Statute Law Revision Act, 1883, s. 12.]

(*n*) Explosive Substances Act, 1875.

# SCHEDULES.

## SCHEDULE I.

### Signals of Distress.

*In the daytime.*—The following signals, numbered 1, 2, and 3, when used or displayed together or separately, shall be deemed to be signals of distress in the daytime:

1. A gun fired at intervals of about a minute;
2. The International Code signal of distress indicated by N C;
3. The distant signal, consisting of a square flag having either above or below it a ball, or anything resembling a ball.

*At night.*—The following signals, numbered 1, 2, and 3, when used or displayed together or separately, shall be deemed to be signals of distress at night:

1. A gun fired at intervals of about a minute;
2. Flames on the ship (as from a burning tar barrel, oil barrel, &c.);
3. Rockets or shells, of any colour or description, fired one at a time, at short intervals.

---

## SCHEDULE II.

### Signals to be made by Ships wanting a Pilot.

*In the daytime.*—The following signals, numbered 1 and 2, when used or displayed together or separately, shall be deemed to be signals for a pilot in the daytime, viz.:

1. To be hoisted at the fore, the Jack or other national colour usually worn by merchant ships, having round it a white border, one fifth of the breadth of the flag; or
2. The International Code pilotage signal indicated by P T.

*At night.*—The following signals, numbered 1 and 2, when used or displayed together or separately, shall be deemed to be signals for a pilot at night, viz.:

1. The pyrotechnic light commonly known as a blue light every fifteen minutes; or
2. A bright white light, flashed or shown at short or frequent intervals just above the bulwarks, for about a minute at a time.

---

## SCHEDULE III.

### Table of Maximum Fees to be paid for the Measurement, Survey, and Inspection of Merchant Ships.

#### 1. *For Measurement of Tonnage.*

|  |  | £ | s. | d. |
|---|---|---|---|---|
| For a ship under 50 tons register tonnage | . . . . . | 1 | 0 | 0 |
| ,, from 50 to 100 tons ,, | . . . . . | 1 | 10 | 0 |
| ,, ,, 100 to 200 ,, ,, | . . . . . | 2 | 0 | 0 |
| ,, ,, 200 to 500 ,, ,, | . . . . . | 3 | 0 | 0 |
| ,, ,, 500 to 800 ,, ,, | . . . . . | 4 | 0 | 0 |
| ,, ,, 800 to 1,200 ,, ,, | . . . . . | 5 | 0 | 0 |
| ,, ,, 1,200 to 2,000 ,, ,, | . . . . . | 6 | 0 | 0 |
| ,, ,, 2,000 to 3,000 ,, ,, | . . . . . | 7 | 0 | 0 |
| ,, ,, 3,000 to 4,000 ,, ,, | . . . . . | 8 | 0 | 0 |
| ,, ,, 4,000 to 5,000 ,, ,, | . . . . . | 9 | 0 | 0 |
| ,, ,, 5,000 and upwards ,, | . . . . . | 10 | 0 | 0 |

2. *For the Inspection of the Berthing or Sleeping Accommodation of the Crew.*

|                             | £ | s. | d. |
|-----------------------------|---|----|----|
| For each visit to the ship  | 0 | 10 | 0  |

Provided as follows:
1. The aggregate amount of the fees for any such inspection shall not exceed one pound (£1) whatever be the number of separate visits.
2. When the accommodation is inspected at the same time with the measurement of the tonnage, no separate fee shall be charged for such inspection.

### 3. *For the Survey of Emigrant Ships.*

|   |   | £ | s. | d. |
|---|---|---|----|----|
| a. For an ordinary survey of the ship, and of her equipments, accommodation, stores, light, ventilation, sanitary arrangements, and medical stores | | 10 | 0 | 0 |
| b. For a special survey | | 15 | 0 | 0 |
| c. In respect of the medical examination of passengers and crew for every hundred persons or fraction of a hundred persons examined | | 1 | 0 | 0 |

### 4. *For the Inspection of Lights and Fog Signals.*

|   | £ | s. | d. |
|---|---|----|----|
| For each visit made to a ship on the application of the owner, and for each visit made where the lights or fittings are found defective | 0 | 10 | 0 |

Provided that the aggregate amount of fees for any such inspection shall not exceed one pound (£1) whatever be the number of separate visits.

---

### 38 & 39 Vict. cap. 90.

*An Act to enlarge the Powers of County Courts in respect of Disputes between Employers and Workmen, and to give other Courts a Limited Civil Jurisdiction in respect of such Disputes.*

[*13th August, 1875.*]

Be it enacted by the Queen's most excellent Majesty, by and with the advice and consent of the Lords spiritual and temporal, and Commons, in this present Parliament assembled, and by the authority of the same, as follows:

#### *Preliminary.*

1. This Act may be cited as the Employers and Workmen Act, 1875. *Short title.*

2. This Act, except so far as it authorizes any rules to be made, or other thing to be done at any time after the passing of this Act, shall come into operation on the first day of September one thousand eight hundred and seventy-five. *Commencement of Act.*

#### Part I.

#### *Jurisdiction—Jurisdiction of County Court.*

3. In any proceeding before a county court in relation to any dispute between an employer and a workman arising out of or incidental to their relation as such (which dispute is hereinafter referred to as a dispute under this Act) the court may, in addition to any jurisdiction it might have exercised if this Act had not passed, exercise all or any of the following powers; (that is to say,) *Power of county court as to ordering of payment of money, set-off, and rescission of contracts and taking security.*

(1.) It may adjust and set off the one against the other all such claims on the part either of the employer or of the workman, arising out of or incidental to the relation between them, as the court may find to be subsisting, whether such claims are liquidated or unliquidated, and are for wages, damages, or otherwise; and,

(2.) If, having regard to all the circumstances of the case, it thinks it just to do so, it may rescind any contract between the employer and the workman upon such terms as to the apportionment of wages or other sums due thereunder, and as to the payment of wages or damages, or other sums due, as it thinks just ; and,

(3.) Where the court might otherwise award damages for any breach of contract it may, if the defendant be willing to give security to the satisfaction of the court for the performance by him of so much of his contract as remains unperformed, with the consent of the plaintiff, accept such security, and order performance of the contract accordingly, in place either of the whole of the damages which would otherwise have been awarded, or some part of such damages.

The security shall be an undertaking by the defendant and one or more surety or sureties that the defendant will perform his contract, subject on non-performance to the payment of a sum to be specified in the undertaking.

Any sum paid by a surety on behalf of a defendant in respect of a security under this Act, together with all costs incurred by such surety in respect of such security, shall be deemed to be a debt due to him from the defendant: and where such security has been given in or under the direction of a court of summary jurisdiction, that court may order payment to the surety of the sum which has so become due to him from the defendant.

### Court of Summary Jurisdiction.

**Jurisdiction of justices in disputes between employers and workmen.**

**4.** A dispute under this Act between an employer and a workman may be heard and determined by a court of summary jurisdiction, and such court, for the purposes of this Act, shall be deemed to be a court of civil jurisdiction, and in a proceeding in relation to any such dispute the court may order payment of any sum which it may find to be due as wages, or damages, or otherwise, and may exercise all or any of the powers by this Act conferred on a county court: Provided that in any proceeding in relation to any such dispute the court of summary jurisdiction—

(1.) Shall not exercise any jurisdiction where the amount claimed exceeds ten pounds ; and

(2.) Shall not make an order for the payment of any sum exceeding ten pounds, exclusive of the costs incurred in the case ; and

(3.) Shall not require security to an amount exceeding ten pounds from any defendant or his surety or sureties.

**Jurisdiction of justices in disputes between masters and apprentices.**

**5.** Any dispute between an apprentice to whom this Act applies and his master, arising out of or incidental to their relation as such (which dispute is hereinafter referred to as a dispute under this Act), may be heard and determined by a court of summary jurisdiction.

**Powers of justices in respect of apprentices.**

**6.** In a proceeding before a court of summary jurisdiction in relation to a dispute under this Act between a master and an apprentice, the court shall have the same powers as if the dispute were between an employer and a workman, and the master were the employer and the apprentice the workman, and the instrument of apprenticeship a contract between an employer and a workman, and shall also have the following powers :

(1.) It may make an order directing the apprentice to perform his duties under the apprenticeship ; and

(2.) If it rescinds the instrument of apprenticeship it may, if it thinks it just so to do, order the whole or any part of the premium paid on the binding of the apprentice to be repaid.

Where an order is made directing an apprentice to perform his duties under the apprenticeship, the court may, from time to time, if satisfied after the expiration of not less than one month from the date of the order that the apprentice has failed to comply therewith, order him to be imprisoned for a period not exceeding fourteen days.

**Order against surety of apprentice, and power to friend of apprentice to give security.**

**7.** In a proceeding before a court of summary jurisdiction in relation to a dispute under this Act between a master and an apprentice, if there is any person liable, under the instrument of apprenticeship, for the good conduct of the apprentice, that person may, if the court so direct, be summoned in like manner as if he were the defendant in such proceeding to attend on the hearing of the proceeding, and the court may, in addition to or in substitution for any order which the court is authorized to make against the apprentice, order the person so summoned to pay damages for any breach of the contract of apprenticeship to an amount not exceeding the limit (if any) to which he is liable under the instrument of apprenticeship.

The court may, if the person so summoned, or any other person, is willing to give security to the satisfaction of the court for the performance by the apprentice of his contract of apprenticeship, accept such security instead of or in mitigation of any punishment which it is authorized to inflict upon the apprentice.

---

## PART II.

### *Procedure.*

**8.** A person may give security under this Act in a county court or court of summary jurisdiction by an oral or written acknowledgment in or under the direction of the court of the undertaking or condition by which and the sum for which he is bound, in such manner and form as may be prescribed by any rule for the time being in force, and in any case where security is so given, the court in or under the direction of which it is given may order payment of any sum which may become due in pursuance of such security. *Mode of giving security.*

The Lord Chancellor may at any time after the passing of this Act, and from time to time make, and when made, rescind, alter, and add to, rules with respect to giving security under this Act (*p*).

**9.** Any dispute or matter in respect of which jurisdiction is given by this Act to a court of summary jurisdiction shall be deemed to be a matter on which that court has authority by law to make an order on complaint in pursuance of the Summary Jurisdiction Act, but shall not be deemed to be a criminal proceeding ; and all powers by this Act conferred on a court of summary jurisdiction shall be deemed to be in addition to and not in derogation of any powers conferred on it by the Summary Jurisdiction Act, except that a warrant shall not be issued under that Act for apprehending any person other than an apprentice for failing to appear to answer a complaint in any proceeding under this Act, and that an order made by a court of summary jurisdiction under this Act for the payment of any money shall not be enforced by imprisonment except in the manner and under the conditions by this Act provided ; and no goods or chattels shall be taken under a distress ordered by a court of summary jurisdiction which might not be taken under an execution issued by a county court. *Summary proceedings.*

A court of summary jurisdiction may direct any sum of money, for the payment of which it makes an order under this Act, to be paid by instalments, and may from time to time rescind or vary such order.

Any sum payable by any person under the order of a court of summary jurisdiction in pursuance of this Act, shall be deemed to be a debt due from him in pursuance of a judgment of a competent court within the meaning of the fifth section of the Debtors Act, 1869, and may be enforced accordingly ; and as regards any such debt a court of summary jurisdiction shall be deemed to be a court within the meaning of the said section.

The Lord Chancellor may at any time after the passing of this Act, and from time to time make, and when made, rescind, alter, and add to, rules for carrying into effect the jurisdiction by this Act given to a court of summary jurisdiction, and in particular for the purpose of regulating the costs of any proceedings in a court of summary jurisdiction, with power to provide that the same shall not exceed the costs which would in a similar case be incurred in a county court, and any rules so made in so far as they relate to the exercise of jurisdiction under the said fifth section of the Debtors Act, 1869, shall be deemed to be prescribed rules within the meaning of the said section.

(*p*) See Chitty's Statutes (Annual Continuation), 2, pt. 1, 51, for the Rules of 1886.

## PART III.

### *Definitions and Miscellaneous.*

#### *Definitions.*

Definitions:
"Workman:"

**10.** In this Act—

The expression "workman" does not include a domestic or menial servant, but save as aforesaid, means any person who, being a labourer, servant in husbandry, journeyman, artificer, handicraftsman, miner, or otherwise engaged in manual labour, whether under the age of twenty-one years or above that age, has entered into or works under a contract with an employer, whether the contract be made before or after the passing of this Act, be express or implied, oral or in writing, and be a contract of service or a contract personally to execute any work or labour.

"The Summary Jurisdiction Act."

The expression "the Summary Jurisdiction Act" means the Act of the session of the eleventh and twelfth years of the reign of her present Majesty, chapter forty-three, intituled "An Act to facilitate the performance of the duties of Justices of the Peace out of sessions within England and Wales with respect to summary convictions and orders," inclusive of any Acts amending the same.

The expression "court of summary jurisdiction" means—

(1.) As respects the city of London, the Lord Mayor or any alderman of the said city sitting at the Mansion House or Guildhall justice room; and

(2.) As respects any police court division in the metropolitan police district, any metropolitan police magistrate sitting at the police court for that division; and

(3.) As respects any city, town, liberty, borough, place, or district for which a stipendiary magistrate is for the time being acting, such stipendiary magistrate sitting at a police court or other place appointed in that behalf; and

(4.) Elsewhere any justice or justices of the peace to whom jurisdiction is given by the Summary Jurisdiction Act: Provided that, as respects any case within the cognizance of such justice or justices as last aforesaid, a complaint under this Act shall be heard and determined and an order for imprisonment made by two or more justices of the peace in petty sessions sitting at some place appointed for holding petty sessions.

Nothing in this section contained shall restrict the jurisdiction of the Lord Mayor or any alderman of the city of London, or of any metropolitan police or stipendiary magistrate in respect of any act or jurisdiction which may now be done or exercised by him out of court.

Set-off in case of factory workers.

**11.** In the case of a child, young person, or woman subject to the provisions of the Factory Acts, 1833 to 1874 (*q*), any forfeiture on the ground of absence or leaving work shall not be deducted from or set off against a claim for wages or other sum due for work done before such absence or leaving work, except to the amount of the damage (if any) which the employer may have sustained by reason of such absence or leaving work.

#### *Application.*

Application to apprentices.

**12.** This Act in so far as it relates to apprentices shall apply only to an apprentice to the business of a workman as defined by this Act upon whose binding either no premium is paid, or the premium (if any) paid does not exceed twenty-five pounds, and to an apprentice bound under the provisions of the Acts relating to the relief of the poor.

#### *Saving Clause.*

Saving of special jurisdiction, and seamen.

**13.** Nothing in this Act shall take away or abridge any local or special jurisdiction touching apprentices.

This Act shall not apply to seamen or to apprentices to the sea service (*r*).

---

(*q*) See Factory and Workshop Act, 1878, s. 102.

(*r*) The Act is extended to seamen and apprentices to the sea service by 43 & 44 Vict. c. 16, s. 11.

## PART IV.

### Application of Act to Scotland.

**14.** This Act shall extend to Scotland, with the modifications following; Application to Scotland.
(that is to say,)

In this Act with respect to Scotland— Definitions.
The expression "county court" means the ordinary sheriff court of the county:

The expression "the court of summary jurisdiction" means the small debt court of the sheriff of the county:

The expression "sheriff" includes sheriff substitute:

The expression "instrument of apprenticeship" means indenture:

The expression "plaintiff" or "complainant" means pursuer or complainer:

The expression "defendant" includes defender or respondent:

The expression "The Summary Jurisdiction Act" means the Act of the seventh year of the reign of his Majesty King William the Fourth and the first year of the reign of her present Majesty, chapter forty-one, intituled "An Act for the more effectual recovery of small debts in the Sheriff Courts, and for regulating the establishment of circuit courts for the trial of small debt causes by the sheriffs in Scotland," and the Acts amending the same.

The expression "surety" means cautioner:

This Act shall be read and construed as if for the expression "the Lord Chancellor," wherever it occurs therein, the expression "the Court of Session by act of sederunt" were substituted.

All jurisdictions, powers, and authorities necessary for the purposes of this Act are hereby conferred on sheriffs in their ordinary or small debt courts, as the case may be, who shall have full power to make any order, on any summons, petition, complaint, or other proceeding under this Act, that any county court or court of summary jurisdiction is empowered to make on any complaint or other proceeding under this Act.

Any decree or order pronounced or made by a sheriff under this Act shall be enforced in the same manner and under the same conditions in and under which a decree or order pronounced or made by him in his ordinary or small debt court, as the case may be, is enforced.

## PART V.

### Application of Act to Ireland.

**15.** This Act shall extend to Ireland, with the modifications following; Application to Ireland.
(that is to say,)

The expression "county court" shall be construed to mean civil bill court:

The expression "Lord Chancellor" shall be construed to mean the Lord Chancellor of Ireland:

The expression "The Summary Jurisdiction Act" shall be construed to mean, as regards the police districts of Dublin metropolis, the Acts regulating the powers and duties of justices of the peace for such district, and elsewhere in Ireland, the Petty Sessions (Ireland) Act, 1851, and any Act amending the same:

The expression "court of summary jurisdiction" shall be construed to mean any justice or justices of the peace or other magistrate to whom jurisdiction is given by the Summary Jurisdiction Act:

The court of summary jurisdiction, when hearing and determining complaints under this Act, shall in the police district of Dublin metropolis be constituted of one or more of the divisional justices of the said district, and elsewhere in Ireland of two or more justices of the peace in petty sessions sitting at a place appointed for holding petty sessions:

The expression "fifth section of the Debtors Act, 1869," shall be constituted to mean "sixth section of the Debtors Act (Ireland), 1872."

39 & 40 VICT. CAP. 80.

*An Act to amend the Merchant Shipping Acts.*
[*15th August,* 1876.]

BE it enacted by the Queen's most excellent Majesty, by and with the advice and consent of the Lords spiritual and temporal, and Commons, in this present Parliament assembled, and by the authority of the same, as follows:

### *Preliminary.*

Short title.　**1.** This Act may be cited as the Merchant Shipping Act, 1876.

Construction of Act.　**2.** This Act shall be construed as one with the Merchant Shipping Act, 1854, and the Acts amending the same ; and the said Acts and this Act may be cited collectively as the Merchant Shipping Acts, 1854 to 1876.

Commencement of Act.　**3.** This Act shall come into operation on the first day of October, 1876 (which day is in this Act referred to as the commencement of this Act) ; nevertheless any Orders in Council and general rules under this Act may be made at any time after the passing of this Act, but shall not come into operation before the commencement of this Act.

### *Unseaworthy Ships.*

Sending unseaworthy ship to sea a misdemeanor.　**4.** Every person who sends or attempts to send, or is party to sending or attempting to send a British ship to sea in such unseaworthy state that the life of any person is likely to be thereby endangered, shall be guilty of a misdemeanor, unless he proves that he used all reasonable means to insure her being sent to sea in a seaworthy state, or that her going to sea in such unseaworthy state was, under the circumstances, reasonable and justifiable, and for the purpose of giving such proof he may give evidence in the same manner as any other witness.

Every master of a British ship who knowingly takes the same to sea in such unseaworthy state that the life of any person is likely to be thereby endangered shall be guilty of a misdemeanor, unless he proves that her going to sea in such unseaworthy state was, under the circumstances, reasonable and justifiable, and for the purpose of giving such proof he may give evidence in the same manner as any other witness.

A prosecution under this section shall not be instituted except by or with the consent of the Board of Trade, or of the governor of the British possession in which such prosecution takes place.

A misdemeanor under this section shall not be punishable upon summary conviction.

Obligation of shipowner to crew with respect to use of reasonable efforts to secure seaworthiness.　**5.** In every contract of service, express or implied, between the owner of a ship and the master or any seaman thereof, and in every instrument of apprenticeship whereby any person is bound to serve as an apprentice on board any ship, there shall be implied, notwithstanding any agreement to the contrary, an obligation on the owner of the ship, that the owner of the ship, and the master, and every agent charged with the loading of the ship, or the preparing thereof for sea, or the sending thereof to sea, shall use all reasonable means to insure the seaworthiness of the ship for the voyage at the time when the voyage commences, and to keep her in a seaworthy condition for the voyage during the same : Provided, that nothing in this section shall subject the owner of a ship to any liability by reason of the ship being sent to sea in an unseaworthy state where, owing to special circumstances, the so sending thereof to sea is reasonable and justifiable.

Power to detain unsafe ships, and procedure for such detention.　**6.** Where a British ship, being in any port of the United Kingdom, is by reason of the defective condition of her hull, equipments or machinery, or by reason of overloading or improper loading, unfit to proceed to sea without serious danger to human life, having regard to the nature of the service for which she is intended, any such ship (hereinafter referred to as "unsafe") may be provisionally detained for the purpose of being surveyed, and either finally detained or released, as follows :

(1.) The Board of Trade, if they have reason to believe on complaint, or otherwise, that a British ship is unsafe, may provisionally order the detention of the ship for the purpose of being surveyed.

(2.) When a ship has been provisionally detained there shall be forthwith served on the master of the ship a written statement of the grounds of her detention, and the Board of Trade may, if they think fit, appoint some competent person or persons to survey the ship and report thereon to the Board.

(3.) The Board of Trade on receiving the report may either order the ship to be released or, if in their opinion the ship is unsafe, may order her to be finally detained, either absolutely, or until the performance of such conditions with respect to the execution of repairs or alterations, or the unloading or reloading of cargo, as the Board think necessary for the protection of human life, and may from time to time vary or add to any such order.

(4.) Before the order for final detention is made a copy of the report shall be served upon the master of the ship, and within seven days after such service the owner or master of the ship may appeal in the prescribed manner to the court of survey (hereinafter mentioned) for the port or district where the ship is detained.

(5.) Where a ship has been provisionally detained, the owner or master of the ship, at any time before the person appointed under this section to survey the ship makes such survey, may require that he shall be accompanied by such person as the owner or master may select out of the list of assessors for the court of survey (nominated as hereinafter mentioned), and in such case if the surveyor and assessors agree, the Board of Trade shall cause the ship to be detained or released accordingly, but if they differ, the Board of Trade may act as if the requisition had not been made, and the owner and the master shall have the like appeal touching the report of the surveyor as is before provided by this section.

(6.) Where a ship has been provisionally detained, the Board of Trade may at any time, if they think it expedient, refer the matter to the court of survey for the port or district where the ship is detained.

(7.) The Board of Trade may at any time, if satisfied that a ship detained under this Act is not unsafe, order her to be released either upon or without any conditions.

(8.) For the better execution of this section, the Board of Trade, with the consent of the Treasury, may from time to time appoint a sufficient number of fit officers, and may remove any of them.

(9.) Any officer so appointed (in this Act referred to as a detaining officer) shall have the same power as the Board of Trade have under this section of provisionally ordering the detention of a ship for the purpose of being surveyed, and of appointing a person or persons to survey her ; and if he thinks that a ship so detained by him is not unsafe may order her to be released.

(10.) A detaining officer shall forthwith report to the Board of Trade any order made by him for the detention or release of a ship.

7. A court of survey for a port or district shall consist of a judge sitting with two assessors.

Constitution of court of survey for appeals.

The judge shall be such person as may be summoned for the case in accordance with the rules made under this Act out of a list (from time to time approved for the port or district by one of her Majesty's Principal Secretaries of State, in this Act referred to as a Secretary of State) of wreck commissioners appointed under this Act, stipendiary or metropolitan police magistrates, judges of county courts, and all other fit persons ; but in any special case in which the Board of Trade think it expedient to appoint a wreck commissioner, the judge shall be such wreck commissioner.

The assessors shall be persons of nautical engineering or other special skill and experience ; one of them shall be appointed by the Board of Trade, either generally or in each case, and the other shall be summoned in accordance with the rules under this Act by the registrar of the court, out of a list of persons periodically nominated for the purpose by the local marine board of the port, or, if there is no such board, by a body of local shipowners or merchants approved for the purpose by a Secretary of State, or if there is no such list, shall be appointed by the judge ; if a Secretary of State think fit at any time, on the recommendation of the government of any British possession or any foreign state, to add any person or persons to any such list, such person or persons shall, until otherwise directed by the Secretary of State, be added to such list, and if there is no such list shall form such list.

The county court registrar, or such other fit person as a Secretary of State may from time to time appoint shall be the registrar of the court, and shall on receiving notice of an appeal on a reference from the Board of Trade, immediately summon the court in the prescribed manner to meet forthwith.

The name of the registrar and his office, together with the rules made under this Act relating to the court of survey, shall be published in the prescribed manner.

**Power and procedure of court of survey.** 8. With respect to the court of survey the following provisions shall have effect :

(1.) The case shall be heard in open court ;

(2.) The judge and each assessor may survey the ship, and shall have for the purposes of this Act all the powers of an inspector appointed by the Board of Trade under the Merchant Shipping Act, 1854 ;

(3.) The judge may appoint any competent person or persons to survey the ship and report thereon to the court ;

(4.) The judge shall have the same power as the Board of Trade have to order the ship to be released or finally detained, but unless one of the assessors concurs in an order for the detention of the ship, the ship shall be released ;

(5.) The owner and master of the ship and any person appointed by the owner or master, and also any person appointed by the Board of Trade, may attend at any inspection or survey made in pursuance of this section ;

(6.) The judge shall send to the Board of Trade the prescribed report, and each assessor shall either sign the report or report to the Board of Trade the reasons for his dissent.

**Rules for procedure of court of survey, &c.** 9. The Lord Chancellor of Great Britain may from time to time (with the consent of the Treasury so far as relates to fees) make, and when made revoke, alter, and add to general rules to carry into effect the provisions of this Act with respect to a court of survey, and in particular with respect to the summoning of and procedure before the court, the requiring on an appeal security for costs and damages, the amount and application of fees, and the publication of the rules.

All such rules while in force shall have effect as if enacted in this Act, and the expression " prescribed " in the provisions of this Act relating to the detention of ships or court of survey means prescribed by such rules.

**Liability of Board of Trade and shipowner for costs and damages.** 10. If it appears that there was not reasonable and probable cause, by reason of the condition of the ship or the act or default of the owner, for the provisional detention of the ship, the Board of Trade shall be liable to pay to the owner of the ship his costs of and incidental to the detention and survey of the ship, and also compensation for any loss or damage sustained by him by reason of the detention or survey.

If a ship is finally detained under this Act, or if it appears that a ship provisionally detained was, at the time of such detention, unsafe within the meaning of this Act, the owner of the ship shall be liable to pay to the Board of Trade their costs of and incidental to the detention and survey of the ship, and those costs shall, without prejudice to any other remedy, be recoverable as salvage is recoverable.

For the purposes of this Act the costs of and incidental to any proceeding before a court of survey, and a reasonable amount in respect of the remuneration of the surveyor or officer of the Board of Trade, shall be deemed to be part of the costs of the detention and survey of the ship, and any dispute as to the amount of costs under this Act may be referred to one of the masters or registrars of the Supreme Court of Judicature, who, on request made to him for that purpose by the Board of Trade, shall ascertain and certify the proper amount of such costs.

An action for any costs or compensation payable by the Board of Trade under this section may be brought against the secretary thereof by his official title as if he were a corporation sole ; and if the cause of action arises in Ireland, it shall be lawful for any of the superior courts of common law in Ireland in which such action may be commenced to order that the summons or writ may be served on the Crown and Treasury Solicitor for Ireland, in such manner and on such terms as to extension of time and otherwise as to the court shall seem fit, and that such service shall be deemed good and sufficient service of such summons or writ upon the Secretary of the Board of Trade.

11. Where a complaint is made to the Board of Trade or a detaining officer that a British ship is unsafe, the Board or officer may, if they or he think fit, require the complainant to give security to the satisfaction of the Board for the costs and compensation which he may become liable to pay as hereinafter mentioned. Power to require from complainant security for costs.

Provided that where the complaint is made by one fourth, being not less than three, of the seamen belonging to the ship, and is not in the opinion of the Board or officer frivolous or vexatious, such security shall not be required, and the Board or officer shall, if the complaint is made in sufficient time before the sailing of the ship, take proper steps for ascertaining whether the ship ought to be detained under this Act.

Where a ship is detained in consequence of any complaint, and the circumstances are such that the Board of Trade are liable under this Act to pay to the owner of the ship any costs or compensation, the complainant shall be liable to pay to the Board of Trade all such costs and compensation as the Board incur or are liable to pay in respect of the detention and survey of the ship.

12. (1.) A detaining officer shall have for the purpose of his duties under this Act the same powers as an inspector appointed by the Board of Trade under the Merchant Shipping Act, 1854. Supplemental provisions as to detention of ship.

(2.) An order for the detention of a ship, provisional or final, and an order varying the same, shall be served as soon as may be on the master of the ship.

(3.) When a ship has been detained under this Act she shall not be released by reason of her British register being subsequently closed.

(4.) For the purposes of a survey of a ship under this Act any person authorized to make the same may go on board the ship and inspect the same and every part thereof, and the machinery, equipments, and cargo, and may require the unloading or removal of any cargo, ballast, or tackle.

(5.) The provisions of the Merchant Shipping Act, 1854, with respect to persons who wilfully impede an inspector, or disobey a requisition or order of an inspector, shall apply as if those provisions were herein enacted, with the substitution for the inspector of any judge, assessor, officer, or surveyor who under this Act has the same powers as an inspector or has authority to survey a ship.

*Foreign Ships, Overloading.*

13. Where a foreign ship has taken on board all or any part of her cargo at a port in the United Kingdom, and is whilst at that port unsafe by reason of overloading or improper loading, the provisions of this Act with respect to the detention of ships shall apply to that foreign ship as if she were a British ship, with the following modifications : Application to foreign ships of provisions as to detention.

(1.) A copy of the order for the provisional detention of the ship shall be forthwith served on the consular officer for the State to which the ship belongs at or nearest to the place where the ship is detained :

(2.) Where a ship has been provisionally detained, the consular officer, on the request of the owner or master of the ship, may require that the person appointed by the Board of Trade to survey the ship shall be accompanied by such person as the consular officer may select, and in such case, if the surveyor and such person agree, the Board of Trade shall cause the ship to be detained or released accordingly, but if they differ, the Board of Trade may act as if the requisition had not been made, and the owner and master shall have the appeal to the court of survey touching the report of the surveyor which is before provided by this Act ; and

(3.) Where the owner or master of the ship appeals to the court of survey, the consular officer, on the request of such owner or master, may appoint any competent person who shall be assessor in such case in lieu of the assessor who, if the ship were a British ship, would be appointed otherwise than by the Board of Trade.

In this section the expression "consular officer" means any consul-general, vice-consul, consular-agent, or other officer recognized by a Secretary of State, as a consular officer of a foreign state.

*Appeal on Refusal of certain Certificates to Ships.*

Appeal on refusal of certain certificates under Merchant Shipping and Passengers Acts.

**14.** Whereas by section three hundred and nine of the Merchant Shipping Act, 1854, and enactments amending the same, the owner of a passenger steamer as defined in that Act (*s*) is required to cause the same to be surveyed by a shipwright surveyor and an engineer surveyor, and those surveyors are required to give declarations of certain particulars with respect to the sufficiency or conformity with the Act of the ship and equipments, and to the limits beyond which the ship is not fit to ply, and to the number of passengers which the ship is fit to carry, and of other particulars in the said section mentioned, and the Board of Trade, under section three hundred and twelve of the same Act, issue a certificate upon such declarations, and the passenger steamer cannot lawfully proceed to sea without obtaining such certificate;

And whereas under sections eleven and fifty of the Passengers Act, 1855, and the enactments amending the same, a passenger ship within the meaning of those sections (in this Act referred to as an emigrant ship) cannot lawfully proceed to sea without a certificate of clearance from an emigration officer, or other officer in those sections mentioned, showing that all the requirements of the said sections and enactments have been complied with, and that the ship is in the officer's opinion seaworthy, and that the passengers and crew are in a fit state to proceed to sea, and otherwise as therein mentioned;

And whereas by section thirty of the Merchant Shipping Act Amendment Act, 1862, provision is made for preventing a ship from proceeding to sea in certain cases without a certificate from a surveyor or person appointed by the Board of Trade to the effect that the ship is properly provided with lights, and with the means of making fog signals;

And whereas it is expedient to give in the said cases such appeal as hereinafter mentioned : Be it therefore enacted that—

If a shipowner feels aggrieved,

(1.) by a declaration of a shipwright surveyor or an engineer surveyor respecting a passenger steamer under the above-recited enactments, or by the refusal of a surveyor to give the said declaration ; or,

(2.) by the refusal of a certificate of clearance for an emigrant ship under the above-recited enactments ; or

(3.) by the refusal of a certificate as to lights or fog signals under the above-recited enactment,

the owner may appeal in the prescribed manner to the court of survey for the port or district where the ship for the time being is.

On such appeal the judge of the court of survey shall report to the Board of Trade on the question raised by the appeal, and the Board of Trade, when satisfied that the requirements of the report and the other provisions of the said enactments have been complied with, may—

(1.) In the case of a passenger steamer give their certificate under section three hundred and twelve of the Merchant Shipping Act, 1854, and

(2.) In the case of an emigrant ship give, or direct the emigration or other officer to give, a certificate of clearance under the above-mentioned enactments, and

(3.) In the case of a refusal of a certificate as to lights or fog signals give or direct a surveyor or other person appointed by them to give a certificate under section thirty of the Merchant Shipping Act Amendment Act, 1862.

Subject to any order made by the judge of the court of survey, the costs of and incidental to an appeal under this section shall follow the event.

Subject as aforesaid, the provisions of this Act with respect to the court of survey and appeals thereto, so far as consistent with the tenour thereof, shall apply to the court of survey when acting under this section, and to appeals under this section.

Where the survey of a ship is made for the purpose of a declaration or certificate under the above-recited enactment, the person appointed to make

(*s*) Sect. 303.

the survey shall, if so required by the owner, be accompanied on the survey by some person appointed by the owner, and in such case, if the said two persons agree, there shall be no appeal to the court of survey in pursuance of this section.

### Scientific Referees.

**15.** If the Board of Trade are of opinion that an appeal under this Act involves a question of construction or design or of scientific difficulty or important principle, they may refer the matter to such one or more out of a list of scientific referees from time to time approved by a Secretary of State, as may appear to possess the special qualifications necessary for the particular case, and may be selected by agreement between the Board of Trade and the appellant, or in default of any such agreement by a Secretary of State, and thereupon the appeal shall be determined by the referee or referees, instead of by the court of survey. *Reference in difficult cases to scientific persons.*

The Board of Trade, if the appellant in any appeal so require and give security to the satisfaction of the Board to pay the costs of and incidental to the reference, shall refer that appeal to a referee or referees so selected as aforesaid.

The referee or referees shall have the same powers as a judge of the court of survey.

### Passenger Steamers and Emigrant Ships.

**16.** Any steamship may carry passengers not exceeding twelve in number although she has not been surveyed by the Board of Trade as a passenger steamer, and does not carry a Board of Trade certificate as provided by the Merchant Shipping Act, 1854, with respect to passenger steamers. *Exemption of certain steamers from passenger certificates.*

**17.** Where the legislature of any British possession provides for the survey of and grant of certificates for passenger steamers, and the Board of Trade report to her Majesty that they are satisfied that the certificates are to the like effect, and are granted after a like survey, and in such manner as to be equally efficient with the certificates granted for the same purpose in the United Kingdom under the Acts relating to merchant shipping, it shall be lawful to her Majesty by Order in Council— *Colonial certificates for passenger steamers.*

(1.) To declare that the said certificates shall be of the same force as if they had been granted under the said Acts ; and

(2.) To declare that all or any of the provisions of the said Acts which relate to certificates granted for passenger steamers under those Acts shall, either without modification or with such modifications as to her Majesty may seem necessary, apply to the certificates referred to in the Order ; and

(3.) To impose such conditions and to make such regulations with respect to the said certificates, and to the use, delivery, and cancellation thereof, as to her Majesty may seem fit, and to impose penalties not exceeding fifty pounds for the breach of such conditions and regulations.

**18.** In every case where a passenger certificate has been granted to any steamer by the Board of Trade under the provisions of the Merchant Shipping Act, 1854, and remain still in force, it shall not be requisite for the purposes of the employment of such steamer under the Passengers Act that she shall be again surveyed in her hull and machinery in order to qualify her for service under the Passengers Act, 1855, and the Acts amending the same ; but for the purposes of employment under those Acts such Board of Trade certificate shall be deemed to satisfy the requirements of the Passengers Acts with respect to such survey, and any further survey of the hull and machinery shall be dispensed with, and so long as a steamship is an emigrant ship that is a passenger ship within the meaning of the Passengers Act, 1855, and the Acts amending the same, and the provisions contained in the said Passengers Acts as to the survey of her hull, machinery, and equipments have been complied with, she shall not be subject to the provisions of the Merchant Shipping Act, 1854, with respect to the survey of and certificate for passenger steamers, or to the enactments amending the same. *Provision against double survey in case of passenger steamers and emigrant ships.*

**19.** Where a foreign ship is a passenger steamer subject to the Merchant Shipping Act, 1854, and the Acts amending the same, or an emigrant ship subject to the Passengers Act, 1855, and the Acts amending the same, and *Provision as to survey of foreign pas-*

senger steamer or emigrant ship.

the Board of Trade are satisfied, by the production of a foreign certificate of survey attested by a British consular officer at the port of survey, that such ship has been officially surveyed at a foreign port, and are satisfied that the requirements of the said Acts, or any of them, are proved by such survey to have been substantially complied with, the Board may, if they think fit, dispense with any further survey of the ship in respect of the requirements so complied with, and give or direct one of their officers to give a certificate, which shall have the same effect as if given upon survey under the said Acts or any of them : Provided that her Majesty may by Order in Council direct that this section shall not apply in the case of an official survey at any foreign port at which it appears to her Majesty that corresponding provisions are not extended to British ships.

Power to modify Passengers Acts as to food, space, and accommodation in emigrant ships.

**20.** It shall be lawful for the Board of Trade, if satisfied that the food, space, accommodation, or any other particular or thing provided in an emigrant ship for any class of passengers is superior to the food, space, accommodation, or other particular or thing required by the Passengers Act, 1855, and the Acts amending the same, to exempt such ship from any of the requirements of those Acts with respect to food, space, or accommodation, or other particular or thing, in such manner and upon such conditions as the Board of Trade may think fit.

Provision of signals of distress, inextinguishable lights, and life buoys in passenger steamers and emigrant ships.

**21.** Every sea-going passenger steamer and every emigrant ship shall be provided to the satisfaction of the Board of Trade —

(1.) With means for making the signals of distress at night specified in the First Schedule to the Merchant Shipping Act, 1873, or in any rules substituted therefor, including means of making flames on the ship which are inextinguishable in water, or such other means of making signals of distress as the Board of Trade may previously approve ; and

(2.) With a proper supply of lights inextinguishable in water and fitted for attachment to life buoys.

If any such steamer or ship goes to sea from any port of the United Kingdom without being so provided as required by this section, for each default in any of the above requisites the owner shall, if he appears to be in fault, incur a penalty not exceeding one hundred pounds, and the master shall, if he appears to be in fault, incur a penalty not exceeding fifty pounds.

*Grain Cargoes.*

**22.** [Repealed by Merchant Shipping (Carriage of Grain) Act, 1880, s. 11.]

*Deck Cargoes.*

Space occupied by deck cargo to be liable to dues

**23.** If any ship, British or foreign, other than home trade ships as defined by the Merchant Shipping Act, 1854, carries as deck cargo, that is to say, in any uncovered space upon deck, or in any covered space not included in the cubical contents forming the ship's registered tonnage, timber, stores, or other goods, all dues payable on the ship's tonnage shall be payable as if there were added to the ship's registered tonnage the tonnage of the space occupied by such goods at the time at which such dues become payable.

The space so occupied shall be deemed to be the space limited by the area occupied by the goods and by straight lines inclosing a rectangular space sufficient to include the goods.

The tonnage of such space shall be ascertained by an officer of the Board of Trade or of Customs, in manner directed by sub-section four of section twenty-one of the Merchant Shipping Act, 1854, and when so ascertained shall be entered by him in the ship's official log-book, and also in a memorandum which he shall deliver to the master, and the master shall, when the said dues are demanded, produce such memorandum in like manner as if it were the certificate of registry, or, in the case of a foreign ship, the document equivalent to a certificate of registry, and in default shall be liable to the same penalty as if he had failed to produce the said certificate or document.

Penalty for carrying deckloads of timber in winter.

**24.** After the first day of November one thousand eight hundred and seventy-six, if a ship, British or foreign, arrives between the last day of October and the sixteenth day of April in any year at any port in the United Kingdom from any port out of the United Kingdom, carrying as deck cargo, that is to say, in any uncovered space upon deck, or in any covered space not included in the cubical contents forming the ship's registered tonnage, any wood goods coming within the following descriptions ; (that is to say,)

(*a*) Any square, round, waney, or other timber, or any pitch, pine, mahogany, oak, teak, or other heavy wood goods whatever ; or

(*b*) Any more than five spare spars or store spars, whether or not made, dressed, and finally prepared for use ; or

(*c*) Any deals, battens, or other light wood goods of any description to a height exceeding three feet above the deck ;

the master of the ship, and also the owner, if he is privy to the offence, shall be liable to a penalty not exceeding five pounds for every hundred cubic feet of wood goods carried in contravention of this section, and such penalty may be recovered by action or on indictment or to an amount not exceeding one hundred pounds (whatever may be the maximum penalty recoverable) on summary conviction.

Provided that a master or owner shall not be liable to any penalty under this section—

(1.) In respect of any wood goods which the master has considered it necessary to place or keep on deck during the voyage on account of the springing of any leak, or of any other damage to the ship received or apprehended ; or

(2 ) If he proves that the ship sailed from the port at which the wood goods were loaded as deck cargo at such time before the last day of October as allowed a sufficient interval according to the ordinary duration of the voyage for the ship to arrive before that day at the said port in the United Kingdom, but was prevented from so arriving by stress of weather or circumstances beyond his control ; or

(3.) If he proves that the ship sailed from the port at which the wood goods were loaded as deck cargo at such time before the sixteenth day of April as allowed a reasonable interval according to the ordinary duration of the voyage for the ship to arrive after that day at the said port in the United Kingdom, and by reason of an exceptionally favourable voyage arrived before that day.

Provided further, that nothing in this section shall affect any ship not bound to any port in the United Kingdom which comes into any port of the United Kingdom under stress of weather, or for repairs, or for any other purpose than the delivery of her cargo.

*Deck and Load Lines.*

**25.** Every British ship (except ships under eighty tons register employed solely in the coasting trade, ships employed solely in fishing, and pleasure yachts) shall be permanently and conspicuously marked with lines of not less than twelve inches in length and one inch in breadth, painted longitudinally on each side amidships, or as near thereto as is practicable, and indicating the position of each deck which is above water.

*Marking of deck-lines.*

The upper edge of each of these lines shall be level with the upper side of the deck plank next the waterway at the place of marking.

The lines shall be white or yellow on a dark ground, or black on a light ground.

**26.** With respect to the marking of a load-line on British ships the following provisions shall have effect :

*Marking of load-line on foreign-going British ships.*

(1.) The owner of every British ship (except ships under eighty tons register employed solely in the coasting trade, ships employed solely in fishing, and pleasure yachts) shall, before entering his ship outwards from any port in the United Kingdom upon any voyage for which he is required so to enter her, or, if that is not practicable, as soon after as may be, mark upon each of her sides amidships, or as near thereto as practicable, in white or yellow on a dark ground, or in black on a light ground, a circular disc twelve inches in diameter, with a horizontal line eighteen inches in length drawn through its centre :

(2.) The centre of this disc shall indicate the maximum load-line in salt water to which the owner intends to load the ship for that voyage :

(3.) He shall also, upon so entering her, insert in the form of entry delivered to the collector or other principal officer of Customs a statement in writing of the distance in feet and inches between the centre of this disc and the upper edge of each of the lines indicating the position of the ship's deck which is above that centre :

(4.) If default is made in delivering this statement in the case of any ship, any officer of Customs may refuse to enter the ship outwards :

(5.) The master of the ship shall enter a copy of this statement in the agreement with the crew before it is signed by any member of the crew, and no superintendent of any mercantile marine office shall proceed with the engagement of the crew until this entry is made :

(6.) The master of the ship shall also enter a copy of this statement in the official log-book :

(7.) When a ship has been marked as by this section required, she shall be kept so marked until her next return to a port of discharge in the United Kingdom.

**Marking of load-line in case of coasting vessels.**
27. With respect to the marking of a load-line on British ships employed in the coasting trade, the following provisions shall have effect :

(1.) The owner of every British ship employed in the coasting trade on the coasts of the United Kingdom (except ships under eighty tons register employed solely in that trade) shall, before proceeding to sea from any port, mark upon each of her sides amidships, or as near thereto as is practicable, in white or yellow on a dark ground or in black on a light ground, a circular disc twelve inches in diameter, with a horizontal line eighteen inches in length drawn through its centre :

(2.) The centre of this disc shall indicate the maximum load-line in salt water to which the owner intends to load the ship, until notice is given of an alteration :

(3.) He shall also once in every twelve months immediately before the ship proceeds to sea, send or deliver to the collector or other principal officer of Customs of the port of registry of the ship a statement in writing of the distance in feet and inches between the centre of the disc and the upper edge of each of the lines indicating the position of the ship's decks which is above that centre :

(4.) The owner, before the ship proceeds to sea after any renewal or alteration of the disc shall send or deliver to the collector or other principal officer of Customs of the port of registry of the ship notice in writing of such renewal or alteration, together with such statement in writing as before mentioned of the distance between the centre of the disc and the upper edge of each of the decklines :

(5.) If default is made in sending or delivering any notice or statement required by this section to be sent or delivered, the owner shall be liable to a penalty not exceeding one hundred pounds :

(6.) When a ship has been marked as by this section required, she shall be kept so marked until notice is given of an alteration.

**Penalty for offences in relation to marks on ships.**
28. Any owner or master of a British ship who neglects to cause his ship to be marked as by this Act required, or to keep her so marked, or who allows the ship to be so loaded as to submerge in salt water the centre of the disc, and any person who conceals, removes, alters, defaces, or obliterates, or suffers any person under his control to conceal, remove, alter, deface, or obliterate, any of the said marks, except in the event of the particulars thereby denoted being lawfully altered, or except for the purpose of escaping capture by an enemy, shall for each offence incur a penalty not exceeding one hundred pounds.

If any of the marks required by this Act is in any respect inaccurate, so as to be likely to mislead, the owner of the ship shall incur a penalty not exceeding one hundred pounds.

*Investigations into Shipping Casualties.*

**Appointment, duties, and powers of wreck commissioners for investigating shipping casualties.**
29. For the purpose of rendering investigations into shipping casualties more speedy and effectual it shall be lawful for the Lord High Chancellor of Great Britain to appoint from time to time some fit person or persons to be a wreck commissioner or wreck commissioners for the United Kingdom, so that there shall not be more than three such commissioners at any one time, and to remove any such wreck commissioner ; and in case it shall become necessary to appoint a wreck commissioner in Ireland the Lord Chancellor of Ireland shall have the appointment and the power of removal of such wreck commissioner.

It shall be the duty of a wreck commissioner, at the request of the Board of Trade, to hold any formal investigation into a loss, abandonment, damage, or casualty (in this Act called a shipping casualty) (*t*) under the Eighth Part of the Merchant Shipping Act, 1854, and for that purpose he shall have the same jurisdiction and powers as are thereby conferred on two justices, and all the provisions of the Merchant Shipping Acts, 1854 to 1876, with respect to investigations conducted under the Eighth Part of the Merchant Shipping Act, 1854, shall apply to investigations held by a wreck commissioner (*u*).

**30.** The wreck commissioner, justices, or other authority holding a formal investigation into a shipping casualty shall hold the same with the assistance of an assessor or assessors of nautical engineering or other special skill or knowledge, to be appointed [by the commissioner, justices, or authority] (*v*) out of a list of persons for the time being approved for the purpose by a Secretary of State. *Assessors and rules of procedure on formal investigations into shipping casualties.*

The commissioner, justices, or authority, when of opinion that the investigation is likely to involve the cancellation or suspension of the certificate of a master or mate, shall, where practicable, appoint a person having experience in the merchant service to be one of the assessors.

Each assessor shall either sign the report made on the investigation, or report to the Board of Trade his reasons for his dissent therefrom.

The Lord High Chancellor of Great Britain may from time to time, with the consent of the Treasury so far as relates to fees, make, and when made revoke, alter, and add to general rules for carrying into effect the enactments relating to formal investigations into shipping casualties, and in particular with respect to the summoning of assessors, the procedure, the parties, the persons allowed to appear, the notice to such parties and persons or to persons affected, and the amount and application of fees.

All such rules, while in force, shall have effect as if enacted in this Act.

Every formal investigation into a shipping casualty shall be conducted in such manner that if a charge is made (*x*) against any person that person shall have an opportunity of making a defence (*y*).

**31.** A wreck commissioner may, at the request of the Board of Trade, by himself, or by some deputy approved by the Board of Trade, institute the same examination as a receiver of wreck under section four hundred and forty-eight of the Merchant Shipping Act, 1854, and shall for that purpose have the powers by that section conferred on a receiver of wreck. *Power for wreck commissioners to institute examination with respect to ships in distress under 17 & 18 Vict. c. 104, s. 448.*

**32.** In the following cases :—

(1.) Whenever any ship on or near the coasts of the United Kingdom or any British ship elsewhere has been stranded or damaged, and any witness is found at any place in the United Kingdom ; or

(2.) Whenever a British ship has been lost or is supposed to have been lost, and any evidence can be obtained in the United Kingdom as to the circumstances under which she proceeded to sea or was last heard of, the Board of Trade (without prejudice to any other powers) may, if they think fit, cause an inquiry to be made or formal investigation to be held, and all the provisions of the Merchant Shipping Acts, 1854 to 1876, shall apply to any such inquiry or investigation as if it had been made or held under the Eighth Part of the Merchant Shipping Act, 1854. *Power to hold inquiries or formal investigations as to stranded and missing ships.*

**33.** A formal investigation into a shipping casualty may be held at any place appointed in that behalf by the Board of Trade, and all enactments relating to the authority holding the investigation shall, for the purpose of the investigation, have effect as if the place so appointed were a place appointed for the exercise of the ordinary jurisdiction of that authority. *Place of investigation.*

## *Miscellaneous.*

**34.** Where under the Merchant Shipping Acts, 1854 to 1876, or any of them, a ship is authorized or ordered to be detained, any commissioned officer on full pay in the naval or military service of her Majesty, or any officer of the Board of Trade or Customs, or any British consular officer may detain the ship, and if the ship after such detention or after service on the master of any notice or order for such detention proceeds to sea before it is released by competent authority, the master of the ship, and also the owner, and any *Enforcing detention of ship.*

---

(*t*) *Ex parte Story*, 3 Q. B. D. 166.
(*u*) Sects. 432—438.
(*v*) The words within brackets repealed by Statute Law Revision Act,

1883.
(*x*) *Ex parte Minto*, 35 L. T. 808.
(*y*) As to rehearing, see 42 & 43 Vict. c. 72.

person who sends the ship to sea, if such owner or person be party or privy to the offence, shall forfeit and pay to her Majesty a penalty not exceeding one hundred pounds.

Where a ship so proceeding to sea when on board thereof in the execution of his duty any officer authorized to detain the ship, or any surveyor or officer of the Board of Trade or Customs, the owner and master of the ship shall each be liable to pay all expenses of and incidental to the officer or surveyor being so taken to sea, and also a penalty not exceeding one hundred pounds, or, if the offence is not prosecuted in a summary manner, not exceeding ten pounds for every day until the officer or surveyor returns, or until such time as would enable him after leaving the ship to return to the port from which he is taken, and such expenses may be recovered in like manner as the penalty.

**Service of order on master, &c.**  **35.** Where any order, notice, statement, or document requires, for the purpose of any provision of this Act, to be served on the master of a ship, the same shall be served, where there is no master, and the ship is in the United Kingdom, on the managing owner of the ship, or if there is no managing owner, on some agent of the owner residing in the United Kingdom, or where no such agent is known or can be found, by affixing a copy thereof to the mast of the ship.

Any such order, notice, statement, or document may be served by delivering a copy thereof personally to the person to be served, or by leaving the same at his last place of abode, or in the case of a master by leaving it for him on board the ship with the person being or appearing to be in command or charge of such ship.

Any person who obstructs the service of any order, notice, statement, or document on the master of a ship shall incur a penalty not exceeding ten pounds, and if the owner or master of the ship is party or privy to such obstruction he shall be guilty of a misdemeanor.

**Ship's managing owner or manager to be registered.**  **36.** The name and address of the managing owner for the time being of every British ship registered at any port or place in the United Kingdom shall be registered at the custom-house of the ship's port of registry.

When there is not a managing owner there shall be so registered the name of the ship's husband or other person to whom the management of the ship is intrusted by or on behalf of the owner; and any person whose name is so registered shall, for the purposes of the Merchant Shipping Acts, 1854 to 1876, be under the same obligations, and subject to the same liabilities, as if he were the managing owner.

If default is made in complying with this section the owner shall be liable, or if there be more owners than one each owner shall be liable in proportion to his interest in the ship, to a penalty not exceeding in the whole one hundred pounds each time the ship leaves any port in the United Kingdom.

**Power for her Majesty by Order in Council to apply certain provisions of Merchant Shipping Acts to foreign ships.**  **37.** Whenever it has been made to appear to her Majesty that the government of any foreign state is desirous that any of the provisions of the Merchant Shipping Acts, 1854 to 1876, or of any Act hereafter to be passed amending the same, shall apply to the ships of such state, her Majesty may by Order in Council declare that such of the said provisions as are in such order specified shall (subject to the limitations, if any, contained in the order) apply, and thereupon, so long as the order remains in force, such provisions shall apply (subject to the said limitations) to the ships of such state, and to the owners, masters, seamen, and apprentices of such ships, when not locally within the jurisdiction of such state, in the same manner in all respects as if such ships were British ships.

**Provisions as to Order in Council.**  **38.** Where her Majesty has power under the Merchant Shipping Act, 1854, or any Act passed or hereafter to be passed amending the same, to make an Order in Council, it shall be lawful for her Majesty from time to time to make such Order in Council, and by Order in Council to revoke, alter, or add to any order so made.

Every such Order in Council shall be published in the *London Gazette*, and shall be laid before both Houses of Parliament within one month after it is made, if Parliament be then sitting, or if not, within one month after the then next meeting of Parliament.

Upon the publication of any such order in the *London Gazette*, the order shall, after the date of such publication, or any later date mentioned in the order, take effect as if it were enacted by Parliament.

**Fees, salaries, and costs.**  **39.** [On and after the first day of January one thousand eight hundred and seventy-seven all fees payable in respect of the survey or measurement of ships under the Merchant Shipping Acts, 1854 to 1876, or in respect of any services performed by any person employed under the authority of the Passengers Act, 1855, shall continue to be paid to the superintendent of a mercantile marine office at such times and in such manner as the Board of Trade from time to time direct, but shall be paid into the receipt of her Majesty's Exchequer in such manner as the Treasury from time to time direct, and shall be carried to and form part of the consolidated fund of the United Kingdom.

On and after the same day the salaries of all surveyors appointed under the Merchant Shipping Acts, 1854 to 1876, and so much of the expenses connected with the survey and measurement of ships under those Acts, and of the salaries and expenses of persons employed under the Passengers Act, 1855, as has heretofore been paid out of the Mercantile Marine Fund, shall be paid out of moneys provided by Parliament, and the Treasury shall have the like control over such salaries and expenses as has heretofore been vested in the Board of Trade] (z).

There may be paid out of moneys provided by Parliament, to any wreck commissioner, judge of a court of survey, assessor, registrar of a court of survey, detaining officer, scientific referee, and other officer or person appointed under this Act, such salary or remuneration (if any) as the Treasury from time to time direct.

[There may be paid out of moneys provided by Parliament all costs and compensation payable by the Board of Trade in pursuance of this Act] (z).

**40.** For the purpose of punishment, jurisdiction, and legal proceedings an offence under this Act shall be deemed to be an offence under the Merchant Shipping Act, 1854. *Legal proceedings in case of offences.*

**41.** In the application of this Act to Scotland,— *Application of Act to Scotland.*

The provision with respect to a prosecution not being instituted except by or with the consent of the Board of Trade shall not apply.

" Judge of a county court " shall be deemed to include a sheriff and sheriff substitute ; and

"Registrar of a county court" shall be deemed to include sheriff clerk; and

" A master of the Supreme Court of Judicature " shall mean the Queen's and Lord Treasurer's Remembrancer.

**42.** In the application of this Act to Ireland,— *Application of Act to Ireland.*

" Judge of a county court " shall be deemed to include chairman of a county and recorder of any borough ;

" Registrar of a county court " shall be deemed to include the clerk of the peace or registrar or other person discharging the duties of registrar of the court, of the chairman of a county, or the recorder of a borough ;

" Stipendiary magistrate " shall be deemed to include any of the justices of the peace in Dublin metropolis and any resident magistrate ; and

" A master of the Supreme Court of Judicature " shall mean one of the masters of the superior courts of common law in Ireland.

**43.** In the application of this Act to the Isle of Man,— *Application of Act to Isle of Man.*

" Judge of a county court " shall mean the water bailiff ;

" Stipendiary magistrate " shall mean a high bailiff ;

"Registrar of a county court " shall mean a clerk to a deemster or a clerk to justices of the peace ;

" A master of the Supreme Court of Judicature " shall mean the clerk of the rolls.

**44.** Nothing in this Act shall apply to any vessel employed exclusively in trading or going from place to place in any river or inland water of which the whole or part is in any British possession ; and the provisions of this Act relating to deck cargo shall not apply to deck cargo carried by a ship while engaged in the coasting trade of any British possession. *Saving for colonial inland waters.*

*Repeal.*

**45.** [Repealed by Statute Law Revision Act, 1883.]

---

### SCHEDULE.

[Repealed by Statute Law Revision Act, 1883.]

(z) The words within brackets repealed by 45 & 46 Vict. c. 55.

## 40 & 41 VICT. CAP. 26.

*An Act to Amend the Companies Acts of 1862 and 1867.*

[*23rd July,* 1877.]

30 & 31 Vict.
c. 131.

WHEREAS doubts have been entertained whether the power given by the Companies Act, 1867, to a company of reducing its capital extends to paid-up capital, and it is expedient to remove such doubts:

Be it enacted by the Queen's most excellent Majesty, by and with the advice and consent of the Lords spiritual and temporal, and Commons, in this present Parliament assembled, and by the authority of the same, as follows:—

Short title.

**1.** This Act may be cited for all purposes as the Companies Act, 1877.

Construction
of Act.
25 & 26 Vict.
c. 89.
30 & 31 Vict.
c. 131.

**2.** This Act shall, so far as is consistent with the tenor thereof, be construed as one with the Companies Acts, 1862 and 1867, and the said Acts and this Act may be referred to as "The Companies Acts, 1862, 1867, and 1877."

Construction of
"capital" and
powers to reduce
capital con-
tained in
30 & 31 Vict.
c. 131.

**3.** The word "capital" as used in the Companies Act, 1867, shall include paid-up capital; and the power to reduce capital conferred by that Act shall include a power to cancel any lost capital, or any capital unrepresented by available assets, or to pay off any capital which may be in excess of the wants of the company; and paid-up capital may be reduced either with or without extinguishing or reducing the liability (if any) remaining on the shares of the company, and to the extent to which such liability is not extinguished or reduced it shall be deemed to be preserved, notwithstanding anything contained in the Companies Act, 1867.

Application of
provisions of
30 & 31 Vict.
c. 131.

**4.** The provisions of the Companies Act, 1867, as amended by this Act, shall apply to any company reducing its capital in pursuance of this Act and of the Companies Act, 1867, as amended by this Act:

Provided that where the reduction of the capital of a company does not involve either the diminution of any liability in respect of unpaid capital or the payment to any shareholder of any paid-up capital,

(1.) The creditors of the company shall not, unless the Court otherwise direct, be entitled to object or required to consent to the reduction; and

(2.) It shall not be necessary, before the presentation of the petition for confirming the reduction, to add, and the Court may, if it thinks it expedient so to do, dispense altogether with the addition of the words "and reduced," as mentioned in the Companies Act, 1867.

30 & 31 Vict.
c. 131.

In any case that the Court thinks fit so to do, it may require the company to publish in such manner as it thinks fit the reasons for the reduction of its capital, or such other information in regard to the reduction of its capital, as the Court may think expedient with a view to give proper information to the public in relation to the reduction of its capital by a company, and, if the Court thinks fit, the causes which led to such reduction.

The minute required to be registered in the case of reduction of capital shall show, in addition to the other particulars required by law, the amount (if any) at the date of the registration of the minute proposed to be deemed to have been paid up on each share.

Power to reduce
capital by the
cancellation of
unissued shares.

**5.** Any company limited by shares may so far modify the conditions contained in its memorandum of association, if authorized so to do by its regulations as originally framed or as altered by special resolution, as to reduce its capital by cancelling any shares which, at the date of the passing of such resolution, have not been taken or agreed to be taken by any person; and the provisions of "The Companies Act, 1867," shall not apply to any reduction of capital made in pursuance of this section.

Reception of
certified copies
of documents as
legal evidence.
25 & 26 Vict.
c. 89.

**6.** And whereas it is expedient to make provision for the reception as legal evidence of certificates of incorporation other than the original certificates, and of certified copies of or extracts from any documents filed and registered under the Companies Acts, 1862 to 1877: Be it enacted, that any certificate of the incorporation of any company given by the registrar or by

any assistant-registrar for the time being shall be received in evidence as if
it were the original certificate ; and any copy of or extract from any of the
documents or part of the documents kept and registered at any of the offices
for the registration of joint stock companies in England, Scotland, or
Ireland, if duly certified to be a true copy under the hand of the registrar or
one of the assistant-registrars for the time being, and whom it shall not be
necessary to prove to be the registrar or assistant-registrar shall, in all legal
proceedings, civil or criminal, and in all cases whatsoever, be received
in evidence as of equal validity with the original document.

30 & 31 Vict.<br>c. 131.<br>40 & 41 Vict.<br>c. 26.

---

## 41 & 42 Vict. cap. 31 (a).

*An Act to consolidate and amend the Law for preventing Frauds upon
Creditors by secret Bills of Sale of Personal Chattels.*

[*22nd July*, 1878.]

Whereas it is expedient to consolidate and amend the law relating to bills of
sale of personal chattels :

Be it enacted by the Queen's most excellent Majesty, by and with the
advice and consent of the Lords spiritual and temporal, and Commons in
this present Parliament assembled, and by the authority of the same, as
follows :

1. This Act may be cited for all purposes as the Bills of Sale Act, 1878. *Short title.*

2. This Act shall come into operation on the first day of January one *Commencement.*
thousand eight hundred and seventy-nine, which day is in this Act referred
to as the commencement of this Act.

3. This Act shall apply to every bill of sale executed on or after the first *Application*
day of January one thousand eight hundred and seventy-nine (whether the *of Act.*
same be absolute, or subject or not subject to any trust) whereby the holder
or grantee has power, either with or without notice, and either immediately
or at any future time, to seize or take possession of any personal chattels
comprised in or made subject to such bill of sale.

4. In this Act the following words and expressions shall have the *Interpretation*
meanings in this section assigned to them respectively, unless there be *of terms.*
something in the subject or context repugnant to such construction ; (that
is to say,)

The expression "bill of sale" shall include bills of sale, assignments,
transfers, declarations of trust without transfer, inventories of goods
with receipt thereto attached, or receipts for purchase-moneys of goods,
and other assurances of personal chattels, and also powers of attorney,
authorities, or licences to take possession of personal chattels as security
for any debt, and also any agreement, whether intended or not to be followed by the execution of any other instrument, by which a right in equity
to any personal chattels, or to any charge or security thereon, shall be
conferred, but shall not include the following documents ; that is to say,
assignments for the benefit of the creditors of the person making or
giving the same, marriage settlements, transfers or assignments of any
ship or vessel or any share thereof, transfers of goods in the ordinary
course of business of any trade or calling. bills of sale of goods in
foreign parts or at sea, bills of lading, India warrants, warehouse-
keepers certificates, warrants or orders for the delivery of goods, or any
other documents used in the ordinary course of business as proof of the
possession or control of goods, or authorising or purporting to authorise,
either by indorsement or by delivery, the possessor of such document to
transfer or receive goods thereby represented :

The expression "personal chattels" shall mean goods, furniture, and other
articles capable of complete transfer by delivery, and (when separately
assigned or charged) fixtures and growing crops, but shall not include
chattel interests in real estate, nor fixtures (except trade machinery as
hereinafter defined), when assigned together with a freehold or leasehold
interest in any land or building to which they are affixed, nor growing
crops when assigned together with any interest in the land on which they

(a) See, also, the Bills of Sale Amendment Act, *infra*, p. 1069.

grow, nor shares or interests in the stock, funds, or securities of any government, or in the capital or property of incorporated or joint stock companies, nor choses in action, nor any stock or produce upon any farm or lands which by virtue of any covenant or agreement or of the custom of the country ought not to be removed from any farm where the same are at the time of making or giving of such bill of sale :

Personal chattels shall be deemed to be in the "apparent possession" of the person making or giving a bill of sale, so long as they remain or are in or upon any house, mill, warehouse, building, works, yard, land, or other premises occupied by him, or are used and enjoyed by him in any place whatsoever, notwithstanding that formal possession thereof may have been taken by or given to any other person :

"Prescribed" means prescribed by rules made under the provisions of this Act.

**Application of Act to trade machinery.**
**5.** From and after the commencement of this Act trade machinery shall, for the purposes of this Act, be deemed to be personal chattels, and any mode of disposition of trade machinery by the owner thereof which would be a bill of sale as to any other personal chattels shall be deemed to be a bill of sale within the meaning of Act.

For the purposes of this Act—

"Trade machinery" means the machinery used in or attached to any factory or workshop ;

1st. Exclusive of the fixed motive powers, such as the water-wheels and steam engines, and the steam-boilers, donkey engines, and other fixed appurtenances of the said motive-powers ; and

2nd. Exclusive of the fixed power machinery, such as the shafts, wheels, drums, and their fixed appurtenances, which transmit the action of the motive-powers to the other machinery, fixed and loose ; and

3rd. Exclusive of the pipes for steam, gas and water in the factory or workshop.

The machinery or effects excluded by this section from the definition of trade machinery shall not be deemed to be personal chattels within the meaning of this Act.

"Factory or workshop" means any premises on which any manual labour is exercised by way of trade, or for purposes of gain, in or incidental to the following purposes or any of them ; that is to say,

(a) In or incidental to the making any article or part of an article ; or

(b) In or incidental to the altering, repairing, ornamenting, finishing, of any article ; or

(c) In or incidental to the adapting for sale any article.

**Certain instruments giving powers of distress to be subject to this Act.**
**6.** Every attornment, instrument, or agreement, not being a mining lease, whereby a power of distress is given or agreed to be given by any person to any other person by way of security for any present, future, or contingent debt or advance, and whereby any rent is reserved or made payable as a mode of providing for the payment of interest on such debt or advance, or otherwise for the purpose of such security only, shall be deemed to be a bill of sale, within the meaning of this Act, of any personal chattels which may be seized or taken under such power of distress.

Provided, that nothing in this section shall extend to any mortgage of any estate or interest in any land, tenement, or hereditament which the mortgagee, being in possession, shall have demised to the mortgagor as his tenant at a fair and reasonable rent.

**Fixtures or growing crops not to be deemed separately assigned when the land passes by the same instrument.**
**7.** No fixtures or growing crops shall be deemed, under this Act, to be separately assigned or charged by reason only that they are assigned by separate words, or that power is given to sever them from the land or building to which they are affixed, or from the land on which they grow, without otherwise taking possession of or dealing with such land or building, or land, if by the same instrument any freehold or leasehold interest in the land or building to which such fixtures are affixed, or in the land on which such crops grow, is also conveyed or assigned to the same persons or person.

The same rule of construction shall be applied to all deeds or instruments, including fixtures or growing crops, executed before the commencement of this Act and then subsisting and in force, in all questions arising under any bankruptcy, liquidation, assignment for the benefit of creditors, or execution of any process of any court, which shall take place or be issued after the commencement of this Act.

**8.** [Repealed by 45 & 46 Vict. c. 43.]

**9.** Where a subsequent bill of sale is executed within or on the expiration of seven days after the execution of a prior unregistered bill of sale, and comprises all or any part of the personal chattels comprised in such prior bill of sale, then, if such subsequent bill of sale is given as a security for the same debt as is secured by the prior bill of sale, or for any part of such debt, it shall, to the extent to which it is a security for the same debt or part thereof, and so far as respects the personal chattels or part thereof comprised in the prior bill, be absolutely void, unless it is proved to the satisfaction of the court having cognizance of the case that the subsequent bill of sale was bonâ fide given for the purpose of correcting some material error in the prior bill of sale, and not for the purpose of evading this Act. *Avoidance of certain duplicate bills of sale.*

**10.** A bill of sale shall be attested and registered under this Act in the following manner : *Mode of registering bills of sale.*

(1.) [The execution of every bill of sale shall be attested by a solicitor of the Supreme Court, and the attestation shall state that before the execution of the bill of sale the effect thereof has been explained to the grantor by the attesting solicitor (*a*) :]

(2.) Such bill, with every schedule or inventory thereto annexed or therein referred to, and also a true copy of such bill and of every such schedule or inventory, and of every attestation of the execution of such bill of sale, together with an affidavit of the time of such bill of sale being made or given, and of its due execution and attestation, and a description of the residence and occupation of the person making or giving the same (or in case the same is made or given by any person under or in the execution of any process, then a description of the residence and occupation of the person against whom such process issued), and of every attesting witness to such bill of sale, shall be presented to and the said copy and affidavit shall be filed with the registrar within seven clear days after the making or giving of such bill of sale, in like manner as a warrant of attorney in any personal action given by a trader is now by law required to be filed :

(3.) If the bill of sale is made or given subject to any defeasance or condition, or declaration of trust not contained in the body thereof, such defeasance, condition, or declaration shall be deemed to be part of the bill, and shall be written on the same paper or parchment therewith before the registration, and shall be truly set forth in the copy filed under this Act therewith and as part thereof, otherwise the registration shall be void.

In case two or more bills of sale are given, comprising in whole or in part any of the same chattels, they shall have priority in the order of the date of their registration respectively as regards such chattels.

A transfer or assignment of a registered bill of sale need not be registered.

**11.** The registration of a bill of sale, whether executed before or after the commencement of this Act, must be renewed once at least every five years, and if a period of five years elapses from the registration or renewed registration of a bill of sale without a renewal or further renewal (as the case may be), the registration shall become void. *Renewal of registration.*

The renewal of a registration shall be effected by filing with the registrar an affidavit stating the date of the bill of sale and of the last registration thereof, and the names, residences, and occupations of the parties thereto as stated therein, and that the bill of sale is still a subsisting security.

Every such affidavit may be in the form set forth in the Schedule (A.) to this Act annexed.

A renewal of registration shall not become necessary by reason only of a transfer or assignment of a bill of sale.

**12.** The registrar shall keep a book (in this Act called " the register") for the purposes of this Act, and shall, upon the filing of any bill of sale or copy *Form of register.*

(*a*) Repealed by 45 & 46 Vict. c. 43, s. 10.

under this Act, enter therein in the form set forth in the second schedule (B.) to this Act annexed, or in any other prescribed form, the name, residence, and occupation of the person by whom the bill was made or given (or in case the same was made or given by any person under or in the execution of process, then the name, residence, and occupation of the person against whom such process was issued, and also the name of the person or persons to whom or in whose favour the bill was given), and the other particulars shown in the said schedule or to be prescribed under this Act, and shall number all such bills registered in each year consecutively, according to the respective dates of their registration.

Upon the registration of any affidavit of renewal the like entry shall be made, with the addition of the date and number of the last previous entry relating to the same bill, and the bill of sale or copy originally filed shall be thereupon marked with the number affixed to such affidavit of renewal.

The registrar shall also keep an index of the names of the grantors of registered bills of sale with reference to entries in the register of the bills of sale given by each such grantor.

Such index shall be arranged in divisions corresponding with the letters of the alphabet, so that all grantors whose surnames begin with the same letter (and no others) shall be comprised in one division, but the arrangement within each such division need not be strictly alphabetical.

**The registrar.** 13. The masters of the Supreme Court of Judicature attached to the Queen's Bench Division of the High Court of Justice, or such other officers as may for the time being be assigned for this purpose under the provisions 36 & 37 Vict. c. 66. of the Supreme Court of Judicature Acts, 1873 and 1875, shall be the regis-38 & 39 Vict. c. 77. trar for the purposes of this Act, and any one of the said masters may perform all or any of the duties of the registrar.

**Rectification of register.** 14 Any judge of the High Court of Justice on being satisfied that the omission to register a bill of sale or an affidavit of renewal thereof within the time prescribed by this Act, or the omission or mis-statement of the name, residence, or occupation of any person, was accidental or due to inadvertence, may in his discretion order such omission or mis-statement to be rectified by the insertion in the register of the true name, residence, or occupation, or by extending the time for such registration on such terms and conditions (if any) as to security, notice by advertisement or otherwise, or as to any other matter, as he thinks fit to direct.

**Entry of satisfaction.** 15. Subject to and in accordance with any rules to be made under and for the purposes of this Act, the registrar may order a memorandum of satisfaction to be written upon any registered copy of a bill of sale, upon the prescribed evidence being given that the debt (if any) for which such bill of sale was made or given has been satisfied or discharged.

**Copies may be taken, &c.** 16. Any person shall be entitled to have an office copy or extract of any registered bill of sale, and affidavit of execution filed therewith, or copy thereof, and of any affidavit filed therewith, if any, or registered affidavit of renewal, upon paying for the same at the like rate as for office copies of judgments of the High Court of Justice, and any copy of a registered bill of sale, and affidavit purporting to be an office copy thereof, shall in all courts and before all arbitrators or other persons, be admitted as primâ facie evidence thereof, and of the fact and date of registration as shown thereon. Any person shall be entitled at all reasonable times to search the register and every registered bill of sale, upon payment of one shilling for every copy of a bill of sale inspected ; such payment shall be made by a judicature stamp.

**Affidavits.** 17. Every affidavit required by or for the purposes of this Act may be sworn before a master of any division of the High Court of Justice, or before any commissioner empowered to take affidavits in the Supreme Court of Judicature.

Whoever wilfully makes or uses any false affidavit for the purposes of this Act shall be deemed guilty of wilful and corrupt perjury.

**Fees.** 18. There shall be paid and received in common law stamps the following fees, viz. :

| | |
|---|---|
| On filing a bill of sale - - - - - - | 2s. |
| On filing the affidavit of execution of a bill of sale - | 2s. |
| On the affidavit used for the purpose of re-registering a bill of sale (to include the fee for filing) - - | 5s. |

**Collection of fees under 38 & 39 Vict. c. 77, s. 26.** 19. Section twenty-six of the Supreme Court of Judicature Act, 1875, and any enactments for the time being in force amending or substituted for that section, shall apply to fees under this Act, and an order under that section may, if need be, be made in relation to such fees accordingly.

20. [Repealed by 45 & 46 Vict. c. 43.]

21. Rules for the purposes of this Act may be made and altered from time to time by the like persons and in the like manner in which rules and regulations may be made under and for the purposes of the Supreme Court of Judicature Acts, 1873 and 1875.

*Rules.*
*36 & 37 Vict.*
*c. 66.*
*38 & 39 Vict.*
*c. 77.*

22. When the time for registering a bill of sale expires on a Sunday, or other day on which the registrar's office is closed, the registration shall be valid if made on the next following day on which the office is open.

*Time for registration.*

23. From and after the commencement of this Act, the Bills of Sale Act, 1854, and the Bills of Sale Act, 1866, shall be repealed: Provided that (except as is herein expressly mentioned with respect to construction and with respect to renewal of registration) nothing in this Act shall affect any bill of sale executed before the commencement of this Act, and as regards bills of sale so executed the Acts hereby repealed shall continue in force.

*Repeal of Acts.*
*17 & 18 Vict.*
*c. 36.*
*29 & 30 Vict.*
*c. 96.*

Any renewal after the commencement of this Act of the registration of a bill of sale executed before the commencement of this Act, and registered under the Acts hereby repealed, shall be made under this Act in the same manner as the renewal of a registration made under this Act.

24. This Act shall not extend to Scotland or to Ireland.

*Extent of Act.*

---

## SCHEDULES.

---

### SCHEDULE A.

I [*A.B.*]                      of                           do swear that a bill of sale, bearing date the                    day of 18      [*insert the date of the bill*], and made between [*insert the names and descriptions of the parties in the original bill of sale*], and which said bill of sale [*or*, and a copy of which said bill of sale, *as the case may be*] was registered on the            day of            18      [*insert date of registration*], is still a subsisting security.

Sworn, *&c.*

---

### SCHEDULE B.

| Satisfaction entered. | No. | By whom given (or against whom process issued). | | | To whom given. | Nature of instrument. | Date. | Date of registration. | Date of registration of affidavit of renewal. |
|---|---|---|---|---|---|---|---|---|---|
| | | Name. | Residence. | Occupation. | | | | | |
| | | | | | | | | | |

---

41 & 42 VICT. CAP. 49.

*An Act to consolidate the Law relating to Weights and Measures.*
[*8th August,* 1878.]

BE it enacted by the Queen's most Excellent Majesty, by and with the advice and consent of the Lords spiritual and temporal, and Commons, in this present Parliament assembled, and by the authority of the same, as follows:

*Preliminary.*

Short title.    **1.** This Act may be cited as the Weights and Measures Act, 1878.

Commencement.    **2.** This Act shall not come into operation until the first day of January one thousand eight hundred and seventy-nine, which day is hereinafter referred to as the commencement of this Act.

## I.—LAW OF WEIGHTS AND MEASURES.

*Uniformity of Weights and Measures.*

Uniformity of weights and measures.    **3.** The same weights and measures shall be used throughout the United Kingdom.

*Standards of Measure and Weight.*

Imperial standards of measure and weight.    **4.** The bronze bar and the platinum weight, more particularly described in the first part of the First Schedule to this Act, and at the passing of this Act deposited in the Standards Department of the Board of Trade in the custody of the Warden of the Standards, shall continue to be the imperial standards of measure and weight, and the said bronze bar shall continue to be the imperial standard for determining the imperial standard yard for the United Kingdom, and the said platinum weight shall continue to be the imperial standard for determining the imperial standard pound for the United Kingdom.

Parliamentary copies of imperial standards.    **5.** The four copies of the imperial standards of measure and weight, described in the second part of the First Schedule to this Act, and deposited as therein mentioned, shall be deemed to be parliamentary copies of the said imperial standards.

The Board of Trade shall as soon as may be after the commencement of this Act cause an accurate copy of the imperial standard of measure and an accurate copy of the imperial standard of weight to be made of the same form and material as the said standards, and it shall be lawful for Her Majesty in Council, on the representation of the Board of Trade, to approve the copies so made, and the copies when so approved shall be of the same effect as the said parliamentary copies, and are in this Act included under the name parliamentary copies of the imperial standards of measure and weight.

Restoration of imperial standards.    **6.** If at any time either of the imperial standards of measure and weight is lost or in any manner destroyed, defaced, or otherwise injured, the Board of Trade may cause the same to be restored by reference to or adoption of any of the parliamentary copies of that standard, or of such of them as may remain available for that purpose.

Restoration of parliamentary copies.    **7.** If at any time any of the parliamentary copies of either of the imperial standards is lost or in any manner destroyed, defaced, or otherwise injured, the Board of Trade may cause the same to be restored by reference either to the corresponding imperial standard, or to one of the other parliamentary copies of that standard.

Secondary (Board of Trade) standards of measure and weight.    **8.** The secondary standards of measure and weight which, having been derived from the imperial standards, are at the commencement of this Act in use under the direction of the Board of Trade, and are mentioned in the Second Schedule to this Act, and no others (save as hereinafter mentioned), shall be secondary standards of measure and weight, and shall be called Board of Trade standards.

If at any time any of such standards is lost or in any manner destroyed, defaced, or otherwise injured, the Board of Trade may cause the same to be restored by reference either to one of the imperial standards or to one of the parliamentary copies of those standards.

The Board of Trade shall from time to time cause such new denominations of standards, being either equivalent to or multiples or aliquot parts of the imperial weights and measures ascertained by this Act, or being equivalent to or multiples of each coin of the realm for the time being, as appear to them to be required, in addition to those mentioned in the Second Schedule to this Act, to be made and duly verified, and those new denominations of standards when approved by Her Majesty in Council shall be Board of Trade standards in like manner as if they were mentioned in the said schedule.

It shall be lawful for Her Majesty by Order in Council to declare that a Board of Trade standard for the time being of any denomination, whether mentioned in the said schedule or approved by Order in Council, shall cease to be such a standard.

Such standards of the Board of Trade as are equivalent to or multiples of any coin of the realm for the time being shall be standard weights for determining the justness of the weight of and for weighing such coin.

9. The standards of measure and weight which are at the commencement of this Act legally in use by inspectors of weights and measures for the purpose of verification or inspection, and all copies of the Board of Trade standards which after the commencement of this Act are compared with those standards and verified by the Board of Trade for the purpose of being used by inspectors of weights and measures under this Act as standards for the verification or inspection of weights and measures, shall be called local standards. *Local standards of measure and weight.*

### Imperial Measures of Length.

10. The straight line or distance between the centres of the two gold plugs or pins (as mentioned in the First Schedule to this Act) in the bronze bar by this Act declared to be the imperial standard for determining the imperial standard yard measured when the bar is at the temperature of sixty-two degrees of Fahrenheit's thermometer, and when it is supported on bronze rollers placed under it in such manner as best to avoid flexure of the bar, and to facilitate its free expansion and contraction from variations of temperature, shall be the legal standard measure of length, and shall be called the imperial standard yard, and shall be the only unit or standard measure of extension from which all other measures of extension, whether linear superficial or solid, shall be ascertained. *Imperial standard yard.*

11. One-third part of the imperial standard yard shall be a foot, and the twelfth part of such foot shall be an inch, and the rod, pole, or perch in length shall contain five such yards and a half, and the chain shall contain twenty-two such yards, the furlong two hundred and twenty such yards, and the mile one thousand seven hundred and sixty such yards. *Linear measures derived from imperial standard yard.*

12. The rood of land shall contain one thousand two hundred and ten square yards according to the imperial standard yard, and the acre of land shall contain four thousand eight hundred and forty such square yards, being one hundred and sixty square rods, poles, or perches. *Superficial measures derived from the imperial standard yard.*

### Imperial Measures of Weight and Capacity.

13. The weight in vacuô of the platinum weight (mentioned in the First Schedule to this Act), and by this Act declared to be the imperial standard for determining the imperial standard pound, shall be the legal standard measure of weight, and of measure having reference to weight, and shall be called the imperial standard pound, and shall be the only unit or standard measure of weight from which all other weights and all measures having reference to weight shall be ascertained. *Imperial standard pound.*

14. One sixteenth part of the imperial standard pound shall be an ounce, and one sixteenth part of such ounce shall be a dram, and one seven thousandth part of the imperial standard pound shall be a grain. *Imperial weights derived from imperial standard pound.*

A stone shall consist of fourteen imperial standard pounds, and a hundredweight shall consist of eight such stones, and a ton shall consist of twenty such hundredweights.

Four hundred and eighty grains shall be an ounce troy.

All the foregoing weights except the ounce troy shall be deemed to be avoirdupois weights.

**Imperial measures of capacity.**

**15.** The unit or standard measure of capacity from which all other measures of capacity, as well for liquids as for dry goods, shall be derived, shall be the gallon containing ten imperial standard pounds weight of distilled water weighed in air against brass weights, with the water and the air at the temperature of sixty-two degrees of Fahrenheit's thermometer, and with the barometer at thirty inches.

The quart shall be one fourth part of the gallon, and the pint shall be one eighth part of the gallon.

Two gallons shall be a peck, and eight gallons shall be a bushel, and eight such bushels shall be a quarter, and thirty-six such bushels shall be a chaldron.

**Measure of capacity for goods formerly sold by heaped measure. 5 & 6 Will. 4, c. 63.**

**16.** [A bushel for the sale of any of the following articles, namely, lime, fish, potatoes, fruit, or any other goods and things which before (the passing of the Weights and Measures Act, 1835, that is to say) the ninth day of September one thousand eight hundred and thirty-five, were commonly sold by heaped measure, shall be a hollow cylinder having a plane base, the internal diameter of which shall be double the internal depth, and every measure used for the sale of any of the above-mentioned articles which is a multiple of a bushel, or is a half bushel or a peck, shall be made of the same shape and proportion as the above-mentioned bushel (*b*).]

**Measure of capacity when used to be stricken or filled up.**

**17.** In using an imperial measure of capacity, the same shall not be heaped, but either shall be stricken with a round stick or roller, straight and of the same diameter from end to end, or if the article sold cannot from its size or shape be conveniently stricken shall be filled in all parts as nearly to the level of the brim as the size and shape of the article will admit.

*Metric Equivalents of Imperial Weights and Measures.*

**Equivalents of metric weights and measures in terms of imperial weights and measures.**

**18.** The table in the Third Schedule to this Act shall be deemed to set forth the equivalents of imperial weights and measures and of the weights and measures therein expressed in terms of the metric system, and such table may be lawfully used for computing and expressing, in weights and measures, weights and measures of the metric system.

*Use of Imperial Weights and Measures.*

**Trade contracts, sales, dealings, &c. to be in terms of imperial weights or measures.**

**19.** Every contract, bargain, sale, or dealing, made or had in the United Kingdom for any work goods wares or merchandise or other thing which has been or is to be done, sold, delivered, carried, or agreed for by weight or measure, shall be deemed to be made and had according to one of the imperial weights or measures ascertained by this Act, or to some multiple or part thereof, and if not so made or had shall be void; and all tolls and duties charged or collected according to weight or measure shall be charged and collected according to one of the imperial weights or measures ascertained by this Act, or to some multiple or part thereof.

Such contract, bargain, sale, dealing, and collection of tolls and duties as is in this section mentioned is in this Act referred to under the term "trade."

No local or customary measures, nor the use of the heaped measure, shall be lawful.

Any person who sells by any denomination of weight or measure other than one of the imperial weights or measures, or some multiple or part thereof, shall be liable to a fine not exceeding forty shillings for every such sale.

**Sale by avoirdupois weight, with exceptions.**

**20.** All articles sold by weight shall be sold by avoirdupois weight; except that—

(1.) Gold and silver, and articles made thereof, including gold and silver thread, lace, or fringe, also platinum, diamonds, and other precious metals or stones, may be sold by the ounce troy or by any decimal parts of such ounce; and all contracts, bargains, sales, and dealings in relation thereto shall be deemed to be made and had by such weight, and when so made or had shall be valid; and

(2.) Drugs, when sold by retail, may be sold by apothecaries weight.

Every person who acts in contravention of this section shall be liable to a fine not exceeding five pounds.

**Exception for contract, &c. in metric weights and measures.**

**21.** A contract or dealing shall not be invalid or open to objection on the ground that the weights or measures expressed or referred to therein **are**

(*b*) Repealed : 52 & 53 Vict. c. 21, s. 5.

weights or measures of the metric system, or on the ground that decimal subdivisions of imperial weights and measures, whether metric or otherwise, are used in such contract or dealing.

**22.** Nothing in this Act shall prevent the sale, or subject a person to a fine under this Act for the sale, of an article in any vessel, where such vessel is not represented as containing any amount of imperial measure, nor subject a person to a fine under this Act for the possession of a vessel where it is shown that such vessel is not used nor intended for use as a measure.

**23.** Any person who prints, and any clerk of a market or other person who makes, any return, price list, price current, or any journal or other paper containing price list or price current, in which the denomination of weights and measures quoted or referred to denotes or implies a greater or less weight or measure than is denoted or implied by the same denomination of the imperial weights and measures under this Act, shall be liable to a fine not exceeding ten shillings for every such return, price list, price current, journal, or other paper which he publishes.

**24.** Every person who uses or has in his possession for use for trade a weight or measure which is not of the denomination of some Board of Trade standard, shall be liable to a fine not exceeding five pounds, or in the case of a second offence ten pounds, and the weight or measure shall be liable to be forfeited.

### Unjust Weights and Measures.

**25.** Every person who uses or has in his possession for use for trade any weight measure scale balance steelyard or weighing machine which is false or unjust, shall be liable to a fine not exceeding five pounds, or in the case of a second offence [twenty] pounds (c), and any contract bargain sale or dealing made by the same shall be void, and the weight measure scale balance or steelyard shall be liable to be forfeited.

**26.** Where any fraud is wilfully committed in the using of any weight measure scale balance steelyard or weighing machine, the person committing such fraud, and every person party to the fraud, shall be liable to a fine not exceeding five pounds, or in the case of a second offence [twenty] pounds (c), and the weight measure scale balance or steelyard shall be liable to be forfeited.

**27.** A person shall not wilfully or knowingly make or sell, or cause to be made or sold, any false or unjust weight measure scale balance steelyard or weighing machine.

Every person who acts in contravention of this section shall be liable to a fine not exceeding ten pounds, or in the case of a second offence fifty pounds.

### Stamping and Verification of Weights and Measures.

**28.** Every weight, except where the small size of the weight renders it impracticable, shall have the denomination of such weight stamped on the top or side thereof in legible figures and letters.

Every measure of capacity shall have the denomination thereof stamped on the outside of such measure in legible figures and letters.

A weight or measure not in conformity with this section shall not be stamped with such stamp of verification under this Act as is hereinafter mentioned.

**29.** Every measure and weight whatsoever used for trade shall be verified and stamped by an inspector with a stamp of verification under this Act.

Every person who uses or has in his possession for use for trade any measure or weight not stamped as required by this section, shall be liable to a fine not exceeding five pounds, or in the case of a second offence ten pounds, and shall be liable to forfeit the said measure or weight, and any contract bargain sale or dealing made by such measure or weight shall be void.

**30.** A weight made of lead or pewter, or of any mixture thereof, shall not be stamped with a stamp of verification or used for trade, unless it be wholly and substantially cased with brass copper or iron, and legibly stamped or marked "cased":

Provided that nothing in this section shall prevent the insertion into a weight of such a plug of lead or pewter as is bonâ fide necessary for the purpose of adjusting it and of affixing thereon the stamp of verification.

A person guilty of any offence against or disobedience to the provisions of

(c) 52 & 53 Vict. c. 21, ss. 3, 4.

this section, shall be liable to a penalty not exceeding five pounds, or in case of a second offence ten pounds.

**Stamping of verification on weights for coin.**  **31.** Every coin weight, not less in weight than the weight of the lightest coin for the time being current, shall be verified and stamped by the Board of Trade with a mark of verification under this Act, and otherwise shall not be deemed a just weight for determining the weight of gold and silver coin of the realm.

Every person who uses any weight declared by this section not to be a just weight shall be liable to a fine not exceeding fifty pounds.

**Forgery, &c. of stamps on measures or weights.**  **32.** If any person forges or counterfeits any stamp used for the stamping under this Act of any measure or weight, or used before the commencement of this Act for the stamping of any measure or weight, under any enactment repealed by this Act, or wilfully increases or diminishes a weight so stamped, he shall be liable to a fine not exceeding fifty pounds.

Any person who knowingly uses, sells, utters, disposes of, or exposes for sale any measure or weight with such forged or counterfeit stamp thereon, or a weight so increased or diminished, shall be liable to a fine not exceeding ten pounds.

All measures and weights with any such forged or counterfeit stamp shall be forfeited (*d*).

## II.—Administration.

### (a.) *Central.*

#### *Board of Trade.*

**Powers and duties of Board of Trade as to standards of weights and measures, &c.**  **33.** The Board of Trade shall have all such powers and perform all such duties relative to standards of measure and weight, and to weights and measures, as are by any Act or otherwise vested in or imposed on the Treasury, or the Comptroller-General of the Exchequer, or the Warden of the Standards; and all things done by the Board of Trade, or any of their officers, or at their office, in relation to standards of weights and measures in pursuance of this Act shall be as valid, and have the like effect and consequences, as if the same had been done by the Treasury, or by the Comptroller-General or other officer of the Exchequer, or by the Warden of the Standards, or at the office of the Exchequer.

It shall be the duty of the Board of Trade to conduct all such comparisons, verifications, and other operations with reference to standards of measure and weight, in aid of scientific researches or otherwise, as the Board of Trade from time to time thinks expedient, and to make from time to time a report to Parliament on their proceedings and business under this Act.

#### *Custody and Verification of Standards and Copies.*

**Custody of imperial and Board of Trade standards to remain with Board of Trade.**  **34.** The imperial standards of measure and weight, the Board of Trade standards of measure and weight, and all balances, apparatus, books, documents, and things used in connection therewith or relating thereto, deposited at the passing of this Act in the Standards Department, or in any other office of the Board of Trade, shall remain and be in the custody of the Board of Trade.

**Custody and periodical verification of parliamentary copies of imperial standards.**  **35.** The parliamentary copies of the imperial standards of measure and weight mentioned in part two of the First Schedule to this Act shall continue to be deposited as therein mentioned.

The copies of the imperial standards of measure and weight made in pursuance of this Act, when approved by Her Majesty in Council, shall be deposited at some office of the Board of Trade, and be in the custody of the Board of Trade.

The Board of Trade shall cause the parliamentary copies of the imperial standards of measure and weight, except the copy immured in the new palace at Westminster, to be compared once in every ten years with each other, and once in every twenty years with the imperial standards of measure and weight.

**Periodical verification of Board of Trade standards.**  **36.** Once at least in every five years the Board of Trade shall cause the Board of Trade standards for the time being to be compared with the parliamentary copies of the imperial standards of measure and weight made and approved in pu u        of this Act and with each other, and to be adjusted or renewed, if requisite.

. (*b*) **This** section now applies to weighing machines: 52 & 53 Vict. c. 21, s. 1 (4).

**37.** The Board of Trade shall cause to be compared with the Board of Trade standards and verified at such places as the Board of Trade in each case direct all copies of any of those standards which are submitted for the purpose by any local authority, and have been used or are intended to be used as local standards, and if they find the same fit for the purpose of being used by inspectors of weights and measures under this Act as standards for the verification and inspection of weights and measures, shall cause them to be stamped as verified or reverified in such manner as to show the date of such verification or re-verification, and every such verification shall be evidenced by an indenture, and every such re-verification shall be evidenced by an indorsement upon the original indenture of verification, or by a new indenture of verification.

Any such indenture or indorsement, if purporting to be signed (either before or after the passing of this Act) by an officer of the Board of Trade, shall be evidence of the verification or re-verification of the weights and measures therein referred to.

Any such indenture or indorsement shall not be liable to stamp duty, nor shall any fee be payable on the verification or re-verification of any local standard.

An account shall be kept by the Board of Trade of all local standards verified or re-verified.

**38.** Whereas the Board of Trade have obtained accurate copies of the metric standards mentioned in part two of the Third Schedule to this Act, and it is expedient to make the provision hereinafter mentioned for the verification of metric weights and measures, be it therefore enacted as follows:

The Board of Trade may, if they think fit, cause to be compared with the metric standards in their custody and verified all metric weights and measures which are submitted to them for the purpose, and are of such shape and construction as may be from time to time in that behalf directed by the Board of Trade, and which the Board of Trade are satisfied are intended to be used for the purpose of science or of manufacture, or for any lawful purpose not being for the purpose of trade within the meaning of this Act.

**39.** The Board of Trade, on payment of such fee, not exceeding five shillings, as they from time to time prescribe, shall cause all coin weights required by this Act to be verified, to be compared with the standard weights for weighing coin, and, if found to be just, stamped with a mark approved of by the Board, and notified in the London Gazette.

All fees under this section shall be paid into the Exchequer.

*Side notes:* Verification by Board of Trade of local standards. — Power of Board of Trade to verify metric weights and measures. — Verification and stamping of coin weights.

### (b.) *Local Administration.*

#### *Local Standards.*

**40.** The local authority (mentioned in the Fourth Schedule to this Act) of every county and borough from time to time shall provide such local standards of measure and weight as they deem requisite for the purpose of the comparison by way of verification or inspection, in accordance with this Act, of all weights and measures in use in their county or borough, and shall fix the places at which such standards are to be deposited.

The said local authority shall also provide from time to time proper means for verifying weights and measures by comparison with the local standards of such authority and for stamping the weights and measures so verified.

**41.** A local standard of weight shall not be deemed legal nor be used for the purposes of this Act unless it has been verified or re-verified within five years before the time at which it is used.

A local standard of measure shall not be deemed legal nor be used for the purposes of this Act unless it has been verified or re-verified within ten years before the time at which it is used.

A local standard of weight or measure which has become defective in consequence of any wear or accident, or has been mended, shall not be legal nor be used for the purpose of this Act until it has been re-verified by the Board of Trade.

A local standard may, save as aforesaid, be re-verified, for the purpose of this section, by such local comparison thereof as is hereinafter mentioned, if on that local comparison it is found correct, but otherwise shall be, and in any case may be, re-verified by the Board of Trade.

*Side notes:* Provision of local standards by local authority. — Periodical verification of local standards.

A local comparison of a local standard shall be made by an inspector of weights and measures for the county or borough in which such standard is used comparing the same, in the presence of a justice of the peace, with some other local standard which has been verified or re-verified by the Board of Trade, in the case of a weight within the previous five years, and in the case of a measure within the previous ten years.

Upon a local comparison where the local standard is found correct the justice shall sign an indorsement upon the indenture of verification of that standard, stating such local comparison and verification, and the error, if any, found thereon, and the indorsement so signed shall be transmitted to the Board of Trade to be recorded in the account of the verification of local standards. The indorsement when so recorded shall be evidence of the local comparison and verification, and a statement of the record thereof, if purporting to be signed by an officer of the Board of Trade, shall be evidence of the same having been so recorded.

It shall be lawful for Her Majesty from time to time, by Order in Council, to define the amount of error to be tolerated in local standards when verified or re-verified by the Board of Trade, or when re-verified by such a local comparison as is authorised by this section.

**Production of local standards.** **42.** The local standards shall be produced by the person having the custody thereof, upon reasonable notice, at such reasonable time and place within the county, borough, or place for which the same have been provided, as any person by writing under his hand requires, upon payment by the person requiring such production of the reasonable charges of producing the same.

### Local Verification and Inspection of Weights and Measures.

**Appointment of inspectors of weights and measures.** **43.** Every local authority shall from time to time appoint a sufficient number of inspectors of weights and measures for safely keeping the local standards provided by such authority, and for the discharge of the other duties of inspectors under this Act; and where they appoint more than one such inspector, shall allot to each inspector (subject to any arrangement made for a chief inspector or inspectors) a separate district, to be distinguished by some name, number, or mark; and the local authority may suspend or dismiss any inspector appointed by them or appoint additional inspectors, as occasion may require, and shall assign reasonable remuneration to each inspector for his duties.

A local authority may, if they think fit, appoint different persons to be inspectors for verification and for inspection respectively of weights and measures under this Act.

[A maker or seller of weights or measures, or a person employed in the making or selling thereof, shall not be an inspector of weights and measures under this Act (e).]

An inspector of weights and measures shall forthwith on his appointment enter into a recognizance to the Crown (to be sued for in any court of record) in the sum of two hundred pounds for the due performance of the duties of his office, and for the due payment, at the times fixed by the local authority appointing him, of all fees received by him under this Act, and for the safety of the local standards and the stamps and appliances for verification committed to his charge, and for their due surrender immediately on his removal or other cessation from office to the person appointed by the local authority to receive them.

**Verification and stamping by inspectors of weights and measures.** **44.** The local authority shall from time to time fix the times and places within their jurisdiction at which each inspector appointed by them is to attend for the purpose of the verification of weights and measures; and the inspector shall attend, with the local standards in his custody, at each time and place fixed, and shall examine every measure or weight which is of the same denomination as one of such standards and is brought to him for the purpose of verification, and compare the same with that standard, and if he find the same correct shall stamp it with a stamp of verification in such manner as best to prevent fraud; and in the case of a measure or of a weight of a quarter of a pound or upwards, shall further stamp thereon a name, number, or mark distinguishing the district for which he acts.

He shall also enter in a book kept by him minutes of every such verification, and give, if required, a certificate under his hand of every such stamping.

(e) Repealed: see 52 & 53 Vict. c. 21, ss. 12, 36.

An inspector appointed by the local authority for a county may enter a place within the district of an inspector appointed by any other local authority, and there verify and stamp the weights and measures of any person residing within his own district, but if he knowingly stamp a weight or measure of any person residing in the district of an inspector legally appointed by another local authority, he shall be liable to a fine not exceeding twenty shillings for every weight or measure which he so stamps.

45. A weight or measure duly stamped by an inspector under this Act shall be a legal weight or measure throughout the United Kingdom, unless found to be false or unjust, and shall not be liable to be re-stamped because used in any place other than that in which it was originally stamped.

46. [Where a measure for liquids is constructed with a small window or transparent part through which the contents, whether to the brim or to any other index thereof, may be seen without impediment, such measure may be verified and stamped by inspectors under this Act, although such measure is made partly of metal and partly of glass or other transparent medium, and that whether such measure corresponds exactly to a Board of Trade standard, or whether it exceeds such standard, but has the capacity of such standard indicated by a level line drawn through the centre of the window or transparent part (f).]

47. [An inspector under this Act may take in respect of the verification and stamping of weights and measures such fees not exceeding those specified in the Fifth Schedule to this Act as the authority appointing him from time to time fix, and shall at such times not less often than once a quarter as the said authority direct, account for and pay over to the treasurer of the local rate or such person as the said authority direct all fees taken by him (g).]

Where the Board of Trade, upon the application of any local authority from time to time represent to Her Majesty that it would be expedient to alter the fees taken by the inspectors of such authority under this Act (whether specified in the said schedule or in any order previously made under this section) or, for the purpose of adapting those fees to the local standards provided by such authority, to add to the said fees, it shall be lawful for Her Majesty by Order in Council from time to time to alter or add to the said fees.

48. Every inspector under this Act authorized in writing under the hand of a justice of the peace, also every justice of the peace, may at all reasonable times inspect all weights measures scales balances steelyards and weighing machines within his jurisdiction which are used or in the possession of any person or on any premises for use for trade, and may compare every such weight and measure with some local standard, and may seize and detain any weight measure scale balance or steelyard which is liable to be forfeited in pursuance of this Act, and may for the purpose of such inspection enter any place, whether a building or in the open air, whether open or enclosed, where he has reasonable cause to believe that there is any weight measure scale balance steelyard or weighing machine which he is authorised by this Act to inspect.

Any person who neglects or refuses to produce for such inspection all weights measures scales balances steelyards and weighing machines in his possession or on his premises, or refuses to permit the justice or inspector to examine the same or any of them, or obstructs the entry of the justice or inspector under this section, or otherwise obstructs or hinders a justice or inspector acting under this section, shall be liable to a fine not exceeding five, or, in the case of a second offence, ten pounds.

49. If an inspector under this Act stamps a weight or measure in contravention of any provision of this Act, or without duly verifying the same by comparison with a local standard, or is guilty of a breach of any duty imposed on him by this Act, or otherwise misconducts himself in the execution of his office, he shall be liable to a fine not exceeding five pounds for each offence.

### Local Authorities.

50. For the purposes of this Act "the local authority" and "the local rate" shall mean in each of the different areas mentioned in the first column of the Fourth Schedule to this Act the authority and the rate or fund mentioned in that schedule in connexion with that area:

Provided that in England the council of a borough which has not a separate

(f) Repealed: 52 & 53 Vict. c. 21, ss. 5, 36.
(g) Repealed: 52 & 53 Vict. c. 21, s. 36.

---

Margin notes:

Validity of weights and measures stamped throughout the United Kingdom.

Power to stamp measures made partly of metal and partly of glass.

Fees for comparison and stamping.

Power to inspect measures, weights, scales, &c., and to enter shops, &c., for that purpose.

Penalty on inspector for misconduct.

Local authorities and local rate.

court of quarter sessions shall not, unless they so resolve, be the local authority for the purposes of this Act, and if they so resolve and provide local standards and appoint inspectors after the commencement of this Act, they shall forthwith give notice of such resolution and appointment, under the corporate seal of the borough, to the clerk of the peace of the county in which the borough is situate, and after the expiration of one month from the day on which that notice of the said appointment is given the powers of inspectors of weights and measures appointed by the justices of the county shall, as to such borough and the weights and measures of persons residing therein, cease ; but until such notice is given the borough shall be deemed to form part of the said county in like manner as if the same were not a borough.

Where at the commencement of this Act legal local standards are provided and inspectors are appointed by the council of a borough not having a separate court of quarter sessions, that council shall continue to be the local authority until they otherwise resolve.

**Expenses of local authority.**
51. The expense of providing and re-verifying local standards, the salaries of the inspectors, and all other expenses incurred by the local authority under this Act shall be paid out of the local rate.

The treasurer of the county in which a borough in England having a separate court of quarter sessions is situate shall exclude from the account kept by him of all sums expended out of the county rate to which the borough is liable to contribute all sums expended in pursuance of this Act.

**Power of local authorities to combine for purposes of Act.**
52. Any two or more local authorities may combine, as regards either the whole or any part of the areas within their jurisdiction, for all or any of the purposes of this Act, upon such terms and in such manner as may be from time to time mutually agreed upon.

An inspector appointed in pursuance of an agreement for such combination shall, subject to the terms of his appointment, have the same authority, jurisdiction and duties as if he had been appointed by each of the authorities who are parties to such agreement.

**Power to local authority to make byelaws as to local verification, &c.**
53. Any local authority from time to time, with the approval of the Board of Trade, may make, and when made, revoke, alter, and add to, byelaws for regulating the comparison with the local standards of such authority, and the verification and stamping of weights and measures in use in their county or borough, and for regulating the local comparison of the local standards of such authority, and generally for regulating the duties under this Act of the inspectors appointed by the local authority or of any of those inspectors. Such byelaws may impose fines not exceeding twenty shillings for the breach of any byelaw, to be recovered on summary conviction. The Board of Trade before approving any such byelaws shall cause them to be published in such manner as they think sufficient for giving notice thereof to all persons interested (h).

**Appointment of inspectors in towns and other places.**
54. Where a town or other place has been or may hereafter be authorised under any Act, whether local or otherwise, to appoint inspectors or examiners of weights and measures, or where any other place has been or may hereafter be, by charter Act of Parliament or otherwise, possessed of legal jurisdiction, and such town or place is for the time being provided with legal local standards, the magistrates of such town or place, or other persons authorised as aforesaid, may appoint inspectors of weights and measures within the limits of their jurisdiction, and suspend and dismiss such inspectors, and such inspectors shall within such limits exclusively have the same power and discharge the same duties as inspectors of weights and measures appointed under this Act by the local authority for the county, and shall pay over and account for the fees received by them under this Act, to such persons as may be duly authorised by the magistrates or other persons appointing them (i).

**Power of vestry, &c. in Metropolis to put an end to appointment of inspectors of weights and measures under Local Act.**
55. Where in any place in the Metropolis—that is to say, in the parishes and places in which the Metropolitan Board of Works have power to levy the consolidated rate—any vestry commissioners or other body have any duties or powers, under any Local Act charter or otherwise, in relation to the appointment of inspectors or examiners of weights and measures, such vestry commissioners or body may, at a meeting specially convened for the purpose of which not less than fourteen days' notice has been given, resolve that it is expedient that their said duties and powers should cease in such place.

The clerk or other like officer of such vestry commissioners or body shall give notice of such resolution to the clerk of the peace for the county in

(h) See 52 & 53 Vict. c. 21, s. 1 (3).
(i) As to the county of London, see 52 & 53 Vict. c. 21, s. 16.

which such place is situate, and the clerk of the peace shall lay such notice before the next practicable court of quarter sessions for the county, and after the receipt of such notice by the court of quarter sessions the appointment, and all powers of appointment, of any inspector or examiner appointed under such Local Act charter or otherwise, shall cease in the said place, without prejudice to any proceedings then pending for penalties or otherwise (*k*).

### Legal Proceedings.

**56.** All offences under this Act may be prosecuted and all fines and forfeitures under this Act may be recovered on summary conviction before a court of summary jurisdiction in manner provided by the Summary Jurisdiction Act. *Prosecution of offences and recovery of fines.*

The court when hearing and determining an information or complaint under this Act shall be constituted either of two or more justices of the peace in petty sessions sitting at a place appointed for holding petty sessions, or of some magistrate or officer sitting alone or with others at some court or other place appointed for the administration of justice and for the time being empowered by law to do alone any act authorised to be done by more than one justice of the peace.

**57.** The following enactments shall apply to proceedings under this Act before a court of summary jurisdiction ; (that is to say,) *Provisions as to summary proceedings.*

1. The description of any offence in the words of this Act, or in similar words, shall be sufficient in law ; and

2. Any exception, exemption, proviso, excuse, or qualification, whether it does or does not accompany in the same section the description of the offence, may be proved by the defendant but need not be specified or negatived in the information or complaint, and, if so specified or negatived, no proof in relation to the matter so specified or negatived shall be required on the part of the informant or complainant ; and

3. A warrant of commitment shall not be held void by reason of any defect therein, if it be therein alleged that the offender has been convicted, and there is a good and valid conviction to sustain the same.

4. Such portion of any fine under this Act, not exceeding a moiety, as the court of summary jurisdiction before whom a person is convicted think fit to direct, may, if the court in their discretion so order, be paid to the informer.

5. All weights measures scales balances and steelyards forfeited under this Act shall be broken up, and the materials thereof may be sold or otherwise disposed of as a court of summary jurisdiction direct, and the proceeds of such sale shall be applied in like manner as fines under this Act.

**58.** A person shall not be liable to any increased penalty for a second offence under any section of this Act unless that offence was committed after a conviction within five years previously for an offence under the same section. *Limitation as to conviction for second offences.*

**59.** Where any weight measure scale balance steelyard or weighing machine is found in the possession of any person carrying on trade within the meaning of this Act, or on the premises of any person which, whether a building or in the open air, whether open or enclosed, are used for trade within the meaning of this Act, such person shall be deemed for the purposes of this Act, until the contrary is proved, to have such weight measure scale balance steelyard or weighing machine in his possession for use for trade. *Evidence as to possession.*

**60.** Any person who feels himself aggrieved by a conviction or order of a court of summary jurisdiction under this Act may appeal therefrom, subject in England to the conditions following ; that is to say, *Appeal from conviction.*

(1.) The appeal shall be made to the next practicable court of general or quarter sessions having jurisdiction in the county or place in which the decision of the court was given, and holden not less than twenty-one days after the day on which such decision was given ; and

(2.) The appellant shall, within ten days after the day on which the decision was given, serve notice on the other party and on the clerk of the court of summary jurisdiction of his intention to appeal, and of the general grounds of such appeal ; and

(3.) The appellant shall, within three days after the day on which he gave

*λ*) Now as to the County of London, see 52 & 53 Vict. c. 21, s. 16.

notice of appeal, enter into a recognizance before a court of summary jurisdiction, with or without a surety or sureties as the court may direct, conditioned to appear at the said sessions and to try such appeal, and to abide the judgment of the court thereon, and to pay such costs as may be awarded by the court, or the appellant may, if the court of summary jurisdiction thinks it expedient, instead of entering into a recognizance, give such other security, by deposit of money with the clerk of the court of summary jurisdiction or otherwise, as the court deems sufficient ; and

(4.) Where the appellant is in custody a court of summary jurisdiction may, if it seem fit, on the appellant entering into such recognizance or giving such other security as aforesaid, release him from custody ; and

(5.) The court of appeal may adjourn the hearing of the appeal, and upon the hearing thereof may confirm, reverse, or modify the decision of the court of summary jurisdiction, or remit the matter to the court of summary jurisdiction with the opinion of the court of appeal thereon, or make such other order in the matter as the court thinks just. The court of appeal may also make such order as to costs to be paid by either party as the court thinks just ; and

(6.) Whenever a decision is reversed by the court of appeal the clerk of the peace shall indorse on the conviction or order appealed against a memorandum that such conviction or order has been quashed, and whenever any copy or certificate of such conviction or order is made, a copy of such memorandum shall be added thereto, and shall be sufficient evidence that the conviction or order has been quashed in every case where such copy or certificate would be sufficient evidence of such conviction or order ; and

(7.) Every notice in writing required by this section to be given by an appellant may be signed by him, or by his agent on his behalf, and may be transmitted in a registered letter by the post in the ordinary way, and shall be deemed to have been served at the time when it would be delivered in the ordinary course of the post.

**Provision as to action against person acting in execution of Act.** 61. In an action for any act done in pursuance or execution or intended execution of this Act, or in respect of any alleged neglect or default in the execution of this Act, tender of amends before the action is commenced may in lieu of or in addition to any other plea be pleaded, if the action was commenced after such tender, or is proceeded with after payment into court of any money in satisfaction of the plaintiff's claim. If the action is commenced after such tender, or is proceeded with after such payment, and the plaintiff does not recover more than the sum tendered or paid respectively, the plaintiff shall not recover any costs incurred after such tender or payment, and the defendant shall be entitled to his costs, to be taxed as between solicitor and client, as from the time of such tender or payment; but this provision shall not affect costs on any injunction in the action.

### III.—MISCELLANEOUS.

**Continuance of inquisition recorded for ascertaining rents and tolls payable.** 62. Every inquisition which, in pursuance of any Act hereby repealed, has been taken for ascertaining the amount of contracts to be performed or rents to be paid in grain or malt, or in any other commodity or thing, or with reference to the measure or weight of any grain, malt or other commodity or thing, and the amount of any toll, rate or duty payable according to any weight or measure in use before the passing of the said Act, and has been enrolled of record in her Majesty's Court of Exchequer, shall continue in force, and may be given in evidence in any legal proceeding, and the amount ascertained by such inquisition shall, when converted into imperial weights and measures, continue to be the rule of payment in regard to all such contracts rents tolls rates or duties.

**Orders in Council.** 63. It shall be lawful for her Majesty in Council from time to time to make orders for the purposes of this Act, and to revoke and vary any such order.

All Orders in Council made under this Act shall be published in the London Edinburgh and Dublin Gazettes, and shall be forthwith laid before both Houses of Parliament, and shall have full effect as part of this Act.

**Effect of schedules.** 64. The schedules to this Act, with the notes thereto, shall be construed and have effect as part of this Act.

**65.** Where an enactment refers to any Act repealed by this Act, or to any enactment thereof, the same shall be construed to refer to this Act or to the corresponding enactment of this Act.

*Construction of Acts referring to repealed enactments.*

### Savings and Definitions.

**66.** Nothing in this Act shall affect the validity of the models of gas holders verified and deposited in the standards department of the Board of Trade in pursuance of the Act of the session of the twenty-second and twenty-third years of the reign of her present Majesty, chapter sixty-six, intituled "An Act for regulating measures used in sales of gas," and of the Acts amending the same, and the provisions of this Act with respect to Board of Trade standards shall apply to such models; and the provisions of this Act with respect to defining the amount of error to be tolerated in local standards when verified or re-verified, shall apply to defining the amount of error to be tolerated in such copies of the said models of gas holders as are provided by any justices council commissioners or other local authority in pursuance of the said Acts.

*Saving as to models of gas holders under 22 & 23 Vict. c. 66.*

**67.** Nothing in this Act shall extend to prohibit, defeat, injure, or lessen the rights granted by charter to the master, wardens, and commonalty of the mystery of Founders of the City of London.

*Saving as to rights of the Founders Company.*

**68.** Nothing in this Act shall prohibit, defeat, injure, or lessen the right of the mayor and commonalty and citizens of the City of London, or of the lord mayor of the City of London for the time being, with respect to the stamping or sealing of weights and measures, or with respect to the gauging of wine or oil, or other gaugeable liquors.

*Saving as to London.*

**69.** Nothing in this Act shall extend to supersede, limit, take away, lessen, or prevent the authority which any person or body politic or corporate, or any person appointed at any court leet for any hundred or manor, or any jury or ward inquest, may have or possess for the examining, regulating, seizing, breaking, or destroying any weights, balances, or measures within their respective jurisdictions, and for the purposes of this section the court of burgesses of the City of Westminster shall be deemed to be a body politic, and nothing in this Act shall be deemed to repeal or supersede the Acts relating to that court, or lessen, diminish, or alter the powers of the same.

*Act not to abridge the power of the leet jury, &c.*

**70.** In this Act, unless the context otherwise requires,—

*Definitions:*

The expression "the Summary Jurisdiction Act" means the Act of the session of the eleventh and twelfth years of the reign of her present Majesty, chapter forty-three, intituled "An Act to facilitate the performance of the duties of justices of the peace out of sessions within England and Wales with respect to summary convictions and orders," inclusive of any Acts amending the same:

*"Summary Jurisdiction Act:"*

The expression "court of summary jurisdiction" means any justice or justices of the peace, metropolitan police magistrate, stipendiary or other magistrate or officer, by whatever name called, to whom jurisdiction is given by the Summary Jurisdiction Act or any Acts therein referred to:

*"Court of summary jurisdiction:"*

The expression "quarter sessions" includes general sessions:

*"Quarter sessions:"*

The expression "Treasury" means the Commissioners of her Majesty's Treasury:

*"Treasury:"*

The expression "person" includes a body corporate:

*"Person:"*

The expression "stamping" includes casting, engraving, etching, branding, or otherwise marking, in such manner as to be so far as practicable indelible, and the expression "stamp" and other expressions relating thereto shall be construed accordingly:

*"Stamping:"*

The expression "coin weight" means a weight used or intended to be used for weighing coin:

*"Coin weight:"*

The expression "Weights and Measures Act, 1835," means the Act of the fifth and sixth years of the reign of King William the Fourth, chapter sixty-three, intituled "An Act to repeal an Act of the fourth and fifth year of his present Majesty, relating to weights and measures, and to make other provisions instead thereof."

*"Weights and Measures Act, 1835."*

### IV.—APPLICATION OF ACT TO SCOTLAND.

This Act shall apply to Scotland, with the following modifications:—

**71.** In the application of this Act to Scotland, the expression "rents and

*Application of imperial weights*

and measures to tolls, &c.

tolls " includes all stipends, feu duties, customs, casualties, and other demands whatsoever payable in grain, malt, or meal, or any other commodity or thing.

The fiars prices of all grain in every county shall be struck by the imperial quarter, and all other returns of the prices of grain shall be set forth by the same, without reference to any other measure whatsoever.

Any person who acts in contravention of this provision shall be liable to a fine not exceeding five pounds.

Recovery and application of penalties.

**72.** All offences under this Act which may be prosecuted, and all fines and forfeitures under this Act which may be recovered on summary conviction, may in Scotland be prosecuted or recovered, with expenses, before the sheriff or sheriff substitute or two or more justices of the peace of the county, or the magistrates of the burgh wherein the offence was committed or the offender resides, at the instance either of the procurator fiscal or of any person who prosecutes.

Every person found liable in Scotland in any fine recoverable summarily under this Act shall, failing payment thereof immediate or within a specified time, as the case may be, and expenses, be liable to be imprisoned for a term not exceeding sixty days, and the conviction and warrant may be in the form

27 & 28 Vict. c. 53.

number three of Schedule K. of the Summary Procedure Act, 1864.

All fines and forfeitures so recovered, subject to any payment made to the informer, shall be paid as follows:

(a) To the Queen's and Lord Treasurer's Remembrancer, on behalf of her Majesty, when the court is the sheriff court:

(b) To the collector of county rates, in aid of the county general assessment, when the court is the justice of the peace court:

(c) To the treasurer of the burgh, in aid of the funds of the burgh, when the court is a burgh court:

(d) To the treasurer of the board of police, or commissioners of police, in aid of the police funds, when the court is a police court.

Appeal.

**73.** An appeal against a conviction under this Act in Scotland shall be to the Court of Justiciary at the next circuit court, or where there are no circuit courts, to the High Court of Justiciary at Edinburgh, and not otherwise, and such appeal may be made in the manner and under the rules, limitations, and conditions contained in the Act of the twentieth year of the reign of King George the Second, chapter forty-three, intituled " An Act for taking away and abolishing heritable jurisdictions in Scotland," or as near thereto as circumstances admit; with this variation, that the appellant shall find caution to pay the fine and expenses awarded against him by the conviction or order appealed from, together with any additional expenses awarded by the court dismissing the appeal.

Definitions as regards Scotland.

**74.** In the application of this Act to Scotland,—

The expression " enter into a recognizance " means grant a bond of caution:

The expression " any court of record " includes the Court of Session and the ordinary sheriff court:

The expression " burgh " shall include royal burgh and parliamentary burgh:

The expression " plaintiff " means pursuer, and the expression " defendant " means defender:

The expression " solicitor " means writer or agent:

27 & 28 Vict. c. 53.

The expression " Summary Jurisdiction Act " means the Summary Procedure Act, 1864, inclusive of any Act amending the same.

Power of sheriff.

**75.** A sheriff or sheriff substitute shall have the same power in relation to a local comparison of standards, and to the inspection comparison seizure and detention of weights and measures, and to entry for that purpose, as is given by this Act to a justice of the peace.

## V.—Application of Act to Ireland.

This Act shall apply to Ireland with the following modifications:—

Contracts to be made by denominations of imperial weight, otherwise to be void.

**76.** In Ireland every contract bargain sale or dealing—

For any quantity of corn, grain, pulses, potatoes, hay, straw, flax, roots, carcases of beef or mutton, butter, wool, or dead pigs, sold, delivered, or agreed for;

Or for any quantity of any other commodity sold, delivered, or agreed for

by weight (not being a commodity which may by law be sold by the troy ounce or by apothecaries weight),
shall be made or had by one of the following denominations of Imperial weight; namely:—

the ounce avoirdupois;
the imperial pound of sixteen ounces;
the stone of fourteen pounds;
the quarter-hundred of twenty-eight pounds;
the half-hundred of fifty-six pounds;
the hundredweight of one hundred and twelve pounds; or
the ton of twenty hundredweight;

and not by any local or customary denomination of weight whatsoever, otherwise such contract bargain sale or dealing shall be void:

Provided always, that nothing in the present section shall be deemed to prevent the use in any contract bargain sale or dealing of the denomination of the quarter, half, or other aliquot part of the ounce pound or other denomination aforesaid, or shall be deemed to extend to any contract bargain sale or dealing relating to standing or growing crops.

77. In Ireland every article sold by weight shall, if weighed, be weighed in full net standing beam; and for the purposes of every contract bargain sale or dealing the weight so ascertained shall be deemed the true weight of the article, and no deduction or allowance for tret or beamage, or on any other account, or under any other name whatsoever, the weight of any sack vessel or other covering in which such article may be contained alone excepted, shall be claimed or made by any purchaser on any pretext whatever under a penalty not exceeding five pounds. *Mode of weighing.* *Deductions prohibited.*

A proceeding for the recovery of a penalty under this section shall be begun within three months after the offence is committed.

78. (1.) The local authority in Ireland shall provide one complete set of local standards for their county or borough; also so many copies in iron or other sufficient material of the local standards. *Providing of local standards and sub-standards.*

(2.) The said copies of the local standards when duly verified as hereinafter mentioned shall be the local sub-standards, and shall be used for the verification of weights and measures brought by the public for verification as if they were local standards.

(3.) Not less than one set of local sub-standards, and one set of accurate scales, shall be provided for each petty sessions district in a county, and not less than two such sets shall be provided for a borough.

(4.) The local authority shall have the local standards from time to time duly compared and re-verified in manner directed by this Act.

(5.) The Commissioners of the Dublin Metropolitan Police shall not be under any obligation to provide local standards, but they may, with the assent of the Chief Secretary or Under-Secretary to the Lord Lieutenant, procure such sub-standards scales and stamps as they think necessary for the purposes of this Act in the district for which they are the local authority.

79. In Ireland, in every year— *Inquiry by judge of assize and chairman of quarter sessions as to provision of local standards and sub-standards.*

(a) In the case of a county, the judge of assize at the first assizes held for the county by inquiry of the foreman of the grand jury; and

(b) In the case of every borough in a county, the recorder of the borough, or, if there be no recorder, the chairman of the quarter sessions for that county at the quarter sessions, held next after the twenty-fifth day of March,

shall inquire whether one complete set of local standards, and a sufficient number of local sub-standards of weights and measures, and a sufficient number of scales and stamps (for verification), have been provided in such county or in such borough.

If it appear to the judge or chairman upon such inquiry that the same have not been so provided, he shall forthwith order the proper officer to provide a complete set of local standards and such sub-standards scales and stamps as appear to the judge or chairman making the order to be sufficient for the purposes of this Act, and that order shall have the effect in the case of a county of a presentment on the county for, and in the case of a borough, of an order on the council of the borough to raise by way of rate, the sum necessary to execute the order, and the said officer shall within three months after he receives the order fully execute the same, and in default shall be liable to a fine not exceeding twenty pounds.

The proper officer shall, in the case of a county, be the treasurer of the county, and in the case of a borough, the town clerk or other proper officer of the borough.

**Expenses of ex-officio inspectors.** **80.** Expenses incurred by any member of the Royal Irish constabulary as an ex-officio inspector of weights and measures in the execution of this Act shall be payable to such inspector by the person acting as treasurer of the local authority of the district on presentation of accounts of such expenses, to be furnished quarterly certified to be correct by the county inspector of the county.

The secretary of every grand jury being a local authority under this Act shall, at each assizes or presenting term, and the clerk of every other local authority shall once in every year lay before each such grand jury or other local authority an estimate of the sum which may appear to be necessary to meet such expenses until the next assizes or presenting term, or for the ensuing year; and every such grand jury or other local authority shall, without previous application to presentment sessions or other preliminary proceedings, present in advance to the person acting as treasurer the sum specified in such estimate, to be raised and paid out of the local rate; and if the sum so raised proves more than sufficient for the purpose, the balance shall be carried to the credit of the local rate by the person acting as treasurer, and if the sum so raised proves insufficient, the person acting as treasurer shall apply for payment of such expenses any other available funds in his hands.

**Ex-officio inspectors of weights and measures.** **81.** Nothing in this Act shall authorise the local authority in Ireland, except the local authority of the borough of Dublin, to appoint inspectors of weights and measures, but such head or other constables in each petty sessions district as may be from time to time selected by the inspector general of constabulary, with the approval of the Lord Lieutenant, shall be ex-officio inspectors of weights and measures under this Act within that district, and shall perform their duties under this Act under the direction of the justices of petty sessions, without fee or reward, and notwithstanding any manorial jurisdiction or claim of jurisdiction within such district:

Provided that if within one month from the date of such selection the justices signify their disapproval of the selection of any head or other constable, another selection shall be made by the same authority, subject to the same conditions, and the inspector general of constabulary shall within three days after any selection has been made in a petty sessions district, give or cause to be given to the clerk of that district notice of such selection, and the clerk shall immediately make known the said selection to the justices of the district.

An ex-officio inspector of weights and measures may exercise, without any authority from a justice of the peace, the powers given by this Act to an inspector of weights and measures having such authority.

In the district in which the commissioners of the Dublin metropolitan police are the local authority under this Act, such of the superintendents inspectors or acting inspectors of the said police as may be selected by the local authority with the approval of the Lord Lieutenant shall be ex-officio inspectors of weights and measures within the said district (a).

**Custody and use of local standards.** **82.** The local standards of every county or borough in Ireland shall be in the custody of such sub-inspector of constabulary as may be from time to time appointed for that county or borough by the inspector-general of constabulary, with the approval of the Lord Lieutenant.

Such sub-inspector shall, subject to such regulations as the inspector general of constabulary, with the approval of the Lord Lieutenant, from time to time makes, compare with the local standards in his custody, and adjust and verify the local sub-standards sent to him for the purpose, and when the same are correct shall stamp the same with a stamp of verification, and for the purpose of such verification and stamping, and of the verification of local standards, such sub-inspector of constabulary shall be deemed to be an inspector of weights and measures appointed under this Act.

**Custody and periodical verification of local sub-standards.** **83.** The local sub-standards shall be deposited in the custody of the ex-officio inspector of weights and measures, and shall at least once in every year, and also at other times when required by the county inspector of con-

(a) Amended: 52 & 53 Vict. c. 21, s. 19.

stabulary of the county, or by the justices in petty sessions of the county, be compared with the local standards of the county and verified, and when so verified shall until the expiration of one year or any shorter period at which the next comparison of the same under this section is made be deemed to be local sub-standards and be valid local standards for the purpose of the comparison by way of verification or inspection of weights and measures under this Act.

The sub-standards provided by the commissioners of the Dublin metropolitan police shall be verified by comparison with the local standards of the city of Dublin, as directed by this section, with this qualification, that the said commissioners, and not the county inspector or the justices, shall have authority to require the same to be verified oftener than once a year.

Any person who uses any sub-standard for any purpose other than that authorized by this Act shall be liable to a fine not exceeding five pounds.

**84.** For the purpose of the prosecution of offences and the recovery of fines under this Act, in Ireland,— *Recovery of fines, &c.*

(1.) The expression "Summary Jurisdiction Acts" in this Act means, within the police district of Dublin metropolis, the Acts regulating the powers and duties of justices of the peace for such district, or of the police of such district, and elsewhere in Ireland the Petty Sessions (Ireland) Act, 1851, and any Act amending or affecting the same ; and *14 & 15 Vict. c. 93.*

(2.) A court of summary jurisdiction when hearing and determining an information or complaint in any matter arising under this Act shall be constituted within the police district of Dublin metropolis of one of the divisional justices of that district sitting at a police court within the district, and elsewhere of a stipendiary magistrate sitting alone, or with others, or of two or more justices of the peace sitting in petty sessions at a place appointed for holding petty sessions ; and

(3.) Appeals from a court of summary jurisdiction shall lie in the manner and subject to the conditions and regulations prescribed in the twenty-fourth section of the Petty Sessions (Ireland) Act, 1851, and any Acts amending the same. *14 & 15 Vict. c. 93.*

**85.** In this Act, unless the context otherwise requires, *Definitions.*
The expression "Lord Lieutenant" means the lieutenant or other chief governor or governors of Ireland for the time being :
The expression "treasurer" includes the finance committee and the secretary of the grand jury for the county of Dublin.

## VI.—REPEAL.

**86.** The Acts mentioned in the first part of the Sixth Schedule to this Act are hereby repealed to the extent in the third column of that schedule mentioned ; subject to the following qualification, that is to say, that so much of the said Acts as is set forth in the second part of that schedule shall be re-enacted (b) in manner therein appearing, and shall be in force as if enacted in the body of this Act. *Repeal.*

Provided that,—

(1.) Every inspector appointed in pursuance of any enactment hereby repealed shall continue in office as if he had been appointed in pursuance of this Act ; and

(2.) Any person holding office as examiner of weights and measures under any enactment repealed by this Act, and not being an inspector of weights and measures within the meaning of this Act, shall continue in office and receive the same remuneration, and have the same powers and duties and be subject to the same liabilities and to the same power of dismissal as if this Act had not passed.

(3.) Every notice published in a Gazette in relation to coin weights in pursuance of any enactment hereby repealed shall continue in force.

(4.) All weights and measures duly verified and stamped in pursuance of any enactment hereby repealed, shall continue and be as valid as if they had been verified and stamped in pursuance of this Act, and that although such weights or measures could not have been verified and stamped in pursuance of this Act ; and all weights and measures which at the commencement of this Act may lawfully be used without being stamped with a stamp of verification or a stamp

(h) See 52 & 53 Vict. c. 21, s. 36, and 5th Sched.

3 z 2

of their denomination, and which are required by this Act to be stamped with such a stamp, may, notwithstanding they are not so stamped, be used until the expiration of six months after the commencement of this Act, without being subject to be seized or forfeited, and without rendering the person using or having possession of the same subject to any fine.

(5.) This repeal shall not affect—

(a) The past operation of any enactment hereby repealed, nor anything duly done or suffered under any enactment hereby repealed ; nor

(b) Any right, privilege, obligation, or liability acquired, accrued, or incurred under any enactment hereby repealed ; nor

(c) Any penalty, forfeiture, or punishment incurred in respect of any offence committed against any enactment hereby repealed ; nor

(d) Any investigation, legal proceeding, or remedy in respect of any such right, privilege, obligation, liability, penalty, forfeiture, or punishment as aforesaid ; and any such investigation, legal proceeding, and remedy may be carried on as if this Act had not passed ; and

(6.) This repeal shall not revive any enactment, right, office, privilege, matter, or thing not in force or existing at the commencement of this Act.

## SCHEDULES.

### FIRST SCHEDULE.

### PART I.

#### IMPERIAL STANDARDS.

Sections
4, 10, 13, 64.

The following standards were constructed under the direction of the Commissioners of her Majesty's Treasury, after the destruction of the former imperial standards in the fire at the Houses of Parliament.

The imperial standard for determining the length of the imperial standard yard is a solid square bar, thirty-eight inches long and one inch square in transverse section, the bar being of bronze or gun-metal ; near to each end a cylindrical hole is sunk (the distance between the centres of the two holes being thirty-six inches) to the depth of half an inch, at the bottom of this hole is inserted in a smaller hole a gold plug or pin, about one-tenth of an inch in diameter, and upon the surface of this pin there are cut three fine lines at intervals of about the one-hundreth part of an inch transverse to the axis of the bar, and two lines at nearly the same interval parallel to the axis of the bar ; the measure of length of the imperial standard yard is given by the interval between the middle transversal line at one end and the middle transversal line at the other end, the part of each line which is employed being the point midway between the longitudinal lines ; and the said points are in this Act referred to as the centres of the said gold plugs or pins ; and such bar is marked "copper 16 oz., tin 2½, zinc 1. Mr. Baily's metal. No. 1 standard yard at 62°·00 Fahrenheit. Cast in 1845. Troughton & Simms, London."

The imperial standard for determining the weight of the imperial standard pound is of platinum, the form being that of a cylinder nearly 1·35 inch in height and 1·15 inch in diameter, with a groove or channel round it, whose middle is about 0·34 inch below the top of the cylinder, for insertion of the points of the ivory fork by which it is to be lifted ; the edges are carefully rounded off, and such standard pound is marked, P.S. 1844, 1 lb.

### PART II.

#### PARLIAMENTARY COPIES OF IMPERIAL STANDARDS.

Sections
5, 35, 64.

The following copies of the standards above mentioned in part one of this Schedule were constructed at the same time as the above standards. They are of the same construction and form as the above standards, and they are respectively marked and deposited as follows :—

(1.) One of the copies of the imperial standard for determining the imperial standard yard, being a bronze bar, marked "copper 16 oz., tin 2½, zinc 1. Mr. Baily's metal. No. 2. Standard yard at 61°·94 Fahrenheit. Cast in 1845. Troughton & Simms, London;" and one of the copies of the imperial standard for determining the imperial standard pound marked No. 1., P.C. 1844, 1 lb., have been deposited at the Royal Mint;

(2.) One other of the copies of the imperial standard for determining the imperial standard yard, being a bronze bar, marked "copper 16 oz., tin 2½, zinc 1. Mr. Baily's metal. No. 3. Standard yard at 62°·10 Fahrenheit. Cast in 1845. Troughton & Simms, London," and one other of the copies of the imperial standard for determining the imperial standard pound marked No. 2., P.C. 1844, 1 lb., have been delivered to the Royal Society of London;

(3.) One other of the copies of the imperial standard for determining the imperial standard yard, being a bronze bar, marked "copper 16 oz., tin 2½, zinc 1. Mr. Baily's metal. No. 5. Standard yard at 62°·16 Fahrenheit. Cast in 1845. Troughton & Simms, London," and one other of the copies of the imperial standard for determining the imperial standard pound marked No. 3., P.C. 1844, 1 lb., have been deposited in the Royal Observatory of Greenwich;

(4.) The other of the copies of the imperial standard for determining the imperial standard yard, being a bronze bar, marked "copper 16 oz., tin 2½, zinc 1. Mr. Baily's metal. No. 4. Standard yard at 61°·98 Fahrenheit. Cast in 1845. Troughton & Simms, London," and the other of the copies of the imperial standard for determining the imperial standard pound marked No. 4., P.C. 1844, 1 lb., have been immured in the New Palace at Westminster.

---

## SECOND SCHEDULE.
### Board of Trade Standards.

Sections 8, 64.

Standards of the measures and weights following are at the commencement of this Act in use under the direction of the Board of Trade.

| Measures of Length. | Measures of Capacity. |
|---|---|
| Denomination of Standard. | Denomination of Standard. |
| **MEASURE OF LENGTH.** | **MEASURES OF CAPACITY.** |
| 100 feet. | Bushel. |
| 66 feet, or a chain of 100 links. | Half-bushel. |
| Rod, pole, or perch. | Peck. |
| 10 feet. | Gallon. |
| 6 feet, or 2 yards. | Half-gallon. |
| 5 feet. | Quart. |
| 4 feet. | Pint. |
| 3 feet, or 1 yard. | Half-pint. |
| 2 feet. | Gill. |
| 1 foot. | Half-gill. |
| 1 inch divided into 12 duodecimal, 10 decimal, and 16 binary equal parts. | Quarter-gill. |
| | **MEASURES USED IN THE SALE OF DRUGS.** |
| | Fluid ounces:— |
| | 4, 3, 2, 1. |
| | Fluid drachms:— |
| | 4, 3, 2, 1. |
| | Minims:— |
| | 30, 20, 10, 5, 4, 3, 2, 1. |

---

Note.—The brass gallon marked "Imperial Standard Gallon, Anno Domini MDCCCXXIV., Anno V G^iv Regis," which has a diameter equal to its height, and was made in pursuance of 5 Geo. 4, c. 74, s. 6, and is at the passing of this Act in the custody of the Warden of the Standards, shall be deemed to be a Board of Trade standard for the gallon.

WEIGHTS.

| Denomination of Standard. | Denomination of Standard. | Denomination of Standard. |
|---|---|---|
| AVOIRDUPOIS WEIGHTS. | TROY BULLION WEIGHTS. | DECIMAL GRAIN WEIGHTS. |
| 56 pounds. | 500 ounces. | 4,000 grains. |
| 28 ,, | 400 ,, | 2,000 ,, |
| 14 ,, | 300 ,, | 1,000 ,, |
| 7 ,, | 200 ,, | 500 ,, |
| 4 ,, | 100 ,, | 300 ,, |
| 2 ,, | 50 ,, | 200 ,, |
| 1 pound. | 40 ,, | 100 ,, |
| 8 ounces. | 30 ,, | 50 ,, |
| 4 ,, | 20 ,, | 30 ,, |
| 2 ,, | 10 ,, | 20 ,, |
| 1 ounce. | 5 ,, | 10 ,, |
| 8 drams. | 4 ,, | 5 ,, |
| 4 ,, | 3 ,, | 3 ,, |
| 2 ,, | 2 ,, | 2 ,, |
| 1 dram. | 1 ounce. | 1 ,, |
| ½ ,, | 0·5 ,, | 0·5 grain. |
| 240 grains, commonly called 10 pennyweights. | 0·4 ,, | 0·3 ,, |
| 120 grains, commonly called 5 pennyweights. | 0·3 ,, | 0·2 ,, |
| 72 grains, commonly called 3 pennyweights. | 0·2 ,, | 0·1 ,, |
| 48 grains, commonly called 2 pennyweights. | 0·1 ,, | 0·05 ,, |
| 24 grains, commonly called 1 pennyweight. | 0·05 ,, | 0·03 ,, |
| | 0·04 ,, | 0·02 ,, |
| | 0·03 ,, | 0·01 ,, |
| | 0·02 ,, | |
| | 0·01 ,, | |
| | 0·005 ,, | |
| | 0·004 ,, | |
| | 0·003 ,, | |
| | 0·002 ,, | |
| | 0·001 ,, | |

COIN WEIGHTS.

| Denomination of Coin. | Standard Weight. | |
|---|---|---|
| | Imperial Weight. | Metric Weight. |
| GOLD : | *Grains.* | *Grams.* |
| Five pound | 616·37239 | 39·94028 |
| Two pound | 246·54895 | 15·97611 |
| Sovereign | 123·27447 | 7·98805 |
| Half Sovereign | 61·63723 | 3·99402 |
| SILVER : | | |
| Crown | 436·36363 | 28·27590 |
| Half-crown | 218·18181 | 14·13795 |
| Florin | 174·54545 | 11·31036 |
| Shilling | 87·27272 | 5·65518 |
| Sixpence | 43·63636 | 2·82759 |
| Groat, or fourpence | 29·09090 | 1·88506 |
| Threepence | 21·81818 | 1·41379 |
| Twopence | 14·54545 | 0·94253 |
| Penny | 7·27272 | 0·47126 |
| BRONZE : | | |
| Penny | 145·83333 | 9·44984 |
| Halfpenny | 87·50000 | 5·66990 |
| Farthing | 43·75000 | 2·83495 |

## THIRD SCHEDULE.

### PART I.

#### Metric Equivalents.

Sections 18, 61.

Table of the Values of the Principal Denominations of Measures and Weights on the Metric System expressed by means of Denominations of Imperial Measures and Weights, and of the Values of the Principal Denominations of Measures and Weights of the Imperial system expressed by means of Metric Weights and Measures.

#### Measures of Length.

| Metric Denominations and Values. | | Equivalents in Imperial Denominations. | | | |
|---|---|---|---|---|---|
| — | Metres. | Miles. | Yards. | Feet. | Ins. Decimals. |
| Myriametre | 10,000 | 6 | 376 | 0 | 11·9 |
| | | or | 10,936 | 0 | 11·9 |
| Kilometre | 1,000 | | 1,093 | 1 | 10·79 |
| Hectometre | 100 | | 109 | 1 | 1·079 |
| Dekametre | 10 | | 10 | 2 | 9·7079 |
| Metre | 1 | | 1 | 0 | 3·3708 |
| Decimetre | $\frac{1}{10}$ | | | | 3·9371 |
| Centimetre | $\frac{1}{100}$ | | | | 0·3937 |
| Millimetre | $\frac{1}{1000}$ | | | | 0·0394 |

#### Measure of Surface.

| Metric Denominations and Values. | | Equivalents in Imperial Denominations. | |
|---|---|---|---|
| — | Square Metres. | Acres. | Square Yards. Decimals. |
| Hectare, i.e., 100 Ares | 10,000 | 2 | 2280·3326 |
| | | or | 11,960·3326 |
| Dekare, i.e., 10 Ares | 1,000 | | 1196·0333 |
| Are | 100 | | 119·6033 |
| Centiare, i.e., $\frac{1}{100}$·Are | 1 | | 1·1960 |

#### Measures of Capacity.

| Metric Denominations and Values. | | Equivalents in Imperial Denominations. | | | | | | |
|---|---|---|---|---|---|---|---|---|
| — | Cubic Metres. | Quarters. | Bushels. | Pecks. | Gallons. | Quarts. | Pints. | Decimals. |
| Kilolitre, i.e., 1,000 Litres | 1 | 3 | 3 | 2 | 0 | 0 | 0·77 | |
| Hectolitre, i.e., 100 Litres | $\frac{1}{10}$ | | 2 | 3 | 0 | 0 | 0·077 | |
| Dekalitre, i.e., 10 Litres | $\frac{1}{100}$ | | | 1 | 0 | 0 | 1·6077 | |
| Litre | $\frac{1}{1000}$ | | | | | | 1·76077 | |
| Decilitre, i.e., $\frac{1}{10}$·Litre | $\frac{1}{10000}$ | | | | | | 0·176077 | |
| Centilitre, i.e., $\frac{1}{100}$·Litre | $\frac{1}{100000}$ | | | | | | 0·0176077 | |

WEIGHTS.

| Metric Denominations and Values. | | Equivalents in Imperial Denominations. | | | | | |
| --- | --- | --- | --- | --- | --- | --- | --- |
| — | Grams. | Cwts. | Stones. | Pounds. | Ounces. | Drams. | Decimals. |
| Millier ................. | 1,000,000 | 19 | 5 | 6 | 9 | 15·04 | |
| Quintal ............... | 100,000 | 1 | 7 | 10 | 7 | 6·304 | |
| Myriagram ............. | 10,000 | | 1 | 8 | 0 | 11·8304 | |
| Kilogram ............ | 1,000 | | | | 2 | 3 | 4·3830 |
| | | \{ (or 15432·3487 grains) | | | | | |
| Hectogram ............. | 100 | | | | | 3 | 8·4383 |
| Dekagram ............. | 10 | | | | | | 5·6438 |
| Gram ................. | 1 | | | | | | 0·56438 |
| Decigram ............. | $\frac{1}{10}$ | | | | | | 0·056438 |
| Centigram ............. | $\frac{1}{100}$ | | | | | | 0·0056438 |
| Milligram ............. | $\frac{1}{1000}$ | | | | | | 0·00056438 |

MEASURES OF LENGTH.

| Imperial Measures. | Equivalents in Metric Measures. | | | |
| --- | --- | --- | --- | --- |
| | Millimetre. | Decimetre. | Metre. | Kilometre. |
| Inch ............... | = 25·39954 | | | |
| Foot or 12 inches ...... | .. | = 3·04794 | = 0·30479 | |
| YARD, or 3 feet, or 36 Inches ............. | .. | .. | = 0·91438 | |
| Fathom, or 2 yards, or 6 feet ............. | .. | .. | = 1·82877 | |
| Pole or 5½ yards ...... | .. | .. | = 5·02911 | |
| Chain, or 4 poles, or 22 yards ............. | .. | .. | = 20·11644 | |
| Furlong 40 poles, or 220 yards ............. | .. | .. | = 201·16437 | = 0·20116 |
| Mile, 8 furlongs, or 1,760 yards ............. | .. | .. | = 1,609·31493 | = 1·60931 |

MEASURES OF SURFACE.

| Imperial Measures. | Equivalents in Metric Measures. | | | |
| --- | --- | --- | --- | --- |
| | Square Decimetres. | Square Metres. | Ares. | Hectares. |
| Square inch ............ | = 0·06451 | | | |
| Square foot or 144 square inches ............. | = 9·28997 | = 0·092900 | | |
| Square yard, or 9 square feet, or 1,296 square inches ............. | = 83·60971 | = 0·836097 | | |
| Pole or perch, or 30¼ square yards.......... | .. | = 25·291939 | | |
| Rood, or 40 perches, or 1,210 square yards .... | .. | .. | = 10·116776 | |
| ACRE, or 4 roods, or 4,840 square yards ........ | .. | .. | .. | = 0·40467 |
| Square mile or 640 acres | .. | .. | .. | = 258·98946 |

## MEASURES OF CAPACITY.

| Imperial Measures. | Equivalents in Metric Measures. | | | |
|---|---|---|---|---|
| | Decilitres. | Litres. | Dekalitres. | Hectolitres. |
| Gill .................. | = 1·41983 | = 0·14198 | | |
| Pint or 4 gills .......... | = 5·67932 | = 0·56793 | | |
| Quart or 2 pints ........ | .. | = 1·13587 | | |
| GALLON or 4 quarts .... | .. | = 4·54346 | | |
| Peck or 2 gallons........ | .. | = 9·08692 | = 0·90869 | |
| Bushel, or 8 gallons, or 4 pecks .............. | .. | .. | = 3·63477 | |
| Quarter or 8 bushels .... | .. | .. | .. | = 2·90781 |

## CUBIC MEASURE.

| Imperial Measures. | Equivalents in Metric Measures. | | |
|---|---|---|---|
| | Cubic Centimetres. | Cubic Decimetres. | Cubic Metres. |
| Cubic inch ......................... | 16·38618 | | |
| Cubic foot or 1,728 cubic inches ...... | .. | 28·31531 | |
| Cubic yard or 27 cubic feet .......... | .. | .. | 0·76451 |

## WEIGHTS.

| Imperial Weights. | Equivalents in Metric Weights. | | | |
|---|---|---|---|---|
| | Grams. | Dekagrams. | Kilograms. | Millier or Metric Ton. |
| Grain .............. | = 0·06479895 | | | |
| Dram .............. | = 1·77185 | | | |
| Ounce, avoirdupois, or 16 drams, or 437·5 grains ............ | = 28·34954 | = 2·83495 | ... .. ..... | .. |
| POUND, or 16 ounces, or 256 drams, or 7,000 grains ...... | = 453·59265 | = 45·35927 | = 0·45359 | |
| Hundredweight or 112 lbs. .............. | .. | .. | = 50·80238 | |
| Ton or 20 cwt. ...... | .. | .. | = 1016·04754 | = 1·01605 |
| Ounce, troy, or 480 grains ............ | = 31·103496 | = 3·11035 | | |

## PART II.

### METRIC STANDARDS.

List of metric standards in the custody of the Board of Trade at the passing of this Act:—

#### *Measures of Length.*

Double metre or 2 metres.
METRE or 1 metre.
Decimetre or 0·1 ,,
Centimetre or 0·01 ,,
Millimetre or 0·001 ,,

#### *Weights.*

20, 10, 5, 2 kilograms.
KILOGRAM.
500, 200, 100, 50, 20, 10, 5, 2, 1 grams.
5, 2, 1 decigrams.
5, 2, 1, 0·5 milligrams.

#### *Measures of Capacity.*

20, 10, 5, 2 litres.
LITRE.
0·5 litre or 500 cubic centimetres.
0·2 ,, 200 ,,
0·1 ,, 100 ,,
0·05 ,, 50 ,,
0·02 ,, 20 ,,
0·01 ,, 10 ,,
0·005 ,, 5 ,,
0·002 ,, 2 ,,
0·001 ,, 1 ,,

## FOURTH SCHEDULE.

### LOCAL AUTHORITIES.

### ENGLAND.

| Area. | Local Authority. | Local Rate. |
| --- | --- | --- |
| County .............. | The justices in general or quarter sessions assembled. | The county rate. |
| County of the city of London. | The court of the Lord Mayor and aldermen of the city. | The consolidated rate. |
| Borough .............. | The mayor, aldermen, and burgesses acting by the council. | The borough fund and borough rate. |

### SCOTLAND.

| County .............. | The justices in general or quarter sessions assembled. | The county general assessment. |
| --- | --- | --- |
| Burgh ................ | The magistrates........ | The police assessment. |

## IRELAND.

| Area. | Local Authority. | Local Rate. |
|---|---|---|
| County .............. | The grand jury acting at any assizes or presenting term. | The presentments to be made by the grand jury. |
| Such portion of the police district of Dublin metropolis as is without the municipal boundary of the borough of Dublin. | The Commissioners of the Dublin metropolitan police. | The funds applicable to defray the expenses of the Dublin metropolitan police. |
| Borough .............. | Town Council.......... | Rate to be levied by the council, or if the borough is liable to county cess and no rate is levied in the borough, the county cess of the county in which the borough or the larger part thereof is situate. |

NOTES.

For the purposes of this schedule—

The expression " county," as regards England, does not include a county of a city or a county of a town, but includes every riding, division, or parts of a county having a separate court of quarter sessions. The Soke of Peterborough shall be deemed to be a county, but every other liberty of a county not forming part of the City of London shall be deemed to form part of the county in which the same is situate or which it adjoins, and if it adjoins more than one county, then of the county with which it has the longest common boundary.

The expression "borough," as regards England, means any place for the time being subject to the Municipal Corporation Act, 1835, and any Act amending the same, which has a separate commission of the peace.

The expression " county," as regards Ireland, includes a riding and a county of a city and a county of a town.

The county of Dublin shall be deemed not to include any portion of the police district of Dublin metropolis.

The two constabulary districts of the county of Galway shall respectively be deemed to be counties for the purposes of this Act.

The expression " borough," as regards Ireland, means any borough or town corporate.

In the borough of Dublin the rate to be levied by the council shall mean the improvement rate.

---

## [FIFTH SCHEDULE (a).

### FEES OF INSPECTORS.

Sections 47, 64.

The following fees are the maximum fees which, unless altered as authorised by this Act, may be taken by any inspector of weights and measures appointed under this Act.

| For comparing and stamping all brass weights :— | s. | d. |
|---|---|---|
| Each half hundredweight ............................... | 0 | 9 |
| Each quarter of a hundredweight ......................... | 0 | 6 |
| Each stone .................................... | 0 | 4 |
| Each weight under a stone to a pound inclusive ............. | 0 | 1 |
| Each weight under a pound ................................ | 0 | 0½ |
| Each set of weights of a pound and under.................. | 0 | 2 |

(a) Now repealed: 52 & 53 Vict. c. 21, s. 36.

For comparing and stamping all iron weights, or weights of other descriptions not made of brass:—

|  | s. | d. |
|---|---|---|
| Each half hundredweight | 0 | 3 |
| Each quarter of a hundredweight | 0 | 2 |
| Each stone | 0 | 1 |
| Each weight under a stone | 0 | 0½ |
| Each set of weights of a pound and under | 0 | 2 |

For comparing and stamping all wooden measures:—

|  | s. | d. |
|---|---|---|
| Each bushel | 0 | 3 |
| Each half bushel | 0 | 2 |
| Each peck, and all under | 0 | 1 |
| Each yard | 0 | 0½ |

For comparing and stamping all measures of capacity of liquids made of copper or other metal:—

|  | s. | d. |
|---|---|---|
| Each four gallon | 0 | 9 |
| Each two gallon | 0 | 4 |
| Each gallon | 0 | 2 |
| Each half gallon | 0 | 1 |
| Each quart and under | 0 | 0½ (b).] |

---

**SIXTH SCHEDULE.**

**FIRST PART.**

*Enactments repealed.*

Section 64, 86.

A description or citation of a portion of an Act is inclusive of the word, section, or other part first or last mentioned, or otherwise referred to as forming the beginning or as forming the end of the portion described in the description or citation.

Portions of Acts which have already been specifically repealed are in some instances included in the repeal in this schedule, in order to preclude henceforth the necessity of looking back to previous Acts.

| Session and chapter. | Title or short title of Act. | Extent of repeal. |
|---|---|---|
| 31 Edw. 3, st. 1 .. | The statute made at Westminster on the Monday next after the feast of Easter, in the thirty-first year, statute the first. | Chapter two. |
| 6 Anne, c. 11...... (5 & 6 Anne, c. 8. in Ruffhead.) | An Act for the union of the two kingdoms of England and Scotland. | Article seventeen. |
| 15 Geo. 2, c. 20 .. | An Act to prevent the counterfeiting of gold and silver lace, and for settling and adjusting the proportions of fine silver and silk, and for the better making of gold and silver thread. | Section five. |
| 35 Geo. 3, c. 102 .. | An Act for the more effectual prevention of the use of defective weights, and of false and unequal balances. | The whole Act. |

(b) This schedule is repealed: 52 & 53 Vict. c. 21, s. 36.

| Session and chapter. | Title or short title of Act. | Extent of repeal. |
|---|---|---|
| 36 Geo. 3, c. 85.... | An Act for the better regulation of mills. | Section one from "and any person or persons appointed" down to "with respect to weights and balances," and from "and every miller or other persons as aforesaid, in whose mill shall be found any weight or weights" to the end of the section. |
| 37 Geo. 3, c. 143 .. | An Act to explain and amend an Act made in the thirty-fifth year of the reign of his present Majesty, intituled "An Act for the more effectual prevention of the use of defective weights and of false and unequal balances." | The whole Act. |
| 55 Geo. 3, c. 43 .. | An Act for the more effectual prevention of the use of false and deficient measures. | The whole Act. |
| 5 Geo. 4, c. 74 .... | An Act for ascertaining and establishing uniformity of weights and measures. | The whole Act, except section twenty-five. |
| 6 Geo. 4, c. 12 .... | An Act to prolong the time of the commencement of an Act of the last session of Parliament for ascertaining and establishing uniformity of weights and measures, and to amend the said Act. | The whole Act. |
| 5 & 6 Will. 4, c. 63 | An Act to repeal an Act of the fourth and fifth year of his present Majesty relating to weights and measures, and to make other provisions instead thereof. | The whole Act. |
| 16 & 17 Vict. c. 29 | An Act for regulating the weights used in sales of bullion. | The whole Act. |
| 16 & 17 Vict. c. 79 | An Act for making sundry provisions with respect to municipal corporations in England. | Section five. |
| 18 & 19 Vict. c. 72 | An Act for legalizing and preserving the restored standards of weights and measures. | The whole Act. |
| 22 & 23 Vict. c. 56 | An Act to amend the Act of the fifth and sixth years of king William the Fourth, chapter sixty-three, relating to weights and measures. | The whole Act. |
| 23 & 24 Vict. c. 119 | An Act to amend the law relating to weights and measures in Ireland. | The whole Act. |
| 24 & 25 Vict. c. 75 | An Act for amending the Municipal Corporations Act. | Section six. |

| Session and chapter. | Title or short title of Act. | Extent of repeal. |
| --- | --- | --- |
| 25 & 26 Vict. c. 76 | The Weights and Measures (Ireland) Amendment Act, 1862. | The whole Act except section two, and Part three and so much of Part four as relates to Part three. |
| 25 & 26 Vict. c. 102 | The Metropolis Management Amendment Act, 1862. | Section one hundred and one. |
| 27 & 28 Vict. c. 117 | The Metric Weights and Measures Act, 1864. | The whole Act. |
| 29 & 30 Vict. c. 82 | An Act to amend the Acts relating to the standard weights and measures, and to the standard trial pieces of the coin of the realm. | The whole Act. |
| 30 & 31 Vict. c. 94 | An Act to provide for the inspection of weights and measures, and to regulate the law relating thereto, in certain parts of the police district of Dublin metropolis. | The whole Act. |
| 33 & 34 Viet. e. 10 | The Coinage Act, 1870 .......... | Section seventeen, from the beginning of the section down to "weight of and for weighing such coin," and from "all weights which are not less in weight," to the end of the section. |

## SECOND PART.

### *Enactments re-enacted.*

### 5 & 6 Will. 4, c. 63, s. 9.

Sale of coals by weight and not by measure.

[All coals, slack, culm, and cannel of every description shall be sold by weight, and not by measure. Every person who sells any coals, slack, culm, or cannel of any description by measure, and not by weight, shall be liable on summary conviction to a fine not exceeding forty shillings for every such sale (c).]

### 5 & 6 Will. 4, c. 63, s. 26.

Supply of weigh-masters in Ireland with scales, and copies of local standards.

In Ireland, in every city or town, not being a county of itself, every person, persons, or body corporate exercising the privilege of appointing a weigh-master, shall supply him with accurate scales, and with an accurate set of copies of the local standards, and in default shall be liable on summary conviction to a fine of twenty pounds, and the accuracy of such set of copies shall be certified under the hand of some inspector of weights and measures. They shall also, once at least in every five years, cause such copies to be readjusted by comparison with some local standards which have been verified by the Board of Trade, and in default shall be liable on summary conviction to a fine of five pounds.

Such set of copies shall for the purpose of comparison and verification be considered local standards, and shall be used for no other purpose whatever, and if they are so used the person using the same shall be liable on summary conviction to a fine of five pounds.

(c) Now repealed : 52 & 53 Vict. c. 21, s. 36, and 5th Scbed.

22 & 23 Vict. c. 56, ss. 6, 8, 12.

The owners or managers of any public market in Great Britain where goods are exposed or kept for sale shall provide proper scales and balances and weights and measures or other machines, for the purpose of weighing or measuring all goods sold, offered, or exposed for sale in any such market, and shall deposit the same at the office of the clerk or toll collector of such market, or some other convenient place, and shall have the accuracy of all such scales and balances and weights and measures or other machines tested at least twice in every year by the inspector of weights and measures of and for the county, borough, or place where the market is situate ;

All expenses attending the purchase, adjusting, and testing thereof shall be paid out of the moneys collected for tolls in the market ;

Such clerk or toll collector shall at all reasonable times, whenever called upon so to do, weigh or measure all goods which have been sold, offered, or exposed for sale in any such market, upon payment of such reasonable sum as may from time to time be decided upon by the said owners or managers, subject to the approval and revision of the justices in general or quarter sessions assembled if such market be in England, or of the sheriff if it be in Scotland ;

For every contravention of this section the offender shall be liable, on summary conviction, to a fine not exceeding five pounds.

*Owners of markets to provide scales, &c.*

22 & 23 Vict. c. 56, ss. 7, 8, 12.

Every clerk or toll collector of any public market in Great Britain, at all reasonable times, may weigh or measure all goods sold, offered, or exposed for sale in any such market ; and if upon such weighing or measuring any such goods are found deficient in weight or measure or otherwise contrary to the provisions of this Act, such clerk or toll collector shall take the necessary proceedings for recovering any fine, to which the person selling, offering, or exposing for sale, or causing to be sold, offered, or exposed for sale, such goods, is liable, and the court convicting the offender may award out of the fine to such clerk or toll collector such reasonable remuneration as to the court seems fit.

For every offence against or disobedience to this section the offender shall be liable on summary conviction to a fine not exceeding five pounds.

*Power to clerks of markets to inspect goods sold, &c. and if weighing found deficient to summon the offender.*

---

## 42 & 43 VICT. C. 72.

*An Act to provide for the re-hearing of Investigations into Shipping Casualties, and to amend the Rules as to the mode of holding, and procedure at, such Investigations.* [15th August, 1879.]

---

## 42 & 43 VICT. C. 76.

*An Act to amend the Law with respect to the Liability of Members of Banking and other Joint Stock Companies ; and for other purposes.*
[15th August, 1879.]

BE it enacted by the Queen's most Excellent Majesty, by and with the advice and consent of the Lords Spiritual and Temporal, and Commons, in this present Parliament assembled, and by the authority of the same, as follows :

1. This Act may be cited as the Companies Act, 1879. *Short title.*

2. This Act shall not apply to the Bank of England. *Act not to apply to Bank of England.*

**3.** This Act shall, so far as is consistent with the tenor thereof, be construed as one with the Companies Acts, 1862, 1867, and 1877, and those Acts together with this Act may be referred to as the Companies Acts, 1862 to 1879.

**4.** Subject as in this Act mentioned, any company registered before or after the passing of this Act as an unlimited company may register under the Companies Acts, 1862 to 1879, as a limited company, or any company already registered as a limited company may re-register under the provisions of this Act.

The registration of an unlimited company as a limited company in pursuance of this Act shall not affect or prejudice any debts, liabilities, obligations, or contracts incurred or entered into by, to, with, or on behalf of such company prior to registration, and such debts, liabilities, contracts, and obligations may be enforced in manner provided by Part VII. of the Companies Act, 1862, in the case of a company registering in pursuance of that Part.

**5.** An unlimited company may, by the resolution passed by the members when assenting to registration as a limited company under the Companies Acts, 1862 to 1879, and for the purpose of such registration or otherwise, increase the nominal amount of its capital by increasing the nominal amount of each of its shares.

Provided always, that no part of such increased capital shall be capable of being called up, except in the event of and for the purposes of the company being wound up.

And, in cases where no such increase of nominal capital may be resolved upon, an unlimited company may, by such resolution as aforesaid, provide that a portion of its uncalled capital shall not be capable of being called up, except in the event of and for the purposes of the company being wound up.

A limited company may by a special resolution declare that any portion of its capital which has not been already called up shall not be capable of being called up, except in the event of and for the purpose of the company being wound up; and thereupon such portion of capital shall not be capable of being called up, except in the event of and for the purposes of the company being wound up.

**6.** Section one hundred and eighty-two of the Companies Act, 1862, is hereby repealed, and in place thereof it is enacted as follows:—A bank of issue registered as a limited company, either before or after the passing of this Act, shall not be entitled to limited liability in respect of its notes; and the members thereof shall continue liable in respect of its notes in the same manner as if it had been registered as an unlimited company; but in case the general assets of the company are, in the event of the company being wound up, insufficient to satisfy the claims of both the note-holders and the general creditors, then the members, after satisfying the remaining demands of the note-holders, shall be liable to contribute towards payment of the debts of the general creditors a sum equal to the amount received by the note-holders out of the general assets of the company.

For the purposes of this section the expression "the general assets of the company" means the funds available for payment of the general creditor as well as the note-holder.

It shall be lawful for any bank of issue registered as a limited company to make a statement on its notes to the effect that the limited liability does not extend to its notes, and that the members of the company continue liable in respect of its notes in the same manner as if it had been registered as an unlimited company.

**7.** (1.) Once at the least in every year the accounts of every banking company registered after the passing of this Act as a limited company shall be examined by an auditor or auditors, who shall be elected annually by the company in general meeting.

(2.) A director or officer of the company shall not be capable of being elected auditor of such company.

(3.) An auditor on quitting office shall be re-eligible.

(4.) If any casual vacancy occurs in the office of any auditor the surviving auditor or auditors (if any) may act, but if there is no surviving auditor, the directors shall forthwith call an extraordinary general meeting for the purpose of supplying the vacancy or vacancies in the auditorship.

(5.) Every auditor shall have a list delivered to him of all books kept by the company, and shall at all reasonable times have access to the books and accounts of the company ; and any auditor may, in relation to such books and accounts, examine the directors or any other officer of the company : Provided that if a banking company has branch banks beyond the limits of Europe, it shall be sufficient if the auditor is allowed access to such copies of and extracts from the books and accounts of any such branch as may have been transmitted to the head office of the banking company in the United Kingdom.

(6.) The auditor or auditors shall make a report to the members on the accounts examined by him or them, and on every balance sheet laid before the company in general meeting during his or their tenure of office ; and in every such report shall state whether, in his or their opinion, the balance sheet referred to in the report is a full and fair balance sheet properly drawn up, so as to exhibit a true and correct view of the state of the company's affairs, as shown by the books of the company ; and such report shall be read before the company in general meeting.

(7.) The remuneration of the auditor or auditors shall be fixed by the general meeting appointing such auditor or auditors, and shall be paid by the company.

**8.** Every balance sheet submitted to the annual or other meeting of the members of every banking company registered after the passing of this Act as a limited company shall be signed by the auditor or auditors, and by the secretary or manager (if any), and by the directors of the company, or three of such directors at the least. *Signature of balance sheet.*

**9.** On the registration, in pursuance of this Act, of a company which has been already registered, the registrar shall make provision for closing the former registration of the company, and may dispense with the delivery to him of copies of any documents with copies of which he was furnished on the occasion of the original registration of the company (*b*) ; but, save as aforesaid, the registration of such a company shall take place in the same manner and have the same effect as if it were the first registration of that company under the Companies Acts, 1862 to 1879, and as if the provisions of the Acts under which the company was previously registered and regulated had been contained in different Acts of Parliament from those under which the company is registered as a limited company. *Application of 25 & 26 Vict. c. 89, 30 & 31 Vict. c. 131, and 40 & 41 Vict. c. 26. 25 & 26 Vict. c. 89, 30 & 31 Vict. c. 131, 40 & 41 Vict. c. 26, and 42 & 43 Vict. c. 76.*

**10.** A company authorised to register under this Act may register thereunder and avail itself of the privileges conferred by this Act, notwithstanding any provisions contained in any Act of Parliament, royal charter, deed of settlement, contract of copartnery, cost book, regulations, letters patent, or other instrument constituting or regulating the company. *Privileges of Act available notwithstanding constitution of company.*

---

## 43 VICT. c. 19.

*An Act to amend the Companies Acts of 1862, 1867, 1877, and 1879.*
[*24th March*, 1880.]

BE it enacted by the Queen's most Excellent Majesty, by and with the advice and consent of the Lords Spiritual and Temporal, and Commons, in this present Parliament assembled, and by the authority of the same, as follows :

**1.** This Act may be cited for all purposes as the Companies Act, 1880. *Short title.*

**2.** This Act shall, so far as is consistent with the tenor thereof, be construed as one with the Companies Acts, 1862, 1867, 1877, and 1879, and the said Acts and this Act may be referred to as the Companies Acts, 1862 to 1880. *Construction of Acts. 25 & 26 Vict. c. 89. 30 & 31 Vict. c. 131. 40 & 41 Vict. c. 26. 42 & 43 Vict. c. 76.*

**3.** When any company has accumulated a sum of undivided profits, which with the consent of the shareholders may be distributed among the shareholders in the form of a dividend or bonus, it shall be lawful for the company, by special resolution, to return the same, or any part thereof, to the shareholders in reduction of the paid-up capital of the company, the unpaid capital being thereby increased by a similar amount. The powers vested in the directors of making calls upon the shareholders in respect of moneys *Accumulated profits may be returned to shareholders in reduction of paid-up capital.*

(*b*) 25 & 26 Vict. c. 89, s. 184, *supra.*

unpaid upon their shares shall extend to the amount of the unpaid capital as augmented by such reduction.

No resolution to take effect till particulars have been registered.

4. No such special resolution as aforesaid shall take effect until a memorandum, showing the particulars required by law in the case of a reduction of capital by order of the court, shall have been produced to and registered by the Registrar of Joint Stock Companies.

Power to any shareholder within one month after passing of resolution to require company to retain moneys paid upon shares held by such person.

5. Upon any reduction of paid-up capital made in pursuance of this Act, it shall be lawful for any shareholder, or for any one or more of several joint shareholders, within one month after the passing of the special resolution for such reduction, to require the company to retain, and the company shall retain accordingly, the whole of the moneys actually paid upon the shares held by such person, either alone or jointly with any other person or persons, and which, in consequence of such reduction, would otherwise be returned to him or them, and thereupon the shares in respect of which the said moneys shall be so retained shall, in regard to the payment of dividends thereon, be deemed to be paid up to the same extent only as the shares on which payment as aforesaid has been accepted by the shareholders in reduction of their paid-up capital, and the company shall invest and keep invested the moneys so retained in such securities authorised for investment by trustees as the company shall determine, and upon the money so invested, or upon so much thereof as from time to time exceeds the amount of calls subsequently made upon the shares in respect of which such moneys shall have been retained, the company shall pay such interest as shall be received by them from time to time on such securities, and the amount so retained and invested shall be held to represent the future calls which may be made to replace the capital so reduced on those shares, whether the amount obtained on sale of the whole or such proportion thereof as represents the amount of any call when made, produces more or less than the amount of such call.

Company to specify amounts which shareholders have required them to retain under s. 5; also to specify amounts of profits returned to shareholders.
25 & 26 Vict. c. 89.

6. From and after such reduction of capital the company shall specify in the annual lists of members, to be made by them in pursuance of the twenty-sixth section of the Companies Act, 1862, the amounts which any of the shareholders of the company shall have required the company to retain, and the company shall have retained accordingly, in pursuance of the fifth section of this Act, and the company shall also specify in the statements of account laid before any general meeting of the company the amount of the undivided profits of the company which shall have been returned to the shareholders in reduction of the paid-up capital of the company under this Act.

Power of registrar to strike names of defunct companies off register.

7.—(1.) Where the Registrar of Joint Stock Companies has reasonable cause to believe that a company, whether registered before or after the passing of this Act, is not carrying on business or in operation, he shall send to the company by post a letter inquiring whether the company is carrying on business or in operation.

(2.) If the registrar does not within one month of sending the letter receive any answer thereto, he shall within fourteen days after the expiration of the month send to the company by post a registered letter referring to the first letter, and stating that no answer thereto has been received by the registrar, and that if an answer is not received to the second letter within one month from the date thereof, a notice will be published in the Gazette with a view to striking the name of the company off the register.

(3.) If the registrar either receives an answer from the company to the effect that it is not carrying on business or in operation, or does not within one month after sending the second letter receive any answer thereto, the registrar may publish in the Gazette and send to the company a notice that at the expiration of three months from the date of that notice the name of the company mentioned therein will, unless cause is shown to the contrary, be struck off the register and the company will be dissolved.

(4.) At the expiration of the time mentioned in the notice the registrar may, unless cause to the contrary is previously shown by such company, strike the name of such company off the register, and shall publish notice thereof in the Gazette, and on the publication in the Gazette of such last-mentioned notice the company whose name is so struck off shall be dissolved. Provided that the liability (if any) of every director, managing officer, and member of the company shall continue and may be enforced as if the company had not been dissolved.

(5.) If any company or member thereof feels aggrieved by the name of such company having been struck off the register in pursuance of this section, the company or member may apply to the superior court in which the company is liable to be wound up ; and such court, if satisfied that the company was at the time of the striking off carrying on business or in operation, and that it is just so to do, may order the name of the company to be restored to the register, and thereupon the company shall be deemed to have continued in existence as if the name thereof had never been struck off; and the court may by the order give such directions and make such provisions as seem just for placing the company and all other persons in the same position as nearly as may be as if the name of the company had never been struck off.

(6.) A letter or notice authorised or required for the purposes of this section to be sent to a company may be sent by post addressed to the company at its registered office, or, if no office has been registered, addressed to the care of some director or officer of the company, or if there be no director or officer of the company whose name and address are known to the registrar, the letter or notice (in identical form) may be sent to each of the persons who subscribed the memorandum of association, addressed to him at the address mentioned in that memorandum.

(7.) In the execution of his duties under this section the registrar shall conform to any regulations which may be from time to time made by the Board of Trade.

(8.) In this section the Gazette means, as respects companies whose registered office is in England, the London Gazette ; as respects companies whose registered office is in Scotland, the Edinburgh Gazette ; and as respects companies whose registered office is in Ireland, the Dublin Gazette.

---

### 43 & 44 VICT. C. 16.

*An Act to amend the Law relating to the Payment of Wages and Rating of Merchant Seamen.*         [*2nd August*, 1880.]

BE it enacted by the Queen's most excellent Majesty, by and with the advice and consent of the Lords spiritual and temporal, and Commons, in this present Parliament assembled, and by the authority of the same, as follows ; (that is to say,)

1. This Act may be cited as the Merchant Seamen (Payment of Wages and Rating) Act, 1880. *Short title and construction.*

This Act shall be construed as one with the Merchant Shipping Acts, 1854 to 1876, and those Acts and this Act may be cited collectively as the Merchant Shipping Acts, 1854 to 1880. *17 & 18 Vict. c. 104, &c.*

2.—[(1.) After the first day of August one thousand eight hundred and eighty-one, any document authorising or promising, or purporting to authorise or promise, the future payment of money on account of a seaman's wages conditionally on his going to sea from any port in the United Kingdom, and made before those wages have been earned, shall be void. *Conditional advance notes illegal.*

(2.) No money paid in satisfaction or in respect of any such document shall be deducted from a seaman's wages, and no person shall have any right of action, suit, or set-off against the seaman or his assignee in respect of any money so paid or purporting to have been so paid.

(3.) Nothing in this section shall affect any allotment note made under the Merchant Shipping Act, 1854 (c).] *17 & 18 Vict. c. 104.*

3.—(1.) Every agreement with a seaman which is required by the Merchant Shipping Act, 1854, to be made in the form sanctioned by the Board of Trade shall, if the seaman so require, stipulate for the allotment of any part not exceeding one half of the wages of the seaman in favour of one or more of the persons mentioned in section one hundred and sixty-nine of the Merchant Shipping Act, 1854, as amended by this section. *Amendment of 17 & 18 Vict. c. 104, s. 169, as to allotment notes.*

(2.) The allotment may also be made in favour of a savings bank, and in that case shall be in favour of such persons and carried into effect in such manner as may be for the time being directed by regulations of the Board of Trade, and section one hundred and sixty-nine of the Merchant Shipping Act, 1854, shall be construed as if the said persons were named therein. *17 & 18 Vict. c. 104.*

(c) Repealed : see 52 & 53 Vict. c. 46, s. 2.

(3.) The sum received in pursuance of such allotment by a savings bank shall be paid out only on an application made, through a superintendent of a mercantile marine office or the Board of Trade, by the seaman himself, or, in case of death, by some person to whom the same might be paid under section one hundred and ninety-nine of the Merchant Shipping Act, 1854.

17 & 18 Vict.
c. 104.

(4.) A payment under an allotment note shall begin at the expiration of one month, or, if the allotment is in favour of a savings bank, of three months, from the date of the agreement, or at such later date as may be fixed by the agreement, and shall be paid at the expiration of every subsequent month, or of such other periods as may be fixed by the agreement, and shall be paid only in respect of wages earned before the date of payment.

(5.) For the purposes of this section "savings bank" means a savings bank established under one of the Acts mentioned in the First Schedule to this Act.

Rules as to pay-
ment of wages.

4. In the case of foreign-going ships—

(1.) The owner or master of the ship shall pay to each seaman on account, at the time when he lawfully leaves the ship at the end of his engagement, two pounds, or one fourth of the balance due to him, whichever is least; and shall pay him the remainder of his wages within two clear days (exclusive of any Sunday, Fast Day in Scotland, or Bank holiday) after he so leaves the ship.

17 & 8 Vict.
c. 104.

(2.) The master of the ship may deliver the account of wages mentioned in section one hundred and seventy-one of the Merchant Shipping Act, 1854, to the seaman himself at or before the time when he leaves the ship instead of delivering it to a superintendent of a mercantile marine office.

(3.) If the seaman consents, the final settlement of his wages may be left to the superintendent of a mercantile marine office under regulations to be made by the Board of Trade, and the receipt of the superintendent shall in that case operate as a release by the seaman under section one hundred and seventy-five of the Merchant Shipping Act, 1854.

17 & 18 Vict.
c. 104.

(4.) In the event of the seaman's wages or any part thereof not being paid or settled as in this section mentioned, then, unless the delay is due to the act or default of the seaman, or to any reasonable dispute as to liability, or to any other cause not being the act or default of the owner or master, the seaman's wages shall continue to run and be payable until the time of the final settlement thereof.

(5.) Where a question as to wages is raised before the superintendent of a mercantile marine office between the master or owner of a ship, and a seaman or apprentice, if the amount in question does not exceed five pounds, the superintendent may adjudicate, and the decision of the superintendent in the matter shall be final; but if the superintendent is of opinion that the question is one which ought to be decided by a court of law he may refuse to decide it.

Penalty for
being on board
ship without
permission
before seamen
leave. See
17 & 18 Vict.
c. 104, s. 237.

5. Where a ship is about to arrive, is arriving, or has arrived at the end of her voyage, every person, not being in her Majesty's service or not being duly authorised by law for the purpose, who—

(a) goes on board the ship, without the permission of the master, before the seamen lawfully leave the ship at the end of their engagement, or are discharged (whichever last happens); or,

(b) being on board the ship, remains there after being warned to leave by the master, or by a police officer, or by any officer of the Board of Trade or of the customs,

shall for every such offence be liable on summary conviction to a fine not exceeding twenty pounds, or, at the discretion of the court, to imprisonment for any term not exceeding six months; and the master of the ship or any officer of the Board of Trade may take him into custody, and deliver him up forthwith to a constable to be taken before a court or magistrate capable of taking cognizance of the offence, and dealt with according to law.

Provisions con-
tained in section
five to apply to
ships belonging
to foreign
countries in
certain cases.

6. Whenever it is made to appear to her Majesty—

(1.) That the government of any foreign country has provided that unauthorised persons going on board of British ships which are about to arrive or have arrived within its territorial jurisdiction shall be subject to provisions similar to the provisions contained in the last preceding section as applicable to persons going on board British ships at the end of their voyages; and

(2.) That the government of such foreign country is desirous that the provisions of the said section shall apply to unauthorised persons going on board of ships belonging to such foreign country within the limits of British territorial jurisdiction ;

her Majesty may, by Order in Council, declare that the provisions of the said last preceding section shall apply to the ships of such country ; and thereupon so long as the order remains in force those provisions shall apply and have effect as if the ships of such country were British ships arriving, about to arrive, or which had arrived at the end of their voyage.

7. A seaman shall not be entitled to the rating of A.B., that is to say, of an able-bodied seaman, unless he has served at sea for four years before the mast, but the employment of fishermen in registered decked fishing vessels shall only count as sea service up to the period of three years of such employment; and the rating of A.B. shall only be granted after at least one year's sea service in a trading vessel in addition to three or more years' sea service on board of registered decked fishing vessels. *Rating of seamen.*

Such service may be proved by certificates of discharge, by a certificate of service from the Registrar-General of Shipping and Seamen (which certificate the registrar shall grant on payment of a fee not exceeding sixpence), and in which shall be specified whether the service was rendered in whole or in part in steam ship or in sailing ship, or by other satisfactory proof.

Nothing in this section shall affect a seaman who has been rated and has served as A.B. before the passing of this Act.

8. Where a proceeding is instituted in or before any court in relation to any dispute between an owner or master of a ship and a seaman or apprentice to the sea service, arising out of or incidental to their relation as such, or is instituted for the purpose of this section, the court, if, having regard to all the circumstances of the case, they think it just so to do, may rescind any contract between the owner or master and the seaman or apprentice, or any contract of apprenticeship, upon such terms as the court may think just, and this power shall be in addition to any other jurisdiction which the court can exercise independently of this section. *Power of court to rescind contract between owner or master and seaman or apprentice.*

For the purposes of this section the term "Court" includes any magistrate or justice having jurisdiction in the matter to which the proceeding relates.

9. It shall be lawful for the sanitary authority of any seaport town to pass bye-laws for the licensing of seamen's lodging-houses, for the periodical inspection of the same, for the granting to the persons to whom such licences are given, the authority to designate their houses as seamen's licensed lodging-houses, and for prescribing the penalties for the breach of the provisions of the bye-laws: provided always, that no such bye-laws shall take effect till they have received the approval of the Board of Trade. *Licensing of seamen's lodging-houses.*

10. The following provisions shall from the commencement of this Act have operation within the United Kingdom : — *Desertion and absence without leave.*

A seaman or apprentice to the sea service shall not be liable to imprisonment for deserting or for neglecting or refusing without reasonable cause to join his ship or to proceed to sea in his ship, or for absence without leave at any time within twenty-four hours of his ship's sailing from any port, or for absence at any time without leave and without sufficient reason from his ship or from his duty.

Whenever either at the commencement or during the progress of any voyage any seaman or apprentice neglects or refuses to join or deserts from or refuses to proceed to sea in any ship in which he is duly engaged to serve, or is found otherwise absenting himself therefrom without leave, the master or any mate, or the owner, ship's husband, or consignee may, with or without the assistance of the local police officers or constables, who are hereby directed to give the same, if required, convey him on board : Provided that if the seaman or apprentice so requires he shall first be taken before some court capable of taking cognizance of the matters to be dealt with according to law; and that if it appears to the court before which the case is brought that the seaman or apprentice has been conveyed on board or taken before the court on improper or insufficient grounds, the master, mate, owner, ship's husband, or consignee, as the case may be, shall incur a penalty not exceeding twenty pounds, but such penalty, if inflicted, shall be a bar to any action for false imprisonment.

If a seaman or apprentice to the sea service intends to absent himself from his ship or his duty, he may give notice of his intention either to the owner

17 & 18 Vict.
c. 104.

or to the master of the ship, not less than forty-eight hours before the time at which he ought to be on board his ship; and in the event of such notice being given, the court shall not exercise any of the powers conferred on it by section two hundred and forty seven of the Merchant Shipping Act, 1854.

17 & 18 Vict.
c. 104.

Subject to the foregoing provision of this section, the powers conferred by section two hundred and forty-seven of the Merchant Shipping Act, 1854, may be exercised, notwithstanding the abolition of imprisonment for desertion and similar offences, and of apprehension without warrant.

17 & 18 Vict.
c. 104.

Nothing in this section shall affect section two hundred and thirty-nine of the Merchant Shipping Act, 1854.

Extension to
seamen of
38 & 39 Vict.
c. 90.

11. The thirteenth section of the Employers and Workmen Act, 1875, shall be repealed in so far as it operates to exclude seamen and apprentices to the sea service from the said Act, and the said Act shall apply to seamen and apprentices to the sea service accordingly; but such repeal shall not, in the absence of any enactment to the contrary, extend to or affect any provision contained in any other Act of Parliament passed, or to be passed, whereby workman is defined by reference to the persons to whom the Employers and Workmen Act, 1875, applies.

38 & 39 Vict.
c. 90.

Repeal of
enactments in
Second Schedule.

12. The enactments described in the Second Schedule to this Act shall be repealed as from the commencement of this Act within the United Kingdom.

Provided that this repeal shall not affect—

(1.) Anything duly done or suffered before the commencement of this Act under any enactment hereby repealed; or

(2.) Any right, or privilege acquired or any liability incurred before the commencement of this Act, under any enactment hereby repealed; or

(3.) Any imprisonment, fine, or forfeiture, or other punishment incurred or to be incurred, in respect of any offence committed before the commencement of this Act, under any enactment hereby repealed; or

(4.) The institution or prosecution to its termination of any investigation or legal proceeding, or any other remedy for prosecuting any such offence, or ascertaining, enforcing, or recovering any such liability imprisonment, fine, forfeiture, or punishment as aforesaid, and any such investigation, legal proceeding, and remedy may be carried on as if this repeal had not been enacted.

## SCHEDULES.

### FIRST SCHEDULE.

Chapter.                                Savings Banks.

| | |
|---|---|
| 24 & 25 Vict. c. 14  ............ | Post Office Savings Banks. |
| 26 & 27 Vict. c. 87  .......... ⎫ | |
| 17 & 18 Vict. c. 104, s. 180.... ⎬ | Trustee Savings Banks. |
| 19 & 20 Vict. c. 41  .......... ⎭ | Seamen's Savings Banks. |

### SECOND SCHEDULE.

(17 & 18 Vict. c. 104, in part.)

The Merchant Shipping Act, 1854,
in part: namely,

In section two hundred and forty-three, sub-section (1), the words " to imprisonment for any period not exceeding twelve weeks with or without hard labour; and also."

In section two hundred and forty-three, sub-section (2), the words " to imprisonment for any period not exceeding ten weeks with or without hard labour, and also at the discretion of the court."

Section two hundred and forty-six.

In section two hundred and forty-seven the words " instead of committing the offender to prison; "

And section two hundred and forty-eight.

### 43 & 44 VICT. C. 42.

*An Act to extend and regulate the Liability of Employers to make Compensation for Personal Injuries suffered by Workmen in their service.* [*7th September*, 1880.]

BE it enacted by the Queen's most excellent Majesty, by and with the advice and consent of the Lords spiritual and temporal, and Commons, in this present Parliament assembled, and by the authority of the same, as follows:

1. Where after the commencement of this Act personal injury is caused to a workman — *(Amendment of law.)*

(1.) By reason of any defect in the condition of the ways, works, machinery, or plant connected with or used in the business of the employer; or

(2.) By reason of the negligence of any person in the service of the employer who has any superintendence entrusted to him whilst in the exercise of such superintendence; or

(3.) By reason of the negligence of any person in the service of the employer to whose orders or directions the workman at the time of the injury was bound to conform, and did conform, where such injury resulted from his having so conformed; or

(4.) By reason of the act or omission of any person in the service of the employer done or made in obedience to the rules or byelaws of the employer, or in obedience to particular instructions given by any person delegated with the authority of the employer in that behalf; or

(5.) By reason of the negligence of any person in the service of the employer who has the charge or control of any signal, points, locomotive engine, or train upon a railway,

the workman, or in case the injury results in death, the legal personal representatives of the workman, and any persons entitled in case of death, shall have the same right of compensation and remedies against the employer as if the workman had not been a workman of nor in the service of the employer, nor engaged in his work.

2. A workman shall not be entitled under this Act to any right of compensation or remedy against the employer in any of the following cases; that is to say, *(Exceptions to amendment of law.)*

(1.) Under sub-section one of section one, unless the defect therein mentioned arose from, or had not been discovered or remedied owing to the negligence of the employer, or of some person in the service of the employer, and entrusted by him with the duty of seeing that the ways, works, machinery, or plant were in proper condition.

(2.) Under sub-section four of section one, unless the injury resulted from some impropriety or defect in the rules, byelaws, or instructions therein mentioned; provided that where a rule or byelaw has been approved or has been accepted as a proper rule or byelaw by one of her Majesty's Principal Secretaries of State, or by the Board of Trade or any other department of the Government, under or by virtue of any Act of Parliament, it shall not be deemed for the purposes of this Act to be an improper or defective rule or byelaw.

(3.) In any case where the workman knew of the defect or negligence which caused his injury, and failed within a reasonable time to give, or cause to be given, information thereof to the employer or some person superior to himself in the service of the employer, unless he was aware that the employer or such superior already knew of the said defect or negligence.

3. The amount of compensation recoverable under this Act shall not exceed such sum as may be found to be equivalent to the estimated earnings, during the three years preceding the injury. of a person in the same grade employed during those years in the like employment and in the district in which the workman is employed at the time of the injury. *(Limit of sum recoverable as compensation.)*

4. An action for the recovery under this Act of compensation for an injury shall not be maintainable unless notice that injury has been sustained is given within six weeks, and the action is commenced within six months from *(Limit of time for recovery of compensation.)*

the occurrence of the accident causing the injury, or, in case of death, **within** twelve months from the time of death: Provided always, that in case of death the want of such notice shall be no bar to the maintenance of such action if the judge shall be of opinion that there was reasonable excuse for such want of notice.

Money payable under penalty to be deducted from compensation under Act.

**5.** There shall be deducted from any compensation awarded to any workman, or representatives of a workman, or persons claiming by, under, or through a workman in respect of any cause of action arising under this Act, any penalty or part of a penalty which may have been paid in pursuance of any other Act of Parliament to such workman, representatives, or persons in respect of the same cause of action ; and where an action has been brought under this Act by any workman, or the representatives of any workman, or any persons claiming by, under, or through such workman, for compensation in respect of any cause of action arising under this Act, and payment has not previously been made of any penalty or part of a penalty under any other Act of Parliament in respect of the same cause of action, such workman, representatives, or person shall not be entitled thereafter to receive any penalty or part of a penalty under any other Act of Parliament in respect of the same cause of action.

Trial of actions.

**6.**—(1.) Every action for recovery of compensation under this Act shall be brought in a county court, but may, upon the application of either plaintiff or defendant, be removed into a superior court in like manner and upon the same conditions as an action commenced in a county court may by law be removed.

(2.) Upon the trial of any such action in a county court before the judge without a jury one or more assessors may be appointed for the purpose of ascertaining the amount of compensation.

(3.) For the purpose of regulating the conditions and mode of appointment and remuneration of such assessors, and all matters of procedure relating to their duties, and also for the purpose of consolidating any actions under this Act in a county court, and otherwise preventing multiplicity of such actions, rules and regulations may be made, varied, and repealed from time to time in the same manner as rules and regulations for regulating the practice and procedure in other actions in county courts.

"County Court" shall, with respect to Scotland, mean the " Sheriff's Court," and shall, with respect to Ireland, mean the " Civil Bill Court."

In Scotland any action under this Act may be removed to the Court of Session at the instance of either party, in the manner provided by, and subject to the conditions prescribed by, section nine of the Sheriff Courts (Scotland) Act, 1877.

40 & 41 Vict. c. 50.

In Scotland the sheriff may conjoin actions arising out of the same occurrence or cause of action, though at the instance of different parties and in respect of different injuries.

Mode of serving notice of injury.

**7.** Notice in respect of an injury under this Act shall give the name and address of the person injured, and shall state in ordinary language the cause of the injury and the date at which it was sustained, and shall be served on the employer, or, if there is more than one employer, upon one of such employers.

The notice may be served by delivering the same to or at the residence or place of business of the person on whom it is to be served.

The notice may also be served by post by a registered letter addressed to the person on whom it is to be served at his last known place of residence or place of business; and, if served by post, shall be deemed to have been served at the time when a letter containing the same would be delivered in the ordinary course of post ; and, in proving the service of such notice, it shall be sufficient to prove that the notice was properly addressed and registered.

Where the employer is a body of persons corporate or unincorporate, the notice shall be served by delivering the same at or by sending it by post in a registered letter addressed to the office, or, if there be more than one office, any one of the offices of such body.

A notice under this section shall not be deemed invalid by reason of any defect or inaccuracy therein, unless the judge who tries the action arising from the injury mentioned in the notice shall be of opinion that the defendant in the action is prejudiced in his defence by such defect or inaccuracy, and that the defect or inaccuracy was for the purpose of misleading.

8. For the purposes of this Act, unless the context otherwise requires,— *Definitions.*
The expression "person who has superintendence entrusted to him" means a person whose sole or principal duty is that of superintendence, and who is not ordinarily engaged in manual labour :
The expression "employer" includes a body of persons corporate or unincorporate :
The expression "workman" means a railway servant and any person to whom the Employers and Workmen Act, 1875, applies. *38 & 39 Vict.*

*c. 90.*

9. This Act shall not come into operation until the first day of January one thousand eight hundred and eighty-one, which date is in this Act *Commencement* referred to as the commencement of this Act. *of Act.*

10. This Act may be cited as the Employers' Liability Act, 1880, and *Short title.* shall continue in force till the thirty-first day of December one thousand eight hundred and eighty-seven, and to the end of the then next session of Parliament, and no longer, unless Parliament shall otherwise determine, and all actions commenced under this Act before that period shall be continued as if the said Act had not expired.

---

### 43 & 44 Vict. c. 43.

*An Act to provide for the safe carriage of Grain Cargoes by Merchant Shipping.*                              [*7th September, 1880.*]

Be it enacted by the Queen's most excellent Majesty, by and with the advice and consent of the Lords spiritual and temporal, and Commons, in this present Parliament assembled, and by the authority of the same, as follows :

1. This Act may be cited as the Merchant Shipping (Carriage of Grain) *Short title and* Act, 1880, and shall be construed as one with the Merchant Shipping Act, *construction.* 1854, and the Acts amending the same, and together with those Acts may be *17 & 18 Vict.* cited as the Merchant Shipping Acts, 1854 to 1880. *c. 104, &c.*

2. This Act shall come into operation on the first day of January one *Commencement* thousand eight hundred and eighty-one (which day is in this Act referred to *of Act.* as the commencement of this Act).

3. Where a grain cargo is laden on any British ship all necessary and *Obligation to* reasonable precautions (whether prescribed by this Act or not) shall be taken *take precautions* in order to prevent the grain cargo from shifting. *to prevent grain cargo from shifting.*
If such precautions have not been taken in the case of any such ship, the master of the ship and any agent of the owner who was charged with the loading of the ship or the sending her to sea, shall each be liable to a penalty not exceeding three hundred pounds, and the owner of the ship shall also be liable to the same penalty, unless he shows that he took all reasonable means to enforce the observance of this section, and was not privy to the breach thereof.

4. Where a British ship laden with a grain cargo at any port in the *Precautions* Mediterranean or Black Sea is bound to ports outside the Straits of Gibraltar, *against shifting* or where a British ship is laden with a grain cargo on the coast of North *of grain cargo* America, the following precautions to prevent the grain cargo from shifting *laden in port in* shall be adopted; that is to say, *Mediterranean or Black Sea, or*
(a) There shall not be carried between the decks, or, if the ship has more *on coast of* than two decks, between the main and upper decks, any grain in bulk, *North America.* except such as may be necessary for feeding the cargo in the hold, and is carried in properly constructed feeders.
(b) Where grain (except such as may be carried in properly constructed feeders) is carried in bulk in any hold or compartment, and proper provision for filling up the same by feeders is not made, not less than one-fourth of the grain carried in the hold or compartment (as the case may be) shall be in bags supported on suitable platforms laid upon the grain in bulk :   Provided that this regulation with respect to bags shall not apply—
(i) To oats, or cotton seed ; nor
(ii) To a ship which is a sailing ship of less than four hundred tons registered tonnage, and is not engaged in the Atlantic trade ; nor

(iii) To a ship laden at a port in the Mediterranean or Black Sea if the ship is divided into compartments which are formed by substantial transverse partitions, and are fitted with longitudinal bulkheads or such shifting boards as hereafter in this section mentioned, and if the ship does not carry more than one-fourth of the grain cargo, and not more than one thousand five hundred quarters, in any one compartment, bin, or division, and provided that each division of the lower hold is fitted with properly constructed feeders from the between decks; nor

(iv) To a ship in which the grain cargo does not exceed one-half of the whole cargo of the ship, and the rest of the cargo consists of cotton, wool, flax, barrels or sacks of flour, or other suitable cargo so stowed as to prevent the grain in any compartment, bin, or division from shifting.

(c) Where grain is carried in the hold or between the decks, whether in bags or bulk, the hold or the space between the decks shall be divided by a longitudinal bulkhead or by sufficient shifting boards which extend from deck to deck or from the deck to the keelson and are properly secured, and if the grain is in bulk are fitted grain-tight with proper fillings between the beams.

(d) In loading, the grain shall be properly stowed, trimmed, and secured.

In the event of the contravention of this section in the case of any ship, reasonable precautions to prevent the grain cargo of that ship from shifting shall be deemed not to have been taken, and the owner and master of the ship and any agent charged with loading her or sending her to sea shall be liable accordingly to a penalty under this Act.

Provided that nothing in this section shall exempt a person from any liability, civil or criminal, to which he would otherwise be subject for failing to adopt any reasonable precautions which, although not mentioned in this section, are reasonably required to prevent grain cargo from shifting.

**Exemption from precautions specified in this Act for ships laden in Mediterranean or Black Sea, or on coast of North America.**

5. The precautions required by this Act to be adopted by ships laden with a grain cargo at a port in the Mediterranean or Black Sea, or on the coast of North America, shall not apply to ships loaded in accordance with regulations for the time being approved by the Board of Trade; nor to any ship constructed and loaded in accordance with any plan approved by the Board of Trade.

**Notice by master of kind and quantity of grain cargo.**

6. Before a British ship laden with grain cargo at any port in the Mediterranean or Black Sea, bound to ports outside the Straits of Gibraltar, or laden with grain cargo on the coast of North America, leaves her final port of loading, or within forty-eight hours after leaving such port, the master shall deliver or cause to be delivered to the British consular officer, or, if it is in her Majesty's dominions, to the principal officer of customs at that port, a notice stating—

**34 & 35 Vict. c. 110.**
**36 & 37 Vict. c. 85.**

(1.) The draught of water and clear side, as defined by section five of the Merchant Shipping Act. 1871, and section four of the Merchant Shipping Act, 1873, of the said ship after the loading of her cargo has been completed at the said last port of loading;

(2.) And also stating the following particulars in respect to the grain cargo; namely,

(a) The kind of grain and the quantity thereof, which quantity may be stated in cubic feet, or in quarters, or bushels, or in tons weight; and

(b) The mode in which the grain cargo is stowed; and

(c) The precautions taken against shifting.

The master shall also deliver a similar notice to the principal collector or other proper officer of customs in the United Kingdom, together with the report required to be made by the Customs Consolidation Act, 1876, on the arrival of the ship in the United Kingdom.

**39 & 40 Vict. c. 36, ss. 50, 51.**

Every such notice shall be sent to the Board of Trade as soon as practicable by the officer receiving the same.

If the master fails to deliver any notice required by this section he shall be liable to a penalty not exceeding one hundred pounds: Provided always, that the Board of Trade may, by notice published in the London Gazette, or in such other way as it may deem expedient, exempt ships laden at any particular port or any class of such ships from the provisions of this section.

**Penalty for false**

7. Any master of a ship, who in any notice required by this Act wilfully

makes any false statement or wilfully omits any material particular, shall be liable to a penalty not exceeding one hundred pounds.

**8.** For the purpose of securing the observance of this Act, any officer having authority in that behalf from the Board of Trade, either general or special, shall have the same power as an inspector appointed under the Merchant Shipping Act, 1854, and shall also have power to inspect any grain cargo, and the mode in which the same is stowed.

**9.** Every offence punishable under this Act may be prosecuted summarily and every penalty under this Act may be recovered and enforced summarily in like manner as offences and penalties under the Merchant Shipping Act, 1854, and the Acts amending the same.

**10.** For the purposes of this Act—
The expression "grain" means any corn, rice, paddy, pulse, seeds, nuts, or nut kernels.
The expression "ship laden with a grain cargo" means a ship carrying a cargo of which the portion consisting of grain is more than one-third of the registered tonnage of the ship, and such third shall be computed, where the grain is reckoned in measures of capacity, at the rate of one hundred cubic feet for each ton of registered tonnage, and where the grain is reckoned in measures of weight, at the rate of two tons weight for each ton of registered tonnage.

**11.** Section twenty-two of the Merchant Shipping Act, 1876, is hereby repealed as from the commencement of this Act:
Provided that any offence against that section committed before the commencement of this Act may be prosecuted, and the penalty recovered and enforced, in like manner as if the said section had continued to remain in force.

*Statement in notice.*
*Power of Board of Trade for enforcing of Act. 17 & 18 Vict. c. 104.*
*Prosecution of offences and recovery of penalties. 17 & 18 Vict. c. 104.*
*Definitions.*
*Repeal of 39 & 40 Vict. c. 80, s. 22.*

---

### 45 & 46 VICT. C. 43 (a).

*An Act to amend the Bills of Sale Act, 1878.*
[*18th August,* 1882.]

WHEREAS it is expedient to amend the Bills of Sale Act, 1878:
Be it enacted by the Queen's most excellent Majesty, by and with the advice and consent of the Lords Spiritual and Temporal, and Commons, in this present Parliament assembled, and by the authority of the same, as follows:

**1.** This Act may be cited for all purposes as the Bills of Sale Act (1878) Amendment Act, 1882; and this Act and the Bills of Sale Act, 1878, may be cited together as the Bills of Sale Acts, 1878 and 1882.

**2.** This Act shall come into operation on the first day of November one thousand eight hundred and eighty-two, which date is hereinafter referred to as the commencement of this Act.

**3.** The Bills of Sale Act, 1878, is hereinafter referred to as "the principal Act," and this Act shall, so far as it is consistent with the tenor thereof, be construed as one with the principal Act; but unless the context otherwise requires shall not apply to any bill of sale duly registered before the commencement of this Act so long as the registration thereof is not avoided by non-renewal or otherwise.
The expression "bill of sale," and other expressions in this Act, have the same meaning as in the principal Act, except as to bills of sale or other documents mentioned in section four of the principal Act, which may be given otherwise than by way of security for the payment of money, to which last-mentioned bills of sale and other documents this Act shall not apply.

**4.** Every bill of sale shall have annexed thereto or written thereon a schedule containing an inventory of the personal chattels comprised in the bill of sale; and such bill of sale, save as hereinafter mentioned, shall have effect only in respect of the personal chattels specifically described in the said schedule; and shall be void, except as against the grantor, in respect of any personal chattels not so specifically described.

*41 & 42 Vict. c. 31.*
*Short title.*
*Commencement of Act.*
*Construction of Act. 41 & 42 Vict. c. 31.*
*Bill of sale to have schedule of property attached thereto.*

(a) See, also, the Bills of Sale Act, *supra*, p. 1025.

Bill of sale not
to affect after
acquired
property.

**5.** Save as hereinafter mentioned, a bill of sale shall be void, except as against the grantor, in respect of any personal chattels specifically described in the schedule thereto of which the grantor was not the true owner at the time of the execution of the bill of sale.

**6.** Nothing contained in the foregoing sections of this Act shall render a bill of sale void in respect of any of the following things ; (that is to say),

(1.) Any growing crops separately assigned or charged where such crops were actually growing at the time when the bill of sale was executed.

(2.) Any fixtures separately assigned or charged, and any plant, or trade machinery where such fixtures, plant, or trade machinery are used in, attached to, or brought upon any land, farm, factory, workshop, shop, house, warehouse, or other place in substitution for any of the like fixtures, plant, or trade machinery specifically described in the schedule to such bill of sale.

Bill of sale with
power to seize
except in certain
events to be
void.

**7.** Personal chattels assigned under a bill of sale shall not be liable to be seized or taken possession of by the grantee for any other than the following causes :—

(1.) If the grantor shall make default in payment of the sum or sums of money thereby secured at the time therein provided for payment, or in the performance of any covenant or agreement contained in the bill of sale and necessary for maintaining the security ;

(2.) If the grantor shall become a bankrupt, or suffer the said goods or any of them to be distrained for rent, rates, or taxes ;

(3.) If the grantor shall fraudulently either remove or suffer the said goods, or any of them, to be removed from the premises ;

(4.) If the grantor shall not, without reasonable excuse, upon demand in writing by the grantee, produce to him his last receipts for rent, rates, and taxes ;

(5.) If execution shall have been levied against the goods of the grantor under any judgment at law :

Provided that the grantor may within five days from the seizure or taking possession of any chattels on account of any of the above-mentioned causes, apply to the High Court, or to a judge thereof in chambers, and such court or judge, if satisfied that by payment of money or otherwise the said cause of seizure no longer exists, may restrain the grantee from removing or selling the said chattels, or may make such other order as may seem just.

Bill of sale to
be void unless
attested and
registered.

**8.** Every bill of sale shall be duly attested, and shall be registered under the principal Act within seven clear days after the execution thereof, or if it is executed in any place out of England, then within seven clear days after the time at which it would in the ordinary course of post arrive in England if posted immediately after the execution thereof ; and shall truly set forth the consideration for which it was given ; otherwise such bill of sale shall be void in respect of the personal chattels comprised therein.

**9.** A bill of sale made or given by way of security for the payment of money by the grantor thereof shall be void unless made in accordance with the form in the Schedule to this Act annexed.

**10.** The execution of every bill of sale by the grantor shall be attested by one or more credible witness or witnesses, not being a party or parties thereto. So much of section 10 of the principal Act as requires that the execution of every bill of sale shall be attested by a solicitor of the Supreme Court, and that the attestation shall state that before the execution of the bill of sale the effect thereof has been explained to the grantor by the attesting witness, is hereby repealed.

Local registra-
tion of contents
of bills of sale.

32 & 33 Vict.
c. 71, s. 60.

**11.** Where the affidavit (which under section ten of the principal Act is required to accompany a bill of sale when presented for registration) describes the residence of the person making or giving the same, or of the person against whom the process is issued to be in some place outside the London bankruptcy district as defined by the Bankruptcy Act, 1869, or where the bill of sale describes the chattels enumerated therein as being in some place outside the said London bankruptcy district, the registrar under the principal Act shall forthwith and within three clear days after registration in the principal registry, and in accordance with the prescribed directions, transmit an abstract in the prescribed form of the contents of such bill of sale to the county court registrar in whose district such places are situate, and if such places are in the districts of different registrars to each such registrar.

Every abstract so transmitted shall be filed, kept, and indexed by the registrar of the county court in the prescribed manner, and any person may search, inspect, make extracts from, and obtain copies of the abstract so registered in the like manner and upon the like terms as to payment or otherwise as near as may be as in the case of bills of sale registered by the registrar under the principal Act.

**12.** Every bill of sale made or given in consideration of any sum under thirty pounds shall be void.

*Bill of sale under 30l. to be void.*

**13.** All personal chattels seized or of which possession is taken after the commencement of this Act, under or by virtue of any bill of sale (whether registered before or after the commencement of this Act), shall remain on the premises where they were so seized or so taken possession of, and shall not be removed or sold until after the expiration of five clear days from the day they were so seized or so taken possession of.

*Chattels not to be removed or sold.*

**14.** A bill of sale to which this Act applies shall be no protection in respect of personal chattels included in such bill of sale which but for such bill of sale would have been liable to distress under a warrant for the recovery of taxes and poor and other parochial rates.

*Bill of sale not to protect chattels against poor and parochial rates.*

**15.** The eighth and the twentieth sections of the principal Act, and also all other enactments contained in the principal Act which are inconsistent with this Act are repealed, but this repeal shall not affect the validity of anything done or suffered under the principal Act before the commencement of this Act.

*Repeal of part of Bills of Sale Act, 1878.*

**16.** So much of the sixteenth section of the principal Act as enacts that any person shall be entitled at all reasonable times to search the register and every registered bill of sale upon payment of one shilling for every copy of a bill of sale inspected is hereby repealed, and from and after the commencement of this Act any person shall be entitled at all reasonable times to search the register, on payment of a fee of one shilling, or such other fee as may be prescribed, and subject to such regulations as may be prescribed, and shall be entitled at all reasonable times to inspect, examine, and make extracts from any and every registered bill of sale without being required to make a written application, or to specify any particulars in reference thereto, upon payment of one shilling for each bill of sale inspected, and such payment shall be made by a judicature stamp : Provided that the said extracts shall be limited to the dates of execution, registration, renewal of registration, and satisfaction, to the names, addresses, and occupations of the parties, to the amount of the consideration, and to any further prescribed particulars.

*Inspection of registered bills of sale.*

**17.** Nothing in this Act shall apply to any debentures issued by any mortgage, loan, or other incorporated company, and secured upon the capital stock or goods, chattels, and effects of such company.

*Debentures to which Act not to apply.*

**18.** This Act shall not extend to Scotland or Ireland.

*Extent of Act.*

---

## SCHEDULE.

### FORM OF BILL OF SALE.

This Indenture made the                day of                , between *A. B.*, of                , of the one part, and *C. D.*, of                , of the other part, witnesseth that in consideration of the sum of £                now paid to *A. B.* by *C. D.*, the receipt of which the said *A. B.* hereby acknowledges [*or whatever else the consideration may be*], he the said *A. B.* doth hereby assign unto *C. D.*, his executors, administrators, and assigns, all and singular the several chattels and things specifically described in the schedule hereto annexed by way of security for the payment of the sum of £                , and interest thereon at the rate of                per cent. per annum [*or whatever else may be the rate*]. And the said *A. B.* doth further agree and declare that he will duly pay to the said *C. D.* the principal sum aforesaid, together with the interest then due, by equal                payments of £                on the            day of            [*or whatever else may be the stipulated times or time of payment*]. And the said *A. B.* doth also agree with the said *C. D.* that he will [*here insert terms as to insurance, payment of rent, or otherwise, which the parties may agree to for the maintenance or defeasance of the security*].

Provided always, that the chattels hereby assigned shall not be liable to seizure or to be taken possession of by the said *C. D.* for any cause other than those specified in section seven of the Bills of Sale Act (1878) Amendment Act, 1882.

In witness, &c.

Signed and sealed by the said *A. B.* in the presence of me *E. F.* [*add witness' name, address, and description*].

---

45 & 46 VICT. C. 61.

*An Act to codify the law relating to Bills of Exchange, Cheques, and Promissory Notes.*

[*18th August*, 1882.]

BE it enacted by the Queen's most excellent Majesty, by and with the advice and consent of the Lords spiritual and temporal, and Commons, in this present Parliament assembled, and by the authority of the same, as follows:

## PART I.

### PRELIMINARY.

Short title.  
1. This Act may be cited as the Bills of Exchange Act, 1882.

Interpretation of terms.  
2. In this Act, unless the context otherwise requires,—

"Acceptance" means an acceptance completed by delivery or notification.

"Action" includes counter-claim and set off.

"Banker" includes a body of persons whether incorporated or not who carry on the business of banking.

"Bankrupt" includes any person whose estate is vested in a trustee or assignee under the law for the time being in force relating to bankruptcy.

"Bearer" means the person in possession of a bill or note which is payable to bearer.

"Bill" means bill of exchange, and "note" means promissory note.

"Delivery" means transfer of possession, actual or constructive, from one person to another.

"Holder" means the payee or indorsee of a bill or note who is in possession of it, or the bearer thereof.

"Indorsement" means an indorsement completed by delivery.

"Issue" means the first delivery of a bill or note, complete in form to a person who takes it as a holder.

"Person" includes a body of persons whether incorporated or not.

"Value" means valuable consideration.

"Written" includes printed, and "writing" includes print.

---

## PART II.

### BILLS OF EXCHANGE.

*Form and Interpretation.*

Bill of exchange defined.  
3.—(1.) A bill of exchange is an unconditional order in writing, addressed by one person to another, signed by the person giving it, requiring the

person to whom it is addressed to pay on demand or at a fixed or determinable future time a sum certain in money to or to the order of a specified person, or to bearer.

(2.) An instrument which does not comply with these conditions, or which orders any act to be done in addition to the payment of money, is not a bill of exchange.

(3.) An order to pay out of a particular fund is not unconditional within the meaning of this section ; but an unqualified order to pay, coupled with (a) an indication of a particular fund out of which the drawee is to re-imburse himself or a particular account to be debited with the amount, or (b) a statement of the transaction which gives rise to the bill, is unconditional.

(4.) A bill is not invalid by reason—
  (a.) That it is not dated ;
  (b.) That it does not specify the value given, or that any value has been given therefor ;
  (c.) That it does not specify the place where it is drawn or the place where it is payable.

**4.**—(1.) An inland bill is a bill which is or on the face of it purports to be (a) both drawn and payable within the British Islands, or (b) drawn within the British Islands upon some person resident therein. Any other bill is a foreign bill. *Inland and foreign bills.*

For the purposes of this Act " British Islands" mean any part of the United Kingdom of Great Britain and Ireland, the islands of Man, Guernsey, Jersey, Alderney, and Sark, and the islands adjacent to any of them being part of the dominions of Her Majesty.

(2.) Unless the contrary appear on the face of the bill the holder may treat it as an inland bill.

**5.**—(1.) A bill may be drawn payable to, or to the order of, the drawer ; or it may be drawn payable to, or to the order of, the drawee. *Effect where different parties to bill are the same person.*

(2.) Where in a bill drawer and drawee are the same person, or where the drawee is a fictitious person or a person not having capacity to contract, the holder may treat the instrument, at his option, either as a bill of exchange or as a promissory note.

**6.**—(1.) The drawee must be named or otherwise indicated in a bill with reasonable certainty. *Address to drawee.*

(2.) A bill may be addressed to two or more drawees whether they are partners or not, but an order addressed to two drawees in the alternative or to two or more drawees in succession is not a bill of exchange.

**7.**—(1.) Where a bill is not payable to bearer, the payee must be named or otherwise indicated therein with reasonable certainty. *Certainty required as to payee.*

(2.) A bill may be made payable to two or more payees jointly, or it may be made payable in the alternative to one of two, or one or some of several payees. A bill may also be made payable to the holder of an office for the time being.

(3.) Where the payee is a fictitious or non-existing person the bill may be treated as payable to bearer.

**8.**—(1.) When a bill contains words prohibiting transfer, or indicating an intention that it should not be transferable, it is valid as between the parties thereto, but is not negotiable. *What bills are negotiable.*

(2.) A negotiable bill may be payable either to order or to bearer.

(3.) A bill is payable to bearer which is expressed to be so payable, or on which the only or last indorsement is an indorsement in blank.

(4.) A bill is payable to order which is expressed to be so payable, or which is expressed to be payable to a particular person, and does not contain words prohibiting transfer or indicating an intention that it should not be transferable.

(5.) Where a bill, either originally or by indorsement, is expressed to be payable to the order of a specified person, and not to him or his order, it is nevertheless payable to him or his order at his option.

**9.**—(1.) The sum payable by a bill is a sum certain within the meaning of this Act, although it is required to be paid— *Sum payable.*
  (a) With interest.
  (b) By stated instalments.
  (c) By stated instalments, with a provision that upon default in payment of any instalment the whole shall become due.

(d) According to an indicated rate of exchange or according to a rate of exchange to be ascertained as directed by the bill.

(2.) Where the sum payable is expressed in words and also in figures, and there is a discrepancy between the two, the sum denoted by the words is the amount payable.

(3.) Where a bill is expressed to be payable with interest, unless the instrument otherwise provides, interest runs from the date of the bill, and if the bill is undated from the issue thereof.

**Bill payable on demand.** 10.—(1.) A bill is payable on demand—

(a) Which is expressed to be payable on demand, or at sight, or on presentation ; or

(b) In which no time for payment is expressed.

(2.) Where a bill is accepted or indorsed when it is overdue, it shall, as regards the acceptor who so accepts, or any indorser who so indorses it, be deemed a bill payable on demand.

**Bill payable at a future time.** 11. A bill is payable at a determinable future time within the meaning of this Act which is expressed to be payable—

(1.) At a fixed period after date or sight.

(2.) On or at a fixed period after the occurrence of a specified event which is certain to happen, though the time of happening may be uncertain.

An instrument expressed to be payable on a contingency is not a bill, and the happening of the event does not cure the defect.

**Omission of date in bill payable after date.** 12. Where a bill expressed to be payable at a fixed period after date is issued undated, or where the acceptance of a bill payable at a fixed period after sight is undated, any holder may insert therein the true date of issue or acceptance, and the bill shall be payable accordingly.

Provided that (1) where the holder in good faith and by mistake inserts a wrong date, and (2) in every case where a wrong date is inserted, if the bill subsequently comes into the hands of a holder in due course the bill shall not be avoided thereby, but shall operate and be payable as if the date so inserted had been the true date.

**Ante-dating and post-dating.** 13.—(1.) Where a bill or an acceptance or any indorsement on a bill is dated, the date shall, unless the contrary be proved, be deemed to be the true date of the drawing, acceptance, or indorsement, as the case may be.

(2.) A bill is not invalid by reason only that it is ante-dated or post-dated, or that it bears date on a Sunday.

**Computation of time of payment.** 14. Where a bill is not payable on demand the day on which it falls due is determined as follows :

(1.) Three days, called days of grace, are, in every case where the bill itself does not otherwise provide, added to the time of payment as fixed by the bill, and the bill is due and payable on the last day of grace : Provided that—

(a.) When the last day of grace falls on Sunday, Christmas Day, Good Friday, or a day appointed by Royal proclamation as a public fast or thanksgiving day, the bill is, except in the case hereinafter provided for, due and payable on the preceding business day ;

**34 & 35 Vict. c. 17.** (b.) When the last day of grace is a bank holiday (other than Christmas Day or Good Friday) under the Bank Holidays Act, 1871, and Acts amending or extending it, or when the last day of grace is a Sunday and the second day of grace is a Bank Holiday, the bill is due and payable on the succeeding business day.

(2.) Where a bill is payable at a fixed period after date, after sight, or after the happening of a specified event, the time of payment is determined by excluding the day from which the time is to begin to run and by including the day of payment.

(3.) Where a bill is payable at a fixed period after sight, the time begins to run from the date of the acceptance if the bill be accepted, and from the date of noting or protest if the bill be noted or protested for non-acceptance, or for non-delivery.

(4.) The term " month " in a bill means calendar month.

**Case of need.** 15. The drawer of a bill and any indorser may insert therein the name of a person to whom the holder may resort in case of need, that is to say, in case the bill is dishonoured by non-acceptance or non-payment. Such person is called the referee in case of need. It is in the option of the holder to resort to the referee in case of need or not as he may think fit.

16. The drawer of a bill, and any indorser, may insert therein an express stipulation—
(1.) Negativing or limiting his own liability to the holder :
(2.) Waiving as regards himself some or all of the holder's duties.

Optional stipulations by drawer or indorser.

17.—(1.) The acceptance of a bill is the signification by the drawee of his assent to the order of the drawer.
(2.) An acceptance is invalid unless it complies with the following conditions, namely :
(a.) It must be written on the bill and be signed by the drawee. The mere signature of the drawee without additional words is sufficient.
(b.) It must not express that the drawee will perform his promise by any other means than the payment of money.

Definition and requisites of acceptance.

18. A bill may be accepted
(1.) Before it has been signed by the drawer, or while otherwise incomplete :
(2.) When it is overdue, or after it has been dishonoured by a previous refusal to accept, or by non-payment :
(3.) When a bill payable after sight is dishonoured by non-acceptance, and the drawee subsequently accepts it, the holder, in the absence of any different agreement, is entitled to have the bill accepted as of the date of first presentment to the drawee for acceptance.

Time for acceptance.

19.—(1.) An acceptance is either (a) general or (b) qualified.
(2.) A general acceptance assents without qualification to the order of the drawer. A qualified acceptance in express terms varies the effect of the bill as drawn.
In particular an acceptance is qualified which is—
(a.) conditional, that is to say, which makes payment by the acceptor dependent on the fulfilment of a condition therein stated :
(b.) partial, that is to say, an acceptance to pay part only of the amount for which the bill is drawn :
(c.) local, that is to say, an acceptance to pay only at a particular specified place :
An acceptance to pay at a particular place is a general acceptance, unless it expressly states that the bill is to be paid there only and not elsewhere :
(d.) qualified as to time :
(e.) the acceptance of some one or more of the drawees, but not of all.

General and qualified acceptances.

20.—(1.) Where a simple signature on a blank stamped paper is delivered by the signer in order that it may be converted into a bill, it operates as a primâ facie authority to fill it up as a complete bill for any amount the stamp will cover, using the signature for that of the drawer, or the acceptor, or an indorser ; and, in like manner when a bill is wanting in any material particular the person in possession of it has a primâ facie authority to fill up the omission in any way he thinks fit.
(2.) In order that any such instrument when completed may be enforceable against any person who became a party thereto prior to its completion, it must be filled up within a reasonable time, and strictly in accordance with the authority given. Reasonable time for this purpose is a question of fact.
Provided that if any such instrument after completion is negotiated to a holder in due course it shall be valid and effectual for all purposes in his hands, and he may enforce it as if it had been filled up within a reasonable time and strictly in accordance with the authority given.

Inchoate instruments.

21.—(1.) Every contract on a bill, whether it be the drawer's, the acceptor's, or an indorser's, is incomplete and revocable, until delivery of the instrument in order to give effect thereto.
Provided that where an acceptance is written on a bill, and the drawee gives notice to or according to the directions of the person entitled to the bill that he has accepted it, the acceptance then becomes complete and irrevocable.
(2.) As between immediate parties, and as regards a remote party other than a holder in due course, the delivery—
(a) in order to be effectual must be made either by or under the authority of the party drawing, accepting, or indorsing, as the case may be :

Delivery.

(b) may be shown to have been conditional or for a special purpose only, and not for the purpose of transferring the property in the bill.

But if the bill be in the hands of a holder in due course a valid delivery of the bill by all parties prior to him so as to make them liable to him is conclusively presumed.

(3.) Where a bill is no longer in the possession of a party who has signed it as drawer, acceptor, or indorser, a valid and unconditional delivery by him is presumed until the contrary is proved.

### Capacity and Authority of Parties.

**Capacity of parties.**  **22.**—(1.) Capacity to incur liability as a party to a bill is co-extensive with capacity to contract.

Provided that nothing in this section shall enable a corporation to make itself liable as drawer, acceptor, or indorser of a bill unless it is competent to it so to do under the law for the time being in force relating to corporations.

(2.) Where a bill is drawn or indorsed by an infant, minor, or corporation having no capacity or power to incur liability on a bill, the drawing or indorsement entitles the holder to receive payment of the bill, and to enforce it against any other party thereto.

**Signature essential to liability.**  **23.** No person is liable as drawer, indorser, or acceptor of a bill who has not signed it as such : provided that

(1.) Where a person signs a bill in a trade or assumed name, he is liable thereon as if he had signed it in his own name:

(2.) The signature of the name of a firm is equivalent to the signature by the person so signing of the names of all persons liable as partners in that firm.

**Forged or unauthorized signature.**  **24.** Subject to the provisions of this Act, where a signature on a bill is forged or placed thereon without the authority of the person whose signature it purports to be, the forged or unauthorised signature is wholly inoperative, and no right to retain the bill or to give a discharge therefor or to enforce payment thereof against any party thereto can be acquired through or under that signature, unless the party against whom it is sought to retain or enforce payment of the bill is precluded from setting up the forgery or want of authority.

Provided that nothing in this section shall affect the ratification of an unauthorised signature not amounting to a forgery.

**Procuration signatures.**  **25.** A signature by procuration operates as notice that the agent has but a limited authority to sign, and the principal is only bound by such signature if the agent in so signing was acting within the actual limits of his authority.

**Persons signing as agent or in representative capacity.**  **26.**—(1.) Where a person signs a bill as drawer, indorser, or acceptor, and adds words to his signature, indicating that he signs for or on behalf of a principal, or in a representative character, he is not personally liable thereon; but the mere addition to his signature of words describing him as an agent, or as filling a representative character, does not exempt him from personal liability.

(2.) In determining whether a signature on a bill is that of the principal or that of the agent by whose hand it is written, the construction most favourable to the validity of the instrument shall be adopted.

### The Consideration for a Bill.

**Value and holder for value.**  **27.**—(1.) Valuable consideration for a bill may be constituted by,—

(a) Any consideration sufficient to support a simple contract;

(b) An antecedent debt or liability. Such a debt or liability is deemed valuable consideration whether the bill is payable on demand or at a future time.

(2.) Where value has at any time been given for a bill the holder is deemed to be a holder for value as regards the acceptor and all parties to the bill who became parties prior to such time.

(3.) Where the holder of a bill has a lien on it, arising either **from contract** or by implication of law, he is deemed to be a holder for value to the extent of the sum for which he has a lien.

**Accommodation bill or party.**  **28.**—(1.) An accommodation party to a bill is a person who has signed a bill as drawer, acceptor, or indorser, without receiving value therefor, and for the purpose of lending his name to some other person.

(2.) An accommodation party is liable on the bill to a holder for value; and it is immaterial whether, when such holder took the bill, he knew such party to be an accommodation party or not.

29.—(1.) A holder in due course is a holder who has taken a bill, complete and regular on the face of it, under the following conditions; namely, Holder in due course.

(a) That he became the holder of it before it was overdue, and without notice that it had been previously dishonoured, if such was the fact :

(b) That he took the bill in good faith and for value, and that at the time the bill was negotiated to him he had no notice of any defect in the - title of the person who negotiated it.

(2.) In particular the title of a person who negotiates a bill is defective within the meaning of this Act when he obtained the bill, or the acceptance thereof, by fraud, duress, or force and fear, or other unlawful means, or for an illegal consideration, or when he negotiates it in breach of faith, or under such circumstances as amount to a fraud.

(3.) A holder (whether for value or not), who derives his title to a bill through a holder in due course, and who is not himself a party to any fraud or illegality affecting it, has all the rights of that holder in due course as regards the acceptor and all parties to the bill prior to that holder.

30.—(1.) Every party whose signature appears on a bill is primâ facie deemed to have become a party thereto for value. Presumption of value and good faith.

(2.) Every holder of a bill is primâ facie deemed to be a holder in due course; but if in an action on a bill it, is admitted or proved that the acceptance, issue, or subsequent negotiation of the bill is affected with fraud, duress, or force and fear, or illegality, the burden of proof is shifted, unless and until the holder proves that, subsequent to the alleged fraud or illegality, value has in good faith been given for the bill.

### Negotiation of Bills.

31.—(1.) A bill is negotiated when it is transferred from one person to another in such a manner as to constitute the transferee the holder of the bill. Negotiation of bill.

(2.) A bill payable to bearer is negotiated by delivery.

(3.) A bill payable to order is negotiated by the indorsement of the holder completed by delivery.

(4.) Where the holder of a bill payable to his order transfers it for value without indorsing it, the transfer gives the transferee such title as the transferor had in the bill, and the transferee in addition acquires the right to have the indorsement of the transferor.

(5.) Where any person is under obligation to indorse a bill in a representative capacity, he may indorse the bill in such terms as to negative personal liability.

32. An indorsement in order to operate as a negotiation must comply with the following conditions, namely :— Requisites of a valid indorsement.

(1.) It must be written on the bill itself and be signed by the indorser. The simple signature of the indorser on the bill, without additional words, is sufficient.

An indorsement written on an allonge, or on a " copy " of a bill issued or negotiated in a country where "copies" are recognised, is deemed to be written on the bill itself.

(2.) It must be an indorsement of the entire bill. A partial indorsement, that is to say, an indorsement which purports to transfer to the indorsee a part only of the amount payable, or which purports to transfer the bill to two or more indorsees severally, does not operate as a negotiation of the bill.

(3.) Where a bill is payable to the order of two or more payees or indorsees who are not partners all must indorse, unless the one indorsing has authority to indorse for the others.

(4.) Where, in a bill payable to order, the payee or indorsee is wrongly designated, or his name is mis-spelt, he may indorse the bill as therein described, adding, if he think fit, his proper signature.

(5.) Where there are two or more indorsements on a bill, each indorsement is deemed to have been made in the order in which it appears on the bill, until the contrary is proved.

(6.) An indorsement may be made in blank or special. It may also contain terms making it restrictive.

Conditional indorsement.

**33.** Where a bill purports to be indorsed conditionally the condition may be disregarded by the payer, and payment to the indorsee is valid whether the condition has been fulfilled or not.

Indorsement n blank and special indorsement.

**34.**—(1.) An indorsement in blank specifies no indorsee, and a bill so indorsed becomes payable to bearer.

(2.) A special indor-ement specifies the person to whom, or to whose order, the bill is to be payable.

(3.) The provisions of this Act relating to a payee apply with the necessary modifications to an indorsee under a special indorsement.

(4.) When a bill has been indorsed in blank, any holder may convert the blank indorsement into a special indorsement by writing above the indorser's signature a direction to pay the bill to or to the order of himself or some other person.

Restrictive indorsement.

**35.**—(1.) An indorsement is restrictive which prohibits the further negotiation of the bill or which expresses that it is a mere authority to deal with the bill as thereby directed and not a transfer of the ownership thereof, as, for example, if a bill be indorsed "Pay D. only," or "Pay D. for the account of X.," or "Pay D. or order for collection."

(2.) A restrictive indorsement gives the indorsee the right to receive payment of the bill and to sue any party thereto that his indorser could have sued, but gives him no power to transfer his rights as indorsee unless it expressly authorise him to do so.

(3.) Where a restrictive indorsement authorises further transfer, all subsequent indorsees take the bill with the same rights and subject to the same liabilities as the first indorsee under the restrictive indorsement.

Negotiation of overdue or dishonoured bill.

**36.**—(1.) Where a bill is negotiable in its origin it continues to be negotiable until it has been (a) restrictively indorsed or (b) discharged by payment or otherwise.

(2.) Where an overdue bill is negotiated, it can only be negotiated subject to any defect of title affecting it at its maturity, and thenceforward no person who takes it can acquire or give a better title than that which the person from whom he took it had.

(3.) A bill payable on demand is deemed to be overdue within the meaning and for the purposes of this section when it appears on the face of it to have been in circulation for an unreasonable length of time. What is an unreasonable length of time for this purpose is a question of fact.

(4.) Except where an indorsement bears date after the maturity of the bill, every negotiation is primâ facie deemed to have been effected before the bill was overdue.

(5.) Where a bill which is not overdue has been dishonoured any person who takes it with notice of the dishonour takes it subject to any defect of title attaching thereto at the time of dishonour, but nothing in this sub-section shall affect the rights of a holder in due course.

Negotiation of bill to party already liable thereon.

**37.** Where a bill is negotiated back to the drawer, or to a prior indorser or to the acceptor, such party may, subject to the provisions of this Act, re-issue and further negotiate the bill, but he is not entitled to enforce payment of the bill against any intervening party to whom he was previously liable.

Rights of the holder.

**38.** The rights and powers of the holder of a bill are as follows :

(1.) He may sue on the bill in his own name :

(2.) Where he is a holder in due course, he holds the bill free from any defect of title of prior parties, as well as from mere personal defences available to prior parties among themselves, and may enforce payment against all parties liable on the bill :

(3.) Where his title is defective (a) if he negotiates the bill to a holder in due course, that holder obtains a good and complete title to the bill, and (b) if he obtains payment of the bill the person who pays him in due course gets a valid discharge for the bill.

### General Duties of the Holder.

When presentment for acceptance is necessary.

**39.**—(1.) Where a bill is payable after sight, presentment for acceptance is necessary in order to fix the maturity of the instrument.

(2.) Where a bill expressly stipulates that it shall be presented for acceptance, or where a bill is drawn payable elsewhere than at the residence or place of business of the drawee, it must be presented for acceptance before it can be presented for payment.

(3.) In no other case is presentment for acceptance necessary in order to render liable any party to the bill.

(4.) Where the holder of a bill, drawn payable elsewhere than at the place of business or residence of the drawee, has not time, with the exercise of reasonable diligence, to present the bill for acceptance before presenting it for payment on the day that it falls due, the delay caused by presenting the bill for acceptance before presenting it for payment is excused, and does not discharge the drawer and indorsers.

**40.**—(1.) Subject to the provisions of this Act, when a bill payable after sight is negotiated, the holder must either present it for acceptance or negotiate it within a reasonable time. *Time for presenting bill payable after sight.*

(2.) If he do not do so, the drawer and all indorsers prior to that holder are discharged.

(3.) In determining what is a reasonable time within the meaning of this section, regard shall be had to the nature of the bill, the usage of trade with respect to similar bills, and the facts of the particular case.

**41.**—(1.) A bill is duly presented for acceptance which is presented in accordance with the following rules : *Rules as to presentment for acceptance, and excuses for non-presentment.*

(a) The presentment must be made by or on behalf of the holder to the drawee or to some person authorised to accept or refuse acceptance on his behalf at a reasonable hour on a business day and before the bill is overdue :

(b) Where a bill is addressed to two or more drawees, who are not partners, presentment must be made to them all, unless one has authority to accept for all, then presentment may be made to him only :

(c) Where the drawee is dead presentment may be made to his personal representative :

(d) Where the drawee is bankrupt, presentment may be made to him or to his trustee :

(e) Where authorised by agreement or usage, a presentment through the post office is sufficient.

(2.) Presentment in accordance with these rules is excused, and a bill may be treated as dishonoured by non-acceptance—

(a) Where the drawee is dead or bankrupt, or is a fictitious person or a person not having capacity to contract by bill :

(b) Where, after the exercise of reasonable diligence, such presentment cannot be effected :

(c) Where, although the presentment has been irregular, acceptance has been refused on some other ground.

(3.) The fact that the holder has reason to believe that the bill, on presentment, will be dishonoured does not excuse presentment.

**42.**—(1.) When a bill is duly presented for acceptance and is not accepted within the customary time, the person presenting it must treat it as dishonoured by non-acceptance. If he do not, the holder shall lose his right of recourse against the drawer and indorsers. *Non-acceptance.*

**43.**—(1.) A bill is dishonoured by non-acceptance— *Dishonour by non-acceptance and its consequences.*

(a) when it is duly presented for acceptance, and such an acceptance as is prescribed by this Act is refused or cannot be obtained ; or

(b) when presentment for acceptance is excused and the bill is not accepted.

(2.) Subject to the provisions of this Act when a bill is dishonoured by non-acceptance, an immediate right of recourse against the drawer and indorsers accrues to the holder, and no presentment for payment is necessary.

**44.**—(1.) The holder of a bill may refuse to take a qualified acceptance, and if he does not obtain an unqualified acceptance may treat the bill as dishonoured by non-acceptance. *Duties as to qualified acceptances.*

(2.) Where a qualified acceptance is taken, and the drawer or an indorser has not expressly or impliedly authorised the holder to take a qualified acceptance, or does not subsequently assent thereto, such drawer or indorser is discharged from his liability on the bill.

The provisions of this sub-section do not apply to a partial acceptance, whereof due notice has been given. Where a foreign bill has been accepted as to part, it must be protested as to the balance.

(3.) When the drawer or indorser of a bill receives notice of a qualified acceptance, and does not within a reasonable time express his dissent to the holder he shall be deemed to have assented thereto.

**45.** Subject to the provisions of this Act a bill must be duly presented for payment. If it be not so presented the drawer and indorsers shall be discharged.

A bill is duly presented for payment which is presented in accordance with the following rules:—

(1.) Where the bill is not payable on demand, presentment must be made on the day it falls due.

(2.) Where the bill is payable on demand, then, subject to the provisions of this Act, presentment must be made within a reasonable time after its issue in order to render the drawer liable, and within a reasonable time after its indorsement, in order to render the indorser liable.

In determining what is a reasonable time, regard shall be had to the nature of the bill, the usage of trade with regard to similar bills, and the facts of the particular case.

(3.) Presentment must be made by the holder or by some person authorised to receive payment on his behalf at a reasonable hour on a business day, at the proper place as hereinafter defined, either to the person designated by the bill as payer, or to some person authorised to pay or refuse payment on his behalf if with the exercise of reasonable diligence such person can there be found.

(4.) A bill is presented at the proper place—

(a) Where a place of payment is specified in the bill and the bill is there presented.

(b) Where no place of payment is specified, but the address of the drawee or acceptor is given in the bill, and the bill is there presented.

(c) Where no place of payment is specified and no address given, and the bill is presented at the drawee's or acceptor's place of business if known, and if not, at his ordinary residence, if known.

(d) In any other case if presented to the drawee or acceptor wherever he can be found, or if presented at his last known place of business or residence.

(5.) Where a bill is presented at the proper place, and after the exercise of reasonable diligence no person authorized to pay or refuse payment can be found there, no further presentment to the drawee or acceptor is required.

(6.) Where a bill is drawn upon, or accepted by two or more persons who are not partners, and no place of payment is specified, presentment must be made to them all.

(7.) Where the drawee or acceptor of a bill is dead, and no place of payment is specified, presentment must be made to a personal representative, if such there be, and with the exercise of reasonable diligence he can be found.

(8.) Where authorized by agreement or usage, a presentment through the post office is sufficient.

**46.** (1.) Delay in making presentment for payment is excused when the delay is caused by circumstances beyond the control of the holder, and not imputable to his default, misconduct or negligence. When the cause of delay ceases to operate presentment must be made with reasonable diligence.

(2.) Presentment for payment is dispensed with—

(a) Where, after the exercise of reasonable diligence presentment, as required by this Act, cannot be effected.

The fact that the holder has reason to believe that the bill will, on presentment, be dishonoured, does not dispense with the necessity for presentment.

(b) Where the drawee is a fictitious person.

(c) As regards the drawer, where the drawee or acceptor is not bound, as between himself and the drawer, to accept or pay the bill, and the drawer has no reason to believe that the bill would be paid if presented.

(d) As regards an indorser, where the bill was accepted or made for the accommodation of that indorser, and he has no reason to expect that the bill would be paid if presented.

(e) By waiver of presentment, express or implied,

**47.**—(1.) A bill is dishonoured by non-payment (a) when it is duly pre- Dishonour by sented for payment and payment is refused or cannot be obtained, or non-payment. (b) when presentment is excused and the bill is overdue and unpaid.

(2.) Subject to the provisions of this Act, when a bill is dishonoured by non-payment, an immediate right of recourse against the drawer and indorsers accrues to the holder.

**48.** Subject to the provisions of this Act, when a bill has been dishonoured Notice of dis-by non-acceptance or by non-payment, notice of dishonour must be given to honour and the drawer and each indorser, and any drawer or indorser to whom such effect of non-notice is not given is discharged; provided that— notice.

(1.) Where a bill is dishonoured by non-acceptance, and notice of dishonour is not given, the rights of a holder in due course subsequent to the omission, shall not be prejudiced by the omission.

(2.) Where a bill is dishonoured by non-acceptance and due notice of dishonour is given, it shall not be necessary to give notice of a subsequent dishonour by non-payment unless the bill shall in the meantime have been accepted.

**49.** Notice of dishonour in order to be valid and effectual, must be given Rules as to in accordance with the following rules:— notice of dis-

honour.

(1.) The notice must be given by or on behalf of the holder, or by or on behalf of an indorser who, at the time of giving it, is himself liable on the bill.

(2.) Notice of dishonour may be given by an agent either in his own name or in the name of any party entitled to give notice whether that party be his principal or not.

(3.) Where the notice is given by or on behalf of the holder, it enures for the benefit of all subsequent holders and all prior indorsers who have a right of recourse against the party to whom it is given.

(4.) Where notice is given by or on behalf of an indorser entitled to give notice as hereinbefore provided, it enures for the benefit of the holder, and all indorsers subsequent to the party to whom notice is given.

(5.) The notice may be given in writing or by personal communication, and may be given in any terms which sufficiently identify the bill, and intimate that the bill has been dishonoured by non-acceptance or non-payment.

(6.) The return of a dishonoured bill to the drawer or an indorser is, in point of form, deemed a sufficient notice of dishonour.

(7.) A written notice need not be signed, and an insufficient written notice may be supplemented and validated by verbal communication. A misdescription of the bill shall not vitiate the notice unless the party to whom the notice is given is in fact misled thereby.

(8.) Where notice of dishonour is required to be given to any person, it may be given either to the party himself, or to his agent in that behalf.

(9.) Where the drawer or indorser is dead, and the party giving notice knows it, the notice must be given to a personal representative if such there be, and with the exercise of reasonable diligence he can be found.

(10.) Where the drawer or indorser is bankrupt, notice may be given either to the party himself or to the trustee.

(11.) Where there are two or more drawers or indorsers who are not partners, notice must be given to each of them, unless one of them has authority to receive such notice for the others.

(12.) The notice may be given as soon as the bill is dishonoured and must be given within a reasonable time thereafter.

In the absence of special circumstances notice is not deemed to have been given within a reasonable time, unless—

(a.) where the person giving and the person to receive notice reside in the same place, the notice is given or sent off in time to reach the latter on the day after the dishonour of the bill.

(b.) where the person giving and the person to receive notice reside in different places, the notice is sent off on the day after the dishonour of the bill, if there be a post at a convenient hour on that day, and if there be no such post on that day then by the next post thereafter.

(13.) Where a bill when dishonoured is in the hands of an agent, he may either himself give notice to the parties liable on the bill, or he may give notice to his principal. If he give notice to his principal, he must do so within the same time as if he were the holder, and the principal upon receipt of such notice has himself the same time for giving notice as if the agent had been an independent holder.

(14.) Where a party to a bill receives due notice of dishonour, he has after the receipt of such notice the same period of time for giving notice to antecedent parties that the holder has after the dishonour.

(15.) Where a notice of dishonour is duly addressed and posted, the sender is deemed to have given due notice of dishonour, notwithstanding any miscarriage by the post office.

**Excuses for non-notice and delay.** **50.**—(1.) Delay in giving notice of dishonour is excused where the delay is caused by circumstances beyond the control of the party giving notice, and not imputable to his default, misconduct, or negligence. When the cause of delay ceases to operate the notice must be given with reasonable diligence.

(2.) Notice of dishonour is dispensed with—

(a.) When, after the exercise of reasonable diligence, notice as required by this Act cannot be given to or does not reach the drawer or indorser sought to be charged :

(b.) By waiver express or implied. Notice of dishonour may be waived before the time of giving notice has arrived, or after the omission to give due notice :

(c.) As regards the drawer in the following cases, namely, (1) where drawer and drawee are the same person, (2) where the drawee is a fictitious person or a person not having capacity to contract, (3) where the drawer is the person to whom the bill is presented for payment, (4) where the drawee or acceptor is as between himself and the drawer under no obligation to accept or pay the bill, (5) where the drawer has countermanded payment :

(d) As regards the indorser in the following cases, namely, (1) where the drawee is a fictitious person or a person not having capacity to contract and the indorser was aware of the fact at the time he indorsed the bill, (2) where the indorser is the person to whom the bill is presented for payment, (3) where the bill was accepted or made for his accommodation.

**Noting or protest of bill.** **51.**—(1.) Where an inland bill has been dishonoured it may, if the holder think fit, be noted for non-acceptance or non-payment, as the case may be ; but it shall not be necessary to note or protest any such bill in order to preserve the recourse against the drawer or indorser.

(2.) Where a foreign bill, appearing on the face of it to be such, has been dishonoured by non-acceptance it must be duly protested for non-acceptance, and where such a bill, which has not been previously dishonoured by non-acceptance, is dishonoured by non-payment it must be duly protested for non-payment. If it be not so protested the drawer and indorsers are discharged. Where a bill does not appear on the face of it to be a foreign bill, protest thereof in case of dishonour is unnecessary.

(3.) A bill which has been protested for non-acceptance may be subsequently protested for non-payment.

(4.) Subject to the provisions of this Act, when a bill is noted or protested, it must be noted on the day of its dishonour. When a bill has been duly noted, the protest may be subsequently extended as of the date of the noting.

(5.) Where the acceptor of a bill becomes bankrupt or insolvent or suspends payment before it matures, the holder may cause the bill to be protested for better security against the drawer and indorsers.

(6.) A bill must be protested at the place where it is dishonoured : Provided that—

(a) When a bill is presented through the post office, and returned by post dishonoured, it may be protested at the place to which it is returned and on the day of its return if received during business hours, and if not received during business hours, then not later than the next business day :

(b) When a bill drawn payable at the place of business or residence of some person other than the drawee, has been dishonoured by non-acceptance, it must be protested for non-payment at the place where it is expressed to be payable, and no further presentment for payment to, or demand on, the drawee is necessary.

(7.) A protest must contain a copy of the bill, and must be signed by the notary making it, and must specify—

(a) The person at whose request the bill is protested :

(b) The place and date of protest, the cause or reason for protesting the bill, the demand made, and the answer given, if any, or the fact that the drawee or acceptor could not be found.

(8.) Where a bill is lost or destroyed, or is wrongly detained from the person entitled to hold it, protest may be made on a copy or written particulars thereof.

(9.) Protest is dispensed with by any circumstance which would dispense with notice of dishonour. Delay in noting or protesting is excused when the delay is caused by circumstances beyond the control of the holder, and not imputable to his default, misconduct, or negligence. When the cause of delay ceases to operate the bill must be noted or protested with reasonable diligence.

**52.**—(1.) When a bill is accepted generally presentment for payment is not necessary in order to render the acceptor liable. *Duties of holder as regards drawee or acceptor.*

(2.) When by the terms of a qualified acceptance presentment for payment is required, the acceptor, in the absence of an express stipulation to that effect, is not discharged by the omission to present the bill for payment on the day that it matures.

(3.) In order to render the acceptor of a bill liable it is not necessary to protest it, or that notice of dishonour should be given to him.

(4.) Where the holder of a bill presents it for payment, he shall exhibit the bill to the person from whom he demands payment, and when a bill is paid the holder shall forthwith deliver it up to the party paying it.

*Liabilities of Parties.*

**53.**—(1.) A bill, of itself, does not operate as an assignment of funds in the hands of the drawee available for the payment thereof, and the drawee of a bill who does not accept as required ·by this Act is not liable on the instrument. This sub-section shall not extend to Scotland. *Funds in hands of drawee.*

(2.) In Scotland, where the drawee of a bill has in his hands funds available for the payment thereof, the bill operates as an assignment of the sum for which it is drawn in favour of the holder, from the time when the bill is presented to the drawee.

**54.** The acceptor of a bill, by accepting it— *Liability of acceptor.*

(1.) Engages that he will pay it according to the tenor of his acceptance :

(2.) Is precluded from denying to a holder in due course :

(a) The existence of the drawer, the genuineness of his signature, and his capacity and authority to draw the bill ;

(b) In the case of a bill payable to drawer's order, the then capacity of the drawer to indorse, but not the genuineness or validity of his indorsement ;

(c) In the case of a bill payable to the order of a third person, the existence of the payee and his then capacity to indorse, but not the genuineness or validity of his indorsement.

**55.**—(1.) The drawer of a bill by drawing it— *Liability of drawer or indorser.*

(a) Engages that on due presentment it shall be accepted and paid according to its tenor, and that if it be dishonoured he will compensate the holder or any indorser who is compelled to pay it, provided that the requisite proceedings on dishonour be duly taken :

(b) Is precluded from denying to a holder in due course the existence of the payee and his then capacity to indorse.

(2.) The indorser of a bill by indorsing it—

(a) Engages that on due presentment it shall be accepted and paid according to its tenor, and that if it be dishonoured he will compensate the holder or a subsequent indorser who is compelled to pay it, provided that the requisite proceedings on dishonour be duly taken ;

(b) Is precluded from denying to a holder in due course the genuineness and regularity in all respects of the drawer's signature and all previous indorsements ;

(c) Is precluded from denying to his immediate or a subsequent indorsee that the bill was at the time of his indorsement a valid and sub-sisting bill, and that he had then a good title thereto.

*Stranger signing bill liable as indorser.*

**56.** Where a person signs a bill otherwise than as drawer or acceptor, he thereby incurs the liabilities of an indorser to a holder in due course.

*Measure of damages against parties to dishonoured bill.*

**57.** Where a bill is dishonoured, the measure of damages, which shall be deemed to be liquidated damages, shall be as follows:

(1.) The holder may recover from any party liable on the bill, and the drawer who has been compelled to pay the bill may recover from the acceptor, and an indorser who has been compelled to pay the bill may recover from the acceptor or from the drawer, or from a prior indorser—

(a) The amount of the bill:

(b) Interest thereon from the time of presentment for payment if the bill is payable on demand, and from the maturity of the bill in any other case:

(c) The expenses of noting, or, when protest is necessary, and the protest has been extended, the expenses of protest.

(2.) In the case of a bill which has been dishonoured abroad, in lieu of the above damages, the holder may recover from the drawer or an indorser, and the drawer or an indorser who has been compelled to pay the bill may recover from any party liable to him, the amount of the re-exchange with interest thereon until the time of payment.

(3.) Where by this Act interest may be recovered as damages, such interest may, if justice require it, be withheld wholly or in part, and where a bill is expressed to be payable with interest at a given rate, interest as damages may or may not be given at the same rate as interest proper.

*Transferor by delivery and transferee.*

**58.**—(1.) Where the holder of a bill payable to bearer negotiates it by delivery without indorsing it, he is called a "transferor by delivery."

(2.) A transferor by delivery is not liable on the instrument.

(3.) A transferor by delivery who negotiates a bill thereby warrants to his immediate transferee being a holder for value that the bill is what it purports to be, that he has a right to transfer it, and that at the time of transfer he is not aware of any fact which renders it valueless.

### Discharge of Bill.

*Payment in due course.*

**59.**—(1.) A bill is discharged by payment in due course by or on behalf of the drawee or acceptor.

"Payment in due course" means payment made at or after the maturity of the bill to the holder thereof in good faith and without notice that his title to the bill is defective.

(2.) Subject to the provisions hereinafter contained, when a bill is paid by the drawer or an indorser it is not discharged; but

(a) Where a bill payable to, or to the order of, a third party is paid by the drawer, the drawer may enforce payment thereof against the acceptor, but may not re-issue the bill.

(b) Where a bill is paid by an indorser, or where a bill payable to drawer's order is paid by the drawer, the party paying it is remitted to his former rights as regards the acceptor or antecedent parties, and he may, if he thinks fit, strike out his own and subsequent indorsements, and again negotiate the bill.

(3.) Where an accommodation bill is paid in due course by the party accommodated the bill is discharged.

*Banker paying demand draft whereon indorsement is forged.*

**60.** When a bill payable to order on demand is drawn on a banker, and the banker on whom it is drawn pays the bill in good faith and in the ordinary course of business, it is not incumbent on the banker to show that the indorsement of the payee or any subsequent indorsement was made by or under the authority of the person whose indorsement it purports to be, and the banker is deemed to have paid the bill in due course, although such indorsement has been forged or made without authority.

*Acceptor the holder at maturity.*

**61.** When the acceptor of a bill is or becomes the holder of it at or after its maturity, in his own right, the bill is discharged.

*Express waiver.*

**62.**—(1.) When the holder of a bill at or after its maturity absolutely and unconditionally renounces his rights against the acceptor the bill is discharged.

The renunciation must be in writing, unless the bill is delivered up to the acceptor.

(2.) The liabilities of any party to a bill may in like manner be renounced by the holder before, at, or after its maturity ; but nothing in this section shall affect the rights of a holder in due course without notice of the renunciation.

63.—(1.) Where a bill is intentionally cancelled by the holder or his agent, and the cancellation is apparent thereon, the bill is discharged. Cancellation.

(2.) In like manner any party liable on a bill may be discharged by the intentional cancellation of his signature by the holder or his agent. In such case any indorser who would have had a right of recourse against the party whose signature is cancelled, is also discharged.

(3.) A cancellation made unintentionally, or under a mistake, or without the authority of the holder is inoperative ; but where a bill or any signature thereon appears to have been cancelled the burden of proof lies on the party who alleges that the cancellation was made unintentionally, or under a mistake, or without authority.

64.—(1.) Where a bill or acceptance is materially altered without the assent of all parties liable on the bill, the bill is avoided except as against a party who has himself made, authorised, or assented to the alteration, and subsequent indorsers. Alteration of bill.

Provided that,

Where a bill has been materially altered, but the alteration is not apparent, and the bill is in the hands of a holder in due course, such holder may avail himself of the bill as if it had not been altered, and may enforce payment of it according to its original tenor.

(2.) In particular the following alterations are material, namely, any alteration of the date, the sum payable, the time of payment, the place of payment, and, where a bill has been accepted generally, the addition of a place of payment without the acceptor's assent.

### *Acceptance and Payment for Honour.*

65.—(1.) Where a bill of exchange has been protested for dishonour by non-acceptance, or protested for better security, and is not overdue, any person, not being a party already liable thereon, may, with the consent of the holder, intervene and accept the bill suprà protest, for the honour of any party liable thereon, or for the honour of the person for whose account the bill is drawn. Acceptance for honour suprà protest.

(2.) A bill may be accepted for honour for part only of the sum for which it is drawn.

(3.) An acceptance for honour suprà protest in order to be valid must—
(a) be written on the bill, and indicate that it is an acceptance for honour:
(b) be signed by the acceptor for honour.

(4.) Where an acceptance for honour does not expressly state for whose honour it is made, it is deemed to be an acceptance for the honour of the drawer.

(5.) Where a bill payable after sight is accepted for honour, its maturity is calculated from the date of the noting for non-acceptance, and not from the date of the acceptance for honour.

66.—(1.) The acceptor for honour of a bill by accepting it engages that he will, on due presentment, pay the bill according to the tenor of his acceptance, if it is not paid by the drawee, provided it has been duly presented for payment, and protested for non-payment, and that he receives notice of these facts. Liability of acceptor for honour.

(2.) The acceptor for honour is liable to the holder and to all parties to the bill subsequent to the party for whose honour he has accepted.

67.—(1.) Where a dishonoured bill has been accepted for honour suprà protest, or contains a reference in case of need, it must be protested for non-payment before it is presented for payment to the acceptor for honour, or referee in case of need. Presentment to acceptor for honour.

(2.) Where the address of the acceptor for honour is in the same place where the bill is protested for non-payment, the bill must be presented to him not later than the day following its maturity ; and where the address of the acceptor for honour is in some place other than the place where it was protested for non-payment, the bill must be forwarded not later than the day following its maturity for presentment to him.

(3.) Delay in presentment or non-presentment is excused by any circumstance whioh would excuse delay in presentment for payment or non-presentment for payment.

(4.) When a bill of exchange is dishonoured by the acceptor for honour it must be protested for non-payment by him.

Payment for<br>honour suprà<br>protest.

**68.**—(1.) Where a bill has been protested for non-payment, any person may intervene and pay it suprà protest for the honour of any party liable thereon, or for the honour of the person for whose account the bill is drawn.

(2.) Where two or more persons offer to pay a bill for the honour of different parties, the person whose payment will discharge most parties to the bill shall have the preference.

(3.) Payment for honour suprà protest, in order to operate as such and not as a mere voluntary payment, must be attested by a notarial act of honour which may be appended to the protest or form an extension of it.

(4.) The notarial act of honour must be founded on a declaration made by the payer for honour, or his agent in that behalf, declaring his intention to pay the bill for honour, and for whose honour he pays.

(5.) Where a bill has been paid for honour, all parties subsequent to the party for whose honour it is paid are discharged, but the payer for honour is subrogated for, and succeeds to both the rights and duties of, the holder as regards the party for whose honour he pays, and all parties liable to that party.

(6.) The payer for honour on paying to the holder the amount of the bill and the notarial expenses incidental to its dishonour is entitled to receive both the bill itself and the protest. If the holder do not on demand deliver them up he shall be liable to the payer for honour in damages.

(7.) Where the holder of a bill refuses to receive payment suprà protest he shall lose his right of recourse against any party who would have been discharged by such payment.

*Lost Instruments.*

Holder's right<br>to duplicate of<br>lost bill.

**69.** Where a bill has been lost before it is overdue, the person who was the holder of it may apply to the drawer to give him another bill of the same tenor, giving security to the drawer if required to indemnify him against all persons whatever in case the bill alleged to have been lost shall be found again.

If the drawer on request as aforesaid refuses to give such duplicate bill, he may be compelled to do so.

Action on lost<br>bill.

**70.** In any action or proceeding upon a bill, the court or a judge may order that the loss of the instrument shall not be set up, provided an indemnity be given to the satisfaction of the court or judge against the claims of any other person upon the instrument in question.

*Bill in a Set.*

Rules as to sets.

**71.**—(1.) Where a bill is drawn in a set, each part of the set being numbered, and containing a reference to the other parts, the whole of the parts constitute one bill.

(2.) Where the holder of a set indorses two or more parts to different persons, he is liable on every such part, and every indorser subsequent to him is liable on the part he has himself indorsed as if the said parts were separate bills.

(3.) Where two or more parts of a set are negotiated to different holders in due course, the holder whose title first accrues is as between such holders deemed the true owner of the bill ; but nothing in this sub-section shall affect the rights of a person who in due course accepts or pays the part first presented to him.

(4.) The acceptance may be written on any part, and it must be written on one part only.

If the drawee accepts more than one part, and such accepted parts get into the hands of different holders in due course, he is liable on every such part as if it were a separate bill.

(5.) When the accepter of a bill drawn in a set pays it without requiring the part bearing his acceptance to be delivered up to him, and that part at maturity is outstanding in the hands of a holder in due course, he is liable to the holder thereof.

(6.) Subject to the preceding rules, where any one part of a bill drawn in a set is discharged by payment or otherwise, the whole bill is discharged.

### *Conflict of Laws.*

**72.** Where a bill drawn in one country is negotiated, accepted, or payable in another, the rights, duties, and liabilities of the parties thereto are determined as follows : Rules where laws conflict.

(1.) The validity of a bill as regards requisites in form is determined by the law of the place of issue, and the validity as regards requisites in form of the supervening contracts, such as acceptance, or indorsement, or acceptance suprà protest, is determined by the law of the place where such contract was made.

Provided that—

(*a.*) Where a bill is issued out of the United Kingdom it is not invalid by reason only that it is not stamped in accordance with the law of the place of issue :

(*b.*) Where a bill, issued out of the United Kingdom, conforms, as regards requisites in form, to the law of the United Kingdom, it may, for the purpose of enforcing payment thereof, be treated as valid as between all persons who negotiate, hold, or become parties to it in the United Kingdom.

(2.) Subject to the provisions of this Act, the interpretation of the drawing, indorsement, acceptance, or acceptance suprà protest of a bill, is determined by the law of the place where such contract is made.

Provided that where an inland bill is indorsed in a foreign country the indorsement shall as regards the payer be interpreted according to the law of the United Kingdom.

(3.) The duties of the holder with respect to presentment for acceptance or payment and the necessity for or sufficiency of a protest or notice of dishonour, or otherwise, are determined by the law of the place where the act is done or the bill is dishonoured.

(4.) Where a bill is drawn out of but payable in the United Kingdom and the sum payable is not expressed in the currency of the United Kingdom, the amount shall, in the absence of some express stipulation, be calculated according to the rate of exchange for slight drafts at the place of payment on the day the bill is payable.

(5.) Where a bill is drawn in one country and is payable in another, the due date thereof is determined according to the law of the place where it is payable.

---

## PART III.

### CHEQUES ON A BANKER.

**73.** A cheque is a bill of exchange drawn on a banker payable on demand. Cheque defined.
Except as otherwise provided in this Part, the provisions of this Act applicable to a bill of exchange payable on demand apply to a cheque.

**74.** Subject to the provisions of this Act— Presentment of cheque for payment.

(1.) Where a cheque is not presented for payment within a reasonable time of its issue, and the drawer or the person on whose account it is drawn had the right at the time of such presentment as between him and the banker to have the cheque paid and suffers actual damage through the delay, he is discharged to the extent of such damage, that is to say, to the extent to which such drawer or person is a creditor of such banker to a larger amount than he would have been had such cheque been paid.

(2.) In determining what is a reasonable time regard shall be had to the nature of the instrument, the usage of trade and of bankers, and the facts of the particular case.

(3.) The holder of such cheque as to which such drawer or person is discharged shall be a creditor, in lieu of such drawer or person, of such banker to the extent of such discharge, and entitled to recover the amount from him.

*Revocation of banker's authority.*
**75.** The duty and authority of a banker to pay a cheque drawn on him by his customer are determined by—

(1.) Countermand of payment:

(2.) Notice of the customer's death.

### Crossed Cheques.

*General and special crossings defined.*
**76.**—(1.) Where a cheque bears across its face an addition of—

(*a.*) The words "and company" or any abbreviation thereof between two parallel transverse lines, either with or without the words "not negotiable"; or

(*b.*) Two parallel transverse lines simply, either with or without the words "not negotiable";

that addition constitutes a crossing, and the cheque is crossed generally.

(2.) Where a cheque bears across its face an addition of the name of a banker, either with or without the words "not negotiable," that addition constitutes a crossing, and the cheque is crossed specially and to that banker.

*Crossing by drawer or after issue.*
**77.**—(1.) A cheque may be crossed generally or specially by the drawer.

(2.) Where a cheque is uncrossed, the holder may cross it generally or specially.

(3.) Where a cheque is crossed generally the holder may cross it specially.

(4.) Where a cheque is crossed generally or specially, the holder may add the words "not negotiable."

(5.) Where a cheque is crossed specially, the banker to whom it is crossed may again cross it specially to another banker for collection.

(6.) Where an uncrossed cheque, or a cheque crossed generally, is sent to a banker for collection, he may cross it specially to himself.

*Crossing a material part of cheque.*
**78.** A crossing authorized by this Act is a material part of the cheque; it shall not be lawful for any person to obliterate or, except as authorized by this Act, to add to or alter the crossing.

*Duties of banker as to crossed cheques.*
**79.**—(1.) Where a cheque is crossed specially to more than one banker except when crossed to an agent for collection being a banker, the banker on whom it is drawn shall refuse payment thereof.

(2.) Where the banker on whom a cheque is drawn which is so crossed nevertheless pays the same, or pays a cheque crossed generally otherwise than to a banker, or if crossed specially otherwise than to the banker to whom it is crossed, or his agent for collection being a banker, he is liable to the true owner of the cheque for any loss he may sustain owing to the cheque having been so paid.

Provided that where a cheque is presented for payment which does not at the time of presentment appear to be crossed, or to have had a crossing which has been obliterated, or to have been added to or altered otherwise than as authorized by this Act, the banker paying the cheque in good faith and without negligence shall not be responsible or incur any liability, nor shall the payment be questioned by reason of the cheque having been crossed, or of the crossing having been obliterated or having been added to or altered otherwise than as authorized by this Act, and of payment having been made otherwise than to a banker, or to the banker to whom the cheque is or was crossed, or to his agent for collection being a banker, as the case may be.

*Protection to banker and drawer where cheque is crossed.*
**80.** Where the banker, on whom a crossed cheque is drawn, in good faith and without negligence pays it, if crossed generally, to a banker, and if crossed specially, to the banker to whom it is crossed, or his agent for collection being a banker, the banker paying the cheque, and, if the cheque has come into the hands of the payee, the drawer, shall respectively be entitled to the same rights and be placed in the same position as if payment of the cheque had been made to the true owner thereof.

*Effect of crossing on holder.*
**81.** Where a person takes a crossed cheque which bears on it the words "not negotiable," he shall not have and shall not be capable of giving a better title to the cheque than that which the person from whom he took it had.

*Protection to collecting banker.*
**82.** Where a banker in good faith and without negligence receives payment for a customer of a cheque crossed generally or specially to himself, and the customer has no title or a defective title thereto, the banker shall not incur any liability to the true owner of the cheque by reason only of having received such payment.

## PART IV.

### PROMISSORY NOTES.

**83.**—(1.) A promissory note is an unconditional promise in writing made by one person to another signed by the maker, engaging to pay, on demand or at a fixed or determinable future time, a sum certain in money, to, or to the order of, a specified person or to bearer. *Promissory note defined.*

(2.) An instrument in the form of a note payable to maker's order is not a note within the meaning of this section unless and until it is indorsed by the maker.

(3.) A note is not invalid by reason only that it contains also a pledge of collateral security with authority to sell or dispose thereof.

(4.) A note which is, or on the face of it purports to be, both made and payable within the British Islands is an inland note. Any other note is a foreign note.

**84.** A promissory note is inchoate and incomplete until delivery thereof to the payee or bearer. *Delivery necessary.*

**85.**—(1.) A promissory note may be made by two or more makers, and they may be liable thereon jointly, or jointly and severally according to its tenour. *Joint and several notes.*

(2.) Where a note runs "I promise to pay," and is signed by two or more persons, it is deemed to be their joint and several note.

**86.**—(1.) Where a note payable on demand has been indorsed, it must be presented for payment within a reasonable time of the indorsement. If it be not so presented the indorser is discharged. *Note payable on demand.*

(2.) In determining what is a reasonable time, regard shall be had to the nature of the instrument, the usage of trade, and the facts of the particular case.

(3.) Where a note payable on demand is negotiated, it is not deemed to be overdue, for the purpose of affecting the holder with defects of title of which he had no notice, by reason that it appears that a reasonable time for presenting it for payment has elapsed since its issue.

**87.**—(1.) Where a promissory note is in the body of it made payable at a particular place, it must be presented for payment at that place in order to render the maker liable. In any other case, presentment for payment is not necessary in order to render the maker liable. *Presentment of note for payment.*

(2.) Presentment for payment is necessary in order to render the indorser of a note liable.

(3.) Where a note is in the body of it made payable at a particular place, presentment at that place is necessary in order to render an indorser liable; but when a place of payment is indicated by way of memorandum only, presentment at that place is sufficient to render the indorser liable, but a presentment to the maker elsewhere, if sufficient in other respects, shall also suffice.

**88.** The maker of a promissory note by making it— *Liability of maker.*

(1.) Engages that he will pay it according to its tenour;

(2.) Is precluded from denying to a holder in due course the existence of the payee and his then capacity to indorse.

**89.**—(1.) Subject to the provisions in this part and, except as by this section provided, the provisions of this Act relating to bills of exchange apply, with the necessary modifications, to promissory notes. *Application of, Part II. to notes.*

(2.) In applying those provisions the maker of a note shall be deemed to correspond with the acceptor of a bill, and the first indorser of a note shall be deemed to correspond with the drawer of an accepted bill payable to drawer's order.

(3.) The following provisions as to bills do not apply to notes; namely, provisions relating to—

(a) Presentment for acceptance;

(b) Acceptance;

(c) Acceptance suprà protest;

(d) Bills in a set.

(4.) Where a foreign note is dishonoured, protest thereof is unnecessary.

## PART V.

### SUPPLEMENTARY.

**Good faith.** 90. A thing is deemed to be done in good faith, within the meaning of this Act, where it is in fact done honestly, whether it is done negligently or not.

**Signature.** 91.—(1.) Where, by this Act, any instrument or writing is required to be signed by any person, it is not necessary that he should sign it with his own hand, but it is sufficient if his signature is written thereon by some other person, by or under his authority.

(2.) In the case of a corporation, where, by this Act, any instrument or writing is required to be signed, it is sufficient if the instrument or writing be sealed with the corporate seal.

But nothing in this section shall be construed as requiring the bill or note of a corporation to be under seal.

**Computation of time.** 92. Where, by this Act, the time limited for doing any act or thing is less than three days, in reckoning time, non-business days are excluded.

"Non-business days" for the purposes of this Act mean—

(a) Sunday, Good Friday, Christmas Day :

(b) A bank holiday under the Bank Holidays Act, 1871, or Acts amending it :

(c) A day appointed by Royal proclamation as a public fast or thanksgiving day.

Any other day is a business day.

**When noting equivalent to protest.** 93. For the purposes of this Act, where a bill or note is required to be protested within a specified time or before some further proceeding is taken, it is sufficient that the bill has been noted for protest before the expiration of the specified time or the taking of the proceeding ; and the formal protest may be extended at any time thereafter as of the date of the noting.

**Protest when notary not accessible.** 94. Where a dishonoured bill or note is authorised or required to be protested, and the services of a notary cannot be obtained at the place where the bill is dishonoured, any householder or substantial resident of the place may, in the presence of two witnesses, give a certificate, signed by them, attesting the dishonour of the bill, and the certificate shall in all respects operate as if it were a formal protest of the bill.

The form given in Schedule 1 to this Act may be used with necessary modifications, and if used shall be sufficient.

**Dividend warrants may be crossed.** 95. The provisions of this Act as to crossed cheques shall apply to a warrant for payment of dividend.

**Repeal.** 96. The enactments mentioned in the second schedule to this Act are hereby repealed as from the commencement of this Act to the extent in that schedule mentioned.

Provided that such repeal shall not affect anything done or suffered, or any right, title, or interest acquired or accrued before the commencement of this Act, or any legal proceeding or remedy in respect of any such thing, right, title, or interest.

**Savings.** 97.—(1.) The rules in bankruptcy relating to bills of exchange, promissory notes, and cheques, shall continue to apply thereto notwithstanding anything in this Act contained.

(2.) The rules of common law including the law merchant, save in so far as they are inconsistent with the express provisions of this Act, shall continue to apply to bills of exchange, promissory notes, and cheques.

(3.) Nothing in this Act or in any repeal affected thereby shall affect—

**33 & 34 Vict. c. 97.** (a) The provisions of the Stamp Act, 1870, or Acts amending it, or any law or enactment for the time being in force relating to the revenue :

**25 & 26 Vict. c. 89.** (b) The provisions of the Companies Act, 1862, or Acts amending it, or any Act relating to joint stock banks or companies :

(c) The provisions of any Act relating to or confirming the privileges of the Bank of England or the Bank of Ireland respectively :

(d) The validity of any usage relating to dividend warrants, or the indorsements thereof.

**Saving of summary diligence in Scotland.** 98. Nothing in this Act or in any repeal effected thereby shall extend or restrict, or in any way alter or affect the law and practice in Scotland in regard to summary diligence.

99. Where any Act or document refers to any enactment repealed by this Act, the Act or document shall be construed, and shall operate, as if it referred to the corresponding provisions of this Act.    *Construction with other Acts, &c.*

100. .In any judicial proceeding in Scotland, any fact relating to a bill of exchange, bank cheque, or promissory note, which is relevant to any question of liability thereon, may be proved by parole evidence: provided that this enactment shall not in any way affect the existing law and practice whereby the party who is, according to the tenour of any bill of exchange, bank cheque, or promissory note, debtor to the holder in the amount thereof, may be required, as a condition of obtaining a sist of diligence, or suspension of a charge, or threatened charge, to make such consignation, or to find such caution as the Court or judge before whom the cause is depending may require.    *Parole evidence allowed in certain judicial proceedings in Scotland.*

This section shall not apply to any case where the bill of exchange, bank cheque, or promissory note has undergone the sesennial prescription.

---

## SCHEDULES.

### FIRST SCHEDULE.

Form of protest which may be used when the services of a notary cannot be obtained.    *Section 94.*

Know all men that I, A. B. [householder], of    , in the county of    , in the United Kingdom, at the request of C. D., there being no notary public available, did on the     day of    , 188 , at    , demand payment [*or* acceptance] of the bill of exchange hereunder written, from E. F., to which demand he made answer [state answer, if any] wherefore I now, in the presence of G. H. and J. K. do protest the said bill of exchange.

(Signed)    A. B.

G. H. &#125;<br>J. K. &#125; Witnesses.

N.B.—The bill itself should be annexed, or a copy of the bill and all that is written thereon should be underwritten.

---

### SECOND SCHEDULE.

#### ENACTMENTS REPEALED.

| Session and Chapter. | Title of Act and extent of Repeal. |
| --- | --- |
| 9 Will. 3, c. 17 ......... | An Act for the better payment of inland bills of exchange. |
| 3 & 4 Anne, c. 8 ........ | An Act for giving like remedy upon promissory notes as is now used upon bills of exchange, and for the better payment of inland bills of exchange. |
| 17 Geo. 3, c. 30 ......... | An Act for further restraining the negotiation of promissory notes and inland bills of exchange under a limited sum within that part of Great Britain called England. |
| 39 & 40 Geo. 3, c. 42 .... | An Act for the better observance of Good Friday in certain cases therein mentioned. |
| 48 Geo. 3, c. 88 ......... | An Act to restrain the negotiation of promissory notes and inland bills of exchange under a limited sum in England. |

| Session and Chapter. | Title of Act and extent of Repeal. |
| --- | --- |
| 1 & 2 Geo. 4, c. 78 ...... | An Act to regulate acceptances of bills of exchange. |
| 7 & 8 Geo. 4, c. 15 ...... | An Act for declaring the law in relation to bills of exchange and promissory notes becoming payable on Good Friday or Christmas Day. |
| 9 Geo. 4, c. 24 .......... | An Act to repeal certain Acts, and to consolidate and amend the laws relating to bills of exchange and promissory notes in Ireland, in part; that is to say, Sections two, four, seven, eight, nine, ten, eleven. |
| 2 & 3 Will. 4, c. 98 ...... | An Act for regulating the protesting for non-payment of bills of exchange drawn payable at a place not being the place of the residence of the drawee or drawees of the same. |
| 6 & 7 Will. 4, c. 58 ...... | An Act for declaring the law as to the day on which it is requisite to present for payment to acceptor, or acceptors suprà protest for honour, or to the referee or referees, in case of need, bills of exchange which have been dishonoured. |
| 8 & 9 Vict. c. 37 ........ in part. | An Act to regulate the issue of bank notes in Ireland, and to regulate the repayment of certain sums advanced by the Governor and Company of the Bank of Ireland for the public service, in part; that is to say, Section twenty-four. |
| 19 & 20 Vict. c. 97 ...... in part. | The Mercantile Law Amendment Act, 1856, in part; that is to say, Sections six and seven. |
| 23 & 24 Vict. c. 111 ...... in part. | An Act for granting to her Majesty certain duties of stamps, and to amend the laws relating to the stamp duties, in part; that is to say, Section nineteen. |
| 34 & 35 Vict. c. 74 ...... | An Act to abolish days of grace in the case of bills of exchange and promissory notes payable at sight or on presentation. |
| 39 & 40 Vict. c. 81 ...... | The Crossed Cheques Act, 1876. |
| 41 & 42 Vict. c. 13 ...... | The Bills of Exchange Act, 1878. |

ENACTMENT REPEALED AS TO SCOTLAND.

| | |
| --- | --- |
| 19 & 20 Vict. c. 60 ...... in part. | The Mercantile Law (Scotland) Amendment Act, 1856, in part; that is to say, Sections ten, eleven, twelve, thirteen, fourteen, fifteen, and sixteen. |

---

45 & 46 VICT. C. 76.

*An Act to amend the Merchant Shipping Act, 1854, with respect to Colonial Courts of Inquiry.*      [*18th August*, 1882.]

## 46 & 47 VICT. C. 28.

*An Act to amend the Companies Acts, 1862 and 1867.*

[*20th August, 1883.*]

BE it enacted by the Queen's most excellent Majesty, by and with the advice and consent of the Lords Spiritual and Temporal, and Commons, in this present Parliament assembled, and by the authority of the same, as follows:

1. This Act may be cited for all purposes as the Companies Act, 1883. Short title.

2. This Act shall, so far as is consistent with the terms thereof, be construed as one with the Companies Acts, 1862 and 1867. Construction of Act.

3. This Act shall come into force on the first day of September one thousand eight hundred and eighty-three. Commencement of Act.

4. In the distribution of the assets of any company being wound up under the Companies Acts, 1862 and 1867, there shall be paid in priority to other debts (*a*),— Wages and salary to be preferential claims.

   (a) All wages or salary of any clerk or servant in respect of service rendered to the company during four months before the commencement of the winding up not exceeding fifty pounds; and

   (b) All wages of any labourer or workman in respect of services rendered to the company during two months before the commencement of the winding up.

5. The foregoing debts shall rank equally among themselves, and shall be paid in full, unless the assets of the company are insufficient to meet them, in which case they shall abate in equal proportions between themselves. Such claims to rank equally.

6. Subject to the retention of such sums as may be necessary for the costs of administration or otherwise, the liquidator or liquidators or official liquidator shall discharge the foregoing debts forthwith, so far as the assets of the company are and will be sufficient to meet them, as and when such assets come into the hands of such liquidator or liquidators or official liquidator. Liquidator to discharge same upon receipt of sufficient assets.

---

## 46 & 47 VICT. C. 31.

*An Act to prohibit the Payment of Wages to Workmen in Public-houses and certain other places.*

[*20th August, 1883.*]

WHEREAS by the Coal Mines Regulations Act, 1872, and the Metalliferous Mines Regulation Act, 1872, the payment in public-houses, beershops, or other places in the said Acts mentioned of wages to persons employed in or about any mines to which the said Acts apply is prohibited, and it is expedient to extend such prohibition to the payment in public-houses, beershops, and other places in England and Scotland of wages to all workmen as defined by this Act: 35 & 36 Vict. c. 76.<br>35 & 36 Vict. c. 77.

Be it therefore enacted by the Queen's most Excellent Majesty, by and with the advice and consent of the Lords Spiritual and Temporal, and Commons, in this present Parliament assembled, and by the authority of the same, as follows:

1. This Act may be cited as the Payment of Wages in Public-houses Prohibition Act, 1883. Short title.

2. In this Act the expression "workman" means any person who is a labourer, servant in husbandry, journeyman, artificer, handicraftsman, or is otherwise engaged in manual labour, whether under the age of twenty-one years or above that age, but does not include a domestic or menial servant, nor any person employed in or about any mine to which the Coal Mines Regulation Act, 1872, or the Metalliferous Mines Regulation Act, 1872, applies. Definition of workman.

(*a*) See Bankruptcy Act, 1883, s. 40.

4 c 2

No wages to be
paid within
public-house.

**3.** From and after the passing of this Act no wages shall be paid to any workman at or within any public-house, beershop, or place for the sale of any spirits, wine, cyder, or other spirituous or fermented liquor, or any office, garden, or place belonging thereto or occupied therewith, save and except such wages as are paid by the resident owner or occupier of such public-house, beershop, or place to any workman bonâ fide employed by him.

Every person who contravenes or fails to comply with or permits any person to contravene or fail to comply with this Act shall be guilty of an offence against this Act.

And in the event of any wages being paid by any person in contravention of the provisions of this Act for or on behalf of any employer, such employer shall himself be guilty of an offence against this Act, unless he prove that he had taken all reasonable means in his power for enforcing the provisions of this Act and to prevent such contravention.

Penalties.

**4.** Every person who is guilty of an offence against this Act shall be liable to a penalty not exceeding ten pounds for each offence ; and all offences against this Act may be prosecuted and all penalties under this Act may be recovered by any person summarily in England in the manner provided by the Summary Jurisdiction Acts, and in Scotland in the manner provided by the Summary Jurisdiction (Scotland) Acts, 1864 and 1881.

Act not to apply
to Ireland.

**5.** This Act shall not apply to Ireland.

---

## 46 & 47 VICT. C. 41.

*An Act to amend the Merchant Shipping Acts, 1854 to 1880, with respect to Fishing Vessels and Apprenticeship to the Sea Fishing Service and otherwise.*

[*25th August,* 1883.]

---

## 46 & 47 VICT. C. 52.

*An Act to amend and consolidate the Law of Bankruptcy.*

[*25th August,* 1883.]

BE it enacted by the Queen's most excellent Majesty, by and with the advice and consent of the Lords spiritual and temporal, and Commons, in this present Parliament assembled, and by the authority of the same, as follows :—

### *Preliminary.*

Short title.

**1.** This Act may be cited as the Bankruptcy Act, 1883.

Extent of Act.

**2.** This Act shall not, except so far as is expressly provided, extend to Scotland or Ireland.

Commencement
of Act.

**3.** This Act shall, except as by this Act otherwise provided, commence and come into operation from and immediately after the thirty-first day of December, one thousand eight hundred and eighty-three.

---

## PART I.

### PROCEEDINGS FROM ACT OF BANKRUPTCY TO DISCHARGE.

#### *Acts of Bankruptcy.*

Acts of
bankruptcy.

**4.** (1.) A debtor commits an act of bankruptcy in each of the following cases :—

(a) If in England or elsewhere he makes a conveyance or assignment of his property to a trustee or trustees for the benefit of his creditors generally :

(b) If in England or elsewhere he makes a fraudulent conveyance, gift, delivery, or transfer of his property, or of any part thereof :

(c) If in England or elsewhere he makes any conveyance or transfer of his property or any part thereof, or creates any charge thereon which would under this or any other Act be void as a fraudulent preference if he were adjudged bankrupt :

(d) If with intent to defeat or delay his creditors he does any of the following things, namely, departs out of England, or being out of England remains out of England, or departs from his dwelling-house, or otherwise absents himself, or begins to keep house :

(e) If execution issued against him has been levied by seizure and sale of his goods under process in an action in any court, or in any civil proceeding in the High Court :

(f) If he files in the Court a declaration of his inability to pay his debts or presents a bankruptcy petition against himself :

(g) If a creditor has obtained a final judgment against him for any amount, and execution thereon not having been stayed, has served on him in England, or, by leave of the Court, elsewhere, a bankruptcy notice under this Act, requiring him to pay the judgment debt in accordance with the terms of the judgment, or to secure or compound for it to the satisfaction of the creditor or the Court, and he does not, within seven days after service of the notice, in case the service is effected in England, and in case the service is effected elsewhere, then within the time limited in that behalf by the order giving leave to effect the service, either comply with the requirements of the notice, or satisfy the Court that he has a counter-claim set off or cross demand which equals or exceeds the amount of the judgment debt, and which he could not set up in the action in which the judgment was obtained :

(h) If the debtor gives notice to any of his creditors that he has suspended, or that he is about to suspend, payment of his debts.

(2.) A bankruptcy notice under this Act shall be in the prescribed form, and shall state the consequences of non-compliance therewith, and shall be served in the prescribed manner.

*Receiving Order.*

**5.** Subject to the conditions hereinafter specified, if a debtor commits an act of bankruptcy the Court may, on a bankruptcy petition being presented either by a creditor or by the debtor, make an order, in this Act called a receiving order, for the protection of the estate. Jurisdiction to make receiving order.

**6.** (1.) A creditor shall not be entitled to present a bankruptcy petition against a debtor unless— Conditions on which creditor may petition.

(a.) The debt owing by the debtor to the petitioning creditor, or, if two or more creditors join in the petition, the aggregate amount of debts owing to the several petitioning creditors, amounts to fifty pounds, and

(b.) The debt is a liquidated sum, payable either immediately or at some certain future time, and

(c.) The act of bankruptcy on which the petition is grounded has occurred within three months before the presentation of the petition, and

(d.) The debtor is domiciled in England, or, within a year before the date of the presentation of the petition, has ordinarily resided or had a dwelling-house or place of business in England.

(2.) If the petitioning creditor is a secured creditor, he must, in his petition, either state that he is willing to give up his security for the benefit of the creditors in the event of the debtor being adjudged bankrupt, or give an estimate of the value of his security. In the latter case, he may be admitted as a petitioning creditor to the extent of the balance of the debt due to him, after deducting the value so estimated in the same manner as if he were an unsecured creditor.

**7.** (1.) A creditor's petition shall be verified by affidavit of the creditor, or of some person on his behalf having knowledge of the facts, and served in the prescribed manner. Proceedings and order on creditor's petition.

(2.) At the hearing the Court shall require proof of the debt of the petitioning creditor of the service of the petition, and of the act of bankruptcy, or, if more than one act of bankruptcy is alleged in the petition, of some one of the alleged acts of bankruptcy, and, if satisfied with the proof, may make a receiving order in pursuance of the petition.

(3.) If the Court is not satisfied with the proof of the petitioning creditor's debt, or of the act of bankruptcy, or of the service of the petition, or is satisfied by the debtor that he is able to pay his debts, or that for other sufficient cause no order ought to be made, the Court may dismiss the petition.

(4.) When the act of bankruptcy relied on is non-compliance with a bankruptcy notice to pay, secure, or compound for a judgment debt, the Court may, if it thinks fit, stay or dismiss the petition on the ground that an appeal is pending from the judgment.

(5.) Where the debtor appears on the petition, and denies that he is indebted to the petitioner, or that he is indebted to such an amount as would justify the petitioner in presenting a petition against him, the Court, on such security (if any) being given as the Court may require for payment to the petitioner of any debt which may be established against him in due course of law, and of the costs of establishing the debt, may instead of dismissing the petition stay all proceedings on the petition for such time as may be required for trial of the question relating to the debt.

(6.) Where proceedings are stayed, the Court may, if by reason of the delay caused by the stay of proceedings or for any other cause it thinks just, make a receiving order on the petition of some other creditor, and shall thereupon dismiss, on such terms as it thinks just, the petition in which proceedings have been stayed as aforesaid.

(7.) A creditor's petition shall not, after presentment, be withdrawn without the leave of the Court.

Debtor's petition and order thereon.

**8.** (1.) A debtor's petition shall allege that the debtor is unable to pay his debts, and the presentation thereof shall be deemed an act of bankruptcy without the previous filing by the debtor of any declaration of inability to pay his debts, and the Court shall thereupon make a receiving order.

(2.) A debtor's petition shall not, after presentment, be withdrawn without the leave of the Court.

Effect of receiving order.

**9.** (1.) On the making of a receiving order an official receiver shall be thereby constituted receiver of the property of the debtor, and thereafter, except as directed by this Act, no creditor to whom the debtor is indebted in respect of any debt provable in bankruptcy shall have any remedy against the property or person of the debtor in respect of the debt, or shall commence any action or other legal proceedings unless with the leave of the Court and on such terms as the Court may impose.

(2.) But this section shall not affect the power of any secured creditor to realize or otherwise deal with his security in the same manner as he would have been entitled to realize or deal with it if this section had not been passed.

Discretionary powers as to appointment of receiver and stay of proceedings.

**10.** (1.) The Court may, if it is shown to be necessary for the protection of the estate, at any time after the presentation of a bankruptcy petition, and before a receiving order is made, appoint the official receiver to be interim receiver of the property of the debtor, or of any part thereof, and direct him to take immediate possession thereof or of any part thereof.

(2.) The Court may at any time after the presentation of a bankruptcy petition stay any action, execution, or other legal process against the property or person of the debtor, and any Court in which proceedings are pending against a debtor may, on proof that a bankruptcy petition has been presented by or against the debtor, either stay the proceedings or allow them to continue on such terms as it may think just.

Service of order staying proceedings.

**11.** Where the Court makes an order staying any action or proceeding, or staying proceedings generally, the order may be served by sending a copy thereof, under the seal of the Court, by prepaid post letter to the address for service of the plaintiff or other party prosecuting such proceeding.

Power to appoint special manager.

**12.** (1.) The official receiver of a debtor's estate may, on the application of any creditor or creditors, and if satisfied that the nature of the debtor's estate or business or the interests of the creditors generally require the appointment of a special manager of the estate or business other than the official receiver, appoint a manager thereof accordingly to act until a trustee is appointed, and with such powers (including any of the powers of a receiver) as may be entrusted to him by the official receiver.

(2.) The special manager shall give security and account in such manner as the Board of Trade may direct.

(3.) The special manager shall receive such remuneration as the creditors may, by resolution at an ordinary meeting, determine, or in default of any such resolution, as may be prescribed.

13. Notice of every receiving order, stating the name, address, and description of the debtor, the date of the order, the Court by which the order is made, and the date of the petition, shall be gazetted and advertised in a local paper in the prescribed manner. *Advertisement of receiving order.*

14. If in any case where a receiving order has been made on a bankruptcy petition it shall appear to the Court by which such order was made, upon an application by the official receiver, or any creditor or other person interested, that a majority of the creditors in number and value are resident in Scotland or in Ireland and that from the situation of the property of the debtor, or other causes, his estate and effects ought to be distributed among the creditors under the Bankrupt or Insolvent Laws of Scotland or Ireland, the said Court, after such inquiry as to it shall seem fit, may rescind the receiving order and stay all proceedings on, or dismiss the petition upon such terms, if any, as the Court may think fit. *Power to Court to annul receiving order in certain cases.*

### Proceedings consequent on Order.

15. (1.) As soon as may be after the making of a receiving order against a debtor a general meeting of his creditors (in this Act referred to as the first meeting of creditors) shall be held for the purpose of considering whether a proposal for a composition or scheme of arrangement shall be entertained, or whether it is expedient that the debtor shall be adjudged bankrupt, and generally as to the mode of dealing with the debtor's property. *First and other meetings of creditors.*

(2.) With respect to the summoning of and proceedings at the first and other meetings of creditors, the rules in the First Schedule shall be observed.

16. (1.) Where a receiving order is made against a debtor, he shall make out and submit to the official receiver a statement of and in relation to his affairs in the prescribed form, verified by affidavit, and showing the particulars of the debtor's assets, debts, and liabilities, the names, residences, and occupations of his creditors, the securities held by them respectively, the dates when the securities were respectively given, and such further or other information as may be prescribed or as the official receiver may require. *Debtor's statement of affairs.*

(2.) The statement shall be so submitted within the following times, namely :

(i.) If the order is made on the petition of the debtor, within three days from the date of the order.

(ii.) If the order is made on the petition of a creditor, within seven days from the date of the order.

But the Court may, in either case, for special reasons, extend the time.

(3.) If the debtor fails without reasonable excuse to comply with the requirements of this section, the Court may, on the application of the official receiver, or of any creditor, adjudge him bankrupt.

(4.) Any person stating himself in writing to be a creditor of the bankrupt may, personally or by agent, inspect this statement at all reasonable times, and take any copy thereof or extract therefrom, but any person untruthfully so stating himself to be a creditor shall be guilty of a contempt of Court, and shall be punishable accordingly on the application of the trustee or official receiver.

### Public Examination of Debtor.

17. (1.) Where the Court makes a receiving order it shall hold a public sitting, on a day to be appointed by the Court, for the examination of the debtor, and the debtor shall attend thereat, and shall be examined as to his conduct, dealings, and property. *Public examination of debtor.*

(2.) The examination shall be held as soon as conveniently may be after the expiration of the time for the submission of the debtor's statement of affairs.

(3.) The Court may adjourn the examination from time to time.

(4.) Any creditor who has tendered a proof, or his representative authorised in writing, may question the debtor concerning his affairs and the causes of his failure.

(5.) The official receiver shall take part in the examination of the debtor ;

· and for the purpose thereof, if specially authorised by the Board of Trade, may employ a solicitor with or without counsel.

(6.) If a trustee is appointed before the conclusion of the examination he may take part therein.

(7.) The Court may put such questions to the debtor as it may think expedient.

(8.) The debtor shall be examined upon oath, and it shall be his duty to answer all such questions as the Court may put or allow to be put to him. Such notes of the examination as the Court thinks proper shall be taken down in writing, and shall be read over to and signed by the debtor, and may thereafter be used in evidence against him; they shall also be open to the inspection of any creditor at all reasonable times.

(9.) When the Court is of opinion that the affairs of the debtor have been sufficiently investigated, it shall, by order, declare that his examination is concluded, but such order shall not be made until after the day appointed for the first meeting of creditors.

### Composition or Scheme of Arrangement.

**Power for creditors to accept and Court to approve composition or arrangement.**

**18.** (1.) The creditors may at the first meeting or any adjournment thereof, by special resolution, resolve to entertain a proposal for a composition in satisfaction of the debts due to them from the debtor, or a proposal for a scheme of arrangement of the debtor's affairs.

(2.) The composition or scheme shall not be binding on the creditors unless it is confirmed by a resolution passed (by a majority in number representing three fourths in value of all the creditors who have proved) at a subsequent meeting of the creditors, and is approved by the Court.

Any creditor who has proved his debt may assent to or dissent from such composition or scheme by a letter addressed to the official receiver in the prescribed form, and attested by a witness, so as to be received by such official receiver not later than the day preceding such subsequent meeting, and such creditor shall be taken as being present and voting at such meeting.

(3.) The subsequent meeting shall be summoned by the official receiver by not less than seven days notice, and shall not be held until after the public examination of the debtor is concluded. The notice shall state generally the terms of the proposal, and shall be accompanied by a report of the official receiver thereon.

(4.) The debtor or the official receiver may, after the composition or scheme is accepted by the creditors, apply to the Court to approve it, and notice of the time appointed for hearing the application shall be given to each creditor who has proved.

(5.) The Court shall, before approving a composition or scheme, hear a report of the official receiver as to the terms of the composition or scheme and as to the conduct of the debtor, and any objections which may be made by or on behalf of any creditor.

(6.) If the Court is of opinion that the terms of the composition or scheme are not reasonable, or are not calculated to benefit the general body of creditors, or in any case in which the Court is required under this Act where the debtor is adjudged bankrupt to refuse his discharge, the Court shall, or if any such facts are proved as would under this Act justify the Court in refusing, qualifying, or suspending the debtor's discharge, the Court may, in its discretion, refuse to approve the composition or scheme.

(7.) If the Court approves the composition or scheme, the approval may be testified by the seal of the Court being attached to the instrument containing the terms of the composition or scheme, or by the terms being embodied in an order of the Court.

(8.) A composition or scheme accepted and approved in pursuance of this section shall be binding on all the creditors so far as relates to any debts due to them from the debtor and provable in bankruptcy.

(9.) A certificate of the official receiver that a composition or scheme has been duly accepted and approved shall, in the absence of fraud, be conclusive as to its validity.

(10.) The provisions of a composition or scheme under this section may be enforced by the Court on application by any person interested, and any disobedience of an order of the Court made on the application shall be deemed a contempt of Court.

(11.) If default is made in payment of any instalment due in pursuance of the composition or scheme, or if it appears to the Court, on satisfactory evidence, that the composition or scheme cannot in consequence of legal difficulties, or for any sufficient cause, proceed without injustice or undue delay to the creditors or to the debtor, or that the approval of the Court was obtained by fraud, the Court may, if it thinks fit, on application by any creditor, adjudge the debtor bankrupt, and annul the composition or scheme, but without prejudice to the validity of any sale, disposition, or payment duly made, or thing duly done under or in pursuance of the composition or scheme. Where a debtor is adjudged bankrupt under this sub-section any debt provable in other respects, which has been contracted before the date of the adjudication, shall be provable in the bankruptcy.

(12.) If, under or in pursuance of a composition or scheme, a trustee is appointed to administer the debtor's property or manage his business, Part V. of this Act shall apply to the trustee as if he were a trustee in a bankruptcy, and as if the terms "bankruptcy," "bankrupt," and "order of adjudication" included respectively a composition or scheme of arrangement, a compounding or arranging debtor, and order approving the composition or scheme.

(13.) Part III. of this Act shall, so far as the nature of the case and the terms of the composition or scheme admit, apply thereto, the same interpretation being given to the words "trustee," "bankruptcy," "bankrupt," and "order of adjudication," as in the last preceding sub-section.

(14.) No composition or scheme shall be approved by the Court which does not provide for the payment in priority to other debts of all debts directed to be so paid in the distribution of the property of a bankrupt.

(15.) The acceptance by a creditor of a composition or scheme shall not release any person who under this Act would not be released by an order of discharge if the debtor had been adjudged bankrupt.

19. Notwithstanding the acceptance and approval of a composition or scheme, such composition or scheme shall not be binding on any creditor so far as regards a debt or liability from which, under the provisions of this Act, the debtor would not be discharged by an order of discharge in bankruptcy, unless the creditor assents to the composition or scheme.

*Effect of composition or scheme.*

### Adjudication of Bankruptcy.

20. (1.) Where a receiving order is made against a debtor, then, if the creditors at the first meeting or any adjournment thereof by ordinary resolution resolve that the debtor be adjudged bankrupt, or pass no resolution, or if the creditors do not meet, or if a composition or scheme is not accepted or approved in pursuance of this Act within fourteen days after the conclusion of the examination of the debtor or such further time as the Court may allow, the Court shall adjudge the debtor bankrupt ; and thereupon the property of the bankrupt shall become divisible among his creditors and shall vest in a trustee.

*Adjudication of bankruptcy where composition not accepted or approved.*

(2.) Notice of every order adjudging a debtor bankrupt, stating the name, address, and description of the bankrupt, the date of the adjudication, and the Court by which the adjudication is made, shall be gazetted and advertised in a local paper in the prescribed manner, and the date of the order shall for the purposes of this Act be the date of the adjudication.

21. (1.) Where a debtor is adjudged bankrupt, or the creditors have resolved that he be adjudged bankrupt, the creditors may, by ordinary resolution, appoint some fit person, whether a creditor or not, to fill the office of trustee of the property of the bankrupt ; or they may resolve to leave his appointment to the committee of inspection hereinafter mentioned.

*Appointment of trustee.*

(2.) The person so appointed shall give security in manner prescribed to the satisfaction of the Board of Trade, and the Board, if satisfied with the security, shall certify that his appointment has been duly made, unless they object to the appointment on the ground that it has not been made in good faith by a majority in value of the creditors voting, or that the person appointed is not fit to act as trustee, or that his connexion with or relation to the bankrupt or his estate or any particular creditor makes it difficult for him to act with impartiality in the interests of the creditors generally.

(3.) Provided that where the Board make any such objection they shall, if so requested by a majority in value of the creditors, notify the objection to the High Court, and thereupon the High Court may decide on its validity.

(4.) The appointment of a trustee shall take effect as from the date of the certificate.

(5.) The official receiver shall not, save as by this Act provided, be the trustee of the bankrupt's property.

(6.) If a trustee is not appointed by the creditors within four weeks from the date of the adjudication, or, in the event of negotiations for a composition or scheme being pending at the expiration of those four weeks, then within seven days from the close of those negotiations by the refusal of the creditors to accept, or of the Court to approve, the composition or scheme, the official receiver shall report the matter to the Board of Trade, and thereupon the Board of Trade shall appoint some fit person to be trustee of the bankrupt's property, and shall certify the appointment.

(7.) Provided that the creditors or the committee of inspection (if so authorized by resolution of the creditors) may, at any subsequent time, if they think fit, appoint a trustee, and on the appointment being made and certified the person appointed shall become trustee in the place of the person appointed by the Board of Trade.

(8.) When a debtor is adjudged bankrupt after the first meeting of creditors has been held, and a trustee has not been appointed prior to the adjudication, the official receiver shall forthwith summon a meeting of creditors for the purpose of appointing a trustee.

**Committee of inspection.**

**22.** (1.) The creditors, qualified to vote, may at their first or any subsequent meeting, by resolution, appoint from among the creditors qualified to vote, or the holders of general proxies or general powers of attorney from such creditors, a committee of inspection for the purpose of superintending the administration of the bankrupt's property by the trustee. The committee of inspection shall consist of not more than five nor less than three persons.

(2.) The committee of inspection shall meet at such times as they shall from time to time appoint, and failing such appointment, at least once a month; and the trustee or any member of the committee may also call a meeting of the committee as and when he thinks necessary.

(3.) The committee may act by a majority of their members present at a meeting, but shall not act unless a majority of the committee are present at the meeting.

(4.) Any member of the committee may resign his office by notice in writing signed by him, and delivered to the trustee.

(5.) If a member of the committee becomes bankrupt, or compounds or arranges with his creditors, or is absent from five consecutive meetings of the committee, his office shall thereupon become vacant.

(6.) Any member of the committee may be removed by an ordinary resolution at any meeting of creditors of which seven days notice has been given, stating the object of the meeting.

(7.) On a vacancy occurring in the office of a member of the committee, the trustee shall forthwith summon a meeting of creditors for the purpose of filling the vacancy, and the meeting may, by resolution, appoint another creditor or other person eligible as above to fill the vacancy.

(8.) The continuing members of the committee, provided there be not less than two such continuing members, may act notwithstanding any vacancy in their body; and where the number of members of the committee of inspection is for the time being less than five, the creditors may increase that number, so that it do not exceed five.

(9.) If there be no committee of inspection, any act or thing or any direction or permission by this Act authorized or required to be done or given by the committee may be done or given by the Board of Trade on the application of the trustee.

**Power to accept composition or scheme after bankruptcy adjudication.**

**23.** (1.) Where a debtor is adjudged bankrupt the creditors may, if they think fit, at any time after the adjudication, by special resolution, resolve to entertain a proposal for a composition in satisfaction of the debts due to them under the bankruptcy, or for a scheme of arrangement of the bankrupt's affairs; and thereupon the same proceedings shall be taken and the same consequences shall ensue as in the case of a composition or scheme accepted before adjudication.

(2.) If the Court approves the composition or scheme it may make an order annulling the bankruptcy and vesting the property of the bankrupt in him

or in such other person as the Court may appoint, on such terms, and subject to such conditions, if any, as the Court may declare.

(3.) If default is made in payment of any instalment due in pursuance of
the composition or scheme, or if it appears to the Court that the composition
or scheme cannot proceed without injustice or undue delay, or that the
approval of the Court was obtained by fraud, the Court may, if it thinks fit,
on application by any person interested, adjudge the debtor bankrupt,
and annul the composition or scheme, but without prejudice to the validity
of any sale, disposition, or payment duly made, or thing duly done, under
or in pursuance of the composition or scheme. Where a debtor is adjudged
bankrupt under this sub-section, all debts, provable in other respects, which
have been contracted before the date of such adjudication shall be provable
in the bankruptcy.

*Control over Person and Property of Debtor.*

**24.** (1.) Every debtor against whom a receiving order is made shall, unless prevented by sickness or other sufficient cause, attend the first meeting
of his creditors, and shall submit to such examination and give such information as the meeting may require.

(2.) He shall give such inventory of his property, such list of his creditors
and debtors, and of the debts due to and from them respectively, submit to
such examination in respect of his property or his creditors, attend such other
meetings of his creditors, wait at such times on the official receiver, special
manager, or trustee, execute such powers of attorney, conveyances, deeds,
and instruments, and generally do all such acts and things in relation to his
property and the distribution of the proceeds amongst his creditors, as may be
reasonably required by the official receiver, special manager, or trustee, or
may be prescribed by general rules, or be directed by the Court by any special
order or orders made in reference to any particular case, or made on the occasion of any special application by the official receiver, special manager,
trustee, or any creditor or person interested.

(3.) He shall, if adjudged bankrupt, aid, to the utmost of his power, in the
realisation of his property and the distribution of the proceeds among his
creditors.

(4.) If a debtor wilfully fails to perform the duties imposed on him by this
section, or to deliver up possession of any part of his property, which is divisible amongst his creditors under this Act, and which is for the time being in
his possession or under his control, to the official receiver or to the trustee, or
to any person authorized by the Court to take possession of it, he shall, in
addition to any other punishment to which he may be subject, be guilty of a
contempt of court, and may be punished accordingly.

**25.** (1.) The Court may, by warrant addressed to any constable or
prescribed officer of the Court, cause a debtor to be arrested, and any books,
papers, money, and goods in his possession to be seized, and him and them to
be safely kept as prescribed until such time as the Court may order under the
following circumstances:

(a.) If after a bankruptcy notice has been issued under this Act, or after
presentation of a bankruptcy petition by or against him, it appears
to the Court that there is probable reason for believing that he
is about to abscond with a view of avoiding payment of the debt in
respect of which the bankruptcy notice was issued, or of avoiding
service of a bankruptcy petition, or of avoiding appearance to any
such petition, or of avoiding examination in respect of his affairs, or
of otherwise avoiding, delaying, or embarrassing proceedings in
bankruptcy against him.

(b.) If, after presentation of a bankruptcy petition by or against him, it
appears to the Court that there is probable cause for believing that
he is about to remove his goods with a view of preventing or delaying
possession being taken of them by the official receiver or trustee, or
that there is probable ground for believing that he has concealed or
is about to conceal or destroy any of his goods, or any books, documents, or writings, which might be of use to his creditors in the
course of his bankruptcy.

(c.) If, after service of a bankruptcy petition on him, or after a receiving
order is made against him, he removes any goods in his possession

*Marginal notes:*

Duties of debtor
as to discovery
and realization
of property.

Arrest of debtor
under certain
circumstances.

above the value of five pounds, without the leave of the official receiver or trustee.

(*d.*) If, without good cause shown, he fails to attend any examination ordered by the Court.

Provided that no arrest upon a bankruptcy notice shall be valid and protected unless the debtor before or at the time of his arrest shall be served with such bankruptcy notice.

(2.) No payment or composition made or security given after arrest made under this section shall be exempt from the provisions of this Act relating to fraudulent preferences.

Re-direction of debtor's letters.
    **26.** Where a receiving order is made against a debtor, the Court, on the application of the official receiver or trustee, may from time to time order that for such time, not exceeding three months, as the Court thinks fit, post letters addressed to the debtor at any place, or places, mentioned in the order for re-direction shall be re-directed, sent or delivered by the Postmaster-General, or the officers acting under him, to the official receiver, or the trustee, or otherwise as the Court directs, and the same shall be done accordingly.

Discovery of debtor's property.
    **27.** (1.) The Court may, on the application of the official receiver or trustee, at any time after a receiving order has been made against a debtor, summon before it the debtor or his wife, or any person known or suspected to have in his possession any of the estate or effects belonging to the debtor, or supposed to be indebted to the debtor, or any person whom the Court may deem capable of giving information respecting the debtor, his dealings or property, and the Court may require any such person to produce any documents in his custody or power relating to the debtor, his dealings or property.

(2.) If any person so summoned, after having been tendered a reasonable sum, refuses to come before the Court at the time appointed, or refuses to produce any such document, having no lawful impediment made known to the Court at the time of its sitting and allowed by it, the Court may, by warrant, cause him to be apprehended and brought up for examination.

(3.) The Court may examine on oath, either by word of mouth or by written interrogatories, any person so brought before it concerning the debtor, his dealings or property.

(4.) If any person on examination before the Court admits that he is indebted to the debtor, the Court may, on the application of the official receiver or trustee, order him to pay to the receiver or trustee, at such time and in such manner as to the Court seems expedient, the amount admitted, or any part thereof, either in full discharge of the whole amount in question or not, as the Court thinks fit, with or without costs of the examination.

(5.) If any person on examination before the Court admits that he has in his possession any property belonging to the debtor, the Court may, on the application of the official receiver or trustee, order him to deliver to the official receiver or trustee such property, or any part thereof, at such time, and in such manner, and on such terms as to the Court may seem just.

(6.) The Court may, if it think fit, order that any person who if in England would be liable to be brought before it under this section shall be examined in Scotland or Ireland, or in any other place out of England.

### *Discharge of Bankrupt.*

Discharge of bankrupt.
    **28.** (1.) A bankrupt may, at any time after being adjudged bankrupt, apply to the Court for an order of discharge, and the Court shall appoint a day for hearing the application, but the application shall not be heard until the public examination of the bankrupt is concluded. The application shall be heard in open Court.

(2.) On the hearing of the application the Court shall take into consideration a report of the official receiver as to the bankrupt's conduct and affairs, and may either grant or refuse an absolute order of discharge, or suspend the operation of the order for a specified time, or grant an order of discharge subject to any conditions with respect to any earnings or income which may afterwards become due to the bankrupt, or with respect to his after-acquired property : Provided that the Court shall refuse the discharge in all cases where the bankrupt has committed any misdemeanor under this Act, or Part II. of the Debtors Act, 1869, or any amendment thereof, and shall, on proof of any of the facts hereinafter mentioned, either refuse the order, or suspend the operation of the order for a specified time, or grant an order of discharge, subject to such conditions as aforesaid.

(3.) The facts hereinbefore referred to are—

(a) That the bankrupt has omitted to keep such books of account as are usual and proper in the business carried on by him and as sufficiently disclose his business transactions and financial position within the three years immediately preceding his bankruptcy :

(b) That the bankrupt has continued to trade after knowing himself to be insolvent :

(c) That the bankrupt has contracted any debt provable in the bankruptcy, without having at the time of contracting it any reasonable or probable ground of expectation (proof whereof shall lie on him) of being able to pay it :

(d) That the bankrupt has brought on his bankruptcy by rash and hazardous speculations or unjustifiable extravagance in living :

(e) That the bankrupt has put any of his creditors to unnecessary expense by a frivolous or vexatious defence to any action properly brought against him :

(f) That the bankrupt has within three months preceding the date of the receiving order, when unable to pay his debts as they become due, given an undue preference to any of his creditors :

(g) That the bankrupt has on any previous occasion been adjudged bankrupt, or made a [statutory] (a) composition or arrangement with his creditors :

(h) That the bankrupt has been guilty of any fraud or fraudulent breach of trust :

(4.) For the purposes of this section the report of the official receiver shall be primâ facie evidence of the statements therein contained.

(5.) Notice of the appointment by the Court of the day for hearing the application for discharge shall be published in the prescribed manner and sent fourteen days at least before the day so appointed to each creditor who has proved, and the Court may hear the official receiver and the trustee, and may also hear any creditor. At the hearing the Court may put such questions to the debtor and receive such evidence as it may think fit.

(6.) The Court may, as one of the conditions referred to in this section, require the bankrupt to consent to judgment being entered against him by the official receiver or trustee for any balance of the debts provable under the bankruptcy which is not satisfied at the date of his discharge ; but in such case execution shall not be issued on the judgment without leave of the Court, which leave may be given on proof that the bankrupt has since his discharge acquired property or income available for payment of his debts.

(7.) A discharged bankrupt shall, notwithstanding his discharge, give such assistance as the trustee may require in the realization and distribution of such of his property as is vested in the trustee, and if he fails to do so he shall be guilty of a contempt of Court ; and the Court may also, if it thinks fit, revoke his discharge, but without prejudice to the validity of any sale, disposition, or payment duly made or thing duly done subsequent to the discharge, but before its revocation.

29. In either of the following cases ; that is to say,

Fraudulent settlements.

(1.) In the case of a settlement made before and in consideration of marriage where the settlor is not at the time of making the settlement able to pay all his debts without the aid of the property comprised in the settlement ; or

(2.) In the case of any covenant or contract made in consideration of marriage for the future settlement on or for the settlor's wife or children of any money or property wherein he had not at the date of his marriage any estate or interest (not being money or property of or in right of his wife) ;

If the settlor is adjudged bankrupt or compounds or arranges with his creditors, and it appears to the Court that such settlement, covenant, or contract was made in order to defeat or delay creditors, or was unjustifiable having regard to the state of the settlor's affairs at the time when it was made, the Court may refuse or suspend an order of discharge, or grant an

(a) See 50 & 51 Vict. c. 57, s. 16.

order subject to conditions, or refuse to approve a composition or arrangement, as the case may be, in like manner as in cases where the debtor has been guilty of fraud.

Effect of order of discharge.

**30.** (1.) An order of discharge shall not release the bankrupt from any debt on a recognizance nor from any debt with which the bankrupt may be chargeable at the suit of the Crown or of any person for any offence against a statute relating to any branch of the public revenue, or at the suit of the sheriff or other public officer on a bail bond entered into for the appearance of any person prosecuted for any such offence: and he shall not be discharged from such excepted debts unless the Treasury certify in writing their consent to his being discharged therefrom. An order of discharge shall not release the bankrupt from any debt or liability incurred by means of any fraud or fraudulent breach of trust to which he was a party, nor from any debt or liability whereof he has obtained forbearance by any fraud to which he was a party.

(2.) An order of discharge shall release the bankrupt from all other debts provable in bankruptcy.

(3.) An order of discharge shall be conclusive evidence of the bankruptcy, and of the validity of the proceedings therein, and in any proceedings that may be instituted against a bankrupt who has obtained an order of discharge in respect of any debt from which he is released by the order, the bankrupt may plead that the cause of action occurred before his discharge, and may give this Act and the special matter in evidence.

(4.) An order of discharge shall not release any person who at the date of the receiving order was a partner or co-trustee with the bankrupt or was jointly bound or had made any joint contract with him, or any person who was surety or in the nature of a surety for him.

Undischarged bankrupt obtaining credit to extent of 20l. to be guilty of misdemeanor.

**31.** Where an undischarged bankrupt who has been adjudged bankrupt under this Act obtains credit to the extent of twenty pounds or upwards from any person without informing such person that he is an undischarged bankrupt, he shall be guilty of a misdemeanor, and may be dealt with and punished as if he had been guilty of a misdemeanor under the Debtors Act, 1869, and the provisions of that Act shall apply to proceedings under this section.

---

# PART II.

## DISQUALIFICATIONS OF BANKRUPT.

Disqualifications of bankrupt.

**32.** (1.) Where a debtor is adjudged bankrupt he shall, subject to the provisions of this Act, be disqualified for—

(a) Sitting or voting in the House of Lords, or on any committee thereof, or being elected as a peer of Scotland or Ireland to sit and vote in the House of Lords ;

(b) Being elected to, or sitting or voting in, the House of Commons, or on any committee thereof ;

(c) Being appointed or acting as a justice of the peace ;

(d) Being elected to or holding or exercising the office of mayor, alderman, or councillor ;

(e) Being elected to or holding or exercising the office of guardian of the poor, overseer of the poor, member of a sanitary authority, or member of a school board, highway board, burial board, or select vestry.

(2.) The disqualifications to which a bankrupt is subject under this section shall be removed and cease if and when,—

(a) the adjudication of bankruptcy against him is annulled ; or

(b) he obtains from the Court his discharge with a certificate to the effect that his bankruptcy was caused by misfortune without any misconduct on his part.

The Court may grant or withhold such certificate as it thinks fit, but any refusal of such certificate shall be subject to appeal.

(3.) The disqualifications imposed by this section shall extend to all parts of the United Kingdom.

**33.** (1.) If a member of the House of Commons is adjudged bankrupt, and the disqualifications arising therefrom under this Act are not removed within six months from the date of the order, the Court shall, immediately after the expiration of that time, certify the same to the Speaker of the House of Commons, and thereupon the seat of the member shall be vacant.

*Vacating of seat in House of Commons.*

(2.) Where the seat of a member so becomes vacant, the Speaker, during a recess of the House, whether by prorogation or by adjournment, shall forthwith, after receiving the certificate, cause notice thereof to be published in the London Gazette; and after the expiration of six days after the publication shall (unless the House has met before that day, or will meet on the day of the issue), issue his warrant to the clerk of the Crown to make out a new writ for electing another member in the room of the member whose seat has so become vacant.

(3.) The powers of the act of the twenty-fourth year of the reign of King George the Third, chapter twenty-six, "to repeal so much of two Acts made in the tenth and fifteenth years of the reign of his present Majesty as authorises the Speaker of the House of Commons to issue his warrant to the clerk of the Crown for making out writs for the election of members to serve in Parliament in the manner therein mentioned; and for substituting other provisions for the like purposes," so far as those powers enable the Speaker to nominate and appoint other persons, being members of the House of Commons, to issue warrants for the making out of new writs during the vacancy of the office of Speaker, or during his absence out of the realm, shall extend to enable him to make the like nomination and appointment for issuing warrants, under the like circumstances and conditions, for the election of a member in the room of any member whose seat becomes vacant under this Act.

**34.** If a person is adjudged bankrupt whilst holding the office of mayor, alderman, councillor, guardian, overseer, or member of a sanitary authority, school board, highway board, burial board, or select vestry, his office shall thereupon become vacant.

*Vacating of municipal and other offices.*

**35.** (1.) Where in the opinion of the Court a debtor ought not to have been adjudged bankrupt, or where it is proved to the satisfaction of the Court that the debts of the bankrupt are paid in full, the Court may, on the application of any person interested, by order, annul the adjudication.

*Power for court to annul adjudication in certain cases.*

(2.) Where an adjudication is annulled under this section all sales and dispositions of property and payments duly made, and all acts theretofore done, by the official receiver, trustee, or other person acting under their authority, or by the Court, shall be valid, but the property of the debtor who was adjudged bankrupt shall vest in such person as the Court may appoint, or in default of any such appointment revert to the debtor for all his estate or interest therein on such terms and subject to such conditions, if any, as the Court may declare by order.

(3.) Notice of the order annulling an adjudication shall be forthwith gazetted and published in a local paper.

**36.** For the purposes of this part of this Act, any debt disputed by a debtor shall be considered as paid in full, if the debtor enters into a bond, in such sum and with such sureties as the Court approves, to pay the amount to be recovered in any proceeding for the recovery of or concerning the debt, with costs, and any debt due to a creditor who cannot be found or cannot be identified shall be considered as paid in full if paid into Court.

*Meaning of payment of debts in full.*

---

## PART III.

### Administration of Property.

### *Proof of Debts.*

**37.** (1.) Demands in the nature of unliquidated damages arising otherwise than by reason of a contract, promise, or breach of trust, shall not be provable in bankruptcy.

*Description of debts provable in bankruptcy.*

(2.) A person having notice of any act of bankruptcy available against the debtor shall not prove under the order for any debt or liability contracted by the debtor subsequently to the date of his so having notice.

(3). Save as aforesaid, all debts and liabilities, present or future, certain or contingent, to which the debtor is subject at the date of the receiving order, or to which he may become subject before his discharge by reason of any obligation incurred before the date of the receiving order, shall be deemed to be debts provable in bankruptcy.

(4.) An estimate shall be made by the trustee of the value of any debt or liability provable as aforesaid, which by reason of its being subject to any contingency or contingencies, or for any other reason, does not bear a certain value.

(5.) Any person aggrieved by any estimate made by the trustee as aforesaid may appeal to the Court.

(6.) If, in the opinion of the Court, the value of the debt or liability is incapable of being fairly estimated, the Court may make an order to that effect, and thereupon the debt or liability shall, for the purposes of this Act, be deemed to be a debt not provable in bankruptcy.

(7.) If, in the opinion of the Court, the value of the debt or liability is capable of being fairly estimated, the Court may direct the value to be assessed, before the Court itself without the intervention of a jury, and may give all necessary directions for this purpose, and the amount of the value when assessed shall be deemed to be a debt provable in bankruptcy.

(8.) "Liability" shall for the purposes of this Act include any compensation for work or labour done, any obligation or possibility of an obligation to pay money or money's worth on the breach of any express or implied covenant, contract, agreement, or undertaking, whether the breach does or does not occur, or is or is not likely to occur or capable of occurring before the discharge of the debtor, and generally it shall include any express or implied engagement, agreement, or undertaking, to pay, or capable of resulting in the payment of money, or money's worth, whether the payment is, as respects amount, fixed or unliquidated; as respects time, present or future, certain or dependent on any one contingency or on two or more contingencies; as to mode of valuation capable of being ascertained by fixed rules, or as matter of opinion.

**Mutual credit and set-off.**

38. Where there have been mutual credits, mutual debts, or other mutual dealings between a debtor against whom a receiving order shall be made under this Act, and any other person proving or claiming to prove a debt under such receiving order, an account shall be taken of what is due from the one party to the other in respect of such mutual dealings, and the sum due from the one party shall be set off against any sum due from the other party, and the balance of the account, and no more, shall be claimed or paid on either side respectively; but a person shall not be entitled under this section to claim the benefit of any set-off against the property of a debtor in any case where he had at the time of giving credit to the debtor, notice of an act of bankruptcy committed by the debtor, and available against him.

**Rules as to proof of debts.**

39. With respect to the mode of proving debts, the right of proof by secured and other creditors, the admission and rejection of proofs, and the other matters referred to in the Second Schedule, the rules in that schedule shall be observed.

**Priority of debts.**

40. (1.) In the distribution of the property of a bankrupt there shall be paid in priority to all other debts,—

(a) All parochial or other local rates due from the bankrupt at the date of the receiving order, and having become due and payable within twelve months next before such time, and all assessed taxes, land tax, property or income tax, assessed on him up to the fifth day of April next before the date of the receiving order, and not exceeding in the whole one year's assessment;

(b) All wages or salary of any clerk or servant in respect of services rendered to the bankrupt during four months before the date of the receiving order, not exceeding fifty pounds; and

(c) All wages of any labourer or workman, not exceeding fifty pounds, whether payable for time or piece-work, in respect of services rendered to the bankrupt during four months before the date of the receiving order.

(2.) The foregoing debts shall rank equally between themselves, and shall be paid in full, unless the property of the bankrupt is insufficient to meet them, in which case they shall abate in equal proportions between them-- selves.

(3.) In the case of partners the joint estate shall be applicable in the first instance in payment of their joint debts, and the separate estate of each partner shall be applicable in the first instance in payment of his separate debts. If there is a surplus of the separate estates it shall be dealt with as part of the joint estate. If there is a surplus of the joint estate it shall be dealt with as part of the respective separate estates in proportion to the right and interest of each partner in the joint estate.

(4.) Subject to the provisions of this Act all debts proved in the bankruptcy shall be paid pari passu.

(5.) If there is any surplus after payment of the foregoing debts, it shall be applied in payment of interest from the date of the receiving order at the rate of four pounds per centum per annum on all debts proved in the bankruptcy.

(6.) Nothing in this section shall alter the effect of section five of the Act twenty-eight and twenty-nine Victoria, chapter eighty-six, "to amend the Law of Partnership," or shall prejudice the provisions of the Friendly Societies Act, 1875. *38 & 39 Vict. c. 60.*

**41.** (1.) Where at the time of the presentation of the bankruptcy petition any person is apprenticed or is an articled clerk to the bankrupt, the adjudication of bankruptcy shall, if either the bankrupt or apprentice or clerk gives notice in writing to the trustee to that effect, be a complete discharge of the indenture of apprenticeship or articles of agreement; and if any money has been paid by or on behalf of the apprentice or clerk to the bankrupt as a fee, the trustee may, on the application of the apprentice or clerk, or of some person on his behalf, pay such sum as the trustee, subject to an appeal to the Court, thinks reasonable, out of the bankrupt's property, to or for the use of the apprentice or clerk, regard being had to the amount paid by him or on his behalf, and to the time during which he served with the bankrupt under the indenture or articles before the commencement of the bankruptcy, and to the other circumstances of the case. *Preferential claim in case of apprenticeship.*

(2.) Where it appears expedient to a trustee, he may, on the application of any apprentice or articled clerk to the bankrupt, or any person acting on behalf of such apprentice or articled clerk, instead of acting under the preceding provisions of this section, transfer the indenture of apprenticeship or articles of agreement to some other person.

**42.** (1.) The landlord or other person to whom any rent is due from the bankrupt may at any time either before or after the commencement of the bankruptcy, distrain upon the goods or effects of the bankrupt for the rent due to him from the bankrupt, with this limitation, that if such distress for rent be levied after the commencement of the bankruptcy it shall be available only for one year's rent accrued due prior to the date of the order of adjudication, but the landlord or other person to whom the rent may be due from the bankrupt may prove under the bankruptcy for the surplus due for which the distress may not have been available. *Power to landlord to distrain for rent.*

(2.) For the purposes of this section the term "order of adjudication" shall be deemed to include an order for the administration of the estate of a debtor whose debts do not exceed fifty pounds, or of a deceased person who dies insolvent.

### *Property available for Payment of Debts.*

**43.** The bankruptcy of a debtor, whether the same takes place on the debtor's own petition or upon that of a creditor or creditors, shall be deemed to have relation back to, and to commence at, the time of the act of bankruptcy being committed on which a receiving order is made against him, or, if the bankrupt is proved to have committed more acts of bankruptcy than one, to have relation back to, and to commence at, the time of the first of the acts of bankruptcy proved to have been committed by the bankrupt within three months next preceding the date of the presentation of the bankruptcy petition; but no bankruptcy petition, receiving order, or adjudication shall be rendered invalid by reason of any act of bankruptcy anterior to the debt of the petitioning creditor. *Relation back of trustee's title.*

**44.** The property of the bankrupt divisible amongst his creditors, and in this *Description of* bankrupt's property divisible amongst creditors.

Act referred to as the property of the bankrupt, shall not comprise the following particulars :

(1.) Property held by the bankrupt on trust for any other person :

(2.) The tools (if any) of his trade and the necessary wearing apparel and bedding of himself, his wife and children, to a value, inclusive of tools and apparel and bedding, not exceeding twenty pounds in the whole :

But it shall comprise the following particulars :

(i.) All such property as may belong to or be vested in the bankrupt at the commencement of the bankruptcy, or may be acquired by or devolve on him before his discharge ; and

(ii.) The capacity to exercise and to take proceedings for exercising all such powers in or over or in respect of property as might have been exercised by the bankrupt for his own benefit at the commencement of his bankruptcy or before his discharge, except the right of nomination to a vacant ecclesiastical benefice ; and,

(iii.) All goods being, at the commencement of the bankruptcy, in the possession, order or disposition of the bankrupt, in his trade or business, by the consent and permission of the true owner, under such circumstances that he is the reputed owner thereof ; provided that things in action other than debts due or growing due to the bankrupt in the course of his trade or business, shall not be deemed goods within the meaning of this section.

### Effect of Bankruptcy on antecedent Transactions.

Restriction of rights of creditor under execution or attachment.

**45.** (1.) Where a creditor has issued execution against the goods or lands of a debtor, or has attached any debt due to him, he shall not be entitled to retain the benefit of the execution or attachment against the trustee in bankruptcy of the debtor, unless he has completed the execution or attachment before the date of the receiving order, and before notice of the presentation of any bankruptcy petition by or against the debtor, or of the commission of any available act of bankruptcy by the debtor.

(2.) For the purposes of this Act, an execution against goods is completed by seizure and sale ; an attachment of a debt is completed by receipt of the debt ; and an execution against land is completed by seizure, or, in the case of an equitable interest, by the appointment of a receiver.

Duties of sheriff as to goods taken in execution.

**46.** (1.) Where the goods of a debtor are taken in execution, and before the sale thereof notice is served on the sheriff that a receiving order has been made against the debtor, the sheriff shall, on request, deliver the goods to the official receiver or trustee under the order, but the costs of the execution shall be a charge on the goods so delivered, and the official receiver or trustee may sell the goods or an adequate part thereof for the purpose of satisfying the charge.

(2.) Where the goods of a debtor are sold under an execution in respect of a judgment for a sum exceeding twenty pounds, the sheriff shall deduct the costs of the execution from the proceeds of sale, and retain the balance for fourteen days, and if within that time notice is served on him of a bankruptcy petition having been presented against or by the debtor, and the debtor is adjudged bankrupt thereon or on any other petition of which the sheriff has notice, the sheriff shall pay the balance to the trustee in the bankruptcy, who shall be entitled to retain the same as against the execution creditor, but otherwise he shall deal with it as if no notice of the presentation of a bankruptcy petition had been served on him.

(3.) An execution levied by seizure and sale on the goods of a debtor is not invalid by reason only of its being an act of bankruptcy, and a person who purchases the goods in good faith under a sale by the sheriff shall in all cases acquire a good title to them against the trustee in bankruptcy.

Avoidance of voluntary settlements.

**47.** (1.) Any settlement of property not being a settlement made before and in consideration of marriage, or made in favour of a purchaser or incumbrancer in good faith and for valuable consideration, or a settlement made on or for the wife or children of the settlor of property which has accrued to the settlor after marriage in right of his wife, shall, if the settlor becomes bankrupt within two years after the date of the settlement, be void against the trustee in the bankruptcy, and shall, if the settlor becomes bankrupt at any subsequent time within ten years after the date of the settlement, be void against the trustee in the bankruptcy, unless the parties claiming under the settlement can prove that the settlor was at the time of making the settlement able to pay all his debts without the aid of the property comprised in the settlement, and that the interest of the settlor in such property had passed to the trustee of such settlement on the execution thereof.

(2.) Any covenant or contract made in consideration of marriage, for the future settlement on or for the settlor's wife or children of any money or property wherein he had not at the date of his marriage any estate or interest, whether vested or contingent in possession or remainder and not being money or property of or in right of his wife, shall, on his becoming bankrupt before the property or money has been actually transferred or paid pursuant to the contract or covenant, be void against the trustee in the bankruptcy.

(3.) "Settlement" shall for the purposes of this section include any conveyance or transfer of property.

**48.** (1.) Every conveyance or transfer of property, or charge thereon made, every payment made, every obligation incurred, and every judicial proceeding taken or suffered by any person unable to pay his debts as they become due from his own money in favour of any creditor, or any person in trust for any creditor, with a view of giving such creditor a preference over the other creditors shall, if the person making, taking, paying, or suffering the same is adjudged bankrupt on a bankruptcy petition presented within three months after the date of making, taking, paying, or suffering the same, be deemed fraudulent and void as against the trustee in the bankruptcy. *Avoidance of preferences in certain cases.*

(2.) This section shall not affect the rights of any person making title in good faith and for valuable consideration through or under a creditor of the bankrupt.

**49.** Subject to the foregoing provisions of this Act with respect to the effect of bankruptcy on an execution or attachment, and with respect to the avoidance of certain settlements and preferences, nothing in this Act shall invalidate, in the case of a bankruptcy— *Protection of bonâ fide transactions without notice.*

(a) Any payment by the bankrupt to any of his creditors,

(b) Any payment or delivery to the bankrupt,

(c) Any conveyance or assignment by the bankrupt for valuable consideration,

(d) Any contract, dealing, or transaction by or with the bankrupt for valuable consideration,

Provided that both the following conditions are complied with, namely—

(1.) The payment, delivery, conveyance, assignment, contract, dealing, or transaction, as the case may be, takes place before the date of the receiving order: and

(2.) The person (other than the debtor) to, by, or with whom the payment, delivery, conveyance, assignment, contract, dealing, or transaction was made, executed, or entered into, has not at the time of the payment, delivery, conveyance, assignment, contract, dealing, or transaction, notice of any available act of bankruptcy committed by the bankrupt before that time.

### Realisation of Property.

**50.** (1.) The trustee shall, as soon as may be, take possession of the deeds, books, and documents of the bankrupt, and all other parts of his property capable of manual delivery. *Possession of property by trustee.*

(2.) The trustee shall, in relation to and for the purpose of acquiring or retaining possession of the property of the bankrupt, be in the same position as if he were a receiver of the property appointed by the High Court, and the Court may on his application, enforce such acquisition or retention accordingly.

(3.) Where any part of the property of the bankrupt consists of stock, shares in ships, shares, or any other property transferable in the books of any company, office, or person, the trustee may exercise the right to transfer the property to the same extent as the bankrupt might have exercised it if he had not become bankrupt.

(4.) Where any part of the property of the bankrupt is of copyhold or customary tenure, or is any like property passing by surrender and admittance or in any similar manner, the trustee shall not be compellable to be admitted to the property, but may deal with it in the same manner as if it had been capable of being and had been duly surrendered or otherwise conveyed to such uses as the trustee may appoint; and any appointee of the trustee shall be admitted to or otherwise invested with the property accordingly.

(5.) Where any part of the property of the bankrupt consists of things in action, such things shall be deemed to have been duly assigned to the trustee.

(6.) Any treasurer or other officer, or any banker, attorney, or agent of a bankrupt, shall pay and deliver to the trustee all money and securities in his possession or power, as such officer, banker, attorney, or agent, which he is not by law entitled to retain as against the bankrupt or the trustee. If he does not he shall be guilty of a contempt of court, and may be punished accordingly on the application of the trustee.

**51.** Any person acting under warrant of the Court may seize any part of the property of a bankrupt in the custody or possession of the bankrupt, or of any other person, and with a view to such seizure may break open any house, building, or room of the bankrupt where the bankrupt is supposed to be, or any building or receptacle of the bankrupt where any of his property is supposed to be; and where the Court is satisfied that there is reason to believe that property of the bankrupt is concealed in a house or place not belonging to him, the Court may, if it thinks fit, grant a search warrant to any constable or officer of the Court, who may execute it according to its tenor.

**52.** (1.) Where a bankrupt is a beneficed clergyman, the trustee may apply for a sequestration of the profits of the benefice, and the certificate of the appointment of the trustee shall be sufficient authority for the granting of sequestration without any writ or other proceeding, and the same shall accordingly be issued as on a writ of levari facias founded on a judgment against the bankrupt, and shall have priority over any other sequestration issued after the commencement of the bankruptcy in respect of a debt provable in the bankruptcy, except a sequestration issued before the date of the receiving order by or on behalf of a person who at the time of the issue thereof had not notice of an act of bankruptcy committed by the bankrupt, and available for grounding a receiving order against him.

(2.) The bishop of the diocese in which the benefice is situate may, if he thinks fit, appoint to the bankrupt such or the like stipend as he might by law have appointed to a curate duly licensed to serve the benefice in case the bankrupt had been non-resident, and the sequestrator shall pay the sum so appointed out of the profits of the benefice to the bankrupt, by quarterly instalments while he performs the duties of the benefice.

(3.) The sequestrator shall also pay out of the profits of the benefice the salary payable to any duly licensed curate of the church of the benefice in respect of duties performed by him as such during four months before the date of the receiving order not exceeding fifty pounds.

(4.) Nothing in this section shall prejudice the operation of the Ecclesiastical Dilapidations Act, 1871, or the Sequestration Act, 1871, or any mortgage or charge duly created under any Act of Parliament before the commencement of the bankruptcy on the profits of the benefice.

**53.** (1.) Where a bankrupt is an officer of the army or navy, or an officer or clerk or otherwise employed or engaged in the civil service of the Crown, the trustee shall receive for distribution amongst the creditors so much of the bankrupt's pay or salary as the Court, on the application of the trustee, with the consent of the chief officer of the department under which the pay or salary is enjoyed, may direct. Before making any order under this subsection the Court shall communicate with the chief officer of the department as to the amount, time, and manner of the payment to the trustee, and shall obtain the written consent of the chief officer to the terms of such payment.

(2.) Where a bankrupt is in the receipt of a salary or income other than as aforesaid, or is entitled to any half pay, or pension, or to any compensation granted by the Treasury, the Court, on the application of the trustee, shall from time to time make such order as it thinks just for the payment of the salary, income, half pay, pension, or compensation, or of any part thereof, to the trustee to be applied by him in such manner as the Court may direct.

(3.) Nothing in this section shall take away or abridge any power of the chief officer of any public department to dismiss a bankrupt, or to declare the pension, half pay, or compensation of any bankrupt to be forfeited.

---

*Margin notes:*

Seizure of property of bankrupt.

Sequestration of ecclesiastical benefice.

34 & 35 Vict. c. 43.
34 & 35 Vict. c. 45.

Appropriation of portion of pay or salary to creditors.

**54.** (1.) Until a trustee is appointed the official receiver shall be the trustee Vesting and transfer of property. for the purposes of this Act, and immediately on a debtor being adjudged bankrupt, the property of the bankrupt shall vest in the trustee.

(2.) On the appointment of a trustee the property shall forthwith pass to and vest in the trustee appointed.

(3.) The property of the bankrupt shall pass from trustee to trustee, including under that term the official receiver when he fills the office of trustee, and shall vest in the trustee for the time being during his continuance in office, without any conveyance, assignment, or transfer whatever.

(4 ) The certificate of appointment of a trustee shall, for all purposes of any law in force in any part of the British dominions requiring registration, enrolment, or recording of conveyances or assignments of property, be deemed to be a conveyance or assignment of property, and may be registered, enrolled, and recorded accordingly.

**55.** (1.) Where any part of the property of the bankrupt consists of land of Disclaimer of onerous property. any tenure burdened with onerous covenants, of shares or stock in companies, of unprofitable contracts, or of any other property that is unsaleable, or not readily saleable, by reason of its binding the possessor thereof to the performance of any onerous act, or to the payment of any sum of money, the trustee, notwithstanding that he has endeavoured to sell or has taken possession of the property, or exercised any act of ownership in relation thereto, but subject to the provisions of this section, may, by writing signed by him, at any time within three months after the first appointment of a trustee, disclaim the property.

Provided that where any such property shall not have come to the knowledge of the trustee within one month after such appointment, he may disclaim such property at any time within two months after he first became aware thereof.

(2.) The disclaimer shall operate to determine, as from the date of disclaimer, the rights, interests, and liabilities of the bankrupt and his property in or in respect of the property disclaimed, and shall also discharge the trustee from all personal liability in respect of the property disclaimed as from the date when the property vested in him, but shall not, except so far as is necessary for the purpose of releasing the bankrupt and his property and the trustee from liability, affect the rights or liabilities of any other person.

(3.) A trustee shall not be entitled to disclaim a lease without the leave of the Court, except in any cases which may be prescribed by general rules, and the Court may, before or on granting such leave, require such notices to be given to persons interested, and impose such terms as a condition of granting leave, and make such orders with respect to fixtures, tenant's improvements, and other matters arising out of the tenancy as the Court thinks just.

(4.) The trustee shall not be entitled to disclaim any property in pursuance of this section in any case where an application in writing has been made to the trustee by any person interested in the property requiring him to decide whether he will disclaim or not, and the trustee has for a period of twenty-eight days after the receipt of the application, or such extended period as may be allowed by the Court, declined or neglected to give notice whether he disclaims the property or not; and, in the case of a contract, if the trustee, after such application as aforesaid, does not within the said period or extended period disclaim the contract, he shall be deemed to have adopted it.

(5.) The Court may, on the application of any person who is, as against the trustee, entitled to the benefit or subject to the burden of a contract made with the bankrupt, make an order rescinding the contract on such terms as to payment by or to either party of damages for the non-performance of the contract, or otherwise, as to the Court may seem equitable, and any damages payable under the order to any such person may be proved by him as a debt under the bankruptcy.

(6.) The Court may, on application by any person either claiming any interest in any disclaimed property, or under any liability not discharged by this Act in respect of any disclaimed property, and on hearing such persons as it thinks fit, make an order for the vesting of the property in or delivery thereof to any person entitled thereto, or to whom it may seem just that the same should be delivered by way of compensation for such liability as aforesaid, or a trustee for him, and on such terms as the Court thinks just; and on any such vesting order being made, the property comprised therein shall vest accordingly in the person therein named in that behalf without any conveyance or assignment for the purpose.

Provided always, that where the property disclaimed is of a leasehold nature, the Court shall not make a vesting order in favour of any person claiming under the bankrupt, whether as under-lessee or as mortgagee by demise except upon the terms of making such person subject to the same liabilities and obligations as the bankrupt was subject to under the lease in respect of the property at the date when the bankruptcy petition was filed, and any mortgagee or under-lessee declining to accept a vesting order upon such terms shall be excluded from all interest in and security upon the property, and if there shall be no person claiming under the bankrupt who is willing to accept an order upon such terms, the Court shall have power to vest the bankrupt's estate and interest in the property in any person liable either personally or in a representative character, and either alone or jointly with the bankrupt to perform the lessee's covenants in such lease, freed and discharged from all estates, incumbrances, and interests created therein by the bankrupt.

(7.) Any person injured by the operation of a disclaimer under this section shall be deemed to be a creditor of the bankrupt to the extent of the injury, and may accordingly prove the same as a debt under the bankruptcy.

Powers of trustee to deal with property.
**56.** Subject to the provisions of this Act, the trustee may do all or any of the following things:—

(1.) Sell all or any part of the property of the bankrupt (including the goodwill of the business, if any, and the book debts due or growing due to the bankrupt), by public auction or private contract, with power to transfer the whole thereof to any person or company, or to sell the same in parcels:

(2.) Give receipts for any money received by him, which receipts shall effectually discharge the person paying the money from all responsibility in respect of the application thereof:

(3.) Prove, rank, claim, and draw a dividend in respect of any debt due to the bankrupt:

(4.) Exercise any powers the capacity to exercise which is vested in the trustee under this Act, and execute any powers of attorney, deeds, and other instruments, for the purpose of carrying into effect the provisions of this Act:

(5.) Deal with any property to which the bankrupt is beneficially entitled as tenant in tail in the same manner as the bankrupt might have dealt with it; and sections fifty-six to seventy-three (both inclusive) of the Act of the session of the third and fourth years of the reign of King William the Fourth (chapter seventy-four), "for the abolition of fines and recoveries, and for the substitution of more simple modes of assurance," shall extend and apply to proceedings under this Act, as if those sections were here re-enacted and made applicable in terms to those proceedings.

Powers exerciseable by trustee with permission of committee of inspection.
**57.** The trustee may, with the permission of the committee of inspection, do all or any of the following things:

(1.) Carry on the business of the bankrupt, so far as may be necessary for the beneficial winding up of the same:

(2.) Bring, institute, or defend any action or other legal proceeding relating to the property of the bankrupt:

(3.) Employ a solicitor or other agent to take any proceedings or do any business which may be sanctioned by the committee of inspection:

(4.) Accept as the consideration for the sale of any property of the bankrupt a sum of money payable at a future time subject to such stipulations as to security and otherwise as the committee think fit:

(5.) Mortgage or pledge any part of the property of the bankrupt for the purpose of raising money for the payment of his debts:

(6.) Refer any dispute to arbitration, compromise all debts, claims, and liabilities, whether present or future, certain or contingent, liquidated or unliquidated, subsisting or supposed to subsist between the bankrupt and any person who may have incurred any liability to the bankrupt, on the receipt of such sums, payable at such times, and generally on such terms as may be agreed on :

(7.) Make such compromise or other arrangement as may be thought expedient with creditors, or persons claiming to be creditors, in respect of any debts provable under the bankruptcy :

(8.) Make such compromise or other arrangement as may be thought expedient with respect to any claim arising out of or incidental to the property of the bankrupt, made or capable of being made on the trustee by any person or by the trustee on any person :

(9.) Divide in its existing form amongst the creditors, according to its estimated value, any property which from its peculiar nature or other special circumstances cannot be readily or advantageously sold.

The permission given for the purposes of this section shall not be a general permission to do all or any of the above-mentioned things, but shall only be a permission to do the particular thing or things for which permission is sought in the specified case or cases.

### *Distribution of Property.*

**58.** (1.) Subject to the retention of such sums as may be necessary for the costs of administration, or otherwise, the trustee shall, with all convenient speed, declare and distribute dividends amongst the creditors who have proved their debts. *Declaration and distribution of dividends.*

(2.) The first dividend, if any, shall be declared and distributed within four months after the conclusion of the first meeting of creditors, unless the trustee satisfies the committee of inspection that there is sufficient reason for postponing the declaration to a later date.

(3.) Subsequent dividends shall, in the absence of sufficient reason to the contrary, be declared and distributed at intervals of not more than six months.

(4.) Before declaring a dividend the trustee shall cause notice of his intention to do so to be gazetted in the prescribed manner, and shall also send reasonable notice thereof to each creditor mentioned in the bankrupt's statement who has not proved his debt.

(5.) When the trustee has declared a dividend he shall send to each creditor who has proved a notice showing the amount of the dividend and when and how it is payable, and a statement in the prescribed form as to the particulars of the estate.

**59.** (1.) Where one partner of a firm is adjudged bankrupt, a creditor to whom the bankrupt is indebted jointly with the other partners of the firm, or any of them, shall not receive any dividend out of the separate property of the bankrupt until all the separate creditors have received the full amount of their respective debts. *Joint and separate dividends.*

(2.) Where joint and separate properties are being administered, dividends of the joint and separate properties shall, subject to any order to the contrary that may be made by the Court on the application of any person interested, be declared together : and the expenses of and incident to such dividends shall be fairly apportioned by the trustee between the joint and separate properties, regard being had to the work done for and the benefit received by each property.

**60.** In the calculation and distribution of a dividend the trustee shall make provision for debts provable in bankruptcy appearing from the bankrupt's statements, or otherwise, to be due to persons resident in places so distant from the place where the trustee is acting that in the ordinary course of communication they have not had sufficient time to tender their proofs, or to establish them if disputed, and also for debts provable in bankruptcy, the subject of claims not yet determined. He shall also make provision for any disputed proofs or claims, and for the expenses necessary for the administration of the estate or otherwise, and, subject to the foregoing provisions, he shall distribute as dividend all money in hand. *Provision for creditors residing at a distance, &c.*

**61.** Any creditor who has not proved his debt before the declaration of any dividend or dividends shall be entitled to be paid out of any money for the time being in the hands of the trustee any dividend or dividends he may have failed to receive before that money is applied to the payment of any future dividend or dividends, but he shall not be entitled to disturb the *Right of creditor who has not proved debt before declaration of a dividend.*

distribution of any dividend declared before his debt was proved by reason that he has not participated therein.

Final dividend.

**62.** When the trustee has realised all the property of the bankrupt, or so much thereof as can, in the joint opinion of himself and of the committee of inspection, be realised without needlessly protracting the trusteeship, he shall declare a final dividend, but before so doing he shall give notice in manner prescribed to the persons whose claims to be creditors have been notified to him, but not established to his satisfaction, that if they do not establish their claims to the satisfaction of the Court within a time limited by the notice, he will proceed to make a final dividend, without regard to their claims. After the expiration of the time so limited, or, if the Court on application by any such claimant grant him further time for establishing his claim, then on the expiration of such further time, the property of the bankrupt shall be divided among the creditors who have proved their debts, without regard to the claims of any other persons.

No action for dividend.

**63.** No action for a dividend shall lie against the trustee, but if the trustee refuses to pay any dividend the Court may, if it thinks fit, order him to pay it, and also to pay out of his own money interest thereon for the time that it is withheld, and the costs of the application.

Power to allow bankrupt to manage property.

**64.** (1.) The trustee, with the permission of the committee of inspection, may appoint the bankrupt himself to superintend the management of the property of the bankrupt or of any part thereof, or to carry on the trade (if any) of the bankrupt for the benefit of his creditors, and in any other respect to aid in administering the property in such manner and on such terms as the trustee may direct.

Allowance to bankrupt for maintenance or service.

(2.) The trustee may from time to time, with the permission of the committee of inspection, make such allowance as he may think just to the bankrupt out of his property for the support of the bankrupt and his family, or in consideration of his services if he is engaged in winding up his estate, but any such allowance may be reduced by the Court.

Right of bankrupt to surplus.

**65.** The bankrupt shall be entitled to any surplus remaining after payment in full of his creditors, with interest, as by this Act provided, and of the costs, charges, and expenses of the proceedings under the bankruptcy petition.

---

## PART IV.

### OFFICIAL RECEIVERS AND STAFF OF BOARD OF TRADE.

Appointment by Board of Trade of official receivers of debtors' estates.

**66.** (1.) The Board of Trade may, at any time after the passing of this Act, and from time to time, appoint such persons as they think fit to be official receivers of debtors' estates, and may remove any person so appointed from such office. The official receivers of debtors' estates shall act under the general authority and directions of the Board of Trade, but shall also be officers of the courts to which they are respectively attached.

(2.) The number of official receivers so to be appointed, and the districts to be assigned to them, shall be fixed by the Board of Trade, with the concurrence of the Treasury. One person only shall be appointed for each district unless the Board of Trade, with the concurrence of the Treasury, shall otherwise direct ; but the same person may, with the like concurrence, be appointed to act for more than one district.

(3.) Where more than one official receiver is attached to the Court, such one of them as is for the time being appointed by the Court for any particular estate shall be the official receiver for the purposes of that estate. The Court shall distribute the receiverships of the particular estates among the official receivers in the prescribed manner.

Deputy for official receiver.

**67.** (1.) The Board of Trade may from time to time, by order direct that any of its officers mentioned in the order shall be capable of discharging the duties of any official receiver during any temporary vacancy in the office, or during the temporary absence of any official receiver through illness or otherwise.

(2.) The Board of Trade may, on the application of an official receiver, at any time by order nominate some fit person to be his deputy, and to act for him for such time not exceeding two months as the order may fix, and under such conditions as to remuneration and otherwise as may be prescribed.

**68.** (1.) The duties of the official receiver shall have relation both to the conduct of the debtor and to the administration of his estate. Status of official receiver.

(2.) An official receiver may, for the purpose of affidavits verifying proofs, petitions, or other proceedings under this Act, administer oaths.

(3.) All expressions referring to the trustee under a bankruptcy shall, unless the context otherwise requires, or the Act otherwise provides, include the official receiver when acting as trustee.

(4.) The trustee shall supply the official receiver with such information, and give him such access to, and facilities for inspecting the bankrupt's books and documents and generally shall give him such aid, as may be requisite for enabling the official receiver to perform his duties under this Act.

**69.** As regards the debtor, it shall be the duty of the official receiver— Duties of official receiver as regards the debtor's conduct.

(1.) To investigate the conduct of the debtor and to report to the Court, stating whether there is reason to believe that the debtor has committed any act which constitutes a misdemeanor under the Debtors Act, 1869, or any amendment thereof, or under this Act, or which would justify the Court in refusing, suspending or qualifying an order for his discharge.

(2.) To make such other reports concerning the conduct of the debtor as the Board of Trade may direct.

(3.) To take such part as may be directed by the Board of Trade in the public examination of the debtor.

(4.) To take such part, and give such assistance, in relation to the preseention of any fraudulent debtor as the Board of Trade may direct.

**70.** (1.) As regards the estate of a debtor it shall be the duty of the official receiver— Duties of official receiver as to debtor's estate.

(a.) Pending the appointment of a trustee, to act as interim receiver of the debtor's estate, and, where a special manager is not appointed, as manager thereof :

(b.) To authorise the special manager to raise money or make advances for the purposes of the estate in any case where, in the interests of the creditors, it appears necessary so to do :

(c.) To summon and      at the first meeting of creditors :

(d.) To issue forms of proxity for use at the meetings of creditors :

(e.) To report to the creditors as to any proposal which the debtor may have made with respect to the mode of liquidating his affairs :

(f.) To advertise the receiving order, the date of the creditors first meeting and of the debtor's public examination, and such other matters as it may be necessary to advertise :

(g.) To act as trustee during any vacancy in the office of trustee.

(2.) For the purpose of his duties as interim receiver or manager the official receiver shall have the same powers as if he were a receiver and manager appointed by the High Court, but shall, as far as practicable, consult the wishes of the creditors with respect to the management of the debtor's property, and may for that purpose, if he thinks it advisable, summon meetings of the persons claiming to be creditors, and shall not, unless the Board of Trade otherwise order, incur any expense beyond such as is requisite for the protection of the debtor's property or the disposing of perishable goods.

Provided that when the debtor cannot himself prepare a proper statement of affairs, the official receiver may, subject to any prescribed conditions, and at the expense of the estate, employ some person or persons to assist in the preparation of the statement of affairs.

(3.) Every official receiver shall account to the Board of Trade and pay over all moneys and deal with all securities in such manner as the Board from time to time direct.

**71.** The Board of Trade may, at any time after the passing of this Act, and from time to time, with the approval of the Treasury, appoint such additional officers, including official receivers, clerks, and servants (if any) as may be required by the Board for the execution of this Act, and may dismiss any person so appointed. Power for Board of Trade to appoint officers.

## PART V.

### TRUSTEES IN BANKRUPTCY.

#### *Remuneration of Trustee.*

Remuneration of trustee.

**72.** (1.) Where the creditors appoint any person to be trustee of a debtor's estate, his remuneration (if any) shall be fixed by an ordinary resolution of the creditors or if the creditors so resolve by the Committee of Inspection, and shall be in the nature of a commission or percentage, of which one part shall be payable on the amount realised, after deducting any sums paid to secured creditors out of the proceeds of their securities, and the other part on the amount distributed in dividend.

(2.) If one fourth in number or value of the creditors dissent from the resolution, or the bankrupt satisfies the Board of Trade that the remuneration is unnecessarily large, the Board of Trade shall fix the amount of the remuneration.

(3.) The resolution shall express what expenses the remuneration is to cover, and no liability shall attach to the bankrupt's estate, or to the creditors, in respect of any expenses which the remuneration is expressed to cover.

(4.) Where no remuneration has been voted to a trustee he shall be allowed out of the bankrupt's estate such proper costs and expenses incurred by him in or about the proceedings of the bankruptcy as the taxing officer may allow.

(5.) A trustee shall not, under any circumstances whatever, make any arrangement for or accept from the bankrupt, or any solicitor, auctioneer, or any other person that may be employed about a bankruptcy, any gift, remuneration, or pecuniary or other consideration or benefit whatever beyond the remuneration fixed by the creditors and payable out of the estate, nor shall he make any arrangement for giving up, or give up, any part of his remuneration, either as receiver, manager, or trustee to the bankrupt, or any solicitor or other person that may be employed about a bankruptcy.

#### *Costs.*

Allowance and taxation of costs.

**73.** (1.) Where a trustee or manager receives remuneration for his services as such no payment shall be allowed in his accounts in respect of the performance by any other person of the ordinary duties which are required by statute or rules to be performed by himself.

(2.) Where the trustee is a solicitor he may contract that the remuneration for his services as trustee shall include all professional services.

(3.) All bills and charges of solicitors, managers, accountants, auctioneers, brokers, and other persons, not being trustees, shall be taxed by the prescribed officer, and no payments in respect thereof shall be allowed in the trustee's accounts without proof of such taxation having been made. The taxing master shall satisfy himself before passing such bills and charges that the employment of such solicitors and other persons, in respect of the particular matters out of which such charges arise, has been duly sanctioned.

(4.) Every such person shall, on request by the trustee (which request the trustee shall make a sufficient time before declaring a dividend), deliver his bill of costs or charges to the proper officer for taxation, and if he fails to do so within seven days after receipt of the request, or such further time as the Court, on application, may grant, the trustee shall declare and distribute the dividend without regard to any claim by him, and thereupon any such claim shall be forfeited as well against the trustee personally as against the estate.

#### *Receipts, Payments, Accounts, Audit.*

Payment of money into Bank of England.

**74.** (1.) An account called the Bankruptcy Estates Account shall be kept by the Board of Trade with the Bank of England, and all moneys received by the Board of Trade in respect of proceedings under this Act shall be paid to that account.

(2.) The account of the Accountant in Bankruptcy at the Bank of England shall be transferred to the Bankruptcy Estates Account.

(3.) Every trustee in bankruptcy shall, in such manner and at such times as the Board of Trade with the concurrence of the Treasury direct, pay the money received by him to the Bankruptcy Estates Account at the Bank of England, and the Board of Trade shall furnish him with a certificate of receipt of the money so paid.

(4.) Provided that if it appears to the committee of inspection that for the purpose of carrying on the debtor's business, or of obtaining advances, or because of the probable amount of the cash balance, or if the committee shall satisfy the Board of Trade that for any other reason it is for the advantage of the creditors that the trustee should have an account with a local bank, the Board of Trade shall, on the application of the committee of inspection, authorise the trustee to make his payments into and out of such local bank as the committee may select.

Such account shall be opened and kept by the trustee in the name of the debtor's estate ; and any interest receivable in respect of the account shall be part of the assets of the estate.

The trustee shall make his payments into and out of such local bank in the prescribed manner.

(5.) Subject to any general rules relating to small bankruptcies under Part VII. of this Act, where the debtor at the date of the receiving order has an account at a bank, such account shall not be withdrawn until the expiration of seven days from the day appointed for the first meeting of creditors, unless the Board of Trade, for the safety of the account, or other sufficient cause, order the withdrawal of the account.

(6.) If a trustee at any time retains for more than ten days a sum exceeding fifty pounds, or such other amount as the Board of Trade in any particular case authorise him to retain, then, unless he explains the retention to the satisfaction of the Board of Trade, he shall pay interest on the amount so retained in excess at the rate of twenty pounds per centum per annum, and shall have no claim for remuneration, and may be removed from his office by the Board of Trade, and shall be liable to pay any expenses occasioned by reason of his default.

(7.) All payments out of money standing to the credit of the Board of Trade in the Bankruptcy Estates Account shall be made by the Bank of England in the prescribed manner.

**75.** No trustee in a bankruptcy or under any composition or scheme of arrangement shall pay any sums received by him as trustee into his private banking account. *Trustee not to pay into private account.*

**76.** (1.) Whenever the cash balance standing to the credit of the Bankruptcy Estates Account is in excess of the amount which in the opinion of the Board of Trade is required for the time being to answer demands in respect of bankrupts' estates, the Board of Trade shall notify the same to the Treasury, and shall pay over the same or any part thereof as the Treasury may require to the Treasury, to such account as the Treasury may direct, and the Treasury may invest the said sums or any part thereof in Government securities to be placed to the credit of the said account. *Investment of surplus funds.*

(2.) Whenever any part of the money so invested is, in the opinion of the Board of Trade, required to answer any demands in respect of bankrupts' estates, the Board of Trade shall notify to the Treasury the amount so required, and the Treasury shall thereupon repay to the Board of Trade such sum as may be required to the credit of the Bankruptcy Estates Account, and for that purpose may direct the sale of such part of the said securities as may be necessary.

(3.) The dividends on the investments under this section shall be paid to such account as the Treasury may direct, and regard shall be had to the amount thus derived in fixing the fees payable in respect of bankruptcy proceedings.

**77.** The Treasury may from time to time issue to the Board of Trade in aid of the votes of Parliament, out of the receipts arising from fees, fee stamps, and dividends on investments under this Act, any sums which may be necessary to meet the charges estimated by the Board of Trade in respect of salaries and expenses under this Act. *Certain receipts and fees to be applied in aid of expenditure.*

**78.** (1.) Every trustee shall, at such times as may be prescribed, but not less than twice in each year during his tenure of office, send to the Board of Trade, or as they direct, an account of his receipts and payments as such trustee. *Audit of trustee's accounts.*

(2.) The account shall be in a prescribed form, shall be made in duplicate, and shall be verified by a statutory declaration in the prescribed form.

(3.) The Board of Trade shall cause the accounts so sent to be audited, and for the purposes of the audit the trustee shall furnish the Board with such vouchers and information as the Board may require, and the Board may at any time require the production of and inspect any books or accounts kept by the trustee.

(4.) When any such account has been audited one copy thereof shall be filed and kept by the Board, and the other copy shall be filed with the Court, and each copy shall be open to the inspection of any creditor, or of the bankrupt, or of any person interested.

**79.** The trustee shall, whenever required by any creditor so to do, and on payment by such creditor of the prescribed fee, furnish and transmit to such creditor by post a list of the creditors, showing in such list the amount of the debt due to each of such creditors.

**80.** The trustee shall keep, in manner prescribed, proper books, in which he shall from time to time cause to be made entries or minutes of proceedings at meetings, and of such other matters as may be prescribed, and any creditor of the bankrupt may, subject to the control of the Court, personally or by his agent inspect any such books.

**81.** (1.) Every trustee in a bankruptcy shall from time to time, as may be prescribed, and not less than once in every year during the continuance of the bankruptcy, transmit to the Board of Trade a statement showing the proceedings in the bankruptcy up to the date of the statement, containing the prescribed particulars, and made out in the prescribed form.

(2.) The Board of Trade shall cause the statements so transmitted to be examined, and shall call the trustee to account for any misfeasance, neglect, or omission which may appear on the said statements or in his accounts or otherwise, and may require the trustee to make good any loss which the estate of the bankrupt may have sustained by the misfeasance, neglect, or omission.

## Release of Trustee.

**82.** (1.) When the trustee has realised all the property of the bankrupt, or so much thereof as can, in his opinion, be realised without needlessly protracting the trusteeship, and distributed a final dividend, if any, or has ceased to act by reason of a composition having been approved, or has resigned, or has been removed from his office, the Board of Trade shall, on his application, cause a report on his accounts to be prepared, and, on his complying with all the requirements of the Board, shall take into consideration the report, and any objection which may be urged by any creditor or person interested against the release of the trustee, and shall either grant or withhold the release accordingly, subject nevertheless to an appeal to the High Court.

(2.) Where the release of a trustee is withheld the Court may, on the application of any creditor or person interested, make such order as it thinks just, charging the trustee with the consequences of any act or default he may have done or made contrary to his duty.

(3.) An order of the Board releasing the trustee shall discharge him from all liability in respect of any act done or default made by him in the administration of the affairs of the bankrupt, or otherwise in relation to his conduct as trustee, but any such order may be revoked on proof that it was obtained by fraud or by suppression or concealment of any material fact.

(4.) Where the trustee has not previously resigned or been removed, his release shall operate as a removal of him from his office, and thereupon the official receiver shall be the trustee.

## Official Name.

**83.** The trustee may sue and be sued by the official name of "the trustee of the property of     a bankrupt," inserting the name of the bankrupt, and by that name may in any part of the British dominions or elsewhere hold property of every description, make contracts, sue and be sued, enter into any engagements binding on himself and his successors in office, and do all other acts necessary or expedient to be done in the execution of his office.

*Appointment and Removal.*

**84.** (1.) The creditors may, if they think fit, appoint more persons than one to the office of trustee, and when more persons than one are appointed they shall declare whether any act required or authorized to be done by the trustee is to be done by all or any one or more of such persons, but all such persons are in this Act included under the term "trustee," and shall be joint tenants of the property of the bankrupt. Power to appoint joint or successive trustees.

(2.) The creditors may also appoint persons to act as trustees in succession in the event of one or more of the persons first named declining to accept the office of trustee, or failing to give security, or not being approved of by the Board of Trade.

**85.** If a receiving order is made against a trustee, he shall thereby vacate his office of trustee. Office of trustee vacated by insolvency.

**86.** (1.) The creditors may, by ordinary resolution, at a meeting specially called for that purpose, of which seven days notice has been given, remove a trustee appointed by them, and may at the same or any subsequent meeting appoint another person to fill the vacancy as hereinafter provided in case of a vacancy in the office of trustee. Removal of trustee.

(2.) If the Board of Trade are of opinion that a trustee appointed by the creditors is guilty of misconduct, or fails to perform his duties under this Act, the Board may remove him from his office, but if the creditors, by ordinary resolution, disapprove of his removal, he or they may appeal against it to the High Court.

**87.** (1.) If a vacancy occurs in the office of a trustee the creditors in general meeting may appoint a person to fill the vacancy, and thereupon the same proceedings shall be taken as in the case of a first appointment. Proceedings in case of vacancy in office of trustee.

(2.) The official receiver shall, on the requisition of any creditor, summon a meeting for the purpose of filling any such vacancy.

(3.) If the creditors do not within three weeks after the occurrence of a vacancy appoint a person to fill the vacancy, the official receiver shall report the matter to the Board of Trade, and the Board may appoint a trustee; but in such case the creditors or committee of inspection shall have the same power of appointing a trustee as in the case of a first appointment.

(4.) During any vacancy in the office of trustee the official receiver shall act as trustee.

*Voting powers of Trustee.*

**88.** The vote of the trustee, or of his partner, clerk, solicitor, or solicitor's clerk, either as creditor or as proxy for a creditor, shall not be reckoned in the majority required for passing any resolution affecting the remuneration or conduct of the trustee. Limitation of voting powers of trustee.

*Control over Trustee.*

**89.** (1.) Subject to the provisions of this Act the trustee shall, in the administration of the property of the bankrupt and in the distribution thereof amongst his creditors, have regard to any directions that may be given by resolution of the creditors at any general meeting, or by the committee of inspection, and any directions so given by the creditors at any general meeting shall in case of conflict be deemed to override any directions given by the committee of inspection. Discretionary powers of trustee and control thereof.

(2.) The trustee may from time to time summon general meetings of the creditors for the purpose of ascertaining their wishes, and it shall be his duty to summon meetings at such times as the creditors, by resolution, either at the meeting appointing the trustee or otherwise may direct, or whenever requested in writing to do so by one-fourth in value of the creditors.

(3.) The trustee may apply to the Court in manner prescribed for directions in relation to any particular matter arising under the bankruptcy.

(4.) Subject to the provisions of this Act the trustee shall use his own discretion in the management of the estate and its distribution among the creditors.

**90.** If the bankrupt or any of the creditors, or any other person, is aggrieved by any act or decision of the trustee, he may apply to the Court, and the Court may confirm, reverse, or modify the act or decision complained of, and make such order in the premises as it thinks just. Appeal to Court against trustee.

Control of Board of Trade over trustees.

**91.** (1.) The Board of Trade shall take cognizance of the conduct of trustees, and in the event of any trustee not faithfully performing his duties, and duly observing all the requirements imposed on him by statute, rules or otherwise, with respect to the performance of his duties, or in the event of any complaint being made to the Board by any creditor in regard thereto, the Board shall inquire into the matter and take such action thereon as may be deemed expedient.

(2.) The Board may at any time require any trustee to answer any inquiry made by them in relation to any bankruptcy in which the trustee is engaged, and may, if the Board think fit, apply to the Court to examine on oath the trustee or any other person concerning the bankruptcy.

(3.) The Board may also direct a local investigation to be made of the books and vouchers of the trustee.

## PART VI.

### CONSTITUTION, PROCEDURE, AND POWERS OF COURT.

#### *Jurisdiction.*

Jurisdiction to be exercised by High Court and county courts.

**92.** (1.) The Courts having jurisdiction in bankruptcy shall be the High Court and the county courts.

(2.) But the Lord Chancellor may from time to time, by order under his hand, exclude any county court from having jurisdiction in bankruptcy, and for the purposes of bankruptcy jurisdiction may attach its district or any part thereof to the High Court, or to any other county court or courts, and may from time to time revoke or vary any order so made. The Lord Chancellor may, in like manner and subject to the like conditions, detach the district of any county court or any part thereof from the district and jurisdiction of the High Court.

(3.) The term "district," when used in this Act with reference to a county court, means the district of the court for the purposes of bankruptcy jurisdiction.

(4.) A county court which, at the commencement of this Act, is excluded from having bankruptcy jurisdiction, shall continue to be so excluded until the Lord Chancellor otherwise orders.

(5.) Periodical sittings for the transaction of bankruptcy business by county courts having jurisdiction in bankruptcy shall be holden at such times and at such intervals as the Lord Chancellor shall prescribe for each such court.

Consolidation of London Bankruptcy Court with Supreme Court of Judicature.

**93.** (1.) From and after the commencement of this Act the London Bankruptcy Court shall be united and consolidated with and form part of the Supreme Court of Judicature, and the jurisdiction of the London Bankruptcy Court shall be transferred to the High Court.

(2.) For the purposes of this union, consolidation, and transfer, and of all matters incidental thereto and consequential thereon, the Supreme Court of Judicature Act, 1873, as amended by subsequent Acts, shall, subject to the provisions of this Act, have effect as if the union, consolidation, and transfer had been effected by that Act, except that all expressions referring to the time appointed for the commencement of that Act shall be construed as referring to the commencement of this Act, and, subject as aforesaid, this Act and the said above-mentioned Acts shall be read and construed together.

Transaction of bankruptcy business by special judge of High Court.

**94.** (1.) Subject to general rules, and to orders of transfer made under the authority of the Supreme Court of Judicature Act, 1873, and Acts amending it, —

(a) All matters pending in the London Bankruptcy Court at the commencement of this Act ; and

(b) All matters which would have been within the exclusive jurisdiction of the London Bankruptcy Court, if this Act had not passed ; and

(c) All matters in respect of which jurisdiction is given to the High Court by this Act,

shall be assigned to such Division of the High Court as the Lord Chancellor may from time to time direct.

(2.) All such matters shall, subject as aforesaid, be ordinarily transacted and disposed of by or under the direction of one of the judges of the High Court, and the Lord Chancellor shall from time to time assign a judge for that purpose.

(3.) Provided that during vacation, or during the illness of the judge so assigned, or during his absence or for any other reasonable cause such matters, or any part thereof, may be transacted and disposed of by or under the directions of any judge of the High Court named for that purpose by the Lord Chancellor.

(4.) Subject to the provisions of this Act, the officers, clerks, and subordinate persons who are, at the commencement of this Act, attached to the London Bankruptcy Court, and their successors, shall be officers of the Supreme Court of Judicature, and shall be attached to the High Court.

(5.) Subject to general rules, all bankruptcy matters shall be entitled, "In bankruptcy."

**95.** (1.) If the debtor against or by whom a bankruptcy petition is presented has resided or carried on business within the London bankruptcy district as defined by this Act for the greater part of the six months immediately preceding the presentation of the petition, or for a longer period during those six months than in the district of any county court, or is not resident in England, or if the petitioning creditor is unable to ascertain the residence of the debtor, the petition shall be presented to the High Court. *Petition, where to be presented.*

(2.) In any other case the petition shall be presented to the county court for the district in which the debtor has resided or carried on business for the longest period during the six months immediately preceding the presentation of the petition.

(3.) Nothing in this section shall invalidate a proceeding by reason of its being taken in a wrong court.

**96.** The London Bankruptcy District shall, for the purposes of this Act, comprise the city of London and the liberties thereof, and all such parts of the metropolis and other places as are situated within the district of any county court described as a metropolitan county court in the list contained in the Third Schedule. *Definition of the London Bankruptcy District.*

**97.** (1.) Subject to the provisions of this Act, every court having orignal jurisdiction in bankruptcy shall have jurisdiction throughout England. *Transfer of proceedings from court to court.*

(2.) Any proceedings in bankruptcy may at any time, and at any stage thereof, and either with or without application from any of the parties thereto, be transferred by any prescribed authority and in the prescribed manner from one court to another court, or may by the like authority be retained in the court in which the proceedings were commenced, although it may not be the court in which the proceedings ought to have been commenced.

(3.) If any question of law arises in any bankruptcy proceeding in a county court which all the parties to the proceeding desire, or which one of them and the judge of the county court may desire, to have determined in the first instance in the High Court, the judge shall state the facts, in the form of a special case, for the opinion of the High Court. The special case and the proceedings, or such of them as may be required, shall be transmitted to the High Court for the purposes of the determination.

**98.** Subject to the provisions of this Act and to general rules the judge of the High Court exercising jurisdiction in bankruptcy may exercise in chambers the whole or any part of his jurisdiction. *Exercise in chambers of High Court jurisdiction.*

**99.** (1.) The registrars in bankruptcy of the High Court, and the registrars of a county court having jurisdiction in bankruptcy, shall have the powers and jurisdiction in this section mentioned, and any order made or act done by such registrars in the exercise of the said powers and jurisdiction shall be deemed the order or act of the Court. *Jurisdiction in bankruptcy of registrar.*

(2.) Subject to general rules limiting the powers conferred by this section, a registrar shall have power—

(a) To hear bankruptcy petitions, and to make receiving orders and adjudications thereon:

(b) To hold the public examination of debtors:

(c) To grant orders of discharge where the application is not opposed:

(d) To approve compositions or schemes of arrangement when they are not opposed:

(e) To make interim orders in any case of urgency:

(f) To make any order or exercise any jurisdiction which by any rule in that behalf is prescribed as proper to be made or exercised in chambers :

(g) To hear and determine any unopposed or ex parte application :

(h) To summon and examine any person known or suspected to have in his possession effects of the debtor or to be indebted to him, or capable of giving information respecting the debtor, his dealings or property.

(3.) The registrars in bankruptcy of the High Court shall also have power to grant orders of discharge and certificates of removal of disqualifications, and to approve compositions and schemes of arrangement.

(4.) A registrar shall not have power to commit for contempt of Court.

(5.) The Lord Chancellor may from time to time by order direct that any specified registrar of a county court shall have and exercise all the powers of a bankruptcy registrar of the High Court.

Powers of county court.

**100.** A county court shall, for the purposes of its bankruptcy jurisdiction, in addition to the ordinary powers of the Court, have all the powers and jurisdiction of the High Court, and the orders of the Court may be enforced accordingly in manner prescribed.

Board of Trade to make payments in accordance with directions of Court.

**101.** Where any moneys or funds have been received by an official receiver or by the Board of Trade, and the Court makes an order declaring that any person is entitled to such moneys or funds the Board of Trade shall make an order for the payment thereof to the person so entitled as aforesaid.

General power of bankruptcy courts.

**102.** (1.) Subject to the provisions of this Act, every Court having jurisdiction in bankruptcy under this Act shall have full power to decide all questions of priorities, and all other questions whatsoever, whether of law or fact, which may arise in any case of bankruptcy coming within the cognizance of the Court, or which the Court may deem it expedient or necessary to decide for the purpose of doing complete justice or making a complete distribution of property in any such case.

Provided that the jurisdiction hereby given shall not be exercised by the county court for the purpose of adjudicating upon any claim, not arising out of the bankruptcy, which might heretofore have been enforced by action in the High Court, unless all parties to the proceeding consent thereto, or the money, money's worth, or right in dispute does not in the opinion of the judge exceed in value two hundred pounds.

(2.) A Court having jurisdiction in bankruptcy under this Act shall not be subject to be restrained in the execution of its powers under this Act by the order of any other Court, nor shall any appeal lie from its decisions, except in manner directed by this Act.

(3.) If in any proceeding in bankruptcy there arises any question of fact which either of the parties desire to be tried before a jury instead of by the Court itself, or which the Court thinks ought to be tried by a jury, the Court may if it thinks fit direct the trial to be had with a jury, and the trial may be had accordingly, in the High Court in the same manner as if it were the trial of an issue of fact in an action, and in the county court in the manner in which jury trials in ordinary cases are by law held in that Court.

(4.) Where a receiving order has been made in the High Court under this Act, the judge by whom such order was made shall have power, if he sees fit, without any further consent, to order the transfer to such judge of any action pending in any other division, brought or continued by or against the bankrupt.

(5.) Where default is made by a trustee, debtor, or other person in obeying any order or direction given by the Board of Trade or by an official receiver or any other officer of the Board of Trade under any power conferred by this Act, the Court may, on the application of the Board of Trade or an official receiver or other duly authorised person order such defaulting trustee, debtor, or person to comply with the order or direction so given ; and the Court may also, if it shall think fit, upon any such application make an immediate order for the committal of such defaulting trustee, debtor, or other person ; provided that the power given by this subsection shall be deemed to be in addition to and not in substitution for any other right or remedy in respect of such default.

*Judgment Debtors.*

**103.** (1.) It shall be lawful for the Lord Chancellor by order to direct that the jurisdiction and powers under section five of the Debtors Act, 1869, now vested in the High Court, shall be assigned to and exercised by the judge to whom bankruptcy business is assigned. *Judgment debtor's summons to be bankruptcy business.*

(2.) It shall be lawful also for the Lord Chancellor in like manner to direct that the whole or any part of the said jurisdiction and powers shall be delegated to and exercised by the bankruptcy registrars of the High Court.

(3.) Any order made under this section may, at any time, in like manner, be rescinded or varied.

(4.) Every county court within the jurisdiction of which a judgment debtor is or resides shall have jurisdiction under section five of the Debtors Act, 1869, although the amount of the judgment debt may exceed fifty pounds.

(5.) Where, under section five of the Debtors Act, 1869, application is made by a judgment creditor to a Court, having bankruptcy jurisdiction, for the committal of a judgment debtor, the Court may, if it thinks fit, decline to commit, and in lieu thereof, with the consent of the judgment creditor, and on payment by him of the prescribed fee, make a receiving order against the debtor. In such case the judgment debtor shall be deemed to have committed an act of bankruptcy at the time the order is made.

(6.) General rules under this Act may be made for the purpose of carrying into effect the provisions of the Debtors Act, 1869.

*Appeals.*

**104.** (1.) Every Court having jurisdiction in bankruptcy under this Act may review, rescind, or vary any order made by it under its bankruptcy jurisdiction. *Appeals in bankruptcy.*

(2.) Orders in bankruptcy matters shall, at the instance of any person aggrieved, be subject to appeal as follows:

(*a.*) An appeal shall lie from the order of a county court to Her Majesty's Court of Appeal:

(*b.*) An appeal shall lie from the order of the High Court to Her Majesty's Court of Appeal:

(*c.*) An appeal shall, with the leave of Her Majesty's Court of Appeal, but not otherwise, lie from the order of that Court to the House of Lords:

(*d.*) No appeal shall be entertained except in conformity with such general rules as may for the time being be in force in relation to the appeal.

*Procedure.*

**105.** (1.) Subject to the provisions of this Act and to general rules, the costs of and incidental to any proceeding in Court under this Act shall be in the discretion of the Court: Provided that where any issue is tried by a jury the costs shall follow the event, unless, upon application made at the trial, for good cause shown, the judge before whom such issue is tried shall otherwise order. *Discretionary powers of the Court.*

(2.) The Court may at any time adjourn any proceedings before it upon such terms, if any, as it may think fit to impose.

(3.) The Court may at any time amend any written process or proceeding under this Act upon such terms, if any, as it may think fit to impose.

(4.) Where by this Act or by general rules, the time for doing any act or thing is limited, the Court may extend the time either before or after the expiration thereof, upon such terms, if any, as the Court may think fit to impose.

(5.) Subject to general rules, the Court may in any matter take the whole or any part of the evidence either vivâ voce, or by interrogatories, or upon affidavit, or by commission abroad.

(6.) For the purpose of approving a composition or scheme by joint debtors, the Court may, if it thinks fit, and on the report of the official receiver that it is expedient so to do, dispense with the public examination of one of such joint debtors if he is unavoidably prevented from attending the examination by illness or absence abroad.

Consolidation of petitions.

**106.** Where two or more bankruptcy petitions are presented against the same debtor or against joint debtors, the court may consolidate the proceedings, or any of them, on such terms as the court thinks fit.

Power to change carriage of proceedings.

**107.** Where the petitioner does not proceed with due diligence on his petition, the court may substitute as petitioner any other creditor to whom the debtor may be indebted in the amount required by this Act in the case of the petitioning creditor.

Continuance of proceedings on death of debtor.

**108.** If a debtor by or against whom a bankruptcy petition has been presented dies, the proceedings in the matter shall, unless the court otherwise orders, be continued as if he were alive.

Power to stay proceedings.

**109.** The court may at any time, for sufficient reason, make an order staying the proceedings under a bankruptcy petition, either altogether or for a limited time, on such terms and subject to such conditions as the court may think just.

Power to present petition against one partner.

**110.** Any creditor whose debt is sufficient to entitle him to present a bankruptcy petition against all the partners of a firm may present a petition against any one or more partners of the firm without including the others.

Power to dismiss petition against some respondents only.

**111.** Where there are more respondents than one to a petition the court may dismiss the petition as to one or more of them, without prejudice to the effect of the petition as against the other or others of them.

Property of partners to be vested in same trustee.

**112.** Where a receiving order has been made on a bankruptcy petition against or by one member of a partnership, any other bankruptcy petition against or by a member of the same partnership shall be filed in or transferred to the court in which the first-mentioned petition is in course of prosecution, and, unless the court otherwise directs, the same trustee or receiver shall be appointed as may have been appointed in respect of the property of the first-mentioned member of the partnership, and the court may give such directions for consolidating the proceedings under the petitions as it thinks just.

Actions by trustee and bankrupt's partners.

**113.** Where a member of a partnership is adjudged bankrupt, the court may authorise the trustee to commence and prosecute any action in the names of the trustee and of the bankrupt's partner; and any release by such partner of the debt or demand to which the action relates shall be void; but notice of the application for authority to commence the action shall be given to him, and he may show cause against it, and on his application the court may, if it thinks fit, direct that he shall receive his proper share of the proceeds of the action, and if he does not claim any benefit therefrom he shall be indemnified against costs in respect thereof as the court directs.

Actions on joint contracts.

**114.** Where a bankrupt is a contractor in respect of any contract jointly with any person or persons, such person or persons may sue or be sued in respect of the contract without the joinder of the bankrupt.

Proceedings in partnership name.

**115.** Any two or more persons, being partners, or any person carrying on business under a partnership name, may take proceedings or be proceeded against under this Act in the name of the firm, but in such case the court may, on application by any person interested, order the names of the persons who are partners in such firm, or the name of such person to be disclosed in such manner, and verified on oath, or otherwise as the court may direct.

### Officers.

Disabilities of officers.

**116.** (1.) No registrar or other officer attached to any court having jurisdiction in bankruptcy shall, during his continuance in office, be capable of being elected or sitting as a member of the House of Commons.

(2.) No registrar or official receiver or other officer attached to any such court shall, during his continuance in office, either directly or indirectly, by himself, his clerk, or partner, act as solicitor in any proceeding in bankruptcy or in any prosecution of a debtor by order of the court, and if he does so act he shall be liable to be dismissed from office.

Provided that nothing in this section shall affect the right of any registrar or officer appointed before the passing of this Act to act as solicitor by himself, his clerk, or partner to the extent permitted by section sixty-nine of the Bankruptcy Act, 1869.

### Orders and Warrants of Court.

Enforcement of orders of courts throughout the United Kingdom.

**117.** Any order made by a court having jurisdiction in bankruptcy in England under this Act shall be enforced in Scotland and Ireland in the courts having jurisdiction in bankruptcy in those parts of the United Kingdom respectively, in the same manner in all respects as if the order had been made by the court hereby required to enforce it; and in like manner any order made by a court having jurisdiction in bankruptcy in Scotland shall be enforced in England and Ireland, and any order made by a court having jurisdiction in bankruptcy in Ireland shall be enforced in England and Scotland by the courts respectively having jurisdiction in bankruptcy in the part of the United Kingdom where the orders may require to be enforced, and in the same manner in all respects as if the order had been made by the court required to enforce it in a case of bankruptcy within its own jurisdiction.

**118.** The High Court, the county courts, the courts having jurisdiction in bankruptcy in Scotland and Ireland, and every British court elsewhere having jurisdiction in bankruptcy or insolvency, and the officers of those courts respectively, shall severally act in aid of and be auxiliary to each other in all matters of bankruptcy, and an order of the court seeking aid, with a request to another of the said courts, shall be deemed sufficient to enable the latter court to exercise, in regard to the matters directed by the order, such jurisdiction as either the court which made the request, or the court to which the request is made, could exercise in regard to similar matters within their respective jurisdictions. *[margin: Courts to be auxiliary to each other.]*

**119.** (1.) Any warrant of a court having jurisdiction in bankruptcy in England may be enforced in Scotland, Ireland, the Isle of Man, the Channel Islands, and elsewhere in Her Majesty's dominions, in the same manner and subject to the same privileges in and subject to which a warrant issued by any justice of the peace against a person for an indictable offence against the laws of England may be executed in those parts of Her Majesty's dominions respectively in pursuance of the Acts of Parliament in that behalf. *[margin: Warrants of Bankruptcy Courts.]*

(2.) A search warrant issued by a court having jurisdiction in bankruptcy for the discovery of any property of a debtor may be executed in manner prescribed or in the same manner and subject to the same privileges in and subject to which a search warrant for property supposed to be stolen may be executed according to law.

**120.** Where the court commits any person to prison, the commitment may be to such convenient prison as the court thinks expedient, and if the gaolor of any prison refuses to receive any prisoner so committed he shall be liable for every such refusal to a fine not exceeding one hundred pounds. *[margin: Commitment to prison.]*

---

## PART VII.

### SMALL BANKRUPTCIES.

**121.** When a petition is presented by or against a debtor, if the court is satisfied by affidavit or otherwise, or the official receiver reports to the court that the property of the debtor is not likely to exceed in value three hundred pounds, the court may make an order that the debtor's estate be administered in a summary manner, and thereupon the provisions of this Act shall be subject to the following modifications : *[margin: Summary administration in small cases.]*

(1.) If the debtor is adjudged bankrupt the official receiver shall be the trustee in the bankruptcy :

(2.) There shall be no committee of inspection, but the official receiver may do with the permission of the Board of Trade all things which may be done by the trustee with the permission of the committee of inspection :

(3.) Such other modifications may be made in the provisions of this Act as may be prescribed by general rules (a) with the view of saving expense and simplifying procedure; but nothing in this section shall permit the modification of the provisions of this Act relating to the examination or discharge of the debtor.

Provided that the creditors may at any time, by special resolution, resolve that some person other than the official receiver be appointed trustee in the bankruptcy, and thereupon the bankruptcy shall proceed as if an order for summary administration had not been made.

(a) Rules of Dec. 1, 1883, have been made.

4 F 2

Power for
county court to
make adminis-
tration order
instead of order
for payment by
instalments.

**122.** (1.) Where a judgment has been obtained in a county court and the debtor is unable to pay the amount forthwith, and alleges that his whole indebtedness amounts to a sum not exceeding fifty pounds, inclusive of the debt for which the judgment is obtained, the county court may make an order providing for the administration of his estate, and for the payment of his debts by instalments or otherwise, and either in full or to such extent as to the county court under the circumstances of the case appears practicable, and subject to any conditions as to his future earnings or income which the court may think just.

(2.) The order shall not be invalid by reason only that the total amount of the debts is found at any time to exceed fifty pounds, but in such case the county court may, if it thinks fit, set aside the order.

(3.) Where, in the opinion of the county court in which the judgment is obtained, it would be convenient that that court should administer the estate, it shall cause a certificate of the judgment to be forwarded to the county court in the district of which the debtor or the majority of the creditors resides or reside, and thereupon the latter county court shall have all the powers which it would have under this section, had the judgment been obtained in it.

(4.) Where it appears to the registrar of the county court that property of the debtor exceeds in value ten pounds, he shall, at the request of any creditor, and without fee, issue execution against the debtor's goods, but the household goods, wearing apparel, and bedding of the debtor or his family, and the tools and implements of his trade to the value in the aggregate of twenty pounds, shall to that extent be protected from seizure.

(5.) When the order is made no creditor shall have any remedy against the person or property of the debtor in respect of any debt which the debtor has notified to a county court, except with the leave of that county court, and on such terms as that court may impose; and any county court or inferior court in which proceedings are pending against the debtor in respect of any such debt shall, on receiving notice of the order, stay the proceedings, but may allow costs already incurred by the creditor, and such costs may, on application, be added to the debt notified.

(6.) If the debtor makes default in payment of any instalment payable in pursuance of any order under this section, he shall, unless the contrary is proved, be deemed to have had since the date of the order the means to pay the sum in respect of which he has made default and to have refused or neglected to pay the same.

(7.) The order shall be carried into effect in such manner as may be prescribed by general rules.

(8.) Money paid into court under the order shall be appropriated first in satisfaction of the costs of the plaintiff in the action, next in satisfaction of the costs of administration (which shall not exceed two shillings in the pound on the total amount of the debts) and then in liquidation of debts in accordance with the order.

(9.) Notice of the order shall be sent to the registrar of county court judgments, and be posted in the office of the county court of the district in which the debtor resides, and sent to every creditor notified by the debtor, or who has proved.

(10.) Any creditor of the debtor, on proof of his debt before the registrar, shall be entitled to be scheduled as a creditor of the debtor for the amount of his proof.

(11.) Any creditor may in the prescribed manner object to any debt scheduled, or to the manner in which payment is directed to be made by instalments.

(12.) Any person who after the date of the order becomes a creditor of the debtor, shall, on proof of his debt before the registrar, be scheduled as a creditor of the debtor for the amount of his proof, but shall not be entitled to any dividend under the order until those creditors who are scheduled as having been creditors before the date of the order have been paid to the extent provided by the order.

(13.) When the amount received under the order is sufficient to pay each creditor scheduled to the extent thereby provided, and the costs of the plaintiff and of the administration, the order shall be superseded, and the debtor shall be discharged from his debts to the scheduled creditors.

(14.) In computing the salary of a registrar under the County Courts Acts every creditor scheduled, not being a judgment creditor, shall count as a plaint.

## PART VIII.

### SUPPLEMENTAL PROVISIONS.

#### *Application of Act.*

**123.** A receiving order shall not be made against any corporation, or against any partnership or association, or company registered under the Companies Act, 1862. Exclusion of partnerships and companies.

**124.** If a person having privilege of Parliament commits an act of bankruptcy, he may be dealt with under this Act in like manner as if he had not such privilege. Privilege of Parliament.

**125.** (1.) Any creditor of a deceased debtor whose debt would have been sufficient to support a bankruptcy petition against such debtor, had he been alive, may present to the court a petition in the prescribed form praying for an order for the administration of the estate of the deceased debtor, according to the Law of Bankruptcy. Administration in bankruptcy of estate of person dying insolvent.

(2.) Upon the prescribed notice being given to the legal personal representative of the deceased debtor, the court may, in the prescribed manner, upon proof of the petitioner's debt, unless the court is satisfied that there is a reasonable probability that the estate will be sufficient for the payment of the debts owing by the deceased, make an order for the administration in bankruptcy of the deceased debtor's estate, or may upon cause shown dismiss such petition with or without costs.

(3.) An order of administration under this section shall not be made until the expiration of two months from the date of the grant of probate or letters of administration, unless with the concurrence of the legal personal representative of the deceased debtor, or unless the petitioner proves to the satisfaction of the court that the debtor committed an act of bankruptcy within three months prior to his decease.

(4.) A petition for administration under this section shall not be presented to the court after proceedings have been commenced in any court of justice for the administration of the deceased debtor's estate, but that court may in such case, on the application of any creditor, and on proof that the estate is insufficient to pay its debts, transfer the proceedings to the court exercising jurisdiction in bankruptcy, and thereupon such last-mentioned court may, in the prescribed manner, make an order for the administration of the estate of the deceased debtor, and the like consequences shall ensue as under an administration order made on the petition of a creditor.

(5.) Upon an order being made for the administration of a deceased debtor's estate, the property of the debtor shall vest in the official receiver of the court, as trustee thereof, and he shall forthwith proceed to realise and distribute the same in accordance with the provisions of this Act.

(6.) With the modifications hereinafter mentioned, all the provisions of Part III. of this Act, relating to the administration of the property of a bankrupt, shall, so far as the same are applicable, apply to the case of an administration order under this section in like manner as to an order of adjudication under this Act.

(7.) In the administration of the property of the deceased debtor under an order of administration, the official receiver shall have regard to any claim by the legal personal representative of the deceased debtor to payment of the proper funeral and testamentary expenses incurred by him in and about the debtor's estate, and such claims shall be deemed a preferential debt under the order, and be payable in full, out of the debtor's estate, in priority to all other debts.

(8.) If, on the administration of a deceased debtor's estate, any surplus remains in the hands of the official receiver, after payment in full of all the debts due from the debtor, together with the costs of the administration and interest as provided by this Act in case of bankruptcy, such surplus shall be paid over to the legal personal representative of the deceased debtor's estate, or dealt with in such other manner as may be prescribed.

(9.) Notice to the legal personal representative of a deceased debtor of the presentation by a creditor of a petition under this section shall, in the event of an order for administration being made thereon, be deemed to be equivalent to notice of an act of bankruptcy, and after such notice no payment or transfer of property made by the legal personal representative shall operate as a discharge to him as between himself and the official receiver; save as aforesaid nothing in this section shall invalidate any payment made or any act or thing done in good faith by the legal personal representative before the date of the order for administration.

(10.) Unless the context otherwise requires, "court," in this section, means the court within the jurisdiction of which the debtor resided or carried on business for the greater part of the six months immediately prior to his decease ; "creditor" means one or more creditors qualified to present a bankruptcy petition, as in this Act provided.

(11.) General rules, for carrying into effect the provisions of this section, may be made in the same manner and to the like effect and extent as in bankruptcy.

**Saving as to debts contracted before Act of 1861.** 126. No person, not being a trader within the meaning of the Bankruptcy Act, 1861, shall be adjudged bankrupt in respect of a debt contracted before the passing of that Act.

### General Rules.

**Power to make general rules.** 127. (1.) The Lord Chancellor may from time to time, with the concurrence of the President of the Board of Trade, make, revoke, and alter general rules for carrying into effect the objects of this Act (*a*).

(2.) All general rules made under the foregoing provisions of this section shall be laid before Parliament within three weeks after they are made if Parliament is then sitting, and if Parliament is not then sitting, within three weeks after the beginning of the then next session of Parliament, and shall be judicially noticed, and shall have effect as if enacted by this Act.

(3.) Such general rules as may be required for purposes of this Act may be made at any time after the passing of this Act.

(4.) Provided always, that the said general rules, so made, revoked, or altered, shall not extend the jurisdiction of the court.

(5.) After the commencement of this Act no general rule under the provisions of this section shall come into operation until the expiration of one month after the same has been made and issued.

### Fees, Salaries, Expenditure, and Returns.

**Fees and remuneration.** 128. (1.) The Lord Chancellor may, with the sanction of the Treasury, from time to time prescribe a scale of fees and percentages to be charged for or in respect of proceedings under this Act ; and the Treasury shall direct by whom and in what manner the same are to be collected, accounted for, and to what account they shall be paid. The Board of Trade, with the concurrence of the Treasury, shall direct whether any and what remuneration is to be allowed to any officer of, or person attached to, the Board of Trade, performing any duties under this Act, and may from time to time vary, increase, or diminish such remuneration as they may see fit.

(2.) This section shall come into operation on the passing of this Act.

**Judicial salaries, &c.** 129. (1.) The Lord Chancellor, with the concurrence of the Treasury, shall direct whether any and what remuneration is to be allowed to any person (other than an officer of the Board of Trade) performing any duties under this Act, and may from time to time vary, increase, or diminish such remuneration as he may think fit.

(2.) This section shall come into operation on the passing of this Act.

**Annual accounts of receipts and expenditure in respect of bankruptcy proceedings.** 130. (1.) The Treasury shall annually cause to be prepared and laid before both houses of Parliament an account for the year ending with the thirty-first day of March, showing the receipts and expenditure during that year in respect of bankruptcy proceedings, whether commenced under this or any previous Act, and the provisions of section twenty-eight of the Supreme Court of Judicature Act, 1875, shall apply to the account as if the account had been required by that section.

(2.) The accounts of the Board of Trade, under this Act, shall be audited

---

(*a*) Under this section the Bankruptcy Rules, 1886, have been made. They are divided into five parts:— Part I. (rr. 6—134) deals with "Court Procedure" ; Part II. (rr. 135—271) with "Proceedings from Act of Bankruptcy to Discharge" ; Part III. (rr. 271—279) with "Special Procedures:" viz., (a) small bankruptcies, under sect. 121, *supra ;* and (b) administration of estate of persons dying intestate, under sect. 125, *supra ;* Part IV. (rr. 280—346) with "Officers, Trustees, Audit, &c. ;" and Part V. (rr. 347—362) with "Miscellaneous Matters."

Non-compliance with the rules does not render any proceeding void unless the court so directs, but such proceeding may be set aside, or amended, or otherwise dealt with in such manner and upon such terms as the court may think fit : rule 350.

Rules as to Administration Orders, under sect. 122, *supra,* have also been made. They are dated Dec. 1, 1883.

in such manner as the Treasury from time to time direct, and, for the purpose of the account to be laid before Parliament, the Board of Trade shall make such returns, and give such information as the Treasury may from time to time direct.

131. The registrars and other officers of the courts acting in bankruptcy shall make to the Board of Trade such returns of the business of their respective courts and offices, at such times and in such manner and form as may be prescribed, and from such returns the Board of Trade shall cause books to be prepared which shall, under the regulations of the Board, be open for public information and searches. *{Returns by bankruptcy officers.}*

The Board of Trade shall also cause a general annual report of all matters, judicial and financial, within this Act, to be prepared and laid before both houses of Parliament.

*Evidence.*

132. (1.) A copy of the London Gazette containing any notice inserted therein in pursuance of this Act shall be evidence of the facts stated in the notice. *{Gazette to be evidence.}*

(2.) The production of a copy of the London Gazette containing any notice of a receiving order, or of an order adjudging a debtor bankrupt, shall be conclusive evidence in all legal proceedings of the order having been duly made, and of its date.

133. (1.) A minute of proceedings at a meeting of creditors under this Act, signed at the same or the next ensuing meeting, by a person describing himself as, or appearing to be, chairman of the meeting at which the minute is signed, shall be received in evidence without further proof. *{Evidence of proceedings at meetings of creditors.}*

(2.) Until the contrary is proved, every meeting of creditors in respect of the proceedings whereof a minute has been so signed shall be deemed to have been duly convened and held, and all resolutions passed or proceedings had thereat to have been duly passed or had.

134. Any petition or copy of a petition in bankruptcy, any order or certificate or copy of an order or certificate made by any Court having jurisdiction in bankruptcy, any instrument or copy of an instrument, affidavit, or document made or used in the course of any bankruptcy proceedings, or other proceedings had under this Act, shall, if it appears to be sealed with the seal of any court having jurisdiction in bankruptcy, or purports to be signed by any judge thereof, or is certified as a true copy by any registrar thereof, be receivable in evidence in all legal proceedings whatever. *{Evidence of proceedings in bankruptcy.}*

135. Subject to general rules, any affidavit to be used in a bankruptcy court may be sworn before any person authorised to administer oaths in the High Court, or in the Court of Chancery of the county palatine of Lancaster, or before any registrar of a bankruptcy court, or before any officer of a bankruptcy court authorised in writing on that behalf by the judge of the court, or, in the case of a person residing in Scotland or in Ireland, before a judge ordinary, magistrate, or justice of the peace, or, in the case of a person who is out of the Kingdom of Great Britain and Ireland, before a magistrate or justice of the peace or other person qualified to administer oaths in the country where he resides (he being certified to be a magistrate or justice of the peace, or qualified as aforesaid by a British minister or British consul, or by a notary public). *{Swearing of affidavits.}*

136. In case of the death of the debtor or his wife, or of a witness whose evidence has been received by any court in any proceeding under this Act, the deposition of the person so deceased, purporting to be sealed with the seal of the court, or a copy thereof purporting to be so sealed, shall be admitted as evidence of the matters therein deposed to. *{Death of witness.}*

137. Every court have jurisdiction in bankruptcy under this Act shall have a seal describing the court in such manner as may be directed by order of the Lord Chancellor, and judicial notice shall be taken of the seal, and of the signature of the judge or registrar of any such court, in all legal proceedings. *{Bankruptcy Courts to have seals.}*

138. A certificate of the Board of Trade that a person has been appointed trustee under this Act, shall be conclusive evidence of his appointment. *{Certificate of appointment of trustee.}*

139. Where by this Act an appeal to the High Court is given against any decision of the Board of Trade, or of the official receiver, the appeal shall be brought within twenty-one days from the time when the decision appealed against is pronounced or made. *{Appeal from Board of Trade to High Court.}*

140. (1.) All documents purporting to be orders or certificates made or *{Proceedings of Board of Trade.}*

issued by the Board of Trade, and to be sealed with the seal of the Board, or to be signed by a secretary or assistant secretary of the Board, or any person authorised in that behalf by the President of the Board, shall be received in evidence, and deemed to be such orders or certificates without further proof unless the contrary is shown.

(2.) A certificate signed by the President of the Board of Trade that any order made, certificate issued, or act done, is the order, certificate, or act of the Board of Trade shall be conclusive evidence of the fact so certified.

### Time.

Computation of time.

**141.** (1.) Where by this Act any limited time from or after any date or event is appointed or allowed for the doing of any act or the taking of any proceeding, then in the computation of that limited time the same shall be taken as exclusive of the day of that date or of the happening of that event, and as commencing at the beginning of the next following day ; and the act or proceeding shall be done or taken at latest on the last day of that limited time as so computed, unless the last day is a Sunday, Christmas Day, Good Friday, or Monday or Tuesday in Easter Week, or a day appointed for public fast, humiliation, or thanksgiving, or a day on which the court does not sit, in which case any act or proceeding shall be considered as done or taken in due time if it is done or taken on the next day afterwards, which shall not be one of the days in this section specified.

(2.) Where by this Act any act or proceeding is directed to be done or taken on a certain day, then if that day happens to be one of the days in this section specified, the act or proceeding shall be considered as done or taken in due time if it is done or taken on the next day afterwards, which shall not be one of the days in this section specified.

### Notices.

Service of notices.

**142.** All notices and other documents for the service of which no special mode is directed may be sent by prepaid post letter to the last known address of the person to be served therewith.

### Formal Defects.

Formal defect not to invalidate proceedings.

**143.** (1.) No proceeding in bankruptcy shall be invalidated by any formal defect or by any irregularity, unless the court before which an objection is made to the proceeding is of opinion that substantial injustice has been caused by the defect or irregularity, and that the injustice cannot be remedied by any order of that court.

(2.) No defect or irregularity in the appointment or election of a receiver, trustee, or member of a committee of inspection shall vitiate any act done by him in good faith.

### Stamp Duty.

Exemption of deeds, &c. from stamp duty.

**144.** Every deed, conveyance, assignment, surrender, admission, or other assurance relating solely to freehold, leasehold, copyhold, or customary property, or to any mortgage, charge, or other incumbrance on, or any estate, right, or interest in any real or personal property which is part of the estate of any bankrupt, and which, after the execution of the deed, conveyance, assignment, surrender, admission, or other assurance, either at law or in equity, is or remains the estate of the bankrupt or of the trustee under the bankruptcy, and every power of attorney, proxy paper, writ, order, certificate, affidavit, bond, or other instrument or writing relating solely to the property of any bankrupt, or to any proceeding under any bankruptcy, shall be exempt from stamp duty, except in respect of fees under this Act.

### Executions.

Sales under executions to be public.

**145.** Where the sheriff sells the goods of a debtor under an execution for a sum exceeding twenty pounds (including legal incidental expenses), the sale shall, unless the court from which the process issued otherwise orders, be made by public auction, and not by bill of sale or private contract, and shall be publicly advertised by the sheriff on and during three days next preceding the day of sale.

Writ of elegit not to extend to goods.

**146.** (1.) The sheriff shall not under a writ of elegit deliver the goods of a debtor, nor shall a writ of elegit extend to goods.

(2.) No writ of *levari facias* shall hereafter be issued in any civil proceeding.

### Bankrupt Trustee.

**147.** Where a bankrupt is a trustee within the Trustee Act, 1850, section thirty-two of that Act shall have effect so as to authorise the appointment of a new trustee in substitution for the bankrupt (whether voluntarily resigning or not), if it appears expedient to do so, and all provisions of that Act, and of any other Act relative thereto, shall have effect accordingly.

*Application of Trustee Act to bankruptcy of trustee.*

### Corporations, &c.

**148.** For all or any of the purposes of this Act a corporation may act by any of its officers authorised in that behalf under the seal of the corporation, a firm may act by any of its members, and a lunatic may act by his committee or curator bonis.

*Acting of corporations, partners, &c.*

### Construction of former Acts, &c.

**149.** (1.) Where in any Act of Parliament, instrument, or proceeding passed, executed, or taken before the commencement of this Act mention is made of a commission of bankruptcy or fiat in bankruptcy, the same shall be construed, with reference to the proceedings under a bankruptcy petition, as if a commission of or a fiat in bankruptcy had been actually issued at the time of the presentation of such petition.

*Construction of Acts mentioning commission of bankruptcy, &c.*

(2.) Where by any Act or instrument, reference is made to the Bankruptcy Act, 1869, the Act or instrument shall be construed and have effect as if reference were made therein to the corresponding provisions of this Act.

**150.** Save as herein provided the provisions of this Act relating to the remedies against the property of a debtor, the priorities of debts, the effect of a composition or scheme of arrangement, and the effect of a discharge shall bind the Crown.

*Certain provisions to bind the Crown.*

**151.** Nothing in this Act, or in any transfer of jurisdiction effected thereby shall take away or affect any right of audience that any person may have had at the commencement of this Act, and all solicitors or other persons who had the right of audience before the Chief Judge in Bankruptcy shall have the like right of audience in bankruptcy matters in the High Court.

*Saving for existing rights of audience.*

**152.** Nothing in this Act shall affect the provisions of the Married Women's Property Act, 1882.

*Married women.*

### Transitory Provisions.

**153.** (1.) The existing comptroller in bankruptcy and his officers, clerks, and servants shall not be attached to the Supreme Court, but shall in all respects act under the directions of the Board of Trade.

*Comptroller of bankruptcy, &c. and their staff.*

(2.) The existing official assignee, provisional and official assignee of the estates and effects of insolvent debtors, and receiver of the Insolvent Debtors' Court, together with his staff, the official solicitors and the messenger in bankruptcy, together with his staff, and the accountant in bankruptcy and his staff, and also such other officers and clerks of the London Bankruptcy Court as the Lord Chancellor, with the concurrence of the Board of Trade, may at any time select, shall be transferred to and become officers of the Board of Trade; provided that the Board of Trade, with the concurrence of the Lord Chancellor, may at any time transfer any such officer or clerk from the Board of Trade to the Supreme Court.

(3.) Subject to the provisions of this Act they shall hold their offices by the same tenure and on the same terms and conditions, and be entitled to the same rights in respect of salary and pension as heretofore, and their duties shall, except so far as altered with their own consent, be such as in the opinion of the Board of Trade are analogous to those performed by them at the commencement of this Act.

(4.) On the occurrence, at any time after the passing of this Act, of any vacancy in the office of any of the said persons the Board of Trade may, with the approval of the Treasury, make such arrangement as they think fit, either for the abolition of the office, or for its continuance under modified conditions, and may appoint a fit person to perform the remaining duties thereof, and the person so appointed shall have all the powers and authorities of the person who is at the passing of this Act the holder of such office;

and all estates, rights, and effects vested at the time of the vacancy in any such officer shall by virtue of such appointment become vested in the person so appointed, and the like appointment on a vacancy shall be made, and the like vesting shall have effect from time to time as occasion requires: Provided that any person so appointed shall be an officer of the Board of Trade, and shall in all respects act under the directions of the Board of Trade.

(5.) The Board of Trade may, with the approval of the Lord Chancellor, from time to time direct that any duties or functions, not of a judicial character, relating to any bankruptcies, insolvencies, or other proceedings under any Act prior to the Bankruptcy Act, 1869, which were, at the time of the passing of this Act, performed or exercised by registrars of county courts, shall devolve on and be performed by the official receiver, and thereupon all powers and authorities of the registrar, and all estates, rights, and effects vested in the registrar shall become vested in the official receiver.

**Power to abolish existing offices.** 154. (1.) If the Lord Chancellor is of opinion that any office attached to the London Bankruptcy Court at the passing of this Act is unnecessary, he may, with the concurrence of the Treasury, at any time after the passing of this Act, abolish the office.

(2.) The Treasury may, on the petition of any person whose office or employment is abolished by or under this Act, on the commencement of this Act or on any other event, inquire whether any, and if any, what compensation ought to be made to the petitioner, regard being had to the conditions on which his appointment was made, the nature of his office or employment, and the duration of his service; and if they think that his claim to compensation is established, may award to him, out of moneys to be provided by Parliament, such compensation, by annuity or otherwise, as under the circumstances of the case they think just and reasonable.

(3.) The Board of Trade may, under the like conditions and on the like terms, abolish any of the offices in the last preceding section mentioned.

**Performance of new duties by persons whose offices are abolished.** 155. (1.) The Lord Chancellor or Board of Trade may, at any time after the passing of this Act appoint any person whose office is abolished under this Act to some other office under this Act, the duties of which he is in the opinion of the Lord Chancellor or Board competent to perform. Provided that the person so appointed shall during his tenure of the new office receive an amount of annual remuneration which, together with the compensation for the loss of the abolished office, is not less than the emoluments of the abolished office.

(2.) When, after the commencement of this Act, any officer is continued in the performance of any duties relating to bankruptcy or insolvency, under any previous Act, the Lord Chancellor, or, as the case may be, the Board of Trade may order that such officer may, in addition to such duties, perform any analogous duties under this Act, without being entitled to receive any additional remuneration.

**Selection of persons from holders of abolished offices.** 156. Every person appointed to any office or employment under this Act shall in the first instance be selected from the persons (if any) whose office or employment is abolished under this Act, unless in the opinion of the Lord Chancellor, or in the case of persons to be appointed by the Board of Trade, of that Board, none of such persons are fit for such office or employment: Provided that the person so appointed or employed shall during his tenure of the new office be entitled to receive an amount of remuneration which, together with the compensation (if any) for loss of the abolished office, shall be not less than the emolument of the abolished office.

**Acceptance of public employment by annuitants.** 157. If any person to whom a compensation annuity is granted under this Act accepts any public employment, he shall, during the continuance of that employment, receive only so much (if any) of that annuity as, with the remuneration of that employment, will amount to a sum not exceeding the salary or emoluments in respect of the loss whereof the annuity was awarded, and if the remuneration of that employment is equal to or greater than such salary or emoluments the annuity shall be suspended so long as he receives that remuneration.

**Superannuation of registrars, &c.** 158. The registrars, clerks, and other persons holding their offices at the passing of this Act who may be continued in their offices, shall, on their retirement therefrom, be allowed such superannuation as they would have been entitled to receive if this Act had not been passed, and they had continued in their offices under the existing Acts.

**Transfer of estates on** 159. In every liquidation by arrangement under the Bankruptcy Act,

1869, pending at the commencement of this Act, if at any time after the commencement of this Act there is no trustee acting in the liquidation by reason of death, or for any other cause, such of the official receivers of bankrupts estates as is appointed by the Board of Trade for that purpose shall become and be the trustee in the liquidation, and the property of the liquidating debtor shall pass to and vest in him accordingly (a); but this provision shall not prejudice the right of the creditors in the liquidation to appoint a new trustee, in manner directed by the Bankruptcy Act, 1869, or the rules thereunder; and on such appointment the property of the liquidating debtor shall pass to and vest in the new trustee. *vacancy of office of trustee in liquidation under the Bankruptcy Act, 1869.*

The provisions of this Act with respect to the duties and responsibilities of and accounting by a trustee in a bankruptcy under this Act shall apply, as nearly as may be, to a trustee acting under the provisions of this section.

**160.** Where a bankruptcy or liquidation by arrangement under the Bankruptcy Act, 1869, has been or is hereafter closed, any property of the bankrupt or liquidating debtor which vested in the trustee and has not been realised or distributed shall vest (a) in such person as may be appointed by the Board of Trade for that purpose, and he shall thereupon proceed to get in, realise, and distribute the property in like manner and with and subject to the like powers and obligations as far as applicable, as if the bankruptcy or liquidation were continuing, and he were acting as trustee thereunder. *Transfer of outstanding property on close of bankruptcy or liquidation.*

**161.** In every bankruptcy under the Bankruptcy Act, 1869, pending at the commencement of this Act, where a registrar of the London Bankruptcy Court, or of any county court, is or would hereafter but for this enactment become the trustee under the bankruptcy, such of the official receivers of bankrupts estates as may be appointed by the Board of Trade for that purpose shall from and after the commencement of this Act be the trustee in the place of the registrar, and the property of the bankrupt shall pass to and vest (a) in the official receiver accordingly. *Transfer of estates from registrars of London Court to official receiver.*

### Unclaimed Funds or Dividends.

**162.** (1.) Where the trustee, under any bankruptcy, composition or scheme pursuant to this Act, shall have under his control any unclaimed dividend which has remained unclaimed for more than six months, or where, after making a final dividend, such trustee shall have in his hands or under his control any unclaimed or undistributed moneys arising from the property of the debtor, he shall forthwith pay the same to the Bankruptcy Estates Account at the Bank of England. The Board of Trade shall furnish him with a certificate of receipt of the money so paid, which shall be an effectual discharge to him in respect thereof. *Unclaimed and undistributed dividends or funds under this and former Acts.*

(2.) (a.) Where, after the passing of this Act, any unclaimed or undistributed funds or dividends in the hands or under the control of any trustee or other person empowered to collect, receive, or distribute any funds or dividends under any Act of Parliament mentioned in the Fourth Schedule, or any petition, resolution, deed, or other proceeding under or in pursuance of any such Act, have remained or remain unclaimed or undistributed for six months after the same became claimable or distributable, or in any other case for two years after the receipt thereof by such trustee or other person, it shall be the duty of such trustee or other person forthwith to pay the same to the Bankruptcy Estates Account at the Bank of England. The Board of Trade shall furnish such trustee or other person with a certificate of receipt of the money so paid, which shall be an effectual discharge to him in respect thereof.

(b.) The Board of Trade may at any time order any such trustee or other person to submit to them an account verified by affidavit of the sums received and paid by him under or in pursuance of any such petition, resolution, deed, or other proceeding as aforesaid, and may direct and enforce an audit of the account.

(c.) The Board of Trade, with the concurrence of the Treasury, may from time to time appoint a person to collect and get in all such unclaimed or undistributed funds or dividends, and for the purposes of this section any court having jurisdiction in bankruptcy shall have and at the instance of the

(a) See 50 & 51 Vict. c. 66, s. 6 (1).

person so appointed, or of the Board of Trade, may exercise all the powers conferred by this Act with respect to the discovery and realisation of the property of a debtor, and the provisions of Part I. of this Act with respect thereto shall, with any necessary modifications, apply to proceedings under this section.

(3.) The provisions of this section shall not, except as expressly declared herein, deprive any person of any larger or other right or remedy to which he may be entitled against such trustee or other person.

(4.) Any person claiming to be entitled to any moneys paid in to the Bankruptcy Estates Account pursuant to this section may apply to the Board of Trade for payment to him of the same, and the Board of Trade, if satisfied that the person claiming is entitled, shall make an order for the payment to such person of the sum due.

Any person dissatisfied with the decision of the Board of Trade in respect of his claim may appeal to the High Court.

(5.) The Board of Trade may at any time after the passing of this Act open the account at the Bank of England referred to in this Act as the Bankruptcy Estates Account.

### Punishment of Fraudulent Debtors.

Extension of penal provisions of 32 & 33 Vict. c. 62, to petitioning debtors, &c.

**163.** (1.) Sections eleven and twelve of the Debtors Act, 1869, relating to the punishment of fraudulent debtors and imposing a penalty for absconding with property, shall have effect as if there were substituted therein for the words " if after the presentation of a bankruptcy petition against him," the words, " if after the presentation of a bankruptcy petition by or against him."

(2.) The provisions of the Debtors Act, 1869, as to offences by bankrupts shall apply to any person whether a trader or not in respect of whose estate a receiving order has been made as if the term " bankrupt" in that Act included a person in respect of whose estate a receiving order had been made.

Power for Court to order prosecution on report of official receiver.

**164.** Section sixteen of the Debtors Act, 1869, shall be construed and have effect as if the term " a trustee in any bankruptcy " included the official receiver of a bankrupt's estate, and shall apply to offences under this Act as well as to offences under the Debtors Act, 1869.

Power for Court to commit for trial.

**165.** (1.) Where there is, in the opinion of the court, ground to believe that the bankrupt or any other person has been guilty of any offence which is by statute made a misdemeanor in cases of bankruptcy, the court may commit the bankrupt or such other person for trial.

(2.) For the purpose of committing the bankrupt or such other person for trial the court shall have all the powers of a stipendiary magistrate as to taking depositions, binding over witnesses to appear, admitting the accused to bail, or otherwise.

Nothing in this sub-section shall be construed as derogating from the powers or jurisdiction of the High Court.

Public Prosecutor to act in certain cases.

**166.** Where the court orders the prosecution of any person for any offence under the Debtors Act, 1869, or Acts amending it, or for any offence arising out of or connected with any bankruptcy proceedings, it shall be the duty of the Director of Public Prosecutions to institute and carry on the prosecution.

Criminal liability after discharge or composition.

**167.** Where a debtor has been guilty of any criminal offence he shall not be exempt from being proceeded against therefor by reason that he has obtained his discharge or that a composition or scheme of arrangement has been accepted or approved.

### Interpretation.

Interpretation of terms.

**168.** (1.) In this Act, unless the context otherwise requires—

" The court " means the court having jurisdiction in bankruptcy under this Act :

" Affidavit " includes statutory declarations, affirmations, and attestations on honour :

" Available act of bankruptcy " means any act of bankruptcy available for a bankruptcy petition at the date of the presentation of the petition on which the receiving order is made :

"Debt provable in bankruptcy" or "provable debt" includes any debt or liability by this Act made provable in bankruptcy:

"Gazetted" means published in the London Gazette:

"General rules" include forms:

"Goods" includes all chattels personal:

"High Court" means Her Majesty's High Court of Justice:

"Local bank" means any bank in or in the neighbourhood of the bankruptcy district in which the proceedings are taken:

"Oath" includes affirmation, statutory declaration, and attestation on honour:

"Ordinary resolution" means a resolution decided by a majority in value of the creditors present, personally or by proxy, at a meeting of creditors and voting on the resolution:

"Person" includes a body of persons corporate or unincorporate:

"Prescribed" means prescribed by general rules within the meaning of this Act:

"Property" includes money, goods, things in action, land, and every description of property, whether real or personal, and whether situate in England or elsewhere; also, obligations, easements, and every description of estate, interest and profit, present or future, vested or contingent, arising out of or incident to property as above defined:

"Resolution" means ordinary resolution:

"Secured creditor" means a person holding a mortgage charge or lien on the property of the debtor, or any part thereof, as a security for a debt due to him from the debtor:

"Schedule" means schedule to this Act:

"Sheriff" includes any officer charged with the execution of a writ or other process:

"Special resolution" means a resolution decided by a majority in number and three fourths in value of the creditors present, personally or by proxy, at a meeting of creditors and voting on the resolution:

"Treasury" means the Commissioners of Her Majesty's Treasury:

"Trustee" means the trustee in bankruptcy of a debtor's estate.

(2.) The schedules to this Act shall be construed and have effect as part of this Act.

### *Repeal.*

**169.** (1.) The enactments described in the Fifth Schedule are hereby repealed as from the commencement of this Act to the extent mentioned in that Schedule. *Repeal of enactments.*

(2.) The repeal effected by this Act shall not affect—

(a) anything done or suffered before the commencement of this Act under any enactment repealed by this Act; nor

(b) any right or privilege acquired, or duty imposed, or liability, or disqualification incurred, under any enactment so repealed; nor

(c) any fine, forfeiture, or other punishment incurred or to be incurred in respect of any offence committed or to be committed against any enactment so repealed; nor

(d) the institution or continuance of any proceeding or other remedy, whether under any enactment so repealed, or otherwise, for ascertaining any such liability or disqualification, or enforcing or recovering any such fine, forfeiture, or punishment, as aforesaid.

(3.) Notwithstanding the repeal effected by this Act, the proceedings under any bankruptcy petition, liquidation by arrangement, or composition with creditors under the Bankruptcy Act, 1869, pending at the commencement of this Act shall, except so far as any provision of this Act is expressly applied to pending proceedings, continue, and all the provisions of the Bankruptcy Act, 1869, shall, except as aforesaid, apply thereto, as if this Act had not passed.

**170.** After the passing of this Act no composition or liquidation by arrangement under sections 125 and 126 of the Bankruptcy Act, 1869, shall be entered into or allowed without the sanction of the court or registrar having jurisdiction in the matter; such sanction shall not be granted unless the composition or liquidation appears to the court or registrar to be reasonable and calculated to benefit the general body of creditors. *Proceedings under 32 & 33 Vict. c. 71, ss. 125, 126 (a).*

(a) See 50 & 51 Vict. c. 66.

## SCHEDULES.

## THE FIRST SCHEDULE.

### Meetings of Creditors.

1. The first meeting of creditors shall be summoned for a day not later than fourteen days after the date of the receiving order, unless the court for any special reason deem it expedient that the meeting be summoned for a later day.

2. The official receiver shall summon the meeting by giving not less than seven days notice of the time and place thereof in the London Gazette and in a local paper.

3. The official receiver shall also, as soon as practicable, send to each creditor mentioned in the debtor's statement of affairs, a notice of the time and place of the first meeting of creditors, accompanied by a summary of the debtor's statement of affairs, including the causes of his failure, and any observations thereon which the official receiver may think fit to make; but the proceedings at the first meeting shall not be invalidated by reason of any such notice or summary not having been sent or received before the meeting.

4. The meeting shall be held at such place as is in the opinion of the official receiver most convenient for the majority of the creditors.

5. The official receiver or the trustee may at any time summon a meeting of creditors, and shall do so whenever so directed by the court, or so requested in writing by one-fourth in value of the creditors.

6. Meetings subsequent to the first meeting shall be summoned by sending notice of the time and place thereof to each creditor at the address given in his proof, or if he has not proved, at the address given in the debtor's statement of affairs, or at such other address as may be known to the person summoning the meeting.

7. The official receiver, or some person nominated by him, shall be the chairman at the first meeting. The chairman at subsequent meetings shall be such person as the meeting by resolution appoint.

8. A person shall not be entitled to vote as a creditor at the first or any other meeting of creditor unless he has duly proved a debt provable in bankruptcy to be due to him from the debtor, and the proof has been duly lodged before the time appointed for the meeting.

9. A creditor shall not vote at any such meeting in respect of any unliquidated or contingent debt, or any debt the value of which is not ascertained.

10. For the purpose of voting, a secured creditor shall, unless he surrenders his security, state in his proof the particulars of his security, the date when it was given, and the value at which he assesses it, and shall be entitled to vote only in respect of the balance (if any) due to him, after deducting the value of his security. If he votes in respect of his whole debt he shall be deemed to have surrendered his security unless the court on application is satisfied that the omission to value the security has arisen from inadvertence.

11. A creditor shall not vote in respect of any debt on or secured by a current bill of exchange or promissory note held by him unless he is willing to treat the liability to him thereon of every person who is liable thereon antecedently to the debtor, and against whom a receiving order has not been made, as a security in his hands, and to estimate the value thereof, and for the purposes of voting, but not for the purposes of dividend, to deduct it from his proof.

12. It shall be competent to the trustee or to the official receiver, within twenty-eight days after a proof estimating the value of a security as aforesaid has been made use of in voting at any meeting, to require the creditor to give up the security for the benefit of the creditors generally on payment of the value so estimated, with an addition thereto of twenty per centum. Provided, that where a creditor has put a value on such security, he may, at any time before he has been required to give up such security as aforesaid, correct such valuation by a new proof, and

deduct such new value from his debt, but in that case such addition of twenty per centum shall not be made if the trustee requires the security to be given up.

13. If a receiving order is made against one partner of a firm, any creditor to whom that partner is indebted jointly with the other partners of the firm, or any of them, may prove his debt for the purpose of voting at any meeting of creditors, and shall be entitled to vote thereat.

14. The chairman of a meeting shall have power to admit or reject a proof for the purpose of voting, but his decision shall be subject to appeal to the court. If he is in doubt whether the proof of a creditor should be admitted or rejected he shall mark the proof as objected to and shall allow the creditor to vote, subject to the vote being declared invalid in the event of the objection being sustained.

15. A creditor may vote either in person or by proxy.

16. Every instrument of proxy shall be in the prescribed form, and shall be issued by the official receiver, or, after the appointment of a trustee, by the trustee, and every insertion therein shall be in the handwriting of the person giving the proxy.

17. A creditor may give a general proxy to his manager or clerk, or any other person in his regular employment. In such case the instrument of proxy shall state the relation in which the person to act thereunder stands to the creditor.

18. A creditor may give a special proxy to any person to vote at any specified meeting, or adjournment thereof, for or against any specific resolution, or for or against any specified person as trustee, or member of a committee of inspection.

19. A proxy shall not be used unless it is deposited with the official receiver or trustee before the meeting at which it is to be used.

20. Where it appears to the satisfaction of the court that any solicitation has been used by or on behalf of a trustee or receiver in obtaining proxies or in procuring the trusteeship or receivership, except by the direction of a meeting of creditors, the court shall have power, if it think fit, to order that no remuneration shall be allowed to the person by whom or on whose behalf such solicitation may have been exercised, notwithstanding any resolution of the committee of inspection or of the creditors to the contrary.

21. A creditor may appoint the official receiver of the debtor's estate to act in manner prescribed as his general or special proxy.

22. The chairman of a meeting may, with the consent of the meeting, adjourn the meeting from time to time, and from place to place.

23. A meeting shall not be competent to act for any purpose, except the election of a chairman, the proving of debts, and the adjournment of the meeting, unless there are present, or represented thereat, at least three creditors, or all the creditors if their number does not exceed three.

24. If within half an hour from the time appointed for the meeting a quorum of creditors is not present or represented, the meeting shall be adjourned to the same day in the following week at the same time and place, or to such other day as the chairman may appoint, not being less than seven or more than twenty-one days.

25. The chairman of every meeting shall cause minutes of the proceedings at the meeting to be drawn up, and fairly entered in a book kept for that purpose, and the minutes shall be signed by him or by the chairman of the next ensuing meeting.

26. No person acting either under a general or special proxy shall vote in favour of any resolution which would directly or indirectly place himself, his partner or employer, in a position to receive any remuneration out of the estate of the debtor otherwise than as a creditor rateably with the other creditors of the debtor. Provided that where any person holds special proxies to vote for the appointment of himself as trustee he may use the said proxies and vote accordingly.

Section 39.

## THE SECOND SCHEDULE.

### PROOF OF DEBTS.

#### *Proof in ordinary Cases.*

1. Every creditor shall prove his debt as soon as may be after the making of a receiving order.

2. A debt may be proved by delivering or sending through the post in a prepaid letter to the official receiver, or, if a trustee has been appointed, to the trustee, an affidavit verifying the debt.

3. The affidavit may be made by the creditor himself, or by some person authorised by or on behalf of the creditor. If made by a person so authorised it shall state his authority and means of knowledge.

4. The affidavit shall contain or refer to a statement of account showing the particulars of the debt, and shall specify the vouchers, if any, by which the same can be substantiated. The official receiver or trustee may at any time call for the production of the vouchers.

5. The affidavit shall state whether the creditor is or is not a secured creditor.

6. A creditor shall bear the cost of proving his debt, unless the court otherwise specially orders.

7. Every creditor who has lodged a proof shall be entitled to see and examine the proofs of other creditors before the first meeting, and at all reasonable times.

8. A creditor proving his debt shall deduct therefrom all trade discounts, but he shall not be compelled to deduct any discount, not exceeding five per centum on the net amount of his claim, which he may have agreed to allow for payment in cash.

#### *Proof by secured Creditors.*

9. If a secured creditor realises his security, he may prove for the balance due to him, after deducting the net amount realised.

10. If a secured creditor surrenders his security to the official receiver or trustee for the general benefit of the creditors, he may prove for his whole debt.

11. If a secured creditor does not either realise or surrender his security, he shall, before ranking for dividend, state in his proof the particulars of his security, the date when it was given, and the value at which he assesses it, and shall be entitled to receive a dividend only in respect of the balance due to him after deducting the value so assessed.

12. (a.) Where a security is so valued, the trustee may at any time redeem it on payment to the creditor of the assessed value.

(b.) If the trustee is dissatisfied with the value at which a security is assessed, he may require that the property comprised in any security so valued be offered for sale at such times and on such terms and conditions as may be agreed on between the creditor and the trustee, or as, in default of such agreement, the court may direct. If the sale be by public auction the creditor, or the trustee on behalf of the estate, may bid or purchase.

(c.) Provided that the creditor may at any time, by notice in writing, require the trustee to elect whether he will or will not exercise his power of redeeming the security or requiring it to be realised, and if the trustee does not, within six months after receiving the notice, signify in writing to the creditor his election to exercise the power, he shall not be entitled to exercise it; and the equity of redemption, or any other interest in the property comprised in the security which is vested in the trustee, shall vest in the creditor, and the amount of his debt shall be reduced by the amount at which the security has been valued.

13. Where a creditor has so valued his security, he may at any time amend the valuation and proof on showing to the satisfaction of the trustee, or the court, that the valuation and proof were made bonâ fide on a mistaken estimate, or that the security has diminished or increased in value since its previous valuation; but every such amendment shall be made at the cost of the creditor, and upon such terms as the court shall order, unless the trustee shall allow the amendment without application to the court.

14. Where a valuation has been amended in accordance with the foregoing rule, the creditor shall forthwith repay any surplus dividend which he may have received in excess of that to which he would have been entitled on the amended valuation, or, as the case may be, shall be entitled to be paid out of any money for the time being available for dividend any dividend or share of dividend which he may have failed to receive by reason of the inaccuracy of the original valuation, before that money is made applicable to the payment of any future dividend, but he shall not be entitled to disturb the distribution of any dividend declared before the date of the amendment.

15. If a creditor after having valued his security subsequently realises it, or if it is realised under the provisions of Rule 12, the net amount realised shall be substituted for the amount of any valuation previously made by the creditor, and shall be treated in all respects as an amended valuation made by the creditor.

16. If a secured creditor does not comply with the foregoing rules he shall be excluded from all share in any dividend.

17. Subject to the provisions of Rule 12, a creditor shall in no case receive more than twenty shillings in the pound, and interest as provided by this Act.

### Proof in respect of Distinct Contracts.

18. If a debtor was at the date of the receiving order liable in respect of distinct contracts as a member of two or more distinct firms, or as a sole contractor, and also as member of a firm, the circumstance that the firms are in whole or in part composed of the same individuals, or that the sole contractor is also one of the joint contractors, shall not prevent proof in respect of the contracts, against the properties respectively liable on the contracts.

### Periodical Payments.

19. When any rent or other payment falls due at stated periods, and the receiving order is made at any time other than one of those periods, the person entitled to the rent or payment may prove for a proportinate part thereof up to the date of the order, as if the rent or payment grew due from day to day.

### Interest.

20. On any debt or sum certain, payable at a certain time or otherwise, whereon interest is not reserved or agreed for, and which is overdue at the date of the receiving order and provable in bankruptcy, the creditor may prove for interest at a rate not exceeding four per centum per annum to the date of the order from the time when the debt or sum was payable, if the debt or sum is payable by virtue of a written instrument at a certain time, and if payable otherwise, then from the time when a demand in writing has been made giving the debtor notice that interest will be claimed from the date of the demand until the time of payment.

### Debt payable at a future time.

21. A creditor may prove for a debt not payable when the debtor committed an act of bankruptcy as if it were payable presently, and may receive dividends equally with the other creditors, deducting only thereout a rebate of interest at the rate of five pounds per centum per annum computed from the declaration of a dividend to the time when the debt would have become payable, according to the terms on which it was contracted.

### Admission or Rejection of Proofs.

22. The trustee shall examine every proof and the grounds of the debt, and in writing admit or reject it, in whole or in part, or require further evidence in support of it. If he rejects a proof he shall state in writing to the creditor the grounds of the rejection.

23. If the trustee thinks that a proof has been improperly admitted, the court may, on the application of the trustee, after notice to the creditor who made the proof, expunge the proof or reduce its amount.

24. If a creditor is dissatisfied with the decision of the trustee in respect of a proof, the court may, on the application of the creditor, reverse or vary the decision.

25. The court may also expunge or reduce a proof upon the application of

a creditor if the trustee declines to interfere in the matter, or, in the case of a composition or scheme, upon the application of the debtor.

26. For the purpose of any of his duties in relation to proofs, the trustee may administer oaths and take affidavits.

27. The official receiver, before the appointment of a trustee, shall have all the powers of a trustee with respect to the examination, admission, and rejection of proofs, and any act or decision of his in relation thereto shall be subject to the like appeal.

---

Section 96.

## THE THIRD SCHEDULE.

### LIST OF METROPOLITAN COUNTY COURTS.

The Bloomsbury County Court of Middlesex.
The Bow County Court of Middlesex.
The Brompton County Court of Middlesex.
The Clerkenwell County Court of Middlesex.
The Lambeth County Court of Surrey.
The Marylebone County Court of Middlesex.
The Shoreditch County Court of Middlesex.
The Southwark County Court of Surrey.
The Westminster County Court of Middlesex.
The Whitechapel County Court of Middlesex.

---

Section 162.

## THE FOURTH SCHEDULE.

### STATUTES RELATING TO UNCLAIMED DIVIDENDS.

| Session and Chapter. | Title of Act. |
| --- | --- |
| 7 & 8 Vict. c. 70 . | An Act for facilitating arrangements between debtors and creditors. |
| 12 & 13 Vict. c. 106 . | The Bankruptcy Law Consolidation Act, 1849. |
| 24 & 25 Vict. c. 134 . | The Bankruptcy Act, 1861. |
| 32 & 33 Vict. c. 71 . | The Bankruptcy Act, 1869. |

---

Section 169.

## THE FIFTH SCHEDULE.

### ENACTMENTS REPEALED AS TO ENGLAND.

| | |
| --- | --- |
| 13 Edw 1 c. 18. in part. | The statutes of Westminster the second, chapter eighteen, Execution either by levying of the lands and goods, or by delivery of goods and half the land; at the choice of the creditor; in part; namely, the words " all the chattels of the debtor saving only his oxen and beasts of the plough, and " |
| 32 & 33 Vict. c. 62. in part. | The Debtors Act, 1869. in part; namely, Sub-section (b) of section five, and Sections twenty-one and twenty-two. |
| 32 & 33 Vict. c. 71. | The Bankruptcy Act, 1869. |
| 32 & 33 Vict. c. 83. in part. | The Bankruptcy Repeal and Insolvent Court Act, 1869. in part; namely, Section nineteen. |
| 33 & 34 Vict. c. 76. | The Absconding Debtors Act, 1870. |
| 34 & 35 Vict. c. 50. | The Bankruptcy Disqualification Act, 1871. Except sections six, seven, and eight. |
| 38 & 39 Vict. c. 77. in part. | The Supreme Court of Judicature Act, 1875. in part; namely, Sections nine and thirty-two. |

46 & 47 VICT. C. 57.

*An Act to amend and consolidate the Law relating to Patents for Inventions, Registration of Designs, and of Trade Marks.*
[*25th August*, 1883.]

BE it enacted by the Queen's most Excellent Majesty, by and with the advice and consent of the Lords Spiritual and Temporal, and Commons, in this present Parliament assembled, and by the authority of the same, as follows:

## PART I.

### PRELIMINARY.

1. This Act may be cited as the Patents, Designs, and Trade Marks Act, 1883. *Short title.*

2. This Act is divided into parts, as follows:— *Division of Act into parts.*
    Part I.—PRELIMINARY.
    Part II.—PATENTS.
    Part III.—DESIGNS.
    Part IV.—TRADE MARKS.
    Part V.—GENERAL.

3. This Act, except where it is otherwise expressed, shall commence from and immediately after the thirty-first day of December one thousand eight hundred and eighty-three. *Commencement of Act.*

---

## PART II.

### PATENTS.

*Application for and Grant of Patent.*

4.—(1.) Any person, whether a British subject or not, may make an application for a patent. *Persons entitled to apply for patent.*

(2.) Two or more persons may make a joint application for a patent, and a patent may be granted to them jointly.

5.—(1.) An application for a patent must be made in the form set forth in the First Schedule to this Act, or in such other form as may be from time to time prescribed; and must be left at, or sent by post to, the patent office in the prescribed manner. *Application and specification.*

(2.) An application must contain a declaration (*a*) to the effect that the applicant is in possession of an invention, whereof he, or in the case of a joint application, one or more of the applicants, claims or claim to be the true and first inventor or inventors, and for which he or they desires or desire to obtain a patent; and must be accompanied by either a provisional or complete specification.

(3.) A provisional specification must describe the nature of the invention, and be accompanied by drawings, if required.

(4.) A complete specification, whether left on application or subsequently, must particularly describe and ascertain the nature of the invention, and in what manner it is to be performed, and must be accompanied by drawings, if required (*b*).

(5.) A specification, whether provisional or complete, must commence with the title, and in the case of a complete specification must end with a distinct statement of the invention claimed.

6. The comptroller shall refer every application to an examiner, who shall ascertain and report to the comptroller whether the nature of the invention has been fairly described, and the application, specification, and draw- *Reference of application to examiner.*

(*a*) See 48 & 49 Vict. c. 63, s. 2.    (*b*) See 49 & 50 Vict. c. 37, s. 2.

4 F 2

ings (if any) have been prepared in the prescribed manner, and the title sufficiently indicates the subject-matter of the invention.

Power for comptroller to refuse application or require amendment.

7.—(1.) If the examiner reports that the nature of the invention is not fairly described, or that the application, specification or drawings has not or have not been prepared in the prescribed manner, or that the title does not sufficiently indicate the subject-matter of the invention, the comptroller may require that the application, specification or drawings be amended before he proceeds with the application.

(2.) Where the comptroller requires an amendment, the applicant may appeal from his decision to the law officer.

(3.) The law officer shall, if required, hear the applicant and the comptroller, and may make an order determining whether and subject to what conditions, if any, the application shall be accepted.

(4.) The comptroller shall, when an application has been accepted, give notice thereof to the applicant.

(5.) If after an application has been made, but before a patent has been sealed, an application is made, accompanied by a specification bearing the same or a similar title, it shall be the duty of the examiner to report to the comptroller whether the specification appears to him to comprise the same invention; and, if he reports in the affirmative, the comptroller shall give notice to the applicants that he has so reported.

(6.) Where the examiner reports in the affirmative, the comptroller may determine, subject to an appeal to the law officer, whether the invention comprised in both applications is the same, and if so he may refuse to seal a patent on the application of the second applicant.

Time for leaving complete specification.

8.—(1.) If the applicant does not leave a complete specification with his application, he may leave it at any subsequent time within nine months (a) from the date of application.

(2.) Unless a complete specification is left within that time the application shall be deemed to be abandoned.

Comparison of provisional and complete specification.

9.—(1.) Where a complete specification is left after a provisional specification, the comptroller shall refer both specifications to an examiner for the purpose of ascertaining whether the complete specification has been prepared in the prescribed manner, and whether the invention particularly described in the complete specification is substantially the same as that which is described in the provisional specification.

(2.) If the examiner reports that the conditions hereinbefore contained have not been complied with, the comptroller may refuse to accept the complete specification unless and until the same shall have been amended to his satisfaction; but any such refusal shall be subject to appeal to the law officer.

(3.) The law officer shall, if required, hear the applicant and the comptroller, and may make an order determining whether and subject to what conditions, if any, the complete specification shall be accepted.

(4.) Unless a complete specification is accepted within twelve months (a) from the date of application, then (save in the case of an appeal having been lodged against the refusal to accept) the application shall, at the expiration of those twelve months, become void.

(5.) Reports of examiners shall not in any case be published or be open to public inspection, and shall not be liable to production or inspection in any legal proceeding, other than an appeal to the law officer under this Act, unless the court or officer having power to order discovery in such legal proceeding shall certify that such production or inspection is desirable in the interests of justice, and ought to be allowed.

Advertisement on acceptance of complete specification.

10. On the acceptance of the complete specification the comptroller shall advertise the acceptance; and the application and specification or specifications with the drawings (if any) shall be open to public inspection.

Opposition to grant of patent.

11.—(1.) Any person may at any time within two months from the date of the advertisement of the acceptance of a complete specification give notice at the patent office of opposition to the grant of the patent on the ground of the applicant having obtained the invention from him, or from a person of whom he is the legal representative, or on the ground that the invention has been patented in this country on an application of prior date, or on the

(a) See 48 & 49 Vict. c. 63, s. 3.

ground of an examiner having reported to the comptroller that the specification appears to him to comprise the same invention as is comprised in a specification bearing the same or a similar title and accompanying a previous application, but on no other ground.

(2.) Where such notice is given the comptroller shall give notice of the opposition to the applicant, and shall, on the expiration of those two months, after hearing the applicant and the person so giving notice, if desirous of being heard, decide on the case, but subject to appeal to the law officer.

(3.) The law officer shall, if required, hear the applicant and any person so giving notice and being, in the opinion of the law officer, entitled to be heard in opposition to the grant, and shall determine whether the grant ought or ought not to be made.

(4.) The law officer may, if he thinks fit, obtain the assistance of an expert, who shall be paid such remuneration as the law officer, with the consent of the Treasury, shall appoint.

**12.**—(1.) If there is no opposition, or, in case of opposition, if the determination is in favour of the grant of a patent, the comptroller shall cause a patent to be sealed with the seal of the patent office. *Sealing of patent.*

(2.) A patent so sealed shall have the same effect as if it were sealed with the Great Seal of the United Kingdom.

(3.) A patent shall be sealed as soon as may be, and not after the expiration of fifteen months (a) from the date of application, except in the cases hereinafter mentioned, that is to say—

(a) Where the sealing is delayed by an appeal to the law officer, or by opposition to the grant of the patent, the patent may be sealed at such time as the law officer may direct.

(b) If the person making the application dies before the expiration of the fifteen months aforesaid, the patent may be granted to his legal representative and sealed at any time within twelve months after the death of the applicant.

**13.** Every patent shall be dated and sealed as of the day of the application: *Date of patent.* Provided that no proceedings shall be taken in respect of an infringement committed before the publication of the complete specification: Provided also, that in case of more than one application for a patent for the same invention, the sealing of a patent on one of those applications shall not prevent the sealing of a patent on an earlier application.

### Provisional Protection.

**14.** Where an application for a patent in respect of an invention has been accepted, the invention may during the period between the date of the application and the date of sealing such patent be used and published without prejudice to the patent to be granted for the same: and such protection from the consequences of use and publication is in this Act referred to as provisional protection. *Provisional protection.*

### Protection by Complete Specification.

**15.** After the acceptance of a complete specification and until the date of sealing a patent in respect thereof, or the expiration of the time for sealing, the applicant shall have the like privileges and rights as if a patent for the invention had been sealed on the date of the acceptance of the complete specification: Provided that an applicant shall not be entitled to institute any proceeding for infringement unless and until a patent for the invention has been granted to him. *Effect of acceptance of complete specification.*

### Patent.

**16.** Every patent when sealed shall have effect throughout the United Kingdom and the Isle of Man. *Extent of patent.*

**17.**—(1.) The term limited in every patent for the duration thereof shall be fourteen years from its date. *Term of patent.*

(2.) But every patent shall, notwithstanding anything therein or in this Act, cease if the patentee fails to make the prescribed payments within the prescribed times.

(a) 48 & 49 Vict. c. 63, s. 3.

(3.) If, nevertheless, in any case, by accident, mistake or inadvertence, a patentee fails to make any prescribed payment within the prescribed time, he may apply to the comptroller for an enlargement of the time for making that payment.

(4.) Thereupon the comptroller shall, if satisfied that the failure has arisen from any of the above-mentioned causes, on receipt of the prescribed fee for enlargement, not exceeding ten pounds, enlarge the time accordingly, subject to the following conditions:—

(a) The time for making any payment shall not in any case be enlarged for more than three months.

(b) If any proceeding shall be taken in respect of an infringement of the patent committed after a failure to make any payment within the prescribed time, and before the enlargement thereof, the court before which the proceeding is proposed to be taken may, if it shall think fit, refuse to award or give any damages in respect of such infringement.

### Amendment of Specification.

**Amendment of specification.**

**18.**—(1.) An applicant or a patentee may, from time to time, by request in writing left at the patent office, seek leave to amend his specification, including drawings forming part thereof, by way of disclaimer, correction, or explanation, stating the nature of such amendment and his reasons for the same.

(2.) The request and the nature of such proposed amendment shall be advertised in the prescribed manner, and at any time within one month from its first advertisement any person may give notice at the patent office of opposition to the amendment.

(3.) Where such notice is given the comptroller shall give notice of the opposition to the person making the request, and shall hear and decide the case subject to an appeal to the law officer.

(4.) The law officer shall, if required, hear the person making the request and the person so giving notice, and being in the opinion of the law officer entitled to be heard in opposition to the request, and shall determine whether and subject to what conditions, if any, the amendment ought to be allowed.

(5.) Where no notice of opposition is given, or the person so giving notice does not appear, the comptroller shall determine whether and subject to what conditions, if any, the amendment ought to be allowed.

(6.) When leave to amend is refused by the comptroller, the person making the request may appeal from his decision to the law officer.

(7.) The law officer shall, if required, hear the person making the request and the comptroller, and may make an order determining whether, and subject to what conditions, if any, the amendment ought to be allowed.

(8.) No amendment shall be allowed that would make the specification, as amended, claim an invention substantially larger than or substantially different from the invention claimed by the specification as it stood before amendment.

(9.) Leave to amend shall be conclusive as to the right of the party to make the amendment allowed, except in case of fraud; and the amendment shall in all courts and for all purposes be deemed to form part of the specification.

(10.) The foregoing provisions of this section do not apply when and so long as any action for infringement or other legal proceeding in relation to a patent is pending.

**Power to disclaim part of invention during action, &c.**

**19.**—(1.) In an action for infringement of a patent, and in a proceeding for revocation of a patent, the court or a judge may at any time order that the patentee shall, subject to such terms as to costs and otherwise as the court or a judge may impose, be at liberty to apply at the patent office for leave to amend his specification by way of disclaimer, and may direct that in the meantime the trial or hearing of the action shall be postponed.

**Restriction on recovery of damages.**

**20.** Where an amendment by way of disclaimer, correction, or explanation, has been allowed under this Act, no damages shall be given in any action in respect of the use of the invention before the disclaimer, correction, or explanation, unless the patentee establishes to the satisfaction of the court that his original claim was framed in good faith and with reasonable skill and knowledge.

21. Every amendment of a specification shall be advertised in the pre- Advertisement<br>of amendment. scribed manner.

### Compulsory Licences.

22. If on the petition of any person interested it is proved to the Board of Power for Board<br>to order grant<br>of licences. Trade that by reason of the default of a patentee to grant licences on reasonable terms—

(a.) The patent is not being worked in the United Kingdom ; or

(b.) The reasonable requirements of the public with respect to the invention cannot be supplied ; or

(c.) Any person is prevented from working or using to the best advantage an invention of which he is possessed,

the Board may order the patentee to grant licences on such terms as to the amount of royalties, security for payment, or otherwise, as the Board, having regard to the nature of the invention and the circumstances of the case, may deem just, and any such order may be enforced by mandamus.

### Register of Patents.

23.—(1.) There shall be kept at the patent office a book called the Register Register of<br>patents. of Patents, wherein shall be entered the names and addresses of grantees of patents, notifications of assignments and of transmissions of patents, of licences under patents, and of amendments, extensions, and revocations of patents, and such other matters affecting the validity or proprietorship of patents as may from time to time be prescribed.

(2.) The register of patents shall be primâ facie evidence of any matters by this Act directed or authorized to be inserted therein.

(3.) Copies of deeds, licences, and any other documents affecting the proprietorship in any letters patent or in any licence thereunder, must be supplied to the comptroller in the prescribed manner for filing in the patent office.

### Fees.

24.—(1.) There shall be paid in respect of the several instruments described Fees in schedule. in the Second Schedule to this Act, the fees in that schedule mentioned, and there shall likewise be paid, in respect of other matters under this part of the Act, such fees as may be from time to time, with the sanction of the Treasury, prescribed by the Board of Trade ; and such fees shall be levied and paid to the account of her Majesty's Exchequer in such manner as the Treasury may from time to time direct.

(2.) The Board of Trade may from time to time, if they think fit, with the consent of the Treasury, reduce any of those fees.

### Extension of Term of Patent.

25.—(1.) A patentee may, after advertising in manner directed by any Extension of<br>term of patent<br>on petition to<br>Queen in<br>Council. rules made under this section his intention to do so, present a petition to her Majesty in Council, praying that his patent may be extended for a further term; but such petition must be presented at least six months before the time limited for the expiration of the patent.

(2.) Any person may enter a caveat, addressed to the Registrar of the Council at the Council Office, against the extension.

(3.) If her Majesty shall be pleased to refer any such petition to the Judicial Committee of the Privy Council, the said committee shall proceed to consider the same, and the petitioner and any person who has entered a caveat shall be entitled to be heard by himself or by counsel on the petition.

(4.) The Judicial Committee shall, in considering their decision, have regard to the nature and merits of the invention in relation to the public, to the profits made by the patentee as such, and to all the circumstances of the case.

(5.) If the Judicial Committee report that the patentee has been inadequately remunerated by his patent, it shall be lawful for Her Majesty in Council to extend the term of the patent for a further term not exceeding seven, or in exceptional cases fourteen, years; or to order the grant of a new patent for the term therein mentioned, and containing any restrictions, conditions, and provisions that the Judicial Committee may think fit.

(6.) It shall be lawful for Her Majesty in Council to make, from time to time, rules of procedure and practice for regulating proceedings on such petitions, and subject thereto such proceedings shall be regulated according to the existing procedure and practice in patent matters of the Judicial Committee.

(7.) The costs of all parties of and incident to such proceedings shall be in the discretion of the Judicial Committee; and the orders of the Committee respecting costs shall be enforceable as if they were orders of a division of the High Court of Justice.

### Revocation.

**Revocation of patent.**

**26.**—(1.) The proceeding by scire facias to repeal a patent is hereby abolished.

(2.) Revocation of a patent may be obtained on petition to the court.

(3.) Every ground on which a patent might, at the commencement of this Act, be repealed by scire facias shall be available by way of defence to an action of infringement and shall also be a ground of revocation.

(4.) A petition for revocation of a patent may be presented by—

(a) The Attorney-General in England or Ireland, or the Lord Advocate in Scotland.

(b) Any person authorised by the Attorney-General in England or Ireland, or the Lord Advocate in Scotland.

(c) Any person alleging that the patent was obtained in fraud of his rights, or of the rights of any person under or through whom he claims:

(d) Any person alleging that he, or any person under or through whom he claims was the true inventor of any invention included in the claim of the patentee:

(e) Any person alleging that he, or any person under or through whom he claims an interest in any trade, business, or manufacture, had publicly manufactured, used, or sold, within this realm, before the date of the patent, anything claimed by the patentee as his invention.

(5.) The plaintiff must deliver with his petition particulars of the objections on which he means to rely, and no evidence shall, except by leave of the court or a judge, be admitted in proof of any objection of which particulars are not so delivered.

(6.) Particulars delivered may be from time to time amended by leave of the court or a judge.

(7.) The defendant shall be entitled to begin, and give evidence in support of the patent, and if the plaintiff gives evidence impeaching the validity of the patent the defendant shall be entitled to reply.

(8.) Where a patent has been revoked on the ground of fraud, the comptroller may, on the application of the true inventor made in accordance with the provisions of this Act, grant to him a patent in lieu of and bearing the same date as the date of revocation of the patent so revoked, but the patent so granted shall cease on the expiration of the term for which the revoked patent was granted.

### Crown.

**Patent to bind Crown.**

**27.**—(1.) A patent shall have to all intents the like effect as against Her Majesty the Queen, her heirs and successors, as it has against a subject.

(2.) But the officers or authorities administering any department of the service of the Crown may, by themselves, their agents, contractors, or others, at any time after the application, use the invention for the services of the Crown on terms to be before or after the use thereof agreed on, with the approval of the Treasury, between those officers or authorities and the patentee, or, in default of such agreement, on such terms as may be settled by the Treasury after hearing all parties interested.

### Legal Proceedings.

**Hearing with assessor.**

**28.**—(1.) In an action or proceeding for infringement or revocation of a patent, the court may, if it thinks fit, and shall, on the request of either of the parties to the proceeding, call in the aid of an assessor specially qualified, and try and hear the case wholly or partially with his assistance; the action shall be tried without a jury, unless the court shall otherwise direct.

(2.) The Court of Appeal or the Judicial Committee of the Privy Council may, if they see fit, in any proceeding before them respectively, call in the aid of an assessor as aforesaid.

(3.) The remuneration, if any, to be paid to an assessor under this section shall be determined by the court or the Court of Appeal or Judicial Committee, as the case may be, and be paid in the same manner as the other expenses of the execution of this Act.

29.—(1.) In an action for infringement of a patent the plaintiff must deliver with his statement of claim, or by order of the court or the judge, at any subsequent time, particulars of the breaches complained of. *Delivery of particulars.*

(2.) The defendant must deliver with his statement of defence, or, by order of the court or a judge, at any subsequent time, particulars of any objections on which he relies in support thereof.

(3.) If the defendant disputes the validity of the patent, the particulars delivered by him must state on what grounds he disputes it, and if one of those grounds is want of novelty, must state the time and place of the previous publication or user alleged by him.

(4.) At the hearing no evidence shall, except by leave of the court or a judge, be admitted in proof of any alleged infringement or objection of which particulars are not so delivered.

(5.) Particulars delivered may be from time to time amended, by leave of the court or a judge.

(6.) On taxation of costs regard shall be had to the particulars delivered by the plaintiff and by the defendant; and they respectively shall not be allowed any costs in respect of any particular delivered by them unless the same is certified by the court or a judge to have been proven or to have been reasonable and proper, without regard to the general costs of the case.

30. In an action for infringement of a patent, the court or a judge may, on the application of either party, make such order for an injunction, inspection, or account, and impose such terms and give such directions respecting the same and the proceedings thereon as the court or a judge may see fit. *Order for inspection, &c., in action.*

31. In an action for infringement of a patent, the court or a judge may certify that the validity of the patent came in question; and if the court or a judge so certifies, then in any subsequent action for infringement, the plaintiff in that action on obtaining a final order or judgment in his favour, shall have his full costs, charges and expenses as between solicitor and client, unless the court or judge trying the action certifies that he ought not to have the same. *Certificate of validity questioned and costs thereon.*

32. Where any person claiming to be the patentee of an invention, by circulars, advertisements, or otherwise threatens any other person with any legal proceedings or liability in respect of any alleged manufacture, use, sale, or purchase of the invention, any person or persons aggrieved thereby, may bring an action against him, and may obtain an injunction against the continuance of such threats, and may recover such damage (if any) as may have been sustained thereby, if the alleged manufacture, use, sale, or purchase to which the threats related was not in fact an infringement of any legal rights of the person making such threats: Provided that this section shall not apply if the person making such threats with due diligence commences and prosecutes an action for infringement of his patent. *Remedy in case of groundless threats of legal proceedings.*

*Miscellaneous.*

33. Every patent may be in the form in the First Schedule to this Act, and shall be granted for one invention only, but may contain more than one claim; but it shall not be competent for any person in an action or other proceeding to take any objection to a patent on the ground that it comprises more than one invention. *Patent for one invention only.*

34.—(1.) If a person possessed of an invention dies without making application for a patent for the invention, application may be made by, and a patent for the invention granted to, his legal representative. *Patent on application of representative of deceased inventor.*

(2.) Every such application must be made within six months of the decease of such person, and must contain a declaration by the legal representative that he believes such person to be the true and first inventor of the invention.

35. A patent granted to the true and first inventor shall not be invalidated by an application in fraud of him, or by provisional protection obtained thereon, or by any use or publication of the invention subsequent to that fraudulent application during the period of provisional protection. *Patent to first inventor not invalidated by application in fraud of him.*

36. A patentee may assign his patent for any place in or part of the United Kingdom, or Isle of Man, as effectually as if the patent were originally granted to extend to that place or part only. *Assignment for particular places.*

**Loss or destruction of patent.**

**37.** If a patent is lost or destroyed, or its non-production is accounted for to the satisfaction of the comptroller, the comptroller may at any time cause a duplicate thereof to be sealed.

**Proceedings and costs before law officer.**

**38.** The law officers may examine witnesses on oath and administer oaths for that purpose under this part of this Act, and may from time to time make, alter, and rescind rules regulating references and appeals to the law officers and the practice and procedure before them under this part of this Act ; and in any proceeding before either of the law officers under this part of this Act, the law officer may order costs to be paid by either party, and any such order may be made a rule of the court.

**Exhibition at industrial or international exhibition not to prejudice patent rights.**

**39.** The exhibition of an invention at an industrial or international exhibition, certified as such by the Board of Trade, or the publication of any description of the invention during the period of the holding of the exhibition, or the use of the invention for the purpose of the exhibition in the place where the exhibition is held, or the use of the invention during the period of the holding of the exhibition by any person elsewhere, without the privity or consent of the inventor, shall not prejudice the right of the inventor or his legal personal representative to apply for and obtain provisional protection and a patent in respect of the invention or the validity of any patent granted on the application, provided that both the following conditions are complied with, namely,—

(a) The exhibitor must, before exhibiting the invention, give the comptroller the prescribed notice of his intention to do so ; and

(b) The application for a patent must be made before or within six months from the date of the opening of the exhibition (a).

**Publication of illustrated journal, indexes, &c.**

**40.**—(1.) The comptroller shall cause to be issued periodically an illustrated journal of patented inventions, as well as reports of patent cases decided by courts of law, and any other information that the comptroller may deem generally useful or important.

(2.) Provision shall be made by the comptroller for keeping on sale copies of such journal, and also of all complete specifications of patents for the time being in force, with their accompanying drawings, if any.

(3.) The comptroller shall continue, in such form as he may deem expedient, the indexes and abridgments of specifications hitherto published, and shall from time to time prepare and publish such other indexes, abridgments of specifications, catalogues, and other works relating to inventions, as he may see fit.

**Patent Museum.**

**41.** The control and management of the existing Patent Museum, and its contents shall from and after the commencement of this Act, be transferred to and vested in the Department of Science and Art, subject to such directions as Her Majesty in Council may see fit to give.

**Power to require models on payment.**

**42.** The Department of Science and Art may at any time require a patentee to furnish them with a model of his invention on payment to the patentee of the cost of the manufacture of the model ; the amount to be settled, in case of dispute, by the Board of Trade.

**Foreign vessels in British waters.**

**43.**—(1.) A patent shall not prevent the use of an invention for the purposes of the navigation of a foreign vessel within the jurisdiction of any of Her Majesty's Courts in the United Kingdom, or Isle of Man, or the use of an invention in a foreign vessel within that jurisdiction, provided it is not used therein for or in connection with the manufacture or preparation of anything intended to be sold in or exported from the United Kingdom or Isle of Man.

(2.) But this section shall not extend to vessels of any foreign state of which the laws authorise subjects of such foreign state, having patents or like privileges for the exclusive use or exercise of inventions within its territories, to prevent or interfere with the use of such inventions in British vessels while in the ports of such foreign state, or in the waters within the jurisdiction of its courts, where such inventions are not so used for the manufacture or preparation of anything intended to be sold in or exported from the territories of such foreign state.

**Assignment to Secretary for War of certain inventions.**

**44.**—(1.) The inventor of any improvement in instruments or munitions of war, his executors, administrators, or assigns (who are in this section comprised in the expression the inventor) may (either for or without valuable

(a) See 49 & 50 Vict. c. 37, s. 3.

consideration) assign to Her Majesty's Principal Secretary of State for the War Department (hereinafter referred to as the Secretary of State), on behalf of Her Majesty, all the benefit of the invention and of any patent obtained or to be obtained for the same ; and the Secretary of State may be a party to the assignment.

(2.) The assignment shall effectually vest the benefit of the invention and patent in the Secretary of State for the time being on behalf of Her Majesty, and all covenants and agreements therein contained for keeping the invention secret and otherwise shall be valid and effectual (notwithstanding any want of valuable consideration), and may be enforced accordingly by the Secretary of State for the time being.

(3.) Where any such assignment has been made to the Secretary of State, he may at any time before the application for a patent for the invention, or before publication of the specification or specifications, certify to the comptroller his opinion that, in the interest of the public service, the particulars of the invention and of the manner in which it is to be performed should be kept secret.

(4.) If the Secretary of State so certifies, the application and specification or specifications with the drawings (if any), and any amendment of the specification or specifications, and any copies of such documents and drawings, shall, instead of being left in the ordinary manner at the patent office, be delivered to the comptroller in a packet sealed by authority of the Secretary of State.

(5.) Such packet shall until the expiration of the term or extended term during which a patent for the invention may be in force, be kept sealed by the comptroller, and shall not be opened save under the authority of an order of the Secretary of State, or of the law officers.

(6.) Such sealed packet shall be delivered at any time during the continuance of the patent to any person authorised by writing under the hand of the Secretary of State to receive the same, and shall if returned to the comptroller be again kept sealed by him.

(7.) On the expiration of the term or extended term of the patent, such sealed packet shall be delivered to any person authorised by writing under the hand of the Secretary of State to receive it.

(8.) Where the Secretary of State certifies as aforesaid, after an application for a patent has been left at the patent office, but before the publication of the specification or specifications, the application specification or specifications, with the drawings (if any), shall be forthwith placed in a packet sealed by authority of the comptroller, and such packet shall be subject to the foregoing provisions respecting a packet sealed by authority of the Secretary of State.

(9.) No proceeding by petition or otherwise shall lie for revocation of a patent granted for an invention in relation to which the Secretary of State has certified as aforesaid.

(10.) No copy of any specification or other document or drawing, by this section required to be placed in a sealed packet, shall in any manner whatever be published or open to the inspection of the public, but save as in this section otherwise directed, the provisions of this part of this Act shall apply in respect of any such invention and patent as aforesaid.

(11.) The Secretary of State may, at any time by writing under his hand, waive the benefit of this section with respect to any particular invention, and the specifications, documents and drawings shall be thenceforth kept and dealt with in the ordinary way.

(12.) The communication of any invention for any improvement in instruments or munitions of war to the Secretary of State, or to any person or persons authorised by him to investigate the same or the merits thereof, shall not, nor shall anything done for the purposes of the investigation, be deemed use or publication of such invention so as to prejudice the grant or validity of any patent for the same.

### *Existing Patents.*

**45.**—(1.) The provisions of this Act relating to applications for patents and proceedings thereon shall have effect in respect only of applications made after the commencement of this Act. Provisions respecting existing patents.

(2.) Every patent granted before the commencement of this Act, or on an application then pending, shall remain unaffected by the provisions of this Act relating to patents binding the Crown, and to compulsory licenses.

(3.) In all other respects (including the amount and time of payment of fees) this Act shall extend to all patents granted before the commencement of this Act, or on applications then pending, in substitution for such enactments as would have applied thereto if this Act had not been passed.

(4.) All instruments relating to patents granted before the commencement of this Act required to be left or filed in the Great Seal Patent Office shall be deemed to be so left or filed if left or filed before or after the commencement of this Act in the patent office.

*Definitions.*

Definitions of patent, patentee, and invention.

**46.** In and for the purposes of this Act—

" Patent" means letters patent for an invention:

" Patentee" means the person for the time being entitled to the benefit of a patent:

" Invention" means any manner of new manufacture the subject of letters patent and grant of privilege within section six of the Statute of Monopolies (that is, the Act of the twenty-first year of the reign of King James the First, chapter three, intituled "An Act concerning Monopolies and Dispensations with Penal Laws and the Forfeiture thereof"), and includes an alleged invention.

In Scotland "injunction" means "interdict."

---

## PART III.

### Designs.

*Registration of Designs.*

Application for registration of designs.

**47.**—(1.) The comptroller may, on application by or on behalf of any person claiming to be the proprietor of any new or original design not previously published in the United Kingdom, register the design under this part of this Act.

(2.) The application must be made in the form set forth in the first schedule to this Act, or in such other form as may be from time to time prescribed, and must be left at, or sent by post to, the patent office in the prescribed manner.

(3.) The application must contain a statement of the nature of the design, and the class or classes of goods in which the applicant desires that the design be registered.

(4.) The same design may be registered in more than one class.

(5.) In case of doubt as to the class in which a design ought to be registered, the comptroller may decide the question.

(6.) The comptroller may, if he thinks fit, refuse to register any design presented to him for registration, but any person aggrieved by any such refusal may appeal therefrom to the Board of Trade.

(7.) The Board of Trade shall, if required, hear the applicant and the comptroller, and may make an order determining whether, and subject to what conditions, if any, registration is to be permitted.

Drawings, &c., to be furnished on application.

**48.**—(1.) On application for registration of a design the applicant shall furnish to the comptroller the prescribed number of copies of drawings, photographs, or tracings of the design sufficient, in the opinion of the comptroller, for enabling him to identify the design ; or the applicant may, instead of such copies, furnish exact representations or specimens of the design.

(2.) The comptroller may, if he thinks fit, refuse any drawing, photograph, tracing, representation, or specimen which is not, in his opinion, suitable for the official records.

Ceatificate of registration.

**49.**—(1.) The comptroller shall grant a certificate of registration to the proprietor of the design when registered.

(2.) The comptroller may, in case of loss of the original certificate, or in any other case in which he deems it expedient, grant a copy or copies of the certificate.

*Copyright in registered Designs.*

**50.**—(1.) When a design is registered, the registered proprietor of the design shall, subject to the provisions of this Act, have copyright in the design during five years from the date of registration.

(2.) Before delivery on sale of any articles to which a registered design has been applied, the proprietor must (if exact representations or specimens were not furnished on the application for registration), furnish to the comptroller the prescribed number of exact representations or specimens of the design; and if he fails to do so, the comptroller may erase his name from the register, and thereupon his copyright in the design shall cease.

**51.** Before delivery on sale of any articles to which a registered design has been applied, the proprietor of the design shall cause each such article to be marked with the prescribed mark, or with the prescribed word or words or figures, denoting that the design is registered; and, if he fails to do so, the copyright in the design shall cease, unless the proprietor shows that he took all proper steps to ensure the marking of the article.

**52.**—(1.) During the existence of copyright in a design, the design shall not be open to inspection except by the proprietor, or a person authorised in writing by the proprietor, or a person authorised by the comptroller or by the court, and furnishing such information as may enable the comptroller to identify the design, nor except in the presence of the comptroller, or of an officer acting under him, nor except on payment of the prescribed fee; and the person making the inspection shall not be entitled to take any copy of the design, or of any part thereof.

(2.) When the copyright in a design has ceased, the design shall be open to inspection, and copies thereof may be taken by any person on payment of the prescribed fee.

**53.** On the request of any person producing a particular design, together with its mark of registration, or producing only its mark of registration, or furnishing such information as may enable the comptroller to identify the design, and on payment of the prescribed fee, it shall be the duty of the comptroller to inform such person whether the registration still exists in respect of such design, and if so, in respect of what class or classes of goods, and stating also the date of registration, and the name and address of the registered proprietor.

**54.** If a registered design is used in manufacture in any foreign country and is not used in this country within six months of its registration in this country, the copyright in the design shall cease.

*Margin notes: Copyright on registration. Marking registered designs. Inspection of registered designs. Information as to existence of copyright. Cesser of copyright in certain events.*

*Register of Designs.*

**55.**—(1.) There shall be kept at the patent office a book called the Register of Designs, wherein shall be entered the names and addresses of proprietors of registered designs, notifications of assignments and of transmissions of registered designs, and such other matters as may from time to time be prescribed.

(2.) The register of designs shall be primâ facie evidence of any matters by this Act directed or authorised to be entered therein.

*Margin note: Register of designs.*

*Fees.*

**56.** There shall be paid in respect of applications and registration and other matters under this part of this Act such fees as may be from time to time, with the sanction of the Treasury, prescribed by the Board of Trade; and such fees shall be levied and paid to the account of Her Majesty's Exchequer in such manner as the Treasury shall from time to time direct.

*Margin note: Fees on registration, &c.*

*Industrial and International Exhibitions.*

**57.** The exhibition at an industrial or international exhibition certified as such by the Board of Trade, or the exhibition elsewhere during the period of the holding of the exhibition, without the privity or consent of the proprietor, of a design, or of any article to which a design is applied, or the publication, during the holding of any such exhibition, of a description of a design, shall not prevent the design from being registered, or invalidate the

*Margin note: Exhibition at industrial or international exhibition not to prevent or invalidate registration.*

registration thereof, provided that both the following conditions are complied with; namely,—

(a.) The exhibitor must, before exhibiting the design or article, or publishing a description of the design, give the comptroller the prescribed notice of his intention to do so; and

(b.) The application for registration must be made before or within six months from the date of the opening of the exhibition (a).

### Legal Proceedings.

Penalty on piracy of registered design.

**58.** During the existence of copyright in any design—

(a.) It shall not be lawful for any person without the license or written consent of the registered proprietor to apply such design or any fraudulent or obvious imitation thereof, in the class or classes of goods in which such design is registered, for purposes of sale to any article of manufacture or to any substance artificial or natural or partly artificial and partly natural; and

(b.) It shall not be lawful for any person to publish or expose for sale any article of manufacture or any substance to which such design or any fraudulent or obvious imitation thereof shall have been so applied, knowing that the same has been so applied without the consent of the registered proprietor.

Any person who acts in contravention of this section shall be liable for every offence to forfeit a sum not exceeding fifty pounds to the registered proprietor of the design, who may recover such sum as a simple contract debt by action in any court of competent jurisdiction.

Action for damages.

**59.** Notwithstanding the remedy given by this Act for the recovery of such penalty as aforesaid, the registered proprietor of any design may (if he elects to do so) bring an action for the recovery of any damages arising from the application of any such design, or of any fraudulent or obvious imitation thereof for the purpose of sale, to any article of manufacture or substance, or from the publication sale or exposure for sale by any person of any article or substance to which such design or any fraudulent or obvious imitation thereof shall have been so applied, such person knowing that the proprietor had not given his consent to such application.

### Definitions.

Definition of "design," "copyright."

**60.** In and for the purposes of this Act—

"Design" means any design applicable to any article of manufacture, or to any substance artificial or natural, or partly artificial and partly natural, whether the design is applicable for the pattern, or for the shape or configuration, or for the ornament thereof, or for any two or more of such purposes, and by whatever means it is applicable, whether by printing, painting, embroidering, weaving, sewing, modelling, casting, embossing, engraving, staining, or any other means whatever, manual, mechanical, or chemical, separate or combined, not being a design for a sculpture, or other thing within the protection of the Sculpture Copyright Act of the year 1814 (fifty-fourth George the Third, chapter fifty-six).

"Copyright" means the exclusive right to apply a design to any article of manufacture or to any such substance as aforesaid in the class or classes in which the design is registered.

Definition of proprietor.

**61.** The author of any new and original design shall be considered the proprietor thereof, unless he executed the work on behalf of another person for a good or valuable consideration, in which case such person shall be considered the proprietor, and every person acquiring for a good or valuable consideration a new and original design, or the right to apply the same to any such article or substance as aforesaid, either exclusively of any other person or otherwise, and also every person on whom the property in such design or such right to the application thereof shall devolve, shall be considered the proprietor of the design in the respect in which the same may have been so acquired, and to that extent, but not otherwise.

49 & 50 Vict. c. 37, s. 3.

## PART IV.

### Trade Marks.

*Registration of Trade Marks.*

**62.**—(1.) The comptroller may, on application by or on behalf of any person claiming to be the proprietor of a trade mark, register the trade mark.

*Application for registration.*

(2.) The application must be made in the form set forth in the First Schedule to this Act, or in such other form as may be from time to time prescribed, and must be left at, or sent by post to, the Patent Office in the prescribed manner.

(3.) The application must be accompanied by the prescribed number of representations of the trade mark, and must state the particular goods or classes of goods in connexion with which the applicant desires the trade mark to be registered.

(4.) The comptroller may, if he thinks fit, refuse to register a trade mark, but any such refusal shall be subject to appeal to the Board of Trade, who shall, if required, hear the applicant and the comptroller, and may make an order determining whether, and subject to what conditions, if any, registration is to be permitted.

(5.) The Board of Trade may, however, if it appears expedient, refer the appeal to the Court; and in that event the Court shall have jurisdiction to hear and determine the appeal and may make such order as aforesaid.

**63.** Where registration of a trade mark has not been or shall not be completed within twelve months from the date of the application, by reason of default on the part of the applicant, the application shall be deemed to be abandoned.

*Limit of time for proceeding with application.*

**64.**—(1.) For the purposes of this Act, a trade mark must consist of or contain at least one of the following essential particulars:—

*Conditions of registration of trade mark.*

(a) A name of an individual or firm printed, impressed, or woven in some particular and distinctive manner; or

(b) A written signature or copy of a written signature of the individual or firm applying for registration thereof as a trade mark; or

(c) A distinctive device, mark, brand, heading, label, ticket, or fancy word or words not in common use.

(2.) There may be added to any one or more of these particulars any letters words or figures, or combination of letters words or figures, or of any of them.

(3.) Provided that any special and distinctive word or words letter, figure, or combination of letters or figures or of letters and figures used as a trade mark before the thirteenth day of August one thousand eight hundred and seventy-five may be registered as a trade mark under this part of this Act.

**65.** A trade mark must be registered for particular goods or classes of goods.

*Connection of trade mark with goods.*

**66.** When a person claiming to be the proprietor of several trade marks which, while resembling each other in the material particulars thereof, yet differ in respect of (a) the statement of the goods for which they are respectively used or proposed to be used, or (b) statements of numbers, or (c) statements of price, or (d) statements of quality, or (e) statements of names of places, seeks to register such trade marks, they may be registered as a series in one registration. A series of trade marks shall be assignable and transmissible only as a whole, but for all other purposes each of the trade marks composing a series shall be deemed and treated as registered separately.

*Registration of a series of marks.*

**67.** A trade mark may be registered in any colour, and such registration shall (subject to the provisions of this Act) confer on the registered owner the exclusive right to use the same in that or any other colour.

*Trade marks may be registered in any colour.*

**68.** Every application for registration of a trade mark under this part of this Act shall as soon as may be after its receipt be advertised by the comptroller.

*Advertisement of application.*

**69.**—(1.) Any person may within two months of the first advertisement of the application, give notice in duplicate at the patent office of opposition to registration of the trade mark, and the comptroller shall send one copy of such notice to the applicant.

*Opposition to registration.*

(2.) Within two months after receipt of such notice or such further time as the comptroller may allow, the applicant may send to the comptroller a counter statement in duplicate of the grounds on which he relies for his application, and if he does not do so, shall be deemed to have abandoned his application.

(3.) If the applicant sends such counter statement, the comptroller shall furnish a copy thereof to the person who gave notice of opposition, and shall require him to give security in such manner and to such amount as the comptroller may require for such costs as may be awarded in respect of such opposition ; and if such security is not given within fourteen days after such requirement was made or such further time as the comptroller may allow, the opposition shall be deemed to be withdrawn.

(4.) If the person who gave notice of opposition duly gives such security as aforesaid, the comptroller shall inform the applicant thereof in writing, and thereupon the case shall be deemed to stand for the determination of the court.

**Assignment and transmission of trade mark.**

70. A trade mark, when registered, shall be assigned and transmitted only in connexion with the goodwill of the business concerned in the particular goods or classes of goods for which it has been registered, and shall be determinable with that goodwill.

**Conflicting claims to registration.**

71. Where each of several persons claims to be registered as proprietor of the same trade mark, the comptroller may refuse to register any of them until their rights have been determined according to law, and the comptroller may himself submit or require the claimants to submit their rights to the court.

**Restrictions on registration.**

72.—(1.) Except where the court has decided that two or more persons are entitled to be registered as proprietors of the same trade mark, the comptroller shall not register in respect of the same goods or description of goods a trade mark identical with one already on the register with respect to such goods or description of goods.

(2.) The comptroller shall not register with respect to the same goods or description of goods a trade mark so nearly resembling a trade mark already on the register with respect to such goods or description of goods as to be calculated to deceive.

**Further restriction on registration.**

73. It shall not be lawful to register as part of or in combination with a trade mark any words the exclusive use of which would by reason of their being calculated to deceive or otherwise, be deemed disentitled to protection in a court of justice, or any scandalous design.

**Saving for power to provide for entry on register of common marks as additions to trade marks.**

74.—(1.) Nothing in this Act shall be construed to prevent the comptroller entering on the register, in the prescribed manner, and subject to the prescribed conditions, as an addition to any trade mark—

(a) In the case of an application for registration of a trade mark used before the thirteenth day of August, one thousand eight hundred and seventy-five—

Any distinctive device, mark, brand, heading, label, ticket, letter, word, or figure, or combination of letters, words, or figures, though the same is common to the trade in the goods with respect to which the application is made ;

(b) In the case of an application for registration of a trade mark not used before the thirteenth day of August one thousand eight hundred and seventy-five—

Any distinctive word or combination of words, though the same is common to the trade in the goods with respect to which the application is made ;

(2.) The applicant for entry of any such common particular or particulars must, however, disclaim in his application any right to the exclusive use of the same, and a copy of the disclaimer shall be entered on the register.

(3.) Any device, mark, brand, heading, label, ticket, letter, word, figure, or combination of letters, words, or figures, which was or were, before the thirteenth day of August one thousand eight hundred and seventy-five, publicly used by more than three persons on the same or a similar description of goods shall, for the purposes of this section, be deemed common to the trade in such goods.

### Effect of Registration.

**Registration equivalent to public use.**

75. Registration of a trade mark shall be deemed to be equivalent to public use of the trade mark.

76. The registration of a person as proprietor of a trade mark shall be primâ facie evidence of his right to the exclusive use of the trade mark, and shall, after the expiration of five years from the date of the registration, be conclusive evidence of his right to the exclusive use of the trade mark, subject to the provisions of this Act.

*Right of first proprietor to exclusive use of trade mark.*

77. A person shall not be entitled to institute any proceeding to prevent or to recover damages for the infringement of a trade mark unless, in the case of a trade mark capable of being registered under this Act, it has been registered in pursuance of this Act, or of an enactment repealed by this Act, or, in the case of any other trade mark in use before the thirteenth of August one thousand eight hundred and seventy-five, registration thereof under this part of this Act, or of an enactment repealed by this Act, has been refused. The comptroller may, on request and on payment of the prescribed fee, grant a certificate that such registration has been refused.

*Restrictions on actions for infringement, and on defence to action in certain cases.*

### Register of Trade Marks.

78. There shall be kept at the patent office a book called the Register of Trade Marks, wherein shall be entered the names and addresses of proprietors of registered trade marks, notifications of assignments and of transmissions of trade marks, and such other matters as may be from time to time prescribed.

*Register of trade marks.*

79.—(1.) At a time not being less than two months nor more than three months before the expiration of fourteen years from the date of the registration of a trade mark, the comptroller shall send notice to the registered proprietor that the trade mark will be removed from the register unless the proprietor pays to the comptroller before the expiration of such fourteen years (naming the date at which the same will expire) the prescribed fee ; and if such fee be not previously paid, he shall at the expiration of one month from the date of the giving of the first notice send a second notice to the same effect.

*Removal of trade mark after fourteen years unless fee paid.*

(2.) If such fee be not paid before the expiration of such fourteen years the comptroller may after the end of three months from the expiration of such fourteen years remove the mark from the register, and so from time to time at the expiration of every period of fourteen years.

(3.) If before the expiration of the said three months the registered proprietor pays the said fee together with the additional prescribed fee, the comptroller may without removing such trade mark from the register accept the said fee as if it had been paid before the expiration of the said fourteen years.

(4.) Where after the said three months a trade mark has been removed from the register for non-payment of the prescribed fee, the comptroller may, if satisfied that it is just so to do, restore such trade mark to the register on payment of the prescribed additional fee.

(5.) Where a trade mark has been removed from the register for nonpayment of the fee or otherwise, such trade mark shall nevertheless for the purpose of any application for registration during the five years next after the date of such removal, be deemed to be a trade mark which is already registered.

### Fees.

80. There shall be paid in respect of applications and registration and other matters under this part of this Act, such fees as may be from time to time, with the sanction of the Treasury, prescribed by the Board of Trade ; and such fees shall be levied and paid to the account of Her Majesty's Exchequer in such manner as the Treasury may from time to time direct.

*Fees for registration, &c.*

### Sheffield Marks.

81. With respect to the master, wardens, searchers, assistants, and commonalty of the Company of Cutlers in Hallamshire, in the county of York (in this Act called the Cutlers' Company) and the marks or devices (in this Act called Sheffield marks) assigned or registered by the master, wardens, searchers, and assistants of that company, the following provisions shall have effect:

*Registration by Cutlers' Company of Sheffield marks.*

(1.) The Cutlers' Company shall establish and keep at Sheffield a new register of trade marks (in this Act called the Sheffield register) :

(2.) The Cutlers' Company shall enter in the Sheffield register, in respect of cutlery, edge tools, or raw steel and the goods mentioned in the next sub-section all the trade marks entered before the commencement of this Act in respect of cutlery, edge tools, or raw steel, and such goods in the register established under the Trade Marks Registration Act, 1875, belonging to persons carrying on business in Hallamshire, or within six miles thereof, and shall also enter in such register, in respect of the same goods, all the trade marks which shall have been assigned by the Cutlers' Company and actually used before the commencement of this Act, but which have not been entered in the register established under the Trade Marks Registration Act, 1875 :

(3.) An application for registration of a trade mark used on cutlery, edge tools, or on raw steel, or on goods made of steel, or of steel and iron combined, whether with or without a cutting edge, shall, if made after the commencement of this Act by a person carrying on business in Hallamshire, or within six miles thereof, be made to the Cutlers' Company :

(4.) Every application so made to the Cutlers' Company shall be notified to the comptroller in the prescribed manner, and unless the comptroller within the prescribed time gives notice to the Cutlers' Company that he objects to the acceptance of the application, it shall be proceeded with by the Cutlers' Company in the prescribed manner :

(5.) If the comptroller gives notice of objection as aforesaid, the application shall not be proceeded with by the Cutlers' Company, but any person aggrieved may appeal to the court :

(6.) Upon the registration of a trade mark in the Sheffield register the Cutlers' Company shall give notice thereof to the comptroller, who shall thereupon enter the mark in the register of trade marks ; and such registration shall bear date as of the day of application to the Cutlers' Company, and have the same effect as if the application had been made to the comptroller on that day :

(7.) The provisions of this Act, and of any general rules made under this Act, with respect to application for registration in the register of trade marks, the effect of such registration, and the assignment and transmission of rights in a registered trade mark shall apply in the case of applications and registration in the Sheffield register ; and notice of every entry made in the Sheffield register must be given to the comptroller by the Cutlers' Company, save and except that the provisions of this sub-section shall not prejudice or affect any life, estate, and interest of a widow of the holder of any Sheffield mark which may be in force in respect of such mark at the time when it shall be placed upon the Sheffield register :

(8.) Where the comptroller receives from any person not carrying on business in Hallamshire or within six miles thereof an application for registration of a trade mark used on cutlery, edge tools, or on raw steel, or on goods made of steel, or of steel and iron combined, whether with or without a cutting edge, he shall in the prescribed manner notify the application and proceedings thereon to the Cutlers' Company :

(9.) At the expiration of five years from the commencement of this Act the Cutlers' Company shall close the Cutlers' register of corporate trade marks, and thereupon all marks entered therein shall, unless entered in the Sheffield register, be deemed to have been abandoned :

(10.) A person may (notwithstanding anything in any Act relating to the Cutlers' Company) be registered in the Sheffield register as proprietor of two or more trade marks :

(11.) A body of persons, corporate or not corporate, may (notwithstanding anything in any Act relating to the Cutlers' Company) be registered in the Sheffield register as proprietor of a trade mark or trade marks :

(12.) Any person aggrieved by a decision of the Cutlers' Company in respect of anything done or omitted under this Act may, in the prescribed manner, appeal to the comptroller, who shall have power to confirm reverse or modify the decision, but the decision of the comptroller shall be subject to a further appeal to the court:

(13.) So much of the Cutlers' Company's Acts as applies to the summary punishment of persons counterfeiting Sheffield corporate marks, that is to say, the fifth section of the Cutlers' Company's Act of 1814, and the provisions in relation to the recovery and application of the penalty imposed by such last-mentioned section contained in the Cutlers' Company's Act of 1791, shall apply to any mark entered in the Sheffield register.

---

## PART V.

### GENERAL.

*Patent Office and Proceedings thereat.*

**82.**—(1.) The Treasury may provide for the purposes of this Act an office Patent Office. with all requisite buildings and conveniences, which shall be called, and is in this Act referred to as, the Patent Office.

(2.) Until a new patent office is provided, the offices of the Commissioners of Patents for inventions and for the registration of designs and trade marks existing at the commencement of this Act shall be the patent office within the meaning of this Act.

(3.) The patent office shall be under the immediate control of an officer called the comptroller general of patents, designs, and trade marks, who shall act under the superintendence and direction of the Board of Trade.

(4.) Any act or thing directed to be done by or to the comptroller may, in his absence, be done by or to any officer for the time being in that behalf authorized by the Board of Trade.

**83.**—(1.) The Board of Trade may at any time after the passing of this Officers and Act, and from time to time, subject to the approval of the Treasury, appoint clerks. the comptroller-general of patents, designs, and trade marks, and so many examiners and other officers and clerks, with such designations and duties as the Board of Trade think fit, and may from time to time remove any of those officers and clerks.

(2.) The salaries of those officers and clerks shall be appointed by the Board of Trade, with the concurrence of the Treasury, and the same and the other expenses of the execution of this Act shall be paid out of money provided by Parliament.

**84.** There shall be a seal for the patent office, and impressions thereof Seal of patent shall be judicially noticed and admitted in evidence. office.

**85.** There shall not be entered in any register kept under this Act, or be Trust not to be receivable by the comptroller, any notice of any trust expressed implied or entered in constructive. registers.

**86.** The comptroller may refuse to grant a patent for an invention, or to Refusal to grant register a design or trade mark, of which the use would, in his opinion, be patent, &c., in contrary to law or morality. certain cases.

**87.** Where a person becomes entitled by assignment, transmission, or other Entry of as- operation of law to a patent, or to the copyright in a registered design, or to signments and a registered trade mark, the comptroller shall on request, and on proof of transmissions in title to his satisfaction, cause the name of such person to be entered as registers. proprietor of the patent, copyright in the design, or trade mark, in the register of patents, designs, or trade marks, as the case may be. The person for the time being entered in the register of patents designs or trade-marks, as proprietor of a patent, copyright in a design or trade mark as the case may be, shall, subject to any rights appearing from such register to be vested in any other person, have power absolutely to assign, grant licences as to, or otherwise deal with, the same and to give effectual receipts for any consideration for such assignment, licence, or dealing. Provided that any equities in respect of such patent, design, or trade mark may be enforced in like manner as in respect of any other personal property.

**88.** Every register kept under this Act shall at all convenient times be Inspection of open to the inspection of the public, subject to such regulations as may be and extracts from registers.

4 G 2

prescribed; and certified copies, sealed with the seal of the patent office, of any entry in any such register shall be given to any person requiring the same on payment of the prescribed fee.

**Sealed copies to be received in evidence.**

**89.** Printed or written copies or extracts, purporting to be certified by the comptroller and sealed with the seal of the patent office, of or from patents specifications disclaimers and other documents in the patent office, and of or from registers and other books kept there, shall be admitted in evidence in all courts in Her Majesty's dominions, and in all proceedings, without further proof or production of the originals.

**Rectification of registers by court.**

**90.**—(1.) The court may on the application of any person aggrieved by the omission without sufficient cause of the name of any person from any register kept under this Act, or by any entry made without sufficient cause in any such register, make such order for making expunging or varying the entry, as the court thinks fit; or the court may refuse the application; and in either case may make such order with respect to the costs of the proceedings as the court thinks fit.

(2.) The court may in any proceeding under this section decide any question that it may be necessary or expedient to decide for the rectification of a register, and may direct an issue to be tried for the decision of any question of fact, and may award damages to the party aggrieved.

(3.) Any order of the court rectifying a register shall direct that due notice of the rectification be given to the comptroller.

**Power for comptroller to correct clerical errors.**

**91.** The comptroller may, on request in writing accompanied by the prescribed fee,—

(a) Correct any clerical error in or in connection with an application for a patent, or for registration of a design or trade mark; or

(b) Correct any clerical error in the name style or address of the registered proprietor of a patent, design, or trade mark.

(c) Cancel the entry or part of the entry of a trade mark on the register: Provided that the applicant accompanies his request by a statutory declaration made by himself, stating his name, address, and calling, and that he is the person whose name appears on the register as the proprietor of the said trade mark.

**Alteration of registered mark.**

**92.**—(1.) The registered proprietor of any registered trade mark may apply to the court for leave to add to or alter such mark in any particular, not being an essential particular within the meaning of this Act, and the court may refuse or grant leave on such terms as it may think fit.

(2.) Notice of any intended application to the court under this section shall be given to the comptroller by the applicant; and the comptroller shall be entitled to be heard on the application.

(3.) If the court grants leave, the comptroller shall, on proof thereof and on payment of the prescribed fee, cause the register to be altered in conformity with the order of leave.

**Falsification of entries in registers.**

**93.** If any person makes or causes to be made a false entry in any register kept under this Act, or a writing falsely purporting to be a copy of an entry in any such register, or produces or tenders or causes to be produced or tendered in evidence any such writing, knowing the entry or writing to be false, he shall be guilty of a misdemeanor.

**Exercise of discretionary power by comptroller.**

**94.** Where any discretionary power is by this Act given to the comptroller, he shall not exercise that power adversely to the applicant for a patent, or for amendment of a specification, or for registration of a trade mark or design, without (if so required within the prescribed time by the applicant) giving the applicant an opportunity of being heard personally or by his agent.

**Power of comptroller to take directions of law officers.**

**95.** The comptroller may, in any case of doubt or difficulty arising in the administration of any of the provisions of this Act, apply to either of the law officers for directions in the matter.

**Certificate of comptroller to be evidence.**

**96.** A certificate purporting to be under the hand of the comptroller as to any entry, matter, or thing which he is authorised by this Act, or any general rules made thereunder, to make or do, shall be prima facie evidence of the entry having been made, and of the contents thereof, and of the matter or thing having been done or left undone.

**Applications and notices by post.**

**97.**—(1.) Any application, notice, or other document authorised or required to be left made or given at the patent office, or to the comptroller, or to any other person under this Act, may be sent by a prepaid letter through the post; and if so sent shall be deemed to have been left made or given respectively at the time when the letter containing the same would be delivered in the ordinary course of post.

(2.) In proving such service or sending, it shall be sufficient to prove that the letter was properly addressed and put into the post.

**98.** Whenever the last day fixed by this Act, or by any rule for the time being in force, for leaving any document or paying any fee at the patent office shall fall on Christmas Day, Good Friday, or on a Saturday or Sunday, or any day observed as a holiday at the Bank of England, or any day observed as a day of public fast or thanksgiving, herein referred to as excluded days, it shall be lawful to leave such document or to pay such fee on the day next following such excluded day, or days if two or more of them occur consecutively.

Provision as to days for leaving documents at office.

**99.** If any person is by reason of infancy lunacy or other inability, incapable of making any declaration or doing anything required or permitted by this Act or by any rules made under the authority of this Act, then the guardian or committee (if any) of such incapable person, or if there be none, any person appointed by any court or judge possessing jurisdiction in respect of the property of incapable persons, upon the petition of any person on behalf of such incapable person, or of any other person interested in the making such declaration or doing such thing, may make such declaration or a declaration as nearly corresponding thereto as circumstances permit, and do such thing in the name and on behalf of such incapable person, and all acts done by such substitute shall, for the purposes of this Act, be as effectual as if done by the person for whom he is substituted.

Declaration by infant, lunatic, &c.

**100.** Copies of all specifications, drawings, and amendments left at the patent office after the commencement of this Act, printed for and sealed with the seal of the patent office, shall be transmitted to the Edinburgh Museum of Science and Art, and to the Enrolments Office of the Chancery Division in Ireland, and to the Rolls Office in the Isle of Man, within twenty-one days after the same shall respectively have been accepted or allowed at the patent office; and certified copies of or extracts from any such documents shall be given to any person requiring the same on payment of the prescribed fee: and any such copy or extract shall be admitted in evidence in all Courts in Scotland and Ireland, and in the Isle of Man, without further proof or production of the originals.

Transmission of certified printed copies of specifications, &c.

**101.—(1.)** The Board of Trade may from time to time make such general rules and do such things as they think expedient, subject to the provisions of this Act—

Power for Board of Trade to make general rules for classifying goods and regulating business of patent office.

(a) For regulating the practice of registration under this Act:

(b) For classifying goods for the purposes of designs and trade marks:

(c) For making or requiring duplicates of specifications, amendment, drawings, and other documents:

(d) For securing and regulating the publishing and selling of copies, at such prices and in such manner as the Board of Trade think fit, of specifications drawings amendments and other documents:

(e) For securing and regulating the making printing publishing and selling of indexes to, and abridgments of, specifications and other documents in the patent office; and providing for the inspection of indexes and abridgments and other documents:

(f) For regulating (with the approval of the Treasury) the presentation of copies of patent office publications to patentees and to public authorities, bodies, and institutions at home and abroad;

(g) Generally for regulating the business of the patent office, and all things by this Act placed under the direction or control of the comptroller, or of the Board of Trade.

(2.) Any of the forms in the First Schedule to this Act may be altered or amended by rules made by the Board as aforesaid.

(3.) General rules may be made under this section at any time after the passing of this Act, but not so as to take effect before the commencement of this Act, and shall (subject as hereinafter mentioned) be of the same effect as if they were contained in this Act, and shall be judicially noticed.

(4.) Any rules made in pursuance of this section shall be laid before both Houses of Parliament, if Parliament be in session at the time of making thereof, or, if not, then as soon as practicable after the beginning of the then next session of Parliament, and they shall also be advertised twice in the official journal to be issued by the comptroller.

(5.) If either House of Parliament, within the next forty days after any rules have been so laid before such House, resolve that such rules or any of them ought to be annulled, the same shall after the date of such resolution be of no effect, without prejudice to the validity of anything done in the meantime under such rules or rule or to the making of any new rules or rule.

**Annual reports of comptroller.**

102. The comptroller shall, before the first day of June in every year, cause a report respecting the execution by or under him of this Act to be laid before both Houses of Parliament, and therein shall include for the year to which each report relates all general rules made in that year under or for the purposes of this Act, and an account of all fees, salaries, and allowances, and other money received and paid under this Act.

*International and Colonial Arrangements.*

**International arrangements for protection of inventions, designs, and trade marks.**

103.—(1.) If Her Majesty is pleased to make any arrangement with the government or governments of any foreign state or states for mutual protection of inventions, designs, and trade marks, or any of them, then any person who has applied for protection for any invention, design, or trade mark in any such state, shall be entitled to a patent for his invention or to registration of his design or trade mark (as the case may be) under this Act, in priority to other applicants; and such patent or registration shall have the same date as the date of the protection obtained (a) in such foreign state :

Provided that his application is made, in the case of a patent within seven months, and in the case of a design or trade mark within four months, from his applying for protection in the foreign state with which the arrangement is in force :

Provided that nothing in this section contained shall entitle the patentee or proprietor of the design or trade mark to recover damages for infringements happening prior to the date of the actual acceptance of his complete specification, or the actual registration of his design or trade mark in this country, as the case may be :

(2.) The publication in the United Kingdom, or the Isle of Man during the respective periods aforesaid of any description of the invention, or the use therein during such periods of the invention, or the exhibition or use therein during such periods of the design, or the publication therein during such periods of a description or representation of the design, or the use therein during such periods of the trade mark, shall not invalidate the patent which may be granted for the invention, or the registration of the design or trade mark :

(3.) The application for the grant of a patent, or the registration of a design, or the registration of a trade mark under this section, must be made in the same manner as an ordinary application under this Act : Provided that, in the case of trade marks, any trade mark the registration of which has been duly applied for in the country of origin may be registered under this Act :

(4.) The provisions of this section shall apply only in the case of those foreign states with respect to which Her Majesty shall from time to time by Order in Council declare them to be applicable, and so long only in the case of each state as the Order in Council shall continue in force with respect to that state.

**Provision for colonies and India.**

104.—(1.) Where it is made to appear to Her Majesty that the legislature of any British possession has made satisfactory provision for the protection of inventions, designs, and trade marks, patented or registered in this country, it shall be lawful for Her Majesty from time to time, by Order in Council, to apply the provisions of the last preceding section, with such variations or additions, if any, as to Her Majesty in Council may seem fit, to such British possession.

(2.) An Order in Council under this Act shall, from a date to be mentioned for the purpose in the Order, take effect as if its provisions had been contained in this Act; but it shall be lawful for Her Majesty in Council to revoke any Order in Council made under this Act.

(a) 48 & 49 Vict. c. 63, s. 6.

*Offences.*

**105.**—(1.) Any person who represents that any article sold by him is a patented article, when no patent has been granted for the same, or describes any design or trade mark applied to any article sold by him as registered which is not so, shall be liable for every offence on summary conviction to a fine not exceeding five pounds.

*Penalty on falsely representing articles to be patented.*

(2.) A person shall be deemed, for the purposes of this enactment, to represent that an article is patented or a design or a trade mark is registered, if he sells the article with the word "patent," "patented," "registered," or any word or words expressing or implying that a patent or registration has been obtained for the article stamped, engraved, or impressed on, or otherwise applied to, the article.

**106.** Any person who, without the authority of Her Majesty, or any of the Royal Family, or of any Government Department, assumes or uses in connexion with any trade, business, calling, or profession, the Royal arms, or arms so nearly resembling the same as to be calculated to lead other persons to believe that he is carrying on his trade, business, calling, or profession by or under such authority as aforesaid, shall be liable on summary conviction to a fine not exceeding twenty pounds.

*Penalty on unauthorised assumption of Royal arms.*

*Scotland ; Ireland ; &c.*

**107.** In any action for infringement of a patent in Scotland the provisions of this Act, with respect to calling in the aid of an assessor, shall apply, and the action shall be tried without a jury, unless the court shall otherwise direct, but otherwise nothing shall affect the jurisdiction and forms of process of the courts in Scotland in such an action, or in any action or proceeding respecting a patent hitherto competent to those courts.

*Saving for courts in Scotland.*

For the purposes of this section "court of appeal" shall mean any court to which such action is appealed.

**108.** In Scotland any offence under this Act declared to be punishable on summary conviction may be prosecuted in the sheriff court.

*Summary proceedings in Scotland.*

**109.**—(1.) Proceedings in Scotland for revocation of a patent shall be in the form of an action of reduction at the instance of the Lord Advocate, or at the instance of a party having interest with his concurrence, which concurrence may be given on just cause shown only.

*Proceedings for revocation of patent in Scotland.*

(2.) Service of all writs and summonses in that action shall be made according to the forms and practice existing at the commencement of this Act.

**110.** All parties shall, notwithstanding anything in this Act, have in Ireland their remedies under or in respect of a patent as if the same had been granted to extend to Ireland only.

*Reservation of remedies in Ireland.*

**111.**—(1.) The provisions of this Act conferring a special jurisdiction on the court as defined by this Act, shall not, except so far as the jurisdiction extends, affect the jurisdiction of any court in Scotland or Ireland in any proceedings relating to patents or to designs or to trade marks; and, with reference to any such proceedings in Scotland, the term "the court" shall mean any Lord Ordinary of the Court of Session, and the term "Court of Appeal" shall mean either Division of the said Court ; and, with reference to any such proceedings in Ireland, the terms "the Court," and "the Court of Appeal," respectively mean the High Court of Justice in Ireland and Her Majesty's Court of Appeal in Ireland.

*General saving for jurisdiction of courts.*

(2.) If any rectification of a register under this Act is required in pursuance of any proceeding in a court in Scotland or Ireland, a copy of the order, decree, or other authority for the rectification, shall be served on the comptroller, and he shall rectify the register accordingly.

**112.** This Act shall extend to the Isle of Man, and—

*Isle of Man.*

(1.) Nothing in this Act shall affect the jurisdiction of the courts in the Isle of Man, in proceedings for infringement or in any action or proceeding respecting a patent, design, or trade mark competent to those courts ;

(2.) The punishment for a misdemeanor under this Act in the Isle of Man shall be imprisonment for any term not exceeding two years, with or without hard labour, and with or without a fine not exceeding one hundred pounds, at the discretion of the court ;

(3.) Any offence under this Act committed in the Isle of Man which would in England be punishable on summary conviction may be prosecuted, and any fine in respect thereof recovered at the instance of any person aggrieved, in the manner in which offences punishable on summary conviction may for the time being be prosecuted.

### Repeal; Transitional Provisions; Savings.

**Repeal and saving for past operation of repealed enactments, &c.**

**113.** The enactments described in the Third Schedule to this Act are hereby repealed. But this repeal of enactments shall not—

(a) Affect the past operation of any of those enactments, or any patent or copyright or right to use a trade mark granted or acquired, or application pending, or appointment made, or compensation granted, or order or direction made or given, or right, privilege, obligation, or liability acquired, accrued, or incurred, or anything duly done or suffered under or by any of those enactments before or at the commencement of this Act ; or

(b) Interfere with the institution or prosecution of any action or proceeding, civil or criminal, in respect thereof, and any such proceeding may be carried on as if this Act had not been passed ; or

(c) Take away or abridge any protection or benefit in relation to any such action or proceeding.

**Former registers to be deemed continued.**

**114.**—(1.) The registers of patents and of proprietors kept under any enactment repealed by this Act shall respectively be deemed parts of the same book as the register of patents kept under this Act.

(2.) The registers of designs and of trade marks kept under any enactment repealed by this Act shall respectively be deemed parts of the same book as the register of designs and the register of trade marks kept under this Act.

**Saving for existing rules.**

**115.** All general rules made by the Lord Chancellor or by any other authority under any enactment repealed by this Act, and in force at the commencement of this Act, may at any time after the passing of this Act be repealed altered or amended by the Board of Trade, as if they had been made by the Board under this Act, but so that no such repeal alteration or amendment shall take effect before the commencement of this Act ; and, subject as aforesaid, such general rules shall, so far as they are consistent with and are not superseded by this Act, continue in force as if they had been made by the Board of Trade under this Act.

**Saving for prerogative.**

**116.** Nothing in this Act shall take away abridge or prejudicially affect the prerogative of the Crown in relation to the granting of any letters patent or to the withholding of a grant thereof.

### General Definitions.

**General definitions.**

**117.**—(1.) In and for the purposes of this Act, unless the context otherwise requires,—

"Person" includes a body corporate :

"The court" means (subject to the provisions for Scotland, Ireland, and the Isle of Man) her Majesty's High Court of Justice in England :

"Law officer" means her Majesty's Attorney-General or Solicitor-General for England :

"The Treasury" means the Commissioners of her Majesty's Treasury :

"Comptroller" means the Comptroller-General of Patents, Designs, and Trade Marks :

"Prescribed" means prescribed by any of the schedules to this Act, or by general rules under or within the meaning of this Act :

"British possession" means any territory or place situate within her Majesty's dominions, and not being or forming part of the United Kingdom, or of the Channel Islands, or of the Isle of Man, and all territories and places under one legislature, as hereinafter defined, are deemed to be one British possession for the purposes of this Act :

"Legislature" includes any person or persons who exercise legislative authority in the British possession ; and where there are local legislatures as well as a central legislature, means the central legislature only.

In the application of this Act to Ireland, "summary conviction" means a conviction under the Summary Jurisdiction Acts, that is to say, with reference to the Dublin Metropolitan Police District the Acts regulating the duties of justices of the peace and of the police for such district, and elsewhere in Ireland the Petty Sessions (Ireland) Act, 1851, and any Act amending it.

---

# SCHEDULES.

---

## THE FIRST SCHEDULE.

### FORMS OF APPLICATION, &C.

| £1 Stamp. |
|---|

### FORM A.                                    Section 5.

#### FORM OF APPLICATION FOR PATENT.

I, (a) *John Smith*, of 29, *Perry Street, Birmingham*, in the county of *Warwick, Engineer*, do solemnly and sincerely declare that I am in possession of an invention for (b) *"Improvements in Sewing Machines;"* that I am the true and first inventor thereof ; and that the same is not in use by any other person or persons to the best of my knowledge and belief ; and I humbly pray that a patent may be granted to me for the said invention.

    And I make the above solemn declaration conscientiously believing the same to be true, and by virtue of the provisions of the Statutory Declarations Act, 1835.

(c) John Smith.

Declared at *Birmingham*, in the county of *Warwick*, this      day of , 18 .

Before me,
(d) James Adams,
Justice of the Peace.

NOTE.—Where the above declaration is made out of the United Kingdom, the words " and by virtue of the Statutory Declarations Act, 1835," must be omitted ; and the declaration must be made before a British consular officer, or where it is not reasonably practicable to make it before such officer, then before a public officer duly authorized in that behalf.

*(a) Here insert name, address and calling of inventor.*

*(b) Here insert title of invention.*

*(c) Signature of inventor.*

*(d) Signature and title of the officer before whom the declaration is made.*

---

### FORM B.

#### FORM OF PROVISIONAL SPECIFICATION.

Improvements in Sewing Machines (a).

I, (b) *John Smith*, of 29, *Perry Street, Birmingham*, in the county of *Warwick, Engineer*, do hereby declare the nature of my invention for *"Improvements in Sewing Machines,"* to be as follows (c) :—

    ＊    ＊    ＊    ＊    ＊    ＊

(d) John Smith.

Dated this      day of , 18 .

NOTE.—No stamp is required on this document.

*(a) Here insert title as in declaration.*

*(b) Here insert name, address, and calling of inventor as in declaration.*

*(c) Here insert short description of invention.*

*(d) Signature of inventor.*

Form C.

| £3 Stamp. | Form of Complete Specification. |

*Improvements in Sewing Machines.*  (a)

(a) Here insert title, as in declaration.

(b) Here insert name, address, and calling of inventor, as in declaration.

I, (b) *John Smith*, of 29, *Perry Street, Birmingham*, in the county of *Warwick, Engineer*, do hereby declare the nature of my invention for " *Improvements in Sewing Machines*," and in what manner the same is to be performed, to be particularly described and ascertained in and by the following statement (c) :—

(c) Here insert full description of invention.

＊          ＊          ＊          ＊          ＊

Having now particularly described and ascertained the nature of my said invention and in what manner the same is to be performed, I declare that what I claim is (d).

(d) Here state distinctly the features of novelty claimed.

1.
2.
3, &c.

(e) Signature of inventor.

(e) *John Smith.*

Dated this          day of          , 18   .

———

Form D.

Form of Patent.

Victoria, by the grace of God, of the United Kingdom of Great Britain and Ireland, Queen, defender of the faith : to all to whom these presents shall come greeting :

Whereas *John Smith*, of 29, *Perry Street, Birmingham*, in the county of *Warwick, Engineer*, hath by his solemn declaration represented unto us that he is in possession of an invention for "*Improvements in Sewing Machines*," that he is the true and first inventor thereof, and that the same is not in use by any other person to the best of his knowledge and belief :

And whereas the said inventor hath humbly prayed that we would be graciously pleased to grant unto him (hereinafter together with his executors, administrators, and assigns, or any of them, referred to as the said patentee) our royal letters patent for the sole use and advantage of his said invention :

And whereas the said inventor hath by and in his complete specification particularly described the nature of his invention :

And whereas we being willing to encourage all inventions which may be for the public good, are graciously pleased to condescend to his request :

Know ye, therefore, that we, of our especial grace, certain knowledge, and mere motion do by these presents, for us, our heirs and successors, give and grant unto the said patentee our especial license, full power, sole privilege, and authority, that the said patentee by himself, his agents, or licensees, and no others, may at all times hereafter during the term of years herein mentioned, make, use, exercise, and vend the said invention within our United Kingdom of Great Britain and Ireland, and Isle of Man, in such manner as to him or them may seem meet, and that the said patentee shall have and enjoy the whole profit and advantage from time to time accruing by reason of the said invention, during the term of fourteen years from the date hereunder written of these presents : And to the end that the said patentee may have and enjoy the sole use and exercise and the full benefit of the said invention, we do by these presents for us, our heirs and successors, strictly command all our subjects whatsoever within our United Kingdom of Great Britain and Ireland, and the Isle of Man, that they do not at any time during the continuance of the said term of fourteen years either directly or indirectly make use of or put in practice the said invention, or any part of the same, nor in anywise imitate the same, nor make or cause to be made any addition thereto or subtraction therefrom, whereby to pretend themselves the inventors thereof, without the consent, licence or agreement of the said patentee in writing under his hand and seal, on pain of incurring such penalties as may be justly inflicted on such offenders for their contempt of this our royal command, and of being answerable to the patentee according to law for his damages thereby occasioned: provided that these our letters patent are on this condition, that, if at any time during the said term it be made to appear to us, our heirs, or successors, or any six or more of our privy council, that this our grant is contrary to law, or prejudicial or inconvenient to our subjects in general, or that the said invention is not a new invention as to the public use and exercise thereof within our United Kingdom of Great Britain and Ireland, and Isle of Man, or that the said patentee is not the first and true inventor thereof within this realm as aforesaid, these our letters patent shall forthwith determine, and be void to all intents and purposes, notwithstanding anything hereinbefore contained: provided also, that if the said patentee shall not pay all fees by law required to be paid in respect of the grant of these letters patent, or in respect of any matter relating thereto at the time or times, and in manner for the time being by law provided; and also if the said patentee shall not supply or cause to be supplied, for our service, all such articles of the said invention as may be required by the officers or commissioners administering any department of our service in such manner, at such times, and at and upon such reasonable prices and terms as shall be settled in manner for the time being by law provided, then, and in any of the said cases, these our letters patent, and all privileges and advantages whatever hereby granted shall determine and become void notwithstanding anything hereinbefore contained: Provided also that nothing herein contained shall prevent the granting of licences and in such manner and for such considerations as they may by law be granted: And lastly, we do by these presents for us, our heirs and successors, grant unto the said patentee that these our letters patent shall be construed in the most beneficial sense for the advantage of the said patentee. In witness whereof we have caused these our letters to be made patent this                    one thousand eight hundred and            and to be sealed as of the         one thousand eight hundred and                             .

Seal
of Patent
Office.

---

FORM E.                                                      Section 47.

FORM OF APPLICATION FOR REGISTRATION OF DESIGN.

                                          day of         , 18  .
You are hereby requested to register the accompanying      design, in   (a) Here insert
Class        , in the name of (a)         of         , who claims to be the pro-   legibly the name
prietor thereof, and to return the same to      .                and address of
Statement of nature of design        .                          the individual
*Registration fees enclosed, £       ,,      s.*                or firm.

To the Comptroller,
        Patent Office,
            25, *Southampton Buildings, Chancery Lane, W.C.*
                        (Signed)

Section 62.

## FORM F.

### FORM OF APPLICATION FOR REGISTRATION OF TRADE MARK.

(One representation to be fixed within this square, and two others on separate sheets of foolscap of same size.)

(Representations of a larger size may be folded, but must be mounted upon linen and affixed hereto.)

You are hereby requested to register the accompanying trade mark [*In Class*    , *iron in bars, sheets, and plates ; in Class*    , *steam engines and boilers ; and in Class*    , *warming apparatus*], in the name of (*a*), who claims to be the proprietor thereof.

*(a)* Here insert legibly the name, address, and business of the individual or firm.

*Registration fees enclosed, £*    *,,*    *s.*

To the Comptroller,
     Patent Office,
        25, *Southampton Buildings, Chancery Lane, W.C.*
                  (Signed)

*Note.*—If the trade mark has been in use before August 13, 1875, state length of user.

---

## THE SECOND SCHEDULE.

Section 24.

*Fees on instruments for obtaining Patents, and renewal.*

(*a*) *Up to sealing.*

|  | £ | s. | £ | s. | d. |
|---|---|---|---|---|---|
| On application for provisional protection............ | 1 | 0 | | | |
| On filing complete specification .................... | 3 | 0 | | | |
|  |  |  | 4 | 0 | 0 |

*or*

| On filing complete specification with first application ......... | 4 | 0 | 0 |
|---|---|---|---|

(*b*) *Further before end of four years from date of patent.*

| On certificate of renewal ............................. | 50 | 0 | 0 |
|---|---|---|---|

(*c*) *Further before end of seven years, or in the case of patents granted after the commencement of this Act, before the end of eight years from date of patent.*

| On certificate of renewal ............................. | 100 | 0 | 0 |
|---|---|---|---|

*Or in lieu of the fees of £50 and £100 the following annual fees :—*

| | £ | s. | d. |
|---|---|---|---|
| Before the expiration of the fourth year from the date of the patent | 10 | 0 | 0 |
| ,,    ,,    fifth    ,,    ,, | 10 | 0 | 0 |
| sixth   ,, | 10 | 0 | 0 |
| seventh   ,, | 10 | 0 | 0 |
| eighth   ,, | 15 | 0 | 0 |
| ninth | 15 | 0 | 0 |
| tenth   ,, | 20 | 0 | 0 |
| eleventh   ,, | 20 | 0 | 0 |
| twelfth   ,, | 20 | 0 | 0 |
| thirteenth   ,, | 20 | 0 | 0 |

THE THIRD SCHEDULE.                    Section 113.

*Enactments repealed.*

| | |
|---|---|
| 21 James I. c. 3 .... [1623.] | The Statute of Monopolies. In part ; namely,— Sections, ten, eleven, and twelve. |
| 5 & 6 Will. 4, c. 62.. [1835.] In part. | The Statutory Declarations Act, 1835. In part ; namely,— Section eleven. |
| 5 & 6 Will. 4, c. 83.. [1835.] | An Act to amend the law touching letters patent for inventions. |
| 2 & 3 Vict. c. 67 .... [1839.] | An Act to amend an Act of the fifth and sixth years of the reign of King William the Fourth, intituled "An Act to amend the law touching letters patent for inventions." |
| 5 & 6 Vict. c. 100 .. [1842.] | An Act to consolidate and amend the laws relating to the copyright of designs for ornamenting articles of manufacture. |
| 6 & 7 Vict. c. 65 .... [1843.] | An Act to amend the laws relating to the copyright of designs. |
| 7 & 8 Vict. c. 69 (a).. [1844.] In part. | An Act for amending an Act passed in the fourth year of the reign of his late Majesty, intituled "An Act for the better administration of justice in his Majesty's Privy Council, and to extend its jurisdiction and powers." In part ; namely,— Sections two to five, both included. |
| 13 & 14 Vict. c. 104.. [1850.] | An Act to extend and amend the Acts relating to the copyright of designs. |
| 15 & 16 Vict. c. 83 .. [1852.] | The Patent Law Amendment Act, 1852. |
| 16 & 17 Vict. c. 5 .. [1853.] | An Act to substitute stamp duties for fees on passing letters patent for inventions, and to provide for the purchase for the public use of certain indexes of specifications. |
| 16 & 17 Vict. c. 115.. [1853. ] | An Act to amend certain provisions of the Patent Law Amendment Act, 1852, in respect of the transmission of certified copies of letters patent and specifications to certain offices in Edinburgh and Dublin, and otherwise to amend the said Act. |
| 21 & 22 Vict. c. 70 .. [1858.] | An Act to amend the Act of the fifth and sixth years of her present Majesty, to consolidate and amend the laws relating to the copyright of designs for ornamenting articles of manufacture. |
| 22 Vict. c. 13 ...... [1859.] | An Act to amend the law concerning patents for inventions with respect to inventions for improvements in instruments and munitions of war. |
| 24 & 25 Vict. c. 73 .. [1861.] | An Act to amend the law relating to the copyright of designs. |
| 28 & 29 Vict. c. 3 .. [1865.] | The Industrial Exhibitions Act, 1865. |
| 33 & 34 Vict. c. 27 .. [1870.] | The Protection of Inventions Act, 1870. |
| 33 & 34 Vict. c. 97 .. [1870.] | The Stamp Act, 1870. In part ; namely,— Section sixty-five, and in the schedule the words and figures. "Certificate of the registration of a design ..£5  0  0 And see section 65." |

(a) *Note.*—Sections six and seven of this Act are repealed by the Statute Law Revision (No. 2) Act, 1874.

| | |
|---|---|
| 38 & 39 Vict. c. 91 .. [1875.] | The Trade Marks Registration Act, 1875. |
| 38 & 39 Vict. c. 93 .. [1875.] | The Copyright of Designs Act, 1875. |
| 39 & 40 Vict. c. 33 .. [1876.] | The Trade Marks Registration Amendment Act, 1876. |
| 40 & 41 Vict. c. 37 .. [1877.] | The Trade Marks Registration Extension Act, 1877. |
| 43 & 44 Vict. c. 10 .. [1880.] | The Great Seal Act, 1880. In part ; namely,— Section five. |
| 45 & 46 Vict. c. 72 .. [1882.] | The Revenue, Friendly Societies, and National Debt Act, 1882. In part ; namely,— Section sixteen. |

## 48 & 49 VICT. C. 63.

### An Act to Amend the Patents, Designs, and Trade Marks Act, 1883.

[14th August, 1885.]

BE it enacted by the Queen's most Excellent Majesty, by and with the advice and consent of the Lords Spiritual and Temporal, and Commons, in this present Parliament assembled, and by the authority of the same, as follows :

Construction and short title.

1. This Act shall be construed as one with the Patents, Designs, and Trade Marks Act, 1883 (in this Act referred to as the principal Act).

This Act may be cited as the Patents, Designs, and Trade Marks (Amendment) Act, 1885, and this Act and the principal Act may be cited together as the Patents, Designs, and Trade Marks Acts, 1883 and 1885.

Amendment of s. 5 of 46 & 47 Vict. c. 57.

2. Whereas subsection two of section five of the principal Act requires a declaration to be made by an applicant for a patent to the effect in that subsection mentioned, and doubts have arisen as to the nature of that declaration, and it is expedient to remove such doubts : Be it therefore enacted that:

5 & 6 Will. 4, c. 62.

The declaration mentioned in subsection two of section five of the principal Act may be either a statutory declaration under the Statutory Declarations Act, 1835, or not, as may be from time to time prescribed.

Amendment of ss. 8, 9, and 12 of 46 & 47 Vict. c. 57.

3. Whereas under the principal Act, a complete specification is required (by section eight) to be left within nine months, and (by section nine) to be accepted within twelve months, from the date of application, and a patent is required by section twelve to be sealed within fifteen months from the date of application, and it is expedient to empower the comptroller to extend in certain cases the said times : Be it therefore enacted as follows :

A complete specification may be left and accepted within such extended times, not exceeding one month and three months respectively after the said nine and twelve months respectively as the comptroller may on payment of the prescribed fee allow, and where such extension of time has been allowed, a further extension of four months after the said fifteen months shall be allowed for the sealing of the patent ; and the principal Act shall have effect as if any time so allowed were addded to the said periods specified in the principal Act.

Specifications, &c. not to be published unless application accepted.

4. Where an application for a patent has been abandoned, or become void, the specification or specifications and drawings (if any) accompanying or left in connexion with such application, shall not at any time be open to public inspection or be published by the comptroller.

Power to grant patents to several persons jointly.

5. Whereas doubts have arisen whether under the principal Act a patent may lawfully be granted to several persons jointly, some or one of whom only are or is the true and first inventors or inventor ; be it therefore

enacted and declared that it has been and is lawful under the principal Act to grant such a patent.

6. In subsection one of section one hundred and three of the principal Act, the words " date of the application " shall be substituted for the words " date of the protection obtained."

Amendment of s. 103 of 46 & 47 Vict. c. 57.

---

## 49 Vict. c. 23.

*An Act to amend the Companies Acts of* 1862, 1867, 1870, 1877, 1879, 1880, *and* 1883.

[*4th June,* 1886.]

Whereas it has become expedient to amend the provisions of the Companies Act, 1862, and of the other Acts amending the same hereinafter recited, in so far as the said provisions relate to the liquidation of companies in Scotland:

25 & 26 Vict. c. 89.

Be it therefore enacted by the Queen's most excellent Majesty, by and with the advice and consent of the Lords spiritual and temporal, and Commons, in this present Parliament assembled, and by the authority of the same, as follows :

1. This Act may be cited for all purposes as the Companies Act, 1886.

Short title.

2. This Act shall, so far as consistent with the tenor thereof, be construed as one with the Companies Acts, 1862, 1867, 1877, 1879, 1880, and 1883, and the Joint Stock Companies Arrangement Act, 1870, and the said Acts and this Act may be referred to as the Companies Acts, 1862 to 1886.

Construction of Acts.
25 & 26 Vict. c. 89.
30 & 31 Vict.

3. In the winding up, by or subject to the supervision of the court, of any company under the Companies Acts, 1862 to 1886, whose registered office is in Scotland, where the winding up shall commence after the passing of this Act, the following provisions shall have effect :

c. 131.
40 & 41 Vict. c. 26.
42 & 43 Vict. c. 76.

(1.) Such winding up shall, in the case of a winding up by the court as at the commencement thereof, and in the case of a winding up subject to the supervision of the court as at the date of the presentation of the petition, on which a supervision order is afterwards pronounced, be equivalent to an arrestment in execution and decree of forth-coming, and to an executed or completed poinding ; and no arrest-ment or poinding of the funds or effects of the company, executed on or after the sixtieth day prior to the commencement of the winding up by the court, or to the presentation of the petition on which a supervision order is made, as the case may be, shall be effectual ; and such funds or effects, or the proceeds of such effects, if sold, shall be made forthcoming to the liquidator : Provided that any arrester or poinder, before the date of such winding up, or of such petition, as the case may be, who shall be thus deprived of the benefit of his diligence, shall have preference out of such funds or effects for the expense bonâ fide incurred by him in such diligence.

43 Vict. c. 19.
46 & 47 Vict. c. 28.
33 & 34 Vict. c. 104.
Effect of diligence within 60 days of wind-ing-up by or subject to super-vision of court.

(2.) Such winding up shall, as at the respective dates aforesaid, be equivalent to a decree of adjudication of the heritable estates of the company for payment of the whole debts of the company, principal and interest, accumulated at the said dates respectively, subject always to such preferable heritable rights and securities as existed at the said dates and are valid and unchallengeable, and the right to poind the ground hereinafter provided.

(3.) The provisions of sections one hundred and twelve to one hundred and seventeen inclusive, and also of section one hundred and twenty, of the Bankruptcy (Scotland) Act, 1856, shall, so far as consistent with the tenor of the recited Acts, apply to the realization of heritable estates affected by such heritable rights and securities as aforesaid ; and for the purposes of this Act the words " sequestra-tion " and " trustee " occurring in said sections of the Bankruptcy (Scotland) Act, 1856, shall mean respectively " liquidation " and " liquidator " ; and the expression " the lord ordinary or the court " shall mean " the court " as defined by this Act.

19 & 20 Vict. c. 79.

(4.) No poinding of the ground which has not been carried into execution by sale of the effects sixty days before the respective dates aforesaid shall, except to the extent hereinafter provided, be available in any question with the liquidator : Provided that no creditor who holds a security over the heritable estate preferable to the right of the liquidator shall be prevented from executing a poinding of the ground after the respective dates aforesaid, but such poinding shall in competition with the liquidator be available only for the interest on the debt for the current half-yearly term, and for the arrears of interest for one year immediately before the commencement of such term.

**Ranking of claims.**   **4.** In the winding up of any company under the Companies Acts, 1862 to 1886, whose registered office is in Scotland, and where the winding up shall commence after the passing of this Act, the general and special rules in regard to voting and ranking for payment of dividends, provided by the Bankruptcy (Scotland) Act, 1856, sections forty-nine to sixty-six inclusive, or any other rules in regard thereto which may be in force for the time being in the sequestration of the estates of bankrupts in Scotland, shall, so far as consistent with the tenor of the said recited Acts, apply to creditors of such companies voting in matters relating to the winding up, and ranking for payment of dividends ; and for this purpose sequestration shall be taken to mean liquidation, trustee to mean liquidator, and sheriff to mean the court.

**Jurisdiction of the Lord Ordinary on the Bills in vacation.**   **5.** Wherever the expression "the court of session" occurs in the said recited Acts, or the expression "the court" occurring therein or in this Act refers to the court of session in Scotland, it shall mean and include either division thereof, or, in the event of a remit to a permanent Lord Ordinary, as hereinafter provided, such Lord Ordinary, during session, and in time of vacation the Lord Ordinary on the Bills ; and in regard to orders or judgments pronounced by the said Lord Ordinary on the Bills in vacation, the following provisions shall have effect :—

(1.) No order or judgment pronounced by the said Lord Ordinary in vacation, under or by virtue, in whole or in part, of the following sections of the said recited Acts, shall be subject to review, reduction, suspension, or stay of execution, videlicet, of the Companies Act, 1862, sections ninety-one, one hundred and seven, one hundred and fifteen, one hundred and seventeen, and one hundred and twenty-seven, and section one hundred and forty-nine so far as it authorises the court to direct meetings of creditors or contributories to be held, and that portion of section two of the Joint Stock Companies Arrangement Act, 1870, which authorises the court to order that a meeting of creditors or class of creditors shall be summoned ; and also sections one hundred and twenty-two and one hundred and twenty-three of the Companies Act, 1862, so far as they may affect the sections above enumerated.

**25 & 26 Vict. c. 89.**

**33 & 34 Vict. c. 104.**

(2.) All other orders or judgments pronounced by the said Lord Ordinary in vacation (except as after mentioned) shall be subject to review only by reclaiming note, in common form, presented (notwithstanding the terms of section one hundred and twenty-four of the Companies Act, 1862,) within fourteen days from the date of such order or judgment : Provided always, that such orders or judgments pronounced by the said Lord Ordinary in vacation, under or by virtue, in whole or in part, of the following sections of the Companies Act, 1862, shall, from the dates of such orders or judgments, and notwithstanding any reclaiming note against the same, be carried out and receive effect till such reclaiming note be disposed of by the court, videlicet, sections eighty-five, eighty-seven, eighty-nine, ninety-three (except in regard to the removal or remuneration of liquidators), ninety-five, ninety-six (except in regard to the power to sell), one hundred, one hundred and eighteen, first part of one hundred and forty-one, one hundred and forty-seven, one hundred and fifty (except in regard to the removal of liquidators and the filling up of vacancies caused by such removal), one hundred and ninety-seven, one hundred and ninety-eight, and two hundred and one ; and also sections one hundred and twenty-two, and one hundred and twenty-three of the Companies Act, 1862, so far as they may affect the sections above enumerated.

. Provided that nothing in this section contained shall in any way affect the provisions of section one hundred and twenty-one of the Companies Act, 1862, in reference to decrees for payment of calls in the winding up of companies, whether voluntary or by or subject to the supervision of the court.

6. When the court makes a winding up or a supervision order, or at any time thereafter, it shall be lawful for the court, in either division thereof, if it thinks fit, to direct all subsequent proceedings in the winding up to be taken before one of the permanent Lords Ordinary, and to remit the winding up to him accordingly ; and thereupon such Lord Ordinary shall, for the purposes of the winding up, be deemed to be "the court," within the meaning of the recited Acts and this Act, and shall have, for the purposes of such winding up, all the jurisdiction and powers of the court of session : Provided always, that all orders or judgments pronounced by such Lord Ordinary shall be subject to review only by reclaiming note in common form, presented (notwithstanding the terms of section one hundred and twenty-four of the Companies Act, 1862,) within fourteen days from the date of such order or judgment. But, should a reclaiming note not be presented and moved during session, the provisions of section five of this Act shall apply to such orders or judgments : Provided also, that the said Lord Ordinary may report to the division of the court any matter which may arise in the course of the winding up. This section and the immediately preceding section shall come into force from the passing of this Act, and shall include companies then in the course of being wound up.

*Winding up may be remitted to Lord Ordinary.*

---

## 49 & 50 VICT. C. 37.

*An Act to remove certain Doubts respecting the construction of the Patents, Designs, and Trade Marks Act, 1883, so far as respects the Drawings by which Specifications are required to be accompanied, and as respects Exhibitions,*

[*25th June,* 1886.]

WHEREAS by section five of the Patents, Designs, and Trade Marks Act, 1883, specifications, whether provisional or complete, must be accompanied by drawings if required, and doubts have arisen as to whether it is sufficient that a complete specification refers to the drawings by which the provisional specification was accompanied, and it is expedient to remove such doubts :

Be it therefore enacted by the Queen's most excellent Majesty, by and with the advice and consent of the Lords Spiritual and Temporal, and Commons, in this present Parliament assembled, and by the authority of the same, as follows :

*46 & 47 Vict. c. 57.*

1. This Act may be cited as the Patents Act, 1886, and shall be construed as one with the Patents, Designs, and Trade Marks Acts, 1883 and 1885, and, together with those Acts, may be cited as the Patents, Designs, and Trade Marks Acts, 1883 to 1886.

*Short title and construction. 46 & 47 Vict. c. 57. 48 & 49 Vict. c. 63.*

2. The requirement of sub-section four of section five of the Patents, Designs, and Trade Marks Act, 1883, as to drawings shall not be deemed to be insufficiently complied with by reason only that instead of being accompanied by drawings the complete specification refers to the drawings which accompanied the provisional specification. And no patent heretofore sealed shall be invalid by reason only that the complete specification was not accompanied by drawings, but referred to those which accompanied the provisional specification.

*The same drawings may accompany both specifications.*

Protection of
patents and
designs ex-
hibited at
international
exhibitions.

**3.** Whereas by section thirty-nine of the Patents, Designs, and Trade Marks Act, 1883, as respects patents, and by section fifty-seven of the same Act as respects designs, provision is made that the exhibition of an invention or design at an industrial or international exhibition, certified as such by the Board of Trade, shall not prejudice the rights of the inventor or proprietor thereof, subject to the conditions therein mentioned, one of which is that the exhibitor must, before exhibiting the invention, design, or article, or publishing a description of the design, give the controller the prescribed notice of his intention to do so :

And whereas it is expedient to provide for the extension of the said sections to industrial and international exhibitions held out of the United Kingdom, be it therefore enacted as follows :

It shall be lawful for Her Majesty, by Order in Council, from time to time to declare that sections thirty-nine and fifty-seven of the Patents, Designs, and Trade Marks Act, 1883, or either of those sections, shall apply to any exhibition mentioned in the Order in like manner as if it were an industrial or international exhibition certified by the Board of Trade, and to provide that the exhibitor shall be relieved from the conditions, specified in the said sections, of giving notice to the controller of his intention to exhibit, and shall be so relieved either absolutely or upon such terms and conditions as to Her Majesty in Council may seem fit.

---

50 & 51 Vict. c. 28.

*An Act to consolidate and amend the Law relating to Fraudulent Marks on Merchandise.*

[*23rd August,* 1887.]

Be it enacted by the Queen's most excellent Majesty, by and with the advice and consent of the Lords Spiritual and Temporal, and Commons, in this present Parliament assembled, and by the authority of the same, as follows :

Short title.
**1.** This Act may be cited as the Merchandise Marks Act, 1887.

Offences as to
trade marks and
trade descrip-
tions.
**2.**—(1.) Every person who—

(a) Forges any trade mark ; or

(b) Falsely applies to goods any trade mark or any mark so nearly resembling a trade mark as to be calculated to deceive ; or

(c) Makes any die, block, machine, or other instrument for the purpose of forging, or for being used for forging, a trade mark ; or

(d) Applies any false trade description to goods ; or

(e) Disposes of or has in his possession any die, block, machine, or other instrument for the purpose of forging a trade mark ; or

(f) Causes any of the things above in this section mentioned to be done,

shall, subject to the provisions of this Act, and unless he proves that he acted without intent to defraud, be guilty of an offence against this Act.

(2.) Every person who sells, or exposes for, or has in his possession for, sale, or any purpose of trade or manufacture, any goods or things to which any forged trade mark or false trade description is applied, or to which any trade mark or mark so nearly resembling a trade mark as to be calculated to deceive is falsely applied, as the case may be, shall, unless he proves—

(a) That having taken all reasonable precautions against committing an offence against this Act, he had at the time of the commission of the alleged offence no reason to suspect the genuineness of the trade mark, mark, or trade description; and

(b) That on demand made by or on behalf of the prosecutor, he gave all the information in his power with respect to the persons from whom he obtained such goods or things; or

(c) That otherwise he had acted innocently;

be guilty of an offence against this Act.

(3.) Every person guilty of an offence against this Act shall be liable—

(i) On conviction on indictment, to imprisonment, with or without hard labour, for a term not exceeding two years, or to fine, or to both imprisonment and fine; and

(ii) On summary conviction to imprisonment, with or without hard labour, for a term not exceeding four months, or to a fine not exceeding twenty pounds, and in the case of a second or subsequent conviction to imprisonment, with or without hard labour, for a term not exceeding six months, or to a fine not exceeding fifty pounds; and

(iii) In any case, to forfeit to her Majesty every chattel, article, instrument, or thing by means of or in relation to which the offence has been committed.

(4.) The court before whom any person is convicted under this section may order any forfeited articles to be destroyed or otherwise disposed of as the court thinks fit.

(5.) If any person feels aggrieved by any conviction made by a court of summary jurisdiction, he may appeal therefrom to a court of quarter sessions.

(6.) Any offence for which a person is under this Act liable to punishment on summary conviction may be prosecuted, and any articles liable to be forfeited under this Act by a court of summary jurisdiction may be forfeited, in manner provided by the Summary Jurisdiction Acts: Provided that a 42 & 43 Vict. person charged with an offence under this section before a court of summary c. 49. jurisdiction shall, on appearing before the court, and before the charge is gone into, be informed of his right to be tried on indictment, and if he requires be so tried accordingly.

3.—(1.) For the purposes of this Act—

The expression "trade mark" means a trade mark registered in the Definitions. register of trade marks kept under the Patents, Designs, and Trade 46 & 47 Vict. Marks Act, 1883, and includes any trade mark which, either with or c. 57. without registration, is protected by law in any British possession or foreign State to which the provisions of the one hundred and third section of the Patents, Designs, and Trade Marks Act, 1883, are, under Order in Council, for the time being applicable:

The expression "trade description" means any description, statement, or other indication, direct or indirect,

(a) as to the number, quantity, measure, gauge, or weight of any goods, or

(b) as to the place or country in which any goods were made or produced, or

(c) as to the mode of manufacturing or producing any goods, or

(d) as to the material of which any goods are composed, or

(e) as to any goods being the subject of an existing patent, privilege, or copyright,

and the use of any figure, word, or mark which, according to the custom of the trade, is commonly taken to be an indication of any of the above matters, shall be deemed to be a trade description within the meaning of this Act:

The expression "false trade description" means a trade description which is false in a material respect as regards the goods to which it is applied, and includes every alteration of a trade description, whether by way of addition, effacement, or otherwise, where that alteration makes the description false in a material respect, and the fact that a trade description is a trade mark, or part of a trade mark, shall not prevent such trade description being a false trade description within the meaning of this Act:

The expression "goods" means anything which is the subject of trade, manufacture, or merchandise:

The expressions "person," "manufacturer, dealer, or trader," and "proprietor" include any body of persons corporate or unincorporate:

4 H 2

· The expression "name" includes any abbreviation of a name.

(2.) The provisions of this Act respecting the application of a false trade description to goods shall extend to the application to goods of any such figures, words, or marks, or arrangement or combination thereof, whether including a trade mark or not, as are reasonably calculated to lead persons to believe that the goods are the manufacture or merchandise of some person other than the person whose manufacture or merchandise they really are.

(3.) The provisions of this Act respecting the application of a false trade description to goods, or respecting goods to which a false trade description is applied, shall extend to the application to goods of any false name or initials of a person, and to goods with the false name or initials of a person applied, in like manner as if such name or initials were a trade description, and for the purpose of this enactment the expression false name or initials means as applied to any goods, any name or initials of a person which—

(a) are not a trade mark, or part of a trade mark, and

(b) are identical with, or a colourable imitation of the name or initials of a person carrying on business in connexion with goods of the same description, and not having authorised the use of such name or initials, and

(c) are either those of a fictitious person or of some person not bonâ fide carrying on business in connexion with such goods.

**Forging trade mark.**

4. A person shall be deemed to forge a trade mark who either—

(a) without the assent of the proprietor of the trade mark makes that trade mark or a mark so nearly resembling that trade mark as to be calculated to deceive; or

(b) falsifies any genuine trade mark, whether by alteration, addition, effacement, or otherwise;

and any trade mark or mark so made or falsified is in this Act referred to as a forged trade mark.

Provided that in any prosecution for forging a trade mark the burden of proving the assent of the proprietor shall lie on the defendant.

**Applying marks and descriptions.**

5.—(1.) A person shall be deemed to apply a trade mark or mark or trade description to goods who—

(a) applies it to the goods themselves; or

(b) applies it to any covering, label, reel, or other thing in or with which the goods are sold or exposed or had in possession for any purpose of sale, trade, or manufacture; or

(c) places, encloses, or annexes any goods which are sold or exposed or had in possession for any purpose of sale, trade, or manufacture, in, with, or to any covering, label, reel, or other thing to which a trade mark or trade description has been applied; or

(d) uses a trade mark or mark or trade description in any manner calculated to lead to the belief that the goods in connexion with which it is used are designated or described by that trade mark or mark or trade description.

(2.) The expression " covering " includes any stopper, cask, bottle, vessel, box, cover, capsule, case, frame, or wrapper; and the expression "label" includes any band or ticket.

A trade mark, or mark, or trade description, shall be deemed to be applied whether it is woven, impressed, or otherwise worked into, or annexed, or affixed to the goods, or to any covering, label, reel, or other thing.

(3.) A person shall be deemed to falsely apply to goods a trade mark or mark, who without the assent of the proprietor of a trade mark 'applies such trade mark, or a mark so nearly resembling it as to be calculated to deceive, but in any prosecution for falsely applying a trade mark or mark to goods the burden of proving the assent of the proprietor shall lie on the defendant.

**Exemption of certain persons employed in ordinary course of business.**

6. Where a defendant is charged with making any die, block, machine, or other instrument for the purpose of forging, or being used for forging, a trade mark, or with falsely applying to goods any trade mark or any mark so nearly resembling a trade mark as to be calculated to deceive, or with applying to goods any false trade description, or causing any of the things in this section mentioned to be done, and proves—

(a) That in the ordinary course of his business he is employed, on behalf of other persons, to make dies, blocks, machines, or other instruments for making, or being used in making, trade marks, or as the case may be, to apply marks or descriptions to goods, and that in the case which is the subject of the charge he was so employed by some person resident in the United Kingdom, and was not interested in the goods by way of profit or commission dependent on the sale of such goods ; and

(b) That he took reasonable precautions against committing the offence charged ; and

(c) That he had, at the time of the commission of the alleged offence, no reason to suspect the genuineness of the trade mark, mark, or trade description ; and

(d) That he gave to the prosecutor all the information in his power with respect to the persons on whose behalf the trade mark, mark, or description was applied—

he shall be discharged from the prosecution, but shall be liable to pay the costs incurred by the prosecutor, unless he has given due notice to him that he will rely on the above defence.

**7.** Where a watch case has thereon any words or marks which constitute, or are by common repute considered as constituting, a description of the country in which the watch was made, and the watch bears no description of the country where it was made, those words or marks shall primâ facie be deemed to be a description of that country within the meaning of this Act, and the provisions of this Act with respect to goods to which a false trade description has been applied, and with respect to selling or exposing for or having in possession for sale, or any purpose of trade or manufacture, goods with a false trade description, shall apply accordingly, and for the purposes of this section the expression "watch" means all that portion of a watch which is not the watch case. *[margin: Application of Act to watches.]*

**8.**—(1.) Every person who after the date fixed by Order in Council sends or brings a watch case, whether imported or not, to any assay office in the United Kingdom for the purpose of being assayed, stamped, or marked, shall make a declaration declaring in what country or place the case was made. If it appears by such declaration that the watch case was made in some country or place out of the United Kingdom, the assay office shall place on the case such a mark (differing from the mark placed by the office on a watch case made in the United Kingdom), and in such a mode as may be from time to time directed by Order in Council. *[margin: Mark on watch case.]*

(2.) The declaration may be made before an officer of an assay office, appointed in that behalf by the office (which officer is hereby authorised to administer such a declaration), or before a justice of the peace, or a commissioner having power to administer oaths in the Supreme Court of Judicature in England or Ireland, or in the Court of Session in Scotland, and shall be in such form as may be from time to time directed by Order in Council.

(3.) Every person who makes a false declaration for the purposes of this section shall be liable, on conviction on indictment, to the penalties of perjury, and on summary conviction to a fine not exceeding twenty pounds for each offence.

**9.** In any indictment, pleading, proceeding, or document, in which any trade mark or forged trade mark is intended to be mentioned, it shall be sufficient, without further description and without any copy or facsimile, to state that trade mark or forged trade mark to be a trade mark or forged trade mark. *[margin: Trade mark, how described in pleading.]*

**10.** In any prosecution for an offence against this Act,— *[margin: Rules as to evidence.]*

(1.) A defendant, and his wife or her husband, as the case may be, may, if the defendant thinks fit, be called as a witness, and, if called, shall be sworn and examined, and may be cross-examined and re-examined in like manner as any other witness.

(2.) In the case of imported goods, evidence of the port of shipment shall be primâ facie evidence of the place or country in which the goods were made or produced.

**11.** Any person who, being within the United Kingdom, procures, counsels, aids, abets, or is accessory to the commission, without the United Kingdom, of any act, which, if committed in the United Kingdom, would under this Act be a misdemeanour, shall be guilty of that misdemeanour as a principal, and be liable to be indicted, proceeded against, tried, and convicted in any county or *[margin: Punishment of accessories.]*

place in the United Kingdom in which he may be, as if the misdemeanour had been there committed.

12.—(1.) Where, upon information of an offence against this Act, a justice has issued either a summons requiring the defendant charged by such information to appear to answer to the same, or a warrant for the arrest of such defendant, and either the said justice on or after issuing the summons or warrant, or any other justice, is satisfied by information on oath that there is reasonable cause to suspect that any goods or things by means of or in relation to which such offence has been committed are in any house or premises of the defendant, or otherwise in his possession or under his control in any place, such justice may issue a warrant under his hand by virtue of which it shall be lawful for any constable named or referred to in the warrant, to enter such house, premises, or place at any reasonable time by day, and to search there for and seize and take away those goods or things; and any goods or things seized under any such warrant shall be brought before a court of summary jurisdiction for the purpose of its being determined whether the same are or are not liable to forfeiture under this Act.

(2.) If the owner of any goods or things which, if the owner thereof had been convicted, would be liable to forfeiture under this Act, is unknown or cannot be found, an information or complaint may be laid for the purpose only of enforcing such forfeiture, and a court of summary jurisdiction may cause notice to be advertised stating that, unless cause is shown to the contrary at the time and place named in the notice, such goods or things will be forfeited, and at such time and place the court, unless the owner or any person on his behalf, or other person interested in the goods or things, shows cause to the contrary, may order such goods or things or any of them to be forfeited.

(3.) Any goods or things forfeited under this section, or under any other provision of this Act, may be destroyed or otherwise disposed of, in such manner as the court by which the same are forfeited may direct, and the court may, out of any proceeds which may be realised by the disposition of such goods (all trade marks and trade descriptions being first obliterated), award to any innocent party any loss he may have innocently sustained in dealing with such goods.

13. The Act of the session of the twenty-second and twenty-third years of the reign of her present Majesty, chapter seventeen, intituled "An Act to prevent vexatious indictments for certain misdemeanours," shall apply to any offence punishable on indictment under this Act, in like manner as if such offence were one of the offences specified in section one of that Act, but this section shall not apply to Scotland.

14. On any prosecution under this Act the court may order costs to be paid to the defendant by the prosecutor, or to the prosecutor by the defendant, having regard to the information given by and the conduct of the defendant and prosecutor respectively.

15. No prosecution for an offence against this Act shall be commenced after the expiration of three years next after the commission of the offence, or one year next after the first discovery thereof by the prosecutor, whichever expiration first happens.

16. Whereas it is expedient to make further provision for prohibiting the importation of goods which, if sold, would be liable to forfeiture under this Act; be it therefore enacted as follows:

(1.) All such goods, and also all goods of foreign manufacture bearing any name or trade mark being or purporting to be the name or trade mark of any manufacturer, dealer, or trader in the United Kingdom, unless such name or trade mark is accompanied by a definite indication of the country in which the goods were made or produced, are hereby prohibited to be imported into the United Kingdom, and, subject to the provisions of this section, shall be included among goods prohibited to be imported as if they were specified in section forty-two of the Customs Consolidation Act, 1876.

(2.) Before detaining any such goods, or taking any further proceedings with a view to the forfeiture thereof under the law relating to the Customs, the Commissioners of Customs may require the regulations under this section, whether as to information, security, conditions, or other matters, to be complied with, and may satisfy themselves in accordance with those regulations that the goods are such as are prohibited by this section to be imported.

(3.) The Commissioners of Customs may from time to time make, revoke, and vary regulations, either general or special, respecting the detention and forfeiture of goods the importation of which is prohibited by this section, and the conditions, if any, to be fulfilled before such detention and forfeiture, and may by such regulations determine the information, notices, and security to be given, and the evidence requisite for any of the purposes of this section, and the mode of verification of such evidence.

(4.) Where there is on any goods a name which is identical with or a colourable imitation of the name of a place in the United Kingdom, that name, unless accompanied by the name of the country in which such place is situate, shall be treated for the purposes of this section as if it were the name of a place in the United Kingdom.

(5.) Such regulations may apply to all goods the importation of which is prohibited by this section, or different regulations may be made respecting different classes of such goods or of offences in relation to such goods.

(6.) The Commissioners of Customs, in making and in administering the regulations, and generally in the administration of this section, whether in the exercise of any discretion or opinion, or otherwise, shall act under the control of the Commissioners of her Majesty's Treasury.

(7.) The regulations may provide for the informant reimbursing the Commissioners of Customs all expenses and damages incurred in respect of any detention made on his information, and of any proceedings consequent on such detention.

(8.) All regulations under this section shall be published in the "London Gazette" and in the "Board of Trade Journal."

(9.) This section shall have effect as if it were part of the Customs Consolidation Act, 1876, and shall accordingly apply to the Isle of Man as if it were part of the United Kingdom.

(10.) Section two of the Revenue Act, 1883, shall be repealed as from a day fixed by regulations under this section, not being later than the first day of January one thousand eight hundred and eighty-eight, without prejudice to anything done or suffered thereunder. 46 & 47 Vict. c. 55.

**17.** On the sale or in the contract for the sale of any goods to which a trade mark, or mark, or trade description has been applied, the vendor shall be deemed to warrant that the mark is a genuine trade mark and not forged or falsely applied, or that the trade description is not a false trade description within the meaning of this Act, unless the contrary is expressed in some writing signed by or on behalf of the vendor and delivered at the time of the sale or contract to and accepted by the vendee. Implied warranty on sale of marked goods.

**18.** Where, at the passing of this Act, a trade description is lawfully and generally applied to goods of a particular class, or manufactured by a particular method, to indicate the particular class or method of manufacture of such goods, the provisions of this Act with respect to false trade descriptions shall not apply to such trade description when so applied: Provided that where such trade description includes the name of a place or country, and is calculated to mislead as to the place or country where the goods to which it is applied were actually made or produced, and the goods are not actually made or produced in that place or country, this section shall not apply unless there is added to the trade description, immediately before or after the name of that place or country, in an equally conspicuous manner, with that name, the name of the place or country in which the goods were actually made or produced, with a statement that they were made or produced there. Provisions of Act as to false description not to apply in certain cases.

**19.**—(1.) This Act shall not exempt any person from any action, suit, or other proceeding which might, but for the provisions of this Act, be brought against him. Savings.

(2.) Nothing in this Act shall entitle any person to refuse to make a complete discovery, or to answer any question or interrogatory in any action, but such discovery or answer shall not be admissible in evidence against such person in any prosecution for an offence against this Act.

(3.) Nothing in this Act shall be construed so as to render liable to any prosecution or punishment any servant of a master resident in the United

Kingdom who bonâ fide acts in obedience to the instructions of such master, and, on demand made by or on behalf of the prosecutor, has given full information as to his master.

**False representation as to Royal Warrant.**

20. Any person who falsely represents that any goods are made by a person holding a royal warrant, or for the service of her Majesty, or any of the Royal Family, or any Government department, shall be liable, on summary conviction, to a penalty not exceeding twenty pounds.

**Application of Act to Scotland.**

21. In the application of this Act to Scotland, the following modifications shall be made :—

The expression "Summary Jurisdiction Acts" means the Summary Procedure Act, 1864, and any Acts amending the same.

The expression "justice" means sheriff.

The expression "court of summary jurisdiction" means the Sheriff Court, and all jurisdiction necessary for the purpose of this Act is hereby conferred on sheriffs.

**Application of Act to Ireland.**

22. In the application of this Act to Ireland the following modifications shall be made :—

The expression "Summary Jurisdiction Acts," means, so far as respects the police district of Dublin metropolis, the Acts regulating the powers and duties of justices of the peace of such district, and as regards the rest of Ireland means the Petty Sessions (Ireland) Act, 1851, and any

**14 & 15 Vict. c. 93.**

Act amending the same.

The expression "court of summary jurisdiction" means justices acting under those Acts.

**Repeal of 25 & 26 Vict. c. 88.**

23. The Merchandise Marks Act, 1862, is hereby repealed, and any unrepealed enactment referring to any enactment so repealed shall be construed to apply to the corresponding provision of this Act; provided that this repeal shall not affect—

(a) Any penalty, forfeiture, or punishment incurred in respect of any offence committed against any enactment hereby repealed; nor

(b) The institution or continuance of any proceeding or other remedy under any enactment so repealed for the recovery of any penalty incurred, or for the punishment of any offence committed, before the commencement of this Act; nor

(c) Any right, privilege, liability, or obligation acquired, accrued, or incurred under any enactment hereby repealed.

---

50 & 51 Vict. c. 46.

*An Act to amend and extend the Law relating to Truck.*

[16*th September*, 1887.]

Be it enacted by the Queen's most excellent Majesty, by and with the advice and consent of the Lords Spiritual and Temporal, and Commons, in this present Parliament assembled, and by the authority of the same, as follows :

**Short title.**

1. This Act may be cited as the Truck Amendment Act, 1887. The Act of the session of the first and second years of the reign of King William the Fourth, chapter thirty-seven, intituled "An Act to prohibit the payment in certain trades of wages in goods or otherwise than in the current coin of the

**1 & 2 Will. 4, c. 37.**

realm" (in this Act referred to as the principal Act (*a*) ), may be cited as the Truck Act, 1831, and that Act and this Act may be cited together as the Truck Acts, 1831 and 1887, and shall be construed together as one Act.

**Application of principal Act to workman as defined by 38 & 39 Vict. c. 90.**

2. The provisions of the principal Act shall extend to, apply to, and include any workman as defined in the Employers and Workmen Act, 1875, section ten (*a*), and the expression "artificer" in the principal Act shall be construed to include every workman to whom the principal Act is extended and applied by this Act, and all provisions and enactments in the principal Act inconsistent herewith are hereby repealed.

**Advance of wages.**

3. Whenever by agreement, custom, or otherwise a workman is entitled to receive in anticipation of the regular period of the payment of his wages an advance as part or on account thereof, it shall not be lawful for the employer to withhold such advance or make any deduction in respect of such

(*a*) *Supra.*

advance on account of poundage, discount, or interest, or any similar charge.

4. Nothing in the principal Act or this Act shall render illegal a contract with a servant in husbandry for giving him food, drink, not being intoxicating, a cottage, or other allowances or privileges in addition to money wages as a remuneration for his services. *Saving for servant in husbandry.*

5. In any action brought by a workman for the recovery of his wages, the employer shall not be entitled to any set off or counterclaim in respect of any goods supplied to the workman by any person under any order or direction of the employer, or any agent of the employer, and the employer of a workman or any agent of the employer, or any person supplying goods to the workman under any order or direction of such employer or agent, shall not be entitled to sue the workman for or in respect of any goods supplied by such employer or agent, or under such order or direction, as the case may be.

Provided that nothing in this section shall apply to anything excepted by section twenty-three of the principal Act (b). *Order for goods as a deduction from wages illegal.*

6. No employer shall, directly or indirectly, by himself or his agent, impose as a condition, express or implied, in or for the employment of any workman any terms as to the place at which, or the manner in which, or the person with whom, any wages or portion of wages paid to the workman are or is to be expended, and no employer shall by himself or his agent dismiss any workman from his employment for or on account of the place at which, or the manner in which, or the person with whom, any wages or portion of wages paid by the employer to such workman are or is expended or fail to be expended (c). *No contracts with workman as to spending wages at any particular shop, &c.*

7. Where any deduction is made by an employer from a workman's wages for education, such workman on sending his child to any state-inspected school selected by the workman shall be entitled to have the school fees of his child at that school paid by the employer at the same rate and to the same extent as the other workmen from whose wages the like deduction is made by such employer (c). *Deduction for education.*

In this section "state-inspected school" means any elementary school inspected under the direction of the Education Department in England or Scotland or of the Board of National Education in Ireland.

8. No deduction shall be made from a workman's wages for sharpening or repairing tools, except by agreement not forming part of the condition of hiring (c). *Deduction for sharpening tools, &c.*

9. Where deductions are made from the wages of any workmen for the education of children or in respect of medicine, medical attendance, or tools, once at least in every year the employer shall, by himself or his agent, make out a correct account of the receipts and expenditure in respect of such deductions, and submit the same to be audited by two auditors appointed by the said workmen, and shall produce to the auditors all such books, vouchers, and documents, and afford them all such other facilities as are required for such audit. *Audit of deductions.*

10. Where articles are made by a person at his own home, or otherwise, without the employment of any person under him except a member of his own family, the principal Act (b) and this Act shall apply as if he were a workman, and the shopkeeper, dealer, trader, or other person buying the articles in the way of trade were his employer, and the provisions of this Act with respect to the payment of wages shall apply as if the price of an article were wages earned during the seven days next preceding the date at which any article is received from the workman by the employer. *Artificer to be paid in cash and not by way of barter for articles made by him.*

This section shall apply only to articles under the value of five pounds knitted or otherwise manufactured of wool, worsted, yarn, stuff, jersey, linen, fustian, cloth, serge, cotton, leather, fur, hem, flax, mohair, or silk, or of any combination thereof, or made or prepared of bone, thread, silk, or cotton lace, or of lace made of any mixed materials. Where it is made to appear to her Majesty the Queen in Council that, in the interests of persons making articles to which this section applies in any county or place in the United Kingdom, it is expedient so to do, it shall be lawful for her Majesty, by Order in Council, to suspend the operation of this section in such county or place, and the same shall accordingly be suspended, either wholly or in

---

(b) See sect. 1, *supra*.          (c) See sect. 11, *infra*.

part, and either with or without any limitations or exceptions, according as is provided by the order.

Offences.

**11.** If any employer or his agent contravenes or fails to comply with any of the foregoing provisions of this Act, such employer or agent, as the case may be, shall be guilty of an offence against the principal Act (a), and shall be liable to the penalties imposed by section nine of that Act as if the offence were such an offence as in that section mentioned.

Fine on person committing offence for which employer is liable, and power of employer to exempt himself from penalty on conviction of actual offender.'

**12.**—(1.) Where an offence for which an employer is, by virtue of the principal Act (a) or this Act, liable to a penalty has in fact been committed by some agent of the employer or other person, such agent or other person shall be liable to the same penalty as if he were the employer.

(2.) Where an employer is charged with an offence against the principal Act (a) or this Act he shall be entitled, upon information duly laid by him, to have any other person whom he charges as the actual offender brought before the court at the time appointed for hearing the charge, and if, after the commission of the offence has been proved the employer proves to the satisfaction of the court that he had used due diligence to enforce the execution of the said Acts, and that the said other person had committed the offence in question without his knowledge, consent, or connivance, the said other person shall be summarily convicted of such offence, and the employer shall be exempt from any penalty.

When it is made to appear to the satisfaction of an inspector of factories or mines, or in Scotland a procurator fiscal, at the time of discovering the offence, that the employer had used due diligence to enforce the execution of the said Acts, and also by what person such offence had been committed, and also that it had been committed without the knowledge, consent, or connivance of the employer, then the inspector or procurator fiscal shall proceed against the person whom he believes to be the actual offender in the first instance without first proceeding against the employer.

Recovery of penalties.

**13.**—(1.) Any offence against the principal Act (a) or this Act may be prosecuted, and any penalty therefor recovered in manner provided by the Summary Jurisdiction Acts, so, however, that no penalty shall be imposed on summary conviction exceeding that prescribed by the principal Act for a second offence.

(2.) It shall be the duty of the inspectors of factories and the inspectors of mines to enforce the provisions of the principal Act (a) and this Act within their districts so far as respects factories, workshops, and mines inspected by them respectively, and such inspectors shall for this purpose have the same powers and authorities as they respectively have for the purpose of enforcing the provisions of any Acts relating to factories, workshops, or mines, and all expenses incurred by them under this section shall be defrayed out of moneys provided by Parliament.

(3.) In England all penalties recovered under the principal Act (a) and this Act shall be paid into the receipt of her Majesty's Exchequer, and be carried to the Consolidated Fund.

(4.) In Scotland—

(a) The procurators fiscal of the sheriff court shall, as part of their official duty, investigate and prosecute offences against the principal Act or this Act, and such prosecution may also be instituted in the sheriff court at the instance of any inspector of factories or inspector of mines ;

(b) All offences against the said Acts shall be prosecuted in the sheriff court.

Definitions.

**14.** In this Act, unless the context otherwise requires,—

The expression "Summary Jurisdiction Acts" means, as respects England, the Summary Jurisdiction Acts as defined by the Summary Jurisdiction Act, 1879 ; and, as respects Scotland, means the Summary Jurisdiction (Scotland) Acts, 1864 and 1881, and any Acts amending the same :

Other expressions have the same meaning as in the principal Act.

Disqualification of justice.

**15.** So much of the principal Act as disqualifies any justice from acting as such under the principal Act is hereby repealed.

A person engaged in the same trade or occupation as an employer charged with an offence against the principal Act or this Act shall not act as a justice of the peace in hearing and determining such charge.

(a) See sect. 1, *supra*.

**16.** The provisions of the principal Act (b) conferring powers on any over-seers or overseer of the poor shall be deemed to confer those powers in the case of England on the guardians of a union, and in the case of Scotland on the inspectors of the poor. Amendment of 1 & 2 Will. 4, c. 37, as to over-seers.

**17.** The Acts mentioned in the schedule to this Act are hereby repealed to the extent in the third column of the said schedule mentioned without pre-judice to anything heretofore done or suffered in respect thereof. Repeal.

**18.** The principal Act (b), so far as it is not hereby repealed, and this Act shall extend to Ireland, subject to the following provisions: Application of Acts to Ireland.

(1.) Any offence against the principal Act or this Act may be prosecuted and any penalty therefor may be recovered in the manner pro-vided by the Summary Jurisdiction (Ireland) Acts; (that is to say,) within the Dublin Metropolitan Police District the Acts regulating the powers and duties of justices of the peace and of the police of that district, and elsewhere in Ireland the Petty Sessions (Ireland) Act, 1851, and the Acts amending the same;

(2.) Penalties recovered under the principal Act or this Act shall be applied in the manner directed by the Fines (Ireland) Act, 1851, and the Acts amending the same.

## SCHEDULE.

| Session and Chapter. | Title of Act. | Extent of Repeal. |
| --- | --- | --- |
| 12 Geo. 1, c. 34.. | An Act to prevent unlawful combinations of workmen employed in the woollen manufactures, and for better payment of their wages. | Section three, and so much of section eight as applies section three. |
| 22 Geo. 2, c. 27.. | An Act, the title of which begins with "An Act for the more effectual pre-venting of frauds," and ends with the words "and for the better pay-ment of their wages." | So much of section twelve as applies to any enactment re-pealed by this Act. |
| 30 Geo. 2, c. 12.. | An Act, the title of which begins with the words "An Act to amend an Act," and ends with the words "payment of the workmen's wages in any other manner than in money." | Sections two and three. |
| 57 Geo. 3, c. 115.. | An Act, the title of which begins with the words "An Act to extend the provisions of an Act," and ends with the words "articles of cutlery." | The whole Act. |
| 57 Geo. 3, c. 122.. | An Act, the title of which begins with the words "An Act to extend the provisions," and ends with the words "extend-ing the provisions of the said Acts to Scotland and Ireland." | The whole Act. |

(b) See sect. 1, *supra.*

| Session and Chapter. | Title of Act. | Extent of Repeal. |
|---|---|---|
| 1 & 2 Will. 4, c. 37 | An Act to prohibit the payment in certain trades of wages in goods or otherwise than in the current coin of the realm. | Section ten, down to "be produced to the court and jury" inclusive ; section eleven, section twelve, section fifteen, section sixteen, section eighteen, section nineteen, in section twenty the words "or servant in husbandry"; section twenty-one, section twenty-two, section twenty-four from "and unless the agreement" inclusive to end of section, and section twenty-five from "all workmen" to "purposes aforesaid," both inclusive, and the schedules. |

## 50 & 51 VICT. C. 57.

*An Act to provide for the Registration of Deeds of Arrangement.*
[*16th September*, 1887.]

BE it enacted by the Queen's most excellent Majesty, by and with the advice and consent of the Lords spiritual and temporal, and Commons, in this present Parliament assembled, and by the authority of the same, as follows :

**Short title.** **1.** This Act may be cited for all purposes as the Deeds of Arrangement Act, 1887.

**Extent of Act.** **2.** This Act shall not extend to Scotland.

**Commencement of Act.** **3.** This Act shall, except as in this Act specially provided, come into operation on the first day of January one thousand eight hundred and eighty-eight, which date is in this Act referred to as the commencement of this Act.

**Application of Act.** **4.**—(1.) This Act shall apply to every deed of arrangement, as defined in this section, made after the commencement of this Act.

(2.) A deed of arrangement to which this Act applies shall include any of the following instruments, whether under seal or not, made by, for, or in respect of the affairs of a debtor for the benefit of his creditors generally (otherwise than in pursuance of the law for the time being in force relating to bankruptcy), that is to say :—

(a) An assignment of property ;
(b) A deed of or agreement for a composition ;

And in cases where creditors of a debtor obtain any control over his property or business :—

(c) A deed of inspectorship entered into for the purpose of carrying on or winding up a business ;
(d) A letter of license authorising the debtor or any other person to manage, carry on, realise, or dispose of a business, with a view to the payment of debts ; and
(e) Any agreement or instrument entered into for the purpose of carrying on or winding up the debtor's business, or authorising the debtor or any other person to manage, carry on, realise, or dispose of the debtor's business, with a view to the payment of his debts.

**Avoidance of unregistered deeds of arrangement.** **5.** From and after the commencement of this Act a deed of arrangement to which this Act applies shall be void unless the same shall have been registered under this Act within seven clear days after the first execution thereof by the debtor or any creditor, or if it is executed in any place out of England or Ireland respectively, then within seven clear days after the time at which it would, in the ordinary course of post, arrive in England or Ireland respectively, if posted within one week after the execution thereof, and unless the same shall bear such ordinary and ad valorem stamp as is under this Act provided.

**6.** The registration of a deed of arrangement under this Act shall be effected in the following manner :— *Mode of registration.*

(1.) A true copy of the deed, and of every schedule or inventory thereto annexed, or therein referred to, shall be presented to and filed with the registrar within seven clear days after the execution of the said deed (in like manner as a bill of sale given by way of security for the payment of money is now required to be filed), together with an affidavit verifying the time of execution, and containing a description of the residence and occupation of the debtor, and of the place or places where his business is carried on, and an affidavit by the debtor stating the total estimated amount of property and liabilities included under the deed, the total amount of the composition (if any) payable thereunder, and the names and addresses of his creditors ;

(2.) No deed shall be registered under this Act unless the original of such deed, duly stamped with the proper inland revenue duty, and in addition to such duty a stamp denoting a duty computed at the rate of one shilling for every hundred pounds or fraction of a hundred pounds of the sworn value of the property s , or (where no property passes under the deed) the amount of composition payable under the deed, is produced to the registrar at the time of such registration.

**7.** The registrar shall keep a register wherein shall be entered, as soon as conveniently may be after the presentation of a deed for registration, an abstract of the contents of every deed of arrangement registered under this Act, containing the following and any other prescribed particulars :— *Form of register.*

(a) The date of the deed :

(b) The name, address, and description of the debtor, and the place or places where his business is carried on, and the title of the firm or firms under which the debtor carries on business, and the name and address of the trustee (if any) under the deed :

(c) A short statement of the nature and effect of the deed, and of the composition in the pound payable thereunder :

(d) The date of registration :

(e) The amount of property and liabilities included under the deed, as estimated by the debtor.

**8.**—(1.) The registrar of bills of sale in England and Ireland respectively shall be the registrar for the purposes of this Act. *Registrar and office for registration.*

(2.) In England the Bills of Sale Department of the Central Office of the Supreme Court of Judicature, and in Ireland the Bills of Sale Office of the Queen's Bench Division of the High Court of Justice, shall be the office for the registration of deeds of arrangement.

**9.** The court or a judge upon being satisfied that the omission to register a deed of arrangement within the time required by this Act or that the omission or mis-statement of the name, residence, or description of any person was accidental or due to inadvertence, or to some cause beyond the control of the debtor and not imputable to any negligence on his part, may on the application of any party interested, and on such terms and conditions as are just and expedient, extend the time for such registration, or order such omission or mis-statement to be supplied or rectified by the insertion in the register of the true name, residence, or description. *Rectification of register.*

**10.** When the time for registering a deed of arrangement expires on a Sunday, or other day on which the registration office is closed, the registration shall be valid if made on the next following day on which the office is open. *Time for registration.*

**11.** Subject to the provisions of this Act, and to any rules made thereunder, any person shall be entitled to have an office copy of, or extract from, any deed registered under this Act upon paying for the same at the like rate as for office copies of judgments of the High Court of Justice, and any copy or extract purporting to be an office copy or extract shall, in all courts *Office copies.*

and before all arbitrators or other persons, be admitted as primâ facie evidence thereof, and of the fact and date of registration as shown thereon.

**12.**—(1.) Any person shall be entitled, at all reasonable times, to search the register on payment of one shilling, or such other fee as may be prescribed, and subject to such regulations as may be prescribed, and shall be entitled, at all reasonable times, to inspect, examine, and make extracts from any registered deed of arrangement, without being required to make a written application or to specify any particulars in reference thereto, upon payment of one shilling, or such other fee as may be prescribed, for each deed of arrangement inspected.

(2.) Provided that the said extracts shall be limited to the dates of execution and of registration, the names, addresses, and descriptions of the debtor and of the parties to the deed, a short statement of the nature and effect of the deed, and any other prescribed particulars.

**13.**—(1.) When the place of business or residence of the debtor who is one of the parties to a deed of arrangement, or who is referred to therein, is situate in some place outside the London bankruptcy district, as defined by the Bankruptcy Act, 1883, the registrar shall within three clear days after registration, and in accordance with the prescribed directions, transmit a copy of such deed to the registrar of the county court in the district of which such place of business or residence is situate.

(2.) Every copy so transmitted shall be filed, kept, and indexed by the registrar of the county court in the prescribed manner, and any person may search, inspect, make extracts from, and obtain copies of, the registered copy, in the like manner and upon the like terms, as to payment or otherwise, as near as may be, as in the case of deeds registered under this Act.

(3.) This section shall not apply to Ireland.

**14.** Every affidavit required by or for the purposes of this Act may be sworn before a master of the Supreme Court of Judicature in England or Ireland, or before any person empowered to take affidavits in the Supreme Courts of Judicature of England or Ireland.

**15.**—(1.) There shall be taken, in respect of the registration of deeds of arrangement, and in respect of any office copies or extracts, or official searches made by the registrar, such fees as may be from time to time prescribed ; and nothing in this Act contained shall make it obligatory on the registrar to do, or permit to be done, any act in respect of which any fee is specified or prescribed. except on payment of such fee.

(2.) The twenty-sixth section of the Supreme Court of Judicature Act, 1875, as regards England, and the eighty-fourth section of the Supreme Court of Judicature Act (Ireland), 1877, as regards Ireland, and any enactments for the time being in force amending or substituted for those sections respectively shall apply to fees under this Act, and orders under those sections may, if need be, be made in relation to such fees accordingly.

**16.**—(1.) The third sub-section, paragraph (g) of the twenty-eighth section of the Bankruptcy Act, 1883, which enacts, amongst other things that one of the facts on proof of which the court shall either refuse an order of discharge to a bankrupt, or suspend the operation of the order for a specified time, or grant the bankrupt an order of discharge subject to the conditions mentioned in the section, is that the bankrupt has on any previous occasion made a statutory composition or arrangement with his creditors, shall be read and construed with the word "statutory" omitted therefrom.

(2.) This section shall not apply to Ireland.

**17.** Nothing contained in this Act shall be construed to repeal or shall affect any provision of the law for the time being in force in relation to bankruptcy, or shall give validity to any deed or instrument which by law is an act of bankruptcy, or void or voidable.

**18.**—(1.) Rules for carrying this Act into effect may be made, revoked, and altered from time to time by the like persons and in the like manner in which rules may be made under and for the purposes of the Supreme Court of Judicature Acts, 1873 to 1884, as regards England, and the Supreme Court of Judicature Act (Ireland), 1877, as regards Ireland.

(2.) Such rules as may be required for the purposes of this Act may be made at any time after the passing of this Act.

**19.** In this Act, unless the context otherwise requires,—

"Court or a judge" means the High Court of Justice and any judge thereof ;

" Creditors generally" includes all creditors who may assent or take the benefit of a deed of arrangement ;

" Person " includes a body of persons corporate or unincorporate ;

"Prescribed " means prescribed by rules to be made under this Act ;

" Property " has the same meaning as the same expression has in the Bankruptcy Act, 1883 ;

" Rules " includes forms.

---

50 & 51 VICT. C. 62.

*An Act to amend in certain minor particulars some of the Enactments relating to Merchant Shipping and Seamen.*

[*16th September*, 1887.]

BE it enacted by the Queen's most excellent Majesty, by and with the advice and consent of the Lords spiritual and temporal, and Commons, in this present Parliament assembled, and by the authority of the same, as follows :—

1.—(1.) This Act may be cited as the Merchant Shipping (Miscellaneous) Act, 1887.

(2.) This Act shall be construed as one with the Merchant Shipping Act, 1854, and the Acts amending the same, and this Act and those Acts may be cited collectively as the Merchant Shipping Acts, 1854 to 1887.

2. Whereas by section seven of the Merchant Shipping Act Amendment Act, 1862, it is provided that the fees payable by applicants for examination for certificates of competency as engineers shall be carried to the account of the Mercantile Marine Fund, and at the time of the passing of that Act the salaries of the surveyors by whom the examinations are conducted were paid out of the Mercantile Marine Fund :

And whereas by section thirty-nine of the Merchant Shipping Act, 1876, it was provided that the salaries of the said surveyors should be paid out of moneys provided by Parliament, and by section four of the Merchant Shipping (Fees and Expenses) Act, 1880, it was provided that the fees paid by the said applicants for examination for certificates of competency as engineers should be paid into the Exchequer :

And whereas under section three of the Merchant Shipping (Expenses) Act, 1882, the salaries of the said surveyors are charged on and paid out of the Mercantile Marine Fund, and it is expedient that the fees paid by the said applicants for examination should be carried to the account of the Mercantile Marine Fund ; be it therefore enacted as follows :

The fees payable in pursuance of section seven of the Merchant Shipping Act Amendment Act, 1862, shall cease to be payable into the Exchequer, and all such of those fees as have been levied since the first day of April one thousand eight hundred and eighty-three, or are hereafter levied, shall be carried to the account of the Mercantile Marine Fund.

3. Whereas doubts have been expressed as to the extent of the powers conferred by section thirty-one of the Merchant Shipping Act, 1854, on certain colonial authorities, and it is expedient to remove those doubts : Be it therefore enacted that the powers conferred by that section on the governor, lieutenant-governor, or other person administering the government in a British possession shall include and be deemed to have always included the following powers, namely :—

(a.) Power to approve a port or place within the possession for the registry of ships ; and

(b.) Power to appoint surveyors within the limits of the possession to survey and measure ships for registry or re-registry as British ships in accordance with the provisions of the Merchant Shipping Acts, 1854 to 1887.

*Margin notes:*

Short title and construction.

Fees on examinations of engineers to be paid to Mercantile Marine Fund.
25 & 26 Vict. c. 63, s. 7.
39 & 40 Vict. c. 80, s. 39.
43 & 44 Vict. c. 22, s. 4.

45 & 46 Vict. c. 55, s. 3.

Explanation of 17 & 18 Vict. c. 104, s. 31, as to powers of colonial governors.

Public Record Acts to apply to records in custody of Registrar-General of Seamen.

**4.** All documents which, under section two hundred and seventy-seven of the Merchant Shipping Act, 1854, or any enactment amending the same, are required to be recorded and preserved by the Registrar-General of Seamen shall be deemed to be public records and documents within the meaning of the Public Record Offices Acts, 1838 and 1877, and those Acts shall, where applicable, apply to such documents in all respects as if such documents had been specifically referred to in the said Acts.

Explanation of meaning of lighthouses.

**5.** In the Merchant Shipping Act, 1854, and the Acts amending the same, the expression "lighthouses" shall, in addition to the meaning assigned to it by the Merchant Shipping Act, 1854, include sirens and all other descriptions of fog signals, and the expression "new lighthouse" shall include the addition to any existing lighthouse of any improved light, or any siren, or any description of fog signal.

Repeal.

**6.** The enactments mentioned in the Schedule to this Act are hereby repealed to the extent appearing in the third column of that Schedule :

Provided that the repeal of any enactment by this Act shall not affect the validity of anything done, or any right acquired or liability incurred, before the commencement of this Act under the repealed enactment, and that proceedings for enforcing any such right or liability may be commenced, continued, and completed as if this Act had not passed.

Section 6.

## SCHEDULE.

### REPEAL.

| Session and Chapter. | Title. | Extent of repeal. |
|---|---|---|
| 14 & 15 Vict. c. 102 .. | The Seamen's Fund Winding-up Act, 1851. | Section forty-eight. |
| 43 & 44 Vict. c. 22  .. | The Merchant Shipping (Fees and Expenses) Act, 1880. | Section four. |

## 50 & 51 Vict. c. 66.

*An Act to amend the Law relating to the discharge of Bankrupts and the closure of Bankruptcy Proceedings.*

[*16th September*, 1887.]

BE it enacted by the Queen's most Excellent Majesty, by and with the advice and consent of the Lords Spiritual and Temporal, and Commons, in this present Parliament assembled, and by the authority of the same, as follows :

Short title and construction.

**1.**—(1.) This Act may be cited as the Bankruptcy (Discharge and Closure) Act, 1887.

(2.) Expressions used in this Act shall, unless a contrary intention appears, have the same meaning as in the Bankruptcy Act, 1883.

Proceedings for discharge of bankrupt under repealed Bankruptcy Acts. 32 & 33 Vict. c. 71.

**2.**—(1.) A debtor who has been adjudged bankrupt, or whose affairs have been liquidated by arrangement under the Bankruptcy Act, 1869, or any previous Bankruptcy Act, and who has not obtained his discharge, may apply to the court for an order of discharge, and thereupon the court shall appoint a day for hearing the application in open court.

(2.) Notice of the appointment by the court of the day for hearing the application for discharge shall twenty-one days at least before the day so appointed be sent by the debtor to each creditor who has proved in the bankruptcy or liquidation, or to those of them whose addresses appear in the debtor's statement of affairs or are known to the debtor, and shall also, fourteen days at least before the day so appointed, be published in the London Gazette.

(3.) On the hearing of the application the court may hear any creditor, and may put such questions to the debtor and receive such evidence as the court thinks fit, and, on being satisfied that the notice required by this section has been duly sent and published, may either grant or refuse the order of discharge or suspend the operation of the order for a specified time, or grant the order of discharge subject to any conditions with respect to any earnings or income which may afterwards become due to the debtor, or with respect to his after-acquired property : Provided that the court shall refuse the discharge in all cases where the court is satisfied by evidence that the debtor has committed any misdemeanour under Part Two of the Debtors Act, 1869, or any amendment thereof. 32 & 33 Vict.<br>c. 62.

(4.) The court may, as one of the conditions referred to in this section, require the debtor to consent to judgment being entered against him in the court having jurisdiction in the bankruptcy or liquidation by the official receiver of the court, or the trustee or assignee in the bankruptcy or liquidation, for any balance of the debts provable under the bankruptcy or liquidation which is not satisfied at the date of the discharge, or for such sum as the court shall think fit, but in such case execution shall not be issued on the judgment without the leave of the court, which leave may be given on proof that the debtor has since his discharge acquired property or income available for payment of his debts.

(5.) A discharge granted under this section shall have the same effect as if it had been granted in pursuance of the Act under which the debtor was adjudged bankrupt or liquidated his affairs by arrangement.

3.—(1.) Every bankruptcy under the Bankruptcy Act, 1869, which is pending on the thirty-first day of December one thousand eight hundred and eighty-seven shall, by virtue of this Act, be closed on that day unless the court otherwise orders. Proceedings for<br>closing bank-<br>ruptcies under<br>Bankruptcy Act,<br>1869.

(2.) Subject to the provisions of this section, the court may, on the application of the trustee under any such bankruptcy, and on being satisfied that there are special circumstances rendering it expedient to postpone the close of the bankruptcy, make an order postponing the close of the bankruptcy until such date as the court may from time to time determine.

(3.) The order may be made either before or after the said day, but an application under this section shall not be entertained unless made before the said day.

(4.) The trustees shall, before making an application under this section, give notice to the Board of Trade of his intention to do so, and shall supply the Board with such information as the Board may require as to the position of the bankruptcy, and the court before making an order under this section shall consider any representation which may be made by or on behalf of the Board of Trade with respect thereto.

4.—(1.) In each of the following cases, that is to say :
(a) Any insolvency under any Act for the relief of insolvent debtors ;
(b) Any commission, fiat, or adjudication in bankruptcy within the jurisdiction of the old London Bankruptcy Court, under any Act prior to the Bankruptcy Act, 1869 ;
(c) Any administration by way of arrangement pursuant to an Act of the session held in the seventh and eighth years of the reign of Her Majesty, chapter seventy, entitled "An Act for facilitating arrangements between debtors and creditors," or pursuant to the provisions of the Bankrupt Law Consolidation Act, 1849, or the hundred and ninety-second section of the Bankruptcy Act, 1861, within the jurisdiction of the old London Bankruptcy Court,
In bankruptcies,<br>insolvencies, or<br>arrangements<br>under Acts prior<br>to 1869 in the<br>London district,<br>official assignee<br>may be ap-<br>pointed to super-<br>sede creditors<br>assignee.

in which the estate is now vested in a creditors assignee, or trustee, or inspector, either alone or jointly with the official assignee, the court may at any time after the passing of this Act, upon the application of any creditor, and upon being satisfied that there is good ground for removing such creditors assignee, trustee, or inspector, or in any other case in which it shall appear to the court just or expedient, appoint the official assignee, or any person appointed under the one hundred and fifty-third section of the Bankruptcy Act, 1883, to perform the remaining duties of the office of official 46 & 47 Vict.<br>c. 52.

assignee, to be sole assignee, or trustee, or inspector of the estate in the place of such creditors assignee, trustee, or inspector, as the case may be.

(2.) Such appointment shall operate as a removal of the creditors assignee, trustee, or inspector of the estate, and shall vest the whole of the property of the bankrupt or debtor in the official assignee or person appointed by the Board of Trade as aforesaid alone ; and all estate, rights, powers, and duties of such former creditors assignee, trustee, or inspector shall thereupon vest in and devolve upon the official assignee or person appointed by the Board of Trade as aforesaid alone.

Provision to release trustee.

**5.** An application by a trustee in a bankruptcy under the Bankruptcy Act, 1869, to the comptroller in bankruptcy for a report on his accounts with a view to his release shall not be entertained unless made within twelve months after the close of the bankruptcy.

Effect of release.

**6.**—(1.) Where on the close of a bankruptcy or liquidation, or on the release of a trustee, a registrar or official receiver or official assignee is or is acting as trustee, and where under section one hundred and fifty-nine, section one hundred and sixty, or section one hundred and sixty-one of the Bankruptcy Act, 1883, an official receiver is or is acting as trustee, no liability shall attach to him personally in respect of any act done or default made or liability incurred by any prior trustee.

(2.) Section eighty-two of the Bankruptcy Act, 1883 (which section relates to the release of a trustee), shall, with the exception of sub-section four thereof, apply to an official receiver or official assignee when he is or is acting as trustee, and when an official receiver or official assignee has been released under that section he shall continue to act as trustee for any subsequent purposes of the administration of the debtor's estate, but no liability shall attach to him personally by reason of his so continuing in respect of any act done, default made, or liability incurred before his release.

Disposal of old books and papers.

40 & 41 Vict. c. 55.

**7.** All books and papers in the custody of an official receiver or official assignee, or of the acting comptroller in bankruptcy, and relating to any bankruptcy under the Bankruptcy Act, 1869, may, on the expiration of one year after the close of the bankruptcy, be disposed of in accordance with rules made under section one of the Public Records Office Act, 1877, and that section shall apply accordingly.

Power to make rules and prescribe fees.

**8.**—(1.) General rules for carrying into effect the objects of this Act may from time to time be made, revoked, or altered by the same authority and subject to the same provisions as general rules for carrying into effect the objects of the Bankruptcy Act, 1883.

(2.) There shall be paid in respect of proceedings under this Act such fees as the Lord Chancellor may, with the sanction of the Treasury, from time to time prescribe, and the Treasury may direct by whom and in what manner the same are to be collected and accounted for, and to what account they are to be paid.

---

## 51 & 52 VICT. c. 25.

*An Act for the better regulation of Railway and Canal Traffic, and for other purposes.*

[*10th August,* 1888.]

BE it enacted by the Queen's most Excellent Majesty, by and with the advice and consent of the Lords Spiritual and Temporal, and Commons, in this present Parliament assembled, and by the authority of the same, as follows :

Short title and construction.

36 & 37 Vict. c. 48.

**1.** This Act may be cited as the Railway and Canal Traffic Act, 1888.

This Act shall be construed as one with the Regulation of Railways Act, 1873, and the Acts amending it ; and those Acts and this Act may be cited together as the Railway and Canal Traffic Acts, 1873 and 1888.

# PART I.

## COURT AND PROCEDURE OF RAILWAY AND CANAL COMMISSIONERS.

### *Establishment of Railway and Canal Commission.*

**2.** On the expiration of the provisions of the Regulation of Railways Act, 1873, with respect to the commissioners therein mentioned, there shall be established a new Commission, styled the Railway and Canal Commission (in this Act referred to as the commissioners), and consisting of two appointed and three ex officio commissioners ; and such commission shall be a court of record, and have an official seal, which shall be judicially noticed. The commissioners may act notwithstanding any vacancy in their body. *Establishment of new Railway and Canal Commission.*

**3.**—(1.) The two appointed commissioners may be appointed by her Majesty at any time after the passing of this Act, and from time to time as vacancies occur. *Appointment and tenure of office of appointed commissioners.*

(2.) They shall be appointed on the recommendation of the President of the Board of Trade, and one of them shall be of experience in railway business.

(3.) Section five of the Regulation of Railways Act, 1873, shall apply to each appointed commissioner.

(4.) There shall be paid to each appointed commissioner such salary not exceeding three thousand pounds a year as the President of the Board of Trade may, with the concurrence of the Treasury, determine.

(5.) It shall be lawful for the Lord Chancellor, if he think fit, to remove for inability or misbehaviour any appointed commissioner.

**4.**—(1.) Of the three ex officio commissioners of the Railway and Canal Commission one shall be nominated for England, one for Scotland, and one for Ireland ; and an ex officio commissioner shall not be required to attend out of the part of the United Kingdom for which he is nominated. *Appointment and attendance of ex officio commissioners.*

(2.) The ex officio commissioner in each case shall be such judge of a superior court as—
(a) in England the Lord Chancellor ; and
(b) in Scotland the Lord President of the Court of Session ; and
(c) in Ireland the Lord Chancellor of Ireland ;
may from time to time by writing under his hand assign, and such assignment shall be made for a period of not less than five years.

(3.) For the purpose of the attendance of the ex officio commissioners, regulations shall be made from time to time by the Lord Chancellor, the Lord President of the Court of Session, and the Lord Chancellor of Ireland respectively, in communication with the ex officio commissioners for England, Scotland, or Ireland, as the case may be, as to the arrangements for securing their attendance, as to the times and place of sitting in each case, and otherwise for the convenient and speedy hearing thereof.

**5.**—(1.) Subject to the provisions of this Act, and to general rules under this Act, the commissioners may hold sittings in any part of the United Kingdom, in such place or places as may be most convenient for the determination of proceedings before them. *Sittings of commissioners.*

(2.) The central office of the commissioners shall be in London, and the commissioners when holding a public sitting in London shall hold the same at the Royal Courts of Justice, or at such other place as the Lord Chancellor may from time to time appoint.

(3.) Not less than three commissioners shall attend at the hearing of any case, and the ex officio commissioner shall preside, and his opinion upon any question which in the opinion of the commissioners is a question of law shall prevail.

(4.) Save as aforesaid, section twenty-seven of the Regulation of Railways Act, 1873, shall apply, and any act may be done by any two commissioners. *36 & 37 Vict. c. 48.*

(5.) Every judge who may with his consent be assigned to hold the office of ex officio commissioner shall attend to hear any cases before the commission, which as ex officio commissioner he is required to hear, when and as soon as the cases are ready to be heard, or as soon thereafter as reasonably may be ; and any such judge shall be required to perform any of the other duties of a judge of a superior court only when his attendance on the commission is not required.

(6.) If and when any judge who may be assigned to hold the office of ex officio commissioner is temporarily unable to attend, the Lord Chancellor in England, the Lord President of the Court of Session in Scotland, and the Lord Chancellor in Ireland, may respectively nominate any judge of a superior court to sit as ex officio commissioner in place of the judge who is so temporarily unable to attend as aforesaid, and the judge so nominated shall for the purpose of any case which he may hear be an ex officio commissioner.

(7.) If the President of the Board of Trade is satisfied either of the inability of an appointed commissioner to attend at the hearing of any case, or of there being a vacancy in the office, and in either case of the necessity of a speedy hearing of the case, he may appoint a temporary commissioner to hear such case, and such commissioner, for all purposes connected with such case, shall, until the final determination thereof, have the same jurisdiction and powers as if he were an appointed commissioner. A temporary commissioner shall be paid such sum by the commissioner so unable to sit, or, if the office is vacant, out of the salary of the office, as the President of the Board of Trade may assign.

*Appointment of additional judge.*

6. On an address from both Houses of Parliament representing that, regard being had to the duties imposed by this Act on the ex officio commissioners, the state of business of the High Court in England requires the appointment of an additional judge of that court, it shall be lawful for her Majesty to appoint an additional judge of such court, and from time to time, on a like address but not otherwise, to fill any vacancy in such judgeship, and the law relating to the appointment and qualification of the judges of such superior court, to their duties and tenure of office, to their precedence, salary and pension, and otherwise, shall apply to any judge so appointed under this section, and a judge so appointed under this section shall be attached to such division or branch of the court as her Majesty may direct, subject to such power of transfer as may exist in the case of any other judge of such division or branch.

*Provision for complaints by public authority in certain cases.*

7.—(1.) Any of the following authorities, that is to say—

(a) any of the following local authorities, namely, any harbour board, or conservancy authority, the common council of the city of London, any council of a city or borough, any representative county body which may be created by an Act passed in the present or any future session of Parliament, any justices in quarter sessions assembled, the commissioners of supply of any county in Scotland, the Metropolitan Board of Works, or any urban sanitary authority not being a council as aforesaid, or any rural sanitary authority ; or

(b) any such association of traders or freighters, or chamber of commerce or agriculture as may obtain a certificate from the Board of Trade that it is, in the opinion of the Board of Trade, a proper body to make such complaint,

may make to the commissioners any complaint which the commissioners have jurisdiction to determine, and may do so without proof that such authority is aggrieved by the matter complained of, and any of such authorities may appear in opposition to any complaint which the commissioners have jurisdiction to determine in any case where such authority, or the persons represented by them, appear to the commissioners to be likely to be affected by any determination of the commissioners upon such complaint.

(2.) The Board of Trade may, if they think fit, require, as a condition of giving a certificate under this section, that security be given in such manner and to such amount as they think necessary for any costs which the complainants may be ordered to pay or bear.

(3.) Any certificate granted under this section shall, unless withdrawn, be in force for twelve months from the date on which it was given.

### *Jurisdiction.*

*Jurisdiction of Railway Commissioners transferred to the Commission.*

8. There shall be transferred to and vested in the commissioners all the jurisdiction and powers which at the commencement of this Act were vested in, or capable of being exercised by the Railway Commissioners, whether under the Regulation of Railways Act, 1873, or any other Act, or otherwise, and any reference to the Railway Commissioners in the Regulation of Railways Act, 1873, or in any other Act, or in any document, shall, from and after the commencement of this Act, be construed to refer to the Railway and Canal Commission established by this Act.

**9.** Where any enactment in a special Act—
Jurisdiction of commissioners under special Acts. 17 & 18 Vict. c. 31.
- (a) contains provisions relating to traffic facilities, undue preference, or other matters mentioned in section two of the Railway and Canal Traffic Act, 1854 (a), or
- (b) requires a company to which this part of this Act applies to provide any station, road, or other similar work for public accommodation, or
- (c) otherwise imposes on a company to which this part of this Act applies any obligation in favour of the public or any individual,

or where any Act contains provisions relating to private branch railways or private sidings, the commissioners shall have the like jurisdiction to hear and determine a complaint of a contravention of the enactment as the commissioners have to hear and determine a complaint of a contravention of section two of the Railway and Canal Traffic Act, 1854, as amended by subsequent Acts.

**10.** Where any question or dispute arises, involving the legality of any toll, rate, or charge, or portion of a toll, rate, or charge, charged or sought to be charged for merchandise traffic by a company to which this part of this Act applies, the commissioners shall have jurisdiction to hear and determine the same, and to enforce payment of such toll, rate, or charge, or so much thereof as the commissioners decide to be legal.
Jurisdiction over tolls and rates.

**11.** Nothing in any agreement, whether made before or after the passing of this Act, which has not been confirmed by Act or by the Board of Trade, or by the commissioners under the Regulation of Railways Act, 1873, or this Act, shall render a company to which this part of this Act applies unable to afford, or shall authorise such company to refuse, such reasonable facilities for traffic as may in the opinion of the commissioners be required in the interests of the public, or shall prevent the commissioners from making or enforcing any order with respect to such facilities.
Jurisdiction to order traffic facilities, notwithstanding agreements.

**12.** Where the commissioners have jurisdiction to hear and determine any matter, they may, in addition to or in substitution for any other relief, award to any complaining party who is aggrieved such damages as they find him to have sustained; and such award of damages shall be in complete satisfaction of any claim for damages, including repayment of overcharges, which, but for this Act, such party would have had by reason of the matter of complaint.
Power to award damages.

Provided that such damages shall not be awarded unless complaint has been made to the commissioners within one year from the discovery by the party aggrieved of the matter complained of.

The commissioners may ascertain the amount of such damages either by trial before themselves, or by directing an inquiry to be taken before one or more of themselves or before some officer of their court.

**13.** In cases of complaint of undue preference no damages shall be awarded if the commissioners shall find that the rates complained of have, for the period during which such rates have been in operation, been duly published in the rate books of their railway company kept at their stations in accordance with section fourteen of the Regulation of Railways Act, 1873, as amended by this Act, unless and until the party complaining shall have given written notice to the railway company requiring them to abstain from or remedy the matter of complaint, and the railway company shall have failed, within a reasonable time, to comply with such requirements in such a manner as the commissioners shall think reasonable.
No damages where rates published under certain conditions.

**14.** The commissioners may order two or more companies to which this part of this Act applies to carry into effect an order of the commissioners, and to make mutual arrangements for that purpose, and may further order the companies or, in case of difference, any of them, to submit to the commissioners for approval a scheme for carrying into effect the order, and when the commissioners have finally approved the scheme, they may order each of the companies to do all that is necessary on the part and within the power of such company to carry into effect the scheme, and may determine the proportions in which the respective companies are to defray the expense of so doing, and may for the above purposes make, if they think fit, separate orders on any one or more of such companies.
Orders on two or more companies.

(a) *Supra.*

Provided that nothing in this section shall authorise the commissioners to require two companies to do anything which they would not have jurisdiction to require to be done if such two companies were a single company.

**Amendment of 36 & 37 Vict. c. 48, s. 8, as to references to arbitration.**

15. For the purposes of section eight of the Regulation of Railways Act, 1873, and any other enactment relating to the reference to the Railway Commission of any difference between companies which under the provisions of any general or special Act is required or authorised to be referred to arbitration, the provisions of any agreement confirmed or authorised by any such Act shall be deemed to be provisions of such Act.

**Power to apportion expenses between railway company and applicants for works.**

16.—(1.) Where the Board of Trade or the commissioners, in the exercise of any power given by any general or special Act, on application order a company to which this part of this Act applies, to provide a bridge, subway, or approach, or any work of a similar character, the Board of Trade or the Commissioners, as the case may be, may require as a condition of making the order that an agreement to pay the whole or a portion of the expenses of complying with the order shall be entered into by the applicants or some of them, or such other persons as the Board of Trade or commissioners think fit, and any of the following local authorities, namely, any sanitary authority, highway board, surveyor of highways acting with the consent of the vestry of his parish, or any other authority having power to levy rates, shall have power, if such authority think fit, to enter into any such agreement as is sanctioned by the Board of Trade or commissioners for the purpose of the order.

(2.) In such case any question respecting the persons by whom or the proportions in which the expenses of complying with the order are to be defrayed may, on the application of any party to the application, or on a certificate of the Board of Trade, be determined by the commissioners.

(3.) In this section the expression "parish" shall have the same meaning as the same expression has in the Acts relating to highways; and the expression "the consent of the vestry of his parish" shall, in any place where there is no vestry meeting, mean the consent of a meeting of inhabitants contributing to the highway rates, provided that the same notice shall have been given of such a meeting as would be required by law for the assembling of a meeting in vestry.

### Appeals.

**Appeals on certain questions to superior court of appeal.**

17.—(1.) No appeal shall lie from the commissioners upon a question of fact, or upon any question regarding the locus standi of a complainant.

(2.) Save as otherwise provided by this Act, an appeal shall lie from the commissioners to a Superior Court of Appeal.

(3.) An appeal shall not be brought except in conformity with such rules of court as may from time to time be made in relation to such appeals by the authority having power to make rules of court for the Superior Court of Appeal.

(4.) On the hearing of an appeal the Court of Appeal may draw all such inferences as are not inconsistent with the facts expressly found, and are necessary for determining the question of law, and shall have all such powers for that purpose as if the appeal were an appeal from a judgment of a Superior Court, and may make any order which the commissioners could have made, and also any such further or other order as may be just, and the costs of and incidental to an appeal shall be in the discretion of the Court of Appeal, but no commissioner shall be liable to any costs by reason or in respect of any appeal.

(5.) The decision of the Superior Court of Appeal shall be final: provided that where there has been a difference of opinion between any two of such Superior Courts of Appeal, any Superior Court of Appeal in which a matter affected by such difference of opinion is pending may give leave to appeal to the House of Lords, on such terms as to costs as such court shall determine.

(6.) Save as provided by this Act, an order or proceeding of the commissioners shall not be questioned or reviewed, and shall not be restrained or removed by prohibition, injunction, certiorari, or otherwise, either at the instance of the Crown or otherwise.

### Supplemental.

**General powers and enforcement of orders.**

18.—(1.) For the purposes of this Act the commissioners shall have full jurisdiction to hear and determine all matters whether of law or of fact, and shall as respects the attendance and examination of witnesses, the production and inspection of documents, the enforcement of their orders, the entry on and inspection of property, and other matters necessary or proper for the due exercise of their jurisdiction under this Act, or otherwise for carrying this Act into effect, have all such powers, rights, and privileges as are vested in a Superior Court : provided that no person shall be punished for contempt of court, except with the consent of an ex officio commissioner.

(2.) The commissioners may review and rescind or vary any order made by them ; but, save as is by this Act provided, every decision or order of the commissioners shall be final.

19. The costs of and incidental to every proceeding before the commissioners shall be in the discretion of the commissioners, who may order by whom and to whom the same are to be paid, and by whom the same are to be taxed and allowed. *Costs.*

20.—(1.) The commissioners may from time to time, with the approval of the Lord Chancellor and the President of the Board of Trade, make, rescind, and vary general rules for their procedure and practice under this Act, and generally for carrying into effect this part of this Act. *Power to make rules.*

(2.) All rules made under this section shall be laid before Parliament within three weeks after they are made, if Parliament is then sitting, and if Parliament is not then sitting within three weeks after the beginning of the then next session of Parliament, and shall be judicially noticed, and shall have effect as if they were enacted by this Act.

21.—(1.) There shall be attached to the Railway and Canal Commission such officers, clerks, and messengers as the Lord Chancellor, with the consent of the Treasury as to number, from time to time appoints. *Appointment of officers, clerks, &c.*

(2.) There shall be paid to each of such officers, clerks, and messengers, such salaries as the Treasury from time to time determine.

22. The salaries of the appointed commissioners, and of all officers, clerks, and messengers attached to the Railway and Canal Commission, and all the expenses of the said commission of and incidental to the carrying out of this Act, shall be paid out of moneys to be provided by Parliament. *Salaries, expenses, &c.*

23. This part of this Act shall apply to any railway company, and to any canal company, and to any railway and canal company. *Company to which Part I. applies.*

## PART II.

### TRAFFIC.

24.—(1.) Notwithstanding any provision in any general or special Act, every railway company shall submit to the Board of Trade a revised classification of merchandise traffic, and a revised schedule of maximum rates and charges applicable thereto, proposed to be charged by such railway company, and shall fully state in such classification and schedule the nature and amounts of all terminal charges proposed to be authorised in respect of each class of traffic, and the circumstances under which such terminal charges are proposed to be made. In the determination of the terminal charges of any railway company regard shall be had only to the expenditure reasonably necessary to provide the accommodation in respect of which such charges are made, irrespective of the outlay which may have been actually incurred by the railway company in providing that accommodation. *Revised classification of traffic and schedule of rates.*

(2.) The classification and schedule shall be submitted within six months from the passing of this Act, or such further time as the Board of Trade may, in any particular case, permit, and shall be published in such manner as the Board of Trade may direct.

(3.) The Board of Trade shall consider the classification and schedule, and any objections thereto, which may be lodged with them on or before the prescribed time and in the prescribed manner, and shall communicate with the railway company and the persons (if any) who have lodged objections, for the purpose of arranging the differences which may have arisen.

(4.) If, after hearing all parties whom the Board of Trade consider to be entitled to be heard before them respecting the classification and schedule, the Board of Trade come to an agreement with the railway company as to the classification and schedule, they shall embody the agreed classification and schedule in a Provisional Order, and shall make a report thereon, to be submitted to Parliament, containing such observations as they think fit in relation to the agreed classification and schedule.

(5.) When any agreed classification and schedule have been embodied in a Provisional Order, the Board of Trade, as soon as they conveniently can after the making of the Provisional Order (of which the railway company shall be deemed to be the promoters), shall procure a Bill to be introduced into either House of Parliament for an Act to confirm the Provisional Order, which shall be set out at length in the schedule to the Bill.

(6.) In any case in which a railway company fails within the time mentioned in this section to submit a classification and schedule to the Board of Trade, and also in every case in which a railway company has submitted to the Board of Trade a classification and schedule, and after hearing all parties whom the Board of Trade consider to be entitled to be heard before them, the Board of Trade are unable to come to an agreement with the railway company as to the railway company's classification and schedule, the Board of Trade shall determine the classification of traffic which, in the opinion of the Board of Trade, ought to be adopted by the railway company, and the schedule of maximum rates and charges, including all terminal charges proposed to be authorised applicable to such classification which would, in the opinion of the Board of Trade, be just and reasonable, and shall make a report, to be submitted to Parliament, containing such observations as they may think fit in relation to the said classification and schedule, and calling attention to the points therein on which differences which have arisen have not been arranged.

(7.) After the commencement of the session of Parliament next after that in which the said report of the Board of Trade has been submitted to Parliament, the railway company may apply to the Board of Trade to submit to Parliament the question of the classification and schedule which ought to be adopted by the railway company, and the Board of Trade shall on such application, and in any case may, embody in a Provisional Order such classification and schedule as in the opinion of the Board of Trade ought to be adopted by the railway company, and procure a Bill to be introduced into either House of Parliament for an Act to confirm the Provisional Order, which shall be set out at length in the schedule to the Bill.

(8.) If, while any Bill to confirm a Provisional Order made by the Board of Trade under this section is pending in either House of Parliament, a petition is presented against the Bill or any classification and schedule comprised therein, the Bill, so far as it relates to the matter petitioned against, shall be referred to a Select Committee, or if the two Houses of Parliament think fit so to order, to a joint committee of such Houses, and the petitioner shall be allowed to appear and oppose as in the case of a private Bill.

(9.) In preparing, revising, and settling the classifications and schedules of rates and charges, the Board of Trade may consult and employ such skilled persons as they may deem necessary or desirable ; and they may pay to such persons such remuneration as they may think fit and as the Treasury may approve.

(10.) The Act of Parliament confirming any Provisional Order made under this section shall be a public general Act, and the rates and charges mentioned in a Provisional Order as confirmed by such Act shall, from and after the Act coming into operation, be the rates and charges which the railway company shall be entitled to charge and make.

(11.) At any time after the confirmation of any Provisional Order under this section any railway company may, and any person, upon giving not less than twenty-one days notice to the railway company may, apply in the prescribed manner to the Board of Trade to amend any classification and schedule by adding thereto any articles, matters, or things, and the Board of Trade may hear and determine such application, and classify and deal with the articles, matters, or things referred to therein in such manner as the Board of Trade shall think right. Every determination of the Board of Trade under this sub-section shall forthwith be published in the "London Gazette," and shall take effect as from the date of the publication thereof.

(12.) Nothing in this section shall apply to any remuneration payable by the Postmaster-General to any railway company for the conveyance of mails, letter bags, or parcels under any general or special Act relating to the conveyance of mails, or under the Post Office (Parcels) Act, 1882. 45 & 46 Vict. c. 74.

(13.) Nothing in this section shall apply to any remuneration payable by the Secretary of State for War to any railway company for the conveyance of War Office stores under the powers conferred by the Cheap Trains Act, 1883. 46 & 47 Vict. c. 34.

25. Whereas by section two of the Railway and Canal Traffic Act, 1854 (*a*), it is enacted that every railway company and canal company, and railway and canal company shall, according to their respective powers, afford all reasonable facilities for the receiving and forwarding and delivering of traffic upon and from the several railways and canals belonging to or worked by such companies respectively, and for the return of carriages, trucks, boats, and other vehicles; and that no such company shall make or give any undue or unreasonable preference or advantage to or in favour of any particular person or company, or any particular description of traffic, in any respect whatsoever, or shall subject any particular person or company, or any particular description of traffic, to any undue or unreasonable prejudice or disadvantage in any respect whatsoever; and that every railway company and canal company and railway and canal company having or working railways or canals which form part of a continuous line of railway, or canal or railway and canal communication, or which have the terminus station or wharf of the one near the terminus station or wharf of the other, shall afford all due and reasonable facilities for receiving and forwarding by one of such railways or canals all the traffic arriving by the other, without any unreasonable delay, and without any such preference or advantage or prejudice or disadvantage as aforesaid, and so that no obstruction may be offered to the public desirous of using such railways or canals or railways and canals as a continuous line of communication, and so that all reasonable accommodation may by means of the railways and canals of the several companies be at all times afforded to the public in that behalf: Provisions as to through traffic.

And whereas it is expedient to explain and amend the said enactment:

Be it therefore enacted, that—

Subject as hereinafter mentioned, the said facilities to be so afforded are hereby declared to and shall include the due and reasonable receiving, forwarding, and delivering by every railway company and canal company and railway and canal company, at the request of any other such company, of through traffic to and from the railway or canal of any other such company at through rates, tolls, or fares (in this Act referred to as through rates); and also the due and reasonable receiving, forwarding, and delivering by every railway company and canal company and railway and canal company, at the request of any person interested in through traffic, of such traffic at through rates: Provided that no application shall be made to the commissioners by such person until he has made a complaint to the Board of Trade under the provisions of this Act as to complaints to the Board of Trade of unreasonable charges, and the Board of Trade have heard the complaint in the manner herein provided.

Provided as follows:

(1.) The company or person requiring the traffic to be forwarded shall give written notice of the proposed through rate to each forwarding company, stating both its amount and the route by which the traffic is proposed to be forwarded; and when a company gives such notice it shall also state the apportionment of the through rate. The proposed through rate may be per truck or per ton:

(2.) Each forwarding company shall, within ten days, or such longer period as the commissioners may from time to time by general order prescribe, after the receipt of such notice, by written notice inform the company or persons requiring the traffic to be forwarded, whether they agree to the rate and route; and if they object to either, the grounds of the objection:

(3.) If at the expiration of the prescribed period no such objection has been sent by any forwarding company, the rate shall come into operation at such expiration:

(4.) If an objection to the rate or route has been sent within the

(*a*) *Supra.*

prescribed period, the matter shall be referred to the commissioners for their decision:

(5.) If an objection be made to the granting of the rate or to the route, the commissioners shall consider whether the granting of a rate is a due and reasonable facility in the interest of the public, and whether, having regard to the circumstances, the route proposed is a reasonable route, and shall allow or refuse the rate accordingly, or fix such other rate as may seem to the commissioners just and reasonable:

(6.) Where, upon the application of a person requiring traffic to be forwarded, a through rate is agreed to by the forwarding companies, or is made by order of the commissioners, the apportionment of such through rate, if not agreed upon between the forwarding companies, shall be determined by the commissioners:

(7.) If the objection be only to the apportionment of the rate, the rate shall come into operation at the expiration of the prescribed period, but the decision of the commissioners, as to its apportionment, shall be retrospective; in any other case the operation of the rate shall be suspended until the decision is given:

(8.) The commissioners, in apportioning the through rate, shall take into consideration all the circumstances of the case, including any special expense incurred in respect of the construction, maintenance, or working of the route, or any part of the route, as well as any special charges which any company may have been entitled to make in respect thereof:

(9.) It shall not be lawful for the commissioners in any case to compel any company to accept lower mileage rates than the mileage rates which such company may for the time being legally be charging for like traffic carried by a like mode of transit on any other line of communication between the same points, being the points of departure and arrival of the through route.

Where a railway company or canal company use, maintain, or work, or are party to an arrangement for using, maintaining, or working steam vessels for the purpose of carrying on a communication between any towns or ports, the provisions of this section shall extend to such steam vessels, and to the traffic carried thereby.

When any company, upon written notice being given as aforesaid, refuses or neglects without reason to agree to the proposed through rates, or to the route, or to the apportionment, the commissioners, if an order is made by them upon an application for through rates, may order the respondent company or companies to pay such costs to the applicants as they think fit.

**Powers of commissioners as to through rates.**

26. Subject to the provisions in the last preceding section contained, the commissioners shall have full power to decide that any proposed through rate is just and reasonable, notwithstanding that a less amount may be allotted to any forwarding company out of such through rate than the maximum rate such company is entitled to charge, and to allow and apportion such through rate accordingly.

**Undue preference in case of unequal tolls, rates, and charges, and unequal services performed.**

27.—(1.) Whenever it is shown that any railway company charge one trader or class of traders, or the traders in any district, lower tolls, rates, or charges for the same or similar merchandise, or lower tolls, rates, or charges for the same or similar services, than they charge to other traders, or classes of traders, or to the traders in another district, or make any difference in treatment in respect of any such trader or traders, the burden of proving that such lower charge or difference in treatment does not amount to an undue preference shall lie on the railway company.

(2.) In deciding whether a lower charge or difference in treatment does or does not amount to an undue preference, the court having jurisdiction in the matter, or the commissioners, as the case may be, may, so far as they think reasonable, in addition to any other considerations affecting the case, take into consideration whether such lower charge or difference in treatment is necessary for the purpose of securing in the interests of the public the traffic in respect of which it is made, and whether the inequality cannot be removed without unduly reducing the rates charged to the complainant: Provided that no railway company shall make, nor shall the court, or the commissioners, sanction any difference in the tolls, rates, or charges made for, or any difference in the treatment of, home and foreign merchandise, in respect of the same or similar services.

(3.) The court or the commissioners shall have power to direct that no higher charge shall be made to any person for services in respect of merchandise carried over a less distance than is made to any other person for similar services in respect of the like description and quantity of merchandise carried over a greater distance on the same line of railway.

28. The provisions of section two of the Railway and Canal Traffic Act, 1854 (a), and of section fourteen of the Regulation of Railways Act, 1873 (b), and of any enactments amending and extending those enactments, shall apply to traffic by sea in any vessels belonging to or chartered or worked by any railway company, or in which any railway company procures merchandise to be carried, in the same manner and to the like extent as they apply to the land traffic of a railway company.

*Extension of enactments as to undue preference to goods carried by sea.*

29.—(1.) Notwithstanding any provision in any general or special Act, it shall be lawful for any railway company, for the purpose of fixing the rates to be charged for the carriage of merchandise to and from any place on their railway, to group together any number of places in the same district, situated at various distances from any point of destination or departure of merchandise, and to charge a uniform rate or uniform rates of carriage for merchandise to and from all places comprised in the group from and to any point of destination or departure.

*Group rates to be chargeable by railway companies.*

(2.) Provided that the distances shall not be unreasonable, and that the group rates charged and the places grouped together shall not be such as to create an undue preference.

(3.) Where any group rate exists or is proposed, and in any case where there is a doubt whether any rates charged or proposed to be charged by a railway company may not be a contravention of section two of the Railway and Canal Traffic Act, 1854, and any Acts amending the same, the railway company may, upon giving notice in the prescribed manner, apply to the commissioners, and the commissioners may, after hearing the parties interested and any of the authorities mentioned in section seven of this Act, determine whether such group rate or any rate charged or proposed to be charged as aforesaid does or does not create an undue preference. Any persons aggrieved, and any of the authorities mentioned in section seven of this Act, may, at any time after the making of any order under this section, apply to the commissioners to vary or rescind the order, and the commissioners, after hearing all parties who are interested, may make an order accordingly.

30. Any port or harbour authority or dock company which shall have reason to believe that any railway company is by its rates or otherwise placing their port, harbour, or dock, at an undue disadvantage as compared with any other port, harbour, or dock to or from which traffic is or may be carried by means of the lines of the said railway company, either alone or in conjunction with those of other railway companies, may make complaint thereof to the commissioners, who shall have the like jurisdiction to hear and determine the subject-matter of such complaint as they have to hear and determine a complaint of a contravention of section two of the Railway and Canal Traffic Act, 1854, as amended by subsequent Acts.

*Power to dock companies and harbour boards to complain of undue preference.*

31.—(1.) Whenever any person receiving or sending or desiring to send goods by any railway is of opinion that the railway company is charging him an unfair or an unreasonable rate of charge, or is in any other respect treating him in an oppressive or unreasonable manner, such person may complain to the Board of Trade.

*Complaints to Board of Trade of unreasonable charges by railway companies.*

(2.) The Board of Trade, if they think that there is reasonable ground for the complaint, may thereupon call upon the railway company for an explanation, and endeavour to settle amicably the differences between the complainant and the railway company.

(3.) For the purpose aforesaid, the Board of Trade may appoint either one of their own officers or any other competent person to communicate with the complainant and the railway company, and to receive and consider such explanations and communications as may be made in reference to the complaint; and the Board of Trade may pay to such last-mentioned person such remuneration as they may think fit, and as may be approved by the Treasury.

(4.) The Board of Trade shall from time to time submit to Parliament

(a) *Supra.*          (b) *Supra.*

reports of the complaints made to them under the provisions of this section, and the results of the proceedings taken in relation to such complaints, together with such observations thereon as the Board of Trade shall think fit.

(5.) A complaint under this section may be made to the Board of Trade by any of the authorities mentioned in section seven of this Act, in any case in which, in the opinion of any of such authorities, they or any traders or persons in their district are being charged unfair or unreasonable rates by a railway company ; and all the provisions of this section shall apply to a complaint so made as if the same had been made by a person entitled to make a complaint under this section.

Annual returns by railway companies to contain such statistics as the Board of Trade shall require.<br>34 & 35 Vict. c. 78, s. 9.<br><br>36 & 37 Vict. c. 76.

32.—(1.) The returns required of a railway company under section nine of the Railways Regulation Act, 1871, shall include such statements as the Board of Trade may from time to time prescribe, and the forms referred to in that section may from time to time be altered by the Board of Trade in such manner as they think expedient for giving effect to this section, and the said section nine of the Railways Regulation Act, 1871, shall apply accordingly.

(2.) The Board of Trade may from time to time alter the times fixed by the said Act or by the Railways Regulation Act (Returns of Signal Arrangements, Workings, &c.), 1873, for the forwarding of any of the returns required by the said Act or this Act.

Classification table to be open for inspection. Copies to be sold.

33 —(1.) The book, tables, or other document in use for the time being containing the general classification of merchandise carried on the railway of any company, shall, during all reasonable hours, be open to the inspection of any person without the payment of any fee at every station at which merchandise is received for conveyance, or where merchandise is received at some other place than a station then at the station nearest such place, and the said book, tables, or other document as revised from time to time shall be kept on sale at the principal office of the company at a price not exceeding one shilling.

(2.) Printed copies of the classification of merchandise traffic, and schedule of maximum tolls, rates, and charges of every railway company authorised, as provided by this Act, shall be kept for sale by the railway company at such places and at such reasonable price as the Board of Trade may by any general or special order prescribe.

(3.) The company shall within one week after application in writing made to the secretary of any railway company by any person interested in the carriage of any merchandise which has been or is intended to be carried over the railway of such company, render an account to the person so applying in which the charge made or claimed by the company for the carriage of such merchandise shall be divided, and the charge for conveyance over the railway shall be distinguished from the terminal charges (if any), and from the dock charges (if any), and if any terminal charge or dock charge is included in such account the nature and detail of the terminal expenses or dock charges in respect of which it is made shall be specified.

(4.) Every railway company shall publish at every station at which merchandise is received for conveyance, or where merchandise is received at some other place than a station then at the station nearest to such place, a notice, in such form as may be from time to time prescribed by the Board of Trade, to the effect that such book, tables, and document touching the classification of merchandise and the rates as they are required by this section and section fourteen of the Regulation of Railways Act, 1873, to

36 & 37 Vict c. 48.

keep at that station, are open to public inspection, and that information as to any charge can be obtained by application to the secretary or other officer at the address stated in such notice.

(5.) Where a railway company carries merchandise partly by land and partly by sea, all the books, tables, and documents, touching the rates of charge of the railway company, which are kept by the railway company at any port in the United Kingdom used by the vessels which carry the sea traffic of the railway company, shall, besides containing all the rates charged for the sea traffic, state what proportion of any through rate is appropriated to conveyance by sea, distinguishing such proportion from that which is appropriated to the conveyance by land on either side of the sea.

(6.) Where a railway company intend to make any increase in the tolls, rates, or charges published in the books required to be kept by the company for public inspection, under section fourteen of the Regulation of Railways Act, 1873, or this Act, they shall give by publication in such manner as the

Board of Trade may prescribe at least fourteen days notice of such intended increase, stating in such notice the date on which the altered rate or charge is to take effect ; and no such increase in the published tolls, rates, or charges of the railway company shall have effect unless and until the fourteen days notice required under this section has been given.

(7.) Any company failing to comply with the provisions of this section shall, for each offence, and in the ease of a continuing offence for every day during which the offence continues, be liable, on summary conviction, to a penalty not exceeding five pounds.

**34.** When traffic is received or delivered at any place on any railway other than a station within the meaning of section fourteen of the Regulation of Railways Act, 1873, the railway company on whose line such place is, shall keep at the station nearest such place a book or books showing every rate for the time being charged for the carriage of traffic other than passengers and their luggage, from such place to any place to which they book, including any rates charged under any special contract, and stating the distance from that place of every station, wharf, siding, or place to which such rate is charged. *Place of publication of rates in respect of traffic at places other than stations.*

Every such book shall, during all reasonable hours, be open to the inspection of any person without the payment of a fee.

**35.**—(1.) The Board of Trade may from time to time make, rescind, and vary rules with respect to the following matters :— *Power to make rules for purposes of Part II. of Act.*

  (a) The form and manner in which classifications and schedules under this part of this Act are to be prepared and submitted to the Board of of Trade and to Parliament, and the publication, advertisement, and settlement (by the Board of Trade) of such classifications and schedules, and of provisional orders ;

  (b) All proceedings before the Board of Trade under this part of this Act ;

  (c) The fees to be paid in respect of such proceedings ; and

  (d) Any matter authorized by this Act to be prescribed.

(2.) Any rules made by the Board of Trade in pursuance of this section shall be laid before Parliament within three weeks after they are made, if Parliament be then sitting, and if Parliament be not then sitting, within three weeks after the beginning of the then next session of Parliament, and shall be judicially noticed, and shall have effect as if they were enacted by this Act.

---

## PART III.

### Canals.

**36.** All the provisions of Part II. of this Act relating to any railway company shall, so far as applicable, apply to every canal company, and to every railway and canal company ; and in Part II. of this Act, unless the context otherwise requires, the expression " railway company " shall include a canal company and railway and canal company, and the expression " railway " shall include a canal, and the expression "rate" shall include tolls and dues of every description chargeable for the use of any canal or by any canal company. *Part II. to extend to canal companies.*

**37.**—(1.) Section fifteen of the Regulation of Railways Act, 1873, shall apply to the terminal charges of a canal company. *Application of 36 & 37 Vict. c. 48, to canals.*

(2.) The Railway and Canal Traffic Act, 1854, as amended by the Regulation of Railways Act, 1873, shall extend to any person whose consent is required to any variation of the rates, tolls, or dues charged for the use of any canal, or by any canal company, in like manner as if such person were a canal company, and the expressions "canal company" and "railway and canal company" in the said Acts and this Act shall be construed accordingly to include such person.

(3.) The provisions of the Railway and Canal Traffic Act, 1854, and the Regulation of Railways Act, 1873, with respect to rates, shall apply to tolls and dues of every description chargeable for the use of any canal or by any canal company. And nothing in any agreement, whether made before or after the passing of this Act, and whether confirmed by Act of Parliament or not, and nothing in this Act shall prevent the commissioners from making or enforcing any order for a through rate or toll which may in their opinion be required in the interest of the public.

(4.) Any company allowing traffic to pass from a canal on to any other canal or any railway, or from a railway on to a canal, shall be deemed to be a forwarding company, and the allowing of traffic so to pass shall be deemed to be the forwarding of traffic within the meaning of the above-mentioned Acts.

(5.) The provisions of the Railway and Canal Traffic Act, 1854, and of the Regulation of Railways Act, 1873, and of this Act, with respect to through rates, shall extend to any canals which, in connection with any river or other waterway, form part of a continuous line of water communication, notwithstanding that tolls may not be leviable by authority of Parliament upon such river or other waterway.

Powers of commissioners over canal tolls, rates, and charges where a railway company or its officers own or control the traffic of a canal.

**38.** Where a railway company, or the directors or officers of a railway company, or any of them or any persons on their behalf, have the control over, or the right to interfere in or concerning the traffic conveyed, or the tolls, rates, or charges levied on the traffic of or for the conveyance of merchandise on a canal, or any part of a canal, and it is proved to the satisfaction of the commissioners that the tolls, rates, or charges levied on the traffic of or for the conveyance of merchandise on the canal are such as are calculated to divert the traffic from the canal to the railway, to the detriment of the canal or persons sending traffic over the canal or other canals adjacent to it—

(1.) The commissioners may, on the application of any person interested in the traffic of the canal, make an order requiring the tolls, rates, and charges levied on the traffic of or for the conveyance of merchandise on the canal, to be altered and adjusted in such a manner that the same shall be reasonable as compared with the rates and charges for the conveyance of merchandise on the railway :

(2.) If within such time as may be prescribed by the order of the commissioners, the tolls, rates, and charges levied on the traffic of or for the conveyance of merchandise on the canal are not altered and adjusted as required by such order, the commissioners may themselves by an order make such alterations in and adjustment of the tolls, rates, and charges levied on the traffic of or for the conveyance of merchandise on the canal as they shall think just and reasonable, and the tolls, rates, and charges as altered and adjusted by the order of the commissioners shall be binding on the company or persons owning or having the control over the traffic of, or the tolls, rates, and charges levied on the traffic of, or for the conveyance of merchandise on the canal :

(3.) No application shall be made to the commissioners under this section until the Board of Trade have certified that the applicant is a fit person to make the application, and that the application is a proper one to be submitted for the adjudication of the commissioners ; and no order shall be made by the commissioners under this section unless notice of the application has been served upon such company and persons, and in such manner as the Board of Trade may direct :

(4.) The commissioners may at any time, upon the application of any company or person affected by any order made under this section, and after notice to and hearing such companies and persons as the commissioners may by any general rules or special order prescribe, rescind or vary any order made under this section.

Returns by canal companies.

**39.**—(1.) Every canal company shall, on or before the first day of January in every year, beginning on the first day of January next after the passing of this Act, send to the registrar of joint stock companies a return stating the name of the company, a short description of their canal, the name of their principal officer, and the place of their office, or, if they have more than one office, of their principal office.

(2.) Every canal company shall within such time as may be prescribed by the Board of Trade, and afterwards from time to time whenever required by the Board of Trade, not being oftener than once in every year, forward to the Board of Trade in such form and manner as the Board may from time to time prescribe, such returns as the Board of Trade may require for the purpose of showing the capacity of such canal for traffic, and the capital, revenue, expenditure, and profits of the canal company.

(3.) When the canal of a canal company, or any part thereof, is intended to be stopped for more than two days, the company shall report to the Board of Trade, stating the time during which such stoppage is intended to last, and when the same is re-opened the company shall so report to the Board of Trade.

(4.) A company failing to comply with this section, shall be liable, on summary conviction, to a fine not exceeding five pounds for every day during which their default continues, and any director, manager, and officer of the company who knowingly and wilfully authorises or permits the default shall be liable, on summary conviction, to the like fine.

40.—(1.) Every canal company shall, before such date as the Board of Trade may prescribe, forward to the Board of Trade true copies, certified in such manner as the Board of Trade direct, of any byelaws or regulations of such company which are in force at the commencement of this Act; and the byelaws of any canal company, copies of which are not forwarded to the Board of Trade as provided by this section, shall from and after the said date cease to have any operation, save in so far as any penalty may have been already incurred under the same. *Byelaws of canal companies.*

(2.) A byelaw or regulation of any canal company hereafter to be made under any power which has before or at the time of the passing of this Act been, or which may hereafter be, conferred on any canal company, shall not have any force or effect until two months after a true copy of such byelaw or regulation, certified in such manner as the Board of Trade direct, has been forwarded to the Board of Trade, unless the Board of Trade before the expiration of such period have signified their approbation thereof.

(3.) The Board of Trade may, at any time after any existing or future byelaws or regulations of a canal company have been forwarded to them, notify to the company their disallowance thereof, or of any of them, and in case such byelaws or regulations are in force at the time of the disallowance, the time at which the said byelaws or regulations shall cease to be in force. A byelaw or regulation disallowed by the Board of Trade shall not after such disallowance have any force or effect whatever, save (as regards any byelaw or regulation which may be in force at the time of the disallowance thereof) in so far as any penalty may have been then already incurred under the same.

(4.) The Board of Trade may from time to time make, rescind, and vary such regulations as they think fit with respect to the publication by canal companies of their byelaws and regulations, and with respect to the publication by canal companies of their intention to apply to the Board of Trade for the allowance of any intended byelaws and regulations. Any regulations so made which are for the time being in force, shall have effect as if they had been enacted in this Act.

41. Whenever the Board of Trade are, through their officers or otherwise, informed that the works of any canal are in such a condition as to be dangerous to the public, or to cause serious inconvenience or hindrance to traffic, the Board of Trade may direct such officer or other person as they appoint for the purpose to inspect the said canal and report thereon to the Board of Trade, and for the purpose of making any inspection under this section the officer or person appointed for the purpose shall, in relation to the canal or works to be inspected, have all the powers of an inspector appointed under the Regulation of Railways Act, 1871. *Inspection of canals.*

*34 & 35 Vict. c. 78.*

42.—(1.) No railway company, or director, or officer of a railway company shall, without express statutory authority, apply or use or authorise or permit the application or use of any part of the company's funds for the purpose of acquiring either in the name of the railway company, or of any director or officer of the railway company, or other person, any canal interest, or of enabling any director or officer of the railway company, or other person, to purchase or acquire any canal interest, or of guaranteeing or repaying to any director or officer of the railway company or other person who has purchased or acquired any canal interest the sums of money expended or liability incurred by such director, officer, or person, in the purchase or acquisition of such canal interest, or any part of such money or liability. *Misapplication of a railway company's funds for acquisition of unauthorised interest in canal.*

(2.) In the event of any contravention of the provisions of this section, the canal interest purchased in such contravention shall be forfeited to the Crown, and the directors or officers of the company who so applied or used, or authorised or permitted such application or use of the company's funds, shall be liable to repay to the company the sums so applied or used, and the value of the canal interest so forfeited; and proceedings to compel such repayment may be taken by any shareholder in the company.

(3.) In this section the expression " company's funds " means the corporate funds of any railway company, and includes any funds which are under the control of or administered by a railway company; the expression "officer" includes any person having any control over a company's funds or any part thereof; and the expression " canal interest " means shares in the capital of a canal company, and includes any interest of any kind in a canal company or canal.

**Canal companies may agree for through tolls, &c.**
**43.**—(1.) Any canal company may make and enter into contracts and arrangements with any other canal company or canal companies for the passage over and along their respective canals, or any of them, of boats, barges, vessels, and other through traffic, and for the use, by such traffic, of the wharves, landing-places, and other works of any such canal, upon payment of such through tolls, rates, and charges, and subject to such conditions and restrictions as may be agreed upon between such companies; and for the collection and recovery by any one of the companies on behalf of themselves and the other companies interested of the tolls, rates, and charges payable in respect of such through traffic; and for the division and apportionment of the tolls, rates, and charges; and any such contract may contain provisions for the erection and maintenance of or otherwise for providing warehouses, offices, and other buildings and conveniences, and any other provisions for the purpose of carrying into effect any such arrangement, and any company may apply their funds or moneys for the same purpose.

(2.) Notwithstanding any enactments providing for the charge of equal tolls, rates, and charges, such through tolls, rates, and charges as above mentioned may respectively be computed at a lower toll or rate per mile than the tolls, rates, or charges charged for the passage over and along the same canals of like traffic, not being through traffic, without necessitating or occasioning any reduction of the last-mentioned tolls, rates, or charges.

(3.) Any like contracts and arrangements existing at the passing of this Act shall be, and from the respective dates of the making thereof shall be deemed to have been, as valid as if the same had been made after the commencement of this Act.

**Canal companies may establish clearing system.**
**44.** For the purpose of facilitating through traffic upon canals, any canal companies upon whose canals through tolls, rates, or charges may be in operation, may establish a canal clearing system, on such principles, in such manner, and subject to such regulations as to the admission of other companies to such system, the retirement of members, the appointment of a committee to conduct the business of the system, and of a secretary or other necessary officers, the mode of conducting business, and such other regulations for carrying into effect such system as may from time to time be approved by the Board of Trade in writing under the hand of the secretary or one of the assistant secretaries of that Board; and any company may apply any funds or money belonging to them, for the purpose of establishing or carrying into effect any such system, and the provisions of sections **13 & 14 Vict. c. xxxiii.;** eleven to twenty-six inclusive of the Railway Clearing Act, 1850, shall, mutatis mutandis, apply to any canal clearing system when so established.

**Abandonment of canal.**
**45.**—(1.) Where, on the application of a canal company, it appears to the Board of Trade that any canal or part of a canal belonging to the applicants (hereinafter referred to as an unnecessary canal) is at the time of making the application unnecessary for the purposes of public navigation, or where, on the application of any local authority, or of three or more owners of lands adjoining or near to any canal or part of a canal, it appears to the Board of Trade that that canal or part of a canal (hereinafter referred to as a derelict canal) has for at least three years previously to the making of the application been disused for navigation, or, by reason of the default of the proprietors thereof, has become unfit for navigation, or that the lands adjoining or near thereto have suffered injury by water that has escaped from the derelict canal, and that the proprietors of the derelict canal decline or are unable to effect the repairs necessary to prevent further injury, the Board of Trade may by warrant signed by their secretary authorise the abandonment by the existing proprietors of such unnecessary canal or such derelict canal, and after the granting of the warrant, and the due publication as required

by the Board of Trade of a notice of the granting thereof, the Board of Trade may make an order releasing the canal company or other the proprietors of the unnecessary or derelict canal from all liability to maintain the same canal, and from all statutory and other obligations in respect thereof, or of or consequent on the abandonment thereof.

(2.) In the case of an unnecessary canal no warrant of abandonment shall be granted unless the Board of Trade are satisfied—

(a) That it is unnecessary for the purposes of public navigation ;

(b) That the application has been expressly authorised by a resolution of a majority of the shareholders of the canal company owning the canal present and voting at an extraordinary or special general meeting of that company;

(c) That such public and other notices of the application have been given as the Board of Trade may require;

(d) That compensation (the amount thereof to be determined in case of difference as the Board of Trade may prescribe) has been made to all persons entitled to compensation by reason of the proposed abandonment of the canal.

(3.) In the case of a derelict canal the warrant may be granted on the condition that the canal or any part thereof, with all or any of the powers relating thereto, be transferred to any person, body of persons, or local authority, and where any such condition is imposed the Board of Trade may, if they think fit, frame and embody in a Provisional Order a scheme for the management of the canal or any part thereof.

(4.) The Provisional Order may provide for the constitution of a body to manage the canal or any part thereof, for the transfer to that body or any local authority of the canal or any part thereof, and of all or any of the powers relating thereto, for the limitation or discharge of any liabilities affecting the canal or the owners thereof for the time being, and for any other matters which may appear to the Board of Trade to be necessary or proper for carrying this section into effect.

(5.) The Board of Trade may submit to Parliament for confirmation any Provisional Order made by it in pursuance of this section, but any such order shall be of no force unless and until it is confirmed by Act of Parliament.

(6.) If while the Bill confirming any such order is pending in either House of Parliament, a petition is presented against any order comprised therein, the Bill, so far as it relates to the order, may be referred to a select committee, and the petitioner shall be allowed to appear and oppose as in the case of private Bills.

(7.) In this section the expression "local authority" means any one of the local authorities mentioned in section seven of this Act.

(8.) For the purpose of giving effect to the provisions of this section, the Board of Trade may require the applicants to furnish any evidence in their possession or under their control relative to the application, and may at the expense of the applicants appoint and send an officer to inspect the canal referred to in the application, and to obtain information and evidence in the neighbourhood thereof relative to the proposed abandonment, and may from time to time make regulations as to the mode of making applications, and the nature and mode of publication of notices, and generally as to the conduct of proceedings.

**46.** In this part of this Act the expression "canal company" shall include a "railway and canal company," so far as relating to any canal of any such last-mentioned company.

*Definition of "canal company."*

---

## PART IV.

### MISCELLANEOUS.

**47.** So much of the Regulation of Railways Act, 1873, as limits the time during which that Act shall continue in force shall, save so far as it relates to the appointment of the Commission, be repealed, and the said Act, save as aforesaid, shall be perpetual.

*Perpetuation of 36 & 37 Vict. c. 48.*

Evidence on
rating appeals.
**48.** On any rating appeal, and before any court, where it may be material to show the receipts or profits of a railway company or canal company, or railway and canal company, it shall be lawful for the company to prove the same by written statements or returns verified by the affidavit or statutory declaration of the manager or other responsible officer, and any such statements or returns shall be primâ facie evidence of the facts therein stated with respect to such receipts or profits: Provided that the person by whom any such affidavit or statutory declaration is made shall in every case, if required, attend to be cross-examined thereon.

Recovery and
application of
penalties.
**49.** Every penalty recoverable on summary conviction under this Act may be prosecuted and recovered in the manner directed by the Summary Jurisdiction Acts before a court of summary jurisdiction.

Parties may
appear in person
or by counsel,
&c.
**50.** In any proceedings under this Act any party may appear before the Commissioners either by himself in person or by counsel or solicitor.

Parliamentary
agents entitled
to practise
before Commissioners.
**51.** Any person who shall be certified by the Chairman of Committees of the House of Lords or the Speaker of the House of Commons to have practised for two years before the passing of this Act in promoting or opposing Bills in Parliament shall be entitled to practise in any proceedings under this Act as an attorney or agent before the Commissioners: Provided that every such person so practising as aforesaid shall, in respect of such practice and everything relating thereto, be subject to the jurisdiction and orders of the Commissioners, and further provided that no such person shall practise as aforesaid until his name shall have been entered in a roll to be made and kept, and which is hereby authorised to be made and kept, by the Commissioners.

Saving of
powers conferred on Commissioners and
Board of Trade.
**52.** The powers and jurisdiction conferred by this Act on the Commissioners or Board of Trade shall be in addition to and not in substitution for any powers and jurisdiction vested in the Commissioners or Board of Trade by any statute.

Proceedings of
Board of Trade.
**53.**—(1.) All documents purporting to be rules, orders, or certificates made or issued by the Board of Trade, and to be sealed with the seal of the Board, or to be signed by a secretary or assistant secretary of the Board, or any person authorised in that behalf by the President of the Board, shall be received in evidence, and deemed to be such orders, rules, or certificates without further proof, unless the contrary is shown.

(2.) A certificate signed by the President of the Board of Trade that any order made, certificate issued, or act done, is the order, certificate, or act of the Board of Trade, shall be conclusive evidence of the fact so certified.

Expenses of
local authorities.
**54.**—(1.) Where any local authority having power under this Act to make or oppose any complaint to the Commissioners, or the Board of Trade, or to enter into any agreement to pay the whole or a portion of the expenses of complying with an order of the Commissioners or the Board of Trade, or to make any application for the abandonment or acquisition of a canal under this Act, incur any expenses in or incidental to such complaint, opposition, agreement, or application, such expenses may be defrayed out of the rates or funds out of which the expenses incurred by such authority in the execution of their ordinary duties are defrayed, and if such authority is a rural sanitary authority in England, shall be defrayed as general expenses, unless the Local Government Board direct that they shall be defrayed as special expenses.

(2.) A local authority may enter into any contract involving the payment by themselves and their successors of any expenses authorised by this section to be defrayed.

(3.) Where any such local authority have no power to borrow money for the purpose of defraying any expenses authorised by this section, such authority, if other than a surveyor of highways, may, with the consent of the Board of Trade in the case of any harbour board or conservancy authority, and with the consent of the Local Government Board in the case of any other authority, borrow money in manner provided by the Local Loans
38 & 39 Vict.
c. 83.
Act, 1875, on the security of the rates or funds out of which the expenses are authorised to be defrayed, and the prescribed period for the loan shall be such period as the Board giving such consent may approve.

(4.) On the request of any board whose consent is required for such loan, the Board of Trade or Commissioners shall certify such particulars respecting the amount of the said expenses and the propriety of incurring the same and of borrowing for the payment thereof as may be requested by such board.

(5.) In Ireland, any authority borrowing in pursuance of this section may borrow in manner provided by the Public Health (Ireland) Act, 1878, in like manner as if the provisions of that Act with respect to borrowing were re-enacted in this section, and in terms made applicable thereto.    41 & 42 Vict. c. 52.

**55.** In this Act, unless the context otherwise requires,—    Definitions.

Terms defined by the Regulation of Railways Act, 1873, have the meanings thereby assigned to them:

The term "conservancy authority" means any persons who are otherwise than for private profit intrusted with the duty or invested with the power of conserving, maintaining, or improving the navigation of any tidal or inland water or navigation:

The term "harbour board" means any persons who are otherwise than for private profit intrusted with the duty or invested with the power of constructing, improving, managing, regulating, and maintaining a harbour, whether natural or artificial, or any dock:

The term "Lord Chancellor" means the Lord High Chancellor of Great Britain:

The term "undue preference" includes an undue preference, or an undue or unreasonable prejudice or disadvantage, in any respect, in favour of or against any person or particular class of persons or any particular description of traffic:

The term "terminal charges" includes charges in respect of stations, sidings, wharves, depots, warehouses, cranes, and other similar matters, and of any services rendered thereat:

The term "merchandise" includes goods, cattle, live stock, and animals of all descriptions:

The term "trader" includes any person sending, receiving, or desiring to send merchandise by railway or canal:

The term "home," in relation to merchandise, includes the United Kingdom, the Channel Islands, and the Isle of Man:

The term "rating appeal" means an appeal against any valuation list or against any poor rate or any other local rate:

The term "Summary Jurisdiction Acts" in Scotland means the Summary Procedure Act, 1864, the Summary Jurisdiction (Process) Act, 1881, and any Act or Acts amending the same; and in Ireland, within the police district of Dublin metropolis, the Acts regulating the powers and duties of justices of the peace for such district, or of the police of such district, and elsewhere, the Petty Sessions (Ireland) Act, 1851, and any Act amending the same:    27 & 28 Vict. c. 53. 44 & 45 Vict. c. 24. 14 & 15 Vict. c. 93.

The term "superior court" means, as regards England, the High Court of Justice, as regards Scotland, the Court of Session, and as regards Ireland, the High Court of Justice:

The term "superior court of appeal" means, as regards England, Her Majesty's Court of Appeal; as regards Scotland, the Court of Session in either division of the Inner House; and as regards Ireland, Her Majesty's Court of Appeal.

The term "rules of court" means, as regards Scotland, acts of sederunt.

In the application of this Act to Ireland, the expression "council of a borough," includes town or township commissioners, and any reference to justices in quarter sessions shall be construed to refer to a grand jury; and any reference to the Local Government Board or to an urban or rural sanitary authority, shall be construed to refer to the Local Government Board for Ireland, and to an urban or rural sanitary authority in Ireland.

**56.** This Act shall come into operation on the first day of January one thousand eight hundred and eighty-nine, which day is in this Act referred to as the commencement of this Act: provided that at any time after the passing of this Act any appointment and rules may be made, and other things done for the purpose of bringing this Act into operation at such commencement.    Commencement of Act.

**57.** Subject to general rules to be made under this Act, all proceedings which, at the commencement of this Act, under the Regulation of Railways Act, 1873, and Acts amending it, or under any other Acts, are pending before the Railway Commissioners, shall be transferred to the Railway and Canal Commission under this Act, and may thereupon be continued and concluded in all respects as if such proceedings had been originally instituted before that Commission.    Pending business. 36 & 37 Vict. c. 48.

**Transfer of pending business from superior courts.**

**58.** Every action or proceeding which might have been brought before the Railway Commissioners if this Act had been in force at the time when such action or proceeding was begun, and is at the commencement of this Act pending before any superior court, may, upon the application of either party, be transferred by any judge of such superior court to the Railway and Canal Commissioners under this Act, and may thereupon be continued and concluded in all respects as if such action or proceeding had been originally instituted before that Commission : Provided that no such transfer, nor anything herein contained, shall vary or affect the rights or liabilities of any party to such action or proceeding.

**Repeal.**

**59.**—(1.) The enactments mentioned in the schedule to this Act are hereby repealed to the extent therein specified.

(2.) The repeal effected by this Act shall not affect—

(a) Anything done or suffered before the commencement of this Act under any enactment repealed by this Act, or the expiration of any office which would otherwise have expired by virtue of any enactment repealed by this Act ; nor

(b) Any right or privilege acquired, or duty imposed, or liability or disqualification incurred, under any enactment so repealed ; nor

(c) Any fine, forfeiture, or other punishment incurred or to be incurred in respect of any offence committed or to be committed against any enactment so repealed ; nor

(d) The institution or continuance of any proceeding or other remedy, whether under any enactment so repealed, or otherwise, for ascertaining or enforcing any such liability or disqualification, or enforcing or recovering any such fine, forfeiture, or punishment as aforesaid.

---

## SCHEDULE.

### ACTS REPEALED.

**Section 59.**

*Note.*—A description or citation in this schedule of a portion of an Act is inclusive of the words, section, or other part first and last mentioned, or otherwise referred to as forming the beginning or as forming the end of the portion described in the description or citation.

| Session and Chapter of Act. | Short Title. | Extent of Repeal. |
| --- | --- | --- |
| 17 & 18 Vict. c. 31 | The Railway and Canal Traffic Act, 1854. | Section four and section five. |
| 31 & 32 Vict. c. 119 | The Regulation of Railways Act, 1868. | Section sixteen, paragraph two, from "The provisions of" to the end of the section. |
| 36 & 37 Vict. c. 48 | The Regulation of Railways Act, 1873. | Section three, from "The term 'superior court'" to the end of the section, section four, section eleven, section twelve, section thirteen, section twenty-one, section twenty-two, section twenty-three, section twenty-four, section twenty-five, section twenty-six, from the words "The Commissioners may review" to the end of the section, section twenty-eight, section twenty-nine, section thirty-four, and section thirty-seven. |
| 37 & 38 Vict. c. 40 | The Board of Trade Arbitrations, &c. Act, 1874. | Section eight, from "and shall continue in force" to "expiration." |

## 51 & 52 VICT. C. 62.

*An Act to amend the Law with respect to Preferential Payments in Bankruptcy, and in the winding-up of Companies.*

[*24th December,* 1888.]

**1.**—(1.) In the distribution of the property of a bankrupt, and in the distribution of the assets of any company being wound up under the Companies Act, 1862, and the Acts amending the same, there shall be paid in priority to all other debts— *Priority of debts.*

(a) All parochial or other local rates due from the bankrupt or the company at the date of the receiving order or, as the case may be, the commencement of the winding-up, and having become due and payable within twelve months next before that time, and all assessed taxes, land tax, property or income tax assessed on the bankrupt or the company up to the fifth day of April next before the date of the receiving order, or, as the case may be, the commencement of the winding-up, and not exceeding in the whole one year's assessment;

(b) All wages or salary of any clerk or servant in respect of services rendered to the bankrupt or the company during four months before the date of the receiving order, or, as the case may be, the commencement of the winding-up, not exceeding fifty pounds; and

(c) All wages of any labourer or workman not exceeding twenty-five pounds, whether payable for time or for piece work, in respect of services rendered to the bankrupt or the company during two months before the date of the receiving order or, as the case may be, the commencement of the winding-up: Provided that where any labourer in husbandry has entered into a contract for the payment of a portion of his wages in a lump sum at the end of the year of hiring, he shall have priority in respect of the whole of such sum, or a part thereof, as the Court may decide to be due under the contract, proportionate to the time of service up to the date of the receiving order, or, as the case may be, the commencement of the winding-up.

(2.) The foregoing debts shall rank equally between themselves and shall be paid in full, unless the property of the bankrupt is, or the assets of the company are, insufficient to meet them, in which case they shall abate in equal proportions between themselves.

(3.) Subject to the retention of such sums as may be necessary for the costs of administration or otherwise, the foregoing debts shall be discharged forthwith so far as the property of the debtor, or the assets of the company, as the case may be, is or are sufficient to meet them.

(4.) In the event of a landlord or other person distraining or having distrained on any goods or effects of a bankrupt or a company being wound up within three months next before the date of the receiving order or the winding-up order respectively, the debts to which priority is given by this section shall be a first charge on the goods or effects so distrained on, or the proceeds of the sale thereof.

Provided, that in respect of any money paid under any such charge the landlord or other person shall have the same rights of priority as the person to whom such payment is made.

(5.) This section, so far as it relates to the property of a bankrupt, shall have effect as part of section forty of the Bankruptcy Act, 1883.

(6.) This section shall apply, in the case of a deceased person who dies insolvent, as if he were a bankrupt, and as if the date of his death were substituted for the date of the receiving order.

**2.**—(1.) Nothing in this Act shall alter the effect of section five of the Act twenty-eight and twenty-nine Victoria, chapter eighty-six, "To amend the law of partnership," or shall prejudice the provisions of the Friendly Societies Act, 1875, or shall affect the priority given to the payment of funeral and testamentary expenses by section one hundred and twenty-five of the Bankruptcy Act, 1883. *Savings.*

(2.) Nothing in this Act shall affect the provisions of the Stannaries Act, 1887.

Application of Act.

**3.** This Act shall apply only in the case of receiving orders and orders for the administration of the estates of deceased debtors according to the law of bankruptcy made and windings-up commenced after the commencement of this Act.

Extent of Act.

**4.** This Act shall not apply to Ireland.

Repeal.

**5.** The enactments specified in the schedule hereto are hereby repealed to the extent in the third column of that schedule mentioned.

Short title.

**6.** This Act may be cited as the Preferential Payments in Bankruptcy Act, 1888.

## SCHEDULE.
### ENACTMENTS REPEALED.

| Session and Chapter. | Title. | Extent of Repeal. |
| --- | --- | --- |
| 46 & 47 Vict. c. 28 | The Companies Act, 1883. | The whole Act except as regards its application to Ireland. |
| 46 & 47 Vict. c. 52 | The Bankruptcy Act, 1883. | Section forty, sub-sections one and two. |
| 49 & 50 Vict. c. 28 | The Bankruptcy (Agricultural Labourers' Wages) Act, 1886. | The whole Act. |

---

## 52 & 53 VICT. c. 21.

*An Act for amending the Law relating to Weights and Measures, and for other purposes connected therewith.*

[26th July, 1889.]

### PART I.

#### Weights and Measures.

Verification of weighing instruments.

**1.**—(1.) Every weighing instrument used for trade shall be verified and stamped by an inspector of weights and measures with a stamp of verification under this Act.

(2.) Every person who, after the expiration of twelve months from the commencement of this Act, uses, or has in his possession for use, for trade any weighing instrument not stamped as required by this Act, shall be liable to a fine not exceeding two pounds, or in the case of a second offence five pounds.

(3.) The power of making bye-laws conferred by section fifty-three of the principal Act (a) shall extend to the making of bye-laws for giving effect to this section.

(4.) Section thirty-two of the principal Act (a) shall apply to weighing instruments in like manner as it applies to weights and measures.

Local verification of metric weights and measures.

**2.** The Board of Trade may, if they think fit, at the expense of the local authority, deposit with any inspector of weights and measures copies of any of the metric standards in their custody, and cause to be verified with any copy so deposited any metric weights and measures which can under section thirty-eight of the principal Act be compared with the metric standards in their custody.

Amendment of 41 & 42 Vict. c. 49, ss. 25 and 26.

**3.** The fine for a second or a subsequent offence under section twenty-five or section twenty-six of the principal Act (a) shall be a sum not exceeding twenty pounds, and the provisions of the said section twenty-six with respect to forfeiture shall apply to weighing instruments in like manner as they apply to weights, measures, scales, balances, and steelyards.

(a) 41 & 42 Vict. c. 49, *supra*.

**4.** Where a person is convicted under any section of the principal Act or this Act of a second or subsequent offence, and the Court by which he is convicted is of opinion that such offence was committed with intent to defraud, he shall be liable, in addition to or in lieu of any fine, to be imprisoned with or without hard labour for a term not exceeding two months.

*Liability to imprisonment in cases of fraud.*

**5.** [Repeal of 41 & 42 Vict. c. 49, ss. 16, 46.]

**6.** [New denominations of standards.]

**7.** Any local authority may provide for the use of their officers working standards of measure and weight, and scale-beams of such material and in such form as the Board of Trade may approve, and those standards may, if verified in such manner as the Board of Trade from time to time direct, be used for the inspection and verification of weights and measures as if they were local standards.

*Working standards.*

**8.** [Power for Board of Trade to take fees.]

**9.** [Local authorities or persons having power to appoint inspectors of weights and measures, with the approval of the Board of Trade, to make general regulations for the guidance of inspectors.]

**10.** [Provision as to local inquiries.]

**11.** [Qualification of inspectors of weights and measures.]

**12.**—(1.) An inspector of weights and measures shall not, during the time he holds office, be a person deriving any profit from or employed in the making, adjusting, or selling of weights, measures, or measuring or weighing instruments :

*Inspector not to be maker, seller, or adjuster of weights, measures, or weighing instruments.*

(2.) Provided that in any district where, on the representation of the local authority, it appears to be desirable for an inspector of weights and measures to be allowed to adjust weights and measures, the Board of Trade may, if they think fit, authorise an inspector appointed by that local authority to act as an adjuster of weights and measures.

(3.) An inspector so authorised may for any such adjustment make such charges as the local authority approve, and shall account for and pay any money received by him in respect of such charges in such manner as the local authority direct.

**13.** [Inspectors may take in respect of the verification and stamping of weights, measures, and weighing instruments the fees specified in the First Schedule.]

**14.** Where a person is convicted before any Court of any offence under the principal Act or this Act, the Court may, if it thinks fit, cause the conviction to be published in such manner as it thinks desirable.

*Publication of convictions.*

**15.** The provisions of the principal Act and of this Act as to the verification and re-verification of local and working standards shall apply to the standards used by any local authority in testing meters under the Act of the Session held in the twenty-second and twenty-third years of the reign of Her present Majesty, chapter sixty-six, intituled "An Act for regulating measures used in sales of gas," and the Acts amending the same.

*Application of 41 & 42 Vict. c. 49, s. 66, to gas standards.*

**16.** [Powers to London County Council to exercise jurisdiction throughout the county.]

**17.** [Provision as to city of London.]

**18.** [Provision of copies of local standards in Ireland.]

**19.** [Amendment of 41 & 42 Vict. c. 49, as to inspectors in Ireland.]

---

## PART II.

### *Sale of Coal.*

**20.**—(1.) All coal shall be sold by weight only, except where by the written consent of the purchaser it is sold by boat load or by waggons or tubs delivered from the colliery into the works of the purchaser.

*Coal to be sold by weight.*

(2.) If any person sells coal otherwise than is required by this section he shall be liable to a fine not exceeding five pounds for every such sale.

**21.** [Weight ticket or note to be delivered on delivery of coal over two hundredweight.]

**22.** [Tare weight of vehicle where coal sold in bulk.]

**23.** [Frauds by drivers of coal carts.]

**24.** [Penalty on deficiency in weight of coal on small sales.]
**25.** [Weighing instrument to be kept in place where coal sold by retail.]
**26.** [Local authorities may erect and maintain fixed weighing instruments at convenient places for the purpose of weighing coal, and may provide portable weighing instruments for the same purpose.]
**27.** [Power to require weighment of coal or vehicle.]
**28.** [Local authorities may make byelaws.]
**29.** [Power to weigh coal in shop or vehicle.]
**30.** [Power to make local exemptions.]
**31.** This part of this Act, except the provision requiring coal to be sold by weight only, shall not extend to Scotland.

---

## PART III.

### *Bread.*

Explanation of law as to bakers.

**32.** Nothing in the enactments referred to in the Fourth Schedule to this Act shall render any baker or seller of bread, or the journeyman, servant, or other person employed by such baker or seller of bread, liable to any forfeiture or penalty for refusing to weigh in the presence of the purchaser any bread conveyed or carried out in any cart or other carriage, unless he is requested so to do by or on behalf of the purchaser.

---

## PART IV.

### *Supplemental.*

Saving for liabilities otherwise than under Act.

**33.**—(1.) No proceeding or conviction for any offence punishable under this Act shall affect any civil remedy to which any person aggrieved by the offence may be entitled.

(2.) This Act shall not exempt any person from any indictment or other proceeding for an offence which is punishable at common law or under some Act of Parliament other than this Act, so that no person be punished twice for the same offence.

(3.) Where proceedings are taken before any Court against any person in respect of any offence punishable under this Act, and the offence is also punishable at common law or under some Act of Parliament other than this Act, the Court may direct that, instead of those proceedings being continued, proceedings shall be taken against that person at common law or under some Act of Parliament other than this Act.

Construction of Act.

**34.** This Act and the principal Act shall be construed together as one Act.

Definitions.

**35.** In this Act, unless the context otherwise requires,—

"Weighing instrument" includes scales, with the weights belonging thereto, scale-beams, balances, spring-balances, steelyards, weighing machines, and other instruments for weighing:

"Measuring instrument" includes any instrument for the measurement of length, capacity, volume, temperature, pressure, or gravity, or for the measurement and determination of electrical quantities:

"Vehicle" means any carriage, cart, waggon, truck, barrow, or other means of carrying coal by land, in whatever manner the same may be drawn or propelled, but does not include a railway truck or waggon:

"Inspector" means an inspector under the principal Act:

Other expressions have the same meaning as in the principal Act: Provided that the expression "local authority" shall, in its application to England, be construed subject to the provisions of the Local Government Act, 1888, and the expression "weighing machine" in the principal Act shall include any weighing instrument as defined by this Act.

51 & 52 Vict. c. 41.

**36.**—(1.) The enactments specified in the Fifth Schedule to this Act are Repeal. hereby repealed to the extent mentioned in the third column of that schedule.

(2.) The repeal of any enactment by this Act shall not affect—

(a) the past operation of any enactment so repealed, or anything duly done or suffered under any enactment so repealed; or

(b) any right or liability acquired or incurred under any enactment so repealed; or

(c) any penalty, forfeiture, or punishment incurred in respect of any offence committed against any enactment so repealed; or

(d) any power, legal proceeding, or remedy in respect of any such right, liability, penalty, forfeiture, or punishment as aforesaid; and any such power, legal proceeding, and remedy may be exercised and carried on as if this Act had not passed.

**37.** This Act shall come into operation on the first day of January one Commencement. thousand eight hundred and ninety, which date is in this Act referred to as the commencement of this Act:

Provided as follows:

(a) At any time after the passing of this Act any appointment, byelaw, or regulation may be made, and any other thing may be done, which appears to a local authority to be necessary or proper for the purpose of bringing this Act into operation at the commencement thereof;

(b) In Ireland, where a grand jury is the local authority, so much of this Act as concerns the powers and duties of the local authority and the consequences of the exercise of such powers and duties shall come into operation on the first day of May one thousand eight hundred and ninety.

**38.** [Saving for corporation of Dublin.]

---

## FIRST SCHEDULE.

Section 13.

*Fees to be taken on the verification and stamping of Weights, Measures, and Weighing Instruments by Inspectors of Local Authorities.*

### Weights.

|  | s. | d. |
|---|---|---|
| Avoirdupois: |  |  |
| Each weight of 100 lb. (cental) | 0 | 4 |
| ,, ,, ,, 56 lb. and 28 lb. | 0 | 3 |
| ,, ,, ,, 14 lb. and 7 lb. | 0 | 2 |
| ,, ,, from 4 lb. to 1 lb., inclusive | 0 | 1 |
| ,, ,, ,, 8 oz. to $\frac{1}{2}$ dram, inclusive | 0 | $0\frac{1}{4}$ |
| ,, ,, ,, 4,000 grains to $\frac{1}{100}$th of a grain, inclusive | 0 | $0\frac{1}{2}$ |
| ,, ,, ,, 240 to 24 grains, inclusive, commonly called pennyweights | 0 | $0\frac{1}{2}$ |
| Troy: |  |  |
| Each weight from 500 oz. to 100 oz., inclusive | 0 | 4 |
| ,, ,, ,, 50 oz. to 10 oz., inclusive | 0 | 2 |
| ,, ,, ,, 5 oz. to $\frac{1}{1000}$th of an oz., inclusive | 0 | 1 |
| Apothecaries: |  |  |
| Each weight from 10 oz. to 1 oz., inclusive | 0 | 2 |
| ,, ,, ,, 4 drachms to $\frac{1}{2}$ grain, inclusive | 0 | 1 |

### Measures.

|  | s. | d. |
|---|---|---|
| Length: |  |  |
| Each measure from 100 feet to 7 feet, inclusive | 0 | 3 |
| ,, ,, ,, 6 feet to 4 feet, inclusive | 0 | 2 |
| ,, ,, of a yard, 2 feet, foot, and inch respectively, including their subdivisions | 0 | 1 |
| Measures from 0·500 to 0·001 inch, in the form of wire-gauge plates: |  |  |
| For each notch, or for each internal gauge or separate size, from half an inch to $\frac{1}{1000}$th of an inch | 0 | $0\frac{1}{4}$ |

Capacity:

| | *s.* | *d.* |
|---|---|---|
| Dry and liquid measures : | | |
| Each measure of 4 bushels (32 gallons) and 1 bushel (8 gallons).. | 0 | 6 |
|   ,,     ,,   from 5 gallons to 2 gallons (peck), inclusive .... | 0 | 3 |
|   ,,     ,,   ,, 1 gallon to a $\frac{1}{4}$ gill, inclusive.............. | 0 | 1 |

Apothecaries :

| | *s.* | *d.* |
|---|---|---|
| Each subdivided measure containing : | | |
| Not more than twelve subdivisions ........................ | 0 | 1 |
| More than twelve subdivisions but not more than fifteen ...... | 0 | $1\frac{1}{4}$ |
| More than fifteen subdivisions but not more than eighteen .... | 0 | $1\frac{1}{2}$ |
| More than eighteen subdivisions but not more than twenty-one | 0 | $1\frac{3}{4}$ |
| More than twenty-one subdivisions but not more than twenty-four ...... | 0 | 2 |
| More than twenty-four subdivisions but not more than thirty .. | 0 | $2\frac{1}{2}$ |
| More than thirty subdivisions but not more than thirty-six .... | 0 | 3 |
| More than thirty-six subdivisions but not more than forty-two.. | 0 | $3\frac{1}{2}$ |
| More than forty-two subdivisions but not more than fifty...... | 0 | 4 |
| More than fifty subdivisions but not more than one hundred .. | 0 | 6 |
| More than one hundred subdivisions but not more than one hundred and fifty ...................................... | 0 | 9 |
| More than one hundred and fifty................‚............. | 1 | 0 |
| Each separate measure from 40 fluid oz. to 10 fluid oz., inclusive.. | 0 | 2 |
|   ,,    ,,    ,,    ,, 10 fluid oz. ..................... | 0 | $0\frac{1}{2}$ |

*Weighing Instruments.*

| | *s.* | *d.* |
|---|---|---|
| For 10 tons and above ................................... | 10 | 0 |
| For under 10 tons and above 1 ton ........................ | 5 | 0 |
| For 1 ton and above 5 cwt. ............................... | 2 | 0 |
| For 5 cwt. and above 1 cwt.............................. | 1 | 6 |
| For 1 cwt. and above 56 lbs............................... | 1 | 0 |
|   exclusive of cost of cartage and lifting of standards in each of the above cases. | | |
| For 56 lb. and above 14 lb. .............................. | 0 | 6 |
| For 14 lbs. and above 1 lb. .............................. | 0 | 3 |
| For 1 lb. or under ...................................... | 0 | 2 |

Section 21.

## THIRD SCHEDULE.

*Weight Ticket or Consignment Note on delivery of Coal over Two Hundredweight.*

Mr. *A. B.* [*here insert the name of the buyer*].

| Take notice that you are to receive herewith | tons | cwt. | lbs. |
|---|---|---|---|

of coal.

[*When sold in sacks, add*]

| in    sacks, each containing | cwt. |
|---|---|

[*When sold in bulk, add*]

| | tons | cwts. | lbs. |
|---|---|---|---|
| Weight of coal and vehicle .............. | | | |
| Tare weight of vehicle.................. | | | |
| Net weight of coal herewith delivered to purchaser ........................ | | | |

*C. D.* [*here insert the name of the seller*].

*E. F.* [*here insert the name of the person in charge of the vehicle*].

Where coal is delivered by means of a vehicle, the seller must deliver or send by post or otherwise to the purchaser or his servant, before any part of the coal is unloaded, a ticket or note in this form.

Any seller of coal who delivers a less quantity than is stated in this ticket or note is liable to a fine.

Any person attending on a vehicle used for the delivery of coal who, having received a ticket or note for delivery to the purchaser, refuses or neglects to deliver it to the purchaser or his servant, is liable to a fine.

## FOURTH SCHEDULE. Section 32.

| Session and Chapter. | Title. | Enactments referred to. |
|---|---|---|
| 3 Geo. 4, c. cvi..... | An Act to repeal the Acts now in force relating to bread to be sold in the city of London and the liberties thereof, and within the weekly bills of mortality, and ten miles of the Royal Exchange; and to provide other regulations for the making and sale of bread, and preventing the adulteration of meal, flour, and bread, within the limits aforesaid. | Section nine. |
| 6 & 7 Will. 4, c. 37.. | An Act to repeal the several Acts now in force relating to bread to be sold out of the city of London and the liberties thereof, and beyond the weekly bills of mortality, and ten miles of the Royal Exchange; and to provide other regulations for the making and sale of bread, and for preventing the adulteration of meal, flour, and bread, beyond the limits aforesaid. | Section seven. |

## FIFTH SCHEDULE.
### ENACTMENTS REPEALED. Section 36.

| Session and Chapter. | Short Title. | Extent of Repeal. |
|---|---|---|
| 41 & 42 Vict. c. 49.. | The Weights and Measures Act, 1878. | Section sixteen. Section forty-three, from "A maker or seller of weights" to "measures under this Act." Section forty-six. Section forty-seven. Section eighty-six, so far as it re-enacts section nine of the Weights and Measures Act, 1835. The Fifth Schedule. |

### 52 & 53 VICT. C. 24.

*An Act to repeal certain Statutes, relating to Master and Servants in particular Manufactures, which have ceased to be put in force, or have become unnecessary by the enactment of subsequent Statutes.*

[26th July, 1889.]

### 52 & 53 VICT. C. 43.

*An Act to Amend the Law relating to the Measurement of the Tonnage of Merchant Ships.*     [26th August, 1889.]

1.—(1.) In the measurement of a ship for the purpose of ascertaining her register tonnage, no deduction shall be allowed in respect of any space which has not been first included in the measurement of her tonnage. Amendment of rules for measurement of tonnage.

(2.) In section twenty-one, paragraph (4), of the Merchant Shipping Act, 1854, the words "First, that nothing shall be added for a closed-in space solely appropriated to the berthing of the crew, unless such space exceeds one-twentieth of the remaining tonnage of the ship, and in case of such excess the excess only shall be added; and secondly"; and in section twenty-two, paragraph (2), of the same Act the words "subject to the deduction for a closed-in space appropriated to the crew, as mentioned in Rule I." shall be repealed.

Provided that this section shall not apply until after the expiration of five years from the date of the passing of this Act to any ship in the measurement or re-measurement of which the deductions prohibited by this section have been made before the tenth day of March one thousand eight hundred and eighty-nine, or to any ship the building of which was commenced before the tenth day of March one thousand eight hundred and eighty-nine, and which is registered for the first time between that date and the last day of December one thousand eight hundred and eighty-nine, unless in either case the ship is, before the expiration of the said five years, measured or re-measured in accordance with the provisions of this Act, and any such ship may be measured or re-measured at the request of the owner.

But this exemption shall not extend to any ship in the case of which the allowance for propelling-power space exceeds fifty per cent. of the gross tonnage of the ship.

Subject as aforesaid, the tonnage of every ship shall be estimated for all purposes as if any deduction prohibited by this section had not been made, and the particulars relating to the ship's tonnage in the register book, and in her certificate of registry, shall be corrected accordingly.

Rule as to allowance for engine-room in steamers.

2. In the case of any ship built or measured after the passing of this Act, such portion of the space or spaces above the crown of the engine room and above the upper deck as is framed in for the machinery or for the admission of light and air, shall not be included in the measurement of the space occupied by the propelling power, except in pursuance of a request in writing to the Board of Trade by the owner of the ship, and shall not be included in pursuance of such request unless:—

(a) that portion is first included in the measurement of the gross tonnage; and

(b) a surveyor appointed under the Fourth Part of the Merchant Shipping Act, 1854, certifies that the portion so framed in is reasonable in extent and is so constructed as to be safe and seaworthy, and that it cannot be used for any purpose other than the machinery or for the admission of light and air to the machinery or boilers of the ship.

Deductions for navigation spaces, &c.

3.—(1.) In measuring or re-measuring a ship for the purpose of ascertaining her register tonnage, the following deductions shall be made from the space included in the measurement of the tonnage:—

(a) In the case of a ship wholly propelled by sails, any space set apart and used exclusively for the storage of sails:

(b) In the case of any ship—

(i.) Any space used exclusively for the accommodation of the master;

(ii.) Any space used exclusively for the working of the helm, the capstan, and the anchor gear, or for keeping the charts, signals, and other instruments of navigation, and boatswain's stores; and

(iii.) The space occupied by the donkey engine and boiler, if connected with the main pumps of the ship.

(2.) The deductions allowed under this section shall be subject to the following provisions, namely :—

(a) The space deducted must be certified by a surveyor appointed by the Board of Trade as reasonable in extent and properly and efficiently constructed for the purpose for which it is intended;

(b) There must be permanently marked in or over every such space a notice stating the purpose to which it is to be applied and that whilst so applied it is to be deducted from the tonnage of the ship;

(c) The deduction on account of space for storage of sails must not exceed two and a half per cent. of the tonnage of the ship.

**4.** In the case of a screw steamship which, at the passing of this Act, has an engine-room allowance of thirty-two per cent. of the gross tonnage of the ship, and in which any crew space on deck has not been included in the gross tonnage, whether its contents have been deducted therefrom or not, the crew space shall be, on the application of the owner of the ship, or by direction of the Board of Trade, measured and its contents ascertained and added to the registered tonnage of the ship; and if it appears that with such addition to the tonnage the engine room does not occupy more than thirteen per cent. of the tonnage of the ship, the existing allowance for engine room of thirty-two per cent. of the tonnage shall be continued, notwithstanding anything in this Act. *(Provisions as to deductions in case of certain steamships.)*

**5.** In the case of a ship constructed with a double bottom for water ballast, if the space between the inner and outer plating thereof is certified by a surveyor appointed by the Board of Trade to be not available for the carriage of cargo, stores, or fuel, then the depth required by section twenty-one, paragraph (2), of the Merchant Shipping Act, 1854, shall be taken to be the upper side of the inner plating of the double bottom, and that upper side shall, for the purposes of measurement, be deemed to represent the floor timber referred to in that section. *(Measurement of ships with double bottoms for water ballast.)*

**6.** If and whenever it is made to appear to Her Majesty that the tonnage of any foreign ship, as measured by the rules of the country to which she belongs, materially differs from that which would be her tonnage if measured under the Merchant Shipping Act, 1854, and the Acts amending the same, Her Majesty may from time to time, by Order in Council, direct that, notwithstanding any Order in Council for the time being in force under those Acts, any of the ships of that country may, for all or any of the purposes of those Acts, be re-measured in accordance with the provisions of those Acts, and Her Majesty may revoke any Order so made. *(Re-measurement of foreign ships.)*

---

## 52 & 53 VICT. C. 45.

*An Act to amend and consolidate the Factors Acts.*

[*26th August*, 1889.]

### *Preliminary.*

**1.** For the purposes of this Act— *(efinitions.)*

(1.) The expression "mercantile agent" shall mean a mercantile agent having in the customary course of his business as such agent authority either to sell goods, or to consign goods for the purpose of sale, or to buy goods, or to raise money on the security of goods:

(2.) A person shall be deemed to be in possession of goods or of the documents of title to goods, where the goods or documents are in his actual custody or are held by any other person subject to his control or for him or on his behalf:

(3.) The expression "goods" shall include wares and merchandise :

(4.) The expression "document of title" shall include any bill of lading, dock warrant, warehouse-keeper's certificate, and warrant or order for the delivery of goods, and any other document used in the ordinary course of business as proof of the possession or control of goods, or authorising or purporting to authorise, either by endorsement or by delivery, the possessor of the document to transfer or receive goods thereby represented :

(5.) The expression "pledge" shall include any contract pledging, or giving a lien or security on, goods, whether in consideration of an original advance or of any further or continuing advance or of any pecuniary liability :

(6.) The expression "person" shall include any body of persons corporate or unincorporate.

### *Dispositions by Mercantile Agents.*

**2.**—(1.) Where a mercantile agent is, with the consent of the owner, in possession of goods or of the documents of title to goods, any sale, pledge, or other disposition of the goods, made by him when acting in the ordinary course of business of a mercantile agent, shall, subject to the provisions of this Act, be as valid as if he were expressly authorised by the owner of the goods to make the same; provided that the person taking under the disposition acts in good faith, and has not at the time of the disposition notice that the person making the disposition has not authority to make the same. *(Powers of mercantile agent with respect to disposition of goods.)*

(2.) Where a mercantile agent has, with the consent of the owner, been in possession of goods or of the documents of title to goods, any sale, pledge, or other disposition, which would have been valid if the consent had continued, shall be valid notwithstanding the determination of the consent: provided that the person taking under the disposition has not at the time thereof notice that the consent has been determined.

(3.) Where a mercantile agent has obtained possession of any documents of title to goods by reason of his being or having been, with the consent of the owner, in possession of the goods represented thereby, or of any other documents of title to the goods, his possession of the first-mentioned documents shall, for the purposes of this Act, be deemed to be with the consent of the owner.

(4.) For the purposes of this Act the consent of the owner shall be presumed in the absence of evidence to the contrary.

**Effect of pledges of documents of title.** 3. A pledge of the documents of title to goods shall be deemed to be a pledge of the goods.

**Pledge for antecedent debt.** 4. Where a mercantile agent pledges goods as security for a debt or liability due from the pledgor to the pledgee before the time of the pledge, the pledgee shall acquire no further right to the goods than could have been enforced by the pledgor at the time of the pledge.

**Rights acquired by exchange of goods or documents.** 5. The consideration necessary for the validity of a sale, pledge, or other disposition, of goods, in pursuance of this Act, may be either a payment in cash, or the delivery or transfer of other goods, or of a document of title to goods, or of a negotiable security, or any other valuable consideration; but where goods are pledged by a mercantile agent in consideration of the delivery or transfer of other goods, or of a document of title to goods, or of a negotiable security, the pledgee shall acquire no right or interest in the goods so pledged in excess of the value of the goods, documents, or security when so delivered or transferred in exchange.

**Agreements through clerks, &c.** 6. For the purposes of this Act an agreement made with a mercantile agent through a clerk or other person authorised in the ordinary course of business to make contracts of sale or pledge on his behalf shall be deemed to be an agreement with the agent.

**Provisions as to consignors and consignees.** 7.—(1.) Where the owner of goods has given possession of the goods to another person for the purpose of consignment or sale, or has shipped the goods in the name of another person, and the consignee of the goods has not had notice that such person is not the owner of the goods, the consignee shall, in respect of advances made to or for the use of such person, have the same lien on the goods as if such person were the owner of the goods, and may transfer any such lien to another person.

(2.) Nothing in this section shall limit or affect the validity of any sale, pledge, or disposition, by a mercantile agent.

### Dispositions by Sellers and Buyers of Goods.

**Disposition by seller remaining in possession.** 8. Where a person, having sold goods, continues, or is, in possession of the goods or of the documents of title to the goods, the delivery or transfer by that person, or by a mercantile agent acting for him, of the goods or documents of title under any sale, pledge, or other disposition thereof, or under any agreement for sale, pledge, or other disposition thereof, to any person receiving the same in good faith and without notice of the previous sale, shall have the same effect as if the person making the delivery or transfer were expressly authorised by the owner of the goods to make the same.

**Disposition by buyer obtaining possession.** 9. Where a person, having bought or agreed to buy goods, obtains with the consent of the seller possession of the goods or the documents of title to the goods, the delivery or transfer, by that person or by a mercantile agent acting for him, of the goods or documents of title, under any sale, pledge, or other disposition thereof, or under any agreement for sale, pledge, or other disposition thereof, to any person receiving the same in good faith and without notice of any lien or other right of the original seller in respect of the goods, shall have the same effect as if the person making the delivery or transfer were a mercantile agent in possession of the goods or documents of title with the consent of the owner.

**Effect of transfer of documents on vendor's lien or right of stoppage in transitu.** 10. Where a document of title to goods has been lawfully transferred to a person as a buyer or owner of the goods, and that person transfers the document to a person who takes the document in good faith and for valuable consideration, the last-mentioned transfer shall have the same effect for defeating any vendor's lien or right of stoppage in transitu as the transfer of a bill of lading has for defeating the right of stoppage in transitu.

### *Supplemental.*

**11.** For the purposes of this Act, the transfer of a document may be by endorsement, or, where the document is by custom or by its express terms transferable by delivery, or makes the goods deliverable to the bearer, then by delivery. *Mode of transferring documents.*

**12.**—(1.) Nothing in this Act shall authorise an agent to exceed or depart from his authority as between himself and his principal, or exempt him from any liability, civil or criminal, for so doing. *Saving for rights of true owner.*

(2.) Nothing in this Act shall prevent the owner of goods from recovering the goods from an agent or his trustee in bankruptcy at any time before the sale or pledge thereof, or shall prevent the owner of goods pledged by an agent from having the right to redeem the goods at any time before the sale thereof, on satisfying the claim for which the goods were pledged, and paying to the agent, if by him required, any money in respect of which the agent would by law be entitled to retain the goods or the documents of title thereto, or any of them, by way of lien as against the owner, or from recovering from any person with whom the goods have been pledged any balance of money remaining in his hands as the produce of the sale of the goods after deducting the amount of his lien. .

(3.) Nothing in this Act shall prevent the owner of goods sold by an agent from recovering from the buyer the price agreed to be paid for the same, or any part of that price, subject to any right of set off on the part of the buyer against the agent.

**13.** The provisions of this Act shall be construed in amplification and not in derogation of the powers exercisable by an agent independently of this Act. *Saving for common law powers of agent.*

**14.** The enactments mentioned in the schedule to this Act are hereby repealed as from the commencement of this Act, but this repeal shall not affect any right acquired or liability incurred before the commencement of this Act under any enactment hereby repealed. *Repeal.*

**15.** This Act shall commence and come into operation on the first day of January one thousand eight hundred and ninety. *Commencement.*

**16.** This Act shall not extend to Scotland. *Extent of Act.*

**17.** This Act may be cited as the Factors Act, 1889. *Short title.*

### SCHEDULE.
#### ENACTMENTS REPEALED.

*Section 14.*

| Session and Chapter. | Title. | Extent of Repeal. |
|---|---|---|
| 4 Geo. 4, c. 83 .. | An Act for the better protection of the property of merchants and others who may hereafter enter into contracts or agreements in relation to goods, wares, or merchandises entrusted to factors or agents. | The whole Act. |
| 6 Geo. 4, c. 94 .. | An Act to alter and amend an Act for the better protection of the property of merchants and others who may hereafter enter into contracts or agreements in relation to goods, wares, or merchandise entrusted to factors or agents. | The whole Act. |
| 5 & 6 Vict. c. 39.. | An Act to amend the law relating to advances bonâ fide made to agents entrusted with goods. | The whole Act. |
| 40 & 41 Vict. c. 39 | An Act to amend the Factors Acts. | The whole Act. |

52 & 53 VICT. c. 46.

*An Act to amend the Merchant Shipping Act, 1854, and the Acts amending the same.*

[*26th August,* 1889.]

**Remedies for recovery of master's disbursements.**

**1.** Every master of a ship and every person lawfully acting as master of a ship by reason of the decease or incapacity from illness of the master of the ship, shall, so far as the case permits, have the same rights, liens, and remedies for the recovery of disbursements properly made by him on account of the ship, and for liabilities properly incurred by him on account of the ship, as a master of a ship now has for the recovery of his wages; and if in any proceeding in any Court of Admiralty or Vice Admiralty, or in any County Court having Admiralty jurisdiction, touching the claim of a master or any person lawfully acting as master to wages or such disbursements or liabilities as aforesaid, any right of set-off or counterclaim is set up, it shall be lawful for the Court to enter into and adjudicate upon all questions, and to settle all accounts then arising or outstanding and unsettled between the parties to the proceeding, and to direct payment of any balance which is found to be due.

**Restrictions on advance notes.**

**2.**—(1.) Any agreement with a seaman made under section one hundred and forty-nine of the Merchant Shipping Act, 1854 (*a*), may contain a stipulation for payment to or on behalf of the seaman, conditionally on his going to sea in pursuance of the agreement, of a sum not exceeding the amount of one month's wages payable to the seaman under the agreement.

(2.) Save as authorised by this section, any agreement by or on behalf of the employer of a seaman for the payment of money to or on behalf of the seaman conditionally on his going to sea from any port in the United Kingdom shall be void, and no money paid in satisfaction or in respect of any such agreement shall be deducted from the seaman's wages, and no person shall have any right of action, suit, or set-off against the seaman or his assignee in respect of any money so paid or purporting to have been so paid.

(3.) Nothing in this section shall affect any allotment made under the Merchant Shipping Act, 1854, or the Acts amending the same.

(4.) Section two of the Merchant Seamen (Payment of Wages and Rating) Act, 1880, is hereby repealed.

**Register of deserters.**

**3.** Every superintendent of a mercantile marine office shall keep at his office a list of the seamen who, to the best of his knowledge and belief, have deserted or failed to join their ships after signing an agreement to proceed to sea in them, and shall on request show this list to any master of a ship.

A superintendent of a mercantile marine office shall not be liable in respect of any entry made in good faith in the list so kept.

**Rule as to payment of British seamen in foreign money.**

**4.** Where a seamen has agreed with the master of a British ship for payment of his wages in British sterling or any other money, any payment of, or on account of, his wages if made in any other currency than that stated in the agreement shall, notwithstanding anything in the agreement, be made at the rate of exchange for the money stated in the agreement for the time being current at the place where the payment is made.

**Provisions as to steamships to apply to ships propelled by electricity, &c.**

**5.** The provisions of the Merchant Shipping Act, 1854, and the Acts amending the same, with respect to steamships, shall apply to ships propelled by electricity or other mechanical power, with such modifications as the Board of Trade may from time to time prescribe for purposes of adaptation.

(*a*) *Supra.*

## 52 & 53 VICT. c. 49.

*An Act for amending and consolidating the Enactments relating to Arbitration.*    [*26th August,* 1889.]

### *References by Consent out of Court.*

**1.** A submission, unless a contrary intention is expressed therein, shall be irrevocable, except by leave of the Court or a Judge, and shall have the same effect in all respects as if it had been made an order of Court.
*Submission to be irrevocable, and to have effect as an order of Court.*

**2.** A submission, unless a contrary intention is expressed therein, shall be deemed to include the provisions set forth in the First Schedule to this Act, so far as they are applicable to the reference under the submission.
*Provisions implied in submissions.*

**3.** Where a submission provides that the reference shall be to an official referee, any official referee to whom application is made shall, subject to any order of the Court or a Judge as to transfer or otherwise, hear and determine the matters agreed to be referred.
*Reference to official referee.*

**4.** If any party to a submission, or any person claiming through or under him, commences any legal proceedings in any Court against any other party to the submission, or any person claiming through or under him, in respect of any matter agreed to be referred, any party to such legal proceedings may at any time after appearance, and before delivering any pleadings or taking any other steps in the proceedings, apply to that Court to stay the proceedings, and that Court or a Judge thereof if satisfied that there is no sufficient reason why the matter should not be referred in accordance with the submission, and that the applicant was, at the time when the proceedings were commenced, and still remains, ready and willing to do all things necessary to the proper conduct of the arbitration, may make an order staying the proceedings.
*Power to stay proceedings where there is a submission.*

**5.** In any of the following cases:—
*Power for the Court in certain cases to appoint an arbitrator, umpire, or third arbitrator.*

(a) Where a submission provides that the reference shall be to a single arbitrator, and all the parties do not after differences have arisen concur in the appointment of an arbitrator:

(b) If an appointed arbitrator refuses to act, or is incapable of acting, or dies, and the submission does not show that it was intended that the vacancy should not be supplied, and the parties do not supply the vacancy:

(c) Where the parties or two arbitrators are at liberty to appoint an umpire or third arbitrator and do not appoint him:

(d) Where an appointed umpire or third arbitrator refuses to act, or is incapable of acting, or dies, and the submission does not show that it was intended that the vacancy should not be supplied, and the parties or arbitrators do not supply the vacancy:

any party may serve the other parties or the arbitrators, as the case may be, with a written notice to appoint an arbitrator, umpire, or third arbitrator.

If the appointment is not made within seven clear days after the service of the notice, the Court or a Judge may, on application by the party who gave the notice, appoint an arbitrator, umpire, or third arbitrator, who shall have the like powers to act in the reference and make an award as if he had been appointed by consent of all parties.

**6.** Where a submission provides that the reference shall be to two arbitrators, one to be appointed by each party, then, unless the submission expresses a contrary intention—
*Power for parties in certain cases to supply vacancy.*

(a) If either of the appointed arbitrators refuses to act, or is incapable of acting, or dies, the party who appointed him may appoint a new arbitrator in his place;

(b) If, on such a reference, one party fails to appoint an arbitrator, either originally or by way of substitution as aforesaid, for seven clear days after the other party, having appointed his arbitrator, has served the party making default with notice to make the appointment, the party who has appointed an arbitrator may appoint that arbitrator to act as sole arbitrator in the reference, and his award shall be binding on both parties as if he had been appointed by consent:

Provided that the Court or a Judge may set aside any appointment made in pursuance of this section.

**Powers of arbitrator.**

7. The arbitrators or umpire acting under a submission shall, unless the submission expresses a contrary intention, have power—

(a) to administer oaths to or take the affirmations of the parties and witnesses appearing ; and

(b) to state an award as to the whole or part thereof in the form of a special case for the opinion of the Court ; and

(c) to correct in an award any clerical mistake or error arising from any accidental slip or omission.

**Witnesses may be summoned by subpœna.**

8. Any party to a submission may sue out a writ of subpœna ad testificandum, or a writ of subpœna duces tecum, but no person shall be compelled under any such writ to produce any document which he could not be compelled to produce on the trial of an action.

**Power to enlarge time for making award.**

9. The time for making an award may from time to time be enlarged by order of the Court or a Judge, whether the time for making the award has expired or not.

**Power to remit award.**

10.—(1.) In all cases of reference to arbitration the Court or a Judge may from time to time remit the matters referred, or any of them, to the reconsideration of the arbitrators or umpire.

(2.) Where an award is remitted, the arbitrators or umpire shall, unless the order otherwise directs, make their award within three months after the date of the order.

**Power to set aside award.**

11.—(1.) Where an arbitrator or umpire has misconducted himself, the Court may remove him.

(2.) Where an arbitrator or umpire has misconducted himself, or an arbitration or award has been improperly procured, the Court may set the award aside.

**Enforcing award.**

12. An award on a submission may, by leave of the Court or a Judge, be enforced in the same manner as a judgment or order to the same effect.

### References under Order of Court.

**Reference for report.**

13.—(1.) Subject to Rules of Court and to any right to have particular cases tried by a jury, the Court or a Judge may refer any question arising in any cause or matter (other than a criminal proceeding by the Crown) for inquiry or report to any official or special referee.

(2.) The report of an official or special referee may be adopted wholly or partially by the Court or a Judge, and if so adopted may be enforced as a judgment or order to the same effect.

**Power to refer in certain cases.**

14. In any cause or matter (other than a criminal proceeding by the Crown),—

(a) If all the parties interested who are not under disability consent: or,

(b) If the cause or matter requires any prolonged examination of documents or any scientific or local investigation which cannot in the opinion of the Court or a Judge conveniently be made before a jury or conducted by the Court through its other ordinary officers: or,

(c) If the question in dispute consists wholly or in part of matters of account ;

the Court or a Judge may at any time order the whole cause or matter, or any question on issue of fact arising therein, to be tried before a special referee or arbitrator respectively agreed on by the parties, or before an official referee or officer of the Court.

**Powers and remuneration of referees and arbitrators.**

15.—(1.) In all cases of reference to an official or special referee or arbitrator under an order of the Court or a Judge in any cause or matter, the official or special referee or arbitrator shall be deemed to be an officer of the Court, and shall have such authority, and shall conduct the reference in such manner, as may be prescribed by Rules of Court, and subject thereto as the Court or a Judge may direct.

(2.) The report or award of any official or special referee or arbitrator on any such reference shall, unless set aside by the Court or a Judge, be equivalent to the verdict of a jury.

(3.) The remuneration to be paid to any special referee or arbitrator to whom any matter is referred under order of the Court or a Judge shall be determined by the Court or a Judge.

16. The Court or a Judge shall, as to references under order of the Court or a Judge, have all the powers which are by this Act conferred on the Court or a Judge as to references by consent out of Court.

*Court to have powers as in references by consent.*

17. Her Majesty's Court of Appeal shall have all the powers conferred by this Act on the Court or a Judge thereof under the provisions relating to references under order of the Court.

*Court of Appeal to have powers of Court.*

### General.

18.—(1.) The Court or a judge may order that a writ of subpœna ad testificandum or of subpœna duces tecum shall issue to compel the attendance before an official or special referee, or before any arbitrator or umpire, of a witness wherever he may be within the United Kingdom.

*Power to compel attendance of witness in any part of the United Kingdom, and to order habeas corpus to issue.*

(2.) The Court or a judge may also order that a writ of habeas corpus ad testificandum shall issue to bring up a prisoner for examination before an official or special referee, or before any arbitrator or umpire.

19. Any referee, arbitrator, or umpire may at any stage of the proceedings under a reference, and shall, if so directed by the Court or a Judge, state in the form of a special case for the opinion of the Court any question of law arising in the course of the reference.

*Statement of case pending arbitration.*

20. Any order made under this Act may be made on such terms as to costs, or otherwise, as the authority making the order thinks just.

*Costs.*

21. Provision may from time to time be made by Rules of Court for conferring on any master, or other officer of the Supreme Court, all or any of the jurisdiction conferred by this Act on the Court or a judge.

*Exercise of powers by masters and other officer*

22. Any person who wilfully and corruptly gives false evidence before any referee, arbitrator, or umpire shall be guilty of perjury, as if the evidence had been given in open Court, and may be dealt with, prosecuted, and punished accordingly.

*Penalty for perjury.*

23. This Act shall, except as in this Act expressly mentioned, apply to any arbitration to which her Majesty the Queen, either in right of the Crown, or of the Duchy of Lancaster or otherwise, or the Duke of Cornwall, is a party, but nothing in this Act shall empower the Court or a judge to order any proceedings to which her Majesty or the Duke of Cornwall is a party, or any question or issue in any such proceedings, to be tried before any referee, arbitrator, or officer without the consent of her Majesty or the Duke of Cornwall, as the case may be, or shall affect the law as to costs payable by the Crown.

*Crown to be bound.*

24. This Act shall apply to every arbitration under any Act passed before or after the commencement of this Act as if the arbitration were pursuant to a submission, except in so far as this Act is inconsistent with the Act regulating the arbitration or with any rules or procedure authorised or recognised by that Act.

*Application of Act to references under statutory powers.*

25. This Act shall not affect any arbitration pending at the commencement of this Act, but shall apply to any arbitration commenced after the commencement of this Act under any agreement or order made before the commencement of this Act.

*Saving for pending arbitrations.*

26.—(1.) The enactments described in the Second Schedule to this Act are hereby repealed to the extent therein mentioned, but this repeal shall not affect anything done or suffered, or any right acquired or duty imposed or liability incurred, before the commencement of this Act, or the institution or prosecution to its termination of any legal proceeding or other remedy for ascertaining or enforcing any such liability.

*Repeal.*

(2.) Any enactment or instrument referring to any enactment repealed by this Act shall be construed as referring to this Act.

27. In this Act, unless the contrary intention appears,—

*Definitions.*

  "Submission" means a written agreement to submit present or future differences to arbitration, whether an arbitrator is named therein or not.

"Court" means Her Majesty's High Court of Justice.

"Judge" means a judge of Her Majesty's High Court of Justice.

"Rules of Court" means the Rules of the Supreme Court made by the proper authority under the Judicature Acts.

Extent.    **28.** This Act shall not extend to Scotland or Ireland.

Commencement.    **29.** This Act shall commence and come into operation on the first day of January one thousand eight hundred and ninety.

Short title.    **30.** This Act may be cited as the Arbitration Act, 1889.

# SCHEDULES.

## THE FIRST SCHEDULE.

### PROVISIONS TO BE IMPLIED IN SUBMISSIONS.

(a) If no other mode of reference is provided, the reference shall be to a single arbitrator.

(b) If the reference is to two arbitrators, the two arbitrators may appoint an umpire at any time within the period during which they have power to make an award.

(c) The arbitrators shall make their award in writing within three months after entering on the reference, or after having been called on to act by notice in writing from any party to the submission, or on or before any later day to which the arbitrators, by any writing signed by them, may from time to time enlarge the time for making the award.

(d) If the arbitrators have allowed their time or extended time to expire without making an award, or have delivered to any party to the submission, or to the umpire a notice in writing, stating that they cannot agree, the umpire may forthwith enter on the reference in lieu of the arbitrators.

(e) The umpire shall make his award within one month after the original or extended time appointed for making the award of the arbitrators has expired, or on or before any later day to which the umpire by any writing signed by him may from time to time enlarge the time for making his award.

(f) The parties to the reference, and all persons claiming through them respectively, shall, subject to any legal objection, submit to be examined by the arbitrators or umpire, on oath or affirmation, in relation to the matters in dispute, and shall, subject as aforesaid, produce before the arbitrators or umpire, all books, deeds, papers, accounts, writings, and documents within their possession or power respectively which may be required or called for, and do all other things which during the proceedings on the reference the arbitrators or umpire may require.

(g) The witnesses on the reference shall, if the arbitrators or umpire thinks fit, be examined on oath or affirmation.

(h) The award to be made by the arbitrators or umpire shall be final and binding on the parties and the persons claiming under them respectively.

(i) The costs of the reference and award shall be in the discretion of the arbitrators or umpire, who may direct to and by whom and in what manner those costs or any part thereof shall be paid, and may tax or settle the amount of costs to be so paid or any part thereof, and may award costs to be paid as between solicitor and client.

## THE SECOND SCHEDULE.

ENACTMENTS REPEALED.

| Session and Chapter. | Title or Short Title. | Extent of Repeal. |
|---|---|---|
| 9 Will. 3, c. 15 ...... | An Act for determining differences by arbitration. | The whole Act. |
| 3 & 4 Will. 4, c. 42 .. | An Act for the further amendment of the law and the better advancement of justice. | Sections thirty-nine to forty-one, both inclusive. |
| 17 & 18 Vict. c. 125 .. | The Common Law Procedure Act, 1854. | Sections three to seventeen, both inclusive. |
| 36 & 37 Vict. c. 66 .. | The Supreme Court of Judicature Act, 1873. | Section fifty-six from "Subject to any Rules of Court" down to "as a judgment by the Court," both inclusive, and the words "special referees or." Sections fifty-seven to fifty-nine, both inclusive. |
| 47 & 48 Vict. c. 61 .. | The Supreme Court of Judicature Act, 1884. | Sections nine to eleven, both inclusive. |

---

### 52 & 53 VICT. C. 68.
*An Act to amend the Law relating to Pilotage.*
[*30th August*, 1889.]

---

### 52 & 53 VICT. C. 73.
*An Act to amend the Law relating to the use of Flags in the British Merchant Service.* [*30th August*, 1889.]

# GENERAL INDEX.

———◆———

ABANDONMENT, 461. See *Maritime Insurance.*

ACCEPTANCE,
    of bills of exchange, 256. See *Bills of Exchange.*
        requisites of, 256
        may be before bill complete, *ib.*
        may be conditional, 256, 257
        what it admits, 257, 258
    for honour, *supra protest*, 258, 259
    of goods within meaning of Statute of Frauds, 620, 622, 623. See
      *Sale.*

ACCOMMODATION BILL. See *Bills of Exchange.*
    meaning of, 260
    presentment of, when dispensed with, 267
    notice of dishonour to drawer of, when dispensed with, 274, 275
    acceptor of, when discharged by indulgence to drawer, 294

ACCOUNT,
    between partners, taking of by the Court, 29, 30
    under builder's hand, to be produced on registry of a ship, 192

ACQUITTANCE, 681. See *Receipt.*

ACTION,
    against joint stock company stayed on winding up, 102
    against bankrupt may be stayed after petition, 725
                Court may permit to proceed, 728
    not maintainable for dividends under bankruptcy, 779

ACT OF GOD,
    carrier not responsible for, 304, 305, 361, 362. See *Carriers.*

ACTS OF BANKRUPTCY, 711—721. See *Bankruptcy.*

ADJUDICATION. See *Bankruptcy.*
    in bankruptcy, what and how obtained, 733, 734
        effect of, *ib.*
        when it may be annulled, 788, 789
        consequences of annulling, *ib.*

ADJUSTMENT. See *Maritime Insurance.*
    what, 477
    how far binding, *ib.*

AFFREIGHTMENT—*continued.*
 *Duties of Shipper, under Contract of Affreightment*—continued.
  part payment of freight may be claimed, when, 378, 379
  what freight payable in case of transhipment, *ib.*
  advance freight, 368, 379
  " dead freight," 369
  duty of shipper to name port of delivery with diligence, 379
   port must be safe, 380
  shipper or consignee must unload in reasonable time, *ib.*

 *General Average.* See *General Average.*

 *Salvage.* See *Salvage.*

AGENCY. See *Principal and Agent.*

AGENT. See *Principal and Agent.*
 concealment of material fact by, when avoids policy of insurance,
  480, 485
 signature by, under Statute of Frauds, 629—633. See *Sale.*
  in guaranty, 577, 578
 right of, to stop in transitu, 687, n.

AGREEMENT. See *Guaranties.*
 construction of the word, when used in Statute of Frauds, 574
 comprehends *Parties, Consideration, and Promise, ib.*
  consideration need not be expressed in guaranty now, 574, 575
  but must exist, and what sufficient, 575
 may be collected from distinct papers, when, 577
  from letters to third parties, *ib.*

AGRICULTURAL HOLDINGS ACT, 1883 (46 & 47 Vict. c. 61),
 exemption of live stock from distress under, 185

ALIEN,
 friend, rights of, 4
 enemy, rights of, 4, 5
 enemy cannot insure, 397. See *Maritime Insurance.*
  except by royal licence, *ib.*
 not entitled to be owner of British ship, 188, 189. See *Shipping.*
 interest of, in British ship when forfeited, 196

ALLOTMENT,
 of shares in joint stock company, 77

ALLOWANCE,
 to bankrupt, 786. See *Bankruptcy.*

ALTERATION,
 of bill or note, effect of, 290, 291. See *Bills of Exchange.*
 in policy of insurance, may be made without fresh stamp, when,
  443, 444. See *Maritime Insurance.*

APPEAL IN BANKRUPTCY, 726. See *Bankruptcy.*

APPOINTMENT,
 *of Agent,* how made, 117, 118. See *Principal and Agent.*
  when may be by parol, *ib.*
  when must be in writing, *ib.*
  when by deed, *ib.*
 *of Trustee,* 759 et *seq.* See *Bankruptcy.*

DEBTOR. See *Debt*.

DEBTORS ACT, 1869,
powers of commitment under, 784—786

DECLARATION. See *Shipping*.
on *Registry of Ship*, its contents, 191, 192
by and before whom to be made, *ib.*
ship forfeited for false, 191, n.
on registry of transfer of ship, its contents, 201, 202
by and before whom to be made, *ib.*
of interest in insurance, when requisite, 415
does not require underwriter's assent, *ib.*
but ought to be communicated to him, *ib.*

DEED,
requisite, in general, to bind corporations, 92
when dispensed with, 92, 93
of composition, 789. See *Bankruptcy*.
of sale. See *Bill of Sale*.

DEEDS OF ARRANGEMENT ACT, 1887,
provisions of, 789, 790

"DEFECT OF TITLE,"
meaning of, in Bills of Exchange Act, 253

DEL CREDERE. See *Principal and Agent*.
what, 127
need not be in writing, 568, 569

DELAY. See *Maritime Insurance*.
when in the nature of deviation, 453

DELIVERY,
of goods, constructive, takes place, when, 620, 621
to agent, binds principal, 167

DEMURRAGE. See *Affreightment*.
what, 330, 331, 332
clause respecting it in charter-party, how construed, 330—334
action for, lies against consignee, when, 347
lien for, 336

DESERTER,
seaman may be carried on board, when, 538, 539

DESERTION,
forfeiture of seaman's wages by, 536, 552. See *Seaman*.
summary power of apprehending for, 538, 539
what amounts to, 553

DEVIATION,
under contract of affreightment, 356
its effect on policy of insurance, 420. See *Maritime Insurance*.
what constitutes, 451, 452, 453

DIRECTOR,
of joint stock company, duties of, 80
to register transfer of shares, 83, 84, 86
misappropriation or misfeasance by, 80, 113, 114

## G.

## M.

MARITIME INSURANCE,
  early history of, INTRODUCTION, lxviii, lxix
  1. *Definition and Nature of the Contract*, 394—396
    is a contract of indemnity, 394
    construed liberally for benefit of assured, 396
    valued policy, what is, 394
  2. *Parties to Contract of Insurance*, 396—399
    " insurer," meaning of, 395
    " underwriter," meaning of, *ib.*
    " insured " or " assured," meaning of, *ib.*
    at common law any person might have been an insurer, 396
    monopoly of Royal Exchange and London Assurance Companies,
      396
      its abolition, *ib.*
    policies by mutual insurances, requirements as to, 397
    who can be insured, *ib.*
    alien enemies cannot be insured, *ib.*
      unless by royal licence, *ib.*
    English subject, when looked on as an enemy, *ib.*
    occupation of a neutral territory by enemies, its effect, 397, 398
    brokers, their character, 398, 399
  3. *Subject-Matter of Insurance*, 399—408
    insured must, generally speaking, be interested, 399
    at common law, effect of the words *interest or no interest, ib.*
    statute 19 Geo. 2, c. 37, *ib.*
    in what cases the insured need not have an interest, 399, 400
    wager policy, what, 400
    statute 8 & 9 Vict. c. 109, s. 18..407
    insurable interest, what constitutes, 400—405
      special property in ship or goods, 401, 402
      right to freight, 402
      defeasible or inchoate interest, 403
      goods to be shipped from abroad to purchaser, 403—405
    policy must describe the interest, 406
    interest must not be too remote, 406, 407
    interest presumed, 407
    reassurance formerly illegal, now valid, 405
    illegal voyage, or goods employed in illegal commerce uninsur-
      able, 407, 416
    trading with an enemy, generally illegal, *ib.*
      unless by royal licence, *ib.*
      breach of revenue laws of another country, not, 407
      nor conveying contraband of war, *ib.*
      nor running blockade, *ib.*
    infirmity in any part of an integral voyage vitiates the whole, 408
  4. *The Policy*, 395, 408—461
    every marine insurance in England must be contained in a policy,
      408, 409
    no claim sustainable on a slip, 409
    legal nature of slip, *ib.*
    difference between the effect of the printed and the written part,
      408
    parol evidence cannot be received to control meaning of, 409
    usage admitted to explain it, 409, 410
    usage of Lloyd's not binding on non-subscribers, 410
    open policy, what, *ib.*
    valued policy, what, *ib.*

PARTNERSHIP—*continued.*
5. *Rights of third Persons against Partners*—continued.
representative of deceased partner discharged at law, 47
joint securities, when construed joint and several against him, 50
not in equity, 47—49
unless barred by Statute of Limitations, 52
rights of separate and partnership creditors against separate estate of deceased partner, 49, 50
liability of late partner or his representative reduced by payments made since dissolution, 50, 51
not discharged by an agreement with the other partners, 52
unless creditor of firm consent, *ib.*
such consent, when binding, 52—54
firm, when discharged by act of one partner, 54
payment by one, payment by all, *ib.*
release to one, release to all, *ib.*
covenant not to sue one, no release, *ib.*
proof in bankruptcy, 742—745. See *Bankruptcy.*
6. *Rights of Partners against Third Persons,* 55—57
on loan of partnership money by a single partner, 55
sale of partnership goods by single partner, *ib.*
guaranty given to one for benefit of all, *ib.*
when considered to be so given, *ib.*
effect of change in firm on partnership securities, 55, 56
liabilities to firm may be released by one partner, 56
satisfied by payment to one, *ib.*
suspended by indulgence by one, *ib.*
cannot be enforced, if enforcement would be unconscientious in one, *ib.*
*Mode of Administering the effects of Partnership under the Bankruptcy of the entire Firm or of one Partner.* See *Bankruptcy.*
creditors of partners may petition against some or one, 724
joint petition dismissed as to some, good against rest, *ib.*
proof between partners in case of bankruptcy, 745—747
power of partner to transfer joint property after co-partner's bankruptcy, 772

PART-OWNERS,
of ship. See *Shipping.*

PATENTS, DESIGNS, AND TRADE MARKS ACT, 1883 (46 & 47 Vict. c. 57), 215, 216

PAYEE,
of bill or note. See *Bill of Exchange.*

PAYMENT,
how generally to be made, 666—671. See *Debt.*
in bill or note, effect of, 669, 670
in goods, 666
of price by vendee generally condition precedent, 640. See *Sale.*
agreement for by bill, not mean approved bill, *ib.*
by approved bill, meaning of, *ib.*
when goods to be delivered without, 640, 641
appropriation of, 678—680. See *Appropriation of Payments.*
of bill or note, 278—282. See *Bill of Exchange.*
*supra protest,* 280
to agent, is payment to principal, 154—156
by one partner, is payment by all, 54
to one partner, payment to all, 56

## U.

UNDERWRITER. See *Maritime Insurance.*

UNDISCLOSED PRINCIPAL, 149—156, 163—171, 173. See *Principal and Agent.*

UNDUE PREFERENCE. See *Carriers.*

USAGE,
    of trade, admissible to explain terms of policy, 408, 409
    of Lloyd's not binding on non-subscribers, 409
    interest payable by, 676

USANCE,
    signification of, 264

USURY,
    laws now repealed, 677

## V.

VALUED POLICY, 393, 409. See *Policy of Insurance.*

VENDEE. See *Sale.*

VENDOR. See *Sale.*

VENDOR'S LIEN, 642—644, 699, n. See *Sale.*

VOLUNTARY CONVEYANCES,
    · of bankrupt, when void against trustee, 776, 777

VOYAGE,
    description of, in policy, 415, 416. See *Maritime Insurance.*

## W.

WAGER POLICY,
    meaning of term, 399
    generally illegal, 399, 406

WAGES,
    of seamen. See *Seamen.*
    of servants, 520 *et seq.* See *Hiring and Service.*

WAIVER,
    of bill or note, when effectual, 292

WARRANTY,
    on sale of goods, 644 *et seq.*
        in policy, 444 *et seq.* See *Insurance.*
    on sale, 645 *et seq.* See *Sale.*

THE END.

PRINTED BY C. F. ROWORTH, GREAT NEW STREET, FETTER LANE— E.C.

# A CATALOGUE

OF

# LAW WORKS

PUBLISHED BY

# STEVENS AND SONS,

LIMITED,

## 119 & 120, CHANCERY LANE, LONDON,

(*And at* 14, *Bell Yard, Lincoln's Inn*).

Telegraphic Address—"**RHODRONS**, London."

**A Catalogue of Modern Law Works,** *together with a complete Chronological List of all the English, Irish, and Scotch Reports, an Alphabetical Table of Abbreviations used in reference to Law Reports and Text Books, and an Index of Subjects corrected to end of* 1890. Demy 8*vo.* (114 *pages*), *limp binding. Post free,* 6*d.*

**Acts of Parliament.**—*Public and Local Acts from an early date may be had of the Publishers of this Catalogue, who have also on sale the largest collection of Private Acts, relating to Estates, Enclosures, Railways, Roads, &c., &c.*

ACCOUNT STAMP DUTY.—Gosset.—*Vide* "Stamp Duty."

ACTION AT LAW.—Foulkes' Elementary View of the Proceedings in an Action in the Supreme Court, with a Chapter on Matters and Arbitrations.—(Founded on "SMITH'S ACTION AT LAW.") By W. D. I. FOULKES, Esq., Barrister-at-Law. Third Edition. Demy 12mo. 1884. 7*s.* 6*d.*

ADMIRALTY.—Roscoe's Admiralty Practice.—A Treatise on the Jurisdiction and Practice of the Admiralty Division of the High Court of Justice, and on Appeals therefrom, with a chapter on the Admiralty Jurisdiction of the Inferior and the Vice-Admiralty Courts. With an Appendix containing Statutes, Rules as to Fees and Costs, Forms, Precedents of Pleadings and Bills of Costs. By E. S. ROSCOE, Esq., Barrister-at-Law. Second Edition. Demy 8vo. 1882. 1*l.* 4*s.*

ADVOCACY.—Harris' Hints on Advocacy.—Conduct of Cases Civil and Criminal. Classes of Witnesses and Suggestions for Cross-examining them, &c., &c. By RICHARD HARRIS, one of her Majesty's Counsel. Ninth Edition (with a new chapter on "Tactics"). Royal 12mo. 1889. 7*s.* 6*d.*

"The work is not merely instructive, it is exceedingly interesting and amusing. . . . . We know of no better mode at present of learning some at least of an advocate's duties than in studying this book and the methods of the most distinguished advocates of the day."—*The Jurist.*

"Full of good sense and just observation. A very complete Manual of the Advocate's art in Trial by Jury."—*Solicitors' Journal.*

"A book at once entertaining and really instructive. . . Deserves to be carefully read by the young barrister whose career is yet before him."—*Law Magazine.*

"We welcome it as an old friend, and strongly recommend it to the would-be advocate."—*Law Student's Journal.*

\*₄\* *All standard Law Works are kept in Stock, in law calf and other bindings.*

A

**AGRICULTURAL LAW.**—Beaumont's Treatise on Agricultural Holdings and the Law of Distress as regulated by the Agricultural Holdings (England) Act, 1883, with Appendix containing Full Text of the Act, and Precedents of Notices and Awards. By JOSEPH BEAUMONT, Esq., Solicitor. Royal 12mo. 1883. 10s. 6d.

Cooke's Treatise on the Law and Practice of Agricultural Tenancies.—New edition, in great part re-written with especial reference to Unexhausted Improvements, with Modern Forms and Precedents. By G. PRIOR GOLDNEY and W. RUSSELL GRIFFITHS, Esqs., Barristers-at-Law. Demy 8vo. 1882. 1l. 1s.

Dixon.—Vide "Farm."

Griffiths' Agricultural Holdings (England) Act, 1883, containing an Introduction ; a Summary of the Act, with Notes ; the complete text of the Act, with Forms, and a specimen of an Award under the Act. By W. RUSSELL GRIFFITHS, Esq., of the Midland Circuit. Demy 8vo. 1883. 5s.

Spencer's Agricultural Holdings (England) Act, 1883, with Explanatory Notes and Forms ; together with the Ground Game Act, 1880. Forming a Supplement to "Dixon's Law of the Farm." By AUBREY J. SPENCER, B.A., Barrister-at-Law. Demy 8vo. 1883. 6s.

**ALLOTMENTS.**—Hall's Allotments Acts, 1887, with the Regulations issued by the Local Government Board, and Introductory Chapters, Notes, and Forms. By T. HALL HALL, Barrister-at-Law. Author of "The Law of Allotments." Royal 12mo. 1888. 7s. 6d.

**ANNUAL DIGEST.**—Mews'.—Vide "Digest."

**ANNUAL PRACTICE (THE).** — The Annual Practice for 1890-91. Edited by THOMAS SNOW, Barrister-at-Law ; CHARLES BURNEY, a Chief Clerk of the Hon. Mr. Justice Chitty, Editor of "Daniell's Chancery Forms "; and F. A. STRINGER, of the Central Office. 2 vols. Demy 8vo.

"A book which every practising English lawyer must have."—Law Quarterly Review.
"Every member of the bar, in practice, and every London solicitor, at all events, finds the last edition of the Annual Practice a necessity."—Solicitors' Journal.

**ANNUAL STATUTES.**—Lely.—Vide "Statutes."

**ARBITRATION.**—Russell's Treatise on the Power and Duty of an Arbitrator, and the Law of Submissions and Awards ; with an Appendix of Forms, and of the Statutes relating to Arbitration. By FRANCIS RUSSELL, Esq., M.A., Barrister-at-Law. Sixth Edition. By the Author and HERBERT RUSSELL, Esq., Barrister-at-Law. Royal 8vo. 1882. 36s.

"This edition may be commended to the profession as comprehensive, accurate and practical."—Solicitors' Journal.

**ARCHITECTS.**—Macassey and Strahan.—Vide "Civil Engineers."

**ARTICLED CLERKS.**—Rubinstein and Ward's Articled Clerks' Handbook.—Being a Concise and Practical Guide to all the Steps Necessary for Entering into Articles of Clerkship, passing the Preliminary, Intermediate, Final, and Honours Examinations, obtaining Admission and Certificate to Practise, with Notes of Cases Third Edit. By J. S. RUBINSTEIN and S. WARD, Solicitors. 12mo. 1881. 4s.

"No articled clerk should be without it."—Law Times.

**ASSETS, ADMINISTRATION OF.**—Eddis' Principles of the Administration of Assets in Payment of Debts.—By ARTHUR SHELLY EDDIS, one of Her Majesty's Counsel. Demy 8vo. 1880. 6s.

**AVERAGE.**—Hopkins' Hand-Book of Average, to which is added a Chapter on Arbitration.—Fourth Edition. By MANLEY HOPKINS, Esq. Demy 8vo. 1884. 1l. 1s.

\*\*\* All standard Law Works are kept in Stock, in law calf and other bindings.

AVERAGE—*continued.*

Lowndes' Law of General Average.—English and Foreign. Fourth Edition. By RICHARD LOWNDES, Average Adjuster. Author of "The Law of Marine Insurance," &c. Royal 8vo. 1888. 1*l.* 10*s.*

"The book is one which shows a mastery of its subject."—*Solicitors' Journal.*

"The author has worked in with that skill which has given him his reputation the recent cases which are by no means easy to deal with, and present difficulties to the lawyer."—*Law Times.*

"It may be confidently asserted that, whether for the purposes of the adjuster or the lawyer, Mr. Lowndes' work presents (in a style which is a model of clear and graceful English) the most complete store of materials relating to the subject in every particular, as well as an excellent exposition of its principles."—*Law Quarterly Review.*

BALLOT.—Fitzgerald's Ballot Act.—With an Introduction. Forming a Guide to the Procedure at Parliamentary and Municipal Elections. Second Edition. By GERALD A. R. FITZGERALD, Esq., Barrister-at-Law. Fcap. 8vo. 1876. 5*s.* 6*d.*

BANKING.—Walker's Treatise on Banking Law.—Second Edition. By J. D. WALKER, Esq., Barrister-at-Law. Demy 8vo. 1885. 15*s.*

BANKRUPTCY.—Chitty's Index, Vol. I.—*Vide* "Digests."

Lawrance's Precedents of Deeds of Arrangement between Debtors and their Creditors; including Forms of Resolutions for Compositions and Schemes of Arrangement under the Bankruptcy Act, 1883. Third Edition. With Introductory Chapters; also the Deeds of Arrangement Act, 1887, with Notes. By G. W. LAWRANCE, Esq., Barrister-at-Law. 8vo. 1888. 7*s.* 6*d.*

"The new edition of Mr. Lawrance's work is as concise, practical, and reliable as its predecessors."—*Law Times,* Feb. 11, 1888.

Williams' Law and Practice in Bankruptcy.—Comprising the Bankruptcy Acts, 1883 to 1890, the Bankruptcy Rules, 1886, 1890, the Debtors Acts, 1869, 1878, the Bankruptcy (Discharge and Closure) Act, 1887, and the Deeds of Arrangement Act, 1887. By the Hon. Sir ROLAND VAUGHAN WILLIAMS, one of the Justices of Her Majesty's High Court of Justice. Fifth Edition. By EDWARD WM. HANSELL, Esq., Barrister-at-Law. Roy. 8vo. 1891. 25*s.*

"Almost indispensable to the general practitioner."—*Law Gazette,* April 23, 1891.

"Mr. Hansell has done his editorial work with evident care and industry."—*Law Times,* May 2, 1891.

BILLS OF EXCHANGE.—Chalmers' Digest of the Law of Bills of Exchange, Promissory Notes, Cheques and Negotiable Securities. Fourth Edition. By His Honour Judge CHALMERS, Draughtsman of the Bills of Exchange Act, 1882, &c. Demy 8vo.
(*In the press.*)

"This excellent work is unique. As a statement and explanation of the law, it will be found singularly useful."—*Solicitors' Journal.*

BILLS OF SALE.—Fithian's Bills of Sale Acts, 1878 and 1882. With an Introduction and Explanatory Notes, together with an Appendix of Precedents, Rules of Court, Forms, and Statutes. Second Edition. By EDWARD WILLIAM FITHIAN, Esq., Barrister-at-Law. Royal 12mo. 1884. 6*s.*

BOOK-KEEPING.—Matthew Hale's System of Book-keeping for Solicitors, containing a List of all Books necessary, with a comprehensive description of their objects and uses for the purpose of Drawing Bills of Costs and the rendering of Cash Accounts to clients; also showing how to ascertain Profits derived from the business; with an Appendix. Demy 8vo. 1884. 5*s.* 6*d.*

"We think this is by far the most sensible, useful, practical little work on solicitors' book-keeping that we have seen."—*Law Students' Journal.*

*。* *All standard Law Works are kept in Stock, in law calf and other bindings.*

**BRITISH GUIANA.**—Pound's Supplement to "The Magisterial Law of British Guiana" published in 1877. With a combined Index to both works. By ALFRED JOHN POUND, Barrister-at-Law, and formerly a Stipendiary Magistrate in and for the Colony of British Guiana. Demy 8vo. 1888.                    *Net*, 2*l*. 10*s*.

**BUILDING SOCIETIES.**—Wurtzburg on Building Societies.— The Acts relating to Building Societies, comprising the Act of 1836 and the Building Societies Acts, 1874, 1875, 1877, and 1884, and the Treasury Regulations, 1884 ; with an Introduction, copious Notes, and Precedents of Rules and Assurances. By E. A. WURTZBURG, Esq., Barrister-at-Law. Royal 12mo. 1886.            7*s*. 6*d*.
" The work presents in brief, clear, and convenient form the whole law relating to Building Societies."

**CANALS.**—Webster's Law Relating to Canals : Comprising a Treatise on Navigable Rivers and Canals, together with the Procedure and Practice in Private Bill Legislation ; with a coloured Map of the existing Canals and Navigations in England and Wales. By ROBERT G. WEBSTER, M.P., Barrister-at-Law. Demy 8vo. 1885. 1*l*. 1*s*.

Street.—*Vide* " Company Law."

**CARRIERS.**—Carver's Treatise on the Law relating to the Carriage of Goods by Sea.—Second Edition. By THOMAS GILBERT CARVER, Esq., Barrister-at-Law. Royal 8vo. 1891.        1*l*. 12*s*.
" A careful and accurate treatise."—*Law Quarterly Review.*

Macnamara's Law of Carriers.—A Digest of the Law of Carriers of Goods and Passengers by Land and Internal Navigation, including the Railway and Canal Traffic Act, 1888.—By WALTER HENRY MACNAMARA, of the Inner Temple, Barrister-at-Law, Registrar to the Railway Commission. Royal 8vo. 1888.            1*l*. 8*s*.
" Mr. Macnamara seems to have done his work soundly and industriously, and to have produced a book which will be useful to practitioners in a large class of cases."— *Saturday Review*, June 15, 1889.
" A complete *epitome* of the law relating to carriers of every class."—*Railway Press.*
" We cordially approve of the general plan and execution of this work. . . . . The general arrangement of the book is good."—*Solicitors' Journal*, March 9, 1889.
" Should find a place in the library of all railway men. The work is written in a terse, clear style, and is well arranged for speedy reference."—*Railway News*, Dec. 8, 1888.

**CHAMBER PRACTICE.**—Archibald's Practice at Judges' Chambers and in the District Registries in the Queen's Bench Division, High Court of Justice ; with Forms of Summonses and Orders. Second Edition. By W. F. A. ARCHIBALD, Esq., Barrister-at-Law, and P. E. VIZARD, of the Summons and Order Department, Royal Courts of Justice. Royal 12mo. 1886.        15*s*.

**CHANCERY,** *and Vide* " Equity."

Daniell's Chancery Practice.—The Practice of the Chancery Division of the High Court of Justice and on appeal therefrom. Sixth Edit. By L. FIELD, E. C. DUNN, and T. RIBTON, assisted by W. H. UPJOHN, Barristers-at-Law. 2 vols. in 3 parts. Demy 8vo. 1882-84. 6*l*. 6*s*.

Daniell's Forms and Precedents of Proceedings in the Chancery Division of the High Court of Justice and on Appeal therefrom. Fourth Edition. With Summaries of the Rules of the Supreme Court, Practical Notes and References to the Sixth Edition of "Daniell's Chancery Practice." By CHARLES BURNEY, B.A. Oxon., a Chief Clerk of the Hon. Mr. Justice Chitty. Royal 8vo. 1885. 2*l*. 10*s*.

Morgan's Chancery Acts and Orders.—The Statutes, Rules of Court and General Orders relating to the Practice and Jurisdiction of the Chancery Division of the High Court of Justice and the Court of Appeal. With Copious Notes. Sixth Edition. By the Right Hon. GEORGE OSBORNE MORGAN, one of Her Majesty's Counsel, and E. A. WURTZBURG, Barrister-at-Law. Royal 8vo. 1885. 1*l*. 10*s*.

*** All standard Law Works are kept in Stock, in law calf and other bindings.*

**CHANCERY**—*continued.*

Peel's Chancery Actions.—A Concise Treatise on the Practice and Procedure in Chancery Actions under the Rules of the Supreme Court, 1883. Third Edition. By SYDNEY PEEL, Esq., Barrister-at-Law. Demy 8vo. 1883.     8s. 6d.

**CHARITABLE TRUSTS.**—Mitcheson's Charitable Trusts.—The Jurisdiction of the Charity Commission; being the Acts conferring such jurisdiction, 1853—1883, with Introductory Essays and Notes on the Sections. By RICHARD EDMUND MITCHESON, Esq., Barrister-at-Law. Demy 8vo. 1887.     18s.

"A very neat and serviceable hand-book of the Law of the Charity Commissioners."
—*Law Journal.*

**CHARTER PARTIES.**—Carver.—*Vide* "Carriers." Wood.—*Vide* "Mercantile Law."

**CIVIL ENGINEERS.**—Macassey and Strahan's Law relating to Civil Engineers, Architects and Contractors.—Primarily intended for their own use. By L. LIVINGSTON MACASSEY and J. A. STRAHAN, Esqrs., Barristers-at-Law. Demy 8vo. 1890.     10s. 6d.

**COAL MINES.**—Chisholm's Manual of the Coal Mines Regulation ACT, 1887.—With Introduction, Explanatory and Practical Notes and References to Decisions in England and Scotland, Appendix of Authorized Forms, Particulars as to Examinations for Certificates, &c., and a copious Index. By JOHN C. CHISHOLM, Secretary to the Midland and East Lothian Coalmasters' Association. Demy 8vo. 1888.   7s. 6d.

**COLLISIONS.**—Marsden's Treatise on the Law of Collisions at Sea.—With an Appendix containing Extracts from the Merchant Shipping Acts, the International Regulations for preventing Collisions at Sea; and local Rules for the same purpose in force in the Thames, the Mersey, and elsewhere. By REGINALD G. MARSDEN, Esq., Barrister-at-Law. Third Edition. By the Author and the Hon. J. W. MANSFIELD, Barrister-at-Law. Demy 8vo. 1891. 1l. 5s.

**COMMERCIAL LAW.**—The French Code of Commerce and most usual Commercial Laws.—With a Theoretical and Practical Commentary, and a Compendium of the Judicial Organization and of the Course of Procedure before the Tribunals of Commerce; together with the text of the law; the most recent decisions, and a glossary of French judicial terms. By L. GOIRAND, Licencié en droit. Demy 8vo. 1880.     2l. 2s.

**COMMON LAW.**—Ball's Short Digest of the Common Law; being the Principles of Torts and Contracts. Chiefly founded upon the Works of Addison, with Illustrative Cases, for the use of Students. By W. EDMUND BALL, LL.B., Barrister-at-Law. Demy 8vo. 1880.   16s.

Chitty's Archbold's Practice of the Queen's Bench Division of the High Court of Justice and on Appeal therefrom to the Court of Appeal and House of Lords in Civil Proceedings. Fourteenth Edition. By THOMAS WILLES CHITTY, assisted by J. ST. L. LESLIE, Barristers-at-Law. 2 vols. Demy 8vo. 1885. 3l. 13s. 6d.

Napier's Concise Practice of the Queen's Bench and Chancery Divisions and of the Court of Appeal, with an Appendix of Questions on the Practice, and intended for the use of Students. By T. BATEMAN NAPIER, Esq., Barrister-at-Law. Demy 8vo. 1884. 10s.

Shirley.—*Vide* "Leading Cases."

Smith's Manual of Common Law.—For Practitioners and Students. Comprising the Fundamental Principles, with useful Practical Rules and Decisions. By JOSIAH W. SMITH, B.C.L., Q.C. Tenth Edition. By J. TRUSTRAM, LL.M., Esq., Barrister-at-Law. 12mo. 1887. 14s.

Chitty's Forms.—*Vide* "Forms."

*⁎* *All standard Law Works are kept in Stock, in law calf and other bindings.*

**COMMON LAW**—*continued.*

Fisher's Digest of Reported Decisions in all the Courts, with a Selection from the Irish; and references to the Statutes, Rules and Orders of Courts from 1756 to 1883. Compiled and arranged by JOHN MEWS, assisted by C. M. CHAPMAN, HARRY H. W. SPARHAM and A. H. TODD, Barristers-at-Law. In 7 vols. Royal 8vo. 1884. *12l. 12s.*

Mews' Consolidated Digest of all the Reports in all the Courts, for the years 1884–88, inclusive. By JOHN MEWS, Barrister-at-Law. Royal 8vo. 1889. *1l. 11s. 6d.*

The Annual Digest for 1889 and 1890. By JOHN MEWS. *Each, 15s.*

*\*\** The above works bring Fisher's Common Law and Chitty's Equity Digests down to end of 1890.

**COMMONS AND INCLOSURES.**—Chambers' Digest of the Law relating to Commons and Open Spaces, including Public Parks and Recreation Grounds. By GEORGE F. CHAMBERS, Esq., Barrister-at-Law. Imperial 8vo. 1877. *6s. 6d.*

**COMPANY LAW.**—Hamilton's Manual of Company Law: For Directors and Promoters. Being a Treatise upon the nature of Trading Corporations, the Rights, Duties, and Liabilities of Directors and Promoters (including their Liabilities under the Directors Liability Act, 1890), the Appointment and Removal of Directors, the Powers of Directors, and the Law of Ultra Vires. By WILLIAM FREDERICK HAMILTON, LL.D. (Lond.), assisted by KENNARD GOLBORNE METCALFE, M.A., Esqrs., Barristers-at-Law. Demy 8vo. 1891. *12s. 6d.*

" The work is executed throughout with great care and accuracy . . . . may be safely recommended as a most useful manual of the law with which it deals."—*Law Gazette.*

Palmer's Private Companies, their Formation and Advantages; being a Concise Popular Statement of the Mode of Converting a Business into a Private Company, and the Benefit of so doing. With Notes on "Single Ship Companies." Eighth Edition. By F. B. PALMER, Esq., Barrister-at-Law. 12mo. 1890. *Net 2s.*

Palmer.—*Vide* "Conveyancing" and "Winding-up."

Palmer's Shareholders' and Directors' Legal Companion.—A Manual of Every-day Law and Practice for Promoters, Shareholders, Directors, Secretaries, Creditors and Solicitors of Companies under the Companies Acts, 1862 to 1890, with an Appendix on the Conversion of Business Concerns into Private Companies, and on the Directors Liability Act, 1890. 11th edit. By F. B. PALMER, Esq., Barrister-at-Law. 12mo. 1890. *Net, 2s. 6d.*

Street's Law relating to Public Statutory Undertakings: comprising Railway Companies, Water, Gas, and Canal Companies, Harbours, Docks, &c., with special reference to Modern Decisions. By J. BAMFIELD STREET, Esq., Barrister-at-Law. Demy 8vo. 1890. *10s. 6d.*

" This book contains in a small compass a large amount of useful information : its style is clear and its arrangement good."—*Solicitors' Journal,* November 1, 1890.

Thring.—*Vide* "Joint Stocks."

**COMPENSATION.**—Cripps' Treatise on the Principles of the Law of Compensation. Second Edition. By C. A. CRIPPS, Esq., Barrister-at-Law. Demy 8vo. 1884. *16s.*

**COMPOSITION DEEDS.**—Lawrance.—*Vide* "Bankruptcy."

**CONTINGENT REMAINDERS.**—An Epitome of Fearne on Contingent Remainders and Executory Devises. Intended for the Use of Students. By W. M. C. Post 8vo. 1878. *6s. 6d.*

**CONTRACTS.**—Addison on Contracts. Being a Treatise on the Law of Contracts. Eighth Edition. By HORACE SMITH, Esq., Barrister-at-Law. Royal 8vo. 1883. *2l. 10s.*

"To the present editor must be given all praise which untiring industry and intelligent research can command."—*Law Times.*

"A satisfactory guide to the vast storehouse of decisions on contract law." *Sol. Jour.*

*\*\** *All standard Law Works are kept in Stock, in law calf and other bindings.*

CONTRACTS—*continued.*

Fry.—*Vide* "Specific Performance."

Leake on Contracts.—An Elementary Digest of the Law of Contracts. By STEPHEN MARTIN LEAKE, Barrister-at-Law. Demy 8vo. 1878.                                                                  1*l.* 18*s.*

Pollock's Principles of Contract.—Being a Treatise on the General Principles relatng to the Validity of Agreements in the Law of England. Fifth Edition, with a new Chapter. By Sir FREDERICK POLLOCK, Bart., Barrister-at-Law, Professor of Common Law in the Inns of Court, &c. Demy 8vo. 1889.                          1*l.* 8*s.*

"The reputation of the book stands so high that it is only necessary to announce the publication of the fifth edition, adding that the work has been thoroughly revised."— *Law Journal,* Dec. 14, 1889.

Smith's Law of Contracts.—Eighth Edition. By V. T. THOMPSON, Esq., Barrister-at-Law. Demy 8vo. 1885.                              1*l.* 1*s.*

CONVEYANCING.—Dart.—*Vide* "Vendors and Purchasers."

Greenwood's Manual of Conveyancing. — A Manual of the Practice of Conveyancing, showing the present Practice relating to the daily routine of Conveyancing in Solicitors' Offices. To which are added Concise Common Forms and Precedents in Conveyancing. Eighth Edition. Edited by HARRY GREENWOOD, M.A., LL.D., Esq., Barrister-at-Law. Demy 8vo. 1891.                            16*s.*

"That this work has reached its eighth edition is sufficient evidence of the fact that it is one of those books which no lawyer's bookshelf should be without. Recent Acts have necessitated several changes which have been carried out, and cases are cited up to date. The book is a complete guide to Conveyancing, and, though the author says that it is intended for students and articled and other clerks, we can fearlessly assert that those who would perhaps consider it an insult to be mistaken for students will find in it very much that is useful. The Table of Precedents could not, we imagine, be made more complete than it is. Where and how the author obtained his information is a perfect puzzle to us, and no conceivable state of affairs seems to have been left unprovided for."—*Law Gazette,* December 4, 1890.

"We should like to see it placed by his principal in the hands of every articled clerk. One of the most useful practical works we have ever seen."—*Law Students' Journal.*

Morris's Patents Conveyancing.—Being a Collection of Precedents in Conveyancing in relation to Letters Patent for Inventions. Arranged as follows:—Common Forms, Agreements, Assignments, Mortgages, Special Clauses, Licences, Miscellaneous; Statutes, Rules, &c. With Dissertations and Copious Notes on the Law and Practice. By ROBERT MORRIS, M.A., Barrister-at-Law. Royal 8vo. 1887.                                                               1*l.* 5*s.*

"Contains valuable dissertations, and useful notes on the subject with which it deals. . . . . We think it would be difficult to suggest a form which is not to be met with or capable of being prepared from the book before us. To those whose business lies in the direction of letters patent and inventions it will be found of great service. . . . Mr. Morris' forms seem to us to be well selected, well arranged, and thoroughly practical."—*Law Times.*

Palmer's Company Precedents.—For use in relation to Companies subject to the Companies Acts, 1862 to 1890. Arranged as follows:—Promoters, Prospectus, Agreements, Memoranda and Articles of Association, Resolutions, Notices, Certificates, Private Companies, Power of Attorney, Debentures and Debenture Stock, Petitions, Writs, Pleadings, Judgments and Orders, Reconstruction, Amalgamation, Arrangements, Special Acts, Provisional Orders, Winding-up. With Copious Notes and an Appendix containing the Acts and Rules. Fifth Edition. By FRANCIS BEAUFORT PALMER, assisted by CHARLES MACNAGHTEN, Esqrs., Barristers-at-Law. Royal 8vo. 1891.                                           1*l.* 16*s.*

"No company lawyer can afford to be without it."—*Law Journal,* April 25, 1891.

"As regards company drafting—as we remarked on a former occasion—it is unrivalled."—*Law Times.*

\*\*\* *All standard Law Works are kept in Stock, in law calf and other bindings.*

**CONVEYANCING**—*continued.*

**Prideaux's Precedents in Conveyancing—With Dissertations on** its Law and Practice. Fourteenth Edition. By FREDERICK PRIDEAUX, late Professor of the Law of Real and Personal Property to the Inns of Court, and JOHN WHITCOMBE, Esqrs., Barristers-at-Law. 2 vols. Royal 8vo. 1889. * 3*l*. 10*s*.

"The most useful work out on Conveyancing."—*Law Journal.*
"This work is accurate, concise, clear, and comprehensive in scope, and we know of no treatise upon conveyancing which is so generally useful to the practitioner."—*Law Times.*

**Turner's Duties of Solicitor to Client as to Partnership Agreements, Leases, Settlements, and Wills.** — By EDWARD F. TURNER, Solicitor, Lecturer on Real Property and Conveyancing, Author of "The Duties of Solicitor to Client as to Sales, Purchases, and Mortgages of Land." (Published by permission of the Council of the Incorporated Law Society.) Demy 8vo. 1884. 10*s*. 6*d*.

"The work has our full approval, and will, we think, be found a valuable addition to the student's library."—*Law Students' Journal.*

**CONVICTIONS.—Paley's Law and Practice of Summary Convictions under the Summary Jurisdiction Acts, 1848 and 1879;** including Proceedings preliminary and subsequent to Convictions, and the responsibility of convicting Magistrates and their Officers, with Forms. Sixth Edition. By W. H. MACNAMARA, Esq., Barrister-at-Law. Demy 8vo. 1879. 1*l*. 4*s*.

**COPYRIGHT.—Slater's Law relating to Copyright and Trade Marks, treated more particularly with Reference to Infringement;** forming a Digest of the more important English and American decisions, together with the Practice of the English Courts, &c. By JOHN HERBERT SLATER, Esq., Barrister-at-Law. 8vo. 1884. 18*s*.

**CORONERS.—Jervis on the Office and Duties of Coroners.—** The Coroners Act, 1887. With Forms and Precedents. By R. E. MELSHEIMER, Esq., Barrister-at-Law. Being the Fifth Edition of "Jervis on Coroners." Post 8vo. 1888. 10*s*. 6*d*.

"The present edition will hold the place of that occupied by its predecessors, and will continue to be the standard work on the subject."—*Law Times.*

**COSTS.—Morgan and Wurtzburg's Treatise on the Law of Costs in the Chancery Division.—**Second Edition. With Forms and Precedents. By the Rt. Hon. GEORGE OSBORNE MORGAN, Q.C., and E. A. WURTZBURG, Esq., Barrister-at-Law. Demy 8vo. 1882. 1*l*. 10*s*.

**Summerhays and Toogood's Precedents of Bills of Costs in the Chancery, Queen's Bench, Probate, Divorce and Admiralty Divisions of the High Court of Justice;** in Conveyancing; the Crown Office; Bankruptcy; Lunacy; Arbitration under the Lands Clauses Consolidation Act; the Mayor's Court, London; the County Courts; the Privy Council; and on Passing Residuary and Succession Accounts; with Scales of Allowances and Court Fees; Rules of Court relating to Costs; Forms of Affidavits of Increase, and of Objections to Taxation. By WM. FRANK SUMMERHAYS, and THORNTON TOOGOOD, Solicitors. Sixth Edition. By THORNTON TOOGOOD, Solicitor. Royal 8vo. 1889. 1*l*. 8*s*.

**Summerhays and Toogood's. Precedents of Bills of Costs in the County Courts.** Royal 8vo. 1889. 5*s*.

**Scott's Costs in the High Court of Justice and other Courts.** Fourth Edition. By JOHN SCOTT, of the Inner Temple, Esq., Barrister-at-Law. Demy 8vo. 1880. 1*l*. 6*s*.

**Webster's Parliamentary Costs.—**Private Bills, Election Petitions, Appeals, House of Lords. Fourth Edition. By C. CAVANAGH, Esq., Barrister-at-Law. Post 8vo. 1881. 20*s*.

*** *All standard Law Works are kept in Stock, in law calf and other bindings.*

**COUNTY COUNCILS.**—Bazalgette and Humphreys, Chambers.
—*Vide* "Local and Municipal Government."

**COUNTY COURTS.**—Pitt-Lewis' County Court Practice.—A
Complete Practice of the County Courts, including that in Admiralty
and Bankruptcy, embodying the County Courts Act, 1888, and other
existing Acts, Rules, Forms and Costs, with Full Alphabetical Index
to Official Forms, Additional Forms and General Index. Fourth
Edition. With Supplementary Volume containing the NEW WINDING-
UP PRACTICE. By G. PITT-LEWIS, Esq., Q.C., M.P., Recorder of
Poole. 3 vols. Demy 8vo. 1890-91.   2*l.* 10*s.*
   *\*\* The Supplement sold separately.*   7*s.* 6*d.*
"A complete practice of the County Courts."—*Law Journal*, March 22, 1890.
"The present edition of this work fully maintains its reputation as the standard
County Court Practice."—*Solicitors' Journal*, March 29, 1890.

Pitt-Lewis' County Courts Act, 1888.—With Introduction, Tabular
Indices to consolidated Legislation, Notes, and an Index to the Act.
Second Edition. By GEORGE PITT-LEWIS, Esq., Q.C., Author of "A
Complete Practice of the County Courts." Imperial 8vo. 1889. 5*s.*
   *\*\** The above, with THE COUNTY COURT RULES, 1889. Official
copy. *Limp binding.*   10*s.* 6*d.*
Summerhays and Toogood.—*Vide* "Costs."

**COVENANTS.**—Hamilton's Law of Covenants.—A Concise Treatise
on the Law of Covenants. By G. BALDWIN HAMILTON, of the Inner
Temple, Esq., Barrister-at-Law. Demy 8vo. 1888.   7*s.* 6*d.*
"A handy volume written with clearness, intelligence, and accuracy, and will be
useful to the profession."—*Law Times.*

**CRIMINAL LAW.**—Archbold's Pleading and Evidence in Criminal
Cases.—With the Statutes, Precedents of Indictments, &c., and the
Evidence necessary to support them. Twentieth Edition. By
WILLIAM BRUCE, Esq., Stipendiary Magistrate for the Borough of
Leeds. Royal 12mo. 1886.   1*l.* 11*s.* 6*d.*

Mews' Digest of Cases relating to Criminal Law from 1756 to
1883, inclusive.—By JOHN MEWS, assisted by C. M. CHAPMAN,
HARRY H. W. SPARHAM, and A. H. TODD, Barristers-at-Law. Royal
8vo. 1884.   1*l.* 1*s.*

Phillips' Comparative Criminal Jurisprudence.—Vol. I. Penal
Law. Vol. II. Criminal Procedure. By H. A. D. PHILLIPS, Bengal
Civil Service. 2 vols. Demy 8vo. 1889.   1*l.* 4*s.*

Roscoe's Digest of the Law of Evidence in Criminal Cases.—
Eleventh Edition. By HORACE SMITH and GILBERT GEORGE KEN-
NEDY, Esqrs., Metropolitan Magistrates. Demy 8vo. 1890. 1*l.* 11*s.* 6*d.*
"To the criminal lawyer it is his guide, philosopher and friend. What Roscoe says
most judges will accept without question. . . . Every addition has been made necessary
to make the digest efficient, accurate, and complete."—*Law Times.*

Russell's Treatise on Crimes and Misdemeanors.—Fifth Edition. By SAMUEL PRENTICE, Esq., one of Her Majesty's Counsel,
3 vols. Royal 8vo. 1877.   5*l.* 15*s.* 6*d.*
"What better Digest of Criminal Law could we possibly hope for than 'Russell on
Crimes'?"—*Sir James Fitzjames Stephen's Speech on Codification.*

Shirley's Sketch of the Criminal Law.—By W. S. SHIRLEY, Esq.,
Barrister-at-Law. Second Edition. By CHARLES STEPHEN HUNTER,
Esq., Barrister-at-Law. Demy 8vo. 1889.   7*s.* 6*d.*
As a primary introduction to Criminal Law, it will be found very acceptable to
students."—*Law Students' Journal.*

Shirley.—*Vide* "Leading Cases." Thring.—*Vide* "Navy."

*\*\* All standard Law Works are kept in Stock, in law calf and other bindings.*

B

**DECISIONS OF SIR GEORGE JESSEL.**—Peter's Analysis and Digest of the Decisions of Sir George Jessel; with Notes, &c. By APSLEY PETRE PETER, Solicitor. Demy 8vo. 1883. 16*s.*

**DIARY.**—Lawyer's Companion (The), Diary, and Law Directory for 1891.—For the use of the Legal Profession, Public Companies, Justices, Merchants, Estate Agents, Auctioneers, &c., &c. Edited by J. TRUSTRAM, LL.M., of Lincoln's Inn, Barrister-at-Law; and contains Tables of Costs in Conveyancing, &c.; Monthly Diary of County, Local Government, and Parish Business; Oaths in Supreme Court; Summary of Legislation of 1890; Alphabetical Index to the Practical Statutes; a Copious Table of Stamp Duties; Legal Time, Interest, Discount, Income, Wages and other Tables; Probate, Legacy and Succession Duties; and a variety of matters of practical utility: together with a complete List of the English Bar, and London and Country Solicitors, with date of admission and appointments. PUBLISHED ANNUALLY. Forty-fifth Issue. 1891. (*Pub. about Nov.* 1.)

Issued in the following forms, octavo size, strongly bound in cloth :—

1. Two days on a page, plain . . . . . . . 5*s.*0*d.*
2. The above, INTERLEAVED for ATTENDANCES . . . 7 0
3. Two days on a page, ruled, with or without money columns . 5 6
4. The above, with money columns, INTERLEAVED for ATTENDANCES . 8 0
5. Whole page for each day, plain . . . . . . 7 6
6. The above, INTERLEAVED for ATTENDANCES . . . 9 6
7. Whole page for each day, ruled, with or without money columns 8 6
8. The above, INTERLEAVED for ATTENDANCES . . . 10 6
9. Three days on a page, ruled blue lines, without money columns . 5 0

*The Diary contains memoranda of Legal Business throughout the Year.*

" Contains all the information which could be looked for in such a work, and gives it in a most convenient form and very completely."—*Solicitors' Journal.*

" The ' Lawyer's Companion and Diary ' is a book that ought to be in the possession of every lawyer, and of every man of business."

" The ' Lawyer's Companion ' is, indeed, what it is called, for it combines everything required for reference in the lawyer's office."—*Law Times.*

" The practitioner will find in these pages, not only all that he might reasonably expect to find, but a great deal more."—*Law Journal,* December 6, 1890.

" It should be in the hands of all members of both branches of the profession."—*Law Gazette,* November 27, 1890.

" The thousand and one things that one needs constantly to know and yet can never remember, will be found handily arranged for immediate reference."—*Pump Court.*

" This legal Whitaker is a noble work, and no lawyer has any right to want to know anything—except law, which it would not tell him."—*Saturday Review.*

**DICTIONARY.**—The Pocket Law Lexicon.—Explaining Technical Words, Phrases and Maxims of the English, Scotch and Roman Law, to which is added a complete List of Law Reports, with their Abbreviations. Second Edition, Enlarged. By HENRY G. RAWSON, Esq., Barrister-at-Law. Fcap. 8vo. 1884. 6*s.* 6*d.*

" A wonderful little legal Dictionary."—*Indermaur's Law Students' Journal.*
" A very handy, complete, and useful little work."—*Saturday Review.*

Wharton's Law Lexicon.—Forming an Epitome of the Law of England, and containing full Explanations of the Technical Terms and Phrases thereof, both Ancient and Modern; including the various Legal Terms used in Commercial Business. Together with a Translation of the Latin Law Maxims and selected Titles from the Civil, Scotch and Indian Law. Ninth Edition. By J. M. LELY, Esq., Barrister-at-Law. Super-royal 8vo. (*In preparation.*)

" On almost every point both student and practitioner can gather information from this invaluable book, which ought to be in every lawyer's office."—*Gibson's Law Notes.*

" One of the first books which every articled clerk and bar student should procure."—*Law Students' Journal.*

" As it now stands the Lexicon contains all it need contain, and to those who value such a work it is made more valuable still."—*Law Times.*

" Edited with industry, learning, and judgment."—*Saturday Review.*

*\*\* All standard Law Works are kept in Stock, in law calf and other bindings.*

DIGESTS.—Chitty's Index to all the Reported Cases decided in the several Courts of Equity in England, the Privy Council, and the House of Lords, with a selection of Irish Cases, on or relating to the Principles, Pleading, and Practice of Equity and Bankruptcy from the earliest period. Fourth Edition. Wholly Revised, Re-classified, and brought down to the End of 1883. By HENRY EDWARD HIRST, Barrister-at-Law. Complete in 9 vols. Roy. 8vo. 1883-89. 12*l.* 12*s.*

\*\* The volumes sold separately; Vols. I., II., III., V., VI., VII. and VIII. *Each*, 1*l.* 11*s.* 6*d.* Vol. IV., 2*l.* 2*s.* Vol. IX., Names of Cases, 1*l.* 1*s.*

" A work indispensable to every bookcase in Lincoln's Inn."—*Law Quarterly Review*, January, 1890.

" The practitioner can hardly afford to do without such a weapon as Mr. Hirst supplies, because if he does not use it probably his opponent will."—*Law Journal.*

" On the whole the work is thoroughly well done. The laborious care bestowed upon the fourth edition of ' Chitty ' deserves all praise."—*Law Quarterly Review.*

" We think that we owe it to Mr. Hirst to say that on each occasion when a volume of his book comes before us we exert some diligence to try and find an omission in it, and we apply tests which are generally successful with ordinary text-writers, but not so with Mr. Hirst. At present we have not been able to find a flaw in his armour. We conclude, therefore, that he is an unusually accurate and diligent compiler."—*Law Times.*

" Mr. Hirst has done his work with conspicuous ability and industry, and it is almost unnecessary to add that the modern cases are digested with the perspicuity and conciseness which have always been features of Chitty's Equity Index."—*Law Journal.*

Dale and Lehmann's Digest of Cases, Overruled, Not Followed, Disapproved, Approved, Distinguished, Commented on and specially considered in the English Courts from the Year 1756 to 1886 inclusive, arranged according to alphabetical order of their subjects ; together with Extracts from the Judgments delivered thereon, and a complete Index of the Cases, in which are included all Cases reversed from the year 1856. By CHAS. WM. MITCALFE DALE, and RUDOLF CHAMBERS LEHMANN, assisted by CHAS. H. L. NEISH, and HERBERT H. CHILD, Barristers-at-Law. Royal 8vo. 1887. 2*l.* 10*s.*

(*Forms a Supplement to Chitty's Equity Index and Fisher's Common Law Dig.*)

" One of the best works of reference to be found in any library."—*Law Times.*

" The work has been carefully executed, and is likely to be of much service to the practitioner."—*Solicitors' Journal.*

" So far as we have tested the work, it seems very well done, and the mechanical execution is excellent. As for the utility of such a book as this, it is too obvious to be enlarged upon. One could wish that there had been a ' Dale & Lehmann' some years sooner."—*Law Quarterly Review.*

" The book is divided into two parts, the first consisting of an alphabetical index of the cases contained in the Digest presented in a tabular form, showing at a glance how, where, and by what judges they have been considered. The second portion of the book comprises the Digest itself, and bears marks of the great labour and research bestowed upon it by the compilers."—*Law Journal.*

Fisher's Digest of the Reported Decisions of the Courts of Common Law, Bankruptcy, Probate, Admiralty, and Divorce, together with a Selection from those of the Court of Chancery and Irish Courts from 1756 to 1883 inclusive. Founded on Fisher's Digest. By J. MEWS, assisted by C. M. CHAPMAN, H. H. W. SPARHAM, and A. H. TODD, Barristers-at-Law. 7 vols. Roy. 8vo. 1884. 12*l.* 12*s.*

" To the common lawyer it is, in our opinion, the most useful work he can possess.—*Law Times.*

Mews' Consolidated Digest of all the Reports in all the Courts, for the Years 1884-88 inclusive.—By JOHN MEWS, Barrister-at-Law. Royal 8vo. 1889. 1*l.* 11*s.* 6*d.*

" This work is an indispensable companion to the new edition of Chitty's Digest, which ends with 1883, and also Fisher's Digest ending with the same year. . . . . The work appears to us to be exceedingly well done."—*Solicitors' Journal*, Nov. 2, 1889.

The Annual Digest for 1889 and 1890. By JOHN MEWS. *Each*, 15*s.*

\*\* The above Works bring Fisher's Common Law and Chitty's Equity Digests down to end of 1890.

\*\* *All standard Law Works are kept in Stock, in law calf and other bindings.*

**DISCOVERY.**—Hare's Treatise on the Discovery of Evidence.— Second Edition. By SHERLOCK HARE, Barrister-at-Law. Post 8vo. 1877. *12s.*

Sichel and Chance's Discovery.—The Law relating to Interrogatories, Production, Inspection of Documents, and Discovery, as well in the Superior as in the Inferior Courts, together with an Appendix of the Acts, Forms and Orders. By WALTER S. SICHEL, and WILLIAM CHANCE, Esqrs., Barristers-at-Law. Demy 8vo. 1883. *12s.*

**DISTRESS.**—Oldham and Foster on the Law of Distress.—A Treatise on the Law of Distress, with an Appendix of Forms, Table of Statutes, &c. Second Edition. By ARTHUR OLDHAM and A. LA TROBE FOSTER, Esqrs., Barristers-at-Law. Demy 8vo. 1889. *18s.*

"This is a useful book, because it embraces the whole range of the remedy by distress, not merely distress for rent, but also for *damage feasant*, tithes, poor and highway rates and taxes, and many other matters."—*Solicitors' Journal.*

**DISTRICT REGISTRIES.**—Archibald.—*Vide* "Chamber Practice."

**DIVORCE.**—Browne and Powles' Law and Practice in Divorce and Matrimonial Causes. Fifth Edition. By L. D. POWLES, Esq., Barrister-at-Law. Demy 8vo. 1889. *1l. 6s.*

"The practitioner's standard work on divorce practice."—*Law Quarterly Review.*

"Mr. Powles' edition cites all the necessary information for bringing the book down to date, supplies an excellent index, on which he has spent much pains, and maintains the position which Browne's Divorce Treatise has held for many years."—*Law Journal.*

Winter's Manual of the Law and Practice of Divorce.—By DUNCAN CLERK WINTER, Solicitor. (Reprinted from "The Jurist.") Crown 8vo. 1889. *Net, 2s. 6d.*

**DOGS.**—Lupton's Law relating to Dogs.—By FREDERICK LUPTON, Solicitor. Royal 12mo. 1888. *5s.*

"Within the pages of this work the reader will find every subject connected with the law relating to dogs touched upon, and the information given appears to be both exhaustive and correct."—*Law Times.*

**DOMICIL.**—Dicey's Le Statut Personnel anglais ou la Loi du Domicile.—Ouvrage traduit et complété d'après les derniers arrêts des Cours de Justice de Londres, et par la comparaison avec le Code Napoléon et les Diverses Législations du Continent. Par EMILE STOCQUART, Avocat à la Cour d'Appel de Bruxelles. 2 Tomes. Demy 8vo. 1887-88. *1l. 4s.*

**EASEMENTS.**—Goddard's Treatise on the Law of Easements.— By JOHN LEYBOURN GODDARD, Esq., Barrister-at-Law. Fourth Edition. Demy 8vo. 1891. *1l. 1s.*

"An indispensable part of the lawyer's library."—*Solicitors' Journal.*

"The book is invaluable: where the cases are silent the author has taken pains to ascertain what the law would be if brought into question."—*Law Journal.*

"Nowhere has the subject been treated so exhaustively, and, we may add, so scientifically, as by Mr. Goddard. We recommend it to the most careful study of the law student, as well as to the library of the practitioner."—*Law Times.*

Innes' Digest of the English Law of Easements. Third Edition. By Mr. JUSTICE INNES, lately one of the Judges of Her Majesty's High Court of Judicature, Madras. Royal 12mo. 1884. *6s.*

**ECCLESIASTICAL LAW.**—Phillimore's Ecclesiastical Law of the Church of England. With Supplement. By the Right. Hon. Sir ROBERT PHILLIMORE, D.C.L. 2 vols. 8vo. 1873-76. (Published at 3l. 7s. 6d.) *Reduced to net, 1l. 10s.*

**ELECTION IN EQUITY.**—Serrell's Equitable Doctrine of Election. By GEORGE SERRELL, M.A., LL.D., Esq., Barrister-at-Law. Royal 12mo. 1891. *7s. 6d.*

"The work is well executed, and will be of service to all who desire to master the doctrine of election."—*Law Journal.*

\*\*\* *All standard Law Works are kept in Stock, in law calf and other bindings.*

**ELECTIONS.**—Loader's The Candidate's and Election Agent's Guide; for Parliamentary and Municipal Elections, with an Appendix of Forms and Statutes. By JOHN LOADER, Esq., Barrister-at-Law. Demy 12mo. 1885. 7*s.* 6*d.*

" The book is a thoroughly practical one."—*Solicitors' Journal.*

Rogers on Elections.—In two parts.

Part I. REGISTRATION, including the Practice in Registration Appeals; Parliamentary, Municipal, and Local Government; with Appendices of Statutes, Orders in Council, and Forms. Fifteenth Edition. By MAURICE POWELL, of the Inner Temple, Esq., Barrister-at-Law. Royal 12mo. 1890. 1*l.* 1*s.*

" The practitioner will find within these covers everything which he can be expected to know, well arranged and carefully stated."—*Law Times,* July 12, 1890.

Part II. ELECTIONS AND PETITIONS. Parliamentary and Municipal, with an Appendix of Statutes and Forms. Fifteenth Edition. Incorporating all the Decisions of the Election Judges, with Statutes to June, 1886, and a new and exhaustive Index. By JOHN CORRIE CARTER, and J. S. SANDARS, Esqrs., Barristers-at-Law. Royal 12mo. 1886. 1*l.* 1*s.*

" A very satisfactory treatise on election law . . . . his chapters on election expenses and illegal practices are well arranged, and tersely expressed. The completeness and general character of the book as regards the old law are too well known to need description."—*Solicitors' Journal.*

**ELECTRIC LIGHTING.** — Bazalgette and Humphreys.—*Vide* "Local and Municipal Government."

Cunynghame's Treatise on the Law of Electric Lighting, with the Acts of Parliament, and Rules and Orders of the Board of Trade, a Model Provisional Order, and a set of Forms, to which is added a Description of the Principal Apparatus used in Electric Lighting, with Illustrations. By HENRY CUNYNGHAME, Barrister-at-Law. Royal 8vo. 1883. 12*s.* 6*d.*

**EMPLOYERS' LIABILITY.**—Firth's Law relating to the Liability of Employers for Injuries suffered by their Servants in the course of their Employment.—By T. W. STAPLEE FIRTH, Solicitor (The Sir Henry James Prize Essay). Demy 8vo. 1890. *Net* 2*s.* 6*d.*

**EQUITY,** *and Vide* **CHANCERY.**

Chitty's Index.—*Vide* "Digests."

Mews' Digest.—*Vide* "Digests."

Serrell.—*Vide* "Election in Equity."

Seton's Forms of Decrees, Judgments, and Orders in the High Court of Justice and Courts of Appeal, having especial reference to the Chancery Division, with Practical Notes. Fourth Edition. 2 vols. in 3. Royal 8vo. 1877—1879. *Reduced to net* 30*s.*

Shearwood's Introduction to the Principles of Equity. By JOSEPH A. SHEARWOOD, Author of "A Concise Abridgment of Real and Personal Property," &c., Barrister-at-Law. 8vo. 1885. 6*s.*

Smith's Manual of Equity Jurisprudence.—A Manual of Equity Jurisprudence for Practitioners and Students, founded on the Works of Story, Spence, and other writers, comprising the Fundamental Principles and the points of Equity usually occurring in General Practice. By JOSIAH W. SMITH, Q.C. Fourteenth Edition. By J. TRUSTRAM, LL.M., Esq., Barrister-at-Law. 12mo. 1889. 12*s.* 6*d.*

" Still holds its own as the most popular first book of equity jurisprudence, and one which every student must of necessity read."—*Law Journal,* September 21, 1889.

" It will be found as useful to the practitioner as to the student."—*Solicitors' Journal.*

" A book that must very nearly be learnt by heart."—*The Jurist,* September, 1889.

" We still think that the student of Equity will do well to read the book of the late Mr. Josiah Smith, especially now that a new edition has appeared."—*Law Notes,* September, 1889.

*•\** *All standard Law Works are kept in Stock, in law calf and other bindings.*

**EQUITY**—*continued.*

Smith's Practical Exposition of the Principles of Equity, illustrated by the Leading Decisions thereon. For the use of Students and Practitioners. Second Edition. By H. ARTHUR SMITH, M.A., LL.B., Esq., Barrister-at-Law. Demy 8vo. 1888.        21s.

"This excellent practical exposition of the principles of equity is a work one can well recommend to students either for the bar or the examinations of the Incorporated Law Society. It will also be found equally valuable to the busy practitioner. It contains a mass of information well arranged, and is illustrated by all the leading decisions. All the legislative changes that have occurred since the publication of the first edition have been duly incorporated in the present issue."—*Law Times.*

**ESTOPPEL.**—Everest and Strode's Law of Estoppel. By LANCELOT FIELDING EVEREST, and EDMUND STRODE, Esqrs., Barristers-at-Law. Demy 8vo. 1884.        18s.

" A useful repository of the case law on the subject."—*Law Journal.*

**EXAMINATION GUIDES.**—Bedford's Digest of the Preliminary Examination Questions in Latin Grammar, Arithmetic, French Grammar, History and Geography, with the Answers. Second Edition. Demy 8vo. 1882.        18s.

Bedford's Student's Guide to the Ninth Edition of Stephen's New Commentaries on the Laws of England.—Third Edition. Demy 8vo. 1884.        7s. 6d.

Haynes and Nelham's Honours Examination Digest, comprising all the Questions in Conveyancing, Equity, Common Law, Bankruptcy, Probate, Divorce, Admiralty, and Ecclesiastical Law and Practice asked at the Solicitors' Honours Examinations, with Answers thereto. By JOHN F. HAYNES, LL.D., and THOMAS A. NELHAM, Solicitor (Honours). Demy 8vo. 1883.        15s.

" Students going in for honours will find this one to their advantage."—*Law Times.*

Napier's Modern Digest of the Final Examinations; a Modern Digest of the Law necessary to be known for the Final Examination of the Incorporated Law Society, done into Questions and Answers; and a Guide to a Course of Study for that Examination. By T. BATEMAN NAPIER, LL.D., London, of the Inner Temple, Barrister-at-Law. Demy 8vo. 1887.        18s.

" As far as we have tested them we have found the questions very well framed, and the answers to them clear, concise and accurate. If used in the manner that Dr. Napier recommends that it should be used, that is, together with the text-books, there can be little doubt that it will prove of considerable value to students."—*The Jurist.*

Napier & Stephenson's Digest of the Subjects of Probate, Divorce, Bankruptcy, Admiralty, Ecclesiastical and Criminal Law necessary to be known for the Final Examination, done into Questions and Answers. With a Preliminary Chapter on a Course of Study for the above Subjects. By T. BATEMAN NAPIER and RICHARD M. STEPHENSON, Esqrs., Barristers-at-Law. Demy 8vo. 1888. 12s.

" It is concise and clear in its answers, and the questions are based on points, for the most part, material to be known."—*Pump Court.*

Napier & Stephenson's Digest of the Leading Points in the Subject of Criminal Law necessary to be known for Bar and University Law Examinations. Done into Questions and Answers. By T. BATEMAN NAPIER and RICHARD M. STEPHENSON, Esqrs.; Barristers-at-Law. Demy 8vo. 1888.        5s.

" We commend the book to candidates for the Bar and University Legal Examinations."—*Pump Court.*

Shearwood's Guide for Candidates for the Professions of Barrister and Solicitor.—Second Edition. By JOSEPH A. SHEARWOOD, Esq., Barrister-at-Law. Demy 8vo. 1887.        6s.

" A practical little book for students."—*Law Quarterly Review.*

\*\*\* *All standard Law Works are kept in Stock, in law calf and other bindings.*

**EXECUTIONS.**—Edwards' Law of Execution upon Judgments and Orders of the Chancery and Queen's Bench Divisions of the High Court of Justice.—By C. JOHNSTON EDWARDS, of Lincoln's Inn, Esq., Barrister-at-Law. Demy 8vo. 1888.     16s.

"Will be found very useful, especially to solicitors. . . . In addition to the other good points in this book, it contains a copious collection of forms and a good index."—*Solicitors' Journal.*

"Mr. Edwards writes briefly and pointedly, and has the merit of beginning in each case at the beginning, without assuming that the reader knows anything. He explains who the sheriff is; what the Queen, in a writ *Elegit*, for example, orders him to do; how he does it; and what consequences ensue. The result is to make the whole treatise satisfactorily clear and easy to apprehend. If the index is good—as it appears to be—practitioners will probably find the book a thoroughly useful one."—*Law Quarterly Review.*

**EXECUTORS.**—Macaskie's Treatise on the Law of Executors and Administrators, and of the Administration of the Estates of Deceased Persons. With an Appendix of Statutes and Forms. By S. C. MACASKIE, Esq., Barrister-at-Law. 8vo. 1881.     10s. 6d.

Williams' Law of Executors and Administrators.—Ninth Edition. By the Hon. Sir ROLAND VAUGHAN WILLIAMS, a Justice of the High Court. 2 vols. Roy. 8vo.     (*In the press.*)

**EXTRADITION.**—Kirchner's L'Extradition.—Recueil Renfermant in Extenso tous les Traités conclus jusqu'au 1er Janvier, 1883, entre les Nations civilisées, et donnant la solution précise des difficultés qui peuvent surgir dans leur application. Avec une Préface de Me GEORGES LACHAUD, Avocat à la Cour d'Appel de Paris. Publié sous les auspices de M. C. E. HOWARD VINCENT, Directeur des Affaires Criminelles de la Police Métropolitaine de Londres. Par F. J. KIRCHNER, Attaché à la Direction des Affaires Criminelles. In 1 vol. (1150 pp.). Royal 8vo. 1883.     2l. 2s.

**FACTORS ACTS.**—Boyd and Pearsons Factors Acts (1823 to 1877). With an Introduction and Explanatory Notes. By HUGH FENWICK BOYD and ARTHUR BEILBY PEARSON, Barristers-at-Law. Royal 12mo. 1884.     6s.

Neish & Carter's Factors Act, 1889: with Commentary and Notes; designed particularly for the use and guidance of Mercantile Men. By CHARLES H. L. NEISH and A. T. CARTER, Esqrs., Barristers-at-Law. Royal 12mo. 1890.     4s.

**FACTORY ACTS.**—Notcutt's Law relating to Factories and Workshops. Second Edition. 12mo. 1879.     9s.

**FARM, LAW OF.**—Dixon's Law of the Farm.—A Digest of Cases connected with the Law of the Farm, and including the Agricultural Customs of England and Wales. Fourth Edition. By HENRY PERKINS, Esq., Barrister-at-Law. 8vo. 1879.     1l. 6s.

"It is impossible not to be struck with the extraordinary research that must have been used in the compilation of such a book as this."—*Law Journal.*

**FIXTURES.**—Amos and Ferard on the Law of Fixtures and other Property partaking both of a Real and Personal Nature. Third Edition. By C. A. FERARD and W. HOWLAND ROBERTS, Esqrs., Barristers-at-Law. Demy 8vo. 1883.     18s.

"An accurate and well written work."—*Saturday Review.*

**FORMS.**—Allen.—*Vide* "Pleading."

Archibald.—*Vide* "Chamber Practice."

Bullen and Leake.—*Vide* "Pleading."

Chitty's Forms of Practical Proceedings in the Queen's Bench Division of the High Court of Justice. Twelfth Edition. By T. W. CHITTY, Esq., Barrister-at-Law. Demy 8vo. 1883.     1l. 18s.

"The forms themselves are brief and clear, and the notes accurate and to the point.—*Law Journal.*

\*\*\* *All standard Law Works are kept in Stock, in law calf and other bindings.*

FORMS—*continued.*

Daniell's Forms and Precedents of Proceedings in the Chancery Division of the High Court of Justice and on Appeal therefrom.—Fourth Edition, with Summaries of the Rules of the Supreme Court, Practical Notes and References to the Sixth Edition of "Daniell's Chancery Practice." By CHARLES BURNEY, B.A. (Oxon.), a Chief Clerk of the Hon. Mr. Justice Chitty. Royal 8vo. 1885. 2*l*.10*s*.

" Mr. Burney appears to have performed the laborious task before him with great success."—*Law Journal.*

" The standard work on Chancery Procedure."—*Law Quarterly Review.*

FRAUD AND MISREPRESENTATION.—Moncreiff's Treatise on the Law relating to Fraud and Misrepresentation.—By the Hon. FREDERICK MONCREIFF, of the Middle Temple, Barrister-at-Law. Demy 8vo. 1891. 21*s*.

GOLD COAST.—Smith's Analytical Index to the Ordinances Regulating the Civil and Criminal Procedure of the Gold Coast Colony and of the Colony of Lagos. By SMALMAN SMITH, Esq., Barrister-at-Law, Judge of the Supreme Court of the Colony of Lagos. Royal 8vo. 1888. *Net*, 10*s*.

GOODWILL.—Allan's Law relating to Goodwill.—By CHARLES E. ALLAN, M.A., LL.B., Esq., Barrister-at-Law. Demy 8vo. 1889. 7*s*. 6*d*.

" A work of much value upon a subject which is by no means easy."—*Solicitors' Journal.*

HIGHWAYS.—Baker's Law of Highways in England and Wales, including Bridges and Locomotives. Comprising a succinct Code of the several Provisions under each Head, the Statutes at length in an Appendix ; with Notes of Cases, Forms, and copious Index. By THOMAS BAKER, Esq., Barrister-at-Law. Royal 12mo. 1880. 15*s*.

Bazalgette and Humphreys.—*Vide* " Local and Municipal Government."

Chambers' Law relating to Highways and Bridges, being the Statutes in full and brief Notes of 700 Leading Cases. By GEORGE F. CHAMBERS, Esq., Barrister-at-Law. 1878. 7*s*. 6*d*.

HOUSE TAX.—Ellis' Guide to the House Tax Acts, for the use of the Payer of Inhabited House Duty in England.—By ARTHUR M. ELLIS, LL.B. (Lond.), Solicitor, Author of "A Guide to the Income Tax Acts." Royal 12mo. 1885. 6*s*.

" We have found the information accurate, complete and very clearly expressed."—*Solicitors' Journal.*

HUSBAND AND WIFE.—Lush's Law of Husband and Wife; within the Jurisdiction of the Queen's Bench and Chancery Divisions. By C. MONTAGUE LUSH, Esq., Barrister-at-Law. 8vo. 1884. 20*s*.

"Mr. Lush has one thing to recommend him most strongly, and that is his accuracy."—*Law Magazine.*

INCOME TAX.—Ellis' Guide to the Income Tax Acts.—For the use of the English Income Tax Payer. Second Edition. By ARTHUR M. ELLIS, LL.B. (Lond.), Solicitor. Royal 12mo. 1886. 7*s*. 6*d*.

" Contains in a convenient form the law bearing upon the Income Tax."—*Law Times.*

INLAND REVENUE CASES.—Highmore's Summary Proceedings in Inland Revenue Cases in England and Wales.—Second Edition. By N. J. HIGHMORE, Esq., Barrister-at-Law, and of the Solicitors' Department, Inland Revenue. Roy. 12mo. 1887. 7*s*. 6*d*.

" Is very complete. Every possible information is given."—*Law Times.*

INSURANCE.—Arnould on the Law of Marine Insurance.—Sixth Edition. By DAVID MACLACHLAN, Esq., Barrister-at-Law. 2 vols. Royal 8vo. 1887. 3*l*.

" As a text book, 'Arnould' is now all the practitioner can want."—*Law Times.*

Lowndes' Practical Treatise on the Law of Marine Insurance.—By RICHARD LOWNDES. Author of " The Law of General Average," &c. Second Edition. Demy 8vo. 1885. 12*s*. 6*d*.

\*\*\* *All standard Law Works are kept in Stock, in law calf and other bindings.*

**INSURANCE**—*continued.*
Lowndes' Insurable Interest and Valuations. — By RICHARD
LOWNDES. Demy 8vo. 1884.     5*s.*
McArthur on the Contract of Marine Insurance.—Second Edition.
By CHARLES MCARTHUR, Average Adjuster. Demy 8vo. 1890.   16*s.*

**INTERNATIONAL LAW.**—Kent's International Law.—Kent's Com-
mentary on International Law. Edited by J. T. ABDY, LL.D.,
Judge of County Courts. Second Edition. Crown 8vo. 1878. 10*s.* 6*d.*
Nelson's Private International Law.—Selected Cases, Statutes, and
Orders illustrative of the Principles of Private International Law as
Administered in England, with Commentary. By HORACE NELSON,
M.A., B.C.L., Barrister-at-Law. Roy. 8vo. 1889.     21*s.*
"The notes are full of matter, and avoid the vice of discursiveness, cases being cited
for practically every proposition."—*Law Times.*
Wheaton's Elements of International Law; Third English Edition.
Edited with Notes and Appendix of Statutes and Treaties. By
A. C. BOYD, Esq., Barrister-at-Law. Royal 8vo. 1889.   1*l.* 10*s.*
"A handsome and useful edition of a standard work."—*Law Quarterly Review.*
"Wheaton stands too high for criticism, whilst Mr. Boyd's merits as an editor are
almost as well established."—*Law Times,* November 30, 1889.

**INTERROGATORIES.**—Sichel and Chance.—*Vide* "Discovery."

**JOINT STOCKS.**—Palmer.—*Vide* "Company Law," "Conveyanc-
ing," and "Winding-up."
Thring's Joint Stock Companies' Law.—The Law and Practice of
Joint Stock and other Companies, including the Companies Acts,
1862 to 1886, with Notes, Orders, and Rules in Chancery, a Collection
of Precedents of Memoranda and Articles of Association, and other
Forms required in Making and Administering a Company. Also
the Partnership Law Amendment Act, the Life Assurance Companies
Acts, and other Acts relating to Companies. By LORD THRING,
K.C.B., formerly the Parliamentary Counsel. Fifth Edition. By
J. M. RENDEL, Esq., Barrister-at-Law. Royal 8vo. 1889. 1*l.* 10*s.*
"The highest authority on the subject."—*The Times.*
"The book has long taken its place among the authoritative expositions of the law
of companies. Its very useful forms are a special feature of the book, which will be of
great value to practitioners."—*Law Journal,* September 14, 1889.

**JUDGES' CHAMBER PRACTICE.**—Archibald.—*Vide* "Chamber
Practice."

**JUDICATURE ACTS.**—Wilson's Practice of the Supreme Court
of Judicature : containing the Acts, Orders, Rules, and Regulations
relating to the Supreme Court. With Practical Notes. Seventh
Edition. By CHARLES BURNEY, a Chief Clerk of the Hon. Mr. Justice
Chitty, Editor of "Daniell's Chancery Forms;" M. MUIR MACKENZIE,
and C. A. WHITE, Esqrs., Barristers-at-Law. Roy. 8vo. 1888. 1*l.*
"A thoroughly reliable and most conveniently arranged practice guide."—*Law Times*

**JUSTICE OF THE PEACE.**—Stone's Practice for Justices of the
Peace, Justices' Clerks and Solicitors at Petty and Special Sessions,
in Summary matters, and Indictable Offences, with a list of Summary
Convictions, and matters not Criminal. With Forms. Ninth Edit.
By W. H. MACNAMARA, Esq., Barrister-at-Law. Demy 8vo. 1882. 1*l.* 5*s.*
Wigram's Justice's Note Book.—Containing a short account of the
Jurisdiction and Duties of Justices, and an Epitome of Criminal Law.
By the late W. KNOX WIGRAM, Esq., Barrister-at-Law, J. P. Mid-
dlesex and Westminster. Fifth Edition. Revised by WALTER S.
SHIRLEY, Esq., Barrister-at-Law. Royal 12mo. 1888.   12*s.* 6*d.*
"The style is clear, and the expression always forcible, and sometimes humorous.
The book will repay perusal by many besides those who, as justices, will find it an
indispensable companion."—*Law Quarterly Review.*
"We can thoroughly recommend the volume to magistrates."—*Law Times.*

*\*\** *All standard Law Works are kept in Stock, in law calf and other bindings.*

**LAND TAX.**—Bourdin's Land Tax.—An Exposition of the Land Tax. Third Edition. Including the Recent Judicial Decisions, and the Incidental Changes in the Law effected by the Taxes Management Act, with other Additional Matter. Thoroughly revised and corrected. By SHIRLEY BUNBURY, of the Inland Revenue Department, Assistant Registrar of the Land Tax. Royal 12mo. 1885.        6*.

**LANDLORD AND TENANT.**—Woodfall's Law of Landlord and Tenant.—With a full Collection of Precedents and Forms of Procedure; containing also a collection of Leading Propositions. Fourteenth Edit. By J. M. LELY, Esq., Barrister-at-Law, Editor of "Chitty's Statutes," "Wharton's Law Lexicon," &c. Roy. 8vo. 1889. 1*l.* 18*s*.
" The editor has expended elaborate industry and systematic ability in making the work as perfect as possible."—*Solicitors' Journal.*
Lely and Peck.—*Vide* " Leases."

**LANDS CLAUSES ACTS.**—Jepson's Lands Clauses Consolidation Acts ; with Decisions, Forms, and Table of Costs. By ARTHUR JEPSON, Esq., Barrister-at-Law. Demy 8vo. 1880.        18*s*.

**LAW LIST.**—Law List (The).—Comprising the Judges and **Officers** of the different Courts of Justice, Counsel, Special Pleaders, Conveyancers, Solicitors, Proctors, Notaries, &c., in England and Wales ; the Circuits, Judges, Treasurers, Registrars, and High Bailiffs of the County Courts ; Metropolitan and Stipendiary Magistrates, Official Receivers under the Bankruptcy Act, Law and Public Officers in England and the Colonies, Foreign Lawyers with their English Agents, Clerks of the Peace, Town Clerks, Coroners, &c., &c., and Commissioners for taking Oaths, Conveyancers Practising in England under Certificates obtained in Scotland. Compiled, so far as relates to Special Pleaders, Conveyancers, Solicitors, Proctors and Notaries, by JOHN SAMUEL PURCELL, C.B., Controller of Stamps, and Registrar of Joint Stock Companies, Somerset House, and Published by the Authority of the Commissioners of Inland Revenue. 1891. (*Published about March* 1.)  (*Net cash*, 9*s*.)   10*s*. 6*d*.

**LAW QUARTERLY REVIEW**—Edited by Sir FREDERICK POLLOCK, Bart., M.A., LL.D., Corpus Professor of Jurisprudence in the University of Oxford. Vols. I., II., III., IV., V. and VI. Royal 8vo. 1885-90.        *Each*, 12*s*.
☞ *Subscription* 10*s. per annum, post free.* (*Foreign postage* 2*s. 6d. extra.*) ·
The Review includes :—The discussion of current decisions of importance in the Courts of this country, and (so far as practicable) of the Colonies, the United States, British India, and other British Possessions where the Common Law is administered ; the consideration of topics of proposed legislation before Parliament ; the treatment of questions of immediate political and social interest in their legal aspect ; inquiries into the history and antiquities of our own and other systems of law and legal institutions. Endeavour is also made to take account of the legal science and legislation of Continental States in so far as they bear on general jurisprudence, or may throw light by comparison upon problems of English or American legislation. The current legal literature of our own country receives careful attention ; and works of serious importance, both English and foreign, are occasionally discussed at length.

**LAWYER'S ANNUAL LIBRARY.**—(1) The Annual Practice.—By SNOW, BURNEY, and STRINGER. (2) The Annual Digest.—By MEWS. (3) The Annual Statutes.—By LELY. (4) The Annual County Court Practice.—By His Honour JUDGE HEYWOOD.
The Complete Series, as above, delivered on the day of publication, *net*, 2*l*. Nos. 1, 2, and 3 only, *net*, 1*l*. 10*s*. Nos. 2, 3, and 4 only, *net*, 1*l*. 10*s*. (*Carriage extra*, 2*s*.)
☞ *Subscriptions, payable on or before August* 1*st in each year.*
*Full prospectus forwarded on application.*

**LAWYER'S COMPANION.**—*Vide* " Diary."

*\** *All standard Law Works are kept in Stock, in law calf and other bindings.*

**LEADING CASES.**—Ball's Leading Cases. *Vide* " Torts."
Haynes' Student's Leading Cases. Being some of the Principal
Decisions of the Courts in Constitutional Law, Common Law, Con-
veyancing and Equity, Probate, Divorce, and Criminal Law. With
Notes for the use of Students. Second Edition. By JOHN F.
HAYNES, LL.D. Demy 8vo. 1884.                    16s.
" Will prove of great utility, not only to students, but practitioners. The notes are
clear, pointed and concise."—*Law Times.*

Shirley's Selection of Leading Cases in the Common Law.
With Notes. By W. SHIRLEY SHIRLEY, Esq., Barrister-at-Law.
Third Edition. Demy 8vo. 1886.                    16s.
" If any words of praise of ours can add to its well-deserved reputation, we give the
reader carte blanche to supply them on our behalf out of his own thrilling eloquence
and vivid imagination, and we will undertake to ratify them."—*The Jurist.*

Shirley's Selection of Leading Cases in the Criminal Law. With
Notes. By W. S. SHIRLEY, Esq., Barrister-at-Law. 8vo. 1888. 6s.
" Will undoubtedly prove of value to students."—*Law Notes.*

**LEASES.**—Lely and Peck's Precedents of Leases for Years,
and other Contracts of Tenancy, and Contracts relating thereto;
mainly selected or adapted from existing Collections, including many
additional Forms, with a short Introduction and Notes. By J. M.
LELY and W. A. PECK, Barristers-at-Law. Royal 8vo. 1889. 10s. 6d.
" Varied, well considered, and thoroughly practical . . . while a useful addition to
the library of the conveyancing counsel, will be still more useful to conveyancing
solicitors and estate agents."—*Law Times,* November 9, 1889.

**LEXICON.**—*Vide* " Dictionary."

**LIBEL AND SLANDER.**—Odgers on Libel and Slander.—A
Digest of the Law of Libel and Slander: the Evidence, Procedure
and Practice, both in Civil and Criminal Cases, and Precedents of
Pleadings. Second Edition, with a SUPPLEMENT, bringing the Law
down to June, 1890. By W. BLAKE ODGERS, LL.D., Barrister-at-
Law. Royal 8vo. 1890.                    1l. 12s.
*⁎* *The Supplement, containing the Law of Libel Amendment Act, 1888, with
Notes and Addenda of Cases, separately. Net,* 1s. 6d.
" The best modern book on the law of libel."—*Daily News.*
" A full, accurate, and satisfactory guide."—*Solicitors' Journal.*

**LIBRARIES AND MUSEUMS.**—Chambers' Digest of the Law
relating to Public Libraries and Museums, and Literary and
Scientific Institutions: with much Practical Information useful to
Managers, Committees and Officers of all classes of Associations and
Clubs connected with Literature, Science and Art; including Prece-
dents of By-Laws and Regulations, the Statutes in Full, and brief
Notes of Leading Cases. Third Edition. By GEO. F. CHAMBERS, Esq.,
Barrister-at-Law. Roy. 8vo. 1889.                    8s. 6d.

**LICENSING.**—Lely and Foulkes' Licensing Acts, 1828, 1869,
and 1872–1874; with Notes to the Acts, a Summary of the Law,
and an Appendix of Forms. Third Edit. By J. M. LELY and W. D. I.
FOULKES, Esqrs., Barristers-at-Law. Roy. 12mo. 1887. 10s. 6d.
" We do not know of a more compact or useful treatise on the subject."—*Sol. Jour.*

**LOCAL AND MUNICIPAL GOVERNMENT.**—Bazalgette and
Humphreys' Law relating to County Councils: being the Local
Government Act, 1888, County Electors Act, 1888, the Incorporated
Clauses of the Municipal Corporations Act, 1882, and a compendious
Introduction and Notes; with Analysis of Statutes affecting the same,
Orders in Council, Circulars, and a Copious Index. By C. N. BAZAL-
GETTE and GEORGE HUMPHREYS, Barristers-at-Law, Joint Authors of
" The Law of Local and Municipal Government." Third Edition.
By GEORGE HUMPHREYS, Esq. Royal 8vo. 1889.                    7s. 6d.
" The most stately as regards size, and the best in point of type of all the works.
There is a good introduction . ⁘ . the notes are careful and helpful."—*Solicitors' Journal.*

*⁎* *All standard Law Works are kept in Stock, in law calf and other bindings.*

LOCAL AND MUNICIPAL GOVERNMENT—*continued.*

Bazalgette and Humphreys' Law relating to Local and Municipal Government. Comprising the Statutes relating to Public Health, Municipal Corporations, Highways, Burial, Gas and Water, Public Loans, Compulsory Taking of Lands, Tramways, Electric Lighting, Artizans' Dwellings, &c., Rivers' Pollution, the Clauses Consolidation Acts, and many others, fully annotated with cases up to date, a selection of the Circulars of the Local Government Board, with a Table of upwards of 2,500 Cases, and full Index. With Addenda containing the Judicial Decisions and Legislation relating to Local and Municipal Government since 1885. By C. NORMAN BAZALGETTE and GEORGE HUMPHREYS, Esqrs., Barristers-at-Law. Sup. royal 8vo. 1888. *3l. 3s.*

*** The Addenda may be had separately. Net, 2s. 6d.*
"The book is thoroughly comprehensive of the law on all points of which it professes to treat."—*Law Journal.*
"The work is one that no local officer should be without; for nothing short of a whole library of statutes, reports, and handbooks could take its place."—*Municipal Review.*

Chambers' Popular Summary of the Law relating to Local Government, forming a complete Guide to the new Act of 1888. Second Edition. By G. F. CHAMBERS, Barrister-at-Law. Imp. 8vo. 1888. (*Or bound in Cloth with copy of Act, 5s. 6d.*) *Net, 2s. 6d.*

MAGISTERIAL LAW.—Shirley's Elementary Treatise on Magisterial Law, and on the Practice of Magistrates' Courts.—By W. S. SHIRLEY, Esq., Barrister-at-Law. Roy. 12mo. 1881. *6s. 6d.*

Wigram.—*Vide* "Justice of the Peace."

MALICIOUS PROSECUTIONS. — Stephen's Law relating to Actions for Malicious Prosecutions.—By HERBERT STEPHEN, LL.M., of the Inner Temple, Barrister-at-Law, part Author of "A Digest of the Criminal Law Procedure." Royal 12mo. 1888. *6s.*
"A reliable text-book upon the law of malicious prosecution."—*Law Times.*

MARITIME DECISIONS.—Douglas' Maritime Law Decisions.— An Alphabetical Reference Index to Recent and Important Maritime Decisions. Compiled by ROBT. R. DOUGLAS. Demy 8vo. 1888. *7s. 6d.*

Marine Insurance.—*Vide* "Insurance."

MARRIAGE.—Kelly's French Law of Marriage, and the Conflict of Laws that arises therefrom. By E. KELLY, M.A., of the New York Bar, Licencié en Droit de la Faculté de Paris. Roy. 8vo. 1885. *6s.*

MARRIAGE SETTLEMENTS.—Banning's Concise Treatise on the Law of Marriage Settlements; with an Appendix of Statutes. By H. T. BANNING, Esq., Barrister-at-Law. Demy 8vo. 1884. *15s.*

MARRIED WOMEN'S PROPERTY.—Lush's Married Women's Rights and Liabilities in relation to Contracts, Torts, and Trusts. By MONTAGUE LUSH, Esq., Barrister-at-Law, Author of "The Law of Husband and Wife." Royal 12mo. 1887. *5s.*
"Well arranged, clearly written, and has a good index."—*Law Times.*

Smith's Married Women's Property Acts, 1882 and 1884, with an Introduction and Critical and Explanatory Notes, together with the Married Women's Property Acts, 1870 and 1874, &c. 2nd Edit. Revised. By H. A. SMITH, Esq., Barrister-at-Law. Roy. 12mo. 1884. *6s.*

MASTER AND SERVANT.—Macdonell's Law of Master and Servant. Part I. Common Law. Part II. Statute Law. By JOHN MACDONELL, M.A., Esq., Barrister-at-Law. Demy 8vo. 1883. *1l. 5s.*
"A work which will be of real value to the practitioner."—*Law Times.*

MAYOR'S COURT PRACTICE.—Candy's Mayor's Court Practice.—The Jurisdiction, Process, Practice and Mode of Pleading in Ordinary Actions in the Mayor's Court in London. By GEORGE CANDY, Esq., one of Her Majesty's Counsel. Demy 8vo. 1879. *14s.*

*** All standard Law Works are kept in Stock, in law calf and other bindings.*

**MERCANTILE LAW.**—Russell's Treatise on Mercantile Agency. Second Edition. 8vo. 1873. 14s.

Smith's Compendium of Mercantile Law.—Tenth Edition. By JOHN MACDONELL, Esq., a Master of the Supreme Court of Judicature, assisted by GEO. HUMPHREYS, Esq., Barrister-at-Law. 2 vols. Royal 8vo. 1890. 2l. 2s.

"Of the greatest value to the mercantile lawyer."—*Law Times*, March 22, 1890.

"We have no hesitation in recommending the work before us to the profession and the public as a reliable guide to the subjects included in it, and as constituting one of the most scientific treatises extant on mercantile law."—*Solicitors' Journal*, May 10, 1890.

Tudor's Selection of Leading Cases on Mercantile and Maritime Law.—With Notes. By O. D. TUDOR, Esq., Barrister-at-Law. Third Edition. Royal 8vo. 1884. 2l. 2s.

Wilson's Mercantile Handbook of the Liabilities of Merchant, Shipowner, and Underwriter on Shipments by General Vessels.—By A. WILSON, Solicitor and Notary. Royal 12mo. 1883. 6s.

Wood's Mercantile Agreements.—The Interpretation of Mercantile Agreements: A Summary of the Decisions as to the Meaning of Words and Provisions in Written Agreements for the Sale of Goods, Charter-Parties, Bills of Lading, and Marine Policies. With an Appendix containing a List of Words and Expressions used in, or in connection with, Mercantile Agreements, and a List of Mercantile Usages. By JOHN DENNISTOUN WOOD, Esq., Barrister-at-Law Royal 8vo. 1886. 18s.

"A book of great use in the interpretation of written mercantile agreements."— *Law Journal.*

**MERCHANDISE MARKS ACT.**—Payn's Merchandise Marks Act, 1887.—With special reference to the Important Sections and the Customs Regulations and Orders made thereunder, together with the Conventions with Foreign States for Protection of Trade Marks, and Orders in Council, &c. By HOWARD PAYN, Barrister-at-Law, and of the Secretary's Department of the Board of Customs. Royal 12mo. 1888. 3s. 6d.

"Mr. Payn's lucid introduction places the subject very clearly before the reader, and his book must be a safe guide to all who are interested in the act."—*Law Times*, Feb. 1888.

**METROPOLIS BUILDING ACTS.** — Woolrych's Metropolitan Building Acts, together with such clauses of the Metropolis Management Acts as more particularly relate to the Building Acts, with Notes and Forms. Third Edition. By W. H. MACNAMARA, Esq., Barrister-at-Law. 12mo. 1882. 10s.

**MINES.**—Rogers' Law relating to Mines, Minerals and Quarries in Great Britain and Ireland, with a Summary of the Laws of Foreign States, &c. Second Edition Enlarged. By His Honor Judge ROGERS. 8vo. 1876. 1l. 11s. 6d.

**MORTGAGE.**—Coote's Treatise on the Law of Mortgage.—Fifth Edition. Thoroughly revised. By WILLIAM WYLLYS MACKESON, Esq., one of Her Majesty's Counsel, and H. ARTHUR SMITH, Esq., Barrister-at-Law. 2 vols. Royal 8vo. 1884. 3l.

"A complete, terse and practical treatise for the modern lawyer."—*Solicitors' Journal.*

**MUNICIPAL CORPORATIONS.**—Bazalgette and Humphreys.— *Vide* "Local and Municipal Government."

Lely's Law of Municipal Corporations.—Containing the Municipal Corporation Act, 1882, and the Enactments incorporated therewith. With Notes. By J. M. LELY, Esq., Barrister-at-Law. Demy 8vo. 1882. 15s.

*** All standard Law Works are kept in Stock, in law calf and other bindings.*

**NAVY.**—Thring's Criminal Law of the Navy, with an Introductory Chapter on the Early State and Discipline of the Navy, the Rules of Evidence, and an Appendix comprising the Naval Discipline Act and Practical Forms. Second Edition. By THEODORE THRING, Esq., Barrister-at-Law, and C. E. GIFFORD, Assistant-Paymaster, Royal Navy. 12mo. 1877. 12s. 6d.

**NEGLIGENCE.**—Smith's Treatise on the Law of Negligence Second Edition. By HORACE SMITH, Esq., Barrister-at-Law, Editor of "Addison on Contracts, and Torts," &c. 8vo. 1884. 12s. 6d.

" Of great value both to the practitioner and student of law."—*Solicitors' Journal.*

**NISI PRIUS.**—Roscoe's Digest of the Law of Evidence on the Trial of Actions at Nisi Prius.—Sixteenth Edition. By MAURICE POWELL, Esq., Barrister-at-Law. 2 vols. Demy 8vo. 1891.

*(Nearly ready.)*

" Continues to be a vast and closely packed storehouse of information on practice at Nisi Prius."—*Law Journal.*

**NONCONFORMISTS.**—Winslow's Law Relating to Protestant Nonconformists and their Places of Worship; being a Legal Handbook for Nonconformists. By REGINALD WINSLOW, Esq., Barrister-at-Law. Post 8vo. 1886. 6s.

**NOTARY.**—Brooke's Treatise on the Office and Practice of a Notary of England.—With a full collection of Precedents. Fifth Ed. By G. F. CHAMBERS, Esq., Barrister-at-Law. Demy 8vo. 1890. 1l. 1s.

**OATHS.**—Stringer's Oaths and Affirmations in Great Britain and Ireland; being a Collection of Statutes, Cases, and Forms, with Notes and Practical Directions for the use of Commissioners for Oaths, and of all Courts of Civil Procedure and Offices attached thereto. [In succession to "Braithwaite's Oaths."] By FRANCIS A. STRINGER, of the Central Office, Supreme Court of Judicature, one of the Editors of the "Annual Practice." Crown 8vo. 1890. 3s. 6d.

" Indispensable to all commissioners."—*Solicitors' Journal*, Jan. 11, 1890.
" A most excellent little handbook."—*Law Times*, Feb. 1, 1890.

**PARISH LAW.**—Steer's Parish Law; being a Digest of the Law relating to the Civil and Ecclesiastical Government of Parishes and the Relief of the Poor. Fifth Edition. By W. H. MACNAMARA, Esq., Barrister-at-Law. Demy 8vo. 1887. 18s.

" An exceedingly useful compendium of Parish Law."—*Law Times.*
" A very complete and excellent guide to Parish Law."—*Solicitors' Journal.*
" Every subject that can be considered parochial is, we think, contained in this volume, and the matter is brought down to date. It is a compendium which is really compendious."—*Law Journal*, Jan. 21, 1888.

**PARTNERSHIP.**—Pollock's Digest of the Law of Partnership; incorporating the Partnership Act, 1890. Fifth Edition. By Sir FREDERICK POLLOCK, Bart., Barrister-at-Law. Author of "Principles of Contract," "The Law of Torts," &c. Demy 8vo. 1890. 8s. 6d.

" What Sir Frederick Pollock has done he has done well, and we are confident this book will be most popular as well as extremely useful."—*Law Times*, Dec. 13, 1890.

Turner.—*Vide* "Conveyancing."

**PATENTS.**—Aston's (T.) Patents, Designs and Trade Marks Act, 1883, with Notes and Index to the Act, Rules and Forms. By THEODORE ASTON, Q.C. Royal 12mo. 1884. 6s.

Edmunds' Patents, Designs and Trade Marks Acts, 1883 to 1888, Consolidated, with an Index. By LEWIS EDMUNDS, D.Sc., LL.B., Barrister-at-Law. Imp. 8vo. 1889. *Net* 2s. 6d.

*\*\* All standard Law Works are kept in Stock, in law calf and other bindings.*

**PATENTS**—*continued.*

**Edmunds on Patents.**—The Law and Practice of Letters Patent for Inventions; with the Patents Acts and Rules annotated, and the International Convention, a full collection of Statutes, Forms, and Precedents, and an Outline of Foreign and Colonial Patent Laws, &c. By LEWIS EDMUNDS, assisted by A. WOOD RENTON, Esqrs., Barristers-at-Law. Royal 8vo. (992 pp.). 1890. *1l. 12s.*

"We have nothing but commendation for the book. Conceived in a large and comprehensive spirit, it is well and thoroughly carried out. . . . The statement of the existing law is accurate and clear. . . . The book is one to be recommended."—*Solicitors' Journal*, June 14, 1890.

"We have no hesitation in saying that the book is a useful and exhaustive one, and one which could not have been produced without much labour and considerable research. It describes the law of letters patent and its history, including proceedings in the Privy Council, international arrangements, and an abridgment of foreign laws on the subject. It would be difficult to make it more complete, and it is printed on good paper."—*Law Times*, June 21, 1890.

"Taking the book as a whole, it is undoubtedly the most comprehensive book that has yet been written upon the special branch of law, and, having examined it in some detail, we can commend it as answering well to the many tests we have applied."—*Law Journal*, June 21, 1890.

**Johnson's Patentees' Manual.**—A Treatise on the Law and Practice of Patents for Inventions. With an Appendix of Statutes, Rules, and Foreign and Colonial Patent Laws, International Convention, and Protocol. Sixth Edition. By JAMES JOHNSON, Esq., Barrister-at-Law; and J. HENRY JOHNSON, Solicitor and Patent Agent. Demy 8vo. 1890. *10s. 6d.*

**Morris's Patents Conveyancing.**—Being a Collection of Precedents in Conveyancing in relation to Letters Patent for Inventions. Arranged as follows :—Common Forms, Agreements, Assignments, Mortgages, Special Clauses, Licences, Miscellaneous; Statutes, Rules, &c. With Dissertations and Copious Notes on the Law and Practice. By ROBERT MORRIS, Esq., Barrister-at-Law. Royal 8vo. 1887. *1l. 5s.*

"Mr. Morris' forms seem to us to be well selected, well arranged, and thoroughly practical."—*Law Times.*

"The dissertations contain a large amount of valuable and accurate information. The Index is satisfactory."—*Solicitors' Journal.*

**Munro's Patents, Designs and Trade Marks Act, 1883,** with the Rules and Instructions, together with Pleadings, Orders and Precedents. By J. E. CRAWFORD MUNRO, Esq., Barrister-at-Law. Royal 12mo. 1884. *10s. 6d.*

**Thompson's Handbook of Patent Law of all Countries.**—By WM. P. THOMPSON, Head of the International Patent Office, Liverpool. Eighth Edition. 12mo. 1889. *Net, 2s. 6d.*

**PERPETUITIES.**—Marsden's Rule against Perpetuities.—A Treatise on Remoteness in Limitation; with a chapter on Accumulation and the Thelluson Act. By REGINALD G. MARSDEN, Esq., Barrister-at Law. Demy 8vo. 1883. *16s.*

**PERSONAL PROPERTY.**—Shearwood's Concise Abridgment of the Law of Personal Property; showing analytically its Branches and the Titles by which it is held. By J. A. SHEARWOOD, Esq., Barrister-at-Law. 1882. *5s. 6d.*

"Will be acceptable to many students, as giving them, in fact, a ready-made note book."—*Indermaur's Law Students' Journal.*

**Smith.**—*Vide* "Real Property."

**PLEADING.**—Allen's Forms of Indorsements of Writs of Summons, Pleadings, and other Proceedings in the Queen's Bench Division prior to Trial, pursuant to the Rules of the Supreme Court, 1883; with Introduction, &c. By GEORGE BAUGH ALLEN, Esq., Special Pleader, and WILFRED B. ALLEN, Esq., Barrister-at-Law. Royal 12mo. 1883. *18s.*

*\*\** *All standard Law Works are kept in Stock, in law calf and other bindings.*

PLEADING—*continued*.

Bullen and Leake's Precedents of Pleadings, with Notes and Rules relating to Pleading. Fourth Edition. By THOMAS J. BULLEN, Esq., Special Pleader, and CYRIL DODD, Esq., Barrister-at-Law. Part I. Statements of Claim. Royal 12mo. 1882. 1*l* 4*s*.

Part II. Statements of Defence. By THOMAS J. BULLEN and C.W. CLIFFORD, Esqrs., Barristers-at-Law. Royal 12mo. 1888. 1*l*. 4*s*.

" A very large number of precedents are collected together, and the notes are full and clear."—*Law Times*.

POISONS.—Reports of Trials for Murder by Poisoning; by Prussic Acid, Strychnia, Antimony, Arsenic and Aconitine; including the trials of Tawell, W. Palmer, Dove, Madeline Smith, Dr. Pritchard, Smethurst, and Dr. Lamson. With Chemical Introductions and Notes. By G. LATHAM BROWNE, Esq., Barrister-at-Law, and C. G. STEWART, Senior Assistant in the Laboratory of St. Thomas's Hospital, &c. Demy 8vo. 1883. 12*s*. 6*d*.

POWERS.—Farwell on Powers.—A Concise Treatise on Powers. By GEORGE FARWELL, Esq., Barrister-at-Law. 8vo. 1874. 1*l*. 1*s*.

PRINTERS, PUBLISHERS, &c.—Powell's Laws specially affecting Printers, Publishers and Newspaper Proprietors. By ARTHUR POWELL, Esq., Barrister-at-Law. Demy 8vo. 1889. 4*s*.

PROBATE.—Browne's Probate Practice: A Treatise on the Principles and Practice of the Court of Probate, in Contentious and Non-Contentious Business. By L. D. POWLES, Barrister-at-Law. Including Practical Directions to Solicitors for Proceedings in the Registry. By T. W. H. OAKLEY, of the Principal Registry, Somerset House. 8vo. 1881. 1*l*. 10*s*.

PUBLIC HEALTH.—Bazalgette and Humphreys.—*Vide* "Local and Municipal Government."

Chambers' Digest of the Law relating to Public Health and Local Government.—With Notes of 1,260 leading Cases. The Statutes in full. A Table of Offences and Punishments, and a Copious Index. Eighth Edition (with Supplement corrected to May 21, 1887). Imperial 8vo. 1881. 16*s*.

*Or*, the above with the Law relating to Highways and Bridges. 1*l*.

Smith's Public Health Acts Amendment Act, 1890.—With Introduction, Notes, and References to Cases; also an Appendix, containing all the Material Sections of the Public Health Act, 1875 ; The Public Health (Rating of Orchards) Act, 1890 ; and The Infectious Diseases (Prevention) Act, 1890: and a Copious Index. By BOVILL SMITH, M.A., of the Inner Temple and Western Circuit, Barrister-at-Law. Royal 12mo. 1891. 6*s*.

PUBLIC MEETINGS.—Chambers' Handbook for Public Meetings, including Hints as to the Summoning and Management of them. Second Edition. By GEORGE F. CHAMBERS, Esq., Barrister-at-Law. Demy 8vo. 1886. *Net*, 2*s*. 6*d*.

QUARTER SESSIONS.—Archbold.—*Vide* "Criminal Law."

Leeming & Cross's General and Quarter Sessions of the Peace.—Their Jurisdiction and Practice in other than Criminal matters. Second Edition. By HORATIO LLOYD, Esq., Judge of County Courts, and H. F. THURLOW, Esq., Barrister-at-Law. 8vo. 1876. 1*l*. 1*s*.

Pritchard's Quarter Sessions.—The Jurisdiction, Practice and Procedure of the Quarter Sessions in Criminal, Civil, and Appellate Matters. By THOS. SIRRELL PRITCHARD, Esq., Barrister-at-Law. 8vo. 1875. (Published at 2*l*. 2*s*.) Reduced to *net* 12*s*.

*⁎* *All standard Law Works are kept in Stock, in law calf and other bindings.*

**RAILWAYS.**—Browne and Theobald's Law of Railway Companies.—Being a Collection of the Acts and Orders relating to Railway Companies in England and Ireland, with Notes of all the Cases decided thereon, and Appendix of Bye-Laws and Standing Orders of the House of Commons.    Second Edition.    By J. H. BALFOUR BROWNE, Esq., one of Her Majesty's Counsel, and H. S. THEOBALD, Esq., Barrister-at-Law.    Royal 8vo.    1888.        1*l*. 15*s*.

" Contains in a very concise form the whole law of railways."—*The Times*.

" The learned authors seem to have presented the profession and the public with the most ample information to be found whether they want to know how to start a railway, how to frame its bye-laws, how to work it, how to attack it for injury to person or property, or how to wind it up."—*Law Times*.

Macnamara.—*Vide* " Carriers."

Street.—*Vide* " Company Law."

**RATES AND RATING.**—Castle's Practical Treatise on the Law of Rating.—Second Edition.    By EDWARD JAMES CASTLE, Esq., one of Her Majesty's Counsel.    Demy 8vo.    1886.        25*s*.

" A correct, exhaustive, clear and concise view of the law."—*Law Times*.

Chambers' Law relating to Local Rates; with especial reference to the Powers and Duties of Rate-levying Local Authorities, and their Officers ; comprising the Statutes in full and a Digest of 718 Cases.    Second Edition.    By G. F. CHAMBERS, Esq., Barrister-at-Law.    Royal 8vo.    1889.        10*s*. 6*d*.

" A complete repertory of the statutes and case law of the subject."—*Law Journal*.

**REAL ESTATE.**—Foster's Law of Joint Ownership and Partition of Real Estate.—By EDWARD JOHN FOSTER, M.A., late of Lincoln's Inn, Barrister-at-Law.    8vo.    1878.        10*s*. 6*d*.

**REAL PROPERTY.**—Greenwood's Real Property Statutes; comprising those passed during the years 1874—1884, inclusive, consolidated with the earlier statutes thereby amended. With copious notes.    Second Edition.    By HARRY GREENWOOD, assisted by LEES KNOWLES, Esqrs., Barristers-at-Law.    Demy 8vo.    1884.    1*l*. 5*s*.

" The second edition of this useful collection of statutes relating to real property will be heartily welcomed by conveyancers and real property lawyers.    In referring to it as a collection of statutes, however, we do not fully describe it, because the method adopted by the author of grouping together the provisions of the various Acts, which are in *pari materiâ*, combined with the fullness and accuracy of the notes, entitles the book to rank high amongst treatises on the law of real property."—*Law Journal*.

Leake's Elementary Digest of the Law of Property in Land.— Containing : Introduction.    Part I.    The Sources of the Law.— Part II.    Estates in Land.    By STEPHEN MARTIN LEAKE, Barrister-at-Law.    Demy 8vo.    8vo.    1874.        1*l*. 2*s*.

Leake's Digest of the Law of Property in Land.—Part III. The Law of Uses and Profits of Land.    By STEPHEN MARTIN LEAKE, Barrister-at-Law, Author of " A Digest of the Law of Contracts." Demy 8vo.    1888.        1*l*. 2*s*.

Shearwood's Real Property.—A Concise Abridgment of the Law of Real Property and an Introduction to Conveyancing. Designed to facilitate the subject for Students preparing for examination. By JOSEPH A. SHEARWOOD, Esq., Barrister-at-Law.    Third Edition. Demy 8vo.    1885.        8*s*. 6*d*.

" We heartily recommend the work to student's for any examination on real property and conveyancing, advising them to read it after a perusal of other works and shortly before going in for the examination."—*Law Student's Journal*.

" A very useful little work, particularly to students just before their examination." —*Gibson's Law Notes*.

" One of the most obvious merits of the book is its good arrangement.    The author evidently understands ' the art of putting things.'    All important points are so printed as to readily catch the eye."—*Law Times*.

Shelford's Real Property Statutes.—Ninth Edition. By T. H. CARSON, Esq., Barrister-at-Law.        (*In preparation*.)

*⁎⁎* *All standard Law Works are kept in Stock, in law calf and other bindings.*

REAL PROPERTY—*continued.*

Smith's Real and Personal Property.—A Compendium of the Law of Real and Personal Property, primarily connected with Conveyancing. Designed as a second book for Students, and as a digest of the most useful learning for practitioners. By JOSIAH W. SMITH, B.C.L., Q.C. Sixth Edition. By the AUTHOR and J. TRUSTRAM, LL.M., Barrister-at-Law. 2 vols. Demy 8vo. 1884. 2*l.* 2*s.*

" A book which he (the student) may read over and over again with profit and pleasure."—*Law Times.*

" Will be found of very great service to the practitioner."—*Solicitors' Journal.*

" The book will be found very handy for reference purposes to practitioners, and very useful to the industrious student as covering a great deal of ground."—*Law Notes.*

" A really useful and valuable work on our system of Conveyancing. We think this edition excellently done."—*Law Student's Journal.*

REGISTRATION.—Rogers.—*Vide* "Elections."

Coltman's Registration Cases.—Vol. I. (1879—1885). Royal 8vo. Calf.                                                          *Net,* 2*l.* 8*s.*

Fox's Registration Cases.—Vol. I., Part I. (1886), *net,* 4*s.* Part II. (1887), *net,* 6*s.* 6*d.* Part III. (1888), *net,* 4*s.* Part IV. (1889), *net,* 4*s.* (In continuation of Coltman.)

RENTS.—Harrison's Law Relating to Chief Rents and other Rentcharges and Lands as affected thereby, with a chapter on Restrictive Covenants and a selection of Precedents. By WILLIAM HARRISON, Solicitor. Demy 12mo. 1884.                    6*s.*

ROMAN LAW.—Goodwin's XII. Tables.—By FREDERICK GOODWIN, LL.D. London. Royal 12mo. 1886.                               3*s.* 6*d.*

Greene's Outlines of Roman Law.—Consisting chiefly of an Analysis and Summary of the Institutes. For the use of Students. By T. WHITCOMBE GREENE, Barrister-at-law. Fourth Edition. Foolscap 8vo. 1884.                                          7*s.* 6*d.*

Ruegg's Student's "Auxilium" to the Institutes of Justinian.— Being a complete synopsis thereof in the form of Question and Answer. By ALFRED HENRY RUEGG, Esq., Barrister-at-Law. Post 8vo. 1879.                                                      5*s.*

SALES.—Blackburn on Sales. A Treatise on the Effect of the Contract of Sale on the Legal Rights of Property and Possession in Goods, Wares, and Merchandise. By Lord BLACKBURN. Second Edition. By J. C. GRAHAM, Esq., Barrister-at-Law. Royal 8vo. 1885.                                                            1*l.* 1*s.*

" We have no hesitation in saying that the work has been edited with remarkable ability and success, and if we may hazard a speculation on the cause, we should say that the editor has so diligently studied the excellent methods and work of his author as to have made himself a highly competent workman in the same kind."—*Law Quarterly Review.*

SALES OF LAND.—Clerke and Humphry's Concise Treatise on the Law relating to Sales of Land. By AUBREY ST. JOHN CLERKE, and HUGH M. HUMPHRY, Esqrs., Barristers-at-Law. Royal 8vo. 1885.                                                        1*l.* 5*s.*

Webster's Particulars and Conditions of Sale.—The Law relating to Particulars and Conditions of Sale on a Sale of Land. By WM. FREDK. WEBSTER, Esq., Barrister-at-Law. Royal 8vo. 1889. 1*l.* 1*s.*

" Characterized by clearness of arrangement and careful and concise statement ; and we think it will be found of much service to the practitioner."—*Solicitors' Journal.*

" A full account of case law, well arranged under convenient headings, together with a few precedents. The book is fit to be of practical service to a practical man."—*Law Quarterly Review.*

" It forms an admirable digest, evidently prepared with great care, and selected and arranged in a manner likely to be of great practical value. Its treatment has the air of thoroughness, and, although it hardly claims originality, it may be credited with utility."—*Law Journal.*

" A complete and accurate representation of the law. Nothing is shirked or slurred over."—*Law Times.*

\*\*\* *All standard Law Works are kept in Stock, in law calf and other bindings.*

**SETTLED ESTATES STATUTES.**—Middleton's Settled Estates Statutes, including the Settled Estates Act, 1877, Settled Land Act, 1882, Improvement of Land Act, 1864, and the Settled Estates Act Orders, 1878, with Introduction, Notes and Forms. Third Edition. By JAMES W. MIDDLETON, Esq., Barrister-at-Law. Royal 12mo. 1882.                                                            7s. 6d.

**SHERIFF LAW.**—Churchill's Law of the Office and Duties of the Sheriff, with the Writs and Forms relating to the Office. Second Edition. By CAMERON CHURCHILL, Esq., Barrister-at-Law. Demy 8vo. 1882.                                                                            1l. 4s.

"A very complete treatise."—*Solicitors' Journal.*
" Under-sheriffs, and lawyers generally, will find this a useful book."—*Law Mag.*

**SHIPPING.**—Boyd's Merchant Shipping Laws; being a Consolidation of all the Merchant Shipping and Passenger Acts from 1854 to 1876, inclusive, with Notes of all the leading English and American Cases, and an Appendix. By A. C. BOYD, LL.B., Esq., Barrister-at-Law. 8vo. 1876.                                                            1l. 5s.

Foard's Treatise on the Law of Merchant Shipping and Freight. —By J. T. FOARD, Barrister-at-Law. Roy. 8vo. 1880. *Hf. cf.* 1l. 1s.

**SLANDER.**—Odgers.—*Vide* " Libel and Slander."

**SOLICITORS.**—Cordery's Law relating to Solicitors of the Supreme Court of Judicature. With an Appendix of Statutes and Rules, and Notes on Appointments open to Solicitors, and the Right to Admission to the Colonies. Second Edition. By A. CORDERY, Esq., Barrister-at-Law. Demy 8vo. 1888.                                    16s.

"The book is very clear, accurate, and practical, and will be found of much value. Without being bulky, it contains in a concise and intelligible form all the matters usually occurring in a solicitor's practice."—*Solicitors' Journal*, July 28, 1888.
" This is a very valuable work, and being the only one on the subject, the appearance of its second edition will be welcomed by the profession."—*Law Journal*, Jan. 21, 1888.

Turner.—*Vide* " Conveyancing " and " Vendors and Purchasers."

Whiteway's Hints to Solicitors.—Being a Treatise on the Law relating to their Duties as Officers of the High Court of Justice; with Notes on the Recent Changes affecting the Profession. By A. R. WHITEWAY, M.A., of the Equity Bar and Midland Circuit. Royal 12mo. 1883.                                                                    6s.

**SPECIFIC PERFORMANCE.**—Fry's Treatise on the Specific Performance of Contracts. By the Hon. Sir EDWARD FRY, a Lord Justice of Appeal. Second Edition. By the Author and W. DONALDSON RAWLINS, of Lincoln's Inn, Esq., Barrister-at-Law. Royal 8vo. 1881.                                                            1l. 16s.

**STAMP DUTY.**—Gosset's Practical Guide to Account Stamp Duty, Customs, and Inland Revenue Act, 1881 (44 Vict. c. 12, s. 38). By J. A. GOSSET, of the Legacy and Succession Duty Office. Post 8vo. 1887.                                                        5s.

"The author, by reason of his official position and the experience of six years' working of this section of the Act of 1881 (which imposed an entirely new duty), has been enabled to produce an exceptionally valuable guide."—*Law Times.*

**STATUTE LAW.**—Wilberforce on Statute Law. The Principles which govern the Construction and Operation of Statutes. By E. WILBERFORCE, Esq., Barrister-at-Law. 1881.                                18s.

\*\*\* *All standard Law Works are kept in Stock, in law calf and other bindings.*

STATUTES, and *vide* " Acts of Parliament."

Chitty's Collection of Statutes from Magna Charta to 1890.—A Collection of Statutes of Practical Utility, arranged in Alphabetical and Chronological order, with Notes thereon. The Fourth Edition, with Supplement. By J. M. LELY, Esq., Barrister-at-Law. In 8 vols. Royal 8vo. 1880-90. Published at 17*l.* 11*s.* 6*d.*, reduced to *Net* 10*l.* 10*s.*

The following may still be had separately—

| | |
|---|---|
| 6 vols. To end of the year 1880. | *Net* 6*l.* 6*s.* |
| 50 & 51 Vict. 1887. | 10*s.* 6*d.* |
| 51 & 52 Vict. 1888. | 12*s.* 6*d.* |
| 51 & 52 Vict. 1888. (Second Session.) | *Net* 2*s.* 6*d.* |
| 52 & 53 Vict. 1889. | 10*s.* |
| 53 & 54 Vict. 1890. | 15*s.* |

" It is needless to enlarge on the value of 'Chitty's Statutes' to both the Bar and to Solicitors, for it is attested by the experience of many years."—*The Times.*

" A very satisfactory edition of a time-honoured and most valuable work, the trusty guide of present, as of former, judges, jurists, and of all others connected with the administration or practice of the law."—*Justice of the Peace.*

" 'Chitty' is pre-eminently a friend in need. Those who do not possess a complete set of the Statutes turn to its chronological index when they wish to consult a particular Act of Parliament. Those who wish to know what Acts are in force with reference to a particular subject turn to that head in 'Chitty,' and at once find all the material of which they are in quest. Moreover, they are, at the same time, referred to the most important cases which throw light on the subject."—*Law Journal.*

SUCCESSION.—Potts' Principles of the Law of Succession to Deceased Persons.—By T. RADFORD POTTS, B.C.L., M.A., Barrister-at-Law. Demy 8vo. 1885. 7*s.* 6*d.*

" We should have no hesitation in recommending it to a student who was to have a paper set on Succession generally."—*Saturday Review,* June 15th, 1889.

SUMMARY CONVICTIONS.—Paley's Law and Practice of Summary Convictions under the Summary Jurisdiction Acts, 1848 and 1879; including Proceedings preliminary and subsequent to Convictions, and the responsibility of Convicting Magistrates and their Officers, with Forms. Sixth Edition. By W. H. MACNAMARA, Esq., Barrister-at-Law. Demy 8vo. 1879. 1*l.* 4*s.*

Wigram.—*Vide* " Justice of the Peace."

SUMMONSES & ORDERS.—Archibald.—*Vide* "Chamber Practice."

TAXES ON SUCCESSION.—Trevor's Taxes on Succession.— A Digest of the Statutes and Cases (including those in Scotland and Ireland) relating to the Probate, Legacy and Succession Duties, with Practical Observations and Official Forms. Fourth Edition. By EVELYN FREETH and R. J. WALLACE, of the Legacy and Succession Duty Office. Royal 12mo. 1881. 12*s.* 6*d.*

" Contains a great deal of practical information."—*Law Journal.*

TAXPAYERS' GUIDES.—*Vide* "House Tax," "Income Tax," and " Land Tax."

THEATRES AND MUSIC HALLS.—Geary's Law of Theatres and Music Halls, including Contracts and Precedents of Contracts.—By W. N. M. GEARY, J.P. With Historical Introduction. By JAMES WILLIAMS, Esqrs., Barristers-at-Law. 8vo. 1885. 5*s.*

TITHES.—Bolton's Tithe Acts; including the Recent Act for the Limitation and Redemption of Extraordinary Tithe; with an Introduction and Observations and copious Index. By T. H. BOLTON, Solicitor. Royal 12mo. 1886. 6*s.*

Studd's Law of Tithes and Tithe Rent-Charge.—Being a Treatise on the Law of Tithe Rent-Charge, with a sketch of the History and Law of Tithes prior to the Commutation Acts. Second Edition. By EDWARD FAIRFAX STUDD, Esq., Barrister-at-Law. (*In the press.*)

" We can recommend it for professional use."—*Law Times.*

*\*\* All standard Law Works are kept in Stock, in law calf and other bindings.*

**TORTS.**—Addison on Torts; being a Treatise on Wrongs and their Remedies. Sixth Edition. By HORACE SMITH, Esq., Bencher of the Inner Temple, Editor of "Addison on Contracts," &c. Royal 8vo. 1887. *1l. 18s.*

"Upon a careful perusal of the editor's work, we can say that he has done it excellently."—*Law Quarterly Review.*

"As now presented, this valuable treatise must prove highly acceptable to judges and the profession."—*Law Times.*

"An indispensable addition to every lawyer's library."—*Law Magazine.*

Ball's Leading Cases-on the Law of Torts, with Notes. Edited by W. E. BALL, LL.D., Esq., Barrister-at-Law, Author of "Principles of Torts and Contracts." Royal 8vo. 1884. *1l. 1s.*

"The notes are extremely, and as far as we have been able to discover uniformly, good. . . There is much intelligent and independent criticism."—*Solicitors' Journal.*

"All the cases given are interesting, and most of them are important, and the comments in the notes are intelligent and useful."—*Law Journal.*

Pollock's Law of Torts: a Treatise on the Principles of Obligations arising from Civil Wrongs in the Common Law. Second Edition, to which is added the draft of a Code of Civil Wrongs prepared for the Government of India. By Sir FREDERICK POLLOCK, Bart., Barrister-at-Law. Author of "Principles of Contract," "A Digest of the Law of Partnership," &c. Demy 8vo. 1890. *21s.*

"Concise, logically arranged, and accurate."—*Law Times.*

"A book which is well worthy to stand beside the companion volume on 'Contracts.' Unlike so many law-books, especially on this subject, it is no mere digest of cases, but bears the impress of the mind of the writer from beginning to end."—*Law Journal.*

Shearwood's Sketch of the Law of Tort for the Bar and Solicitors Final Examinations. By JOSEPH A. SHEARWOOD, Esq., Barrister-at-Law. Author of "Concise Abridgments of the Law of Real and Personal Property," &c. Royal 12mo. 1886. *3s.*

**TRADE MARKS.**—Aston.—*Vide* "Patents."

Graham's Designs and Trade Marks.—By JOHN CAMERON GRAHAM, of the Middle Temple, Barrister-at-Law. Demy 8vo. 1889. *6s.*

Sebastian on the Law of Trade Marks and their Registration, and matters connected therewith, including a chapter on Goodwill; together with the Patents, Designs and Trade Marks Acts, 1883-8, and the Trade Marks Rules and Instructions thereunder; Forms and Precedents; the Merchandize Marks Act, 1887, and other Statutory Enactments; the United States Statutes, 1870-81, and the Rules and Forms thereunder; and the Treaty with the United States, 1877. Third Edition. By LEWIS BOYD SEBASTIAN, Esq., Barrister-at-Law. Demy 8vo. 1890. *1l. 5s.*

"The work stands alone as an authority upon the law of trade-marks and their registration."—*Law Journal,* August 2, 1890.

"It is hardly necessary to tell anyone who has consulted the last edition of this book that it is characterized by mastery of the subject, exemplary industry, and completeness and accuracy of statement It is rarely we come across a law book which embodies the results of years of careful investigation and practical experience in a branch of law, or that can be unhesitatingly appealed to as a standard authority. This is what can be said of Mr. Sebastian's book."—*Solicitors' Journal,* Nov. 1, 1890.

Sebastian's Digest of Cases of Trade Mark, Trade Name, Trade Secret, Goodwill, &c., decided in the Courts of the United Kingdom, India, the Colonies, and the United States of America. By LEWIS BOYD SEBASTIAN, Esq., Barrister-at-Law. 8vo. 1879. *1l. 1s.*

"A digest which will be of very great value to all practitioners who have to advise on matters connected with trade marks."—*Solicitors' Journal.*

Hardingham's Trade Marks: Notes on the British, Foreign, and Colonial Laws relating thereto. By GEO. GATTON MELHUISH HARDINGHAM, Consulting Engineer and Patent Agent. Royal 12mo. 1881. *Net, 2s. 6d.*

\*\*\* *All standard Law Works are kept in Stock, in law calf and other bindings.*

**TRAMWAYS.**—Sutton's Tramway Acts of the United Kingdom; with Notes on the Law and Practice, an Introduction, including the Proceedings before the Committees, Decisions of the Referees with respect to Locus Standi, and a Summary of the Principles of Tramway Rating, and an Appendix containing the Standing Orders of Parliament. Rules of the Board of Trade relating to Tramways, &c. Second Edition. By HENRY SUTTON, assisted by ROBERT A. BENNETT, Barristers-at-Law. Demy 8vo. 1883.     15*s.*

**TRUST FUNDS.**—Geare's Investment of Trust Funds.—Incorporating the Trustee Act, 1888. By EDWARD ARUNDEL GEARE, Esq., Barrister-at-Law. Second Edition. Including the Trusts Investment Act, 1889. Royal 12mo. 1889.     7*s.* 6*d.*

"The work is written in an easy style, it can very well be read by all trustees, whether they are lawyers or not; and if they will take our advice, and invest their money here before they invest other people's elsewhere, they may be spared much trouble in the future."—*The Jurist.*

**TRUSTS AND TRUSTEES.**—Godefroi's Law Relating to Trusts and Trustees.—Second Edition. By HENRY GODEFROI, of Lincoln's Inn, Esq., Barrister-at-Law. Royal 8vo. 1891.     1*l.* 12*s.*

"The second edition of this work which lies before us is a model of what a legal text-book ought to be. It is clear in style and clear in arrangement, and we can have little doubt that it will soon take the foremost place among text-books dealing with trusts. Moreover, it is brought up to date by including in its scope the Trust Investment Act of 1889, and the Settled Land Act, 1890. The chapter on Precatory Trusts in Mr. Godefroi's work seems to us particularly good and clear, and the many judicial decisions as to what expressions are sufficient and what are insufficient to import a trust are marshalled with great care and accuracy."—*Law Times,* April 18, 1891.

Hamilton's Trustee Acts.—Containing the Trustee Act, 1850; the Trustee Extension Act, 1852; and the Trustee Act, 1888; with Supplement of the Lunacy Act, 1890 (53 Vict. c. 5), so far as relates to Vesting Orders. By G. BALDWIN HAMILTON, Esq., Barrister-at-Law, Author of "A Concise Treatise on the Law of Covenants." Demy 8vo. 1890.     6*s.*

"This is a very useful little book. We have perused it with much care, and we have come to the conclusion that it may be safely trusted to as a guide to the complicated law to which it relates."—*Law Quarterly Review.*

**VENDORS AND PURCHASERS.** — Dart's Vendors and Purchasers.—A Treatise on the Law and Practice relating to Vendors and Purchasers of Real Estate. By the late J. HENRY DART, Esq., one of the Six Conveyancing Counsel of the High Court of Justice, Chancery Division. Sixth Edition. By WILLIAM BARBER, Esq., one of Her Majesty's Counsel, RICHARD BURDON HALDANE, and WILLIAM ROBERT SHELDON, both of Lincoln's Inn, Esqrs., Barristers-at-Law. 2 vols. Royal 8vo. 1888.     3*l.* 15*s.*

"The new edition of Dart is far ahead of all competitors in the breadth of its range, the clearness of its exposition, and the soundness of its law."—*Law Times.*

"The extensive changes and numerous improvements which have been introduced are the result of assiduous labour, combined with critical acumen, sound knowledge, and practical experience."—*Law Quarterly Review.*

Turner's Duties of Solicitor to Client as to Sales, Purchases, and Mortgages of Land.—By EDWARD F. TURNER, Solicitor, Lecturer on Real Property and Conveyancing. Demy 8vo. 1883.     10*s.* 6*d.*

*See also* Conveyancing.—"Turner."

"A careful perusal of these lectures cannot fail to be of great advantage to students, and more particularly, we think, to young practising solicitors."—*Law Times.*

**WAR, DECLARATION OF.**—Owen's Declaration of War.—A Survey of the Position of Belligerents and Neutrals, with relative considerations of Shipping and Marine Insurance during War. By DOUGLAS OWEN, Barrister-at-Law. Demy 8vo. 1889.     21*s.*

\*\*\* *All standard Law Works are kept in Stock, in law calf and other bindings.*

WATERS.—Musgrave's Dissertation on the Common Law of Waters and its Application to Natural Circumstances other than those of England.—By W. A. B. MUSGRAVE, D.C.L., of the Inner Temple, Barrister-at-Law. Demy 8vo. 1890. *Net, 2s.*

WILLS.—Theobald's Concise Treatise on the Law of Wills.— Third Edition. By H. S. THEOBALD, Esq., Barrister-at-Law. Royal 8vo. 1885. *1l. 10s.*

" A book of great ability and value. It bears on every page traces of care and sound judgment. It is certain to prove of great practical usefulness."—*Solicitors' Journal.*

Weaver's Precedents of Wills.—A Collection of Concise Precedents of Wills, with Introduction, Notes, and an Appendix of Statutes. By CHARLES WEAVER, B.A. Post 8vo. 1882. *5s.*

WINDING UP.—Palmer's Winding-up Forms.—A Collection of 580 Forms of Summonses, Affidavits, Orders, Notices and other Forms relating to the Winding-up of Companies. With Notes on the Law and Practice, and an Appendix containing the Acts and Rules. By FRANCIS BEAUFORT PALMER, Esq., Barrister-at-Law, Author of "Company Precedents," &c. 8vo. 1885. *12s.*

Pitt-Lewis' Winding-up Practice.—A Manual of the Practice as to Winding-up in the High Court and in the County Court; being the Companies (Winding-up) Act, 1890, and the Winding-up of Companies and Associations (Part IV. of the Companies Act, 1862), as now amended, with Notes, and the Companies Winding-up Rules, 1890. Forming a SUPPLEMENT to "A Complete Practice of the County Courts." By G. PITT-LEWIS, Q.C., M.P., Recorder of Poole. Demy 8vo. 1891. *7s. 6d.*

"This is a book that we can cordially recommend, and forms a fitting supplement to the aptly-named larger work of the same author."—*Law Gazette,* March 5, 1891.

WRECK INQUIRIES.—Murton's Law and Practice relating to Formal Investigations in the United Kingdom, British Possessions and before Naval Courts into Shipping Casualties and the Incompetency and Misconduct of Ships' Officers. With an Introduction. By WALTER MURTON, Solicitor to the Board of Trade. Demy 8vo. 1884. *1l. 4s.*

WRONGS.—Addison, Ball, Pollock, Shearwood.—*Vide* "Torts."

---

REPORTS.—A large Stock, New and Second-hand. Prices on application.

BINDING.—Executed in the best manner at moderate prices and with dispatch.

## The Law Reports, Law Journal, and all other Reports, bound to Office Patterns, at Office Prices.

PRIVATE ACTS.—*The Publishers of this Catalogue possess the largest known collection of Private Acts of Parliament (including Public and Local), and can supply single copies commencing from a very early period.*

*LICENSED VALUERS* for Probate, Partnership, &c.

## LIBRARIES PURCHASED OR EXCHANGED.

STEVENS AND SONS, LD., 119 & 120, CHANCERY LANE, LONDON.

# NEW WORKS AND NEW EDITIONS.

Carver's Carriage by Sea: a Treatise on the Law relating to the Carriage of Goods by Sea.—Second Edition. By THOMAS GILBERT CARVER, Esq., Barrister-at-Law. Royal 8vo. (*Nearly ready.*)

Chalmers' Digest of the Law of Bills of Exchange, Promissory Notes, Cheques, and Negotiable Securities. Fourth Edition. By His Honour Judge CHALMERS, Draughtsman of the Bills of Exchange Act, 1882, &c. Demy 8vo. (*In the press.*)

Kennedy's Law of Civil Salvage.—By WILLIAM RANN KENNEDY, Esq., one of Her Majesty's Counsel. (*In the press.*)

Phillimore's Ecclesiastical Law of the Church of England.— Second Edition. Edited by Sir WALTER GEO. FRANK PHILLIMORE, Bart., D.C.L., Chancellor of the Diocese of Lincoln. (*In preparation.*)

Rawson's Profit-Sharing Precedents, with Notes.—By HENRY G. RAWSON, of the Inner Temple, Esq., Barrister-at-Law.
(*In the press.*)

Roscoe's Admiralty Practice.—Third Edition. By E. S. ROSCOE and T. LAMBERT MEARS, Esqrs., Barristers-at-Law. (*In preparation.*)

Roscoe's Digest of the Law of Evidence on the Trial of Actions at Nisi Prius.—Sixteenth Edition. By MAURICE POWELL, Esq., Barrister-at-Law. 2 vols Demy 8vo. (*Nearly ready.*)

Russell's Treatise on the Power and Duty of an Arbitrator, and the Law of Submissions and Awards.—7th Edit. By the Author and HERBERT RUSSELL, Esq., Barrister-at-Law. (*In the press.*)

Selwyn's Abridgment of the Law of Nisi Prius.—14th Edition. By W. H. MACNAMARA, Esq., Barrister-at-Law. (*In preparation.*)

Seton's Forms of Judgments and Orders in the High Court of Justice and Courts of Appeal, having especial reference to the Chancery Division, with Practical Notes. Fifth Edition. By C. C. M. DALE, of Lincoln's Inn, Esq., Barrister-at-Law, and W. CLOWES, Esq., one of the Registrars of the Supreme Court. (*In the press.*)

Studd's Law of Tithes and Tithe Rent-Charge.—Being a Treatise on the Law of Tithe Rent-Charge, with a sketch of the History and Law of Tithes prior to the Commutation Acts. Second Edition. By EDWARD FAIRFAX STUDD, Esq., Barrister-at-Law. (*In the press.*)

Talbot and Fort's Index of Cases Judicially noted (1865—1890); being a List of all Cases cited in Judgments reported in the "Law Reports," "Law Journal," "Law Times," and "Weekly Reporter," from Michaelmas Term, 1865 to the end of 1890, with the places where they are so cited.—By GEORGE JOHN TALBOT and HUGH FORT, Barristers-at-Law. (*Nearly ready.*)

Theobald and Schuster's Lunacy Act, 1890, with Notes.—By H. S. THEOBALD and E. J. SCHUSTER, Barristers-at-Law. (*In preparation.*)

Wharton's Law Lexicon.—Forming an Epitome of the Law of England, and containing full Explanations of the Technical Terms and Phrases thereof, both Ancient and Modern; including the various Legal Terms used in Commercial Business. Together with a Translation of the Latin Law Maxims and selected Titles from the Civil, Scotch and Indian Law. Ninth Edition. By J. M. LELY, Esq., Barrister-at-Law. Super-royal 8vo. (*In preparation.*)

Whitehead's Church Law.—Being a Concise Dictionary of Statutes, Canons and Regulations affecting the Clergy and Laity. By BENJAMIN WHITEHEAD, B.A., Esq., Barrister-at-Law. (*In preparation.*)

Williams' Law of Executors and Administrators.—Ninth Edition. By the Hon. Sir ROLAND VAUGHAN WILLIAMS, a Justice of the High Court. 2 vols. Royal 8vo. (*In the press.*)

STEVENS AND SONS, LD., 119 & 120, CHANCERY LANE, LONDON.

## Stringer's Oaths and Affirmations in Great Britain and

Ireland; being a Collection of Statutes, Cases, and Forms, with Notes and Practical Directions for the use of Commissioners for Oaths, and of all Courts of Civil Procedure and Offices attached thereto. [In succession to "Braithwaite's Oaths."] By FRANCIS A. STRINGER, of the Central Office, Supreme Court of Judicature, one of the Editors of the "Annual Practice." *Crown 8vo.* 1890. *Price 3s. 6d. cloth.*
"Indispensable to all Commissioners."—*Solicitors' Journal.*

## Thring's Joint Stock Companies' Law.—The Law and

Practice of Joint Stock and other Companies, including the Companies Acts, 1862 to 1886, with Notes, Orders, and Rules in Chancery, a Collection of Precedents of Memoranda and Articles of Association, and other Forms required in Making and Administering a Company. By Lord THRING, K.C.B. *Fifth Edition.* By J. M. RENDEL, Esq., Barrister-at-Law. *Royal 8vo.* 1889. *Price 1l. 10s. cloth.*
"The highest authority on the subject."—*The Times.*

## Woodfall's Law of Landlord and Tenant.—With a full

Collection of Precedents and Forms of Procedure; containing also a Collection of Leading Propositions. *Fourteenth Edition.* By J. M. LELY, Esq., Barrister-at-Law. *Royal 8vo.* 1889. *Price 1l. 18s. cloth.*

## Lely and Peck's Precedents of Leases for Years, and other

Contracts of Tenancy, and Contracts relating thereto, mainly selected or adapted from existing Collections, including many additional Forms, with a short Introduction and Notes. By J. M. LELY and W. A. PECK, Esqrs., Barristers-at-Law. *Royal 8vo.* 1889. *Price 10s. 6d. cloth.*

## Oldham and Foster on the Law of Distress —A Treatise

on the Law of Distress, with an Appendix of Forms, Table of Statutes, &c. *Second Edition.* By ARTHUR OLDHAM and A. LA TROBE FOSTER, Esqrs., Barristers-at-Law. *Demy 8vo.* 1889. *Price 18s. cloth.*

## Daniell's Chancery Forms.—*Fourth Edition.* Forms and

Precedents of Proceeding in the Chancery Division of the High Court of Justice and on Appeal therefrom. *Fourth Edition.* With Summaries of the Rules of the Supreme Court, Practical Notes and References to the Sixth Edition of "Daniell's Chancery Practice." By CHARLES BURNEY, B.A. (Oxon.), a Chief Clerk of the Hon. Mr. Justice Chitty. *Royal 8vo.* (1260 pp.) 1885. *Price 2l. 10s. cloth.*

## Chambers' Law relating to Local Rates, with especial

reference to the Powers and Duties of Rate-levying Local Authorities, and their Officers. Comprising the Statutes in full and a Digest of 718 Cases. By G. F. CHAMBERS, Esq., Barrister-at-Law. *Royal 8vo.* 1889. *Price 10s. 6d. cloth.*

## Bullen and Leake's Precedents of Pleadings, with Notes

and Rules relating to Pleading. Revised and adapted to the Present Practice in the Queen's Bench Division of the High Court of Justice. *Fourth Edition.* Part II. By THOMAS J. BULLEN and CHARLES WALTER CLIFFORD, Esqrs., Barristers-at-Law. *Royal 12mo.* 1888. *Price 24s. cloth.*
\*.\* Part I., "Statements of Claim," may still be had, price 24s.

## Macnamara's Law of Carriers.—A Digest of the Law of

Carriers of Goods and Passengers by Land and Internal Navigation. By WALTER HENRY MACNAMARA, Esq., Barrister-at-Law, Registrar to the Railway Commission. *Royal 8vo.* 1888. *Price 1l. 8s. cloth.*
"We cordially approve of the general plan and execution of this work."—*Solicitors' Journal.*

## Browne and Theobald's Law of Railway Companies.—

Being a Collection of the Acts and Orders relating to Railway Companies in England and Ireland, with Notes of all the Cases decided thereon, and Appendix of Bye-Laws and Standing Orders of the House of Commons. *Second Edition.* By J. H. BALFOUR BROWNE, Esq., one of Her Majesty's Counsel, and H. S. THEOBALD, Esq., Barrister-at-Law. *Royal 8vo.* 1883. *Price 1l. 15s. cloth.*
"Contains in a very concise form the whole law of railways."—*The Times.*

## Geare's Investment of Trust Funds.—Incorporating the

Trustee Act, 1888. *Second Edition.* Including the Trusts Investment Act, 1889. By EDWARD ARUNDEL GEARE, Esq., Barrister-at-Law. *Royal 12mo.* 1889. *Price 7s. 6d. cloth.*

## Brooke's Notary.—A Treatise on the Office and Practice of

a Notary of England. With a full Collection of Precedents. *Fifth Edit.* By GEORGE F. CHAMBERS, Esq., Barrister-at-Law. *Demy 8vo.* 1890. *Price 1l. 1s. cloth.*

\*.\* *A large stock of Second-hand Law Reports and Text-books on Sale.*

**Marsden's Treatise on the Law of Collisions at Sea.—** With an Appendix containing Extracts from the Merchant Shipping Acts, the International Regulations for preventing Collisions at Sea; and Local Rules for the same purpose in force in the Thames, the Mersey, and elsewhere. By REGINALD G. MARSDEN, Esq., Barrister-at-Law. *Third Edition.* By the Author and the Hon. J. W. MANSFIELD, Barrister-at-Law. *Demy 8vo.* 1891. *Price 1l. 5s. cloth.*

**Webster on Conditions of Sale.—**The Law relating to Particulars and Conditions of Sale on a Sale of Land. By WILLIAM FREDERICK

. 1s. *cloth.*
together with a few
*Quarterly Review.*

Divorce and
Barrister-at-Law.

*Third English*
*Royal 8vo.* 1889.

Collection of
Conventions, arranged
as, Special Clauses,
and Copious Notes
Barrister-at-Law.

*Law Times.*
—*Second Edition.*
1886. *Price 25s. cloth.*
."—*Law Times.*

iciples of Equity,
use of Students and Practi-
Esq., M.A., LL.B. (Lond.),

*r.—Second Edition.*
-at-Law. *Demy 8vo.* 1889.

he Criminal Law,
ster-at-Law. *Demy 8vo.*

Law.—With
Barrister-at-Law.

tioners and
ractical Rules and
*Edition.* By J.
. *Price 14s. cloth.*

Manual of
on the Works of
Principles and the
AH W. SMITH,
Barrister-at-Law.

s Civil and
ng them, &c., &c.,
By RICHARD HARRIS, one of Her Majesty's Counsel. *Ninth Edition.* With a
New Chapter on "Tactics." *Royal 12mo.* 1889. *Price 7s. 6d. cloth.*
"Full of good sense and just observation. A very complete Manual of the Advocate's art in Trial by Jury."—*Solicitors' Journal.*

**The Pocket Law Lexicon.—**Explaining Technical Words, Phrases and Maxims of the English, Scotch and Roman Law, to which is added a complete List of Law Reports, with their Abbreviations. *Second Edition.* Revised and Enlarged. By HENRY G. RAWSON, B.A., of the Inner Temple, Esq., Barrister-at-Law. *Fcap. 8vo.* 1884. *Price 6s. 6d. limp binding.*
"**A** wonderful little legal **Dictionary.**"—*Indermaur's Law Students' Journal.*

*\*\** *A Catalogue of New Law Works* (1891) *gratis on application.*

CPSIA information can be obtained
at www.ICGtesting.com
Printed in the USA
BVHW052154051118
532208BV00013B/801/P